SERBIA

MARKO ATTILA HOARE

Serbia

A Modern History

Oxford University Press is a department of the
University of Oxford. It furthers the University's objective
of excellence in research, scholarship, and education
by publishing worldwide.

Oxford New York

Auckland   Cape Town   Dar es Salaam   Hong Kong   Karachi
Kuala Lumpur   Madrid   Melbourne   Mexico City   Nairobi
New Delhi   Shanghai   Taipei   Toronto

With offices in

Argentina   Austria   Brazil   Chile   Czech Republic   France   Greece
Guatemala   Hungary   Italy   Japan   Poland   Portugal   Singapore
South Korea   Switzerland   Thailand   Turkey   Ukraine   Vietnam

Oxford is a registered trade mark of Oxford University Press
in the UK and certain other countries.

Published in the United States of America by
Oxford University Press
198 Madison Avenue, New York, NY 10016

Copyright © Marko Attila Hoare, 2024

All rights reserved. No part of this publication may be reproduced,
stored in a retrieval system, or transmitted, in any form or by any means,
without the prior permission in writing of Oxford University Press,
or as expressly permitted by law, by license, or under terms agreed with
the appropriate reproduction rights organization. Inquiries concerning
reproduction outside the scope of the above should be sent to the
Rights Department, Oxford University Press, at the address above.

You must not circulate this work in any other form
and you must impose this same condition on any acquirer.
Library of Congress Cataloging-in-Publication Data is available

ISBN: 9780197769423

Printed in the United Kingdom by Bell and Bain Ltd, Glasgow.

*For my children,
Maximilian, Cecilia and Hector*

CONTENTS

Glossary — xi

List of Abbreviations — xvii

Maps — xix

Acknowledgements — xxi

Introduction: Rise and Fall of the First Modern Serbia — 1

PART I
SERBIA IN THE OTTOMAN EMPIRE

1. Serbia and the Serbs Before the Nineteenth Century — 9
   Rise of medieval Serbia 9 – *Battle of Kosovo and Ottoman conquest* 16 – *Serbia under Ottoman rule and creation of a Serb diaspora* 22 – *Ottoman decline and origins of the Serbian revolution* 28 – *Twilight of Ottoman rule in Serbia* 34

2. The Serbian Uprisings, 1804–1815 — 37
   Serbia on the eve of the uprisings 37 – *Tyranny of the deys* 40 – *Rebellion against the deys* 43 – *Rebellion against the Sultan* 46 – *Ottoman reconquest* 55 – *Second Serbian Uprising* 59

3. Prince Miloš and the Founding of Modern Serbia, 1815–1839 — 65
   Prince Miloš establishes his absolutism 65 – *Rebellion at home and crisis abroad* 69 – *Ottoman recognition of Serbia's autonomy* 75 – *Regaining of the six nahijas and expulsion of the Muslims* 79 – *Foundation of a modern society* 83 – *Mileta's rebellion and Presentation Constitution* 89 – *Turkish Constitution and fall of Prince Miloš* 94

4. The Constitutionalist Era, 1839–1858 — 101
   Prince Mihailo's first reign 101 – *Birth of a modern elite* 108 – *Vuk Karadžić and linguistic nationalism* 115 – *Ilija Garašanin and the Plan* 122 – *Austrian Serbs, populist reaction and the revolutions of 1848* 126 – *Between Austria and Russia* 133 – *Tenka's plot* 135

CONTENTS

5. The National Liberation Struggle Resumes, 1858–1867   139
   Birth of Serbian liberalism 139 – *St Andrew's Day parliament* 143 – *Second reign of Prince Miloš* 147 – *Prince Mihailo's domestic counter-revolution* 154 – *Transfiguration Day parliament* 156 – *National liberation 'from above'* 160 – *Downfall of the Great Court and liberation of Belgrade* 165

6. Liberals, Socialists and Nationalism from Below, 1867–1872   171
   United Serb Youth and Court Liberals 171 – *Assassination of Prince Mihailo and Court Liberal coup* 178 – *Regency Constitution* 182 – *Origins of Serbian socialism* 186 – *Svetozar Marković and anti-state nationalism* 188 – *Socialists and Liberals split* 195

PART II
INDEPENDENCE AND THE TWO SERBIAS

7. Achievement of Independence, 1872–1880   201
   Prince Milan attains his majority 201 – *Birth of the Radical party* 206 – *Rebellion in Bosnia and Radical agitation in Serbia* 209 – *Serbia prepares for war* 213 – *First Serbo-Ottoman war* 215 – *Second Serbo-Ottoman war* 220 – *Expulsion of the Albanians* 222 – *Independence and vassalage under Austria-Hungary* 224

8. Court and Radicals, 1880–1892   233
   Establishment of the Progressive regime 233 – *Formal establishment of political parties* 237 – *Progressive government and Radical opposition* 241 – *Timok rebellion* 244 – *Serbo-Bulgarian war* 249 – *Constitution of 1889 and abdication of King Milan* 253 – *Radical-regent condominium* 259

9. Court–Radical Collaboration and Praetorian Reaction, 1892–1903   267
   Ex-queen Natalija is expelled from Serbia 267 – *Liberal coup and Royal-Radical counter-coup* 270 – *Anti-Radical counter-revolution* 274 – *Southward expansionism and pivot to Russia* 279 – *Aleksandar's marriage to Draga Mašin* 288 – *Radical-Progressive 'fusion' and April Constitution* 295

10. A Royal 'Honour Killing', 1903   303
    Regicidal conspiracy 303 – *Socio-economic change and evolution of socialist thought* 308 – *'March disturbances'* 314 – *'May putsch'* 317 – *Historical autopsy of the regicide* 321 – *Restoration of the 1889 constitution and Karađorđević dynasty* 325

11. Radical–Conspirator Condominium, 1903–1912   331
    Counter-conspiracy 331 – *Guerrilla war and irredentism in the south* 336 – *Radical party formally splits* 339 – *Conspirators crisis and Pig War* 342 – *Annexation crisis* 350 – *Black Hand and White Hand* 356

CONTENTS

12. The Balkan Wars and the Road to World War I, 1912–1914 — 363
    Serbian nationalism and South Slav cooperation before 1914 363 – *Road to the Balkan Wars* 370 – *First Balkan War* 373 – *Second Balkan War* 377 – *War against the Albanians* 380 – *Social Democratic opposition to militarism* 383 – *Priority question* 385 – *Sarajevo assassination and outbreak of World War I* 391

PART III
NATIONAL UNIFICATION AND YUGOSLAVIA

13. Defeat and Occupation, 1914–1917 — 399
    Self-defence and revolutionary war 399 – *Initial victory and Niš Declaration* 402 – *Third Balkan War* 407 – *Central Powers conquer Serbia* 412 – *Serbia under Central Power occupation* 416 – *Volunteer units* 422

14. Liberation and Unification, 1917–1918 — 425
    Salonika trial 425 – *Corfu Declaration* 431 – *Collapse of the Central Powers* 436 – *Geneva Declaration* 440 – *Annexation of Montenegro* 442 – *Establishment of Yugoslavia* 445

15. Establishment of the Yugoslav State, 1918–1921 — 451
    International position of the new state 451 – *Yugoslav unification on a Serbian model* 455 – *Repression in the periphery* 462 – *Formation of the Democratic Party* 469 – *People's Radical Party expands beyond Serbia* 472 – *Yugoslav Communist Party* 476 – *Radical-Democrat conflict and collaboration* 478 – *St Vitus's Day Constitution* 481

16. Reign of the Second King Aleksandar, 1921–1934 — 487
    Collapse of prečani-Serbian unity 487 – *The court finally breaks Pašić and the Radicals* 494 – *Assassination of Stjepan Radić* 498 – *6 January Regime* 504 – *Socio-economic change and Radical decline* 513 – *Resistance and repression under the dictatorship* 517 – *Foreign policy of the 6 January Regime* 523

17. Fascism and Court Radicalism, 1934–1939 — 527
    Serbia's far right 527 – *Milan Stojadinović and the Court Radical renaissance* 534 – *Concordat crisis* 542 – *Green shirts and new friendships* 545 – *Cvetković-Maček Agreement* 549

18. End of the Yugoslav Kingdom, 1939–1941 — 557
    Serb-nationalist backlash 557 – *Serb Cultural Club* 559 – *Reborn military conspiracy* 563 – *Return to official anti-Semitism* 566 – *Yugoslavia joins the Tripartite Pact* 569 – *Putsch of 26–27 March and government of Dušan Simović* 572 – *April War* 578

Conclusion — 585

CONTENTS

Notes 589
Select Bibliography 665
Index 671

GLOSSARY

aga:	Ottoman Muslim lord, lower in status than a bey (q.v.)
anterija:	long, embroidered, wide-sleeved Turkish gown
Arnaut:	Albanian
ayan:	senior Ottoman Muslim town official
baba:	granny
baklava:	sweet made with layered pastry, nuts and syrup eaten in (post-)Ottoman Balkans
ban:	ruler or governor of Croatia or Bosnia (-Hercegovina); governor of a banovina (q.v.)
banovina:	Yugoslav province governed by a ban (q.v.)
bashibazouk:	Ottoman irregular soldier
bastinado:	whipping of the soles of the feet
beg:	*see* bey
berat:	decree of the Sultan
bey, beg:	Ottoman Muslim lord, in particular a sipahi (q.v.)
beyler-bey:	governor of a beylerbeylik (q.v.)
beylerbeylik, eyalet, pashalik:	the largest Ottoman unit of territorial administration
beylik:	fiefdom of a bey (q.v.)
buljubaša:	commander of fifty men
čaksire:	traditional Serbian men's trousers, baggy above the knee but tight from the knee down
čarsija:	elite or bourgeoisie of a (post-)Ottoman town
chetnik:	member of an armed band; Serb guerrilla or irregular soldier
chibouk:	Turkish tobacco pipe

GLOSSARY

chiftlik:	heritable landholding owned outright
cift:	plot of arable land
Cincar:	member of the Vlach ethnic group living among Serbs
dahija:	*see* dey
danak:	local tax
desetak:	tenth; payment in kind owed by peasants to their Ottoman lord
devşirme:	blood levy of Christian boys
dey, dahija:	commander of janissaries (q.v.)
dimije:	baggy Turkish britches
dinar:	Serbian national currency
domnitor:	prince of Romania
Drang nach Osten:	drive to the east (by German imperialism)
ducat:	coin used in the Habsburg Empire
džumruk:	tariffs for produce sold at town market
eyalet:	*see* beylerbeylik
firman:	Sultan's written command
freikorps:	Austrian auxiliary soldiers
glavarina, harač:	head tax
great national parliament:	Serbian parliament convened for exceptional purposes, with about three or four times the usual number of delegates
great župan:	ruler of medieval Raška (Serbia); governor of an oblast in the Yugoslav kingdom
groschen:	monetary unit equal to one tenth of a thaler (q.v.)
gusle:	Serb one-stringed musical instrument
hacılık:	hajj; pilgrimage to Jerusalem if Orthodox or Mecca if Muslim
hadži:	denoting someone who has made the hacılık (q.v.)
hajduk:	brigand
hajj:	*see* hacılık

GLOSSARY

harač:	*see* glavarina
has:	large estate held by beyler-bey (q.v.) or sanjak-bey (q.v.)
hatt-ı şerif:	Sultan's written decree
hećimi:	traditional travelling folk healers
hodja:	Muslim cleric
hospodar:	prince or governor of Wallachia or Moldavia
internuncius:	Austrian envoy at the Ottoman court
janissary:	Ottoman infantryman originally recruited as a slave from the Christian subject population
kadi:	Islamic law judge
kadiluk:	jurisdiction of a kadi (q.v.)
kajmakam:	Ottoman governor or regent
kajmakamlije:	jurisdiction of a kajmakam (q.v.)
kapetan:	Ottoman military governor
kapetanija:	jurisdiction of a kapetan (q.v.)
kara (adj.):	black
kmet:	village headman or head of a municipality
knez:	leader of the Serb population in a given locality or territory; prince
knežina:	jurisdiction of a knez (q.v.), equivalent to srez (q.v.)
kođabaša:	Ottoman Christian notable
komitadji, komita:	guerrilla in Macedonia
komovica:	grape brandy
konak:	palace or tavern
krajina:	borderland
kuluk:	corvée; labour duty owed by a peasant to his Ottoman lord
kum:	best man at wedding; god-brother
Kutzovlach:	*see* Vlach
Magyar:	ethnic Hungarian
mekteb:	Islamic seminary

GLOSSARY

metropolitan:	senior Orthodox bishop
millet:	Christian or Jewish community enjoying autonomous rights in the Ottoman Empire
millet-başi:	head of a millet (q.v.), e.g. the Orthodox Patriarch
muezzin:	one who calls Muslims to prayer
muhafiz:	Ottoman fortress commander
müsellim, mütesellim:	Ottoman military governor of a nahija (q.v.)
nahija:	large Ottoman administrative district equivalent to okrug (q.v.)
Nemačkari:	derogatory Serbian term for Serbs from the Habsburg Empire
oblast:	large administrative district, equal to or larger than an okrug (q.v.)
obor-knez:	a knez (q.v.) with jurisdiction over a nahija (q.v.)
okrug:	large administrative district, larger than a srez (q.v.)
open city:	a city declared in wartime to be undefended, so exempt from enemy destruction under international law
opština:	municipality
pandur:	Serb soldier in Ottoman or Habsburg service; derogatory Serbian term for a policeman
pasha:	Ottoman lord or governor
pashalik:	domain of a pasha (q.v.), in particular a beylerbeylik (q.v.)
Patriarch:	head of the Orthodox Church
Porte, Sublime:	government of the Ottoman Empire (from the 'High Gate' to its premises)
posela:	social gathering of the post-Ottoman Serbian urban elite
prečani:	Serbs who come 'from across' (the Sava and Danube rivers), from present-day Vojvodina, Croatia, Hungary or Romania
raya:	Christian commoners under Ottoman rule

GLOSSARY

reis-ul-ulema:	head of the Bosnian or Yugoslav Islamic religious community
ruskoslovenski:	Russian Church Slavonic; script used by Serbian Orthodox Church
sabor:	Croatian parliament
salvare:	baggy Turkish britches
sanjak:	Ottoman province, smaller than a beylerbeylik (q.v.) but larger than a nahija (q.v.)
sanjak-bey:	Ottoman governor of a sanjak (q.v.)
scudi:	Italian coins
sejmeni:	body of Ottoman troops or gendarmes
serdar:	Serbian governor of an oblast (q.v.)
serhat:	Ottoman border region with a particular military organisation
sipahi:	Ottoman cavalryman supported by a timar (q.v.); later simply a landlord
slava:	celebration of a saint's day
slavenosrpski:	Serbian script blending non-standardised vernacular and Russian Church Slavonic
šljivovica:	plum brandy
srez:	district, smaller than an okrug (q.v.)
subaşa:	Ottoman territorial commander of a larger settlement; zaim (q.v.)
Sublime Porte:	see Porte
tekke:	dervish lodge; Sufi monastery
thaler:	monetary unit equal to ten groschen (q.v.)
timar:	fief supporting, but not owned outright by, a sipahi (q.v.)
unitarism:	the principle that the state be organised as a single unit with a uniform administration and power devolved from the centre, rather than as a federation
Ustasha:	rebel; Croat fascist
vakif:	Ottoman charitable endowment

GLOSSARY

vilayet:	eyalet (q.v.) or beylerbeylik (q.v.) from 1864
vizier:	Ottoman governor
Vlach:	member of a Latin ethnic group descended from pre-Slavic inhabitants of the Balkans
vladika:	Montenegrin prince-bishop
vojvoda:	senior Serb military leader
yataghan:	Turkish sabre
zadruga:	pre-modern Balkan rural commune based on the extended family
zaim:	commander of a group of sipahis (q.v.), holding a zeâmet (q.v.)
zeâmet:	larger timar (q.v.) held by a zaim (q.v.)
župa:	medieval South Slav fiefdom ruled by a župan (q.v.)
župan:	medieval South Slavic chieftain ruling a župa (q.v.)

LIST OF ABBREVIATIONS

CUP:	Committee of Union and Progress; Young Turks
HRSS:	Croat Republican Peasant Party
HSS:	Croat Peasant Party
JMO:	Yugoslav Muslim Organisation
JNS:	Yugoslav National Party
JRSD:	Yugoslav Radical Peasant Democracy
JRZ:	Yugoslav Radical Union
JUGORAS:	Yugoslav Workers' Union
KPJ:	Communist Party of Yugoslavia
NCO:	non-commissioned officer
ORJUNA:	Organisation of Yugoslav Nationalists
SKK:	Serb Cultural Club
SLS:	Slovene People's Party
SOE:	Special Operations Executive
SPC:	Serbian Orthodox Church
VMRO:	Internal Macedonian Revolutionary Organisation
ZBOR:	Cooperative, Combative, Association, Work

MAPS

1. **Medieval Serbia under Tsar Dusan, c. 1350**
   University of Belgrade, 1922 (https://commons.wikimedia.org/wiki/File:Map_of_the_Serbian_Empire,_University_of_Belgrade,_1922.jpg)

2. **Ottoman Empire after 1815**
   Mladifilozof, own work, https://sh.m.wikipedia.org/wiki/Datoteka:Balkans_1815.png

3. **Serbia, 1815-1833**
   Panonian, own work, https://commons.wikimedia.org/wiki/File:Serbia1817.png

4. **Serbia, 1833-1878**
   Panonian, own work, https://commons.wikimedia.org/wiki/File:Serbia1817.png

5. **Serbia and Vojvodina, 1848**
   Panonian, own work, https://en.m.wikipedia.org/wiki/File:Serbia_and_Vojvodina_1848.png

6. **Great Bulgaria of the Treaty of San Stefano, 1878**
   Pakko, own work, https://commons.wikimedia.org/wiki/File:Sanstefanska_Bulgaria.png

7. **Balkans after the Treaty of Berlin, 1878**
   J. G. Bartholomew: A literary & historical atlas of Europe, 1910, https://commons.wikimedia.org/wiki/File:Balkans_1878.png

8. **Serbia, 1878-1912**
   Pakko, own work, https://commons.wikimedia.org/wiki/File:Principality_of_Serbia_in_1878_EN.png

9. **Disputed and undisputed zones of Macedonia, 1912-1913**
   Avidius, own work, https://commons.wikimedia.org/wiki/File:Uncontested_zone.JPG

MAPS

10. **Balkan Wars, 1912-1913**
    Report of the International Commission To Inquire into the Causes and Conduct of the Balkan Wars, 1914, https://commons.wikimedia.org/wiki/File:Balkan_Wars_Boundaries.jpg

11. **Serbia after the Balkan Wars, 1913**
    Panonian, own work, https://commons.wikimedia.org/wiki/File:Serbia1913.png

12. **Austria-Hungary and the Balkan States, 1914**
    Niusereset, own work, Political map of Europe 1914 (cropped), https://commons.wikimedia.org/wiki/File:Europe_1914_(coloured).png

13. **Central Powers' conquest of Serbia, 1915**
    Aeengath, own work, https://commons.wikimedia.org/wiki/File:Serbian_Campaign_1915.jpg

14. **Lands of the Kingdom of Serbs, Croats and Slovenes, 1920**
    Panonian, own work, https://commons.wikimedia.org/wiki/File:Scs_kingdom_provinces_1920_1922_en.png

15. **Oblasts of the Kingdom of Serbs, Croats and Slovenes, 1922**
    Panonian, own work, https://commons.wikimedia.org/w/index.php?curid=27887913

16. **Banovinas of the Kingdom of Yugoslavia, 1931-1939**
    NordNordWest, own work, Banovinas of the Kingdom of Yugoslavia 1929-1931, https://creativecommons.org/licenses/by-sa/3.0/de/legalcode

17. **Banovina of Croatia and proposed Serb Country, 1939-1941**
    Panonian, own work, https://commons.wikimedia.org/wiki/File:Yugoslavia_proposed_banovinas_1939_1941.png

18. **Axis conquest of Yugoslavia, 1941**
    US Army, November 1953, https://commons.wikimedia.org/wiki/File:Operation25yu.jpg

19. **Axis dismemberment of Yugoslavia, 1941**
    Direktor, own work, https://commons.wikimedia.org/wiki/File:Axis_occupation_of_Yugoslavia_1941-43.png

ACKNOWLEDGEMENTS

This book has been many years in the making. The funding for the research originated with a British Academy Postdoctoral Fellowship in 2001 and a British Academy Small Research Grant in 2005; I should like to thank the British Academy for their support and apologise for the slowness in bringing the project to fruition. The writing and research began at Robinson College and the Faculty of History, University of Cambridge, and were completed at the Sarajevo School of Science and Technology, and I should like to thank these institutions for their support, in particular Professor Ejup Ganić and the late Jack Lewis, Baron Lewis of Newnham. My late mentor and friend, Professor Ivo Banac, was tireless in his support, and I should like to thank him and express my sorrow that he never saw the book in print. The Institute for Contemporary History in Belgrade was generous in its support and allowing me the use of its space and library, and I should like to thank in particular my colleagues Ljubodrag Dimić, the late Petar Kačavenda, Momčilo Pavlović and Nikola B. Popović, and Branka Srdanović, Dragić and Mlađa. I should like to thank Belgrade's Archive of Yugoslavia, Military Archive, Historical Archive of Belgrade and Josip Broz Tito Archive and their staff for making their collections available to me, though much of the material I gathered in these archives will only be used for the sequel to the current volume. I should like to thank Sonja Biserko, Branka Panić, the late Latinka Perović and the late Olga Popović-Obradović for their support and advice during my research in Belgrade. I have benefited in the course of my research in Belgrade from conversations with colleagues, including Milivoj Bešlin, Mile Bjelajac, Đorđe Borozan, the late Slavoljub Cvetković, Smiljana Đurović, Ranka Gašić, Predrag Marković, the late Olivera Milosavljević, Branka Prpa, Mira Radojević and Dubravka Stojanović. I should like to thank the online bookseller Knjizara.com for invaluable assistance in providing most of the books used to produce this volume. I should like to thank Michael Dwyer and Hurst Publishers for their willingness to publish this lengthy book and their patience in awaiting the completed manuscript. Three anonymous reviewers provided thoughtful and constructive comments that improved the manuscript and for which I am grateful. Above all, very special thanks go to Sarah Correia, Nicola Gollan, Branka Magaš and Quintin Hoare for their intellectual input and emotional support throughout.

1

INTRODUCTION

RISE AND FALL OF THE FIRST MODERN SERBIA

Serbia is a country that has inspired exceptional intellectual interest. It was centrally involved in the crises marking both the start and the end of Europe's twentieth century: the outbreak of World War I in 1914 and the Wars of Yugoslav Succession beginning in 1991. Yet this interest has not translated into a large English-language historiography of the country. There is no substantial general English-language history of Serbia; existing short histories provide only an introductory overview.[1] The best introduction to modern Serbian history for an English-language reader is Michael Boro Petrovich's two-volume *History of Modern Serbia*, now over forty-five years old and covering the period only up to 1918.[2] It is beautifully written and acquaints the reader unforgettably with the main events and characters in modern Serbian history, though it left the present author still wondering how to explain it. A more recent attempt by a foreign author is Holm Sundhaussen's *A History of Serbia from the 19th to the 21st Centuries*, published first in German in 2007 and in Serbian translation the following year.[3] It contains some valuable observations but also significant factual errors and omissions. Most recently, there is Dejan Djokić's *A Concise History of Serbia*, published in 2023. It successfully identifies many interesting historical details and key secondary sources but appears overwhelmed by them; its narrative has little structure or coherent analysis and also significant errors and omissions.[4] For example, both Sundaussen and Djokić barely touch upon the era of King Aleksandar of Serbia (r. 1889–1903), when the country not only acquired an effective modern army but also witnessed the birth of the military-praetorian phenomenon that conditioned the subsequent four decades of its history. Neither author carried out or digested sufficient research for such a monumental project.

Most serious research and writing on modern Serbian history is, and has always been, the work of Serbian historians writing in Serbian. The reader of Serbian can choose from numerous works providing an introduction to modern Serbian history, often extending to the pre-modern period and to the history of the entire Serb people (i.e. including the Serbs outside Serbia). They range from short summaries to weighty multi-author, multi-volume collections.⁵ The quality of these works is variable but generally high. The present author does not seek to rival the efforts of such Serbian historians. Instead, my aim has been to synthesise as much as possible of their findings so as to transmit them to the English-language reader, while providing a foreign historian's alternative perspective. This Serbian-language historiography is vast, and attempting to master it has taken me many years. A further difficulty is that until 1919 Serbia used the Julian rather than the Gregorian calendar (the two have a disparity of 12–13 days in this period), but not all its historians say which calendar they are using. The present author has used the Gregorian calendar but noted dates in the Julian where necessary.

This book aims to explain what were the principal determinants of Serbia's political evolution and its principal long-term political trends. It examines the period 1804–1941: from the start of the First Serbian Uprising, which began the process of constructing the first modern Serbia, to the fall of this state—in its extended, Yugoslav form—through conquest by Nazi Germany. The People's Republic of Serbia, which arose from the Communist-led revolution in Yugoslavia during and immediately after World War II and evolved into the Serbia of today, was a state reconstituted by new forces with new rules, so should be considered effectively a second modern Serbia requiring a separate volume, although the question of how much continuity there was between the first and second modern Serbias is fascinating.

The period 1804–1941 constitutes a unity, insofar as the birth of modern Serbian statehood after 1804 set forces in motion that played themselves out over the next century and a third, culminating in the catastrophe of 1941. This catastrophe was not predestined by Serbia's internal nature: Nazi Germany's readiness and ability to conquer such countries was, from Serbia's perspective, a historical accident. Yet internal forces at work in Serbia led to not just one but two such catastrophes of defeat and foreign occupation; the first being Serbia's conquest by the Central Powers of Germany, Austria-Hungary and Bulgaria during World War I. This was no coincidence: to be dragged into one world war by one's internal conflicts may be regarded as a misfortune, but to be dragged into both, as Lady Bracknell might have noted, suggests something more. This book challenges the view prevalent in the West that modern Serbia's history has been driven primarily by nationalism and expansionism, and instead interprets these as subordinate to conditions and conflicts within the country. Serbia's nationalism and expansionism were less about the strategies of Serbian leaders, politicians and intellectuals in relation to the outside world and more about their mutual power struggles and conflicting visions of what it meant to be Serb. That is why they proved so self-destructive.

Serbia was wiped off the map of Europe by its conquest by the Ottoman Empire in the fifteenth century, which destroyed not only its statehood and borders but its native, Christian elite, turning the Serbian nation into a nation of peasants. Serbia re-

INTRODUCTION

emerged following uprisings against the Ottomans in 1804–1815 and was formally recognised by the Sultan as an autonomous state within the empire in 1830. This reborn Serbia was built upon the limited institutions permitted the Serbs under Ottoman rule, and its founder and first prince, Miloš Obrenović, the first of five monarchs of the Obrenović dynasty, resembled an Ottoman pasha in his style of rule. The new state supported itself by taxing the peasants, who made up most of its population, in much the same way that the Ottomans had taxed them, consequently it was widely perceived by the peasants as embodying not so much national liberation as the continuation of Ottoman oppression. Serbia's standing army was created less to defend it from foreign foes than to keep its peasant population down. As the youthful Serbian elite increasingly adopted the culture of central and western Europe, it catalysed the rise of a populist nationalism directed against its oppression, exploitation and seemingly alien values. The division extended to foreign policy, for the monarchical regime looked to the Habsburg Austrian Empire, later Austria-Hungary, while the populist nationalists eventually looked to Russia.

The populist-nationalist reaction eventually coalesced in the 1870s and 1880s as the People's Radical Party under Nikola Pašić, which formed a counter-elite opposing the original Serbian elite. Considering themselves the only true representative of the Serbian peasant nation, the Radicals regarded the Serbian state as alien and parasitical and other parties as unnational and illegitimate. But though this Radical counter-elite won the loyalty of the overwhelming majority of Serbians, it could not overthrow the old elite headed by the Obrenović monarch controlling the army. Instead, from the second half of the 1880s, the court began to co-opt the Radical counter-elite, leading to the gradual establishment of a synthetic or composite elite, whereby monarchs came to rule in partnership with the Radicals or factions of them. This was a partnership of an authoritarian monarchy and an anti-pluralist party that left little space for constitutional political alternatives. Serbia adopted its first constitutions in 1835 and 1838, a form of controlled parliamentary government with its constitution of 1869, and something closer to formal liberal democracy with its constitutions of 1889 and 1903, but the new state lacked long-established constitutional norms and procedures that commanded respect and obedience. This meant the political struggle did not remain within constitutional bounds but would bend or break Serbia's institutions. Serbia's frequent, usually extra-constitutional changes of ruler, dynasty and constitution during the nineteenth and early twentieth centuries, for which it was notorious, reflected rather than caused its internal divisions. The institution whose warping by politics from the 1890s would prove most fateful was the army.

The emerging synthetic elite of court and Radicals from the 1890s engendered opponents 'on the left', in the form of purist or 'Independent' Radicals opposed to any alliance with the court, and 'on the right', in the form of the most authoritarian, anti-Radical, Austrophile elements of the old elite. These two groups would, somewhat paradoxically, eventually coalesce into a counter-synthesis, united by opposition to the regime. Consequently, in 1903, a clique of army officers, allied to anti-Radical hardline politicians yet fired by the Independents' denunciations of royal 'tyranny', murdered Serbia's last Obrenović ruler in a grisly putsch that restored to the throne the rival Karađorđević dynasty. Yet the power struggle continued: some of the putschist officers sought to control Serbian political life after 1903 and resisted government by the Radicals, eventually constituting themselves as a political-militarist organisation known as the Black Hand. Its power struggle with the Radicals extended to the field of foreign policy, contributing decisively to the outbreak of war between Serbia and Austria-Hungary in 1914, which began World War I.

Serbia emerged as an autonomous state in 1830 and became formally independent in 1878, but most ethnic Serbs as well as other South Slavs whom its elites perceived either as Serbs or as kindred peoples—Croats, Muslim Bosniaks, Slovenes, Montenegrins, Macedonians, Bulgarians—inhabited lands still under foreign rule, either Habsburg or Ottoman. Increasingly after 1844, with Ilija Garašanin's famous 'Plan', and especially after 1858, when a dynastic revolution catalysed by liberal nationalism triumphed, the goal of Serbia's princes, kings, ministers and politicians was expansion and unification with some or most of these lands, the precise combination varying. Serbia's internal conflict superimposed itself upon this national mission. Eventually, after the 1903 putsch, it manifested itself in a difference between what could, to simplify somewhat, be referred to as a 'Great Serbian' and a 'Yugoslav' strategy. This was not so much a difference in the lands to be unified, which tended to be broadly the same in both cases: those inhabited by Serbs, Croats, Muslim Bosniaks and Montenegrins plus part of Macedonia, with the Slovenes sometimes included. It was rather a difference over whether to impose Serbia's political order on the unified state, as Pašić's more conservative or 'Old' Radicals wished, or whether to submerge Serbia in a new, 'Yugoslav' whole for the purpose of overturning this order, as the more liberal Independents wished. The political opponents of Pašić and the Old Radicals, above all the Independents, sought allies among the South Slavs in Austria-Hungary to counter their hegemony in Serbia. Thus, as World War I drew to a close and the South Slav lands moved toward unification, and particularly after the common state (Yugoslavia) was established in 1918 under Serbia's leadership, Serbia's political factions co-opted political factions in the lands joined to Serbia—Montenegro, Vojvodina, Bosnia-Hercegovina, Dalmatia, Croatia-Slavonia and Slovenia—and the Serbian power struggle continued much as before.

The Yugoslavia established in 1918 was a centralised monarchy on the Serbian model, essentially an expanded Serbia under the same Karađorđević dynasty. The creation of a much larger political arena for Serbia's power struggle, with many more competing factions, weakened the position of Serbia's parties—Radicals and Democrats (heirs to the Independent Radicals)—and rejuvenated the monarch's power, which had been crippled by the 1903 putsch. Yugoslavia's ruler, the Prince

INTRODUCTION

Regent later King Aleksandar Karađorđević, successfully played Yugoslavia's mutually hostile factions off against each other to increase his own power, breaking Pašić and the Radicals and eventually establishing a royal dictatorship in 1929 that reconstituted the authoritarian regime of his Obrenović predecessors. He sought to bend Serbia and Yugoslavia as a whole to his rule by building a new regime from co-opted factions of Radicals, Democrats and others, and promoting a homogeneous 'Yugoslav' national identity in place of the narrower identities of the Serbs, Croats and his other South Slav subjects, which were to be suppressed. Yet this merely meant that the decisive reaction in Serbia against the regime would take a form that was both Serb nationalist and extra-parliamentary.

The Karađorđević regime liberalised somewhat following Aleksandar's assassination in 1934, but it remained a form of controlled parliamentarism on Serbia's traditional model. It was finally overthrown in 1941 in a putsch by largely the same combination that had brought down the Obrenović regime in 1903: praetorian army officers from the Black Hand tradition encouraged by politicians and other civilians from the anti-Radical tradition. As the 1903 putsch unleashed forces that dragged Serbia into World War I, so the 1941 putsch hurled Serbia into World War II, ending the life of the first Yugoslavia and, by extension, the first modern Serbia. The army, supposed to defend the country from foreign enemies, for the second time in 27 years was the cause of its conquest by foreign enemies. For all that the first Yugoslavia's failure is frequently blamed on its national conflict, particularly between Serbs and Croats, the putsch that triggered its destruction involved Serb putschists from Serbia overthrowing a regime dominated by Serbs from Serbia. It represented the latest blow in a struggle predating Yugoslavia—the outcome of a long-term historical process that this book traces.

This is a history of the first modern Serbia, meaning the state that arose in 1804–1815 and the country and people it encompassed. It is primarily a political history, in which social, economic and cultural developments are discussed to provide context to political developments, while developments in art, literature and science are mostly outside its scope. The history of the Serbs outside Serbia and of the other South Slav lands is considered only insofar as it impacts upon the history of Serbia. The Yugoslav state that existed between 1918 and 1941 was effectively an extension of Serbia, but the focus remains on the political classes, institutions and territory of pre-1912 Serbia and on their relationship to territories that were in some sense 'Serbian' or 'Serb' by virtue of conquest, annexation or ethnicity, over and above being Yugoslav (Macedonia, Kosovo, Montenegro, Vojvodina, Bosnia-Hercegovina). In general, the adjective or noun 'Serbian' (srbijanski, Srbijanac, Srbijanka) pertains to the land of Serbia and its inhabitants while 'Serb' (srpski, Srbin, Srpkinja) pertains to the Serb people irrespective of land; for example, Serbs from Bosnia were 'Serb' but not 'Serbian'. That these terminological distinctions are not absolute is reflective of the blurred borders of the reality. The book is divided into three parts corresponding to three periods in the history of the first modern Serbia: the first part concerns Serbia as an autonomous principality within the Ottoman Empire, the second the independent Principallity and Kingdom of Serbia, and the third Serbia within the Yugoslav kingdom. Each of these periods was launched by an armed struggle against a foreign enemy with which the corresponding part of the book begins.

Serbia is a country with which I fell in love during my PhD research and in whose capital city I lived for over two years, from the end of 1998 until the start of 2001, including, for over a month, during its bombardment by NATO in 1999. Too often today, the history of Serbia is reduced to the background to the Wars of Yugoslav Succession in the 1990s. I hope that, while this book may throw some light on those wars, it will also contribute to a better understanding of the country by looking at history that is distant from those wars. The reader familiar with contemporary Serbia may recognise, in this history, facts about the country that remain true today: a remarkably egalitarian culture; a popular suspicion of state authority; a socialist tradition that embraces rather than opposes nationalism. I seek to explain such phenomena. But this is also a story of a world that is lost. And the resulting sense of loss is central to the story.

PART I

SERBIA IN THE OTTOMAN EMPIRE

1

SERBIA AND THE SERBS BEFORE THE NINETEENTH CENTURY

Medieval Serbia arose with the Roman Empire's decline and the accompanying migrations of so-called barbarians—Slavs and Serbs—into Roman territory. It rose to become the most powerful state in the Balkans by the first half of the fourteenth century, then declined, finally disappearing from the map of Europe when conquered by the Ottoman Empire in the mid-fifteenth. The modern Serbian state that arose in the early nineteenth century was not straightforwardly the continuation of medieval Serbia, but the latter left a foundation on which the former could be built. The long Ottoman occupation added a layer to this foundation, decisively shaping the character of the eventual modern nation-state.

Rise of medieval Serbia

Before the arrival of the Romans, the northern and central Balkans had been primarily inhabited by peoples referred to in ancient sources as Illyrians, Dacians and Thracians, themselves heterogeneous groups. The land that eventually became Serbia was a borderland between the closely related Illyrians and Dacians. Other peoples migrated through the Balkans, in particular Celts during the fourth and third centuries BC. Rome's conquest of the Balkans, beginning in the third century BC, romanised the languages of the Balkan peoples, except for the forerunners of modern Albanians and Greeks. Roman veterans settled in the Balkans, adding to the genetic mix.[1] The Romans in 378 were heavily defeated at the Battle of Adrianople by the Goths, who were consequently permitted to remain in the Roman Balkans. Goths were one of several 'barbarian' peoples to conquer the Roman city of Singidunum, the future Belgrade, in the following centuries; others included Huns, Sarmatians, Gepids and Avars.[2] The Goths were finally expelled from the Balkans by Emperor Justinian (r. 527–565). They, too, may have added to the region's genetic mix.[3]

Justinian launched major wars to reconquer territories lost to 'barbarian' invaders, above all in North Africa and Italy and including the city of Rome itself.

This exhausted the empire and diverted resources away from the defence of the Balkans, enabling their invasion by barbarian peoples from further north that copied the Romans' own military techniques.[4] These included Turkic Avars, who left traces of their presence in the region's nomenclature, but the most significant were Slavs, who began arriving in the sixth century AD. Whereas the empire, in its prime, could Romanise 'barbarian' peoples like the Illyrians, Thracians and Gauls, in its decline it could not do so with the Slavs.[5] Consequently, the lands today comprising Slovenia, Croatia, Bosnia-Hercegovina, Serbia, Montenegro, Macedonia and Bulgaria acquired the Slavic languages spoken by most of their inhabitants.

The original Serbs were not part of the first Slavic invasion; along with a related people, the Croats, they migrated to the territory of the future Yugoslavia in the seventh century AD, during Emperor Heraclius's reign (610–641). Like the Croats, they may originally have been an Iranian people that assumed leadership of part of the Slavs and migrated with them to the Balkans, eventually being assimilated by them but bequeathing them their name. Another Slavic group fell under a Turkic people, the Bulgars, which they likewise assimilated, so that the three South Slav nations that eventually emerged—Croats, Serbs and Bulgarians—may have all derived their names from non-Slavic peoples which originally ruled them. The origins of the Serb name are disputed, however: scholars have variously speculated that it may have derived from a word 'ser' (pl. 'ser-b') in a Caucasian language meaning 'man' or 'people'; or from an Indo-European root ('ser', 'serv') meaning 'guard' or 'protect', relating in particular to herds or flocks of domesticated animals; or to the Slavic root 'srb-', 'sbf', related to the drinking of fluids, hence 'those who sucked the same maternal milk', hence 'members of the same family or tribal community'.[6] According to the mid-tenth-century historical account of Emperor Constantine VII Porphyrogenitus (r. 913–959), the Serbs originally dwelt north of the Balkans, adjacent to Francia, land of the Franks. 'But when two brothers succeeded their father in the rule of Serbia, one of them, taking one half of the folk, claimed the protection of Heraclius, the emperor of the Romans, and the same emperor Heraclius received him and gave him a place in the province of Thessalonica to settle in, namely Serbia, which from that time has acquired this denomination.'[7] While historians do not accept all of Constantine's account, traces of the presence of those original Serbs survive today in place names in eastern Germany and Poland and most notably in the name of the Sorbs, a small Slavic minority inhabiting the region of Lusatia, in Germany adjacent to Poland.[8] Though Constantine referred to 'Serbia', this name was only slowly adopted by its rulers and people.

The Serbs settled in the area between the Lim River in the east and the Pliva River in the west, an area later known as 'Baptised Serbia', roughly corresponding to present-day eastern and central Bosnia, eastern Hercegovina, western Serbia, southern Dalmatia, Montenegro and the Sanjak.[9] Locally, power among the Serbs was divided between clans under chieftains—župans—whose territories were called župas. As some župans dominated others, they left to them or granted them lands and prerogatives in exchange for recognition of their authority and military support. Thus was Serbian feudalism founded.[10] The Serbs did not initially form a single state; the dominant župans recognised Roman (Byzantine) overlordship, so that in the mid-ninth century the principalities of Duklja, Hum and Raška were established, roughly corresponding to modern Montenegro, Hercegovina and Serbia. Raška emerged from eastern Baptised Serbia, centred on the town of Ras (probably located near the town of Novi Pazar in modern Serbia's Sanjak region), during the first half of the ninth century under a prince (župan or knez) called Vlastimir, in response to the threat from Bulgaria, as a counterweight to which the Byzantines encouraged its unity.[11]

The pre-Slavic, Romance-speaking population retreated to the mountainous interior to escape the Slavic invaders, eventually acquiring the name Vlachs. They based their society on animal husbandry and were gradually slavicised over centuries while bequeathing the Slavs some cultural traits, such as inhabiting stone houses. As the historian Vladimir Ćorović notes, 'the Vlach animal husbandmen intermingled completely with the Serbs'.[12] Eventually, the Ottoman conquest from the fifteenth century would in turn drive Serbs into the mountainous regions to which the Vlachs had previously retreated, outnumbering them and mostly completing their assimilation.[13] The modern populations of the South Slav lands are thus syntheses of their pre-Slavic, Slavic and other inhabitants, though on account of their languages they have been referred to in modern times simply as 'South Slavic'. The ethnic heterogeneity and chequered history of barbarian invasion bequeathed to Balkan feudalism a diverse nomenclature: the term 'župan' may have derived from the Huns; the title of Bosnia's ruler, 'ban', from the Avars; and the Serbian word for king, 'kralj', from Charlemagne.[14]

The Byzantine Empire in the last third of the ninth century reaffirmed its authority over the eastern Adriatic coast, which catalysed the interior's conversion to Christianity.[15] The Byzantine missionaries Constantine and Methodius, subsequently canonised as SS Cyril and Methodius, undertook in 863 a mission to Great Moravia, to Serbia's north, at its prince's request, aimed at resisting the Frankish Roman clergy's spiritual influence. To this end, they founded a literary language, today called Old Church Slavonic, probably based on the Slavic dialect of the hinterland of Thessalonika, their home town, which they bolstered with Greek words and grammatical forms. They devised a new alphabet, the Glagolitic, to enable them to translate the Bible and other religious texts into this language. This facilitated the conversion of the Serbs; Raška was Christian from about 870. The bishopric of Ras was founded soon after 871.[16] Somewhat later, following the establishment of Bulgaria's capital in Preslav in 893, scholars there devised the Cyrillic alphabet, based on the Greek uncial script adapted to the needs of Slavic.[17] Named after St Cyril, this emerged as the principal Serbian, Bulgarian and Russian alphabet. With the Eastern

SERBIA

and Western Christian churches definitely separating in 1054, Serbia fell firmly on the Eastern, Byzantine side.

Powerful Bulgaria made Raška its vassal in 897 and fully conquered it by 924. But Byzantine–Bulgarian conflict facilitated its escape from Bulgarian domination. Following the death of Bulgaria's strong ruler Simeon I in 927, Raška reasserted its independence under Časlav Klonimirović, accepting Byzantine overlordship. In the 930s, it extended its authority to the River Sava and began Serbianising the adjacent territory immediately to its south.[18] Traditional historiography claims Časlav's rule extended also over Bosnia, based on Constantine Porphyrogenitus's account, though this claim has been challenged.[19] Nevertheless, following Časlav's death in 960, Duklja emerged as the leading Serb state. The Pope recognised its ruler Mihailo as king in 1077.[20] Byzantium's conflict with Duklja allowed Raška to escape Duklja's domination and emerge as the most powerful Serb state by the eleventh century's end under Great Župan Vukan, centred on the area around modern Novi Pazar.

In the twelfth century, frequent warfare between Hungary and Byzantium permitted Raška, as a borderland, to achieve some independence. In 1165, Emperor Manuel I Comnenus (r. 1143–1180) arrested his vassal Desa, great župan of Raška, for collaboration with Hungary. He replaced him in 1168 with a relative of previous great župans, Tihomir, required to rule together with his brothers Sracimir, Miroslav and Nemanja. Each ruled part of the territory, with Nemanja ruling in eastern Raška, probably in the Toplica region. Nemanja attacked Tihomir's domain in 1169 and killed him in battle at Pantino, near Zvečan in present-day northern Kosovo, after which his other brothers recognised him as great župan of Raška. Encouraged by Venice and supported by Hungary, Nemanja then warred against Manuel in 1172 to free himself from Byzantium's domination, but his support from his allies collapsed and he was forced to surrender: 'he came and approached the tribunal, with head uncovered and arms bare to the elbow, his feet unshod; a rope haltered his neck and a sword in his hand. He offered himself to the emperor for whatever treatment he desired.' Captured and paraded by Manuel in his triumphal procession in Constantinople, he was nevertheless released and returned to Raška.[21]

Following Manuel's death in 1180, Nemanja asserted his independence from Byzantium, exploiting civil conflict there and allied with Hungary. He expanded his domain over such territories as the plains of Kosovo including Prizren, part of northern Macedonia including Skopje, and the coastal towns of Kotor, Ulcinj and Bar in present-day Montenegro. He also expanded north-east along the River Morava and established Niš as his capital by 1188. An attack on Ragusa (Dubrovnik) in 1185 failed, but Zeta (Duklja) was conquered by 1189 and his son Vukan appointed to rule it, while his brother Miroslav was appointed to rule Hum. This period also witnessed Bulgaria's successful revolt against Byzantium and restoration of its independence, recognised in 1188, after which Raška's independence was recognised in 1190. Although Byzantium defeated Nemanja in battle in 1191 or 1192 and forced him to acknowledge its supreme authority, Raška remained effectively independent. This was confirmed following the Latin conquest of Constantinople in 1204, which precipitated the collapse of Byzantine power in the Balkans. The fact that Nemanja's state was founded in rebellion against Byzantium conditioned its expansion for the subsequent century and a half: southwards, into Byzantine territory, ultimately including the part inhabited by Albanians and Greeks, instead of westwards into ethnically kindred Bosnia, which was consequently lost to Serbian statehood—permanently as it turned out.[22]

Nemanja abdicated in 1196 in favour of his son Stefan Nemanjić, taking monastic vows along with his younger son Ratko, who adopted the name Sava. Travelling to Mt Athos in present-day Greece, Nemanja was granted the Hilandar monastery there by the emperor and, along with Sava, restored and expanded it, making it the principal Serbian cultural centre.[23] Nemanja died in 1199 on Mt Athos and was canonised the following year as St Simeon, known as the 'myrrh-bearer' in the cult established around him. His relics were returned to Serbia, to the monastery of Studenica which he had founded. Both his sons, Stefan and Sava, authored lives of St Simeon; Sava's described him as 'our lord and autocrat, and ruler of the entire Serbian land'. These two lives formed the basis for the cult of Nemanja, viewed as having founded a 'dynasty of sacred roots'. This precluded further partitioning of Raška between the ruling family's members, making possible its subsequent rise.[24] Zeta, under first Vukan, then his son, sought independence from Raška. Vukan in 1202 actually deposed Stefan and himself assumed the title of great župan of Raška. In return for Hungary's support, he recognised its suzerainty. This foreshadowed the rivalry between Serbia's and Montenegro's dynasties in modern times. But Stefan subsequently regained Raška and by 1216 Zeta was fully integrated into it, its separatism crushed.[25] Meanwhile, the conflict between Vukan and Stefan enabled Bulgaria to attack Serbia in 1203 and occupy Niš, Skopje and Prizren.

Stefan was granted the title of autocrat by the Pope in 1217. He called himself 'First-Crowned', hence was viewed subsequently as Serbia's first king, though this was disputed by Hungary's king, who had claimed the title since 1202. To affirm Raška's independence, Sava succeeded in 1219 in persuading the Orthodox Patriarch to make him primate and archbishop of an autocephalous Serbian Orthodox archbishopric, freeing Raška from the authority of the archbishopric of Ohrid, which was then rebelling against the Patriarch. The Patriarch was in a weak position, having been expelled to Nicaea in Anatolia following the Latin conquest of Constantinople, so was ready to recognise Serbian autocephaly in return for the Serbian church's recognition of his supremacy, which boosted the prestige of both parties. The arrangement militated against any Catholic influence in Serbia and consolidated the Serb identity in Stefan's lands, including Zeta and Hum.[26] Sava established his see at the Žiča monastery near Kraljevo, whose construction Stefan had begun. The establishment of an autocephalous Serbian archbishopric facilitated expansion of the Orthodox Church's authority westward at the expense of the Papacy's, up to the River Neretva and the Adriatic coast.

Confluence of state and church in Serbia consolidated foundations for the Serb nation. To achieve his soul's salvation, each Serbian king built at least one monastery church and tended to be generous in his endowments to the church. The church reciprocated by supporting the dynasty, endowing it with a sacred aura greater than that of any other royal dynasty in Eastern Europe.[27] The name 'Serbia' itself was first used in the country in relation to Sava's burial at the Mileševa monastery in 1237.[28] Because Serbia before Sava had been a borderland between the Catholic and Orthodox churches, the Serbian church did not consolidate itself along the lines of either and its hierarchy remained underdeveloped; it never attained the economic power or independence from the state of its counterparts elsewhere in Europe. This militated against any church–state conflict, consolidated the church's 'national' character and ensured its subordination to the dynasty. It also permitted it to remain closer to the pagan-influenced folkloric Christianity of the ordinary people, who consequently identified readily with it. It was not the Serbian Orthodox Church that determined the Serbian nation's character, but the nation that determined the church's character.[29]

Stefan First-Crowned's title was 'Crowned first king of all Serb lands, Dioklitije [Duklja] and Travunija [Trebinje] and Dalmatia and Zahumlje [Hum]'; his son Vladislav, upon becoming king, bore the title 'King of all Raška's lands and Dioklitije and Dalmatia and Travunija and Zahumlje', suggesting that 'Serb lands' and 'Raška's lands' were initially viewed by Serbia's rulers as coterminous. Serb nationhood in Raška's lands was consolidated in 1219, when Sava founded eight bishoprics—Moravica, Toplica, Raška, Dabar, Hvosno, Hum, Zeta, Budimlja—roughly corresponding to modern central and southern Serbia, Sanjak, northern Kosovo, eastern Hercegovina and Montenegro.[30] The Serb national character of these lands consequently largely survived the medieval period, Ottoman conquest and, to an extent, up to the present. Conversely, in Bosnia, where members of the original Serb people had settled from the seventh century but which was not encompassed by Stefan's state or Sava's church, the Serb identity died out by the late Middle Ages.[31] The modern Bosnian Serb identity arose not from primordial medieval ethnicity but from expansion of the Serbian church into Bosnia following the Ottoman conquest.

Serbia underwent economic growth from the mid-thirteenth until well into the fourteenth century thanks to the opening of silver mines in the region of the upper Lim River. Under Uroš I, king from 1243, old family appanages like Zeta and Hum lost all remnants of their former autonomy.[32] Uroš dropped all reference to Hum, Zeta and Travunija from his title and called himself simply 'King of all Serbian land and the Coast'. To centralise his realm, he did not create appanages for his sons.[33] Yet Serbian feudalism at its height was characterised by powerful nobles; without a strong monarch, the state was prone to degenerate into squabbling between them.

SERBIA AND THE SERBS BEFORE THE NINETEENTH CENTURY

Serfs meanwhile enjoyed security of hereditary tenure of their plots, shaping the Serbian peasantry's identity. Meanwhile, a population of Vlachs inhabited pastoral villages in feudal Serbia; enjoying a nomadic or quasi-nomadic life, they remained free of feudal obligations and had their status legally recognised.[34] Other minorities with recognised legal statuses included Ragusan merchants, Saxon miners and Albanian shepherds. Indeed, in medieval Serbia, which from the late twelfth century included present-day Kosovo, Serbs and Albanians were not wholly distinct and widely intermarried.[35] Uroš was overthrown in 1276 by his son Stefan Dragutin, who became king but who was then himself forced to abdicate in 1282 and replaced as king by his younger brother Stefan Milutin.

The city of Belgrade—'White City'—is first mentioned in the historical records in 878 under that name, which it probably received from the limestone used originally to build it which, particularly in sunlight, appeared white. It came under a Serb ruler for the first time in 1284, when along with other territories it was passed to former Serbian king Stefan Dragutin by his father-in-law, Hungary's king. Dragutin now became king of Srem (Syrmia) and Hungary's vassal.[36] Milutin and Dragutin gained mastery of Braničevo some years later, thereby moving the border of the Serbian-ruled lands to the Sava and Danube rivers. Milutin also expanded southwards to establish Serbian control of northern Macedonia and, by marrying a daughter of the Byzantine emperor in 1299, was permitted to keep these conquests as dowry. Milutin by 1315–1317 had subordinated Dragutin's Serbian lands and occupied the Adriatic coast as far south as Durrës, making him the most powerful ruler in the Balkans.[37] He oriented Serbia much more toward Byzantium, copied its institutions and court life, and undertook an ambitious church-building process, laying the foundations for a Serbian empire.[38] Following Dragutin's death, Belgrade came under the rule of Serbia itself for the first time in 1316, though only briefly, as Milutin tried to claim all his deceased brother's lands.[39] Belgrade remained a contested border outpost between Serbia and Hungary.

Milutin died in 1321 and, following a brief civil war between his sons, was succeeded in 1322 by one of them, Stefan Dečanski, whose name derives from the Visoko Dečani monastery in present-day Kosovo, which he built. Dynastic conflict continued, weakening the kingdom and permitting neighbouring Bosnia to annex the Serbian part of Hum in 1326, laying the basis for the eventual Bosnia-Hercegovina. Dečanski and his son Stefan Dušan crushingly defeated the Bulgarians at the Battle of Velbužd on 28 July 1330, ensuring Serbian control of Macedonia and pre-eminence in the Balkans more generally. But the following year Stefan Dečanski was overthrown, apparently due to his unwillingness to war against Byzantium, which alienated the warlike nobility.[40] Under Dušan, who replaced him as king as Stefan Uroš IV Dušan (r. 1331–1355), medieval Serbia reached its apogee. Exploiting civil war in Byzantium, Dušan, who focused on southern expansion, conquered the rest of Macedonia, almost all present-day Albania and most of mainland Greece,

15

plus part of present-day Bulgaria. His empire was multinational, above all Serbian, Greek and Albanian; different laws applied in his Serbian and Greek lands while the Albanians were largely left under their chiefs to manage their lands according to their customs. The army he used to conquer northern Greece was mostly Albanians; he also employed German mercenaries.[41]

Dušan was an ambitious state- and empire-builder. He added Albania to his title in 1340, becoming 'King of Serbia, Albania and the Coast'. Three years later, he also proclaimed himself king of the Romans.[42] He convened in 1346, at his capital of Skopje, an assembly of senior Orthodox clergy, including the Bulgarian Patriarch, which promoted the Serbian primate—the Archbishop of Peć—to Patriarch of Serbia. Simultaneously, several bishoprics were promoted to metropolitanates (including Zeta, laying another foundation stone of modern Montenegro). To copy and rival Byzantium's emperor, Dušan then had himself crowned 'Emperor of the Serbs and Greeks' by the Serbian Patriarch in the same year at a synod held at Skopje, becoming recorded for posterity as Tsar Stefan Dušan 'the Mighty'. Dušan's son Uroš was then named king (kralj) of the Serbian lands, though in practice Dušan governed them himself. Dušan was eventually recognised as Emperor of the Serbs by Byzantium's emperor in 1352. Near the end of his life he was apparently planning to conquer Constantinople, but could not do so since he lacked a fleet.[43] He convened parliaments, comprising representatives of the aristocracy, clergy and government officials, relatively frequently with much pomp and solemnity, but purely to ratify his decisions.[44] He issued a state law-code for his Serbian lands in 1349 aimed at consolidating his realm—practically the first Serbian code of public law. A greatly expanded version was issued in 1354. His forces also fought and lost the Serbs' first battle with the Ottomans, at Demotika in Thrace in 1352, after which he recognised the threat they posed and attempted unsuccessfully to assemble a European coalition against them. Nevertheless Dušan, though successful in his own lifetime, laid the basis for medieval Serbia's subsequent decline. In Ćorović's words, 'Carried away by victories, Dušan encompassed a much larger circle of territories than that which he could have, without major crisis, joined and assimilated to the new state. His politics were too imperialistic.' Territorial over-expansion produced a more heterogeneous and less cohesive population and state under a weaker central authority.[45] It portended Serbia's twentieth-century experience.

Battle of Kosovo and Ottoman conquest

Serbia declined under Dušan's son and successor, Tsar Uroš V 'the Weak'. Dušan's southern territories seceded, including most of his Greek and Albanian lands, so Uroš's realm was reduced to central Serbia, Zeta and the greater part of Macedonia. Furthermore, the regional lords successfully asserted their power, defying his authority. Lords emerged who would play a central role in Serbian national mythology. Prince Lazar Hrebeljanović, subsequently the Kosovo legend's hero, made Kruševac in present-day central Serbia his base. A Serbian lord called Branko took control of part of Macedonia; his son would be Vuk Branković, also of the Kosovo legend. Uroš appointed one of his officials, Vukašin Mrnjavčević, from a family from Hum, as his subordinate co-ruler, crowning him king of the Serbian lands in 1365 while Uroš remained tsar. Vukašin's son would be Kraljević Marko, one of Serbian folklore's most important heroes, albeit as the Ottoman Sultan's warrior.[46] Though Tsar Uroš was in principle more senior, King Vukašin dominated the partnership.[47]

The Ottomans emerged as a new, overwhelming force on mainland Europe in 1354 with their capture of Kallipolis (Gallipoli). Vukašin and his brother Uglješa, despot of Serres in Macedonia, marched against them but were crushingly defeated on 26 September 1371 at the Battle of Maritsa near Chernomen, near where today Greece, Bulgaria and Turkey meet; both were killed. The defeat was due to the weakening of the state and rise of lordly independence following Dušan's death; Serbian lords mostly failed to follow their king into battle. Maritsa broke Serbia, which lost half its territory. Uroš died shortly afterwards, ending the Nemanjid dynasty. The new king, Marko, lacked authority; the lords encroached upon his domains and fought among themselves, leaving the country vulnerable to Ottoman conquest.[48] Marko recognised Ottoman suzerainty after Maritsa, as did Bulgaria and Byzantium in the years following. Prince Lazar established himself as Serbia's dominant lord in the uncertain situation following Uroš's death, aided by Kruševac's relative distance from the Ottomans, whose ravages he was consequently spared until the mid-1380s. This shifted the centre of power in Serbia northwards.[49]

Lazar renounced the Serbs' right to hold the imperial title in 1375 in return for the Patriarch of Constantinople's recognition of the Serbian Patriarch and the Serbian church's autocephaly. Bosnia's ruler Tvrtko, a Hungarian vassal, in 1377 crowned himself 'King of Bosnia and Serbia', but Serbia's real ruler remained Lazar, though he recognised Tvrtko's overlordship. Lazar did not seek the title of king for himself but accurately adopted the title 'Lord of the Serbs', and when in 1378 the Serbian church honoured him for ending the schism with Constantinople, it crowned him 'Lord of the Serbs and the Danube, Stefan Prince Lazar, autocrat of all the Serbs'.[50] But at the legendary Battle of Kosovo, usually dated to 28 June 1389, which was less militarily significant than Maritsa, both Lazar and Ottoman Sultan Murad I were killed. The historical battle was probably a tactical draw, but Serbia's losses at Kosovo left it unable to resist the Ottomans further, so it became an Ottoman vassal under the regency of Lazar's widow, Princess Milica, on behalf of her young son Stefan Lazarević, while she married her daughter Olivera to Murad's son and successor, Bayezid I ('the Thunderbolt').

The Ottomans' military success owed much to their relatively generous treatment of the soldiers and subjects of the Christian states. They removed the right of the increasingly exploitative Christian feudal lords to determine peasant dues and transferred it to the central Ottoman administration, which considerably lightened them. Whereas Dušan's law-code had determined that the peasant should provide his lord with two days' labour service (corvée) a week, Ottoman regulations reduced this to only three days a year. Thousands of Serbian and other Christian soldiers were retained in Ottoman service and permitted to enjoy the usufruct of state land and exemption from taxation, while Orthodoxy was tolerated.[51] Conversely, Serbia loyally contributed troops, led by Stefan himself, to Ottoman campaigns. Under Bayezid these were successful against Christian opponents, and in 1393 the Ottomans completed Bulgaria's conquest. But at the Battle of Ankara on 20 July 1402, Bayezid was defeated and captured by the Mongol emperor Timur ('Tamerlane'). The latter's forces included 32 Indian elephants, but Bayezid was defeated partly because not all his Muslim troops would fight fellow Muslims; recent unwilling Seljuk conscripts from Anatolia deserted, although the regular Ottoman corps fought well. The Serbian contingent under Stefan, Bayezid's brother-in-law, fought bravely and loyally; witnessing this, Timur allegedly exclaimed, 'The wretches fight like lions!'[52] When Bayezid was captured in the battle, Stefan valiantly but unsuccessfully tried thrice to free him.[53]

Stefan visited Byzantium's emperor following the defeat at Ankara and was granted the title of despot; the Principality of Serbia thus became the Despotate of Serbia. With the Ottoman Empire in chaos following Bayezid's death after the battle, Stefan became vassal in 1404 to Sigismund, king of Hungary, who awarded him Belgrade, which became Serbia's capital for the first time, distant as it was from the Ottomans. However, the Ottomans continued to benefit from internal Serbian divisions and allied with Stefan's nephew Đurađ Branković against him. Stefan himself returned to Ottoman vassalage in 1409. He recognised the suzerainty of both Hungary and the Ottomans to avoid trouble from both. Sigismund awarded him in 1411 the Bosnian town of Srebrenica ('Silver Mine') with its rich silver mines, creating a territorial dispute between Serbia and Bosnia that prevented them uniting against the Ottomans.[54] Stefan, with Ottoman support, suppressed the unruly nobles and effectively centralised state power under himself. Serbia thus experienced a temporary resurgence.

Stefan was a patron of the church and of literature and built several monasteries, including Manasija. Literary revival was spurred by the influx of Greek and Bulgarian émigrés fleeing Ottoman conquest. Both church and intelligentsia promoted the cult of Stefan's dynasty, focusing on the legend of the Battle of Kosovo at which his father had died heroically, in what was interpreted as martyrdom. Conversely, chronicles from this period negatively portrayed the dynasty's rivals, the Branković family and Marko Kraljević. The more important Battle of Maritsa, at which Marko's father and uncle had died heroically, was neglected in favour of Kosovo, while Vuk Branković became the traitor of the Kosovo legend, blamed for Serbia's defeat; his name remains today a Serbian byword for treachery, although the historical Branković had fought loyally and heroically.⁵⁵ There was less interest in sustaining the cult of Lazar and Kosovo following the Lazarević dynasty's extinction in 1427, and by the end of the seventeenth century the Ravanica monastery, which Lazar had founded, was the only place where his cult was still celebrated.⁵⁶ The foundations were nevertheless laid of the Kosovo legend that became central to the Serb identity. The legend was nurtured through oral folklore, above all of Serbs who fled westwards and northwards from the Ottoman advance over subsequent centuries. It was recounted and reworked by writers from outside Serbia, including Benedikt Kuripešić, a Latin translator to the Austrian embassy in Constantinople, who heard it from soldiers on the Habsburg Military Border, and Ludovik Crijević and Mavro Orbini, historians from the Republic of Ragusa, and was brought to southern Hungary (present-day Vojvodina) by Serb refugees in the early eighteenth century, where it assumed roughly its final form.⁵⁷ The legend may have been influenced by the events of the second Battle of Kosovo in 1448, when the Ottomans, with assistance from Branković's son Đurađ, defeated a Hungarian–Wallachian army under János Hunyadi; this may be a reason for the unjustified identification of the older Branković as a traitor in the first battle.⁵⁸

The Kosovo legend was thus shaped by the Catholic frontier states facing the Ottomans—Venice, Hungary, Austria—which appropriated the heritage of the Serb struggle against the Ottomans. The legend was not created by Serbs living under direct Ottoman rule, for whom such a story was less relevant. It was then reimported into the Ottoman Serb world during the late seventeenth and eighteenth centuries, via the Serbs of southern Hungary, autonomous Montenegro and, above all, the Bay of Kotor, a Venetian territory inhabited by South Slavs, adjacent to Montenegro, that Austria acquired in the Napoleonic Wars and which Vuk Stefanović Karadžić (1787–1864), the great anthologist of Serb poems, eventually visited in 1835.⁵⁹ By the time the First Serbian Uprising erupted in 1804, the Kosovo legend formed a major part of the consciousness of Orthodox priests and monks in what was to become modern Serbia, something of which they would frequently remind their peasant flock.⁶⁰ The association of the battle with St Vitus's Day, 28 June in the Gregorian calendar, was a late accretion dating from the eighteenth century and the beginnings of Serb national awakening and resistance; it drew upon folk memory of Dajbog, the pagan god of war and the sun, associated with St Vitus and with Miloš Obilić, the Kosovo legend's principal hero, embodying martial prowess and valour appropriate to the age.⁶¹

According to the legend in its ultimate form, Lazar was visited by a grey falcon on the eve of the battle, which transformed into St Elias and delivered him a message from the Mother of God, containing a question:

> Tsar Lazar, noble prince!
> Which empire will you conquer?
> Either you love the earthly kingdom,

> Or you love the heavenly kingdom,
> If you love the earthly kingdom,
> Saddle the horses, buckle the belts,
> Gird the swords of your knights,
> And charge into the Turks,
> All the Turkish army will perish;
> But if you love the heavenly kingdom,
> And you build a church at Kosovo,
> Its foundations not built of marble,
> But of pure silk and scarlet,
> And take communion and command your army,
> All your army will perish,
> And you will, prince, be slain with them.

To which Lazar concluded:

> The earthly kingdom is but fleeting
> But the heavenly is always and forever.[62]

Another key part of the legend concerns Lazar's son-in-law Vuk Branković slandering Miloš Obilić, his other son-in-law, accusing him of treachery. Consequently, at the banquet on the eve of the battle, Lazar accused Obilić: 'Tomorrow you will betray me at Kosovo; And flee to the Turkish emperor Murat.' To which Obilić replied: 'I have never been a renegade; Neither have I been, nor will I ever be; But tomorrow I intend to die for the Christian faith ... I will go tomorrow at Kosovo; And I shall slay the Turkish emperor Murat.'[63] True to his word, he assassinated the Sultan at the end of the battle, which was lost through Branković's treachery.

The Kosovo legend was preserved both by the Serbian Orthodox Church and in popular epic poetry, but these would interpret it differently. While the church canonised Lazar and built the myth around his person, thereby memorialising the Serbian medieval state in explicitly religious form, popular epic poetry would eventually focus primarily on Obilić, who was, unlike Lazar, a hero rather than a saint, thus of greater popular appeal.[64] He was a possibly mythical figure first mentioned in a short addition to a 1390 epic poem by the Turkish poet Ahmedi, as an unnamed but cowardly assassin, later by a Bulgarian writing in the period 1413–1421, who presented him as a hero called Miloš, subsequently named Miloš Kobila in 1497 by the Bosnian chronicler Konstantin Mihailović, then living in Poland and writing for the Polish and Hungarian kings, under the influence of renewed conflict between vassal Serbia and the Ottomans in the second half of the fifteenth century, with the aim of making propaganda for an anti-Ottoman crusade. The actual name 'Miloš Obilić' was an eighteenth-century innovation. Obilić is also claimed as a hero by the Albanians, who attribute Albanian origin to him under the name of Millosh

Kopiliq, and his home as the Albanian village of Kopiliq in Kosovo's Drenica region. In reality, there is no historical evidence that he was either Serb or Albanian, and the ethnic border between the two peoples in pre-modern times was blurred. The legend may have been based on a Hungarian knight who, some accounts suggest, killed Murat; the legend's Miloš Obilić was Lazar's son-in-law, and the historical Lazar had a Hungarian son-in-law who likely contributed a contingent to his army.[65]

Serbia in its final years served as a battlefield in the long struggle between the Ottomans and Hungary; its ruling elite torn between them.[66] The Ottomans in 1425 resumed incursions into Serbia, which Stefan and his successors attempted to stall through conciliation and collaboration. Stefan died in 1427 and was succeeded by his nephew Đurađ Branković, while the Ottomans invaded Serbia and seized several towns. Đurađ had to return Belgrade to Hungary, so transferred his capital to nearby Smederevo on the Danube. Threatened with invasion, Đurađ in 1435 married his daughter Mara to Ottoman Sultan Murad II, while for balance he married his other daughter, Catherine, to a leading Hungarian nobleman. The Ottomans nevertheless resumed their incursions and by 1441 had occupied all Serbia except Zeta, installing their first governor of the country the following year. Serbia having fallen, Zeta effectively re-emerged as an independent state, increasingly referred to as Montenegro. Meanwhile, the Ottomans abducted many Serbs into slavery, above all in Anatolia; according to a contemporary Franciscan source, 60,000 were so abducted from Serbia in 1438 alone. Emulating this, Hungary's king and his allied Serb magnates evacuated large numbers of Serbs to Hungary as part of their military campaigns, peaking in 1480–1481, when 110,000 were so removed.[67] These actions and counter-actions depopulated large areas of the country, permanently changing its social and demographic character.

A Polish–Hungarian–Serbian crusade in 1443, sponsored by the Pope, liberated much of Serbia and reached Sofia. Consequently, Đurađ won restoration of a small Despotate of Serbia, including Smederevo, from the Ottomans at the Peace of Szeged in 1444. Murad agreed to this in return for Đurađ's abandonment of the Hungarian alliance. Đurađ refused to support the continuation of the Polish–Hungarian crusade when it resumed later that year, facilitating its crushing defeat by the Ottomans at Varna on 10 November. He then collaborated in the subsequent Ottoman warfare against the Hungarians and, with his detachment numbering 1,500, assisted Sultan Mehmed II's conquest of Constantinople in 1453.[68] However, Mehmed resumed the offensive against Serbia the following year and steadily conquered it. Đurađ died in 1456 and Stjepan Tomašević, son of King Tomaš of Bosnia, became despot in 1459. Mehmed then completed the conquest of Serbia by capturing Smederevo on 20 June. The Sanjak of Smederevo was established as an Ottoman administrative unit in place of the Serbian state, within the framework of the Eyalet of Rumelia ('Land of the Romans').

SERBIA

Serbia under Ottoman rule and creation of a Serb diaspora

Ottoman occupation of the Balkans forged the modern Serb nation. Unlike neighbouring Bosnia, Serbia did not continue to exist as an Ottoman administrative unit. The conquest destroyed not only medieval Serbia's statehood and borders but its ruling elite and social structure. The Ottoman Empire was an Islamic empire based upon Muslim supremacy, in which non-Muslims were generally second-class subjects. Consequently, the Christian Serbian nobility was destroyed and replaced by a new, predominantly Muslim ruling elite. Many members of the Serbian nobility were absorbed into the latter by converting to Islam; thus, Mahmud-pasha Anđelović, a scion of the Byzantine–Serbian nobility from Novo Brdo in present-day Kosovo, was captured as a youth by the Ottomans, converted to Islam and raised by them, becoming head of the Ottoman government by late 1453 and going on to be the longest-serving grand vizier in the empire's history, serving altogether seventeen years. Similarly, Gedik Ahmed Pasha, appointed grand vizier in 1473 by Sultan Mehmed II, had been a member of the lesser Serbian aristocracy from near Vranje. The Ottoman state authority and administrative presence were centred on the towns, which were consequently much more solidly Islamised than the countryside. The towns—in terms of size, mostly little more than villages—thus became inhabited primarily by non-Serbs and their inhabitants owed fewer fiscal or other obligations. These were mostly Muslims, but included Jews, gypsies, Greeks, Cincars, Armenians and others, engaging in trade and craft and coexisting economically with the dominant Muslims. The Serbian Orthodox population became ruralised; the bulk of it inhabited the countryside and tended to view the towns as alien, non-Serb territory.

In the Balkan countryside, land was divided into plots held in trust for the Sultan by a hierarchy of Muslim landlords, whose duties were also military and administrative. The basic rank of landlord was a sipahi or bey: a cavalryman who received his fiefdom (timar) with its mostly Christian tenants in return for military service to the Sultan and collection of imperial taxes, part of which he would retain for himself. By the mid-eighteenth century there were about 900 timars in the Smederevo sanjak, mostly covering the territory of one village each, occasionally two. This figure did not change until they were finally abolished in the 1830s.[69] Although Christian sipahis were permitted to exist in some parts of the empire, they were almost everywhere in the minority and often converted to Islam to secure their positions. The last Christian sipahis in the territory of the former Despotate of Serbia are recorded in the first half of the seventeenth century.[70] Larger landholdings were called zeâmets, held by zaims—commanders of groups of sipahis. Alongside these landlords were local Islamic judges (kadis), each responsible for administering sharia law in a territory called a kadiluk, each of which could cover multiple nahijas (large districts), whose governors were from the eighteenth century called mütesellim or müsellim. A group of nahijas formed a sanjak ('flag'), such as the Sanjak of Smederevo.

Sanjaks were administered by sanjak-beys, in turn subordinate to beyler-beys ('beys of beys'), who governed beylerbeyliks (eyalets, pashaliks)—large provinces such as Rumelia or, from 1580, Bosnia. Sanjak-beys and beyler-beys held estates still larger than zeâmets, called 'has'.[71] Thus, a new, Muslim ruling elite emerged in Ottoman Serbia. Religious and class distinctions overlapped.

The subordinate peasantry (raya) owned their own houses and gardens and had hereditary tenure over plots of arable land (cift). In return for use of these they owed various taxes and duties. To the Sultan, they owed a head-tax (harač or glavarina), legally originating as payment in lieu of military service which, as non-Muslims, they were spared, but which also symbolised their subordination, as Christians, to Muslim rule. To the sipahi they owed a share of their harvest, formally about a tenth (desetak) but often more; another head-tax; labour services (kuluk or corvée); an inheritance tax, to enable them to pass their family plots to their heirs; and additional minor fees. Serb women were required to perform labour services—'women's work' such as washing, knitting, embroidering and the like—at the sipahis' homes, where they were often subject to rape and other abuse.[72] An institution that caused particular trauma and won lasting notoriety in folk memory was the janissaries: elite Ottoman infantrymen recruited in part through the devşirme—the blood levy of Christian boys aged between about ten and twenty, forcibly taken from their families and converted to Islam. The last such levy was exacted in Serbia in 1638.[73] Muslim peasants also owed taxes and duties, but they were lighter than for Christians.

With the Ottoman conquest of the independent Balkan states effectively completed and the devşirme system fully established, the Serbian nobility's recruitment into the Ottoman elite tailed off from the early sixteenth century and senior positions in the administration were instead filled with former Christian peasant children converted to Islam. Whereas the reigns of Mehmed II, Bayezid II and Selim I between 1451 and 1520 saw several grand viziers of Serbian or Bosnian noble descent, 1536–1579 was a period of pre-eminence of South Slavs from humble backgrounds at the Ottoman court, in particular with grand viziers Rustem-pasha Okupović (in office 1544–1553, 1555–1561), who was from Bosnia or Croatia and was described as Serb or Croat, and Mehmed-pasha Sokolović (in office 1565–1579), from a Bosnian Orthodox family.[74] Yet whether of noble or peasant background, Ottoman Muslim officials recruited from Serbia and the other Balkan peoples became indistinguishable from other Ottoman Muslim officials and lost their native national identities.[75] The Serbian Orthodox Church nevertheless obstructed Serbia's Islamisation, in contrast to neighbouring Bosnia, which lacked a unifying national church and whose Christian population was more confessionally fragmented. Thus, in 1520–1535, 97.8 per cent of households in the Sanjak of Smederevo were Christian and 2.2 per cent Muslim, compared with 54 per cent and 46 per cent respectively in the Sanjak of Bosnia.[76]

Christians were not allowed legally to testify against Muslims. They could not erect new churches or use church bells. Although the burden on the Ottoman Christian peasantry was initially lighter than for peasants in Christian Europe, their discriminatory treatment, in relation to Muslims, would stimulate the emergence of their nationalism, which consequently took an anti-Muslim form. Nevertheless, the Serbian Orthodox community, along with other Ottoman Christian and Jewish communities, was permitted some autonomy: the right to administer its own tax collection and justice involving its members and manage its churches and eventually, where they existed, schools. Historians have sometimes called such Christian and Jewish autonomy under Muslim supremacy the millet system—a 'millet' being a non-Muslim religious community. It provided an institutional basis upon which the autonomous statehoods of Serbs and other Christian subject peoples (Greeks, Bulgarians) was eventually built.

Vlach communities, not subject to feudal obligations in medieval Serbia, remained privileged following the Ottoman conquest and did not originally pay the head-tax or perform kuluk but paid lighter taxes in money or kind. By around 1516 there were over 12,000 Vlach households in the Smederevo sanjak, suggesting the Ottoman authorities deliberately settled them there for military and strategic reasons given the territory's depopulation.[77] Their elders representing them before the Ottoman authorities were called knezes (knezovi). Following the Ottoman conquest of most of Hungary in 1526, when the Smederevo sanjak ceased to be a frontier territory, and the transition of the Vlachs in the Smederevo sanjak from animal husbandmen into farmers, they were subsumed within the Christian raya, with the Vlach status formally abolished in 1536. The institution of knez as a hereditary office was territorialised and extended to the raya generally, with jurisdiction over groups of villages or localities. Knez was originally a senior rank but the term gradually came to denote Christian community leaders of different levels, whether representing municipalities or whole districts. Knezes had to guarantee order in areas under their jurisdiction and raise soldiers from the households and families there for service in the empire's wars. These troops remained free of the head-tax; they were from the end of the sixteenth century known as panduri—a word that survives in Serbia today as a derogatory term for policemen, similar to 'pigs' in English. A grand vizier's report from 1602 records thousands of these troops from the Smederevo sanjak being sent to fight the Austrians.[78] Because there were relatively few Muslims in this sanjak compared with other Ottoman territories, knezes there performed the administrative and military functions that were, in Bosnia for example, performed by Muslim officials (ayans).[79]

The Ottomans continued to expand westward and northward following their conquest of Serbia. They captured Belgrade from the Hungarians in 1521, to which the seat of the Smederevo sanjak was then transferred; the city was renamed Dar ul Jihad ('House of Holy War').[80] This laid the basis for Belgrade becoming modern

SERBIA AND THE SERBS BEFORE THE NINETEENTH CENTURY

Serbia's capital. It marked also the definite origins of Serbia's Jewish community, in the form of Sephardim expelled from Spain in 1492 who arrived in Belgrade following the Ottoman conquest; they spoke their own language, Ladino, derived from medieval Spanish, predominantly retaining it as their first language until the twentieth century. Favourably located at the confluence of the Sava and Danube rivers, Belgrade thrived under Ottoman rule. The Prussian traveller Reinhold Lubenau noted at the end of the sixteenth century, 'Belgrade now has mostly low houses, the roads are of mud, but nevertheless long and broad ... The whole town is full of little shops, caravanserais and pretty mosques and Turkish churches, as well as various Christian churches and Jewish synagogues. It is similarly full of wonderful fountains and baths, and everything a person could want can be bought in the shops, just as in the most ordinary towns of Spain or Germany.'[81] The Ottoman explorer Evliya Çelebi, who visited Belgrade repeatedly in the second half of the seventeenth century, described it as 'beautiful as a jewel in a ring' and noted its Turkish cuisine: 'Such baklava as we ate at the Belgrade feasts we truly had seen nowhere, neither in Rumelia nor in Arabia nor in Persia. Belgrade itself is the Egypt of Rumelia.'[82] Serbian scholar Milan Đakov Milićević, writing in 1876, noted: 'Several decades ago, the principal town of Serbia was partly Turkish, partly Greek, partly cosmopolitan, and probably least of all Serbian. In the streets were spoken Turkish and corrupted Serbian, in the shops principally Greek, and in the churches and schools more Greek than Serbian. Houses, shops, workshops, clothes, way of life and all customs were eastern.'[83]

The Ottomans completed the conquest and destruction of the Kingdom of Bosnia in 1463, conquered most of Hungary following the Battle of Mohács in 1526 and besieged Vienna in 1529. Following their capture of the Hungarian town of Buda in 1541, they established the Eyalet of Buda as an administrative unit encompassing primarily Hungarian territory and transferred to it the Smederevo sanjak. The Ottomans occupied a large part of what was then Croatia, and these territories would form the westernmost outpost of the modern Serb nationality. Perhaps 200,000 Orthodox Christian refugees fleeing Ottoman conquest settled in Slavonia and Srem, in present-day northern Croatia and western Vojvodina, by 1483, and by the early sixteenth century the first Orthodox settlements were established in unoccupied Croatia around Ogulin, Otok and Modruša, where their security and certain rights were recognised by Emperor Ferdinand I in May 1540.[84] These refugees were not just Slavs but also Vlachs, who retained their distinct language and identity but who in Croatia would be assimilated into the Serbs by the nineteenth century. Vlachs in Ottoman Serbia and Serb areas of the Habsburg Empire were called Cincars. Their strength peaked in the 1780s and 1790s, and in the town of Temesvár (Timișoara), a major centre of Serb life in historic Hungary, the town assembly was the scene of a major clash in 1790 between Cincar and Serb demands relating to the financing of schools and churches, but thereafter Cincar strength declined as the group increasingly and smoothly assimilated into the Serbs, providing many of Serbia's leading political figures and families, though a small minority of self-identifying Cincars still exists in Serbia today.[85]

Following the Hungarian king's death at the Battle of Mohács in 1526, Hungary's crown passed to the Habsburg dynasty, as did Croatia's the following year. The Habsburgs' military weakness in Croatia led them to co-opt the Orthodox refugees for their defence. The refugee forces were subordinated to Habsburg command, which by 1553 placed them under its own appointed officers and integrated them into the state service. In that year, Archduke Ferdinand of Austria, younger brother of Emperor Charles V, appointed a general officer to command the two borderland military districts in Croatia and Slavonia. Thus arose the institution of the Austrian Military Border, whose strongest portion lay in Habsburg Croatia. It not only guarded the Habsburg border from the Ottomans but provided troops for Habsburg campaigns elsewhere. Orthodox migrants continued arriving in Croatia throughout the sixteenth and seventeenth centuries; those settling in what is today central Croatia in the 1660s were granted favourable conditions by Emperor Leopold I in July 1659.[86] The Military Border's population was granted extensive autonomy in the election of its own captains (vojvodas) and magistrates (knezes) and was freed from regular feudal obligations. This borderland and refugee population was both Catholic and Orthodox; Orthodox freedom of worship was recognised. These privileges attracted more Orthodox settlers. Administration of the Croatian and Slavonian Borders was exclusively under the Habsburg crown rather than the Croatian civil authorities; the frontiersmen's privileges led them to resist full incorporation into Croatia.[87] Although the Croatian and Hungarian nobility resisted recognising the privileges of the Orthodox settlers, the Habsburg emperors enforced them; for example, by the Statuta Valachorum, which confirmed the rights of Orthodox settlers in the Varaždin frontier region. Although the Military Border was not a nationally Serb institution and its population not solely Orthodox, it obstructed Croatian assimilation of its Orthodox population.

Under the Ottoman umbrella, the Serbian church expanded its jurisdiction over the Orthodox population west of the River Drina—inhabitants of territories that would be incorporated into the Eyalet of Bosnia, formed in 1580, which included large parts of what is today Croatia. From the first decades of the Ottoman conquest of Bosnia and Serbia, with the encouragement of the new rulers, Orthodox herdsmen from Raška, Zeta, Hercegovina and East Bosnia migrated to settle in what is today Serbia's heartland as well as parts of Bosnia, Croatia and Dalmatia. In Bosnia, they settled in first the northern and north-central and subsequently north-western parts of the country, territory depopulated by the Austro-Turkish warfare and indigenous Catholic population's exodus. These settlers were ethnic Vlachs and Serbs who merged to form a single ethno-national group through their shared Orthodoxy. This produced a Serb majority that persists in north-western Bosnia today. This

SERBIA AND THE SERBS BEFORE THE NINETEENTH CENTURY

Orthodox population was important to the Ottomans as a frontier people against the Christian states; for example, the Ottoman commander of the offensive into Banat in Hungary in 1551, Mehmed-pasha Sokolović, relied on Serb troops, who fought very effectively. In these circumstances, Ottoman occupation produced widespread conversion from Catholicism to Orthodoxy; the Ottomans favoured the Orthodox Church, which they controlled through the Patriarch in Constantinople, over the Catholic Church—the church of the Habsburg enemy, independent under the Pope.[88] Bosnians in Ottoman service, in particular, promoted a pro-Orthodox policy in Bosnia to exploit Catholic–Orthodox antagonism in the country.[89] In the nineteenth century, particularly following Austria-Hungary's occupation of Bosnia-Hercegovina in 1878 and the resulting exodus of the Muslim population, Orthodox Serbs would emerge as the largest nationality in the country, remaining so until after World War II.

The Serbian Patriarchate effectively ceased to exist following the Serbian Despotate's fall in 1459 and the death of Patriarch Arsenios II in 1463. Its dioceses eventually reverted, probably in the 1520s, to the original authority of the archbishopric of Ohrid, subordinate to the Patriarch in Constantinople, in what is today Macedonia.[90] The Serbian church nevertheless resisted Ohrid's authority, culminating in an unsuccessful attempt in the early 1530s by Pavle, bishop of Smederevo, unilaterally to re-establish Serbian church independence. The Ottomans sought to appease their Serb subjects, and at Sokolović's initiative, after he became third vizier in 1555, the Serbian Patriarchate was re-established in 1557, with its see in Peć in present-day Kosovo. Sokolović used his own familial links to facilitate this policy; the re-established Patriarchate's first Patriarch was his cousin Makarije Sokolović.[91] Mehmed-pasha became grand vizier in 1565. The Patriarchate's re-establishment produced something of a Serb spiritual and national revival over the next thirty-five years, coinciding somewhat with Europe's Renaissance.[92] The restored Serbian Patriarch was a fully-fledged ethnarch, or millet-başi, whose authority extended beyond the Ottoman border to the Orthodox inhabiting the Military Border and Venetian Dalmatia. Consequently, Orthodox monks from the Military Border regularly claimed they came from 'Serb lands'.[93] In Ćorović's words: 'Only under the government of the Peć Patriarchate was for the first time the unification achieved of the Serb nation on the whole of its ethnic territory, for its government reached everywhere where they went, among the Serbs, in the borders of the Turkish state. Never up till then had the Serb borders, either of the state or of the church, coincided with the territory of the whole of the Serb nation.'[94] The Ottoman Empire thus provided an umbrella under which a Serb people with a shared national consciousness emerged, descended from Slavs, Vlachs and others and stretching into present-day Bosnia-Hercegovina, Croatia and Vojvodina.

The Serbian church preserved the memory of the Serbian medieval state, canonised Serbian kings and promoted the cult of its founder, St Sava. Priests and monks transmitted the memory of Serbian national independence before the Ottoman conquest to the people. The Patriarch was sometimes referred to in the church as 'Lord of the Serbs', as the only remnant of the former medieval state, while at the Porte the institution was recorded as 'the Patriarchate of the Serb unbelievers in the oblast of Peć' ('and in the Buda, Temeşvar, Bosnian, Győr, Eğri and Kanizsa eyalets, and the Shkodër and Prizren sanjaks, and the oblasts that fall to them').[95] The Orthodox religion and heritage of medieval statehood therefore became inseparable parts of Serb national identity under Ottoman rule. Kuripešić, who travelled through Serbia in 1530, noted: 'The land of Serbia (Seruia), which we Germans call Surffen, has its own language that is called Serbian (surffisch). That is likewise a Slavic (Wendian) language. The people in this country are very God-fearing (pious) and protect themselves (as much as that is possible) from evil and sin.'[96] Nevertheless, Serb national identity was far from fully formed. Dress, speech and music differed between regions and local identity was strong. A peasant's native village could be identified by the clothes he or she wore. As the historian Milorad Ekmečić notes, 'Even in Serbia itself, the transformation of peasants into Serbs was not completed by 1914.'[97]

Ottoman decline and origins of the Serbian revolution

From the late sixteenth century, Ottoman expansion into Europe stalled and the empire began stagnating. The Ottoman military and landholding elite evolved into a more sedentary class. Serb soldiers were increasingly excluded from its armies and Serb sipahis and knezes from its elite. There were no longer plentiful conquered territories to distribute to the sipahi class, whose members had increasingly to subdivide existing timars among their descendants. They came to view themselves less as soldiers and more as landowners; their lordship over their Christian tenants became more exploitative as they sought to maximise their revenue from their landholdings, in part by converting them into hereditable property (chiftliks). Frano Stojimirović, bishop of Prizren, noted in 1652: 'the Christians are every day burdened with new taxes and tributes, because of which the poor flee hither and thither'.[98] Peasants resisted their loss of a legally guaranteed status and demotion to mere private tenants on landlord-dictated terms.[99] This process was paralleled by the degeneration of the janissary corps from soldiers feared by the empire's enemies into militarily worthless gangs of local mafiosi feared only by the empire's own populace, particularly non-Muslims, whom they terrorised and from whom they extorted tribute. Furthermore, the empire after 1577 sharply increased the head-tax on its Christian subjects, which did not stabilise until after 1690.[100] The Serbian Patriarchate increasingly sought protection from foreign Christian powers, conducting its own foreign policy with the Habsburgs, the Russians, the Pope and others.[101] Consequently, Ottoman Christians were increasingly likely to look upon invading Christian powers as liberators.

SERBIA AND THE SERBS BEFORE THE NINETEENTH CENTURY

The Ottoman Empire's siege of Vienna of 1683 marked its last attempt at significant expansion in Europe and was a turning point also for its relationship with its Serb subjects. As in previous wars, the Ottomans mobilised Serbs under their knezes to fight for them. But when the Holy Roman Empire's forces, after repelling the siege, decisively defeated the Ottomans at the second Battle of Mohács on 12 August 1687 (close to today's Hungarian border with Vojvodina), liberated Hungary and in 1688 went on to invade the land that would become Serbia, thousands of Serbs flocked to join them, driven by worsening oppression at Ottoman hands. These Serbs were organised into a militia, led from 1689 by Pavle Nestorović Deak and Antonije Znorić, which fought alongside the Holy Roman Empire's regular army. The Austrians also toyed with a pretender, Đorđe Branković, a minor Hungarian Serb nobleman who claimed to be Đorđe II, legitimate heir to the Despotate of Serbia. He wanted the Habsburgs' support to re-establish the Serbian state, and they made him a duke following their capture of Belgrade on 6 September 1688, hoping he could encourage further Serb rebellion. He failed at this, and they came to view him as a threat, arrested him and removed him from the region. He nevertheless won considerable support from the Serbs of Hungary and remained inspirational for later Serb rebels.[102] Meanwhile, local Ottoman forces responded to the Serb rebellion with large-scale massacres of the Serb population. The situation was worsened for both the Serbs and the Porte by the fact that Belgrade's governor (serdar) appointed in 1688, Yeğen Osman-pasha, resisted Constantinople's authority and treated the area as his personal fiefdom. He persecuted the Serbian church, whose bishops were accused of inciting rebellion in collusion with the Habsburgs, causing several of them to flee to Vienna, and extorted money from the Patriarch, Arsenije III Čarnojević.[103] Yeğen Osman-pasha was the prototype for future rebellious Ottoman officials, up to and including Ali Pasha of Janina and the dahijas (deys) in Serbia, whose misrule there would eventually provoke full-scale national revolution.[104]

The administrative seat of what was left of the former Eyalet of Buda was transferred to Belgrade in December 1687, marking the establishment of what became known informally as the 'Belgrade pashaluk'. Its core was the Sanjak of Smederevo and what was left of the Sanjak of Srem.[105] These were formally transferred to the Eyalet of Temeşvar, while Belgrade remained formally merely the seat of the Smederevo sanjak, but, given the city's central strategic importance as a serhat (border territory), its administrative authority was greater than this in practice. Although the Smederevo sanjak's sanjak-bey was lord of only this sanjak, as military commander (muhafiz) his authority extended into three other sanjaks.[106] Under him, a Belgrade chancellery was subsequently established and the treasuries of the former Buda, Eğri and Kanizsa eyalets absorbed into it, and it was the recipient also of state income from a wide area to support the corresponding fortresses and garrisons; as a result the sanjak-bey had a degree of military authority similar to an actual beyler-bey, or pasha, hence the nickname 'Belgrade pashaluk'.[107] For the next half-century, Serbia would be a central battlefield of the Habsburg–Ottoman struggle. After capturing Belgrade, which they would hold for two years, Habsburg forces penetrated deep into the Ottoman Balkans. The imperial forces defeated the Ottomans at the Battle of Batočina in present-day central Serbia on 29 August 1689, with Nestorović's Serb militia defeating an Ottoman vanguard unit. The imperial army defeated the Ottomans again at Niš on 24 September 1689 to capture the city, then reached Macedonia and present-day Bulgaria. Meanwhile, Russia under Tsar Peter I ('the Great') entered the anti-Ottoman war. Serbs began looking to it as a potential saviour preferable to Austria.[108]

The Holy Roman Emperor Leopold I, on 6 April 1690 called upon 'all peoples who inhabit Albania, Serbia, Mizija, Bulgaria, Silistria, Illyria, Macedonia and Rajcija, and other lands that once depended on our Kingdom of Hungary, and all other peoples that suffer under the Turkish yoke', to join his imperial army.[109] Patriarch Arsenije avoided collaborating with the invaders, but when the Ottomans counter-attacked and began expelling the imperial forces from the future Serbia, he and the Serbs faced the prospect of their bloody retribution. Consequently, a gathering of Serbian religious and national leaders, under Arsenije's stewardship, met in Belgrade on 18 June 1690 and resolved to recognise Leopold as king of Serbia, in response to the emperor's exhortation. Leopold recognised the Serbian Orthodox Church on 21 August 1690 as a separate legal body within his empire. Then, in what became known as the Great Migration, approximately 60,000–70,000 Serbs under Arsenije retreated alongside the Austrian forces and settled in the Habsburg lands, mostly in Hungary, while the Ottomans retook Niš on 6 September and Belgrade on 8 October 1690. Arsenije was pilloried for this by later Serbian nationalists, on the grounds that it contributed to the Serb demographic loss of territory in and around present-day Kosovo. Yet the exodus was not the result of a conscious decision on his part but a spontaneous flight in terror of death over which he had little control and little choice but to participate.[110]

The great imperial victory at Slankamen, just north of Belgrade, on 19 October 1691 ended the Ottoman recovery. The war continued, with Eugene of Savoy's great victory at Zenta, in what is today northern Vojvodina, on 11 September 1697 clinching the Habsburg triumph. Their expansion southward gave the Habsburgs possession of Hungary and turned Belgrade into a border town, which it would remain until World War I. The peace treaty was signed on 26 January 1699 at Sremski Karlovci (Karlowitz), in Srem in Habsburg Croatia. The Serb community in Hungary would thenceforth be swelled by refugees following subsequent Habsburg incursions into, and retreats from, the Ottoman Balkans. Unlike earlier waves of Orthodox refugees, those arriving in the 1690s possessed a definite Serb ethnic consciousness centred on the Patriarch who came with them, while the Habsburg emperor, in four decrees between 1690 and 1695, for the first time recognised the right of the Serbian church to minister to its flock throughout the empire.[111]

SERBIA AND THE SERBS BEFORE THE NINETEENTH CENTURY

Responding to imperial efforts at mobilising them to fight the Ottomans, the Serbs in Hungary requested the right to elect themselves a military leader (vojvoda) and the Habsburg court permitted them to convene an assembly for this purpose, which occurred on 20–22 March 1691. However, the assembly chose the imprisoned pretender Branković and sought to proclaim him not merely vojvoda but despot. This was unacceptable to the court, which instead imposed an officer of the imperial army of Cincar background, Jovan Monasterlija, as Serb military leader with the title 'vice-vojvoda'.[112] The Serb province that eventually emerged in southern Hungary would consequently be called Vojvodina. Southern Hungary thus became the principal centre of Serb national life until the nineteenth century, though owing to Habsburg colonisation policies the Serbs would share the region with diverse other peoples. A Serbian Orthodox metropolitanate for the Habsburg lands was eventually established in 1708 at Krušedol and moved in 1713 to Sremski Karlovci; its autonomy was recognised by the Patriarch in Peć. It was in this period, the late seventeenth and early eighteenth century, when Serb literary life in the Habsburg Empire was undergoing a renaissance, that the term 'Serbia' first came to be widely used by educated Austrian Serbs, though not yet by Serbs in the Ottoman Empire.[113] Among those migrating to Hungary were the monks of Ravanica monastery, who brought with them Prince Lazar's remains. There, the cult of St Lazar was rejuvenated.[114]

Another centre of Serbian national life lay in Montenegro, broadly corresponding to medieval Zeta, previously Duklja. Its ruler, Ivan Crnojević, formally accepted the Ottomans' suzerainty in 1470 but resisted them until finally crushed and forced to accept their rule over the tiny territory left to him as their vassal. He established his capital in 1482 at the village of Cetinje, which would become Montenegro's capital, and founded a monastery. The Metropolitan of Zeta moved his seat to Cetinje in 1485; the bishopric would provide the backbone of the future Montenegrin state. Though the Ottomans converted Montenegro into a sanjak by 1513 under Ivan's son, an Islamic convert,[115] it retained in practice broad autonomy not enjoyed by Serbia. The regular Ottoman administrative system based on timars was not imposed on Montenegro; Ottoman suzerainty involved little more than irregular payment of a tribute. The Metropolitan of Cetinje, elected by the monastery of Cetinje's monks following the last Crnojević ruler's disappearance, became prince-bishop (vladika) in 1516, a major step toward Montenegrin statehood. The vladikas were elected by an assembly representing all Montenegro's tribes, subject to confirmation prior to 1766 by the Patriarch of Peć. The prince-bishopric became hereditary in the Petrović family from the Njegoš tribe from 1697.[116] Autonomous Montenegro became the increasing object of international diplomatic efforts as the empire declined.

The Ottoman loss in the war of territories in Hungary, Croatia and Dalmatia to the Christian powers led to the expulsion of large numbers of sipahis, janissaries and other Ottoman officials to Bosnia and Serbia in the Ottoman Balkan rump. There they sought to acquire or expropriate a shrinking share of fiefdoms of exploitable land, joining the ranks of the Serbs' oppressors and fuelling Serb resistance.[117] Serb peasants responded to this increased oppression with migration, either into the mountains of the interior or to the Habsburg lands to the north and west. Some peasants turned to brigandage, becoming hajduks, a group that entered popular legend for its resistance to Ottoman authority. Meanwhile, the Austrian incursion into Serbia of the 1680s and 1690s showed the population there that Ottoman rule would not last forever.

In the Habsburg–Ottoman war of 1716–1718, the Austrians were again militarily successful. Eugene defeated the Ottomans at Petrovaradin, to the north of Belgrade in present-day Vojvodina, on 5 August 1716, capturing Belgrade on 17 August 1717. In the subsequent Treaty of Passarowitz (Požarevac in present-day Serbia) of 21 July 1718, they annexed Belgrade and the surrounding territory, which they administered as the Kingdom of Serbia. It was at the time, according to Mary Montague, the British envoy's wife, 'a beautiful, abandoned country, all just forests and mountains ... We travelled through whole regions of Serbia, almost completely covered in forests, though the land is naturally fertile.'[118] The Habsburgs kept northern Serbia for two decades until the Habsburg–Ottoman war of 1737–1739, while the Ottomans transferred the seat of the Belgrade pashaluk to the town of Niš, which consequently grew. During their two decades of rule in northern Serbia, the Habsburgs divided the country into fifteen to seventeen districts, each presided over by a leader called an obor-knez, beneath which were junior knezes. Through these, the Serbian population enjoyed significant self-management of its communal affairs, establishing a tradition that decisively shaped its future national character and politics.[119] The Serbian Orthodox Church in the new Kingdom of Serbia was recognised by the Habsburgs as an autonomous metropolitanate of Belgrade separate from the metropolitanate of Sremski Karlovci and recognised by the Serbian Patriarch in Peć. Mojsije Petrović was elected metropolitan of the combined metropolitanates of Belgrade and Sremski Karlovci on 7 February 1726, thereby unifying the Serbian church on Habsburg territory.[120] A new palace was built for him in Belgrade. He did not live to see its completion, but he noted that Belgrade had become the 'celebrated and leading place in our country and fatherland'. Thus, the city began to be perceived as the Serb national centre.[121]

The Serbian Patriarch's defection to the Habsburgs during the Vienna War began the re-subordination of the Serbian church in the Ottoman Empire to the Patriarch in Constantinople. A Greek was appointed Patriarch in Arsenije III's place; the Serbian bishops refused to support him and unity was restored only when a Serb was again appointed. But the Serbian church was increasingly crushed by Ottoman financial demands. Consequently, upon the war's renewal, when the Austrians advanced south from Belgrade in 1737, they met on 24 July near Niš a joint Orthodox–Catholic delegation led by the Serbian Patriarch Arsenije IV Jovanović Šakabenta, who pledged his support. The Austrians captured Niš on the 28th, by which time the

Serbian church establishment was apparently united in believing that the war was an opportunity for liberation from the Ottomans.[122] But the Ottoman victory at Banja Luka in Bosnia on 4 August turned the war's tide and the Austrians abandoned Niš again in October. Following their victories, the Ottomans regained Belgrade by the Treaty of Belgrade of 18 September 1739.

The Austrians destroyed many Belgrade mosques during their 22-year rule, and largely demolished the city before returning it to the Ottomans who, consequently angered, destroyed all Catholic and Orthodox churches and many other buildings that the Austrians had built, including the Belgrade metropolitan's new palace. They heavily damaged the Orthodox cathedral in its vicinity and converted the new Church of St John the Baptist into a mosque dedicated to the victorious grand vizier.[123] The Serbs did not remember Austrian rule fondly; the Belgrade metropolitan Viđentije Jovanović wrote: 'Of the aberrations and impositions carried out by the Austrian generals Valis and Najpreg and other generals, commanders and even soldiers—that is not something that a human tongue can relate, and that is the case both in the homes and other properties and in the churches; furthermore, they did not leave in peace even the dead, but they dug them out of their graves and took from them everything of value that they found.' In their treatment of the Serbian poor, the Austrians 'dishonoured their girls, raped women and committed other misdeeds. Not a single fortress, not a single town, not a single village, moreover not a single church was safe from them.'[124] Nevertheless, the Austrian administrative system of large districts (nahijas) and obor-knezes was mostly retained following the Ottoman reoccupation. Given the weakness of the restored Ottoman system, the Serbs were permitted to retain their system of communal self-management. Four more nahijas were added to produce a sanjak of 21 nahijas; a structure persisting until the late eighteenth century.[125] The Smederevo sanjak was now definitely reincorporated into the Eyalet of Rumelia, of which it remained part until the early nineteenth-century Serbian uprisings.

Restoration of Ottoman rule prompted another great migration of Serbs to Habsburg territory, which augmented their numbers there. The renewed Serbian defection to the Austrians strengthened the Greeks' hand in the struggle for control of the Serbian church; a Greek Patriarch was again installed. The Serbian church was absorbed into the patronage system of the Patriarchate of Constantinople, which exploited the Serbian clergy mercilessly. By 1760, according to one source, the Serbian Patriarch was paying 10,000 scudi a year to the Patriarch in Constantinople. The last Serb to head the Patriarchate, Vasilije Jovanović-Brkić, was denounced before the Sultan by his Greek rival Kalinik and exiled to Cyprus, but this did not end the Serbian church's exploitation. To escape this, Kalinik, who succeeded to the Patriarchate as Kalinik II, and several Serbian bishops petitioned the Sultan in 1766 for their church's formal reintegration with the Orthodox Church under the Patriarch of Constantinople.[126] Consequently, in September, and at the latter's request too, the Ottomans abolished the Patriarchate of Peć, replaced the Serbian bishops with Greeks and ended the Serbian church's autonomy. This meant future Serbian uprisings could not be led by a Serbian national church but would have secular leadership. Nevertheless, the Greek ethnicity of the new church hierarchy separated it from the lower clergy, whose identification consequently increased with the Serb peasantry,[127] from which it was not culturally distinct. In the 1830s, one eyewitness testified that the monks included 'criminals, bandits, murderers, pimps, homosexuals, drunkards, thugs; beggars who beg without leave and for their own account and who curse if they are not given; and charlatans who heal [patients] without any [medical] knowledge and take the money'.[128]

As the Serbian church in the Ottoman Empire declined, so in the Habsburg Empire it flourished under Sremski Karlovci's metropolitanate. The Serbs' demands for a specific territory and secular government of their own within the empire were not granted, but they were permitted to convene an assembly concerned with exercising and affirming their privileges and relations within the Serb community. It elected the metropolitan as the community's head. Composition of the assembly from 1749 was regulated to comprise the bishops and 25 additional clergymen, 25 representatives of the Military Border and 25 representatives of other territories and towns.[129] When Serb rights clashed with Hungarian rights, the Serbs appealed to the emperor. In 1745 Empress Maria Theresa (Queen of Hungary and Croatia, 1717–1780) established the Illyrian Court Commission, renamed Deputation in 1747, to safeguard Serb rights. The Serbian coat of arms was legalised within the Habsburg Empire in 1776, although the Deputation was abolished under Hungarian pressure in 1777.

Twilight of Ottoman rule in Serbia

Increasing Ottoman oppression in the Sanjak of Smederevo in the second half of the eighteenth century ensured a steady flow of refugees into the Habsburg Empire, where as many as 18,000 may have volunteered to fight against the Ottomans. In the last Habsburg–Ottoman war of 1788–1791, the Austrians infiltrated the territory of the Smederevo sanjak with agents tasked with surveying the terrain and winning over the local population to collaboration, 'above all priests and monks, and after that some of the more minor merchants'. Local priests distributed Austrian proclamations to the Serbs.[130] Local Serbs fought alongside the Austrians in unsuccessful attempts to capture Belgrade in late 1787 and early 1788, after which they retreated with them onto Austrian territory and formed the basis of a Serb 'Free Corps', organised by the Austrians and fighting under their command, which eventually grew to over 10,000 men, recruited with the Serb clergy's assistance. This was a proto-national movement spearheaded by Serbs from the Habsburg Empire, in which, for the first time, the area today corresponding approximately to Serbia, Bosnia, Slavonia, Vojvodina and Montenegro was treated as Serb ethnic territory.

The Free Corps' activity gained its participants valuable military experience; many of its veterans went on to active roles in the First Serbian Uprising of 1804–1813, providing the majority of its leaders, in particular Karađorđe Petrović.[131] The Austrians appointed as captain a distinguished Serb fighter, Koča Anđeljković, and sent him to wage guerrilla warfare in the Smederevo sanjak. He established the rebel territory his men called 'Koča's Krajina' (Koča's Borderland). He liberated Požarevac and Kragujevac, encouraging uprisings in several areas of northern Serbia, and was awarded a gold medal by the Austrian emperor, though the Ottomans counter-attacked and killed him on 7 September 1788. The outbreak of the French Revolution the following year may have further encouraged Serb belief in rebellion and liberty; once again, Serbs of the Habsburg Empire, conscious of events beyond the Balkans, transmitted this seditious spirit to their brethren in the Smederevo sanjak.[132] The Austrians, assisted by the Free Corps, now under Mihailo Mihaljević, took Belgrade on 8 October 1789, followed by Smederevo, Ćuprija and Paraćin, and occupied the whole of the territory soon known as Serbia.[133] They held it until the Treaty of Sistova of 4 August 1791, which restored it to Ottoman rule and required both sides to maintain order on their respective sides of the border, which the Ottomans attempted to do by banning the janissaries' return to the Belgrade pashaluk. Serbs who had rebelled against the Ottomans were granted amnesty and those who had fled to Austria were recognised as Habsburg subjects. Allegedly, when one Ottoman official beheld a Serbian troop march out of a fortress due to be returned by the Austrians, he exclaimed, 'Neighbours! What have you made of our *Raya*?'[134] The treaty was the first that referred to the contested territory as 'Serbia', thereby linking the name for the first time to the Sanjak of Smederevo—until then, there was no definite understanding of what territory it referred to; it had more generally been associated with land further south, corresponding to medieval Serbia's heartland.[135]

The treaty was viewed as a betrayal by Serbs from Serbia who had fought with the Austrians; Free Corps Lieutenant Aleksa Nenadović told Mihaljević he would 'go from monastery to monastery and call upon every monk and priest to write in every monastery: that nobody who is Serb should ever again trust a German'.[136] Another wave of Serb refugees left Ottoman for Austrian territory during and after this war. Mihaljević later fought in Austria's war against Revolutionary France and was killed in 1794. Nevertheless, the fact that the Austrians had largely fought their war using Serbs, who had temporarily freed their homeland, boosted their self-confidence and belief that national liberation could be near. Meanwhile, the constant occupation and reoccupation of the Smederevo sanjak by Habsburg and Ottoman armies in 1688–1792 had uprooted its Muslim population, which consequently numbered only about 40,000 by 1804, weakening the foundations there of Ottoman statehood. This marked a difference with the neighbouring Eyalet of Bosnia, which the Ottomans and local Muslims more successfully defended and which was consequently much more firmly rooted by the nineteenth century's start. Hence, the Smederevo sanjak would prove a more conducive location for founding Serb statehood than Bosnia, even though the latter's Serb population was of comparable size to the former's and may at one point have exceeded it.[137]

Hopes for Serbia's liberation were accompanied by awakened Serb political activity in Hungary. Under the enlightened emperors Joseph II (King of Hungary and Croatia, 1780–1790) and Leopold II (King of Hungary and Croatia, 1790–1792), the Orthodox Church's rights in the Habsburg lands were improved.[138] At the initiative of the Serbian metropolitan, an assembly of a hundred Serb representatives, including some from the Smederevo sanjak, was held at Temesvár between 26 August and 22 November 1790 with the Habsburg court's blessing. It submitted a demand to the emperor for Serb equality with Germans and Hungarians and territorial autonomy for Banat in Hungary as a Serb unit. This was not granted so as not to offend the Hungarians, but the emperor did restore the Deputation as the Illyrian Court Chancellery. Although abolished again in 1792, it was a step on the road to the formation of Vojvodina; politically conscious Serbs at this time saw their national centre as this area within Habsburg Hungary rather than as the Ottoman territory that would emerge as Serbia. Unable to grant their Serb subjects' national demands at home, the Habsburgs considered appeasing them by liberating Serbian territory in the Ottoman Empire.[139] Briefly but crucially, the Habsburgs supported the Serb national cause. Permitted by the emperor their own gymnasium, printing press and newspapers, the Habsburg Serbs underwent a new renaissance whose sons would contribute significantly to building the future Serbian state. Dositej Obradović (1739–1811), a Serb from Banat, promoted Serb educational institutions and Western learning in Hungary and became education minister in Serbia's rebel government shortly before his death. He was the pioneer of the modern Serb intellectual.

2

THE SERBIAN UPRISINGS

1804–1815

Modern Serbia arose from the Sanjak of Smederevo. This Ottoman administrative unit roughly corresponded to the region of Šumadija ('Sylvania', or 'Land of Forest'), modern Serbia's heartland. The social, economic and geopolitical circumstances of this region, on the Habsburg Empire's border, combined explosively: its Orthodox Serbs were increasingly oppressed, exploited and fractious yet retained the residual communal autonomy granted them by the Ottomans—a starting point for their bid for statehood. Meanwhile, across the border in Austria, Serb national life flourished. Austria, which since 1687 incorporated Hungary and which in 1804 would be formally constituted as the Empire of Austria, served as a wrecking ball to weaken Ottoman rule in the sanjak while mobilising Serbs to fight it. These factors produced a revolution in the sanjak in the first two decades of the nineteenth century. Historiography traditionally divides this into the First and Second Serbian Uprisings, though they formed a continuous process of resistance divided by a briefly successful episode of Ottoman repression. When this revolution began, the name 'Serbia' itself was not used by the inhabitants to refer to their country; they referred to themselves simply as the Serb people (srpski narod). In the nineteenth-century Serbian scholar Vladimir Karić's words, 'the name "Serbia" was unknown, almost until the start of this century, not only to the Serb people around our contemporary kingdom but to those Serbs who lived at the time in this bit of the Serb Lands.'[1] 'Serbia' as a concept in its modern sense was created by these uprisings.

Serbia on the eve of the uprisings

Šumadija was, at the nineteenth century's start, socially and economically underdeveloped by European standards. It almost wholly lacked proper roads, and the oak forests covering it were full of wolves, bears and other wild animals, but were ideal for farming pigs, which lived off the acorns; this formed the basis of livelihood for much of the Serbian Orthodox population. Decades of Ottoman–Serbian warfare had driven many peasants to shift from agricultural to pastoral husbandry, allowing them to migrate with their animals to the mountains to avoid the violence.[2] The great Serbian ethnographer Jovan Cvijić (1865–1927) calculated that in the nineteenth century only 20 per cent of Serbia's population was indigenous, the rest having migrated there from neighbouring lands since the start of the eighteenth, reducing any sense of difference between Serbs in Serbia and those in the neighbouring regions today comprising Bosnia, Hercegovina, Montenegro, Kosovo and Macedonia. Šumadija, depopulated by the war ending in 1739, with a weak Ottoman administration, few Muslims outside the towns and forests suitable for grazing, attracted the migrant husbandmen, many coming from mountainous areas where Ottoman authority had been weak, from which they brought the tradition of freer communal life.[3]

Šumadija's villages were small, rarely larger than twenty homes, usually dispersed over a wide area of up to five or six kilometres; houses in neighbouring villages were often closer to each other than houses in the same village.[4] Karadžić noted that 'some villages of forty houses are larger than Vienna', reflecting the husbandmen's needs.[5] Animal husbandry, primarily involving pigs, sheep, goats and to a lesser extent cattle, was largely subsistence, though those living closer to the Sava and Danube rivers in the north had greater opportunities for livestock trade. Most peasant huts were made of logs or bark with thatched roofs and a single room; windows were small apertures covered with oiled paper when available. Furniture was mostly unknown apart from three-legged stools by the hearth. Peasants followed the Turkish practice of sleeping and eating on the floor, using wooden spoons, with the whole family eating from the same pot. The inner walls were hung with firearms, tools and food like slabs of bacon, strings of peppers and wreaths of garlic. Stables were often attached to the house for warmth. Multiple rooms, furniture, ceramic roof tiles and glass windows began to appear during the 1830s. Peasants tended to begin each day with a shot of home-brewed šljivovica (plum brandy); the more prosperous ones had orchards to produce it.[6] The primitive nature of farming in Šumadija made it highly vulnerable to the weather; drought in 1802 and 1803 produced widespread hunger, more people becoming hajduks (brigands) and greater popular rebelliousness.

Rural society centred on the zadruga, or extended family commune, in which different generations of the same family and multiple married brothers, averaging four or five married men, cohabited in a homestead with a meticulous division of labour, creating communal self-sufficiency.[7] Since Ottoman taxes and kuluk duties were imposed on homesteads rather than on individuals or married couples, zadrugas lightened the burden.[8] The zadruga protected its members from loneliness, economic insecurity and material hardship, giving them a social support network and status.[9] The senior male from every zadruga of a village, or more rarely the village's entire male population, would periodically assemble to discuss and determine village business, such as election of a kmet (headman), distribution of taxes, management of communal property, resolution of disputes between villagers, punishment of miscreants, maintenance of public morality and relations with the Ottoman authorities.[10] The calendar was marked by saints' days which had once numbered 170 per year, the majority of them holidays when peasants did not work. The Serbian church's canonisation of its saints by 1787 reduced these holidays to 81 per year, while there were at least 55 others when peasants did not work for reasons of folk religion, though many of these were in the winter when peasants could not work in the fields anyway.[11] Serbs individually prayed to God in the morning when awaking, together as a family before supper and again individually at bedtime.[12] Lingering pagan influence on folk Christianity was strong; the pagan practice whereby each household paid tribute to a household god had evolved into worship of a household patron saint, the celebration of whose saint's day—'slava'—was a major event in every Serbian family's year and largely remains so today. Each village also had its patron saint, whose day was celebrated and who was supposed to protect it and bring it a bountiful year. The Serbian custom of eating roast pork for Christmas dinner may also have originated in pagan times, with the sacrificing of pigs to the sun god, Dajbog, although another theory is that it was adopted under the Ottomans to prevent Turkish lords entering Serb homes during Christmas and appropriating the meal.[13]

Zadrugas were rigidly hierarchical by age and sex. Fathers were due enormous respect; sons in their presence were required to be quiet and calm, avoid expressions of merriment, not to smoke or look at their wives or sit without their permission, and had to keep some steps behind them when out walking. Women were entirely subordinate to men: considered unclean, they rarely appeared in the streets and never at public gatherings. They could not enter churches until 1730 and adulteresses were sometimes stoned to death. In the zadruga, all adult men were considered senior to all women. Wives, like children, were considered property of their husbands, who could legitimately beat them. It was considered disgraceful for a wife to refer to her husband by name; she could refer to him only as 'he'. Wives were widely required to kiss the hands and wash the feet of male relatives, particularly fathers-in-law, and of visitors; children also had to kiss adults' hands. Like Ottoman Muslims, Serb Christians sometimes practised polygamy and, if of sufficient status, kept harems. Serb Christian women, like Muslim women, were required by Ottoman law until 1830 to veil their faces and keep their shoulders and bodies covered in public.[14] When Serb women in Belgrade left the house, they would dress to be as inconspicuous as possible and take the backstreets to avoid the male gaze; foreign visitors remarked how rare it was to see women in the street, particularly Christian women.[15] When European-style furniture was introduced into Serbian homes in the 1830s, women initially could not eat at the table alongside males, but were required to wait upon them and were seated apart in the Ottoman manner. Young women were nevertheless protected and valued as marriage partners; monetary purchase and abduction of girls were widespread, while a young man who impregnated his unmarried lover would probably be pressed by the community into marrying her.[16]

There were no qualified doctors in Šumadija until 1819; for medical treatment, people relied upon folk healers or so-called hećimi—Ottoman Muslim or ethnic-Greek travelling doctors of often dubious medical proficiency.[17] The habit, introduced by the Turks, of smoking tobacco in pipes (chibouks) was widespread, and combined with the lack of proper medical care helps explain why, until the twentieth century, even Serbian statesmen tended to die before they reached their seventies. Even today, Serbians are among Europe's heaviest smokers.[18] Alongside the church there existed a lively and colourful set of folk beliefs and superstitions, some of which originated in pagan times. People believed in spirits, vampires, fairies, witches and other supernatural beings, and there were cases of witch-burning until 1803. Common customs included opening doors and windows of a house following a death to allow the spirit to leave, and burying money alongside the dead to allow their souls to pay for crossing the river in the underworld. It was widely believed that spirits of the dead could either aid or punish the living, depending on how respectfully their mortal remains were treated and their memory preserved.[19] Epic poems, recounting the exploits of legendary or mythical heroes of the Middle Ages and early Ottoman era and sung by bards while playing the gusle, a one-stringed instrument, provided escape from the reality of peasant life under the Ottomans, while preserving, in mythologised form, folk memory of medieval Serbia.[20] The practice of making a pilgrimage to Jerusalem arose among Serbs and other Balkan Orthodox Christians in emulation of the Muslim hajj to Mecca; they referred to it by the Turkish word for its Muslim counterpart, hacılık.[21] Serbs who had made the hajj added the prefix 'Hadži' to their name, for example Hadži Milutin Savić Garašanin, father of the famous nineteenth-century statesman Ilija Garašanin.

Tyranny of the deys

Selim III was Sultan from 1789. Following the disastrous losses of the war ending in 1791, primarily to the Russians, he resolved to reform the Ottoman Empire. Given the empire's poor military performance and the perennial readiness of Ottoman Christians to revolt in support of its foreign enemies, he sought both to reform the Ottoman armed forces and improve conditions for the Christian peasantry. This meant attacking the vested interests of some segments of the Ottoman establishment and population, above all the janissaries. These had degenerated by the end of the eighteenth century into a parasitic class, swollen by the influx of Muslim poor seeking to evade civilian taxes. It terrorised and exploited ordinary people—both Christians and Muslims—and obstructed the government and state.[22] What followed was a power struggle in the empire between Selim and the reformers on the one hand and

THE SERBIAN UPRISINGS

the janissaries and other conservative elements on the other, in which the Serbs and other Christian subjects became involved.

Following the Treaty of Sistova, the muhafiz of Belgrade's jurisdiction was reduced to the Sanjak of Smederevo and the town of Šabac; the so-called Belgrade pashaluk now corresponded almost completely to this single sanjak. This was organised as twelve nahijas, each with a müsellim commanding a body of troops (sejmeni) and a kadi with a scribe. Each nahija was divided into knežinas, each headed by a knez. Selim appointed the reformer Abu-Bekir Pasha governor of the Smederevo sanjak in 1793, mandated to mobilise the Serbs behind his goal of restoring Constantinople's authority over the janissaries. Abu-Bekir consequently forbade the janissaries to reside in the sanjak, amnestied Serbs who had supported the Habsburgs in the war, promised to restore the possessions of those who returned to their homes and generally took steps to improve conditions for the Christians. The knežinas were granted autonomy ('self-management') over their own affairs by a firman (decree) of the Sultan in 1793. Thus, each village elected a kmet, while groups of villages elected a knez, though the post tended in practice to become hereditary. The knezes presided over popular assemblies at the knežina level, composed of kmets and other local notables and genuinely representative of local opinion, where matters such as tax collection, maintenance of religious buildings and relations with the Ottoman authorities were discussed. The knezes in 1739–1804 were not landlords as in earlier times; they 'were peasants and in their domestic lives differed little from the other peasants', according to Karadžić.[23] The obor-knezes, likewise elected by the populace, served as intermediaries between the Serbs and Ottoman authorities. The knezes and obor-knezes were confirmed in office by the pasha. Taxes were reduced and capped and Muslims forbidden to enter Serb villages. In principle, Serbs could accuse their knezes of wrongdoing before the müsellims or the vizier in Belgrade, but unsurprisingly this was rare. New firmans in 1794 banned the sipahis in the pashalik from residing anywhere outside Belgrade, and Serbs were permitted to build churches in all areas where they resided. This led to the building or renewal of ten churches or monasteries in the following six years.[24]

The janissaries and their supporters counter-attacked. Abu-Bekir Pasha was replaced in 1795 by Shashit Pasha, who moved to restore janissary authority in the Smederevo sanjak. This was but a brief interlude, however, as Selim used the knezes' complaints in July of that year to replace Shashit with Hadži Mustafa Pasha, who had previously served as Belgrade's custodian, when he mobilised the Serbs to resist the janissaries. His reign would be fondly remembered by the Serbs; he was popularly dubbed 'Serb mother'.[25] Another firman in 1796 reaffirmed knežina autonomy and transferred to the knezes the right to collect the Sultan's tribute. According to an Austrian report, a majority of the sanjak's knezes gathered in April 1796 and elected a 'supreme knez'—a certain Petar, probably from Ćuprija.[26] Janissaries fled the sanjak in large numbers, many of them taking refuge with Pasvanoglu Osman Pasha, the conservative governor of Vidin in what is today Bulgaria. There followed a virtual civil war in the region between conservatives and reformists, in which Pasvanoglu raided the sanjak and was then attacked by loyalist Ottoman forces led by the governor of Rumelia.[27] In 1797–1798, Serbian knezes were permitted to collect their own taxes and raise a militia, which came to number 15,000–16,000, armed with muskets, pistols and yataghans (sabres), to help the governor maintain order against the janissaries.

Mustafa Pasha supplied munitions to the Serb militia and ordered town criers to announce in all marketplaces on market day, 'Hear men! Whoever is a Serb and has not a long musket, two pistols and a long knife, let him sell a cow and buy himself arms. Whoever does not obey shall receive 50 strokes of the bastinado and pay 50 groschen in fine. Hear and heed well, for this is the vizier's command!'[28] He rewarded Serbs with a bounty of two ducats for the head of every rebel janissary they delivered and four ducats for a live rebel.[29] The militia was organised on the basis of the sanjak's twelve nahijas, under overall command of Stanko Arambašić. It would form the basis of the future Serb rebel army and the Serbian autonomous state that would emerge from it. Meanwhile, the reforms improved social conditions, enabling prosperous Serb peasants to engage profitably in the export trade, producing between the early 1790s and early 1800s a new class of pig and cattle merchants, who exported yearly around 4,000 heads of cattle and 160,000 pigs to Austria and central Germany. Their prosperity compared with that of ordinary peasants led them to consider themselves the most important members of the community. This class provided many leaders of the rebellion beginning in 1804, such as Karađorđe Petrović, Miloš Obrenović and Hajduk Veljko (Petrović).[30]

However, a conservative reaction in Constantinople and the danger represented by Pasvanoglu's fractious activities led to a reversal of Ottoman policy. Arambašić was murdered in 1798 and the following year Mustafa Pasha was forced to permit the janissaries to return and increase taxes on the Christians. This produced a tyranny of the janissaries, headed by their four dahijas (deys)—Küçük-Ali, Aganlija Husein Bayraktar, Mehmed Foça-oglu and Mülla Yusuf—who divided the sanjak between themselves. In 1800–1801, after Ottoman forces had been transferred from the Balkans to counter the French invasion of Egypt, Pasvanoglu attacked the sanjak, capturing Požarevac, Smederevo and Belgrade except the citadel, where Mustafa Pasha held out. Serb forces under the knezes then counter-attacked, driving the janissaries from the sanjak and restoring Mustafa Pasha's authority.[31] Resentment at the deys' behaviour united Christians and Muslims; the bey of the village of Urovci near Belgrade allegedly told Knez Aleksa Nenadović, a Free Corps veteran and member of the powerful Nenadović family: 'You see, knez, what those four dogs are doing both to the *raya* and to the honourable Turks ... if they could, they would take this village from me and appropriate it for themselves, but the flint in me is still strong. I tell you: they will not last long.'[32] Nevertheless, under pressure from domestic conservatives, Selim was forced to pardon the janissaries and permit them to return to Belgrade. They seized the city on 20 August 1801 and, after Pasvanoglu's forces had intervened to ensure their victory, captured the citadel and murdered Mustafa Pasha. He died with plans formulated for a joint movement of Serbs and Turks loyal to the Sultan to resist the deys, while the deys, having crushed their Turkish opponents, now prepared to move against the Serbs.[33]

The janissaries terrorised and killed both Serb Christians and sipahis. Self-management of the knežinas was once again abolished. Serbs complained to the Sultan who, following the end of his war with France, sent an expedition to restore order in the Smederevo sanjak, inviting the Serbs to join him in crushing the rebellious janissaries and restoring his rule. Consequently, from early 1803, the Serbs began preparing for an uprising; in February of that year, all twelve obor-knezes met for this purpose. The deys learned that this would enjoy the Sultan's support, so sought to pre-empt this by a systematic massacre of all potential Serb rebel leaders, subsequently known as the 'chopping of the knezes'. They hoped to replace the Sanjak's administration by knezes with a tighter Muslim order, as in neighbouring Bosnia, in which they would become ayans.[34] On 4–10 February 1804 they killed about 140 Serb notables—obor-knezes, knezes, buljubašas (a buljubaša being a commander of fifty men), kmets, priests, monks and merchants—including Aleksa Nenadović, who had been at the centre of resistance preparations. This prompted other intended victims to flee to the woods to join the hajduks, who spearheaded the armed resistance under Stanoje Glavaš, Hajduk Veljko and others. Thus, the First Serbian Uprising began as part of a conflict between Ottoman factions, with the Serbs defending the reforming Sultan's authority against local reactionaries defying it.

Rebellion against the deys

The figure of pig-trader Karađorđe Petrović (1768?–1817), from the village of Viševac near Topola, would become synonymous with the uprising as rebel Serbia's 'Chief'. His family had migrated to the Smederevo sanjak from Montenegro in the first half of the eighteenth century. There is great disagreement among historians about when he was born; the year 1768 is perhaps most likely, but estimates range from 1749 to 1770.[35] His nickname Karađorđe meant 'Black Đorđe'—'kara' being a Turkish loanword. Prior to leading the uprising, his biography exemplified the experience of his generation of Serbs. He had married in autumn 1785 or spring 1786, and his Muslim landlord had apparently wanted to sleep with his bride; either to avoid this, or because he actually killed the landlord and wanted to avoid punishment, he trekked with his family across the border into Srem in Austria, accompanied by some other families. An incident on this trek, highlighting his steely character, occurred when his father abandoned the refugee column. According to folk legend, his mother Marica then said: 'Đorđe, you dishonour the milk that you suckled from these breasts if you do not kill that dog. Kill him so that he does not inform on us to the Turks. Better that he alone should die than that thirty souls should fall into slavery.' Karađorđe consequently killed his father. But a decade later, returning from exile, he sought the church's forgiveness for doing so. This he received in the presence of many people from his locality, who knew what he had done and whom he needed to witness his penitence. He distributed to the crowd a large quantity of brandy, wine and bread, which they consumed, saying, 'May God forgive him for having, out of necessity, ordered the killing of his father.' The archimandrite read the pardon and received five ducats from Karađorđe, who also donated an ox to the monastery.[36]

Karađorđe consequently made a natural recruit for Austria's Free Corps.[37] He served with distinction against the Ottomans and the Austrians decorated him for bravery. This gained him both status and military experience. When the Austrians withdrew from Ottoman territory, he continued the struggle as a hajduk and was known to kidnap Serb women as wives for his men, in which he was resisted by Aleksa Nenadović. Muslim janissaries and Christian hajduks collaborated against the Ottoman authorities and in terrorising the Serb population, but with the Peace of Sistova, Karađorđe switched sides and joined Mustafa Pasha's militia to fight for the knezes against the hajduks. He attained senior rank but, following Arambašić's murder, returned to brigandage.[38] As a mere hajduk rather than a knez, Karađorđe was not targeted by the deys during the chopping of the knezes, which may have saved him. Nevertheless, after janissaries attacked his home, he formed a rebel band on 11 February. Leaders of the Serbs in his locality, driven into rebellion by the massacre, gathered in Orašac near Aranđelovac in mid-February, probably on the 14th, to elect a commander; the first choice, hajduk leader Stanoje Glavaš, declined in the belief that he lacked the appropriate military experience, while the second choice, Teodosije Maričević, knez of Orašac, declined on the grounds that he was a knez, not a hajduk leader. Karađorđe was elected as the third choice; he allegedly tried to decline, on the grounds that 'I am a person angry and wicked, and whoever doesn't obey me, or goes off to one side, or tries to push his own thing, I will kill that person, and you will hate me for that and everyone for their part will try to undermine me, so that there will be nothing left of us, and the Turks will be only waiting for this, so that we will collapse worse than before', to which the refrain came from the assembly, 'We want you and we need someone like you, and if we have such a strict chief, we will all help you in everything.'[39] Archpriest Mateja Nenadović, son of murdered Aleksa, who himself became an important rebel leader, provided the rebels on 15 February with what was probably their first flag: the banner of his church in Brankovina, of red, white and blue muslin with three crosses.[40]

The Sultan's firman arrived in the sanjak on 12 March, legitimising resistance to the janissaries and inviting all Ottoman officials and Serb and Muslim inhabitants to join the rebels. Arms flowed to the rebels from the loyalist Ottoman authorities and from Serbs in the Habsburg Empire, whose officials acquiesced, given the 'rebellion' was defending the Sultan's authority.[41] As Ekmečić writes, 'When it broke out in 1804, the Serbian revolution was not exclusively Serb nor exclusively peasant. Part of the Muslim population joined the uprising and with the Christians fought against the janissaries. The Sultan himself, initially, gave support to this movement.'[42] Within a month, the rebels had liberated almost all Šumadija. Their leaders held an assembly at Ostružnica near Belgrade during May to formulate their demands to the deys. These centred on restoration of the Serbs' autonomous rights conceded in the 1790s, the end of the deys' rule in the sanjak, and the election of a supreme knez as the Serbs' representative before the Sultan. On this occasion, Maričević, apparently regretting ceding the rebellion's leadership to Karađorđe, whom he despised as an illiterate hajduk, and after prolonged tension between the two, openly challenged him. This led to a gunfight in which Karađorđe killed Maričević, which served as a warning to other Serb notables and confirmed the leader's authority.[43]

Negotiations between the Serbs and Ottomans, mediated by the Austrians, occurred on 10 May at Zemun, a town in Austria across the river from Belgrade, resulting in the Ottomans accepting the Serb demands. But the deys rejected them and continued fighting.[44] The rebels under Karađorđe and Jakov Nenadović captured Požarevac in mid-June. Abu-Bekir Pasha, now vizier of Bosnia, intervened with his army against the deys on 12 July and, with his blessing, the latter were pursued to the Danubian island of Ada Kaleh by Karađorđe's officer Milenko Stojković. The island's Ottoman commander informed the Serbs of their arrival, and, with his assistance, all four were executed on 5–6 August after a fierce struggle. Their heads were cut off as proof of the act; when the gypsy tasked with washing the heads accidentally let Aganlija's be washed away by the river, the Serbs beat him so badly in punishment that he died.[45] That summer, all of the Smederevo sanjak except Belgrade was in Serb rebel hands, although with the destruction of the janissaries, the rebels were abandoned by the sipahis. The rebels and Ottomans were by September able to agree on most points: Karađorđe's recognition as Serb supreme knez; complete Serb autonomy in taxation; a ban on Muslims residing in the sanjak outside Belgrade without Karađorđe's permission; all Ottoman customs and justice officials to be replaced by Serbs; all forts in the sanjak to be garrisoned by equal numbers of Serb and Ottoman troops; Karađorđe to be permitted a 500-strong personal guard; and the Serbs to pay the Sultan an annual tribute of half a million piasters and provide sufficient money to maintain the governor's administration. But the Ottomans were unable to accept the rebels' demand that the terms be guaranteed by a foreign power. They attempted to appease the Serbs by unilaterally implementing their demands for autonomy of tax collection in the sanjak under the knezes and confinement of the sipahis to the towns. But Selim also demanded that the rebels lay down their arms and rely for protection on the new vizier, Süleyman Pasha, and on 4 October his firman was read in Belgrade demanding the rebels go home. In refusing to do so, the rebels defied the Sultan's will for the first time, transforming a rebellion in defence of his authority into a rebellion against him.[46] Nevertheless, negotiations continued, and in December 1804 the Serbs conceded the sipahis' right to continue exploiting their estates.

Rebellion against the Sultan

Selim was under increasing pressure from conservatives at home to cease supporting the Serb rebels, particularly given the rebellion's spread southward to the towns of Kruševac and Niš, while the rebels were turning for support to foreign powers. The Serbs had appealed to the Habsburg emperor for protection already in April 1804, and Serb Free Corps veterans arrived from Austria to join the uprising as officers. Since the Austrians would not intervene, Karađorđe sent a delegation to St Petersburg in September to seek the Tsar's support. Both the Sultan and the rebels from late May or June 1805 were preparing for war against each other; the rebels captured Kruševac on 15 June and Karanovac (Kraljevo) on 11 July. Consequently, with the rebels planning to extend the uprising beyond the Smederevo sanjak, Selim in August 1805 ordered their suppression, thereby transforming the anti-dey rebellion into a Serbian war of independence. The first battle, at Ivankovac near Ćuprija on 18 August, occurred when the rebels attempted to prevent the newly appointed vizier of Belgrade moving there from Skopje, which he intended to do as prelude to the planned offensive against them. The rebels won the battle, killing the vizier, and Selim proclaimed a holy war against them.

The rebels held an assembly or parliament at Borak on 27 August 1805 which established a Governing Council, whose name was subsequently shortened simply to 'Council', intended to comprise elected representatives of all twelve nahijas of their embryonic state. Archpriest Mateja, a member of the delegation to St Petersburg, was behind this move, which he subsequently claimed had been suggested to him by Russia's foreign minister. Russia would consistently, for the next few decades, support such an institution in Serbia, believing it could be more reliably manipulated to support Russian policy than an individual Serbian autocrat. Similarly, Archpriest Mateja and other notables, including his uncle Jakov Nenadović, Milan Obrenović and Sima Marković, hoped to use the Council to curtail Karađorđe's power and maximise their own. Archpriest Mateja was supported by Boža Grujović (real name, Todor Filipović), a doctor of law and professor of legal history from the Austrian Empire, who arrived on rebel territory from Russia alongside Mateja. He favoured the Council, believing it would shape the fledgling state both on the Hungarian administrative model and in the spirit of French Revolutionary ideas of justice and legality. The Council's establishment was backed furthermore by Stefan Stratimirović, Metropolitan of Karlovac in the Austrian Empire and an ally of Jakov's, and by Karađorđe himself, to provide the rebellion with proper government.

Thus, the Council, an institution destined to play a central role in Serbian politics over the next half-century, was from the start intended to fulfil conflicting purposes by its various supporters.[47] Its first members, only four in number and representing only the four nahijas from which it was possible to select candidates at this time, were chosen by Archpriest Mateja on Karađorđe's authority. It expanded to ten members by autumn.

The Council's first seat was Voljavča monastery near Kragujevac, chosen by Karađorđe because it was in his own nahija. However, it soon moved to Bogovađa monastery, further to the north-west, where on 16 October it elected Karađorđe as its president, tasked with implementing its decisions, which had no validity without his signature. On 22 October, it decreed an inventory of the nation's wealth so as to apportion taxes, and the following day established a system of courts at the village, knežina, nahija and national level—the last being the Council itself—with a parallel system of religious courts.[48] The Council was transferred to Smederevo following its liberation on 20 November 1805; there, in the first half of December, a major assembly or parliament convened of the most prominent rebel leaders. On the 1st, it resolved to establish a national army. The head-tax was to be collected from both Serbs and Turks to finance it. Indeed, the Ottoman system of taxation was largely retained, with Serbs in part paying the traditional taxes to the rebel state rather than to the Ottomans, and in part to individual rebel commanders. These commanders frequently aspired to the privileges previously enjoyed by the former Muslim elite, and frequently similarly abused the peasants; for example, by extracting from them kuluk for their personal needs. As the historian Dragoslav Janković writes, 'almost all the warlords—some more, some less—behaved inhumanely with the people, oppressing and plundering them.'[49]

The Serbian people, meanwhile, were given a voice through assemblies periodically summoned and initially dominated by the knezes and kmets but increasingly by the same, often abusive rebel commanders. The question was therefore posed (and remained relevant for decades) whether or to what extent the new order based on Serb national freedom was an improvement on the old Ottoman order. Accounts differ over whether a struggle occurred at this time between Karađorđe and the Council, occasioned by the opposition's attempts to have the Council proclaimed supreme authority over the rebellion, and it almost led Karađorđe to abandon the parliament. Nevertheless, it was agreed on 7 December that Karađorđe would be supreme commander with Archpriest Mateja as Council president; the division of competencies between them was unclear. The Council consequently proclaimed its supreme authority over the land. The parliament dissolved itself after sending appeals to the Tsar and Sultan, whose authority it still formally recognised; the latter appeal was signed by Karađorđe as 'supreme commander of the Serbs', by Nenadović as Council president and by five other Council members representing the Valjevo,

Belgrade, Požarevac, Šabac and Rudnik nahijas. In practice, Karađorđe's leadership over Council, parliament and rebellion was generally supreme.[50]

Karađorđe's rebel army was spearheaded by hajduks and Free Corps veterans, its principal instructors being Serbs from the Military Border and elsewhere in the Habsburg Empire. But the army was organised on the basis of the traditional Ottoman administration. Thus, each of the Smederevo sanjak's twelve nahijas had one rebel army, organised into forces corresponding to the knežinas and under their knezes. In turn, each village in a knežina contributed a band of about ten to twelve men.[51] Thus, the Serbian rebellion represented a synthesis of the influences of the two empires, Habsburg and Ottoman. Although the two Serbian bishops of the dioceses of Belgrade and Šabac were Greeks who did not identify with the rebellion, a particular role in it was played by more junior Serbian Orthodox clergy: religious buildings were used as rebel bases, church flags became rebel flags, and priests blessed the rebels and themselves became leading rebel fighters and leaders, including Archpriest Mateja, Archimandrite Melentije Nikšić, the Reverend Luka Lazarević and others.[52] Archpriest Mateja recalled, 'When our army [in April 1806] gathered at the inn at Ub, I saw among our soldiers many sabres, bloody and battered knives, gun-butts likewise battered and broken, and every plunder taken from the Turks. Then I was very sorry that I had not managed to make it to the battle. But thanks to God and to our brother Serbs, we avenged our church and our homes.'[53]

Karađorđe brutally enforced martial discipline; he periodically beat, shot and killed his own chieftains and men to assert his authority. He humiliated cowardly Serbs by hanging Turks on the thresholds of their homes. He punished one defiant Serb by killing not only him but all his children as well. He did not discriminate; in June 1806, he made an example of his own brother Marinko, who was frequently guilty of acts of violence and theft, after a woman apparently complained to him that Marinko had assaulted her daughter: 'You are driving the Turks from Serbia, yet you've left behind in Topola Marinko, who is worse than any Turk.' The allusion to Turkish rapes of Serb women shamed Karađorđe; he hanged Marinko himself in the family courtyard in Topola. Marinko apparently did not attempt to deny the accusations, seek forgiveness or defend himself, although he was physically as strong as his brother. According to one account, Karađorđe then asked their mother what the punishment for rapists should be; she replied that only hanging could satisfy justice, so he pointed out her hanged son through the window. He allegedly banned his mother, wife and children from mourning his brother's death, threatening that anyone who did would suffer the same fate.[54] He then invited the Council, his military chieftains and a metropolitan to dine at his house with the corpse dangling outside.[55] Despite, or perhaps partly because of such brutality, his rebel army was highly successful; under his command, it defeated the Ottoman Bosnian army on 12–15 August 1806 at the Battle of Mišar. By summer 1806, it had liberated almost the entire sanjak. In September, it defeated a large Ottoman force under the vizier

THE SERBIAN UPRISINGS

of Shkodër, Ibrahim Pasha, at the Battle of Deligrad. After a long siege, it finally captured Belgrade on 13 December, though not its fortress. Karađorđe's biographer Milenko Vukičević wrote in 1912: 'After so many hundred years, the Serbs had again become masters of the town that constituted for them the door at the entrance from Central Europe to the Balkan peninsula.'[56]

The rebels continued to pay lip service to their loyalty to the Sultan; in the summer of 1806, rebuked for his disloyalty during negotiations with the Ottoman authorities in Bosnia, Archpriest Mateja replied, 'We are everywhere obedient to our emperor as our grandfathers and fathers were ... But all the lords and all Bosnia know, how the deys became; they killed Hadži Mustafa Pasha ...'[57] But this fiction was becoming harder to sustain. The transition from a war against the deys to a war against the Sultan ended rebel collaboration with sympathetic Muslims, who instead were killed in large-scale massacres. This was opposed by the great scholar Dositej Obradović, who wrote to the rebels on 10 August 1806: 'I advise you not to drive out and expel from your homeland all those Turks who are not soldiers (that is, janissaries and sipahis) ... ordinary Turks, peaceful traders, craftsmen, farmers, paupers and every Turk who lives for themselves and does not wish to rule over the *raya*; leave them to live in their homeland, as they have up till now, only place them under your administration, government and court, as you have up till now been under theirs.'[58] This advice was disregarded. In his history of the uprising, written with Karadžić's help, the great German historian Leopold von Ranke describes the intentions of the Serbian rebels, as they prepared to occupy Belgrade in late 1806: 'Nevertheless, it is probable that even at this time all the Turks were destined to be put to death.'[59]

The uprising became bound up with Great Power politics during 1806 as Selim adopted a pro-French policy, Napoleon penetrated the Balkan peninsula by annexing Dalmatia to his Kingdom of Italy, and Russia responded by occupying the Danubian Principalities of Moldavia and Wallachia. French officers advised the Ottoman commanders on operations against the Serbs. But when the Ottomans declared war on Russia in December 1806, Selim was prompted to conciliate them. A peace agreement had been negotiated in June and July by the rebels' diplomat Petar Ičko in Constantinople ('Ičko's Peace'), issued to the Serbs in August and accepted by their parliament in November; this was now ratified by the Sultan and the Serbs on 27 January 1807. Selim gave his blessing to the surrender to them of the Belgrade fortress, which they seized from the recalcitrant vizier Süleyman Pasha on 6–8 January, and of the Šabac fortress, which was delivered to them in February. The agreement granted the rebels amnesty; turned over Serbia to the administration of the knezes under the supreme knez, whose position would be hereditary; pledged the removal of all janissaries from the sanjak and all Ottoman troops except for a token force in the Belgrade citadel, and the removal of all sipahis from the countryside; granted the Serbs complete religious freedom with the right to found and restore churches, monasteries and schools; and turned over tax collection in the sanjak exclusively to the Serbian administration. In return, the Serbs would recognise the Sultan's suzerainty and pay him an annual tribute.

This peace agreement granted the Serbs their key demands but was undermined by Russian diplomacy, which sought to keep them fighting the Ottomans. The Serbian parliament was convened in Belgrade from 25 February to 6 March 1807 and resolved to repudiate the agreement, declare full independence and resume fighting alongside Russia. Consequently, on 6 March 1807 Karađorđe's forces attacked and massacred the vizier Süleyman Pasha and his entourage, after which most adult Turks in Belgrade and Šabac were massacred other than converts to Christianity, breaking their promise of a safe evacuation.[60] In Vukičević's words: 'There immediately then erupted on all sides an attack on the remaining Turks in Belgrade and on their families, sparing neither old nor young, male nor female, apart from those who agreed to be christened. The same such fate befell the remaining Turks in Šabac ...'[61] Muslims not slaughtered were expelled or forcibly converted to Christianity.[62] So were Jews, who, as an ethnically and religiously alien minority inhabiting the towns alongside the Muslims, were conflated with them by the rebels.[63] The massacre was encouraged by Russia's representatives with the rebels, to drive a permanent wedge between them and the Porte.[64] As many as 6,000 Muslims and Jews may have been forcibly converted to Christianity at this time, including Aganlija's principal widow, who changed her name from Runisha to Ljubica.[65] Most mosques in Belgrade and other towns held by the rebels were converted into churches.[66] In Belgrade, Muslims, Jews, Cincars and Greeks were conscripted into forced labour while Muslim girls were widely made available to young Serb men.[67] Some Muslim women and girls were taken into slavery: Milenko Stojković acquired many of them, relatives and wives of the men killed, and established his own harem for which he became famous.[68] The city changed demographically from Ottoman to Serb.

Russia sent officers, troops and funds to Serbia to help it establish a functioning army and administration; the Serbs launched offensives to link up with Russia's army in the Danubian Principalities. Serbian forces advanced on several fronts; on 18 July they captured Užice, in the fighting for which Miloš Obrenović, Serbia's future ruler, was heavily wounded. Meanwhile, Selim was overthrown by his conservative opponents on 29 May and replaced by Mustafa IV, and the regime in Constantinople descended into chaos. Russia's envoy Philip Paulucci travelled to Negotin and secured the rebels' signature for a Russo-Serbian convention on 10 July 1807 whose goal was a nominally independent Serbia under Russian protection and administration. A Russian gubernator was to organise the state and grant it a constitution in the name of the Tsar, in whose name all civilian and military officials would also be appointed, while Serbia's military occupation and control by Russia was also envisaged. Karađorđe opposed this since it envisaged his displacement in favour of the gubernator, while the opposition under Stojković supported it for that very reason. Karađorđe nevertheless felt unable to resist this alliance between the

Russians and Serbian opposition, and abandoned Negotin for the front, allowing his opponents to sign the convention in his absence. According to the historian Radoš Ljušić, 'Paulucci's convention brought to the fore Karađorđe's flaws: lack of tenacity in political talks, weakness in the face of Russian officials and military figures and insufficient motivation in the struggle with opponents from the opposition.'[69]

Karađorđe signed on 20 August 1807 the draft 'Foundation of a Serbian Administration' brought to Belgrade by another Russian agent, Konstantin Rodofinikin, which recognised him, as prince, merely as head of the Senate, not as the supreme executive power. This amounted to his capitulation before the Serbian opposition, while the draft's recognition of Serbia as remaining in the Ottoman Empire as an autonomous principality amounted to a major rebel climbdown. However, by this time, Napoleon had decisively defeated the Russians at the Battle of Friedland and signed with them the Treaty of Tilsit on 7 July, requiring them to end offensive operations against the Ottomans. Consequently, the Tsar no longer needed military cooperation with the Serbs, who were not mentioned at Tilsit, and did not sign the convention brought him by Paulucci, or Rodofinikin's draft.[70] Russia signed a truce with the Ottomans at Slobozia on 25 August. This period nevertheless came to be viewed as a duumvirate of Rodofinikin and Karađorđe; the Serbian priesthood began to speak of the Tsar as Serbia's ruler. Karađorđe was grateful for Rodofinikin's assistance, since 'my job is to wage war against the Turks; I don't understand other things'; he tended to leave management of the civilian administration to Rodofinikin while he concentrated on military affairs.[71] Consequently, Mladen Milovanović, who became Council president, emerged as the principal opposition to Rodofinikin and Russian hegemony. On Milovanović's prompting, the Serbs looked for support, in place of Russia, to Austria, which, it was hoped, would among other things help them alleviate Serbia's chronic food shortage. Karađorđe negotiated on 4 April 1808 with Austria's representative for Serbia's annexation to the Habsburg Empire. The Serbs divided into pro-Austrian and pro-Russian factions. But Russian diplomacy led by Rodofinikin counter-attacked and the vacillating Karađorđe quickly repudiated the mooted Austrian protectorate.

Ottoman military operations in 1808 were paralysed by the chaos convulsing Constantinople: Mustafa IV was overthrown in July by supporters of the reformist faction under Mustafa Pasha Bayraktar and replaced by Mahmud II. Mustafa Pasha Bayraktar became grand vizier, but the janissaries then counter-attacked in November and killed him. The Ottomans were consequently again ready to recognise most Serb demands, but negotiations failed on 4 December on account of Serb insistence that any agreement be guaranteed by Russia. In encouraging Serb intransigence on this point, the Russians, through Rodofinikin, once again torpedoed a peace settlement.[72] The Russians sought to determine Serbia's internal organisation and external relations, given their contempt for the Serb leaders. As Rodofinikin wrote to Russia's commander-in-chief, Alexander Prozorovsky, in November 1808, 'Almost all the native chiefs, except two or three, as I had the honour of reporting to Your Excellency, were previously hajduks or swine-herds, who have not left the forest and whose ideas are very limited. These people now, by force of circumstance, are ruling Serbia, and, I can say, ruling as they want.' Rodofinikin believed it necessary to remove Karađorđe and Milovanović from Serbia before a proper state order could be introduced.[73] Nevertheless, the Council strove to establish a uniform system of courts and town commanders across the entire country, enforce the rule of law against unruly elders, impose universal military service, take control of the property of expelled Muslims, and regulate the clergy's income. It approved and funded the establishment by Jovan Savić, known as Ivan Jugović, a Serb from Sombor in Hungary, of a college for the training of state officials, known as the 'Great School' and modelled on the Hungarian Royal Academy, in Belgrade on 12 September 1808. Its first director was Dositej Obradović. Its students, numbering twenty in its first year and forty the next, were largely sons and nephews of members of the rebel elite, including Karađorđe's son Aleksa. Karadžić studied there too.[74]

Opposition to Karađorđe's increasingly arbitrary lordship meanwhile grew among the leading Serbian notables such as Milovanović, Jakov and Mateja Nenadović, and Stojković. The opposition was spurred by tales of his periodic murders. Once, a penniless widow complained to him that a priest had refused to bury her husband without financial reimbursement, so Karađorđe apparently went to the village, ordered two graves to be dug at his own expense, ordered the priest to bury the deceased in one of them, then ordered those present to bury the priest alive in the other. On another occasion, Karađorđe caught a pauper growing corn on one of his unused fields, so shot him dead; when the man's wife then screamed at him, he killed her with his sabre, leaving their six children orphaned. On a third occasion, he apparently permitted the killing of three of his baptised Turkish mistress's children and two other Turkish women by his secretary and the throwing of their bodies into the Danube at night. Whether or not the details of all these murders were accurate, they reflected the essence of Karađorđe's behaviour. Miloš Obrenović later recalled that there was not a single rebel commander, himself included, who did not 'shiver in his britches' when summoned before Karađorđe.[75] At the request of Rodofinikin, under pressure from the terrified and angry Council members, Prozorovsky wrote to Karađorđe on 25 May 1808, ordering that nobody could be punished without a trial.[76] Increasingly isolated among the rebellion's top figures, Karađorđe depended for his survival on the loyalty of his military commanders such as Petar Dobrnjac, Hajduk Veljko and Stanoje Glavaš.

Karađorđe and Council president Milovanović united to assert their leadership over the uprising in the face of Russian domination. A Serbian rebel parliament was convened at Topola on 7–12 December 1808 which proclaimed Karađorđe hereditary 'Supreme National Serb Leader'; all orders were to be given by him and the Council acting in agreement, and to pass from the leader through the Council to the subordinate commanders. The conservative scholar and statesman Stojan Novaković later characterised this as a 'coup d'état' and 'the first act of a modern centralised monarchical order' in Serbia.[77] With centrally appointed commanders as the senior officials at the nahija and knežina level, the traditional self-management of the Serbian people was ended in favour of a centralised national military leadership.[78] This was a strike against the influence of the Russians and their supporters among the rebels, depriving them of the power to influence who the leader of Serbia would be.[79] These decisions were confirmed on 26 December by the Council, which was reduced to a pliant body in Karađorđe's hands. These moves established in principle his absolute mastery over rebel Serbia, though in practice the rebel chieftains remained autonomous in their own localities.

Russia announced the resumption of offensive operations against the Ottomans in April 1809 and encouraged Serbia to fight alongside it. Seeking full independence, the Serbs consequently resumed offensive operations, ending a period of military inactivity by both sides since autumn 1807. They advanced in four directions: toward Vidin, under Stojković's command, into what is today the Sanjak of Novi Pazar, where forces under Karađorđe's personal command captured Stari Vlah, Nova Varoš, Sjenica, Prijepolje and Novi Pazar (except for the fortress); across the Drina into Bosnia, where Jakov Nenadović's forces seized Višegrad, Srebrenica, Janj and Bijeljina; and toward Niš. Alongside the rebel forces organised by locality, Karađorđe's leadership established a regular uniformed army which peaked at just over 4,300 troops in summer 1812.[80] Serbian forces may have peaked at somewhere between 38,000 and 49,000. Karađorđe in this period attempted to restrain his forces from massacring Muslim civilians so as to encourage the Ottoman surrender of strongholds, though massacres continued occurring against his wishes. Meanwhile, Napoleon signed the Treaty of Schönbrunn with Austria on 14 October 1809 and established the Illyrian Provinces, primarily from Slovene and Croatian territory taken from the Habsburgs, as a counterweight to rebel Serbia.[81]

This period of the uprising was memorable for several reasons. Filip Višnjić, a blind gusle player, joined the rebels following their incursion into Bosnia and became the uprising's bard: 'Ha, heroes! All for the holy guns. You with guns, and I with the gusle ...' Advancing on Niš, the Serbs were decisively defeated on 31 May at the Battle of Čegar; after fierce fighting, their commander, Vojvoda Stevan Sinđelić, realising further resistance was futile, fired into his own powder store, 'and went into the sky along with many Serbs and Turks'. Following this victory, the Ottoman commander, Huršid Ahmed Pasha, built the notorious 'Skull Tower' of Niš with the skulls of 952 slain rebels, to cow the local population. On another occasion, after the Serbs retreated from a village following an Ottoman counter-attack, abandoning fifty wounded whom the Ottomans immediately decapitated, Karađorđe blamed Milovanović and personally beat him up in front of the rebel leaders. Ljušić notes: 'The beating up of the second figure of the state left a terrible impression, not only among the elders but among the soldiers.'[82] Karađorđe ended by drawing his pistol and shooting Milovanović, narrowly failing to kill him but severely wounding him in the scrotum, after which he could not perform sexually or have children.[83]

Karađorđe's relations with the Russians broke down during 1809 in the face of the Ottoman victory at Čegar and recapture of Deligrad and Ćuprija and due to increasing rebel disillusionment with the Russian army's failure to defend Serbia. The Russians were blamed for preventing the Serbs from accepting the Ottomans' offers of amnesty and peace terms. The Council, under Karađorđe's and Milovanović's leadership, increasingly resisted Rodofinikin. After Rodofinikin learned that Karađorđe had said of him, 'I'm going to Belgrade to kill that dog,' he fled Serbia for Austrian territory in August and himself plotted Karađorđe's assassination.[84] The Russians became a pole of attraction for the swelling opposition to Karađorđe, embracing Stojković, Dobrnjac, Hajduk Veljko, Jakov and Mateja Nenadović and, eventually, Milan Obrenović; the Council re-emerged as a body in opposition to him. Encouraged by the Russians, Karađorđe's opponents among the local commanders withheld taxes and even resisted his officials by force; Stojković claimed he did not recognise Karađorđe's authority, but only the Tsar's. Karađorđe responded by sending on 28 August 1809 simultaneous offers to both France and Austria of a protectorate over Serbia. The offer to Austria was subsequently repeated on 10 January 1810, but none of these was accepted. Internationally isolated and facing growing domestic opposition, Karađorđe had to summon a parliament, which assembled in Belgrade in late November and early December and forced him to retreat; he had to dismiss his principal supporters, Milovanović and Miloje Petrović, accept Jakov Nenadović as the new Council president, and sign a new appeal to the Russians for military assistance. Nenadović now appeared to have gained the upper hand over Karađorđe and become the most powerful man in Serbia.[85] The Serbian parliament on 13 May 1810 forced Karađorđe to renounce any further intention of seeking Austrian protection. It required him instead to send Serbia's forces to join the Russians in their operations against the Ottomans. Russian and Serbian forces consequently met on the Danube on 17 June and proceeded to attack Ottoman positions in the region, liberating Prahovo, Kladovo, Negotin, Banja, Knjaževac and the whole of the Timok region, and, with Karađorđe in command of the Serbs, defeating the Ottomans at Varvarin on 18–22 September. The Ottomans were then pushed across the Drina.

Taking advantage in autumn 1810 of the fortuitous absence, incapacity or death of several leading members of the opposition including Stojković, Dobrnjac, Jakov Nenadović, Milan Obrenović and Hajduk Veljko, Karađorđe retaliated, purging its members from the Council and replacing them with his supporters, so that this body now definitely became simply an instrument of his rule. His absolute authority was then confirmed in a rebel parliament—the most representative one of the entire uprising—that convened in 19–25 January 1811. A small opposition current was represented by Luka Lazarević, Vujica Vuličević and Miloš Obrenović, but Karađorđe manipulated the body to do his bidding. He pledged before it to maintain the Russian alliance in perpetuity and govern on the basis of agreement with the (neutered) Council, now named once again the 'Governing Council'. This body now became a government with Karađorđe himself as president (prime minister), while other members had specific ministries: Milovanović became war minister; Stojković foreign minister; Obradović education minister; Jakov Nenadović interior minister; Marković finance minister; and Petar Todorović justice minister. Its premises displayed the imperial Russian coat of arms with the Serbian coat of arms beneath it.[86] The idea for such a government had originated with Mihailo Grujović, an ally of Karađorđe and Milovanović, who aimed thereby to limit the power of the Council and the assembly of rebel leaders, so as to strengthen Karađorđe's authority.[87] But while Karađorđe remained unassailable, he failed to reconcile his opponents among the warlords or maintain rebel unity.

The assembly bestowed on Karađorđe the power to appoint all military commanders at the level of town and knežina. Thus, the Serbian state-building process evolved into an assault on the very system of local autonomy that the Serbs had risen against the deys to defend. Two of Karađorđe's remaining opponents, Stojković and Dobrnjac, summoned the assembly of the Požarevac nahija in late February 1811, immediately to Belgrade's east, sparking a rebellion against him, which Karađorđe pacified, after which the pair fled Serbia permanently for exile in Wallachia. Karađorđe's attempt in March 1812 to recruit a contingent of Serbs to act as armed escort to the Russian commander, Mikhail Kutuzov, sparked a rebellion at the village of Garaši, near Kragujevac. Karađorđe crushed the rebellion and burned down the family home of the rebellion's leader, Hadži Milutin Savić Garašanin, whose family, including his two-month-old son, Ilija, was forced to relocate to Belgrade. But widespread resistance to the recruitment nevertheless prevented Karađorđe from providing the escort to Kutuzov.[88] Meanwhile, Serbs living in Ottoman-held territories—Montenegro, Kosovo and Macedonia and, to a lesser extent, Bosnia and Hercegovina—fled Ottoman terror in huge numbers to take refuge in rebel Serbia, joined by Serbs from Austria wishing to join the national struggle; the population of rebel Serbia may have increased from 180,000 at the uprising's start to about half a million by 1811. This helped dissolve local particularism among Serbs and consolidate their sense of common identity, even as Karađorđe's tyranny undermined the struggle.[89]

Ottoman reconquest

Russia ended its war against the Ottomans with the Treaty of Bucharest on 28 May 1812. Despite its victory, its impending invasion by Napoleon forced it to offer moderate terms. The Ottomans granted an amnesty to the Serb rebels but were permitted to reoccupy the Serbian towns. The Serbs gained a legally recognised status and a vague promise of autonomy, but without any mechanism or oversight to guarantee Ottoman compliance. Autonomous Serbia was to include six nahijas that were not part of the Sanjak of Smederevo but that had been encompassed by the uprising. When Napoleon's Grande Armée the following month invaded Russia, the latter withdrew its forces from Serbia in August. Sultan Mahmud then saw no reason to abide by the terms of the treaty. Although the French invasion collapsed by December when Napoleon's last troops left Russia, the Russians remained preoccupied with the war against him; as late as August 1813 he scored a great victory over them and their allies at the Battle of Dresden. Mahmud consequently commenced a full-scale reconquest of Serbia in July 1813 while the Serbs were demoralised and weakened by the conflict between Karađorđe and the opposition.[90]

Karađorđe and the Governing Council fled Serbia in October as part of another large exodus of Serbs numbering about 110,000. Karađorđe crossed on the 3rd to Zemun, two days before the Ottomans retook Belgrade. The rebellion was drowned in blood. The Ottomans carried out the systematic mass extermination of Serbian males and mass enslavement of women and children. Approximately another 100,000 Serbs may have disappeared from Serbia as a result; Mahmud Pasha of Prizren sent about 300 Serb children to Constantinople as gifts to dignitaries of the Porte and kept up to 30 women and children for himself, while in a single day in Belgrade in October 1,800 women and children were exhibited for sale.[91] Almost the entire Serb population fled Belgrade. Gibbets and decapitated rebel heads were displayed everywhere in and around the city. Visiting in 1829, the Prussian travel-writer Otto Ferdinand Dubislav von Pirch noted: 'The old town of Belgrade was burned down and is so ruined that, apart from one or two houses, only ruins of the old buildings built of stone are to be seen. Such as it is now, Belgrade does not look like towns such as we see in civilised lands ...'[92]

The Ottoman *ancien régime* was harshly reimposed on Serbia; knezes and obor-knezes were restored as mere Ottoman functionaries, without self-management for the knežinas or nahijas. Karađorđe's revolution thus ended in disaster. His defeat and flight irreparably destroyed his and his commanders' standing among the Serbian population, ensuring they would never hold power in Serbia again.[93] Most rebel leaders fled to Austria, and as regards those who remained, 'They were not thought of well by the people either; they hid from the people as from the Turks; blame for the past and for the suffering of misfortune was heaped upon the elders; they were everywhere followed by curses and the desire for revenge'.[94] From exile, Karađorđe accepted responsibility for the disaster, in part because of his rebels' brutality towards the Ottoman Muslims: 'If we had not killed the pasha at Emekluk [behind Belgrade]; if we had not Christened Turks; if we had not taken their wives and girls for our Serbs; and if we had not gone to Sjenica, we would not have collapsed, nor would we have so enraged the Turks.'[95] But one rebel commander who refused to flee and bravely remained in Serbia, Miloš Obrenović, was thenceforth favourably compared with Karađorđe and would replace him as the Serbian national leader.[96]

Karađorđe became an archetype for future Serb rebels and nationalists: fearless, charismatic, brutal and terrifying. Vladimir Stojančević, a leading Serbian historian of nineteenth-century Serbia, displays typical reverence:

> Of all the personal strengths and qualities that Karađorđe manifested during the First Insurrection, three were outstanding—manliness, military genius and statesmanship. In the historical tradition of the Serbian people, Karađorđe has been regarded as a man of exceptionally great courage. He was tall, slightly stooped in the shoulders, and had powerful biceps ... On the battlefield Karađorđe personified the collective will of the Serbian people and their perseverance in the centuries-long struggle with the Turks. Regardless of the degree of danger posed by the presence of hostile forces, the 'supreme leader' remained fearless and confident of the outcome. According to contemporary accounts, Karađorđe decisively and boldly engaged the Turks in battle, and so excelled in fierce combat with a yatagan, rifle and pistol that among contemporaries he had no equal.[97]

But he was self-destructive and destined to heroic failure, while his ready use of brutality in pursuit of the national interest set a dangerous precedent. He was an ambiguous role model.

The catastrophe of 1813 cost Serbia about a third of its population, which in 1815 numbered around 300,000 inhabiting about 1,400 settlements. The Sanjak of Smederevo was reduced to its original size, without the six nahijas. The catastrophe had one benefit for the Serbs: the exodus of many rebel leaders allowed the subsequent concentration of national leadership in fewer and more capable hands, namely those of Miloš Obrenović (1780–1860). He was born in the village of Gornja Dobrinja near Požega in western Serbia to parents of Hercegovinian descent whose families had migrated to the region in the late seventeenth or early eighteenth century. As his father died when he was very young, leaving his mother a widow for the second time, Miloš grew up in extreme poverty and worked as a farmhand and eventually a salesman for his older half-brother Milan, a livestock trader, whose surname he took, from Milan's father Obren Martinović, Miloš's mother's first husband. Despite his humble beginnings, he became a skilled livestock trader in his own right and a self-made man. His work during his youth took him to towns across the Sanjak of Smederevo, Bosnia and the Adriatic coast, including Sarajevo, Zadar, Dubrovnik and, perhaps, Venice.[98] He fought in the First Serbian Uprising alongside Milan until the latter's death in late 1810, and was appointed commander of south-western Serbia by Karađorđe, who had been kum (best man) at his wedding. However, relations between the two soured after Miloš quarrelled with another prominent rebel who had lost Miloš's horse during a battle with the Turks; Karađorđe was so angered by Miloš's small-mindedness that he warned him, 'If I hear you once more, in any way, mention the horse to him again, I'll cut your head off.' Miloš was not given the rewards under Karađorđe he felt he deserved, and may have suspected him of having his brother murdered. He joined the opposition to Karađorđe and was arrested by him in 1811 for plotting rebellion, tried before the Council but pardoned, though he remained in disfavour, and Karađorđe sent back the medal awarded Miloš by the Tsar.[99]

Miloš refused to flee into exile following the rebellion's defeat, instead surrendering to the vizier Ali-aga Serčesmi, who spared his life, guaranteed his safety and, as a token of respect, permitted him to keep his weapons except for his sabre. He was then appointed obor-knez of the Rudnik nahija and persuaded other Serb rebels to surrender.[100] Belgrade's new vizier, Süleyman Pasha Skopljak, even adopted Miloš as his son. He immediately made himself useful to the Ottomans by joining a mission of prominent Serbs sent in February 1814 to Austria to arrange the return of the refugees who had fled the Ottoman reconquest. These were living in terrible poverty and feared being conscripted to serve in Austria's wars against France, while the Ottomans wanted to restore the Smederevo sanjak's economy and eliminate the potential threat posed by having so many of their subjects in Austrian hands. The mission facilitated the return of 30,000 refugees with their livestock by April.[101] Meanwhile, the Russians had arranged Karađorđe's release from Austrian prison and his transport to Bessarabia, and it was expected they would employ him for further intrigues. Miloš, fearing both Karađorđe and Ottoman reprisal, wrote to the Tsar, telling him the Serbian people would never accept back Karađorđe and his elders, who had been 'worse than the Turks'.[102]

The situation in reconquered Serbia was unstable. The Ottomans feared a renewed attack by Austria and Russia and viewed the discontented Serbian population as a security threat, while efforts at collaboration between Turks and Serbs were undermined by mutual mistrust. A key incident involved Hadži Prodan Gligorijević, a rebel who surrendered to the Ottomans and who was rewarded with a pardon, becoming a collaborator of the müsellim of Čačak in the Požega nahija. When men led by his cousin captured and robbed some Turks at the village of Trnava on 26 September 1814, he secured their release, but the Ottomans believed him responsible while local Serbs gathered around him, so that he was reluctantly compelled to head the new spontaneous revolt. Miloš refused the invitation to join it, instead assisting the Ottomans in suppressing it, encouraging the local population to remain calm and joining a combined Serb–Ottoman force to pursue the rebels. At the town of Knić in central Šumadija, he persuaded a group of about a thousand rebels to surrender or disperse.[103] He was rewarded by being made obor-knez also of the Kragujevac and Požega nahijas.

Nevertheless, the repression that followed the defeat of Hadži Prodan's uprising encompassed even Serbian collaborators. Miloš led a delegation of knezes to Belgrade in November, only to be told by Süleyman Pasha: 'These are all culprits!' Miloš replied, 'There are some who are guilty, but not all.' The knezes were required to provide names of all who were inciting disorder and collectively to guarantee the peace. Over a hundred prisoners, including women and children, taken following the collapse of the revolt, were massacred in Belgrade in January 1815.[104] A new reign of terror descended on Serbia as the Turks attempted to instil docility through murders and torture. A man was roasted alive in the Kragujevac nahija to force him to reveal his hidden weapons. In Ranke's words, 'the Turks would fill bags, like those out of which horses eat, with ashes, tie them under the chins of the women, and, by beating upon them, cause the dust to ascend into their mouths and nostrils. Some were bound hand and foot, and thus suspended by the extremities, with heavy stones hung from the middle of their bodies. Some were flogged to death; others roasted alive on spits.'[105] Turks spoke openly of a new 'chopping of the knezes' to encompass everyone who had fought under Karađorđe. Miloš and other collaborators were caught between desperate people seeking their protection and Ottoman authorities seeking blood.[106] In February, Süleyman Pasha had Stanoje Glavaš murdered; he was a great hajduk commander of the First Serbian Uprising who had, like Miloš, surrendered to the Ottomans and become their loyal collaborator. Knezes feared that if someone like Glavaš could be murdered, then any of them could be next.

When Miloš and other knezes in February answered a summons to Belgrade from Süleyman Pasha, he noticed Glavaš's head displayed at the city gate. A Turkish friend warned him that his head could be next, to which Miloš claimed he replied, 'I put my head in a bag ages ago and I am already wearing someone else's!' He noticed another twenty or so heads similarly displayed and saw the writing on the wall.[107] He was kept hostage by Süleyman Pasha while the other knezes were released after pledging they would write to the Sultan to request his mercy. At a meeting at Rudovci to the south of Belgrade, representatives of the Belgrade, Valjevo and Rudnik nahijas, among them Garašanin, resolved to offer Miloš leadership of a new uprising, not because they were particularly devoted to him but because they recognised his popular standing. A second rebel gathering, at the nearby settlement of Breoci, resolved to seek help from the Austrians. Miloš thus faced a choice: be killed by Süleyman Pasha, join with him in crushing the new impending revolt or lead the revolt himself. He consequently escaped to join the rebels.

Second Serbian Uprising

Miloš announced the revolt on 23 April 1815 at a popular gathering before the church of the village of Takovo in the Rudnik nahija, with the support of the elders of several neighbouring nahijas.[108] The revolt was presented as against not the Porte but merely Süleyman Pasha's brutality. Nevertheless, some knezes initially remained loyal to the vizier and fought with him against the rebels, including the Belgrade nahija's knez. In May, the rebels won an important victory at Palež, giving them access to the Austrian border through which munitions then reached them along with further recruits from among the émigré former rebels from the first uprising. The vizier sent his forces to crush the rebels, but they were surrounded at Čačak. The revolt rapidly spread throughout the Smederevo sanjak. The rebels succeeded by July in defeating Süleyman Pasha's forces in the sanjak, confining him to Belgrade. Miloš treated captured Muslim civilians and Ottoman soldiers relatively humanely and threatened punishment against rebels who harmed them, as Karadžić noted. This encouraged Turks to surrender to him and won him sympathy from Muslim civilians and goodwill and respect from the Ottoman commanders.[109] It laid the basis for Miloš's strategy of collaboration with the Ottomans, resulting in his uprising succeeding where Karađorđe's had failed. He treated captured Ottoman commander Ibrahim Pasha with great respect and courtesy while explaining to him the legitimacy of the Serbs' grievances, turning him from an enemy into a partner in the quest for a negotiated peace.[110]

The Porte responded to Miloš's defeat of Süleyman Pasha by ordering the Ottoman forces under the beyler-beys of Bosnia and Rumelia, Huršid Pasha and Maraşli Ali Pasha, to move against him. However, with Ibrahim Pasha's blessing, Miloš visited Huršid Pasha with a delegation of his knezes and kmets and negotiated with him over a period of four days in August, after which the beyler-bey granted him a twenty-day ceasefire. He then negotiated a peace agreement with Maraşli Ali. The rebels permitted the latter to send a detachment into Belgrade while they maintained their positions and sent a delegation to Constantinople led by Archimandrite Melentije Nikšić, on Maraşli Ali's recommendation, to request that Maraşli Ali replace Süleyman Pasha as vizier of Belgrade and that the rebellion be pardoned. Miloš's delegation assured the Sultan of his loyalty, blamed the 1807 peace agreement's failure on 'swindling by the Russians', and denounced Karađorđe.[111] The requests were granted. However, one of his demands, that he be named 'Great Knez', with the position hereditary in his family and with the right in conjunction with the vizier to select the obor-knezes, was removed by Nikšić from the list of demands before it was submitted, since he did not wish to empower Miloš further.[112] The delegation returned triumphantly in September.

Napoleon's final defeat at Waterloo on 18 June 1815 freed Russia to renew pressure on the Porte, giving the latter an incentive to settle the Serbian question promptly. Consequently, it appointed Maraşli Ali governor of Belgrade. Following an agreement between the latter and Miloš, probably on 5 November 1815, the two entered the city's Kalemegdan fortress together; Miloš sacrificed several rams in the Muslim Kurban style to honour the agreement. Maraşli Ali transferred tax collection in the Smederevo sanjak to the Serb knezes' exclusive authority, in which the Ottoman authorities would not interfere. A Serb obor-knez would be elected to every nahija alongside the müsellim; without him the latter would not be permitted to prosecute Serbs. The sipahis would be banned from extracting from their tenants more than their legal entitlement. Bosniaks and Albanians would be barred from the sanjak-bey's service. A National Chancellery would be established, comprising the twelve obor-knezes, which would prosecute Serbs for major crimes, sentence them to death where necessary and deliver to the vizier the taxes, customs duties and other monies owed. Serbs were permitted to carry small arms. In December, Maraşli Ali authorised Miloš to announce the uprising's end and organise the organs of government in the nahijas to maintain law and order.[113] These terms were then broadly confirmed and elaborated upon in a series of decrees issued by the Porte in February 1816.

Maraşli Ali had, from his perspective, simply reaffirmed Ottoman authority in the Smederevo sanjak based on the traditional arrangement with the knezes, with abuses curbed in the interest of stability and efficiency. He undertook to ensure that all Ottoman customs, taxes and dues would be exacted only in the legally prescribed way; that the Ottoman garrisons would be limited to the towns and would not burden the populace, with the janissaries (Bosniaks and Albanians) excluded from the garrisons with their families and their place taken by actual Turks; that Serbs would be permitted to travel and trade throughout the empire; that in the towns, a Serb knez would sit beside the Turkish officials to assist them in their duties; that the National Chancellery would be constituted as a permanent body; and that the Serbs would be pardoned for all past actions. The head-tax was reduced from thirteen to three groschen. The purely oral arrangement suited him since it promised smooth collection of taxes and dues and their steady flow into his coffers, which was his primary concern; the losers were the janissaries and other lower Ottoman officials who had milked the Christian population and siphoned off money due to the governor and state.[114]

Miloš became the vizier's top tax-collector and policeman. He was wary of Belgrade, seat of the vizier and his garrison and home to a heterogeneous population including thousands of Muslims, Jews and other non-Serbs.[115] Consequently, he chose for his capital Kragujevac, which was more safely in Serbian hands and at the geographical heart of his state; it was then little more than a village, with 193 houses, 378 head-tax payers and about 1,300 inhabitants overall.[116] It remained the capital until the end of his reign, though he maintained also a court in Požarevac where his family lived. He ruled from 1815 until 1839 and is the single most significant figure in Serbia's modern history. He embodied the Ottoman Serb past: he was, like Karađorđe, a pig-trader and remained illiterate all his life. With limited experience of the world outside Serbia, he learned his governing style from his former masters, ruling like an Ottoman pasha, his Serbia resembling an Ottoman pashalik run by Christians. Meanwhile, completion of the uprising and establishment of an autonomous Serbia began the process of differentiating it as a land from neighbouring Ottoman lands. In Ekmečić's words, 'Only the great battles of the Serbian revolution divided, in a political sense, Serbia from Bosnia, Old Serbia and Bulgaria. The chain of great war zones will, in the consciousness of the subsequent nation, create a conception of a border. Before them, that border was only administrative and geographic, not ethnic, cultural and linguistic.'[117] The name 'Serbia' was not immediately used by ordinary people after 1815 but was increasingly imported by educated Austrian Serbs recruited to staff the fledgling state's bureaucracy, and it gradually diffused into the population's consciousness.[118]

The Serbs in 1815 formally settled for much less than the Treaty of Bucharest had promised, but in practice the change was more radical than it seemed. Miloš succeeded in subordinating not only the knezes and Serbs generally but also the Muslim civilians and officials—sipahis, müsellim and kadis—whom the vizier would dismiss at his request. The sipahis, numbering approximately 500 at the time of the agreement, were aggressively encouraged to migrate from the countryside under Miloš's control to the Ottoman garrison towns. This was achieved by imposing a legal regime that invariably took the side of their Christian tenants against them, cutting their dues from tenants to below even what they were legally entitled to and, where necessary, even physically assaulting them. Although Miloš did not have the right to arrest Muslims, he could and did frequently intervene with the Ottoman authorities to have them arrested. The next five years, until the outbreak of the Greek War of independence in 1821, would be, in the words of Miloš's biographer Mihailo Gavrilović, 'a golden age of Serb–Muslim relations' in Serbia, as the country's two rulers, Maraşli Ali and Miloš, collaborated to ensure that neither group hurt the other; Miloš even repaired the mosque at Jagodina.[119] The newly liberated Serbs now began to wear Turkish dress previously forbidden to Christians: men and women in the towns wore, in the Turkish style, long, embroidered, wide-sleeved gowns (anterije) and baggy britches (salvare, dimije) while men also wore turbans. The Porte complained about the Serb appropriation of the turban; Miloš, who himself long dressed in the Turkish style, replied that 'by wearing the cloth, we speak, and show to the whole world the freedom that the Sultan has gifted us'.[120] Years later, in 1830, the Russian diplomat Alexander Ribeaupierre complained to Miloš's envoy Dimitrije Davidović about his master's habit of always wearing Turkish dress. He recommended that he adopt European-style dress and introduce uniforms for his officials while allowing his ordinary subjects to continue to dress as they had always done.[121] The fledgling Serbian state was very Ottoman.

Reborn Serbian statehood began as little more than limited autonomy based on the existing Ottoman framework and its traditional Serb institutions, whose enhancement the Ottomans permitted so as to re-establish order. This did not, at the time, seem a radical break with the existing order. The Serbs could have obtained a settlement soon after the start of their struggle similar to what Miloš ultimately achieved, had not Karađorđe pursued more radical goals. The dilemma was therefore posed and would remain with the Serbs for the next hundred years: whether to achieve their national goals slowly and incrementally, through collaboration with the imperial hegemon, or to try to achieve them much more quickly and fully through radical, aggressive action. Miloš's achievement suggested the first approach was superior, and his successors would continue to pursue Serbian national goals by collaborating with the Ottomans and, later, with the Austrians. Yet for future radicals disappointed by a Serbian state that seemed to combine authoritarianism at home with collaborationism abroad, the example of Karađorđe and the 1804 uprising remained inspirational.[122]

3

PRINCE MILOŠ AND THE FOUNDING OF MODERN SERBIA

1815–1839

The agreement between Miloš Obrenović and Maraşli Ali Pasha in 1815 ended the Second Serbian Uprising, but it remained tenuous, limited and informal, apparently amounting to little more than recognition of traditional Serb autonomy and rights. Miloš's rule was insecure, wedged as he was between the Ottoman regime and domestic rivals who sought to share his power. He nevertheless built upon this shaky foundation as he sought more powers from the Ottomans while cementing his authority. Albeit tyrannical, his regime launched a dynamic that would transform Serbia over the next quarter-century, securing its statehood.

Prince Miloš establishes his absolutism

The National Chancellery proclaimed Miloš on 21 November 1815 'supreme knez and leader of the Serbian people'. His title 'knez' meant both a traditional elected peasant leader of a group of villages and a Serbian prince—the two meanings combined in his person. His assumption of this title had not been agreed with Maraşli Ali. His power seemed tenuous, both resting on Ottoman goodwill and challenged by other Serbs who had achieved status in the uprisings. Miloš had been forced to appoint such notables to high office to secure his accession; they saw him as merely one of them, with no right to be absolute master. Pavle Nikolajević Moler, a commander on the Drina front in the First Serbian Uprising who had represented the Serb rebels before Russia and Austria and served as the National Chancellery's supervisor in 1815–1816—alongside Miloš, who was president—saw himself as Miloš's equal if not superior—he was, unlike Miloš, a literate polyglot. He consequently requested of Miloš that Serbia be governed as a quadrumvirate of himself, Miloš, Pavle Cukić and Archpriest Mateja. But Miloš craved exclusive absolute power and was terrified that Moler or some other rival might collaborate with the Ottomans against him. Many of his actual or potential rivals, as former rebel leaders or obor-knezes, had either their own relations with members of the Ottoman administration or popular power bases, or both.

As the National Chancellery's supervisor, Moler lived in Belgrade, in close contact with the Ottoman authorities. Miloš consequently sought to bypass the Chancellery, and deal directly with the vizier, which in turn Moler considered affronting and threatening. The fledgling Serbian elite divided into pro-Miloš and pro-Moler camps. At an assembly of elders on 6 May 1816, Miloš struck against Moler, accusing him of embezzlement, which was true, and of being a traitor and Austrian agent, which was false. He had him declared an enemy of the people and sentenced to death; rumours were spread that he lived in sin with two women and violated the fast. Miloš subsequently turned Moler over to Maraşli Ali for execution, telling him Moler had been plotting a new uprising. The vizier fulfilled this request reluctantly, after considerable vacillation; unwilling to return Moler and lacking sufficient evidence to have him legally executed, he had him quietly murdered. Miloš then arranged the murder of another rival, Bishop Melentije Nikšić; he spread rumours that Nikšić and Moler had been plotting with the Turks to disarm the Serbs again.[1]

With the Serbian opposition to Miloš attracting former leaders of the First Serbian Uprising, linked to the Serbian emigration in Russian Bessarabia, the Ottomans shared Miloš's interest in his winning this power struggle and in preventing the émigrés' return. This became increasingly serious for the Ottomans as the Filiki Eteria nationalist movement based around the Greek Phanariot ruling elite in the Danubian Principalities, in preparation for launching what would become the Greek War of Independence, made common cause with the Serbian émigrés for anti-Ottoman action. Miloš crushed a rebellion to the south of Belgrade in March 1817 led by Sima Marković and Pavle Cukić, two former friends or associates of Moler's. He delivered Marković and another rebel leader to Maraşli Ali, who executed them, while Miloš then had Cukić assassinated. Finally, after Miloš had refused to cooperate with Filiki Eteria, the organisation sent Karađorđe to Serbia to rekindle its anti-Ottoman resistance.[2] Hearing this, Miloš summoned the knezes then present in Belgrade to an assembly, which resolved unanimously that Karađorđe should be killed. Miloš then informed Maraşli Ali of Karađorđe's arrival; the vizier reminded him he must remain loyal to the Sultan and offered help, but warned him that if he refused, the Ottoman army would be deployed in Serbia.[3]

Karađorđe arrived in Serbia with his close associate Naum Krnar, a Cincar from what is today Albania. Educated in a Greek school, Naum considered himself Greek and belonged to Filiki Eteria.[4] They stayed with Karađorđe's kum Vujica Vulićević, obor-knez of the Smederevo nahija and formerly one of his leading commanders. Miloš sent an order to Vulićević specifying, 'If Karađorđe's head is not now brought to Belgrade, that will mean that yours and mine will be lost and the ruin of the whole nation will follow from that.'[5] The order was delivered by three men, including Toma

PRINCE MILOŠ AND THE FOUNDING OF MODERN SERBIA

Vučić-Perišić (1788–1859), who was to become one of the most important men in Serbia during the next four decades.[6] In the early hours of 25 July 1817, while Karađorđe slept, he was attacked with an axe by one of Vuličević's young men, Nikola Novaković, whose brother Karađorđe had killed during the uprising. Novaković killed Karađorđe and decapitated him while Naum was shot dead.[7] Demonstrating his loyalty to the Ottoman Empire, Miloš sent Karađorđe's head to Maraşli Ali, who in turn had it stuffed and sent to Constantinople as a gift to the Sultan. The Greek rebel leadership concluded that 'as regards Serbia, on no account should its support be counted on' because 'Miloš, who governs it, killed Black Đorđe' and was 'a worse Turk than the Turks'.[8]

Having eliminated his key opponents, Miloš induced an assembly of obor-knezes and other notables in November 1817 to proclaim him hereditary prince of Serbia for life; the act was signed by the obor-knezes and leading clergymen. The National Chancellery was rapidly sidelined and lost all meaningful influence in Serbia's government; it was effectively converted into Belgrade's judicial court. However, Miloš needed a male heir to cement his dynasty. Since his wife Princess Ljubica had failed to produce a surviving male child after more than ten years of marriage, it seemed he might divorce her and marry his mistress, Petrija Pljakić, who had recently borne him a daughter. This possibility was ended by a dramatic incident in March 1819. According to one colourful account, Ljubica surprised Pljakić in her husband's bedroom, making two beds.

'For whom are you making two beds, Petrija?'
'I'm making one for the lord, the other for myself.'
'And where will I sleep tonight?'
'Thank god, there's plenty of space in the house.'

The exchange ended with Ljubica picking up Miloš's pistol and shooting Pljakić dead.[9] Miloš wept and sincerely mourned Pljakić, but Ljubica was spared his anger because she was pregnant with the future Prince Milan, whose birth secured her position. Michael Boro Petrovich evaluates Miloš: 'Though an adulterer, he was far more considerate toward his wife than many a European monarch; he even forgave her when she murdered one of his mistresses.'[10] Ljubica apparently came to regret the murder: 'I have many sins and they will be forgiven by the merciful Lord, but that I killed that woman with my own hand, I fear, he never will! Why did my woman's intelligence let me down? If I had killed all his girlfriends, I could have killed much of the world! Guilty conscience, what do I do?'[11] She adopted Miloš's and Pljakić's baby daughter, treating her like one of her own children.

Miloš's multiple mistresses strengthened his resemblance to an Ottoman pasha. After Pljakić, his next significant mistress was Stanka, who had begun as his table servant. Ljubica planned to shoot her too and waited for her with her pistol, but Miloš, learning of this, sent his men to stop her. She was punished with a beating in which her head was cracked. Stanka aborted several of Miloš's babies, wrecking her health, but eventually bore him a son, who died in infancy, after which he found her a husband at her request.[12] After Stanka came Jelenka, a Turk who had belonged to Stojković's harem. She bore Miloš an illegitimate son in 1826 and effectively became his second wife, residing with him in Kragujevac while Ljubica resided in Belgrade and Požarevac, and appearing with him in public.[13] Visiting Miloš in 1829, Otto von Pirch was shocked that Ljubica did not sit at the dining table with her husband and the other men, instead waiting upon him, pouring him his šljivovica. Pirch noted that, since their marriage, she had never eaten at the table with him.[14] Ljubica was eventually allowed to sit at the dining table with her husband in 1834, but only when there were no guests. Even then, she was still required to kiss his hand and serve him šljivovica.[15] She addressed him as 'lord', used the formal 'you' and usually began her letters to him with 'Your majesty, merciful lord'.[16] Soon after, in 1835, Miloš bought two Cherkess slave girls in Constantinople, eventually fathering a child with one of them.[17] He meanwhile mercilessly policed the sexual conduct of his family's women; learning of his sixteen-year-old daughter Jelizaveta's love affair with his secretary, Popovski, whom he had loved as a son, Miloš employed two of his men to murder him, after which they robbed his body and buried it in a bush.[18]

Miloš's tyranny over his own family extended to Serbia as a whole, which he treated as his personal fiefdom. Self-management had been restored to the knežinas and nahijas and rejuvenated by the victory of the Second Serbian Uprising, yet now, in the late 1810s, Miloš moved to curb it, as Ottoman reactionaries had done before him. As the historian Vasa Čubrilović said of Miloš's regime, 'In building this government, he struck to the right against the Turkish administrative organs and to the left against the people's self-management.'[19] He systematically eliminated notables with independent bases of authority to end the threat of rebellions. The twelve obor-knezes and, beneath them, the regular knezes ceased to be hereditary or elected and were now appointed by Miloš, becoming simply his officials through whom he transmitted orders to the people; each had his own staff of clerks and gendarmes. Members of this fledgling bureaucratic class were the prince's servants, not the state's as such, and were indistinct from his personal servants. They had no formal positions or hierarchy and Miloš arbitrarily moved them between roles.[20] The knežina and nahija parliaments lost their consultative function and became simply assemblies at which the people could be informed of Miloš's will. He ensured the loyalty of his officialdom by imposing as obor-knezes and knezes his brothers, cousins, friends and other minions. He made his younger brother Jovan obor-knez of the Rudnik nahija and his youngest brother Jevrem obor-knez of the Šabac and subsequently also the Valjevo and Sokol nahijas. These appointees did not enjoy relations with their constituents based on mutual trust and respect established over generations; widely distrusted by them and owing their positions entirely to Miloš, they distinguished themselves by harshness in imposing the prince's authority and exploiting the population for kuluk and taxes.[21]

PRINCE MILOŠ AND THE FOUNDING OF MODERN SERBIA

The grateful Ottomans rewarded Miloš for Karađorđe's murder by granting him in 1818 the right to sentence Christians to death, thereby cementing his authority over the Serb population. He used this power liberally, particularly in 1820–1826, when almost every week he decreed several death sentences, particularly for hajduks and their collaborators but also for many others whom he resented or who had resisted his authority. Brigandage peaked in Serbia around 1820, partly reflecting the desperate population's resistance, but by 1824 Miloš had largely crushed it through liberal use of the death penalty, torture, confiscation of property, internment of family members, killing of collaborators and treating villages as collectively culpable.[22] Punishments imposed by the courts, often on Miloš's orders, included mob beatings, amputation of hands and parts of the tongue, death by torture and public display of corpses after execution.[23] At the close of 1820 Miloš ended the involvement of Muslim officials in trying legal cases between Serbs, and transferred this authority to the obor-knezes; these appointed courts and magistrates in the nahija centres, except Belgrade, which already had a court that had evolved from the National Chancellery, and Kragujevac, where the court evolved from the prince's personal chancellery.

With the ending of Ottoman military occupation and administrative and judicial authority over Serbia's countryside went the taxes and tolls that supported them, so the weight of direct Ottoman exploitation of Serbia's people was considerably reduced.[24] Eventually, in 1821, the Christian tenants' labour dues to the sipahis were ended altogether. This agrarian revolution transformed the Smederevo sanjak from an integral part of the Ottoman socio-political order into what was in effect just a vassal state with Ottoman garrisons. Miloš continued cultivating Maraşli Ali, who cherished him, calling him 'son'; he was effectively the vizier's deputy, running the pashalik for him.[25] Between 1816 and 1826, with Maraşli Ali's connivance, Miloš bought up all the imperial (not privately held) landholdings in the sanjak, whose tenants had to continue paying him the desetak, and diverted an increasing part of the customs and taxes due the imperial state into his own coffers, amassing a vast personal fortune while continuing to pay Serbia's tribute directly. Both in the people's eyes and in actual fact, the new state was inseparable from the prince's person.

Rebellion at home and crisis abroad

The Serbian revolution was by the start of the 1820s doubly incomplete: the new state continued to tyrannise over and exploit the peasantry, much as the old Ottoman order had done, while its status as an autonomous entity was still not formally recognised by Constantinople. Miloš therefore followed a difficult path, maintaining power while alleviating popular discontent and maintaining Ottoman goodwill while agitating for Serbian statehood. Whereas formalising Serbia's autonomy remained a Russian foreign-policy goal, the Ottomans sought to minimise Russian interference in the Serbian question and treat it as their domestic matter, thereby preferring to reach agreement with the Serbs directly and grant them autonomy via an imperial firman. Miloš had to navigate between the two states to consolidate Serbia's autonomy while also lobbying for his position as prince to be made hereditary in his own family. Self-interest and raisons d'état coincided; a hereditary prince was less open to foreign manipulation than one elected by elders buyable by foreign powers. The Porte consequently balked at recognising a hereditary prince. While the Russians recognised the need for such a prince as a foundation for Serbia's statehood, they preferred him to share power with a senate or council to restrain his autocracy and give them leverage over him. In these circumstances, the Serbian elders around Miloš divided into Turcophile and Russophile currents: the first was more conservative, favouring the status quo with Serbia effectively an Ottoman pashalik; the second had a more forward-looking vision of Serbia as *Rechtsstaat*.[26]

Miloš remained collaborationist in his relations with the Porte. At Maraşli Ali's prompting, he sent an expression of devotion in June 1817 to the Sultan:

> We pledge, our faces to the ground: kodabašas, knezes, kmets and all paupers, the raya of your Smederevo sanjak, come with these short words of thanks to you, great emperor, for the excessive mercy you show us ... The Great Knez and all knezes and kmets and all paupers, kissing your foot, pray to you, that in future too the heavenly sun of your look will alight upon us and that beneath your gaze we remain, so that treachery may never again befall us. In your health and excessive mercy we pray to most merciful God that he guide and strengthen your empire to eternal amen.[27]

This declaration strengthened the Ottomans' hand in negotiations regarding Serbia, enraging Russia's ambassador to Constantinople, Baron Grigory Alexandrovich Stroganov, who detested the Turcophile Miloš, a feeling that Karađorđe's murder only exacerbated. Miloš nevertheless subsequently concluded he could only achieve his goals with Russian assistance. On 26 August 1820, with Stroganov's blessing, he rejected the Sultan's firman affirming Serbia's rights since it did not recognise him as hereditary prince.[28] However, by rejecting Ottoman concessions to consolidate his oppressive personal regime, he catalysed opposition among Serbia's fledgling elite.[29]

Miloš's tyranny and exploitation of the peasantry through heavy taxes meanwhile provoked peasant resistance, which anticipated the conflicts that would dominate nineteenth-century Serbia. For while his administration had reduced the taxes and services owed the landlords—the desetak and kuluk—the state's tax burden on the peasants was increased. Peasants were also required to provide the knezes with kuluk labour of several days a year for their private needs while their wives now performed 'women's work' at the homes of the obor-knezes and other officials, reinforcing the perception that the new Serbian administrators were simply heirs of the sipahis.[30] To avoid having to pay the kmets out of the state treasury, Miloš granted them the right to extract one day's kuluk labour annually from every household in their jurisdiction.[31] Kuluk labour was exploited by higher officials up to and including the prince himself. The abolition of kneževina self-government and the absence of any legal protection or recourse for the peasants gave them few means for redress.[32] Consequently, Miloš's administration was widely viewed as worse than the Turks and faced the same peasant resistance that had generated the First and Second Serbian Uprisings.

Trade, particularly in the livestock upon which many peasants depended, was heavily restricted in favour of the large merchants and others close to Miloš. Trade permits were difficult to acquire and credit-based trade was banned. Miloš did not pay customs duties on his own imports. Knezes appointed by him had the right to sell their produce at the town markets for a set period without competition from ordinary peasants. Miloš made his officials work for his trading business, buying cattle on his behalf. He eventually acquired a vastly profitable monopoly on the sale in Serbia of salt imported from Wallachia in 1829 and from Moldavia in 1834. His trading privileges were greatly resented by other merchants.[33] Another measure, arguably tyrannical but perhaps reflecting enlightened concern for public health, safety and morality, was a decree of 3 December 1824: 'That nobody must dare to smoke in the street, or walk along the street with a chibouk, or in front of Toma's tavern, or to light up in church; to smoke, dishonouring and disrespecting the church.' This and future anti-smoking measures failed, but they did allegedly lead to one location in Belgrade outside the centre, where smoking was permitted, being named Palilula ('Light the Pipe'), which remains the municipality's name to this day.[34]

The Greek rebellion began in Wallachia in February 1821, led by Filiki Eteria under Alexander Ypsilantis, thereby launching the Greek War of Independence. It was linked to a revolt among the Romanian population of Wallachia against the Greek Phanariot administration. This renewed conflict in the Ottoman Empire between rebels and loyalists reopened fissures in Serbia. Ypsilantis's revolt was supported by the anti-Miloš Serbian emigration in Bessarabia, which viewed it as continuing their own anti-Ottoman struggle. Miloš, conversely, feared both rebellion, as his Ottoman masters did, and the possibility that the Ottomans might extend their repression of the Greeks to a renewed assault upon Serbia. Serbian fears increased as Muslims across the empire carried out pogroms against Christians in retaliation for the Greek uprising, including in Niš, on the doorstep of Miloš's realm. Serbia's deputies in Constantinople were interned. Many Serbs and Turks in Serbia fled from areas where they lived close to each other, and as a result much of Belgrade and other places on the ethnic frontlines were deserted. Miloš and Maraşli Ali consequently collaborated to maintain peace and order and calm both communities. After Maraşli Ali died on 21 August, Miloš ensured the new vizier was courteously received by Serbs as well as Turks when he arrived in Belgrade in September.

Two knezes, Marko Todorović Abdula, obor-knez of the Požarevac nahija, and Stevan Todorović Dobrnjac, knez of the nahija's Morava kneževinas, rebelled on 6 April 1821. They were unhappy with Miloš's rejection of the 1820 firman and angered when his administrative reorganisation threatened their positions. They knew Miloš was appropriating to himself tax income from the populace that had previously gone to the vizier, and may have sought to establish a direct relationship between their nahija and the vizier, bypassing Miloš.[35] They were linked to the Serbian emigration in Bessarabia, among whom was Dobrnjac's brother Petar. However, their revolt was crushed in just over two weeks; Abdula and Dobrnjac surrendered to Miloš and received his pardon, but Abdula died shortly afterwards in suspicious circumstances, after which Dobrnjac fled to Austria, fearing for his life.[36] Miloš curried favour with the Ottomans by claiming he had preserved Serbia from a revolt originating in Wallachia, despite the rebels' actual Turcophilia.[37] He targeted members of the Russophile faction too, and in the same year arrested two of its members, Nikola Nikolajević and Lazar Teodorović, his two chief advisers on foreign affairs, for real or suspected seditious activities; he eventually had Nikolajević murdered.

Miloš's sense of insecurity increased as evidence surfaced of another planned rebellion in the Rudnik nahija. In the fallout from the suppression of its preparations, Obor-Knez Petar Vuličević of the Smederevo nahija (Miloš's wife's brother-in-law and son of Karađorđe's assassin, Vujica Vuličević, whose office he had inherited) had a peasant arrested from the village of Selevac, on suspicion of involvement. This triggered a rebellion of the Selevac villagers on 23 January 1825, under the leadership of Miloje Popović Đak, which was consequently known as Đak's rebellion. Miloš ordered his brother Jovan, then administering the Požarevac nahija, Milutin Savić Garašanin, knez of Jasenica, and another knez from the Belgrade nahija to crush the rebellion. But the rebellion struck them first, spreading to the villages around Selevac, then to the Belgrade, Kragujevac and Požarevac nahijas. Jovan fled with his family and his home was plundered. It was the first major expression of popular peasant resistance to the high taxes and oppressive bureaucracy of the new state. Portentously, rebel anger was channelled through an educated leader: Đak, a nickname meaning 'student', was a former clerk of Vujica Vuličević's and had spent time abroad.

The rebellion seriously threatened Miloš's regime. Đak's rebel host alone numbered about 5,000 men and the prince lacked sufficient reliable local forces to defeat it. He was forced tactically to accommodate the rebels while preparing to crush them, so agreed to Đak's appointment as Smederevo's knez in place of Vuličević and to other appointments the rebels favoured. The rebels convened a popular assembly at the town of Topola, Karađorđe's former base, on 1 February and sent Miloš a list of demands: that the 'oppression by the knezes be ended' and the 'criminals [be] removed from the vilayet'; that their replacements be chosen by the people and approved by Miloš; that taxes and kuluk be reduced to what the peasants could afford; that traders be free to trade among the people; and that people's fear of arbitrary execution by the authorities be addressed, centring on the abolition of new taxes and an end to the knezes' abuses. A conservative side to the rebellion was manifested in the denunciation of Miloš's 'representatives' who 'go about the country cursing to the people the law and the cross and eat meat on Wednesdays and Fridays' in violation of Orthodox Christian custom.[38]

Reflecting his role as intermediary between the Ottoman authorities and Serbian Christian population, while preparing to crush the rebellion, Miloš denounced Đak before the Serbs as a Turkish hireling and before the vizier as a hireling of the Greek revolutionaries.[39] He assembled loyal forces from outside the area affected by the rebellion, under his brother Jevrem and Vučić-Perišić, knez of Gruža, near Knić. They crushed the rebellion with great brutality within ten days of its outbreak: after the poorly armed, ill-prepared rebel host was routed, the captured rebels were force-marched naked and participating villages were burned and looted on Miloš's orders. In Ranke's words, 'The victors threw themselves upon the villages where the insurrection had originated, or through which it had spread, and committed the same atrocities that the Turks had been accustomed to commit on similar occasions.'[40] Jevrem was tasked with retrieving the corpse of Đak's brother, killed during the uprising, in order to fix his head on a stake in front of Selevac, where the rebellion had started. Đak himself was captured, brought before Miloš on 7 February and allowed to explain himself:

> Lord, I myself see that I will not live, and I will tell it all to you truthfully. As much, Lord, as you fine the people and impose forced labour on them, your brothers do twice as much; as much as your brothers do, Lord, your knezes do as much; and your tax collectors, and your toll collectors; and your retainers, and your gendarmes; a thousand times worse than what the subaşas did. And you gave a command that no one is allowed to complain. Now the way it is, Lord, the people would not let me eat my bread in peace, and they arose together to tell you what they were enduring from your brothers and the knezes and your other minions. And truly I say to you, had I known that you would treat the poor this way; do not even think of the gunpowder and lead and guns and cannon that you have, for it would not help you, for you have made yourself bitter to Serbia, and whatever army that you could assemble, it would all beat you, just so you know, so that not even the foundations of your home would be recognisable, just so you know.[41]

Miloš had Đak put on a horse and sent him before a firing squad, allowing his soldiers to decide his fate. When none was willing to kill him, Jevrem rode after him and shot him dead. His head was cut off and sent to the vizier in Belgrade, who had it mounted on a stake at the Kalemegdan fortress. However, for propaganda purposes, Miloš highlighted his merciful side by sparing Đak's wife and children, who were permitted to keep his property. Đak's wife and one-year-old son were received as guests by Miloš in Kragujevac, where Ljubica gave the boy some of her son Mihailo's old clothes.[42]

The rebellion shook Miloš and his regime. He learned that in some areas, including Belgrade, Smederevo and Čačak, the populace had appealed to the Ottoman authorities to restore the rights they had enjoyed at the time of Mustafa

Pasha—much as they had once appealed for an end to the tyranny of the deys.[43] The rebellion showed that while the Serbian 'nation-in-arms' that had arisen from the Second Serbian Uprising could be trusted to resist Ottoman depredations, it could not be trusted to enforce the prince's authority over the masses: mobilised men from Jasenica and Lepenica had refused to fight the rebels and joined them instead.[44] Consequently, a month after the rebellion was suppressed, Miloš founded a standing army by requiring village elders to conscript one or two young men per village and organise them into companies. There were 1,147 such soldiers by May 1825, armed with Austrian carbines and officered by Serb veterans of Austria's army. This fledgling force in 1827 was organised into regiments, divisions and companies. Miloš had the two knezes elected at the initiative of the rebels assassinated. His proclamation of 9 March demanded that 'every village to its kmet, and the kmets all at an assembly at the church, pledge their loyalty and obedience to our government'.[45] This decree was to be obeyed throughout his administration and the kmets were compelled to participate; he demanded reports on how well it had been executed.

Miloš nevertheless attempted to address some of the grievances that had fuelled the rebellion. He recognised some failings on his administration's part, dismissed many officials and allowed knežina and nahija assemblies to present popular complaints. He convened on 5 May 1825 a parliament of elders from the nahijas, knežinas and courts, including a significant number of kmets from every nahija, which expressed regret at the rebellion and pledged its continued loyalty to him; it also, on his instructions, decreed the lowering of taxes, thereby creating the impression of a body representing the people and addressing its grievances.[46] However, the Jagodina nahija's assembly, in his view, 'gave an opinion deadly for the people, that the sipahis be permitted back according to the old ways', indicating that some, at least, considered restoration of the old Ottoman order the lesser evil. He consequently took steps to restrain the tyranny of the knezes and ensure they would not arbitrarily punish those under their authority, and that the courts would function properly. His all-national court in Kragujevac issued a decree on 6 June 1825 detailing rules that magistrates had to follow in criminal court proceedings, which was eventually augmented by a further decree on 3 March 1829. This was the first step in regulating judicial procedure at the village and knežina levels, whose arbitrary nature had galvanised peasant discontent, and in establishing the rule of law. In August 1825 he established the institution of people's attorneys, tasked with asking the people if they had reasons for dissatisfaction and informing Miloš and the national court.[47] By 1827 courts had been established for each of the twelve nahijas, the court in Kragujevac having become by 1823 a superior court of appeals. Miloš's legal reforms of 1825 were followed by measures to restrict corporal punishment, further reduce taxes, grant greater commercial freedom, and ensure peasant complaints were properly investigated. This appeased the population, so the next ten years of his reign passed without popular rebellion. However, the reforms aroused the opposition of the sipahi class, whose members began agitating against his regime. In August 1825, one of them murdered a Serb at Miloš's home in Belgrade. He consequently began viewing them as hostile and a threat.[48]

Miloš remained wary of the Serbian emigration in Bessarabia. In May 1823, after Milovanović, former Council president under Karađorđe, returned to Serbia, Miloš had him murdered, using his death as a warning to other émigrés not to try to come home.[49] But Karađorđe's oldest surviving son, Aleksa Karađorđević, a Russian officer, was a source of opposition until his premature death from tuberculosis in Kishinev in 1830: responding to his father's murder by placing a bounty on Miloš's head, he declared a dynastic war against the Obrenovićes that would continue until the start of the twentieth century. Two malcontents, brothers Đorđe and Marko Čarapić, nephews of Vasa Čarapić, hero of the First Serbian Uprising, who were linked to the emigration and supported by Aleksa, launched another revolt in April 1826 near Mt Avala close to Belgrade, seeking to overthrow Miloš and bring back the émigré leaders. This was not a major popular revolt like Đak's rebellion but the conspiracy of a small circle of individuals. It was rapidly suppressed and the Čarapić brothers killed. The participants had their homes burned down, families evicted and property confiscated, though the families were later pardoned and had their property restored. One prominent participant was punished by having both his hands cut off above the wrists, along with part of his tongue, emulating Turkish punishments.[50] Miloš nevertheless felt compelled to establish a five-member Serbian Council to provide a form of primitive government, a fig leaf for his autocracy and a semblance of legality. Archimandrite Melentije Pavlović was appointed Council member for church affairs, Aleksa Simić for finance, Dimitrije Davidović for foreign affairs, and Vučić-Perišić for military affairs as well as chief officer of the army and head of the prince's royal guard.[51] This initiative was short-lived and in 1827 the Serbian Council was converted into a national court, but the question of a council—a consultative or governing body existing alongside the prince—remained central to Serbian politics.

Ottoman recognition of Serbia's autonomy

The Greek revolt's outbreak in 1821 interrupted the normal course of Russo-Ottoman diplomacy, halting progress toward formal recognition of the Serbian principality. The Serbian delegation in Constantinople remained interned for years. Tsar Alexander I sympathised somewhat with the Greek rebels and terminated relations with the Porte following the anti-Orthodox pogroms in Constantinople that killed the Patriarch and other priests, but he deferred to Austria's Chancellor Klemens von Metternich and other European statesmen who viewed the revolt as a revolutionary threat to the established order. Miloš consequently sought to put pressure on both Russia and the Porte. At his parliament of 5 May 1825 following Đak's rebellion, he elicited the elders' expression of support for his efforts to secure the liberation of the Serbian delegation, forwarding the message to the vizier. At a subsequent parliament on 27–28 May, Miloš expressed his alignment with Russian policy abroad and elicited a declaration from the deputies requesting that he obtain from the Porte all the rights that the Serbs had been promised in the Treaty of Bucharest and the return of the six nahijas lost in 1813, and that if they were not granted, he lead them into war against the Sultan alongside the Greeks. He then transmitted to the Russians the message that the Serbian people did not approve of their policy of passivity towards the Ottomans but that he would follow it nonetheless. He simultaneously sent a message to the delegation in Constantinople, telling it to inform the Porte that, unless it freed the delegation and granted the Serbs their rights, given the extent of popular disquiet and the presence of Greek agents, he would not be able to guarantee peace in Serbia.[52] Ðak's rebellion was cited as a warning of what could follow if the Porte remained intransigent.

Miloš reinforced his absolutism by regularly summoning parliaments to inform the people's representatives of his decisions and consult with them over policy. Members were elected by village, town, district and nahija assemblies and by the lower clergy, with kmets representing their villages and representatives of the guilds elected in towns. Miloš could also appoint others: members of his family, higher clergy, senior officials of state, or representatives of district or nahija government. They tended to meet semi-annually at the prince's meadow in Kragujevac during the mid- to late 1820s, where they sat for two to three days in the open air until the prince dismissed them. For exceptionally important decisions, like accepting a hatt-ı şerif (written decree) from the Porte or, eventually, a constitution, a 'great national parliament' would be summoned, which had about four times the usual number of deputies. In principle, parliaments ratified budgets as well as decisions and decrees made by the prince or Porte; in practice, since Miloš could invariably manipulate them through a combination of authority, charisma and intimidation, they served to rubber-stamp steps he had already taken, giving them the seal of popular approval.[53]

Miloš's triumph over his domestic opponents by 1826 freed him to focus on obtaining Serbia's formal recognition by the Ottomans. This coincided fortuitously with Alexander I's death and the accession in December 1825 of Tsar Nicholas I, who was readier to confront the Ottomans over Balkan Christian rights. A Russian ultimatum forced the Ottoman Empire on 7 October 1826 to sign the so-called Akkerman Convention. Among other things, this required it to respect the terms of the 1812 Treaty of Bucharest regarding the 'Serbian nation': a fully autonomous Serbian administration, return to Serbia of territory taken from it in 1813, the conversion of Serbia's dues to the Ottoman Empire into a lump sum, a prohibition on Muslims not connected with the Ottoman garrisons from residing in Serbia and the transfer of all Muslim estates in Serbia to Serbian hands. On 27 January 1827 Miloš summoned a parliament at Kragujevac, at which he cited this foreign policy triumph to demonstrate his policy's correctness while denouncing the legacy of

Karađorđe and of the Đak and other recent rebellions. The parliament responded enthusiastically by praying, 'Let God give life to you, Lord, and to the Sultan and Tsar Nicholas!' It reaffirmed its loyalty to him as hereditary prince of Serbia.[54]

The Ottomans' persisting failure to suppress the Greek revolt prompted Britain, France and Russia to dispatch a joint fleet to coerce them to accept an armistice. The allied fleet destroyed the Ottoman fleet at the Battle of Navarino on 20 October 1827, prompting the outraged Ottomans to retaliate by closing the Straits to Russian shipping and repudiating the Akkerman Convention, in turn precipitating a Russo-Turkish war lasting until 1829. Nicholas required Serbia to remain neutral, since he did not wish to be seen inciting a rebellion of subjects against their lawful ruler and since Serbia's involvement would militarily have been more a hindrance than a help. All parties—Russia, the Ottomans and Serbia—shared an interest in keeping Serbia out of the war, which Miloš's cordial relations with the Ottomans made possible. The Porte did force Serbia to accept a temporary occupation by its troops, which Miloš was unable to resist, but their behaviour was restrained. With Serbia occupied by Ottoman armies from Bosnia and Rumelia, Miloš' maintained friendly relations with Belgrade's vizier, seeing him as Serbia's protector from the neighbouring viziers.[55] Following the Ottoman Empire's defeat by Russia, the Treaty of Adrianople of 14 September 1829 required it to respect the autonomous rights granted Serbia in the Akkerman Convention and to restore to it the six nahijas, while Russia's protectorate of Serbia was reaffirmed.[56] The Porte codified these terms in a hatt-ı şerif on 30 September 1829. It was received on 6 February 1830 by a parliament summoned by Miloš both to announce his success to the Serbian people and to impress upon the Porte the popular support for his demand to be made hereditary prince. The parliament declared him 'Saviour and Father of Serbia'. It expressed gratitude to the Sultan while requesting again that Miloš's hereditary status be recognised.[57]

Extensive, arduous three-way negotiations between the Porte, Russia and the Serbian delegation about the precise terms to be granted the Serbs ended with the Sultan signing a second hatt-ı şerif on 20 October 1830, codifying them more precisely. It was announced to the Serbian public in Belgrade on 12 December and read in Turkish before the Ottoman officials, after which Miloš visited the cathedral to receive a blessing from the metropolitan. The next day—chosen by Miloš as the anniversary of the rebel liberation of Belgrade in 1806—the hatt-ı şerif was read in Serbian in full to a great national parliament of the Serbian people. It was followed by a speech delivered by Davidović in Miloš's name, stating:

> Thus, brothers, we too have become since yesterday a nation; a nation dependent upon the Sultan, it is true, but a nation that has its own rights. Since yesterday we have become a nation that has its own administration, not simply in practice and taken by force, as up till now, but by law ... Now we resemble the Hungarians under Austria and the Poles under Russia ... Happy Serb nation, happy Serbia; who would ever have thought that you would come to this point?! Who would ever have thought that

SERBIA

Serbia, reduced to slavery both on the Field of Kosovo and in later times, namely at its final collapse in 1813, would ever raise its head again?! Now it raises it![58]

During this ceremony, the Serbs displayed a coat of arms that Miloš would thenceforth increasingly display in place of Ottoman symbols. It featured a white cross with four Cs in the corners. This device dated back to the time of Princess Milica, was preserved by the seventeenth-century Dubrovnik historian Mavro Orbini, adopted by the Sremski Karlovci metropolitanate, passed to the Belgrade metropolitanate when the two branches of the church were united during the Austrian occupation of Serbia in the 1720s, so reintroduced to the country and adopted by Miloš. It was then interpreted to stand for 'Saint Sava Serbian Glory' (the 'C' in Cyrillic being equivalent to the Latin 'S'). At the head of the cross was a turban, eventually replaced with a crown.[59]

The hatt-ı şerif formally established the Principality of Serbia. It pledged that 'the current Prince Miloš Obrenović, as hereditary prince of Serbia, will be as a reward for his loyalty to my Sublime Porte, by the voice of the berat [decree], which has been supplied, recognised as the prince of the said people, and this honour will belong to his family', thereby making him hereditary prince of Serbia. It reaffirmed, strengthened or clarified previous concessions from the Sultan: Serbian freedom of religion was guaranteed; a Russo-Turkish commission was to determine the borders of the six nahijas to be returned to Serbia; Muslims outside the Ottoman garrisons were banned from residing in Serbia and given a year to sell their property there; and the size of the Serbian tribute to the Sultan was to be determined, along with the income from the sipahi holdings to be transferred to Serbian hands. Furthermore, 'To prevent disorder and punish the guilty, Prince Miloš will have in his service the necessary force of soldiers.'[60] The Belgrade church's bells, forbidden under Ottoman rule, were restored. Muslim property around Belgrade was bought on a massive scale by Serbs. Serbia took formal control of the Belgrade customs house through which most of the country's trade with Austria passed. This marked the zenith of Miloš's regime, and he was now at the height of his power and prestige.[61] Yet the settlement also permitted the return to Serbia of émigré veterans of the First Serbian Uprising. Marginalised in Miloš's Serbia, many of them and their family members aligned themselves with his opponents in the coming years.[62]

The hatt-ı şerif permitted Serbia to have its own printing press. The following year Serbia's emissaries in St Petersburg, Avram Petronijević and Cvetko Rajović, bought one there. It arrived in Serbia on 24 May 1831, commencing operation on 9 September. This was inevitably followed on 22 December 1832 by a censorship decree, banning the printing of blasphemy or anti-government sedition. The press was soon being used to print newspapers, calendars, magazines and books for schools and churches. The first printed public placards appeared in 1832, used to advertise the visit to Belgrade of an adult circus elephant and its foreign female owner, Emilija Leserf, which caused something of a sensation; superstitious locals blamed it for creating excess rainfall by spraying water from the River Sava from its trunk and for raising the price of bread through its gluttony.[63]

Regaining of the six nahijas and expulsion of the Muslims

The hatt-ı şerif of 1830 was a concession extracted from the Ottomans following their defeat in war, and the Porte immediately procrastinated on its implementation regarding both the return of the six nahijas and the evacuation of the Muslims. Miloš consequently achieved these goals by his usual combination of collaboration and pressure. Thus, he gave the Sultan a gift of two hundred horses to secure his goodwill. But when the Albanian vizier of Shkodër, Hussein Pasha, launched a rebellion against the Sultan in March 1831, Miloš loaned Hussein Pasha half a million groschen, hoping the conflict would weaken the Porte and make it keener to conciliate Serbia. When the revolt was quickly defeated and the Porte learned of the loan, Miloš was embarrassed.[64] Meanwhile, a Muslim uprising against Ottoman rule erupted in the Eyalet of Bosnia under Husein-kapetan Gradaščević, motivated partly by opposition to the surrender of the six nahijas to Serbia.[65] In a change of policy following his embarrassment with Hussein Pasha, Miloš acted as the Porte's loyal vassal. Gradaščević's victory over the Sultan's army at Shtime in Kosovo on 18 July led Miloš to attempt mediation, even suggesting that Bosnia, like Serbia, be granted autonomy within the empire. However, once the Porte moved decisively to crush the Bosnians, Miloš supported it resolutely, sending Petronijević in mid-March 1832 to negotiate a common strategy with the grand vizier and offer him extensive military and material assistance. Serbia mobilised 30,000 men to resist the Bosnians, though in the event the Sultan's forces decisively defeated them in May without direct Serbian participation. Nevertheless, Serbia contributed significantly to the Sultan's victory by supplying his army with food, and because news of Serbia's mobilisation demoralised the Bosnians and dissuaded the Montenegrins from intervening on their side. Miloš then used his influence with the grand vizier to moderate the Porte's retribution and secure amnesty for many of the rebels.[66]

Only after the Bosnian rebels had been crushed could the Ottomans in mid-1832 relinquish to Miloš administration of the Jadar-Rađevina nahija and additional territory, as reward for his loyalty. Miloš followed this up at the end of the year by exploiting the disorder created by Albanian lords in the Kruševac and Aleksinac nahijas to occupy them unilaterally. Since this was perpetrated against the same unlawful elements that the grand vizier had been fighting in the Albanian and Bosnian lands, it could reasonably be presented as part of the restoration of order in the empire. Miloš first incited uprisings in these territories by local Serbs, who were just waiting for the opportunity to throw off the oppressive rule of their Albanian lords.[67] The occasion for the rebellion in Kruševac was the kidnapping of two local Serb girls by two Albanian beys in November 1832; the consequent

Ottoman investigation ruled in favour of the Serbs, thereby confirming the reality of Albanian misrule, though Miloš was careful to reward the Belgrade vizier and other Ottoman officials with generous gifts.[68] When further negotiations with the Ottomans failed to produce results, Miloš incited further rebellion in the disputed territories in May 1833, then invaded them with his forces to protect the local Serbs from Muslim retaliation. This completed his liberation of what remained of the six nahijas, whose annexation increased the size of Serbia's territory from approximately 22,440 to 37,740 square kilometres.[69] Expansion on this model—external invasion combined with local uprisings—would be emulated by future Serbian leaders for at least the next 160 years.

Pursuit of territorial reunification was accompanied by measures to remove the Muslim population from Serbia. Since the outbreak of the Greek revolt, Miloš had increasingly tolerated harassment and murder of Muslims. The hatt-ı şerif of 1830 greatly restricted their residency and property rights. As soon as it reached Belgrade, Miloš instructed the Serbian people to boycott Muslim shops and businesses, to make economic life impossible for them. The announcement of the hatt-ı şerif on 12 December prompted the large-scale sale of Muslim extramural property in Belgrade, most of which was transferred to Serb hands within three days. The Porte sought to stem the exodus, encouraging Muslims to remain in defiance of the agreement. As the Muslims resisted, Miloš threatened to remove them forcibly.[70] He forbade Muslims to till the land, arguing they would not be able to collect the harvest before the deadline for their departure specified in the hatt-ı şerif. He banned sipahis from collecting their tribute from Serb peasants. From 1831, kuluk was ended and Serbs banned from employment on Muslim private holdings. Miloš assumed the right and duty to collect the tribute from the peasants and deliver it to the sipahis and Sultan; in practice, this meant peasants paid somewhat less than they had previously while the sipahis and Sultan received still less, with the balance going to the Serbian treasury, paving the way for the complete abolition of the peasants' 'feudal' dues.[71]

The Porte was by 1833 preoccupied with its war with Muhammad Ali of Egypt and unable to contest the six nahijas, so it quickly recognised the fait accompli. Miloš proclaimed their annexation on 9 June. Consequently, in a hatt-ı şerif in November 1833, 'wanting to reward the Serbian nation', the Porte formally recognised the transfer of all six nahijas (listed as Krajina, Crna Reka, Aleksinac, Kruševac, part of Stari Vlah, and Jadar-Rađevina) to Serbia.[72] It also set Serbia's annual tribute at 2.3 million Ottoman groschen, increased to 2.345 million from 1835. All feudal dues owed to the sipahis and the Sultan by the Serb peasants were definitely ended. Nevertheless, the signing of a Russo-Ottoman alliance with the Treaty of Unkiar-Skelessi on 8 July 1833, directed against Muhammad Ali, reduced Russia's willingness to put pressure on the Ottomans, who could consequently afford to be less generous to the Serbs. Thus, the deadline for Muslims outside the Ottoman garrison towns to leave Serbia was extended by a further five years and the Muslim civilian population was once again permitted to reside extramurally in Belgrade. Compensation for the lost landholdings would be deducted from Serbia's annual tribute to the Sultan, which nevertheless accounted for 47.5 per cent of Serbia's state budget in the mid-1830s, though only 11 per cent by 1838 owing to Miloš's successful financial management.

The hatt-ı şerif of 1833 also determined Serbia's border with the empire, which was then to be demarcated by a joint Serbian–Ottoman commission. Since the local Muslims of Serbia's part of the Podrinje region linking Serbia to Bosnia refused to evacuate, Serbia's forces commanded by Vučić-Perišić, with Stevan Petrović Knićanin as his adjutant, expelled them in July 1834. Those living close to the Ottoman fortress in Soko near the Bosnian border were particularly recalcitrant, so their villages were burned and destroyed. But the villages of Mali Zvornik and Sakar were sufficiently close to the Ottoman fortress in Zvornik in Bosnia to be impregnable, and in November 1834 they attacked and drove off the Serbian–Ottoman commission attempting to arrange the sale of local Muslim property to Serbs. Consequently, these villages remained under Muslim control until 1878.[73] With these exceptions, Miloš succeeded in encouraging most of the Muslim landlords to leave Serbia. The departure of the Muslims definitely freed the Serbian Orthodox peasants of their 'feudal' obligations to their former landlords, creating a rural society of free peasant holdings.[74]

This emancipation of the peasants was ambiguous. In place of dues owed to Muslim landlords, they were faced with higher state taxes than they had paid under the Ottomans: a head-tax of 34 groschen twice a year between 1828 and 1834, payable in coin rather than in kind, rising to 60 groschen (six thalers) from 1835. To pay it, peasants were forced to sell part of their produce for money, thereby stimulating the rise of a money economy. They were then hit heavily by indirect taxes, above all tariffs for produce sold at the town market (džumruk), so were economically worse off than under the old Ottoman order.[75] Miloš's ambitious project, launched by a decree on 20 March 1837, to modernise Serbia's dispersed villages through their consolidation and the construction of proper village roads, could not everywhere be completed so increased peasant discontent.[76] The vanished Muslim shopkeepers and artisans were replaced by a new class of Serb Christian shopkeepers and artisans, including those who emigrated from the Austrian Empire, bringing with them a demand for Central European clothes and other goods requiring money for their purchase. As this new class was much more present in the villages than its Muslim predecessor had been, there was a rapid spread of village shops. The growing market economy led to increased peasant demand for products of handicrafts and factories such as textiles, footwear, jewellery, household utensils, cosmetics, sugar and coffee, which could not be produced adequately or at all within the zadruga but required further cash for their purchase. As the peasantry was increasingly integrated into the market economy, it began to differentiate into richer, middling and poor peasants, thus producing losers as well as winners and, eventually, a new rural proletariat. There was an increasing division of labour among the peasantry as particular households specialised in newly profitable economic activities. These factors accelerated the zadruga's decay, as successful small family units left the collective to go it alone.[77] Many peasant households fell into debt and a new class of usurers arose, many of whom were also government officials. The transition therefore involved a sense of loss that would dramatically influence Serbian politics.

In the short term, the emergence of a new Serbian elite from the peasant and merchant ranks produced a culturally homogeneous, egalitarian society in which differences in wealth, though they existed, did not reflect long-standing class divisions. Around 97 per cent of the Serb Christian population already inhabited the countryside in 1815. The Muslim exodus further ruralised Serbia; market towns regressed to mere villages or were wholly deserted.[78] The Muslim question was nevertheless not ended in Serbia. The expulsion of 8,000 Muslims across the Drina into Bosnia in 1834 aggravated relations with that eyalet. The refugees, sometimes accompanied by Bosnian Muslims, regularly re-crossed the river to burn Serb villages, kill the inhabitants and steal their livestock.[79] Furthermore, the principality's formal establishment left five Ottoman garrisons on Serbian territory: Belgrade, Šabac and Smederevo, located along the Sava and Danube rivers on Serbia's northern border, and Užice and Soko, on or close to the River Drina on Serbia's western border. The territorial expansion of 1833 added a sixth garrison, Feth-i Islam (Kladovo) on the Danube. These all included Muslim civilian populations, which in Belgrade and Užice outnumbered Christian Serbs. The garrisons remained thorns in the side of the Serbian state for the next three and a half decades, with periodic clashes between their Muslim soldiers and civilians and local Serbs. In February 1832, Muslims in Užice perpetrated a pogrom against the Serbs, killing several and causing almost the entire Serb population to flee, leaving Užice almost solely inhabited by Muslims for the next couple of years, after which Miloš and the vizier reached an agreement that allowed the Serb population to return.[80]

The towns remaining in Miloš's Serbia were predominantly inhabited by migrants from other parts of the Ottoman Empire, the Balkan peninsula, Austria and Wallachia. This meant there was little shared identity between peasants and townsmen. In Karadžić's words, 'the Serb nation has no other people but the peasants. That small number of Serbs who live in the towns, like merchants ... and craftsmen ... are called townsmen; they dress like Turks and live according to Turkish customs, and during uprisings or wars either enclose themselves with the Turks in the towns or with their money flee to Germany. Thus not only are they not counted among the Serb people, but the people despise them ...'[81] Serb migrants from other parts of the Ottoman Empire and Austria were also resented for the privileges granted them by Miloš, who encouraged them to settle in Serbia in large numbers with considerable tax exemptions, even confiscating land from native Serbs to give them. Natives consequently persecuted settlers, tore down their houses and plundered their possessions.[82]

Some Serbian notables, in particular Petronijević and Stojan Simić, had wished to acquire timar land from the departing Muslims, so replace Ottoman Muslim with Serbian Christian feudalism and obtain wealth and status similar to the boyar class in neighbouring Wallachia. That country, highly socially stratified and under oligarchic rule, was an inspirational model for members of Serbia's new elite, particularly since some owned timar estates there themselves, including Stojan and Aleksa Simić, Jevrem and Miloš himself.[83] Miloš, however, viewed the potential emergence of a new class of Serbian large landowners as a threat to his power and was supported in his opposition by Russia and the Porte. He promoted instead an egalitarian rural population of small peasant freeholders and family farms, thus strengthening his hold on peasant loyalties.[84] Miloš protected their rights against their former Muslim landlords, Serbian notables, merchants and moneylenders alike. However, he did not formally legalise the peasants' possession of their plots. This created a degree of insecurity among them that his opponents would exploit.[85] Overall, while Serbian peasants would resent and periodically resist the tax burden, venality of officials and brutality of the police, there would be no straightforward class struggle on the European model.

Foundation of a modern society

Miloš developed his armed forces on the basis of the 1830 hatt-ı şerif. He established a new force, the guard or cadets, which was not territorially based but accompanied the prince wherever he was located, and which was garrisoned in Kragujevac and Požarevac. Enrolling 149 cadets in its first year, it was recruited from youths of families select 'in stature and reputation', who were trained in their own special guards' school first established at Požarevac on 7 May 1830. Miloš founded a cavalry in 1832. Although the guards' school closed in autumn 1833, Miloš then sent 30 cadets to Russia to receive military training as infantry, cavalry and artillery officers.[86] In 1835, Sultan Mahmud gifted six cannon to Miloš, who then established an artillery section for his army. Soldiers wore a uniform of round caps, dark red vests, dark blue trousers and yellow buttons, thereby introducing European-style dress into Serbia.[87] The army was initially disguised as part of the police, given Austria's and the Porte's opposition to its existence.[88] Its commander was Vučić-Perišić.

To cow his population further, Miloš requested the Ottomans to strengthen their forces on Serbia's borders. They eventually agreed that the Ottoman garrison in Belgrade should be reinforced by a thousand troops, signifying the empire's readiness to crush further revolts.[89] Sixteen more cannon were obtained from Austria in 1837. Miloš established the Military Academy of the Principality of Serbia, staffed by Austrian Serb instructors, on 27 December 1837, initially in Požarevac and subsequently relocated to Belgrade, then Kragujevac. This was, however, even shorter-lived than the guards' school and closed in June 1838, apparently owing to logistical difficulties and insufficient commitment from Miloš.[90] Nevertheless, the guard numbered 2,417 by 1838, stationed in the Belgrade, Kragujevac, Požarevac and smaller garrisons, subsequently peaking at 4,307 before the end of Miloš's first reign in June 1839.[91] Meanwhile, a workshop for repairing hand arms began work in Kragujevac in 1836, employing twenty engineers. At a meeting of Serbia's military commanders there on 5 February 1837, the idea was mooted of establishing a cannon foundry in the town, though it would be over a decade before this happened.[92]

The guard was augmented by the principle of a 'nation-in-arms'; from 1833, taxpayers were required to own a gun and appropriate equipment and respond to military summons when required. The hatt-ı şerif of 1830 recognised the Serbian prince's right to build schools and hospitals, and the army's establishment was followed by the building of military hospitals. These were almost Serbia's first hospitals; the very first was founded by Jevrem in Šabac in 1826 along with the first apothecary, while apothecaries were opened in Belgrade and Kragujevac in 1830 and 1835 respectively.[93] In 1835, Serbia was divided between four military commands: Podrinje-Sava, based in Šabac under Jevrem; Morava-Podrinje, based in Čačak under Jovan; Danube-Timok, based in Negotin under Stevan Stojanović-Čosa; and Šumadija, based in Kragujevac under Petar Tucaković. These commands constituted the national militia, numbering between 70,000 and 100,000 men and responsible for maintaining public order, while the standing army remained under Miloš's exclusive command.[94] By 1837, the Serbian border was properly established, with a border police and customs and sanitation services.

There had been only three schools in Serbia in 1815 and the number increased only slowly between then and the start of the 1830s. However, in 1831, Dimitrije Isailović, an Austrian Serb from Dalj in Croatia-Slavonia, educated in Sremski Karlovci and Pest and formerly a professor at the teacher-training college in Sombor in Hungary, was brought to Belgrade by Miloš to establish a high school named, like its predecessor under Karađorđe, the Great School, and was tasked with educating cadres for the new bureaucracy. Isailović was subsequently joined by a second Austrian Serb teacher, Atanasije Teodorović. The City Library of Belgrade was founded on 28 February 1832 on Miloš's orders at the bookshop of Gligorije Bozarović, a Serb from near Sremska Mitrovica in the Austrian Empire, who had learned his trade in Vienna. It would be officially renamed the National Library in 1858. The first law on public elementary education in Serbia was passed in 1833. As part of the government's efforts at public education, it launched Serbia's first newspaper, *Novine Srbske* (Serb Newspaper), in January 1834; its first editor was Davidović. He was born in Zemun, founded the first Serbian-language newspaper in Vienna in 1813, moved to Serbia in 1821 and became secretary of Miloš's chancellery until 1829. An Austrian Serb gymnasium professor, Petar Radovanović, was appointed superintendent for Serbia's schools in 1836. The school system in Serbia expanded more rapidly thereafter, with the teachers being overwhelmingly Austrian Serbs. The Great School was transferred to Kragujevac in 1833, promoted to the status of gymnasium in 1835 and 'Lycée of the Serbian Principality' in 1838, and moved back to Belgrade in 1841. High schools were established between 1833 and 1838 in Šabac, Čačak and Zaječar, and a new gymnasium in 1839 in Belgrade.[95] Meanwhile, the number of state officials grew from 24 in 1815 to 169 in 1830, 492 in 1837 and 672 by the time Miloš abdicated in 1839. Of these 672, 201 were police officials and the rest clerks, secretaries, teachers, judges and others.[96]

Miloš promoted the Orthodox religion and church as important tools of his regime. He took religion very seriously: he financed the construction of churches, promoted religious observance and himself attended church services every weekend and holiday, remaining present from start to finish.[97] This accompanied the church's steady subordination to his regime. He quickly established control of the lower Serbian clergy and greatly reduced the annual payments by the Serbian church to the Patriarchate. He punished monks and priests with beatings, as he did other officials. He lobbied the Patriarchate patiently, over a period of years, for the removal of the two Greek bishops who traditionally held office in the two Serbian dioceses of Belgrade and Šabac, and their replacement with Serb bishops. He had the Serbian archimandrite Melentije Nikšić appointed as bishop in the vacant diocese of Šabac in 1815 following the end of the Second Serbian Uprising, but this proved a false dawn for the Serbianisation of the church when Miloš had him murdered the following year, after which another Greek bishop replaced him. Nevertheless, at Miloš's behest, on 13–14 December 1822, the Serbian parliament established a consistory based in Kragujevac to supervise the bishops, headed by Archimandrite Melentije Pavlović, hero of the Second Serbian Uprising, first cousin of Miloš's henchman Vučić-Perišić and Miloš's own family priest.

Miloš issued a decree on 23 January 1823 which, taking advantage of the replacement of various Ottoman taxes with a lump sum paid by the prince, gave him the right to pay the bishops' wages while largely abolishing their independent revenues.[98] Article 14 of the hatt-ı şerif of 1830 decreed that the Serbs would elect their own metropolitan and bishops, who would then be ordained by the Patriarch. Miloš in December 1830 selected two ethnic Serbs, Melentije Pavlović and Nićifor Maksimović, for the metropolitanate of Belgrade and the new diocese of Užice; and Gerasim Đorđević—an ethnic Vlach from present-day Bulgaria, educated at Studenica monastery and effectively assimilated into Serbdom—for the diocese of Šabac. Melentije and Nićifor were ordained by the Patriarch of Constantinople in August 1831. Lukijan Mušicki, Serbian Orthodox bishop of Gornji Karlovac in Croatia, noted dismissively at the time: 'I don't think it would be necessary to say that not one of these three knows anything, except to read somewhat, whereas to write—in the true sense—not one knows.'[99]

A concordat of the Patriarchate in September 1831 formally recognised the Serbian Orthodox Church's autonomy, though the document's dispatch was delayed until January 1832 to force Miloš to pay the debts of the three Serbian dioceses. The concordat recognised the right of the Serbian clergy, prince and people to elect Serbia's metropolitan and bishops without involvement of the Patriarchate, although the Patriarch retained a veto on the metropolitan's dismissal. The Patriarch would ordain a new metropolitan in return for the sum of 300 imperial ducats and the metropolitan would assume the title of 'Metropolitan of all of Serbia' and mention the Patriarchate in his liturgy.[100] Corresponding to this new status, Belgrade cathedral was constructed, beginning in 1836, replacing a church that had previously stood in the same spot and that was demolished to make way for it. The cathedral's Baroque architectural style was, for the city, unorthodox. It became the place for coronations, royal weddings and funerals.[101]

Following Melentije's death in June 1833, Pavle Jovanović was made Metropolitan of Belgrade and primate of the Serbian church, remaining in the post until 1859; he was an Austrian Serb from Ilok in Croatia and educated at Sremski Karlovci and Szeged in Hungary, where he studied philosophy. He then taught at the Sremski Karlovci gymnasium. A layman who first served as secretary of the national court in Kragujevac, Jovanović was rapidly given holy orders and fast-tracked through the priestly ranks to become metropolitan, adopting the name Petar. He then reorganised the Serbian church, using its counterpart, the Serbian church in Austria, as his model and taking advice from its bishop, Stefan Stratimirović. He worked to establish a church bureaucracy, a code of church laws, an educated priesthood and a system of religious schools paralleling Miloš's state bureaucracy, opening a theological seminary in Belgrade in 1836.[102] Petar regulated marriage: a law in March 1837 established that marriages must be freely entered into by both parties; that parents had to give their consent for marriage; that the minimum legal age for marriage be seventeen for boys and fourteen for girls; that the very old, ill or senile could not marry; and that marriages for women older than forty and men older than fifty had to be approved by the relevant bishop.[103]

The first national census was conducted in 1834 and revealed the principality's population to number around 698,624 inhabiting 2,231 settlements, of whom around 24,000 were Muslims, 12,000 were gypsies, 2,000 were Jews and 1,000 members of other non-Serb minorities. The Serb Christian majority numbered around 659,624, which included around 20,000 ethnic Romanians who were not differentiated from the Serbs; about 338,060 of these were men and 321,564 were women.[104] Belgrade in 1836 had a population of around 14,000, of which 5,704 were Muslims, 5,503 Serb Christians and 1,530 Jews. Nevertheless, the Serb quarter of the town grew, and by the end of the decade Serbs outnumbered Muslims.[105]

PRINCE MILOŠ AND THE FOUNDING OF MODERN SERBIA

Whereas craft production before 1830 had been almost wholly in the hands of Muslims and, to a lesser extent, other ethnic and religious minorities, a class of Serb Orthodox craftsmen was now developing rapidly. By 1838 there were among the Christian population alone in Belgrade nearly 900 craftsmen and merchants and 39 guilds representing about 50 crafts. By this time, a strong craftsman–merchant class had emerged in the provincial towns as well; by 1836 there were 426 craftsmen and merchants in Šabac, 339 in Jagodina, 336 in Kragujevac and 335 in Požarevac, while other towns had under 200. The number of guilds in the country grew from 18 to 79 between 1830 and 1947.[106]

The hatt-ı şerif of 1830 decreed that Miloš was to govern 'with the participation of an assembly composed of heads of the land', i.e. elders. This was, however, perceived not as a parliament but as a much smaller council or 'soviet'—heir to the moribund chancellery abolished in 1823, but originally composed of the twelve knezes of the original twelve Serbian nahijas. It indicated that Miloš, despite his autocracy, had begun not as a monarch in the European sense but as first among equals in a collective body of knezes. The hatt-ı şerif decreed: 'So long as members of the council, of whom there are multiple, are not guilty of a serious offence either against my Sublime Porte or against the law and decrees of the land, they may not be without reason either dismissed or removed from their posts.'[107] The clause was included because both the Porte and the Russians wished to limit Miloš's absolutism and have the means to control him. A precedent existed in the political system in the Romanian principalities of Wallachia and Moldavia. There, the princes (hospodars) were elected by the boyars, whom the Porte could manipulate to ensure the outcome it wanted. Russia's influence in these principalities had grown, however, until the Treaty of Adrianople in 1829, when it gained a veto on any rejection or dismissal of the hospodars by the Porte and a large say in their appointment, so that its control became greater than the Porte's.[108] The hatt-ı şerif, however, left ambiguous precisely what sort of council it envisaged. Miloš interpreted it to mean a government, and ministries were established in April 1834 for law, education and internal affairs, in May for finance, and in June for the army and foreign affairs. The first ministers were Davidović, Đorđe Protić, Lazar Teodorović, Koča Marković and Vučić-Perišić. They did not meet as a government or cabinet but merely executed Miloš's orders.[109] Others, seeking to limit Miloš's power, interpreted the council decreed by the hatt-ı şerif as lying outside his control and sharing power with him. The opposition to Miloš in subsequent years consequently focused on the establishment and defence of such a council.

Serbia at the start of the 1830s was still divided into essentially the same twelve nahijas dating from the end of the eighteenth century: Belgrade, Valjevo, Jagodina, Kragujevac, Požarevac, Požega, Rudnik, Smederevo, Soko, Užice, Ćuprija and Šabac. Following the reacquisition of the six nahijas, its administration was reorganised to produce twenty-one nahijas: the original twelve, some of them

87

expanded, plus Podrinje (soon merged with Šabac), Studenica, Jošanica, Kruševac, Paraćin, Banija, Gurgusovac, Zaječar and Negotin. The nahijas were in turn divided into sixty kapetanijas (before 1830 called kneživas).[110] In February–March 1834, these nahijas were grouped into five larger administrative units, or oblasts, covering the whole principality, based in Belgrade, Šabac, Čačak, Jagodina and Negotin, each headed by an official called a serdar. That summer, Serbia was reorganised again into fifteen units, now renamed okrugs in place of the Ottoman term nahija, which were themselves divided into 61 kapetanijas. The kapetanija was renamed 'srez' (district) the following year, marking the abandonment of Ottoman terminology for territorial administration.[111] In mid-1835, Serbia was divided into four military commanders in place of the five oblasts of the serdars. Two additional okrugs were created in 1836 through the divisions of existing ones, to make seventeen in total. The administrative system was much less democratic than it had been in 1815: the okrug and district governors who replaced the ober-knezes and knezes were directly appointed by the prince, while the district assemblies were rarely convened and played little role in administration. Although villages were generally still allowed to elect their kmets, these had to be formally appointed by the prince either in person or through the district governors, and could only be dismissed by him. The national parliament, which had generally met twice a year during the mid- to late 1820s, met only on average once a year in the 1830s, and in 1838 formally lost its budgetary right to the Council.[112] Yet the institution of local self-management remained in folk memory, and its restoration would one day be demanded by radical—indeed Radical—political activists, who arose against the new bureaucratic order.

The emergence of an autonomous Serbia within the Ottoman Empire influenced the calculations of the Great Powers. David Urquhart, secretary of the British embassy in Constantinople, travelled through Serbia in 1832 and 1833 and spoke with Miloš at length. Miloš expressed to Urquhart his concern at Russian meddling in Serbian affairs. Soon after, Urquhart published an influential book that quickly went through multiple editions, arguing that Serbia along with the Ottoman Empire as a whole should be supported as a bulwark against Russia, and linking this to support for the Poles, who had recently staged a major rebellion against Russian rule. He was impressed by Serbia in its role of loyal vassal:

> its tranquillity and loyalty restrains the Bosniacs and the Albanians, while the independence and the elevation of the social position of the Serbians elevate the character of the Rayas elsewhere, and render impossible former oppression by the refuge it affords, and the respect it commands. Instead of the Porte's having in future to expend its resources, and the blood of its subjects, in quelling revolts produced in Serbia by its maladministration, Serbia becomes the means of restraining commotions elsewhere; and instead of its offering auxiliaries to foreign foes, it has 30,000 brave and warlike troops; and, in case of invasion, 100,000 to defend the empire.[113]

PRINCE MILOŠ AND THE FOUNDING OF MODERN SERBIA

Urquhart collaborated with the Polish émigré Prince Adam Czartoryski, who acquired a copy of the report Urquhart wrote following his meetings with Miloš. Czartoryski adopted Urquhart's strategy of promoting Serbia as a bulwark against Russia. This was eventually expressed in the 1840s in the famous 'Plan' of Serbia's interior minister Ilija Garašanin, the work of Czartoryski's circle.[114]

Another visitor impressed by Miloš's and Serbia's achievements was the French writer Alphonse de Lamartine. Travelling through Ottoman Niš in 1833 en route to Serbia, he was moved by the sight of the Skull Tower built by the Ottomans following the Battle of Čegar:

> I sat down in the shade of the tower to sleep for a while; scarcely had I been seated than, raising my eyes to the monument which lent me its shadow, I saw that its walls, which had seemed to have been built of marble or white stone, were actually formed by rows of human skulls. These skulls and these faces of men, emaciated and whitened by the rain and the sun, cemented by grains of sand and lime, formed entirely the triumphal arch which sheltered me; there may have been fifteen or twenty thousand; to some the hair was still hanging and fluttering like lichens and moss in the wind; the mountain breeze blew lively and fresh and, entering the innumerable cavities of the heads, faces and skulls, made them emit plaintive and lamentable hisses ... Servia, where we were about to enter, is now free, and it is a song of freedom and glory that the mountain winds brought back to the tower of the Servians who died for their country! Soon they will own Niš itself; may they allow this monument to remain! It will teach their children what the independence of a people is worth, by showing them the price their fathers paid for it.[115]

Mileta's rebellion and Presentation Constitution

The successful conclusion of the struggle with the Porte for recognition of Serbian statehood freed members of Serbia's fledgling elite to focus on constitutional reform. Most of them suffered from the abuses of Miloš's despotism one way or another, so wished to curb it. The hatt-ı şerif of 1830, by mandating the formation of a Council with which he was to share power, provided a legal starting point for the constitutional struggle. Serbia's emissaries to St Petersburg, Petronijević and Rajović, returned home at the end of that year with Tsar Nicholas's advice, that 'the time has come for Prince Miloš to issue to the people a statute of state'. Constitutional proposals were subsequently circulated. One was written by Karadžić in a letter to Miloš, dated 24 April 1832 but only dispatched on 25 August, informing him bluntly that 'nobody is satisfied with Your Serene Highness's rule, absolutely *nobody*, apart from your two sons, and if they were a bit older, perhaps they would be dissatisfied like everyone else' (emphasis in the original). Miloš's two sons were aged twelve and eight at the time. Karadžić then presented a thorough critique of Serbia's political, constitutional and legal regime, advocating the rule of law, limitations on the prince's powers and the bureaucracy's professionalisation, which, if implemented, he assured Miloš, 'Then Serbia would become similar to other European statelets of its rank.'[116] Similarly, the French envoy Bois-le-Conte resided in Serbia in the spring of 1834 and conferred with Miloš's secretaries and advisers, conveying to them ideas of constitutionalism.[117]

Miloš considered such ideas but was reluctant to implement any of them. In May 1834, he promised the parliament he would summon a great national parliament to enact a constitution. After further procrastination, he announced on 10 December that he would summon the great national parliament the following month, but on the 31st postponed it until Candlemas (14 February), prompting the opposition to plan an uprising against him. Stojan Simić, principal organiser of the conspiracy, assembled a group of notables at his home in Kruševac on 12 January 1835, ostensibly to attend his son's christening, which was performed there by Metropolitan Petar on the 13th, after which the participants together planned their rebellion. Other notables attending included the conspiracy's second figure, Petronijević, as well as Protić, Mileta Radojković, Milisav Zdravković Resavac, Ranko Majstorović, Milutin Petrović Era, Metropolitan Petar and even Miloš's wife Ljubica and second son, Mihailo.[118] At this time, Miloš's brother Jevrem also joined the opposition while his first son, Milan, came to sympathise with them. Their aim was to force Miloš to grant a constitution and recognise the rule of law, including establishment of a Council.

Some of these men were of powerful independent standing in their own right, but others had risen to prominence in Miloš's service and owed their careers to him, benefiting from his abolition of kneževina autonomy in favour of an authoritarian bureaucratic regime. Stojan Simić was son of a Serb Free Corps officer from Austria who had moved to Serbia in 1805 after the uprising began and become a rebel vojvoda. Stojan had been Miloš's courier; his brother Aleksa had begun as Miloš's scribe and eventually become secretary of his personal chancellery.[119] Petronijević was born in a village on the Serbian side of the Austrian border and educated in Oršova in Transylvania, and had begun as a clerk in Miloš's chancellery, where he owed his employment to his knowledge of Greek. Vučić-Perišić, whose collaboration would prove crucial to the conspiracy's success, was a hero of both the First and Second Serbian Uprisings but only a lowly standard-bearer in the first. They and others in their network were motivated partly by resentment at Miloš's abusive and arbitrary behaviour; Protić, for example, had been beaten on Miloš's orders for dishonouring a knez's sixteen-year-old daughter, while Vučić-Perišić had suffered repeated interference in his family life from the prince, who in 1827 had publicly shamed and dismissed him as knez of Gruža for mistreating his mother.[120] Miloš required even the wives of his high officials to perform the 'women's work' of the household kuluk at his home, enjoying their humiliation.[121] The officials knew they could be dismissed at Miloš's whim, so they sought security for their newly acquired status—their conversion from mere servants of the prince to senior state officials.[122] They also coveted a greater share of rural assets—land, vineyards, inns, shops and so forth—left behind by the retreating Ottoman officials and sipahis.[123]

The conspiracy spawned 'Mileta's rebellion' under Radojković, a veteran of the First and Second Serbian Uprisings who had directed the liberation of the six nahijas in 1833. As serdar of Jagodina, he had authority over the kmets and other elders in a large part of the country, and his high standing stemming from his role in the anti-Ottoman struggle meant the people responded to his summons. He launched his rebellion on 19 January, marching on Miloš's capital of Kragujevac with 5,000 men. Other notables raised rebellions in their respective localities, including in the Danubian oblast under the jurisdiction of the serdar of Belgrade, who was part of the conspiracy. The rebellion encompassed about a third of Serbian territory. Petronijević gave a fiery speech on 20 January to the assembled rebel forces at Taborište outside Kragujevac, assuring them that 'all of Serbia will be with us'. Miloš sent his commander Vučić-Perišić with an army to negotiate with them. But when Radojković and Vučić-Perišić met with their armies at Taborište that day, they collaborated; they were former comrades-in-arms who had fought together against Đak's rebellion. They entered Kragujevac together, ensuring the rebellion's success. The rebels made their base in the office of the national court, most of whose members supported them or were actual leading conspirators—including Stojan Simić, Protić, Resavac and Majstorović. They spoke in the court's name to give their rebellion institutional legitimacy.[124]

Miloš's power thus began crumbling since almost the entire Serbian establishment turned against him, including his own family. Crucially, this included his principal commanders, costing him military control of the country. The pyramidal structure of authority, with the prince's authority resting upon officials with independent local standing, made him peculiarly vulnerable to their revolt. The rebel leaders presented their demands to the assembled multitude on 21 January and the following day their delegation, consisting of Vučić-Perišić, Majstorović and about 35 prominent knezes, presented them to Miloš in Požarevac: the establishment of a Council as an institution representing Serbia's notables that would limit the prince's power; guarantees for the lives and property of all Serbia's inhabitants, including formal recognition of the peasants' ownership of their plots; and fair taxes.[125]

Militarily outgunned as he was, to obtain the withdrawal of the rebels from his capital, Miloš had to accept their demands, and he promised a constitution by Candlemas. Although the rebel leaders were quickly weakened by mutual discord and reawakened fear of Miloš's retribution, this marked the beginning of the end of his autocracy and his regime. Shortly afterwards, the rebel leaders—Radojković, Stojan Simić, Petronijević, Resavac and Protić—met him outside the capital and knelt before him, asking for his forgiveness; he stood them up again and said, 'We are all guilty and I have often erred; we will try to correct everything and mutually forgive one another.'¹²⁶ A great national parliament was consequently summoned by the rebels acting through the national court and sat from 14–16 February 1835: the 'Candlemas Parliament' or 'Presentation Parliament', numbering between 2,400 and 4,000 representatives from every village, district and okrug in Serbia, with apparently another 10,000 onlookers. On the 15th, it formally established the Council and promulgated the constitution, authored by Miloš's secretary Davidović under the influence of Bois-le-Conte.¹²⁷

The so-called Candlemas or Presentation Constitution proclaimed that 'Serbia is an indivisible and, in its administration, independent principality based on the recognition of Sultan Mahmud II and Tsar Nicholas I'; that it was a hereditary principality under Miloš and his heirs; and that Serbia's prince could only be a natural-born Serb of the Orthodox faith, to which his wife and her family also had to belong. The constitution explicitly affirmed Serbia's statehood in formulations such as 'the Serbian prince is the head of state'. It decreed the division of power between a legislature, executive and judiciary, the first two of which would be in the hands of the prince and a Council. The Council would consist of a body of councillors; ministers of law, the interior, finance, foreign affairs, military affairs and education; and a president and secretary. These would be appointed by Miloš; they would debate legislation and decrees proposed by the individual ministers but he would have a veto over them. A popularly elected parliament of 100 members was to meet annually; its approval would be required to pass the annual budget or determine taxes.¹²⁸ This constitution provided merely an oligarchic tempering of and parliamentary window dressing to Miloš's autocracy, but it established judicial independence and the basis for a legal system guaranteeing the rights of individuals and their property. State officials were banned from independently engaging in trade or crafts. Kuluk was formally abolished in most respects, though elements of it lingered.

The three Great Powers with a particular interest in Serbia—Russia, Austria and the Ottoman Empire—were united in their apprehension at the revolutionary outbreak and their readiness to assist Miloš in suppressing it; Austria transferred two regiments to the Serbian border. All three considered the constitution too liberal. Russia and the Porte were offended that it had been promulgated without their permission as protector and suzerain respectively. As the Treaty of Unkiar-Skelessi had transformed Russia into the Ottoman Empire's guardian, St Petersburg did not at this time wish to promote Serbia's independence from it, which the constitution, and the way it had been promulgated, seemed to do. Given their objections, Miloš suspended the constitution at the start of March and dispatched an envoy to Constantinople to consult with the Porte and the Russian ambassador. Their continued objections and those of Austria prompted Miloš, who had not wanted the constitution in the first place, wholly to abrogate it in April, thereby formally restoring his untrammelled autocracy.[129] At his St Peter's Day parliament on 1 June 1835, he passed a law on the Council, recognising its legislative power subject to his absolute veto, but used the occasion to appoint a new Council excluding most of the participants in Mileta's rebellion, so that the body was no longer controlled by the opposition but existed to mollify it.[130] Since the Council had absorbed the national court in 1835, on 10 October 1837 a new Great Court was established to free the Council of legal duties.

Miloš on 15 June 1835 introduced, in place of the old system of multiple feudal dues, a general system of taxation based on a head-tax of six thalers per year for men over twenty years old, something first agreed at the Presentation parliament. The use of kuluk labour by officials was abolished. This definitely stymied the ambitions of the notables to become feudal lords. The tax burden on ordinary peasants was simplified but not lightened. Since they were no longer able to pay part of their taxes in kind, for some it was effectively increased.[131] Miloš sought also to restrict the opening of village shops, partly to protect the commercial interests of the urban merchant class, and on 27 December 1835 he passed a law imposing a punitive tax on them. He bolstered his popular support with a decree on 10 June 1836 forbidding any peasant to pay a debt by selling the minimum part of his freehold needed for his family's economic survival, defined as his house, inherited homestead, two oxen and one cow. A decree in 1837 introduced a legal upper limit of 12 per cent interest per annum on loans.[132] Miloš stopped short of granting the peasants full legal security over their own property, and this enabled the opposition to co-opt part of the peasantry.[133]

Since the hatt-ı şerif of 1833 had apparently resolved the principal outstanding issues between Serbia and the Ottoman Empire, the Porte had been endeavouring to put the seal on their relationship through having Miloš visit Constantinople. Miloš was reluctant to do so since he worried about several things: his personal safety, in particular at the hands of Turkish assassins; what might happen in Serbia in his absence; the trip's huge cost; and that his personal limitations would become plain to the Sultan, his court and the European ambassadors once they met him in the flesh away from his home ground.[134] Nevertheless, under considerable pressure, he made the trip in August 1835 after the resolution of the crisis involving Mileta's rebellion and the Presentation Constitution made his domestic situation somewhat more secure. He met with the Porte and the Sultan, who bestowed gifts upon him; dressed in his general's uniform wearing Ottoman and Russian medals, he knelt before the Sultan and kissed his foot, receiving from him a new medal incorporating Mahmud's portrait and in turn giving him several gifts.[135] The Council responded to the news in a letter to Miloš: 'Mahmud II is truly great. He has endeavoured, under the mercy of his great wisdom, to make the Serbs forget all the misery, all the suffering and all the persecution that his ancestors did to our ancestors. May God fortify him in his intentions!'[136]

Miloš then visited the Patriarch and the Russian ambassador, subsequently also the Austrian internuncius and Prussian ambassador, and attended a ball held by the Russian ambassador in honour of his new British counterpart. During his stay in Constantinople, Miloš also negotiated with the Sultan's ministers the right of Serbia to use a flag; this was formally granted in a firman in December. The Serbian tricolour, originally red-white-blue horizontal stripes, was now redesigned to be red-blue-white, with the Serbian coat of arms in the centre, headed by three crescents symbolising Ottoman overlordship.[137] Following his departure, Miloš sent a message of thanks to the Sultan, 'I begin my journey happy, proud and grateful for the lofty imperial blessing, remaining unwavering and firm, with my poor people, while I exist and the world exists, in humility and faithfulness.'[138] Although given his humble peasant background he was indeed culturally somewhat out of his depth during this trip, the visit crowned his prestige as head of his new state. But back home, oligarchic opposition to his regime was growing.

Turkish Constitution and fall of Prince Miloš

The Great Powers began to establish consulates in Serbia from 1836. The first was Austria, which insisted on the right to do so given its commercial links with Serbia and the large number of its subjects resident there. Although Miloš initially objected to what he saw as unwelcome foreign intrusion and surveillance, he soon changed his mind for a number of reasons: he wished for good relations with Austria to facilitate his import of skilled Austrian Serbs; he wanted Austrian support against the Russian-inclined oligarchic opposition; and he was bribed with a Habsburg imperial decoration, the Order of the Iron Crown, First Class.[139] Russia then appointed its consul to Orşova, further down the Danube from Belgrade on Austrian territory, in an unsuccessful attempt to avoid a precedent for the Western powers to appoint their own consuls in Serbia. Britain's consul, Colonel George Hodges, arrived in Belgrade in 1837.[140]

The consuls meddled in Serbia's political struggle. Russian policymakers favoured Miloš's opponents since they believed an oligarchy would be more amenable to their influence than a despot. In response, the British, while encouraging Miloš to rule according to the law and respect the personal rights and property of his subjects, supported his regime as a bulwark against Russia. Britain's foreign minister, Viscount Palmerston, viewed Serbia as a pawn in the 'Great Game' that was being waged between Britain and Russia across the Near East and Asia. As Metternich noted at the time, paradoxically, liberal Britain was backing the autocrat Miloš while autocratic Russia was backing the opposition seeking constitutional rule.[141] Miloš's position was weakened by the increasing hostility of Russia, which objected to his friendly relations with Hodges. But though Hodges encouraged Miloš to resist the opposition and worked to reconcile him with some of his opponents, Britain could not ensure his victory while the Russians were effective in uniting his opponents. When the Porte resolved to accommodate itself to Russia and abandon Miloš, partly out of fear at the danger of leaving too much power in the prince's hands, his fate was sealed.[142]

The Russians had responded to the Serbian political upheaval of 1835 by seeking to mediate between Miloš and his opponents to achieve a mutually acceptable constitutional arrangement. At their envoy's initiative, Miloš issued a decree on 28 October 1837 that guaranteed security of personal property and vocation, established a wholly free market, confirmed the abolition of kuluk and placed the state treasury under Council control. Yet he ignored the decree in practice and continued to rule as before. Leading members of the opposition—Stojan Simić, Protić, Jevrem, Vučić-Perišić—went into exile to escape Miloš's retribution, whence they lobbied the Russians against him with increasing success. Miloš was compelled to appoint a constitutional committee on 25 February 1838 that included leading members of the opposition, including Jevrem, Petronijević and Archpriest Mateja, tasked with drafting a constitution. However, the continued failure to agree prompted the Porte, with Russia's backing, to issue a firman at the end of March summoning a Serbian delegation to Constantinople to draft a constitution. Miloš retreated, acquiescing in this external intervention.

Mahmud attempted to reform his empire and rein in the autonomy of its dependencies; in 1831–1833, he crushed Gradaščević's Bosnian rebellion and waged an unsuccessful war against Muhammad Ali's Egypt, and in May–June 1835 he dispatched a naval expedition and restored direct rule over Tripoli. He likewise sought to restore Constantinople's influence over Serbia; this shaped both the constitution's terms and the manner in which it was promulgated.[143] Serbia's delegation arrived in Constantinople on 8 May 1838. The constitution's provisions were then negotiated over the succeeding months between Miloš's supporters, his opponents (known as Defenders of the Constitution, or Constitutionalists), the Porte and representatives of the Great Powers. Serbia's new constitution was issued by the Porte in the Sultan's name in the form of a hatt-ı şerif on 24 December 1838, hence remembered as the 'Turkish Constitution'. It was granted to 'my Province of Serbia' and addressed to the vizier in Belgrade, Jusuf-Muhlis Pasha, and only then to Miloš, thus reaffirming Ottoman sovereignty over the country. References to statehood in the constitution were much more muted than they had been in the Presentation Constitution. It was ceremonially delivered by the vizier to Miloš in Kalemegdan on 24 February 1839 before a specially summoned Serbian parliament, opened by a speech from the metropolitan. The hatt-ı şerif was formally read first in Turkish then in Serbian, after which Serbian and Ottoman military forces conducted a joint exercise and the constitution's terms were explained in detail to the parliament. The following day, Miloš formally appointed the Council and government. The Serbian dignitaries assembled in church and, before the metropolitan, pledged allegiance to the constitution.[144]

SERBIA

The constitution proclaimed Serbia a hereditary principality under Miloš and the Obrenović dynasty. It established the Council, 'comprised of the elders and the most important among the Serbs', of seventeen members corresponding to the seventeen okrugs, thereby honouring the hatt-ı şerif of 1830. They would be appointed by the prince but could not be removed by him unless guilty of a misdeed as confirmed by the Porte—this last provision was inserted by the Ottomans and accepted by the Russians over objections from both Serbian factions. Councillors had to be Serbs with Serbian citizenship, older than 35 years, who owned landed property in the country—this requirement was aimed at excluding Miloš's Austrian Serb officials. The Council held legislative power and the right to determine the budget and taxes. Laws passed by majority vote could not be vetoed by the prince. The judiciary was to be independent, establishing Serbia as a legal as well as constitutional state.[145] Serbia's division into seventeen okrugs was confirmed. These were divided into districts (srezes), of which Serbia would have 52 in 1839, which were in turn divided into 1,251 municipalities (opštinas), most of which comprised one to three villages each (an average of 1.7), though some had more. Each municipality had its own court. The okrug and district chiefs were to be organs of the central police administration while the municipalities retained a limited degree of self-management. Kmets were to be elected under the supervision of the district chiefs to ensure state control. The constitution also abolished corporal punishment for state officials, prohibited all forms of kuluk and guaranteed complete freedom of trade.

The councillors and prince were required to swear before the metropolitan 'to do nothing contrary to the interests of the people; to the duties that have been accorded to them on the basis of their rank; to their duties according to their conscience; nor to my Imperial will'. All new laws and taxes had to be approved by the Council. Ministries were established for internal affairs, finance and justice, the last of which had jurisdiction over schools, hospitals and churches. The Serbian church's autonomy was recognised, subject to the prince's supervision and ultimate authority of the Patriarch in Constantinople. Order was to be kept by gendarmes (panduri). The prince was deprived of real control over the security forces. The constitution finally recognised the peasants' absolute ownership of their plots and right to dispose of them.[146] The legal framework for this was eventually finalised by a Law on the Reclamation of Land on 5 August 1839.[147] The fledgling Constitutionalist regime took further measures to win the support of the masses: the head-tax was lowered from six to five thalers; all restrictions were lifted on the number of livestock merchants and their right to trade with peasants; trade permits for these merchants became a mere formality; and villages shops were again permitted, albeit only one per village.[148]

The constitution's authors believed that the oligarchic Council would restrain Miloš more effectively than popular assemblies, which, with his demagogic skill, he had shown he could manipulate.[149] As there was no provision for the election of parliaments, the constitution amounted to a replacement of princely absolutism with oligarchy. It formally transferred budgetary powers from parliament to Council, thereby confirming the former's marginalisation. The precise division of competencies between prince and Council was not clearly defined and the Porte was granted the authority to resolve constitutional disputes between them. This planted the seeds of future power struggles between prince and Council.[150] In January 1839, another Ottoman decree formally confirmed Serbia's right to use its coat of arms and new flag, on which the three crescents, to which the Serbs had objected, were replaced by four stars in the top left-hand corner. Miloš issued a decree on 30 March 1839 adding a constitutional clause giving himself the right to summon parliaments 'according to the old custom, whenever the need for this is recognised', yet these would have a purely consultative role, unlike the fiscal powers which the Presentation Constitution had granted them.

Miloš was by 1839 a broken man who had lost control of the state and was incapable of formulating a strategy either to restore his dictatorship or reconstitute himself as a constitutional monarch. He was the prisoner of the Constitutionalists both physically and politically. He fled on 29 April to Zemun and attempted to extract concessions from the Council, but was forced back four days later under threat of dethronement. The Council then passed a Law on the Organisation of the Council on 9 May, effectively appropriating legislative power from Miloš while depriving him also of executive power. With no other cards left to play, Miloš plotted a rebellion, using his brother Jovan as front man; it was consequently known as Jovan's rebellion. It erupted in the Kragujevac, Ćuprija and Kruševac garrisons on 23 May 1839, involving standing-army soldiers loyal to Miloš; they wrote to him stating that they wanted but one ruler, not seventeen.[151] The military uprising was coupled to an uprising of peasants and officials in central Šumadija, primarily in the Rudnik and Kragujevac okrugs. But Miloš was under the Constitutionalists' physical control, so was unable to lead it.

At a meeting involving the prince, Council, vizier and Russian envoy, the last-mentioned vetoed the Council's suggestion to imprison Miloš in the Belgrade fortress, but he was nevertheless forced to authorise the regime's measures to suppress the rebellion, including granting Vučić-Perišić emergency powers and the title of 'Supreme Lord of the National Army'. Vučić-Perišić used the national militia to defeat the rebels of Miloš's standing army. Vučić-Perišić's greatly superior Constitutionalist forces, armed by the Ottoman garrison in Belgrade and holding Miloš's unwillingly given order to surrender, forced the small rebel army to do so at Trešnja on 28 May, after which the rebellion collapsed. With the Council's approval, Vučić-Perišić deliberately humiliated defeated rebel soldiers by stripping them of their uniforms and forcing them to march in their undergarments so as to destroy the army's prestige, given its institutional loyalty to the prince.[152] Miloš was forced to sign a law on 29 May further strengthening the oligarchy at the prince's expense, by requiring the prince to select his ministers exclusively from Council members.

Finally, Constitutionalists Vučić-Perišić, Stojan Simić, Archpriest Mateja and Lazar Teodorović met at Rakovica on 10 June and resolved to dethrone Miloš.[153] Under the guidance of Vučić-Perišić, who mostly selected its deputies, a parliament was elected in Kragujevac by representatives of the seventeen okrugs. This was the first parliament at which Miloš was not present, as he lacked the resolve to appear before it. It gave the Constitutionalists the authority with which, on 13 June, they compelled him to abdicate in favour of his son Milan, who was seriously ill with tuberculosis, and to leave the country. Power passed to a three-man regency selected by the Council. Since the constitution made no provision for such a body, the Council acted on the basis of the appropriate clauses of the revoked Presentation Constitution: the three selected were prime minister Petronijević, Council president Jevrem, and commander of the army Vučić-Perišić, though the last-mentioned had to resign from that role prior to becoming regent.[154] This regency, in conjunction with the Constitutionalist control of the Council, amounted to a Constitutionalist government.

The Constitutionalists feared the army as an instrument of princely despotism and sought to neuter it; a military law was passed on 10 June, the day Miloš's dethronement was decided upon, depriving the prince of direct control over the standing army, which was placed under the interior ministry's military department, headed by Ilija Garašanin. The army was downgraded to a border and military police force; the cavalry was abolished; and the artillery reduced. Protection of the borders was entrusted to the national militia of the border okrugs.[155] This contributed to the initial military weakness of the Constitutionalists' regime and inclined many soldiers to support their opponents grouped around the Obrenović dynasty in the power struggle that engulfed Serbia during the following three years.[156] The Constitutionalists leaned on the Ottomans, for whom Miloš's overthrow was a victory. It halted the Muslim departure from Serbia decreed by the hatt-ı şerifs of 1830 and 1833; Serbia's Muslim population would actually grow in size and prosperity under the Constitutionalists.[157] The regime change also involved a change in capital cities. Belgrade was unquestionably the largest and most significant town in Serbia, where the foreign consuls and vizier were located. The Constitutionalists on 12 June 1839 moved the capital there from Kragujevac, the Obrenović stronghold, so that their proximity to the vizier and Russian consul would protect them from the Obrenovićes.[158]

In his 24-year rule, Miloš began the construction of a modern state and society. But transforming the obor-knezes, knezes and kmets into his officials and creating a new bureaucratic class, he paradoxically reduced the local freedoms that Serbs had enjoyed in Ottoman times while exploiting them as the Ottomans had. Thus, the new state would be viewed as an alien oppressor by its own people. The emergence of a bureaucratic elite initiated a fissure in Serbian national life between this elite and the peasant populace that would increasingly dominate Serbian political and intellectual life. Eventually, the new class of high officials and the pre-existing Serbian notables sought to end Miloš's autocracy and share power, and these he was unable to defeat, resulting in his abdication. The rule of law was consequently established in Serbia under a constitution and oligarchy that would determine the country's destiny for the next two decades.

4

THE CONSTITUTIONALIST ERA

1839–1858

For all his political genius, Miloš remained an illiterate, patriarchal, Ottoman-style ruler. His overthrow and replacement by an oligarchy of high functionaries, some of them educated and influenced by foreign political ideas, launched the young Serbian nation-state's next stage of development. The Constitutionalist regime presided over the birth of a *Rechtsstaat* involving constitutional government, a modern bureaucracy and full private property rights. Yet this involved the oligarchy and bureaucracy growing culturally apart from the peasantry, dividing Serbia into distinct worlds of elite and people. This division would increasingly influence Serbian politics as the century progressed.

Prince Mihailo's first reign

The Constitutionalist regency summoned a parliament on 12 June 1839 immediately following Miloš's departure from Serbia to inform the deputies of his resignation and of the change in government. The regency permitted the deputies to submit their demands, which it largely accepted so as to strengthen its popular support. These included transferring the taxes on butchers' shops and on pigs feeding on acorns in the forest from state to municipal control, abolishing the fishing tax and permitting free exploitation of the forests. This strengthened the regime's popularity.[1] A decree of 24 July required the administration to employ native Serbians in preference to 'foreigners' (Austrian Serbs), unless sufficiently qualified natives were unavailable. This was, however, only irregularly observed, and parliaments repeatedly sought the exclusion of the Austrian Serbs from state employment.[2]

Prince Milan Obrenović II—the 'II' because he was Serbia's second reigning Obrenović prince—died of tuberculosis on 8 July. The brevity of his reign engendered the myth that he had died without having learned that he had acceded to the throne. He was mourned by the Constitutionalists, with whom he had sympathised and who had entertained high hopes he would be an amenable ruler. He was succeeded by his younger brother, as Prince Mihailo Obrenović III (1823–1868), with whom Constitutionalist relations were much less cordial. Since Miloš still hoped to return to the throne himself, he prevented Mihailo from leaving his side for eight months following Milan's death, retarding his establishment of his authority.[3] This was unfortunate for Mihailo, for his accession had galvanised Constitutionalist machinations to overthrow the Obrenović dynasty altogether. Petronijević and Vučić-Perišić feared Miloš would not permit Mihailo to return from Wallachia to Serbia and that he would endeavour to return to the throne himself. So they resolved to enthrone Aleksandar Karađorđević (1806–1885), Karađorđe's surviving son.

Aleksandar had lived in exile in Khotyn in Russian Bessarabia, where he married Persida Nenadović, granddaughter of both Jakov Nenadović and Mladen Milovanović. As the 1830 hatt-ı şerif permitted the Serbian exiles to return to the Ottoman Empire, Aleksandar moved to Wallachia, finally returning to Serbia in autumn 1839 with Vučić-Perišić's connivance. Following his own return to Serbia some months later, young Prince Mihailo, displaying what would become his characteristic generosity to former opponents, made him his adjutant.[4] The Constitutionalists viewed Aleksandar as more easily controllable than Mihailo, though they could not immediately enthrone him given that the Porte recognised Mihailo's accession. The Council consequently resolved on 31 August to create a commission to travel across Serbia and explain the constitution to the officials and notables of every okrug, while simultaneously listening to their grievances and quietly agitating in favour of Mihailo's replacement by Aleksandar.[5]

Mihailo travelled from Bucharest to Constantinople in November 1839 to receive the Sultan's confirmation of his accession. On their first meeting, sixteen-year-old Sultan Abdulmejid remarked to the Serbian prince that they were about the same age. Sixteen-year-old Mihailo nevertheless received a firman from the Sultan on 3 February 1840 declaring his majority. Before Mihailo's departure, the Sultan decorated him, appointed him a marshal of the empire and gave him the title of '[Your] Grace', which however required him to wear quintessentially Ottoman headwear—a magnificent fez which the Sultan also gave him.[6] Mihailo then travelled to Belgrade at the start of March 1840 to assume government from the regents. At a ceremony at Kalemegdan on the 17th, attended by senior Serbian functionaries, bishops and foreign consuls, before a crowd comprising a parliament summoned to receive him, many other citizens of Belgrade and Serbs who had travelled from other parts of the country and even from the Austrian Empire, the Sultan's decree of his accession was read out in Turkish and Serbian, and he formally assumed government of the country from the regency. Belgrade's church bells pealed and the cannon sounded in celebration.[7] However, it was revealed at the ceremony that Mihailo was acceding as an elected, not hereditary, prince. This contradicted the hatt-ı şerif of 1830 and the constitution, and was due to successful Constitutionalist lobbying of the Porte. Petronijević and Vučić-Perišić had persuaded the Porte to interpret the Obrenović dynasty's hereditary right narrowly, as passing only through Miloš's oldest son, Milan, whose death in 1839 had thereby extinguished it. The hereditary monarchy had been a key underpinning of Serbian statehood, but as Radoš Ljušić writes, 'the Constitutionalists sacrificed a state privilege to achieve their political goals, above all strengthening the rights of the Council in relation to the ruler'.[8] This act of usurpation triggered an outright power struggle between the Obrenovićites and Constitutionalists. So began Serbia's division between parties, presaging the division emerging in the 1850s between liberals and conservatives.

The Obrenovićite camp coalescing around Mihailo included part of Serbia's elite that had abandoned Miloš, including Jevrem and Ljubica, as well as supporters of the old prince. As the two camps sought to rouse the Serbian population against each other, it was the Obrenovićites who were initially more successful. They incited the population against Vučić-Perišić and Petronijević, who had persuaded the Porte to appoint them advisers to the young prince against his wishes; the Obrenovićite refrain against the pair was that the people wanted just one prince, not three—a reference to the three-member regency. Popular opposition to the new bureaucratic-oligarchic elite gelled with support for the prince. Jevrem met with a group of peasants near Belgrade in early May 1840, after which an anti-Constitutionalist movement erupted in Kolubara, then spread across Šumadija and beyond, with popular uprisings at Rudnik, Šabac and Čačak, which grew into a mass gathering at Mihailo's residence at Topčider to the south of Belgrade and a march on the capital in support of him. Councillors were assaulted or forced into hiding. Vučić-Perišić and Petronijević were compelled to resign as the prince's advisers and take refuge with the Ottoman governor Hozrev Pasha in Kalemegdan on 13 May 1840, thus leading the Constitutionalists into open collaboration with the Porte. In a letter to Ottoman foreign minister Reshid Pasha on 23 May, Vučić-Perišić, Petronijević, Stefan Stefanović Tenka, Lazar Teodorović, Archpriest Mateja and Milutin Savić Garašanin sought his help against Mihailo's misrule while Mihailo's police sought to suppress Constitutionalist activity in Belgrade. Under pressure from his restive supporters who wanted to distance him from the Constitutionalists, Mihailo signed a decree on 25 May transferring the Serbian capital back from Belgrade to his father's stronghold, Kragujevac, where his government would be more secure from the vizier and his Constitutionalist protégés. Mihailo also appointed Miloš's bitter enemy Protić as prime minister.[9]

The Porte consequently sent a commission headed by Musa Efendi to defend the Constitutionalist regime and restore order in Serbia. His arrival in Belgrade on 10 July ended Mihailo's repression and allowed the Constitutionalists to counter-attack politically. Serbia's parliament was summoned at Topčider on 2 August to hear the Sultan's firman confirming Mihailo's accession and resolve his conflict with the Constitutionalists. Musa Efendi, Hozrev Pasha and the Russian consul participated in its sessions. The Obrenović-dominated parliament submitted an indictment to Musa Efendi on 4 August, accusing the Constitutionalists of sedition and, paradoxically, collaboration with the Ottomans. The Constitutionalists responded with protestations of loyalty to the Sultan: 'To whom else could we turn to in the case of threats to ourselves and the people, if not our lawful emperor, who has shown that he is the father of the Serb nation and its benefactor.' They stressed the Porte's right to defend the constitution from any revolt against it by Serbia's prince.[10] A crowd of armed peasants, instigated by the Constitutionalists, marched on Mihailo's residence at Topčider on 16 August to prevent his planned relocation to the restored capital of Kragujevac. Mihailo, at the head of his troops, persuaded them to disperse.

Unable to secure a compromise with Mihailo that would protect the Constitutionalists, Musa Efendi left Serbia on 29 October accompanied by their 37 leaders, the majority of whom took up exile in Vidin, close to Serbia's border in present-day Bulgaria. However, Vučić-Perišić, Petronijević, Mateja Nenadović, Teodorović and Milutin Savić Garašanin with his sons Ilija and Luka followed Musa Efendi to Constantinople. The Constitutionalists thus became agents of the Porte, which sought to oust Mihailo and restore a loyal regime in Serbia. Conversely, the Russians sought to reconcile Mihailo with the Constitutionalists, and in March 1841 their envoy brokered negotiations between them, after which Mihailo issued a proclamation on the 26th of that month, summoning all émigrés to return to Serbia and promising them (with the temporary exception of Vučić-Perišić) freedom and personal security. He paid their expenses resulting from their exile and return. To crown the reconciliation, and at the Porte's urging and to earn its goodwill, he issued a decree on 7 May returning the capital to Belgrade, finally moving there himself on 13 May, though some of his supporters cautioned him against this.[11] Thenceforth Belgrade remained Serbia's capital.

Mihailo increasingly alienated the Porte by breaking with his father's cautious policy to pursue more aggressive expansionist plans. Following the Serbian principality's establishment, the Orthodox Christian population of the Ottoman territories around it continued to suffer the same oppression that had fuelled Karađorđe's and Miloš's revolts. Serb notables from the Niš sanjak, to Serbia's south, regularly visited the principality during 1840 to meet with its officials and plan with them an anti-Ottoman uprising. A rebellion in this sanjak was announced by a popular assembly in April 1841 in the village of Gornji Matejevac, near Niš. Involving at least 18,000–20,000 participants, the rebellion stretched from the Niš, Leskovac, Pirot and part of the Vranje nahijas, corresponding to what is today south Serbia, to the Vidin and Skopje sanjaks. It thus encompassed areas that today are part of Bulgaria and Macedonia, the Orthodox South Slav Christian peoples being not yet fully differentiated. A temporary success was the liberation of Bela Palanka, near Pirot, by a local leader who had been Karađorđe's buljubaša.

THE CONSTITUTIONALIST ERA

Mihailo, Ljubica and Protić had known about the preparations since the year before, yet the prince's proclamation concerning the rebellion cautioned Serbia's population against assisting the rebels, although it noted the 'great oppression' that had provoked this 'rebellion of Christians'. Mihailo sought to allay Ottoman suspicions of his involvement while keeping his hands free to act, depending on how the crisis unfolded. Miloš, meanwhile, who was then living in Wallachia and with whom Mihailo was probably in contact, actively supported the rebellion in order to disrupt Ottoman–Serbian relations and create an occasion for his restoration. The revolt was, however, suppressed after ten days; hundreds of villages were burned and looted by the Ottoman forces while people were massacred or enslaved. Rebel leaders and over 11,000 people, mostly civilians, fled to Serbia. Although the Ottoman forces advanced to Serbia's border and threatened to invade if the rebels were not surrendered, Mihailo's regime refused to do so, instead seeking their amnesty and guarantees for the Serb population bordering Serbia. The Porte was angered and alarmed also by Mihailo's strengthening of his army and appointment of a Russian general as its commander. It gave the Constitutionalist exiles its approval to overthrow him.[12]

Mihailo persecuted both Constitutionalists and Miloš's supporters. To strengthen his administration and its finances, he reversed several of the regency's populist measures, introduced new taxes including for religious services, required municipalities to bear the full cost of supporting their schools and provide land to their parish priests (whose houses the peasants were now required to build), introduced a fine for unauthorised cutting of wood in the forests, transferred the tax on pigs feeding on acorns in the forests back from municipal to state administration (severely hurting the merchants) and, most symbolically, on 21 December 1841 raised the head-tax back from five to six thalers. These actions of the administration aroused popular resentment and were highlighted by Constitutionalist agitation, which also condemned its continued employment of Austrian Serbs. The Obrenović camp was further weakened by the division between supporters of Mihailo, including Jevrem, and those seeking Miloš's return, including Ljubica, who now believed only his restoration could end Serbia's crisis. The government suppressed a pro-Miloš rising in the Požarevac okrug in August 1840, instigated by Ljubica and the Obrenovićite strongman Jovan Mićić. Another pro-Miloš conspiracy, led by Ljubica's cousin, was uncovered in mid-1841, while at the end of July another of the old prince's supporters led a band of several hundred Serbs and Bulgarians from Wallachia into Bulgaria to raise a rebellion there, which failed.[13]

Most of the Constitutionalist exiles returned to Serbia in December 1841, followed by Vučić-Perišić and Milutin Savić Garašanin in April 1842. Denied reinstatement in state service by Mihailo, they prepared their putsch in a series of meetings periodically attended by Belgrade vizier Chamil Pasha and an Austrian general.[14] The arrival of a special commissar from the Porte on 26 August 1842 signalled the putsch's start. In close touch with these three senior Ottoman and Austrian officials, Vučić-Perišić crossed from Pančevo in Austria to Smederevo in Serbia on the night of 30–31 August, aiming to march on the Obrenovićes' stronghold of Kragujevac. He was aided by sympathetic local Serbian officials, including Smederevo assistant okrug chief Antonije Majstorović, son of the anti-Miloš conspirator Ranko Majstorović, who received him when he entered Serbia, and Gruža district chief Knićanin, his former adjutant from the campaign against the Podrinje Muslims, who joined him en route.[15] But most importantly, he was a far more effective demagogue than anyone among the Obrenovićites, and his demagogy appealed to Serbia's not fully differentiated officers, soldiers and peasants:

> I fear nobody, not the Prince nor the Council nor the ministers nor the metropolitan, and nobody should fear anyone; we are all equal, the Prince is no different from the swineherd, the swineherd from the Councillor, the Councillor from the tailor, the tailor from the judge; what the judge is so am I, we are all equal; it should not be just one who stands in the sun while the rest of us stand in the shade. I fear nobody, I fear only the Constitution, and I will tell that to Prince Mihailo as I told his father. Let no one think that the Prince may do in the country as he pleases; he must listen to the people and do what the people want and command ...[16]

At Kragujevac, the officials and officers readily defected to him, giving him control of Serbia's artillery. Mihailo responded by marching with his forces on the city. He sent a detachment to deal with 80-year-old Milutin Savić Garašanin, who had joined the revolt. It killed Garašanin outside the village of Barajevo near Belgrade; the prince ordered his head cut off, impaled on a stick and placed by the roadside to deter others. Garašanin's son Luka was captured the next day and likewise decapitated; with a lighted pipe in its mouth, his head was impaled and placed in front of the Garašanins' house at Grocka near Belgrade.[17] Such atrocities alienated Mihailo's supporters and catalysed defections to the Constitutionalists.[18]

Mihailo's roughly 15,000 troops outnumbered Vučić-Perišić's 5,000. But Vučić-Perišić's possession of the artillery gave him a decisive advantage, while his propaganda, according to which he was not fighting to overthrow the prince but merely to change the unpopular administration and reduce taxation, sapped the resolve of Mihailo's troops. Consequently, he repeatedly defeated them. Mihailo was abandoned by the commander of his militia, Milutin Petrović Era, who ordered his men to stop fighting, while one of the majors of his standing army defected to Vučić-Perišić. Mihailo's forces thus disintegrated.[19] As recalled by future prime minister Nikola Hristić, then a young man experiencing his first battle as an official in Mihailo's camp: 'Prince Mihailo himself gave an example of bravery and defied the danger, but it was all for nothing. The regular army was dependable, it would have carried out its duty, which was seen and recognised clearly, but it was few in number; all the rest of the national militia, after the first cannon shots, fled from the heights.'[20]

THE CONSTITUTIONALIST ERA

Mihailo was forced to flee to Zemun on 6–7 September 1842, along with his uncles Jovan and Jevrem, most of his ministers, several state councillors, and various other higher and lower officials. The victory represented the triumph of the traditional form of military mobilisation and Vučić-Perišić's demagoguery over the fledgling standing army pioneered by the Obrenović princes, after which the Constitutionalist regime again sought to neuter the standing army, relying instead on their own armed supporters to maintain order.[21]

The consuls of the Great Powers did not immediately accept the putsch, which they considered revolutionary, and continued to recognise Mihailo as prince. At their intervention, Chamil Pasha was forced to deny Vučić-Perišić entry into Belgrade, so he set up camp at the settlement of Vračar immediately south of the city. There, he was joined by the leading Constitutionalists, who established a Provisional Administration under Petronijević as president and Vučić-Perišić as 'Leader of the People'. A parliament summoned and directed by Vučić-Perišić deposed Mihailo on 14 September and elected his adjutant Aleksandar Karađorđević as the new prince. The last Obrenovićite army, headed by Mićić and Stevča Mihailović, marched against Belgrade in support of Mihailo, but the prince had by this time left Serbia and his support dissipated. Mihailović surrendered this force to Vučić-Perišić on 17 September and asked for pardon. The new regime carried out a purge of Serbian officialdom; according to one source, 241 officials were dismissed, of whom 104 were beaten and tortured. During the first two years of the new regime, 53 recorded Obrenović supporters were killed, though the real number was probably higher. An exodus of Mihailo's supporters left Serbia to join him in Austria.[22] Mićić, a hero of the First and Second Serbian Uprisings, was arrested in 1844 and allowed to die of starvation in a dungeon in Gurgusovac (Knjaževac).

The Sultan immediately confirmed Karađorđević's election with a berat on 14 September. This was announced some weeks later at Kalemegdan, at a ceremony attended by a huge crowd, before Ottoman and Serbian troops and the metropolitan. The Sultan's envoy Emin-efendi handed the berat to Chamil Pasha, who kissed it and handed it to Aleksandar, who also kissed it before returning it to Emin-efendi, who then read its contents aloud in Turkish: Prince Mihailo, having defied the Sultan's will and violated the rights and laws of the people, was removed from the throne and his princely status transferred to Aleksandar. The crowd cheered enthusiastically and the Ottoman cannon fired in salute. The berat was then read to the crowd in Serbian translation, with Chamil Pasha adding that the princely status had been awarded not to Aleksandar personally but to the Serbian people. At this, the crowd applauded still more thunderously and the cannon saluted once more. Then the new prince entered a church where he was awaited by the metropolitan, two bishops and twelve priests. Summoned by the metropolitan, with his hand on the Gospels, he swore to uphold the constitution and the law of the people. The two bishops then led Aleksandar before the altar, where he received the metropolitan's blessing.[23] But Tsar Nicholas was still offended that the putsch had been carried out without his approval, and, under his pressure, the Porte was forced to annul Aleksandar's election. Consequently, parliament was again convened and, again under Vučić-Perišić's direction, re-elected Karađorđević prince on 27 June 1843. This prompted a threat by Nicholas to invade Serbia; he was, among other things, alienated by the links the Constitutionalist exiles in Constantinople had established with émigrés from the 1831 Polish uprising. To avert this, the Constitutionalist regime was forced to accept the resignation of its two leading figures, prime minister and foreign minister Petronijević and interior minister Vučić-Perišić, who were exiled to Constantinople. The Ottoman cannon at Belgrade gave Vučić-Perišić a prolonged salute on the day he left.[24]

In the absence of the two, the new prince, insecure and lacking strongmen on whom to rely, offered the position of prime minister and foreign minister to a young statesman of 32, Ilija Garašanin (1812–1874), the son and brother of the two Constitutionalists recently decapitated by Mihailo's men. He turned down the offer but instead became interior minister, assuming a central position in the regime.[25] Ilija's grandfather Sava had emigrated from Montenegro and settled in the village of Garaši, near Kragujevac, where Ilija's father Milutin Savić was born in 1762, later serving alongside Karađorđe in the Free Corps and fighting in the First and Second Serbian Uprisings. Recognising his son's talents, Milutin Savić, who adopted the surname Garašanin after his native village, sent Ilija to study at the Greek school in Zemun, after which he attended a German school in Orahovica, in Habsburg Slavonia. Miloš appointed him, at his father's request, a customs official in 1834, promoting him to commander of the standing army in July 1837 and to membership of the Council shortly afterward.[26] Ilija was therefore foreign-educated, too young to remember the uprisings but a trailblazing member of the new bureaucratic elite. When his father was killed, Ilija inherited his place in the oligarchy. A younger man than the other leading Constitutionalists and representative of a newer generation, he had a more modern outlook and pioneered a new political course.

Birth of a modern elite

The Constitutionalist regime's establishment marked a departure from Miloš's autocracy and a milestone on the road to a modern Serbia. The oligarchy that had arisen under Miloš now assumed power on the basis of the Turkish Constitution. When Miloš took power, Serbia's people knew only Ottoman oppression, which it was enough for him to end for them to accept his regime. But 24 years later, with the memory of that oppression sufficiently distant, people wanted more: an end to his tyranny and security for their persons and property, above all the Muslim lands they had expropriated.[27] Yet as the price of liberation from him, the Constitutionalists accepted Serbia's continued subordination to the Porte, which had backed their putsch. This subordination was greater than it had been under Miloš, for the Porte's right, under the Turkish Constitution, to resolve constitutional disputes between prince and Council gave it considerable influence in Serbian internal politics. The Constitutionalist regime is often called Turcophile by historians. As Garašanin said in 1844, 'Today's government is extremely enthusiastic about the Porte.'[28] The decree reorganising Serbia's garrison army in January 1845 emphasised its purpose was solely to maintain order in the country and assist the police, as opposed to potentially fighting the Turks or other foreign enemies, and it remained subordinate to the interior ministry. The regime would do little to expand Serbia's independence or borders, yet its internal reforms greatly consolidated and advanced Serbian statehood.

Belgrade in 1839 was still divided between Serb and Turkish quarters, containing eleven mosques and dominated by Kalemegdan fortress. According to Matija Ban, a native of the area near Dubrovnik who lived for a while in Bursa, in Anatolia near Istanbul, before moving to Belgrade in 1844, 'Belgrade is a Turkish small town in which I was able to count barely eighteen houses solidly built in the European style; but this is a town that is being built. The furniture in the houses is oriental but beginning to be mixed with European.'[29] Jovan Avakumović, born in 1841 into a family of Cincar origin and twice prime minister of Serbia, recalls how he grew up in the Turkish quarter of Belgrade: 'Alone among the Turkish inhabitants, I didn't during childhood have Serb friends, so had to hang out with Turkish children as my only neighbours ... we spoke Turkish amongst ourselves.' Every Friday, Serb and Turkish children would arrive from outside the neighbourhood, and 'we would fight like the fiercest thugs. Sometimes the Turks would be more numerous, thus stronger. Then they soundly thrashed us. But sometimes we were greater in number and stronger, so we beat the little Turks soundly and cruelly.' Even when the Serb children were stronger, the Turkish adults would not intervene, saying to themselves, 'Leave them, leave them; they are children.' And 'after, until the next Friday, we would again play like the best of friends'. Years later, during the final military clash between the Serbs and the Ottoman garrison in Belgrade in 1862, Avakumović came upon one of his childhood Turkish friends; armed as he was, the man could have killed him, but instead showed him how to get away safely.[30]

The Constitutionalist regime attempted to modernise Serbia and open it to the world. House numbers were introduced in Belgrade at the start of 1844 and a decision was taken in November 1856 to install street lamps, providing illumination for about 400 houses, shops and taverns.[31] Throughout the country, roads were built or improved, a state postal service established in 1843 and a telegraph system with three lines in 1855, beginning with a line to Zemun. These measures accelerated the pace of socio-economic and cultural change. More stable rural conditions laid the basis for a steady shift in agriculture away from animal husbandry in favour of cereal cultivation, which would accelerate from the late 1850s. Agriculture remained underdeveloped, however; only about 15–22 per cent of the total land surface in Serbia was cultivated or used as meadows during the middle decades of the nineteenth century. The population rose by 21 per cent between 1847 and 1867, but the cultivated area increased by only 6 per cent, meaning a decline in the area of cultivated land per capita. The consequent reduction in the availability of pasture ultimately contributed to the decline of animal husbandry. This trend was exacerbated by chronic deforestation due to unrestricted forest clearance by peasants, which allegedly reduced the forested area of Serbia by half over the twenty years up to 1852, further undermining traditional pig-keeping by diminishing the supply of acorns.

Peasants were generally not yet ready, however, to cultivate crops for sale; selling grain for cash was viewed as a dishonourable activity—'gypsying'—that robbed the household of its basic food.[32] Craftsmen, too, remained pre-modern in their outlook. The law on crafts of 1847, passed under pressure from guild masters, replaced the system of free competition among craftsmen with a regulated system in which guilds would be protected from competition by unqualified outsiders, with the guilds themselves providing certificates of qualification. This law, which remained in force until 1911, retarded the development of craft industry in Serbia; it led to monopolisation in the hands of a small number of recognised producers but ultimately failed to protect them from competition from imported manufactured goods and unregulated production at home.[33] Meanwhile, the tax burden on the population remained: as late as 1857, over two-thirds of state revenue came from direct taxes, with customs duties accounting for about half the remainder, and of those direct taxes, about 90 per cent was raised through the head-tax, in principle determined on the basis of means but in practice collected as a flat rate of five thalers per taxable head. This was insufficient to meet the state's growing needs but sufficient to ensure a permanent reservoir of popular discontent.[34]

The population of the principality rose from about 666,000 in 1834 to perhaps 825,000 in 1846, of which about 783,000 were peasants, 4,200 bureaucrats and their family members, 748 clergy, 6,000 gypsies and 1,300 Jews, who mostly lived in Belgrade. By 1854, the population had risen to about 998,000, of which only about 38,000 lived in the towns.[35] The Serbian nation was thus still small and relatively socially homogeneous. The country lacked, and would never develop, the extreme social divisions along class lines that characterised much of Western and Central Europe. According to Vladimir Karić, writing in 1887, 'Serbia is the only country in which it is perfectly acceptable for a minister and state councillor, in the middle of the street, to kiss and ask after the health of one of his peasants, who has come to town in farm shoes and peasant cloth trousers and jacket, and to speak with him using the informal "you".'[36] It was also a small world for a small elite. Years later, Serbia's former prime minister Vladan Đorđević, who was the same age as Aleksandar's son Petar and attended Belgrade's gymnasium at the same time, recalls that his classmates included Petar's cousin Dragiša Stanojević, who became a leading socialist; Aleksa Jovanović, who succeeded Vladan as prime minister; Lazar Dokić, who was prime minister a few years before him; Milovan Pavlović, who served with him in the wars of the 1870s and later became war minister; and Mihailo Srećković, who became commander of the active army. Đorđević recalls that he saw Petar himself for the first time in school at the age of seven and the second time half a century later, when he was a retired prime minister and Petar was king.[37] This was a close-knit society whose members, irrespective of political orientation, were often related to or knew each other and who were not a world away from the peasant masses, although the gulf between them was widening.

Serbians wore clothes similar to those in the rest of the Ottoman Empire, rather than to those in Christian Europe. This changed only slowly, particularly in the countryside. People carried guns until the end of the 1840s. The fez was the principal headwear for men until the 1860s, considered part of the Serbian national dress. Even Karadžić, who had spent much time in Central Europe, wore the fez his whole life, signalling his unwillingness to ape German cultural behaviour.[38] Some men also wound colourful scarves around their heads, as Prince Miloš did. They wore čaksire—trousers that were baggy above the knee but tight from the knee down. Women wore Turkish-style baggy britches (salvare, dimije), which were more practical than dresses when riding horses. Refugees who fled to Serbia from the violence in the Habsburg lands in 1848–1849 helped shift the fashion to Central European dress, as did pig-traders, who had more contact with foreigners than other native Serbians, and bureaucrats, who were required to wear trousers in the Central European style from 1850 as part of their uniform. Yet only a few prominent Serbian men at mid-century dressed in this style, including Petronijević and Garašanin, while it was only at this time that prosperous Serbian women began to look to Viennese and Parisian fashion.[39] When Serbians did begin to adopt Western and Central European dress, some foreign observers were contemptuous: Wilhelm Gabler, Prince Petar's Bohemian tutor, commented that when Aleksandar received Jovan Ristić following the latter's return from Paris, he was so enthusiastic about his Parisian outfit that he 'saw in his black tailcoat and splendid top-hat the salvation of his fatherland'. Gabler predicted that nothing good would come of Serbia if its craving for Western civilisation meant 'ever more aping while losing the national character'. Gabler's fellow countryman František Aleksandr Zach, who served as attaché to the French consulate in Belgrade, complained that 'the Serb can no longer be recognised ... he blindly follows foreign customs, neglecting his own; he degenerates'. He compared Serbs wearing French tailcoats and gloves to 'dancing bears'.[40]

The new elite, in other words, was just beginning to become 'modern'. Leading Constitutionalists included not only the polyglot diplomat Petronijević and the professional civil servant Garašanin, but also the semi-literate warlord Vučić-Perišić, who never learned to read handwritten script or to write. Petronijević, like Garašanin, had been educated in the Austrian Empire, in Orşova in Hungary. Furthermore, three of the leading Constitutionalists were Serbs from Austria: Metropolitan Petar of Belgrade (Pavle Jovanović), who headed the Serbian Orthodox Church in 1833–1859; and the brothers Stojan and Aleksa Simić, both former protégés of Miloš. Consequently, under the Constitutionalist regime, the new Serbian elite began to appear alien to the Serbian peasant population. Miloš had been able to retain power for 24 years—considerably longer than any subsequent Serbian ruler—because he embodied both the modern Serbia of the bureaucracy and the traditional Serbia of the peasantry; firmly in control of the first, he exercised a hold over the hearts of the second. By contrast, men like Aleksandar, Petronijević and Garašanin could not bridge the gap between the old and new Serbias, but fell on one side of it.

Prince Aleksandar was not an illiterate man of the people like Miloš but a European gentleman who had grown up in Austria and Russian Bessarabia. He and Princess Persida were sufficiently cosmopolitan to give their second daughter the exotic name Kleopatra. At the start of his reign, Aleksandar decided to establish a permanent princely court, something that Miloš and Mihailo had lacked. For that purpose, he bought on behalf of the state a house that Stojan Simić had built for himself outside the town in the fields behind Terazije—though the area is today considered central Belgrade. The house, which became known as the Belgrade Konak, was expanded and the prince's family moved there in 1844. Following the Obrenović dynasty's restoration in 1858, it remained the monarch's residence until 1904, when it was demolished in Petar's reign, ironically because it had become associated with the Obrenovićes. After the Karađorđević family moved into the Konak in 1844, other Serbian notables built their houses around it, including Stojan Simić, who built his new house opposite his old one where the prince now lived.[41] The Konak's interior style was intended to be a mixture of the Central European and the Ottoman; Persida designed her salon to be 'half in the German, half in the oriental style, with covers on the sofas interwoven with golden threads'.[42] But Aleksandar's court was not yet like the court of an old European dynasty; in the words of the prince's sometime son-in-law Đorđe Simić, Stojan's son, it was 'democratic and patriarchal, without great etiquette or ceremony'. It lacked prescribed protocols or permanent officials such as a major domo or master of ceremonies. As a boy, Petar would fight with Turkish children from Kalemegdan, and during summers he would visit the Karađorđević home village of Topola, where he would play in the homes of peasant children his own age.[43] The fact that power was held not by the prince personally but by an oligarchy in which he was merely first among equals ensured that the court would not acquire the weight of formality and ceremony characteristic of royal regimes. Tellingly, alone of Serbia's nineteenth-century rulers, Aleksandar did not give his name in popular memory to the period of his reign; instead it was remembered as the 'Constitutionalist era'.[44]

Prominent prosperous Serbs began holding social gatherings (posela) at their homes at which their peers gathered, musicians sang and played, foreign literature was read, and politics discussed. Persida, in particular, pioneered the posela in the

Belgrade Konak, and hers became famous. Usually compèred by the Austrian-born Catholic Matija Ban, they were intended by the princess to Europeanise and raise the cultural level of the court while impressing foreign visitors, and they usually began with a recital by a female guest on a piano that Persida had imported from Hungary. However, she insisted that her female guests, excepting Ban's Greek wife, wear Serbian national dress.[45] These gatherings raised the social status and influence of women of the elite; no longer expected to be mere silent servants in their husbands' homes, they could make their presence felt, even preside over the gatherings themselves.[46] Characteristic was the treasured presence in court, during her two-year stay in Belgrade, of the great Hungarian Serb painter Katarina Ivanović (1811–1882), educated in Pest, Vienna and Munich; she painted portraits of Persida in Serbian national costumes and a picture depicting Karađorđe's liberation of Belgrade in 1806. Ivanović was thus a female pioneer who assisted the Karađorđević dynasty's self-affirmation.[47]

Miloš's agrarian reforms, by precluding the emergence of a Christian landed elite, had led the Constitutionalist opposition to focus its attention on the bureaucracy, since the new elite could now only be a bureaucratic elite. The constitution transformed the bureaucracy from the prince's personal servants to impersonal servants of the state, their salaries determined by the state budget, with a proper system of ranks, the right to pensions and immunity from corporal punishment.[48] Through successive decrees in the following years, the bureaucracy was transformed into a profession, with definite rules, roles, uniforms and security of tenure. It required qualifications to enter, as opposed simply to personal connections. Bureaucrats were forbidden to engage simultaneously in other professions or trades or to wear beards.[49] The bureaucracy thus became a class apart from the peasantry. To staff the bureaucracy, the school system was expanded: in the school year 1835–1836 there were 72 elementary schools with 2,514 pupils; in 1845–1846, 213 with 6,201; in 1855–1856, 334 with 9,891; and in 1857–1858, 343 with 10,518. The first public elementary school in Serbia for girls was opened in Paraćin in 1845 and the second in Belgrade the following year. In response to large-scale pupil absenteeism, a law was passed in 1857 requiring every school to have at least 25 pupils, with reprimands and fines for parents whose children played truant.[50] The process of creating an educated public was thus in its infancy. Miloš's Serbian principality, at its establishment, had almost wholly lacked literate natives to staff its fledgling administration, so had had to recruit educated bureaucrats largely from among the Serbs of the Austrian Empire— the so-called prečani Serbs, meaning Serbs 'from across [the rivers Sava and Danube, which separated Serbia from Austria]'. These had long exercised an indelible, though ambiguous, influence over Serbia, through men like Dositej Obradović and Dimitrije Davidović, and the trend continued in the Constitutionalist era. Two Hungarian Serb professors at the lycée, Jovan Sterija Popović from the Banat and Atanasije Nikolić from Bačka, founded the Society for Serbian Letters on 19 November 1841.

SERBIA

The following year, Popović became education minister. He established the Serbian Museum on 10 May 1844, subsequently renamed the National Museum. That year, he also authored the Law on the Organisation of Public Instruction.

A civil code was introduced for Serbia on 6 April of the same year, based on Austria's civil code of 1811; its authors were two Austrian Serbs, Vasilije Lazarević, former mayor of Zemun, and Jovan Hadžić, a member of Novi Sad's municipal senate.[51] They had been sent to Serbia at Miloš's request by Austria, which wished to ensure Serbia's civil code was not based on the French. Miloš had considered doing so, but Austria's consul had, with Russian assistance, dissuaded him.[52] The principal purpose of Serbia's civil code was to establish absolute private property rights where none had existed. It thus permitted free division of peasant family plots, accelerating the decline of the zadruga and the rise instead of independent peasant proprietors based on the nuclear family. Since it thus removed the peasants' traditional social safety mechanism, it created losers as well as winners, fuelling rural discontent.[53] The code sanctioned the legal supremacy of husbands over wives: 'The wife is obliged to listen to her husband, to observe his orders, to follow him wherever he goes and to live with him there.' This determined the legally subordinate position of women in Serbia for the next hundred years, whereby wives could not acquire or dispose of property independently of their husbands or work without their permission.[54]

The imposition of a relatively rigid and complex Central European legal code onto the raw and confused system of property that existed in 1840s Serbia, with its multitude of petty disputes between peasant smallholders, produced a judicial logjam. At this time in Serbia, of the presidents of the seventeen okrug courts, three were illiterate, ten were able to sign their own names, three were educated beyond the elementary school level and only one was a lawyer. Among members of the courts, twenty were illiterate, fourteen poorly literate, fifteen educated beyond elementary school level and one was a lawyer. The ability of the judiciary actually to read the new civil code was therefore very limited while lower personnel similarly lacked education. Consequently, for many years the judicial system struggled to cope.[55] Nevertheless, on 21 September 1846 a supreme court was established as the court of third and last instance, which in 1855 assumed the functions of a court of cassation and in 1858 became solely a court of cassation. Meanwhile, a Law on the Establishment of Spiritual Authority in the Serbian Principality of 4 September 1847, brought by Metropolitan Petar, codified more clearly the organisation of the church hierarchy and increased its independence from the state.[56]

This new Serbia was arising while still under Ottoman occupation, and Ottoman soldiers would periodically harass and assault locals. Although local Serbs and Muslims generally lived together amicably in Belgrade, even running shops and businesses together, the overlapping populations inevitably did not match the separate jurisdictions established by the 1830s settlement, producing frequent jurisdictional conflicts between the Ottoman and Serbian police, especially over which was responsible for arresting and punishing Christians from elsewhere in the empire who were resident in Belgrade, or which had jurisdiction over Muslims living outside the Turkish quarter or Serbs living within it. Serbia's regime nevertheless collaborated with the vizier to maintain order. In 1848, when the murder of a Serb by a Muslim prompted angry Serb crowds to gather at Kalemegdan, the vizier's wife Melek Hanum visited Aleksandar to request that he pacify them, which he did by issuing a proclamation stating that the governor had written to Constantinople for permission to punish the killer. He was not punished, as the vizier claimed he had fled. Aleksandar believed the vizier was complicit in his flight, but the unpleasantness was smoothed over with the help of Persida, who was on friendly terms with Melek Hanum. Persida invited her and other ladies from the Ottoman garrison to a banquet with notable Serbian ladies, at which they drank champagne together and toasted Prince Aleksandar and the Sultan, after which Aleksandar sent Melek Hanum a 'very handsome ring and a pair of magnificent earrings'.[57] In 1857, Belgrade's governor, Hristić, himself an Austrian Serb of Cincar background from Sremska Mitrovica, arrested a local troublemaker who enjoyed the vizier's protection. The vizier intervened with Aleksandar to have him released, something that the Austrian consul Teodor Radosavjlević also requested. Aleksandar and his prime minister sided with the vizier; when Hristić nevertheless punished the miscreant with a beating before releasing him, the vizier's secretary berated Aleksandar, who was allegedly so angry he did not speak to Hristić for two or three days.[58] In 1858, Britain's consul in Belgrade was assaulted by Ottoman soldiers after straying too close to the garrison while out walking.[59] Despite efforts by the Serbian and Ottoman authorities to cooperate, the situation was ultimately unsustainable.

Vuk Karadžić and linguistic nationalism

Serbs from Austria spearheaded the development of Serbian intellectual life. According to Ekmečić, of Serbia's 87 most significant intellectuals in 1821–1839, 52 were originally from southern Hungary.[60] Their example encouraged the adoption by native Serbians of Central European dress, furniture, manners and customs. But this also produced a culture clash.[61] Resistance to the new order in Serbia thus focused on these foreigners who appeared to be oppressing and exploiting the native Serbs of Serbia and importing alien ideas inimical to Serbia's traditions. The son of a peasant family from the village of Tršić near Loznica in western Serbia with a keen interest in and affinity for these traditions, Karadžić spearheaded cultural resistance to the Austrian Serbs. As a lame man unable to fight, he had been resident in Sremski Karlovci during the early years of the First Serbian Uprising, where he had come to dislike its wealthy Serb residents. He felt socially inferior to them owing to his humble background, while despising them for their comfortable passivity compared with the Serbs of Serbia fighting for their freedom.[62] He returned to Karađorđe's rebel Serbia, but following its defeat in 1813 he fled again to the Austrian Empire, where the following year he published a collection of Serbian poems and an early attempt at a Serbian grammar. He met Filip Višnjić, the bard who had accompanied Karađorđević's rebels, and recorded several of his poems about the uprising.

Before Karadžić, the language of the Serbian church was Russian Church Slavonic (ruskoslovenski), while people wrote also in the non-standardised vernacular and in Slavonic Serbian (slavenosrpski), a blend of the two languages. Karadžić instead pioneered the use of the Serbian vernacular as spoken by the peasants of Šumadija and the surrounding Ottoman territories as the Serbian literary language, involving the simplification and standardisation of the alphabet on a phonetic basis and the removal of obsolete or foreign (Russian Church Slavonic) words and letters. This was resisted by the Serbian church hierarchy in the Habsburg lands, in particular the Metropolitan of Karlovac, Stefan Stratimirović. He favoured standardisation of Slavonic Serbian as used by Austria's Serb elite, to preserve Serb elite culture and its links with other Slavic peoples, viewing this as essential for Serb survival in the Habsburg Empire. Karadžić's populist nationalism, based on Serbia's peasantry, clashed with the elite patriotism of the Austrian Serb religious establishment.[63]

In the preface to his first published work, *A Small Slavonic Serbian Book of Folk Poems* (Vienna, 1814), Karadžić claimed: 'But still it is above all those Serbs who are slaves [under Ottoman rule] who have up till today retained their nationality, more than those in the enlightened and free [Austrian] Empire, where they freely administer their churches and found schools in their own language, and where nothing is forbidden them that serves to enlighten their nation.'[64] In 1815, he published another anthology of poetry, *National Serb Book of Poems*, which included the subsequently famous 'Prince's dinner', about the mythical confrontation on the eve of the Battle of Kosovo between Prince Lazar and Miloš Obilić. For Karadžić, the moral victory of Obilić over Lazar, the saint venerated by the Orthodox Church establishment, symbolised the triumph of the Serbdom of the people, with its pagan-influenced folklore, over the Austrian Serb elite.[65] His poems about Kosovo published at this time were very prominent for the fledgling Serbian reading public with few books to read, so were instrumental in creating a Serbian national ideology centred on the Kosovo myth.[66] Karadžić published the first edition of his subsequently famous dictionary in 1818.

Back home in Miloš's Serbia, Karadžić continued his struggle against the Austrian Serbs. In his letter to Miloš of April 1832 recommending a constitution, Karadžić warned him not to rely on them to build Serbia's school system: 'Serbs born and educated outside Serbia (in the Austrian states) cannot rectify this deficit, among other reasons, firstly because among the people they cannot enjoy complete confidence and secondly because they have not even done that, which Serbia in its current situation needs.'[67] On another occasion, he quipped that some Austrian Serbs loved Serbia 'the way a swine loves a forest full of acorns'.[68] Karadžić drew close to Miloš, seeking his protection and financial support, subsequently to Mihailo as well. He was consequently out of favour under the Constitutionalists, who viewed him as an Obrenovićite. In particular, Karadžić was targeted by Jovan Hadžić, author of Serbia's civil code and pillar of the Hungarian Serb establishment close to the Metternich regime, against whom he had polemicised. Hadžić denounced Karadžić as Miloš's stooge and helped ensure the cancellation of his pension. Karadžić's struggle against Hadžić and the Constitutionalist regime thus fed into the wider populist reaction against it. In his letter to Serbia's culture minister, which he read out to a meeting of the Society for Serbian Letters in May 1845, Karadžić denounced the spread of books, newspapers and learning produced by the Serb intelligentsia of the Austrian Empire as threatening to corrupt the true Serbian language.[69] By the 1850s, when his works were blacklisted by the Constitutionalist establishment, they were inspirational for rebellious members of the educated younger generation; even a cause of physical fights between pupils from peasant and bureaucratic family backgrounds.[70]

Antipathy to Austrian Serbs, as educated foreigners, was an early manifestation of opposition to Serbia evolving along 'Western' lines. As the new Serbian state began integrating into the international economy and experienced the beginnings of industrialisation, the question of Serbia's path was posed: whether to follow the example of the Western European nations and develop a modern, liberal and capitalist society, or to strike out in a separate direction derived from Serbia's own traditions developed under Ottoman rule. This dilemma, which replicated that between Westernisers and Slavophiles in Russia, would sometimes be posed as the question of 'West' versus 'East'. Later populist politicians and intellectuals would perpetuate Karadžić's negative view of the Austrian Serbs. According to Svetozar Marković, father of Serbian socialism: 'The first who began to bring enlightenment to Serbia were the Austrian Serbs. That was, in the majority, every kind of scum that did not have more than the most elementary ideas.'[71] Such antipathy was economic as well as cultural; members of craft guilds resented competition from Austrian Serbs. Members of the bootmakers' guild in Belgrade complained in 1832 that Austrian Serbs were setting themselves up as masters of the trade, without requisite qualifications, leaving their own journeymen without work. The Belgrade city administration on 14 June 1840 banned the establishment of a new guild of Central-European-style tailors and shoemakers, ruling that they had to enrol in existing guilds for makers of traditional clothes and makers of slippers. The potters' and small shopkeepers' guilds in Belgrade on 16 December 1841 complained of what they considered unfair trading practices by Austrian Serbs.[72]

Karadžić was not, however, simply an anti-Western reactionary. He was Serbia's leading intellectual representative of the Romantic era, whose conflicting conservative and progressive aspects he embodied. Assimilated into Central European culture by his long stays in the Habsburg Empire, he felt ill at ease back in his native Serbia;

ashamed of his bad leg, he was embarrassed by the custom of Serbian housewives of washing their guests' feet, so avoided going to dinner parties, although he had liked to do so in Austria.[73] He supported the establishment of Christian landed fiefdoms in Serbia to replace the Muslim ones abolished under Miloš, reflecting the prevalent belief of his Austrian milieu that an aristocracy was necessary as a safeguard against monarchical absolutism.[74] His letter of April 1832 to Miloš, arguing for constitutional government, reflected the Enlightenment thinking of the Austrian intellectual circles in which he mixed, presaging the principles that would be set out in Serbia's constitutions of 1835 and 1838, the first of which was written by his sometime friend Davidović, himself an Austrian Serb.

Karadžić was, paradoxically, himself the product of foreign schooling: he studied for several years in Vienna, Sremski Karlovci and elsewhere in the Austrian Empire, as well as in Germany, and published his key works in these lands. While resident in Sremski Karlovci, he had belonged to the pro-Austrian, anti-Russian Serb current; according to his biographer, Miodrag Popović, 'For him, at that time, Austria was simply the land of schools and science, and the German language the path to European culture.'[75] He immersed himself in the intellectual life of religiously bipolar Germany, interacted closely with German, Austro-German, Croat and Slovene intellectuals, and married a Catholic Austrian woman. His campaign for the use of the vernacular as the Serbian literary language reflected the influence of his Romantic-era Austro-German education, not his peasant background. As Popović writes, 'Had there been no Europe, he would, like others, have remained a Slavonic Serbian writer; in truth, somewhat more folkish than the others. Without contact with Europe, he would with difficulty have arrived at the idea, in his thirtieth year, of learning how to write the original people's language.'[76] Thus, Karadžić's ideas reflected a synthesis of cosmopolitan Austro-German and Serbian rural outlooks.

Karadžić consequently posited language rather than religion as the factor defining Serb nationhood. In this, he had been preceded by Obradović, who had pledged in 1783 that he would write in the vernacular: 'I will write for the human mind, heart and nature; for brother Serbs, of whatever law and religion they are.' Consequently, 'My book will be written in pure Serbian just like this letter, so that it can be understood by all Serb sons and daughters, from Montenegro to Smederevo and to Banat'. The endeavour would be supported 'wherever there are Serbs, from the Adriatic Sea to the River Danube'. For 'Who does not know that the Montenegrin, Dalmatian, Hercegovinian, Bosnian, Serbian and Croatian people and the people of Srem, Bačka and Banat (except for the Vlachs) speak the same language? Speaking of the people who live in the kingdom and the provinces, I mean the followers of the Greek church, also the followers of the Latin church, including even the Turks, Bosniaks and Hercegovinians, given that law and religion can be changed but race and language never.'[77]

THE CONSTITUTIONALIST ERA

Karadžić's adoption of this linguistic model of nationhood marked new ground for Serbia's Serbs—a departure from their traditional equation of Serb nationhood with the Orthodox religion. It reflected the influence not only of Obradović but of Karadžić's Slovene mentor Jernej Kopitar (1780–1844) and, through him, of Johann Gottfried Herder (1744–1803), who pioneered the view that the essence of nationhood was to be found in the language and folklore of the common people. Karadžić's concept of linguistic nationhood was at one level a product of the new, revolutionary climate created by the emergence of the Serbian principality. Yet it was also an expression of a wider trend among the contemporary Serb intelligentsia in the Habsburg Empire, whose members likewise adopted a linguistic model of nationhood—men such as Teodor Pavlović (1804–1854), secretary of the Serb cultural and literary body Matica Srpska (Serb Framework), founded in Pest in Hungary in 1826.[78] By rejecting Russian Church Slavonic as the official Serbian language in favour of the Serbian vernacular, Karadžić overturned the linguistic barrier to national unity between Serbs and their non-Orthodox neighbours to the West, Croats and Bosniaks, who spoke essentially the same language. This facilitated the claim that the Bosniaks and at least some of the Croats were, in fact, Serbs. Eminent Slovak scholar Pavel Josef Šafárik (1795–1861) published his *History of the Slavic Language and Literature* in 1826, in which he classified Bosnians, Slavonians and Dalmatians along with Montenegrins as linguistically belonging to the Serbian stem, and Karadžić built his own theory of Serbian linguistic nationhood on the foundation that Šafárik provided.[79]

The Habsburg Empire, as a multinational state in which several Slavic peoples coexisted with varying degrees of institutional autonomy, in subordination to a German monarch and subsequently to a German–Magyar dualist domination, was the incubator of ideas of Slavic kinship, including the kinship of the South Slavs: Slovenes, Croats, Serbs, Bosniaks, Montenegrins, Macedonians and Bulgarians—peoples not fully distinct from each other, who spoke the same or closely related languages and who were geographically separated from the wider Slavic world by the Germans, Magyars and Romanians to their north. Such ideas necessarily had an impact among educated people in neighbouring Serbia, but these viewed them through the prism of their own national identity and cultural worldview, forged by the very different conditions of the Ottoman Empire, which had no equivalent tradition of institutional pluralism along national-territorial lines. For Serbia's Serbs, as for other Ottoman non-Muslim subject peoples, the empire was a religiously alien oppressor that had begun to accept their statehood only as it entered its terminal decline, from which their nation was to be liberated.

The response of Serbia's educated class to ideas of South Slavic kinship emanating from the Habsburg Empire, from the first half of the nineteenth century to the final Habsburg collapse and establishment of Yugoslav unity in 1918 and beyond, would consequently combine sympathy with criticism in varying combinations. When ideas of South Slavic unity were advanced in the Austrian Empire in the 1820s and 1830s by the Croatian linguist Ljudevit Gaj (1809–1872) and his 'Illyrian movement', Karadžić was sympathetic but disagreed. This movement advocated the Illyrian name as one with which Croats and Serbs could build a common nationhood. For Karadžić, it was unacceptable to abandon the Serb name in favour of the archaic name 'Illyrian', which had no resonance among the people. His national identity had been formed in the light of the emphatically Serb popular revolution of 1804–1813, and he saw this popular revolutionary tradition as the only basis for Serb nationhood, central to his struggle against the Austrian Serb hierarchy.[80]

Karadžić consequently upheld a pan-Serb rather than Illyrian or proto-Yugoslav model of nationhood, which he expressed in his essay 'Serbs all and everywhere', written in 1836 but deliberately unpublished until 1849 and the Illyrian movement's evident failure.[81] In it, he claimed as Serbs all speakers of the Štokavian dialect, 'about five million souls', which encompassed the population of Serbia, Montenegro, Bosnia and the best part of Croatia, while admitting: 'Only the first three million [who are Orthodox by religion and follow the 'Greek' law] call themselves "Serbs (Srbi)" or "(Srblji—a variant of Srbi)", and the remainder will not accept this name, but those of the Turkish law think that they are true Turks, and so they call themselves, although not one in a hundred knows Turkish; and those of the Roman law either call themselves by the places in which they live, for example Slavonians, Bosnians (or Bosniaks), Dalmatians, Dubrovnikers, etc., or, as writers in particular do, by an archaic or God knows what name.'[82] Karadžić therefore envisioned a Serb nation whose branches shared no common identity, historical experience, statehood or institutions, but whose boundaries were determined by the 'objective' criterion of language alone. He admitted that, as far as the Serbs and non-Štokavian-speaking Croats (i.e. those who spoke the Čakavian and Kajkavian dialects) were concerned, 'everyone can see that these differences, when one speaks of two different languages and nations, are very minor', suggesting furthermore that it 'may be that the Serbs and Croats, when they settled here [in the South Slav lands during the Middle Ages], were one nation with two different names'. In thus embracing what was subsequently known as a 'Great Serbian' view, Karadžić nevertheless suggested a close Serb–Croat kinship that left the door open to a simultaneous pan-South-Slavic (i.e. Yugoslav) politics.

Karadžić was by the 1840s working for the linguistic unification of Serbs and Croats, including unification of the Cyrillic and Latin alphabets. He was one of the intellectuals—five Croats, two Serbs and a Slovene—who signed on 28 March 1850 the Vienna agreement on linguistic unity, adopting the Bosnian variant of the Serbian and Croatian language(s) as the standard, involving the Štokavian and Ijekavian dialects. He embraced the cause of Serb and Croat patriots during the 1848 revolution, in particular the ban or governor of Croatia, Josip Jelačić, who were ready to ally with Austria's emperor (kaiser) against the German and Hungarian revolutionaries. In November 1848, after Jelačić had crushed the revolution in

Vienna, Karadžić welcomed him and conferred with him for half an hour; the two shared the goal of converting the empire into a federation dominated by its Slavic majority.[83] In his embrace of such conservative proto-Yugoslavist politics, Karadžić reflected the influence of his Slovene mentor, Kopitar. Near the end of his life, he reluctantly accepted that the demarcation between the Serb and Croat nations might have to be religious rather than linguistic: 'If the Croat patriots do not accept this division based on reason, then for now nothing else can be done with this than that we differentiate ourselves by *law* or *religion*: who is by law Greek or Eastern will, wherever he resides, not renounce the Serb name, and of those who are of the Roman law, let anyone who wants to say that they are a *Croat*' (emphasis in original).[84]

Karadžić's activities extended to Montenegro, whose people tended to identify with the Serbs, though the precise form of this identification varied between rulers and individuals. Prince-Bishop Petar I Petrović-Njegoš (r. 1782–1830) and his successor, Petar II Petrović-Njegoš (r. 1830–1851), both viewed Montenegro as a historical part of the Serbian empire unwillingly separated from it by Ottoman conquest, and both favoured Montenegro's eventual absorption in a new, large Christian empire that was to emerge from the Ottoman Empire's overthrow, which would be either Slav, Serbian or Russian—the distinctions between these categories being blurred in this era before modern nationalism.[85] Karadžić befriended Petar II and in spring 1837 in Vienna introduced him to Gaj; that year, the prince-bishop and the Illyrian leader together drafted a plan for the liberation of the South Slavs from Ottoman rule with Russia's help.[86] Indeed, the publication in the vernacular in Vienna in 1847 of Petar II's epic poem *The Mountain Wreath* would be of greater and more lasting influence than Karadžić's own writings on Serb nationhood. The poem recounts the attempts of early eighteenth-century Montenegrin ruler Vladika Danilo—Petar II's ancestor—to resist Ottoman domination, through rejecting coexistence with Muslims in Montenegro and ultimately massacring them on the Orthodox Christmas of 1702, with Miloš Obilić and the Kosovo legend mobilised behind this patriotic endeavour:

> Our Obilić, you fiery dragon,
> the eyes of those who look at you go blind.
> All brave men will always honour your name!
> You did not fail our crown like a coward
> when you set your foot upon the Sultan's throat
> and stepped into the Sultan's torn belly.
> Now I see you riding your stallion, Zdral,
> and dispersing the Turks around the tent.
> What will happen? Who will do the right thing?
> Serb and Turk can never get together.
> The salty sea will sooner change to sweet.[87]

SERBIA

The Mountain Wreath became a key text in the nascent Serb nationalist canon and helped to consolidate the Kosovo legend in its contemporary form. By this point, at mid-century, Karadžić was well on his way to winning the struggle for language reform against his conservative opponents and to becoming Serbia's pre-eminent intellectual.[88]

Ilija Garašanin and the Plan

Serb nationalists and politicians in the first half of the nineteenth century had no contemporary state tradition to fall back on and nothing approaching natural geographical or long-standing administrative borders that could be converted into national borders. Consequently, the formulation of coherent national strategies by Serb leaders, politicians and intellectuals would prove difficult. Meanwhile, the oppressive, bureaucratic state within clear but modest borders that emerged under Miloš would be less appealing than the idealised Serbia of the spirit—the larger or 'Great' Serbia that was to be achieved (though it never was) through 'unification of all Serb lands', whose borders were neither clear nor modest. Miloš himself had wanted eventually to establish an enlarged Serbian state that would have included the Serbs of Bosnia, Hercegovina and the Albanian-majority lands to the south, possibly also Montenegro, and would potentially have expanded into Macedonia and the Bulgarian-inhabited lands. There is no evidence that he envisaged expanding into Austrian territory.[89] These ambitions came to nothing, but Ilija Garašanin operated within the same conceptual framework.

The Constitutionalist regime that took power a few years after Karadžić wrote 'Serbs all and everywhere' was born from a period of turbulence and civil war, in which foreign powers, particularly Russia, Austria and Britain, had interfered callously in Serbia's internal affairs to promote their preferred factions. Petronijević and Vučić-Perišić's forced exile by Russia embittered the Constitutionalists: 'I no longer know who should be deemed your greater enemy, the Turk or the Russian?' wrote Garašanin to the two exiles in Constantinople.[90] During this exile in 1841–1842, the two had come into contact with members of the circle of Polish émigrés from the defeat of the Polish uprising of 1831, led by Paris-based Adam Czartoryski. In 1841, in the hope of intervening in the Eastern Question to Poland's advantage, Czartoryski authorised the formation of an agency in Constantinople headed by Michal Czajkowski.[91] Czartoryski had conspired on an anti-Russian basis in the 1830s with the influential David Urquhart, former secretary of Britain's embassy in Constantinople, and adopted from him the view that Miloš's Serbia could form a bulwark against Russian influence in the Balkans. The Polish émigrés, backed by France, hoped that Serbia under the new Constitutionalist regime would continue Miloš's policy of seeking to establish a strong Serbian state independent of Russia.[92] Consequently, Czajkowski and his fellow émigré Ludwik Zwierkowski, the Polish

THE CONSTITUTIONALIST ERA

circle's envoy in Belgrade, helped to establish the Constitutionalist regime and gain it international recognition, and sought to influence it in an anti-Russian direction. The leading Constitutionalists, for their part, fearing the partnership between Austria and Russia and the possibility that they could divide the Balkans between them, were receptive to the Polish promptings.[93]

Czartoryski wrote a memorandum in January 1843, 'Advice on conduct to be followed by Serbia', advocating South Slav unification under Serbian leadership. This text was communicated in March by Zwierkowski to Garašanin, Serbian interior minister, and would form the basis for his famous 1844 'Plan' (Načertanije), the foundational text of Serbian territorial expansionism. Zwierkowski was replaced in Belgrade from autumn 1843 by Zach, a Czech nationalist émigré recruited by the Polish emigration in Istanbul. Zach was joined in Belgrade in 1844 by Matija Ban, who was apparently converted to the Serb national idea by Czajkowski in Constantinople. Their circle was largely made up of foreigners, including Catholics like Ban from Croatia and Bosnia and a Slovak Protestant, Jan Šafárik, who taught at the Belgrade lycée and whose uncle Pavel Josef Šafárik had heavily influenced Karadžić's nationalism. They propagated the ideal of Serbia as the leading South Slav power and came to exercise a powerful influence over the regime and public opinion, including over Garašanin, while Ban became personal tutor to Aleksandar's daughters.[94] Zach wrote to Czartoryski in January 1844, informing him that Garašanin had commissioned him to 'compose a plan of the means to act upon the Slavs'. He consequently worked for four months on his Plan for South Slavic unification under Serbian leadership, written on the basis of Czartoryski's memorandum of the year before, with the assistance of Atanasije Nikolić and other Serb intellectuals.[95] Zach's Plan reflected his background as an Austrian Slav, in contact with the Illyrian movement's ideas, and his antipathy to Austria and Russia as the enemies of the liberty of Czechs, Poles and their other subject peoples. He was not the only adviser from whom Garašanin sought advice about Serbian state strategy, but it was Zach's plan that Garašanin copied to draw up his own, which he then presented to Aleksandar in December 1844 or January 1845. The title 'Plan' derived from French usage regarding grand state projects; it highlighted the Western orientation of Garašanin's political thought.[96]

The conspiratorial character of the Plan, which was to be pursued covertly by high statesmen in conjunction with a network of select activists, reflected its dissident émigré origins. Czartoryski's circle conspired to free Poland from Russia; this inspired Garašanin's conspiracy to free Serbia from the Ottomans.[97] But whereas Garašanin accepted Zach's model of Serbia as a barrier to Austria and Russia in the Balkans, including his consequent belief in the need to work within and uphold the Ottoman Empire until Serbia was strong enough to replace it, he rewrote Zach's programme in much more exclusively Serbian terms. Thus, whereas Zach's version of the Plan envisioned Serbia as the core of a 'South Slavic state' that would uphold, at some level, the idea of South Slavic reciprocity and cooperation, Garašanin's redraft replaced Zach's references to the 'South Slavic state' and the 'South Slavs' with 'Serbian state' and 'Serbs'.[98] He removed Zach's references to collaboration with the Croats and Czechs to avoid potentially alienating Austria and out of suspicion of Catholicism.[99] Nevertheless, its Serbian nationalism was, like Karadžić's, of the linguistic variety, reflecting its Habsburg Slav origins.

According to Garašanin's Plan, 'the line and foundation of Serbian politics' was 'that it not be limited to its present borders, but that it strive to draw close around it all the Serb peoples that surround it'. He drew upon the existence of the Serbian medieval empire as a precedent for the important role as 'natural protector of all Turkish Slavs' that he envisioned it as assuming: 'The Serb state that has already happily begun but which must expand and strengthen itself, has its foundation and basis in the Serbian empire of the 13th and 14th century and in the rich and illustrious Serbian history.'[100] This was not simple national romanticism. As a conservative, Garašanin preferred to base Serbia's state legitimacy on its medieval state tradition rather than the revolutionary tradition of the First and Second Uprisings. The affirmation of Serbia's medieval legacy, which Garašanin's version of the Plan had copied from Zach's, aimed at legitimising Serbia's expansionism in European eyes; 'we Serbs will then go before the world as the true heirs of our great fathers, who are doing nothing new but restoring our patrimony'.[101] The Plan did not advocate military aggression or territorial conquest nor express chauvinism or hostility toward other peoples or states. It followed instead Miloš's strategy of seeking to establish a powerful, independent Serbian state on a gradual, piecemeal basis, with its expansion broadly modelled on Miloš's annexation of the six nahijas in 1833: 'If Serbia wants to extract itself from its current subordinate status and make itself whole, become a true state, it must aim to eliminate Turkish power bit by bit, and itself appropriate it ...'

The Plan directs Serbian aspirations toward Bosnia, Montenegro and present-day northern Albania and focuses particularly on the promotion of Serbian influence among the Bulgarians, through opening schools and seminaries in Serbia to Bulgarian pupils and students, printing church literature on the Bulgarians' behalf and sending emissaries to Bulgaria to publicise Serbia's friendship for the Bulgarians. However, while a 'close alliance' was to be achieved with the population of Montenegro and northern Albania through their infiltration by Serbia's trading agents and merchants, Bosnia was the only land whose outright annexation the Plan advocated. This annexation was to serve as a model for the future unification of all the Serb lands. However, precisely what the 'Serb lands' were was not defined. The annexation of Bosnia was to be achieved through building close links with it. According to Garašanin, Serbian policy should have as its aim 'that the two peoples, the Eastern Orthodox and the Roman Catholic, understand each other and agree in their national politics'; to this end, Serbian policy should promote 'the tenets of full religious freedom', which 'must appeal to and satisfy all Christians, and—who knows?—from time to time some Mohammedans'.

Bosnia was to be encouraged to unite with Serbia under the latter's own hereditary dynasty; it should avoid establishing a rival dynasty of its own but should 'elect the most important individual from among the whole people, not for life but for a definite time, who would form some kind of council', so that 'with this kind of provincial and departmental government at least, the road would be open to progress; Serbia would in its own time easily be able to link closely and ally with Bosnia'. Garašanin advocated winning over the Bosnian Franciscans: 'For this goal, it would be important to order that certain books of prayers and spiritual songs be published; following that, prayer books for the Orthodox Christians; collections of national songs which would be printed on one side with Latin and on the other with Cyrillic script; apart from that, as the third step a short and general history of Bosnia could be printed, in which there should not be left out the celebration and names of certain past Bosniaks of the Mohammedan religion'. Finally, 'It is at once important also that not only that all basic laws, the constitution and all main structures of the principality of Serbia be disseminated among the people in Bosnia and Hercegovina, but also that in time several young Bosniaks be accepted into Serbian state service' in order to train them in Serbian statecraft and educate them, 'so that their work in all areas is governed by that redeeming idea of general unification and great progress'.

Garašanin envisaged Shkodër in northern Albania as the only outlet to the sea then available to Serbia: 'There, it would therefore be important to establish a Serbian trading agency and to put under its defence and protection the selling of Serbian products and buying of French and English imports.' Regarding Montenegro, Garašanin argued Serbia 'should follow the Russian example and fairly give the prince-bishop an annual support in money—Serbia will in this way have, for a small price, a friendly country, which can field at least 10,000 mountain soldiers.' Garašanin touched only briefly upon Austria's South Slav lands but suggested that publication of patriotic South Slav literature aimed at winning over Bosnia would have repercussions for them too: 'In this way, Dalmatia and Croatia would simultaneously get hold of works whose publication in Austria is impossible, and the close linking of these lands with Serbia and Bosnia would follow.' Finally, with regard to the Serb inhabitants of Srem, Bačka and Banat—present-day Vojvodina—Garašanin argued, 'For now, if nothing else, it should be necessary to become acquainted with the more important persons in these provinces, and establish there a significant Serbian newspaper, which under the constitution of Hungary could favourably work in the Serbian interest ...'[102]

The Plan was the work of a competent, conservative statesman with a realistic appreciation of his state's capacities, working in internationally quiet times and unconstrained by public opinion, which in Serbia was not yet a factor.[103] It was not necessarily representative of the opinion of the Constitutionalists collectively;

among them, Garašanin was something of a nonconformist. He was the only senior figure of the regime who continued supporting Karadžić after the latter's dictionary, whose second edition was published in 1852, was banned in Serbia in February of the following year. Garašanin saw in him a fellow patriot and recruited him to his web of nationalist agents.[104] Nevertheless, the awakening of Serbia's interest in the wider South Slav question, which Garašanin's Plan represented, rapidly began to influence and complicate Serbia's international and domestic relations. Meanwhile, the year following the drafting of his Plan, Garašanin took the first step on the regime's behalf to give Serbia the means to defend its interests internationally, through a Law for the Organisation of the Garrison Military, which re-established a standing army of 2,529 men.[105]

Austrian Serbs, populist reaction and the revolutions of 1848

Garašanin's expansionist programme brought together émigré prečani Serbs from Austria and Bosnia and native Serbians in a common nationalist project, manifesting itself in 1844 in the formation of a secret Slav Society in Belgrade under Ban's leadership. Membership was not restricted to Serbs; in June 1845 it recruited several Bulgarians.[106] It enjoyed the blessing of Aleksandar and of Serbia's military leader, Council member Knićanin. A nativist and populist reaction against the activities of the Society and the regime in general then emerged under Vučić-Perišić, who went into opposition in 1845, focusing on the presence of Austrian Serbs in Serbia and counterposing a pro-Russian stance to the regime's anti-Russian alignment. Like Miloš, he was of peasant background and had the ability to appeal to peasants in terms they understood. His animus against the Austrian Serbs was linked to the so-called Hussar Rebellion of 4–8 October 1844, when an armed band of Obrenovićite Serbs led by the Paris-educated Stojan Jovanović-Cukić invaded Serbia from Austrian territory, seized the towns of Šabac and Loznica and, claiming to enjoy Austrian support, succeeded in raising a rebellion that swelled its numbers to about a thousand. Vučić-Perišić was given command of the army by Aleksandar, with the title of vojvoda, and he mobilised the population of the region against the invaders. Vučić-Perišić's advance guard under another popular strongman—old Archpriest Mateja, hero of the First Serbian Uprising and Persida's first cousin once removed—attacked Jovanović-Cukić's band on 6 October, defeating and killing him. Vučić-Perišić, ably assisted as foreman of his kangaroo court by the young Hristić, then severely punished the defeated rebels. However, Aleksandar's government apparently feared its victorious saviour, Vučić-Perišić, as much as the defeated Hussars, and sent a messenger to strip him of his special powers while on the road back to Belgrade, angering him.[107] Vučić-Perišić then found himself in opposition to the foreign-educated, pro-Austrian Aleksandar, whose court camarilla included two Austrian Serbs, Aleksa Janković and Timotej Knežević. He consequently campaigned to expel

THE CONSTITUTIONALIST ERA

all Austrian Serbs from Serbia, though this failed in the face of Vienna's opposition. A compromise was reached in 1845 whereby all Austrian Serbs in Serbian government service were required either to become Serbian subjects within a year or reach a new contract with Serbia's government.[108]

Popular hostility was not directed only at Serb foreigners. Miloš had been sympathetic to Serbia's small Jewish community, ever since 1815 when Jews had supplied his rebels with arms and munitions. He was something of a philosemite; he liked to visit Belgrade's Jewish quarter frequently and listen to the prayers and choir at the synagogue. He supported the Jewish community materially and morally, guaranteeing the Jews full rights and issuing a decree to protect them, whereby in any conflict between Jews and Serbs, no authority could prosecute the Jews except the prince himself.[109] By contrast, the Constitutionalist regime adopted anti-Semitic measures reminiscent of other Christian European states. It was faced with popular hostility to the growing, increasingly prosperous Jewish community, particularly on the part of Serbian merchants and craftsmen and directed in particular at resident foreign Jews protected by the so-called Capitulations—the system of privileges for foreigners in Ottoman lands, extracted from the Porte by the Great Powers. In Belgrade the tailors' guild on 5 December 1840 and the furriers' guild on 7 March 1841 both complained to the city authorities about the supposedly unfair trading practices of their Jewish competitors, much as other guilds complained about Austrian Serbs, and demanded measures against them.[110] When Jews from Wallachia and Sarajevo sought refuge in Serbia from persecution in February 1844, Garašanin gave strict orders they be denied entry.

The interior ministry on 9 July 1845 informed the Council of the 'great oppression' faced by Serbian merchants on account of the Jews, complaining that they had monopolised all 'outdoor shops, warehouses, goats, turkeys, flour and laundries', and demanded it take measures against them to help 'our citizenry'. Particularly in response to pressure from Serb merchants in Šabac on the Austrian border, the government passed a decree on 12 November 1846 banning Jews from residing or owning property in Serbia outside Belgrade, a measure that forced those living in provincial Serbian towns, numbering in the hundreds, to close their businesses and move to the capital or leave the country altogether. The measure was justified on the grounds that 'the people do not tolerate them, and secondly, because it is in the politics of our liberation that there be no races in the interior that do not have identical interests with us, for liberation'. Although the Treaty of Paris of March 1856 required Serbia to respect freedom of religion and trade, for Jews as well, discrimination against them continued. A subsequent decree of 30 October 1856 banned Jews from conducting trade in the country's interior. Despite the Jewish flight to Belgrade, the Jewish share of the capital's population fell from 9 per cent at the time of Miloš's fall in 1839 to 7 per cent at the time of the Constitutionalist regime's fall in 1858.[111]

SERBIA

While Serbs in Serbia could manifest chauvinism toward Austrian Serbs or Jews, they could also feel solidarity for the unliberated Serbs across the border in Austria. The revolutionary upheavals that began there in 1848 spurred the rise of nationalism among the Habsburg Serbs and Croats, which at this time involved strong currents favouring cooperation with each other against Hungary's government. Although ethnic Hungarians or Magyars comprised only 37 per cent of the Kingdom of Hungary's population, the Hungarian parliament in 1847 proclaimed Hungarian the principal state language, with Serbian and other national languages restricted to churches and schools. The conflict was catalysed by the outbreak of revolution across Europe the following year, beginning in Paris on 22–24 February with the overthrow of France's king Louis Philippe and spreading in March to Vienna, where the notoriously reactionary Chancellor Metternich was forced to resign on 13 March. Revolution then spread to Buda and Pest on 15 March, when the authorities were forced to accept demands not only for an independent national government and democratically elected parliament in Hungary, but also for confirmation of the parliament's previous resolutions, including regarding the Hungarian language. Revolutionary Hungary's aggressive Magyarising policies in turn triggered the opposing revolutions of the Croats and Hungarian Serbs.

Among the Croats, the Illyrian movement spearheaded a revolutionary movement led by Jelačić, aimed at unifying the Croatian lands and freeing them from Hungarian domination.[112] This in turn encouraged Hungary's Serbs to formulate their demands. The Illyrians supported collaboration with Serbia's government; Gaj sent an envoy to Belgrade, who informed it of his idea to proclaim Aleksandar 'King of Illyria'. This idea was favourably received by the prince and by Garašanin.[113] Thus encouraged, Garašanin's collaborator Konstantin Nikolajević, Serbia's envoy in Constantinople and husband of Aleksandar's daughter Poleksija, devised a plan, probably in March or April 1848, for the establishment of a 'Serbian vice-royalty' within the Ottoman Empire. This was the most ambitious attempt to reconcile the Constitutionalist regime's collaboration with the Porte with the pursuit of Serbian national goals, and was motivated by the hope that Serbia could benefit from the European upheavals to achieve these goals, involving the annexation of 'Bosnia, Hercegovina, Montenegro and Upper Albania'. The projected Serbian state would have complete internal autonomy under its own ruler while acknowledging the Sultan's authority. It would have a permanent chancellery representing it before the Sultan in Constantinople, its own army to defend not only its own borders but the empire's as well, a veto on the empire's foreign treaties except in cases of emergency and the right to open commercial but not political consulates in the empire and in foreign states, while 'the Mohammedan inhabitants in Serbia and in all Serbian provinces annexed to Serbia will receive equal political rights with other Serbian citizens'.[114] Garašanin supported Nikolajević's plan, but tentative attempts through unofficial channels to gain the Porte's approval ended in complete failure by October.

THE CONSTITUTIONALIST ERA

Serbia's ministers were divided over whether to collaborate with the Croats. Nikolajević believed the Serbs of the Ottoman and Habsburg lands were fundamentally different and rejected the possibility of Serb unification within the Habsburg rather than the Ottoman Empire, on the grounds that 'the non-coreligionist and non-conational roots of the dynasty; the religious, ethnographic and historical division of the Slavs themselves; and particularly the mixed Magyar and German element in such an empire can never warm the hearts of the Orthodox Turkish Slavs for them to join it themselves'.[115] Plans for a regional insurgent organisation emanating from Garašanin's circle, although they embraced organisational activity in Habsburg Dalmatia and the Military Border, envisaged the actual uprising as being limited to the Ottoman lands—from Bosnia and northern Albania to Bulgaria. Actual attempts at establishing such an organisation in the period 1849–1851 proved abortive.[116] Nevertheless, those Serbians who favoured collaboration with the Habsburg South Slavs were inspired by events. A Serb National Assembly, summoned by the Metropolitan of Sremski Karlovci, Josif Rajačić, and held there on 13–15 May 1848, involved a massive nationalist demonstration and declared the establishment of the 'Serb nation as a nation politically free and independent under the House of Habsburg and the general Crown of Hungary'; consequently, 'Srem with the border, Baranja, Bačka and the Bečej district and Šajkača Battalion, and the Banat with the border and Kikinda District, is proclaimed a Serb Vojvodina'.[117] These were lands of the Hungarian crown and Srem was also part of the Kingdom of Croatia.[118] Vojvodina was to be in political union with the Triune Kingdom of Croatia, Slavonia and Dalmatia. The assembly also proclaimed the restoration of the Serbian Orthodox Patriarchate, and Rajačić assumed the Patriarch's title and leadership of the new province's government. Croatia's parliament meanwhile resolved on 5 June to establish its own government, or 'ban's council', which began operating on 7 July. Croatia then withheld its delegates from Hungary's parliament, formalising the breach. The Croats and Vojvodinian Serbs stood firmly allied against Hungary. By summer, Serb demands were even raised for Vojvodina's annexation to Serbia, and Rajačić wrote about this to the Russian consul in Belgrade.[119]

These acts precipitated military conflict with Hungary in which the Croats and Serbs fought alongside Austria's emperor. Allegedly, after negotiations between Hungary and the Serbs collapsed, the Hungarian leader Lajos Kossuth told the Serb delegation, 'The sword will decide between us', to which one of its members retorted, 'The Serbs were never afraid of that.'[120] Archduchess Sophie, mother of the future emperor Franz Joseph, showed her appreciation by wearing in her hair a ribbon with the Serbian tricolour. The Slavic Congress in Prague, opening on 3 June 1848, brought together representatives of the Slavic peoples from across Europe, including Serbs, Croats, Czechs, Slovaks, Poles, Ukrainians, Russians and others, among them Karadžić, Pavel Josef Šafárik, Mikhail Bakunin and Archpriest Mateja. This was a manifestation of Slavic solidarity against the German and Hungarian nationalist threats. In the Serbs' first battle on 12 June, decisively assisted by armed volunteers from Serbia, they defeated a Hungarian attack on their base at Sremski Karlovci.[121] Jelačić invaded Hungary on 11 September with his army drawn from the Military Border, comprising both Croats and Serbs.

Though conservative in domestic affairs, Garašanin looked geopolitically to the Western liberal powers; he wanted to build links with the Serbs and Croats of the Habsburg lands but feared the side effects of the revolutionary events there. He first sought agreement with Hungary for common action against the Habsburgs but, when this proved impossible owing to Kossuth's inflexibility toward Hungarian Serb demands, Garašanin fell back on an alliance with the Habsburgs against Hungary.[122] He, Aleksandar and the Constitutionalists were under pressure both from liberal nationalists who sympathised with the Habsburg Serbs and from traditionalists opposed to them. For the first time, Serbia now had a generation of young native intellectuals educated in the cities of France, Germany and Austria who had imbibed the Romantic nationalist ideas then popular in Europe. These agitated in favour of support for their Serb brethren in the Habsburg lands. At the same time, the unrest in Austria inspired the Constitutionalist regime's opponents to demand political reforms in Serbia as well, while Slav Society members were inspired with ideas of spreading the revolution to the Ottoman Empire. Members of the Council including Knićanin feared a new incursion by Obrenovićites backed by Vučić-Perišić.

Serbia's government convened the so-called St Peter's Day parliament at Kragujevac on 11 July 1848 in an attempt to defuse popular agitation for change. As the nationalist ambitions of Garašanin and his elite circle had little resonance among Serbia's population at large, he was unable to stage-manage the parliament as he had planned, but was forced to recognise that popular opinion was overwhelmingly with the opposition under Vučić-Perišić.[123] In a weak echo of the revolutionary explosion convulsing Europe, the opposition's representatives demanded that parliament be summoned more regularly in future, that every okrug be represented in parliament and that district governors be selected only from among the local population, while the representatives of eleven of Serbia's okrugs demanded it be summoned annually. Aleksandar replied that the Council had appointed a commission to draw up a law governing the future regular summoning of parliament. Although the Council indeed selected a commission from its ranks to work on such a law, nothing ultimately came of this under the Constitutionalists.[124] Individual representatives also demanded reforms including press freedom and proportional taxation. Various measures restricting the power and privileges of bureaucrats were proposed and the parliament succeeded in obtaining a ban on bureaucrats engaging in commerce.[125] The parliament also unsuccessfully demanded expulsion of all Austrian Serbs from public service and opposed military intervention on their behalf. Serbia's ordinary people were much readier to identify with Serbs in other Ottoman territories and with the anti-Ottoman struggle. Vučić-Perišić's opposition to the volunteer expedition against Hungary that Serbia's government was then preparing gelled with his populist opposition to the regime and struck a chord among the people, at least in areas where his influence was strongest. Finally, the parliament demanded expulsion of all Turks from Serbia by means of a hatt-ı şerif.[126]

The parliament amounted to a partial victory for Vučić-Perišić, who secured the resignations of Knićanin and Aleksa Janković, chief of Aleksandar's chancery and an Austrian Serb.[127] The Constitutionalist regime consequently did not call another parliament for ten years, closing a valve for releasing the pressure of popular discontent. This discontent was not confined to the parliament; some days after it was held, a large demonstration in Belgrade came close to lynching Stojan Simić, president of the Council and another Austrian Serb and opponent of Vučić-Perišić. Simić was rescued by Vučić-Perišić but was nevertheless compelled to resign. Aleksandar replaced him as president with Stefanović without the Council's approval, thereby violating the constitution and marking the start of the conflict between prince and Council that would topple the regime a decade later. In the short term, prince and Council closed ranks to sideline Vučić-Perišić. The latter continued his populist campaign against the regime, condemning its restrictions on the peasantry's exploitation of the forests and its supposed restoration of the Ottoman practice of kuluk in the form of conscription of peasant labour for the repair of roads, and continuing to demand prohibition of the employment of Austrian Serbs as officials.[128] But he was unsuccessful until 1858, when his opposition merged with that of the leading Constitutionalists to Aleksandar's personal regime.

Serbia's government could not stay aloof from the Serb struggle in Austria. News reached it that Miloš was seeking to collaborate with Hungary's government to have himself installed as leader of Hungary's Serbs, who would serve as his base for his return to Serbia. This prompted Serbia's government to support the anti-Hungarian current among Hungary's Serbs.[129] Consequently, it sent a force of several thousand volunteers from the national militia under Knićanin—newly freed by his dismissal from government—to fight the Hungarians.[130] Estimates of the number of these volunteers range from 6,000 to 15,000, yet even the larger figure represented only 1.76 per cent of Serbia's population, reflecting its lack of identification with the Austrian Serbs. The mobilisation achieved was through the efforts of national elders enjoying authority among the people; for example, volunteers from Požarevac were mobilised by Milutin Petrović Era, a vojvoda during the First Serbian Uprising and brother of its hero, Hajduk Veljko.[131] Belgrade also intervened with Vienna to remove both Miloš and Mihailo from Zagreb and Novi Sad respectively and withdraw them to safe distances from the South Slav lands.

The volunteer force experienced its first major engagement with the Hungarians at Bela Crkva in September 1848. Repeatedly defeated following a Hungarian offensive in December, the Serbs decisively defeated the Hungarians at Pančevo, across the river from Belgrade, in January 1849, causing them to retreat, after which the Serbs won further offensive successes in Hungary. However, as the Habsburg military position improved, the Serb cause in Hungary was increasingly subordinated to Habsburg dynastic interests and the volunteers from Serbia came to be seen as a hindrance, so were mostly withdrawn under Austrian and Ottoman pressure in March. The Hungarians then returned to the offensive and occupied almost all of Banat, causing a wave of Serb refugees to flee to Serbia. Knićanin returned to Hungary at Rajačić's request to fight unsuccessfully in defence of local Serbs, while the Russians invaded the country in April. Serbia's war losses may have been over 1,400.[132]

Following Russia's military intervention on the Habsburg side, the Hungarians surrendered on 13 August 1849. The Habsburg government on 18 November rewarded the Serbs' military assistance by recognising Serb Vojvodina, with slightly different borders excluding Sremski Karlovci, as the 'Vojvodstvo of Serbia and Temesvar Banat'. Emperor Franz Joseph I consequently became 'Great Vojvoda of the Vojvodstvo of Serbia'. The Hungarian Serbs' victory was pyrrhic: it was said that the Croats received from the Habsburgs as reward what the Hungarians received as punishment, and the same applied to the Serbs. Thus, the Vojvodstvo was ruled directly from Vienna on an absolutist basis and the Serb population enjoyed no real autonomy. The province was far from having an ethnic majority of Serbs; numbering 321,000, they were outnumbered by both Romanians (397,000) and Germans (335,000), with the Hungarians also being a sizeable group (221,000). Its official language from 1854 was German.[133] Although the absolutism was relaxed somewhat following the Habsburg defeat in the Franco-Austrian war of 1859, in December of the following year the Vojvodstvo was dissolved altogether to appease the Hungarians. Yet Serbia had achieved a victory. Knićanin was decorated by both Aleksandar and the Austrian emperor's court; Aleksandar named him 'vojvoda'—the second after Vučić-Perišić to receive this title—while Franz Joseph appointed him Knight of the Cross of Maria Theresa. Shortly before Knićanin's death, he received a gift from the still-grateful Franz Joseph of 2,000 ducats, and when he died in 1855, the emperor sent a delegation to his funeral consisting of 80 officers representing all Vojvodina's regiments.[134] Similarly, Franz Joseph's court twice offered Garašanin a decoration, which he refused. There was a strengthening of the alliance between the courts of Austria and Serbia, involving a sense of common purpose against any potential domestic opposition in both countries. Serbia's military intervention marked a breakthrough onto the international stage of what was still an Ottoman vassal state and its status as South Slav matrix was greatly enhanced.[135]

Serbia's military expedition catalysed the development of its armed forces. The Council and prince, at Garašanin's initiative, approved the foundation of a cannon foundry, established in Belgrade in October 1848 on the basis of an existing armaments repair workshop; it was intended to serve also as an officer training-school. Knićanin and his fellow commanders, during their service in Austria, realised the need for a modern Serbian military and, on their return home, added to the voices for military development. The cannon foundry failed, after which the project was transferred to Kragujevac and pursued more carefully and methodically. Meanwhile, the Artillery School started work in Belgrade on 6 September 1850, with Zach as director, producing its first cohort of 22 graduates with the rank of sergeant by December. It initially shared a building with the foundry but subsequently moved to its own premises.[136] It served as Serbia's officer training school until 1880, when it was formally converted into the Military Academy.

Between Austria and Russia

In Serbia by the 1850s a modern state apparatus of bureaucracy, police and army was emerging, headed by a regime that looked toward Western Europe both geopolitically and culturally. In light of Austria's military triumph, Garašanin suspended his plans for a Balkan uprising but pursued close relations with France to reduce Serbia's dependence on Russia and Austria. Yet despite his viewing Austria as Serbia's enemy, the elitist character of his regime, rejecting democracy and popular participation in government and ruling through the police, resembled the contemporaneous neo-absolutist regime in Vienna, while Vučić-Perišić's populist opposition looked toward Russia. Garašanin's police law of 1850 bestowed considerable powers on the police, including the right to impose punishments at will, such as flogging. Since this authoritarian measure was directed against the pro-Russian opposition, it was ironically Tsar Nicholas's autocratic Russia that opposed it strongly. That year, the Council rejected Nicholas's suggestion that Serbian officials stop wearing the fez and adopt Western hats or Russian caps.[137] Garašanin continued to strengthen the regime's powers in defiance of the Russians: on 7 October 1851, he placed the police under the control of Knićanin as head of Serbia's army and on 26 March 1852, in the so-called April Circular, he empowered the civil courts to prosecute for sedition.

Petronijević, Serbia's prime minister and foreign minister, died on 22 April 1852 and Garašanin was appointed in his place to both posts in September 1852. Whereas Petronijević had pursued a restrained, Turcophile policy abroad and cooperated amicably with Aleksandar at home, Garašanin was more assertive and conflictual on both fronts. Despite his military support to Austria against the Hungarians and alongside Russia, he pursued independence vis-à-vis both powers. This was manifested in his policy toward Montenegro, where Prince-Bishop Petar II's successor had secularised his office to become Prince Danilo I in 1851–1852, so as to ensure his heirs' hereditary rule over the country.[138] Danilo's move had the support of Russia, which favoured his absolutism in contrast to its preference for oligarchy in Serbia, perhaps to undermine possible independent cooperation between the two states. When a major anti-Ottoman uprising erupted in Hercegovina in 1851–1852, Danilo supported it militarily while Garašanin sought to negotiate an end to the conflict and gain Ottoman acceptance of 'a federation on the model of the Swiss cantons' between Serbia and Montenegro, whereby the Montenegrin bishop would be subordinated to the Serbian church and Serbia would represent Montenegro in its relations with the Porte. This plan was aimed at preventing Austrian and Russian meddling in the conflict in Hercegovina.[139]

Given Russia's support for Vučić-Perišić's opposition, Garašanin viewed that country as his principal enemy. As he wrote in August 1852:

> I eat bread not with Russian teeth but with my own and those of my forefathers; I am not a servant of Russia. When my father fought for the freedom of my country in the first and second uprisings and shed his blood for it, he truly did not know that the Russians existed. Those same Russians were the cause of my father's losing his head in an unnatural manner and also caused much misfortune to other Serbs. They would like me to be their slave or servant as many others here have become, but I will not do that. I serve my country and will continue to serve it truly without the least fear of Russia or anyone else.[140]

After becoming prime minister, he pensioned off Vučić-Perišić, provoking a showdown with Russia. Serbia's government was forced under Russian pressure to revoke the April Circular on 14 October. Further Russian pressure forced Aleksandar to dismiss Garašanin on 14 March 1853, subsequently his close ally, foreign minister Jovan Marinović, as well. The Austrian Serb Aleksa Simić replaced Garašanin, becoming prime minister until December 1855. Serbia's government feared Russian intervention to overthrow it and restore Prince Mihailo.

Both Russia and Austria mobilised diplomatically to oppose the establishment of the Kragujevac cannon foundry. Franz Joseph sent an envoy to Serbia in June 1853 who advised Aleksandar and Serbia's government to drop the project, while Russia intervened in Constantinople to urge the Ottoman government to block it. Nevertheless, the foundry finally began production in October 1853, directed by Charles Loubris, previously supervisor of a cannon foundry in France, whom Napoleon III had authorised to transfer to Serbia. However, following the outbreak of the Crimean War between Russia and the Ottoman Empire on 4 October 1853 and the British and French declaration of war on Russia on 28 March 1854, Paris succumbed to Austrian pressure and prompted Loubris's resignation in August, by which time the foundry had produced 46 cannon. It continued operation under a Serbian director.[141] It proved a permanent fixture and, in the following decades, diversified into producing different types of military hardware. It launched Kragujevac as a major centre of Serbian industry.

Serbia remained neutral in the Crimean War. Of its possible invaders, Garašanin considered Austria the greatest danger: he wrote on 22 June 1854, 'If someone must rule over Serbia, all Serbs agree it should only be the Turks.'[142] A French officer whom Garašanin met in Paris in 1853, Hippolyte Florentain Mondain, was recruited by him to help build Serbia's army. Appointed to France's consulate in

THE CONSTITUTIONALIST ERA

Belgrade with the blessing of its war ministry, he advised Serbia's government on possible defensive measures against possible Russian or Austrian invasion, though he too was soon withdrawn by Paris under Austrian pressure.[143] Russophiles in the Council headed by Stefanović favoured entering the war on Russia's side; in early 1854, Stefanović composed a plan for a Great Serbia that would be established with Russian support, while Russia sought to woo Serbia with promises of territorial expansion and full independence under its protection.[144] Threatened with Austrian or Ottoman occupation, Serbia expanded its army—principally a militia—to about 48,000 infantry and 6,000 cavalry by late 1853.[145] The government's writ of January 1854 emphasised the duty of every Serb to defend the fatherland, based on the principle of the nation-in-arms. A registry of all adult males aged 18–45 was ordered and the number of registered national militiamen rose to 80,000–110,000, recruited and organised through the police apparatus at the district and okrug levels, with the tiny standing army used for training.[146] But in the summer of 1854, Radosavljević formally demanded an end to Serbia's rearmament. Threatened with Austrian invasion, Serbia abandoned it.

The Treaty of Paris of 30 March 1856, ending the Crimean War with Russia's defeat, also ended Russia's protectorate over Serbia, dating back to 1812. It stipulated: 'The Principality of Servia shall continue to hold of the Sublime Porte, in conformity with the Imperial Hats which fix and determine its Rights and Immunities, placed henceforward under the Collective Guarantee of the Contracting Powers. In consequence, the said Principality shall preserve its Independent and National Administration, as well as full Liberty of Worship, of Legislation, of Commerce, and of Navigation.' Furthermore, 'The right of garrison of the Sublime Porte, as stipulated by anterior regulations, is maintained. No armed Intervention can take place in Servia without previous agreement between the High Contracting Powers.' Thus, autonomous Serbia's existence was now guaranteed collectively by the Great Powers.

Tenka's plot

The stability of the Constitutionalist regime depended upon relations between prince and Council. At its birth, the Council had been dominated by notables who enjoyed genuine status in their own right, in the eyes of the people and independently of the prince. In the words of historian Slobodan Jovanović (1869–1958), 'In its first years, the Council could resemble a small people's parliament.' Three members of the Council of 1842 had even been prominent in the First Serbian Uprising. But as members died and were replaced by the prince's appointees, the Council became a bureaucratic elite organ.[147] The prince inserted members of his wife Persida's powerful family, the Nenadovićes, into key posts in the apparatus: her father Jevrem and his brother Aleksandar were members of the Council, chief of staff Jovan Lukavčević was married to Persida's sister, and another family member, Kosta Nenadović, held another senior army post. These relatives, along with Austrian Serbs, formed the mainstay of Aleksandar's embryonic personal regime. Petronijević, Aleksandar's personal friend, had kept the peace between prince and Council; his death in April 1852 removed this linchpin of the duumvirate. With neither prince nor Council having any mooring among the people, there was no popular or constitutional restraint on the struggle for supremacy between them, which escalated from spring 1855.

The Council became afraid in August 1855 that Aleksandar was going to appoint two ministers from outside its ranks to his government, and warned him that this would be unlawful. Intervening in the dispute, the vizier appealed to both sides to resolve matters; this interference was attributed by the Council to Aleksandar's intrigue, though the Council would itself soon seek the Porte's intervention. Once dismissed, Garašanin moved into opposition to Aleksandar and to the presence of Austrian Serbs in government. In autumn, with the Anglo-French victory in the Crimean War assured, he travelled to Paris in an unsuccessful attempt to enlist the support of the Western powers for Aleksandar's dethronement. The prince, who had already capitulated to Austria over the issue of rearmament, responded to Garašanin's intrigues by an increasingly Austrophile stance in the apparent hope of securing his regime through Habsburg support, turning Serbia into an Austrian satellite. Radosavljević's influence became paramount; he was himself an Austrian Serb from Srem, which he had represented in the Serb national movement of 1848–1849.[148]

Aleksandar replaced Simić as prime minister with Aleksa Janković, another Austrian Serb, in December 1855. Simultaneously, he appointed his wife's uncle Aleksandar Nenadović, a non-councillor, as finance minister, in a direct rebuke to the Council, which now itself began seeking the Porte's intervention. From then until 1858, three Austrian Serbs held the post of prime minister: first Janković, then Stefan Marković, then Simić again, then Marković again. There was a corresponding sense of triumphalism among the Ottoman authorities in Serbia and a renewed readiness to assert themselves in its internal affairs, an attitude encouraged by the Austrians.[149] Aleksandar offended the Council again in July 1856 by issuing a proclamation regarding the tenets of the Peace of Paris as they affected Serbia, without consulting it. A highly discontented Garašanin advised him unsuccessfully in August 1856 to establish a cabinet containing no Austrian Serbs. Simić was again appointed prime minister in September, while Aleksandar appointed two non-councillors, Jovan Marinović and his own son-in-law Konstantin Nikolajević, as his new finance minister and interior minister respectively. He also appointed Nenadović to the Council without its permission. Such clashes between prince and Council over priority, appointments and protocol became more numerous. Aleksandar appointed a new government under Marković in June 1857, in which every minister other than the prime minister himself belonged to his family; it was a clear step towards establishing a personal regime. Garašanin complained that year: 'The prince has delivered himself wholly to Austria and the *Nemačkari* [Austrian Serbs], and in alliance with them thinks he can direct the fate of the Serbian people.'[150] Another malcontent was Vučić-Perišić, who articulated a popular Russophile opposition to Aleksandar's excessive and unpopular Austrophilism.[151] Thus, Serbia's internal conflict became once again a question of its international alignment, as it had been at the start of the Constitutionalist era.

The struggle culminated in the revelation in September 1857 of 'Tenka's plot', in which Council president Stefan Stefanović Tenka, three other Council members and the Supreme Court's president were implicated in a plot to assassinate Aleksandar, linked to the exiled Miloš, who was to be restored, and to Russia, whose consul-general in Belgrade encouraged it.[152] Following the plot's discovery, the four implicated Council members were imprisoned; Belgrade's governor Hristić arrested and interrogated them personally.[153] Six others were forced to resign and one other resigned voluntarily, crippling the Council. The imprisoned conspirators were cruelly abused by Aleksandar's panic-stricken regime, causing one of them, Radovan Damjanović, to die, which turned public opinion against it. This arrest and punishment of the councillors was carried out without the Porte's permission and in violation of the constitution, provoking diplomatic intervention with the Porte by the Great Powers—in particular Russia and France, at the time collaborating against Austria, Aleksandar's protector. Consequently, the Porte seized the chance to reassert its authority over Serbia and sent a commissioner, Edhem Pasha, to impose a compromise on the conflict between prince and Council.[154]

Edhem Pasha arrived in Belgrade in March 1858. His readiness to intervene on behalf of the prisoners was linked to his desire to humble their gaoler, Hristić, disliked for his assertive stance against the Ottomans in the Belgrade garrison—according to Hristić's own account.[155] Aleksandar was forced to release the surviving conspirators, restore the dismissed councillors, and appoint a government made up of councillors, including Vučić-Perišić and Garašanin as president of the Council and interior minister respectively. However, Garašanin's hope of enlisting Edhem Pasha to induce Aleksandar to resign went unfulfilled; the Porte handed out honours to Aleksandar's chosen list of state servants to reassure him of its continued support. The crisis nevertheless reasserted the oligarchy's authority, directly protected by the Porte, over that of Aleksandar.[156] A new regulation, imposed through Edhem Pasha's intervention on 3 May 1858, increased the Council's power. The prince's veto on its legislative actions was reduced to the right to suspend, while councillors could no longer be turned over to the court without the prior approval of the Council itself. The principles of ministerial responsibility before the Council and recruitment of ministers from the Council alone were affirmed.[157] However, although the Council was now in principle more powerful than ever, it was divided between Aleksandar's supporters and opponents, thereby paralysing the regime. The failure to convene a parliament for ten years had generated considerable frustration among sections of the population. Vučić-Perišić and Garašanin, conservative populist and conservative elitist, were now united in wishing to overthrow Aleksandar with the populace's help.

In the nineteen years following Miloš's fall, Serbia's transformation was accelerated by its increasing integration into the wider European world—diplomatically, economically and culturally. This found expression in the birth of modern nationalism, pioneered by Garašanin with his 'Plan' and his military intervention to defend the Habsburg Serbs. Nationalism was the preoccupation of Serbs, such as Garašanin and Karadžić, who had been educated abroad or exposed to foreign ideas. Serbia's intervention against the Hungarians marked its emergence as an independent international actor and catalysed the development of its officer corps and military industry along modern European lines. These social, economic and cultural changes provoked a populist backlash against the regime that fuelled an opposition combining conservative oligarchs, the Obrenović dynasty's supporters and a new faction in Serbian politics: the liberals.

5

THE NATIONAL LIBERATION STRUGGLE RESUMES

1858–1867

Serbia by the middle of 1858 was faced with a revolutionary situation. The regime was fatally split by the conflict between prince and Council while liberal activists appeared as a new element on the political scene, spearheading a movement for change fuelled by widespread popular dissatisfaction. A significant portion of Serbia's population remained loyal to the Obrenović dynasty and wished to reverse the outcome of 1842. The upheaval that would engulf Serbia in 1858 combined both liberal-progressive and reactionary pressures for the overthrow of the modernising but conservative and authoritarian Constitutionalist regime. This occurred in a country still part of and occupied by a foreign empire, against which the agitation for change was in part directed. The outcome of the crisis did not resolve Serbia's internal conflicts, but it did launch the next stage of its national liberation struggle.

Birth of Serbian liberalism

The emergence of a Serbian liberal faction reflected the growth in the educated and, in particular, foreign-educated section of the Serbian population, consequently of a public opinion capable of articulating the demand for liberal constitutional reform. The Serbian government issued a decree on 26 September 1839 to send ten students, recruited exclusively from poor families, to study in Hungary and Vienna, of whom two were to transfer to Paris after their first year.[1] Others followed them abroad, as the Serbian school system expanded and produced more students. Prince Aleksandar informed the Russian consul in 1848 that Serbia was permanently maintaining twelve students in foreign universities; when one graduated, another would be recruited in his place.[2] By 1858 there were 23 Serbian students studying abroad at the expense of the Serbian government.[3] By that year, there were at least 200 university graduates in Serbia.[4] The foundations for a liberal intelligentsia in Serbia were thus laid, as the overseas students brought foreign liberal ideas with them when they returned home.

In Belgrade, lycée and gymnasium pupils, schooled by foreign-educated teachers, were at the forefront of political and intellectual developments. The Society of Serb Youth was founded in Belgrade on 28 June 1847 by lycée professor Sergije Nikolić and some lycée students, including Jevrem Grujić and Milovan Janković; it was modelled on similar societies that existed in the Austrian Empire and Germany. The excitement of the revolutionary year of 1848 encouraged the emergence of liberal ideas. Typical was Vladimir Jovanović, who would become one of the leading early Serbian liberals. He arrived in Belgrade to study at the gymnasium in October 1848, aged fifteen; he entered the lycée two years later. He left Serbia to study abroad in the spring of 1854, primarily in Altenburg in Hungary, returning to Belgrade in October 1856, ready to participate in the burgeoning movement of opposition to Aleksandar's regime.[5]

These young liberals were mostly much better educated than their parents. Their reforming zeal partly reflected their sense of superiority vis-à-vis the mostly illiterate older generation.[6] Yet they were shaped by the patriarchal, communal values of the peasantry from which they sprang, with its folk memory of village self-management and for which the authoritarian, bureaucratic new order was alien and oppressive; their liberalism represented at once the embrace of new ideas and the reaction of the old society against the new order.[7] This generation had no direct memory of Miloš's despotism but, not entirely accurately, imagined him as a ruler who had stood up to the Turks, in contrast to the Constitutionalists' perceived obeisance before them.[8] The combination of youthful reformism, nationalism, naivety and impertinence was manifested by students Janković and Grujić while studying in Paris in the early 1850s. Janković was deprived of his stipend after writing the Serbian government a letter with advice on economic reform. The two then published the pamphlet *Slaves du sud, ou le peuple Serbe avec les Croates et les Bulgares, aperçu de leur vie historique, politique et sociale*, in the hope of acquainting the French public with Serbia and the Serbs.[9]

As Garašanin had recommended in the Plan, Janković and Grujić lauded the greatness of Dušan's Serbia so as to give Serbia status. But whereas Garašanin, the responsible senior statesman, put forward a cautious, moderate plan for expansion, the two young liberal activists set out a vastly ambitious definition of 'Serbska—the Serb lands', including Bosnia, Hercegovina, Montenegro, Metohija (including the towns of Priština, Prizren and Novi Pazar), the 'Serb Vojvodstvo' (Srem, Bačka and Banat including Timişoara), Slavonia, Dalmatia and Primorje (the eastern Adriatic coast) including Kotor, Dubrovnik, Istria and Trieste—all with a population of five million, of which only a million lived in Serbia itself, while they reduced Croatia to the territory around Zagreb with a population of a million. On the other hand, they listed Niš—which, unlike most of the aforementioned lands, Serbia *did* eventually succeed in annexing permanently—as part of Bulgaria. They simultaneously affirmed the unity of the Serbian and Croatian written languages. They mocked the

THE NATIONAL LIBERATION STRUGGLE RESUMES

Constitutionalists during the reign of Mihailo for having fled to Turkey 'and sought asylum with the enemy of the country'; Aleksa Simić, soon to become prime minister, was accused of 'meddling in literary questions of which he understands nothing'. Constitutionalist repression in 1844 was graphically described and reference made to the 'tyranny of the Turks'.[10] The Serbian government responded to the pamphlet's publication by depriving Grujić of his stipend too and forcing both authors to return to Serbia.

With reformist ideals went nationalism. The liberals had no memory of direct Ottoman rule yet their national pride was offended by the continued presence of Ottoman garrisons in Serbia. The Constitutionalist regime's acquiescence in this humiliating presence was seen as symbolising its decadence, as was the fact that both prince and Council depended for their positions on the goodwill of the Porte, to which both appealed during their power struggle in 1857–1858.[11] The liberals' attempt to distinguish themselves from the apparently unpatriotic Constitutionalists extended to their dress; in Slobodan Jovanović's words, 'The Constitutionalists wore the fez; the liberals donned the top hat—not just as a symbol of fashion but as a symbol of rebellion.'[12] When the Constitutionalists' delegation led by Garašanin awaited Edhem Pasha in Belgrade to deliver them from Aleksandar's rule, they wore the fez, which Garašanin continued to wear as he drove the Porte's envoy through the city in his official carriage. 'These fezzes, better than any flag, marked the political line of the opposition,' noted Jovan Ristić. Edhem was accommodated in a guest house with the avowedly patriotic name 'By the Serbian Crown', but the nameplate was removed in a further display of obeisance. The behaviour of Garašanin and the Constitutionalists during the crisis of 1858 drew the liberals' patriotic contempt and galvanised their opposition.[13]

The liberals and combined supporters of Vučić-Perišić, Garašanin and the Obrenović dynasty agitated during 1858 for the convening of a parliament to overthrow Aleksandar. These factions represented the different portions of the Serbian population: Garašanin was the most powerful figure of the Constitutionalist oligarchy and sought to ensure bureaucratic leadership of the parliament; Vučić-Perišić gave a voice to the populist opposition to high taxes and oppressive officialdom and, in contrast to Garašanin, sought to ensure the parliament's independence of the bureaucracy; the liberals represented the new educated class; and the Obrenović dynasty provided an alternative princely family with a claim to legitimacy and the loyalty of a significant part of the population. The last two groups were not truly distinct: the young liberals were themselves often members of, or were related to, pro-Obrenović families, which strengthened their anti-regime radicalism.

Jovanović's father, for example, had been a craftsman who had counted Jevrem Obrenović as one of his customers and friends, and was later the business partner of one of Mihailo's ministers; his family fortune had declined when the minister left

Serbia after Mihailo fell.[14] Jovanović later recalled his grief and his mother's tears in 1842, when he was nine and living in his home town of Šabac, after they learned that his mother's brother had been imprisoned by the Constitutionalists following their victory over Mihailo. Other eminent local people were persecuted too:

> My contemporaries and I could not conceive how a Serb could hound other Serbs as enemies, and we asked with amazement and horror what sort of misfortune and power could lead so many honourable people to be persecuted as enemies. And when we also heard that Vučić and company had succeeded, in collusion with the Turks, in expelling the Obrenovićes from Serbia, we began with disbelief and worry to look upon the new order of things in Serbia. The devotion of the people to the liberating Obrenović dynasty was sincere, and that fact also explains why the opponents of that dynasty had the need to come together with foreign intrigues.

Jovanović's negative impression of the regime was strengthened two years later by the harsh treatment meted out indiscriminately to real or suspected supporters of the Hussar Rebellion in Šabac, where it had enjoyed considerable support and which was kept in a state of siege while the repression was in progress; its population deprived of food.[15] Similarly, Grujić's grandfather had been a devoted supporter of Miloš, and although his father joined the opposition to him, he then participated in the uprising against Mihailo only reluctantly and was subsequently disappointed by his experience of service under the Constitutionalists. Grujić was, apparently, much more like his grandfather than like his father, and though he became educated, he retained the patriarchal consciousness of a village boy who grew up working in the fields.[16] He married the daughter of Miloš's much-loved former mistress Jelenka and the husband he had found her.[17] Another prominent young liberal, Ranko Alimpić, was married to one of Princess Ljubica's nieces.

Older members of Obrenovićite families in 1858 still viewed Miloš as their lord, while younger, foreign-educated ones revered young Mihailo as the man they hoped would bring positive change to Serbia.[18] In that year, members of such families, even if they had no background in liberal thinking or agitation, came to identify as liberals as they coalesced into a party in opposition to the Constitutionalists. Stevča Mihailović, commander of the last Obrenovićite army to surrender in 1842, husband of one of Miloš's nieces and head of the Obrenovićite party in 1858, so a Serbian notable of the traditional type, identified as a liberal thenceforth and was subsequently a Liberal prime minister. Todor Tucaković's father Petar had been a supporter of Mihailo's regime in the struggle against the Constitutionalists and had been dismissed from the Council following its fall; Todor became a liberal in 1858 and a Liberal party stalwart thereafter.[19] The liberal movement was thus founded upon an Obrenovićite base, enabling it to grow from a small number of activists defined by their ideas to a party defined by its opposition to the rival Conservatives—from 'liberals' to 'Liberals'. This paradoxically meant that liberals spearheaded a revolution to restore a prince who was considerably more authoritarian than the regime they were overthrowing.

St Andrew's Day parliament

The Council on 3 September approved Garašanin's proposal to convene a parliament. The Porte's attempt, supported by Britain and Austria, to prevent the parliament from being summoned was vetoed by France and Russia, citing the terms of the Treaty of Paris relating to Serbian autonomy from Constantinople.[20] Thus, a law on the national parliament was passed on 9 November 1858. Previously, parliaments had been ad hoc bodies summoned on the basis of custom not law, held in the open air without clear distinction between the deputies and the public, therefore seeming popular rather than constitutional bodies. Under the new law, a parliament would be legally defined: it would comprise 376 elected members each elected by 500 taxpayers, and 63 *ex officio* members including presidents of the higher and lower courts, the governor of the city of Belgrade, okrug chiefs, the archpriests of each okrug and the abbot of a monastery from every diocese. Simultaneously, Council members and other officials and clergymen were barred from election as deputies. Aleksandar's and Garašanin's parties both supported the framing of the law in this way, believing they could use the *ex officio* members to control the parliament, while Vučić-Perišić, as Council president, hence an official, would be barred from entering the parliament and manipulating it, as he had the last parliament in 1848. The institution of parliament was to be tamed and converted into an anchor of the constitutional order.[21] Elections for the parliament were held on 28 November. It convened on 12 December, St Andrew's Day, so became known as the St Andrew's Day parliament. Miša Anastasijević was elected the parliament's president. He was Serbia's richest man and father-in-law of the late Radovan Damjanović, whom he wanted to avenge; also, through his daughter Sarka, of Đorđe Karađorđević, son of Aleksandar's late older brother Aleksa, whom Anastasijević hoped to enthrone in place of Aleksandar. He had also once been Miloš's trading agent in Bucharest. Mihailović was elected the parliament's vice-president and the liberals Grujić and Jovan Ilić its secretaries—Ilić was also a keen supporter of the Obrenovićite party. That party therefore enjoyed a great advantage in the parliament.

The St Andrew's Day parliament was a false dawn for Serbia's liberalisation. The liberals were the largest faction in the parliament so were able to push through constitutional reform, but they lacked the strength to retain control over the proceedings, therefore they allied with other factions. Thus, the liberals in the parliament fused with the populist-conservative supporters of the Obrenović dynasty to form a single caucus. There was ideological common ground, given the liberals' own populist attacks on the Council and bureaucracy, which they portrayed as alien, authoritarian impositions on the supposedly naturally democratic traditional

Serb society. Thus, the liberal movement as it emerged in 1858 was heir to the old Obrenovićite party of Mihailo's first reign, which already in 1839 had channelled popular resentment at the fledgling Constitutionalist-bureaucratic regime. In 1858, in the short term, despite their mutual animosity, the liberal–Obrenovićite faction collaborated with Garašanin's elitist-conservative Constitutionalist faction. On the basis of this broad coalition, the liberals were able to induce the parliament to enact, on 20 December, a law requiring that an elected parliament be convened annually, whose approval would be required for new taxes and which would have the right to impeach ministers. The law, drawn up primarily by the liberal secretaries of the parliament, Grujić and Ilić, was originally more radical but was watered down by the other parliamentary factions upon whose cooperation the liberals relied.

Parliament then voted on 22 December to demand Aleksandar's abdication, notifying him by writing of its decision and requesting that he return his princely authority to it. Aleksandar requested, and was granted, 24 hours to consider. When the rumour reached the parliamentary deputies that he had left for Kragujevac to mobilise the army, panic spread among them. To pre-empt dissolution by the army, they resolved to flee from the 'Prince's Brewery', where they had been based and which was ominously close to the city's principal barracks, to the 'Serbian Crown' tavern, from where they would enjoy the protection of the Ottoman authorities, but they were narrowly dissuaded from doing so by a member of their delegation to the prince, Andrija Stamenković. Yet Aleksandar lacked the resolve to deploy the army to disperse the parliament. When a crowd gathered at his palace, fearing for his life, he did what the parliamentary deputies had almost done and took refuge in Ottoman Kalemegdan, whither he was transported by Garašanin, who thereby helped Aleksandar discredit himself, ensuring the end of his reign.[22] Hristić recalled: 'Karađorđe, on the day of Andrew the First-Called (in the year [1]806), with the Serb nation harried the Turks and entered the city of Belgrade as victor. And his son Aleksandar, Prince of Serbia, collected the representatives of the people on the day of Andrew the First-Called (in the year [1]858), then fled from them to that city of the Turks and there sought their protection. What a strange game is the destiny of man!'[23] This marked virtually the last occasion on which the defeated party in an internal Serbian power struggle took refuge in the Ottoman citadel, therefore the end of an era.

With Aleksandar's deposition assured, the power struggle commenced in earnest between Garašanin's Constitutionalists and the liberal–Obrenovićite party. Aleksandar's flight to Ottoman protection left the army in interior minister Garašanin's hands. But Garašanin's very act of handing Aleksandar over to the Ottoman garrison, though it discredited the prince, appeared unpatriotic and inspired further liberal contempt for him and the Constitutionalists. The Sultan wrote to the vizier in Belgrade, indicating his wish that the Council elect a regency of three kajmakams (Ottoman regents), pending the election of a new prince, which threatened to leave power in Garašanin's hands.²⁴ Aleksandar himself viewed the Constitutionalists as his principal enemy, and wrote to the guaranteeing powers, claiming they were 'seeking to place a third dynasty on the throne, which I shall never permit, even at the cost of my own life', so 'I shall recognise the decision of the parliament only if the Obrenovićes, who have been princes of Serbia, are brought back to the throne and if the guaranteeing powers permit their return, otherwise never'.²⁵

To pre-empt the danger of an Ottoman-backed Constitutionalist regency, the parliament, controlled by the liberal–Obrenovićite party under Grujić's leadership and with Aleksandar's tacit approval, on 23 December combined Aleksandar's deposition and Miloš's restoration in a single act, assumed authority as regent itself, transferred command of the army and police to Mihailović and broadcast its decisions to the populace outside, to produce a fait accompli. Mihailović's assistant Alimpić was placed in charge of the army and his other assistant Jovan Belimarković in charge of the police. Belimarković was a member of the Baba-Dudić family, named after its matriarch Baba (Granny) Duda, whose husband Risto Jovanović had been elected kmet of the Belgrade municipality with Miloš's blessing in 1836.²⁶ The Baba-Dudić family would become the Liberal party's backbone. Garašanin, however, as minister of war and of the interior, retained control over the army and police, while the loyalties of the officer corps remained with Aleksandar and the Karađorđević dynasty. The parliament had assumed sovereign power and abrogated the constitutional rights of the Council, whose consent was legally required to depose the old prince. The Council consequently sent a delegation under Vučić-Perišić and Garašanin to the parliament in an attempt to reassert its authority; when the parliament refused to be cowed by it, the Council ceased to be a leading factor in the power struggle. Mihailović then attempted to take control of Belgrade's garrison and police, but Garašanin refused to surrender them. The liberal–Obrenovićite party therefore mobilised a crowd to defend the parliament from a possible military coup but negotiated a retreat, whereby it would hand over the regency to a triumvirate comprising Mihailović, Garašanin and a third person.

Rumours circulated that Aleksandar's supporters had mobilised sizeable militias and were planning a massacre of their leading opponents reminiscent of the deys' 'chopping of the knezes', though they actually had few armed men.²⁷ Nevertheless, at this point, councillors Antonije Majstorović and Ranko Matejić, diehard supporters of Aleksandar, attempted to stage a coup and restore him. At their instigation, Colonel Jovan Lukavčević, chief of general staff (and one of the military rebels who had overthrown Mihailo in 1842), backed by Kosta Nenadović, chief of artillery and Milivoje Petrović Blaznavac, chief of the military department at the interior ministry, attempted on 24 December to deploy his troops to this end. The putschists appealed to the Council to join them in the garrison, and eleven out of seventeen Council members did so. The Council, repenting of the revolution it had unleashed, now backtracked and sought Aleksandar's restoration, while Lukavčević's Karađorđevićite troops marched on the parliament to confront the Obrenovićite crowd defending it. Serbia stood on the threshold of civil war, with the soldiers crying, 'Long live Prince Aleksandar!' and the crowd outside the parliament crying, 'Long live Prince Miloš!' But the unwillingness of Lukavčević, restrained by Garašanin, to permit his troops to fire on the crowd prevented its outbreak. A subsequent attempt by Majstorović and Matejić with a column of soldiers to break out of the garrison and reach Aleksandar was blocked by the crowds and the two councillors were taken into custody. The parliament's inability to commandeer the army compelled it to respect the transfer of power to the three-man regency comprising Garašanin, Mihailović and Jeftimije Ugričić, president of the court of cassation, while the Council and army leaders now accepted the change of prince and the parliament's decisions.[28] Meanwhile, Aleksandar formally remained prince in the eyes of the Porte and the Great Powers until 2 January 1859 when, still under the vizier's protection, he signed a decree of abdication that the Austrian consul had drafted, handed it over to the Porte's envoy, then placed himself under Austria's protection, crossing the river to Zemun the following day. Only after that, on 14 January, did the Porte confirm Miloš's election.[29]

This abortive armed confrontation before the parliament was the most significant clash since Đak's 1825 rebellion between the new Serbia of the army and bureaucracy and the old Serbia of the 'people'. The 'people' was at this time led by liberals and Obrenovićite populists, but of the two mismatched allied factions, it was the latter that would dominate, as the educated constituency in Serbia favouring liberal reforms was small and the liberals themselves were committed to populist anti-bureaucratic measures that merely laid the basis for a restored Obrenovićite absolutism. The Obrenovićites were conservative populists who favoured a benevolent despotism under Miloš as the best guarantor against the tyranny of oligarchs and bureaucrats; the old prince was remembered fondly as having kept these in their place, while being simultaneously a man of the people who was not afraid to appear before popular assemblies.[30] Serbian politics had divided into two parties: the elitist Conservatives who dominated the Council and upheld the bureaucratic authoritarianism of the Constitutionalist order; and the Liberal–Obrenovićite party, the strongest faction in the parliament, which upheld the principle of parliamentary sovereignty. The contest between the two was exploited by the returning Miloš to ensure the defeat of both Conservatives and Liberals and the re-establishment of his autocracy.

A new law on parliaments was passed by the Council on 17 January 1859, only after it had been watered down by Garašanin so that it lost most of the powers granted in the draft composed by the Liberal-controlled St Andrew's Day parliament. Thus, parliament was to meet only triennially, not annually; it would comprise only one elected deputy for every 1,000 taxpayers instead of every 500; it would not have budgetary control but would merely be consulted over new taxes; it would have no right to change laws, merely to be consulted over their change; it would have no right to repeal laws, merely to suggest their repeal to the Council; and it would have no right to prosecute ministers. It was thus effectively reduced from a legislative to an advisory body. Under pressure from the dissatisfied parliament and Liberals, Mihailović issued a new law on parliaments on 26 January that made minor changes to the previous law, above all increasing the number of deputies back to one for every 500 taxpayers, but this was reversed by Miloš in his law on parliaments of 11 August of the following year, which restored the ratio of one per 1,000.[31] The Liberals, meanwhile, along with other supporters of the new order, sought a purge of the bureaucracy to satisfy popular anti-state feeling, eliminate the problem of a state apparatus loyal to the previous regime and free up jobs in state employment for themselves and their followers. This wish Miloš was, to an extent, ready to grant.

Second reign of Prince Miloš

Prince Miloš's second reign marked a return to his populist autocracy. Following the Porte's confirmation of his election, he dismissed the three-man regency and vested sole power in the hands of Mihailović as his placeholder, pending his own return to Serbia. In the weeks following his formal reinstatement, his 600-strong paid militia under Filip Stanković exercised control in Belgrade, coercing even regent Garašanin and contributing to his decision to resign from government on 21 January and retreat to the Council.[32] In these days, Garašanin met with Grujić, who told him, 'You cannot say anything against the way it was done. The Obrenovićes had to be.' Garašanin complained: 'After all, if you really wanted it that way, why didn't you at least pick Prince Mihailo?' When Grujić replied, 'That could not have been; the people wanted the old man,' Garašanin responded, 'It could very much have been, if only you had been willing to agree. You don't know Prince Miloš, but you will see.'[33] As regent, Garašanin had temporarily been able to prevent the purge of the bureaucracy. But under Mihailović's provisional government, the Liberals launched a purge of the old regime's representatives: ministers, councillors, Austrian Serbs and bureaucrats generally.

Janković declared to parliament on 24 January the need to purge 'enemies of the Serb nation and the Obrenović dynasty', after which parliament voted to dismiss assistant interior minister Atanasije Nikolić, assistant justice minister Jakov Ivanović, court of cassation member Timotije Knežević and Artillery School director František Zach. The first three were Austrian Serbs and the fourth Czech; they were declared 'sworn, bloody malefactors to the people' and all but Ivanović were expelled from the country. Nikolić had been a Constitutionalist pioneer of agricultural modernisation responsible for establishing St Sava's Day, 27 January, as a school holiday in Serbia. Metropolitan Petar was coerced into resigning; he was another Austrian Serb, a personal enemy of Miloš's and was disliked by younger priests trained in Russian seminaries. The new metropolitan, Mihailo, was born in Zaječar in eastern Serbia. Petar's resignation was followed by that of Council president Vučić-Perišić.

Parliament declared on 31 January 1859 that 'the Serb people, truly, neither had nor has confidence in the Council members or the ministers, who are therefore no longer permitted to determine the national destiny'.[34] It voted the same day to deprive officials of security and undertake a general purge, dismissing all ministers and councillors as well as those bureaucrats deemed unworthy, on the grounds that 'the nation is not there for the sake of bureaucrats and officials, but officials and bureaucrats for the nation'.[35]

Miloš supported the purge and threatened those opposing it. Parliament, emboldened by his support, voted two days later to introduce annual elections for village and municipal kmets and to place municipalities under the administration of municipal assemblies alongside the kmets, thus promoting the core principle of nineteenth-century Serbian populism: self-management in the countryside.[36] The Liberals' purge of these officials amounted to a revolution of the new educated generation from Serbia against the Austrian Serbs who had dominated the first stage of the Serbian state's development. This was made possible by the great expansion of the school system under the Constitutionalists, which obviated the need to import educated Serbs from abroad. Whereas in 1836 there had been only 72 elementary schools, 3 gymnasiums and a theological seminary in Serbia, by 1855 there were 330 educational establishments, including 300 elementary schools for boys, 13 for girls, a lycée, a gymnasium, 3 high schools, a school of commerce, an Artillery School and an agricultural school. Whereas in 1836 most elementary schools were either supported by local communes or privately, by 1857 the central government had taken them over entirely. Nevertheless, at this time, roughly two-thirds of Serbia's 1,158 municipalities still had no schools at all, and the peasantry still resisted sending children to them.[37]

Travelling from Wallachia via eastern Serbia, Miloš returned on 6 February 1859 to Belgrade, where the populace welcomed him rapturously with flags, wreaths, flowers and cheers. He first visited the cathedral, where he was greeted by the entire parliament. As with Prince Aleksandar's appointment seventeen years before, the Sultan's decree was read out at Kalemegdan, in the presence of the vizier, high Ottoman and Serbian officials, Serbian parliamentary deputies and a crowd of commoners. The road to Kalemegdan went past Vučić-Perišić's house. As Miloš was afraid of being attacked by him, he took the precaution of stationing a guard around it, ordered to shoot him if he appeared at the window or entrance. Following the ceremony, Miloš received the church's blessing before arriving at the royal palace.[38] His first acts as ruler were to dismiss the St Andrew's Day parliament and appoint a government under Stevan Magazinović, composed of his old, trusted supporters. He reconstituted the government and Council with his own appointees, some of whom had served under the Constitutionalist regime. After Magazinović, he appointed as prime minister Cvetko Rajović, an elderly Obrenović loyalist who had served as secretary of his chancellery during his first reign. Miloš subdued the bureaucratic elite by appealing directly to the people, winning popular support through a nationwide investigation into abuses by, and purge of, local officials—foreshadowing, in some ways, Slobodan Milošević's 'anti-bureaucratic revolution' 130 years later. A law was passed on 27 April establishing four grand commissions to investigate abuses by officials throughout the country, after which the perpetrators would be tried by a special court. This triggered an outpouring of complaints by peasants, directed in particular against kmets and priests and focusing on municipal corruption and abuse.

Following parliamentary elections on 21 August 1859, Miloš summoned on 21 September the first parliament on the basis of the new law on parliaments, known as the Nativity of Mary's Day parliament, at his traditional base of Kragujevac. One of his first moves, in response to petitioning from Belgrade's Jewish community, was to attempt to rescind the Constitutionalist regime's anti-Jewish legislation. However, parliament opposed this, voting on 1 October to uphold the ban on Jews residing or trading outside Belgrade. The Council sought to mobilise the government in support of the ban. Miloš would not retreat, however, and on 9 October issued a Decree on the Equality of the Citizenry, with the aim 'that no Serbian subject, of whatever religion or nationality, shall be restricted in the practice of every kind of business or profession'. It reversed the Constitutionalists' anti-Jewish decree of 1846, permitting Jews once again to reside in Serbia's interior, which they soon did. In this, at least, Miloš was ready to defy both public and elite opinion. The Jewish share of Belgrade's population rose from 7 to 10 per cent during his short second reign and the first Jewish municipality in the country outside Belgrade was established at Šabac.[39]

Parliamentary deputies presented a list of 138 names of higher and lower officials whose removal was demanded, though this was executed only partially, primarily in the interior and justice ministries. Several hundred officials from all ranks ultimately lost their jobs, in violation of the constitution guaranteeing their security of tenure. The uniforms that non-military state employees had previously worn were simplified and made plainer. Their titles—originally copied from their Russian counterparts—were abolished; they were henceforth to be addressed merely as 'Mr Councillor' or 'Mr Clerk'. Bureaucrats were banned from becoming parliamentary deputies. The salaries of all but the lowest-paid were cut.[40] New bureaucrats were appointed from among those the new regime favoured: supporters of the Obrenović dynasty and Liberals. Thus, the emergence of two distinct political factions, Conservatives (supporters of the former Constitutionalist regime) and Liberals (supporters of the 1858–1859 revolution), also reflected the division between winners and losers in the turnover of bureaucratic office.

Miloš's populist assault on the bureaucracy and other institutions of the Constitutionalist regime and the restoration of his autocracy were justified on patriotic grounds. He was aware Aleksandar had fallen partly owing to accusations that he had betrayed the national cause by harnessing his regime to the Ottoman and Austrian empires, and that he, Miloš, needed to pre-empt similar accusations.[41] Furthermore, he sought to harness the nationalist enthusiasm unleashed by the overthrow of the Turcophile Constitutionalist regime. The Nativity of Mary's Day parliament noted on 30 September that state councillors, directly protected by the Porte according to Article 17 of the constitution, are 'prosecuted for crimes differently than all other Serbs, which is contrary to the principle of equality before the law'. It then submitted an address to Miloš, stating that 'the current constitution, which was not granted on the basis of agreement between the Serbian ruler and his people, is not in accordance with a true internally independent administration' and that 'the same Constitution is, because of Article 17, dangerous for the internal independence and peace of the country'; consequently, 'it is the wish of the Serb people that the current Constitution be replaced by a different one, in the spirit of the people and suitable for the country's needs'. The parliament also requested the government to lobby the Great Powers to exempt Serbia, given its autonomy, from any customs treaties made by the Porte without its agreement.[42]

Miloš was not in a position to act on the last demand, but he did seek unsuccessfully both to revoke the constitution, on the grounds that it permitted Turkish control of Serbian affairs, and to convert Serbia from an elected to a hereditary principality under his dynasty, on the grounds that an elected prince would have to be approved by the Porte, similarly giving it a degree of control over Serbia's internal affairs. He also agitated for the removal of the Ottoman troops and Muslim civilians from Serbia's towns, which had been halted following his overthrow in 1839. He disregarded the constitution to dismiss the Council and replace it with one comprising his own nominees, largely veteran notables from his earlier reign. He selected his ministers from outside the Council, so they were wholly dependent upon his patronage. Thus, both Council and government were reduced to his tools. In a small step towards Serbia's full independence, he changed the oath of office for incoming councillors so that they were now required to pledge allegiance only to the prince, no longer to the Sultan.

Miloš expanded the national militia, standing army and gendarmerie. The standing army inherited from the Constitutionalist regime numbered only 2,529 soldiers, many of whom were absent and only about 1,500 actually resident in the garrisons. Miloš in March 1859 transferred it from the interior ministry's jurisdiction to the general staff, thereby definitely separating the army from the police. The following month, he established the General Military Administration by means of which the military would be exclusively under the prince's control. The Belgrade police was likewise removed from the interior ministry's authority and placed under his direct control. His decree of June 1860 stated that the duty of 'the army is the defence of fatherland and support of the legal order'; consequently, 'for the security of the country, the army will be reorganised. It will consist of the standing army and national militia'. The size of the standing army was raised to 3,529 soldiers.[43]

Miloš had entertained expansionist ideas during his first reign but given priority to collaboration with the Ottomans and securing his own rule and dynasty. But his

THE NATIONAL LIBERATION STRUGGLE RESUMES

travels in Europe during his years in exile, in which he had witnessed and dabbled in the revolutionary events of 1848, had turned him into a nationalist. In a fiery speech in November 1859 before the parliament at Kragujevac, he lamented the fact that for so many years since the liberation of Serbia nothing had been done to extend its borders, asserting that now was a favourable time for this. When the deputies responded with overwhelming enthusiasm, he stated that his aim was to unify the Serbs of Austria and inhabitants of Bulgaria, Hercegovina and Bosnia with his principality. This was to begin with a raid into Bosnia near Zvornik, followed by further operations 'against Turkish and Austrian Croatia'. Miloš envisaged a major invasion of Bosnia combined with a general uprising in the province and a Montenegrin invasion of Hercegovina.[44] Armed Serb bands began to make incursions across the border into Ottoman-controlled territory.

Incidents involving Serbs and Turks in Belgrade became more common: Serbian gendarmes and Ottoman soldiers clashed at the Great Piazza in July 1860, when a hodja (Muslim cleric) was stoned by Serb children. A quarrel at the Little Piazza in August 1860 allegedly began when a Serb at a Turkish cafe offered a Turk a coffee and, when the latter responded rudely, slapped him; it grew into an armed fight involving dozens of Turks armed with pistols and Serbs armed with daggers and staves, in which a number of the heavily outnumbered Turks were beaten up and thrown into the Sava, after which enraged Serbs carried out a pogrom of local Turks, leaving several dead. Hristić, governor of Belgrade, deployed police to quell the riot and rescue the Turks, but the vizier nevertheless held him and his police responsible, resulting in a confrontation between the two before the consuls of the Great Powers, who failed to support the vizier. Hristić reported that the city was preparing itself for a bombardment and massacre by the Ottoman garrison—presaging the bombardment that actually occurred two years later.[45]

Miloš presented himself as father of the nation. He passed a series of populist 'reforms' aimed at bolstering his support among the peasant masses. These accelerated the workings of the notoriously slow law courts, greatly improved the legal position of peasant debtors at the expense of usurers, abolished forestry taxes so as to enable peasants to exploit the national forests for the payment of only a nominal fee, and made less onerous the requirement that municipalities maintain grain stockpiles at their own expense to deal with food shortages.[46] But he also dealt harshly with opponents. Vučić-Perišić, the Obrenović dynasty's arch-foe, was unscrupulously singled out for elimination. Having barricaded himself in his fortress-like house, he seemed impervious, so Belgrade's governor Belimarković had his three servants kidnapped in order to starve him out. Miloš then enlisted his militia leader, Stanković, an old friend of Vučić-Perišić's, to trick him into leaving his house on the promise of a reconciliation with the prince, after which he was arrested.[47] Parliament demanded Vučić-Perišić's punishment, but there was no law by which he could be tried. Miloš therefore established a special commission which interrogated him but did not bring him before a court. Instead, he was illegally detained in a military hospital and his property confiscated, to be distributed to his supposed victims from Obrenovićite ranks. This provoked interventions on his behalf from the Porte and Great Powers until he died on 13 July 1859. Miloš was suspected of having him poisoned; he refused the Porte's demand for an autopsy on the grounds that this would constitute interference in Serbia's 'internal affairs'.[48]

Only Vučić-Perišić was assassinated, but other opponents of Miloš including Garašanin, Anastasijević and Metropolitan Petar were forced to take refugee abroad, while Blaznavac was internally exiled to his native village, Blaznava. Miloš could not, however, simply order opponents killed as he had been during his first reign, but was forced to persecute them within the bounds of the law. He arrested several of Aleksandar's relatives and close supporters on 12 July, claiming they were plotting his and Mihailo's assassination: former councillors Jeremija Stanojević, Antonije Majstorović, Aleksandar Nenadović, Gaja Jeremić and Lazar Arsenijević, as well as Atanasije Nenadović, a member of the court of cassation; Jakov Stanojević, a former assistant of the Belgrade district office; and Jovan Marić, a fencing master and the supposed intended assassin. They were eventually released by the courts owing to lack of evidence, but Miloš continued to threaten both them and the judges who had ordered their release. Fearing for their lives, Jeremija and Jakov Stanojević, Antonije Majstorović and Aleksandar Nenadović fled on 15 September to Kalemegdan for protection.[49]

The inherent tension between Miloš and the Liberals inevitably came to a head, for the latter wanted the former to behave as a constitutional ruler on the basis of their advice, while the former wanted the latter to behave as docile supporters of his regime and dynasty. Following the parliamentary elections of 21 August, Miloš instructed the authorities to nullify the elections of all bureaucrats as a strike against the elected Liberal deputies, who were all themselves bureaucrats.[50] Thus, his anti-bureaucratic revolution moved on from purging Conservative office-holders to attacking the political power of Liberal-activist office-holders. Miloš vetoed the election of Grujić and Janković as secretaries of the Nativity of Mary's Day parliament; instead, Živko Karabiberović was elected president and Pantelija Jovanović secretary. Both were also Liberals and, along with Belimarković, represented the three branches of the Baba-Dudić family. But they were less politically experienced or ideologically motivated, hence less dangerous than Grujić or Janković.[51] Todor Tucaković was elected vice-president. This parliament therefore marked a further step in the coalescence of the Obrenovićites into the bedrock of the new Liberal party, with the Baba-Dudić family as its backbone and men like Pantelija Jovanović and Tucaković as its stalwarts. Yet the heads of the dynasty themselves were not behind it.

At this time, the Serbian state newspaper, *Srbske novine*, began publishing a series of attacks on the Liberals—the so-called ducat articles, secretly written by Matija Ban with input from others, above all the ambitious young functionary Jovan Ristić,

THE NATIONAL LIBERATION STRUGGLE RESUMES

who had been Aleksandar's police chief. These articles were signed only with the ducat symbol (#); consequently, the Conservatives at this time referred to themselves as the 'ducatists'. They were instigated by Mihailo Obrenović, who was preparing to succeed his father as prince on the basis of rule in alliance with the Conservatives, whose nascent ideology the ducat articles articulated. Meanwhile, Miloš continued to balance Conservatives and Liberals, and in November 1859 replaced *Srbske novine*'s Conservative editor with Vladimir Jovanović, to enable the Liberal intellectual to respond to the paper's earlier attacks. But the reprieve was only temporary; in January 1860 and continuing over the coming months, Miloš dismissed several prominent Liberal intellectuals from state and government service, including Grujić, Janković, Alimpić, Dimitrije Matić and Stojan Bošković.

Jovanović's tenure as *Srbske novine*'s editor was short-lived and he was exiled from Belgrade. By his own account, he fell victim to Miloš's traditional policy of balancing national affirmation with collaboration with the Ottomans. A Constantinople newspaper had published an article challenging the Obrenović dynasty's right to the throne, and, with the agreement of Miloš and his court, *Srbske novine* had responded with a fiery patriotic editorial affirming that the dynasty's hereditary right had been 'achieved with hand on pistol, and with hand on pistol it will be defended'. The vizier of Belgrade immediately protested to Miloš, who opted to place the newspaper again under the censor as a concession to the vizier, prompting Jovanović to resign.[52] Miloš had not forgotten how to use the Ottomans to dispose of domestic troublemakers. By spring 1860 he was again seeking to mend fences with the Porte, to gain its approval for restoration of his dynasty's hereditary status and for constitutional changes to restore his absolutism. This exacerbated his dissatisfaction with the Liberals, who had been generally inclining toward Russia for nationalistic reasons and, in some cases, intriguing with Russia's consul.[53]

The Obrenović regime had by this time gathered around itself many of the now tamed Conservatives and former Constitutionalist regime officials, including Ban, Marinović, Ristić, Nikola Hristić, Filip Hristić and Kosta Cukić. Some of these were Austrian Serbs, including Ban and Nikola Hristić, while Marinović was from Bosnia. Yet Miloš retained also his alliance with the Liberal party, if not the Liberal intelligentsia, on account of its Obrenovićite dynastic loyalty and popular support; thus Metropolitan Mihailo and Council president Mihailović, both Liberals, retained their positions. Garašanin, the Liberals and Miloš's supporters had combined to topple Aleksandar and restore Miloš; Miloš, his supporters and the Liberals had then combined to defeat Garašanin; and Miloš had then purged the Liberals to restore his autocracy, unchallenged at the time of his death on 26 September 1860. Far from introducing a liberal constitutional order, the Liberals' revolutionary actions in 1858–1860 had merely laid the basis for a more arbitrary and tyrannical regime than the one they had overthrown, with Conservatives and Liberals vying for the prince's favour.

SERBIA

Prince Mihailo's domestic counter-revolution

With Miloš's death on 26 September 1860, power passed for the second time to Prince Mihailo. Since his exile in 1842, Mihailo had lived in Austria, particularly in Vienna, where he had married the Catholic Hungarian noblewoman Júlia Hunyady de Kéthely. He had travelled throughout Europe and learned to speak French and German and, like his father, imbibed the European zeitgeist to become a convinced nationalist. His regime represented a synthesis of his father's personal autocracy and Prince Aleksandar and the Constitutionalists' bureaucratic elitism. He considered himself an enlightened despot standing above party divisions and representing the nation as a whole. Aleksandar had been merely first among equals in the ruling oligarchy, whereas Mihailo's reign marked the full institutionalisation of a monarchy along Central European lines in which the monarch's person was presented as supreme and distinct, with a corresponding court, ceremony and forms of deference. Mihailo was the first modern Serbian ruler who styled himself as ruling not merely by the will of the people but 'by the grace of God'. Whereas Aleksandar's royal residence had simply been a stately home slightly more grand than those of the ministers and councillors, Mihailo's was a copy of European royal palaces.[54] When the Sultan issued a berat confirming Mihailo's accession, it was not read out according to the traditional Ottoman ceremony at the field of Kalemegdan in the presence of the Ottoman and Serbian armies, but on Mihailo's initiative only at the prince's palace, in the presence of the Sultan's envoy, the city's Ottoman warden and senior Serbian officials, though he still pledged 'that I will not cease to express my feelings of loyalty and commitment towards my supreme suzerain the Sultan, nor will I cease to rule as a Prince who firmly safeguards the rights and institutions of the nation'.[55]

Mihailo sought to reconcile not only Conservatives and Liberals but also the Obrenović and Karađorđević dynasties and their supporters. He took sincere steps to rehabilitate and provide restitution to the Karađorđevićites and bureaucrats who had been exiled or purged during his father's reign. In his accession speech, written under the guidance of Karadžić, whose influence was now at its peak, Mihailo pledged his government would, 'scorning revenge and persecution, gather around it all who love their Fatherland and desire its progress'. In 'pardoning them every political fault and forgetting all political transgressions, I summon each and every one to put themselves under the protection of the Laws of the Fatherland', since 'while Prince Mihailo is ruling, let everyone know: that the Law is the highest will in Serbia, to which everyone without distinction must submit.'[56] Hence, a pillar of his regime would be Garašanin, whose father and brother Mihailo's forces had decapitated in 1842; another would be Nikola Hristić, husband of Vučić-Perišić's granddaughter, who had assisted Vučić-Perišić in suppressing the Hussar Rebellion; a third would be Kosta Cukić, whose grandfathers Pavle Cukić and Moler were both killed by, or at the instigation of, Mihailo's father.

THE NATIONAL LIBERATION STRUGGLE RESUMES

Mihailo used the 1858 revolution's momentum to entrench his autocracy under the banner of national unity and liberation. The government he appointed on 9 November 1860, again acting largely on Karadžić's advice, was headed by the court politician and former Karađorđević favourite Filip Hristić, while Karadžić's Liberal admirer Grujić was justice minister and the non-party but decidedly authoritarian Nikola Hristić interior minister.[57] Thus, the old Constitutionalist–Conservative officials had predominance, reflecting Mihailo's preference. The press was censored and tightly controlled and all oppositional political activity suppressed. As Benjamin von Kállay, Austria-Hungary's consul-general in Belgrade, commented in his diary: 'Minister Hristić manages internal affairs with an iron fist and has created an amazing system of espionage so that no one is allowed to speak freely or criticise any action of the government.'[58] The attempt of the liberals Vladimir Jovanović, Bošković and Janković to gain permission to publish a newspaper, *Narodna Skupština* [National Parliament], was rejected on the basis of a 1842 law banning officials from debating government decrees. Their attempt to appeal against this ban resulted in their arrest, imprisonment and trial in April 1861.

Mihailo's regime reversed Miloš's emancipation of the Jews and reverted to the Constitutionalists' anti-Semitic measures. Immediately following the old prince's death, the Council had rescinded his decree permitting Jews to live and trade where they wished. In February 1861, under pressure from Serb merchants and a section of the press, the Council ordered the expulsion of 60 Jewish families from Serbia's interior, though following protests from Britain and other European countries Mihailo refrained from implementing this outright. Under pressure from the merchant community and from Metropolitan Mihailo supported by Russia, the prince on 4 November 1861 ratified parliament's ban on Jews opening shops or owning property in the interior, with limited exemptions for those who had already done so on the basis of Miloš's decree of emancipation. He then resisted pressure from Britain, France, Austria, Prussia and Italy to repeal the ban. Conditions became harder for the Jews; anti-Jewish feeling was particularly strong in Šabac, a border town on the Sava with a strong transit trade and powerful community of merchants and craftsmen. A local Jewish merchant was murdered on 16 January 1865, as was a Bosnian Jew a week later; the local authorities tried to cover up the first of these murders, though this was prevented by the intervention of the international Jewish organisation Alliance Israélite Universelle and of the consuls of the Great Powers. A Jewish girl in the town was forcibly baptised into Orthodoxy three months later, prompting the British, Italian and Ottoman governments to protest and Šabac's Jewish community eventually to appeal to Britain's government for protection and to consider emigrating to Palestine. Mihailo consequently suspended again the expulsion of the Jews from the interior. Nevertheless, Jewish numbers in the interior dropped to thirty families by the time of his death in 1868, of which twenty were in Šabac, while their share of the Belgrade population fell to under 5 per cent, down from 10 per cent at the time of his accession.[59]

SERBIA

Transfiguration Day parliament

Following the appointment of the Filip Hristić government, Nikola Hristić was charged with arranging elections for a parliament to endorse Mihailo's projected laws. In this and subsequent elections, police manipulation ensured a government majority. Ministers now attended all parliamentary sessions to monitor the proceedings. Deputies were deprived of all immunity and could now be tried for sedition in the regular courts, thus neutering their ability to oppose the government. Parliamentary sessions were short and tightly managed. There was consequently little popular interest in the parliament's proceedings and low turnout for elections.[60] Mihailo similarly continued his father's anti-bureaucratic policy by depriving bureaucrats of their security of tenure; his first law on the bureaucracy of 5 April 1861 granted the government the right to pension off any bureaucrat who had earned the right to a pension.

Parliament convened on 18 August 1861 (6 August in the Julian calendar—hence known as the Transfiguration Day parliament) once again in Kragujevac, at the country's geographical centre. This was allegedly to maximise accessibility for the deputies but probably to isolate them from the Belgrade public. The public was kept out of the parliament to prevent it influencing the proceedings; deputies were expected to rubber-stamp decisions already taken. Nevertheless, the Liberals attempted to advance their candidates and agenda in opposition to what they saw as the Conservative old guard in government. Ristić, then associated with the Conservatives, became secretary of the parliament. However, the young Liberal Tucaković was victorious in Kragujevac in opposition to Ristić's friend, the pro-government candidate Pavle Radovanović. Tucaković assumed the position of president of the parliament, where he tried unsuccessfully to advance a law on press freedom. According to Nikola Hristić's recollection, the parliament witnessed hostile agitation on the part of a Liberal opposition led by Mihailović and Belimarković, which accused the government of being hostile to the dynasty. It agitated for restoration of the 1858 law on parliaments and for the prince to act in accordance with parliament's wishes. The government counter-attacked; Tucaković was forced to resign his post after only three days and was replaced by the government's candidate, while Hristić attempted unsuccessfully to prosecute Belimarković and some of his comrades.[61]

Facing down the Liberals and his own traditional dynastic supporters, in alliance with the Conservatives, 'Prince Mihailo carried out a true counter-revolution against the St Andrew's parliament', in the words of historian and sometime Liberal politician Živan Živanović.[62] Mihailo's law on national parliaments of 29 August 1861 determined that deputies would be elected by every 2,000 taxpayers, rather than 1,000 as under Miloš, or 500 as decreed by the St Andrew's Day parliament. This reduced the number of deputies to about 120, making parliament far more manageable than the mass body favoured by the St Andrew's Day liberals; Mihailo justified this on the grounds that 'the nation itself was burdened by the disproportionately large number of parliamentarians relative to our small fatherland'. Parliament was still to meet every three years but was no longer required to meet in the capital, instead meeting wherever the prince chose. Parliament's officials—president, vice-president, secretaries—were no longer elected by it but appointed by the prince, who had the right to dismiss them. The law also affirmed the institution of 'great national parliament': four times larger than an ordinary parliament and elected where necessary to select a prince, confirm the heir to the throne or establish a regency if the new prince was a minor.[63]

Parliament would remain a purely advisory body serving as a safe outlet for airing popular grievances and concerns; with officials excluded from membership, the limited education of the mostly peasant deputies restricted their ability to articulate political opposition. Mihailo once remarked to a parliamentary deputy: 'Did you notice how many crosses there were on the address that you submitted to me? So long as the parliamentarians don't even know how to sign their own names, by God, you young people are fruitlessly rushing to proclaim great freedom!' Another time he observed: 'I can on my fingers count all the European-educated people in my country; there are not more than ten or twelve of them. The institutions of a country are not made for the twelve most educated people; they must correspond to the average level of the people. To grant parliamentarism just so that Milovan Janković and a few others like him can give parliamentary speeches—that would be unserious.'[64]

Mihailo continued his father's policy of combining autocracy with pursuit of national independence by seeking to overturn the Turkish Constitution of 1838 and replace it with one both authentically Serbian and supportive of his autocracy. Since, however, the Porte insisted that it alone could promulgate a new constitution for Serbia, Mihailo was forced to accept a compromise, whereby the 1838 constitution would formally remain but he was permitted to pass laws that changed it in practice. His law on the Council of 29 August 1861 demoted state councillors to the status of regular bureaucrats. They lost their independence from the prince, were appointed solely by him without the Council's agreement, and could be removed by him and tried before regular courts. The Council thereby lost its role as constitutional safeguard limiting princely authority. Mihailo's Council was, furthermore, dominated by ageing Obrenovićite placemen appointed by Miloš who were wholly unable or unwilling to restrain him.[65] An amendment to the Law on the Succession to the Throne, also on 29 August, gave the prince the right to name his successor, thereby finally ending the Porte's interference in this regard.

Serbia had possessed, since Miloš's reign, armed forces based on two wings. The principality had arisen as a nation-in-arms based on the territorial government of nahijas, knežinas and knezes through which the First and Second Serbian Uprisings had been organised. This structure remained as a residual national militia. A regular or standing army had then been established, prompted by Đak's rebellion and the need to suppress internal disorder. Mihailo passed a law on 29 August 1861 introducing compulsory military service in the newly institutionalised national militia 'assembled from all Serbs without distinction' aged between 20 and 50. They were not to be housed in garrisons but trained in their home municipalities, districts and okrugs on Sundays and holidays to accommodate peasant life conditions. This militia was to be developed alongside the standing army, which it was intended to supersede as the state's principal military force. It was organised into seventeen units each of infantry, cavalry and engineers, corresponding to Serbia's seventeen okrugs, plus six batteries of cannon. Although supposed to embody the principle of the nation-in-arms, in practice its soldiers were treated differently according to class: corporal punishment was used to discipline soldiers of peasant or lower-class background, but those from the 'superior class of citizens' were explicitly spared. Broad categories of state official were quickly freed from the obligation of regular training while the lower bureaucrats were required to serve as NCOs for the peasant recruits.[66] Nevertheless, despite the fact that the national militia was a throwback to a pre-modern, Ottoman-era institution of the raya-in-arms, it accelerated the transformation of peasants into Serbs and into modern Europeans. From 1864, militiamen were required to wear a uniform, including Austrian-style military caps, which they were also allowed to wear at home on special occasions such as weddings and funerals. These represented the first tailored clothes in Serbia worn by the peasantry. Since they were cheaper than traditional homemade clothes, they began the transformation of peasant dress along 'European' (Austrian-influenced) lines.[67]

Having passed the laws needed to cement his autocracy and pursue national liberation, Mihailo dissolved the Transfiguration Day parliament on 1 September, only two weeks after it had convened. As the leading Liberals and Conservatives had proved unable to work together, and Filip Hristić's attempt at cross-party government had failed, Mihailo now opted in favour of the Conservatives, whose competence he respected and whose elitism was closer to his own autocratic outlook than was the Liberals' populism. He consequently completed his domestic counter-revolution by appointing Garašanin, mainstay of the old Constitutionalist regime, as prime minister and foreign minister in October 1861. Mihailović, although he had been a loyal, leading supporter of the dynasty since the 1830s, was dismissed as Council president and replaced by Garašanin's friend and fellow Conservative, Marinović, while the interior ministry remained with Nikola Hristić. Grujić having already been removed from government on the eve of parliament's convening, the last Liberal minister, Jovan Gavrilović, was removed as finance minister in December and replaced by the Conservative Cukić. This new Conservative government rapidly removed the leading Liberals from positions of influence, even driving them into exile or imprisoning them. Karadžić also found his influence at court curtailed by the

Conservative elite, to whose bureaucratic absolutism he was deeply unsympathetic. The discarded former members of the old Obrenovićite party, such as Mihailović and Stanković, consequently turned to an alliance with the exiled Karađorđević dynasty against the regime.[68]

Mihailo developed the institution of government along lines that were becoming the European norm. His law of 22 March 1862 severed the link between Council and ministers so that the former lost all authority over the latter, while the latter were now appointed solely by the prince and did not have to be selected from Council ranks. To the four existing ministerial departments (foreign affairs, internal affairs, justice and finance) were added three more (education, construction and war). The competencies of the interior ministry, which for most of his reign was in the hands of loyal hardliner Nikola Hristić, were thereby greatly reduced. Previously, ministers had been state servants managing their respective departments independently of one another, but now they were organised in a ministerial council or cabinet along European lines, based on the principle of collective responsibility; they would thus collectively decide on the policies to be pursued in each department. Previously, the prince had communicated with the ministers through the foreign minister as a 'prince's representative' or intermediary, but now all ministers stood directly before the prince and the 'prince's representative' was replaced by a president of the ministerial council, thereby formalising the status of prime minister. Ministers were for the first time given absolute authority over the bureaucrats in their respective departments.[69] The prince also sought to increase state control over the church; eventually, on 12 October 1862, Metropolitan Mihailo passed a new church law to this end.

Unlike his father, Mihailo consciously wished to modernise Serbia along European lines. This involved educational reforms. In 1863, Mihailo converted Belgrade's lycée into a proto-university, once again named the Great School, with law, justice and technical faculties. In the same year, the first women's high school was opened. Nineteen-year-old Katarina Đorđević (later Katarina Milovuk) was appointed director; born in Novi Sad in Hungary, she obtained her degree in teaching in Odessa. By that year there were 28 girls' schools accounting for 14 per cent of pupils in Serbia.[70] The ban on Karadžić's orthography having been lifted in 1859, his reformed alphabet and orthography became generally accepted by Serbian authors during the 1860s and officially adopted by the Great School in 1868, giving Serbia its modern literary language. Mihailo also developed the National Library, under the directorship of Karadžić's collaborator Đuro Daničić, who was succeeded by Jan Šafárik; the number of its volumes more than doubled during the 1860s to reach 22,909, up from 800 at the time of its foundation in 1832. The government encouraged also the opening of public libraries in provincial Serbian cities, so that there were 37 by 1870.[71] The first Serbian national coinage was minted in 1867—coppers of low denomination, a first step in replacing the confusing mix of Ottoman,

Austrian, Russian, French and other coins with which the Serbian people had had to deal.[72] Serbia's National Theatre was founded in Belgrade on 12 July 1868, shortly after Mihailo's death, holding its first performance, *Đurad Branković*, in a nearby inn on 22 November and its first on-site performance, commemorating Mihailo, on 30 October 1869.

National liberation 'from above'

Garašanin's Plan chimed with the prince's own foreign policy goals regarding the necessity both for expansion and for independence vis-à-vis Austria and Russia, and the reconciliation of Serbia's conflicting factions was intended to unite the nation behind the pursuit of these patriotic goals. The Liberals were initially attracted by Mihailo's promise to fulfil these goals. Thus, as in Bismarck's contemporaneous Prussia, the premier's pursuit of national unification abroad was spurred by competition with the more overtly nationalistic Liberals while justifying domestic authoritarianism.[73] Inspired by Piedmont's success in uniting Italy under its leadership, Mihailo's policy, conducted in partnership with Garašanin until 1867, marked an escalation of the more cautious strategy for expansionism of the 1844 Plan. Mihailo and his government initially viewed Austria as the principal Great Power opponent of his policy. They endeavoured diplomatically to neutralise it by winning the support of its actual or potential opponents: France, Prussia, Italy and, above all, Russia. Whereas in the 1840s the reactionary Russian government under Tsar Nicholas I had restrained Serbia's expansionism, the more nationalist and imperialist Russia of Alexander II in the 1860s encouraged it, so war and insurrection in the Balkans now meant a pro-Russian course. But while Mihailo understood Russian support was essential to restrain Austria, he did not wish to restore Russia's protectorate over Serbia; as he said in 1859, 'we want to be a free, independent nation, but we know that if we were to free ourselves of dependence upon Turkey with the help of Russia that that would also mean that we would be independent only in name, but in reality would depend upon Russia; in other words, that we would simply have changed masters'.[74]

To avoid Serbia's dependence upon any Great Power, Mihailo sought a broad alliance with other Balkan states and peoples. He broadened Serbia's expansionist goal to include potentially Austria's South Slavic territories as well as Macedonia and the Bulgarian-inhabited lands. Garašanin established a secret Serbian Committee in early 1862 tasked with promoting insurrection in the Ottoman lands. Council member Lazar Arsenijević-Batalaka was made its director, assisted by Zach and Atanasije Nikolić. It developed links with insurrectionary groups in Bosnia, Hercegovina and Bulgaria, aiming at a general Balkan anti-Ottoman uprising intended to achieve Serbia's annexation of Bosnia, Hercegovina and part of Macedonia and its union with Bulgaria. Bulgarian representatives were induced

THE NATIONAL LIBERATION STRUGGLE RESUMES

to declare for a Serbo-Bulgarian union under Mihailo as prince, involving a merger of the Bulgarian and Serbian churches.[75] This programme aimed to embrace Croats, Muslim Bosniaks and Albanians. Mihailo approached Montenegro, itself increasingly active in Balkan affairs. In 1858, after a major victory over the Ottomans at the Battle of Grahovac, its previously vague borders were enlarged and clearly delineated by the Great Powers' intercession at Constantinople—a milestone in its road to statehood. Danilo I was assassinated in 1860 and succeeded by Prince Nikola I (r. 1860–1918), whose support for an anti-Ottoman rebellion in Hercegovina in 1861 provoked the Ottomans to war with Montenegro. Nikola was heavily defeated in battle by the brilliant Ottoman commander Omar Pasha Latas in 1862 and forced to acknowledge Ottoman sovereignty. This experience converted Nikola into a firm believer in Montenegrin emancipation through liberation and unification of the entire Serb people, and he and Mihailo drew increasingly close. Meanwhile, according to a draft Serbo-Greek convention of 1861, the 'Serb Kingdom' would encompass the existing Principality of Serbia plus Bosnia, Hercegovina and Upper Albania, as well as Montenegro if it acquiesced, while Greece would receive Thessaly, Epirus, Macedonia, Thrace and the Aegean islands.

Mihailo restored the military administrators that Serbia had had under the Constitutionalists. Zach was reappointed director of the Artillery School; Blaznavac, trained at an artillery school in France, was appointed director of the Kragujevac armaments factory; and Mondain was in October 1861 appointed chief of the General Military Administration, with ministerial rank.[76] The General Military Administration became the war ministry in March 1862 and Mondain the first war minister. Zach was also directly involved in training the new army. However, the project's scale was such that it was beyond the existing military administration's capacity, so it relied on the police to provide the necessary administrative support. The interior ministry under Hristić thus played a central role in developing Serbia's armed forces, which involved also strengthening the gendarmerie. The administration of the militia was formally transferred in 1864 to the seventeen okrug governors and their police. Thus, according to opponents of the regime, the national militia was transformed into a gendarmerie.[77]

Mihailo's policy of developing the military meant his Serbia could field an army of 90,000—easily the largest of any Balkan Christian state. Its size impressed the outside world, raising Serbia's international standing, and incubated patriotic and warlike feelings among the masses serving in it, who became accustomed to the idea of military service and whose nationalistic expectations were raised.[78] But its archaic Ottoman peasant structure meant it was very poorly equipped and trained and wholly inadequate for war against the Ottomans. The standing army that Mondain had attempted to organise on the French model never rose above 3,500 under Mihailo. For all his European aristocratic veneer, Mihailo's basing of his military strategy on the national militia rather than the standing army reflected the inherited wisdom of the son of a peasant guerrilla leader. Omar Pasha Latas, himself Serb by family background, upon witnessing an exercise by the national militia, remarked: 'What does Prince Mihailo want with such soldiers? He is not a military man and does not know what a good army is. These will all flee ...'[79] Major General Josip Filipović, Austrian commander in Zemun, commented on the national militia during the 1862 crisis: 'The Serbs have completely degenerated; they no longer demonstrate any of their known bravery; it has disappeared.'[80]

Serbia's military expansion and increasing national assertiveness were noticed by the Porte, which attempted to enlist the Great Powers to press Serbia to reverse its policy, but Austria and Britain were the only two to agree and they were unable to shift Mihailo. The Porte consequently sought its own showdown with him. Conversely, the officers of Serbia's strengthening armed forces were increasingly assertive towards the occupying Ottomans, who at the start of the 1860s held six garrisons in Serbia, at Belgrade, Šabac, Smederevo, Feth-i Islam (Kladovo), Soko and Užice. These Ottoman garrison towns had, with the permanent end of Austro-Ottoman military conflict after 1815, lost all strategic significance and were in steep economic and demographic decline, but their retention remained important for the Porte's domestic standing, particularly among Balkan Muslims.[81] The Ottomans rearmed the garrisons and strengthened their fortifications along the Serbian border in expectation of war with Serbia.

Confrontations between Serbian and Turkish officials and civilians along the Serbo-Ottoman border and around all of the fortresses became more frequent, with killings on both sides. The inevitable explosion was triggered by a confrontation on 15 June 1862 between a group of Serb civilians and three Ottoman soldiers at one of Belgrade's public fountains, the Kükürt Çeşme (Sulphur Spring), over who would use it first, in which a Serb boy was killed. Belgrade's Serbian governor Mihailo Barlovac sent a detachment of gendarmes to arrest the Ottoman soldiers, whereupon Ottoman reinforcements attacked the gendarmes, killing an officer. This sparked three days of fighting and bloodshed in the city. An assault on the Ottoman city gates by the gendarmerie and citizenry ordered by interior minister Hristić was followed by an unsuccessful attempt by the Ottomans to retake them and what became known to history as the 'bombardment of Belgrade', by the Ottoman artillery in Kalemegdan. This lasted four and a half hours, destroying about twenty houses and damaging 357, with one shell hitting the royal palace. The Serbs erected barricades against the fortress in preparation for the war apparently about to erupt.[82] The Serb and Jewish population of the city largely fled that day. The Jews crossed to Pančevo in Austria; many of them never returned.[83]

Popular excitement was such that, according to one account, when Garašanin warned some members of the militia not to jeopardise the government's diplomatic action aimed at avoiding war, he would have been shot on the spot as a 'Turcophile' if two men present had not stepped in to protect him.[84] The Council responded to the

THE NATIONAL LIBERATION STRUGGLE RESUMES

crisis on 16 June by transferring all power in Serbia to Mihailo, who declared a state of war in Belgrade and the Vračar district. Mihailo wrote to Ristić, his ambassador to the Porte, 'I would say that the dead knot, which exists between us and the Turks, will not be removed until it is cut with the sabre.'[85] Serbia demanded withdrawal of the Ottoman garrisons while the Porte demanded demobilisation of Serbia's militia. Mihailo drafted a speech announcing a resumption of the 1815 uprising: 'My father in 1815 went before your fathers and said: "Here I am; here is war with the Turks for you!" Today, here I am, Miloš's son, who comes before you, the sons of his fellow fighters, a naked sabre in my hand, uncovering myself, until together with you I complete my great, holy task.'[86]

In the resulting international crisis, France and Russia supported Serbia while Austria and Britain supported the Porte. The compromise negotiated by the Great Powers, at a conference at Kanlice Palace in Constantinople in July, required the Ottomans to withdraw their forces from Soko and Užice and the Muslim civilian population from Belgrade, and Serbia to indemnify the Belgrade Muslims for their losses, while the Serbs received no indemnity for the deaths, injuries and damage to property they had suffered. Garašanin had offered to allow the Belgrade Muslim civilian population to remain provided they be placed under Serbia's legal jurisdiction, but this was unacceptable to the Porte, which could not be seen to allow its Muslim subjects to come under the jurisdiction of a Christian vassal and which did not trust Serbia to treat them correctly, so it preferred to evacuate them from Serbia altogether.[87] Serbia's council of ministers met in mid-August and concluded that the country was both financially and technically incapable of waging a successful war against the Ottomans; therefore it had no option but to accept the conclusions of the Kanlice conference. Although Mondain, Garašanin and Marinović all accepted this, Mihailo said he would rather 'bury himself under Serbia's ruins' than make the concessions demanded of him. Only after much agonising did he on 8 October order an end to the state of war and the following day accept the Sultan's firman.[88]

Despite the agreement, fighting broke out at Užice in early September between Serbs and Turks in which the national militia intervened for the first time, marking its baptism of fire. Muslim homes in the outlying localities were systematically burned and the inhabitants driven into the town. For the Serbian citizens and militiamen at Užice, the fighting reflected a genuinely popular desire and effort to expel the Turks from the town. The mobilisation of large numbers of ill-disciplined peasant militiamen hungry for combat threatened to spiral out of the control of the regime. The agreement reached in Constantinople was condemned by the Liberal opposition around Mihailović and Metropolitan Mihailo as a defeat and disgrace for Serbia, for which Garašanin's Conservative government was responsible. Agitators grouped around Stanković were prosecuted for seditious writing at this time; one was sentenced to two years in prison while Stanković himself remained in Austria to avoid justice, there to contemplate more radical measures.[89]

Such agitation was dangerous for the regime because members of the opposition had been, in the course of the national mobilisation, appointed to posts in the military administration, including Mihailović, Belimarković, Alimpić and Alimpije Vasiljević. This had been intended to pacify their opposition and promote national unity but arguably weakened the regime by giving its opponents a significant degree of influence within the unstable military. Service in the expanded national militia gave the peasant recruits a sense of empowerment that increased the potential for popular revolt. The Liberal officers sought to act independently of the war ministry, even to provoke conflict with the Ottomans.[90] In view of the popular passions unleashed, the British consul-general in Belgrade, John Augustus Longworth, envisioned a possible rebellion, even Mihailo's overthrow. Indeed, on 15 September in Belgrade, 200 militiamen abandoned their barricades and trenches toward Kalemegdan fortress, after which militiamen at the Palilula barracks demanded that they either be sent into battle or sent home, since 'they had not come to defend the Belgraders and their women'. When the commanding officers attempted to discipline them, the militiamen 'formally rebelled' and expelled them from the barracks. With the officers unable to restore discipline and the men insisting they would negotiate only with the prince, it required old Mihailović, who had been made general of the national militia by Miloš for largely honorific reasons, to pacify them by promising them they would be sent home in ten days.[91]

Still committed to the national militia as an institution and to the concept of a nation-in-arms, the prince and Council in March 1863 permitted the militiamen to purchase their arms from the state and keep them at home rather than at their barracks, a step which was popular with them but threatened rapidly to disperse the newly acquired armaments. It also increased the danger of indiscipline, which continued in the armed forces following the suspension of the state of war. In June of that year, a group of standing army soldiers in Dorćol, Belgrade, rejected their commanding officer's authority and refused to return to their barracks. The known mutineers were arrested, after which further disorder occurred when some of their fellow soldiers attempted to free one of them. The indiscipline was linked to widespread resentment among soldiers of foreign-born officers, both non-Serbs such as Mondain and Austrian Serbs. Exaggerating somewhat, Longworth at the time reported to London that the peasants were resisting the draft and that both standing army and national militia were showing signs of disintegration. At Mondain's request, the rules were changed in December so that militiamen received their guns for free and could keep them at home, but they remained state property and were required to be kept in good order.[92]

Among conservative Serbs, the disturbances in the armed forces inspired a serious fear of revolution, of whose plotting they variously suspected Liberals, Russophiles and Karađorđevićites. Differing conclusions were drawn among Serbs as to the efficacy of the national militia and the readiness of the peasantry to serve in it, which would increasingly divide them in the following decades.[93] The separation of the war and interior ministries and their joint responsibility for organising the militia produced not only jurisdictional conflict but fear among some senior officials that the state apparatus had been fractured and weakened vis-à-vis the people.[94] Some young Serbian officers, however, were enthused by the militia and became its champions. Two such were Jevrem Marković and Sava Grujić; both were undergoing military training in Prussia in the early 1860s, so missed participating in the heady confrontation of 1862. They would nevertheless write in defence of the militia vis-à-vis the standing army and go on to become leading members of the Radical party, established in the following decade, which upheld the ideal of the nation-in-arms.[95] Eventually, Blaznavac was appointed war minister in April 1865 and sought to reduce discontent in the militia. He evaluated the army's needs on the basis of his military service with Knićanin's Serbian volunteer force in Hungary in the 1840s and on his French military academy training. His experience taught him that Serbian peasant soldiers responded better to elders drawn from their own localities than from professional officers, so he neglected to develop the militia's officer corps. He ordered in March 1868 an end to corporal punishment of soldiers by officers, aiming to inculcate a sense of the army as a 'nation-in-arms' on the French model, in which soldiers were citizens serving their country who deserved dignity.[96]

Downfall of the Great Court and liberation of Belgrade

Mihailo's push for absolute power and his assault on the remains of the Liberal opposition peaked following the confrontation with the Ottomans. The Liberals sought an outlet for their activity in the Society for Serbian Letters but came up against its president, education minister Cukić. Vladimir Jovanović delivered a speech at the Society's annual parliament in January 1864, mocking the supposedly decadent, un-Serbian, foreign-inspired manners and penchant for imported luxuries of the contemporary elite—subsequently published as the political pamphlet *Serbs and Popinjays*.[97] The Liberals also proposed the radical Italian nationalist Giuseppe Garibaldi and the son of the Russian radical Alexander Herzen as members of the society. The government responded by immediately dismissing Jovanović and Stojan Veljković from their posts as professors of the Great School and suspending the Society. It was deemed that for two professors to attack the education minister amounted to an unacceptable violation of the bureaucratic hierarchy.[98] The Society was soon afterwards reconstituted as the Serbian Learned Society.

Mihailo's law of 2 March 1864 permitted the dismissal, by a special court, of bureaucrats deemed physically or morally incapable of continuing to exercise their duties. This was followed by a law of 27 January 1865 permitting the government to dismiss bureaucrats for any reason. Consequently, bureaucrats were transformed from a securely privileged class into one wholly dependent upon government goodwill for its livelihood, and whose members could not therefore engage in opposition politics. On the basis of these laws, opponents of the regime such as Janković, Vladimir Jovanović, Milan Kujundžić and Gliša Geršić were dismissed from service.[99] A law on municipalities passed on 5 April 1866 established the institutions of municipal courts and councils elected by municipal assemblies comprising taxpayers; however, all these organs were wholly subordinate to the central authority which retained the right to overrule their decisions and dismiss municipal court officials, and which had to approve any municipal budget above a certain level.[100]

The government's aggressive authoritarianism was mirrored by an increasing turn to extreme measures on the part of some political outsiders. In the atmosphere of turmoil created by the bombardment of Belgrade, Princess Persida hatched a plot to assassinate Mihailo, stage an uprising, summon an authoritative parliament on the St Andrew's Day model and restore Aleksandar to the throne. The plot was uncovered by the authorities in late 1863. Its principal agent was Miloš's former strongman Stanković, who, like many old Obrenovićites, was alienated by Mihailo's regime. The plot was centred on Stanković's home town of Smederevo, in whose vicinity support for the Karađorđević dynasty was strong, and it included several notables and officials from the former Karađorđević regime and a large number of Karađorđevićites. It drew particular support from the Karađorđevićite heartland in the Jasenica valley region to the south of Smederevo around Topola, where there was considerable discontent among the rural population, both due to the perceived unfairness of the tax burden and the new requirement that peasants train for the militia.[101] It came to be known as Majstorović's Conspiracy, since its leader was suspected of being Antonije Majstorović, the anti-Obrenovićite putschist of 1842 and 1858. The conspiracy implicated Janković, so provided the occasion for Mihailo's final showdown with the remnants of the Liberal movement that had emerged in 1858.

The weakness of the authorities' case resulted in eight of the thirty-four accused being acquitted or released by the Smederevo okrug court in May 1864 and the remainder receiving light sentences of two years or less; after the government responded by taking the case to the Supreme Court, all the accused were acquitted. Since one of the five Supreme Court judges was Jevrem Grujić, demoted to the post from justice minister after the Liberals had fallen into disfavour, the government attributed the acquittal to Liberal sedition. With Mihailo's backing, justice minister Rajko Lešjanin assumed the authority to overrule the Supreme Court on the basis of his own interpretation of the law and to rule the judges' acquittal of the accused as rendering them guilty themselves. The justice ministry passed a law on 23 June 1864 for 'putting the judges before the court'. This established a kangaroo court comprising three members of the Supreme Court who had not ruled in favour of the acquittal of the conspirators plus four members of the Council with no legal qualifications. This court tried and convicted the five Supreme Court judges, who

THE NATIONAL LIBERATION STRUGGLE RESUMES

consequently served just over a year in prison before being pardoned by Mihailo. This affair destroyed his reputation as a ruler who respected the law.[102]

Mihailo summoned the parliament on 27 August 1864 (the 'Assumption Day parliament') to rubber-stamp his actions. He had wanted to convene it at Kragujevac again, but members of the opposition grouped around Mihailović accused him, reasonably, of wanting it so as to keep the deputies isolated and under police control and because he feared the capital. To counter these accusations, and because he was confident he could control the proceedings regardless, he shifted the venue to Belgrade.[103] It was indeed the most supine of parliaments, purged of activist Liberals and retaining only those Liberal deputies that originated from the traditional Obrenovićite base, who disliked the government but remained loyal to the prince. Mihailo, nevertheless, spoke bitterly in his opening address of opponents conspiring against his regime and of the supposed protection given them by the Great Court.[104] The parliament docilely endorsed Mihailo's anti-judicial putsch, thereby signifying the final defeat of Liberal hopes for parliamentary authority under his rule. It unanimously resolved that 'the prince be requested, in the name of the whole nation, to grasp with goodwill the common desire of the Serbian people, which awaits with impatience from His Highness's great wisdom, that the [Ottoman] citadels that remain following the bombardment of Belgrade be removed'.[105] Parliament was dissolved on 18 September.

In the five years following the bombardment of Belgrade, Mihailo and Garašanin continued to prepare for a possible war with the Ottomans and pursue pan-Balkan collaboration. They sent Prince Nikola 3,000 guns and an artillery battery in 1865, followed by several officers to train Montenegro's army. The two princes signed an alliance on 5 October 1866, pledging 'that the entire Serb nation in Turkey liberate and unify in a future Great Serbia'. Montenegro was to 'associate and unify with that great state, recognising Prince Mihailo as ruler of that entire Serb state'. This was the first Serbian official document to use the term 'Great Serbia'. The alliance did not envisage annexation of any Habsburg territory or unification with the Austrian Serbs. At Nikola's request, Mihailo became godfather (kum) to his first three daughters and his young cousin Milan Obrenović godfather to the fourth.[106] Garašanin nevertheless viewed Montenegro as a competitor and troublemaker that could create international difficulties for Serbia, and he sought to supplant Montenegro's influence in Hercegovina and prevent its annexation of the territory.[107] Meanwhile, he sought to collaborate with the Yugoslavist movement in Croatia pioneered by Josip Juraj Strossmayer (1815–1905), Croatian bishop of Đakovo, who founded the Yugoslav Academy of Sciences and Arts in 1866, and Franjo Rački (1828–1894), its first head. They advocated the spiritual union of the South Slavs on the basis of a common culture and literary language, with a federal South Slav state including Serbia and Montenegro as their long-term goal. In a letter to Strossmayer in March 1867, Garašanin proposed unification of the 'Yugoslav tribes' in 'a federal state', with either Belgrade or Zagreb as capital, on the grounds that 'the Croat and Serb nationality is one, *Yugoslav* (Slavic)' (emphasis in original).[108]

Regarding Bosnia and Hercegovina, it was recognised that an insurgency could not succeed if limited to the Bosnian Orthodox population. So Serbia's agents in Bosnia in the 1850s and 1860s attempted to win Catholics and Muslims to their project; the Serbian government was even prepared to recognise the land rights of the Muslim landlords—beys (begs) and agas—though this went against the tradition of Serb rebel nationalism based on the peasant struggle against them. An Ottoman educational reform of 1856 permitted all communities to set up their own public schools, for which funding could come from foreign or vassal states, including Serbia. This facilitated Serbian penetration of other Ottoman lands. In the 1860s, Garašanin and Bosnian émigré Mićo Ljubibratić succeeded in organising a Bosnia-wide organisation with the aim of preparing an anti-Ottoman uprising. Composed mostly of Serb merchants and priests whose relationship with the peasantry and interest in the agrarian question were secondary, it worked for an alliance with the Muslim landlords at the price of recognising and maintaining their property rights.

Political pamphlets directed at Muslims were printed by Serbia's government; one declared that all Bosnians were 'regardless of religious differences brothers: by God, language and fatherland'. While the network succeeded in recruiting many Franciscans and some beys, the price paid was loss of support among the Orthodox peasantry, alienated by the accommodation with the landlords. This choice reflected Garašanin's and Mihailo's conservatism. There were indeed Muslim beys who expressed readiness to accept Serbia's prince as their overlord in return for his assistance against the Ottomans, provided their religion, property and privileges were respected.[109] Thus, Hamzaga Rizvanbegović, who claimed to be 'leader of the Bosnian-Hercegovinian people', in 1868 appealed to a Serbian diplomat in Constantinople, saying that 'the Ottoman oppression can no longer be tolerated and Bosnia and Hercegovina would be much happier if anybody at all ruled over them, and he is eager soon to raise an uprising in Bosnia and Hercegovina and join them with Serbia, if Serbia is willing to help them', on condition that the Muslim landlords' economic and religious rights were preserved.[110]

This diplomatic activity did not end in a pan-Balkan war of liberation, but it may have contributed to the pressure on the Porte to reach a settlement with Serbia, whose government, ably represented in Constantinople by Ristić, simultaneously negotiated with the Porte for the evacuation of the remaining Ottoman garrisons and Muslim population from Serbia. By autumn 1866, the Porte was preoccupied with an uprising in Crete while Austria's military defeat by Prussia had weakened the pro-Ottoman camp among the Great Powers. Mihailo composed a letter to the grand vizier on 29 October, which Ristić delivered to him on 10 November, arguing that 'Serbia peaceful, satisfied and loyal to the Sublime Porte counts for more in case of the need to defend the border of the empire than towns that lie on the border of

THE NATIONAL LIBERATION STRUGGLE RESUMES

the Sava and Danube'. All the principal European powers advised the Porte to grant Serbia's request. The grand vizier consequently informed Ristić on 23 January 1867 that it would hand over the fortresses to Serbia in return for the promise that Serbia would not secede from the empire and for an end to Serbia's rearmament; Ristić assured the vizier that Serbia only wished for security within the empire. The grand vizier wrote to Mihailo on 3 March, adding the condition that the Ottoman flag would continue to fly above the fortresses alongside the Serbian flag. The face-saving fiction was that Serbia's prince would administer the fortresses on behalf of the Sultan. The agreement was sealed by a ten-day visit by Mihailo to Constantinople in April, when he was graciously received by the Sultan as befitted a prince. This caused Mihailo to note how different it had been on his previous visit to Constantinople in 1839–1840, when he had been confined to a modest house in the Christian quarter and kept waiting for weeks before the Sultan would receive him.[111]

The fortresses were consequently handed over to Serbian control between April and May 1867. The handover of the Belgrade fortress of Kalemegdan occurred on 18 April, when the prince arrived for the ceremony on a white Arabian horse given him by the Sultan and wearing a ceremonial general's uniform, and was saluted by the assembled Serbian and Ottoman forces. The Sultan's firman, entrusting Mihailo with the four citadels, that he might 'maintain and increase the security and tranquillity of Serbia, which is a constituent part of my empire', was read out at Kalemegdan before the leading Serbian notables, envoys of the Great Powers, and the Serbian and Ottoman armies. Mihailo was handed the keys by the Ottoman commander on a red velvet cushion edged with a golden cord and he jubilantly raised them for the crowd to see, after which a piece of Serbian patriotic music was played, the firman formally signed and Serbia's flag raised above the citadel alongside the empire's. The ceremony ended with the prince symbolically riding into the citadel to change the guard—Ottoman for Serbian.[112] The rapturous crowds gathering to witness and celebrate the handover included a young man of 21, a certain Nikola Pašić; the impression the spectacle made upon him may have contributed to his subsequent emergence as Serbia's greatest nationalist. The last Ottoman troops left Belgrade on 6 May.

The Ottoman withdrawal involved a thorough de-Ottomanisation of the Serbian towns. Around 8,000 Muslims had left Serbia with the surrender of the first two fortresses, Soko and Užice, in 1862. Official statistics in 1862 gave Serbia's Muslim population as 2,932 soldiers and 9,712 dependent civilians. However, according to the figures of the Russian consulate in Sarajevo, about 30,000 expelled Muslims arrived from Serbia in Bosnia alone, settling mostly in East Bosnia. As Muslim gypsies were not required to leave, some Muslims declared themselves gypsies in order to stay. After Belgrade, Užice had been the largest Muslim urban centre in Serbia with several thousand Muslim inhabitants, known as 'Little Constantinople', and its fate was indicative of the process. A commission was formed to supervise the sale of Muslim property in Užice to Serbs, largely at minimal prices, and in practice much of this property was simply plundered. The Užice fortress was demolished, followed by all seven of the town's remaining mosques, seen as undesirable symbols of Ottoman rule.[113]

Now fully liberated, Belgrade was reconstructed under the direction of Emilijan Josimović (1823–1897), an urban planner educated at the Great School, 'so that the capital would no longer retain the form bequeathed to it by barbarism'. It was remodelled along Austrian lines, with Vienna's Ringstrasse a particular inspiration.[114] The capital's population had grown from 9,245 to 24,612 between 1842 and 1867.[115] It would now continue to expand as a Central European city with little that recalled the Ottoman past, except for the Kalemegdan fortress in the centre and the sole remaining mosque in its vicinity. Writing a few years later, Milan Đakov Milićević, after describing the ethnically and culturally non-Serb, 'Eastern' character of Belgrade in the early nineteenth century, noted: 'Today that is all changed. The Turkish language is heard nowhere; Greek very rarely; the Serbian language is cleansed and corrected every day. Houses, shops, crafts, clothes and customs—all that is modelled according to that which is seen in the West, to be exact, in our closest neighbourhood. In particular women's dress is quickly changing its character, so that it is today very hard to find a girl child, from whatever class of Belgraders, who is not combed and dressed according to the European style.'[116] National development was increasingly channelled toward the capital. It contained 22.4 per cent of Serbia's male population by 1879—over twice the combined population of the two largest towns in the neighbouring Danubian vilayet, roughly corresponding to modern northern Bulgaria. The flip-side was that other Serbian towns were relatively less populous than similar towns in the Danubian vilayet.[117]

With the educated faction genuinely committed to a liberal political order so small and the mass of the population so uneducated and traditional in its way of life, the outcome of the crisis of 1858 was, unsurprisingly, not a liberal order but the replacement of the oligarchy with a new authoritarian regime: Mihailo fused Miloš's patriarchal autocracy with the Constitutionalists' modernising bureaucratic elitism. The energy unleashed by the revolution was channelled first into an assault on Austrian Serbs and Constitutionalist bureaucrats, then into a renewed national liberation movement which the disappointed Liberals could support. Yet the outcome in 1867 was once again ambiguous. Mihailo roused the nation against the imperial overlord but settled for a significant but incomplete victory in collaboration with it, just as his father had done in the Second Serbian Uprising 42 years before. While this may have been the best Serbia could have achieved in the circumstances, it produced Liberal and nationalist frustration, opening a new phase of political conflict.

6

LIBERALS, SOCIALISTS AND NATIONALISM FROM BELOW

1867–1872

The establishment of Mihailo's regime after 1860, as a personal autocracy ruling through Conservative functionaries of the former Constitutionalist regime, gravely disappointed the Liberals, but to an extent they continued to support it in the hope Mihailo would accomplish national liberation and unification. His shift by 1867 to a more moderate, flexible foreign policy, ready to achieve Serbia's national goals through collaboration with the Habsburg Empire, made Liberal disillusionment with him complete. His domestic policy having also created many losers from among the old Obrenovićite camp, his regime was faced by 1867–1868 with a dangerously burgeoning domestic opposition. This catalysed a split in the ruling elite between the Conservatives and a new Court Liberal faction, while from the ranks of the Liberal-nationalist opposition a more radical socialist-nationalist current emerged.

United Serb Youth and Court Liberals

Mihailo and Garašanin's policy before 1867 was insurrectionist abroad but authoritarian at home. Serbia's small size and military weakness vis-à-vis the Ottoman and Austrian empires prevented Mihailo from realising his ambitious maximal goals, and he would not wage a war that would risk his state's annihilation. But other Serb nationalists were more reckless. In the mid-1860s, unlike in the 1840s when Garašanin's Plan was written, an alternative nationalism, articulated by the Liberals, existed to the prince's top-down, authoritarian nationalism. Fusing frustration at the regime's supposedly weak pursuit of national liberation with frustration at its domestic autocracy, they supported both a more militant nationalism abroad and greater liberty at home. This flowed seamlessly into a nationalism directed against Serbia's supposedly alien, un-Serb government and elite, condemned for their supposed subservience to the Turks. Many years, even decades, later, prominent young Liberals like Vasiljević and Vladimir Jovanović would still contemptuously refer to the Conservative-Constitutionalists as the 'Kajmakam party' and 'kajmakamlije', alluding to their alleged attempt to establish a kajmakamlije, or Ottoman governorship, to rule Serbia in place of Aleksandar. In Jovanović's words, 'It is due to them that the Constantinople government in 1838 imposed on Serbia the octroyed constitution, which expunged every idea of national right'; they then allegedly sought in 1858 'on the ruins of national sovereignty to raise in Serbia a Turkish *kajmakamlije* (regency)'.[1]

Following his dismissal from the Great School, Jovanović took refuge in 1864 in Novi Sad in Hungary, where he developed his nationalist ideology directed against an internal enemy inseparable from the external ones—not only the Ottoman Empire but the Great Powers supporting it. He condemned the activities of the foreign consuls in Serbia; he accused them of 'meddling in Serbian domestic affairs' and 'treating Serbia as wholly surrendered to the despotic government of Prince Mihailo, who likes those consuls so much'.[2] He particularly blamed the Russians since the First Serbian Uprising for imposing the oligarchic Council on Serbia, which overlay and suppressed the Serbian people's indigenous, parliament-based folk democracy: 'It is inherently understood, that an "administration, organised and regulated" by the directives of the Russian government could not have been anything other than an *oligarchy*, or *despotism* with *bureaucracy*, all so introduced, that it would poison the entire political framework of Serbia' (emphasis in original). This Russian interference culminated in the imposition of the alien, oligarchic 1838 constitution: 'Of the national parliament there was no mention! In that way, the absolutist powers turned the Serbian Council and ministry into the arms of foreign influence. Prince Miloš made a great mistake and accepted this unconstitutional constitution.'[3] Thus, the 1858 revolution and the liberal movement emerging from it, aimed at restoring true national sovereignty via a freely elected parliament and an authentic Serbian constitution, had to be directed not merely against the oligarchic regime and the Turks, but against Great Power meddling.

Jovanović broadened this into a generalised assault on what he saw as the Serbian elite's corrupted morals and increasing penchant for luxury, counterposing them to the Serb peasantry's rugged integrity:

> The true Serb eats simple but strong, healthy food; the popinjay tastes foods, enjoys 'little cakes', 'ice creams' and other 'sweetmeats'; he drinks 'champagne' and 'Chinese tea'; he smokes 'American cigars'; he empties 'apothecaries'. The true Serb wears modest but clean and long-lasting clothes; the popinjay dresses 'according to fashion', and his 'other half' cannot be seen beneath the silks and the cotton, gold clasps, the 'frills', 'ruffles', 'lace', 'brooches'; and she out of love for 'fashion' throws away almost unworn dresses that could have been worn for much longer. Among the true Serbs, 'work is for a man and thrift is for a woman'. Among the popinjays, 'excess is for a man and profligacy is for a woman.' [And while the elite in Serbia was] 'introducing into

our salons new games' and 'new music' ... our brothers in Montenegro are dying of exposure and hunger, or in Hercegovina, in Bosnia, in Old Serbia and in Bulgaria they in slavery eat bark as their bread.

For Jovanović, this marked a corruption of and divergence from the Serbs' true nature; he looked back in time to a more wholesome national being for the Serbs, in which 'in their *zadrugas*, in their *values* and in their *thrifty modesty*, they found those first foundations for independent life in the country, which it was already decreed had to be defended from wild attackers'. It was these traditions that had to be revitalised, for 'the true Serb gives his soul as a soldier, but the true Serb believes that the main strength of the state consists in *free institutions*, for only for *freedom*, is "every Serb a soldier"; [whereas] the popinjay puts everything into "uniforms"; into "the most splendid coat" and, in the last instance, into the "ribbon"' (emphases in original).[4]

Jovanović condemned the dominant Conservative party as un-Serb and upheld his own Liberal opposition as the only authentic Serbian party, the 'interpreter of the national will' in opposition to foreign influences and other political factions, which he dismissed as 'cliques'. Hence, 'we maintain, that among the Serbs there is just one political party and that is: the Freedom or National party. That is the party that has arisen from the nation itself as the organ of general belief; the organ of public protest and resistance against all intrigues and hostilities that are directed against the national right either from within or from without.'[5] This confidence in the ability of his movement solely to represent the national will accompanied an overconfidence in the ability of the Serbs to lead a Christian Balkan uprising and defeat the Turks: 'If at the time of the Crimean War the Serbs had arisen, the entire Balkan Peninsula would have arisen.' Furthermore, 'there is no doubt that even 50,000 Serb soldiers would be capable of defeating a Turkish army of 100,000 soldiers', and 'without any doubt we can say, that the Serbian, Montenegrin and Hercegovinian army is capable of defeating the Turkish army without seeking foreign assistance'.[6]

A lively émigré press blossomed, with Serbia's Liberals articulating from the safety of Novi Sad and other foreign towns an opposition through their writings to Mihailo's regime. They sought to collaborate with like-minded spirits among the Serbs in Austria. Svetozar Miletić, Hungary's leading Serb Liberal, shared their belief that 'Serbia is the Serb Piedmont' and that while Mihailo deserved credit for rearming Serbia, 'it is important also that the nation is spiritually armed too and that is a candle that needs freer air'.[7] In the freer atmosphere in the Austrian Empire created by its defeat by Prussia the previous month, and on the initiative of Jovanović and the Serb literary societies Preodnica (Morning Star) and Zora (Dawn), based in Pest and Vienna respectively, the first meeting occurred at Novi Sad in Hungary on 27 August 1866 of the United Serb Youth, a national congress of Serb representatives from Serbia and Austria. Attended by 400 deputies, it coincided with meetings held at Novi Sad by two other Serb societies from Austria, Matica Srpska (Serb Matrix) and the Serbian National Theatre. The three meetings together amounted to an unprecedented manifestation of Serb national life in the Habsburg Empire. Allied to Miletić, Jovanović was elected president of the United Serb Youth on 11 November. Soon after, Miletić was elected mayor of Novi Sad. He was also editor of the *Zastava* (Flag) newspaper; Jovanović was his chief editorial assistant.

As heads of this national movement, Jovanović and Miletić criticised Mihailo for not pursuing more bellicose nationalist policies, in particular for his agreement with the Ottomans over the fortresses which averted the war they desired. Although Jovanović had collaborated closely with Mihailo's diplomatic efforts following the bombardment of Belgrade, from 1864 he and the Liberals declared all-out political war against Mihailo's 'politics that were repressive at home and unpatriotic abroad', as Vasiljević subsequently described them.[8] Enthused by Italian and German nationalist successes, Miletić and Jovanović believed Serbia should ally with Prussia and Italy in their 1866 war with Austria and attempt to liberate Bosnia, and were bitterly disappointed when Mihailo failed to do so.

The frustration of the populace mobilised in the national militia at the regime's repressive and supposedly unpatriotic policy provided increasingly fertile ground for subversion by the Liberals, who had been drawn into the militia and administration. Arsenije Tucaković, okrug governor of Ćuprija and brother of Todor, former Liberal president of the parliament, told his fellow Liberals in Belgrade that he was ready to lead his 6,000 militiamen against the regime. When Mihailo scheduled large-scale militia manoeuvres at Požarevac in autumn 1866, Liberal conspirators, including several militia commanders, plotted to use the occasion to lead the militia in an uprising to force Mihailo to dismiss the government and replace it with one more liberal at home and nationalistic abroad; if he refused, he would be dethroned in favour of Montenegro's Prince Nikola. The plan failed when the senior Liberal officer Belimarković refused to participate and threatened to inform Mihailo.[9]

Mihailo felt compelled to accommodate this growing opposition. With his approval, the United Serb Youth's 1,500-strong second congress opened at Belgrade's Great School on 18 August 1867. He prohibited Jovanović and Miletić from attending, but young Nikola Pašić and other future statesmen who subsequently became more conservative, Stojan Novaković and Vladan Đorđević, did attend. The congress approved Jovanović's proposal that the Youth be transformed into a more centralised political organisation, involving the establishment of an executive committee. However, the congress's election of Jevrem Grujić as its president and its oppositional tone prompted the government to end collaboration with it and hasten its termination. This reflected Mihailo's definite shift to a more conservative foreign policy.[10] This in turn ended his reputation among radical nationalists and discredited his autocracy among the Serbian people; they had apparently endured eight years of its heavy taxes and bureaucratic oppression for little in the way of national independence and unification. Mihailo's final break with the United

Serb Youth and Liberals completed their alienation from him, prompting some to consider more radical options.

Mihailo's strategy evolved in a direction opposite to what the Liberals wanted. He secured Austria's goodwill over the fortresses by rejecting all Italian, Hungarian and Prussian offers in previous years of alliances against it, instead informing Vienna of these offers.[11] His success in securing the fortresses convinced him that further national successes could be achieved through collaboration with Austria and the Ottomans rather than by inflexibly pursuing war against the Ottomans as Russia's ally, as Garašanin wanted. At a ministerial meeting in August 1867, war minister Blaznavac explained that Serbia was still not ready for war and that he could not provide a timetable for when it would be.[12] The 8 February 1867 *Ausgleich* (Compromise) which transformed the Austrian Empire into Austria-Hungary made it also a much more attractive collaborator for Serbia, for the Hungarians did not wish to annex any further Slav-inhabited territory that would dilute their new privileged position. Thus, Mihailo—himself married to a Hungarian—found a sympathetic interlocutor in Hungary's prime minister Gyula Andrássy, who sought to win Belgrade away from Russia's influence and preferred at this time to have Serbia rather than Austria-Hungary occupy Bosnia. He met Mihailo on 24–25 August at the latter's estate at Ivanac, where they may have discussed the possibility of a Serbian occupation of part or all of Bosnia and Hercegovina, something Mihailo, fresh from his triumph over the fortresses, had first raised with the Austro-Hungarians in March 1867.[13]

Mihailo did not abandon his plans for a pan-Balkan war of liberation, signing an alliance with Greece on 26 August. Nevertheless, the war's postponement exacerbated the split in the government between the faction behind Garašanin, architect of the old policy and Russia's favourite, and the faction behind Blaznavac, pioneer of the new policy of seeking expansion through accommodation with Austria-Hungary. This was a split between the wing of the regime that wanted to maintain autocracy while appeasing demands for war and that which wanted to maintain peace abroad while appeasing demands for liberalisation at home. At the ministerial meeting in August, Garašanin complained: 'For several years already I have been deceiving people about the start of the war from spring to spring, and this cannot go on indefinitely. The prince must choose between me and the war minister, for I believe the time has come when the war can no longer be postponed.'[14] Garašanin naïvely believed it was sufficient for Serbia's army simply to be better than the Ottomans' bashibazouks (irregular forces).[15] This split became bound up with the controversy over childless Mihailo's wish to divorce his barren wife Julija and marry Katarina, teenage daughter of his first cousin Anka Konstantinović. Garašanin's dominant governmental faction opposed the prince's plan to marry a close relative 25 years younger than himself, which Garašanin argued would offend 'the most sensitive feelings of the Serbian people' and make the government appear like 'a collection of apostates from faith and nation'. Garašanin was supported by the church hierarchy, with Metropolitan Mihailo holding that such a marriage would be 'ungodly' and 'unheard of'. The ambitious Konstantinović consequently allied herself to Blaznavac's dovish faction and worked to undermine Garašanin's standing with the prince.[16]

Bulgarian guerrillas based in Serbia infiltrated the Bulgarian part of the Ottoman Empire during July and August 1867; one was killed by Ottoman troops at Rushchuk on 8 August. Bent upon confrontation, Garašanin exploited the incident to reprimand the Porte and incite Serbian opinion against it. During Mihailo's third parliament, which opened at Kragujevac on 11 October 1867 (the 'Michaelmas parliament'), the deputies' address at Garašanin's instigation urged action against the Turks: 'Sire! We have been deeply moved by the generous response of Your Grace to our National Militia ... But the national representatives must not fail, Your Grace, since they and with them the whole nation maintain: that the National Militia will only be worthy of that satisfaction and that gratitude when it has through its acts contributed to fulfilling the tasks for which it was established ...' It called specifically for ending the disorder in the Ottoman lands to Serbia's south.[17] Mihailo believed Garašanin, by seeking war when Serbia was unprepared, was jeopardising his plan and subordinating Serbia's interests to Russia's. He consequently dismissed him as prime minister and foreign minister on 15 November 1867.[18] This prompted Russian complaints, offending Mihailo sufficiently to push him further toward Austria-Hungary. He pursued a dual strategy, signing an alliance with Romania on 1 February 1868 and a further military convention with Greece on 28 February 1868. Yet when Austria-Hungary's consul-general Kállay, at Vienna's instruction, met with Mihailo in early May 1868 to dissuade him from embarking on a Russian-instigated war, Milailo told him Serbia's goodwill toward Russia would be extended to other powers that gave it similar support.[19]

The Michaelmas parliament spawned a vocal Liberal opposition among the deputies for the first time which proposed reforms, among them that parliament be granted a share of legislative powers; that ministers be responsible to it as well as to the prince; that it be able to elect its own president, vice-president and secretary, instead of having them appointed by the prince; and that a law on press freedom be passed. All these proposals were defeated.[20] The government, in that year, nevertheless permitted the founding of the independent newspaper *Srbija*, which assembled younger intellectuals such as Bošković, Vasiljević, Čedomilj Mijatović and Milan Kujundžić. *Srbija* argued that only by introducing freedom at home could Mihailo achieve Serbian national unification: 'Give the country free institutions, freer than those that our enemies can have, then you will have guaranteed the future. Freedom is stronger than blood. If Serbia becomes a home of true freedom, then Bosnia, Hercegovina etc. will want to unite with it, even if the people in those lands were not Serb.'[21]

LIBERALS, SOCIALISTS AND NATIONALISM FROM BELOW

The division over the prince's marital plans led to the emergence of a Court Liberal faction. Jovan Ristić (1831–1899), Serbian consul in Constantinople and member of the Konstantinović–Blaznavac faction, was chosen by Mihailo to replace Garašanin as prime minister and foreign minister. This marked the entry onto the centre stage of Serbian politics for the first time of the man who was, after Miloš and alongside Mihailo and Garašanin, probably the most significant figure in Serbian political history during the first eighty years of the nineteenth century. His subsequent pre-eminence stemmed from his background of being both Liberal and Conservative. Born in Kragujevac into a very poor family, he had been educated at the Belgrade lycée, joined the Society of Serb Youth, shared a room with Vasiljević while at school, participated in the revolutionary events in Vojvodina and in fighting the Hungarians in the 1840s and was educated in Germany and France. However, he then became a career functionary under the Constitutionalists, chief of police and protégé of Garašanin, who tried unsuccessfully to have him chosen secretary of the St Andrew's Day parliament, after which he joined the Conservatives and participated in drafting the ducatist attacks on the Liberals.[22]

Given Ristić's youthful liberalism, the United Serb Youth congress in Belgrade made an impression on him, convincing him of the need for reform. Mihailo may have appointed him in place of the arch-Conservative Garašanin in part to mollify the Liberal opposition, given the militia's uncertain loyalty.[23] Ristić authorised the composition by the president of the appellate court, Radivoje Milojković, of a draft constitution for a more liberal political order. To Mihailo he argued that the only way for him to achieve his marital ambitions was to liberalise his regime to win popular support and isolate the Conservative old guard. But he did so tactlessly, prompting Mihailo to dismiss him and reconstitute a hardline Conservative government under Nikola Hristić on 3 December 1867. Unsurprisingly, it took no steps to enact Milojković's draft constitution, which neither Mihailo nor Hristić liked.[24] The dismissal of the reformist Ristić and appointment of the arch-reactionary Hristić further damaged Mihailo's credibility and enflamed the radical opposition. As Vasiljević writes, 'His fate was already then sealed, for all his friends lost hope while his enemies had just been waiting for this.'[25]

Ristić's fall, for advocating liberalisation, immediately made him the Liberal opposition's hero. He quickly regained Mihailo's favour and, together with Blaznavac, constituted a Liberal faction at court. Mihailo was thus faced with two court factions: the Conservative old guard supporting autocracy at home but opposing his marital plans and the Liberal Ristić–Blaznavac faction supporting his marital plans but favouring liberalisation at home.[26] The Court Liberals were a group distinct both from the Liberal activists of 1858 such as Grujić and Jovanović and from the old Obrenovićites grouped around Mihailović. Other than Blaznavac, its two principal figures were Ristić and Milojković, both married to daughters of Belgrade merchant Hadži-Toma. Thus, the Hadži-Toma family, of Cincar origin, became the backbone

177

to the Court Liberal faction as the Baba-Dudić family was to the original Liberal party. The two families became rivals.²⁷

Assassination of Prince Mihailo and Court Liberal coup

Mihailo was assassinated at Topčider park outside Belgrade on 10 June 1868 while strolling with his intended bride, Katarina, her mother Anka Konstantinović, his aunt Tomanija Obrenović and his adjutant Svetozar Garašanin, Ilija's son. Konstantinović was killed alongside her would-be son-in-law, valiantly trying to defend him, while young Garašanin was wounded and passed out. The assassination was made possible by Mihailo's naivety, overconfidence and unwillingness to heed the security measures urged by Hristić, his interior minister and prime minister. The perpetrators were a clique headed by Pavle Radovanović, the leading conspirator, with his brothers Kosta and Đorđe (a fourth brother, Ljubomir, was also involved), Lazar Marić and Stanoje Rogić. Another conspirator, Captain Đorđe Mrcajlović, led a small detachment of troops from the Palilula barracks into Belgrade to seize the central police station, but was arrested, while another officer, Mladen Nenadović, Persida's brother, was also supposed to have led a revolt within the army. The socialist Dragiša Stanojević, Persida's cousin, spent the evening before the assassination in Pavle's company, and thereafter he assembled students before the Great School with the aim of proclaiming a republic. Mrcajlović's roommate Ljubomir Kaljević, subsequently a Liberal prime minister, was arrested following the assassination but told a friend to hurry to the piazza before the Great School and wait for the students to rise.²⁸

Pavle, a prominent lawyer, had been the government's defeated candidate for Kragujevac in the election for the Transfiguration Day parliament. Apparently embittered by interior minister Hristić's failure to annul his election defeat, he then joined the opposition. His brother Ljubomir had won the election in Valjevo for the same parliament but had had his victory quashed by Hristić owing to irregularities. Ljubomir was subsequently convicted of a crime of which Pavle believed him innocent, spending time in prison and deepening the grudge. Another conspirator, Vidoje Ivković, had been a district chief in Požarevac dismissed under Mihailo. Another, Ilija Čurčija, had been a loyal Obrenovićite who had already fallen foul of Hristić at the time of the Hussar Rebellion, which he had supported; appointed district chief by Miloš following his return to the throne, Čurčija had then been dismissed by Mihailo, allegedly because he was illiterate.²⁹ Thus, the conspirators were members of the increasingly swollen ranks of embittered Liberal and Obrenovićite former supporters of the prince. In the climate of popular and Liberal frustration following the Hristić government's appointment, the conspirators believed that their act would meet with popular approval, if not an actual rebellion against the unpatriotic and authoritarian regime, that would sweep them to power.

LIBERALS, SOCIALISTS AND NATIONALISM FROM BELOW

The original or 'Old' Liberals, while not actively behind the assassination, helped through their anti-regime agitation to generate an atmosphere that made it possible; they were aware of the conspiracy but took no steps to stop it. The conspirators had planned to create a new government that included the Liberals; their deed was, at some level, a bastard child of Serbian liberalism.[30] The conspirators were personally close to and sympathetic to the Liberals on the one hand and were supported by Aleksandar's agents on the other; they had joined with elements of the moribund Karađorđevićite network from the older Majstorović conspiracy, led lethargically by Stanković. Pavle Radovanović was Aleksandar's cousin by marriage through his wife, a Nenadović; he received money and half-hearted support from Aleksandar himself and more enthusiastic support from Persida.[31] According to the testimony of Jovan Avakumović, a clerk appointed by the court to interrogate the suspects, Pavle claimed a patriotic motivation; he had hoped to replace Mihailo with a republic whose free institutions would attract the other parts of Serbdom.[32]

Mihailo's assassination triggered a power struggle between different factions of his former regime. Garašanin, who, though out of office, retained prestige among the elite, promptly rallied the government to block the conspirators' coup, while Hristić swiftly arrested and prosecuted them. A temporary regency was proclaimed on 12 June consisting of Marinović, Rajko Lešjanin and Đorđe Petrović, hence representing the Conservatives. Sixteen people were tried and executed in total, including all four Radovanović brothers, Marić, Rogić, Mrcajlović, Persida's brothers Mladen and Sima Nenadović, her second cousin Svetozar Nenadović and Majstorović, who was apparently executed to scare the Karađorđevićites, even though it was understood that he had no significant involvement in the plot. Others received lesser sentences, including, in absentia, both Aleksandar himself and Stanković. Still others were acquitted, including former Constitutionalist-era minister Jeremija Stanojević, his son Dragiša and Vladimir Jovanović.[33] The Hungarian authorities, meanwhile, arrested the exiled Aleksandar along with his secretary and Stanković and conducted their own investigation into the assassination, culminating in the trial in Pest of the three arrestees, who were all acquitted. Apparently at the regency's request, Hungary's authorities also arrested the Liberals Miletić and Jovanović, incarcerating them for several months.[34] Kállay lamented in his diary: 'Prince Mihailo's death is a great misfortune for us. He was our sincere friend; a thoughtful, calm man, without a doubt the most educated Serb, an enemy of Russian policy, who did not allow himself to be used as a tool in adventurous plans.'[35]

The fallout from the assassination at one level pitted Court Liberals against Old Liberals, for the latter had created the climate conducive to the murder and had been close to the assassins, while the former conducted the retribution. This was therefore something of a quarrel between two branches of an extended family. Court interrogator Avakumović, as a member of the Baba-Dudić family, had risen quickly in state service and been taken under the wing of Milojković, whom he had met through his uncle Pantelija Jovanović, another leading Liberal and member of the Baba-Dudić family. He found himself interrogating two conspirators, Marić and Ivković, whom he had previously met as good friends of his brother-in-law, Old Liberal activist Vasiljević.[36] The Old Liberals were nevertheless saved by the power struggle between the Court Liberals and Conservatives. Mihailo's militarisation of Serbia had shifted the balance of power from the bureaucracy to the army, so the strongest hand was now held by war minister Blaznavac. He needed allies to ensure the defeat of Garašanin's Conservatives and sought them in the Old Liberals, whom he consequently ensured were exonerated of involvement in the assassination. Garašanin had sought to link the United Serb Youth to the assassination, but Blaznavac ensured that blame and repression were concentrated primarily on Karađorđevićites and socialists.

Serbia's dynastic conflict had seemed to be subsiding under Mihailo who, viewing himself as national unifier, had sought reconciliation with the Karađorđevićes. He and the deposed Aleksandar, his former adjutant, had discussed a possible reconciliation; there was apparently talk of an inter-dynastic marriage that would have cleared the way for a Karađorđević restoration in the event Mihailo died heirless. However, young Prince Petar Karađorđević (1844–1921) had been in contact with members of the conspiracy, so was implicated in the assassination. Since Aleksandar refused to return to Serbia for trial, Serbia's government banned his family's return and confiscated his property in the country, valued at 180,000–250,000 ducats. It could not, however, persuade Romania to confiscate his extensive property there. Thus, the Karađorđevićes gained a new motive to support radical opponents of the regime while retaining the means to continue funding political activity.[37]

The government resolved on 10 June that the throne should remain vacant until a great national parliament could be convened to choose Mihailo's successor, the election of which was set for 20 June. However, Blaznavac staged a *coup d'état*, pre-empting any decision by regents, government or parliament over the succession. Having been in 1858 a diehard opponent of the Obrenović restoration, he had transformed over the following decade into a pillar of the Obrenović regime. He acted quickly to ensure maximum regime continuity by engineering the enthronement of Milan Obrenović, thirteen-year-old grandson of Miloš's brother Jevrem, hence Mihailo's first cousin once removed. Milan's claim to the succession was perhaps better than that of any other non-Karađorđević but was not indisputable. Blaznavac on 20 June issued an order read out to all military units: 'I have called you to arms so that you will, alongside me, stand firm to maintain order and the name of Obrenović, in the person of the legal heir Milan Obrenović IV. The whole Serbian army, like the Serbian nation, has responded with one voice to this summons ... Heroes: I proclaim to you my warmest gratitude for your firm and heroic stance: the army has, on this occasion, maintained order and the Obrenović dynasty and shown the world that it is the great and certain power with which Prince Mihail[o] intended to make the country happy.'[38] Blaznavac thus defined the role and identity of the army as guardian of the nation and its destiny: this would define the mindset of politically minded officers for the next three-quarters of a century.

With the army's loyalty now pledged to Milan, Blaznavac presented the government and regents with the fait accompli of Milan as Serbia's new prince. Prime minister Hristić was the only one with the power to arrest Blaznavac and suppress the coup, but he was unwilling to do so without a clear order from the regents. Since this was lacking, he collaborated instead with Blaznavac to ensure order was maintained. When Milan arrived in Belgrade on 23 June, escorted by Ristić, the regents and government were unwilling to give him a formal ceremonial welcome, but he was greeted instead by Blaznavac, the army and an artillery salute. Slobodan Jovanović notes: 'From his first arrival on Serbian soil, Milan could have had the impression that he was prince of the army.'[39] What followed over the next several months was a controlled, limited Liberal revolution, executed by the opportunistic alliance of army and Liberals. The great national parliament met on 2 July 1868 at Topčider, near where the assassination had occurred; Živko Karabiberović of the Baba-Dudić family was appointed its president and Todor Tucaković vice-president, symbolising the Liberal ascension. But as it was shorn of the power to choose the prince, the parliament's official purpose was merely to proclaim Milan's accession and the appointment of a new three-man regency comprising Blaznavac, Ristić and Jovan Gavrilović. The third was a cipher; Blaznavac and Ristić became Serbia's new real rulers. Blaznavac's troops surrounded the parliament to isolate it from the population outside and ensure the vote's favourable outcome; these 1,600 soldiers outnumbered the 500 deputies themselves by more than three to one. Meanwhile, the regents kept most of Mihailo's Conservative officials in office; for example, Marinović remained Council president. Ristić's inclusion in the regency nevertheless helped win it the support of the original Liberals; the United Serb Youth's third congress, held at Veliki Bečkerek in Hungary on 3–6 September 1868, passed a resolution expressing confidence in it.

This Liberal coup enjoyed the support of Austria-Hungary, France and the Porte, amounting as it did to a defeat for Garašanin's pro-Russian Conservatives and for Russia itself, which had favoured Montenegrin Prince Nikola for Serbia's throne.[40] The Liberals viewed Russia at this time as a threat; Milojković allegedly opposed the idea of seeking a Russian prince on the grounds that 'for us Serbs, it would not be good to come under Russian obduracy and unconstitutionality'.[41] Under Austro-Hungarian pressure, the Porte acquiesced in the revocation of the Turkish Constitution it had previously upheld and in the establishment of a hereditary dynasty it had previously resisted. When Serbia's envoy in Constantinople, Jevrem Grujić, presented a draft of Serbia's new constitution to the grand vizier, the latter simply expressed his thanks.[42] With international support assured, the regents moved quickly to cement their new constitutional order, modelled on the proposal that Ristić had put before Mihailo and on Milojković's constitutional draft. They appointed a new government on 3

July 1868 with a Conservative prime minister, Council member Đorđe Cenić, but it was otherwise dominated by Liberals. A year later, on 29 July 1869, following Cenić's resignation, his place was taken by Milojković, another Liberal.

Regency Constitution

Formally in response to demands from the great national parliament for liberal constitutional reforms, the regents summoned a constitutional committee comprising prominent public figures to draft a new constitution; it began work on St Nicholas's Day, 18 December 1868, hence was known as the St Nicholas Committee.[43] Elections for a new great national parliament tasked with promulgating the new constitution were decreed on 1 June 1869. The resulting great national parliament convened on 22 June at Kragujevac, with Karabiberović and Tucaković once again as president and vice-president. In conjunction with the regents, on 1 July 1869 it promulgated the new constitution, consequently known as the Regency Constitution. It was of dubious legitimacy, engineered by the regents and great national parliament in violation of Serbia's laws. During regencies, constitutional changes were illegal; these were anyway the prerogative of the Council, which the regents had excluded from the constitution-making process. Furthermore, the unilateral promulgation of a new constitution violated the rights of the Sultan as Serbia's legal suzerain. Ristić viewed such a unilateral promulgation as essential for establishing Serbia's independence. By proclaiming Serbia a hereditary principality under the Obrenović dynasty, the constitution deprived the Porte of its ability to meddle in the succession, which it had enjoyed while the prince was elective.[44] The constitution decreed the succession would pass through Milan's male descendants, in the absence of which, 'and if there are no male descendants of the daughters of Prince Miloš, then the Serb nation chooses for itself the hereditary prince that Serb in whom it has most confidence. But never can there be chosen for the Serb prince anyone from the family and descendants of the Karađorđevićes, on whom is thrown a national curse.'

The constitution specified that full political rights were to be enjoyed by Serbs rather than by citizens as such: 'All Serbs are equal before the law.' Serbs had an equal right to all state titles subject to competence and qualification, to freedom of speech and expression and to appeal against unlawful government actions. Conversely, taxes and military service were the duty of all Serbs; 'every Serb is a soldier'. The national militia's existence was guaranteed. The right to vote was granted to all adult Serbs who paid the state tax on property, work or income (women were not explicitly excluded from voting, as they were from succession to the throne, but were excluded in practice). However, to be a parliamentary deputy, a Serb had to be at least 30, pay at least six thalers a year in state tax and have additional means as defined by the electoral law. The state religion was defined as Eastern Orthodox and proselytism at the expense of Orthodoxy alone was banned, although other recognised religions were guaranteed freedom. The prince had to be Orthodox, as did the heir to the throne. Article 132 explicitly upheld the anti-Jewish laws of 1856 and 1861. The great national parliament had apparently come close to proclaiming 'liberty and equality for all, even for the Jews', but had ultimately been dissuaded by Milojković and Karabiberović, who cited the danger of Jewish domination of Serbian commerce and the unacceptability of Jews becoming officers and ministers, so legal restrictions on Jews remained. Jews were consequently legally evicted by the authorities from towns in the Serbian interior in the coming years, including from Šabac, Smederevo and Požarevac in 1873, and eleven more from Smederevo in 1876.[45] Nevertheless, the constitution did permit Jews to serve in the army and they would fight in Serbia's subsequent wars: in 1876, twenty were mobilised to fight against the Ottomans and several more enrolled voluntarily, though without the right to attain rank.[46]

The Regency Constitution established a political order based on supposedly 'moderate'—in fact, controlled—liberalism. Three-quarters of parliamentary deputies were to be elected and a quarter appointed by the prince. As a sop to peasant hostility to state officials and lawyers, these could not be elected as deputies, but they could be appointed deputies by the prince. Ministers could not be parliamentary deputies and were not responsible to the parliament but only to the prince. If the parliament rejected a budget, the government would retain the existing budget. The parliament could express the desire for new laws, but only the prince could actually propose them, and though the parliament could reject them, the government could enact provisional laws when it wished. In practice, parliament enjoyed less legislative authority under the new constitution than the Council had enjoyed under the Turkish Constitution, while the actual Council, which had once ruled Serbia, was now demoted to a mere administrative court with the name State Council. Parliamentary deputies were considered representatives of the nation as a whole, not merely of their constituents, who could not issue instructions to them. The president and vice-president of parliament were chosen by the prince from six candidates elected by parliament.

Parliament could exclude deputies whose statements 'contained attacks on the person of the prince, prince's family, regents, princely dignity, parliament or its individual members'.[47] The mostly uneducated peasant parliamentary deputies could be easily manipulated, given that the prince's appointed deputies were almost the only ones with any education. The use of indirect voting for parliamentary elections in the villages made it difficult for the opposition to win in the countryside; villagers elected electors, who then elected parliamentary representatives for their districts according to the instructions of the district governors. It was somewhat less difficult for the opposition to win in the towns, where voting was direct, but even there it was subject to police repression. Parliaments under the regency were therefore docile.[48] In addition to regular parliaments, the constitution affirmed the institution of the great national parliament, consisting of four times the regular number of deputies and elected for special circumstances: selection of the prince or regents when necessary; changes to the constitution; changes to the national territory; or whatever exceptional circumstances demanded, as determined by the prince.

All state officials were appointed by the prince, who was commander of all armed forces and solely responsible for foreign affairs and foreign treaties, though if they involved payments from the state treasury, changes to the law or restrictions on citizens' rights then parliament's approval was needed. Although state officials were required to pledge to uphold the constitution, this explicitly stated that 'the army does not pledge an oath to the constitution'. Central control of municipalities remained effectively what it had been under Mihailo. Formal censorship, i.e. the police's perusal and suppression of texts before publication, was replaced by the banning of already published texts that contained proscribed material; as authors, editors, publishers and printers were held collectively responsible, this resulted in pre-emptive censorship by printers which was stricter than the former police censorship.[49] Punishment no longer involved confiscation of property, but the police's right to administer corporal punishment for ordinary crimes, established under the Constitutionalists, was now extended to political culprits; intellectuals now suffered the indignity previously endured by peasants.[50] Popular anger at the repression authorised by the constitution focused on interior minister Milojković, as it had on his predecessor Hristić. The constitution effectively restored the Constitutionalist-era oligarchy—in this way it reflected Ristić's background as its former functionary—but cloaked it as a limited parliamentary system. It marked a curtailment of the prince's absolute power: Milan and his successor, Aleksandar Obrenović, would struggle but fail to exercise personal power of the kind enjoyed by Miloš and Mihailo. In contrast to Mihailo, who had attempted to exclude the populace from political life, the regency would seek to mobilise the populace behind its policies. But its tyranny was greater than that of Mihailo or the Constitutionalists.

The regency remained committed to Mihailo's nationalist and state-building policy. It continued developing the army, introducing officers' exams and a central inspectorate for the artillery. The First Serbian Bank was founded on 6 June 1869, followed by the Belgrade Credit Office on 24 September 1870. Under education minister Dimitrije Matić, a teacher training college was established in Kragujevac in October 1870, leading to the emergence of a trained teaching cadre, and import tax was abolished for foreign books, supposedly to diffuse learning among the populace. A law on bookshops of 12 October 1870 established a central bookshop with a monopoly on the sale of schoolbooks, post-free and freely advertised in newspapers to ensure their sale at minimum price.[51] The regency sought to improve economic conditions in the countryside and established a School of Agriculture and Forestry on 19 October 1870. A law on village shops of 15 October 1870 ended the restrictions by which there could be only one shop per village and by which new shops could be opened only with government permission, which had been rarely given. These restrictions had been supported by shopkeepers in the towns, who benefited from the limiting of competition. Their repeal greatly increased the number of village shops, accelerating rural economic development.[52]

The regency pursued a forward policy both southward, vis-à-vis the Ottoman territories of Macedonia and 'Old Serbia' (broadly corresponding to modern Kosovo and the Sanjak), and westward, vis-à-vis Bosnia and Hercegovina. It established a cultural committee in 1868 aimed at establishing Serbian schools in Old Serbia and Macedonia. This policy was further incentivised when the Porte's firman of 28 February 1870 established a Bulgarian Exarchate—effectively an autocephalous national church—with jurisdiction over dioceses to the south of Serbia: Niš, Pirot, Skopje, Debar and Veles. This was motivated by the Porte's desire to promote the Bulgarians, a stateless hence less threatening people, at the expense of the Greeks and Serbs. The population of these territories was not yet properly ethnically differentiated between Serbs and Bulgarians; a group of citizens of Vranje apparently protested against the Ottoman government's inclusion of Vranje under the jurisdiction of the Exarchate, insisting they were neither Bulgarians nor Serbs, but 'Slavs'.[53] It was thus very much open which of the two nations would co-opt this population. The expansion of Bulgarian influence in the lands to Serbia's south in the 1870s was consequently decisive in orienting Serbia away from vaguer plans for supporting anti-Ottoman uprisings in Macedonia and toward straightforward southward expansion. By 1873, there were over 60 Serbian schools in Old Serbia and Macedonia, though they largely disappeared following the Serbian–Ottoman wars of 1876–1878.[54]

Mihailo's death gravely damaged Serbia's credibility among politically conscious Bosnian Serbs. Consequently, from its early days, the regency worked to reconstruct its influence over the irredentist network in Bosnia, to whose activists it sent money. A Bosnian Serb activist, Niko Okan, who was on the Serbian government's payroll, was commissioned to compose a plan to liberate Bosnia, which he completed in September 1868. It envisioned a popular uprising, after which Serbia's army would intervene and play the main role in Bosnia's liberation. Okan and his fellow Serbian government agents worked to establish armed bands.[55] This strategy envisaged co-option of members of the Bosnian Muslim elite as well as Catholics, while Serbia's government simultaneously assisted the spread of Serb schools in Bosnia 'to awaken Serb national consciousness'. Serbia's government negotiated in autumn 1870 with the Porte, Britain and Russia for the peaceful acquisition of all Bosnia-Hercegovina and Old Serbia, which it would 'administer' on the Sultan's behalf; this sought to build on the precedent of the transfer to Serbia of the six fortresses, likewise under the fig leaf of administering them on the Sultan's behalf.[56] Unsurprisingly, nothing came of this.

Austria-Hungary increasingly cultivated Serbia as a satellite, helping move it toward full independence. It signed an agreement on postal services with Serbia on

2 December 1869, disregarding Ottoman objections to treating it as an independent state. It permitted the transit of armaments to Serbia, although it did not permit the same to Romania. Through Kállay's mediation, the Franco-Hungarian Bank of Pest provided half the capital for the founding of the First Serbian Bank. According to Ristić, Austria-Hungary went still further: Kállay offered Serbia a deal, with the blessing of his government and Austria's emperor himself, whereby it would remain neutral in the event of a war between Austria-Hungary and a third party, in return for which, after the war, Vienna would partition Bosnia-Hercegovina with Serbia, with Serbia receiving the two-thirds of the country east of the Vrbas and Neretva rivers and Austria the remaining third. This offer came in autumn 1870 when Ristić was negotiating with the Porte to acquire all Bosnia-Hercegovina. Ristić rejected it, partly out of mistrust of Vienna, partly out of fear of retaliation from the 'third party' (Russia) and partly out of unwillingness to sacrifice a third of the 'Serb lands' of Bosnia-Hercegovina.[57]

Origins of Serbian socialism

The two groups targeted by the regency for retribution for Mihailo's assassination, Karađorđevićites and socialists, overlapped significantly. Socialism arose on a Karađorđevićite base much as liberalism had arisen on an Obrenovićite base. This was possible due to Serbia's social homogeneity and the smallness of its educated stratum. The Serbian socialist movement's founder was Svetozar Marković. His father Radoje had been a supporter of Aleksandar Karađorđević in the 1830s and had participated in the Obrenović dynasty's overthrow in 1842. Radoje's career consequently blossomed during Aleksandar's reign and he allegedly died of shock when Aleksandar was overthrown in 1858, fearing Miloš's vengeance.[58] Another pioneering socialist was Dragiša Stanojević, Petar Karađorđević's former schoolmate. His father Jeremije had been Aleksandar's adviser, while his mother was Persida's second cousin Marija, daughter of Archpriest Mateja. A third prominent early socialist was Vladimir Ljotić. His father Dimitrije was a trader from Smederevo and a loyal Karađorđevićite. Allegedly, this loyalty originated during the First Serbian Uprising when Dimitrije's father Đorđe Ljotić, first of the family to bear that surname, and his brothers had been close to Karađorđe, fought under him and hosted him frequently in their house, as on the occasion when he received Smederevo's surrender from the Turks.[59] Đorđe was forced into exile by Miloš during his first reign; his son Dimitrije joined the Constitutionalist opposition and participated in the overthrow of the Obrenović dynasty in 1842. Dimitrije was then forced into exile, alongside Aleksandar, following the Karađorđević dynasty's overthrow in 1858.

Vladimir Ljotić, a close friend of Svetozar Marković and member of the United Serb Youth, was arrested in 1868 following Mihailo's assassination but released the following year. He resided in Paris at the time of the Commune in 1871 and

LIBERALS, SOCIALISTS AND NATIONALISM FROM BELOW

translated the *Communist Manifesto* into Serbian. Nevertheless, he had remained a close friend of the Karađorđevićes, becoming Aleksandar's secretary and tutor to his two youngest sons.[60] Vladimir was married to Dragiša Stanojević's cousin Ljubica; according to her memoirs, he also acted as informal mentor to Aleksandar's other sons, even introducing them to the United Serb Youth and its ideals, while Persida was a benefactress to socialists, including Stanojević and the Bosnian revolutionary Vaso Pelagić.[61] Ljotić drew the brothers Jevrem and Svetozar Marković into his plans for the Karađorđević dynasty's restoration; Jevrem even received money from Petar.[62] The Karađorđevićites considered Jevrem one of their own; he was eventually arrested in December 1877 after apparently conspiring with them for the Obrenović dynasty's overthrow.[63] Petar himself translated and published a Serbian edition of John Stuart Mill's *On Liberty*, which he distributed through the United Serb Youth. Thus, the old rivalry of the Obrenović dynasty with the Karađorđević dynasty and Nenadović family influenced the birth of the Serbian socialist movement.[64]

Socialism as a movement did not emerge in Serbia as a reaction against established liberalism or capitalism. Rather, in a case of 'combined and uneven development', socialist ideas first became known in Serbia thanks to the 1848 revolutions, but more properly in the 1860s, only a decade or so later than the liberal movement. This was at a time when domestic capitalism was still in its infancy and Serbia was still a relatively egalitarian society, without the stark class divisions characteristic of Western Europe, Germany, Austria-Hungary or Russia and without a large industrial proletariat. Meanwhile, with most Serbs still living under alien rule outside Serbia's borders, the national question inevitably assumed greater importance than the class question for socialists, as for other Serbian political currents.[65] In Serbia, therefore, socialism meant something different from what it meant elsewhere. Rather than advocating that capitalism be superseded in favour of a more socially just system, early Serbian socialists opposed the emergence of capitalism in the first place, believing that the capitalist stage could be skipped and Serbia could move directly to socialism.[66] Serbian socialism was therefore anti-modern.

The conservative turn in European politics following defeat of the 1848–1849 revolutions profoundly affected Serbian intellectual development. Russia's consul in 1849 pressed Serbia's government to desist from sending students to West European universities abroad, rightly fearing they were returning home with liberal ideas. Philosophers, lawyers and historians from the Belgrade lycée were prohibited from studying in the West. Serbian students consequently studied at Russian universities instead, or studied technical subjects like agronomy, engineering and economics rather than the liberal arts.[67] The earliest pioneer of socialist ideas in Serbia was Živojin Žujović (1838–1870), who, though he left little trace on Serbian political thinking, typified what would come later. He studied at the Belgrade seminary, then at Russia's Kiev seminary. He was a fiery nationalist, writing in 1867: 'There is one condition for national survival of the Serbs: that is unification of all Serbs on the Balkan peninsula;

unification of the contemporary Serbian principality with its natural parts: Bosnia, Montenegro, Hercegovina into a single indivisible whole. Without that, we Serbs have no future; we have no life; without that, we are a short-lived fiction.'[68] He viewed Mihailo's suppression of Serbia's Liberal opposition and press as moving it further from its proper goal of national liberation and unification, while at the same time he criticised the Liberals for their capitulation to the prince's autocracy. Thus, socialism began in Serbia in response to the Liberals' betrayal of their principles and accommodation with the regime.[69] Žujović was influenced by the anarchist ideas of Pierre-Joseph Proudhon (1809–1865) and advocated state decentralisation and municipal self-government, but his commitment to Serb national goals prevented him from completely abandoning support for the Serbian state.

Svetozar Marković and anti-state nationalism

Svetozar Marković (1846–1875) is universally acknowledged as the father of Serbian socialism. He began as a nationalist and fundamentally remained so, and the socialism he sired remained inseparably bound up with nationalism and with the defence of Serbia's native society from the corrupting influence of foreign capitalism. Born in the small town of Zaječar in eastern Serbia's Timok region, which had become part of the Serbian principality only in 1833, thirteen years before he was born, he claimed to be of partly Albanian descent and that his principal memory of his father was that he had wanted to kill Svetozar's mother with a pistol but was prevented from doing so by local peasants. He recalled the physically and mentally abusive behaviour of teachers toward pupils at his gymnasium in Kragujevac and their sterile teaching methods, which were perhaps responsible for his lifelong dislike of state authority.[70] He studied at the Great School's Technical Faculty, where he came under the mentorship of his professor, Vladimir Jovanović. Consequently, Marković began as a liberal.[71] However, unlike the previous generation of liberals represented by Jovanović, who were shaped by studying in Western or Central Europe, Marković in 1866 was awarded a scholarship from Russia's foreign ministry to study in St Petersburg. There, in January 1867, he helped establish a Serbian Commune of which he was secretary and Sava Grujić vice-president. This group described itself as the 'Russian wing' of the United Serb Youth, with which it claimed it 'agreed completely'.[72] Marković was shaped by the prevailing Russian radical intellectual climate; according to Slobodan Jovanović, 'Not only were Marković's ideas Russian, but there was something Russian in the way in which Marković propagated them, in which was felt an almost religious depth of belief and a similarly religious intolerance and exclusivity. Through his notes, a breath of Russian political mysticism came to our country.'[73]

Regarding the Serbian government's military preparations, Marković wrote in 1866: 'We rejoice in all this, because we think that the Serbian government has finally realised its task, and its road to achieve it. But how we are shaken when we hear: "The Serbian government pleads with Austria to mediate in the request to the Sultan that the Turkish garrisons be withdrawn from the towns by peaceful means."' He advocated a more radical policy: 'Everyone alive cries, that there is no other path for the solution of the Eastern Question, but a war of life and death between the Christians and the Muslims. What role does Serbia have in this struggle? We ask you this, Serbian government! You are silent ...' He complained that the government was shirking its obligations to wage such a war: 'We believe the Serbian government that in 1862 it was not ready for war, and we can confidently inform it in advance that, being the way it is, it will not even in a century be ready: to avenge Kosovo.' However:

> Serbia has another strength, stronger than all its bayonets, stronger than all the Sultan's armies. Serbia has within itself the power to make the peoples of the Balkan peninsula cry out: we don't want to be Turkey. And that is more than everything; that is the force that overthrows the unjust Turkish rule. For that reason, Serbia is ready both now and forever (and still in today's circumstances the task is made more easy by half). For that reason, it needs neither Bismarck, nor Beust, but only: the fraternal union of all Christians in Turkey, rejoicing in their nation—public and internal freedom.[74]

Marković was only twenty at this time and his views subsequently became more sophisticated. Yet he retained the idea, inherited from Jovanović and the Liberals but radicalised, that the corrupt ruling elite was betraying the national struggle, which the 'people' could better solve, regardless of the actual balance of forces in the world at large.

The following year, 1867, he denounced the Serbian government's peaceful, diplomatic resolution of the question of the Ottoman garrisons, expressing his faith in the Balkan masses' desire for war and revolution, in the Serb people's fighting potential stemming from patriotic enthusiasm regardless of formal military training, and in the readiness of the Ottoman Christian masses to rise in revolution behind Serbia:

> In reality, the Serbian government deemed itself insufficiently strong for its 60,000 soldiers, armed with guns with rifled barrels and considerable artillery, to enter into combat with the exhausted Turkish army that for so long had not been in a condition to subdue a handful of Montenegrins and Hercegovinians armed with the worst weapons and almost without any reserves. It did not trust in the enthusiasm of its nation that (to which history, particularly Serbian history, bears witness) often has much greater meaning than the best reserves in an army without enthusiasm, as the Turkish army was; it did not trust in the forces of the revolution of the Christian population of Turkey, a revolution that was ready to ignite across the whole of the Turkish empire at the first signal from Serbia's side; it did not trust in the sympathy of its Slav brothers, its natural allies.[75]

In Marković's view, the revolution should be Serb and nationalist and result in war:

> In Serbia there exists, on the one hand, the national direction that is the entire Serb nation, full of belief and hope in itself and its future, which seeks for itself all the conditions needed for the life of a nation; it openly and intentionally announces that it can no longer be satisfied with any kind of measures that will keep it in the transitory condition in which it has found itself up till now; it announces that it needs complete freedom and complete unity, and this leads down only one road—to war with Turkey![76]

Ivan Bochkaryov, a Russian who had attended the United Serb Youth's second congress, recruited Marković and Grujić into his radical Russian student group, which followed the revolutionary ideas of Nikolay Chernyshevsky (1828–1889), thus leading Marković increasingly away from the Serbian Liberals. After the United Serb Youth's third congress in September 1868 expressed confidence in the regency, Marković broke decisively with the Liberals and their strategy of achieving national liberation and unification under the regime's leadership. In the months that followed, under the influence of Bochkaryov and of Chernyshevsky's ideas, Marković began seeing himself as leader of a 'radical party' which would head a revolution in Serbia.[77] Fearing persecution by the authorities, he left St Petersburg in April 1869 and moved to Zurich. Switzerland, a relatively liberal and democratic republic organised as a loose, decentralised union of autonomous cantons with a weak central authority, would greatly influence his vision of a Serbia similarly organised.[78]

Marković is often credited by sympathetic scholars for his opposition to the concept of a 'Great Serbia'.[79] Yet what he opposed was not unification of Serbs within and without Serbia—in Bosnia, Hercegovina, Montenegro and beyond—to form a larger unit, but the idea that this could be accomplished 'from above', by Serbia's military expansion led by its prince, and that the outcome should be an expanded, centralised Serbian state. This opposition reflected his reaction against Mihailo's authoritarian rule, which increased the burden on the common people without achieving results. Marković favoured instead Serb unification achieved 'from below', by popular revolt, resulting in a looser, more decentralised union based on popular self-government. In 1868, he distinguished the two types of unification as those championed by 'legitimists' and 'populists' respectively, drawing a parallel between the Piedmontese prime minister, Count Cavour, who had pursued Italian unification through military conquest in alliance with the French emperor, and the rebel adventurer Giuseppe Garibaldi, who had pursued it through revolution.[80] Yet he acknowledged that the division between the two was not absolute, and following Mihailo's assassination he paid a glowing tribute to the fallen champion of '*liberation* and unification of the entire Serb nation [emphasis in original] ... who was the representative of the great idea of the freedom of the whole of Serbdom'.[81]

LIBERALS, SOCIALISTS AND NATIONALISM FROM BELOW

Marković bestowed upon the Serb national idea the leading role in his envisaged Balkan revolution. He wrote in 1871 that 'a single common idea has taken root in our literature as well as, and possibly even more so, among the entire Serb nation, and that is: that the Serb nation should *politically unify*. The Serbs from Montenegro, Dalmatia, Hercegovina, Bosnia, Serbia, Austria-Hungary and elsewhere wish to form a *Serb state*.' Consequently, 'The idea: Serb unity—that is the most revolutionary idea that exists on the whole of the Balkan peninsula from Istanbul to Vienna. That idea already contains within itself: the destruction of Turkey and Austria, the end of Serbia and Montenegro as independent principalities and a revolution in the entire political system of the Serb nation. From parts of those two empires and from two Serb principalities there becomes one, new Serb state—that is what Serb unity means' (emphases in original). These principles were included in the 'Programme of the Serb Socialist Party', adopted by the congress of Serb socialists in Zurich in July 1872: 'That the Serb nation cannot be liberated from social slavery until these states are destroyed: Turkey, Serbia, Montenegro and Austria-Hungary.' This was to be achieved through a revolution led by an alliance of socialists across the Balkan peninsula and southern Austria-Hungary. The states were to be replaced by a 'federation of free municipalities'.[82] As Slobodan Jovanović put it, Marković advocated 'a Serb federation, thus not a Great Serbia.'[83] As Marković outlined in a letter written in November 1873, he viewed the Council of 1807, established during the First Serbian Uprising, as the model for the authority in the liberated Serbia he envisioned, consisting of an elected delegate from each okrug.[84]

Marković contrasted the revolutionary character of the Serb national idea with what he saw as the regressive striving for 'historical-state rights of Hungary, Croatia, Bohemia and other Austrian lands' and for a federation of the historical Habsburg lands under the Habsburg emperor, which he believed represented '*the worst form of state* that it was possible to imagine' (emphasis in original).[85] The issue arose because of the different historical paths followed by Croatia and Serbia: Croatia had passed to the Hungarian crown in 1102 and to the Habsburgs in 1527, but it remained a kingdom in its own right, a fact that underpinned Croat nationalist ideology. By contrast, given the Ottoman destruction of the Serbian medieval kingdom, Serb nationalist ideology had no continuously existing historical statehood to build upon, but based itself upon the legacy of the Serbian revolution of 1804–1815. Marković believed in the superiority of revolutionary Serb nationalism that cut across state borders over supposedly reactionary Croat nationalism based on historical statehood. This would become a staple of Serb nationalist thinking.

Marković nevertheless went beyond Serb nationalism to embrace a broader vision of Balkan unity. He eventually admitted that it was the ideal of Serb unification itself that was revolutionary rather than its realisation: 'We have stated that Serb *state* unity, and the founding of a Great Serb state, is the *most revolutionary idea* of all that have arisen on the Balkan peninsula, for it negates the state right of

Turkey, Serbia, Montenegro, Austria and Hungary, but we have at the same time said that that idea is *impossible, a utopia*, and furthermore: *that it is damaging to the Serb nation.*' Serb unity could only be part of a more general Balkan unity, and while 'contemporary Serbia can be a *lever*, a *bulwark*, for the launching of a revolutionary war in the Balkan peninsula and for the destruction of the existing state order, which divides the Serb nation and holds it in slavery together with the other subordinate nations in Turkey' (emphases in original), this could not happen, he repeated, through the Serbian military occupation of Bosnia and Hercegovina, as Serbian Liberals and Conservatives favoured.[86] Despite opposing a South Slav federation based on historical lands within the Habsburg framework, he was decisively influenced by federalist ideas for solving the national question. These originated with thinkers in Central Europe, above all in the Habsburg lands, whose outlook was shaped by the reality of inhabiting states based upon some degree of multinational pluralism.[87] Noting that the three principal components of the projected Great Serbia among the Ottoman lands—Serbia, Montenegro and Bosnia-Hercegovina—had very different internal conditions, he argued that Serbia's administrative system could not be imposed on the others: 'A *federal system* is much more advantageous for development and progress, in which each of these three principal parts of the Serb nation in Turkey would have its own independent internal organisation and in which it would develop independently' (emphasis in original). This federation would then unite with the Bulgarians to form a 'Serb–Bulgarian federation', which could grow into a 'federation of the nations of the Balkan peninsula'.[88]

Like Karl Marx, Marković developed a model of socialism bound up with his interpretation of history. His fullest work, *Serbia in the East* (1872), was a historical treatise on Serbia before, during and after its liberation from the Ottomans. He presented an idealised picture of traditional Serbian patriarchal society, ironically preserved under Ottoman rule: 'In Serbia, the Turks never lived in the villages; there, the Serb nation remained completely pure.' The life of ordinary Serbian people in this society compared favourably with the conditions of the modern working class in Western Europe: 'In Serbian patriarchal society there is never recorded either prostitution or the pauperism of which thousands of people in the West are suffering; among the Serb nation, celebration never turns into the drunkenness of which the working people in the West suffer, and love never turns into debauchery. Familial ties and communal reciprocity protected every individual from the eventual social illnesses which afflict the working people in the West. This reciprocity within the entire commune is reflected in everyday life, as in the work in the fields.' This pure, patriarchal Serbian society provided the germ for the revolution against the Ottomans: 'Zadruga and commune—those two Serb institutions remained untouched by the Turkish state system. In them, the Serb nation gathered its broken national life and with it resisted the Turks ... For the Serb nation, this was the moral and material source from which seeped the strength for liberation from Turkish rule.'[89]

Marković realised the brutality this liberation involved: 'The Serb nation went simply to *exterminate* the Turks. This was shown later in the Serbian uprisings, when the Serbs killed Turks who surrendered to them in faith. Toward the Turks, the Serbs had a particular conception of justice and morality. Their "conscience" was as if not troubled in the slightest in the carrying out of any kind of acts evil by our contemporary standards, simply in order to avenge the oppression that the Turks had committed for centuries' (emphasis in original). He did not view this negatively: 'The upheaval that the revolution brought about in the Serb nation is so huge that today we literally cannot express its true meaning. This was not simply the division of Turkish state landholdings, nor a change of government, rather, an entire non-working class of people who lived a wholly different life, spoke a different language, practised a different religion and considered the Serb people to be its property was erased ... Thus, at one stroke, the Serb nation became free both socially and politically.' But paradoxically, the Serbs' national liberation also marked the start of their social decay: 'Thus: with the destruction of the Turkish element in Serbia, culture began to change in the Serb nation. From that period, the Serbs began to live in the towns and the Eastern manners, customs, products, taste and so forth, which reigned in the towns, were replaced by European ones. From that period began the economic importance of the towns, and the process of the decay of the patriarchal economic organisation of the Serb nation in the villages began.'[90]

Marković linked Serbian society's decay to several phenomena. He condemned the hatt-ı şerif of 1830, formally establishing Serbia's autonomy, as meaning 'that Turkey determined the state form of the Serb nation, and that in monarchical form'. Hence, 'the *hatt-ı şerif* and *berat* of 1830 were a death blow for the Serbian revolution. The struggle for liberation and unification of the entire Serb nation, and even the very thought of them, was wholly abandoned. Instead of that, in Serbia began the ordering of a monarchical state.' Likewise, 'The *hatt-ı şerif* of 1838 was a death blow for the development of internal freedom in Serbia just as the *hatt-ı şerif* of 1830 was a death blow for the development of external freedom and the struggle with Turkey.'[91] It promoted the rise of the bureaucracy, which replaced the Turks as the new ruling elite in Serbia; the bureaucrats 'primarily relied upon foreign courts and the Porte' and were initially either 'minions and accomplices of Prince Miloš himself' or 'immigrants from Austria who wanted to "civilise" "barbarian" Serbia'. Miloš had therefore, in Marković's view, betrayed Karađorđe's revolutionary struggle and, by collaborating with the Turks, perpetuated their oppression of the Serbs in a new form.

The rise of party politics and accompanying political divisions 'had to have had a terribly bad influence on all true relations of the Serb nation'. Along with the bureaucracy, as a further by-product of the appearance of an urban population, rose the merchant class: 'Together with the increase in wealth of the Serb nation, the very character of production changed. In a patriarchal household, almost every house produced itself what it needed to live. Now a class of people was expanding more and more, who did not directly produce anything that they needed to live, but acquired that through exchange—*buying* and *selling*.' So, 'With such an outlook on economic relations, all previous patriarchal relations that had existed in the extended families and the municipalities had to vanish: the *lending* of work and capital, free help in work when that was needed, assistance in need and sickness—all that disappeared. Work acquired a price like other commodities and capital received a percentage—for every day of work a *wage* was paid; for the use of capital, *interest* was paid' (emphases in original).[92] The emergence of an authoritarian dynastic regime, based on the bureaucracy and army and pursuing the goal of expansion from above, was an expression of this decay.

Marković counterposed the Serbian reality of his day to what he saw as the 'natural' Serbian order—an organic, egalitarian, collectivist order arising from traditional, patriarchal society. As the historian Gale Stokes notes, 'Marković was not a moderniser. He was a populist who believed in the wisdom, virtues and right to govern of the common people, who in Serbia were made up of self-sufficient peasants.'[93] In Marković's words:

> The natural development of Serbian civilisation would have been that those same concepts of relations of members, which already exist in the Serb municipality, be consolidated, extended and institutionally realised; that on that same basis be organised okrugs, as a collection of socio-economic municipalities, and the whole state as a collection of large municipalities—okrugs. In that way, the new Serbian state would have become a social institution—an institution whose goal it was that the general, social strength develop and perfect every particular individual, that it develop and organise the work and production of the nation; in a word, the Serbian state would become that which the contemporary European state is striving to become, and that is: a collective in which people want that every individual should acquire for himself all those provisions, which he is not able to acquire through his own strength.

Unfortunately, 'In Serbia, "civilisation" has begun in that direction that today is called in the West: "bourgeois civilisation"', which 'is measured only by the number of rich people and the quantity of material goods which they can put on display before the outside world; a civilisation that is characterised by the magnificence of the owners; the richness and splendour of their surroundings; and at the same time, the degradation and complete poverty of the majority of the people'.[94] Marković opposed the development of the capitalist class and proletariat which Marx viewed as essential for socialism's eventual triumph. As the historian Latinka Perović notes, 'The whole of his work represents an endeavour that, in the development of the Serbian people, the division into classes be avoided.'[95]

LIBERALS, SOCIALISTS AND NATIONALISM FROM BELOW

Marković approved of the 1848 St Peter's Day parliament's demand for the expulsion of 'foreign bureaucrats', i.e. those who were Austrian Serbs. He argued that a social revolution in Bosnia would 'destroy the local aristocracy', i.e. the Bosnian Muslim landlord class. He believed: 'But when a revolution is recognised as the true basis for a new Serb state, then there disappears the state right of the independent Serb statelets of Serbia and Montenegro; those states themselves disappear, and there remains the entire Serb nation, as a collection of particular individuals, who by general agreement found a new legal order. To create this kind of order on the Balkan peninsula; to destroy all state shackles, which divide and crush the Serb nation, all—*that is the principal task of Serbia*.'[96] Such a revolution would be directed not merely against the existing states and borders of the Balkans, but against the alien, Western civilisational model that he saw as having corrupted the Serb nation: 'Through revolution, the Serb nation liberates its patriarchal institutions, the remnants of its former civilisation, from the pressure of Turkish oppression and equally from the pressure of foreign forms. The Serb nation acquires the possibility of raising on the basis of its national institutions and concepts, and on the basis of contemporary science, an original, Slavic social edifice.'[97]

In sum, Marković argued for a revolt against the Serbian bureaucratic state and embryonic liberal-capitalist socio-economic order with its Western cultural trappings, to restore the traditional Serbian national-patriarchal institutions of the pre-1804 era, skip the capitalist stage of development and achieve socialism. This would be part of a wider pan-Balkan revolt against the Ottomans that would bring about Serb unity 'from below' on the basis of decentralisation, popular local self-government and Balkan federation.

Socialists and Liberals split

The price paid by Serbia's Liberals for the Regency Constitution was the endorsement of a regime dominated by Mihailo's former ministers which continued his pro-Hungarian foreign policy. They therefore abandoned collaboration with Miletić's Serb Liberals of Hungary, who in January 1869 had organised their first political party—the National Liberal Party.[98] At the United Serb Youth's fourth congress at Kikinda in Hungary on 5 September 1869, the Hungarian Serb Liberals blocked a resolution put forward by Serbia's Vasiljević, similar to the one at the third congress, expressing confidence in the regency. Meanwhile, the Liberals' apparent capitulation to the regime led to the blossoming in Serbia itself of the new, left-liberal or socialist current, which during the Congress vocally opposed the older Liberal generation.

The socialist movement in Serbia, distinct from the Liberals, truly took off in 1870. Marković affiliated to Marx's International, subsequently known as the First International, through its Russian section. He became in the second half of 1870 a member of the governing committee of the United Serb Youth and its representative in Belgrade.⁹⁹ In May 1870 in Zurich, Marković and three comrades—Đura Ljočić, Pera Velimirović and Nikola Pašić—agreed to form a new political party, which Marković insisted be called Radical. At the United Serb Youth's fifth congress opening in Novi Sad on 8 September 1870, deputies were not only split between pro- and anti-regency Liberals, broadly corresponding to the geographical division between Serbs in Serbia and Serbs in Hungary, but also between Jovanović's Liberals and Marković's socialists. Neither of these could gain ascendancy over the other, so their struggle for control of the Youth continued. Following the congress, Jovanović linked Marković's followers to the 'red spectre of Panslavism' and the threat of Russian imperialism.¹⁰⁰ A major step had been taken toward Serb nationalism's division into pro- and anti-Western currents.

Marković and his followers became the bitterest critics of the accord between the regency and the Liberals and of the new order established by the Regency Constitution. Marković wrote to Jovanović on 4 December 1870 that 'the greatest misfortune for the Serb people would be to be liberated under the Obrenović dynasty. I want liberation through popular revolt—through revolution.'¹⁰¹ Marković founded the first socialist newspaper in Serbia and the Balkans on 1 June 1871, *Radenik* (Worker). It agitated against the government's plans for building railways that would link Serbia with the railway networks of Austria-Hungary and the Ottoman Empire. While the government spoke of the necessity of ensuring Serbia would not be bypassed by the railways linking the Ottoman Empire with Europe, thereby becoming a backwater, *Radenik* highlighted the danger of Austro-Hungarian economic domination and the advantages the railway links would give the Ottomans in the event of war. Socialist nationalism was thus directed against the international links that modernisation brought. Meanwhile, a voice in Serbia's parliament against the railways was provided by the maverick left-Liberal Ljubomir Kaljević, sometime friend of the socialists and Karađorđević sympathiser.¹⁰²

The United Serb Youth's sixth congress opened at Vršac in Hungary on 26 August 1871. Thereafter, Jovanović's and Marković's followers could no longer cooperate. Because of this and because of Hungarian repression, the United Serb Youth never held another congress.¹⁰³ The Liberal youth mostly defected to Marković's new movement, leaving the Old Liberals as generals without an army.¹⁰⁴ The socialists now became the carriers of revolutionary opposition to the regime of prince, oligarchy, army and bureaucracy. But though he was best remembered by posterity as father of Serbian socialism, Marković's contribution to mainstream Serbian national politics would prove more significant. For his movement spawned the Radical party, which would abandon socialism in favour of pro-peasant populism to become the most important political party in Serbia until the 1920s, while his ideology of Serb nationhood would, through his disciples, particularly Pašić, dominate Serbian nationalist thinking until the twenty-first century.

LIBERALS, SOCIALISTS AND NATIONALISM FROM BELOW

Mihailo's assassination, though executed by fringe malcontents, expressed the strong, widespread opposition to his regime that had developed by 1868. The split that had emerged in it between Conservatives and Court Liberals enabled the latter to take power after his death, through controlling the army and appeasing the desire for liberal constitutional reform, resulting in the Regency Constitution and establishment of controlled parliamentarism. Yet this did not quell pressure for more radical change. The nationalism of the opposition, first Liberal, then socialist, not only demanded a more aggressive reckoning with the Ottoman enemy but was directed against Serbia's own governing institutions created since the 1830s and against cultural Westernisation of its elite. It advocated instead progress based on Serbia's traditional institutions and culture. The resulting Radical party would become the toughest challenger that the regime of prince, oligarchy, army and bureaucracy had so far faced.

PART II

INDEPENDENCE AND THE TWO SERBIAS

7

ACHIEVEMENT OF INDEPENDENCE

1872–1880

Prince Milan, who succeeded to the throne in 1868, would lead Serbia to independence and become its first modern king. As autocratic by inclination as his predecessors, Princes Miloš and Mihailo, he was, thanks to the Regency Constitution, never able to exercise despotism as securely as they had. The first part of his rule witnessed the emergence of the Radical party, which would grow into an organised mass opposition of a kind his predecessors had not faced. Interlinked with this revolutionary threat at home were the revolutionary pressures in the wider Balkans confronting the Ottoman Empire, of which Serbia was still formally part, resulting in major uprisings in Hercegovina and Bosnia in 1875 and in the Bulgarian region in 1876. With danger for the regime went opportunity, for Serbian statesmen, primarily Liberals, sought to exploit these anti-Ottoman rebellions to achieve Serbia's independence and expand its borders, while managing the revolutionary contagion at home. Serbia thus experienced its greatest crisis since the 1810s.

Prince Milan attains his majority

Milan (1854–1901) attained his majority on 22 August 1872. At the ceremony marking this, a new Serbian anthem was introduced, 'God of Justice', composed by Davorin Jenko (1835–1914), a Slovene, with lyrics by Jovan Đorđević (1826–1900), a Hungarian Serb. It was adopted as the Serbian national anthem and, after a long interlude, was readopted as such in the twenty-first century, with minor changes to the lyrics, and remains so today.

> God of justice, you who saved us
> From ruin so far!
> Hear our voices from now on,
> And from now on be our salvation!

SERBIA

> With a powerful hand he leads, he defends
> The future of the Serbian ship;
> God save, God feed
> The Serbian prince, the Serbian race![1]

Yet Milan was not so straightforwardly Serbian as the hymn suggested. His outlook was shaped by his cosmopolitan parentage and upbringing. The Principality of Wallachia ('Land of the Vlachs'), which in 1861 merged with the Principality of Moldavia to become Romania, was Serbia's immediate neighbour, with which the history of the Obrenović dynasty was closely linked. Miloš and his brother Jevrem had owned estates in Wallachia, and Jevrem's son, Milan's father, also called Miloš, served in the Romanian army. The younger Miloš married a Romanian woman from an aristocratic family, Elena Maria Catargiu, who subsequently became mistress to Alexandru Ioan Cuza, first prince (domnitor) of united Romania. As Miloš and Elena's son, Milan was a child of the Romanian aristocracy, so he hailed from a society with a much stronger sense of class distinctions than his father's native land, which may have influenced his attitude toward the Serbian peasantry. But since he was only Mihailo's cousin and Mihailo did not leave a will, he did not inherit any of his wealth, which went instead to Mihailo's closest relatives: his sister Petrija and her children. Milan would not therefore be a wealthy ruler, and lack of money would condition his life.[2]

Milan spent his early childhood in Wallachia and at the age of nine, at Mihailo's initiative, was sent to Paris for education. At his accession he spoke better French than Serbian. He never lost his foreign accent.[3] His father died young and his mother neglected him, so he grew up without parental guidance, developing a huge sense of entitlement and inability to view Serbia except in terms of his personal needs. His sometime prime minister Milan Piroćanac would comment in his diary: 'King Milan did not believe in God, or in people, or in love, or in faithfulness, nor in friendship, nor in justice, but he was firmly convinced that the world was created for the sake of his enjoyment and to satisfy his wishes.'[4] Milan felt little or no patriotic identification with Serbia; as he said to one Austro-Hungarian official, 'I have become accustomed to Western culture and traditions and at home I find only unreliable, petty people'. Were it not for needing to secure his son's eventual accession to the throne, 'I would immediately abandon this damned country that has caused me so many worries.'[5] Allegedly, when he subsequently placed Serbia under an Austro-Hungarian protectorate, some of his dignitaries rebuked him: 'Your Majesty, you've sold Serbia for three thousand ducats!' to which he replied, 'Surely you don't think I could have got more?'[6]

Milan was guided primarily by the aim of preserving his personal authority and dynastic succession. He identified not with the Serbian masses but with the elite, above all the army. According to Piroćanac, 'The Serbian people did not like King Milan.

ACHIEVEMENT OF INDEPENDENCE

They viewed him in general as a foreigner of Vlach blood, and King Milan hated the people, in payback, from the bottom of his soul.[7] Paranoid, temperamental and erratic, he never forgot his predecessor had been assassinated. His sense of insecurity was exacerbated by two incidents occurring when he was sixteen and seventeen. In June 1871, while he was attending the theatre in Belgrade, a bomb exploded in the fountain outside. On 6 October of the same year, he nearly drowned in Smederevo while visiting an outdoor water-closet that collapsed beneath him, depositing him in the sewage below, from which he saved himself by firing his revolver to attract help. The 'Terazije bomb' was too weak to have seriously hurt anyone and may have been merely a prank or an attempt to scare him, while the 'Smederevo plot' may have been merely an accident, but they played on his nervous disposition.[8] He never ceased to be terrified of sedition and conspiracy against his rule or his life.

Milan inherited a dangerous situation in Bosnia-Hercegovina that would soon grow into the principal issue facing Serbia. Sections of the United Serb Youth under Miletić's leadership had resolved during 1871 to plan the start of the national liberation struggle in Bosnia, aimed at establishing a unified state of Serbia, Bosnia, Hercegovina, Montenegro and Bulgaria. Montenegro's participation was envisaged. An envoy from Prince Nikola arrived in Novi Sad in June of that year to begin work on these plans with Miletić and Vaso Pelagić.[9] An Association for Serb Liberation and Unification was formed that year by the executive committee of the United Serb Youth in Cetinje. The regency in Belgrade was also informed of this plan and its support was sought. Despite his harsh criticism of Serbia's regime, Marković and his socialist circle supported such collaboration. Marković's brother Jevrem met with Blaznavac in December 1871 to collaborate over the planned Bosnian uprising, but Blaznavac, under Russian pressure, refused. Yet Blaznavac was not uninterested in harnessing the Serbian radical movement to the regency's expansionist strategy. Early the following year, Marković himself exchanged letters with Blaznavac to discuss collaboration, something that many of his followers considered a hypocritical U-turn.[10]

Ristić was hostile to such collaboration, however, and the involvement of the Montenegrin regime in the project was viewed suspiciously. There were justified fears that the Youth's insurrectionary plans would target the regency itself. Following a press campaign against the radicals spearheaded by the young Vladan Đorđević on behalf of the regime Liberals, the government in March 1872 initiated a clampdown and Marković fled to Novi Sad to avoid arrest. The socialist newspaper *Radenik* was suppressed in May while Ristić stepped up official Serbia's irredentist activity in Bosnia to avoid being outflanked by the Youth.[11] But the threat remained. In Novi Sad, Marković joined with Miletić to found a Central Revolutionary Liberation Committee, including representatives of the 'Serb lands' of Bosnia, Serbia, Montenegro and Slavonia, which worked to prepare an uprising in Bosnia, Hercegovina and Bulgaria. Associated committees were formed in Cetinje, Belgrade and Kragujevac. The purpose of the Kragujevac committee was, in Marković's words, 'by means of the uprising itself to draw Serbia into the struggle'.[12] Meanwhile, Milan's assumption of power undermined the irredentist preparations made by the regency and by Serbia's agents in Bosnia. Consequently, Belgrade's support for insurrectionary groups in Bosnia lapsed wholly by 1873, leaving it unprepared for the crisis erupting two years later.

Milan built his regime initially on the foundations of the regency, which formally ended on the day he attained his majority. That day, he appointed its members to lead his first government: Blaznavac as prime minister and war minister and Ristić as foreign minister. Blaznavac was also appointed general, the first in Serbia's army. Initially the regime's most powerful figure, he was suspected by some of aspiring to the throne himself. He propitiously married Milan's first cousin Katarina, whom Mihailo had wanted to marry. But he died unexpectedly on 5 April 1873, aged 49, apparently owing to his doctor's incompetence.[13] He was succeeded as prime minister by Ristić, now undisputed Liberal leader and Serbia's most powerful politician. Milan was not prepared to defer to him, however. With Blaznavac's death, Milan himself took over management of the army, which thereby became the Obrenović dynasty's principal mainstay—and ultimately its destroyer.

Eager to rid himself of his overbearing former regent, Milan dismissed Ristić's government in October 1873, replacing it with a Conservative administration. Like Mihailo, Milan identified more with the Conservatives than with the Liberals, and he resented the 1869 Liberal constitution. The Conservatives were in government until August 1875, in turn under Jovan Marinović, Aćim Čumić and Danilo Stefanović (brother of Stefan Stefanović Tenka). Their regime advanced Serbia's liberalisation. The Liberal regency's repressiveness had shifted Conservative thinking in favour of greater liberty. Marinović's government consequently introduced several liberal and modernising reforms: police control of the press and corporal punishment were abolished and the metric system of measures and a standardised national silver coinage introduced. The right to select the Great School's rector was transferred from the education minister to the collegium of professors, although it remained an elite institution: only 26.35 per cent of its pupils in 1874 were of peasant background.[14] Measures were introduced to promote industry and protect peasants from debt. Thus, the 1836 ban on the alienation of a peasant's property was extended in 1873; it now encompassed his house, stables and lot around his house up to a 'day of ploughing', or 5,760 metres, as well as a minimum of cropland, vineyards, orchards or forests plus unharvested crops equal to five 'days of ploughing', for a total of 3.5 hectares or 8.5 acres for every taxable head in the household. Minimum inalienable numbers were also specified for different types of livestock, farm equipment and food.[15] However, as the new law left 60 per cent of arable land unprotected, it did not resolve the problem of peasant indebtedness. An increasing number of peasants continued to be left either with unsustainably small plots or wholly landless.[16]

ACHIEVEMENT OF INDEPENDENCE

The Regency Constitution had been intended by Ristić to produce manageable parliaments, but the reality turned out differently. In the elections of October 1874, the Conservative government proved unable to employ the police to manipulate the results effectively because the previous Liberal regime had packed them with its agents. Despite the violence accompanying the election, including the shooting dead of the newly elected deputy for Gornji Milanovac, the new parliament was predominantly Liberal and the government failed to prevent Jevrem Marković's election in Jagodina. The new parliament's first address to the government, drafted by Kujundžić, a Liberal and United Serb Youth member, combined the demand for further liberal reforms with a denunciation of the results of Milan and Marinović's trip to Constantinople that spring, when they had failed to obtain the Sultan's promise to return to Serbia the disputed enclave of Mali Zvornik, on the Bosnian border. Marinović challenged the right of the parliamentary majority to include such political themes in its address, insisting that it be limited to a formal expression of loyalty to the prince. In the vote on this question, the government's victory was so narrow that Marinović had to resign.

Čumić, who served under Marinović as interior minister, succeeded him as prime minister on 7 December 1874, aged only 38. His affiliation with the Conservatives apparently originated less from ideological affinity than from a bitter dispute he had had as a pupil at the lycée with its Liberal professors, which began when he complained to its governing board about one of them, Stojan Veljković. He was thus a rebel against the older Liberal rebels.[17] He had railed against the regency's tyranny whilst in opposition, emerging for a while as the strongest Conservative voice. In 1871, he had even co-signed a political manifesto—Serbia's first—with leading socialists including Ljočić, Jevrem Marković and Pelagić, calling for self-management for municipalities and okrugs, freedom of the press, association and assembly, independence of the courts, rejection of the government's railway plan, complete abolition of the standing army and gendarmerie in favour of the national militia and full parliamentary control over the state budget.[18]

The Liberals remained divided between Old Liberals and Court Liberals, and both Marinović and Čumić attempted to collaborate with the former against the latter. Čumić's government represented a fusion of Young Conservatives, in particular Piroćanac as foreign minister, with young Liberals, in particular Kaljević as finance minister and Stojan Novaković as education minister, while two other Young Conservatives, Mijatović and Ilija Garašanin's son Milutin, had initially intended to be in the government but withdrew over a disagreement with Milan about its composition. The young prince appointed this government in order to exclude the older Conservatives, out of preference for working with those closer to his own age. This government had already collapsed at the start of February due to ministerial disagreements and lack of parliamentary support, but it assembled the politicians who would eventually form the Serbian Progressive Party and preside over a much more radical reform programme in the 1880s.[19] Meanwhile, the resignations of Marinović and Čumić established to a degree the principle of ministerial responsibility to parliament, which the constitution had not envisaged.[20] The parliament was now very powerful, presaging a struggle between left Liberals and Radicals, who wished to extend its competencies, and Prince Milan, who wished to revoke the constitution and return to untrammelled autocracy.

Birth of the Radical party

The city of Kragujevac was a flashpoint: it lay in the geographical heart of the country, whose only true industrial centre it was, with its armaments factory of 600 workers and a teacher training college full of youthful students; it was the usual location of the national parliament; the place where Vučić-Perišić had launched his rebellion that overthrew the Obrenović dynasty in 1842. Workers in Serbia at this time generally worked ten to fourteen hours a day and lacked pensions or health care.[21] For all these reasons, Svetozar Marković made it his base. There, in November 1872, he drafted a programme for a Radical party, under a general council modelled on the Serbian rebel council of 1807, with subsidiary councils at the okrug level, amounting to a solidly structured party organisation with roots among the people in the localities, of a kind new to Serbia. Its goal was to 'destroy completely the contemporary administrative system through a parliamentary decision', abolish the existing court system in favour of a system of elected courts, free the peasantry from debt and place Serbia's wealth at the disposal of the peasant masses through a system of central, okrug and district banks.[22]

The unique personality and outlook of Nikola Pašić (1845–1926), the young man who would come to personify the movement, shaped it from the start. His family originated from the predominantly Albanian Tetovo region in Macedonia and settled in Zaječar in the Timok region. His grandfather, a baker named Paša, bequeathed the family its surname. Nikola's exact date of birth is unknown.[23] He was an inarticulate public speaker, fuelling doubt among some that he was genuinely ethnically Serb,[24] though none of that prevented him from becoming Serbia's most popular politician for decades. That Pašić was Serbian in very much a peripheral sense may have inclined him toward the anti-establishment nationalism that characterised his early political career. He studied in Zurich, where his student community was largely dominated by Russian students whose revolutionary politics influenced him, and he read widely the works of Ferdinand Lassalle (1825–1864), Mikhail Bakunin (1814–1876) and others. This helped forge his peculiar synthesis of French Jacobinical single-chamber anti-pluralism and Slavophile opposition to Serbia's development along Western capitalist lines.

The name 'Radical' indicated inspiration from the French Radicals—the hardline Republicans represented by Alexandre Ledru-Rollin (1807–1874) and

ACHIEVEMENT OF INDEPENDENCE

Louis Blanc (1811–1882), who arose in opposition to the conservative monarchical regime in France during the first half of the nineteenth century. Many positions of the French Radicals would be shared by their Serbian counterparts: constitutional reform, single-chamber parliamentary sovereignty, universal suffrage, democratic freedoms, administrative decentralisation and local self-government, replacement of the standing army by a national militia, and social reform and welfare. The Serbian Radical leaders, who mostly spoke and read French, would by the 1880s be reading the French Radical press regularly.[25] Conversely, the idea that the principal class division in Serbia was between the peasant masses and an oppressive anti-national bureaucratic elite was formulated by Bakunin and heavily influenced Marković and Pašić.[26] Pašić was also close to Ljotić, whom he had known at least since 1872, when they had belonged to the Slavic Union in Zurich.[27] Marković, Pašić and Ljotić formed a 'solid trio' whose close friendship only death would end.[28] The young firebrand Pera Todorović, the third key mind behind the creation of the Radicals after Marković and Pašić, may also have embodied a Russo-French intellectual synthesis; he studied in Zurich along with Pašić and other future Radicals where he came under the same Russian left-wing influences.[29] In particular, Todorović developed the Radical party under the influence of the flowering Narodnik movement in Russia, particularly of its theorists Pyotr Lavrov (1823–1900) and Vasily Bervi-Flerovsky (1829–1918).[30] The Narodniks believed educated socialists should go to the countryside to immerse themselves in peasant life, and this is what the Radicals would do, eventually achieving much greater political success than the Narodniks ever did.

Supporters of Marković, including Sava Grujić, now manager of the armaments factory, and Todorović, active in the plot for an uprising in Bosnia, established in March 1873 the Council of the Kragujevac Social Printing Works, which sought to establish an editorial office, printing press and newspaper in the town. This was followed by the launching by Marković of the newspaper *Javnost* (Public), whose first issue appeared on 20 November. The radical community in Kragujevac grew into a 'commune', involving an influential section of the local citizenry, and established a women's school. The regime retaliated: officers were forbidden to participate in the council of the Kragujevac Social Printing Works and Grujić was dismissed as factory director. Nevertheless, a significant number of workers adopted Marković's ideas.[31] An armed peasant demonstration in Kragujevac in December 1873, 200 strong and led by Jevrem Marković, demanded the government temporarily halt all legal action against the peasantry pending new legislation. Svetozar Marković was arrested in January 1874, tried and sentenced to nine months' imprisonment, while *Javnost* was suppressed.[32] His health was so ruined by the time of his release that, after founding the newspaper *Oslobođenje* (Liberation) to replace *Javnost*, he died of tuberculosis on 10 March 1875.[33] Nevertheless, the socialist threat to the regime only increased, given socialist links to the Karađorđevićes. A lawyer and Karađorđevićite from Šabac, Jovan Milinković, attempted in autumn 1874 to launch a newspaper with

Marković's follower Dimitrije Cenić as editor, resulting in them both being jailed. The following year, the government learned that Prince Aleksandar was funding the Kragujevac commune.[34]

The future Radical deputies came together in the parliament elected in November 1874, marking the parliamentary Radical party's birth. By the time of Marković's death, the Radicals were firmly established as representatives of a Serbian populist reaction against the modern bureaucratic state and embryonic liberal-capitalist order. Liberals and Conservatives had made no effort to mobilise among the disaffected peasantry and Milan lacked his great uncle Miloš's charisma and ability to speak its language. This created a political vacuum that the Radicals filled. They stood in the tradition of earlier anti-bureaucratic populists such as the Liberals of 1858, Vučić-Perišić's rebels of 1842 and Đak's rebels of 1825, but they were the first to build a party organisation to channel peasant anger. This distinguished them from regimes since the regency, which relied on police coercion to win peasant votes, and from regimes before the regency, which had simply sought to keep the peasants in their place.

As they acquired mass peasant support, the Radicals came to equate their party with the nation and other parties with the supposedly alien, non-national elite. As Todorović wrote in spring 1875, 'Today, there stands, armed with learning, an entire mighty party in the country; a national party in it.'[35] The Radical leaders were mostly foreign-educated but none was from Belgrade or a rich family; they were mostly from peasant or craftsman families from the villages or small towns. Whereas the prior Serbian political elite had hailed primarily from western Serbia, the Radical leaders were disproportionately from eastern and southern Serbia—areas that had been under Ottoman rule until 1833—including Svetozar Marković and Pašić themselves, Adam Bogosavljević, Pera Velimirović, Kosta Taušanović, Raša Milošević, Aca Stanojević and Stojan Protić—and this remained their heartland. In particular, Marković, Pašić and Bogosavljević, three of the four principal founders of the party, all came from Zaječar, a town close to the Bulgarian border, while the fourth, Pera Todorović, was from the Karađorđevićite heartland near Topola.[36] The rise of the Radicals thus represented a regional as well as generational shift in Serbian politics.

Following his mentor Marković's death, Pašić broke with the international socialist movement over its unwillingness to support the uprising in Hercegovina that had begun in summer 1875. The uprising was conflated, by Marx and other contemporary socialists, with the aggressive aspirations of Tsarist Russia, their *bête noir*. Pašić would, conversely, come to pin his political hopes for Serbia and Serbdom on Tsarist Russian support against the Obrenović monarchy and Habsburg Empire. He retained Marković's opposition to Serbia's bureaucratic regime and the development of Western-style capitalism; as he wrote in 1876, 'we want to safeguard the people from adopting the erroneous Western industrial society, in which are formed a proletariat and unmeasured wealth, and instead develop industry on a communal basis'. 'The whole of our work has been directed against the contemporary bureaucratic order of our country, and in place of the bureaucratic order we have sought the full administration of the people alone ... the people can be helped only by people who are outside of that bureaucratic system, and for that reason we have left the state service.'[37] It was a message that resonated with the peasantry.

Rebellion in Bosnia and Radical agitation in Serbia

A large-scale, predominantly Serb rebellion erupted in Hercegovina in summer 1875, followed by a second, related rebellion centred on Bosanska Krajina (West Bosnia). The Hercegovinian uprising was oriented toward Montenegro while the Bosnian uprising looked to Serbia. The revolt spread the following spring to the Bulgarian region. These revolts were an expression of social conflict arising from the crushing pressure of taxation on the predominantly Orthodox peasantry, but they grew into a movement for the liberation of Hercegovina, Bosnia and Bulgaria from the Ottoman Empire. The Bosnian peasants' ultimate desire was for an end to serfdom and redistribution of the land held by their Muslim landlords, but it was the urban Bosnian Serb middle classes—the merchants, teachers and priests who formed the politically and nationally conscious element—that provided the rebel leadership. Both the Bosnian agents of official Serbia and Marković's revolutionary followers were quickly drawn into the uprising, turning it into a potential battleground between the two factions.

A movement of support for the rebellion arose in Serbia. Katarina Milovuk, director of the women's high school, in conjunction with other educated and prosperous women, founded a Women's Society on 30 May 1875 to collect material and financial support for the Bosnian rebels; it subsequently established a women's hospital to care for the war-wounded. Its administration elected on 28 August included Milovuk, the painter Poleksija Todorović (Matija Ban's daughter) and the wives of Jevrem Grujić, Čedomilj Mijatović and Filip Hristić. The first issue of its journal, *Domaćica* (Housewife), appeared on 1 July 1879. It would develop as a philanthropic organisation focused on providing education for poor girls, and in the following decades it established a Women Workers' School for teaching tailoring, sewing and embroidery, a library and a home for elderly women.[38]

Conservative prime minister Stefanović, although favouring peace, dispatched volunteers, arms and money across the Drina. Milan himself initially supported this assistance, but he was caught between his nationalist populace and politicians and the Great Powers, which favoured the status quo in the Balkans and to which he looked for his regime's survival. He visited Vienna in June 1875 and agreed with the Hungarian government on coordinated action for suppression of the rebel committees in Novi Sad and Belgrade. However, a committee under Metropolitan Mihailo's leadership was formed in Belgrade at the end of July 1875 to assist the uprising. Milan returned to Vienna in August and was pressed by Austro-Hungarian and Russian representatives to desist from interfering in the uprising. He consequently returned to Belgrade, where his insistence on halting the dispatch of volunteers prompted the Stefanović government's resignation.

Milan favoured peace, fearing the unrest could spread to Serbia and threaten his throne. Marković had, after all, argued that the same revolution needed to target both the Ottomans and the Serb dynasties, and members of his insurrectionist network such as Pelagić were centrally involved in the Bosnian uprising. But popular sympathy in Serbia for the Bosnian rebels, agitation by the more militant Serbian political elements and the pro-war stance of Milan's dynastic rivals Petar Karađorđević and Prince Nikola all made inaction dangerous for him.[39] The government dissolved parliament but failed to manipulate successfully the 15 August 1875 parliamentary election. Radical deputies Bogosavljević and Ranko Tajsić were arrested, but a crowd of peasants arrived at Bogosavljević's prison and forced the police captain to release him, after which the government's attempts to rearrest him failed. In the nationalistic atmosphere created by the Bosnian uprising, the Liberals won the election, forcing Milan to appoint a Liberal government under Stevča Mihailović with Ristić as foreign minister and deputy prime minister—the so-called Action Ministry. Including as it did Jevrem Grujić, Vladimir Jovanović, Milojković and Vasiljević, the government represented the definite convergence of the Liberal party's two wings on a nationalist programme. Ristić was the government's most powerful figure and believed that war was necessary to maintain Serbia's standing in the Balkans and Slavic world, and that even if Serbia lost on the battlefield, its struggle would arouse intense sympathy in Russia, which would ultimately benefit it.[40]

Aware that the Great Powers would not at this time permit Serbia to annex Bosnia, Ristić hoped to lay the foundations for this in the long term. With Milan's acquiescence, the dispatch of volunteers across the River Drina continued and General Ranko Alimpić, former liberal activist of 1858, was appointed to the command of the Serbian border with Bosnia to supervise this. However, these timid efforts had no military effect, causing Alimpić to fear 'loss of faith in Serbia of all Serbs who surround it'.[41] The Liberal-dominated parliament voted for Serbia 'to assist the uprising within the limits of its strength' on the grounds that 'the solution of the Eastern Question is imminent and Serbia has to participate in its solution if it wishes to share in its benefits'. Milan refused to sign this resolution out of fear of the international reaction. He attempted to deflate the pro-war momentum by dramatically addressing parliament in person, over the heads of his ministers, appealing against a precipitate rush to war. This prompted the resignation on 4 October of the Action Ministry, which Milan replaced with a government of left Liberals under Kaljević.[42]

With Serbia on the brink of war and with Milan's regime reeling under popular patriotic pressure, the Radicals and left Liberals, under Kaljević's guidance, pushed through a law for radical municipal self-government on 20 October 1875: the central government lost the right to redraw municipal borders; municipalities gained the right to elect their municipal courts, whose competencies were greatly increased; kmets were elected to fixed one-year instead of indefinite terms and their election no longer depended upon government confirmation; the government was explicitly barred from interfering in the election of kmets and municipal councillors and officers; its right to punish or dismiss kmets and members of the municipal courts was transferred to municipal assemblies; it lost the right to veto legal municipal acts; and the municipalities gained full economic autonomy with greatly increased fiscal and financial competencies.[43] This was followed by the passage of a law that virtually dismantled the powers of the police to control the press.

Kaljević introduced these laws in part to pre-empt more radical populist measures coming from Bogosavljević's Radical parliamentary deputies, who attempted to push through a full-scale dismantling of Serbia's police, bureaucratic and educational regime, including abolition of the gendarmerie, okrug governorships, School of Agriculture and Forestry, teacher training school, stipends for students to study abroad and state financial assistance to the National Theatre. The anti-education measures reflected Bogosavljević's opposition to expending tax money on those who did no physical work. As he said, 'I consider the Theatre as an institution of the rich and lordly, in which lords and rich people, not knowing what to do or how to do it, spend their wasted time and entertain themselves...'[44] The Radicals also attacked the army, demanding a reduction in the length of service in the standing army from two years to one and a ban on officials from becoming officers in the national militia. The government narrowly defeated the first proposal but was unable to prevent the passage of the second. Bogosavljević wanted to go further and allow the national militia to elect its own officers. The Radicals sought a similarly drastic dismantling of the structure and hierarchy of the Serbian Orthodox Church, by abolishing three out of four dioceses and all but six monasteries, the nationalisation of all monastic property and the transfer of marriage litigation to the civil courts.[45] Furthermore, they demanded suspension of the salaries and pensions of all officials and their enrolment in the national militia, and they almost succeeded in forcing a reduction in Council members' salaries. The government was able to resist these demands but parliamentary business was greatly obstructed and slowed.

The Radicals' assault on the bureaucracy gelled with their nationalist enthusiasm for the rebellion in Bosnia and Hercegovina and agitation for Serbia's active support of it. Pašić directed this against Milan's anti-interventionist stance: 'The fate of all Serbdom depends in good measure on the outcome of the Hercegovina uprising'— an uprising against the Ottoman 'gluttons who make up the ruling class ... that lives parasitically on the body of the subjugated people, as does the bourgeoisie in the West'.[46] Pašić travelled in autumn 1875 to Hercegovina on behalf of the Kragujevac Radicals to take the rebels money and advise them on political strategy. The Radicals believed that war, involving the arming of the national militia's peasant soldiers and the peasant parliament's empowerment vis-à-vis the government, would lead to the downfall of tyranny in Serbia as well as in Bosnia.[47] However, their anti-regime and anti-army agitation did not prevent them from actively participating in Serbian military preparations. Pašić sent a draft programme of his fledgling party to a Hungarian Serb interlocutor, highlighting the duality of the Radicals' position on Serb unification: a formal preference that it be carried out 'from below' but a readiness to support it if carried out 'from above': 'As regards "liberation and unification" externally, we always support it, only it would be most amenable to us for that liberation to be carried out by revolution, for with that the people delights in freedom, bears fewer losses and the work of liberation begins for certain, and the work of unification is carried out on the basis of the will of the people not the ruler.' This was coupled with the demand that the 'municipality, district and okrug, and indeed all Serbia, be organised on the basis of self-management', with private ownership of land safeguarded but collective control of industry instituted, to prevent Serbia's stratification along class lines and the peasant nation's transformation into a Western-type proletariat.[48]

Kragujevac remained a power base for the Radicals, grouped around their newspaper *Staro Oslobođenje* (Old Liberation), founded on 27 August 1875 as the successor to Marković's similarly named publication. Sava Grujić was reinstated as director of the armaments factory, where he covertly tolerated Radical political activity. Municipal elections in the city, held in mid-November on the basis of the new law on self-government, were won by the Radicals thanks to their mobilisation of their popular base in the city and factory, giving them control of the municipal court and council, with two factory workers elected as councillors.[49] This prompted a power struggle with the local Liberals and Conservatives. On 27 February 1876, after the municipal assembly overwhelmingly defeated a motion of no confidence in the Radical administration, a triumphal Radical rally took place in the town centre. A red flag, probably made personally by Todorović with a comrade's help and bearing the Radical slogan 'SELF-MANAGEMENT' in capitals, was unfurled; the 'Marseillaise' was sung and cries were heard of 'Long live the Commune! Long live the Republic!' The demonstration degenerated into a riot in which two people were killed. The okrug governor asked for the army to restore order and Milan ordered the war minister to take control of the city, although Kaljević, by threatening to resign, dissuaded Milan from ordering the army to fire upon the crowds. About thirty people were arrested, including eleven workers from the armaments factory; twenty workers from the factory were dismissed; students, professors and many other citizens interrogated; and a Radical priest lost his parish. The army remained on the streets until 4 March. Five people were ultimately sentenced to prison terms, of which the longest was twenty years. Workers from the armaments factor were banned from participation in political or economic protests. In these conditions

ACHIEVEMENT OF INDEPENDENCE

of repression, a new municipal election, which the Radicals boycotted, was held in mid-March and resulted in a Liberal victory.[50] Nevertheless, the affair of the Kragujevac Red Flag, as it subsequently became known, represented the first major political manifestation of Serbia's fledgling proletariat, at a time when the Radicals were still socialist enough to appeal to it. Pašić wrote at the time, 'We want to preserve the nation from the mistakes of Western industrial society, which has produced a proletariat and infinite ostentatious wealth, and instead to raise up industry on the basis of associated labour.'[51] The armaments factory workers would soon be the object of the first government steps to provide social security to industrial workers.[52]

Serbia prepares for war

Kaljević's government, having replaced the pro-war Action Ministry, halted the dispatch of volunteers across the border into Bosnia. However, public opinion in both Serbia and Russia steadily built momentum for war. The powers granted the mostly peasant parliament by the Regency Constitution, combined with the introduction of press freedom, made it difficult for saner statesmen aware of the dangers of war—above all, Milan himself and the Conservatives—to calm nationalist passions or stand against the pro-war agitators, though these were fired by emotion and mostly lacked much strategic or military awareness. Milan was still only in his early twenties and had not yet established his authority as prince. In October 1875 he married his beautiful second cousin Natalija Keshko, the ethnically Romanian daughter of a Bessarabian colonel of the Russian army,[53] who exerted a Russophile influence on Serbian court politics thereafter. Milan was unable to resist being swept up by the nationalistic tide.[54] The apparently revolutionary outburst at Kragujevac convinced him both that Kaljević's government was too liberal at home and that war would be necessary to channel popular passions away from domestic revolt.[55]

Bosnia's rebel leaders, organised in a general council based in the town of Stara Gradiška, were divided between supporters of official Serbia and followers of the deceased Marković. Broadly speaking, the former hoped to limit the uprising to a purely national liberation struggle that would avoid conflict along religious or social lines and co-opt members of the Muslim landed elite. The rebels held an assembly at the village of Jamnica in Croatia on 16–17 December 1875, which reaffirmed the policy of appealing to members of this elite to join them. However, a manifesto entitled 'Project of a Bosnian: On the reorganisation of Bosnia and Hercegovina according to sovereign democratic tenets' appeared in newspapers in January 1876, unsigned but written by Pelagić, proclaiming the goals of the socialists. It advocated not only Bosnia-Hercegovina's independence from the Ottoman Empire and dynastic union with Serbia, but also its decentralised administration through democratically elected municipal self-government and the redistribution to the peasantry of land held by Muslim landlords.⁵⁶ The Serbian government retaliated; at its instigation, Pelagić was arrested by the authorities on Habsburg territory along with about forty other rebels, ending his involvement in the uprising.

Petar Karađorđević's presence in Bosnia represented a further threat to Serbia's regime. Prior to the uprising, the pretender had loosely belonged to the circle of radical agitators plotting to engineer it, and he had his own ambitious though naive plans for a general Balkan Christian uprising. He was drawn into the uprising by his socialist friends and contacts and planned his involvement with his close friend Ljotić. The latter would express their goals in a letter to his comrade Ljočić: 'What do we actually want? The unification of Serbdom. That unification presupposes liberation, and there can be no liberation of Serbdom without the collapse of Turkey and indeed Austria.'⁵⁷ Pašić visited Petar's staff in December 1875 at the village of Bojna on the Habsburg–Bosnian border and was greatly impressed by the pretender's patriotic venture. He delivered money to him through Ljotić, their close mutual friend.⁵⁸ Petar's presence in Bosnia was, however, unwelcome to the rebel general council supported by Serbia's government. At the rebel gathering at Jamnica, the socialists were sidelined and the rebel leaders demanded Petar leave Bosnia.⁵⁹ Soon after, Petar learned they were plotting his murder. He thereupon attempted to fight on against the Ottomans independently of the rebel general council.⁶⁰ His presence added to the pressure on Milan; Hercegovinian rebel leaders issued a proclamation in February 1876 denouncing Serbia for its failure to support the uprising, claiming that it would have already done so if its throne had been occupied by 'a descendant of the immortal Karađorđe or a direct descendant of Miloš Obrenović'—a pointed allusion immediately noted in Belgrade.⁶¹

Mikhail Grigorievich Cherniaev, a retired Russian general and Panslavic agitator, arrived in Belgrade in April 1876 and helped to swing Milan toward war. Milan consequently reinstated the following month a Liberal government under Mihailović as prime minister and Ristić as foreign minister—the so-called Second Action Ministry. Ristić had used Milan's supposedly unpatriotic, anti-war position to bully him into appointing this government. But once in office, he found that the pro-war momentum, which Milan himself was now fuelling, prevented him from managing the entry into war methodically, with the necessary diplomatic preparations. The Army of the Principality of Serbia was woefully unprepared. Since he had placed all his hopes on Russian support, Ristić had not striven to rebuild Mihailo's system of Balkan alliances; his model was the military support France had given Piedmont's Cavour to expel Austria from Italy in 1859. But as official Russia made no pledge to support Serbia at this time, actually counselling restraint, Serbia's government entered the war merely hoping that Russian Panslavic elements would drag Russia into it. Russia—above all, Cherniaev and the Russian ambassador in Constantinople—indeed encouraged Serbian false hopes in this regard. Belgrade dispatched Alimpić to Cetinje to negotiate an alliance with Montenegro, which was signed on 15 June. But Ristić's last-minute diplomacy could not achieve an alliance with Greece or Romania, while Prince Nikola rejected any joint war plan in order to pursue an independent Montenegrin strategy.[62]

Serbia's government was thus left with little more than unjustified romantic hopes of a general Balkan uprising, a gross underestimation of the Ottoman Empire's military capacity and false hopes of dragging in Russia by its example, to give it hope of victory against a state with about twenty-five times its population and a much better trained, better armed and more experienced army. Ristić rationalised his risky strategy on the grounds that passivity in the face of the Christian Slav struggle in Bosnia, Hercegovina and Bulgaria would cost Serbia more, through loss of reputation, than military defeat, which would at least prompt Russia to intervene. At its war council in May 1876, the government adopted a diluted version of a military plan originally drafted by the Radical Major Sava Grujić, while the parliament's standing committee at this time, closely involved in Serbia's war preparations, was dominated by Radicals and left Liberals and headed by Jevrem Marković.[63]

Despite their involvement in the war effort, the Radicals' populist ideological preference for a national militia headed by natural peasant commanders led them to resist the government's efforts, on the eve of war, to strengthen and professionalise the army. They trusted in the supposed revolutionary élan of the Balkan peasants and in the readiness of the Bulgarians to rise in support of the Serbian offensives.[64] Such hopes, by no means restricted to Radicals but shared by Liberals and others, proved illusory and contributed to the coming Serbian military fiasco. Todorović would enthusiastically volunteer for the war; his education and knowledge of foreign languages led to his assignment to the supreme command's staff, where he explained his philosophy to an apparently intrigued Russian colonel. On the one hand, he opined that 'war in my eyes is nothing but an enormous crime' and 'I hate it from the depths of my soul', while war leaders were simply 'the most celebrated robber-bandit chiefs'. On the other, 'Our war has in itself a revolutionary character vis-à-vis Turkey. The Hercegovinian uprising is a plain uprising against the Turkish "legal order". We have leapt to the defence of rebels, joined with them, therefore we too are rebels; revolutionaries ... All my revolutionism consists, you see, in that I recognise for the people this right of rebellion, and then only when there is no other peaceful way out.'[65] It was a naive, contradictory ideology that enthused his generation of activists but did not bring the Serbs any military advantage.

First Serbo-Ottoman war

Serbia and Montenegro declared war on the Ottoman Empire on 30 June. At a hill outside the town of Aleksinac, before an assembly of his soldiers and local people and following a prayer led by Metropolitan Mihailo and his priests, Milan announced war with very similar words to those Prince Mihailo had intended to use in 1862: '"Here

SERBIA

I am, and here is war with the Turks for you!" With these words did my illustrious ancestor Miloš Obrenović go before the Serbian people on that famous day in 1815 and with those words today I come before you, soldiers.' The declaration of war was then made formally at Deligrad on the Morava, a location chosen for its heroic associations with the First Serbian Uprising.[66] Formally, Serbia informed the Porte that it was sending its armed forces into Bosnia to re-establish order. Entry into the war gave the government the opportunity to reassert its authority on various fronts. It suspended the Kaljević government's expansion of press freedom and municipal autonomy, restored full press censorship and police control of the municipalities and moved to assume command of the Bosnian rebel forces. Consequently, it could arrange Petar Karađorđević's expulsion from Bosnia by his own rebel detachment.[67] Army requisitions were authorised in such a way that they largely degenerated into outright plunder, falling disproportionately on the less wealthy proprietors, who found fewer ways to avoid them and were frequently ruined.[68]

Serbia possessed only nineteen army doctors at the start of 1876. The Serbian Red Cross was founded on 6 February 1876 by Dr Vladan Đorđević (1844–1930), Serbia's first and, at the time, only qualified surgeon. He was a Cincar whose father's family had fled to Miloš's Serbia from Epirus, today part of northern Greece, owing to the Albanian Ali Pasha of Janina's revolt in the early 1820s. His father had been an apothecary, who gave him the decidedly Greek and medical name of Hippocrates, subsequently Serbianised to Vladan, and sent him aged eight to Belgrade's Greek school.[69] He trained as a doctor in Vienna, worked in the Prussian army's medical service during the Franco-Prussian War, and founded the Serbian Medical Society in April 1872. While many or most Serbian contemporaries of his social class would die before their seventies, he would live to the ripe old age of 85, testimony to the benefits of modern medical knowledge. Thanks to his efforts, and to the medical missions sent to Serbia at the start of the war by Russia, Britain, Germany, Austria-Hungary, Greece and Romania, Serbia's army was not without field hospitals, but their quality was very poor and medical conditions for military casualties were catastrophic.[70]

The institution of the army general staff was introduced in January 1876, with Zach appointed the first chief of staff. According to the proclamation issued by Generals Zach and Alimpić, 'Arise you all, Orthodox, Catholics and Mohammedans, arise, that we liberate ourselves as united, happy brothers and that we together, fraternally, live defending and respecting one another's family, property and religion.'[71] However, the prioritisation of the national militia over the standing army since Mihailo's reign had left an army of woeful quality overall. Only 147 graduates of Kragujevac's Artillery School served in this conflict with the Ottomans, and though this provided the army with a kernel of trained professional officers, it fell far short of the numbers needed.[72] Russia, meanwhile, resented Serbia's attempt at a fait accompli and quickly made it clear it would not fight Serbia's corner; it reached an agreement at Reichsstadt on 8 July 1876 with Austria-Hungary, whereby in the event of a Serbo-Montenegrin

ACHIEVEMENT OF INDEPENDENCE

victory, the allies would be permitted only relatively small territorial gains, while the lion's share of Bosnia-Hercegovina would go to the Habsburgs. The Russians then informed Serbia that, even if it won, it would be permitted only a slight expansion of its borders and would not be allowed to annex Bosnia.[73]

Officer Mileta Despotović was sent by Belgrade to command the rebellion; he called himself 'Chief Commander of the Bosnian Army and Governor of the Bosnian Nation'.[74] A 'Proclamation to the Bosnian people' was adopted by all rebel bands, whereby 'the lawful representatives of the Serb land of Bosnia, after so much waiting and without hope of any assistance, has decided: that from today and forever, we break with the non-Christian government of Constantinople and wish to share our destiny with our brother Serbs, however that might be.'[75] Consequently, 'we, the entire leadership of the Bosnian rebel detachments as the only legal representatives of the Serb land of Bosnia … proclaim that our homeland Bosnia be joined to the principality of Serbia'.[76] Despotović continued the policy of attempting to co-opt Muslim landlords to the rebellion, while seeking to subordinate the peasant rebels to his command.

Serbia's war plan, adopted in May, divided its forces into four armies: the largest, under General Chernaiev (68,000 troops), would execute the principal offensive, to the south-east against Niš and beyond to Pirot, Bela Palanka and Sofia; armies under Colonel Milojko Lešjanin (25,000) and Alimpić (20,000) would defend the eastern and western borders respectively; while the smallest army, under Zach (11,600) would advance toward Sjenica in the Sanjak of Novi Pazar. The total strength of Serbia's army was 123,000–124,000 men, joined on the eve of the war by 5,000 volunteers, of whom approximately half were Russians while the rest were mostly Serbs from neighbouring Ottoman lands. They faced a total of 178,000 Ottoman regular and irregular troops. Thus, Serbia's forces were outnumbered and their manpower dispersed; Chernaiev's main offensive had too few troops to succeed.[77] Zach's secondary advance was heavily defeated and he was relieved of his command. Alimpić attacked the town of Bijeljina in north-eastern Bosnia; though his troops burned half of it down, they failed to capture it and were forced to withdraw. Lešjanin's attempt to cross the border was quickly repulsed, after which Ottoman forces commanded by Osman Pasha, later the hero of the Siege of Plevna, counter-attacked and captured Veliki Izvor in Serbia. This disrupted Chernaiev's offensive and the supreme command sent him to dislodge the Ottomans from Veliki Izvor, where he was heavily defeated in a pitched battle in July. Serbian offensive operations were therefore halted within two weeks of the start of the war.

The Ottomans then invaded eastern Serbia in late July, capturing Knjaževac and Zaječar. They pursued a scorched-earth strategy, burning the harvest and burning, plundering and ruining the towns and villages they passed through. They treated Serbian civilians with great cruelty; women, children and old people were murdered and their corpses frequently mutilated, and women were raped. For example, according to the Serbian government's investigation, 'Turkish soldiers in the same village captured and took into slavery 12 women, two little girls and two boys. The women they raped every day and the little girl Mirka Radojević was raped by ten soldiers in turn in the course of one hour.' 'The Turks cut both the living and the dead into pieces with their sabres ... Two had their noses cut off and tongues torn out; three were castrated; two had their ears cut off and another two had their sexual organs cut off and put in their mouths; all were extremely mutilated and it was terrible to look at them.' 'They met a woman with a child in a sling. With the same bullet they killed the mother and child. After that, they cut both of them into pieces. They cut off the child's hands, one ear and his sexual organ, which they put in his mouth.'[78] In defence of their country from this brutal invasion, the fighting capacity of the Serbian peasant soldiers improved. In a battle at Šumatovac in late August, Serbia's army under Kosta Protić halted the Ottoman advance in what would be its greatest military success of the war. In recognition, Protić became Serbia's first officer promoted to general during war.[79] This was followed by a failed Ottoman attack on Bobovište on the Morava. Meanwhile, a general advance was launched by Serbia's army on the western front on 20 August, but this failed and in mid-September it was forced back across the Drina.

The Great Powers succeeded at this point in negotiating a one-month ceasefire. Although Ristić, sobered by Serbia's defeats and under no illusions as to its ability to succeed in future offensives, wanted to extend the ceasefire, he was opposed by more warlike members of his government, essentially Old Liberals: Mihailović, Jovanović and Vasiljević. More importantly, despite his defeats and manifest incompetence, Chernaiev wanted to continue the war; his reputation as a Panslavist liberator was not yet achieved. Serbia's government was unable to oppose him given his control over the army and war effort: the influx of Russian officers into Serbia's army meant they now outnumbered Serbian officers, at over 700 to about 460; all the funding gathered by the Panslavist movement in Russia for Serbia's war effort was channelled through Chernaiev, at whose camp only Russian was spoken; 'there, they drank French wine, wallpapered the walls, cavorted with attractive women; that was the full and pleasant life to which Russian officers, soldiers of an aristocratic state, were accustomed in war'. Some Russian adventurers in the army became a public order problem: 'Drunken volunteers created scandals; they fought in taverns, refused to pay bills, assaulted women—and if the authorities reprimanded them even in the mildest way, would immediately draw their sabres.'[80] Meanwhile, Chernaiev and Russia's consul in Belgrade both continued falsely to assure Milan that Russia would soon enter the war. Both to encourage him and to escalate the conflict, Chernaiev arranged the proclamation of Serbia as an independent kingdom by Serbia's military command at a ceremony at Deligrad on 15 September 1876. This was enthusiastically endorsed by the Serbian parliament.

ACHIEVEMENT OF INDEPENDENCE

Milan rejected the offer of the royal crown, given the opposition of the Great Powers, particularly Russia, but this put him at odds with the army and the popular mood.[81] He consequently authorised resumption of Serbia's offensive, although the army was suffering from a crisis of lack of munitions and clothing and the troops were exhausted since there were no reserves. Chernaiev in late September attacked the Ottoman positions at Krevet, on the left bank of the Morava, but, despite heavy losses on both sides, could not dislodge them. The Ottomans resumed their offensive in October; they defeated the Serbians under Colonel Đura Horvatović at Veliki Šiljegovac on 18th–20th and crushingly defeated Chernaiev at Đunis near Kruševac on 28th–29th. Although the Russian officers and soldiers fought well, the discipline of the Serbian peasant troops broke and they fled en masse. Chernaiev telegraphed Belgrade to urge a ceasefire, then ordered his Russian officers and troops to abandon their units, burned down his camp at Deligrad, destroying a large quantity of munitions in the process, and fled with them. Although the Serbian ability to fight on was not broken, Russo-Serbian friendship was; a one-sided account of the battle, according to which the Russians had fought well but the Serbians had fled, reached Russia's court.[82] Tsar Alexander consequently gave a speech at the Kremlin in November: 'In this unequal struggle the Montenegrins revealed themselves always as heroes. Unfortunately, one cannot give the same praise to the Serbs.'[83] The defeat discredited Serbia in the eyes of the Russians, so Bulgaria would replace it as their Balkan favourite.

Russia delivered an ultimatum to the Ottomans, forcing them to halt their military operations, thereby saving Serbia from conquest. Negotiations lasted until early 1877 when a peace agreement was reached. In Slobodan Jovanović's words, 'For years, we lived in the belief that, as soon as our army crossed the border, all the Balkans would arise in arms. Finally, the day came when our army crossed the border—and the Balkans remained quiet, as if nothing were happening. Even that uprising that had already broken out in Bosnia began, after our declaration of war, to languish.'[84] Russia, Greece and Romania failed to come to Serbia's aid and even the Montenegrins and Bulgarian rebels failed to cooperate with Serbia's forces. Although the peace treaty spared Serbia territorial losses, the war had cost it about 15,000 dead, wounded and missing; eastern Serbia was devastated and 200,000 people left homeless.[85] Serbia concluded peace with the Ottomans on 28 February 1877 as a wholly defeated country. The peace treaty discredited Belgrade also in the eyes of the Bosnian rebels, among whom it was felt that 'nothing now links us with Serbia' and whose policy consequently became independent of Serbia.[86] In October, following Despotović's final defeat and surrender, an assembly was convened that included representatives of most Bosnian rebel bands. It elected a Provisional National Bosnian Government and sought to continue the struggle.[87] Serbia's regime, meanwhile, abandoned all attempts to assist or profit from the rebellion. The possibility of any sort of Serbian–Bosnian union was definitely precluded on 15 January 1877 when

SERBIA

Russia reached a secret agreement with Austria-Hungary, permitting the latter to occupy Bosnia-Hercegovina.

Second Serbo-Ottoman war

Milan held elections on 20 February 1877 for a great national parliament, formally in order to ratify the peace treaty but really to shift the blame for the defeat away from himself and provide an opportunity to replace the Liberal government. The Liberals were widely blamed by the populace for the defeat, marking their eclipse as a party.[88] The elections resulted not only in their defeat, but in Conservative–Radical collaboration and widespread success for the Radicals and Karađorđevićites. Not only the Radicals but also the Conservatives sought to expand the role of the great national parliament from rubber-stamping the peace treaty to holding the Liberal government to account.[89] The parliament's subversive character prompted a U-turn on Milan's part; once the treaty was ratified, he dismissed the parliament and retained the Liberals in power. The government in June 1877 reassembled the Liberal-dominated parliament of 1875, which had approved Serbia's entry into the war. It absolved the Liberal ministers of responsibility for the defeat and prolonged the state of war, including the wartime repressive measures regarding the press and municipalities. Led once again by Ristić and Milojković, this amounted to a restoration of the regency's tyranny. The government attributed Serbia's defeat to the 'incapability' of the national militia of meeting the demands of contemporary warfare, in the manner of a properly equipped standing army. The opposition responded by blaming the government for Serbia's military and financial unpreparedness for war. Both positions were essentially correct. In Radical eyes, the government's military policy remained directed against the common people and their representatives. This was demonstrated by the fact that officers continued to employ corporal punishment against soldiers even after it was banned, for which they rarely suffered consequences, and by the fact that a battalion commander in the national militia had been dismissed simply because he was a Radical deputy.[90]

Russia finally declared war on the Ottoman Empire on 23 April 1877. Its army crossed the Danube in July and attacked the Ottoman army defending the town and fortress of Plevna, in present-day Bulgaria. So contemptuous had the Russians become of Serbia's military abilities that they sought to postpone its entry into the war, for fear that a premature Serbian entry would create diplomatic complications with Austria-Hungary and could lead to another rapid Serbian defeat. However, the reverses rapidly suffered by the Russians at Plevna led to a change of heart and to desperate Russian pleas for Serbia to enter the war. Yet Serbia's government was once bitten twice shy and the Russians had made the mistake of terminating military aid to Serbia shortly following its first defeat. Necessary military preparations delayed Serbia's re-entry until 13 December, three days after the belated Russian capture of

ACHIEVEMENT OF INDEPENDENCE

Plevna had made an Ottoman defeat certain. Although this was merely an unfortunate coincidence, the timing created another poor impression in St Petersburg.[91]

Serbia's government was forced to forgo further military requisitions owing to popular exhaustion and anger. Nevertheless, the Karađorđević family and its supporters attempted to capitalise on widespread anti-war feeling among the population and soldiery. Petar issued a proclamation in October 1877, vowing 'to overthrow those who have brought Serbia and her people to the current unheard-of downfall'.[92] In the so-called Topola uprising beginning on 7 December 1877, the majority of soldiers of the 2nd Lepenica Battalion of the Serbian army's Kragujevac Brigade stationed at Stanovljanske Polje near Kragujevac, some 283 strong, refused to take the military oath, mutinied and marched on Topola, traditional home of the Karađorđević dynasty, which they occupied until 11 December when Serbia's standing army arrived and overcame them after a brief exchange of fire. As a participant in the first Serbo-Ottoman war, Sergeant Milan Živić, the leading mutineer, had witnessed its destructiveness and hopelessness, for which he blamed Milan.[93] He and co-conspirator Sergeant Ranko Radivojević acted on the basis of an agreement with Karađorđevićites from Topola and from Azanja near Smederevo, with the aim of igniting a rebellion to replace Milan as prince with Petar. The resulting investigation implicated former Conservative prime minister Čumić and prominent Radical army officer Jevrem Marković. Although the evidence linking them to the mutiny was slender, they were both found to have engaged in seditious plotting with members of the conspiracy, both having met shortly before with Petar's close friend and agent, Ljotić. In a throwback to Miloš's tactics for dealing with domestic opponents, the investigation pointed to Ottoman involvement in the mutiny, based on Petar's contacts with Ottoman agents in Vienna, though there was little evidence of this.

Milan harshly suppressed the mutiny; his troops thoroughly razed Topola. His military tribunal convicted all but four of the seventy accused and handed down twenty-three death sentences of which seven were carried out. Čumić's flirtation with the conspirators appears to have marked the culmination of his collaboration with the Radical opposition since the regency, though the harshness with which the authoritarian Liberal government pursued him, culminating in his death sentence, primarily represented its attempt to destroy a prominent opponent.[94] After Čumić's fellow Young Conservatives and some others petitioned Milan for clemency, his death sentence was commuted to a prison term and he was released in 1880, but never returned to front-line politics. Marković was executed, even though he had been serving successfully on the front at the time of the mutiny. Milan denied him clemency, fearing him as a seditious element in the army and seeking to make an example of him. His execution greatly embittered the Radicals against Milan.[95] Meanwhile, the focus on suppressing the uprising delayed Serbia's re-entry into the war against the Ottomans.[96]

SERBIA

After it was given clearly to understand that Austria-Hungary would not permit it to annex any part of Bosnia-Hercegovina, Serbia's government again resolved to direct its main thrust against Niš. With Protić as chief of staff, five corps were organised, three of which, the Šumadija, Morava and Timok corps (16,000, 18,000 and 13,000 troops under the commands of Belimarković, Lešjanin and Horvatović respectively) were to advance on Niš, while the Drina and Javora corps (19,000 and 15,000 troops) were deployed to guard the borders towards Bosnia and the Sanjak of Novi Pazar respectively; an additional Timok-Zaječar army (8,800) was established to defend positions at Negotin and Zaječar. Serbia's forces totalled 89,800 men—substantially fewer than during the first war in 1876–1877 owing to the losses sustained in it. The Ottoman forces comprised 80,000 positioned toward the Serbian border and another 20,000 in garrisons and fortifications around Niš, Vidin and Belogradiček.[97] Serbia's army took Leskovac on 21 December, Pirot on the 28th, Niš on the 29th and Vranje on 19 January 1878, although the Ottomans successfully resisted its penetration into present-day Kosovo. The ceasefire agreed between Russia and the Ottomans at the end of January ended Serbia's advances, a mere six weeks after its entry into the war. Russia's army had halted at San Stefano, on the outskirts of Constantinople, after the British fleet had appeared there as deterrent. Decades later, elderly World War I hero Živojin Mišić, who had fought as a young man in the 1870s wars, recalled the Serbian frustration at the ceasefire: 'There, by San Stefano, they halted, under the threat of "civilised" Europe, whose selfish interests did not permit the Russians to seize Constantinople and expel the Turks to Asia, whence they had come; they would consequently, until their final years, carry out so many great evils against the Christian nations of Europe!'[98]

Expulsion of the Albanians

Although Serbia's war was fought formally against the Ottoman Empire, it was in practice also a war against the Albanians, who made up much of the regular Ottoman army in the region. In the pre-modern period, Serbian–Albanian relations were not necessarily hostile: Albanians had fought on Serbia's side at the Battle of Kosovo and in both the First and Second Serbian Uprisings; Ilija Garašanin counted on Albanian collaboration as part of his 'Plan'; and co-option of Albanian elements remained part of Serbian strategy for influencing and controlling Albanian-inhabited territories thenceforth.[99] Nevertheless, Serbia's expansion to encompass such territories inevitably resulted in Serbian–Albanian conflict. Serbia's army occupied and ultimately annexed six Ottoman districts: Niš, Pirot, Vranje, Leskovac, Prokuplje and Kuršumlija, with a total pre-war population of about 215,117 Christians and 95,619 Muslims. The Muslim population was concentrated in particular in the cities: the district capitals Niš and Pirot spoke Turkish; Prokuplje and Kuršumlija spoke Albanian; while Vranje and Leskovac spoke both languages.[100] Albanian villages in

ACHIEVEMENT OF INDEPENDENCE

the territories occupied by Serbia's army fought bitterly against it, independently of the Ottoman regular army, so the Serbian war of liberation or conquest became in practice a war against the local Albanian population, involving large-scale atrocities on both sides reminiscent of the Serbian Uprisings.

The Muslim and Albanian population of the conquered area fled before Serbia's advancing army. All but 62 of 900 Muslim families—5,000 individuals—fled from Leskovac, with many parting acts of murder, rape, assault and plunder inflicted on local Serbs in the process, while Serbia's army, for its part, burned and looted Muslim homes in the captured territories. According to a local Serb eyewitness, 'There were many Turks who fled naked, barefoot, in the worst December winter, on foot through the snow, leaving in Leskovac their full houses. Those nights, many children in the wagons or in their mother's arms in cradles died from the great cold, while the Turkish families fled through the valley of the South Morava river, in the greatest winter. By the road through the Grdelica gorge up to Vranje and Kumanovo, whither the Turkish families withdrew, could be seen discarded dead children and rigid old people. The withdrawal was tragic.'[101] Following their capture, Serbia's government decided to deport the Muslim population from the Toplica and Kosanica regions, as a result of which about 71,000 Muslims including 49,000 Albanians were forced to leave and ethnic Serbs settled in their place.

The policy of deportation had some exceptions. General Belimarković felt personally obliged toward the Albanians of Masurica in the Vranje district, who had not resisted the Serbian occupation, and he threatened to resign in protest at their expulsion, but this was consequently merely postponed until he went on leave. The Albanians of the Jablanica valley succeeded in establishing personal contact with Milan, who consequently protected them, and they remained the only compact group of Albanians in Serbia. The expelled Albanians took refuge across the Ottoman border in Kosovo, from which local Serbs were evicted to make way for them. These expulsions and counter-expulsions ensured an ongoing Serbian–Albanian conflict; Albanian refugees resettled in Ottoman frontier regions retaliated against Serbs left under Ottoman rule or carried out raids in their former homeland across the border in Serbia. Albanian bands carried out 73 raids against the territory of the Toplica okrug and 12 against the territory of the Vranje okrug in 1879.[102] The violent border became a thorn in Serbia's side. Meanwhile, even the Christian population of the new territories was alienated by the Serbian army's policy of requisitioning, which fell disproportionately on the poorer classes and for which they were only slowly reimbursed, while being denied compensation for damage sustained in the war. The Radical deputy Raša Milošević would accuse the Serbian parliament, for its failure to offer proper compensation, of 'behaving towards the liberated areas as towards a stepchild'.[103]

The territories emptied of Muslims were rapidly populated by Serb immigrants, particularly from the eastern and southern parts of pre-1878 Serbia and from border territories that remained under Ottoman rule or became part of the new Bulgarian state. The law on settlement of 12 February 1880 granted every settler family four acres and 2,000 square metres for its homestead. Under international pressure to respect the terms of the Treaty of Berlin, which guaranteed the Muslim landlords' property, Serbia passed a law on agrarian relations in the newly liberated territories which provided for the landlords to be bought out. Thus, in principle, Serbs who seized Muslim landholdings were required to pay for them, but they largely evaded this in practice, so the Serbian government eventually had to float a foreign loan to compensate the former landlords.[104] The Albanian bazaar in Niš was razed and twelve of the town's fifteen mosques and about 1,300 of its 4,000 houses were torn down, while the remaining Muslim houses were sold at a fraction of their previous value. This demolition of buildings owned by Muslims, Jews and even recalcitrant Christians was accompanied by the widening of streets and a general attempt to 'modernise' the city, to make it less Ottoman. Albanian merchants who tried to remain in Niš were subjected to a targeted campaign of murder. The tekke (Sufi monastery) at Vranje was also destroyed. Abuses were inflicted by the Serbian authorities on the Jewish inhabitants of Niš, including extortion of money, arbitrary arrests, confiscation of property, forced labour and desecration of graves.[105] Niš, whose population had only been about half Serb before 1878, became 80 per cent Serb by 1884. The Serbian chronicler and sometime government minister Kosta Hristić, Nikola Hristić's son, remarked in 1921 of the Serbian generation that had grown up in the town since its 'liberation':

> To them it would appear inconceivable, if we were to describe to them what Niš looked like in 1878. They simply would not believe it if we told them that King Milan Square was covered in Turkish graves; that today's broad and sunny streets were dense, crooked alleys lined with walls, caked in yellow mud; that the houses were miserable huts with paper taped over the windows, enclosed by trellises. They would not believe that in Niš there had been twenty-two mosques, from whose minarets the muezzins praised the Prophet five times a day, and that there were no bells in the churches.[106]

Independence and vassalage under Austria-Hungary

Despite its eventual victory, Serbia's initial military fiasco and slowness in rejoining the war helped persuade Russia to favour Bulgaria almost exclusively. Serbia's government initially sought annexation of the Sanjak of Novi Pazar, Old Serbia (Kosovo), Vidin in present-day Bulgaria and a portion of Macedonia including Skopje, Veles, Debar and Štip. However, Russia envisaged the creation of a Great Bulgaria, while Serbia was to receive merely some border rectifications. Consequently, it sought to award Niš, Serbia's principal war gain, to Bulgaria; the dioceses of Niš and Vranje had already been placed in 1870 under the Bulgarian Exarchate, to whose borders Russia sought to make its new Bulgarian protégé correspond. Milan sent his envoy to the

ACHIEVEMENT OF INDEPENDENCE

Russian headquarters to declare 'that the Serbian army will not abandon Niš, even if the Russian army attacks it'.[107] The anger he and other Serbian statesmen felt at the injustice was fired by its inexplicability in their eyes; for while 'political reasons of an extremely serious nature' dictated that Serbia be denied Bosnia and Hercegovina, as Milan wrote at the time to Russia's ambassador to Constantinople, he could see no reason for Russia's opposition to Serbia's southward expansion, while the loss of Niš would 'offer the Serbian nation a sad outlook for the future', compared with which the other territories offered to Serbia 'have for us the value only of historical satisfaction, because the land is mountainous and infertile'. Consequently, 'If the annexation of Niš to Bulgaria were to be realised, I would be very painfully hurt by that, and with me the entire Serbian nation deeply confounded.'[108]

Russia relented over Niš. Nevertheless, by the Treaty of San Stefano signed on 3 March 1878 without Serbian involvement, Russia awarded Mali Zvornik and Zakar in Bosnia and Niš, Leskovac, Kuršumlje and Prokuplje to Serbia, but gave Serbia's hard-won gains of Pirot, Vranje, Bela Palanka, Trn and Breznik to Bulgaria. Serbia was therefore to be deprived of territories its army held and supposedly compensated with territories in Kosovo and the Sanjak that it did not hold, which went up to but did not include the important towns of Novi Pazar and Mitrovica and which, on account of Austro-Hungarian opposition, it was anyway unlikely actually to receive. Meanwhile, a huge independent Great Bulgarian state was established, stretching all the way into present-day Albania and including most of Macedonia. As Ristić later put it, 'A nation that contributed nothing to achieving its freedom saw itself at once not only free, but lord of its state of four million inhabitants; a state bigger than every other little national state on the Balkan Peninsula.'[109] Russia's foreign minister responded to Serbian protests: 'First come Russia's interests, then Bulgaria's and only after them come Serbia's, and there are times when Bulgaria's interests stand on the same level as Russia's.'[110] Serbia's envoy in St Petersburg again told the Russians that they would have to expel Serbia's army by force from the towns in question.[111] The Serbians' recalcitrance may have been strengthened by the knowledge that they were not the only Balkan ally feeling betrayed: the Romanians were similarly outraged by being forced to cede southern Bessarabia to Russia in exchange for the much less desirable Ottoman territory of northern Dobrudja.

Serbia refused to withdraw from the territories it was supposed to surrender to Bulgaria, as Ristić correctly calculated that the upcoming Congress of Berlin, which the Great Powers were convening to revise the Treaty of San Stefano, would provide opportunities for Serbia to end up with more territory. Given Russia's betrayal, Ristić and Milan recognised the need to shift to a greater reliance on Austria-Hungary, with which Serbia had anyway been pressed by Russia to reach an agreement. Thus, Ristić met with Austro-Hungarian officials in Vienna on 7–10 June 1878 and obtained their support for Serbia's independence and expansion to include the territories it had occupied in the war, with the understanding that, in return, it would conclude a commercial treaty with Austria-Hungary and integrate their railway networks.[112] The assignment of Serbia to the Austro-Hungarian sphere of influence was in fact readily offered by Russia along with the occupation and future annexation of Bosnia-Hercegovina.[113]

The Congress of Berlin took place during June and July 1878. Ristić sent a memorandum to the participants dated 24 June, setting out deliberately overambitious territorial demands including parts of present-day Bulgaria and Macedonia, while warning of the international complications that would remain 'until the Serb question is resolved satisfactorily; from it will arise heavy misfortunes and it will remain the key to the Eastern Question'. However, he dropped all reference to Serbia's claim to Bosnia-Hercegovina in order to appease Andrássy, now Austria-Hungary's foreign minister, and accepted that the Great Powers 'in their wisdom' would find an appropriate remedy for these lands; in the west, he sought merely annexation of Mali Zvornik, which, as he pointed out, had already been granted to Serbia in 1831.[114] Ristić was extremely frustrated that Serbia was being squeezed between Austria-Hungary and pro-Bulgarian Russia; each wanted to give Serbia territory that the other did not want it to have. He complained to the Russians: 'When the Austrians chase us out of Novi Pazar, you are not in a position to defend us, and when they leave us some compensation, you are opposed to it ... The situation is tragic for us, seeing Russia in a struggle with Austria *against us*'[115] (emphasis in original). Nevertheless, Andrássy's intervention was decisive in ensuring the Congress awarded Pirot to Serbia rather than Bulgaria.[116] Serbia was nevertheless forced to turn over territory to Bulgaria including Trn and Breznik and was not permitted by Austria-Hungary to annex any of the territory in the Sanjak or Kosovo promised it by Russia.

The subsequent Treaty of Berlin of 13 July 1878 confirmed Serbia's possession of most of the territory it had occupied, increasing its size from approximately 37,740 to 48,300 square kilometres. The new territory was organised as four okrugs (Vranje, Pirot, Niš and Toplica), so that Serbia now comprised 21 okrugs with 81 districts.[117] This was achieved by collaboration with the Habsburgs, just as Serbia's previous territorial expansion, in 1833, had been achieved by collaboration with the Ottomans. In return, Serbia accepted Austria-Hungary's occupation of Bosnia-Hercegovina. Furthermore, according to Article 35 of the Treaty:

> In Servia the difference of religious creeds and confessions shall not be alleged against any person as a ground for exclusion or incapacity in matters relating to the enjoyment of civil and political rights, admission to public employments, functions, and honours, or the exercise of the various professions and industries, in any locality whatsoever. The freedom and outward exercise of all forms of worship shall be assured to all persons belonging to Servia, as well as to foreigners, and no hindrance shall be offered either to the hierarchical organisation of the different communions, or to their relations with their spiritual chiefs.

ACHIEVEMENT OF INDEPENDENCE

Similar clauses regarding religious liberty applied to Bulgaria, Romania and Montenegro. In Serbia, this required the government to repeal the anti-Jewish laws upheld by the Regency Constitution, so Ristić wrote to Bismarck on 3 July pledging to do so 'at the first opportunity'.[118] Bulgaria, meanwhile, was cut down to size: Macedonia was returned to direct Ottoman rule, Bulgaria south of the Balkan mountains became the separate autonomous province of Eastern Rumelia under an Ottoman governor, and Bulgaria lost its independent status, remaining formally an Ottoman vassal state. As a corollary of independence, Ristić's government was able to negotiate recognition of the Serbian Orthodox Church's autocephaly in a proclamation by the Patriarchate of Constantinople on 1 November 1879. This was facilitated by the fact that the current Patriarch, Joaquin III, was sympathetic to the Ottoman Slavs and to Metropolitan Mihailo personally. Autocephaly permitted the Serbian church to remove the authority of the Bulgarian Exarchate over the newly annexed territories, including over the dioceses of Niš and Vranje, now directly subordinated to the metropolitan in Belgrade.[119] A new bishopric of Niš was established with jurisdiction over Serbia's four new okrugs.[120]

A census conducted in 1884 indicated that Serbia had a population of 1,901,736 inhabitants, 12.41 per cent of whom lived in towns.[121] The rapid increase since the 1830s was due to its having one of the highest birth rates in Europe, peaking in the first half of the 1880s, and also to high immigration of Serbs from neighbouring lands: 660,000 arrived from Bosnia-Hercegovina, Montenegro, Macedonia and Vojvodina between 1834 and 1874.[122] Yet though larger and formally freer, Serbia was increasingly subordinated to its powerful northern neighbour. An economic agreement was signed with Austria-Hungary on 7 July 1878, requiring Serbia to build a railroad between Belgrade and Niš within three years, to extend in two branches through Pirot and Vranje respectively, thereby eventually linking Vienna with Constantinople and Salonika. Serbia was also required to reach a trade agreement or customs union with Austria-Hungary immediately upon the conclusion of peace. In return, at the Serbian government's request, Petar was interned in Hungary in July 1878 and not released until October. His circle had responded to the suppression of the Topola uprising by launching a new émigré newspaper, entitled *Narodni glasnik* (People's Herald) in Hungary in conjunction with leading Serb socialists and dissidents including Pelagić and Kaljević, which continuously denounced the Belgrade regime's tyranny, particularly Marković's execution.[123]

Austria-Hungary invaded Bosnia-Hercegovina on 29 July, completing its occupation by October. In Slobodan Jovanović's words, 'The Austrian occupation of Bosnia hurt us to our core; Bosnia had been the dream of a whole generation and its loss defeated us like a new Kosovo.'[124] The Treaty of Berlin also approved Austria-Hungary's stationing of garrisons in the Sanjak of Novi Pazar, representing further Austro-Hungarian encroachment into lands Serbia coveted. Serbia's independence was formally declared on 9 August, but it remained a principality rather than a kingdom. In his proclamation the following day announcing to Serbia's people the formal end to the war and the recognition of independence, Milan pledged: 'Relations that are wise abroad and firm at home—those are the only ways that Independent Serbia can flourish.'[125] The Liberal-dominated parliament elected in 1875 convened for the last time; it approved all the government's wartime extraordinary laws and again renewed existing restrictions on press freedom. Wartime restrictions on municipal autonomy were not renewed, but parliament modified the existing laws to grant the government the right to dismiss and punish kmets and members of the municipal courts, and restricted the right to vote in municipal elections to those who paid the full local tax (danak).

Serbia's bureaucratic and police apparatus was extended to the new territories. Okrug and district governors were appointed; kmets were not elected but appointed by the district governors from among local elders. Ristić, who assumed the premiership in Serbia's purely Liberal first post-war government on 13 October 1878, convened the post-war parliament in newly annexed Niš, which he hoped to establish as Serbia's second capital as a bulwark against the Bulgarians, who had established their own capital in Sofia, menacingly just across the border.[126] Liberal politician and historian Živan Živanović subsequently rationalised this on patriotic grounds: 'When the Liberals convened the first parliaments, following the proclamation of independence (1878, 1879), in Niš, they did this so that the representative body of Serb freedom and legislature would hold its meetings on classical land in the middle of its newly liberated brothers.'[127] Their principal motives may have been baser. Access to Niš was restricted by poor roads; its population had no experience of political life and was under a special provisional legal regime. These factors helped maximise the government's ability to manipulate the parliament and harass the opposition.[128] It was an early example of a pattern that would become increasingly apparent as the Serbian state expanded: newly acquired territories increased the scope of regimes for arbitrary, authoritarian behaviour.

Ristić sought to keep a tight rein on Serbian political life and successfully sought from parliament abandonment of the more liberal press law of 1875 and a return to the more restrictive one of 1870, on the grounds that 'the question is not whether we want freedom but how much. Our principle is moderation, not convulsions'. He defended the 1870 press law on the grounds that it resembled the press law of Prussia: 'It seeks to achieve for Serbia the glory and culture that Prussia has achieved.'[129] Pašić, in his first parliamentary speech on 23 December 1878, appealed unsuccessfully in defence of the 1875 press law, complaining: 'Our life, our internal freedom, has recently gone into reverse; and that from the time when we wished to and went to bring freedom to our brothers –we went to liberate our brothers and on the way lost our own freedom.'[130] The government was oppressive toward the people also in the economic sphere: faced with a heavy war debt and required to finance the costs associated with independence, such as opening new foreign embassies, and also to administer the newly acquired territories, it sought to raise new revenues through an unpopular tax on businesses. As part of its attempts at financial reform, the introduction of the Serbian national currency was completed on 22 December 1878 with the issuing of higher-denomination gold coins.[131] But Austro-Hungarian pressure on Serbia continued: Vienna banned the import of Serbian horned cattle in November 1878 and raised its tariff on the import of Serbian pigs in January 1879, to force Serbia to grant further concessions. The Radical-led parliamentary opposition increasingly combined opposition to the Liberal government's supposedly unpatriotic concessions to Austria-Hungary with opposition to its domestic policy, which it portrayed as oppressive, expensive and foreign-inspired.

A law of 19 January 1879 to re-establish the women's high school, with the particular aim of training women teachers, was opposed by the Radical-led opposition on the grounds that it would infect Serbian women with 'foreign accomplishments, contrary to the Serb spirit', when women just needed to be taught how to be 'good housewives and good mothers'.[132] The Radicals similarly opposed a proposal put before parliament on 7 December 1879, originating with Đorđević, for the establishment of a national health fund involving health agencies in every okrug, with a doctor for every district, a municipal doctor for every 10,000 inhabitants, and a medical sister for every 5,000 inhabitants, as well as measures to regulate the medical profession, apothecaries and burials, and prevent the spread of smallpox and cattle plague.[133] It was presented as a necessary measure for the reform of public health in a country still recovering from war. Đorđević explained to the parliament the woeful conditions of public hygiene in Serbia—regarding food, housing, schools, childbirth, the treatment of illness and other areas—that weakened the Serbian population. Yet Bogosavljević condemned it as too expensive, and 'today it is most urgent that the people be cured of hunger', while another opposition deputy argued that the parliament should not be passing laws that were 'copies of foreign laws and institutions; institutions and those countries that are immersed in sin, from which they cannot escape without great change', and a third complained that the suggested doctors were 'foreigners', and 'woe be to the house and those cold walls, in which a foreigner ... sits, let alone the life and health of the people, who are looked after by those who are, at the political level, their sworn enemy ...' The parliament passed the proposal, but only after its implementation was postponed until the start of 1881 and the proposed additional surtax to fund it abandoned.[134]

Bogosavljević, one of two original Radical parliamentary deputies and the man who, more than any other, had brought Svetozar Marković's ideas to the peasantry and given the embryonic party a base, was arrested and imprisoned on 29 March 1880. The police acted on the basis of an old warrant from 1876 when, after Bogosavljević's family home in the village of Koprivnica in Zaječar had been destroyed in a fire, he had apparently stolen a quantity of corn from the municipal depot. In prison, he rapidly developed inflammation of the lungs, was transferred to hospital and died on the 31st. The Radicals accused the government of having poisoned him; although this was almost certainly untrue, it was hard for the government to deny that he had died after being imprisoned on political grounds. Bogosavljević's death at government hands became a sort of foundation myth that catalysed the formal establishment of the Radical party the following year.[135]

Serbia was forced to sign a railway convention with Austria-Hungary on 9 April 1880, requiring it to build its railway all the way to Vranje, near the Ottoman border—something that served Vienna's imperial Balkan goals but was expensive and of questionable economic value for Serbia. In May, when the parliament debated the railway convention, the government's policy was opposed not only by the Radicals and Conservatives but by the Old Liberals under Mihailović and Tucaković.[136] The Radical deputies under Pašić demanded on 1 June that the public be allowed to express its will over the railway convention through new elections, since 'the submitted railway convention contained an international agreement, which is reached eternally between a small state with one of twenty and more times greater population, whose interests are economically and politically opposite, and in our opinion and estimation in Serbia there has not been a more important question, apart from war, nor will there ever be one apart from war'.[137] Ristić replied to the critics that 'whoever wants a Great Serbia and the liberation of the people should not dwell on the fact that they will have afterwards to pay several dinars of surtax' and succeeded in having the railway convention ratified by parliament.[138]

Faced with growing opposition and himself uncomfortable with the policy of excessive subordination to Serbia's powerful neighbour, Ristić was unwilling to submit to Vienna's demands during summer 1880 regarding a trade agreement, which would have required Serbia to grant Austria-Hungary most-favoured-nation status with no reciprocity for itself. His government attempted to create a precedent by signing trade agreements with Britain, Italy, Russia, Switzerland and Belgium, in which the signatories granted each other most-favoured-nation status, but this did not impress Vienna, which demanded unconditional Serbian capitulation.[139] The Serbian government's dilemma was whether to accept Vienna's diktat so as to secure an open market in Austria-Hungary for the export of agricultural produce, thereby appeasing the peasantry at the price of unrestricted Austro-Hungarian imports that would hurt Serbia's fledgling industry, or whether to fight a tariff war with a much more powerful neighbour that would be ruinous for the peasantry but create space for Serbia's industry to develop. The cause of nationalism, self-sufficiency and modernisation stood opposed to the class interests of the peasantry and the future of the primary, agricultural sector of the Serbian economy. Ristić wrote to Milan on 21 October explaining why he was unwilling to submit to Vienna's diktat. Rather than retreating from Ristić's policies, which were pro-Austrian abroad and anti-populist at home, Milan sought to develop them to their logical conclusion. He rejected an invitation to attend the Tsar's jubilee in February 1880, visited Vienna at the end of June and was charmed by the reception the Austrian emperor gave him. He accepted Ristić's resignation on 31 October.[140]

Radicals (with both a small and a capital 'r') influenced by Svetozar Marković's ideas viewed Milan's regime of prince, bureaucracy and army as a continuation of Ottoman oppression, and the struggle against it as part of the wider struggle against the empire; they mobilised against both. Milan's regime under Liberal management navigated between managing this threat and fulfilling Serbia's national mission of liberation and unification. It did so with some success, resulting in an ultimately successful anti-Ottoman war and international recognition of Serbia's independence within modestly expanded borders. Neither the national task abroad nor the radical threat at home ended with independence, however, and they remained linked. Serbia's politics would now be engulfed by the struggle between the old Serbian elite under the prince and the embryonic counter-elite of the Radicals. The national question would be viewed through the prism of this struggle.

8

COURT AND RADICALS

1880–1892

Serbia's achievement of independence and the fall of Jovan Ristić's Liberal government cleared the arena for the battle to begin in earnest between the old Serbian elite of court, army and bureaucracy and the emerging Radical party counter-elite. Milan took power much more directly into his own hands by replacing the domineering Ristić with his protégés, the Young Conservatives, soon renamed Progressives. Yet the Regency Constitution and the Progressive government's liberalising reforms enabled the Radicals, through their populist rhetoric and agitation in the countryside, to emerge rapidly as the party commanding most of the population's support. Thus began a struggle of two Serbias: a struggle between the state and peasant masses, over whether Serbia would modernise along Western lines or preserve its traditional rural society and institutions, and between an Austrophile and a Russophile foreign alignment.

Establishment of the Progressive regime

Milan dismissed Ristić's Liberal government to safeguard Serbia's new Austrophile course. He found a new governmental party in the younger generation of Conservative politicians who came of age following Garašanin's death in 1874 and the retreat of Marinović to diplomatic life in Paris. They would govern Serbia from 31 October 1880 until 13 June 1887. Of the four leading figures in the group soon to be known as Progressives, the new prime minister Milan Piroćanac was 43 in 1880 while Stojan Novaković, Čedomilj Mijatović and Milutin Garašanin were in their late thirties. This was a youthful team with which Prince Milan, himself only 26, felt comfortable.

Milan Piroćanac (1837–1897) personified the new class of highly educated Serbian bureaucrats that had arisen from a patriarchal background. He was born in Jagodina in central Serbia in 1837, to a family that came from the village of Šugrin, near Pirot, whence his surname derived. His mother had been the second wife of

SERBIA

Pavle Cukić, the rebel leader of the First and Second Serbian Uprisings assassinated by Miloš; Cukić had taken her to live bigamously at his home with himself and his first wife, in Ottoman pasha style. She later married Piroćanac's father, a comrade-in-arms of Miloš, who appointed him governor of Knjaževac. Piroćanac *père* apparently then became a supporter of the Constitutionalists, for he was expelled from his post following the regime change in 1858 along with one of his sons (Piroćanac's half-brother) who had been governor of Paraćin. Like members of other families that had lost out from the 1858 upheaval, Piroćanac gravitated to the Conservatives and prospered under Mihailo; having graduated in law in Paris, he joined the state service at the urging of his friend Ilija Garašanin, rising to become chief of the foreign ministry. Considered an enemy by the Liberals, he was demoted under the regency and narrowly escaped prosecution in relation to the Topola uprising alongside his friend Čumić.[1]

Although probably none of the leading Progressives was as fanatical an Austrophile as Milan himself, some of them shared his hostility to Russia. According to Slobodan Jovanović, 'At the basis of Piroćanac's politics was hatred of Russia. Piroćanac was educated in the West and, in his era, every Westerner had to be an opponent of Russia. Russia was then still considered a great state of a barbarian type, closer to Asia than to Europe, incapable of ever adapting itself to Western civilisation ... The question, of whether Serbia would hold to Russia or not, consisted for Piroćanac of whether Serbia would remain in the barbarism and ignorance of the East or attempt to adapt itself to Western civilisation.' This worldview motivated the Progressive government's programme of state modernisation and railway building.[2]

The new government on 10 November 1880 granted Vienna's demand for most-favoured-nation status without reciprocity for Serbia, after which Austria-Hungary immediately lifted its restrictions on the import of Serbian livestock and the two states signed a trade agreement on 17 June 1881. This was aimed at binding Serbia firmly to Austria-Hungary economically: Serbia's agricultural produce would enjoy privileged access to Austro-Hungarian markets in return for unrestricted access to Serbian markets for Austro-Hungarian industrial goods. The treaty was attacked by the Radicals on nationalistic and xenophobic grounds. Speaking against it in parliament on 28 May, Pašić condemned it for violating the anti-Jewish Article 132 of the constitution: 'We have, with this stance, opened the door widely for foreigners and Jews to buy as much land as they wish and wherever they wish ... Austria-Hungary has worked consciously and according to plan to prevent us developing any craft or industry.'[3] In another parliamentary speech two days later days later, Pašić made pointed reference to the ethnic background of one of its supporters—Avram Ozerović, Serbia's first Jewish parliamentary deputy, elected in 1877, and a Progressive: 'The fact that Mr Ozerović has defended this agreement, I understand. Everywhere in the world the Jews represent the principle of freedom of trade. They wish that there be no obstacles to their trading. And it could be that, on the basis of that principle, Mr Ozerović himself supported it and spoke.' Pašić contrasted what he saw as the justified readiness of earlier Serbian statesmen to protect the nation by restricting the settlement of Jews across Serbia with the Progressive government's willingness to give Austro-Hungarians unrestricted access to the country.[4]

Austro-Serbian collaboration culminated in the Secret Convention of 28 June 1881. For ten years, Serbia undertook to conclude no future political agreement with another state without prior agreement with Austria-Hungary, which thereby gained effective control over Serbia's foreign policy. It undertook also to support Austria-Hungary's presence in Bosnia-Hercegovina and the Sanjak of Novi Pazar and suppress any anti-Habsburg activism vis-à-vis Bosnia-Hercegovina on its territory. In return, Austria-Hungary was to suppress Karađorđevićite activism on its own territory, support diplomatically Serbia's proclamation of a kingdom, promote Serbia's interests with other European governments and support its future territorial expansion southwards.[5] Consequently, Milan proclaimed the Kingdom of Serbia on 22 February 1882. This was partly a response to the precedent created by Romania, which had proclaimed itself a kingdom the year before and was undergoing a similar anti-Russian foreign policy reorientation, culminating in its alliance with Austria-Hungary of 30 October 1883. Meanwhile, at the end of 1882, an equestrian statue of Prince Mihailo was erected in Belgrade's Theatre Square (today the Square of the Republic) where the National Theatre stood. The statue's sabre pointed south, at the lands under Ottoman rule that Milan planned to liberate.[6] Today, the statue marks the centre of Belgrade, as Nelson's Column does of London.

The secret convention represented a double blow against the insurgent activities that had shaken the Obrenović regime during the 1870s and secured for it the firm backing of its powerful neighbour. Despite Serbia's proclamation as a kingdom, it was now in practice less independent and more territorially constrained than it had been before 1878 when still in the Ottoman Empire. But for Milan, awareness that the mighty Habsburg Empire had his back gave him confidence to confront his enemies at home and abroad and behave less like a constitutional ruler and more like an autocrat like Mihailo and Miloš. The secret convention was negotiated by Milan in Vienna, alone on Serbia's behalf, then signed in Belgrade by his Austrophile foreign minister Mijatović. Piroćanac and interior minister Garašanin were informed only after the fact; they were so outraged by its terms and the way it had been reached that they offered their resignations, which Milan refused.[7] The value of the secret convention for Vienna was soon demonstrated when on 10–11 January 1882 an armed rebellion broke out in Hercegovina in reaction to the Habsburg army's extension of military conscription to the newly occupied territory. The rebels enjoyed support from Russia's satellites, Bulgaria and Montenegro, while Serbia's government sought to stem the flow of arms and volunteers across its territory to them. Vienna knew that a Liberal or Radical government would not have been so cooperative.[8] Its support of Milan would be permanent.

Austria-Hungary provided the Progressive government with crucial support in its confrontation with the newly autocephalous Serbian Orthodox Church. Both the previous two Obrenović monarchs had sought to control the church, and by the 1880s the imperative to do so was more pressing than ever. The church had evolved, since the modern Serbian state's birth, in parallel to it: the higher clergy were effectively part of the bureaucratic elite while the lower clergy were close to the people—the cultural chasm between them recalled that between Serbia's Greek bishops and lower clergy in Ottoman times. While many junior clergymen were consequently close to the Radicals, who were anti-clerical in relation to the church hierarchy, the primate of the Serbian church himself, Metropolitan Mihailo, was a Liberal and Russophile, formerly a member of the St Nicholas Committee which drafted the Regency Constitution. He received funds from Russian Panslavists for subversive activities in the Balkans and his agitation in Bosnia-Hercegovina, conducted through the Orthodox clergy, provoked an Austro-Hungarian complaint to Milan. The Serbian regime's opponents therefore penetrated the church at both the upper and lower levels, threatening its policy at home and abroad.

The government challenged Metropolitan Mihailo, attempting on 15 April 1881 to impose taxes on several clerical procedures, which he rejected. He summoned a meeting of the synod on 21 September, which declared the taxes uncanonical. Stojan Novaković, minister of education and church affairs, responded by interrogating the bishops, prompting Mihailo to complain to Piroćanac. This in turn prompted Novaković to complain to Milan of Mihailo's behaviour, which he condemned as that of a 'rebel'. Milan consequently dismissed the metropolitan on 31 October 1881 without a pension. Yet the bishops continued to resist the government's policy and uphold the ousted metropolitan's authority. The government consequently passed a new law on church government on 12 January 1883 that broadened the church synod to include, in addition to bishops, two archimandrites and an archpriest from every diocese, to be appointed by the government. The synod lost the right to elect the metropolitan, which was transferred to a new electoral body that included, in addition to the members of the synod, a number of senior secular figures: the prime minister, minister of education and church affairs, president of the Council, president of the court of cassation and parliamentary representatives elected by parliament. This law effectively established state control of the church. The bishops refused to recognise the new law and responded by withdrawing from their functions.

The electoral body in March elected Archimandrite Teodosije Mraović, a Serb from Austria-Hungary, as the new metropolitan. However, it lacked the authority to consecrate him as bishop. Since the Serbian bishops refused to attend the election or consecrate him, he was consecrated in April at Sremski Karlovci in Austria-Hungary by the Serbian Orthodox Patriarch, acting with the Hungarian government's authorisation. The Serbian bishops were in turn dismissed and three new ones selected and consecrated in Belgrade, again with participation of a bishop of the

COURT AND RADICALS

Sremski Karlovci Patriarchate. Two of the new bishops were, like Teodosije, Austro-Hungarian Serbs. The new church hierarchy was recognised by the Patriarchate in Constantinople the following year. According to Slobodan Jovanović, 'With cosseted hair and hands, clean silk frocks and free worldly behaviour, they appeared to our people soft and unserious.' They also heightened the widespread impression of creeping Austrian domination.[9] Metropolitan Mihailo eventually went into exile in Russia, becoming another pole of opposition to Milan's regime. Meanwhile, in October 1883, at the height of the government's confrontation with the Radical party, the synod banned priests from membership of political parties.[10]

Economic development in Serbia before independence had been concentrated on the Sava and Danube rivers, particularly in Belgrade, Šabac and Smederevo, and oriented towards export to Austria-Hungary. Serbia's independence in 1878, its annexation of new lands to the south and the emergence of a railway network linking it to neighbouring countries catalysed development further afield. In the first decade following independence, Serbia signed eleven trade agreements and seven consular conventions. The value of its foreign trade increased from 66,234,116 dinars in 1875 to 90,915,891 in 1884 and 120,500,000 in 1902.[11] The trade convention with Austria-Hungary boosted agricultural exports: crop exports rose from 30,400 tonnes in 1885–1887 to 77,400 in 1888–1890 and 153,600 in 1891–1893.[12] This raised the prosperity of sections of the peasantry. Immigrant businessmen from Austria-Hungary appeared in Serbia and developed trades previously neglected by natives. One example was the production and export of prunes and plum jam, exploiting Serbia's copious plum orchards: the value of plum-based exports rose from virtually nothing in the early 1860s to exceed the value of grain exports by 1914.[13] Meanwhile, the railway-building programme brought employment. Serbia's government on 9 May 1883 signed a four-way railway convention with Austria-Hungary, Bulgaria and the Ottoman Empire, by which Serbia's network would be linked to Bulgaria's via Pirot and to the Ottomans' via Vranje. It promised to integrate Serbia with the outside world. Rising prosperity among sections of the peasantry raised expectations, while accelerating change created losers as well as winners and increased even the winners' sense of insecurity—an explosive combination.

Formal establishment of political parties

The Young Conservatives' political outlook had been shaped by the experience of Liberal tyranny under the regency, against which their pioneer Čumić had agitated in alliance with the socialists. They were more strongly in favour of civil liberty and personal freedom than the Liberals and believed the minority of educated and enlightened Serbs should guide the peasant masses, identifying progress with Western principles and learning. Their belief in liberty was not shared by Milan but, as they were the only political party willing to support his Austrophile foreign policy, he was compelled to accept their liberalising domestic policy in return. When the new government held parliamentary elections on 12 December 1880, the Young Conservatives and Radicals fought them as allies, united by the experience of Liberal tyranny and belief in constitutional change, and the government desisted from using the police to manipulate the voting. The coalition swept to victory, conclusively ending the Liberal regime. This was secured by a hitherto unprecedented purge from the bureaucracy of that regime's supporters: whereas the regency had pensioned off only six bureaucrats, and the Liberal government of 1876–1880 eight as well as dismissing one, the Progressive government pensioned off 65 and dismissed 26 in its first year.[14]

The Radicals retreated from the socialist aspects of Svetozar Marković's ideology, though they saw themselves as loyal to it in other respects. Pašić, a youthful engineer aged 35 in 1880, was emerging as their principal leader. He had been appointed professor at the Great School's Technical Faculty in September 1878, but the Ristić government, fearing his revolutionary activism, had quashed this appointment, thereby creating a sworn enemy of the Obrenović regime. Pašić therefore exemplified the class of bureaucrats whose career frustrations inclined them to opposition politics. In the short term, Pašić's Radicals at the start of the 1880s abandoned their support for agricultural collectivism to represent the class interests of the freeholders who made up most of the Serbian rural population and were committed to private ownership of their plots. The replacement of the moribund Ottoman Empire by the relatively strong, liberal and dynamic Habsburg Empire in Bosnia-Hercegovina meanwhile convinced Pašić that the all-Balkan revolution would be harder to achieve than anticipated and that their revolutionary strategy would have to be tempered accordingly.

The Young Conservatives and Radicals, despite their initial affinity, did not merge into a single party like the Liberals and Obrenovićites in 1858 or the Old Liberals and Court Liberals after 1867. This was largely owing to Milan's hostility to the Radicals. The Radicals published the first issue of their new newspaper *Samouprava* (Self-Management) on 20 January 1881, which presented a formal manifesto for the People's Radical Party. This prompted the Young Conservatives to publish their own manifesto two days later for the Serbian Progressive Party. This marked the emergence in Serbia of formal political parties with official manifestos and newspapers, in contrast to the previous informal groupings. Since the Radical programme was endorsed by 76 of the newly elected parliamentary deputies, Pašić permitted some of these to endorse also the Progressive manifesto, effectively loaning the government some of his Radical deputies, to prevent its fall and the return to power of Ristić's Liberals. This left the Progressives with 113 deputies, the Radicals 40 and the Liberals seven.[15]

The Radicals' manifesto reflected their belief in the indivisible sovereignty of the nation represented by the peasant majority and their desire to dismantle the bureaucratic-military state: it called for parliament to be composed only of deputies directly elected by all adult (male) citizens; abolition of the Council; full legislative power to be entrusted to parliament; abolition of okrug-level administrations and transfer of their power to the lower-level districts and municipalities on the basis of self-management; promotion of the national militia, with the standing army serving merely to train it; introduction of military training in high schools and colleges; reduction of state spending; freedom of the press; and association and security of person and property. The goal was 'national prosperity and freedom at home, and state independence and the liberation and unification of the other parts of Serbdom'. The party advocated also that 'cultural assistance for the dismembered and unliberated parts of Serbdom be organised, and the live awakening of consciousness of our national unity in the distant Serb provinces that are subjected to foreign elements'. What these 'unliberated parts of Serbdom' and 'distant Serb provinces' actually were remained undefined. This form of nationalist discourse quickly came to predominate among Serbia's political classes: concrete expansionist goals and the strategy to achieve them became less important than the emotional rhetoric of populist nationalism as an end in itself. The Radicals favoured also a union of Balkan peoples, advocating in particular ties with Montenegro and Bulgaria.[16]

The Progressive manifesto was classically liberal: 'Law, freedom and progress—those are the three colours in the flag, which we thus develop; those are the three different bases of true constitutionality.' It advocated freedom of speech, voting and association, security of person and property, ministerial responsibility, independence of the judiciary, exclusion of the ruling dynasty from party-political life and municipal self-management. It stressed that 'in the striving for general progress we stand in the ranks of the European nations, whose civilisation we greatly respect', but also pledged to 'assist in spirit the safeguarding of the precious national character of the Serbs outside the borders of the Serbian principality and strengthen the brotherly ties in the great family of Slavic peoples', upholding the principle that 'the East belongs only to the Eastern peoples'.[17] In fact, the Progressives were more pro-Western in their affinities than any other Serbian political faction. In Slobodan Jovanović's words, 'A young generation with an already refined sensibility, the Progressives took from the West not only its learning and its free thinking but its way of life. They felt the sweetness of the West's material culture and marvelled at the elegant and comfortable life of its upper classes. They willingly travelled around Europe and frequently used French phrases in their speech.'[18]

The Progressives and Radicals thus represented two contrasting visions for Serbia: the former sought its development along Western European liberal lines, based on the promotion of civic institutions and personal liberty under elite guidance, while the latter sought to mobilise a populist peasant resistance to dismantle the Serbia of the army, bureaucracy and taxes and execute a radical transfer of power to the countryside and municipalities. The National Liberal Party's manifesto, meanwhile, was initially less precisely expressed; it prioritised 'liberation and unification of the fragmented Serb provinces' while advocating that 'the national representative body, in terms of independence and in terms of expertise, be strengthened'. It called for economic development, so that 'our young productivity be advanced and raised', but also that 'state expenses be reduced to reasonable and true needs'.[19] The party's ideology would develop midway between those of the Radicals and Progressives, reflecting its composite origins.

The Radicals presented themselves as simply expressing the aspirations of the peasant majority, treating disagreement with their manifesto as an assault on the nation itself. They rejected the liberal principle of the division of powers in favour of the Jacobinical ideal of absolute power for a single-chamber parliament, with the monarch constitutionally untouchable but powerless. Since they rapidly won the overwhelming support of the peasant masses, this would in practice have meant their absolute hegemony. They rejected the concept of the state as protector of individual rights and political freedom, in favour of a 'people's state' that would guarantee popular prosperity. As expounded in their 1883 draft constitution, they also supported the idea of a 'great parliament' to be held every seven years, empowered to modify the electoral law and standing orders of the regular parliament, thereby undermining the establishment of regular parliamentary procedure.

The Radicals had no respect for other parties or political voices. They condemned the Liberals and Progressives as 'the proprietors' who stood in conflict with the people. They viewed the correct organisation of state in terms of an association of self-governing districts, whose assemblies' powers would be limited only by the authority of parliament itself. The parliamentary deputies, meanwhile, were to represent their respective districts rather than the nation as a whole and be subject to recall by their districts' voters. This would have transferred all power to the Radical party as the force that controlled the rural districts and had the support of their peasant voters.[20] Meanwhile, in 1878–1879 the parliamentary Radical party had begun to assume a more disciplined form under Pašić's leadership, whereby no Radical deputy could take any initiative in parliament without authorisation from the Radical parliamentary club.[21] The Radicals' revolutionary political ideology and increasingly powerful party machine, combined with their wide support in the countryside, were perceived as mortally threatening by the regime.

Parliament passed a law on 1 March 1880 establishing the Chief Educational Council, tasked with implementing a national education plan at school and university level. The judiciary's independence was established on 21 February 1881, with the government losing the right to dismiss or pension judges. A press law on 9 April introduced almost complete freedom of the press, barring only injuries to the prince's person or incitement to rebellion. The police were now required to obtain judicial approval within 24 hours of any decision to ban a publication. Freedom of assembly and association were introduced and public organisations legalised on 13 April. The police retained the power to ban political associations only when their rules violated the law. This led to the registration on 29 September of the Society for the Support of Serbian Literature, as the National Liberal Party's formal name, with Ristić as president. The Serbian Progressive Party submitted its statutes to the government for registration on 30 September and on 12 October became the first political party legally recognised in Serbia. The People's Radical Party was legally recognised on 12 December. Universal compulsory elementary education was introduced by law on 12 January 1883 while a second teacher-training school was established and the salaries of teachers raised. A National Bank was established on 18 January.[22] The number of schools would rise rapidly in the years to come: 534 in 1885; 1,263 in 1904; and 1,425 in 1911.[23] These liberalising laws enabled free political organisation and agitation, and unintentionally facilitated the Radical party's rapid expansion in the countryside, so that it rapidly became the party supported by the overwhelming majority of Serbian peasants.

Progressive government and Radical opposition

The Progressive government's ambitious modernisation and state-building programme was expensive and it also faced other significant expenditures, some inherited from the Liberal regime. The railway convention with Austria-Hungary required it to finance railway building. The expropriation of Muslim landholdings in the new territories required the Serb peasants to compensate the former landlords, and to ensure the transfer was affordable to both parties, the government in 1882 raised a loan to subsidise the compensation. All this resulted in a large budget deficit and necessitated raising taxes. Meanwhile, the government's military and educational reforms were apparently viewed by some peasants as restored kuluk; Slobodan Jovanović cites a peasant who complained, 'They've taken one of my sons to the army and the other to the school.'[24]

These grievances generated strong opposition to the Progressive regime from wide sections of the population that assumed a nationalist and populist form. The railway-building programme was unpopular with the peasants, who resented the consequent taxes and disruption to their way of life. When the government signed three agreements with Paul Eugène Bontoux's Paris-based General Union to provide credit for the railway building, they were attacked by the Radicals on nationalistic anti-Austrian grounds, because Bontoux was a resident of Vienna, director of the Austrian railway company Südbahn and founder of the Viennese bank Lenderbank. Svetomir Nikolajević stated in parliament in mid-March 1881 that the General Union was 'a company that stood under the direct auspices of Austria'; to support an agreement with it would 'dig the grave of our political freedom; of our state' and make the parliamentary deputies 'traitors to the Balkan peoples'. On this occasion, an angry pro-Radical crowd tried to force its way into the parliament, attacking the gendarmes who restrained them.²⁵ The Radical newspaper *Samouprava* meanwhile complained that German workers were taking all the best railroad jobs.²⁶

The Radical–Progressive war erupted in earnest in January 1882, when parliament convened and the Radical deputies, condemning the government's financial policy at home and Austrophile policy abroad, refused to sign its address. France's stock market crashed that month, causing the General Union to collapse and go bankrupt by February; this appeared to vindicate Radical accusations of governmental financial incompetence and aroused public fear of possible economic repercussions for Serbia. For Pašić, the economic agreements with Austria-Hungary were damned by the very fact that the empire had sought them, because, as he said in parliament on 15 March, 'From the time when the Serb nation arose, from that time until today, I know, and whoever has read the history of our nation and Austria-Hungary knows, that we cannot find a single moment of generosity of Austria-Hungary towards the Serb nation.' Austria-Hungary's goal was 'to have an open road to Old Serbia and Salonika and to prevent us joining with Montenegro'.²⁷ On 17 March, after the government refused to respond to the opposition's interpellation concerning the collapse, the opposition deputies—51 Radicals and two Liberals—resigned, leaving the parliament without a quorum. Resisting calling a new general election out of fear it would lose, the government held a top-up election to replace the opposition deputies while abandoning its restraint about using the police to manipulate the results.

Milan participated in the electoral contest as the Progressives' champion. His proclamation of the kingdom aimed to deflect attention from the General Union scandal. He received delegations from across the country congratulating him on becoming king, to which he preached support for the government and denounced the opposition. Between 20 April and 21 May, he toured Serbia and delivered speeches attacking the Radicals, who in turn organised counter-manifestations. On one of the ceremonial gates set up to greet him at Užice, an inscription was pointedly added: 'Bosnia, Hercegovina and Old Serbia must be ours!'²⁸ The introduction of press freedom unleashed ferocious Radical polemics against the king, whose open party partisanship cost him the deference that political neutrality would have afforded him. Although overt press attacks on the king's person were still illegal, the Radical press could bypass this by denouncing tyrants elsewhere, the allusion to Milan being clear. The top-up election held on 27 May resulted in the Radicals winning 45 of the 50 contested seats. When these deputies immediately resigned, leaving the parliament again without a quorum, Piroćanac attempted to resign on the government's behalf, but Milan rejected this. Instead, the government held a new top-up election on 12 June in which the opposition won 43 of the contested seats. The government responded by declaring that, since the opposition was obstructing parliament, its newly elected deputies had forfeited their mandates and their seats would pass to the runners-up. By this blatant violation of electoral rules, the government achieved a parliamentary quorum. Some of the new government deputies, elected by as few as two votes apiece—hence known as 'two-voters'—were too terrified of their constituents' reaction to attend parliament and had to be coerced to do so by the authorities.[29]

The Progressives thus abandoned their idealistic initial respect for legalism and liberty under pressure from their struggle with the Radicals. Laws were passed in June and July to fine parliamentary deputies who left the parliament without a quorum through resignation or absenteeism; to permit the banning of newspapers that promoted nihilism or communism; to increase heavily the punishment for transgressions in print; and, for the purpose of subjecting villages to gendarme visits for the first time, to establish a flying mounted gendarmerie. These gendarmes were nicknamed 'sejmeni' by the Radicals, after those of the Ottoman era. The Radicals held their first general congress on 7–9 August of that year in Kragujevac, attended by between 350 and 600 delegates from all over the country, who were treated to a series of populist, nationalist and pro-democracy speeches.[30] Pašić complained in his speech: 'In the parliament there is a Turk and a Jew as government deputies, and they have been appointed to committees to make various laws for Serbia, while from our more than fifty people's deputies they have not appointed a single one.'[31] The party formally adopted its statute and manifesto, presented in a fiery speech by Todorović, and elected a general council.[32] The regime responded by reinforcing the Kragujevac garrison and thoroughly purging the police, local administration and teaching profession to ensure their loyalty to the regime and remove Radical sympathisers.

Jelena 'Ilka' Marković, widow of Jevrem Marković whom Milan had judicially murdered, shot at the king on 23 October in Belgrade cathedral in an attempt to avenge her husband, but missed. Milan suspected she had been instigated by the Radicals and sought to use this as a pretext for measures against them, but the investigation implicated only another widow, Jelena Knićanka. In turn, suspicions against the regime were aroused when Knićanka was found hanged in prison on 12 March 1883, supposedly by suicide; this was shortly followed by the fatal shooting of the soldier who had been guarding her by another soldier, supposedly accidentally. Marković herself, having been tried, sentenced to death and granted clemency, was also found dead in prison, again supposedly by suicide. The regime and the Radical opposition may each have been less guilty than the other suspected, but the macabre affair contributed to the growing tension between them.

The government sought to summon a great national parliament to promulgate a more liberal constitution, so restore its popularity and progressive credentials, but it was faced with obstruction from Milan, who felt the existing constitution was already too liberal and who feared the Radicals would win the elections. Milan objected to the Progressives' draft constitution, which involved an upper chamber of parliament restraining what was likely to be a Radical-dominated lower chamber, with both chambers legislatively equal. This upper chamber was reminiscent of the

Council of the Progressives' Constitutionalist predecessors, and Milan, like Miloš before him, did not wish to work with such an institution. The Radicals produced their own draft constitution for a fully parliamentary system involving a wholly directly elected single chamber without any government deputies; districts and municipalities governed wholly through self-management; parliamentary control of the government and army; and the king's demotion to a constitutional monarch. All this was unacceptable to Milan and reinforced his unwillingness to summon the great national parliament. The struggle of the parties was thus also a struggle over different constitutional models.[33]

Timok rebellion

Milan increasingly perceived the Radical party and his foreign enemies as allied against him. Russia disliked both his Austrophile policy and his conflict with the Serbian church. His abandonment of plans for a Balkan uprising and his alienation of Russia also antagonised Prince Nikola, who resented Milan's assumption of the title of king and considered that, since Serbia had abdicated the role, Montenegro should become leader of the Serb national liberation struggle.[34] To strengthen his credentials, Nikola married his eldest daughter Zorka to Petar Karađorđević in August 1883 and, some years later, his second daughter Milica to a Russian grand duke. One Radical reportedly responded to news of Petar's wedding by loudly and drunkenly declaring wherever he went: 'We don't need a Vlach as a king, but a real Serb. We have the Serb Petar Karađorđević and we shall take him as king and crown him.'[35]

Milan developed Serbia's regular army to safeguard his regime. The wars with the Ottoman Empire of the 1870s had highlighted the national militia's deficiency and the need to expand and improve the regular army. A milestone in this respect was reached on 30 January 1880, when the Artillery School was converted into a Military Academy for training an officer corps. Since cadets had to have finished high school, then take an entrance exam, they inevitably came predominantly from the ranks of the educated, bureaucratic and prosperous families of the towns.[36] This emphasised the divide between the army and peasant majority, as did the introduction of new uniforms for officers following the proclamation of the kingdom, modelled on French and German uniforms.[37] One remarkable Serbian officer was an actual Prussian officer: Paulus Sturm, an ethnic Sorb who had fought in the Franco-Prussian War before joining Serbia's army to fight the Turks in 1876, Serbianising his name to Pavle Jurišić-Šturm. He went on to become one of Serbia's greatest commanders in the Balkan Wars and World War I.

The national militia was abolished on 12 January 1883 in favour of compulsory military service in the regular standing army, which was the European norm. The Army of the Kingdom of Serbia was divided between three call-ups: the first was the youngest, divided between the standing army that resided in barracks and the reserves that lived at home, together constituting the 'active army', supposed to be always ready for action; the second was those who had served their term in the active army and now lived at home while performing duties in the rear or serving to replenish the active army when necessary; and the third was only activated in case of extreme need, for the country's defence.[38] A deal was signed with a German company to supply the army with modern weapons. Officers' pay was increased, making them the best-paid profession in the state. These developments were spurred by the Radical party's rapid expansion. With a politically dangerous force conquering the peasant population's loyalties, the militia had become a liability while the dynasty needed a reliable force for self-protection. Officers, meanwhile, were thoroughly alienated by ceaseless Radical attacks on them and identified wholly with Milan's anti-Radical orientation.[39]

The Radicals' vague, emotional ideal of Serb unification went hand in hand with a preference for the idea of the national militia, whereby 'the standing army would be deemed merely as a school for the national militia and, according to this, that only so much of a standing army be maintained as is necessary for the successful and correct training and organisation of the national militia'. Furthermore, their manifesto demanded that 'military training be introduced into middle and high school'.[40] The national militia's purpose was less to pursue concrete military goals than to inculcate the Radical worldview among the people and defend them from tyranny. As Pašić wrote:

> What the gun means to the Serb—that we all know. It is the greatest weapon that the Serb has; it is as dear to him as his wife, brother or sister; the Serb would rather part with his head or his soul than with his weapons. Without guns and weapons there is no freedom. If it be wished to destroy the freedom of a given people; if it be wished to draw them into slavery; then it is necessary to take away their weapons ... The Turks were always ready to promise much so long as the Serbs handed over their weapons—and the Serb always resisted; he was always ready to die in torment rather than surrender his weapons.[41]

In response to the law on the army's reorganisation of December 1882 and January 1883, the Radicals highlighted its huge cost, claiming the police were consuming 18.8 per cent of the budget and the army 36.5 per cent, spent disproportionately on the higher officer corps, while only 10 per cent was spent on education.[42]

The king and the Progressives feared a popular rebellion by the Radicals and militia while the Radicals feared a coup by king, government and army. As each prepared for the other's blow, Serbia moved inexorably towards civil conflict. The Progressives lost elections held on 19 September 1883, which their government treated as a public rejection of their plans for constitutional reform, resigning the following day. The Radicals swept to victory, yet Milan refused to let them form a government, instead appointing Mihailo's former strongman Nikola Hristić prime minister. This choice seemed to presage a coup. The government dissolved parliament on 22 September. The Radical leadership met secretly and 'it was unanimously concluded that King Milan had resolved to begin an open struggle against the people'.[43] The leadership nevertheless did not adopt Todorović's proposal to establish a 'general staff' capable of organising and leading resistance, so it remained without any institutional structure that would have enabled it to do so.[44] Meanwhile, the military law of 12 January was greatly resented by the peasantry: conscription separated them from the fields for two full years and required them after that to undergo annual training as part of the reserves until they turned 37.[45] The government in October 1883 ordered the registration of eligible adult males in the newly established reserve army, involving confiscation of the rifles they had held at home as militiamen. This was motivated by fear of an uprising but threatened to deprive the Radicals and peasant population of the means to resist a coup. It recalled the pre-emptive measures taken by the deys against the Serbs in 1804.

The explosion finally came in the Radical stronghold of the Timok region of eastern Serbia. This had suffered particular material and economic devastation in the wars of the 1870s while a section of its poorer peasantry was becoming proletarianised, as the inability of householders to support themselves on the basis of their plots caused rising indebtedness and their transformation into agricultural labourers, miners, servants or the like.[46] Economic misery and state oppression were lighter than they had been in the late 1870s: the opening of Austria-Hungary's market to Serbian agricultural produce following Milan's convention with Vienna greatly profited the peasantry.[47] But now the Radical party had appeared to channel peasant discontent, based upon a local 'bourgeoisie' of village priests, teachers and traders forming the natural leaders of local resistance.[48] Although the Radical general council had taken no steps to launch an uprising, local Radical organisations in the Timok region, among whose members talk of a rebellion had circulated for months, threw themselves into the fight. They provided organisational backbone for the resistance to the confiscation of arms, by peasants inflamed for months by Radical propaganda. Meanwhile, in Radical-controlled municipalities, it was still legal for them to mobilise the militia, which meant their rebellion was waged through a legitimate state institution.[49]

Several villagers were arrested in the Boljevac district near Zaječar by 23 October, but then freed by a peasant crowd. The Boljevac rebels, led by the Radical deputy the Reverend Marinko Ivković, called for support on neighbouring villages. On 1 November, they surrounded the government force sent to suppress them and forced the colonel in charge to disarm the sejmeni. This prompted the government to declare martial law in the Crnorecki okrug on 3 November. Rebels under Radical deputy Ljubomir Didić arrested the administration of Banja on 6 November. The following day, under Radical deputy Aca Stanojević, rebels seized control of Knjaževac, one of two main towns in the region. Stanojević, like Đak, leader of the 1825 rebellion, was a municipal clerk. He used his experience to establish an effective administration in Knjaževac. In the places they seized, the rebels expelled bureaucrats from their offices and established Radical-led ruling committees.⁵⁰

The Radical general council was now caught between a spontaneous uprising and probable arrest. Pašić, Torodović and other leading Radicals met outside Belgrade to formulate a response. They knew the rising would almost certainly fail but that, if they did not participate, they would forfeit their popular standing and be blamed by the government regardless. They agreed that the foremost Radicals should return to their electoral districts or localities to lead the uprising: Pašić to the Timok region; Todorović to Rudnik; Kosta Taušanović to Aleksinac; and Raša Milošević to Pirot. A meeting of leading Radicals at the newspaper *Samouprava*'s premises on 6 November endorsed this plan, after which Pašić left Belgrade for Zemun; his job as an engineer on the construction of the bridge over the Sava facilitated this. His leaving Serbia was typically cunning: it offered him the possibility either of travelling to the rebel areas if the uprising continued or avoiding arrest if it failed. Yet the other Radical leaders vacillated about leaving Belgrade and that evening were arrested, including Todorović, Taušanović, Milošević, Jovan Đaja and Giga Geršić.⁵¹

The Radical leaders consequently contributed no effective leadership to the rebellion. The rebels failed, on the 8th, to take Zaječar, the region's second principal town, and on the 11th were decisively defeated at Vratarnica. The army retook Knjaževac on the 12th; on the same day the Radical Serafim Negotinac led a belated uprising in the town of Aleksinac and established an administration, but the army immediately suppressed it. Plans to raise rebellions in the vicinity of Kruševac and Negotin came to nothing, as the army appeared in these regions pre-emptively. The Radicals in the Pirot okrug, too, were ready to rise; their local leader claimed Milan wanted to restore the institutions of the tenth, beylik, kuluk 'and everything else that had been imposed during the rule of the Turks'. But the authorities cut communications between Pirot and rebellious Knjaževac and increased their surveillance of Radical party members, thereby preventing them from acting.⁵² Thus the rebellion, having failed to spread beyond eastern Serbia, was defeated.

A special court was established by the government to punish the participants with exemplary severity; its president, Dragomir Rajović, a Progressive, earned the nickname 'Bloody Rajovče'. It completed its proceedings by December 1883: 809 participants were tried of whom 94 were sentenced to death and 640 to prison terms. Of the Radical general council's ten members, Pašić (in absentia), Todorović and Milošević were sentenced to death, Taušanović and Pavle Mihailović received prison terms, and the rest were acquitted. The cost of the rebellion's suppression was to be borne by the municipalities of the okrugs and districts where the state of emergency had been proclaimed.⁵³ Most of those sentenced to death were eventually spared because the legal case against them had been weak. Twenty were eventually executed, including Ivković, Didić and Negotinac. Todorović and Milošević had their death sentences commuted to prison terms after writing to Milan, begging for mercy. Influential voices at home and abroad called for clemency, including Ristić, Queen Natalija and the representatives of Germany, Russia and Austria-Hungary, while European opinion, as expressed in leading newspapers, was shocked at the numerous death sentences for such a minor rebellion. Milan considered all this, as well as the pleas for mercy by some of the convicted, which suggested their possible recruitment as collaborators.[54]

The rebellion's defeat marked the end of the era of peasant uprisings in Serbia and a turning point in the Radical party's history. For Pašić, it was a pivotal experience, after which he abandoned faith in overthrowing the regime by popular revolution. Russia now became the force he looked to for its overthrow. This meant abandonment of the Radicals' early left-wing antipathy toward Tsarist autocracy in favour of a conservative Slavophilism. Pašić also retreated from belief in Balkan federation in favour of a narrower focus on pan-Serb unification. This involved an alliance with Metropolitan Mihailo, a fellow exile and enemy of Milan's, hence a retreat from Radical anti-clericalism in favour of an alliance with the church. Obedience to St Petersburg would remain a hallmark of Pašić's politics until the Bolshevik Revolution.[55] He meanwhile interpreted the Timok rebellion in nationalist terms: 'The struggle, which the opposition is waging against the king, is not simply a personal struggle and a struggle against a worthless and fallen ruler but the struggle of the Serb nation against Austria-Hungary; the struggle of Slavdom against Germanism. Misfortune determined that the Serb nation should for ages and ages expend and break itself against the Turks and Mohammedanism and now that it should fight and expend itself against Germanism.' Indeed, he argued, the Serb nation 'knows that it has spilled more blood for the Austrian court than it has spilled fighting against the Turks, and still the Turk is better and closer than the German. The Serb nation mortally hates Austria.'[56]

Milan cemented his regime in February 1884 with wholly engineered parliamentary elections in which the police selected both candidates and voters who were considered reliable and guided them to participate, resulting in a solid Progressive parliamentary majority. Piroćanac, a genuine believer in liberal government and supporter of constitutional reform, found himself increasingly ill at ease as prime minister, squeezed between a deeply illiberal king and an equally illiberal Radical opposition, prompting his withdrawal from front-line politics. Milan instead appointed Garašanin to head a new Progressive government which would act much more overtly as a front for his personal rule. It returned to Ristić's authoritarian practice of holding parliamentary sessions in Niš instead of Belgrade to reduce the public's involvement in its proceedings. A spate of repressive laws were passed on 23 June: freedom to publish seditious material was restricted and penalties for transgressions toughened; freedom of association was greatly restricted; political associations lost the right to establish subsidiary bodies; and public rallies could no longer be held without official permission and were banned altogether within five days of an election. Municipal self-government was greatly restricted: smaller municipalities were merged into larger ones; direct elections of municipal presidents and kmets were replaced by indirect ones; the resolution of disputes over electoral lists was transferred from the court of first instance to the interior ministry; interior ministry control of municipal courts and councils was increased; the finance ministry was required to approve municipal budgets; the post of municipal president was now generously paid to ensure these officials would be loyal to the government; and the sejmeni were replaced by a regular permanent gendarmerie divided into mounted and infantry branches. These measures were intended to cripple the Radical party and ensure full control by the regime over the countryside.[57] Three days later, the new government, having inherited a huge deficit from the Piroćanac government, overhauled the tax system, abolishing the antiquated head-tax dating back to Miloš's first reign in favour of new taxes on land, homes, capital gains and income.

Serbo-Bulgarian war

Following the Timok rebellion's defeat, about fifty rebels including Pašić and Stanojević fled to Bulgaria. This heightened Milan's sense of encirclement: his principal domestic enemies were now being sheltered by Russia's principal Balkan satellite. Already during 1883, disgruntled Liberals—Ristić, his brother-in-law Nikola Hadži-Toma and Russia-based Metropolitan Mihailo—had established contact with the Karađorđević family and begun receiving from it a monthly subsidy to finance agitation against the Progressive regime. Following his flight to Bulgaria, Pašić, too, for the first time established contact with the Karađorđevićes and the Radicals also began receiving from them a monthly subsidy.[58] The new understanding between the Radicals and Karađorđevićes was facilitated by their shared socialist links or heritage. This was a portentous set of alliances: two decades later, a conspiracy of disgruntled Liberals would destroy the Obrenović regime, restore the Karađorđević monarchy and enable the Radicals to emerge as the dominant governmental party.

The Radical exiles agitated from Bulgaria in Serbia's border areas, even making violent incursions; on one occasion, a Progressive kmet was killed. In the spring of 1884, Serbia's government feared coordinated guerrilla raids from Bulgaria and Montenegro combined with a Radical-backed uprising, organised and funded by Russia in consultation with Pašić and Prince Nikola. Milan felt so threatened that he sought unsuccessfully from Austria-Hungary the deepening of its protectorate over Serbia, even envisaging the possibility of outright occupation, to safeguard both his dynasty and the Austro-Serbian alliance.[59] Meanwhile, this alliance and the consequent abandonment of Serbian expansionist plans vis-à-vis Bosnia-Hercegovina meant renewed interest in expansion southwards into Old Serbia and Macedonia, which also meant conflict with Bulgaria for influence over this region.

Regarding the Bulgarian threat, Milan was arguably more prescient than other Serbs, whose Panslavism and Russophilia militated against any sense of peculiarly Serbian state interests. In Slobodan Jovanović's words: 'King Milan was not a good Slav nor a good Serb. He loved Serbia primarily because it was his state, not because it was the core of Serbdom. But precisely because of those deficiencies in Slavic and pan-Serb sentimentality, he judged with much more political seriousness and state egoism than the majority of contemporary Serbs.'[60]

Foreign minister Mijatović, who shared Milan's Austrophile and Russophobic orientation, raised in early 1881 with the Patriarchate in Constantinople the question of appointing Serb bishops to bishoprics in Old Serbia and Macedonia. Between November 1884 and March 1885, the Serbian government supported the mission of Petar Kostić, director of the Serbian Orthodox seminary in Prizren, who successfully negotiated with the Patriarchate and Porte for permission to use Serbian textbooks in the seminary and Serb schools. During March 1885, in response to Bulgarian nationalist agitation over Macedonia, meetings were held in Belgrade, Niš and Vranje with Serbian governmental support, as was a conference of Great School students, to counter Bulgarian claims and stress the supposedly Serb character of the disputed territory. That month, Garašanin submitted to Milan his plan for Serbian southward action, identifying Bulgaria rather than the Ottoman Empire as Serbia's principal enemy and calling for collaboration with the empire and Greece against Bulgaria, involving negotiation of Greek and Serbian spheres of influence in Macedonia. Garašanin advocated preparation for war with Bulgaria and an alliance with Romania as a precondition for stability in the Balkans, even envisioning Bulgaria's partition between Serbia and Romania. He proposed an additional annual budget of 100,000–150,000 dinars to finance schools, teachers, churches, priests, books, newspapers and other aspects of the irredentist campaign. Diplomatic efforts were to be accelerated for a consular agreement with the Porte and for agreements with the Patriarchate over Serbian bishops in the Ottoman lands and with Albanian leaders.[61]

A unionist coup in Eastern Rumelia's capital Plovdiv led Bulgaria unilaterally to annex the province on 18 September 1885, violating the Treaty of Berlin and threatening dangerously to upset the regional balance of power, even possibly involving Bulgaria's annexation of Macedonia and the establishment of the Great Bulgaria of San Stefano. Milan was determined on a showdown, both to restore this balance in Serbia's favour and to end the Radical emigration's use of Bulgaria as a base. Pašić, from his base in Vidin, wrote to him on behalf of his group of émigrés, pledging that if Milan responded to Bulgaria's annexation by himself annexing the Ottoman territories of Old Serbia and the 'Serbian part' of Macedonia, then the Radicals would stop resisting him and collaborate in this endeavour. Yet Milan was not ready for such collaboration, while Pašić also attempted in autumn 1885 to raise guerrilla forces in Bulgaria for the struggle against Milan's regime. Under pressure

COURT AND RADICALS

from Serbia and to avoid war, the Bulgarian government dispersed these guerrillas and expelled the Radical émigrés, with Pašić moving to Romania. But Milan continued to seek war with Bulgaria to prevent its future use as a Radical base.[62]

After diplomacy failed either to reverse the annexation or win territorial compensation from Bulgaria for Serbia, Milan declared war on 14 November 1885. For the regime of Milan and Garašanin, the resulting war was, like the 1876 war for the Liberals, embarked on overconfidently but poorly prepared militarily and diplomatically. Austria-Hungary's war party encouraged it while the government in Vienna tried to restrain it. Piroćanac, who in the 1870s had cautioned against war with the Ottomans, now opposed this war as well, noting in his diary, 'Now, nothing remains but to see that a clean face comes from this foolish enterprise.'[63] Milan was on personally friendly terms with Bulgaria's Prince Alexander of Battenberg, who was something of a kindred spirit: a German, hence a foreigner in the country where he reigned, just a couple of years younger than Milan, who had similarly rebelled against the Russian yoke. But like many Serbians, Milan had little respect for Bulgarians as soldiers. Unlike the 1876 war, this was a war against a fraternal Orthodox Slavic country for opaque *raisons d'état*. Aloof from Serbia's people, Milan could not convincingly make the case for a war that was arguably in the national interest, but fought it as a cabinet war for the defence of the unpopular Treaty of Berlin. His war effort consequently lacked popular enthusiasm.[64]

Bulgaria's forces were concentrated in Eastern Rumelia, leaving its border with Serbia undefended. Russia's Tsar Alexander III, deeply hostile to Alexander of Battenberg, withdrew the Russian officers from Bulgaria's army to punish him for the unilateral annexation, devastating its command structure. Milan therefore envisaged a 'stroll to Sofia', less than 35 miles from the Serbian border.[65] He nevertheless delayed attacking Bulgaria under pressure from Austria-Hungary, to give it a chance to achieve territorial compensation for Serbia diplomatically. Austria-Hungary failed to achieve this, but the delay enabled Bulgaria to begin transferring its forces to its border with Serbia, which thus lost the chance of a pre-emptive strike.[66] Once the war began, Milan's regime was ineffective at planning and waging it because the regime and army were oriented toward repression of the domestic, Radical enemy rather than combat against a foreign enemy. He employed only a small part of the second call-up of soldiers, as these were members of the former national militia in which he lacked confidence, while part of the standing army remained in Serbia to resist another possible rebellion. Consequently, Serbia's army was considerably outnumbered by Bulgaria's forces. Three Serbian divisions—the Drina, Danube and Šumadija—plus a cavalry brigade were dispatched from Pirot to occupy Sofia. The Morava Division was to converge with them there after occupying Trn (Tran) and Breznik, and the Timok Division was to assemble at Zaječar and march on Vidin. The four divisions sent against Sofia numbered 27,649 and the Timok Division numbered 5,637 while the Bulgarian army proper numbered 56,400 and the Eastern

Rumelian army 36,600. The Bulgarian cannon was superior in quality to the Serbian. Unlike the Serbian soldiers, who were confused about the war's purpose, the Russian-trained Bulgarian soldiers were defending their homeland. Milan's military reforms had yet to bear fruit: Serbia's army was insufficiently organised; its newly trained officer corps was inexperienced; its artillery, intelligence, field fortifications, supplies and other branches were all inadequate. Finally, the Serbian campaign was ineptly directed by Milan himself.[67]

The opposing armies met for the war's decisive clash at Slivnica north of Sofia, where the Bulgarians had entrenched themselves to resist the Serbian advance. In a three-day battle on 17–19 November, the Serbian main force was decisively defeated. Milan's morale broke and he ordered the withdrawal of the Serbian forces back to Serbia, essentially abandoning all plans for an offensive victory. His panicked retreat did not degenerate into a complete rout thanks only to the intervention of Garašanin, who forced him to muster a defence. The Bulgarians took Neškov Vis on the 24th, giving them command of the Pirot basin, then crossed the border and defeated the Serbians again on 26th–27th to occupy Pirot, after which Niš was threatened. Meanwhile, Serbia's Timok Division was still unsuccessfully besieging Vidin. Serbia was rescued from Bulgarian occupation and territorial loss by Austria-Hungary's threat to intervene against Bulgaria. Peace was restored on 3 March 1886 on the basis of the status quo ante bellum. It was an outright Bulgarian victory.

The war was notable for the military service of the first Serbian woman doctor: Draga Ljočić, from a family of Cincar origin, sister of the socialist Đura Ljočić and wife of the Radical Milošević. She had been in 1871 the first woman to enrol at the Great School, completed her studies in Zurich and served as medical assistant in the 1876 war.[68] Despite such signs of modernisation, Milan's Westernising military reforms would not bring victory in his lifetime, though they laid the basis for it after his death. He was Serbia's Sultan Mahmud II, whose reign witnessed repeated Ottoman defeats at the hands of the Great Powers and Egyptians but laid the foundations of the modern Turkey that would eventually achieve victory under Mustafa Kemal. Defeat by Bulgaria led to further Serbian military reforms in the months and years ahead, among them the introduction of formal schooling for NCOs and inclusion of the second call-up in the active army.

The defeat also prompted Milan's regime to promote more aggressively Serbia's expansion of influence in Macedonia. Serbian consulates were opened in the Macedonian cities of Skopje and Salonika in 1886. On 6 September of that year, the Society of St Sava was founded, modelled on the Bulgarians' Society of Cyril and Methodius and headed by the former Radical and future prime minister Svetomir Nikolajević; it renewed the drive to open Serbian schools in the Ottoman lands, so that there were 42 of them by 1889. Serbia's education ministry established in March 1887 a section devoted to 'Serbian Schools and Churches outside Serbia'. This was transferred to the foreign ministry in June 1889. A railway convention was signed with the Ottomans in 1888 to link the Serbian and Ottoman railways via Vranje; it was aimed, on Belgrade's part, at opening Macedonia to Serbia. Two more Serbian consulates were opened in Macedonia and Old Serbia, in Bitola and Priština, in 1889. Serbia's embassy in Constantinople published bilingual Serbian and Macedonian calendars and schoolbooks for Macedonia while the Society of St Sava educated Macedonian pupils.[69] Serbia's government in 1889 also published a German translation of a book on the ethnography of Macedonia by Spiridon Gopčević, arguing that almost all Albanians were 'Albanianised Serbs'—propaganda in support of possible territorial claims.[70]

Ironically, Milan received the greatest encouragement in his Macedonian ambitions from his *bête noire*, Pašić. The latter had, in his Bulgarian exile, realised the danger Bulgaria posed to Serbia's interests in Macedonia: 'For Serbdom, it is not so dangerous that Austria has occupied Bosnia-Hercegovina as Bulgarian propaganda in Macedonia and Old Serbia is dangerous', he wrote in August 1887. 'We cannot redeem Bosnia-Hercegovina, like the other Serb lands in Austria-Hungary, alone, without Russia's military intervention, but we can save Macedonia for Serbia without Russia's military intervention …'[71] Milan and Pašić, bitter foes, pioneered a Macedonian orientation for Serbia when it was unpopular with Serbia's political elite, which was still fixated on Bosnia; the Macedonian orientation would steadily supplant the Bosnian orientation.

Constitution of 1889 and abdication of King Milan

Defeat by the Bulgarians broke the regime of Milan and the Progressives. Milan realised the defeat was partly due to his regime's unpopularity and that he consequently needed reconciliation with the Radicals. He therefore amnestied the Timok rebels on 13 January 1886, other than those in exile, and made 'Bloody Rajovče' scapegoat for his own bloodthirsty response to the rebellion by dismissing him as economics minister.[72] The rebellion's defeat had meanwhile persuaded the chastened Radicals to accept, at least formally, the sort of liberal constitutional models favoured by the Liberals and Progressives, while several of their most eminent figures were ready to sell out to the regime entirely. Todorović, the most influential Radical alongside Pašić, following his near-death experience and pardon by Milan, emerged as the champion of Radical–regime collaboration. He twice wrote to Milan from prison and the latter responded on 27 December 1885 by visiting him there. The two men, broken by the failures of the Timok rebellion and the Bulgarian war respectively, began negotiating a détente between the Obrenović monarchy and the Radical party.[73] At Milan's invitation, about forty senior Radicals met at Niš on 18–19 February 1886. They rejected Todorović's appeal for the alliance with the Progressives that Milan wanted but accepted the need for collaboration with the king to achieve constitutional reform through a great national parliament.[74] The exiled Pašić angrily viewed this as a betrayal that erased the difference between the Radicals and Liberals. Although ready to accept the shift as a fait accompli, he now sought to achieve Radical goals through parliamentary and constitutional rather than revolutionary means, intending that the party should become a wolf in sheep's clothing—liberal on the outside but Radical on the inside.[75]

Following the military defeat, Garašanin's government resigned on 31 March 1886 but was reinstated by Milan in reconstituted form. Of seven ministers, two were reserve and three active officers. These included the new foreign minister, Colonel Dragutin Franasović, indicating Milan's wish to keep foreign policy firmly in his own hands.[76] This immediately prompted a Liberal–Radical agreement on 18 April to form an opposition alliance devoted to constitutional reform at home and a less Austrophile policy abroad. Despite the government's use of police pressure and manipulation, the parliamentary election of 8 May 1886 gave it only a narrow majority. The embattled Progressive regime passed a law in parliament in November to establish the Royal Serbian Academy, an academic body intended to counter Liberal domination among the intelligentsia.[77] Pašić meanwhile worked on a grand alliance to overthrow the regime. He visited Montenegro in July 1886 and, after being assured by another Radical exile that he could count on Prince Nikola's support, negotiated a draft agreement with Petar Karađorđević whereby they would work towards an uprising in Serbia. The conspirators counted on Montenegrin and Russian support and planned to co-opt the Liberals and summon a great national parliament to establish a new order headed by the Karađorđević dynasty. Petar meanwhile reached agreement with the Radicals for a thorough restructuring of Serbia along democratic lines under the great national parliament's aegis, involving a national militia and new constitution. These plans came to nothing because Russia did not wish to support this adventure, and Montenegro would not act without Russia's backing. Furthermore, neither state favoured Serbia's radical democratisation.[78]

The final straw for Milan and the Progressives was his separation from Natalija, which he announced in April 1887, wishing as he did to marry his mistress, Artemis Hristić. The marriage between cynical, amoral, paranoid Milan and proud, scornful, uptight Natalija had long ceased to be loving. The Austrophile king distrusted the Russophile queen; he restricted her movements while taking mistresses himself, and they approached a mutual hatred. In her words:

> Intelligent and cunning, but without substance under the brilliant exterior; spoilt, with a suspicious and dishonest nature; inclined to command, but incompetent to impose his will, while his persistence in his chosen behaviour was more stubbornness than anything else. Moreover ill-bred, uncouth and brutally selfish; a weak character, susceptible to flattery and female influence. Although he thinks that he knows people, he judges them in a biased and unjust manner. Lavish and small; generous more out of profligacy than through any true need of the heart. He does not appear evil, yet he is capable of doing evil out of mistrust. He despises people and is incapable of believing

in noble feelings and loyalty. Petty and unpleasant; incapable of true attachment; he suffers terribly if it seems to him he is insufficiently loved. Spoilt and idle; he feels the need to entertain himself and is constantly bored. He wants to make others happy, but sows tears around him. Fawning before those higher up; churlish to those lower down; a callow nature, unhappy for himself and incompetent to offer happiness to others. Truly worthy of pity. That is Milan.[79]

The dynastic regime, based upon the king's unstable personality and a narrow clique of his friends, imploded along with his marriage. The Progressives were a court party and their leading politicians were closely tied to the queen as well as to the king. She, despite her initial distrust of them, had found them better bred than the preceding Liberals and her relations with them over time had become extremely warm, albeit their Austrophilia did not chime with her Russophilia.[80] So when the royal marriage collapsed in the face of Milan's dishonourable behaviour towards her, they chivalrously took her side. Garašanin finally resigned on 13 June 1887 over his unwillingness to support Milan's measures against her, in particular his attempt to ban her from returning to Serbia.

Milan consequently permitted the formation of a Liberal–Radical coalition government on 13 June 1887 under Ristić, who demanded rapprochement with Russia. The government sought to purge the administration of Progressives, but in the climate of revenge, a much more violent backlash against them occurred in the countryside at the hands of the Radicals and their supporters. Mass lynchings of Progressives, particularly kmets, occurred in the Radical stronghold of eastern Serbia in the okrugs of Požarevac, Ćuprija, Zaječar and Aleksinac. Over 140 Progressives were killed and a similar number beaten and humiliated, while there were about 50 cases of Progressives' homes being destroyed and 70 cases of their properties being burned. Some of the victims were murdered bestially; one had a stake driven through his stomach; another was killed with a knife, then had his corpse stripped naked and thrown into the road; a third was repeatedly beaten until he died, then had his nose and ears cut off and his jaw broken before being thrown onto the road. Meanwhile, crowds in Belgrade shouted 'Long live Russia!' and 'Down with Austria!' The Progressives were terrorised into not participating in the elections of 29 September 1887.[81] This election involved manipulation by the police, controlled by Liberal interior minister Milojković, but the extent of the manipulation was constrained by the coalition with the Radicals, who consequently emerged with a narrow parliamentary majority.

This proved merely a transitional phase, since Austro-Hungarian hostility to pro-Russian Ristić prompted Milan to take his collaboration with the Radicals a step further. The Radicals and Liberals quarrelled over the division of parliamentary seats; when supplementary elections on 23 December produced Liberal victories in all ten contested seats, the Radicals demanded Milojković's resignation. Ristić was ready to agree, but Milan rejected this in order to force his entire government's resignation.⁸² In January 1888 he appointed in its place Serbia's first genuine Radical government under Colonel Sava Grujić, retaining only the foreign ministry for his military confidant, Franasović, to ensure the Radicals would not break the alliance with Austria-Hungary. Milan also amnestied all Radical exiles except Pašić and promoted Grujić to general. In the elections of 4 March 1888, he restrained the Liberal-dominated police, which resulted in an almost entirely Radical parliament.

Grujić's government enacted a series of Radical-inspired laws: the formation of smaller municipalities was permitted; police manipulation of municipal elections was banned; the second and third call-ups of the army were symbolically renamed the 'national militia'; and the tobacco monopoly was nationalised. The Radical press was permitted more freedom and regularly attacked Austria-Hungary, prompting it to complain. Todorović commented cynically on the Radicals: 'They were against generals' epaulettes and privileges but are now grateful that their prime minister has become a general'; although they had fought against state expenditure when in opposition, they had now 'doubled the state budget in almost all fields'; having preached the need for promotion to state service purely on grounds of merit, they now practised nepotism: 'Here a cousin, there a brother-in-law; the whole family is provided for, while the state treasury becomes a disability fund.'⁸³ Unlike the Liberal and Progressive parties, ultimately controlled by their leaderships, the Radical party, as a genuine mass party, was wholly uncontrollable by Grujić's government, which did not include Pašić, the real Radical leader. The government therefore seemed to Milan to facilitate Radical tyranny and anarchy. He dismissed it on 26 April and appointed a government under Hristić, then visited Vienna to consult with his Austro-Hungarian protectors. As Živanović notes, 'After every happening, after every significant change in Serbia, this trip to Vienna became the rule.'⁸⁴

Milan was by this time locked in acrimonious struggle with Natalija over custody of their eleven-year-old son, Prince Aleksandar (1876–1903). Their differences had begun with his birth, for Milan had wanted to name him Miloš while Natalija insisted upon Aleksandar, after the Tsar.⁸⁵ The custody dispute aroused European interest, since whether the prince would be educated according to the wishes of Austrophile Milan or Russophile Natalija, and in which country, had clear implications for Serbia's future alignment. The struggle culminated in the scandalous seizure of Aleksandar from his mother in Wiesbaden by the German police on 14 July 1888, at Milan's instigation, after which he pushed Metropolitan Teodosije into granting him a divorce of questionable legality. This battle with Natalija altered Milan's priorities. He had been preparing to resign since the defeat by Bulgaria, which had cooled Vienna's support for him, upon which he had psychologically depended for the past decade. He now sought an accommodation with his former enemies, involving his abdication and concessions to them domestically, in return for safeguards securing Serbia's pro-Austrian orientation, his son's royal status, his control over him and a degree of continued influence over Serbia. As the Grujić government's deficiencies had highlighted the dangers of a purely Radical regime, Milan moved to establish a hybrid regime. He therefore appointed a constitutional council at the end of October 1888, presided over by himself, numbering over eighty members drawn from all three parties and with the three party leaders, Ristić, Garašanin and Grujić, as vice-presidents. This body elected a twelve-member committee which completed the draft of a new constitution by early December.

The new constitution ended the government's right to appoint a quarter of parliamentary deputies and replaced open, indirect parliamentary elections with direct elections and the secret ballot. The suffrage was extended to all born or naturalised (male) Serbs aged 21 or over who paid at least 15 dinars in direct taxes annually, while parliamentary deputies had to be at least 30 and pay at least 30 dinars annually in direct tax. King and parliament were to exercise legislative powers jointly while executive power remained exclusively with the king, along with the power to appoint and dismiss ministers. The king retained supreme command of the armed forces, the exclusive right to appoint all state officials, declare war, conclude peace and represent the country abroad, although trade agreements and those which involved payments from the treasury or that changed the law or limited the rights of Serbian citizens were subject to parliamentary approval. The king had the right to summon parliament and to postpone its sessions for up to two months, and to dismiss it subject to the obligation to hold new elections within two months and convene the new parliament within three.

Parliament's legislative powers were greatly strengthened. Its deputies, elected for three-year terms, gained the right to propose legislation, submit questions and interpellations, conduct surveys and investigations and receive petitions. Ministers were no longer barred from being parliamentary deputies but selected from their ranks, thereby becoming representatives of the people rather than royal officials. The king lost the power to issue provisional laws. Annual budgets subject to parliamentary approval were introduced and the king lost the right to retain the old budget in the absence of parliamentary approval of the new one; he could now merely extend the budget for four months by edict in case of parliament's suspension or dissolution. Freedom of assembly, speech and of the press were guaranteed except in cases of insults to the monarch or royal house or to foreign rulers and their houses, or of incitement to armed uprising. Equality before the law was still accorded to 'all Serbs', rather than all citizens. The king and regents could only be of the Orthodox faith.[86]

The constitution and subsequent laws ended police control of elections. Full self-government at the municipal, district and okrug levels was introduced, with the establishment of district and okrug assemblies and councils. The size of a municipality was reduced from 500 to 200 taxpayers, with smaller ones permitted in mountainous areas. Organs of self-government were elected by majority public voting at public assemblies. Serbia was divided into fifteen okrugs—Valjevo, Vranje, Kragujevac, Krajina, Kruševac, Morava, Pirot, Podrinje, Podunava, Požarevac,

Rudnik, Timok, Toplica, Užice and Crna Reka—with 72 districts.[87] The constitution guaranteed judicial independence and banned measures restricting freedom of the press, including censorship and administrative cautions. The king lost the right to suspend civil liberties in case of emergencies; they were now wholly inviolable barring the convocation of a new constitutional assembly. Citizens gained the right to take officials to court. True ministerial responsibility was introduced, whereby a minister could be called to account for an act within four years, meaning he could be held accountable by the subsequent parliament, and ministers were required to abide by Council decisions. The new constitution represented a compromise between the Radicals and the king, Liberals and Progressives; the former received a one-chamber parliament that favoured their political hegemony while the latter received an electoral system involving proportional representation, ensuring the presence of the minority parties in parliament. The Radicals had to drop their demand for the restoration of the national militia.

Elections for the great national parliament were held on 2 December; it met on the 23rd. Wholly dominated by Radicals who held nearly 500 out of 600 seats, it contained only about 100 Liberals and no Progressives. It promulgated the constitutional draft on 3 January 1889 virtually without modification, though the Radical deputies were sufficiently unhappy with the constitutional compromises their leaders had made for 73 of them to vote against it. The Radical party's readiness to abandon its maximalist demands and accept such a compromise marked its definite evolution into a parliamentary rather than revolutionary party.[88] Milošević recalled: 'The Serb nation accepted from the hand of King Milan one of the most free-spirited constitutions, which was signed by Nikola Hristić as president of the council of ministers; the most reactionary minister. A political paradox!'[89]

Crushed and exhausted, Milan abdicated on 6 March 1889; his thirteen-year-old son acceded to the throne two days later as Aleksandar I, presided over by a three-man regency comprising Ristić as the dominant figure and two generals, Kosta Protić and Jovan Belimarković, the first a Conservative and the second a Liberal. Their inclusion was meant to ensure Milan's continued influence over the regime.[90] He perhaps intended to return to the throne when circumstances were more propitious, his successors had discredited themselves and there was demand for a firm hand—he allegedly sought to emulate Miloš, who had returned to rule Serbia two decades after abdicating.[91] Aleksander would, some years later, quote to an interlocutor a note Milan had allegedly written him: 'I granted the constitution of 1888 to compromise liberty itself!', meaning he had intended it to fail.[92] Milan meanwhile remained powerful behind the scenes and focused on retaining control over the new king. He was legal guardian of Aleksandar's education, which allowed him continued influence over the court and primacy over Natalija in terms of influence over Aleksandar, including the right to regulate her visits to him.

COURT AND RADICALS

The premiership passed again on 4 March 1889 to Grujić, the moderate Radical whom Milan and the regents trusted, in preference to the actual Radical leader Pašić, whom they did not. Grujić formed a cabinet composed almost wholly of Radicals. Pašić and all participants in the Timok rebellion were amnestied. For Pašić, these events were not simply a victory for democracy and for the Radicals but a patriotic victory for the Serb nation. Returning to Serbia after his amnesty, he gave a speech at Smederevo on 9 March: 'The struggle of the Serb genius, which was shown in unbeatable national achievements and past historical acts; the struggle of that national spirit against the bureaucratic-tutorial system has ended with a victory for the people.' It was a victory for 'that exalted moral character, that is, it seems, most strongly developed among the Serb people, safeguarding it in the course of many centuries from great misery and misfortune; safeguarding it from the cunning Byzantine Empire, from the crude and unbridled Turkish power, giving it the possibility to avoid the snares and cunning of the West. That moral character that was spoken through the mouth of Prince Lazar on the eve of the Battle of Kosovo ... that immeasurable national strength erased like dust its opponents and cleansed the throne of those who, in their weakness, hid behind it.'[93] Since it represented the nation, Pašić deemed it essential that 'the Radical party must not allow its enemies to take power again', thereby affirming the notion that opponents of the governing power and supporters of other parties were enemies of the nation.[94]

Radical–regent condominium

The introduction of a new constitution establishing parliamentary government and Milan's abdication appeared, on paper, a revolutionary change—the end of monarchical rule. Yet this change had not been achieved by a genuine shift of power in society from court to people, merely by an implosion within the court regime that destroyed the reigning king's personal authority. Real power remained with the court, through the army and bureaucracy. The Radical party, though enjoying absolute hegemonic support among the Serbian electorate, which under the 1889 constitution would always translate into electoral victory, was nevertheless only able to remain in government so long as those who really controlled the state—the court and army—permitted it to do so. Consequently, the 1889 constitutional change marked the start of a period of uneasy power-sharing between court and Radicals. The arrangement collapsed within a few years but marked the start of the merging of two formerly antagonistic elements into a new synthesis: although the Radicals never succeeded in replacing the court and army as the real power-holders in Serbia, the court would find it difficult—and from 1903 impossible—to run Serbia except in partnership with either the Radical party or one or more of its offshoots. This court–army–Radical synthesis would gradually become the new regime in Serbia, remaining so until 1941 and, in residual form, until 1944.

The peasants constituting the popular majority had perceived the national state, since its foundation under Miloš, as alien and oppressive; in Slobodan Jovanović's words, 'The people and the state remained for the peasant, as in Turkish times, two enemy forces: the richer the state, the poorer the people—and vice versa.'[95] Now in 1889, for the first time, the state was apparently in the hands of the people's elected representatives. This was therefore a turning point for the Serbian people's identification with the Serbian state, but it was achieved through a single party, hence this identification was dependent on the existence of a 'party-state'—the belief that a single party embodied the nation.[96] In the historian Olga Popović-Obradović's words, 'Thus, in Serbia, the first experience of parliamentarism, under the 1888 constitution, brought with it the first experience of a one-party state.'[97] This was of lasting importance for Serbia's subsequent political development, laying the basis for decades of Radical primacy, followed eventually by decades of Communist and Socialist hegemony ending only in 2000.

The Radical party subscribed formally to a highly democratic ideology, upholding freedom of the press, association and assembly and rejecting interference by the police in elections and by the central state in local and regional government, in favour of maximum municipal self-government. Yet given its hegemony among the peasant masses, this ideology facilitated its quest for absolute mastery of all walks of life. The democratic political order permitted the party to hold public rallies to cement its political hold at the grass-roots level, while free elections permitted it to control parliament and government at the national level and okrug and municipal assemblies at the intermediary levels. The Radicals conquered by combining state decentralisation and fragmentation with party centralisation.[98] The regents were forced to grant the Radicals ten of the sixteen Council seats against the Liberals' five and the Progressives' one, and the Radicals achieved similar dominance in other state institutions. Thus, the constitutional checks and balances that Milan and the regents had hoped would constrain the Radicals were increasingly overridden.

The regents' ability to constrain the Radicals was limited since the latter were guaranteed a victory in any election, hence a parliamentary majority, by their immense popularity and the constitutional constraints on electoral manipulation.[99] With the Progressives broken, the Liberals served as a counterweight. Upon becoming regents, Ristić and Belimarković formally left the Liberal party, which now passed to Avakumović's leadership. Naturally, the two ex-Liberal regents still identified with their former party, but the structural reality of their situation served to drive it away from them. Under the new constitution, the regents and parliament were each to select sixteen candidates for the Council, from which the other was to select eight. When the Radical ministers demanded that the regents choose their candidates in agreement with them, the regents threatened the formation of a Liberal government to coerce them into retreating. This, however, turned the regents—like Milan before them and his son Aleksandar subsequently—into manipulators who played off the parties against one another; it offended their former comrades in the Liberal party, who resented being used as pawns, leaving the regents ultimately friendless.[100]

The new Liberal leader, Avakumović, had been a protégé of the authoritarian Court Liberal Milojković, recently deceased, yet his own political inclinations were more oppositional; he had supported the dissident Liberal opposition to the earlier regency regime of 1868–1872 and opposed the Liberal government in 1878 owing to its brutal response to the Topola uprising and the execution of his childhood friend Jevrem Marković.[101] He consequently steered the party back in an oppositional direction, so that it began to emulate the Radicals' successful model of party-building and popular agitation. It expanded, shifting the initiative within it beyond the traditionally dominant metropolitan high officials to the provincial middle classes. The Liberals now emulated Radical anti-state populism in their attacks on the Radical-dominated government. They denounced high taxes and the salt and tobacco monopolies that the Radicals had opposed in opposition but upheld in government. They demanded a reduction in the salaries of ministers and councillors and other high officials, the extension of municipal self-government and the restoration of the national militia. Avakumović later noted: 'It was extremely interesting at the time to watch the Radicals and their ministers. People who had for the entire century sought the abolition of the State Council and the reduction of senior bureaucratic salaries in general, now, all at once, began to defend both the institution of the State Council and the salaries of members of that Council!!!' This presaged a possible split between the elitist older Liberals, who sought eventual cooperation with the more conservative Radicals, and the younger Liberals, who rejected such cooperation and sought to out-Radical the Radicals to displace them as Serbia's principal party.[102]

Radical-instigated terror against the Progressives continued, involving theft, arson and murder. The Progressives attempted to hold their general congress in central Belgrade on 26 May 1889, with about two thousand participants, but they were attacked, stoned and hounded by a mob; the attacks continued until the following day. When a rioter was killed by a bullet fired by a Progressive, Garašanin was blamed and almost lynched in response. According to official figures, in addition to the dead rioter, twenty gendarmes, eleven Progressives and three other rioters were wounded. The police's response to the riot was lukewarm—interior minister Taušanović appeared on the scene to fraternise with the mob and was unwilling to order firm police action against it—while Garašanin was arrested and charged over the fatality; he consequently fled abroad where he remained for a year. The Progressives claimed fifty of their people were killed through such acts of terror in 1889 alone, though this figure was reached by including deaths from brigands (hajduks), then very active and attributed by the Radicals' enemies to their slack policing; the hajduks depended upon local peasant collaborators, who were in turn likely to be Radical supporters.

The political domination of the Radicals, with their anti-state ideology, produced a climate at the village level in which contempt for the police and courts was widespread, producing lawlessness and intimidation. The local bureaucracy was purged and filled with often unqualified and inept Radical supporters, causing a blurring of boundaries between the official sphere and the general public. Local tax collection was lax. Socialist and Karađorđevićite agitators operated freely under the Radical umbrella. Those few municipalities remaining in the hands of Liberals or Progressives were subjected to pressure both from the Radical-controlled police and from the mob; their supporters were arrested and threatened. The Radical rank and file was not content with dominance but could not tolerate any manifestations of local pluralism or the presence of the opposition anywhere.[103] The electoral law of April 1890 reduced the tax threshold for voting and increased parliamentary representation of the rural population of the okrugs vis-à-vis the towns. It prevented voters from casting separate votes for regular parliamentary candidates on the one hand, and those elected in keeping with the provisions for proportional representation (to ensure the representation of minority parties) on the other. It instead forced voters to cast a single vote for the party lists presented to them. These measures were aimed at strengthening Radical electoral hegemony and undermining the safeguards included in the constitution to protect other parties.[104]

The Radicals were able to enact laws that reflected their populist ideology. Taxes were reduced for the peasant majority and increased for bureaucrats and merchants. After tobacco, the salt monopoly and railways were nationalised between 1888 and 1890, thereby 'liberating' these sectors of the Serbian economy from foreign ownership and control and increasing the state's income. A ban was passed in April 1890 on the opening of shops during holidays, to free the youth employed in them to attend Sunday schools. The sale in village shops of luxury items was prohibited in March 1891, in particular women's beauty products such as makeup and mirrors. This was motivated by the desire to protect, on the one hand, the monopolies of town guilds and traditional village industries from competition from foreign imports and on the other, patriarchal society from foreign-inspired immorality. As the Radical newspaper *Odjek* (Echo) wrote: 'Through village shops are spread foreign tastes and foreign needs ... These shops are the most dangerous intermediaries for foreign economic domination and the worst collaborators in the draining of our national power.'[105] These laws remained in force well into the Yugoslav era after World War I and were renewed as late as 1933–1934, seriously impoverishing material culture in the villages.[106]

The hybrid regime carried out reforms reflective of the ideologies of both its partners, combining efforts at modernisation with steps to protect the interests of the peasant majority. The Progressive-dominated Royal Serbian Academy was merged with the Liberal-dominated Serbian Learned Society in February 1892 to become the Serbian Royal Academy; this measure reflected the Liberal desire to appropriate the Academy. Laws were passed establishing an economic council, trade and craft schools and a state livestock farm to improve the quality of livestock. Somewhat later, as the Radical heyday was ending in late 1893, a young Radical, Mihailo Avramović, with the help of party colleagues, prepared to establish the first peasant cooperative, which was eventually founded at the village of Vranov near Smederevo the following March, after which a countrywide Union of Serbian Farmers' Cooperatives was established at Smederevo on 20 July 1895.[107] By 1899 there would be 167 peasant cooperatives, rising to 654 in 1908. This was a response to the long-standing problem of peasant indebtedness and poverty, though not one that would resolve it.[108]

Metropolitan Mihailo was restored to the head of the Serbian Orthodox Church by a decree of the regency on 9 June 1889, replacing Teodosije, who 'voluntarily' resigned along with his bishops. With Mihailo's assistance, a church law was passed on 9 May 1890 reversing Milan's effort at establishing government control over the church; the non-bishops were expelled from the synod, which gained a veto over future laws and decrees regarding the church and clergy. However, the church law of 12 January 1883 was not wholly revoked. The power to elect the metropolitan remained with the electoral assembly representing the entire clergy, not just the bishops, while a degree of government control over the church courts was also retained, this being insisted upon by the Radicals, who, with their base in the lower clergy, wished to curtail the power of the bishops. The law also abolished the Šabac bishopric and greatly reduced the pay of the metropolitan and bishops. Parliament attempted to transfer the power to elect members of spiritual courts from the synod and bishops to eparchial (diocesan) assemblies, but this encountered fierce resistance from Metropolitan Mihailo and had to be temporarily suspended. In this instance, though they both opposed state control of the church, the metropolitan's desire to defend the church hierarchy's prerogatives clashed with the Radicals' desire to empower the lower clergy, like other grass-roots bodies in which they had strong support.

Military reforms damaged the Serbian army's cohesion. The army had been expanded by Milan following the Serbo-Bulgarian war and the domination of the officer corps by a narrow elite of military families was broken. The Radical government, however, made drastic cuts in the military budget by reducing the terms of service of conscripts and reservists, seeking also to purge the officer corps of the unqualified members who had swelled its ranks since the war.[109] It sought furthermore to win over the army from its absolute loyalty to the Obrenović dynasty. A law on the army in May 1890 formally restored elements of the national militia, in the form of the second and third call-up, but since the weapons remained kept in the barracks rather than in the peasant soldiers' homes, the militia was not truly re-created as it had existed before the Timok rebellion. Given the new regime's Russophile character, increasing numbers of Serbian officers were sent for training to

Russia instead of to Austria-Hungary or Germany. This resulted in a reaction against the older officer class's Prussian drill, and the Military Academy was eventually reorganised in 1895 to reflect this shift.

The result of these changes was that the army itself became susceptible to party-political divisions and prone to indiscipline. Soldiers roamed the streets apparently unsupervised by their officers and clashed with civilians.[110] While the Radical measures helped reduce the budget deficit, they sowed the seeds of the officers' discontent with the post-1889 order, which would have serious consequences in subsequent years. Younger officers were more susceptible to nationalist sentiment directed against Austria-Hungary. A typical example was Dragutin Dimitrijević (1876–1917), son of a tinsmith of Cincar origin, who entered the Military Academy in 1893 and acquired the nickname 'Apis', apparently because he was both large and powerfully built like a bull and energetic like a bee.[111] That year, the Military Academy's director, General Stevan Pantelić, attempted to restore discipline among the cadets by expelling 22 of them after they had completed only their first year; one of these subsequently committed suicide out of despair, after which his mother attempted unsuccessfully to assassinate Pantelić. These events spurred political activity among the cadets, in which the young Apis participated prominently.[112] Thus was launched an activist's career that would have fateful consequences for Serbia.

The court attempted to cement the authority of the king and dynasty by shrouding them in the Kosovo myth. This had become increasingly popular among nationalists since the 1860s, and the government on 20 April 1889 proposed a number of measures to mark the battle's 500th anniversary, including the introduction of an Order of Prince Lazar and the erection of a monument to the battle in Kruševac, Lazar's former capital.[113] It appointed a commission on the 24th to organise the anniversary's official celebrations. The celebratory period was opened at a session of the Serbian Royal Academy on 23 June by Mijatović, who declared that 'Karađorđe breathed with the breath of Kosovo and the Obrenovićes placed Kosovo in their dynasty's coat of arms. We bless Kosovo because the memory of the Kosovo heroes sustained us, encouraged us, taught us and guided us.'[114] On the anniversary itself, 28 June, the king, regents, court and Metropolitan Mihailo visited Kruševac where, at the Lazarica church, the metropolitan delivered an oration calling upon the descendants of the heroes of Kosovo to love their homeland, after which Aleksandar laid the foundation stone of the planned monument. This was followed by a visit to Žiča monastery, where Aleksandar was anointed king in a spectacular ceremony. The king bore the 'crown, sceptre and robe of the new Nemanjić and a new ruler's insignia of the Order of Prince Lazar'. After the anointment, the bells in all the churches in the kingdom tolled to announce 'the all-Serb king, heir to Nemanjić's empire'. The king then went to the Studenica monastery to present himself to the 'holy king', Stefan First-Crowned.[115]

COURT AND RADICALS

The king received congratulations on his anointment from his fellow monarchs from Russia, Britain, Germany, Austria-Hungary, Italy and Belgium and from France's president. This marked the true start of St Vitus's Day (Vid's Day), 28 June, as Serbia's national holiday.[116] Opposition among the clergy to the date's recognition as a church holiday, due to its pagan associations, was finally overcome and the church recognised it in 1892.[117] The Monument to the Kosovo Heroes in Kruševac, by the sculptor Đorđe Jovanović (1861–1953) from Novi Sad in Hungary, was eventually unveiled on St Vitus's Day in 1904. Meanwhile, since Milan had abdicated and power was now shared between similarly Russophile Liberal regents and Radical ministers, Russia viewed Serbia more favourably, particularly given the anti-Russian orientation of contemporary Bulgaria under Stefan Stambolov's government. Aleksandar began his reign with much goodwill both at home and abroad.

The Young Conservative government's idealistic decision to hold elections in 1880 without police manipulation released from the bottle the genie of the People's Radical Party, which emerged as a peasant-based counter-elite to challenge the existing royal, bureaucratic and military elite. It appeared to Milan a mortal threat to his regime on revolutionary, dynastic and foreign policy grounds, and he fought it bitterly. With the Radicals enjoying overwhelming popular support and the Obrenović regime enjoying overwhelming coercive power, the two were like the elephant and the whale, each supreme in their own sphere but unable to conquer the other. Milan with his army could always defeat the Radical party physically, as the Timok rebellion showed, but he had no way of breaking its hold on the loyalty of Serbia's peasant population. The implosion of Milan's regime due to defeat by Bulgaria and the collapse of his marriage led him to reverse course and seek to establish a court–Radical condominium over Serbia, manifested in the relatively liberal-democratic constitution of 1889 and his abdication in favour of a Liberal-dominated regency partnered with a purely Radical government. Yet the condominium was inherently unstable, marking merely a truce in the struggle of the two Serbias.

9

COURT–RADICAL COLLABORATION AND PRAETORIAN REACTION

1892–1903

The modus vivendi between the old elite and Radicals established in 1889 proved unstable given the unwillingness of either party to concede pre-eminence to the other and the opposition of elements in the old elite to the presence of the Radicals in government. The subsequent fourteen years therefore witnessed repeated unsuccessful attempts to make such a hybrid regime work. The old elite divided between those ready to work with the Radicals and those determined to exclude them. King Aleksandar would vacillate between ruling in partnership with the Radicals and ruling against them, reflecting the conflicting influences of his mutually hostile parents but also the dilemma between asserting his authority as king and respecting the Radicals' overwhelming popular support. Serbia consequently experienced a period of instability involving repeated putsches and violations and changes of the constitution.

Ex-Queen Natalija is expelled from Serbia

Elements from the ranks of the old elite of court, army and Liberals quickly began resisting the new order based on the 1889 constitution and the regency–Radical power-sharing arrangement. Yet the Radicals' firm hold on most of the population's loyalty meant they could not be beaten in a free election, so resistance to their hegemony was inevitably elitist and authoritarian. Thus, Radical subversion of the old order provoked an elitist counter-subversion. The court's fracturing triggered by the collapse of Milan's marriage to Natalija created two elite factions, each loosely affiliated with one of the former royal partners. Natalija retained the loyalty of the marginalised Progressives and her 'salon' emerged as initially the principal centre of opposition to the new regime. Prominent army officers, including both Progressive and Liberal sympathisers, visited her regularly.[1] However, Natalija came to support collaboration with the Radicals so as to win popular acceptance for her son's throne and secure Russia's friendship.

A more menacing centre of elite opposition coalesced around ex-king Milan. The first stirrings of what would eventually become a major praetorian reaction emerged in early 1890 in the army, in the form of an officers' movement, in response to its underfunding by the Radical government, which had removed the officers' bonuses. The government responded by pensioning off the ringleaders, but it realised a military coup was a real danger and that Milan, who retained the loyalty of the officer corps, was the biggest threat to the new order.[2] Milan used his status as guardian of King Aleksandar's education to worm his way back into public life, motivated largely by his desire to counter Natalija and her circle. Bankrupted by his dissolute lifestyle and gambling losses, he was prompted by these failures of his personal life to return to Belgrade on 29 May 1890, after which he began meddling again in Serbian politics, hostage once more to his powerful, erratic personality.

The equilibrium of the duumvirate of regents and Radicals appeared very unstable to contemporaries. The Great School's professors held a banquet for Milan on 26 July 1890, at which the rector Svetomir Nikolajević—himself a former Radical—fiercely denounced, to the ex-king's approval, the 'sorry anarchy in the land' since his abdication. The frightened Radical government pensioned off Nikolajević and sought to appease the officers' discontent by restoring their bonuses and reinstating their pensioned colleagues.[3] Fears of a military coup under Milan were so strong that the interior minister, Đaja, took to sleeping in his ministry building so as to be ready to resist with his gendarmes.[4] The Radicals overwhelmingly won parliamentary elections on 26 September. A couple of days later, Milan replaced the Radical Lazar Dokić as Aleksandar's chief tutor with Colonel Jovan Mišković, a Liberal, general staff officer and Ristić's kum. Dokić's appointment as Council president had left him insufficient time to devote to the king, but Milan justified his choice of replacement on the grounds that the tutor should be a soldier. A few days later, Grujić felt compelled to deny press rumours that Milan was sowing sedition among the garrison soldiers.[5]

Grujić's government was weak since he was a compromise figure with little authority. It was caught between Milan's and Natalija's rival elite factions, whose mutual antipathy poisoned the political atmosphere.[6] Milan wished to counter Natalija, who agitated against him, and was upset also by the attacks on him in Belgrade's press, both of which threatened his behind-the-scenes influence. Natalija sought to have her divorce proclaimed illegal by Metropolitan Mihailo, but he retreated from doing so under pressure from Milan and Ristić. She then presented to parliament a memorandum appealing against Milan's restriction of her maternal right to visit her son. Although Grujić was her personal friend, his government and the regents in October 1890 agreed, under pressure from Milan, to suppress press attacks on him as the king's father and have parliament declare itself unauthorised to accept her memorandum, which it did on 11 December.

COURT–RADICAL COLLABORATION

The government was meanwhile seriously constrained by the stranglehold on parliament of the Radical parliamentary deputies' club. Pašić increasingly subordinated the formerly unruly Radical party to the principle of complete centralism and obedience to its general council and to himself personally. This exacerbated the Radicals' hegemonic, anti-pluralist character, particularly since Pašić was now president of parliament, allowing him to control the Radical deputies and, therefore, parliament as a whole. So long as he was outside government, he incited parliament against it.[7] The government was assailed also by purist Radicals, including Ranko Tajsić, young Jaša Prodanović and the socialist infiltrator Dragiša Stanojević, on the questions of ministerial pay, pruning the bureaucracy and press freedom. This threatened to split the party between pro-government moderates and purists, a danger Grujić was too weak to navigate, prompting his resignation on 20 February 1891.

Stanojević at this point published a proclamation calling on parliament to assume full power in the state and appoint a government to carry out a policy of 'National Salvation' involving a revolutionary reorganisation of state and society. This adventurer's pipe dream hardly resonated even among purist Radicals. Nevertheless, Stanojević's accusation, that nothing had really changed in Serbia and that the old order remained intact, embarrassed the party. In parliament, Pašić arranged, in defiance of the opposition, for Stanojević to be deprived of his parliamentary immunity. He was expelled from the party and sentenced to a prison term, serving over a year, after which he withdrew from politics.[8] Concerned by the government's weakness, Regent Ristić decided that a government headed by Pašić himself would have more authority. He hoped to tame the Radicals as he had the Old Liberals, while Pašić was ready to form a government to prevent the collapse of the constitutional order and his party's split. He was consequently appointed prime minister on 24 February 1891.[9]

Pašić ruthlessly negotiated a final settlement with Milan on 12 April at Natalija's expense: Milan's renunciation of his monthly civil-list payment of 30,000 dinars, his privileges as a royal family member and his Serbian citizenship, and his pledge to leave Serbia until his son's majority, in return for a one-off payment and loan totalling three million dinars and the expulsion of Natalija from Serbia if she refused to leave voluntarily. It was signed by Milan, all ministers and regents.[10] Attempts to persuade her to leave Serbia having proven fruitless, the gendarmerie on 18 May tried to deport her. As her gendarme escort left her Belgrade apartment, a large crowd of citizens gathered to defend her, attacked the gendarmes and drove them back. Prominent in this action were members of the Women's Society, whose patron Natalija was and which staunchly supported her against Milan.[11] The government then dispersed the crowd using the army; several civilians were killed and wounded. With Belgrade under virtual army and police occupation, the queen was deported.

Thus the regime, headed by the populist, anti-state Radical party used troops to kill civilians, and to enforce the expulsion of the king's mother, a Serbian citizen, from her own country, in violation of the constitution. This marked the Radicals' transition from a people's party into the new wielders of state repression, and their reputation was severely damaged. 'Pitiful army and more pitiful country', wrote Piroćanac in his diary, expressing the widespread shame about these events.[12] Natalija's expulsion was denounced by both Progressives and Liberals, while public anger focused in particular upon interior minister Đaja, who, as a Catholic from Dubrovnik, made a convenient scapegoat; his political career soon ended. Ristić's and Pašić's reputations also suffered greatly. Years later, told by his father how Pašić had supported the ex-king against the ex-queen, teenage Prince Đorđe Karađorđević's instinctive reaction was: 'Without regard for humanity, he supported the stronger side.'[13] The affair, engineered by Milan and accepted by his son, discredited the Obrenović dynasty at a time when Radical political hegemony was already eroding its authority.

Milan nevertheless remained dissatisfied with the regime. When Ristić, Pašić and Aleksandar travelled to St Petersburg in July 1891 to seek a Russian princess as bride for the king, Milan opposed the trip, fearing Serbia would become a Russian vassal: 'I never wanted Serbia to be a Russian province ...' He feared the long-term outcome would be his dynasty's overthrow and a Karađorđević restoration.[14] But, as Ristić allegedly said, 'We can enter into all kinds of relations with the West, adopt their culture, send our sons to study there, make loan agreements, but we can do nothing to achieve our national ideal, in the sense of the unification and liberation of our tribe, without Russia.'[15] Parliament followed up its agreement with Milan by passing a law on 26 March 1892 stripping him of his Serbian citizenship and membership of the royal family and banning his return to Serbia.

Liberal coup and royal–Radical counter-coup

Removal of the king's parents from Serbia cleared the field for the power struggle between the Liberal regents and Radical government to begin in earnest. Kosta Protić's death on 4 June 1892 left the regency solely in the hands of its two surviving Liberal members while raising the question of who would replace him. Constitutionally, the right to appoint the new regent belonged to parliament, and Pašić sought to ensure Radical domination by becoming the new third regent himself through a parliamentary vote. But Milan advised Ristić to ascertain beforehand that the new regent would behave appropriately rather than simply as the Radicals' representative. So Ristić requested that the Radical government submit a shortlist of possible candidates, to ensure selection of one he deemed suitable; he particularly feared parliament would select a militant Radical. Having violated the constitution to expel Natalija from Serbia, he therefore now violated it again, at the Radicals' expense, posing once again the question whether parliament or the court was pre-eminent.

COURT–RADICAL COLLABORATION

The government insisted on parliament's exclusive constitutional right to select the new regent.[16] Pašić, confident of the Radicals' overwhelming electoral support, threatened to resign and force new elections. But Ristić was under pressure from the increasingly militant Liberal party and in danger of losing its backing, so called his bluff. When Pašić consequently resigned, Ristić on 22 August appointed a Liberal government under Avakumović, initiating open warfare between the two parties.

Avakumović's government called elections for 9 March, made a sop to popular opinion by promising to abolish the state monopolies on tobacco and salt, then sought to engineer a victory through repression and electoral manipulation. This was difficult, given that when they took power, only about 15 of 134 parliamentary deputies were Liberals, the Radicals were firmly supported by most Serbians and the 1889 constitution had ended the government's ability to control voting directly using the police. In the new conditions, involving strong municipal self-management, the government first purged the police of Radical supporters and replaced them with Liberal supporters, then used them to conduct systematic purges of municipal administrations. It exploited constitutional provisions enabling their dismissal at the request of municipal gatherings, which could indeed be mobilised by the police. Elections for replacements likewise involved open-air voting that was manipulable by the police. The government systematically removed, fined and arrested municipal presidents and kmets accused of irregularities and dismissed presidents of voting commissions suspected of Radical sympathies. For particularly entrenched Radical municipal strongholds, when the police proved inadequate, the army was deployed to evict the incumbents.

The regional and local self-management guaranteed by the constitution, for which the Radicals had fought, proved impotent against a hostile government. Okrug assemblies with Radical majorities, democratically elected according to the constitution, found themselves unable to intervene in defence of Radical municipal officials, since the government-appointed chiefs of districts—the administrative level between okrugs and municipalities—obstructed them. The State Council, with a Radical majority, could legally overrule such irregularities by regional and local bodies, but the interior ministry and police refused to enforce its decisions.[17] The president and two other members of the Radical municipal administration of Belgrade were imprisoned on 27 October and held for four days until released owing to lack of evidence of wrongdoing. Government supporters then staged a public vote of no confidence in the Belgrade municipal council; the police dissolved the voting commission on the day of the vote on 3 December and replaced it with one that systematically disenfranchised Radical voters, with the result that the vote of confidence inevitably went against the municipal council, giving the police the pretext to dissolve it and replace it with a provisional council. The dismissed council appealed to the State Council, which ruled its dissolution illegal, but interior minister Stojan Ribarac ordered the police to disregard this ruling and treat the State

Council 'as if it did not exist'. Consequently, elections for a new Belgrade municipal administration were held on 25 December and easily won by the Liberals.[18]

The Liberal government, in sum, waged war against local government and local democracy; with the deployment of mounted police and the army and the use of guns on both sides, this approached actual civil war. A policeman on 8 October fired shots in the vicinity of a carriage carrying Pašić to a Radical rally at Petrovac, which led to a criminal investigation that ultimately absolved the policeman.[19] At the village of Dušanovac near Negotin on 8 January, an attempt by the district clerk to replace the municipal administration was resisted by a Radical crowd, which beat him up along with several of his officials, then drove off police who came to his aid, before the okrug and district chiefs arrived the next day and succeeded in quelling the revolt, whose principal instigators had been two veterans of the Timok rebellion. Around the same time, a Radical crowd including municipal councillors occupied the municipal courtroom in Čačak to prevent a forcible change in municipal government; the police retook the building with the army's help in a battle resulting in several wounded Radical supporters and one dead policeman and the arrest of around a hundred people. At Smederevo, weeks of conflict between Radical municipal councillors and their supporters and the police over control of the municipal office culminated in a battle on 5 December in which shots were exchanged and a policeman killed, after which the police prevailed only with the army's help. Forty-two Radical supporters were arrested and a new election held producing a pro-Liberal administration.[20] The Radical president of Smoljinac municipality in north-eastern Serbia, after resisting attempts to remove him, was seriously wounded on 3 February in an assassination attempt by local Liberals. The pattern was repeated across Serbia. The violence culminated in a confrontation at the village of Goračići near Čačak on 4 March, after the Radical municipal administration refused to accept its replacement by a pro-government one; the army was deployed and fired upon the crowd gathered to defend the administration, resulting in a massacre in which twelve were killed and seven wounded.[21]

The government not only seized control of the majority of Serbia's municipalities prior to the election but undertook additional measures to ensure its favourable outcome. Many voters, particularly those suspected as pro-Radical, were disenfranchised on grounds of non-payment of taxes.[22] Radicals were prevented from paying their taxes by Liberal-controlled municipalities, to justify their disenfranchisement. Ballot papers were regularly withheld from Radical voters; in Belgrade, only 1,200 out of 8,000 eligible voters received them.[23] Pro-Radical voting committee presidents were obstructed by the police. A report reached Ristić that the Radical party's general council was considering an armed uprising in response to such abuses.[24] Nevertheless, when the parliamentary election was held on 9 March, the Radicals won the popular vote with 130,316 to the Liberals' 91,831 and the Progressives' 14,745. After the government manipulated a technicality to annul the election of three Radicals in the Pirot okrug and transfer their seats to the Liberals, the latter were left with a wafer-thin majority of 69 out of 134. It was a moral defeat for the government, which nevertheless proclaimed victory and a new mandate for itself.[25] The election demonstrated that, under the 1889 constitution, the Radicals were effectively unbeatable in a parliamentary election even when in opposition. The resulting Liberal regime had little popular legitimacy. When parliament convened on 6 April, the Radical deputies soon walked out in protest and were even joined by all four Progressive deputies. Lacking a proper majority, Liberals including Avakumović, Ribarac and Belimarković favoured cementing their rule with a coup.[26]

Aleksandar became deeply concerned at the regime's violence against the Radicals, who appealed for his protection. Belimarković threatened 'that he would turn the centre of Terazije into a butcher's shop for Radical meat' and took to walking about publicly with a bearded bodyguard in 'Turkish dress', armed with pistols and a yataghan.[27] Aleksandar was also alienated by the unwillingness of Ristić and, under his influence, of the government to permit his parents to return to Serbia. Consequently, he used the army to stage a coup on 13 April 1893, directed by his first adjutant, Major Ilija Ćirić. The regents and ministers were invited to a formal dinner at the palace to receive a notification from the king regarding the law forbidding his parents' return to Serbia. Ćirić's troops commandeered the palace, interior ministry, foreign ministry, telegraph centre and the two regents' homes and surrounded the parliament. Upon receiving confirmation that all preparations were in place, Aleksandar arose from the dinner table, declaring: 'Messrs Regents and Ministers, I thank you for your service up till now for Serbia and for myself. I consider that today it is in the interests of the fatherland that I assume the royal authority. I count upon your commitment to Serbia and to the dynasty and I expect your resignations.' At this point, soldiers in the entrance hall cried, 'Long live the king!' After an unsuccessful attempt at eliciting their resignations, soldiers then arrested the regents and ministers and held them overnight before escorting them home the following morning, where they remained under house arrest. Avakumović recalled that, while his home was under armed guard, demonstrators outside shouted, 'Down with Avakumović! Down with the Liberals!'[28] Aleksandar visited the military and gendarme garrisons to proclaim the new order. He reported that the army 'stood by me, as always'.[29] The commanders of the gendarmerie and Danube Division were replaced at the same time as the king consolidated his control over the armed forces.

This coup—the '1 April Dinner'—has traditionally been ascribed to Milan's machinations, but historians disagree over whether the ex-king was its real instigator, manipulating its executors like puppets, or merely encouraged and approved it and offered advice on its execution, with the real instigator being Aleksandar himself, who took the initiative following consultations with his friends among the officers and Radicals, above all Ćirić and his former tutor Dokić. Regardless, beyond the king and his father there were powerful elements favouring the coup. Pašić and Garašanin both allegedly knew of it in advance and either blessed it or took no steps to prevent it. It enjoyed the support of the Radicals and broad popular approval, and perhaps pre-empted a violent popular revolution or civil war. Decades later, Milošević recalled 'the minority king was only doing his duty when he overthrew the regents, unworthy representatives of his royal authority; by his act he prevented the people from overthrowing them, and he did well'.[30] The day after the coup, supportive crowds, including many high school pupils, gathered in the palace courtyard to greet and cheer Aleksandar, after which some of them marched to the houses of prominent Radical and Progressive politicians, who blessed the revolution, including Pašić, who shouted, 'Long live the king!'[31]

Aleksandar justified the coup on the grounds that the regents and Liberal government were violating the constitution, which was true, yet the coup itself was unconstitutional, carried out over a year before he attained his majority, when he could legally have assumed power. The army's direct involvement in resolving a political conflict accelerated its politicisation, legitimising future unconstitutional acts by officers. One royal adjutant centrally involved in the coup, Major Aleksandar Mašin, who was also Aleksandar's art teacher, was a decade later centrally involved in another coup that ended Aleksandar's reign and life.[32] The Liberals, for their part, were thoroughly eclipsed and would never again control government or, except briefly in the exceptional circumstances of 1903, hold the premiership. The Radicals, having participated in the coup, helped re-establish an authoritarian Obrenović regime with scant regard for constitutionality, which soon rebounded against them.

Anti-Radical counter-revolution

Aleksandar rode to power on a wave of popular enthusiasm and Radical support. He appointed a Radical government under Dokić which purged Liberal local authorities throughout Serbia and replaced them with Radical ones. This represented a revolution in local government: local Radicals backed by the local population regularly recaptured their municipalities on their own initiatives, not always awaiting the formal outcome of legal processes, often with officialdom's help. For example, Belgrade's Radical governor Stojan Protić (1857–1923) used police to recapture the Belgrade municipality. Presiding over all this, the Radical press called Aleksandar 'Radical king' and 'Aleksandar the Great'. The general elections held on 30 May 1893 involved widespread Radical intimidation of Liberals and Progressives, including violent threats and assaults. The elections were boycotted by the Liberals and naturally won by the Radicals with 88.34 per cent of the vote, resulting in a parliament with 126 Radical, 10 Progressive and no Liberal members. In Aleksandar's speech opening parliament on 16 June, he announced to general acclamation, 'King and people have joined in an equally firm conviction that the fatherland's salvation lies in earnest respect for the constitution and law, which determines for everyone their rights and duties.' Parliament responded with a declaration: 'The national representative body considers it its first and holiest duty, in the name of the Serbian people, to submit to you its deepest gratitude for the great and happy act carried out on 1 April.'[33]

Aleksandar embarked on a policy of 'reconciliation of king and people'. On his birthday on 14 August, he distributed honours, even to Radical firebrand Tajsić. Between 28 August and 21 September, he toured Serbia to general popular enthusiasm, accompanied by Dokić and interior minister Svetozar Milosavljević, making nationalistic speeches alluding to Bosnia-Hercegovina, disquieting the Austro-Hungarians. Visiting Valjevo, he met with old Ljubomir Nenadović, whose brother Svetozar had been executed following Mihailo's assassination; noticing Nenadović had no decorations, he removed a White Eagle medal from his own shoulder and pinned it on him in front of his delegation, moving the old man to tears and creating a powerful impression on those present.[34] He placed a wreath on Karađorđe's grave at Topola, proclaiming 'I place this wreath in honour and memory of that man who first began the uprising for freedom, the great Karađorđe. Glory be to him!'[35] He visited eastern Serbia, the first time an Obrenović had done so since the Timok rebellion, about which he spoke respectfully, saying it had been caused by 'discord between king and people'. But this love-fest was soured by the Radical government's determination to avenge itself on the Liberals and prosecute Avakumović and his former ministers for their breaches of the law and constitution. Proceedings against them were initiated in the state court. The Liberals, who had previously acted as the Obrenović dynasty's mainstay, pivotal in its restoration in 1858 and retention in 1868, were embittered against the king: 'We leave with one prejudice fewer and one lesson more,' they allegedly said.[36]

The establishment of a Radical government through a royal coup marked the definite emergence of the 'Court Radicals': moderate Radicals who sought power through court patronage (Dokić, Grujić), in contrast to those who continued to seek absolute power (Pašić, Taušanović) for their party in opposition to the court. To marginalise Pašić's hardliners, Dokić selected his ministers exclusively from among the moderate Radicals or from those excluded from the party for indiscipline, such as Milošević. Pašić himself was appointed envoy in St Petersburg on 13 May to remove him from Serbia. At the party's annual congress that autumn, several Radical ministers were heavily criticised and only one, Milošević, elected to the general council. Interior minister Milosavljević dismissed Radical hardliner Protić as governor of Belgrade, prompting a power struggle for control of the capital between the two factions, which competed openly against each other in its municipal election.[37]

This second attempt at a court–Radical regime synthesis was rapidly undermined by opposition from within both camps. The Radical party remained committed to its Jacobinical goal of undivided power in its own hands as the nation's sole authentic representative. It sought to reduce the king to a figurehead and crush its Liberal and Progressive opponents. The Radical government consistently retreated before the Radical-dominated parliament while, given Radical control of government, parliament and Council, Aleksandar's wishes were repeatedly overridden. He was frequently reminded by ministers that he was still not an adult, told he should study and sleep and leave affairs of state to them and generally flouted and disrespected. The offended king was consequently receptive to appeals from the Liberals and Progressives for protection and began considering some combination of the two parties as a counterweight to the Radicals. This eventually proved unworkable owing to personal differences and because members of both parties were unwilling to be cannon fodder in Milan's correctly expected assault on the Radicals.[38] Government coalitions involving the Radicals, meanwhile, were stymied by their unwillingness to share power. They were further discredited in Aleksandar's eyes when in November the parliament was summoned for its autumn session and chose to postpone the urgent business of the budget, instead prioritising packing the state administration with their supporters. Radical deputies in parliament proposed re-establishing and arming the national militia, with the soldiers keeping their guns in their homes instead of in magazines, thereby undermining the army, on which royal security depended; Aleksandar viewed this as directed against himself. He battled with the Radicals over military appointments and succeeded in having his candidate appointed head of the Military Academy against their strong opposition, but parliament rejected all his choices of war minister.[39]

Dokić, to whom the king was close, withdrew from the premiership owing to smoking-related illness, from which he soon died.[40] This senior Court Radical had tilted the king in a pro-Radical direction and his death left Aleksandar prey to other influences, above all his father's. Milošević recalled, 'Unfortunately, Dr L. Dokić's death cut the wire of normal development', leading the king instead down an authoritarian, anti-Radical path that had extremely negative consequences for Serbia and for him personally.[41] Dokić's deputy Grujić inherited the government, eventually formally replacing him as prime minister on 5 December. Aleksander thereby defied the Radical parliament, which had favoured Pašić for the post, but Grujić lacked the authority to establish any kind of balance between king and parliament and his government's position was weakened by its struggle with the Radical hardliners, while for Aleksandar, the appointment was merely a temporary measure pending the government's replacement with one composed of 'elements of order'. The Radical press meanwhile began to attack Aleksandar personally. With cooperation collapsing, Aleksandar knew that when parliament reconvened after the Christmas break it would impose on him a Pašić government. He had executed the April coup to strengthen, not diminish, his authority; this clashed with Radical policy. Having collaborated in and endorsed Aleksandar's unconstitutional overthrow of the regency, the Radicals unwittingly prepared the ground for Aleksandar's next coup, against themselves.

COURT–RADICAL COLLABORATION

To bolster his authority in the escalating confrontation with the Radicals, the king informed Grujić and Milosavljević on the night of 20–21 January 1894 that he had invited his father to return to Serbia. This illegal summoning of the Radicals' arch-enemy prompted the ministers to resign immediately. Milan returned to Belgrade on 21 January, possibly with Vienna's encouragement.[42] A 'neutral' government was appointed on the 24th under Đorđe Simić, a diplomat and son of the Constitutionalist grandee Stojan Simić; it was composed mostly of non-party members of the elite without former ministerial experience, though it also included two Progressives. Its first act was to sign the king's decree of amnesty for Avakumović's Liberal ministers—in violation of the constitution, according to which an amnesty had to be first proposed by parliament.[43] The Radical majority in parliament refused to recognise this government while the Radical press savaged Milan. The government responded with a massive purge of Radicals from the administration; 40–60 per cent of all state officials were quickly dismissed, particularly in the police, and replaced largely by Liberals and Progressives.[44]

Simić's government was nevertheless considered by Aleksandar and Milan to be insufficiently anti-Radical, so on 3 April he was replaced as prime minister by Nikolajević, who retained most of the same ministers but included also two Liberals. Nikolajević's government on 29 April decreed the annulment of the law forbidding Milan's return to Serbia. This prompted the Radical general council to launch a nationwide campaign of rallies against Milan. Nikolajević responded on 12 May with a decree banning the rallies—a violation of the constitution and a step towards a coup. Indicative of the aggressive anti-Radical mindset now overtaking the regime was the suggestion of war minister Milovan Pavlović to the Austro-Hungarian envoy: 'When the peasants see how the fire consumes their villages; when hundreds of heads of people's tribunes roll beneath their feet, they will all throw away their arms and beg for mercy. The main thing is that the king gives us permission to trample in blood for a couple of days, after which Serbia will be pacified for fifty or even a hundred years.'[45]

The court of cassation ruled on 17 May that the decree annulling the ban on Milan's return was illegal, thereby handing the Radicals a major victory. Aleksandar responded on 21 May by revoking by fiat the 1889 constitution and restoring the 1869 Regency Constitution. He claimed it was a temporary measure to 'calm party passions', prior to the preparation of a new constitution. Another pretext was provided by the arrest just before of Mihailo Čebinac, allegedly a Karađorđevićite agent plotting an uprising together with prominent Radicals. Several of these were subsequently arrested, including Tajsić and Aca Stanojević, though none ultimately received more than a sentence of a couple of years and those sentenced were quickly amnestied, leading Radical journalists and others to suspect the police had staged the affair.[46] This coup necessarily followed from Aleksandar's anti-Radical policy since, as the Avakumović government's experience had shown, the Radicals would inevitably win any general election held under the 1889 constitution.⁴⁷ The coup, like the previous year's, enjoyed widespread support. But by arbitrarily revoking a constitution composed by a constitutional council and promulgated by a great national parliament, it severely damaged the legitimacy of the Obrenovic monarchy.

Aleksandar aimed to neutralise not only the Radicals but political parties generally, and he encouraged splits in both Liberals and Radicals. He believed party polarisation had damaged Serbia, of whose true interests the court had a better understanding than the party leaders. His authoritarian policy aimed at overcoming party divisions by building a 'neutral' administration assembling the most competent team of ministers drawn from all parties and from non-party people. This was justified on the grounds that the political parties persecuted each other's supporters when in office. His palace commemoration of the anniversary of the start of the Second Serbian Uprising on 22 April 1894 did not involve a single politician, while half the invitees were officers.⁴⁸ Meanwhile, constant purging by each party, when in office, of officials loyal to other parties had reduced bureaucrats from a privileged to an impoverished class. Purged officials became proletarian bureaucratic armies of followers in the hands of their respective parties, living off their savings and awaiting their chance to return to office. Nikolajević's government sought to co-opt Liberal and Progressive bureaucrats and improve the material conditions of the bureaucracy generally, to weaken the bases of both court parties.⁴⁹ It was nevertheless crippled by infighting between officials of the two. Nikolajević wanted to break with the Liberals to resolve the problem, but this brought him into conflict with Milan, who supported them. Although Aleksandar himself preferred the Progressives, he failed to support Nikolajević, who resigned after pointedly asking him 'Who is really the king? Aleksandar or Milan?'⁵⁰

Nikola Hristić, centrally involved in the crushing of the Hussar rebels in 1844, Mihailo's murderers in 1868 and the Timok rebellion in 1883, was appointed prime minister on 28 October 1894 to oversee the next phase of the restoration of royal authoritarianism. His government strengthened the power of the police: investigative criminal courts established under the Radicals were abolished and competence in conducting criminal investigations restored to the police, while the government gained the right to appoint police commissioners in the municipalities. In November, responding to Ristić's hostility and pursuing the policy of curbing party passions, Aleksandar ordered Hristić to 'destroy the Liberal party' in the event it held a planned rally, which was indeed then cancelled.⁵¹ Yet the king knew Hristić could only serve as a stop-gap prime minister, and he sounded out politicians on finding a more lasting replacement. Hristić, aware the king was manoeuvring to replace him, resigned, and a general election was held on 19 April 1895. It was boycotted by the Liberal leaders Avakumović and Ribarac, in response to Aleksandar's efforts to marginalise them, as well as by the Radicals for tactical reasons, so was won by the Progressives with 208 out of 240 seats. The new parliament was convened at Niš, in a throwback to the authoritarian practice of Milan's reign; it ratified the restoration of the Regency Constitution. A Court Liberal faction under Jevrem Andonović, who had been Nikolajević's justice minister, participated in the election and endorsed the 21 May coup; Andonović was consequently expelled by the Liberal general council. Meanwhile, a Radical split emerged, between moderates who remained hostile to Milan but were ready to collaborate in principle with Aleksandar and Natalija and hardliners opposed to the entire Obrenović dynasty. Despite Pašić's hardline record, he was evolving in a conservative direction and increasingly identified with the former current.

Southward expansionism and pivot to Russia

By the time the Obrenović counter-revolution had been completed in spring 1895, Aleksandar was not yet nineteen but had nevertheless come of age politically. He was determined to assert his authority, undermined as it was by his father's presence and political meddling. Aleksandar visited Natalija in Biarritz in France in January 1895 and she began supplanting his father's influence over him. During repeated visits to Biarritz, Aleksandar fell in love with Draga Mašin (1866–1903), Natalija's lady-in-waiting. Draga saved the king from drowning there in summer 1895, when his teacher drowned.[52] Marginalised, Milan left Serbia again and Natalija returned to Belgrade on 10 May 1895 to a magnificent four-day public welcome. Given the Progressive election victory, Aleksandar appointed a Progressive government on 8 July under Stojan Novaković, dominated by Natalija's friends and sharing her opposition to Milan's political interference. Natalija herself favoured a Radical government, believing that her son's regime required an accommodation with the party supported by most of Serbia's population. Nevertheless, pro-Radical steps were taken. The Čebinac conspirators were amnestied.

Novaković's government reversed the Progressives' traditional Austrophilia to adopt a pro-Russian, nationalist foreign policy, reviving Mihailo's plans for pan-Balkan collaboration. This reflected prevailing educated opinion in Serbia that its national goals and economic progress required ending subservience to Austria-Hungary and greater international independence; this was reinforced when Hungary's government closed the border to the importation of Serbian pigs on 3 June 1895, citing swine fever.[53] The secret convention with Vienna expired and was not renewed. Serbia's government sought the opening of Serbian schools and appointment of Serbian bishops in Macedonia with the Porte's agreement. Serbia benefited from worsening Ottoman–Bulgarian relations following Stambolov's fall in May 1894 and the outbreak of fighting between Bulgarian guerrillas and Ottoman forces in Macedonia. Years of Turcophile diplomacy and quiet consular missionary activity in the Ottoman lands to the south paid off when the Ottomans in January 1896 permitted a Serb to become Metropolitan of the Raška-Prizren bishopric. That month, the government passed a law strengthening the army and improving officers' pay and conditions.[54]

On Russian advice, Serbia improved relations with Bulgaria and Montenegro. Bulgaria's Prince Ferdinand visited Belgrade in spring 1896, followed on 28 June by Montenegro's Prince Nikola, who attended the Kosovo dirge at the cathedral. At lunch in the palace he toasted Aleksandar: 'I come to you on Vid's Day ... The whole of Serbdom is with us in spirit today; what it wishes, we two also wish!' Austria-Hungary, meanwhile, punished Serbia by again closing its border to Serbian pigs. In July, Aleksandar gave a copy of the 1881 secret convention to Russia's envoy and authorised him to send his government a copy, asking him to assure the Tsar that he was not responsible for the secret convention, would not have approved it and would not permit anything similar.[55] However, Novaković's government was unsuccessful in negotiating a deal for the prompt purchase of armaments from Russia, given Serbia's inability to pay for them and Russia's then cautious Balkan policy.[56] Meanwhile, the government pursued constitutional reform, seeking to replace the Regency Constitution—universally considered anachronistic by Serbia's political parties—with one more liberal, involving a two-chamber parliament. It produced a draft constitution based on the Progressives' 1883 draft.[57] Although the government did not last long enough to complete this project, Aleksandar accepted the need for constitutional reform and would eventually enact it on the basis of this draft.

The Radicals convened a national congress in Belgrade on 9 August 1896 to impress Aleksandar with the extent of their popular support. Numbering somewhere in the low tens of thousands, its size was unprecedented and it apparently succeeded in its goal.[58] Pašić's speech at the congress exhorted the Radicals to be patient and extolled the need for an agreement with the court. As the court softened toward the Radicals, so they continued their evolution from a once noisily democratic mass party into a more conservative, centralised body under Pašić's firm control: at the party's annual assembly at Kruševac in October, the general council gained the right to nominate parliamentary deputies. This reflected Pašić and Protić's determination that, since the party had to accept the court's constitutional order, it would need to become more disciplined and loyal to its leadership so as not to be emasculated. Although the party had always been anti-pluralist, it had genuinely been pro-democracy.[59] Now, instead of democratising the Serbian monarchical state, the Radical party copied its centralist authoritarianism.

Under Natalija's influence, Aleksandar on 26 December 1896 replaced the Progressive government with one dominated by Court Radicals and led again by Simić, a non-Radical acting as intermediary between party and king, following the king's new policy of taming the Radicals while working with them. This represented the third of four turns by the Obrenovićes toward the Radicals. The court–Radical partnership again proved unstable, for Aleksandar sought a coalition government including representatives of the other two parties, given his opposition to party conflict, while Pašić and the Radical general council wanted a purely Radical government. Following the government's appointment, the Radicals regained control of local government in the countryside through a combination of government action, mob violence and lynchings. About 1,200 out of 1,300 municipal presidents, thirteen out of twenty-one district governors and nine out of fifteen okrug governors were dismissed in the process, while the Radicals also regained control of the Council, diplomatic corps and other institutions.[60] Abandoned by the court upon whose patronage it depended and seeking to save its members from Radical retribution, the Progressive party formally dissolved itself, though it would soon be reactivated in practice.[61] In the parliamentary elections of 4 July 1897, boycotted by the Liberals, the Radicals won 98 per cent of the mandates: of 180 deputies, only three Liberals, one Social Democrat and ten Radical rebels were elected; the Radicals won the rest. Aleksandar again faced the prospect of total Radical hegemony.

The Radicals paradoxically supported a nationalist and Russophile policy abroad while subscribing to an anti-army and low-tax ideology that hampered the state's ability to pursue it. International events made this combination increasingly unattractive for Aleksandar. He was pursuing high-profile Balkan diplomacy and visited the Balkan capitals of Athens, Sofia, Cetinje and Bucharest in 1896–1897, but with little result. An agreement was signed with Bulgaria on 3 March 1897 for the two states to respect each other's interests in Macedonia and cooperate in matters relating to it. However, the Bulgarians were unwilling to agree on a division of Macedonia into Serbian and Bulgarian spheres; they preferred to support autonomy for a unified Macedonia, which Aleksandar opposed for fear it would lead to all Macedonia joining Bulgaria as Eastern Rumelia had done in 1885. Meanwhile, Serbia's military weakness hampered its extraction of concessions from the Ottomans.

War broke out between Greece and the Ottoman Empire in April 1897 over an uprising in Crete. This encouraged the Serbian government to improve its military capacity: military spending and munitions production increased at the Kragujevac armaments factory, a donation of further munitions was negotiated from Russia and a deal signed with the French firm Schneider-Creusot to purchase cannon.[62] However, Emperor Franz Joseph and his foreign minister Count Gołuchowski visited St Petersburg and signed with the Russians an agreement on 5 May, establishing a condominium of the two empires over the Balkans, which committed them to preserving the status quo. This made Russia unwilling to support aggressive moves by Balkan states, so it lessened the attraction for Belgrade of a pro-Russian policy. Meanwhile, Ottoman vulnerability due to the war enabled Serbian diplomacy to arrange the appointment of a Serb administrator to the Skopje bishopric, formally ordained as bishop five years later. The presence of the two Serbian bishops and the Serb school and church network in the region decisively obstructed its Bulgarianisation. Serbia's policy of low-key expansionism progressed under Aleksandar; the number of Serbian schools in the Ottoman Empire increased from 42 in 1889 to 234 by 1901. Bulgaria's unwillingness to agree with Serbia to Macedonia's division into spheres of influence compelled Aleksandar to work with the Porte to maintain the Ottoman Balkan status quo. This was arguably in Serbia's interest but did not satisfy impatient Serbian nationalists.

A new opponent, the Albanian national movement, had arisen since 1878 in response to the threat of partition of the Albanian-inhabited lands between the Balkan Christian states, and was encouraged by Austria-Hungary and Italy.[63] In the predominantly Albanian lands of 'Old Serbia' that remained in the Ottoman Empire after 1878, the Albanians were in the stronger position until 1912. From 1880 to 1889 more than 60,000 Serbs moved under Albanian pressure from the Ottoman Empire to Serbia.[64] Serbia's consul in Priština was murdered on 31 June 1890. The Ottoman victory over Greece in May 1897, won largely by Albanian troops whose lands were threatened by Greek expansionism, was followed by a further upsurge in Albanian aggression against Serbs in the Kosovo vilayet, involving killings, assaults and attacks on property, which resulted in an exodus of refugees into Serbia. The issue damaged Serbia's hitherto friendly relations with the Porte. Tensions in the borderlands were such that when in autumn 1896 Serbia's army undertook military exercises in Kuršumlija in southern Serbia, it induced panic among Muslim and Albanian civilians across the border, who fled in large numbers into the interior; the news spread across Kosovo that Serbia's army had attacked, reaching Constantinople, where the Sultan summoned Serbia's ambassador for an explanation. A border incident in southern Serbia in mid-June 1899 escalated into heavy fighting in which Ottoman forces invaded Serbian territory, several Serbian divisions were dispatched to defend the border and 32 Serbian border guards were killed.[65] Albanian bands occupied the region of Kolašin in the Kosovo vilayet in May 1901 and massacred local Serbs.[66] Unable to intervene militarily or to interest either the Porte or Great Powers in a diplomatic solution, Serbia's king and government began from November 1898 sending arms covertly to the Serbs in Kosovo.[67] Nevertheless, the regime's supposed passivity regarding Albanian attacks on Serbs catalysed a nationalist reaction against it.

Milan, meanwhile, once again mobilised elite resistance to the Radicals in government. He had been building his own clique within the army to the extent that Aleksandar viewed it as a security threat.[68] Đorđe Genčić, governor of the Niš okrug and a non-court Liberal, arranged an address of Niš citizens to Milan in February 1897, begging him to return to Serbia; this prompted his dismissal. Milan did return in October 1897 and soon put pressure on war minister Jovan Mišković to abandon the government. He persuaded his friend Vladan Đorđević, Serbia's ambassador in Constantinople, to write to Aleksandar criticising Simić's foreign policy as insufficiently proactive in extracting concessions from the Ottomans during the Greco-Ottoman war. Aleksandar meanwhile became convinced that the failures of the Radical-dominated government either to strengthen the army or to achieve more significant successes internationally required him to take matters into his own hands regarding the restoration of state finances and reform of the military, and that he would need to entrust the military reform to his father.⁶⁹ He was also convinced of the need to restore good relations with Austria-Hungary by dismissing the Russophile government.

Personal quarrels at court once again catalysed a change of national policy. Aleksandar fell out with his mother following her quarrel with Draga Mašin, who had become his lover in spring 1897. As Slobodan Jovanović notes, had Natalija accepted Aleksandar's relationship with Draga, she would have been guaranteed pre-eminence at court and the victory over Milan she had always sought, but her ego did not permit this, so permanently ending her political influence in Serbia.⁷⁰ Aleksandar's regime needed the support of either his father's or his mother's faction; his quarrel with his mother pushed him back toward his father, in turn necessitating another break with the Radicals.⁷¹ Aleksandar rationalised this, allegedly telling Mijatović at the time: 'You know that by political education I am a Radical as much as my father, by his personal way of thinking, was a Progressive. You know that I have twice delivered myself into the hands of the Radicals, and each time they themselves gave me unmistakable proofs that I ought not to trust them.'⁷²

Aleksandar's turn back toward his father meant a return to an authoritarian personal regime and postponement of constitutional reform. He dismissed Simić's government on 19 October and four days later installed a government under Đorđević, comprised of neutrals, Progressives and one Liberal as a fig leaf for his personal regime (the 'Regime of 11 October'). Đorđević was not a party politician. Like other figures in Serbian politics who were not ethnic Orthodox Serbs or who were not, in terms of recent family background, from Serbia (he was neither), Đorđević occupied a relatively weak position and depended on the patronage of others who were—in this case, the Obrenovićes. Đorđević, the ethnic Cincar with a Greek name, formed a close friendship with the foreign-educated, part-Romanian Milan, arising from their shared sense of being outsiders in Serbia and from Đorđević's services as Milan's personal physician.⁷³ Nevertheless, Đorđević was not permitted to choose his ministers, except the war minister; his government was selected by Aleksandar and Milan from among those less prominent politicians trusted as more loyal to the court than to their parties. Simultaneous with the government's appointment, Aleksandar published his programme, indicating an intention to 'resolve the questions that can ensure the financial, economic and military power of Serbia' since 'Serbia is more important than everything'. The Radicals interpreted this to mean that 'Serbia is more important than Serbdom'; i.e. that it should abandon all nationalist ambitions and focus on domestic affairs.⁷⁴ But though the government purged more Radicals from the administration, it sought to co-opt some of their leading members, offering posts to Đaja, Taušanović and Protić, which only the first two accepted. Pašić, meanwhile, was prosecuted for having stated that in the past he was 'against King Milan' and was sentenced to nine months in prison.[75]

The general election of 4 June 1898, helped by police manipulation, produced a parliament comprising 112 Liberals, 62 Progressives, 19 neutrals and a single Radical. This had been planned by Aleksandar and Milan, who wished to create a court regime based on the dynastic parties, the Liberals and Progressives. Three-quarters of municipalities were also handed to the Liberals. These results were not quite such a Liberal party victory as it seemed, for the court intended to break it along with the Radicals and appropriate the Liberal and Progressive deputies who, fearing the Radicals, naturally inclined toward it. The Liberal leaders were sidelined; Ristić himself died the following year. As Piroćanac had died in March 1897, followed by Garašanin in March 1898, and Novaković had left Serbia to become ambassador in Constantinople, the Progressives, already formally dissolved in 1896, were easily subordinated to the court.[76]

Parliament, meeting in Niš between July 1898 and January 1899, passed several laws entrenching the authoritarian order. Press freedom was restricted. All state employees including teachers, clergymen and even recipients of state benefits were forbidden to belong to political parties or attend political meetings. Political associations were forbidden to hold meetings except in Belgrade or in the okrug capitals, thereby preventing the Radicals from holding meetings in villages. Parliament passed a decree on 29 November 1898 by which 'all political associations that have existed up till now cease to exist'; this included the Radical, Progressive and Liberal parties.[77] Elected municipal presidents were replaced with appointed ones. The mandate of parliamentary deputies was extended from three years to five. Perhaps most indicative of the government's elitism was its closing of ten gymnasiums, so that full gymnasiums remained only in Kragujevac, Niš and Zaječar, plus two in Belgrade. This was intended to reduce the number of peasant youth with anti-state attitudes from entering the bureaucracy, reduce the number of the educated unemployed and re-create a contented elite with privileged access to bureaucratic employment, presiding over a contented peasantry reoriented away from ambitions of state service back towards agricultural work. Within three years of the law's passage in July 1898, the number of secondary school pupils had fallen by almost a third. However, compulsory primary education was extended to girls for the first time. Finally, the parliament partially reversed the Radicals' church law of 1890 to restore the Šabac bishopric and greatly increase the metropolitan's and bishops' pay.[78]

Milan himself was appointed commander of the active army on 7 October 1897, the post that was most senior in the Army of the Kingdom of Serbia after the defence minister, and was made army general—Serbia's first. The army became his personal fiefdom: autonomous within the state, shielded from government control and loyal to him personally. He worked on strengthening, reorganising and re-equipping the army with the assistance of Colonel (later General) Dimitrije Cincar-Marković, who became chief of the general staff on 25 December 1897. Milan increased the number of army battalions from forty to sixty. This required a corresponding rise in the number of officers, which he achieved by increasing the number of cadets at the Military Academy while reducing the length of their study from four to three years. Thus, within four years from the end of 1897 he had turned out 500 new officers. With the closing of the gymnasiums, the Military Academy became an increasingly attractive destination for peasant sons as well as for educated young people. The officer corps was thereby made larger, younger and more socially reflective of the peasant masses, thus less of a conservative and stabilising force in society, as events soon showed.[79]

The military command adopted the idea of war against the Ottoman Empire involving a pan-Balkan alliance of Serbia, Bulgaria, Greece and Montenegro, following German military doctrines. This idea and the army's reform, expansion and strengthening in this period eventually bore fruit in Serbia's spectacular military success and territorial gains in the First Balkan War of 1912–1913. In the short term, tensions with Bulgaria were high owing to competition over Macedonia, leading to war fears in 1898. Military manoeuvres held near Kruševac on 11 October 1898 were Serbia's largest in the nineteenth century, attended by the king, ex-king, most senior officers and thirteen foreign military observers. The foreigners were greatly impressed by the Serbians' professionalism and convinced that they harboured no aggressive designs vis-à-vis Bulgaria, thus reducing tensions between the two states.[80] However, these developments coincided with a dramatic worsening of Serbia's relations with Russia, which loathed Milan. St Petersburg consequently ceased to support Serbia's diplomacy vis-à-vis Macedonia while Serbia's government, increasingly dependent on Austro-Hungarian support, was required to suppress anti-Habsburg irredentist agitation in the press.[81]

Milan's army command sought to extend its power over aspects of civilian government, including the Serb schools and churches in the Ottoman Empire, which aroused Aleksandar's apprehension. The size, power, autonomy and instability of the officer corps rose as nationalist frustration increased. The regime promoted its own nationalist ideology based on the Obrenović dynasty: in 1898 it commemorated the twentieth anniversary of Vranje's liberation, the sixtieth anniversary of the founding of the king's guard and the fortieth anniversary of the St Andrew's Day parliament; it introduced a memorial for the wars of the 1870s and decreed that Miloš be officially known as Miloš the Great.[82] Meanwhile, military needs accelerated the modernisation of the school and medical sectors and their expansion, which in turn promoted social modernisation in general. With this went increased social differentiation; the increased use of mannerisms characteristic of Western and Central European elites, such as the phrases 'It is my honour to say' and 'I humbly state'; the habit of addressing people as 'sir' (gospodin), and the use of the formal 'you' in place of the familiar 'you' ('vi' instead of 'ti').[83]

Aleksandar's personal regime, based on Đorđević's government, ruled in defiance of popular support for the Radicals. Following the elections of June 1898, the Radical general council resolved to resist the regime through inciting the populace against Milan and organising revolts. This policy inspired the so-called St John's Day attempt of 6 July 1899, when an apparently simple-minded, unemployed Bosnian man fired several shots from a revolver at Milan's carriage leaving Belgrade, grazing his back and wounding his adjutant in the shoulder.[84] Although there was no evidence of their complicity, Radicals were arrested en masse, including Pašić, Protić, Taušanović and Stanojević, purged from state employment or placed under police surveillance. Those arrested were treated brutally, frequently denied proper access to food, water or clothing. Many fled abroad. The regime set up a kangaroo court to try the suspects. This draconian approach was approved by Ristić in his last significant political intervention before his death on 4 September, based on his experience of dealing with Mihailo's assassination in 1868 and the Topola mutiny in 1878. Ristić's close political friend Živan Živanović was appointed economics minister and Genčić, another Liberal and personal supporter of Milan, was appointed interior minister in the hope that he would deal with the Radicals more proactively than the previous incumbent, Andonović.[85] Milan intended to use the St John's Day attempt as a pretext finally to crush the Radicals and judicially murder its leaders, above all Pašić and Taušanović, but he was prevented by foreign intervention. Russia and Austria-Hungary were committed to their condominium over the Balkans, which would have been gravely upset had the pro-Austrian Milan extirpated the pro-Russian Radicals. Both powers pressed Belgrade into sparing the Radical leaders.

Pašić was nevertheless forced, on pain of death, publicly to assume responsibility for creating the climate that made the assassination attempt possible. He accepted at his trial 'that I did not succeed in giving sufficient proof of my loyalty and devotion to the throne, and that it was that lack of confidence that put me in prison'. In particular, he had been insufficiently energetic in purging the Radical party of its anti-dynastic elements and failed to follow the regime's instructions in 1897 to disband it after its Liberal and Progressive counterparts had already disbanded. He blamed his comrades in the general council for rejecting his request to do this, but admitted he should have tried harder to persuade them; consequently he had allowed the party struggle to continue, in which 'I personally erred, in insulting His Majesty King Milan in print, and for that I was sentenced. And my error was felt all the more because I did not immediately beg His Majesty King Aleksandar for mercy.' The success of the assassination would, according to Pašić, have led to the fall of the Obrenović dynasty, internal conflict and foreign intervention in Serbia and its partition in the manner of Poland. 'Thank God—he saved the life of King Milan, so saved Serbia and all of us.'[86] Pašić furthermore submitted letters to Aleksandar listing the most prominent Radicals as enemies of the crown: Tajsić, Taušanović, Protić,

COURT–RADICAL COLLABORATION

Đaja, Ljubomir Živković and others. Consequently, the special court's verdict on 25 September sentenced to death only the assassin himself and, in absentia, Tajsić. However, others including Protić, Živković and Taušanović were sentenced to long prison terms for their propaganda activities directed against the Obrenović dynasty and regime. The brutality of the persecution of the Radicals discredited the regime, in particular Milan personally.[87]

Pašić received only a five-year sentence and was immediately pardoned. But his grovelling capitulation and betrayal of his party, which effectively saved the regime's face over what would otherwise have been a fiasco, destroyed his reputation and forced him to retire from party politics. He subsequently rationalised his behaviour in his manuscript 'My political testimony', written in late 1902 and shown to some of his friends, in which he attempted to rebut charges that his political inactivity and capitulation to the court had made possible Aleksandar's personal regime. He claimed that to have bravely died a martyr's death at the trial would only have sparked internal conflict in Serbia which, even if the Obrenović dynasty had been successfully overthrown, would in turn have merely resulted in Great Power intervention and the imposition on Serbia of a foreign dynasty of the kind already installed in Romania, Greece and Bulgaria.[88] But now 'the dynastic question has been resolved once and for all and removed from the order of the day'.[89] His testimony indicated a fundamental shift in his political worldview, undoubtedly related to his personal experience: he now believed that the endless conflict between court and Radicals was distracting Serbs from the pursuit of national unification. Peace between them was therefore necessary: 'We must, in my opinion, hurry, for we are threatened by European culture, whose powerful industrial-trafficking progress crushes small nations and states like an enormous avalanche. National ideas are threatened by the danger from industrial-capitalist-trafficking-trading internationalism.'[90] The urgency of the moment did not permit internal conflict among the Serbs, requiring instead a colossal effort to achieve Serb national unification before the avalanche overwhelmed them.[91]

The St John's Day attempt trial marked the start of the Radical party's split, over the next five years, between a conservative wing under Pašić that collaborated with the regime and a younger, more idealistic faction, disgusted by his capitulation, that sought to remain loyal to the party's rebellious traditions, constituting itself as the Radical Democracy faction and eventually as the Independent Radical Party. As the united Radical party had enjoyed the support of five-sixths of the electorate, democracy in Serbia would have meant one-party rule. Aleksandar, by collaborating with the Radicals, split this monolith into two smaller parties, laying the basis for a functioning multiparty system. This was possible because Aleksandar, unlike previous Obrenović rulers, was not an unbridled autocrat at heart but in principle favoured constitutional government, provided he remained ultimately in control.

SERBIA

Aleksandar's marriage to Draga Mašin

Aleksandar's decision to marry his mother's former lady-in-waiting, Draga Mašin née Lunjevica, announced to members of his court on 15 July 1900 and to his father four days later, was a turning point for Serbia. It provoked widespread hatred in Serbia's elite against Draga and against Aleksandar for marrying her. Her inability to have children, correctly suspected by many, made her a problematic choice in terms of the dynasty's survival.[92] However, to rational political calculations was added the fact that she was a widow twelve years older than Aleksandar, while her familial and personal history, embellished by malicious rumours largely motivated by jealousy, provoked a pathologically snobbish and misogynistic reaction in Serbian public opinion. Not only did she have a (wildly exaggerated) sexual history but she was an educated free-thinker. According to Aleksandar's biographer Suzana Rajić, 'even her enemies did not deny her beauty and intelligence. Some even considered her the most beautiful woman in the capital.'[93] She had worked as a journalist, translator from French and German, short-story writer and member of the editorial board of the Liberal journal *Zastava*, in part to support her younger siblings after the premature deaths of her parents.[94] Following her marriage to Aleksandar, she replaced Natalija as patron of the Women's Society, which she had joined in the 1880s, and she and Aleksandar assiduously donated money to it.[95] She was therefore a trailblazing modern woman, and the hatred she inspired represented, in part, a patriarchal backlash against female emancipation.

The liberal politician and historian Živan Živanović, describing how Milan viewed Draga, referred to her as 'a parvenu in a skirt'.[96] Slobodan Jovanović claims she was widely viewed among officers as a 'harlot'.[97] According to Ljubomir Kaljević,

> Women cannot forgive a citizen for having become queen; they envy her luck and act upon their husbands and relatives in line with their terrible feminine rivalry and hatred. Yet those same women run to the palace and fawn upon that same queen, so that an hour later they can rinse their mouths, criticising her rich toilet, her pride and queenly bearing, that hurt their eyes and eat at their hearts. I hold that in our country there has never up to now been a similar example of such an unseen and lowly campaign by a whole battalion of women, even though they are at the palace most graciously awaited and received, for Queen Draga knows how to lower herself to the level of education and social position of every visitor; to interest herself in that which they are most concerned with; to encourage the downtrodden; to console the sorrowful; and to say to everyone upon parting some nice words by way of goodbye.[98]

In his bitter, hateful polemic against the already murdered Aleksandar and Draga, entitled *End of a Dynasty*, published in 1905, Đorđević recalls how, at the time he was prime minister, Draga sent his wife a book, 'the memoirs of Miss Bashkirtsev, in French', with several passages underlined, including:

COURT–RADICAL COLLABORATION

> One does not need to do anything substantially, in order to achieve happiness once again. One does not need to count on friendship or on generosity or on faithfulness or on honesty; rather, one needs impudently to raise oneself above all human trivialities and place oneself between them and God. One has vigorously to expel from life everything that can separate one from Him; one must not miss a single moment of satisfaction; one must create for oneself a life that is comfortable and magnificent; one must absolutely raise oneself above all others; one must be powerful, yes, very powerful, whatever means one comes to that by … Then the whole world will respect you, because they fear you; then you are strong, and that is the pinnacle of human fortune, because then, although everyone else may have the twitch of treachery in their mouths, they no longer bite you.

Đorđević concluded: 'This nihilistic, feminine-voluptuous and rabidly ambitious philosophy is believed in by the former lady-in-waiting of Queen Natalija; her *Dame d'honneur*! When I saw this, I decided that a woman who likes such a wild expression of egoism is not fit company for honourable women, so Draga Mašin was not invited to the reception that took place at my house following the diplomatic lunch held in honour of Baron Hajdler.'[99] Recalling subsequently visiting her, Đorđević writes:

> As soon as I entered her apartment, I sensed by the scents that filled the atmosphere in it that the woman who lived there well understood the physiological effect of certain perfumes on the *Nervus sacralis medius*. Still more was I convinced of this by the scent that greeted me when Mrs Draga, fresh as if she had just left her bathroom and wearing a morning dress—probably unique in Belgrade—emerged to greet me. With a gracious movement of her hand, the no longer young [she was 35] but still 'piquant' widow of Svetozar Mašin invited me to sit beside her on the sofa …[100]

For many of the court politicians upon whom Aleksandar based his personal regime, the engagement seemed to damage seriously the credibility and future of the dynasty upon which their careers depended. The transfer of the centre of influence at the court to Draga, of whom several had already made an enemy, would have been threatening even without considering her pro-Russian orientation. It occurred at a time when their regime was, in Đorđević's eyes at least, assailed by hostile agitation and propaganda among exiles and other opponents, including Petar Karađorđević himself, as part of a campaign by Russia, stretching across Austria-Hungary, Bulgaria and Montenegro, to subordinate the region to its imperial plans.[101] Aware that they were extremely unpopular among the masses and wholly dependent upon Aleksandar's person for their political standing, their paranoia was inflamed. Đorđević claimed Milan had told him that 'the slut' Draga was a 'common Russian agent' who had co-opted Aleksandar to instigate the St John's Day attempt, telling him that 'today Russia is Serbia's greatest enemy, but if *somehow Milan were to disappear*, then Russia would immediately shower Serbia with its grace and benevolence' (emphasis in original).[102]

In attempting aggressively to dissuade Aleksandar from the marriage, they fell out with him irrevocably.

In protest at the engagement, Đorđević's government resigned and Milan resigned his command of the active army. Aleksandar's publication of the decree of Milan's resignation at the same time as he published the announcement of his engagement informed all Serbia that the engagement had occurred against his father's wishes. Although Aleksandar persuaded Hristić to form a new government, Milan's disapproval caused Hristić to reconsider. Thus, the court regime based on the dual authority of king and king's father was split as the latter abandoned the former. Interior minister Genčić, who had slipped effortlessly into the role of quintessential Court Liberal, attempted at a fraught meeting with Aleksandar on 20 July 1900 to dissuade him from marrying Draga; he told him that he had been her lover himself, for which Aleksandar allegedly slapped him.[103] So began a feud between the two men. On the morning of the 23rd, Genčić met with friends who would form the kernel of the civilian wing of a conspiracy against the king: Vukašin Petrović and General Jovan Atanacković. Petrović suggested that Atanacković should seize control of the army, arrest its chief of staff Cincar-Marković and use it to expel Aleksandar and Draga from Serbia. Atanacković refused: 'I could, but I won't. I won't demoralise the army; I won't encourage it to tread on the road to revolution!' They were restrained too by the fear that Milan, to whose leadership they looked, would avenge himself on them if harm befell his son.[104]

Other senior supporters of the Obrenović regime met at the royal palace itself that night, according to Avakumović's memoirs, to discuss the possible forcible removal of Draga from Serbia. Present were Avakumović, Generals Cincar-Marković, Vasilije Mostić and Luka Lazarević, and Colonels Damjan Popović, Lazar Petrović and Leonid Solarević. Both Petrović and Solarević were the king's adjutants. Mostić allegedly revealed a message from Milan urging that the wedding be prevented at any price: 'But if my son is so enraptured by a harlot that he will not leave her, but wants to dirty the Serbian royal throne and dishonour the Obrenović dynasty, then I must, on the altar of the fatherland, make the sacrifice that I see my misguided son dead.' This was probably a self-exculpatory fabrication on Avakumović's part, though Milan undoubtedly urged Mostić to prevent the wedding. Avakumović claimed that those present were allegedly sympathetic to overthrowing or killing Aleksandar and restoring Milan, but that he, Avakumović, persuaded them to desist from this, owing to the possible domestic and international repercussions and the danger of becoming Milan's expendable pawns: 'Thus was then prevented, fortunately, a great crime.'[105]

Milan left Serbia for Vienna and was forbidden by Aleksandar to return. The Serbian border guard was ordered to arrest him if he tried to do so, using force if necessary, reflecting the king's fear that his father might return and use the army against him. The story that Aleksandar actually ordered the border guard to shoot Milan if he attempted to cross the border was an exaggeration apparently fabricated by members of the conspiracy.¹⁰⁶ When asked by war minister Miloš Vasić what would happen if Milan attempted to break through the border guard by force, Aleksandar replied: 'I think, Mr Vasić, that my father won't try to do that. If he does, force must be resisted by force; and if he should fall on that occasion, he would himself be to blame.'¹⁰⁷ Meanwhile, a letter was published in the Hungarian press and subsequently republished by newspapers across Europe, apparently written by Milan to Aleksandar and from which Milan did not dissociate himself, stating, 'I would be the first to congratulate the government that would expel you from the country after such a reckless act [as marrying Draga].'¹⁰⁸ Natalija was likewise barred from returning to Serbia and threatened with prosecution for treason in absentia for her letters attacking Draga. Aleksandar's threats against his parents violated patriarchal morality in the eyes of many.

Serbia's press was prompted to denounce, as freely as it wished, Milan, Đorđević and the Regime of 11 October (the 'vladanovština'). Aleksandar thereby declared war against his father's court faction. Members of this faction and others opposed to the wedding and to Aleksandar's policies more generally looked to Milan for leadership. The officers revered Milan because of the care he, as the active army's commander, had lavished upon them. They would probably have overthrown Aleksandar and restored him to the throne had he ordered it.¹⁰⁹ Some, including Genčić and Atanacković, indeed congregated around Milan in Vienna and urged him to use the army to prevent the wedding.¹¹⁰ But his abandonment of his powerful position as commander of the active army, followed by his refusal to act, caused them to vacillate. Milan himself eschewed any attempt to overthrow Aleksandar, allegedly keeping his promise to his son that 'he was too good a soldier to rebel against his King; too good a father to take any action against him; and too good a Serb to ignite the torch of civil war in his Fatherland'.¹¹¹ Nevertheless, Milan's resignation and disapproval of the wedding began the process by which Aleksandar lost the support of part of the officer corps.

The king summoned the officers of the Belgrade garrison on 24 July to inform them of his engagement and remind them of their oath of loyalty to him, to which they responded with apparently half-hearted acclaim. He struggled to form a new government and particularly to find a new war minister, not only because leading officers disapproved of his intended marriage but because they feared Milan's reaction to anyone who accepted the post.¹¹² He eventually scraped together the so-called Wedding Cabinet headed by Aleksa Jovanović, with Vasić as war minister, that took office on 25 July. Chief of staff Cincar-Marković reacted to the news of the government's formation by appealing to Metropolitan Inoćentije, to whom he was related and on friendly terms, to try to prevent the wedding, on the grounds that the church's opposition would count for much, but Inoćentije allegedly replied, 'Yes, kum, that is true and I will do everything possible, but I do not however guarantee success. For what can you do, when they love each other so much? Like a dove cock and a dove hen. And aside from that, the Russian Tsar has accepted them as kums.'¹¹³

The wedding occurred on 5 August. The widespread hostility it aroused among the Austrophile section of the elite upon which Aleksandar had based his personal regime necessitated another turn towards the Radicals, whose popular support could sway public opinion on the matter, and other populist measures. Taušanović, Protić and other Radicals imprisoned after the St John's Day attempt as well as prisoners more generally were amnestied or pardoned. The Jovanović government pursued crypto-Radical policies involving lightening the tax burden on the populace and reforming the army. Having become virtually a state within a state under Milan, the army was now subordinated once more by decree on 17 August 1900 to government control through the war minister; then the king's absolute authority over it was reaffirmed and strengthened by the army law of 9 February 1901. The standing army was repackaged as the first call-up of the national army, terms of compulsory military service were shortened and the military budget, expanded to unsustainable levels under Milan, was likewise reduced. This was intended to appeal to the pro-Radical masses.

This pro-Radical policy was also a nationalistic one: Draga was promoted as a true Serb whose grandfather Nikola Milićević Lunjevica, considered the richest Serb in the Smederevo sanjak in 1815,¹¹⁴ had been Miloš's prominent supporter during the Second Serbian Uprising, in contrast to the German princess Milan had been seeking for the king. The marriages of the previous two Obrenović rulers to foreigners—the Hungarian Catholic Julija Hunyadi and the Russian–Romanian Natalija Keshko—had, after all, not been popular or happy. Aleksandar's policy culminated in a turn toward Russia's Tsar Nicholas II, who had consented to be his best man by proxy at his wedding at the price of reconciliation with the Radicals. The Tsar welcomed the marriage, given Draga's background as a lady-in-waiting of the pro-Russian Natalija and the known opposition to it of Milan, leader of Serbia's Austrophile faction. This faction was outflanked as the resulting nationalist and Russophile groundswell helped Aleksandar regain the initiative. Milan could not now return to Serbia to prevent the marriage, for this would have required support from Austria-Hungary, which would not have permitted such an affront to the Tsar.¹¹⁵ The marriage won approval from opponents of Milan's tyranny; as Slobodan Jovanović writes, 'Opponents of King Milan rejoiced that they had, finally, found someone who could flush away the old lord. The Radicals could do nothing to him; Russia could do nothing to him; until a woman arrived who, in the blink of an eye, blew away the first king since Kosovo and the commander of the active army!'¹¹⁶ In Milan's words, as quoted by Đorđević, 'The entire officer corps, *la maison militaire et civile du Roi*, declared against his marriage with the slut, and he would still today not have an assembled government ... if the oldest and most powerful enemy of the Obrenovićes had not helped him carry out this suicide of the dynasty; if Russia had not helped him. Only when it was learned that holy Orthodox Russia had blessed this "marriage"; only then did the last urchins in Serbia consent to form a ministry for such a wedding.'[117]

The traditional historiography, represented by historians who were Aleksandar's political opponents, particularly Slobodan Jovanović and Živan Živanović, portrays Aleksandar's marriage as dooming his regime. Yet without benefit of hindsight, Aleksandar had reason to believe that opposition to his marriage was merely a passing storm. The metropolitan of the Serbian Orthodox Church, the president of the parliament, the president of the Council, representatives of the Belgrade municipality, the commander and other officers of the king's guard and diplomatic representatives of foreign states rapidly declared in support of the marriage. Having toppled Milan and the 11 October regime and produced the pardoning of condemned Radicals and the restoration of relations with Russia, the marriage was welcomed by much of the population and by supporters of all three parties who favoured a return to constitutional government.[118] Pašić welcomed it, because 'for me it was clear that the political direction that had arisen from the wedding would need to seek help from and the support of the Radical party, all the more so since its foreign policy sought and received support from our fraternal Russia'.[119] Parliament in January 1901 approved the king's raising to the throne of a 'Serbian woman of the noble and honourable issue of Vojvoda Nikola Lunjevica'.[120]

Cincar-Marković eventually abandoned the opposition and supported Aleksandar. His readiness, along with that of two other generals, Aleksandar's former tutor Jovan Mišković and Mihailo Srećković, to give the marriage their blessing convinced the king he would have the army behind him. To ensure it remained under his control, he executed a large-scale purge of officers loyal to his father or hostile to Draga, including Solarević, his first adjutant. Four out of six active generals were pensioned off, including Mostić, who was soon after deprived of the right to wear his uniform.[121] Conversely, Aleksandar systematically promoted his favourites and loyalists among the officers. He entrusted the relatively junior Lieutenant Colonel Miloš Vasić with the war ministry, with absolute authority over the army, which Vasić accepted in return for promotion to full colonel. Srećković, a general whom Milan had pensioned, was made commander of the active army, but the post was now downgraded as Aleksandar separated the general staff from it and subordinated it directly to the war ministry. Milan's rank of army general was abolished and a new honorary rank of 'vojvoda' (duke or warlord) was introduced, which a decade later would be awarded to four of Serbia's leading generals in the victorious wars of the 1910s.

Aleksander bolstered the officer corps as a caste apart from the masses: the Law on the Marriage of Officers of 1901 required an officer wishing to marry to demonstrate that his intended bride was a woman of morals, character and family background that accorded with the dignity of the officer corps, and required him also to be free of debts and to provide a sum of 10,000 dinars for his wife and children's upkeep, should he die; the cost in practice fell on the woman's family. This law had the desired effect of binding the officer corps to the social elite consisting of ministers, diplomats, members of the Council, rentiers, industrialists, senior officers, directors of banks and insurance companies, senior judges, university and school professors, doctors and the like: one in four wives of officers came from such families. Yet junior officers still often found themselves struggling financially, given that they were required to buy and maintain their uniforms and, if in the cavalry, their horses.[122] They were a caste apart that resented their lack of means.

Aleksandar's promotions were not without military merit. His first adjutant, Lazar Petrović, was promoted to general ahead of more senior colleagues; nicknamed 'Handsome Laza', he was a brave, outstanding officer genuinely loyal to the king. Lieutenant Colonel Živojin Mišić was appointed chief of the operational department of the general staff, Lieutenant Colonel Petar Bojović was appointed assistant chief of staff of the command of the active army and Stepa Stepanović was appointed commander of the infantry brigade of the Drina Division's permanent cadre; these three first-rate officers would lead Serbia to victory in World War I. But other officers denied the largesse were alienated. Petrović, married to one of the queen's sisters, earned considerable undeserved resentment as her supposed stooge. But outrage was directed particularly at the queen's two officer brothers, Nikodije and Nikola Lunjevica, and the rest of the Lunjevica family—widely deemed too common to deserve such social advancement.

Functionaries who had attempted to prevent the wedding were pensioned off or dismissed, including Genčić. Đorđević lost his military rank. These and other individuals were publicly accused of treason and corruption, causing them to flee abroad in fear for their personal safety. Genčić denounced Aleksandar's regime from abroad; upon returning to Serbia, he was prosecuted and imprisoned for eight months. Milan himself died of pneumonia in Vienna on 11 February 1901, a broken man aged only 46. He allegedly lamented on his deathbed, 'Isn't it terrible, that I should die so young?'—'so long as it isn't in Serbia!'[123] His death ended Austria-Hungary's commitment to the Obrenović dynasty. He was buried at the Krušedol monastery in present-day Vojvodina in Austria-Hungary, against the wishes of Aleksandar, who had wanted him buried in Serbia and who was not granted by the Habsburgs a place in the funeral ceremony that would have permitted him, as king, to attend. This was a calculated Habsburg slight in punishment for Aleksandar's pivot towards Russia; it mortally offended the king, who unleashed Serbia's press against Austria-Hungary in response. Hungary's government further punished Serbia in August 1901 by closing its border once again to the import of Serbian pigs, restrictions on which were only gradually lifted from November.[124] Vienna was increasingly ready to accept a Karađorđević restoration, given Aleksandar Karađorđević's Austrophile record and Petar's own in-and-out residence in the empire throughout his peripatetic life.[125]

COURT–RADICAL COLLABORATION

Conversely, Milan's death removed the threat of restored Austro-Hungarian control of Serbia, which he represented, reducing Russia's need to support Aleksandar.[126]

With the threat of Milan ended, Radical pressure on Aleksandar for further concessions increased while the anti-Draga faction of the court and military, previously restrained by Milan's failure of leadership, was ready to resort to extreme measures. A clique of officers emerged, primarily older men formerly close to Milan or to Aleksandar himself but now in disfavour, who would form the core of a conspiracy against the king: Mašin, Atanacković, Solarević, Petar Mišić, Damjan Popović, Luka Lazarević, Stevan Ilić and others.[127] Other early opponents of the marriage, however, such as Cincar-Marković and Petrović, made their peace with it and would be the victims of the conspiracy alongside Aleksandar. Of those who joined the conspiracy, the case of Colonel Mašin, Draga's former brother-in-law, stands out: he bore a grudge against her for inheriting his late brother's pension. He was also the son of a doctor, Jovan Mašin, whom then Prince Milan was rumoured to have thrown out of his house after he was implicated in Blaznavac's death; he may thus have also had a familial grudge against the dynasty.[128] He had nevertheless risen high in the army, becoming assistant chief of staff and a favourite of Aleksandar, but he was pensioned off for maligning Draga.[129]

Radical–Progressive 'fusion' and April Constitution

Aleksandar sought to build a new governing coalition involving moderate Radicals and left-wing Progressives led by Dimitrije Marinković and his son Pavle. The Jovanović government was expanded on 18 February to include the moderate Radicals Mihailo Vujić and Milovan Milovanović, after which a government under Vujić, containing an equal number of Radicals and Progressives, was appointed on 3 April. This coalition became known as the 'fusion'. The Radicals and Progressives began publishing a common newspaper, *Dnevnik* (Daily), owned by the Progressive legal scholar Živojin Perić and edited by Protić. Aleksandar intended this policy to reconcile the two parties, while the Liberals were to comprise an opposition to counterbalance the government; as Perić pointed out, unification of all three parties in government could have produced tyranny.

The king assembled Radical and Progressive notables at the palace on 20 March, including Pašić, the Marinkovićes and others, and discussed with them a draft constitution, composed by the Radical Milovanović and the Progressive Pavle Marinković, based on the Novaković government's 1896 draft.[130] That draft in turn had been based on the Progressives' draft of 1883. This was therefore essentially a Progressive constitution, as the 1869 constitution had been Liberal and the 1889 constitution Radical. The senate, largely composed of notables, harked back to the oligarchic Council of the 1838 constitution. The draft was sent to other experts for their opinion, including the Liberal leader and lawyer

Avakumović, who initially approved it. It was then put before representatives of the three parties during April, including the Liberals, who generally approved it, though Ribarac was opposed and Avakumović eventually came out in opposition as well. At a conference at the palace on 17 April, representatives of all three parties gave the constitution their blessing. This was then promulgated by royal decree, at an assembly of government ministers and other notables, on 19 April (6 April); a date symbolically chosen as the anniversary of Mihailo's receipt of the keys to the Belgrade fortresses in 1867, intended to signify resumption of his work. It was henceforth known as the April Constitution.

The promulgation of a constitution in this manner was not authorised by the existing Regency Constitution and has traditionally been portrayed as King Aleksandar's third coup, but it occurred on the basis of consultations with representatives of the parties and other experts, so was scarcely an act of arbitrary despotism. None of the previous Serbian constitutions, after all, had been enacted according to legally established rules.[131] Furthermore, the idea for promulgating the constitution in this manner originated with Novaković and was supported by the Progressives and Radicals; the Radicals did not want their arrangement with Aleksandar upset by a great national assembly, nor did they want responsibility before their supporters for the abandonment of the 1889 constitution. The 1901 constitution was an attempt at a working constitutional arrangement on the part of most of the leading state actors, which only the Independent Radicals and one Liberal faction opposed.[132] It was a compromise between the British-type constitutional monarchy favoured by the Radicals and the German type favoured by the Progressives.[133]

The constitution established a bicameral representative body with a lower chamber (parliament) of 130 members democratically elected through direct secret ballot and an upper chamber (senate) enjoying equal legislative authority and control over the budget. The representative body would sit in Belgrade and would be summoned annually by decree. The government would not be responsible to the representative body, ministers could not be members of parliament or elected senators and the king could extend the previous year's budget without parliamentary approval for up to a year. The senate would have fifty-one members: three by right (the heir to the throne, the Belgrade archbishop and the bishop of Niš), eighteen elected democratically by the people, and thirty, or three-fifths of the total, appointed for life by the king. The Council was strengthened and gained the right to rule on appeals against decrees; its members would be selected from the permanent senators. Freedom of speech, the press, assembly and association and judicial independence were guaranteed. In the absence of a male heir from the Obrenović family, the throne would pass to a direct female heir.[134] Aleksandar hoped this constitution would limit the power of the Radical-dominated lower chamber and balance the parties while preserving his royal authority. The Radicals would have a majority in the lower chamber and a minority in the upper; the Progressives would have the reverse; and their coalition would in turn be kept in check by an opposition of hardline Radicals and Liberals.

For the second time in eight years, Pašić's Radicals had endorsed a royal coup. Their support for this constitution's passage marked a further step in their evolution into a conservative monarchist party. They formally abandoned their original ideal of popular democracy to embrace a restrained form of constitutional liberalism, involving support for a second chamber and abandonment of the ideal of the great national assembly. They adopted an increasingly conservative view of constitutional government, resembling that of their Progressive partners, who also became more conservative. Their retreat was justified by the need to concentrate all energies on fulfilling Serbia's national goals—i.e. unification with other Serb or South Slav lands.[135] Acceptance of authoritarianism at home meant heightened support for expansion abroad. This policy of the Radical leadership further split the party, whose younger, 'Independent' wing preferred to remain in opposition. Formally loyal to the 1881 manifesto, the Independents derisively nicknamed Pašić's Radicals 'fusionists'. They were joined by the Liberals, who, excluded from power by Aleksandar, increasingly emulated their hardline pro-democracy stance. This meant the Liberals' ideological return to the principles of the original St Andrew's Day liberals. Thus, party politics divided into two blocs: the conservative governing bloc (Radical–Progressive) supporting the 1901 constitution and the more pro-democracy opposition bloc (Independent–Liberal) demanding a return to the 1889 constitution.[136]

The April Constitution served the Radicals well: they won the elections of 4 August 1901 with the Progressives coming second, earning them 84 and 28 seats in parliament respectively, while the opposition won 17 seats (11 Independents and 6 Avakumović–Ribarac Liberals). Since the king appointed 11 Radical senators and the Radicals won every elected senate seat, they achieved a majority in both chambers. The representative body then passed laws that granted effective press freedom, restored municipal self-government virtually as it had existed under the 1889 constitution and guaranteed freedom of assembly to all except soldiers, the underaged and those without civic rights. The annual military budget was reduced from 25 million dinars a year to just under 18.5 million, thereby continuing the work of the Jovanović government of reducing military expenditure, which had ballooned under Milan.[137] This was necessary given the need to balance the budget, but it led to officers' wages being paid erratically and the quality of soldiers' food suffering. As under the Radical government of 1889–1892, officers' opposition to the regime rose.

Aleksandar attempted to build a new dynastic cult around himself and Draga. Schools and regiments were named after her and her birthday became a major national celebration. She was popular for the first nine months of her reign, particularly among Radicals.[138] Soon after the wedding, a French doctor examined her and concluded she was pregnant. Aleksandar immediately announced this to the public, arousing considerable sympathy, although it constituted acknowledgement that their intimate relations had begun before their marriage. However, in late April 1901, Draga was examined by a Russian doctor at the Russian ambassador Nikolai Charykov's insistence and found not to be pregnant after all. The queen's enemies immediately assumed she had faked her pregnancy to deceive the king and country, though as her sister Ana (Vojka) noted in her memoirs, had she indeed done so she would hardly have allowed the false pregnancy to be discovered by a doctor, when she could easily have faked a miscarriage.[139] Nevertheless, the episode seriously damaged the royal couple's reputation and credibility. Cincar-Marković consequently discussed with the traumatised king the possibility that Draga be removed from Serbia and prevented from returning, to make way for a new queen capable of bearing an heir and saving the dynasty.[140] Draga herself apparently proposed a solution along these lines, but the plan was not realised in time to save the royal couple.

Aleksandar viewed the splitting of the Radicals into pro- and anti-government wings, as the Liberals and Progressives had already split, as a major triumph, but in practice it freed the Independents to wage a ferocious campaign against his regime in parliament and the press. The new constitutional system was insufficiently liberal-democratic to satisfy the Independents but sufficiently so to prevent the regime from suppressing their fierce opposition. Vujić's Radical–Progressive coalition was weak and lacked popular legitimacy; it was seen by the opposition as an extension of the king's personal regime, so opposition attacks were concentrated on Aleksandar and his family rather than on the government. Taušanović died on 8 February 1902; his funeral turned into a popular manifestation of anti-regime anger at which Živković delivered a fiery speech denouncing royal absolutism. A demonstration of high school pupils at the senate in March, directed particularly against Pašić, degenerated into a riot in which gendarmes attacked the demonstrators, after which 186 pupils were suspended and one expelled altogether.[141] The Independents published what they called 'Our first word' in their newspaper *Odjek* in October 1902, in which they called for an end to the 'era of the personal regime' and 'internally national prosperity and freedom and abroad state independence and liberation and unification with the other parts of Serbdom, and we deem the goal of our internal politics a condition for success in foreign politics, for a nation in which there is no freedom or moral and economic strength cannot offer help to oppressed brothers to free themselves from slavery'. They argued such policies could be pursued 'only through maintaining most sincere relations with the great Slavic empire of Russia and fraternal Montenegro'. They claimed these policies represented 'the true Radical programme' that 'some Radical leaders have abandoned'.[142]

This era saw the coming of age of the 'young intellectuals' who, fired by the press opposition to Aleksandar's regime, cut their political teeth opposing it. Some were Independents such as Živković, Prodanović, Ljubomir Stojanović, Jovan Žujović and Radoje Domanović, who considered themselves 'moral gendarmes'. In Žujović's words: 'It seems to me that we are the salt that does not permit Serbian society to rot.'¹⁴³ But others were non-Radicals like Slobodan Jovanović, Svetolik Jakšić and Jovan Jovanović-Pižon. These were men of the elite who aspired to senior service in the state but were frequently dismissed or lived in fear of being dismissed from their posts because of their politics. They were generally hostile both to the regime and to its Old Radical collaborators, instead viewing British or French parliamentarism as a model for Serbia, but they were often inclined to support radical unparliamentary measures to achieve it.¹⁴⁴

To the regime's arbitrary, undemocratic nature was added its supposed failure to defend Serbia's national interests. Unlike Ristić in 1876 or Milan in 1885, Aleksandar did not recklessly start and lose a war, but sought to advance Serbia's national interests more quietly. Thanks to a combination of amicability and pressure toward the Porte, on 10 July 1902 the Serb administrator of the Skopje bishopric, appointed five years before, was formally consecrated bishop by the Patriarch in Constantinople. Serbia's government demanded in August 1902 that the Porte implement measures to protect the Serb population of Old Serbia from Albanian attacks, including strengthening the Ottoman garrisons in mixed Serb–Albanian areas.¹⁴⁵ Under prime minister Cincar-Marković from November 1902 and with Aleksandar's authorisation, Serbia's government established the first guerrilla (Chetnik) bands for action in Macedonia, involving men like Milorad Gođevac and Živojin Rafajlović, son of Draga's kum. Their primary task was to resist the pro-Bulgarian bands already active there, who had killed 43 and wounded 52 Serb schoolmasters, teachers, priests and others between 1897 and 1902.¹⁴⁶ Three battalions of Serbia's regular army were stationed on the southern border in early 1903 for potential action against Bulgarian bands.¹⁴⁷ Aleksandar continued to reform, expand and rearm the military while cementing his direct, exclusive control over it. The institution of Supreme Military Council was introduced on 1 September 1901, comprising the war minister and nine senior officers selected by the king to advise him on military affairs. The military budget was then absorbing 22 per cent of the state budget, the bulk of it spent on the officer corps and military officialdom, though the difficulties in funding military expansion, given the limits of Serbia's state budget, meant that officers' salaries continued to be paid late.¹⁴⁸

Aleksandar was therefore pursuing a national policy as forward as Serbia's limited strength and difficult international position allowed. But this was deemed inadequate by 'patriotic' elements in the army, press and public. The activities of Albanian and Bulgarian guerrillas in the Ottoman lands heightened the feeling that the situation there would soon explode and that Serbia would have to act decisively in defence of its interests, for which a more effective national leadership enjoying Russia's full confidence would be needed. The Society of Serbs from Old Serbia and Macedonia held a demonstration several thousand strong in central Belgrade on 12 October 1902;

this passed a resolution denouncing Albanian crimes against the Serb inhabitants of those areas and demanding that the king and government defend them.[149] The pressure was consequently on Aleksandar to look for successes abroad that would earn national acclamation and restore his popularity. But he was caught between the conflicting demands of nationalist rhetoric, diplomacy and dynastic interest.

Aleksandar sought to improve relations with Austria-Hungary to secure Serbia's rear but came up against the strength of anti-Habsburg feeling in his country. At a banquet commemorating the twenty-fifth anniversary of the Serbo-Ottoman wars of 1876–1878 and the conquest of Niš, he made a fiery speech affirming that he would follow in the footsteps of his father, who had 'liberated half of Serbia': 'Let the whole world know that from now nobody may take a single span of territory in the Balkans without Serbia getting its share.' This rhetoric combining aggressive nationalism with a dynastic cult based on his father was not very popular, given the highly negative views of Milan held by the Radicals and the peasant masses that supported them. Yet it alarmed foreign diplomats, whom Aleksandar then had to reassure that he was not seeking to disturb the peace.[150] Serbia's government in early 1902 aimed to support the movements of Serbs and Muslims in Bosnia-Hercegovina demanding autonomy in the fields of religion and education from the Austro-Hungarian occupation regime, but it failed to win approval for this from Russia, which did not wish to offend Vienna.[151]

The sense of a ridiculous regime, preoccupied with maintaining a facade of patriotic government while ignoring Albanian attacks on Serbs, was articulated by satirist Radoje Domanović in his novella *Stradija*, published in the *Srpski književni glasnik* (Serb Literary Herald) and widely credited with doing more than any other piece of writing to destroy the regime's credibility. It portrayed a Ruritanian stereotype of a country inhabited by citizens overflowing with medals, with an army focused on holding parades, a constitution changed fifteen times in ten years, and a parliament whose elections were arranged by the police. Domanović ridiculed the failure of the authorities to take action against the '*Anuti*, a warlike tribe, who invade the south of our country and carry out hideous depredations'—a thinly veiled reference to the Albanians, who were generally referred to in Serbia at the time as 'Arnauti'. In the words of *Stradija*'s fictitious war minister:

> If I hadn't, as minister of war, acted in this way, one of our commanders in the south of the country could have used the army to come with arms to the defence of our citizens and to spill the blood of the Anuti. All our officers think that that would be the best thing to do, but they won't think about things in a rather deeper and more evenhanded manner. First and foremost, we, today's government, want a peaceful, pious foreign policy; we don't want to be inhumane to our enemies... Secondly... our current government has no supporters among the people, so the army is above all needed for our internal political affairs. For example, if a particular municipality is in the opposition's hands, then it is necessary to use the army to punish such traitors

COURT–RADICAL COLLABORATION

to our ravaged homeland and to turn over the government to the hands of one of our people ...

The fictitious war minister concluded: 'Let enemy detachments attack; those things are not so important; but the main thing is that we parade in the streets with trumpets.'[152] Domanović's implication was that Aleksandar's regime was unpatriotically using the army to control its own population, when it should have been using it to 'spill the blood' of Albanians.

Aleksandar's third attempt to collaborate with the Radicals collapsed for much the same reasons as the first two: neither of the partners was willing to concede ultimate authority in the state to the other. The king, having permitted the Radicals a majority in parliament, senate and Council, resented their attempt further to monopolise power and their failure to tackle the press attacks on him, while the Radicals resented sharing power with the Progressives. Seeking to regain pre-eminence in his party, Pašić was unwilling to permit Vujić's government to consolidate itself; writing in late 1902, he claimed he had from the start opposed the fusion, which was the work of Court Radicals; he nevertheless went along with it to preserve party unity, but was then compelled to oppose it owing to the failure of the Radicals to assert themselves within it.[153] The Radical deputies chafed at the government's failure to restore the legal regime of the 1889 constitution and at the dilution by the king and Progressives of laws they tried to pass. Aleksandar sought to bolster his status by a visit with Draga to the Tsar, but the Tsar, apparently in response to rumours about her past that may have reached him through his Montenegrin in-laws, was unwilling to confirm a date, and this undermined the value, in Aleksandar's eyes, of a regime based on Russia and the Radicals. By autumn 1902, Radical support for the government of the 'fusion' collapsed. After Charykov informed him that the Tsar would not be receiving him, Aleksandar dismissed the Vujić government on 17 October and appointed a reconstituted Radical–Progressive coalition under Pera Velimirović. When this failed to elicit sufficient support in parliament, even among moderate Radicals, Aleksandar abandoned his attempt to work with them.

The king then turned again to a personal regime, appointing on 19 November 1902 the so-called 'government of generals' under Cincar-Marković, up till then army chief of staff and an officer with a tremendous reputation. This government had the backing of loyal factions of the Liberal, Progressive and Radical parties and reflected Aleksandar's favoured long-standing plan: to create a 'fourth party' uniting those loyal to him from the ranks of all three existing parties. A second general, Milovan Pavlović, war minister under Velimirović, was retained under Cincar-Marković; he had been a government minister in 1894 when Aleksandar had abrogated the 1889 constitution. Colonel Vasilije Antonić, foreign minister under Velimirović, was likewise retained under Cincar-Marković, so that the three key portfolios were held by senior officers. The other ministers were four Radicals, one Liberal and one

Progressive.[154] This combination—court generals heading a cross-party coalition in which Court Radicals were prominently represented—was a prototype adopted and further developed by another King Aleksandar in 1929 and by Army General Milan Nedić, puppet prime minister of Nazi-occupied Serbia, in 1941. Yet it marked the twilight of the first King Aleksandar's regime. Milan's old position of commander of the active army was abolished on 30 November 1902 and the active army was subordinated directly to the general staff. The Cincar-Marković government strove to pay officers their salaries, which had fallen into arrears under Vujić. Aleksandar's regime, in its final incarnation, resembled a military dictatorship and sought to build a Serbian army that would loyally defend it against internal enemies and achieve national goals abroad. But it was too late.

While repeated attempts between 1889 and 1903 to establish a functional partnership between court and Radicals proved unworkable, opponents of such a partnership had emerged on the 'right' in the form of Milan's Austrophile faction of the old elite and on the 'left' in the form of the Independents. The peculiar feature of the late Obrenović regime, whereby a king abdicated in favour of his young son but then continued to play a central role in it, resulted in its split into pro-Aleksandar and pro-Milan factions on the occasion of Aleksandar's announcement of his engagement. Wholly excluded from power and any possibility of returning to it, deeply hostile to the Radicals but encouraged by the Independents' fierce opposition to the regime, Milan's faction mutated into a full-blown praetorian reaction, spawning a conspiracy to murder the royal couple.

10

A ROYAL 'HONOUR KILLING'

1903

The conspiracy to murder Aleksandar and Draga united those who sought personal revenge, those who sought to profit from their deaths and some actually motivated by political idealism. The civilian conspirators came predominantly from the authoritarian and anti-democratic or at least anti-Radical segment of the elite, but the younger officer-conspirators reflected a paradoxical synthesis: as children of Milan's army, they inherited his elitism and contempt for political parties, constitutionalism and democracy, but as restless young men they imbibed the zeitgeist from the contemporary opposition press, with its ferocious hostility to the notion of royal tyranny and often demagogic championing of the idea of liberty. Given this mix, the conspiracy lacked clear political goals, focusing on the negative aim simply of killing the king and queen. Formally, the conspirators did not seek a military dictatorship but embraced the demands of the legal opposition to the regime, for constitutional and parliamentary government. In practice, the conspiracy incubated a force in Serbian politics that would obstruct this.

Regicidal conspiracy

On the evening of 20 July 1900, following the confrontation in which Aleksandar allegedly slapped Genčić, Lieutenant Dragutin Dimitrijević 'Apis', whose sister's husband, finance minister Živan Živanović, had told him what had happened, met his friend Lieutenant Antonije Antić, Genčić's nephew. Antić was a cavalry officer personally appointed to the Royal Guard by Milan out of personal friendship with Genčić.[1] Apis asked Antić what should be done in response, to which Antić replied, 'Nothing other than that the cur should be killed.'[2] When Aleksandar announced the wedding to the officer corps on 24 July, the failure of the more senior officers to speak out against it led some of their younger colleagues, born in the 1870s, to consider them cowards. The most outspoken of these was Apis.[3] He and Antić launched a campaign of character assassination against Aleksandar and particularly Draga, spreading malicious gossip about her among their fellow officers to create a climate conducive to their goal.[4] This aimed initially at the elimination of Draga alone but was subsequently expanded to encompass Aleksandar's removal as well.[5]

Draga's opponents were not, however, representative of the entire army, among which the marriage was not unpopular.[6] The minority of irreconcilable officers, lacking the majority's support, turned to extreme measures. According to most accounts, Apis would emerge as their organisational leader. His brother-in-law Živanović claims Apis told him that it had been his, Živanović's, influence that had inspired him to initiate the conspiracy: 'But you, earlier as a minister (1899–1900) and in general, were always expressing the difficulties of the situation and lamenting the actions of the king, who did what he wanted and from everyone required only sacrifices. Thus did I [Apis] begin to consider what to do; to begin first alone, later with my comrades, to ponder the difficult situation of our country and the means of bringing this to an end for good. Thus did this conspiracy come about.'[7] However, the historian Vasa Kazimirović suggests that Apis's central role in the conspiracy may have been a myth constructed by his supporters following his execution in 1917. Kazimirović attributes the moral leadership of the conspiracy to older officers close to Milan or Aleksandar who fell into disfavour due to their opposition to the marriage, including Atanacković, Mašin, Solarević, Petar Mišić, Popović and Lazarević.[8]

The revelation in May 1901 that Draga's pregnancy had been false, followed by the spread of probably baseless rumours that her brother Nikodije Lunjevica would be made royal heir, decisively catalysed the conspiracy. Sitting outside their barracks in mid-September 1901, Antić informed three friends, Captains Radomir Aranđelović and Milan Petrović and Lieutenant Dragutin Dulić, that he had recently followed the king to Draga's flat and considered killing them both. Later that day, the three visited Antić at his flat and suggested that they kill the king together. The following day, the four of them plus Apis and two others, Lieutenants Milan Marinković and Nikodije Popović, met and adopted a plan, suggested by Apis, to murder the royal pair with poisoned daggers at a ball being held to celebrate Draga's birthday on 23 September. This plan as well as a second one came to nothing. Meanwhile Genčić, recently released from prison, agreed with his father-in-law Aleksa Novaković to act against the king. The officer-conspirators agreed on 14 November to enlist the help of politicians. On that day, Antić met with Genčić and they agreed to collaborate, thereby marking the first link between the civilian and military wings of the conspiracy, which thus began largely as familial revenge.[9] Since it was believed that older officers would be unwilling to carry out this putsch, the civilian conspirators chose to rely on the junior officers, among whom Genčić groomed his nephew to organise the plot.[10] Some of the older conspirators, in particular Atanacković, Mašin and Solarević, initially wanted to direct the conspiracy not against Aleksandar but solely against Draga, who would be expelled from Serbia; subsequently, to force Aleksandar to abdicate and expel both him and Draga. They apparently resisted the goal of murder until weeks before the putsch took place, but were eventually outvoted.[11] The younger and more radical conspirators—Apis, Antić and Aranđelović—feared that simply expelling the king would potentially enable him to enlist Austria-Hungary's support to regain his throne.[12] And since the military rank and file was still loyal to the king, the conspirators determined to rely on the junior officers alone, while the latter avoided informing their soldiers of the plot.[13] This chimed with their elitist inclinations: in Apis's words, 'Great ideas have always been the work of a few people.'[14]

Genčić organised a meeting at Novaković's vineyard at Topčider Hill, outside Belgrade, on 18 November, attended by himself, Novaković, Atanacković, Avakumović and Nikola Hadži-Toma, when it was resolved that the fatherland faced collapse, that Aleksandar was the principal culprit and that he would be murdered in punishment if necessary. It was agreed to offer the throne to Petar Karađorđević. He was not a popular choice among the conspirators; he was rumoured to be a drunk, while some of the younger officers had republican sympathies, including Antić, though it was understood that a republic would be unacceptable to the European powers, particularly Russia and Austria-Hungary. Genčić favoured importing a foreign dynasty, as Greece, Romania and Bulgaria had done, but was given to understand that Russia would not accept yet another German Balkan monarch, while Germany and Austria-Hungary would not accept a Russian one. The group entrusted Hadži-Toma with the task of meeting with Petar, whose schoolfriend he had been. Hadži-Toma met with Petar in late November and obtained his assent. Petar nevertheless refused direct involvement, noting it would be difficult to mount a 'bloody throne'. This was the pretender's only meeting with the conspirators prior to the murders.

Genčić met with between about thirteen and twenty young military conspirators in Antić's flat on 5 January 1902 and informed them that Petar 'accepted' the throne. It was agreed that some of them, including Apis and Antić, would be entrusted with recruiting more conspirators. To ensure their loyalty, all conspirators would have their names written on a list and be required to take an oath, composed by Apis: 'Foreseeing the definite collapse of the Fatherland, if the current situation continues for the shortest time, and naming as the principal culprits for everything King Aleksandar and his mistress Draga Mašin, we pledge and by our signatures commit that we shall kill them. On the Serbian throne, cleansed by the blood of these scoundrels, we shall place Petar Karađorđević, grandson of the Chief and son of the lawful Prince, the late Aleksandar Karađorđević.'[15] The young officer-conspirators acted on condition that the political wing of the conspiracy guaranteed there would be no dangerous international repercussions for Serbia. Antić later noted that if Aleksandar had had a brother, it would have been difficult to win acceptance for the Karađorđević dynasty among the largely Obrenovićite conspirators, but in the circumstances Petar was the only option. As for Montenegro's Prince Nikola, Apis and Antić agreed that if anyone tried to substitute him for Petar, they would blow him up in the Belgrade cathedral and blow the cathedral up with him, though a couple of the prominent conspirators apparently favoured his son Prince Mirko.[16] To avoid their suffering the same fate as Mihailo's assassins in 1868, it was agreed that the murders should be accompanied by a revolutionary change of government.

The circle of military conspirators would steadily increase while the civilian conspirators would not greatly expand beyond their initial intake, but the latter gave political focus to the former. The civilian conspirators were primarily former supporters of the personal regimes under Aleksandar and Milan: Genčić had been interior minister under Đorđević, responsible for the special court following the St John's Day attempt; Atanacković had been war minister in Đorđević's government; Novaković was a Progressive and had also supported the personal regime. Hadži-Toma was a Belgrade merchant and mostly unpolitical, but he had also supported the personal regime and had been conspiring with the Karađorđević family since the early 1880s. His father had been patriarch of the great Liberal Hadži-Toma family. The Hadži-Toma family was related by marriage to the Obrenović family, while two of Nikola's late brothers-in-law had been Ristić and Milojković; he thus linked the Liberal and Karađorđevićite wings of the conspiracy, which spread through familial and other personal connections.[17] A late recruit was Novaković's neighbour, the Progressive Dragomir Rajović, formerly president of the special court that tried the Timok rebels in 1883, nicknamed 'Bloody Rajovče', and vice-president of parliament under Đorđević; he had attempted to marshal Progressive support for Cincar-Marković's government, so his change of allegiance was last-minute. Vukašin Petrović, a Progressive on the conspiracy's fringes who had been a Liberal until 1880, had been finance minister in Đorđević's government. Živanović, a senior Liberal and close friend of Ristić's, appears also to have been a conspirator, though less ready than others to admit it. He had been economics minister in Đorđević's government and joined Cincar-Marković's government on 3 May 1903 as education minister; he was therefore a fence-sitter or, like Rajović, a rat deserting the sinking ship. Đorđević himself was not directly involved in the conspiracy but knew of it and gave it his blessing retrospectively.

The conspirators were therefore primarily Liberals seconded by a few Progressives, generally united by hostility to the Radicals; the one prominent civilian conspirator who had not been a supporter of the personal regime, Avakumović, had nevertheless spearheaded the authoritarian anti-Radical reaction in 1892–1893. The conspiracy's composition made Radicals unwilling to support it; both Pašić and the Independent Radical leader Ljubomir Živković resisted attempts to involve them, the latter on the grounds that the Independents did not wish to replace one dynasty with another. Pašić, informed of the date of the putsch, avoided being in Serbia when it happened, instead taking his family to the seaside in Austria-Hungary.

A ROYAL 'HONOUR KILLING'

Conversely, the conspirators viewed the Radicals as opportunistic collaborators who sustained Aleksandar's regime. Among the officers, Antić as Genčić's nephew and Apis as Živanović's brother-in-law were relatives of prominent Liberals, as was Damjan Popović.[18] Apis had been so upset by Aleksandar's 1893 coup toppling the Liberal regime of which his brother-in-law had been part that he had considered quitting the Military Academy.[19] Lieutenant Colonel Petar Mišić was recruited to the conspiracy as Popović's cousin, despite having been promoted and consequently trusted by Aleksandar.[20] Liberal leaders Ribarac and Vojislav Veljković were aware of the conspiracy but did nothing to stop it, despite Veljković having been Aleksandar's private secretary.[21] Aleksandar had begun his rule in 1893 with an anti-Liberal putsch and had thereafter generally sidelined the Liberals. The conspiracy to kill him was to some extent a backlash on their part.

Austria-Hungary had, since Milan's final departure from Serbia and Aleksandar's pivot to Russia, willingly hosted the anti-Aleksandar emigrants. One of the civilian conspirators, Petrović, as former finance minister, had close links with members of the Austro-Hungarian elite, including Austro-Hungarian finance minister Benjamin von Kállay, so could assure Genčić that Vienna would not oppose the putsch, whose organisers were largely Austrophiles. Three weeks before the putsch attempt, Kállay apparently told the British journalist Henry Wickham Steed that he should pay attention to Belgrade, because 'Master Aleksandar' only had perhaps just a few weeks left to live. The indications that neither Austria-Hungary nor Russia cared what happened to Aleksandar and Draga convinced the conspirators that they could kill the royal couple without fear of international ramifications.[22] Indeed, Vienna favoured Petar, son of Serbia's Austrophile ruler Prince Aleksandar. Petar conveyed the impression of being genuinely committed to good relations with Vienna in the event that he acceded to the throne.[23] Two members of Petar's close circle, his private secretary Živojin Balugdžić and his cousin and adjutant Jakov Nenadović, were effectively Austro-Hungarian agents. In a letter to Nenadović, intended for forwarding to the Austro-Hungarian foreign ministry to win Vienna's goodwill prior to the putsch, Petar wrote: 'By its geographic position, Serbia is required to have the best possible relations with the neighbouring Austro-Hungarian monarchy'; were he to become king, 'I will in the foreign policy of the country always maintain the established positions. I would also most energetically take care that the current status quo in the Balkans remain safeguarded.'[24] In return for letting him gain the throne, Petar may have agreed to Austria-Hungary's future annexation of Bosnia-Hercegovina.[25] Austria-Hungary's government also believed the Radicals disliked Petar and preferred his cousin Aleksa Karađorđević, grandson of Karađorđe's son Aleksa, though Vienna evaluated both Aleksa and his younger brother Božidar as being insufficiently capable to be king.[26]

The pro-Milan and Karađorđevićite emigrations on Austro-Hungarian soil consequently collaborated in Aleksandar's demise with Habsburg blessing. The young adventurer Rade Alavantić travelled to Vienna, met with Đorđević and was sent with his recommendation to Nenadović. Funded by the Karađorđevićite emigration, dressed in a general's uniform and with a small retinue, he staged on the night of 19–20 February 1902 a Karađorđevićite replay of the Obrenovićites' Hussar Rebellion of 1844, with an armed incursion from Sremska Mitrovica on Austro-Hungarian soil into Serbia near Šabac. Austria-Hungary's police made no attempt to stop him. He succeeded in putting the border guard under his command, entered Šabac and took control of its municipal office and command of its staff. He then attempted to seize the gendarme station, where he was shot dead by the commander; his dying words were 'Long live Karađorđević!' The fiasco nevertheless highlighted the array of the regime's enemies and the readiness of many junior officials to abandon it.[27]

The conspirators were emboldened by the savage attacks in the opposition—in particular, Independent Radical—press on Aleksandar and his regime, whose apparent unpopularity convinced them that their putsch would receive popular acceptance. They were infected by the nationalistic discourse that presented the king as betraying the Serbian national cause through his cautious and pacific foreign policy. In particular, the pillorying of Aleksandar as a tyrant personally unfit to govern destroyed his legitimacy among a considerable section of the population and created a mental climate conducive to regicide.[28] Those superstitious among the conspirators may also have been encouraged when, in June 1902, a storm of unparalleled strength uprooted the oak tree in Takovo under which Miloš had held the gathering in 1815 that launched the Second Serbian Uprising and the Obrenovićes' transformation into Serbia's ruling dynasty. The indefinite postponement of the king's visit to St Petersburg and the fall of the Vujić government in October 1902 further encouraged and catalysed the conspiracy. The circle of junior military conspirators consequently expanded during 1902 to the provincial garrisons; in particular, the Niš garrison provided recruits who later played leading roles either in the conspiracy itself or in the political faction that grew out of it, including Velimir Vemić and Božin Simić.

Socio-economic change and evolution of socialist thought

The socialist movement in Serbia, as we have seen, properly began with Svetozar Marković in the late 1860s and early 1870s, predating the emergence of an industrial proletariat. Marković's followers were an undifferentiated movement of socialists or radicals broadly subscribing to a populist, collectivist, anti-capitalist and anti-state ideology focusing on the peasantry. However, at the start of the 1880s, to conquer the peasant masses politically, the youthful Radical party abandoned its belief in collectivism to represent the class interests of the freeholders who made up most of the rural population. This presaged a split with those remaining loyal to socialism, represented initially by Dimitrije Cenić who, through his newspaper *Radnik*

(Worker), ignored the Progressive government to concentrate on attacking Pašić and the Radicals for their betrayal, for which he may have received a government subsidy. His socialist ideology found no audience among the peasant masses but did among high school students, workers and craftsmen.[29]

Workers and craftsmen constituted a growing class in Serbia in the 1880s and 1890s. Following Serbia's independence in 1878 and subsequent integration into the international economy, new factories sprang up in the country, financed by foreign capital.[30] An Austro-Hungarian company, at the Serbian government's invitation, established Serbia's first major woollen enterprise at Paraćin in 1882. The trade agreement with Austria-Hungary, by opening the empire to the virtually unfettered import of Serbian agricultural produce, spurred the emergence of factories devoted to the preparation of livestock products. Newly liberated Leskovac emerged as Serbia's third industrial centre alongside Belgrade and Kragujevac, linked to its trade with adjacent Ottoman lands and profits made from the purchase of Muslim property. A cloth spinnery began production there in 1897 and the town, as the heart of Serbia's textile industry, came to be nicknamed 'Serbian Manchester'. A wool mill opened at Karaburma on Belgrade's outskirts in 1898, a cotton-weaving factory opened at Užice at about the same time and a scarf and shawl factory opened at Niš in 1908. Eventually, a cotton-weaving factory with 220 power-looms was established at Leskovac in 1911.[31] Meanwhile in Serbia, between 1893 and 1900, the length of the railways grew from 540 kilometres to 5,708 kilometres, the number of mills rose from 105 to 181 and the number of mines from 16 employing 758 workers to 36 employing 2,190. The number of industrial enterprises increased by 174.5 per cent in 1900–1908 while that of industrial workers rose by 351.1 per cent in the same period.[32]

After independence, Serbia's rural population grew owing to an excess of births over deaths and immigration from neighbouring lands. This resulted in peasant plots both shrinking and multiplying, as family land was divided between sons, and in a growing rural proletariat.[33] The oak forests that had traditionally covered and characterised Serbia had largely disappeared: whereas 25 per cent of the surface area of Serbia comprised forested land in 1867, this had shrunk to 10 per cent by 1897, of which only a quarter was oak.[34] This meant the end of the acorns that had traditionally fed Serbia's pigs, making it harder for smallholders to sustain traditional animal husbandry. The transition from a pastoral to an agricultural economy based on arable farming involved rural economic decline; the per capita output of farming in Serbia fell by 27.5 per cent between the early 1870s and 1910–1912.[35] This transition resulted in a shortage of meat and manure and a consequent drop in the quality of grain as well as of the peasant diet; it was 'a time when the peasant literally lived off bread'.[36] The average lifespan of a man in the countryside in 1903 was 49.69 years and of a woman 41.74 years, while in the towns it was 50.93 and 40.66 respectively; death was particularly common for newborns, small children and women giving birth.[37] At this time, approximately 83 per cent of the population was still illiterate. Despite the laws passed to protect the peasantry and the rise of the agricultural cooperative movement, high taxes and heavy indebtedness forced many peasants to sell their lands.[38] The number of industrial workers was consequently swollen by the growing numbers fleeing rural poverty.[39] The size and number of towns grew steadily, with those such as Niš, Kragujevac, Leskovac, Šabac and Požarevac increasing their population by around 25–40 per cent in the period 1884–1900, while Belgrade nearly doubled in size. Yet the recent peasant background of many of their inhabitants gave many towns a rural character, with townspeople keeping pigs and cows and growing corn in their yards, taking the resulting produce weekly to the marketplace in the town centre.[40]

Serbia was nevertheless witnessing dramatic signs of modernisation. The telephone made its appearance in Belgrade in 1883 because it had been used by the Austro-Hungarian army the year before in Hercegovina during the uprising there; it was initially for purely military use, but a public telephone system was introduced in 1889.[41] An agreement was signed with a Milanese company and adopted by the Belgrade city council on 24–28 July 1891 to begin the installation of electric street lights in Belgrade, though this happened only over years and in the face of considerable opposition, partly due to the poor quality of the lighting introduced. The first tram in Belgrade began to operate on 1 October 1892; although they were initially horse-drawn, electrification of the city's trams began in November 1894.[42] The first loan for the building of a modern infrastructure involving sewers, cobblestoned streets and an aqueduct was raised by Belgrade in 1891, though this reconstruction was not completed until 1911, partly due to social-conservative resistance in parliament to the capital's modernisation along European lines.[43] The first movie in Belgrade, indeed in the Balkans, was shown on 6 June 1896; the first mobile cinemas visited the city in 1898 and 1899.[44] The first permanent cinema was opened in the city in December 1907, providing citizens with a window to the outside world. In 1911, Svetozar Botorić (1857–1916) produced the first Serbian feature film, about Karađorđe's life.[45] The first automobile appeared in Belgrade in April 1903, bought by a rich Serb in Austria-Hungary and delivered by train, much to the citizenry's alarm. It was purchased from its original owner by King Petar in 1906; there were about fifty automobiles owned by rich citizens in 1912.[46] The Great School was formally transformed into the University of Belgrade on 27 February 1905, with faculties of theology, philosophy, law, medicine and technology; female students were permitted to enrol, and in 1912 female graduates in philosophy were permitted to take the exam qualifying them to become professors. By 1914, women comprised 10.7 per cent of students at the university.[47]

Domestic handicrafts such as rope-making, that had been widespread and upon which many households relied, collapsed as the large Ottoman market, to which Serbia belonged until 1878 and across which its craftsmen had peddled their wares, was replaced by smaller states with tariff barriers protecting their producers, while factories arose producing the same goods more cheaply. Foreign mass-produced industrial goods flooded into Serbia; wooden cutlery fashioned by domestic craftsmen was replaced by cheap factory-produced metal alternatives while traditional clothes and shoes made by domestic tailors and shoemakers, particularly from animal hides and furs, were squeezed out by competition from factory-produced European clothes. As a result, Serbs dressed and looked more like other Europeans. The consequent decline of the traditional guild system dating back to Miloš's era involved the beginnings of the modern workers' movement, as guild masters responded to their increasing obsolescence with increased exploitation of their apprentices and journeymen, who frequently went unpaid altogether and responded with strikes and boycotts. The working day in trade and crafts generally lasted ten to sixteen hours, sometimes longer, with fourteen hours considered normal, though in industry and mining it was somewhat shorter at ten to twelve hours. The decreasing ability of the countryside to sustain its population, coupled with a high birth rate, resulted in many children entering the workforce; though the 1910 law on handicraft banned the employment of children younger than fourteen, two years later 60 per cent of apprentices in handicrafts and industry were still under fourteen while children as young as eight were not infrequently employed in factories.[48]

Serbian socialist thought in the 1880s and 1890s, represented by Cenić and his followers, expressed itself as a reaction against the social change that economic development was bringing. Serbian revolutionaries remained heavily influenced by their Russian counterparts; Cenić was influenced by the Russian nihilist revolutionary Sergey Nechayev (1847–1882). His split with the Radicals roughly corresponded to the split in contemporary Russia between the People's Will (Narodnaya Volya) and the Narodniks—the latter were peaceful populists; the former extremist, voluntarist terrorists who assassinated Tsar Alexander II in 1881. Cenić himself had been arrested in Paris in October 1873 on suspicion of planning to assassinate Milan, who was visiting the French capital.[49] His socialism was harsh and xenophobic; he blamed the influx of foreign capital for the phenomenon of 'foreignness' in Serbian society. Lamenting the decline of the zadruga, he looked to the state to protect Serbia from the 'flood from the West', organise social production and prevent Serbian society's division into classes. As Latinka Perović writes, 'Such Serbian socialism was not the expression of the interests of an exploited class, but the necessary means to safeguard the nation.' Cenić wrote in 1887: 'It would not be bad if the members of the union of peasants and craftsmen gave an oath that everyone with their family wore Serbian clothes, made only from Serbian produce; that nobody takes for his wife a girl who does not make her own clothing; who does not sow hemp, weave and knit; who is not a good landlady and hostess. And only the municipality can prohibit dressing up in foreign rags, as our municipalities have often changed fashions and costumes on the basis of agreements between notables and the examples of their women.' Cenić viewed Austro-Hungarian Serbs as degenerate: 'foreignness ... has entered into all the veins of the Serb nation: their language has been corrupted or broken; clothing destroyed; customs perverted; from other Serbs alienated—all that remains of the Austrian Serb is that he is called a Serb, nothing else'.[50]

For Cenić, the struggle against capitalism was Serbia's national struggle against foreign domination and corruption:

> Foreigners will destroy us both economically and politically and in our place will come other nations, economically more developed than us. The economic struggle of Serbia against the foreign flood must be a struggle against the bourgeois order; against bourgeois-ness; and since that bourgeois-ness comes to us from outside, from foreign nations, then this is a national struggle of the Serbian nation against foreignness, equated with the fundamental tenets of socialism. Those socialist statesmen and patriots who want to halt the foreign flood and raise the Serbian nation must, as regards the economy, hold to socialist tenets.[51]

Linked to this, Cenić consistently stressed the need for Serb unification: 'But we want to be master in our own home and to unite in a decisively free state. Montenegro, Serbia, Bosnia, Hercegovina, Old Serbia, Dalmatia, Srem and all Vojvodina must form one state, for they are one nation ... To unite all Serbs in one state, which is to be erected on the basis of equality, freedom and brotherhood: there, that is our programme as regards the national question ...' Following Marković, Cenić believed that the Obrenović state's bureaucratisation and militarism were destroying the Serb spirit outside Serbia, and he favoured a revolution in the Ottoman and Habsburg empires to achieve Serb unity.[52] His hostility to the Serbian dynastic state was aggravated by his experience of police harassment and imprisonment in the 1870s; he had even been held in chains. He published his memoir of these experiences in 1881, listing among his persecutors the man who had jailed him: Panta Lunjevica, Šabac's mayor and Draga's father.[53]

This combined socialist-nationalist opposition to an oppressive state and to foreign capitalist penetration placed Serbia's socialists of the 1880s not in diametric opposition to the 'bourgeois' parties but at one end of a spectrum that it shared with them. Hence the political evolution of Cenić's sometime comrade Dragiša Stanojević, whose family was related to the Karađorđevićes and suffered the regency's repression following Mihailo's assassination. A socialist of a more liberal ideological background, Stanojević agreed with Cenić that the development of capitalism threatened Serbia's independence and that therefore national interests and the need for socialism dovetailed.[54] As he wrote in 1885, 'we Serbs in the front row are faced with being flooded and crushed with the onslaught from the West'; this would 'manifest itself in the form of Western capital', which would be imported by the railways built solely in its interests. Against this, 'We maintain that all who speak Serbian (or Croatian), and all south Slavs except Bulgaria and Rumelia, therefore, all Serb and Croat lands, all Slav regions, all Macedonia, all northern Albania, in a word all lands between Vidin and the Adriatic Sea, between Ljubljana and Salonika, become constituent parts of Great Serbia.' For 'Bulgaria, Rumelia, independent Serbia, Romania, Montenegro and Greece have shown Europe the possibility of Christian, free, modern, legal states on the Balkan peninsula', while the 'further survival of Turkish, non-Christian rule becomes redundant and the end of that Asian regime is simply a matter of time'.[55] Since, 'if modern capitalism ever develops in Serbia it will of necessity be un-Serbian', and given the 'war, peaceful and civil, of foreign capital against Serbia', it was a 'question of national survival' for Serbs to build the 'organisation of Serbian production by state means'. The zadruga was to be protected as society's foundation while 'Education is to be moral and physical, in order to raise a generation of noble, firm and handsome character; a generation of men of heroic hearts and strong muscles and a generation of women worthy of such husbands'.[56] Stanojević differed from Cenić in supporting an entryist strategy in relation to the Radical party, which he joined in 1886, becoming one of its parliamentary representatives.[57]

Cenić and Pelagić established a socialist youth movement in the teacher training school in Belgrade in the early 1880s, paralleling other workers' cooperative societies. These had begun appearing in the early 1870s for different groups of craftsmen and workers such as cobblers, tailors, print workers and others, to support members affected by illness, death, injury at work or unemployment. Cenić died in 1888, but his followers established a craftsmen association in Kragujevac in 1889, from which emerged a craftsmen and workers' union in 1892. Pelagić inherited de facto leadership of the socialist movement, but he was declared mad by Avakumović's Liberal government in March 1893 and imprisoned in the Belgrade lunatic asylum, to be liberated in the popular upsurge following Aleksandar's coup in April. However, two years later, as an archimandrite, he was dragged to the Belgrade cathedral and defrocked. He was released in 1897, but state persecution of the socialist movement increased under Đorđević's government from October of that year and it was effectively crushed following the St John's Day attempt. Pelagić died in prison in Požarevac in 1899 and other prominent socialists were prosecuted or fled abroad. This marked the end of the movement's leadership by Marković's generation. Yet the workers' cooperatives were a rising phenomenon and some were politically radical. For example, the Society of Shoemaking Workers for Mental Development and Fraternal Assistance was founded at Kragujevac on 2 January 1898, for the purpose of resolving disputes between workers and employers and organising the 1 May celebrations; it sent delegates to the international socialist Second International.[58] Strikes increasingly became a feature of labour relations. Serbia at the time of the conspiracy was therefore undergoing significant socio-economic change, reflected in the appearance of a labour movement. These factors contributed to the atmosphere of portentous crisis that enveloped and drove the conspiracy.

SERBIA

'March disturbances'

The socialist movement experienced a rebirth in the liberalising conditions following the fall of the 11 October regime. Rade Dragović founded the Serbian social-democratic movement proper; born in 1878, three years after Svetozar Marković's death, he represented a new generation and outlook. The rebirth involved a growing split between those who favoured a more reformist, cross-class political movement oriented towards collaboration with the Independents as the principal left-wing 'bourgeois' party and those who, influenced by their links with comrades abroad, pursued a revolutionary Marxist path. Dragović, representing the second current, founded the Belgrade Workers' Society in March 1901. An illegal political leadership of the fledgling socialist workers' movement, the Central Council, in which both currents were represented, was founded in May 1902. Soon after, however, the two currents split completely. The principal representatives of the reformist current, Jovan Skerlić and Dragiša Lapčević, drifted towards the Independents and their newspaper *Odjek*, for which Lapčević wrote.[59] Dragović meanwhile rejected cooperation with the Independents, insisting that workers keep their revolutionary class party pure, and his view on the national question evolved in a more internationalist direction. Following anti-Serb riots in Croatia in August–September 1902, Dragović wrote that the 'Serb and Croat peasants had nothing to fight about; they are equally downtrodden, deprived of rights and hungry; their misery is the same and their enemies are the same. And their enemies are those who chant about "Great Serbia" and "Great Croatia", of [Serbian Tsar] Dušan and [Croatian King] Zvonimir, while smothering their own people and keeping them in misery and ignorance. We socialists respect the ideal of national equality.'[60]

Socialists were nevertheless ready to collaborate with radical nationalists against Aleksandar's regime. Fearing another royal coup in early April 1903, the socialist club of students attempted to rally other student clubs to join them in opposing it, but according to the account of one of the ringleaders, Triša Kaclerović, the Radical club refused to participate while the Independent club initially agreed but then dropped out, fearing it would take an extreme form. Thus, the student opposition was left in the hands of a coalition of socialists led by Kaclerović and Dimitrije Tucović and 'a group of nationalist youth around Ljubo Jovanović-Čupa', who resolved to involve Belgrade's workers and citizenry as much as possible.[61] The consequent demonstration of workers, shop assistants and high school students, numbering initially about 150 but swelling to about 5,000, in whose organisation the Central Council played a leading role, rocked Belgrade on 5 April 1903. Jovanović-Čupa later became a guerrilla in Macedonia and founder of the Black Hand, while Tucović became a leading Social Democrat. These two led the crowd, emitting cries of 'Long live the constitution!', 'Down with the king!', 'Down with the queen!' and 'Long live the republic!', right up to the gendarme cordon guarding the palace.[62] When they could advance no further, they began pelting the gendarmes with stones. According to Belgrade police chief Božo Maršićanin's account, 'There was not an official or a gendarme who was not struck at least once!'[63]

On Aleksandar's order, firemen with hoses were deployed to disperse the demonstrators, but these were driven off by a hail of stones. The police acted with restraint; however, after the demonstrators had failed in their goal of reaching the palace and Tucović had declared the demonstration over, a demonstrator was wounded in a confrontation with a policeman, after which shots were fired from the crowd at the police, some of whom returned fire on their own initiative. According to construction minister Pavle Denić's testimony, Aleksandar had not ordered the shooting and was greatly shaken by the sound of gunfire from the streets.[64] Maršićanin, fearing control was being lost, requested the army's assistance. War minister Pavlović ordered the deployment of the army but not the use of force. Prime minister Cincar-Marković, according to his widow's testimony, authorised Maršićanin to allow the gendarmes to use their weapons in self-defence but prohibited any killing.[65] Stevan Ilić, commander of the 6th Regiment and a conspirator, initially disobeyed a verbal order to disperse the demonstrators, demanding that it be put in writing. He subsequently claimed that by the time he appeared with his troops on the street, the demonstrators had already started to disperse because it was already dark, not because of the army. He was sentenced to 30 days' house arrest for insubordination. Some officers, including other conspirators, fraternised with the crowd. A cavalry squadron commander ordered his horsemen not to trample the crowd, earning a cheer from it, and his squadron did not intervene in the fighting. Nevertheless, the army's appearance combined with rain dispersed the demonstrators. In total, four demonstrators were killed and seven wounded, while two gendarmes were wounded heavily and seventeen to nineteen lightly. About 120 demonstrators were arrested but all but about twenty were quickly released.[66]

Tucović's older brother Vladimir was an officer and conspirator; thus, the Tucović brothers linked the conspirators and socialists. A second link was provided by another pair of brothers: conspirator Čedomir Popović and his younger brother Dušan, a gymnasium pupil and friend of Tucović's. A third link was Balugdžić, a socialist, who was Petar's personal secretary and in touch with the conspirators. Apparently, Apis himself enjoyed close links with the high school students, workers and shop assistants and had a cell of collaborators in the Great School.[67] Kaclerović's memoir of the event demonstrates the common ground between the two groups of regime opponents; in his view, the conspirators were 'patriots who loved their country' and viewed Draga as a 'common prostitute'.[68] The laws governing trade unions would be significantly liberalised following the putsch that ended Aleksandar's regime two months later. These factors laid the basis for a peculiar love-hate relationship in the years to come between the socialists and officer-conspirators; bitterly opposed to each other over issues of the day, they shared a commitment to the legacy of the putsch and hostility to its enemies. This had lasting implications for Serbian political culture.

The events of 5 April showed that the army's loyalty to Aleksandar was uncertain; this emboldened the conspirators. Although the security forces had behaved with restraint and had not fired first, the opposition used the bloodshed to damn Aleksandar as a 'bloody' tyrant. The king, shaken by his army's unreliability, carried out his fourth and final *coup d'état* the day after the demonstration, suspending the constitution for three-quarters of an hour, during which he dismissed the majority-Radical senators and state councillors appointed during his alliance with the Radicals and purged the courts and municipalities of their supporters. He appointed twelve new councillors of which six were Liberals, five Progressives and one a soldier, and twenty-four new senators of which ten were Liberals, nine Progressives and five soldiers. He reactivated the laws on the press and municipalities of the Progressive regime of 1881–1885.[69] The royal coup was then proclaimed on 7 April, intended to provide Aleksandar with a loyal administration for him and his new government.

Aleksandar sent his agent, the former Radical firebrand Pera Todorović, on a fact-finding mission across Serbia in late March and early April. Todorović reported back that, whereas the Radical leadership was bent on absolute power, the base was more concerned with municipal self-government and low taxes. The king consequently sought to marginalise the Radical leadership by co-opting the party's local cadres and base, whose demands he sought to meet. This policy was extended to the Liberal and Progressive parties as the king sought a path for his model of enlightened non-party government.[70] It registered some success in parliamentary elections on 1 June, which were boycotted by both Old and Independent Radicals. Despite the apparent scandal of the killing of demonstrators and suspension of the constitution, these elections were undeniably won by the regime, albeit helped by police manipulation: 72 pro-regime Liberals, 34 pro-regime Progressives, 24 Court Radicals and no opposition candidates were elected. This pro-regime coalition secured 180,000 votes—more than had been won by the Radical–Progressive fusion—indicating the regime's success at co-opting much of the Radical electorate.[71]

The reinforced personal regime was nevertheless still incapable of combating the conspiracy. Cincar-Marković and the king's first adjutant General Petrović were unable to believe police reports of their fellow officers' involvement in a plot to kill the royal couple. They considered it their duty to protect their officers from the police. Draga was herself apparently frustrated at Aleksandar's disregard of the police's warnings.[72] However, when Aleksandar eventually demanded that Cincar-Marković court-martial a group of officers whom he suspected of being conspirators, the prime minister refused and threatened to resign.[73] He and Petrović possessed a code of honour not shared by the younger officer-conspirators, and both paid for it with their lives. Apis, through his close friendship with Cincar-Marković's son-in-law Captain Jovan Miljković, and Antić, through his friendship with war minister

A ROYAL 'HONOUR KILLING'

Pavlović, spread the falsehood among the regime notables that the conspiracy did not exist. This reassured Aleksandar, who also rejected security measures suggested by Maršićanin, fearing that innocent officers would be persecuted. These included the suggestion that he dismiss his adjutant, Mihailo Naumović, whom Maršićanin suspected but the king trusted absolutely, to his cost.[74]

'May putsch'

The conspirators resolved to attack the royal palace and murder the royal couple on the night of 10–11 June (28–29 May by the old calendar—hence 'May putsch'). This was the anniversary of Mihailo's assassination 35 years before: it was probably a coincidence, although Vladimir Jovanović claims one of the conspirators told him the date was chosen because it was 'fatal for the Obrenovićes'.[75] The final decision was taken only the night before, 9 June; the conspirators acted quickly and under pressure as they feared being uncovered. Damjan Popović, relocated to Serbia's interior as a suspected conspirator, was supposed to return to the capital to direct the proceedings but did not do so: either he feared alerting the regime, or he was confused over whether the date chosen was the 10th or 11th, or he simply had cold feet.[76] Mašin consequently replaced him. Twenty-eight officer-conspirators gathered on the night at the Officers' Club, where some drank heavily. At about two o'clock, led by Apis, they set off for the palace. They were joined by a detachment of troops under Captain Ljubomir Kostić; he was not wholly trusted by Apis, who assigned Second Lieutenant Josif Kostić to watch over him and kill him if he threatened to betray them.[77] The failure of Mišić to arrive punctually with his own battalion caused some consternation, which Apis overrode to order the operation to proceed regardless.

The posse marched the 550 yards to the palace where they were met by Mišić with his troops. Their late arrival was allegedly due to his last-minute vacillation over whether to participate; one of his subordinate officer-conspirators, Marinković, had apparently threatened to kill the 'dog', as he called him at the time, to make him move.[78] The palace gates into the courtyard were opened for them by Lieutenant Petar Živković (1879–1947), later Yugoslavia's prime minister. He claimed subsequently to have been a late, timid conspirator recruited only in March 1903 by Antić, whose close friend he was, because he had been disgusted by the royal couple's behaviour, such as kissing in front of himself and other officers. Živković was deeply distrusted by the principal officer-conspirators and was coerced into adding his signature to the secret list of participants.[79] Some accounts suggest Živković arrived late to open the gates, was so afraid that he took a long time to unlock them and was then pushed to the ground as the conspirators entered—a humiliation that allegedly planted the seeds for his subsequent break with Apis.[80] But another account has Živković acting resolutely to order the guards away from the gates to allow his fellow conspirators entry, only later manufacturing the tale of his cowardice in order to distance himself from the act.[81]

Entering the palace building, the conspirators confronted duty officer Captain Miljković, whose officer's honour had led him to refuse either to join the conspiracy or to betray his fellow officers who had invited him. The king had offered Miljković the night off since his wife was about to give birth, but he refused, and, refusing also his supposed friend Apis's attempt to persuade him to surrender, he was shot dead while attempting to resist the conspirators. They then shot dead the duty adjutant Naumović, himself a key conspirator whom his fellows had failed to recognise; his last words were allegedly 'Not me!'[82] Naumović's death complicated matters; he had been supposed to unlock the door to the king's chamber but the key was not found on his body. The door was consequently blown open with dynamite; however, the king and queen were not there. While looking for them, Apis came up against two guards who shot and seriously wounded him. The conspirators succeeded in trapping Petrović in his lodge, whence he shot at them until they forced his surrender. They made him help search for the royal couple, but though he knew where they were hidden and though the conspirators threatened to kill him, he did not betray them.

Troops under Mišić and Captain Kostić meanwhile overcame the resistance of Aleksandar's loyal forces outside the palace, which suffered some casualties. Nevertheless, the failure to locate the king and queen caused consternation among the conspirators within, who considered levelling the palace altogether using cannon. Živković later claimed he dissuaded them from this on the grounds that it would cause the deaths of all the soldiers and guardsmen within.[83] Consequently, to prevent any counter-attack by loyalist forces of the kind that had undone Mihailo's murderers, Mašin ordered the assassinations of prime minister Cincar-Marković, war minister Pavlović and the Radical interior minister Velimir Todorović, who had all been placed under surveillance in their homes at the start of the putsch and of whom only the last survived, though heavily wounded. Pavlović's son-in-law Božidar Janković, subsequently a leading Serbian commander in the Balkan Wars, left his house to see what was happening at his father-in-law's, but was threatened with death and led away at gunpoint. Draga's two brothers, officers Nikola and Nikodije Lunjevica, were murdered gratuitously: arrested without a struggle, they were held for a while in a room at a military building, where they were permitted to smoke. Later, Second Lieutenant Vojislav Tankosić, on Mašin's orders, arrived with a group of soldiers, took the brothers out into the courtyard and executed them by firing squad.[84] According to their sister Ana's testimony, their corpses were then looted and their pocket watches, boots and rings stolen; one of Nikola's fingers was cut off to remove its ring.[85] Antić with an infantry platoon, likewise on Mašin's orders, escorted Genčić to the interior ministry, which he commandeered. Genčić immediately began issuing orders by writing and telephone, delivering the state into the conspirators' hands.[86]

A ROYAL 'HONOUR KILLING'

The king and queen were hiding behind a concealed portal in their chamber. According to one account, when Draga looked out of her bedroom window to call for help, Captain Kostić fired at her with his revolver, wounding her in the arm, and her scream alerted the conspirators inside to her location.[87] Another account suggests Second Lieutenant Velimir Vemić noticed the portal by chance after it had already been passed at least once. Petrović tried to distract the conspirators from it, but after they had determined to break into it, he realised the game was up and called to the royal couple: 'Your majesty! It is I, your Laza. Open up to your officers!' The king replied, 'Can I count on the oath of my officers?', to which Vemić replied, 'No way!' and another conspirator, 'You can!', after which the royal couple emerged in their nightclothes, 'tightly holding each other, as if joined in one, two white shadows glimmering in the dark like ghosts'. According to Mišić's account, the king 'held himself bravely and threatened that he would take bloody revenge on them all'. Captain Mihailo Ristić, who had asked from the start to perform the murder personally, attempted to attack Draga, whereupon Petrović pulled out a revolver he had concealed since his capture and fired at and wounded him, then snatched away his pistol, before being cut down by the other conspirators. Mišić recalls: 'It is not true that the king and General Laza Petrović behaved like cowards. They were true heroes and I felt sorry for them, but that was how it had to be.'[88]

Draga and Aleksandar were shot to pieces by Ristić, Vemić and Captain Ilija Radivojević; as she was shot, the queen allegedly fell in front of the king, as if attempting to shield him with her body. After shooting the royal couple to death and riddling the corpses with bullets, the conspirators then stripped them naked and repeatedly slashed them with their sabres until they were mutilated virtually beyond recognition, after which one of them allegedly shouted, 'There, now show your brat; your heir; you cow!'[89] According to Vladimir Jovanović, Radivojević told him how the gunshots had brought other conspirators to the scene, and they agreed that each of them should be allowed one slash of the sabre on the bodies, so that they could claim they had killed them all together.[90] The corpses were then thrown out of the palace window; Ristić subsequently claimed he did this to demonstrate to Aleksandar's troops outside that he was dead, to discourage them from counterattacking.[91] According to the admittedly hostile testimony of a fellow conspirator, Milutin Lazarević, in the aftermath of the 1917 Salonika trial, Mišić had not attended the murder but, upon being informed that the royal couple were dead, 'went to their dead bodies and, growling like a dog, shot at their dead bodies. Milutin was horrified; he completely froze at that savage sight and at Mišić's physiognomy.'[92]

A revolver in each hand, Mišić ran before the troops to inform them that the king and queen were dead, shouting 'Long live Petar Karađorđević!' This helped end resistance from Aleksandar's loyal troops. The royal couple's naked corpses were left where they had fallen for about four hours before being removed and buried at St Mark's Church in Belgrade. The conspirators thoroughly ransacked the palace for treasure until it resembled 'a field of planted potatoes'. The queen's 'intimate wardrobe' was not spared. Rings were removed from the corpses' fingers, some of which were hacked off in the process. One of the conspirators then proudly displayed in public a ring on his hand, saying that he had taken it 'as a memento for Queen Draga'. Vemić was subsequently infamous for carrying about with him as a trophy a piece of her flesh that he had cut from one of her breasts. Draga's possessions were auctioned off as far away as Vienna and London; one of her wardrobes was bought by the Austro-Hungarian ambassador's wife.[93] Antić claims he took nothing himself except one of Aleksandar's royal stamps 'as a memento of that night'.[94]

Maršićanin had, by his own account, been awakened by the gunfire at the palace but suspected it might have been the doing of Aleksandar himself, launching another coup. He phoned the palace, but through some accident of the telephone exchange he was put through to war minister Pavlović, whose presence at the other end of the line reassured him that the palace was not threatened. After he subsequently heard that the interior and war ministers had been murdered, he tried to phone the on-duty member of the general police to dispatch a force of gendarmes to the palace, but the phone was apparently answered by Genčić, who told him that Aleksandar and Draga had been killed and a provisional government had taken power, and warned him to ensure order in the city.[95] As the commander of the Danube Division, Colonel Dimitrije Nikolić, was feared by the conspirators as a brave officer loyal to the king, Lieutenant Ljubomir Vulović was assigned to assassinate him at his home. Nikolić nevertheless evaded Vulović, armed himself and set off to the garrison at Banjica, on the edge of Belgrade, to initiate military counter-measures. By this time, control of the Danube Division had been seized by the conspirators under Solarević, who phoned Nikolić and informed him of Aleksandar's death and of his dismissal. Nikolić requested a personal meeting with representatives of the conspirators as a prerequisite to surrendering. When these representatives approached him, they opened fire; Nikolić was heavily wounded but managed to shoot two of his assailants fatally. One of the two had been a conspirator; the other simply a friend and fellow officer of the first who had met him by chance earlier that morning and decided to accompany him on the adventure, a spur-of-the-moment decision that cost him his life. The third assailant, another conspirator, then took control of Nikolić's troops after informing them that Aleksandar and Draga were dead.[96] Thus ended the resistance of the security forces.

Colonel Živojin Mišić, commander of the Drina Division based in Valjevo and loyal to Aleksandar, sought merely to ensure the security of his troops and the civilians in his charge. He was informed of the regicides at four o'clock in the morning of the putsch by a telegram from Atanacković. He responded by recalling his troops to barracks and appointing guards. The conspirators sent Luka Lazarević's brother-in-law Captain Đuro Dokić with a detachment of troops to Mišić's headquarters to keep a close watch on him. Mišić recalls that as they learned of the regicides,

A ROYAL 'HONOUR KILLING'

the citizens of Valjevo spontaneously hung black flags on their homes. Mišić then received a telegram from the district chief in Obrenovac, who reported that an officer, conspirator Lieutenant Tihomir Stojanović, had appeared there brandishing a revolver and ordered that all black flags be removed and replaced with tricolours, threatening that he was leaving for Šabac but would soon return and that 'insofar as in Obrenovac everything were not carried out as he had ordered, he would kill everyone'. Mišić telephoned Atanacković to complain about the officer and inform him that he would send a battalion to protect Šabac's citizens if necessary. Atanacković was apparently embarrassed but ordered Mišić not to send the battalion.[97]

On the morning after the putsch, 11 June, the city, decked in flags, was in the army's hands, with triumphant, drunken soldiers roaming the streets. Metropolitan Inoćentije was among those who decked his residence in flags, even though he had been related to and friendly with the murdered Cincar-Marković. Although he had enjoyed the king's great sympathy, he refused to perform rites for the deceased and immediately terminated the prayer for them at the church. In a speech at the cathedral, he praised the nation for showing 'maturity' through its 'calm and dignified bearing'—behaviour that earned a sharp protest from the Russian Orthodox Church, which held a dirge for the dead king at the Kazan Cathedral in St Petersburg.[98] The Independent leaders cheered the regicides. Ljubomir Stojanović—released from prison following the announcement of Aleksandar's engagement, when he had gratefully shouted 'Long live Queen Draga!'—was reported in the early morning of the putsch to have run around Belgrade spreading the false story that the king and queen, 'whom the Serb nation had never loved', had killed each other in a gunfight involving their own troops. Prodanović subsequently mocked Draga in *Odjek* as 'a woman, to whom even Justinian's Theodora had not been equal!'—a reference to the sixth-century Byzantine empress demonised for her alleged sexual depravity.[99] Jovan Žujović, an Independent who refused to endorse the murders, nevertheless admitted *Odjek*'s ferocious polemics had created the climate for them: 'The army killed King Aleksandar because we at *Odjek*, with our fire, killed him morally.'[100] The Independents therefore reprised the role of the Old Liberals, whose agitation in the late 1860s had created the climate conducive to Mihailo's assassination. However, power in Serbia did not pass to the moral killers. Foreign observers perceived that real power on the morning after the putsch lay in the hands of Mašin and Petar Mišić and that the city resembled a 'giant madhouse'.[101] In Maršićanin's words, 'When dawn rose properly, hired children crowded the streets and applauded! And over Belgrade, rain fell heavily – God wept!'[102]

Historical autopsy of the regicide

According to Radovan M. Drašković, an early sympathiser and subsequently a critical historian of Apis's circle, 'So many excess bullets fired, mutilation with sabres and the throwing of the corpses through the window, demonstrate not the gentleness and nobility of the people who did this but their savagery and barbarity.'[103] Or as Mijatović wrote a few years after the act, 'The poor woman, Queen Draga, was especially the object of their revolting cruelty. I cannot describe the horrible, disgusting and ferocious conduct of some of those murderers. They seemed to emulate the exploits of Jack-the-Ripper on the dead body of the woman who was their Queen. As I write these lines, I feel utter shame and humiliation that Servian officers could have conducted themselves with such brutal cruelty!'[104] Pera Todorović recalled in his diary how an unnamed conspirator was haunted by the crime to the point of mental illness: 'He as a conspirator played a leading role. Now his mind was tormented. In his delirium, he frequently mentioned Queen Draga: "Oh, my head hurts so much! How my head hurts. I'll go and see Queen Draga; I'll beg her to forgive me and then my head will no longer hurt. She will forgive me!"'[105] Todorović believed the murders were qualitatively different from others in Serbian history: 'The Obrenovićes were not saints. On the contrary, the last two Obrenovićes, King Milan and King Aleksandar, had many faults and weak sides which can seriously be evaluated and criticised. But this criticism cannot justify this bestial massacre of a whole host of people, that ripping up of a dead woman and that brutal throwing through a window of the dead bodies of the slain king and queen.'[106]

The macabre nature of the murders left their mark even upon those not present. Milan Stojadinović, sometime Yugoslav prime minister, recalled sixty years later: 'This tragedy of the royal couple made a deep impression upon me. Only a short time before that, I had seen them in their glory, happy one beside the other, on the balcony of the gymnasium, and now they both lay dead in the street, as in those days mad dogs were dealt with in Užice. And many of those, who had rejoiced in their visit to the town, now equally rejoiced in their death.'[107] The Jerseyan authoress Elinor Glynn was sufficiently moved by Draga's murder to pen her famous romantic novel, *Three Weeks*. Its anonymous heroine was a Russian–Balkan queen modelled on both Draga and Natalija, murdered after having an affair with a much younger man, with the murder's date pointedly given as 29 May: 'And so, as ever, the woman paid the price.'[108] International opinion was outraged and Serbia's reputation seriously damaged. The British newspaper *John Bull* recalled the regicide following the assassination of Franz Ferdinand in 1914, opining on 11 July: 'We have always looked upon Servia as a hot bed of cold-blooded conspiracy and subterfuge—the ringleaders being the scoundrels who compassed the assassination and destruction of the late king and queen of the country', and concluding, 'Servia must be wiped out.' And on 8 August:

> We should like to see Servia receive a trouncing equal to her crimes. We do not forget the utter indifference shown by her people after the bloody infamy of Machin, Mishich, Angelkovich, Kostich, Lazarevich, Dimitrievich, Radivokevich, Saurich and the rest of them, who murdered King Alexander and the beautiful Queen Draga in

A ROYAL 'HONOUR KILLING'

cold blood, hacked, outraged and mutilated their bodies like fiendish butchers, and threw them through the window of the Palace into the grounds below, there to writhe in death agonies unspeakable from darkness until dawn ... Servia must be wiped out. Let Servia be removed from the map of Europe ... To Hell with Servia![109]

During the Salonika trial of 1917 in which Vemić was a defendant, the rumour circulated among Serbian officials, and was picked up by their French counterparts, that he had raped the queen; General Maurice Sarrail, supreme Allied commander on the Salonika front, apparently believed that Vemić 'beat to death, then raped Queen Draga', suggesting a necrophilic act.[110] The biographers of Prince Pavle Karađorđević, Petar's ten-year-old nephew and subsequently Yugoslavia's regent in the 1930s, record that he was 'present when the messenger came in to announce the murders and the memory was to haunt him for the rest of his life'. On his deathbed in September 1976, as his mind faded, Pavle was heard by his wife Princess Olga to 'repeatedly cry out with horror at the memory of the 1903 Obrenović murders in Belgrade and for the last time in her life, and as the terrified ten-year-old must have longed for seventy-three years before, she held his hand in comfort and support'.[111]

The grisly form that the murders took suggests a sexually psychopathic act; a collective act of misogynistic hatred directed against a king viewed as having cuckolded himself and dishonoured his station by marrying a considerably older, barren woman with an allegedly long sexual history from a poor family. The regicide was, in short, akin to an 'honour killing'. By killing the king and queen so brutally, the conspirators symbolically extirpated the sanctity of the royal persons, their dynasty and the cult of their rule. The murders of Cincar-Marković, Pavlović, Petrović and the king himself, and the attempted murder of Nikolić, represented a violation of the honour and respect due from younger officers toward their seniors.[112] Pavlović's corpse was also desecrated. Marinković had not had sufficient confidence in the officers assigned to deal with him and with interior minister Todorović, so he resolved to perform the murders himself, which he did with a band of soldiers including another conspirator.[113] Reports of Pavlović's death stated that his body had been stripped naked and savaged: he was covered in wounds; his fingers had been mutilated and his eye gouged out.[114] With Pavlović's body was found an unopened letter from Major Milosav Živanović, a senior official of the general staff, warning him of the impending putsch. When Živanović learned that Pavlović had failed to open his letter, he shot himself, though he survived.[115]

The Obrenović regime, as a dynastic regime, had been peculiarly dependent upon the personalities of the Obrenović rulers and their relations with family members. In highlighting Aleksandar's undoubted flaws as a ruler, above all his vacillation and repeated changes of course, mainstream historiography has been remarkably reluctant to acknowledge that this was largely due to his parents' interference and the conflicting pressures they exerted upon him. Milan's abdication while still young and energetic, retaining the status of head of the dynasty while continuing to interfere in politics, and Natalija's parallel interference prevented Aleksandar from consolidating either his authority or a dynastic cult around himself. The loyalty of many of the dynasty's senior supporters such as Đorđević and Genčić remained focused on Milan, so rebounded against the actual king when the former king broke with him over his marriage. By abdicating in favour of his son while Aleksandar was still a child, Milan had denied him the opportunity to learn the art of statecraft as an apprentice under the sitting monarch, which Mihailo, for example, had enjoyed. Milan, on his deathbed, allegedly called Aleksandar 'my true killer',[116] but it was Milan who, more than anyone, caused his son's death. Aleksandar's experience recalls Philip Larkin's aphorism 'They fuck you up, your mum and dad'. The peculiar situation, of a dynasty with two heads, in turn arose from Milan's failed marriage. Slobodan Jovanović observed: 'That passion for women, doubly dangerous for those who want to rule men, lay on the Obrenovićes like a family curse and eventually brought the dynasty death.'[117] Miloš, Mihailo and Milan had unstable or failed marriages and problematic romantic interests that destabilised or destroyed their regimes. Aleksandar was the only Obrenović ruler to enjoy a genuinely happy marriage, as he himself pointed out. It cost him his life.

Mainstream historiography remembers Aleksandar as the 'extinguisher' of the Obrenović dynasty, as Slobodan Jovanović put it.[118] But being only 26 at the time of his murder, Aleksander would have had plenty of time to remarry and produce an heir; the true extinguishers of the dynasty were those who plotted his murder. Mihailo, having previously separated from Julija, had died in 1868 without leaving a direct heir, aged 44—considerably older than Aleksandar but without attracting so much opprobrium from posterity. Like Aleksandar, Mihailo had been an unpopular ruler who alienated much of Serbia's political classes irrespective of party and ended his reign with a retreat from liberalisation to hardline personal rule. Like Mihailo, Aleksandar had pursued a sober foreign policy achieving limited gains for the national cause, which he was similarly viewed by the nationalist opposition as having betrayed. Neither ruler could defuse or channel the opposition to him and each was killed by it. That Mihailo was remembered as a great patriot but Aleksandar as a tyrant who brought Serbia to the edge of ruin says less about them than about the regimes that succeeded them and their reconstruction of the past. Yet the parallel between the two murders was noted by contemporaries. Žujović's nephew Mladen recalled how on the morning following the putsch, his father stroked his head and remarked 'I too was not yet eight, as you are now, when Prince Mihailo was killed.'[119]

The Serbian elite at the start of the twentieth century was still a new one, recruited from a nation bitterly divided by the internal conflicts of the previous decades. The army, even individual officers, were internally torn by these conflicts. In Drašković's words, 'the people sent their children into the army, so that these would, when it suited the king, shoot at their fathers'.[120] Of the conspirators, Mihailo Ristić's father had been killed during Milan's suppression of the Timok rebellion. Milutin Lazarević's mother's first husband had been executed following Mihailo's assassination. Vojin Čolak-Antić was the son of a man implicated in the same assassination. Naumović was a descendant of Naum, killed alongside Karađorđe himself by Miloš's agents in 1817; his recruitment was sought by the conspirators in the correct belief that his family history would make him amenable.[121] Luka Lazarević was the grandson of Vojvoda Luka Lazarević, a hero of the First Serbian Uprising and early enemy of the Obrenovićes, who had been imprisoned during Mihailo's first reign. The army that the Obrenovićes had rapidly constructed recruited many children of their dynasty's prior victims with many possible grudges. The dynasty was ultimately the casualty of Serbia's accumulated historical wounds.

Restoration of the 1889 constitution and Karađorđević dynasty

The putsch delivered power into the conspirators' hands. The officer-conspirators immediately arranged public pledges of allegiance by soldiers in Belgrade and elsewhere to Petar as king, thereby pre-empting any possible discussion of a republic or of an alternative royal candidate. The incoming king reciprocated: 'I, Petar Karađorđević, pledge on my honour that, so long as I and my descendants are on the throne of Serbia, not only will the conspirators and their descendants not be prosecuted by the courts, but on the contrary they will be guaranteed the highest positions in the land.' The pledge was eventually published in Vienna in 1908.[122] Consequently, Mašin became chief of staff of the army, Mišić became a senior defence ministry official and Popović became the king's adjutant.[123] Yet according to his son Đorđe, Petar could never approve or forgive the brutal way in which the conspirators had murdered his predecessor and other innocent people, and did not like them, though he understood his debt to them.[124] Shortly after becoming king, he demolished the palace where the murders had occurred.[125]

The older military conspirators initially dominated the younger ones, and consequently the country as a whole. They seriously considered establishing a military dictatorship under Popović but opted instead for a puppet provisional government whose composition they determined. This they formed immediately on the morning after the putsch, 11 June, with Avakumović, a Liberal and conspirator, as prime minister. Ironically, though Aleksandar had been condemned as a 'bloody tyrant', the four people killed by his troops in the March disturbances were considerably fewer than the twelve killed by the army at the behest of Avakumović's previous government at Goračići in March 1893. The new government included Atanacković, a Liberal and conspirator, as war minister; Genčić, a Liberal and conspirator, as economics minister; Kaljević, a Progressive, as foreign minister, chosen because of his known support for the Karađorđević dynasty; Mašin, a conspirator, as construction minister; Protić, a Radical, as interior minister; Veljković, a Liberal, as finance minister; Živković, an Independent, as justice minister; and Stojanović, an

Independent, as church affairs minister. Several of these had served in Aleksandar's governments under his personal rule. Although the post-coup government was supposed to represent all Serbia's political parties and although the Radicals were the most popular party at the time, they were grossly underrepresented. Pašić himself was excluded on account of his refusal to support the conspiracy and his subsequent condemnation of the regicide. This drove a wedge between him and Petar that contributed to the political instability of the subsequent years.[126]

The conspirators nevertheless understood that the Radicals enjoyed the Serbian population's loyalty and that they required a modus vivendi with them. The government reaffirmed the April Constitution and restored the legislative *status quo ante* that existed before Aleksandar's final coup of 7 April. Rejecting the results of Aleksandar's controlled parliamentary elections of 1 June, it restored the Radical-dominated parliament and senate elected on 22 July 1901. Instead of preparing for a constitutional assembly, it authorised the restored regular parliament and senate to choose a new king and constitution, although such a course violated the 1901 constitution, which required the king's participation in any promulgation of a constitution. The putsch thus blossomed as a paradoxical synthesis of court revolution and conservative restoration: the regime that had existed from 19 April 1901 to 7 April 1903, resting upon the Radicals and overthrown by Aleksandar's last putsch, was formally restored while in practice its constitution was trampled over. The post-putsch order was therefore unconstitutional from its birth. As Živojin Perić expressed it a few years later: 'In short, we arrive at this anomalous and dangerous situation: a group of people who have violated the most fundamental rules of Criminal Law remain unpunished. But there is something worse: those people, if not formally then de facto, are ruling. Those who have murdered have been placed at the summit of the social pyramid.'[127]

The Radical-dominated assembly and senate unanimously adopted a joint declaration which 'in evaluating the event of 29 May, accepts and enthusiastically hails the new order that has arisen as a consequence of that event, and in unity and with a single spirit proclaims the complete community of feelings between the Serbian people and the entire Serbian army', while praising the government and approving 'all its decisions and acts'.[128] But this declaration masked major differences between the Radicals, their civilian political rivals and the conspirators. Pašić's Old Radicals had evolved under Aleksandar into a party seeking power through an alliance with the crown, more interested in controlling a strong executive while in power than opposing a strong executive while in opposition. As Pašić had noted shortly before the putsch, the crown would only agree to a constitution as liberal as that of 1889 when sufficiently weakened by internal or external misfortune, but would then seek to overturn it as soon as it had recovered, whereupon the Radicals would not be in a position to resist even if they controlled government and parliament, while the population as a whole was not ready to sacrifice itself in a struggle for a constitution.

A ROYAL 'HONOUR KILLING'

Better, then, to choose a less progressive constitution acceptable to the crown, provided it guaranteed the people legislative control. Serbia would then be spared internal conflict and could preserve its strength for the external struggle for national unification. As Pašić rationalised it: 'I would rather see the Serb a slave in his own state than the slave of a foreign nation, for I am convinced that it will be easier for him when he has his own state, to extract for himself civil liberty, than it will be when he has neither national nor civil liberty.'[129] Following the putsch and faced with an uncertain new political order dominated by elements hostile to them, the Radicals reaffirmed their commitment to the 1901 constitution, which had served them best, based on the principle of limited parliamentarism under a strong crown.

The Liberals and Independents, however, wanted the restoration of the 1889 constitution, which had arisen from the era of Liberal–Radical collaboration at the end of Milan's reign. The Independents associated it with the Radical golden age. The Liberals, opposing Aleksandar, had emulated the Independents as a militantly pro-parliamentary party and favoured the more democratic 1889 constitution, which placed some restrictions on Radical power, above all through the secret ballot which restricted the Radical party machine's ability to sway elections in the countryside. Since the conspirators backed the Liberals and Independents on this question, the Old Radicals had to acquiesce.[130] The question of the 1889 versus the 1901 constitution widened the split between the two Radical factions. The change of constitutions and installation of the new king were enacted by parliamentary deputies acting under military compulsion, as had been the case with the Regency Constitution in 1869.[131] Thus, on 15 June 1903, parliament restored a modified version of the 1889 constitution. It proclaimed Petar king of Serbia on the same day. Yet the putsch had destroyed the authority not only of the Obrenović dynasty but of the institution of monarchy altogether. As the Progressive leader Pavle Marinković noted some years later, 'After 29 May, the day when Serbia saw that a ruler (no matter what he was like) was thrown head first through a window, the monarch's inviolability and prestige were finished.' He added, 'Even if the monarchy in Serbia survives for another 1,000 years, the ruler will no longer be able to achieve its former prestige.'[132] Internationally, the new king was widely perceived as sitting on a 'bloody throne' and it would take years of diplomatic effort before foreign courts and governments consented to receive him, though Austria-Hungary's conspicuously benevolent view and prompt recognition of the dynastic coup facilitated its swift recognition by the Great Powers.[133]

The monarchy's standing would be further diminished by the new king's character. Fifty-nine years old at the time of his accession, he was a weak, uninspiring man with little charisma or authority who had lived most of his life abroad, including dissolute years spent visiting expensive salons, gambling and racking up debts in Paris, Nice, Monte Carlo and Geneva. He had fathered two illegitimate sons with a French mistress, severely damaging his reputation in patriarchal Serbia.

Petar's own tutor, Ljudevit Podhorski, allegedly said that 'he combines in himself the stupidity of his father with the malice and evil of his mother'.[134] Like Milan Obrenović, at the time of his accession, Petar spoke better French than Serbian. Furthermore, Petar had Austro-Hungarian spies in his entourage, while his eldest son and heir, Prince Đorđe, was a cruel, mentally unstable buffoon. Pera Todorović noted in his diary a few weeks after Petar's accession: 'The king passes, and with him his children. Someone whispers "The king! The king!" The people look with disappointment at the king; they look at his weakened children, and on their faces it can be plainly read: "What? Is this really the king?!"'[135] The king's constitutional right to approve, or not, the new constitution was disregarded, despite attempts by the Old Radicals to insist upon it. He was a prisoner of the conspirators who had enthroned him. Suggestions immediately following the putsch by left-wing Independents and those close to them, such as Žujović, Skerlić and others, that a republic be established were abandoned in the face of pressure from the officer-conspirators, and in the years thereafter opponents of the monarchy faced prosecution and censorship.[136] In 1904, Petar awarded all participants in the putsch and other supporters of his dynasty a new medal, the 'Karađorđević Star'.[137] Real power passed to the military conspirators, whose puppet-mastery of Petar enabled them to play monarch.[138] The power struggle between the monarchy and the Radicals therefore continued.

The 1903 constitution was in many ways highly liberal, insofar as it recognised complete freedom of the press and proclaimed an independent judiciary. Both king and parliament shared legislative and budgetary powers, with both possessing the right of legislative initiative; laws had to be passed by the assembly, though the king possessed a veto. But the constitution did not establish a fully parliamentary system of government. Parliament had a more limited right to amend the budget than under the 1889 constitution, since it could now only reduce the budget but not increase it. Furthermore, the king possessed the right, with the Council's agreement, to extend the budget by four months without parliament's approval. He also retained the power to dissolve parliament without its approval and to postpone a parliamentary session for up to two months. Since there was nothing formally preventing the king from repeatedly exercising these powers, they in principle enabled his continuous non-parliamentary government, although in 1910 a law on state accounts limited his right to extend the expired financial year's budget to up to one year only.[139] The suffrage remained restricted: approximately a fifth of adult males (ranging from 22.4 per cent in 1903 to 17.1 per cent in 1908) paid insufficient tax to qualify for the vote while women were entirely disenfranchised. A new provision was introduced whereby votes cast for lists failing to reach the threshold for representation should be added to the list with the most votes. This provision was fiercely denounced by the Radicals' opponents as 'outright theft of votes' and 'proof of the Radicals' Jacobinism'; it cemented their electoral preponderance. In this way, the 1903 constitution's departure from parliamentary and democratic principles resulted in a flawed parliamentary system that would exacerbate Serbia's internal conflicts.[140]

The putsch split the country into two camps: the dominant one, comprising the conspirators and their friends and both wings of the Radicals, which embraced it as overthrowing the Obrenović autocracy and establishing true constitutional parliamentary government; and a much weaker one, represented most prominently by the Progressives and the army's anti-conspirator faction, which lamented it as a 'crime'.[141] This, combined with the unwillingness of the dominant camp to countenance any criticism of the putsch or the conspirators, would retard the development of true constitutional government in the years following. Yet for the socialists, who had been allied with the conspirators, the putsch represented liberation. The founding congress of both the Serbian Social Democratic Party and the General Workers' Union took place in early August 1903 under Dragović's guidance, followed later that month by the Women Workers' Society, subsequently known as Svest (Consciousness). Another event that would change Serbian consciousness took place on 25 January 1904, when Vladislav Ribnikar, from a mixed Slovene–Serb family from the Habsburg Empire, founded the daily newspaper *Politika* (Politics), which would become Serbia's most important, remaining so to this day.

The Radicals dominated parliamentary life and sought to negate Serbia's achievements under the Obrenović dynasty—except for the legacy of their resistance to it. The anniversary of Serbia's proclamation as a kingdom in 1882 was thus erased from the official calendar.[142] As Todorović noted in his diary in 1906, on the 24th anniversary of the proclamation: 'With what joy and enthusiasm in 1882 was this holy moment awaited when the national parliament solemnly proclaimed that, with the assent of Europe, Serbia had joined the ranks of the independent states and stepped up to the level of an independent kingdom. That day was later celebrated as a great national holiday. But 29 May 1903 erased much else, and erased also this beautiful and treasured national ceremony. Petty spirits would even like this to be forgotten: that Serbia under an Obrenović became an independent kingdom.'[143] An article appearing in *Samouprava* in October 1904, attributed to Protić, claimed that Milan had not been fathered by Jevrem Obrenović's son Miloš, as commonly assumed, but illegitimately by another Romanian, and that therefore neither he nor Aleksandar was a Serb or an Obrenović.[144]

The putsch marked the end not only of the Obrenović dynasty but also of the political traditions represented by the civilian conspirators and their friends—Genčić, Đorđević, Vukašin Petrović and company. All future court regimes in Serbia were based on alliances with elements of the Radicals. Though the civilian conspirators dominated the first, short-lived post-putsch government, none of them played a significant role in Serbian politics thereafter. The military conspirators, by contrast, would play a decisive role. One principle established by the putsch would hang like a curse over Serbia: that in the aim of achieving 'patriotic' goals, objectively criminal acts could legitimately be carried out without the perpetrators being held accountable. Speaking in the twenty-first century, Latinka Perović believed, with regard to the killing of Aleksandar and Draga, that 'Serbia still has not healed from those murders'.[145] As the historian Dubravka Stojanović writes, 'Thus, that crime of 1903 is the founding crime; that from which issued all others in the long era from 1903 to 2003; from Obrenović to Đinđić, through the Second World War and the bloodshed of the 1990s, again under the Black Hand's black flag with the skull and crossbones and the unaltered idea of unification or death.'[146] As Edmund Burke commented on another brutal revolutionary persecution of a queen, 'the age of chivalry is gone'.

11

RADICAL-CONSPIRATOR CONDOMINIUM

1903–1912

The May putsch temporarily destroyed the monarchy as a force in Serbian politics. Power was inherited firstly by the military conspirators who had executed the putsch, secondly by the Radical party. In the putsch's immediate aftermath, the Radicals still enjoyed the support of the overwhelming majority of Serbia's population, so were electorally hegemonic now that the Obrenović monarchy was gone. The conspirators, for their part, formally obtained key positions in the army and informally established control over the entire officer corps. Yet like Milan after 1880, they found that, having introduced a major liberalising measure—in this case, the 1903 constitution—they had empowered elected Radical politicians outside their control. Conversely, the Radicals found their path to hegemony over Serbia, previously blocked by the Obrenovićes, now blocked by the conspirators. The Radical party soon completed its division into two separate parties—the 'Old' Radicals and Independent Radicals. Its electoral hegemony was consequently replaced by a bitter rivalry between its two fractions. With Serbia subject to conflicting pressures from Great Powers supporting different Serbian factions, the domestic struggle became also a struggle over international alignment.

Counter-conspiracy

The regicidal conspiracy within the army politicised the officer corps, violated the officers' loyalty oath to their king and corrupted military professionalism. The conspirators privileged themselves in appointments and promotions over other officers. Apis himself enjoyed a meteoric rise, becoming captain in 1905, major in 1908, lieutenant colonel in 1913 and colonel in 1915.[1] The conspirators numbered only about 120 of the army's 1,500 officers yet sought complete power over it. Their friends and relatives benefited from military nepotism worse than that which had existed under the late Aleksandar, while around 300 officers they considered opponents, such as those previously close to Aleksandar, were pensioned off by 1911.[2] Slobodan Jovanović noted the conspirators 'did two things completely contrary to military concepts: they raised their hand against the King, their supreme commander, and they split the army into "ours" and "yours". With military discipline it was all over. Older officers outside of the conspirators' circle had less power and status than younger officers from the conspirators' circle.'[3]

Radomir Putnik, pensioned off by Milan and Aleksandar for suspected disloyalty and later suspected by Milan of being a Radical sympathiser, was restored to duty after the putsch at the rank of general and appointed chief of the general staff and, shortly afterwards, war minister.[4] Putnik was in turn responsible for the appointment of Colonel Živojin Mišić, subsequently one of the great Serbian military heroes of World War I, as the representative of the chief of general staff, tasked with carrying out Putnik's duties as chief of general staff while Putnik served as war minister. But as an Obrenović loyalist, Mišić was quickly pensioned off once more at the conspirators' behest and replaced as representative of the chief of general staff by Mašin. Putnik, apparently afraid of or beholden to the conspirators, acquiesced in the sacrifice of his protégé. As Mišić recalled bitterly nearly two decades later, Putnik summoned him to his office in April 1904 to discuss military affairs, but 'that same Putnik did not have the manhood and boldness, that same day when he summoned me to the ministry of war, to tell me I had been pensioned off ... From all this can be seen how much Putnik at that time was under the influence of the irresponsible factors.' Ostracism followed: 'Those years, the door of my home was closed not only for the conspirators and their adherents, but for many officers of otherwise correct behaviour. All were by some devil afraid even to pass by my house, let alone visit me, although they had previously called on me on the major holidays. Even some officers related to me avoided me, on the grounds that who was visiting and meeting with me was being monitored!'[5]

The conspirators violated military rules and procedures by forcing the revocation of decrees and promotions they disliked. This disgusted officers already shocked by the murder of their king and queen. They found a spokesman in Captain Milan Novaković, who had been studying military science in Paris at the time of the putsch and read about it in the horrified French press. He was a genuine idealist but also had personal grievances: his brother had been a minister in Cincar-Marković's government and his own appointment as Petar's adjutant was blocked by the conspirators.[6] Novaković returned to Belgrade on 18 July 1903 and assumed duty with the 16th Infantry Regiment at Niš on 23 August. There, he agitated against the conspirators, issuing a statement accusing them of having 'entered by force into the royal palace and, in a barbarous way, murdered the reigning royal couple, and after that, in a still more barbarous way, threw their dead, lacerated bodies out of the window'. He accused them of having dishonoured their uniforms and violated their military oaths by the murders, then of having promoted anarchy and corruption in the army. He demanded they be expelled from the army and stripped of their ranks ('uniforms off—theirs or ours!').[7]

Novaković's agitation led to the formation of a counter-conspiracy among the officers, whose supporters would be known as 'contras'. It began in the Niš garrison. Consequently, the interior ministry held an emergency meeting attended by several conspirators, after which Apis was sent to Niš to investigate. He arrived there on 21 August 1903 and obtained a copy of Novaković's statement. On the same day, General Božidar Janković, commander of the Morava Division, ordered the arrest of the officers who had signed it. Eventually, 27 Niš garrison officers were tried before a military court. Novaković himself conducted the defence and used the occasion to denounce the conspirators. Nevertheless, the court on 28 September convicted them, imposing sentences of varying severity that were subsequently upheld by the Supreme Military Court on 8 October. Novaković and his leading collaborator, Dobrivoje Lazarević, each received two years in prison.

The conspirators nevertheless felt compelled to respond, in the sympathetic press, to Novaković's charges. They claimed they had torn up official military decrees of promotion, 'in order not to allow the harmful influence, that had begun, of women, who had succeeded, in them, in promoting their own cavaliers ...' They had also torn up the decree promoting Colonel Ljubomir Lešjanin as marshal of the court because they could not permit someone who had held this post under the Obrenovićes to hold it again under the Karađorđevićes. In practice, the younger conspirators used the occasion to mount an attack on former war minister Atanacković, himself a conspirator, whom they now blamed for the instances of corruption Novaković had cited. The younger conspirators had fallen out with Atanacković because of his slowness in restoring to duty Putnik, whom they considered their friend. Atanacković resigned from the war ministry on 2 August 1903 and was retired from the army on 31 March 1906, aged 58.[8] Meanwhile, prime minister Avakumović attempted to secure the resignations of three leading older conspirators, Mišić, Popović and Lazarević, whom Petar rejected. This produced a ministerial crisis in the putschist government in early August 1903.[9]

The appearance of the counter-conspiracy highlighted the division in Serbian public life between supporters and opponents of the new order. A large rally was held in Belgrade on 31 August 1903 to denounce the anti-conspirator newspapers for their 'treasonous goals' serving 'hostile foreign aspirations' and to call for a boycott of their printing, distribution and sale. The student Ljubomir Jovanović-Čupa declared that 'the head is crushed but the tail remains and it too must be killed ... Surgery is the best means for this. 29 May is not finished. The rubbish must go to the rubbish dump.' The meeting resolved that all 'who buy, read, sell or help these newspapers be taken before the public and marked'. The leading pro-conspirator newspaper *Mali žurnal* (Little Journal) called for the formation of a paramilitary organisation to 'stand on the neck' of the traitors so that 'the revolution of 29 May will be fully completed'. The form of organisation it suggested would eventually emerge as the Black Hand a few years later.[10]

Živojin Perić, a highly respected albeit maverick legal scholar and Progressive, founded the Society for the Legal Settlement of the Conspiratorial Question at the end of 1903, which included some eminent supporters of the former regime, including Colonel Nikolić, wounded during the putsch, and Svetomir Nikolajević. He argued that, since the provisional government and parliament had both affirmed the 1901 constitution in the aftermath of the putsch, it followed that the putsch had not been a revolution, and since that constitution gave the right to pardon solely to the king, the conspirators had not been legally amnestied by parliament's declaration of 2 June. Consequently, he argued that the conspirators remained criminally liable for the royal murders. He would argue over the following years that Serbia's status in Europe required its 'dissociation from the May crime'.[11]

The Radicals still viewed themselves through Jacobinical lenses as embodying the national will, and other political factions as threats to national unity.[12] As Slobodan Jovanović notes, Protić, the Radicals' chief constitutional theoretician, championed the British model of parliamentary sovereignty but misinterpreted this to mean unrestrained power for the majority in the lower chamber, without the checks and balances of the British system.[13] Still formally a single party, they inevitably won the first post-putsch parliamentary elections on 21 September 1903, with 141 out of 160 seats. The victory involved the systematic purging of municipal administrations, the doctoring of electoral registers and intimidation of political opponents—particularly at the expense of the Progressives—but it nevertheless reflected an overwhelming popular mandate and popular rejection of the putschist regime.[14] The 141 Radical deputies were split between the Old Radicals with 76 and the Independents with 65, leaving the party leadership dependent upon the latter for its parliamentary majority. The Independents demanded Pašić be excluded from government. Consequently, the two Radical factions formed a government without Pašić on 4 October 1903, under Sava Grujić, though Pašić joined it as foreign minister in February 1904. Assuming power as still formally a single party, the Radicals felt their long-awaited historical moment had come. In a move that highlighted the vengeful spirit in which they exercised their new hegemony, parliament voted overwhelmingly, with the backing of both wings of the party, to cancel the pensions of the widows of Jovan Ristić and Milutin Garašanin, on the grounds that 'the late Garašanin, Ristić and Vujović did nothing for this country ... theirs was an evil contribution' that only assemblies 'elected by ... assorted Progressive-Liberal riff-raff' could recognise. Objections by Progressive deputies were met with the threat that they would be killed if they tried to reconstitute their party. When former prime minister Nikolajević sought to raise the question of the moral and legal aspects of the putsch, the Radical deputies responded with violent outbursts, including expressions of regret that he 'had not been hanged at Terazije'.[15]

RADICAL–CONSPIRATOR CONDOMINIUM

The Radicals and conspirators were required to share power. They were uneasy bedfellows given their structural and ideological antipathy. The Radicals were traditionally hostile to the standing army from which the conspirators had arisen, developed to keep them and their peasant voters down, something to which the conspirators remained committed. The Radicals were, however, no longer truly 'radical'. Writing in 1890, Todorović had accurately predicted their evolution: 'That which happens with all opposition parties, when they come to power. From fiery champions of freedom they become mere champions of freedom; from moderate champions of freedom moderate conservatives; from moderate conservatives ordinary conservatives; from conservatives reactionaries; and from reactionaries the devil's cousins, to whom you need only give power, for them to be whatever you want.'[16] They had supported two of King Aleksandar's four putsches and served under him, so had no qualms about similarly accommodating themselves to the new order. The violent, unconstitutional nature of the putsch allowed them to present it as a 'revolution' and demagogically justify further illiberal or illegal acts against opponents of the new order.

The Radicals therefore employed extra-legal and demagogic measures to defend the conspirators and the putsch's legacy from legal and legitimate objections. Interior minister Protić responded to the counter-conspiracy by proposing a law, which parliament passed in January 1904, criminalising agitation against individual officers on the part of the press, which he justified by the need 'to defend and protect the state'. All criticism of the May putsch was thus banned and dissenting newspapers were persecuted by the police.[17] The conspirators themselves frequently threatened and assaulted journalists and newspaper editors who criticised them, frequently challenging them to duels. Thus, Vemić attacked the proprietor of a newspaper from behind with his sabre at a tavern in Belgrade on 26 March 1905 because he had refused to reveal the name of a writer who had criticised him.[18] The police as a rule took no action to protect the men of the press, instead joining in harassing them. The leading Social Democrat Dušan Popović noted some years later, 'This regime is a strange melange. The Radical Party is its mother; the officers its father ... Turn it to one side—democratism; turn it to the other side—caesarism! We find ourselves in some sort of strange mixture of political freedom and praetorian excesses.'[19]

Nevertheless, the Radicals understood that the conspirators' unwarranted hegemony over army and state was greatly alienating army officers and members of the establishment who did not support them, that the resulting conflicts and scandals were being reported by the international press and damaging Serbia's reputation and that the Great Powers, especially Britain and Russia, considered this hegemony, particularly over the king, unacceptable. Although the Radicals could not yet break this hegemony, they took the first steps to prune it and, with the support of the foreign diplomatic community, lobbied at the court to this effect. A royal decree on 4 January 1904 limited the term of service of officers at the court to six months, forcing many conspirators to leave. Under heavy pressure from prime minister Grujić and foreign secretary Pašić, the king on 31 March finally signed a decree removing the remaining conspirators from court service.[20] This was the Radicals' first, small victory in their power struggle with the conspirators that would dominate Serbia for years. It was also the first step in breaking the domination of Austrophile elements over the court—which the older conspirators, as remnants of Milan's regime, represented—and reorienting it toward the Russophile policy which the Radicals favoured. The Austro-Hungarians would come to regret joining the Great Power front against the conspirators.

Guerrilla war and irredentism in the south

Opposition to Aleksandar's regime had been catalysed by nationalist frustration at its failure to achieve more vis-à-vis Macedonia. The regime's fall was followed by the flowering of a veritable national movement in Serbia for southward expansion. The Elijah's Day Uprising was launched in Macedonia on 2 August 1903 by what came to be known as the Internal Macedonian Revolutionary Organisation (VMRO), founded by pro-Bulgarian rebels in 1893. A significant number of Serbs participated in the uprising, which met with sympathy from the putschist Serbian government, and there were public calls from the press for volunteers to form Serb guerrilla bands in Macedonia. Though the Ottomans rapidly crushed the uprising, they then recognised the existence of a specifically Serbian Orthodox millet in order to counteract Bulgarian influence in Macedonia, whetting the appetite of official Serbia, which accelerated its financing of guerrilla activity.[21]

Moved by Ottoman brutality in suppressing the uprising, a public meeting was organised at Kalemegdan in Belgrade on 28 August 1903 at which speakers, including Đaja and Živanović, denounced Ottoman tyranny and demanded the Serbian government take action to defend the Serb people in Macedonia. The following month, a meeting was held at the house of Luka Ćelović, a veteran of the Serb struggle in Macedonia from the Obrenović era, and presided over by Atanacković. The participants denounced Aleksandar's policy of collaboration with the Ottomans and advocated the foundation of a revolutionary committee to wage guerrilla warfare in Macedonia. At a second meeting some days later at Atanacković's office, it was resolved to found a Chetnik (guerrilla) organisation: the Serbian Revolutionary Organisation (or Central Revolutionary Secret Council). This was absorbed in the organisation National Defence after 1908. A women's organisation, the Circle of Serbian Sisters, was also established in 1903 to provide the guerrillas and their families with humanitarian assistance, including care for orphans, with committees set up across Serbia. The Serbian Revolutionary Organisation was headed by Atanacković as central committee president. Prominent in it were veterans of the pre-putsch guerrilla movement launched at Aleksandar's behest, including

Ćelović, Milorad Gođevac and Živojin Rafajlović, the last of whom was a Liberal and became head of the movement's executive committee in Vranje near Serbia's border with Macedonia. This was an all-Serbian movement uniting people from across the political spectrum, including for example the Old Radical Ljubomir Jovanović and the Progressive Vojislav Marinković, Pavle's brother. But particularly prominent in it were conspirators and their friends, including Tankosić, Vulović, Jovanović-Čupa and Živanović, and Independents, including Stojanović, Prodanović and Ljubomir Davidović. This movement thus facilitated the conspirator–Independent alliance that would coalesce a few years later.[22]

The Serbian Revolutionary Organisation sent activists into Macedonia to organise Chetnik bands, modelled on VMRO, which was pre-eminent in the Macedonian resistance. The growth of the rural population and the shrinking of peasant plots, from which Serbia suffered, provided an economic incentive for young men to seek their fortunes in this national adventure. Serbian guerrilla leaders were drawn disproportionately from eastern and southern Serbia, liberated in 1833 and 1878 and traditionally both politically and geographically peripheral, and from the Ottoman-ruled lands further south. Typical examples were Mihailo Ristić Džervinac murderer of Aleksandar and Draga, who came from Svrljig, on the far edge of the territory acquired in 1833; Vojin Popović, who came from Sjenica in the Sanjak; and Kosta Milovanović Pećanac, who came from Dečani in Kosovo. Pećanac's father was killed by Albanians when he was a small boy and he fled to Serbia as a teenager in the 1890s to escape Albanian attacks. Dismissed from the regular army for a misdemeanour, he instead built a career with the guerrillas.[23] Such men of the frontier and irredenta spearheaded the struggle for Macedonia, where fighting between rival pro-Serbian and pro-Bulgarian bands in 1903–1912 was bloody and merciless.[24] Nevertheless, the post-putsch governments sought to collaborate with the Bulgarians against the Ottomans, so on 12 April 1904 Serbia signed treaties establishing a close alliance and economic relationship with Bulgaria. A customs agreement between them was then signed on 22 June 1905.

This stepping up of preparations for southward expansion heightened Serbia's regional rivalry with Austria-Hungary, whose interests in Old Serbia and Macedonia clashed with its own. Vienna championed the Albanian national movement, pioneered by Catholics, which sought Catholic–Muslim collaboration, while Belgrade supported the Serbian Orthodox population. Following the defeat of the Elijah's Day uprising, Russia and Austria-Hungary signed the Mürzsteg Agreement on 2 October 1903, whereby each was to appoint a representative to advise Macedonia's Ottoman governor on the implementation of reforms of the administration, judiciary and gendarmerie, while Austria-Hungary, Russia, Britain and France were each to be responsible for overseeing the gendarmerie in a specified part of the region. However, the western part of the Kosovo vilayet, roughly corresponding to present-day Kosovo, was to be excluded from the scheme and remain an exclusively

Austro-Hungarian sphere of influence. With its gendarme officers also in the eastern part of the vilayet and its garrisons still in the Sanjak, Austria-Hungary threatened to place the whole of the vilayet under its control and encircle Serbia to the south, while promoting the Albanians at the expense of the Serbs in areas disputed between them. Belgrade viewed this as a deadly threat.[25] Conversely, the escalating Serbian guerrilla activity in the region alarmed Vienna.

Serbian irredentist activity extended to Montenegro. The Montenegrin rulers and political classes viewed their country as a Serb state but were divided between those asserting a Montenegrin state tradition that set it somewhat apart from Serbia and those favouring its annexation to Serbia outright.[26] Prince Nikola himself formally championed pan-Serb unification and was Petar's father-in-law, but his rivalry with the ruling dynasties of Serbia, first the Obrenović then the Karađorđević, led him to assert Montenegrin independence vis-à-vis Serbia in order to lead the unification struggle himself. Prince Đorđe recalled that as a child, Nikola, his grandfather, told him that although his mother was Montenegrin and he was born in Montenegro, he could never be Montenegrin himself because his father was from Serbia.[27] Nikola's pro-Russian stance, coupled with the political strife in Serbia before 1903, initially gave him the edge in this rivalry and Montenegro served as a refuge for the Obrenovićes' opponents. But Montenegro's great territorial expansion in the 1870s added to the population large numbers of ethnic Serbs with no particular loyalty to the Petrović-Njegoš dynasty. The May putsch and the establishment in Serbia of a relatively democratic regime then turned the tables, with Serbia becoming a centre of agitation against Nikola's authoritarian regime. This fused with pan-Serb agitation for Montenegro's annexation to Serbia, particularly by Montenegrin youth schooled in Serbia.[28] Montenegro divided into two camps: Petrović-Njegoš dynastic loyalists and pro-Serbian annexationists. Nikola granted Montenegro its first constitution on 19 December 1905 in order to defuse popular opposition, but since his regime remained authoritarian, opposition continued.[29]

The poverty of the Montenegrin population and the increasing self-confidence and nationalism of Serbia's political classes fired the annexationists. Supported by the conspirators' circle in Serbia, some turned to violent means. The conspirators Tankosić and Čedomir Popović supplied bombs from the Kragujevac arms factory to Montenegrin rebels for an armed insurgency against Nikola; these were discovered in Cetinje on 5 November 1907 (the 'Bomb Affair'). Belgrade papers published reports of Nikola's assassination the day before the bombs were discovered. The discovery resulted in a trial of over 150 rebels in May–June 1908; several death sentences were delivered though subsequently commuted. The following autumn, Nikola's regime suppressed another attempt at an armed uprising supported by Serbia's conspirators (the 'Kolašin Affair'). The high military tribunal at Kolašin delivered harsh sentences and this time three executions were actually carried out. Demonstrations against this repression occurred in Serbia. One of those sentenced to death at Kolašin, but not executed, was a certain Puniša Račić, a confidant of Pašić's destined to play a fateful role in Yugoslav history.[30] To defend his dynasty and state from the annexationist movement, Nikola promoted himself to king and his state to a kingdom on 28 August 1910.

Radical party formally splits

In this period of apparent absolute electoral hegemony of the formally still-united Radical party, the real opposition to the Grujić government came from within the party's own ranks, not only from Independents but from some who would remain with the Old Radicals following the final split. Pašić himself sought to sabotage the government and replace it with a homogeneous Old Radical government. With Radical infighting paralysing the government, it was reshuffled on 26 January 1904 to include Lazar Paču of the Old Radicals and Davidović of the Independents in an attempt to instil discipline in the parliamentary party. Yet the divisions persisted. Pašić took advantage of this to re-enter the government as foreign minister in February 1904, further alienating the Independents. Opposition coalesced over the January 1904 press law, over Old Radical insistence on linking the raising of international loans on armaments and on railways and over Protić's law on public security, introduced in October 1904 and passed on 31 January 1905, giving the interior minister the right to use the army against domestic unrest.

The Independent deputies consequently seceded to form a separate parliamentary club while the Old Radicals summoned a meeting of the entire party in a final attempt to save its unity. But when the meeting convened on 22 November 1904, representatives of the Independents submitted a statement: 'The Independent Radical club declares that unity of the Radical Party is untenable.' This marked the party's definite split. The Independents would be led in turn by three Ljubomirs—Živković, Stojanović and Davidović. Republican sympathies were strongly present among the Independents and some had also begun as socialists, notably Skerlić. This marked the emergence of a more straightforward division in Serbia between right-wing (Old Radical) and left-wing (Independent) camps, following the European norm.[31] Indeed, in this period the Independents would consciously seek to redefine themselves as a left-wing party, in competition with the Social Democrats. The government resigned on 19 November and Pašić formed a homogeneous Radical government on 10 December. It maintained itself with the collaboration of the Independents, for they continued in the short term to view the Old Radicals as their sister party and defended it from what they still considered the common anti-Radical enemies: Progressives and Liberals, whom they viewed as representing the *ancien régime*.

The Liberals also fragmented, partly owing to bitter differences over the putsch: the party had been an overtly Obrenovićite dynastic party yet its members had also predominated among the conspirators. Under Ribarac's leadership, it renamed itself the National Party in October 1904 to stress that pursuit of the national goal was now its principal purpose.[32] It adopted a new programme, but a minority under Veljković's leadership seceded to form the Liberal Democratic Party. Those involved in the conspiracy, above all Avakumović and Genčić, were effectively driven out of the movement. One Liberal faction launched the newspaper *Opozicija* (Opposition), which became for a while the most vocal anti-conspirator publication.[33] Liberals in parliament, alongside Progressives, spearheaded agitation against the conspirators' interference in Serbian state affairs and against Radical collaboration with them. The two Liberal parties reunited under the name of the National Party in October 1905, with Ribarac as president and Veljković as vice-president, though they continued to be widely referred to as the Liberals. The reconstituted party was, however, a broken reed.

Pašić's government, given its Russophile orientation, sought to re-equip Serbia's army with artillery purchased from the Schneider-Creusot armaments company of France–Russia's ally. Yet the older conspirators retained an Austrophile orientation inherited from Milan's administration of the army, so preferred to purchase the artillery from Austria-Hungary's Škoda company. In particular, Colonel Petar Mišić was an agent of Škoda and stood to benefit personally if it received the contract.[34] The conspirators were supported by the court. Balugdžić, the king's private secretary, who was close to the conspirators, was also the foreign ministry's press bureau chief and a correspondent of Viennese papers; he spied for the Austro-Hungarians, informing their embassy of events in Serbian politics and at court, and tried to steer Petar away from all anti-Austro-Hungarian currents. A similar role was played by Petar's cousin Jakov Nenadović, formerly his representative in Vienna during his exile.[35] The king himself initially agreed with the government position on the 'gun question', but his complete dependence on the conspirators forced him to become their tool to defeat it. The conspirators consequently insisted the government perform parallel tests to determine which company's artillery was superior. They were prepared, if necessary, to topple the government and replace it with a 'neutral' government ready to execute their wishes—reminiscent of the anti-Radical 'neutral' regimes of Aleksandar's reign.

This 'gun question' had clear implications for Serbia's international alignment. Pašić's resistance to the parallel tests led the conspirators, working through their puppet king, to favour the Independents over the Old Radicals. Balugdžić led a press campaign against the government's refusal to conduct parallel tests. This amounted to an extra-constitutional attempt to manipulate the legitimate government. Balugdžić was forced to resign as press bureau chief on 17 January after confidential information that he had leaked appeared in a Viennese newspaper, though he remained Petar's secretary. Nevertheless, the Independent and Liberal opposition sided with the conspirators and king against the government, while Konstantin Dumba, Austria-Hungary's ambassador in Belgrade, responded to Balugdžić's fall by enlisting Nenadović to persuade Petar to dismiss the Pašić government and replace it with a more pro-Austro-Hungarian 'neutral' government, though this intrigue failed.[36]

The government's attempt to link the armaments loan with the railway loan was intended to pre-empt the possibility of the gun contract going to anyone but Schneider-Creusot. But under combined pressure from the king, conspirators, pro-conspirator press and Independents and Liberals in parliament, the government's position weakened and Pašić offered his resignation on 2 February 1905. This amounted to the government's overthrow by extra-parliamentary means, to which even the Independents and Liberals, who had opposed it over the gun issue, objected. Petar refused Pašić's resignation. The Radicals fought hard, seeking not only to expel Balugdžić and Nenadović from court but to place the court gendarmerie under the foreign ministry's control to remove it from control by the army and conspirators. Their intention was to establish physical control over the king, to break his resistance. In the end they apparently capitulated on the issue of parallel tests, gaining in return only Balugdžić's resignation as Petar's secretary as a face-saver. Even this was achieved only through a deal with the leading conspirators. Genčić, Mašin and Popović met at Hadži-Toma's vineyard in late January and agreed to send a delegation to the Radical leaders, Pašić and Protić, consenting to repudiate Balugdžić.

Balugdžić was forced to resign, then prosecuted for leaking government information to the foreign press. He attempted to defend himself in court by turning the tables on the government, claiming that 'Pašić is pursuing a treasonous policy in relation to Bulgaria', the goal of which was the 'subordination of the interests of Serbia and Serbdom to Bulgaria and Bulgardom'. He spoke of 'Pašić's allowing Serbs to continue to be killed in Old Serbia and Macedonia, without him lifting a finger, receiving as reward property in Sofia and diamond rings for his children' and claimed that this collaboration with Bulgaria against Serbia dated back to 1886.[37] His defence was nevertheless unsuccessful and he was convicted and sentenced to a fine of 600 francs and five months in prison, which he evaded by fleeing to Zemun. The conspirators extracted in return another recognition from the government, which praised the officer-conspirators for the putsch. It was, for Pašić, a mere tactical retreat, for at the end of March the government overrode Petar's protests to repudiate its acceptance of parallel tests and on 6 May 1905 finance minister Paču signed a loan agreement in Paris worth 110 million dinars. Balugdžić's defeat was followed by Nenadović's appointment as ambassador to Constantinople, removing the second Austro-Hungarian agent and conspirators' friend from Petar's court.[38]

Meanwhile, the logic of the Independents' position as a separate party increasingly pushed them into full opposition. The government's draft law on okrug and district organisation was aimed at installing a first-past-the-post electoral system and non-secret ballot for the election of okrug officials, measures that would strengthen the Radicals' ability to control regional government, hence manipulate elections. This prompted the Independents' Dragutin Pečić in parliament to label interior minister Protić a 'brazen tyrant' at the head of a coterie of 'gamblers, kapetans' and 'thugs and spies', and to compare the Radical parliamentary majority's 'tyranny' with Aleksandar's. Thus, the intolerant and aggressive Radical rhetoric, directed for the previous two decades against other parties, was now turned against the Radicals themselves; the Independents inherited the Radicals' anti-pluralism and their view of domestic opponents—even their former party comrades—as traitors.[39]

The government's position weakened because of this split with the Independents. Escalating Independent hostility undermined the government and prompted Pašić in May 1905 to ask Petar to dissolve parliament and hold new elections. Prompted by the conspirators, Petar then appointed a minority Independent government under Stojanović on 15 May to supervise the elections. These were conducted in July without any prior purge of the local bureaucracy or significant police interference, so were the only general elections in the period 1903–1914 generally accepted to have been fair. With the pro-Radical electorate not yet having divided neatly into pro-Old and pro-Independent camps, its voters were still floating between them. The Independents won 38.4 per cent of the popular vote against 32.3 per cent for the Old Radicals, 15.2 per cent for the Liberals and 8 per cent for the Progressives. This gave the Independents an absolute majority of 81 seats against 79 for the other parties combined. Yet the fact that the two Radical parties together won only just over 70 per cent of the national vote reflected a considerable decline since the 1890s, when they had enjoyed the loyalty of five-sixths of the electorate.

Conspirators crisis and the Pig War

Stojanović's reconstituted Independent government inherited the problem of the conspirators' extra-constitutional power in Serbia, which by now was an acute international issue. Britain, where public opinion had been horrified by the 1903 regicides and which had no pressing reason to accommodate Serbia, made its re-establishment of diplomatic relations with the post-putsch regime contingent upon the removal of the leading conspirators from positions of influence. This British-led diplomatic blacklisting was a precursor of the pressure that Serbia would come under in the twenty-first century to arrest war criminals indicted by the International Criminal Tribunal for the former Yugoslavia. Jovan Žujović accepted the post of foreign minister with the aim of normalising relations with Britain, while the defence minister was Colonel Antonić, formerly King Aleksandar's foreign minister, considered the conspirators' enemy. The headquarters of the Macedonian guerrilla organisation's executive committee in Vranje were raided in August 1905 by police on the interior minister's orders, unearthing a large quantity of guns and munitions. This prompted the executive committee to resign, in turn prompting the withdrawal in protest from the central committee in Belgrade of its leading members, headed by its president, Atanacković—one of the six conspirators whose retirement the British demanded.⁴⁰ Davidović replaced him as president of the central committee in early 1906. When Petar nevertheless refused in November 1905 to sign the government's decree retiring several conspirators, Žujović resigned on the 28th–29th. The Independent government failed to resign with him, opportunistically capitulating to the conspirators' extra-constitutional authority. The Liberal leaders Ribarac and Veljković submitted to Stojanović's Independent government on 3 December 1905 a new interpellation concerning the re-establishment of diplomatic relations with Britain. Since the government was unable to bring about the retirement of the six conspirators that Britain demanded, it was unable to respond positively to this interpellation, prompting the Liberal and Radical opposition to launch a policy of parliamentary obstruction.

British pressure on Serbia was soon exceeded by a countervailing foreign pressure. Austria-Hungary considered its established relationship with Serbia violated by the latter's customs agreement with Bulgaria. After Serbia resisted Austro-Hungarian pressure to repudiate the customs agreement, Vienna on 22 January 1906 broke off talks on the renewal of its own economic agreement with Serbia and banned imports of Serbian livestock, initiating the so-called Pig War. As Austria-Hungary was at that time the destination of 90 per cent of Serbia's exports and the source of 60 per cent of its imports, Belgrade was exceptionally vulnerable to such pressure. The policy of forging a customs agreement with Bulgaria at the price of economic war with Austria-Hungary was opposed by the Liberals and by the Austrophiles among the civilian conspirators and members of the king's circle—Atanacković, Nenadović and Balugdžić. Đorđević, Balugdžić and Vukašin Petrović even called upon the Austro-Hungarians to close their border with Serbia or keep it closed for as long as possible. Stojanović viewed such activity in terms of representatives of the pre-1903 order seeking to regain power.⁴¹

Serbia's government retaliated by banning or restricting the transit through its territory of Austro-Hungarian goods and seeking trade agreements with Britain, France, Russia, Italy, Romania and Greece.⁴² But it capitulated on 10 February, effectively abandoning the agreement with Bulgaria and reopening its border to Austro-Hungarian goods. Vienna consequently agreed to reopen trade talks but refused to lift its ban on Serbian livestock.⁴³ The Austro-Serbian customs agreement of 1892 expired on 1 March 1906 and Vienna used the opportunity to seek new economic concessions from Belgrade. It finally reopened the frontier on 19 March. But having successfully bullied Serbia over the convention with Bulgaria, it now sought to do the same over Belgrade's choice of Schneider-Creusot's guns over Škoda's. It sought to obstruct reconciliation between Britain and Serbia to increase the latter's dependence on itself. Consequently, and given also that all Serbia's principal parties were by now pro-Russian, Vienna cultivated its friendship with the largely Austrophile conspirators. It defended them against the Serbian politicians' attempts to sacrifice them to appease the British, in return for the conspirators' support on the gun question.[44] Serbia divided over whether to prioritise opposing Austria-Hungary over the gun question or opposing Britain over the conspirators question.

The weakness of the government and crown and Serbia's international difficulties led some of the old civilian conspirators to consider the re-establishment of an authoritarian regime. Genčić proposed this first and met with Petar's sympathy. Genčić, Petrović, Đorđević and Atanacković conspired along these lines during 1904–1905 and considered founding a new conservative party with royal support. However, the plans came to nothing owing to Petar's weak position and passive personality. They were also opposed by the existing conservative party, i.e. the Progressives under Stojan Novaković. They formally reconstituted themselves as a party, after a ten-year hiatus, on 12 February 1906, and viewed the 'Vienna group' under the Viennese-based Petrović and Đorđević as competitors. Đorđević's stubborn agitation against the Independent government ultimately provoked a response. The Independents had not forgiven their persecution at his hands following the St John's Day attempt and took the opportunity to settle the score. The government consequently indicted him for publishing confidential state documents in his memoir, *End of a Dynasty*. His trial began in February 1906 and in March he was sentenced to six months in prison, which he served. The Radical newspaper *Mali žurnal* supported his imprisonment, condemning him derogatorily as a Cincar who, as prime minister, had persecuted Serbs.[45]

Confounded, and abandoning hope in 'Uncle', as they derisively termed Petar, the older conspirators were emboldened by the outbreak of the Pig War. Austria-Hungary's machinations now chimed with theirs. Upholding the tradition of Milan's Austrophile authoritarianism, Genčić and Avakumović had concluded 'that it would have been better if, after the murder of Aleksandar, we had worked for Serbia to become part of the Austro-Hungarian monarchy as an independent kingdom and that to it, in that position, be added Bosnia-Hercegovina, rather than we had done what was done ...'.[46] Vienna raised the gun question with Belgrade on 5 April 1906, informing it that a satisfactory outcome was a precondition for a new customs agreement permitting the continued export of Serbian livestock to Austria-Hungary. Genčić, Mašin, Damjan Popović, Balugdžić and Nenadović opposed the quarrel with Vienna and also the Independents' attempts to sacrifice the conspirators to appease the British; they anticipated the formation of a 'conservative cabinet' that would dissolve parliament, manipulate new elections to give itself a majority and conclude a customs agreement with Austria-Hungary. After three years in Vienna, Petrović returned to Serbia that month to be on hand if summoned to join an Austrophile government. Alarmed by rising socialist and working-class agitation, he and Đorđević during the latter's imprisonment continued fruitlessly to discuss a possible new authoritarian regime to save the existing order.[47]

RADICAL–CONSPIRATOR CONDOMINIUM

The Radical-led opposition attacked the Stojanović government for capitulating to Austria-Hungary, and its parliamentary obstruction forced it to resign. But after securing two defectors from the Radicals, including Grujić, the Independents formed a new government under the latter on 14 March. The opposition's pressure on the government over relations with Britain then continued. Given Petar's continuing refusal to retire the conspirators, Grujić's Independent government finally resigned on 5 April. The conspirators—both the civilians represented by Balugdžić and Nenadović and the officers—warned the king that he could only issue a mandate to a government willing to defer the conspirator question, hence delay the restoration of relations with Britain. Since the Independents were unwilling, the mandate was offered to Pašić and the Radicals, who consequently formed a government on 17 April 1906. This amounted to their capitulation to the conspirators, their puppet king and their Austro-Hungarian allies. The Radicals had to agree furthermore to place half their orders for guns with Austro-Hungarian firms.[48] Petar then retreated from politics and the Radical government took his place as the conspirators' agent and protector.

The contras re-emerged in support of the demand to retire the five conspirators. Following his release from prison, Milan Novaković presided over a meeting of the Society for the Legal Settlement of the Conspiratorial Question on 30 October 1905, when he argued:

> Holding in fact all power in their hands, they [the conspirators] have become the all-powerful factor in the state, destroying all the authority of the responsible elements, meddling in all branches of state administration, making all kinds of pressure on the government, parliament, courts and on certain government offices and officials. In constantly emphasising their services, for which they seek rewards without end, they have become arrogant and intolerable, and because they have monopolised Belgrade exclusively for themselves and their adherents, they decorate, promote and enrich themselves, making scandals from day to day the likes of which are to be found nowhere in the world.[49]

Novaković argued that the May putsch and the conspirators' grip on Serbia had isolated it internationally. He contended that the putsch was a criminal act for which parliament had no right to absolve the perpetrators, but should punish them according to the law. After Novaković, speeches were given by Nikolajević and former education minister Luka I. Lazarević. A council was elected with a Mr Popović, a retired colonel of the military court, as president, Lazarević as vice-president and Novaković as secretary. Its members included Nikolajević, former minister of construction Pavle Denić, retired general Pavle Bošković, retired colonel Nikolić and others, including three former officers of the Niš garrison who had lost their ranks for participating in the counter-conspiracy.

The organisation resolved on 4 December to launch a newspaper, *Za Otadžbinu* (For the Fatherland), which quickly gathered a considerable following within the army.⁵⁰ It found an audience particularly among the NCOs of the Kragujevac garrison for whom conditions were particularly harsh. General Stepa Stepanović, commander of the Šumadija Division, had rejected their demand for an NCOs' reading room and canteen separate from the soldiers. Bitterness was particularly great among those related to the Niš garrison's prosecuted officers. Other potential sympathisers were the Kragujevac socialists, who had spoken out against the harsh treatment of the garrison soldiers and against military brutality more generally. Socialists and workers had been targeted in the so-called Kragujevac riot of 11 July 1904, when they had been physically attacked by officers from the conspirators' circle; dozens were severely injured and 27 imprisoned, some of whom were tortured, after which, at the war minister's request, 180 Social Democratic armaments factory workers were dismissed, though subsequently reinstated in their jobs.⁵¹

Za Otadžbinu supported the NCOs' demands for better conditions. About thirty NCOs met on 25 March 1906 at Stanovljanske Polje, near Kragujevac—site of the 1877 Topola uprising. Sergeant Sreten Sredojević was elected president of the group, which resolved to make a donation to *Za Otadžbinu* and establish contact with Novaković and other sympathetic officers, including retired colonels Živojin Mišić and Miloš Vasić, formerly King Aleksandar's war minister in the 'wedding cabinet' of 1900, and Captain Vojin Maksimović, son-in-law of murdered Cincar-Marković. Sredojević travelled to Belgrade and concluded there was strong support in its garrison for Novaković. Mišić, Vasić and Maksimović pledged their moral support and stated that the Belgrade garrison was behind them, after which the Kragujevac NCOs began preparing for an uprising, to be assisted by the 'working masses' and socialists. They attempted to establish links with the Užice and Čačak garrisons. However, this counter-conspiracy was uncovered and on 29 April a number of contras arrested. A military court on 26 November 1906 handed down sentences to 27 officers and NCOs, which were confirmed by the Supreme Military Court on 8 February 1907. Sredojević was sentenced to twenty years in prison and Maksimović to ten.⁵² Meanwhile, the Society for the Legal Settlement of the Conspiratorial Question was banned in August 1906. *Za Otadžbinu*'s printing press was demolished by the police. The Society dissolved itself on 20 December 1906.

The counter-conspiracy nonetheless helped publicise the conspirators' influence on public life. Pašić's Radicals, unlike Stojanović's Independents, were willing to bargain with the conspirators to negotiate their retirement. Petar finally signed a decree on 17 May 1906 retiring the five conspirators, but only because the decree expressed its gratitude to them and illegally awarded them pensions equivalent to full pay. According to Vojislav Marinković, the decree represented a 'recognition by the government that apart from the royal government, which is based on the national representative body ... there exists in this country also another authority, whose cooperation the royal government needs to implement even a single ordinary bureaucratic decree'. Hence, the 'supremacy of civilian over military authority ... no longer exists'. According to Pavle Marinković, 'all civilian authorities are nothing but puppets in the army's hands'.[53]

The five officers retired were Damjan Popović, Aleksandar Mašin, Petar Mišić, Ljubomir Kostić and Luka Lazarević, while Atanacković had already resigned. This was a defeat merely for the older officer-conspirators who had come of age under King Milan. Vienna viewed their retirement as a further sign, following Balugdžić's and Nenadović's removal from court, that its friends were being excluded from influence in Serbia.[54] It was a victory for the younger officer-conspirators led by Apis, who were ready to sacrifice them to appease Britain. At a fraught meeting at the pavilion of Smutekovac park on the edge of Belgrade, several younger conspirators pressed the older conspirators to resign; the latter reacted angrily, with Popović treating the former as personal enemies. Nevertheless, the meeting ensured their resignations.[55] The now ascendant younger conspirators would reorient Serbia's policy to oppose Austria-Hungary. Meanwhile, the tradition by which the defence minister was an army officer was adopted by the conspirators, and Pašić had to accept their favourite, Putnik, for the post. They then ensured that successive defence ministers always came from among their friends, so that they would determine military policy and have a lever to control government.

The Radicals conducted new elections in June 1906 involving their old techniques of manipulation and intimidation, this time directed in particular against their former Independent comrades, whom they regularly referred to as 'traitors', 'Austrian spies' and 'Brankovićes', against whom stood Pašić, 'the right flank of the Serbian lord [Lazar], whom not even the Sultan can outwit'. Police and municipal officials were purged and replaced en masse and unwilling citizens forced to vote. 'Everywhere we have been placed outside the law,' said Stojanović; 'the fusionists' police ... remind me of the Cincar-Marković period.' The Radicals consequently won 42.9 per cent of the vote, giving them a comfortable majority of 91 seats against 69 for all other parties. The Independents' share of the vote dropped to 29.6 per cent, with 12.5 per cent for the Liberals and 8 per cent for the Progressives. The elections thus firmly established the Old Radicals as Serbia's strongest party, albeit substantially weaker electorally than during their democratic hegemony in the 1880s and 1890s. The Independents were freed from any illusion that they might win over most of the traditional Radical electorate or again form a homogeneous majority government. Dubbing the Radical regime a 'stojanovština' (named after Stojan Protić and reminiscent of the 'vladanovština' under Vladan Đorđević), they increasingly abandoned their traditional hostility to the Liberals and Progressives and instead began closing ranks with them against the Old Radicals. The Independents denounced their Old Radical former comrades in terms such as 'janissary polity', 'state parasite', 'true Turk' and 'villains and criminals', exacerbating the bitterness of the Radical divorce and of the inter-party struggle more generally.[56] Meanwhile, Progressive criticism of the government, though phrased less aggressively than that of the Independents, was equally hard-hitting.[57]

The Radical–conspirator duumvirate was increasingly characterised by political and state terrorism, with the army, police and Radicals working hand in hand. After the counter-conspiracy within the army had been broken by arrests, Captain Novaković was sent to prison for the second time. Protić introduced a writ in August 1906 permitting special measures against labour unrest.[58] The Radicals viewed the Social Democrats, on account of their links with Social Democrats in Germany and Austria-Hungary, as 'Austrian spies' and as people 'who eat frogs, lizards and snakes ... who want to turn the state into a whorehouse; who don't want offspring'.[59] Student demonstrations in Belgrade were brutally suppressed by the police in December 1906 and the army broke up a strike in Čukarica in February 1907, killing four workers in the process.[60] The Radicals' capitulation to the conspirators in 1906 made the latter more brazen in their use of violence and intimidation; early the following year, Pavle Marinković and the Liberal deputy Mihailo Đorđević were attacked by army officers while leaving parliament. The Social Democrat Mihailo Ilić was attacked in Kragujevac and his fellow Social Democrat Dragiša Lapčević, one of the most forthright critics of military interference in politics, received a written threat from 'forty sharp sabres' warning him that 'the boot rules by the highest authority' and that he would suffer Marinković and Đorđević's fate.[61]

The opposition's obstruction of parliament forced Protić's resignation as interior minister in May 1907 and his replacement by Nastas Petrović. On 16 September 1907, Captain Novaković was murdered along with another prisoner on Petrović's orders and in his presence. The opposition, comprising Liberals, Progressives and Independents, responded by organising a mass protest rally in Belgrade, whereupon the Radical government placed the army on alert and brought in additional troops from the interior. Despite the opposition's outrage, the government refused to discuss the murder in parliament on the grounds that it was a matter for the courts. The Social Democratic deputy Triša Kaclerović subsequently wrote sarcastically: 'This murder was one of many evil examples which played themselves out "in the constitutional monarchy with a parliamentary system of government".'[62] Parliament on 28 November rejected by 81 votes to 54 a proposal to condemn the murder and the government's complicity in it. The size of the minority vote reflected widespread disillusion with the new order and revulsion at the murder, which was widely interpreted as dynastic, part of the long history of bloodletting between the Karađorđevićes and Obrenovićes that the 'revolution' of 29 May was supposed to have ended but clearly had not.[63]

The ferocious party strife undermined the government's attempts to resolve the dispute with Austria-Hungary, as the opposition presented its concessions as treason. Pašić's offer to buy part of Serbia's guns from Škoda did not satisfy Vienna, which escalated its economic pressure against Serbia on 7 July 1906, declaring a full tariff war that lasted until January 1911. Petar rebuked Pašić for provoking the conflict with Austria-Hungary and put pressure on him to purchase Serbia's guns from Škoda; when Pašić resisted, the king attempted unsuccessfully to oust him.[64] Nevertheless, Pašić signed a contract on 7 November to purchase guns from Schneider-Creusot and five days later reached agreement for an additional loan of 95 million francs from the French National Bank. Yet when Pašić agreed in March 1907 to meet with Austro-Hungarian foreign minister Count Alois Lexa von Aehrenthal to resolve the dispute, he was bitterly accused by the Independent newspaper *Odjek* of being a 'professional swindler' who had 'treasonously conspired against the country'.[65]

The Pig War forced Serbia to develop alternative economic links with other countries, helping free it from dependence on Austria-Hungary. This was difficult, given that neighbouring countries mostly replicated Serbia's primarily agricultural economy, so trading possibilities with them were limited, while Serbia's agricultural exports—primarily grain, fruit, cattle and pigs—were largely unsuited to long-distance export, a problem exacerbated by Serbia's lack of a seaport. Paču negotiated an agreement in Geneva on 12 November 1906 for a further loan floated with mostly French and partly Swiss capital and Belgrade finalised its contract with Schneider-Creusot on 30 December. During late 1906 and 1907, Serbia established thirteen commercial agencies abroad: in Alexandria, Varna, Brăila, Geneva, Naples, Constantinople, London, Marseilles, Berlin, Brussels, Salonika, Antwerp and Malta.[66] Tariff agreements were reached with Romania, Italy, France, Britain, Russia, Switzerland, Belgium and Sweden in January–April 1907 and in subsequent years with Norway, Denmark and Portugal.[67] Capital investment from other foreign countries filled the vacuum created by Austria-Hungary's withdrawal: British, German, Italian, Belgian and, above all, French. The Pig War sharpened Belgrade's interest in developing a railway link to the Adriatic Sea, something Vienna was determined to resist since it wanted any Serbian outlet to the sea to go via Bosnia-Hercegovina and Dalmatia, to ensure Serbia's continued dependence on Austria–Hungary.[68]

Serbia succeeded in the period 1906–1908 in finding new markets outside Austria-Hungary for most of its exports. Although there were some products for which few or no alternative markets could be found, such as live pigs and fresh fruit, overall Serbian exports actually expanded and industrial production rose. Vienna's tariff war had therefore backfired spectacularly, succeeding only in reducing its own share of the Serbian market to the benefit of other powers and emancipating its smaller neighbour from its economic domination.[69] This prompted Aehrenthal to soften his policy, though he had to contend with Austro-Hungarian agrarian interests that viewed Serbian produce as competition. Pašić meanwhile focused his foreign policy on competing with Bulgaria for influence in Macedonia; on 24 October 1907, in talks with Aehrenthal, he told the latter sincerely that his government had no intentions of any kind toward Bosnia-Hercegovina and that he would assist Vienna regarding those provinces, but that Belgrade wanted in return a free hand over Macedonia.⁷⁰ An agreement on 14 March 1908 permitted Serbia to export a limited amount of processed meat to Austria-Hungary but only on unsatisfactory terms, so that obstruction of Serbia's export of livestock and meat products to the empire continued. The agreement was consequently condemned by the Independent opposition, which called it an 'economic Slivnica' (referring to the defeat by Bulgaria in 1885) and forced the government's resignation.⁷¹

Elections held on 18 May 1908 were marked by widespread Radical violence against supporters of the opposition, causing the Independent newspaper *Odjek* to comment: 'The bloody and barbarous fusionist regime has again engaged in shedding blood.'⁷² They gave the Radicals 44.1 per cent of the vote against 31.2 per cent for the Independents and 23.3 per cent for the Liberals and Progressives. This amounted to 84 seats for the Radicals and 76 for the other parties combined. The Radicals formed a new government, but the Independents continued to undermine it by obstructing approval of the agreement with Austria-Hungary. Lacking a strong majority, the Radicals were forced to accommodate the Independents, leading to the formation on 20 July of a government of moderate Radicals under Velimirović, broadened the following month to include three Independents. This enabled the ratification of the agreement with Austria-Hungary on 18 August. But the new government too was unstable, as Pašić and his Radical hardliners soon began undermining it.

Annexation crisis

The Austro-Serbian conflict was catalysed by shifts in the alignments and policies of the Great Powers. The Anglo-French entente of 1904, Russia's military defeat by Japan in 1905 and the Anglo-Russian entente of 1907 constituted a revolution in international politics that reoriented Russia's imperialist ambition away from Asia and back toward the Balkans, undermining the Mürzsteg entente with Austria-Hungary and reawakening the rivalry between the two empires. In the short term, Anglo-Russian collaboration led to the Reval agreement in June 1908, whereby Macedonia's Ottoman governor was to be appointed with the agreement of the Great Powers and assisted by their officers. This was supported by France but opposed by Germany and Austria-Hungary. To the Turkish opposition organised in the Committee of Union and Progress (CUP– 'Young Turks'), Reval portended a Great Power conflict over Macedonia that would lose the Ottoman Empire that territory as it had lost Bosnia-Hercegovina, Cyprus, Egypt and Crete. To save it, CUP military officers in Macedonia revolted in July.⁷³ Sultan Abdul Hamid II capitulated on 24 July, announcing the restoration of the Ottoman constitution. The CUP assumed power.

The Young Turk revolution galvanised Bosnia-Hercegovina's opposition, comprising the Serb National Organisation and the Muslim National Organisation, to demand that as a constituent part of the Ottoman Empire, Bosnia-Hercegovina also be granted a constitution establishing a parliament and guaranteeing civic and political freedom. Representatives of these two parties submitted this demand to Ban István Burián on 7 September.[74] Austria-Hungary was faced with the threat that Bosnia-Hercegovina might be represented in the new Ottoman parliament or establish its own parliament independently of Vienna, jeopardising its control of the occupied country.[75] Consequently, Austria-Hungary annexed Bosnia-Hercegovina on 5 October 1908. The timing of the annexation, forced upon Vienna by local events, derailed Russian and Serbian diplomacy aimed at avoiding a crisis. Russian foreign minister Alexander Izvolsky had agreed with Aehrenthal to recognise the annexation in return for the opening of the Straits to Russian warships, but had not had time to win the other Great Powers' acceptance of this. Serbian foreign minister Milovan Milovanović had responded to the news that Bosnia-Hercegovina would be annexed by seeking territorial compensation for Serbia in the region of the Sanjak that would provide it with a territorial link with Montenegro; this had been accepted by Izvolsky but not by Aehrenthal. Milovanović informed Petar, Crown Prince Đorđe, the Radical leaders and the government of the impending annexation at a meeting in late September, after which the government adopted his strategy. The annexation presented Russia and Serbia with a fait accompli that affronted public opinion in both countries, while giving them nothing in return.

The annexation therefore came as no surprise to Serbia's political elite. The opposition, however, sought to exploit it at the government's expense, channelling the outburst of anti-Habsburg nationalism to swell its own support. On 6 October, the day the annexation became public knowledge in Serbia, *Odjek* issued an extra issue, calling for Belgrade's population to demonstrate against Austria-Hungary. Consequently, Davidović presided that day over a crowd of over 20,000 people at the National Theatre in Belgrade, at which he called for a fight to the death against the Habsburgs: 'We will struggle until we are victorious, but if we are defeated, we will be defeated knowing that we gave our greatest effort, and that we have the respect not only of all Serbs but also of the whole Slavic race'.[76] Placed on the back foot, Milovanović issued a circular to the Great Powers on 7 October declaring that, if the status quo ante regarding Bosnia-Hercegovina were not restored, an acceptable alternative would be 'that Serbia receive appropriate compensation that would provide guarantees for its independent state life and restore to the Serbian people conditions for its national survival, at least to the degree granted it by the Treaty of Berlin'.[77] He and war minister Stepa Stepanović called up 20,000 reservists, doubling the size of the army.

Milovanović's response failed to appease domestic nationalist opinion. At another demonstration that day at the National Theatre, the crowd of 20,000 shouted not only 'Long live Bosnia, down with Austria!' but 'The government must pack its bags and go home!' At the rally, Protić accused Milovanović of being willing to sell Bosnia-Hercegovina like a 'flea-market vendor'.[78] The crowd marched on the foreign ministry and pelted it with rocks; the police had to be summoned to confront the crowd with bayonets. Skerlić later recalled the 'September days, when the leaders of the Radical party ... assembled a street rabble, and with that unbridled street rabble came before the Ministry of Foreign Affairs, chased the terrorised minister Milovan Milovanović into a small room and themselves appeared on the balcony and gave incendiary speeches to the masses who had gathered before the ministry'.[79] The conspirators were similarly aggressive; Major Tankosić climbed into Milovanović's carriage in the street and threatened him with violence if he did not accept their advice over foreign policy.[80] They reacted particularly strongly against the government's initiative, backed by the leaders of the Radicals, Independents and Progressives and initially also the king, to pardon the imprisoned contras—at a time when national unity appeared crucial. The conspirators threatened Davidović that they would kill his children if he supported this proposal. Petar folded before their pressure and the government was forced to withdraw the proposal, although a few of the imprisoned contras who were ill were pardoned.[81]

Pašić responded to the annexation by calling for secret mobilisation and preparation for war.[82] General Božidar Janković on 8 October 1908 proposed the creation in Serbia of a guerrilla organisation for action against the Austro-Hungarians in Bosnia-Hercegovina. This was founded on 21 October with the name of 'National Defence', headed by Janković as president and Captain Milan Vasić as secretary. Senior officers and prominent conspirators and Chetniks were involved in its establishment.[83] Within a month, National Defence had formed 200 local committees under a central organisation in Belgrade, recruited over 5,000 volunteers, and organised guerrilla bands.[84] Đorđe led a rally in Belgrade on 11 October of over 10,000 people at which he advocated a crusade against Austria-Hungary: 'I am extremely proud to be a soldier and I would be proud to be the one who leads you, the Serbian people, in this desperate struggle for life and death, for our nation and our honour.'[85] Old Vladimir Jovanović, who in 1866 had advocated Serbia joining Prussia and Italy in war against Austria, now reprised his anti-Austrian stance, writing that the 'Austrian annexation of Bosnia-Hercegovina counts as a step in the Austro-German expansion towards the East', representing a 'pan-German peril' and 'Drang nach Osten'; consequently, the 'young and rising Serb nation can perform great services for Europe: powerfully repelling invasion by every military conquering force toward the East; defending and safeguarding the freedom and security of traffic on the great eastern roads; and developing and spreading culture and civilisation'.[86]

Milovanović warned the opposition against its warmongering: 'If the Serbian government adopts your point of view and embarks on such a perilous adventure at this time and provokes war with Austria-Hungary, it would be suicide for us all.' Serbia could not fight a war against Austria-Hungary given Russia's unwillingness to intervene on its side; it should keep in step with Russia and liberate Bosnia-Hercegovina when it was militarily capable of doing so. In a vote of confidence, parliament supported the government: 105 deputies sided with it, including 48

RADICAL–CONSPIRATOR CONDOMINIUM

Independents, 30 Radicals, 20 Liberals and 7 Progressives, while only 54 deputies, all Pašić Radicals, voted against.[87] Thus, the Independents sided with Milovanović and Velimirović's moderate Radicals to isolate and defeat their principal opponents. This support came at a price: Milovanović had to permit parliamentary involvement in his diplomatic response to the annexation, which meant it would be shaped by Serbian nationalist sentiment rather than simply by his interpretation of Serbia's state interest. His nationalist critics complained that abandoning Bosnia-Hercegovina in return for compensation would ruin Belgrade's reputation among the Habsburg South Slavs. Consequently, his note to the Great Powers on 15 October demanded that, failing the annexation's nullification, Bosnia-Hercegovina should receive autonomy within the Habsburg Empire.[88] Temporarily reconciled by shared opposition to the annexation, Serbia and Montenegro signed an agreement on 24 October for 'common and fraternal work on the defence of common national and state interests'.[89]

Milovanović's diplomacy nevertheless remained focused on obtaining compensation for Serbia, above all access to Montenegro and to Austro-Hungarian ports via Bosnian territory and a railway link. Vienna did make a concession to Russia and the Ottoman Empire by withdrawing its garrisons from the Sanjak. This removed an obstacle to the unification of Serbia and Montenegro but also made an eventual Austro-Hungarian attack on Serbia more likely. According to an Austro-Hungarian foreign ministry memorandum of 25 October 1908, the Sanjak had lost its strategic value for the empire, whose further expansion into the Balkans toward Salonika could only proceed via Serbia. Rather than holding the Sanjak to contain Serbia, Austria-Hungary would have to subordinate Serbia itself.[90] But the Great Powers were unwilling to put pressure on Vienna to compensate Serbia. Milovanović's failure left him vulnerable to domestic nationalist criticism. To pre-empt this, in a speech to parliament on 2 January 1909, distributed to Serbian diplomatic staff the following day, he denounced Austro-Hungarian policy in the Balkans and reasserted Serbia's vital interest in a close association with Bosnia-Hercegovina: 'By seizing Bosnia-Hercegovina, throwing Serbia back from the Adriatic Sea and preventing our linking with Montenegro, Austria-Hungary has imposed upon Serbia and Serbdom, either in the nearer or more distant future, a life-and-death struggle.' The speech earned Milovanović a standing ovation and a declaration from Pašić that parliament had confidence in him. But Vienna viewed it as a declaration of hostility, ensuring it would not grant Serbia compensation.[91] It escalated the tariff war to a full-scale economic blockade, preventing Serbia importing the military supplies needed if war had erupted.

Velimirović's government was forced to resign by Pašić's Radicals on 7 February 1909. The Independents' rhetoric descended into full-blown orientalism; contrasting themselves with their former comrades, they claimed that 'today are seen those two Serbias; the old, Balkan, half-wild Serbia ... and the new, reborn, cultured, patriotic Serbia'.[92] The strength of parliamentary opposition prevented Pašić from forming the next government. Given the acute international crisis and under pressure from the king, the Radicals agreed to join a coalition government formed on 24 February, comprising members of all four principal parties, headed by Stojan Novaković, in which Pašić was merely construction minister while Protić was excluded altogether. This closing of ranks between the four parties reflected an almost complete national consensus on foreign policy. A tiny faction of Progressives, comprising Perić and his supporters, remained loyal to their party's traditional Austrophilia; Perić advocated a federal union between Serbia and Austria-Hungary as Serbia's only path to the West, and the achievement of South Slavic unification within the Habsburg framework.[93] This faction established itself as a new Conservative Party on 20 April 1914, advocating strong monarchical authority and a two-chamber parliament.[94] But it was stillborn.

The Ottoman Empire recognised the annexation on 26 February 1909 in return for an indemnity from Austria-Hungary. Under pressure from Vienna, Constantinople now banned the import of military materials into Serbia across its territory. Aehrenthal then issued an ultimatum to Belgrade to recognise the Austro-Ottoman agreement and annexation and to guarantee Vienna a 'correct and peaceful policy'. As Serbia's government resisted and war seemed likely, the Habsburg Empire's Crown Ministerial Council on 27 March 1909 permitted a partial mobilisation of the army. With Russia itself forced by a German ultimatum to recognise the annexation, Serbia had to follow suit on 31 March. It was also forced to undertake to reduce the size of its army to its pre-crisis level, suppress all protests and irregular military activity directed against Austria-Hungary including by National Defence, and alter its policy toward it, to one of good neighbourliness.[95] This capitulation softened Habsburg policy toward Serbia. After further hard bargaining, Vienna and Belgrade signed a treaty on 27 July 1910 regulating Serbian exports to and transit rights across Austria-Hungary, which came into effect in late January 1911, thereby ending the Pig War.

The trade war had, by reducing the economic centrality of Austria-Hungary as an export market for Serbia's farm produce, boosted and diversified its industrial development. The number of Serbian factories doubled between 1906 and 1914 while the number of industrial enterprises rose from 110 to 465 and the number of industrial workers grew by two and a half times to around 16,000. The value of factory products increased from 24 to 59 million dinars between 1898 and 1910—a growth of 146 per cent, or 104 per cent if the population increase is considered. The economic value of the output of Serbia's mines increased tenfold in the same period while the value of industrial production including mining rose from 10.75 to 24.38 dinars per head of population, or by 127 per cent.[96] Although Austria-Hungary's share of Serbian exports subsequently rose again to about 40 per cent, from a low of 18–19 per cent during the dispute, it never again approached its pre-conflict level of about 90 per cent.[97] Thus, Serbia had greatly increased its economic independence from

RADICAL–CONSPIRATOR CONDOMINIUM

Austria-Hungary but was still dangerously dependent upon it. Belgrade continued to seek alternative relations. Finance minister Paču signed a new loan agreement in Paris on 9 November 1909. Another diplomatic success was achieved with Petar's visit to Constantinople and meetings with the Sultan and Patriarch in April 1910, after which a Serb bishop, Petar Rosić, was appointed bishop of Veles Debar, giving Serbia its third bishop in the Ottoman lands to its south.[98]

National Defence survived under the guise of a cultural society. It grew rapidly to 220 branches in Serbia with strong influence in Bosnia-Hercegovina, and provided cover for other, more militant anti-Habsburg factions—particularly the Black Hand.[99] Its central committee published a programme in 1911 calling for 'a new Serbia, in which every Serbian, from child to greybeard, is a rifleman', and declaring, 'If National Defence preaches the necessity of fighting Austria, she preaches a sacred truth of our national position.'[100] In Olga Popović-Obradović's words, there arose a 'widespread mood which from 1908 would grip Serbia like a true war psychosis'.[101] The first Serb shots against Austro-Hungarian rule in Bosnia-Hercegovina were fired on 15 June 1910 by Bogdan Žerajić, a young Hercegovinian who had fled to Serbia following the annexation, joined National Defence and undertaken military training. Attempting to shoot the Habsburg military governor of Bosnia-Hercegovina, Žerajić missed with five bullets from his revolver then used his sixth bullet to kill himself. His attempt inspired subsequent Bosnian radical youths up to and including Gavrilo Princip, who vowed to avenge him.[102]

The atmosphere in Serbia of an impending national liberation war intensified political divisions. Despite their anti-militarist traditions, the Radicals increasingly portrayed themselves as an 'army'. *Samouprava* stated in March 1910, 'In a political struggle it is the same as in a war ... In a struggle that needs successes, everything must be sacrificed, even personal interests ... In days of struggle every soldier must be in his position.'[103] Despite the formation of Novaković's all-party coalition government, Radical terrorism increased, involving frequent murders, in particular of Liberals and Progressives but also of Independents. Novaković's government was allowed to function until after the annexation crisis had passed, after which it collapsed owing to its internal differences. These included Liberal justice minister Ribarac's attempt at a mass amnesty of political prisoners, which the Independents opposed on the grounds that it would involve amnestying contras. Ribarac and Novaković resigned on 8 October 1909 and a new Radical–Independent coalition government was formed under Pašić three days later. This lasted until June 1911, when Protić and Pašić toppled it so as to replace it with a homogeneous Radical government, formed on the 25th under Milovanović, after which Radical terrorism escalated further.[104]

The Radicals' readiness to acquiesce in murder was incontrovertibly demonstrated by their response to the judicial inquiry that found their former interior minister Nastas Petrović guilty of the killing of Milan Novaković. The court of first instance had on 12 May 1908 halted judicial proceedings against Belgrade's mayor and gendarmerie commander on the grounds that Petrović's presence at the crime scene absolved them of responsibility, which was consequently transferred to him. The court ruled that since Petrović was subject to the law on ministerial responsibility, it was up to parliament to bring him before the state court. Ribarac pursued the matter in parliament and eventually, on 18 March 1911, twenty Liberal and Progressive deputies proposed that Petrović be tried before the state court. The Radical ministers, having originally declined to take action against Petrović on the grounds that it was a matter for the courts, now refused to accept the court's prompting to take action against him. Petrović himself admitted ordering Novaković's murder on the grounds that Novaković had been an 'open enemy of the 29 May revolution'. This argument—that the need to defend the outcome of the May putsch by killing one of its enemies overrode the rule of law—was accepted by the Radicals and Independents. Consequently, on 19 April 1911 parliament rejected the motion to indict Petrović.[105]

Black Hand and White Hand

Old King Petar was a gentle man who walked among the citizens of Serbia, chatting to and smoking with them as equals, earning the affectionate nickname 'Our King Uncle Petar'. Nevertheless, he remained unpopular. Despite his spinelessness before the conspirators, Apis did not consider him a suitable leader for the national liberation struggle. He was disappointed by his unwillingness to act decisively against Pašić and the Radicals. Apis wanted a 'fiery king who would raise the nation to its feet, begin the war for the unification of all South Slavs, defeat Austria-Hungary and show the world and Europe who the Serbs were and what a power Serbia was'. He first placed his hopes in Đorđe, and accompanied him on a trip to Italy and Switzerland in order to become better acquainted with him. But this apparently convinced him that Đorđe too would be an unsuitable king, wholly uninterested either in politics or in his future royal duties.[106] Đorđe was mentally unstable and prone to verbal and physical assaults, against his servants, brother and even father. On one occasion, he assaulted his French tutor, threatened to kill him, had to be physically restrained by his adjutants, passed out and, after awakening, continued in his tantrum to break objects in his vicinity, for which his father punished him with ten days in prison.[107] Đorđe was also unwilling to kowtow to Apis and the conspirators, as his father did, and quarrelled violently with them.

The conspirators had, immediately after the putsch, obtained influential positions close to the royal family; Antonije Antić had been appointed escort to Đorđe and Petar Živković to Đorđe's younger brother Prince Aleksandar. The second appointment produced a partnership that would play a decisive role in Serbian politics for the next three decades. According to Apis's biographer David Mackenzie, the relationship between Aleksandar and Živković may have had a homosexual dimension and eventually involved Živković's blackmailing of the prince, although Mackenzie's account is heavily slanted against them both and has homophobic undertones, raising doubts about its reliability. Meanwhile, Josif Kostić became Aleksandar's ordnance officer.[108] The conspirators agitated with Aleksandar's blessing at court and in the popular press against Đorđe, who identified Živković, his brother's leading supporter among the conspirators, as a particular enemy. In October 1907, he obtained Živković's exile to France for fifteen months and a decree relocating Apis to Valjevo. Apis, meanwhile, conspired with Kaclerović to overthrow Đorđe; the Social Democrats misidentified the prince as the principal representative of nationalist militarism.[109] Some conspirators, including Živković and Vemić, apparently plotted with Aleksandar's blessing to poison Đorđe; Vemić recorded in his diary that 'at a meeting of the conspirators it was resolved to give the madman a fluid'.[110] Apis acquired five bottles of poison for this purpose, but apparently had second thoughts and refused to support the plot.[111]

Đorđe nevertheless believed Apis and his circle wanted to kill him. He accused Antić: 'What do you want; you, your Apis and Genčić? You killed King Aleksandar and you want to kill me too.'[112] He became increasingly paranoid. Learning on 27 February 1909 that his own manservant, Stevan Kolaković, had apparently lost or stolen a letter that the prince had written to his girlfriend, he concluded he was involved in the plot against him. Enraged, he savagely beat Kolaković, kicking him in the stomach and rupturing a hernia. Kolaković was hospitalised and died several days later.[113] Guilt-stricken according to own account, Đorđe's resistance to the conspirators collapsed and he renounced his right to the throne on 11 March, which Petar, as the conspirators' prisoner, duly accepted, possibly under threat. Rumours and reports circulated among officialdom in Vienna that the conspirators were planning to overthrow the Karađorđević dynasty altogether; Genčić and Damjan Popović were mentioned in this context. Interior minister Ljubomir Jovanović informed the government that the conspirators, including Apis, Živković, Antić, Josif Kostić and others, had held meetings at which they expressed dissatisfaction with Petar for failing to grant them adequate positions in the state, and sought his replacement.[114]

Apis then turned his attention to the new crown prince. Aleksandar (1888–1934) was much more ambitious and capable than Đorđe. An army officer trained in a St Petersburg military academy, he would prove himself as authoritarian and ruthless as previous Serbian princes and kings. He actively sought to ingratiate himself with Apis so as to enlist his help in becoming heir to the throne. He gifted him rings, gold watches and cigarette cases and made a large financial donation to *Pijemont* (Piedmont), the newspaper of Apis's circle.[115] This strategy succeeded in convincing Apis that Aleksandar would be a more pliant tool than Đorđe. By late 1910 or early 1911, Apis was plotting to force Petar to abdicate in favour of Aleksandar, in order to expel the Radicals from government and replace them with the Independents and Liberals.[116] In fact, the new crown prince, having used Apis's clique to oust his brother and sideline his father, soon turned against it as the next obstacle on his own path to power, cultivating those former conspirators hostile to it. This caused the conspirators to split into two factions: the dominant one, including Apis and the other most eminent regicides, which would become the Black Hand and which sought to dominate Serbian political life in pursuit of its foreign and domestic agenda; and an initially weaker one headed by Živković and Kostić, which rejected such independent military interference in politics and coalesced around Aleksandar, eventually called the White Hand. Though various personal quarrels and disagreements over intrigues have been cited to explain the split,[117] it boiled down to a struggle for pre-eminence between Aleksandar and Apis.

Apis's clique was prompted to act by the 'treason of the government' in accepting the 'conditions of capitulation in March 1909' to the Habsburg diktat and by its curbing of National Defence and, after the Young Turk revolution, of Serb irredentist activities in Macedonia.[118] They formally established a new, more militant and secret nationalist organisation on 3 March 1911, called Unification or Death. The ten founding members included Apis; Bogdan Radenković, chief secretary of the Skopje metropolitanate, an official of the Serb ministry for foreign affairs and a Serb guerrilla leader and activist in Macedonia; the lawyer Ljubomir Jovanović-Čupa, also a guerrilla in Macedonia; Milan Vasić, secretary of National Defence; and two of the actual murderers of Aleksandar and Draga, Vemić and Ilija Radivojević, the second of whom became Unification or Death's president. This group, with four others, formed the organisation's supreme central administration, whose constitution they signed on 9 May.[119] It was principally written by Jovanović-Čupa, who had completed his studies in Brussels, where he had spent three and a half years in the library researching how to be a nationalist activist. The secret Italian and German nationalist organisations and activists of the first half of the nineteenth century, in particular Philippe Buonarroti (1761–1837), inspired Unification or Death's constitution, sections of which were also based on the 1869 text 'Catechism of a Revolutionary' written by Nechayev, possibly in conjunction with Bakunin.[120] The constitution pledged that for the purpose of 'realising the national ideals—the unification of Serbdom', it would 'exercise its influence over all the official factors in Serbia as Piedmont and over all social layers and the entire social life in it' and 'establish a revolutionary organisation in all territories in which Serbs live'. It defined the 'Serb regions' as '1) Bosnia-Hercegovina, 2) Montenegro, 3) Old Serbia and Macedonia, 4) Croatia, Slavonia and Srem, 5) Vojvodina, 6) Primorje [Dalmatia]'. The Slovenian lands were not included. Its coat of arms was 'a skull with crossed bones'—an Orthodox Christian symbol found on churches throughout Serbia.[121] The skull and crossbones featured also on its seal, which also featured a flag, dagger and vial of poison.

Unification or Death was a small body of elite revolutionaries organised on a pyramidal basis, with cells of three to five members each, above which were more senior committees in turn headed by the supreme central administration. Its core was composed predominantly of former conspirators, around 70 to 80 of whom remained grouped around Apis on the eve of the Balkan Wars in 1912, although not all belonged to Unification or Death itself. Contemporary estimates of the organisation's size vary wildly from about 2,500 to 150,000,[122] but by nature the distinction between its formal members and its broader web of sympathisers was vague. One recruit recalled an induction ceremony that took place in a darkened room with a table covered by a black tablecloth on which a small lit candle revealed a cross, dagger and revolver. A member of the supreme central administration wearing a black robe, hood and mask stood silently while the recruit had the organisation's goals read to him and he made his pledge to it. According to its constitution, 'I pledge on the sun that warms me, the earth that feeds me, God, the blood of my father, my honour and life that I will from this moment till death faithfully serve the tasks of this organisation and always be ready to bear any sacrifice for it.'[123] The organisation worked through National Defence, co-opting the latter's network of agents in Bosnia-Hercegovina and other South Slav lands. National Defence performed legal and cultural activities while Unification or Death conducted more militant, secret and illegal actions.[124] After Vasić's death in the Balkan Wars, Unification or Death's direct control over National Defence lessened somewhat, since the latter's president, General Janković, was aligned with Pašić. However, Apis was, on 18 August 1913, appointed chief of the intelligence division of the operational section of the general staff in Belgrade, giving him direct institutional supervision over Serbian military intelligence's network of agents within National Defence.[125] Unification or Death came to be known as the Black Hand, a nickname apparently coined by the Viennese journalist Leopold Mandl then adopted by the Belgrade press.[126]

The Black Hand's goal was not only national liberation and unification but to subordinate Serbia's state, parliament and political life to its will, thereby establishing a praetorian regime. In its first programmatic issue dated 21 August 1911 (3 September 1911), the Black Hand's newspaper *Pijemont* declared its goal was that 'Serbia must, and really as soon as possible, become the Piedmont of the Serb Nation'. Since 'all political parties up till now have displayed their immorality, lack of culture and lack of patriotism ... new political organisations were needed'. Launched to promote such an organisation, 'Pijemont believes that Serbia in its foreign policy has only one goal: national liberation and unification'. Since 'Serbia cannot be Piedmont unless it has an army that is always ready' and since war with Austria-Hungary was unavoidable, 'Pijemont will seek for Serbia to prepare day and night for this war, which will be a life-and-death struggle'. Regarding national liberation and unification, 'whoever is opposed to this idea is our enemy, and who is for is our friend and ally', from which it was clear 'how small is the number of our friends, while the number of our enemies is very large'. To achieve this goal, 'the nurturing of a cult of the state must begin. Without such a cult, Serbia cannot feel itself to be *Pijemont*.' Consequently, 'In opposition to decentralism, Pijemont seeks centralism.' It concluded that 'parliamentarism is not the final word of political wisdom', since 'Demagogy has compromised and misused political freedom'. Consequently, 'There must, on the question of civic freedom, be implemented a middle measure that will correspond to the level of our general culture and civilisation.' A better state administration was needed, whose priority would be 'national health and the racial regeneration of the people' to produce 'better heirs, better people, new Serbs'.[127]

This ideology was the antithesis of Radical anti-state ideology. It could be traced back to Milan's authoritarian, anti-Radical court faction from Aleksandar's reign and to the ethos of the elite forged under Aleksandar, which saw itself as standing above party divisions. Yet it also reflected the influence of the Radicals' anti-pluralist concept of homogeneous nationhood. Like other proto-fascist groups in Europe at that time, the Black Hand sought to channel pressures for social revolution in violent, extreme-nationalist directions. Thus, it upheld the 'economic prosperity of all classes' but specified that 'relations among them [nations] are regulated by force, and it is natural that "Pijemont" seeks that Serbia have an army as large and well armed as possible ... it is the duty of our nation to fight and work to win for itself a dignified place in Europe and in the sun.'[128] The domestic and foreign goals of the Black Hand dovetailed, for the organisation's leadership hoped Serbian military victories would bring it more prestige and supporters, so facilitating the attainment of its domestic agenda.[129] *Pijemont* thundered against the 'immorality', 'barbarity' and 'treachery' of the political parties, yet Protić continued to advocate 'substantial punishment' for anyone publishing criticism of the conspirators. Kaclerović described Serbia in March 1911 as a 'military camp', for which he held the Radicals responsible. The Radicals 'based the whole of this regime on pure military force', said Pavle Marinković in January of that year, 'and the military element has never been stronger in the state, in politics, than it is today'.[130]

The White Hand, although initially weaker than the Black Hand, bolstered itself by recruiting former Obrenović loyalists who had not supported the 1903 putsch, particularly former contras.[131] The organisation was formally founded at a meeting at the Hotel Paris, attended by Živković, Kostić, Antić and the contras Miloš Vasić and Mihailo Rašić.[132] Crown Prince Aleksandar, as chief inspector of the army, launched an investigation in 1911 to determine the Black Hand's existence within the army. The investigation was assisted by White Handers, including Živković and Kostić. The Black Hand retaliated in January 1912 by engineering the transfer of several White Hand officers, including Živković and Kostić, from Belgrade to Serbia's interior. The transfer was ordered by war minister Stepanović, at the suggestion of Black Hand sympathiser General Miloš Božanović, military commander of Belgrade. This temporarily crippled Aleksandar's embryonic officers' clique; the defeat prompted him to offer his resignation as chief inspector of the army, which he was nevertheless persuaded to retract by Serbia's political and military leaders.¹³³ He then sought reconciliation with Apis; when the latter nearly died of food poisoning following a covert trip into Ottoman Macedonia, Aleksandar paid for his medical treatment, even importing a medical specialist from Berlin.

The White Hand gravitated toward the Radicals and the Black Hand to their political opponents, above all the Independents. The Liberals shifted from their earlier position of using the question of the conspirators as a stick with which to beat Radical governments to viewing them as a counterweight to the Radicals. Yet the confidence of the Radicals was strengthened by the support given them by the White Hand, encouraging their increasing rejection of the conspirators' yoke. A personal link between the Radicals and White Hand was provided by Petar Mišić, who, after dismissal from the army at Britain's demand and Apis's behest, became a Radical politician. Rejoining his former conspiratorial comrades at the head of the White Hand, he was restored to duty in the army during the Balkan Wars. Meanwhile, in the months and years following its establishment, the Black Hand systematically bullied and threatened Serbian government ministers and other officials, even warning them they would be killed if they defied it.¹³⁴ An early target of the conspirators' threats, Milovanović in late 1911 reached an accommodation with the Black Hand, hoping he could subordinate it to his policy, 'as if he were following Cavour, who in the pursuit of his national politics utilised Garibaldi and Mazzini, Italian national revolutionaries'. This led to the Black Hand becoming the foreign ministry's executive organ in Macedonia, where irredentist activism was channelled through Black Hand founder Radenković, Serbia's consul in Skopje.¹³⁵ Meanwhile, Milovanović sought to avoid conflict with Austria-Hungary, preferring long-term collaboration with it, whereby Serbia would refrain from seeking unification with the Croats and Slovenes and confine its westward territorial ambitions to Dubrovnik, Boka Kotorska and eastern Bosnia-Hercegovina.¹³⁶

Soon after its foundation, the Black Hand manipulated Serbia's government into establishing a new military institution, the Frontier Guard, which was achieved thanks to the Black Hand's hold over the war ministry through its sympathiser, defence minister Ilija Gojković, and through direct extortion of the necessary funds from an unwilling Radical-controlled finance ministry. Under Black Hand control, the Frontier Guard's purpose was to assist irredentist activity in the Ottoman and Habsburg empires. This was linked to the Black Hand's recruitment among Bosnia-Hercegovina's Serbs, which aimed at expanding its base beyond Serbia, for the sake both of future guerrilla activity in Austria-Hungary and of creating a new base for its political ambitions at home.¹³⁷ The Black Hand commandeered the underground guerrilla channels of National Defence, which served as its fig leaf; collaborators in Bosnia-Hercegovina were enrolled in National Defence rather than the Black Hand.¹³⁸ Black Handers also increasingly led and escalated Serbian guerrilla activity in Macedonia.

SERBIA

The period 1903–1914 has been idealistically viewed as the 'golden age' of Serbian parliamentary democracy. But the reality of first Old Radicals and subsequently Independents collaborating with the conspirators meant both military interference in parliamentary politics and the army's politicisation. The Radicals' electoral hegemony and use of terror against their opponents prompted the latter, particularly Independents and Liberals, to seek allies in the Black Hand, to which the Radicals sought their own counterweight in the White Hand. Meanwhile, Austria-Hungary supported the conspirators in opposition to the pro-Russian, pro-French Radicals, while conservative Serbian politicians supported Austria-Hungary as the Radicals' enemy. With Old Radicals and Independents regularly accusing each other of capitulating to Vienna, governments found it difficult to manage foreign policy independently of nationalist public opinion. These factors intersected dangerously for Serbia as it increasingly clashed with its powerful northern neighbour.

1. Medieval Serbia under Tsar Dusan, c. 1350

2. Ottoman Empire after 1815

3. Serbia, 1815-1833

4. Serbia, 1833-1878

5. Serbia and Vojvodina, 1848

6. Great Bulgaria of the Treaty of San Stefano, 1878

7. Balkans after the Treaty of Berlin, 1878

8. Serbia, 1878-1912

11. Serbia after the Balkan Wars, 1913

12. Austria-Hungary and the Balkan States, 1914

13. Central Powers' conquest of Serbia, 1915

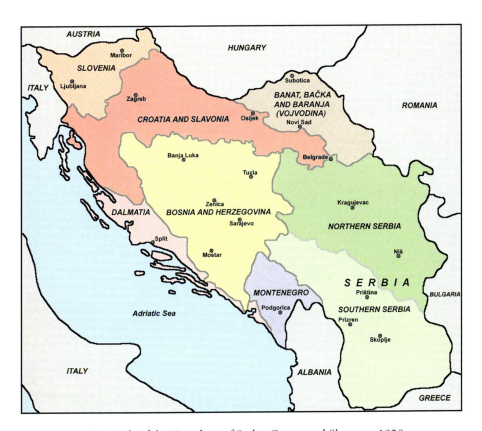

14. Lands of the Kingdom of Serbs, Croats and Slovenes, 1920

15. Oblasts of the Kingdom of Serbs, Croats and Slovenes, 1922

16. Banovinas of the Kingdom of Yugoslavia, 1931-1939

17. Banovina of Croatia and proposed Serb Country, 1939-1941

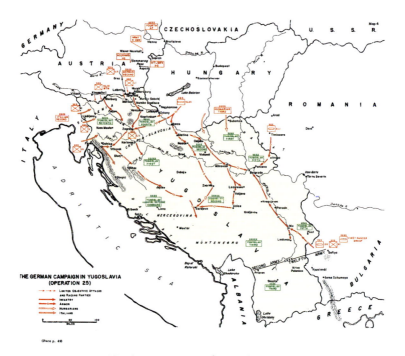

18. Axis conquest of Yugoslavia, 1941

19. Axis dismemberment of Yugoslavia, 1941

12

THE BALKAN WARS AND THE ROAD TO WORLD WAR I

1912–1914

The May putsch ended the long struggle over Serbia's constitutional order, allowing Serbia's political classes in principle to focus more on the pursuit of national goals. After 1903, the Radicals—primarily the Old Radicals and secondarily the Independents—were electorally pre-eminent and their national ideology hegemonic. This ideology was, however, diverging: between a more conservative, Old Radical, 'Great Serbian' current favouring national unification on the basis of the imposition of Serbia's political order on the other South Slav lands; and a more progressivist, Independent Radical, 'Yugoslav' current viewing South Slav unification as an opportunity to transcend the old order in Serbia and the other South Slav lands alike. The Independents' Yugoslavism reflected their opposition to the Old Radicals' hegemony in Serbia and their desire to find new allies against it from among the South Slavs outside Serbia. Meanwhile, Radical governments' pursuit of their national goals faced rivalry and interference from the Black Hand, making a sober and restrained foreign policy, in an increasingly fraught international climate, ever harder to maintain.

Serbian nationalism and South Slav cooperation before 1914

The May putsch coincided with a nationalist upsurge among the Habsburg Empire's South Slav peoples, posing the question of what Serbia's relationship to these peoples should be. The Serbian goal of national liberation and unification has traditionally been presented in terms of two alternative models: a 'Yugoslav' model, whereby Serbs, Croats, Slovenes and other South Slavs were subdivisions of a larger 'Yugoslav' nation or community; and a narrower 'Great Serbian' model, encompassing only those South Slav lands considered Serb. In purely territorial terms, the distinction is anachronistic: Serbian national ideology in the early twentieth century viewed all South Slav lands outside Bulgaria, Istria and present-day Slovenia as Serb lands, while Croatia in the narrow sense (i.e. exclusive of Slavonia and Dalmatia) was sometimes treated as a Serb land and sometimes not. This meant that the coveted territories were not very different whether the project was pan-Serb or Yugoslav. The real difference was over the question of whether Serbia would impose its constitutional order and institutions on the other South Slav lands, making the new state simply a Great Serbia, or whether Serbia and its state and constitutional order would be dissolved in the broader South Slav whole to create something new: Yugoslavia. This question of pan-Serb versus Yugoslav unification superimposed itself on the political divisions within Serbia, with opposing factions posing as champions of each.

Serbia's nationalists consistently opposed any form of South Slav unification that would recognise 'Serb lands' as belonging to other South Slav states, entities or governments. Both Zach and Garašanin feared the emergence of other independent South Slav states separate from Serbia, since 'it would follow that the Serbs would be split up into small provincial principalities under separate dynasts, which would without fail surrender themselves to foreign influence because they would rival and envy each other'.[1] Svetozar Marković condemned Croatian demands for autonomy founded on Croatia's historic right of statehood and the Habsburg Empire's possible federalisation on the basis of Croatia and other historic entities, even suggesting that continued Austro-Hungarian dualist hegemony over the Habsburg Slavs was preferable.[2] Pašić predicated his strategy for national unification on the Serbs in Ottoman and Habsburg lands being unfree in both national and civil terms, since they would be drawn to democratic Serbia: 'Austria would kill the attractive force of the Serbian Piedmont, if it were to unite all the Serb tribes between Trieste and the Kingdom of Serbia and Montenegro and establish a national and cultural centre with its own legislature.'[3]

Following the May putsch, Pašić's strategy for achieving national unification was hegemonic among Serbia's elite. Inspired by the unifications of Italy and Germany under Piedmontese and Prussian leaderships respectively, he concluded that Serbia should be the Piedmont of the South Slavs, implying Serbian leadership over them.[4] As he said in parliament in 1905, 'only a free Serbia; only a Serbia with a free constitutional and parliamentary life can be the centre of Serbdom; can be the Piedmont of the whole of Serbdom'.[5] Pašić believed Serbia's democratic constitutional order should form the basis of the future unified South Slav state, meaning that other South Slavs should accept unification on the Serbian state model. He was not in principle opposed to federalism, provided all Serbs would belong to the Serbian federal unit; this implied Bosnia-Hercegovina's annexation to Serbia along with much of Croatia, which would be reduced to a tiny rump. Since this would be unacceptable to the Croats, Pašić supported a unified, centralised South Slav state as the only alternative.[6]

THE BALKAN WARS AND THE ROAD TO WORLD WAR I

Pašić outlined his views on Serb–Croat relations in his essay 'Unity of the Serbo-Croats', written in the first half of the 1890s. He admitted that the four South Slav groups he recognised (Serbs, Croats, Slovenes and Bulgarians) were a single people whose lands could in principle be unified as a 'Yugoslav' nation on the model of Italy and Germany, but in practice 'prejudices, distinct histories and petty disputes hinder the coalescing of one single people, and that is the coalescing of the Bulgarians-Serbs-Croats-Slovenes as a single nation'. Conversely, he opposed proposals of 'Serb and Croat moderates' for the Serbs and Croats to partition their common lands between themselves: 'The history of the past shows that two independent statelets of a single people governed by different currents cannot survive. Conflict from the past would be renewed in the future.' Consequently, the question was whether unification of the Serbo-Croat lands should be conducted by Croatia or Serbia. This mattered greatly, argued Pašić, because whereas 'the Serb nation has not repudiated any of its sovereign rights in favour of any foreign power or foreign church or foreign dynasty or state', the opposite was true of the Croats.[7]

While the Serb clergy served a national Slavic church, 'the Croat clergy was not and is not now (with few exceptions) a national clergy but a clergy that serves the infallible Pope and executes his regulations and orders', in the service of the 'Vatican's struggle against the Slavic literature and Slavic liturgy'. Support and sympathy for Great Croatian nationalism among Croats were the 'fruit of those ideas which originated with the Catholic religion and Western culture, which are embodied in the expression "*Drang nach Osten*", to which expression the Great Croats are to serve as vanguard'. Ultimately, argued Pašić, 'Western Europe and Eastern Europe are, as we say, two worlds that have been in uninterrupted cultural, religious, national and economic struggle'. The Croats should accept that the 'Serbo-Croat idea' could never be realised under the Habsburg umbrella as the Great Croat nationalists wished, but 'only on the basis of agreement and concord with the two independent Serb states [Serbia and Montenegro] and the protection of mighty Orthodox Russia'.[8] Consequently, unification of the Serbo-Croat lands could and should occur only on the basis of Serbia's leadership and national idea. The point was not simply to acquire maximum territory but to prevent the emergence of a rival, independent, Catholic-led South Slav state.

Serbia's development of a modern school system consolidated the belief among the Serbian population that the South Slav lands to Serbia's north and west were indeed 'Serb lands', albeit there was confusion as to their precise extent. As we have seen, the Chief Educational Council was established on 1 March 1880, tasked with implementing a national plan for education at the school and university level. The first council was appointed by Stojan Novaković, minister of education and religious affairs, who declared that 'the entire future of the nation depends upon schools, and schools will become a strong and powerful organism in the life of the nation only when there is one soul and one goal in every part of the fatherland'.[9] This meant unified school curricula for the Serbian language, history, geography and religion, serving to standardise pupils' conception of nationhood. For example, Vladimir Karić's 1883 geography textbook for the lower grades of secondary schools taught pupils that the Serbian lands included all present-day Croatia, Bosnia-Hercegovina, Vojvodina, Montenegro, Macedonia and Kosovo, and parts of present-day northern Albania, northern Greece, southern Hungary and western Romania.[10] Furthermore, influenced by Vuk Karadžić's linguistic ideas according to which all Štokavian speakers were Serbs, school textbooks of this period included Croat literary texts and authors, presenting them as Serb. With Karadžić's work having popularised among the Serbian intelligentsia the patriotic folklore and poetry of the pre-literate rural masses, pupils were taught poems and stories with overtly patriotic themes and exhorted to be patriots.[11] Serbian nationalists became more ambitious after the 1903 putsch; the 1907 reader for pupils of the fourth level of elementary school authorised by the Chief Educational Council lamented that 'in the beautiful Serbian lands of Bosnia, Hercegovina, Srem, Banat, Bačka, Croatia, Slavonia, Dalmatia, Istria, Old Serbia, Macedonia and the Vidin and Sredac [Sofia] provinces, foreigners rule over the Serbian people ...'[12]

Political parties of the Serbs in Croatia, for their part, were amenable to Yugoslavist politics involving compromise between the Serb and Croat national projects to promote common resistance to Hungary. Several Croat and Serb parties from Austria-Hungary—the Serb Independent Party, Radical Party, Croat Party of Right, Croat Progressive Party and Social Democratic Party—formed the Croat–Serb Coalition on 12 December 1905, supporting Croat–Serb collaboration, Dalmatia's unification with Croatia and universal suffrage. Viewing the Habsburg Empire as the principal enemy and a German *Drang nach Osten* as the principal threat, it aimed to collaborate with the Hungarian opposition and others against them. However, the Radical Party in Croatia, sister party of the Radicals in Serbia, undermined the Coalition. It had followed a trajectory similar to that of its Serbian namesake: beginning as a faction splitting from Svetozar Miletić's Liberal party on left-wing grounds and emphasising socio-economic issues, it had evolved in a conservative direction, upholding the traditional Serbian Orthodox privileges granted by the Habsburgs. It thus focused on the National Church Congress as the principal representative body for Serbs and rejected Serb–Croat kinship and collaboration against the regime. It joined the Croat–Serb Coalition for tactical reasons only and soon left, preferring collaboration with the Habsburg regime.[13]

Pašić's government, committed to peace with Austria-Hungary in the short term, likewise sought to collaborate with Hungary's government against this fledgling movement, joining with it to press the Serb Independent Party of Svetozar Pribićević (1875–1936) to leave the Coalition, albeit unsuccessfully.[14] Habsburg South Slav resistance to Austria-Hungary peaked on 3 March 1909, when the latter launched proceedings against 53 members of the Serb Independent Party, charged with treason as Serbia's agents, while pro-government propaganda vilified all aspects of Serb national life as treasonous. The so-called Zagreb treason trial ended on 5 November in 31 convictions, but all were overturned by the Vienna court of appeal. Also in March, Professor Heinrich Friedjung, in the *Neue Freie Presse*, accused leading South Slav politicians of treason, based upon forged documents, resulting in his defeat in the subsequent libel trial. Despite these legal setbacks for Austria-Hungary's government, the Zagreb trial broke the Serb Independent Party's will to remain in opposition.[15] The turn by the Croat–Serb Coalition, now led by Pribićević, to collaboration with Hungary's government received Serbian government blessing.[16]

Some Independent Radicals, in particular Skerlić, were by contrast interested in Yugoslavist ideas of kinship between Serbs and other South Slavs on a pluralistic basis that suggested a progressive alternative. Independents tended to believe that Serbia's existing order was unworthy of imposition on other South Slav lands, so gravitated towards an ideal of Yugoslavia that would transcend the status quo in all of them.[17] This recalled Marković's belief that revolution needed to overthrow the existing order in the Habsburg and Ottoman empires and the principalities of Serbia and Montenegro alike. The Independents' pro-Yugoslav orientation was consequently linked to more oppositionist Habsburg South Slav currents. In May or June 1905, the Independent Radical Party published its programme, which, in addition to the traditional call for 'Serbia, as the Piedmont of Serbdom, to do everything it is able for unification of all parts of the Serb nation', declared it would 'nurture the spirit of the Yugoslav community'.[18] Independents coalesced around the Yugoslav Club, which grew out of the reading room of the newspaper *Slovenski Jug* (Slavic South) and which became the spiritual centre of Serbia's Yugoslavist movement. Its members included Skerlić and Jovan Cvijić.[19] As Stojanović commented in 1909, 'If similar newspapers appear among the Bulgarians, Croats and Slovenes and if they successfully respond to their tasks, a firm foundation will be laid for the Yugoslav community.'[20]

Jovan Skerlić (1877–1914) was Serbia's leading literary critic. He was born in Belgrade and his father's family originated in what is today Montenegro, but his mother was a Serb from Hungary. Fiercely opposed to Pašić's Old Radicals, he was a Francophile inspired by Yugoslavist currents among the Habsburg South Slavs, in particular by the neo-Slavic Prague congress of July 1908. His Yugoslavist perspective was formed by his study of Habsburg South Slav literature and from the writings of Marković, whose belief in a Balkan federation of equals was closer to Yugoslavism than was Pašić's Great Serbianism. He wrote in 1909: 'Yugoslavism, which from the religious perspective means complete toleration and equality and from the political perspective autonomy and federalism; that modern and progressive Yugoslavism is no longer only a fine wish but a living reality.' Progress and development were bringing the Slovenes, Croats, Serbs and Bulgarians together: 'And with the general spiritual and cultural progress, insofar as the influence of learning and schools weakens religious feeling, insofar as through political education and economic development do new, progressive, free-thinking ideas encompass broad popular layers—so far will the cultural and democratic idea of Yugoslavism increasingly grip minds and capture hearts.'[21] Skerlić proposed in 1913 a Serb–Croat linguistic compromise whereby the Serbs would abandon the Cyrillic script in favour of the Latin script in return for the Croats' adoption of the Serbian Ekavian dialect—a proposal apparently widely welcomed by Serb intellectuals in both Serbia and Austria-Hungary.[22] Skerlić's ideas had lasting influence over the Independent Radical Party and, after 1918, over its heir, the explicitly Yugoslavist Democratic Party.

Cvijić, Serbia's leading ethnographer, was another theorist of Yugoslavism close to the Independents, but his influence among the Serbian political classes went far beyond them. This included Prince Aleksandar, who financed the production of his seminal work, *The Balkan Peninsula and the South Slav Lands*, whose first volume appeared in 1922.[23] Cvijić's beliefs arose from careful research into the geography of the South Slav lands and the customs of its peoples. He came from Loznica in northwestern Serbia, but his family originated in historic Hercegovina and he pioneered the concept of a 'Dinaric type', linked to the Dinaric Mountains stretching across the western Balkans, that was characterised by traits including 'martial prowess', 'energy and impulsiveness' and a 'lively temperament'. Within this Dinaric type he included the 'Šumadija variant', including most of Serbia, characterised by the fact that 'the peasant succeeded in increasingly overcoming his wild democratic instincts. There appeared organisational competence and a strong predisposition to work', as well as 'a healthy reason, measure and sense of reality'. Consequently, 'In Šumadija, the strength was concentrated of the Serb lands, both the Dinaric and the Kosovo-Vardarian. Patriotism became a definite feature of the national character. This national spirit found in the independent Serb state the most favourable terrain.'[24] Thus:

> Every Serb is imbued with a few crystal-clear thoughts: he wants the freedom and independence of all countries that he knows were part of his state and where the 'poor raya' live. By this name, he means all his brothers who do not live within the borders of Serbia and therefore do not have complete moral and intellectual freedom. They should be freed by constant heroism, uninterrupted sacrifice in blood ... The great national achievements of the South Slavs are tied to the Dinaric type: the Church of St Sava, national poems, the creation and expansion of Serbia.[25]

This represented the most sophisticated intellectual expression of the Radical-inspired unitarist, essentialist concept of Serb nationhood, according to which there was only one true Serb national idea, supposedly inseparable from the Serb being.

Cvijić followed Marković and Pašić in his understanding of Serbian democracy and national aspirations, but, in contrast to the Russophile Pašić, he looked toward Western Europe. As he said in a speech to an audience including King Petar, published in February 1907, since Serbia lay on the path between Central Europe and the Near East, it obstructed the imperial aspirations of Austria-Hungary and

Germany, so was the natural ally of the West European powers: 'Western Europe needs a rampart in the northern part of the Balkan peninsula against the economic-political aspirations of Central Europe and against its advance towards Salonika. Turkey can clearly no longer be that rampart ... Now it is known that it is necessary to defend the Balkan peninsula from Central Europe, and because of that, for the politics of Western Europe, the small Danubian states have gained significance; in the first place, Serbia.'[26]

Cvijić's insistence on absolute national unity in the pursuit of Serbia's national goals reflected the Radical rejection of pluralism. To pursue these goals, Serbia had to mobilise itself to 'conduct the process of forming a [single] national thought and work', above all through 'our best intellectuals, who know the most, then among other people of better feeling ... who are required to work on national questions such that they totally lose their individuality and personal vanities, above all their extraneous egos and quests for positions'. Consequently, 'It is necessary to give also other layers of the intelligentsia and the whole people national and patriotic sense; make them so that they are from one forge or plum-tree in their national viewpoint, and that before each of their public actions they consider the interests of the whole; the entire nation ... Every sacrifice that is made must be made naturally, spontaneously, and nobody must even entertain the thought that it could be done otherwise. Each must ceaselessly work and make constant efforts to make their country strong and great.' For this purpose, 'the parties must strive to avoid or at least lessen their internecine strife; as much as possible negate the personal reasons for such strife, and must so arrange their mutual relations that work for the whole is not halted and the country not harmed'.

Cvijić assigned the university a central role in the national mission, emphasising that 'besides intelligent journalists and other people of reason, the most could be achieved by our University, which must become a moral force for our nation; a centre that ceaselessly thinks about national questions and which must not show vacillation'. Furthermore, 'Serbia must have a substantial and well-equipped army; unified, well organised and of high military morale. Without such an army, no country has ever united.'[27] Following Austria-Hungary's annexation of Bosnia-Hercegovina in 1908, Serbia's government published Cvijić's propaganda text 'The annexation of Bosnia-Hercegovina and the Serb problem'. It argued that the annexation struck at Serbia's vital interests, for the provinces were 'the central oblast and heart of a nation' of 9,656,200 'Serbo-Croats' inhabiting a contiguous area 'of the Serbian language' including Serbia, Montenegro, Bosnia-Hercegovina, Banat, Bačka, Baranja, Istria, Rijeka, Dalmatia, Old Serbia (including Kosovo, Metohija and the Sanjak of Novi Pazar) and an indeterminate part of Macedonia, with 1,475,000 Slovenes as a group that 'belong to the Yugoslavs and scarcely differ from the Serbo-Croats'. In Cvijić's view, 'there exists a well-developed trend for the entire Yugoslav complex, from Ljubljana and Trieste to deep into Macedonia, to comprise a single national whole and develop culture on a national basis. And the principal mass of that Yugoslav complex forms the Serb nation ...' Consequently, 'a clash has begun between the idea of Serbo-Croat nationalism and independence and the Austrian conquering policy' in the Balkans. In these circumstances, 'The Serb problem must be solved by force. Both Serb statelets must above all prepare themselves militarily and educationally; sustain the national energy in the oppressed parts of the Serb nation; and use the first half-favourable opportunity to resolve the Serb question with Austria-Hungary.'[28]

Road to the Balkan Wars

With the Radicals in government from June 1911, Serbia's expansionism proceeded unhindered. When prime minister Milovanović died on 18 June 1912, he was replaced provisionally by Marko Trifković, then on 30 August by Pašić, with Protić as interior minister and Paču as finance minister—thus a government such as the Radicals had long sought. Pašić would consequently oversee the era of warfare that began at this time, remaining prime minister for six years until Serbia was submerged in the new Yugoslav state. The patriotism inculcated by schoolbooks became increasingly belligerent; a first-year gymnasium reader of 1911 quoted a poem by Vojislav Ilić (1862–1894): 'My children shed tears; / Because an old enemy torments them; / The enemy drinks their blood; / Turks, Germans and Magyars. / Because he is not free everywhere; / That is why the Serb sheds tears.'[29] Education nevertheless absorbed only 6.7 per cent of the state budget by 1914, compared with 25 per cent for the army.[30] The rise of sports clubs provided another incubator of popular nationalism; apart from the first such club, founded in 1857 with the name Sokol (Falcon) borrowed from its counterpart in Austria, these clubs had patriotic names: Dušan the Mighty, Serbian Knight and Serbian Sword. As the Falcon club's bulletin stated in July 1910: 'The goal of Falcon is not only the culture of flesh but to renounce oneself for the sake of the national ideal. Our goal is to nurture a full consciousness of duties toward our homeland and its role in divided Serbdom.'[31]

Serbian expansionism was encouraged by Russia, which was increasingly proactive in the Balkans following its humiliation in the annexation crisis. Baron Nikolai Hartwig, Russian ambassador to Serbia, played a central role; fiercely pan-Slavic and Austrophobic, his influence earned him the sobriquet 'king of Belgrade'.[32] Prince Aleksandar, meanwhile, had a memorandum drawn up for Russia's Tsar in early 1912, describing the Serbs as the greatest defender of Orthodoxy and Slavdom after Russia itself ('my second Fatherland'):

> For the unification of the Serb lands: Serbia, Old Serbia, part of Macedonia, Bosnia-Hercegovina, Croatia and Montenegro would create a state of 280,000 square kilometres with a purely Slavic population of ten million. Such a state would become an important factor in Europe and a sufficiently strong assistant to Russia for guaranteeing the survival of the other Slavic peoples. Such a state would finally cut

the road for the penetration of Pan-Germanism to the Near East. Slavic domination of the Balkan peninsula would be guaranteed, as well as Slavic domination of the Near East ...'[33]

Italy declared war on the Ottoman Empire on 29 September 1911 and invaded Ottoman Libya, embroiling the Ottomans in a conflict that continued until the following autumn. Meanwhile, the new regime aggressively attempted to centralise the empire. It forced the Great Powers to withdraw their military and civil agents from Macedonia, ending the foreign-sponsored reform programme, abolishing Macedonia's special status and jeopardising the privileges that the Balkan states had accumulated there. As the regime abandoned its initial idealistic belief in Muslim–Christian collaboration on a pan-Ottoman basis, it began suppressing pro-Bulgarian schools, churches, clubs and publications in Macedonia while settling there Muslim refugees from Bosnia-Hercegovina. VMRO, acting independently of the Bulgarian government, responded in December 1911 by initiating a terrorist campaign in Macedonia, in turn provoking Ottoman massacres of Bulgarian civilians.[34]

These developments convinced the Bulgarians that their window for action in Macedonia was closing and that their traditional support for Macedonia's autonomy, with the long-term goal of annexing it as they had done with Eastern Rumelia, would have to be replaced by an agreement with Serbia to partition it.[35] A Serbo-Bulgarian alliance was signed on 13 March 1912, requiring each party to defend the other militarily if it were attacked. Its provisions included a delineation of respective future zones of Macedonia. Territory to the south of the line between Kriva Palanka and Ohrid, including both cities, would go to the Bulgarians while territory to the north would form the so-called disputed zone, whose ownership would be arbitrated by Russia's Tsar.[36] The agreement was Milovanović's initiative; he had concluded from the annexation crisis that Russia could not be relied upon to protect Serbia from Austria-Hungary and that Serbia must therefore promote Balkan solidarity, which meant giving Bulgaria a generous share of Macedonia in return for the promise of Bulgarian assistance against an Austro-Hungarian attack. Pašić disagreed; he still placed his hopes on Russia, believed the pact conceded too much of Macedonia to Bulgaria and was convinced Bulgaria would never honour its commitment to support Serbia in a war with Austria-Hungary. Pašić was not alone; Cvijić was so concerned about Bulgarian ambitions in Macedonia that he went as far as to tell an Austrian politician that he would prefer to see Serbia annexed to Austria-Hungary than allied to Bulgaria.[37] Thus, from the start, the Serbo-Bulgarian agreement was undermined by opposition from within Serbia.

Serbian plans for southward expansion were motivated also by competition with the Albanians. Cvijić estimated that by 1912, 150,000 Serbs had left the Sanjak and Kosovo regions under Albanian pressure since 1876.[38] Milan Nikšić, who worked as a schoolteacher in Kosovo in this period, recalled that 'Anarchy and assassinations were possible only thanks to the bad Turkish administration and inability to maintain order and law in the country' and wrote of 'unheard of terror against the Serbs' and 'beatings and murders that reached such a level' that they moved Serbia's consul in Priština to appeal to the Russian ambassador in Constantinople.[39] Milan Rakić, a Serbian diplomat at the consulate in Priština, reported to Serbia's foreign ministry on 14 January 1907: 'there are two principal factors that are crushing our people and bringing it to ruin. Those are the Turkish government and the Arnauts. The Turkish government because it is creating oppression itself, plundering and killing ... and the Arnauts because on their own account, only to a much greater degree, they annihilate everything that is Serb wherever they can.'[40] In the years preceding the Balkan Wars, the consulate in Priština sent regular reports of Albanians assaulting, killing and plundering local Serbs. Eighteen Serbs were reported to have been killed in the first five months of 1905 in the Peć (İpek), Prizren and Priština sanjaks; eleven more in June 1905 in the Peć nahija; and land belonging to the Serbian monastery of Peć was plundered in January 1907 by a group of over a hundred Albanians. Rakić reported that several more Serbs were killed in summer 1911; others were beaten up and girls were abducted. Rakić nevertheless cautioned against exaggerated reports of atrocities that he noted were reaching Serbia.

Albanians, like Bulgarians, mobilised against the repressive, Turkifying policies of the CUP, forming rebel bands which also terrorised local Serbs, whose livestock they stole.[41] This created common ground between Serb and Turkish nationalists in the Ottoman Balkans, who collaborated temporarily against the Albanians. An Organisation of Ottoman Serbs, linked to National Defence, was established in Skopje in 1908 with CUP support.[42] By spring 1909, Albanians inhabiting present-day Kosovo were rebelling against the CUP regime, provoked by the CUP's deposition of Abdul Hamid on 27 April. A further revolt erupted in northern Albania in spring 1911. The Ottoman authorities, with Serbian support, responded with repression, attempting unsuccessfully to disarm the population. A full-scale Albanian rebellion led by Hasan Prishtina and others erupted on 24 March 1912. By late July, the rebels had taken much of Kosovo including Priština and Kosovska Mitrovica. They took the ethnically mixed Albanian–Macedonian city of Skopje on 14 August.

The Albanian rebels, numbering tens of thousands, threatened to establish an Albanian national state incorporating lands to which Serbia aspired and blocking its further southward expansion. The Ottoman government on 18 August accepted the rebel demands, involving the effective establishment of a unified, autonomous Albania within the empire, recalling Miloš's Serbia.[43] Pašić responded to these developments by attempting to co-opt the Kosovo Albanian notables for his expansionist plans. He composed an 'Agreement on community between Serbs and Albanians in the Kosovo vilayet' in September 1912, offering Albanians who came under Serbian rule 'freedom of religion, the Albanian language and schools; in the realm of courts, in the administration of their municipalities and districts their old

THE BALKAN WARS AND THE ROAD TO WORLD WAR I

judicial customs, and a special Albanian assembly that would pass laws on religious, educational and judicial questions'.[44] But this offer, already difficult to sell given decades of Serb–Albanian enmity, was easily trumped by Austria-Hungary's offer of full Albanian independence.

First Balkan War

Serbian government policy in autumn 1912 consequently became more radical. A Serbo-Montenegrin alliance was concluded on 14 September 1912, while Bulgaria, Greece and Montenegro also concluded alliances with one another. Montenegro declared war on the Ottomans on 8 October 1912, followed by Serbia, Bulgaria and Greece on 17th–18th, thereby initiating the First Balkan War. Simultaneously, a Serbian royal proclamation promised the peasants of Macedonia social and economic freedom along with national liberation: the abolition of serfdom and transfer to them of the land held by Ottoman Muslim landlords.[45] Prince Aleksandar, commanding Serbia's 1st Army, thus presented the war to his soldiers: 'The moment has come for us to continue and complete the great work of liberating and uniting Serbdom which was begun by my great-grandfather, the immortal Karađorđe, with your great-grandfathers, then taken up by Miloš the Great, then by King Milan with your fathers.'[46] The journalist Leon Trotsky, future organiser of Russia's October Revolution, described the war fever engulfing Serbia's media: 'Agitation for war—never mind with whom: Austria, Bulgaria, Turkey, even the whole Concert of Europe—has furnished the uniform political keynote of the entire "independent" press of Belgrade.' He cautioned: 'If the political results of the war do not fulfil the feverishly patriotic expectations of *Politika, Štampa, Pravda* and their stable-mates—and these boundless expectations cannot by their very nature be satisfied—then the whole of the Belgrade press will direct its fire with redoubled vigour against the internal enemy, that is, against all the rudiments of culture, economic development and elementary civic spirit that have begun to appear in Serbian social life.'[47]

The Balkan allies fielded approximately 725,000 troops against roughly 300,000 Ottoman regular troops plus some Albanian irregular forces. Following the principles established under Mihailo and Garašanin, the military conquest was assisted by a revolt in the enemy's rear. Immediately prior to the war's outbreak, the Serbian insurgent organisation in Macedonia possessed three bishops, four representatives in the Ottoman parliament, one senator, many churches and schools, numerous revolutionary councils and three newspapers. Its congress of over seventy delegates elected a Central Revolutionary Council headed by Bogdan Radenković. The organisation assisted Serbia's regular army against the Ottomans.[48] Its paramilitary forces—'Chetniks'—which had arisen from the guerrilla forces active in Macedonia before 1912, were of questionable military value, serving primarily to terrorise and persecute the non-Serb population in the 'liberated' territories. Pašić was nevertheless wary of them, and at his prompting, in response to armed Chetniks leaving their units and roaming around Serbia including Belgrade, war minister Petar Bojović on 17 November ordered that these be disarmed and concentrated in newly liberated Skopje.[49]

Serbia's army performed extremely well. After crossing the Ottoman frontier on 19 October 1912, the 1st Army under Aleksandar and chief of staff Putnik won the decisive Battle of Kumanovo on 23–24 October against an Ottoman force about half its size, allowing the Serbians to take Skopje on the 26th and giving them possession of northern Macedonia. The Bulgarians won a great victory in the Battle of Kirk Kilisse in Eastern Thrace on 24 October over an Ottoman army they were one and a half times larger than. They besieged the city of Adrianople in Thrace and, after defeating the Ottomans again at the Battle of Lule Burgas between 28 October and 2 November, advanced to the Sea of Marmara, while the Ottomans retreated to the Çatalca lines—defensive positions only 30 kilometres from Constantinople. This awakened Russian fears that Bulgaria, with its German monarch and uncertain loyalties, would capture the Ottoman capital. When the Bulgarians commenced their offensive against the Çatalca lines on 17 November, the Russians threatened to intervene militarily against them. They began viewing Serbia as a possible counterweight to Bulgaria.[50] Meanwhile the Greeks, facing the weakest Ottoman forces, advanced rapidly northwards into southern Macedonia and Epirus to take Salonika on 9 November, just before the Bulgarians arrived there the next day.

The Serbians won their second great victory in the Battle of Manastir on 16–19 November against an Ottoman opponent now outnumbered nearly three to one, resulting in the capture of Bitola, Ohrid and Gevgelije and giving them control of south-western Macedonia. This included not only the entire 'disputed zone' but much of Bulgaria's allotted share as well. Meanwhile, Serbia's 3rd Army under Janković took Priština in Kosovo on 22 October, giving the Serbians possession of Kosovo Polje, site of the legendary battle. Units of the 3rd Army subsequently went on to occupy much of Albania, including Lezhë on 18 November and Durrës on 29 November, reaching the Adriatic coast. Serbia's Ibar Army took Novi Pazar in the Sanjak on 23 October, after which the rest of the Sanjak was rapidly occupied, establishing a land link between Serbia and Montenegro. Serbia's army in the Sanjak treated the Muslim Bosniak population correctly.[51] A delegation of Muslims visited General Mihailo Živković in Novi Pazar in October 1912 to pledge their loyalty, and he in turn delivered a message from Petar: 'My army in Old Serbia will, besides Christians, find Muslims, who are equally dear to us, and with them Albanians, both Christians and Muslims ... We are bringing all of them freedom, brotherhood and equality with Serbs in all things.'[52] Serbia's 2nd Army under Stepa Stepanović then assisted the Bulgarian assault on Adrianople.[53]

The war was envisaged by Pašić as a struggle to save Serbia from Austro-Hungarian domination. He therefore prioritised the acquisition of an outlet on the Adriatic Sea in northern Albania. This had been a goal of Serbian statesmen since the first half of the nineteenth century and had featured in Garašanin's Plan. 'Northern Albania' meant territory to which Serbian statesmen believed they had a legitimate claim on medieval historical grounds; it was consequently labelled 'Old Serbia'.[54] Pašić believed that 'without it, Serbia would extinguish itself and cook as in some sort of boiler which is everywhere closed'. Conversely, the arrival of Serbia's army on the Albanian coast alarmed Austria-Hungary. Pašić on 6 November 1912 rejected Austria-Hungary's offer to recognise its expansion into northern Albania in exchange for a customs union between the two states. Austria-Hungary consequently viewed the establishment of an independent Albania as essential to keep pro-Russian Serbia away from the Adriatic Sea, so gave its blessing to Albania's declaration of independence on 28 November. Austria-Hungary found an ally of the moment in Italy, its long-standing rival for patronage over the Albanian national movement, which likewise opposed a Serbian presence on the Adriatic. Thus, the enmity between Vienna and Belgrade grew into a bitter conflict between Serbian and Albanian national aspirations, with Vienna and Rome backing the latter.

The disputed territory was overwhelmingly ethnic Albanian. Pašić told Austria-Hungary's envoy that 'the Arnauts in these territories are recently Albanianised Serbs who speak Serbian'.[55] In practice, the weakness of Serbia's ethnic claim on northern Albanian territory was admitted in December 1912 by Cvijić, who wrote that owing to 'processes of assimilation and migration, the population in that part of northern Albania which the Serbian army has seized is almost completely Albanian. But Serbia must, for the sake of its economic independence, gain an outlet on the Adriatic Sea and one part of the Albanian coast', which meant 'seizing an oblast that is, truthfully, ethnographically foreign, but it must be taken for economic interests, indeed for needs of survival. Such a seizure could perhaps be called an *anti-ethnographic necessity*. In this case, this is still more justified because the Albanians of northern Albania are descended from the merging of Albanians and Serbs.'[56]

The Balkan allies, having occupied the whole of Turkey-in-Europe except Ioannina, Shkodër, Adrianople and Constantinople itself, but temporarily unable to make further progress, signed an armistice with the Ottomans on 3 December. The London peace conference, involving the Balkan allies, Ottoman Empire and Great Powers, opened on 17 December 1912 and immediately recognised Albania's independence, necessary to avert an Austro-Hungarian attack on Serbia. The new state's borders with Serbia and Montenegro were determined by fierce haggling between Austria-Hungary and Russia. Austria-Hungary initially demanded Ohrid, Debar, Prizren, Đakovica and Peć for Albania, but conceded them to the Serbians and Montenegrins in return for Russia's concession to Albania of Shkodër and Luma.[57] Austria-Hungary thus successfully denied Serbia an outlet on the Adriatic. For Pašić, obtaining such an outlet had been the priority; redeeming 'historically' Serbian land was merely a supporting argument and back-up plan.[58] Forced to retain what he could of the occupied Albanian-inhabited territories, Pašić wrote in a telegram to the Serbian envoys at the conference:

> Those territories are indissolubly joined to Old Serbia and separated by high mountains from Albania, which form an economic, geographic, strategic and communications border between Old Serbia and Albania. The Albanians in those territories are Serbs by origin and today still speak Serbian and have no links with the coastal Albanians. Peć, Đakovica, Prizren lie in the heart of Old Serbia and are full of Serbian monasteries, churches, schools and sancties. The Serbian army has liberated these territories with great losses and nothing can force it to relinquish them, other than some foreign army, and then only if it could destroy the Serbian army.[59]

Thus were the foundations laid for the territory that came to be known as Kosovo. For all that the region came to be imbued with Serbian nationalist symbolism, Pašić negotiated its borders with remarkable lack of sentimentality; in negotiations over its division with Montenegro, he eventually abandoned not only Đakovica and Dečani, where one of the greatest Serbian monasteries was located, but also Peć, former seat of the Serbian Patriarch.[60]

The Balkan states completed their victory in spring 1913. The Greeks took Ioannina on 6 March 1913 and the Bulgarians, assisted by the Serbians, finally captured Adrianople on 26 March. While the Bulgarians engaged in prolonged, ultimately unsuccessful heavy fighting at the Çatalca lines, the final great victory of the Balkan allies was the Montenegrin capture of Shkodër on 23 April, following a lengthy siege. This provoked another international crisis resulting in a four-power naval demonstration by Britain, France, Germany and Austria-Hungary, at Vienna's insistence, to force Montenegro to evacuate the city. In reality, this demonstration was for show, and it was Austria-Hungary's threat to use its army that led Montenegro on 3 May to agree to surrender Shkodër to Albania. The Balkan allies had conquered the whole of Ottoman Europe except Constantinople itself—a crushing victory recognised by the Great Powers in the Treaty of London of 30 May 1913, which ended the war. Even without Constantinople, the pre-war Ottoman Balkans had had a Muslim majority for which conquest by the Balkan Christian states was very far from an act of liberation: according to Justin McCarthy's study, 27 per cent of this Ottoman Muslim population, or 632,408 people, died as a result of the war.[61] Similarly, the Christian Macedonians found their patriotic dreams shattered as their homeland was partitioned between the victors.

Serbia's victory was nevertheless pyrrhic. The conquered territory was ethnically overwhelmingly non-Serb: Macedonian, Albanian and Muslim Bosniak. The first two groups in particular resisted incorporation into Serbia. In an era when nationalists sought to justify claims on territory by pseudo-scientific 'proofs' of ethnic kinship with its population, this was problematic. Cvijić wrote in March 1913 that on linguistic grounds, the northern part of the conquered territory, 'the vicinity of Skoplje, Kratovo and Tetovo ... must be labelled as Serb'. But Cvijić did not even pretend to believe that the population living to the south of Skopje was Serb; its 'national consciousness was so vacillating' between Serb and Bulgarian, he wrote, that 'maybe it would be most precise to define the whole of this Slavic, nationally vacillating mass by a neutral name: Macedonian Slavs'.[62] Cvijić's view of the Macedonians as 'standing in the middle between the Serbian and the Bulgarian colouring'[63] was adopted by Pašić. Trotsky wrote in July 1913:

> Serbian imperialism found itself quite unable to advance along the 'normal', that is the national line: its path was barred by Austria-Hungary, which included within its borders more than half of all the Serbs. Hence Serbia's push down the line of least resistance, towards Macedonia. The national achievements of Serbian propaganda in that quarter were quite insignificant, but all the more sweeping for that reason seem the territorial conquests made by Serbian imperialism. Serbia now includes within her borders about half a million Macedonians, just as she already included half a million Albanians. A dizzy success! Actually, this hostile million may prove fatal to the historical existence of Serbia.[64]

It was a fairly accurate prediction. Conquest of this large territory inhabited by a mostly unassimilable population poisoned Serbia's democracy at home and its relationship with Bulgaria abroad, which in World War I nearly proved fatal for Serbia. Serbia lost the part of Macedonia it had conquered when it was made a separate republic by Josip Broz Tito's Yugoslav Partisans in the 1940s, while Kosovo was reassigned to the Serbian state but as an autonomous unit. It became the weak spot where Yugoslavia's final dissolution began in the 1980s and over which Serbia was bombarded by NATO in 1999, resulting in its final loss of the territory.

Second Balkan War

The Balkan alliance came unstuck as the allies quarrelled over division of the spoils. Because Austria-Hungary had deprived it of northern Albania and an Adriatic outlet, Serbia sought compensation by reneging upon its March 1912 agreement with Bulgaria for Macedonia's division and seeking to keep all the territory it had occupied. This reflected not merely expansionist greed but Serbian fears of being encircled by Austria-Hungary, Germany and their satellites (Albania, Bulgaria) and consequent determination to prevent the territorial linking of Albania and Bulgaria and the closing of Serbia's route to Salonika.[65] Conversely, the Bulgarians, who had borne the brunt of the fighting with the Ottomans, were aggrieved that most of Macedonia had been occupied by the Serbians and Greeks and sought a larger share than they had achieved in battle. Beginning even before the war with the Ottomans had formally ended, Greece and Serbia signed a series of agreements directed against Bulgaria, culminating in a formal alliance on 1 June 1913, the day after the Treaty of London was signed.

SERBIA

The Russian Tsar's proposal to arbitrate between its Bulgarian and Serbian clients was resisted by the Black Hand, which petitioned Serbia's government to reject it. The Black Hand agitated instead for a pre-emptive attack on Bulgaria, before the latter could reposition its forces for the correctly expected attack on Serbia and as the only way to resolve the dispute. This sentiment was shared by Serbia's supreme command, which noted that Bulgaria's army was concentrated on the Ottoman front and its border with Serbia was undefended, but it was beginning to reposition there. A golden opportunity to defeat a militarily superior enemy was thus being squandered. Pašić resisted this pressure for a pre-emptive strike as he prioritised maintaining Russian goodwill, which would have been lost if Serbia had attacked Bulgaria first.[66] He himself was bitterly opposed to the territorial demarcation in Macedonia that his predecessor Milovanović had agreed to, but believed that rectification could and should occur through Russian arbitration.

The Black Hand consequently accused the Radicals of being ready to surrender Macedonia to the Bulgarians. *Pijemont* stated on 15 March 1913: 'Let not the Serbian government dare to order us to abandon these territories, for not only will we not obey but we will punish it for treason. And if the Bulgarians think they can expel us from here—let them try.'[67] Seventeen leading Black Handers, including Apis and Jovanović-Čupa, delivered an ultimatum to Pašić on 30 May warning him not to accept Russian arbitration or they would kill him.[68] Pašić on 15 June offered his resignation in order to put pressure on both Petar and the Russians, prompting the alarmed Baron Hartwig to persuade Petar to refuse it and Pašić to accept Russian arbitration.[69] Yet fear that the arbitration might favour Bulgaria apparently so worried Pašić that he told Austria-Hungary's military attaché on 24 June: 'Now we have truly had enough of the Russian tutelage. If now the Monarchy, whose stance towards us we are only now beginning to appreciate, leaps to our assistance and pulls us out of the hole we are in, then she may be certain that we shall join her completely and shake off forever the Russian tutelage ...'[70] The Independent opposition enjoyed the regime's plight. Jovan Žujović told Milorad Drašković that Pašić ought to commit suicide; when Drašković suggested Petar should too, Žujović responded that the king was unworthy of such a fine gesture.[71]

Pašić's dilemmas were resolved for him when on 29–30 June the Bulgarian 4th and 2nd Armies attacked the Serbians and Greeks to enforce Bulgaria's Macedonian claims. Pašić's passivity in the face of the Bulgarian threat meant that Serbia entered this war with international goodwill toward it intact but with its strategic position seriously jeopardised, and it was only a combination of gross Bulgarian errors and fortuitous actions by other Balkan states that enabled Serbia to win. The Bulgarian general who had initiated the attack did so with the authorisation of Bulgaria's Tsar Ferdinand but not of Bulgaria's government, which ordered him to halt his offensive immediately. The general did suspend his attack and was dismissed by Ferdinand for having done so; paradoxically, his dismissal was simultaneously ordered by Bulgaria's government for having launched the attack in the first place. Meanwhile, Bulgaria's 5th Army remained passive because, in the confusion reigning in the Bulgarian headquarters, its commander had not been authorised to act. The Bulgarian forces' temporary halt, the dismissal of their general, the 5th Army's passivity and the resulting confusion in their ranks crippled their offensive.

Facing a Bulgarian attack on the River Bregalnica in Macedonia, all the Serbian commanders favoured a tactical withdrawal except deputy chief of staff Živojin Mišić, who feared this would recall Serbia's retreat before the Bulgarians in 1885, thus damage troop morale and discourage intervention by the Romanians and Ottomans. He favoured fighting on the Bregalnica. After some hesitation, Putnik took Mišić's advice.[72] In the ensuing Battle of Bregalnica, ending on 8 July, the Serbians heavily defeated the Bulgarians. Meanwhile, to the south, the Bulgarians were also heavily defeated by the Greeks. On both fronts, the active Bulgarian forces were outnumbered by the allies; on the Greek front by more than three to one. After suffering considerable territorial losses, the Bulgarians eventually stabilised their lines against the Serbians and Greeks, but their defeat was ensured by Romania's declaration of war on them on 10 July and invasion of their undefended rear, threatening Sofia and ending any possibility that Austria-Hungary might intervene on their side. A renewed Ottoman offensive on 12 July and the reoccupation of Adrianople on the 23rd completed Bulgaria's catastrophe. The war was ended by the Treaty of Bucharest of 10 August 1913, confirming Serbia's possession both of the so-called disputed zone of Macedonia and of the zone Bulgaria was to have received.[73]

The Balkan Wars resulted in Serbia nearly doubling its territory, from about 48,300 to 87,000 square kilometres, and its population, from an estimated 2,911,701 to 4,527,992. The new territory was organised as eleven new okrugs (Bitola, Debar, Kavadar, Kumanovo, Novi Pazar, Pljevlja, Prizren, Priština, Skopje, Tetovo, Štip) with 46 districts.[74] Serbia's seizure of Albanian-inhabited territory in Old Serbia curtailed Austria-Hungary's influence there; its possibility for further expansion toward Salonika ended. Serbia's military capabilities, once derided, were made brutally apparent, and with 1.6 million new inhabitants these capabilities were likely only to increase.[75] Britain's ambassador to Vienna, Sir Fairfax Cartwright, predicted in January 1913 that 'Servia will someday set Europe by the ears, and bring about a general war on the continent ... I cannot tell you how exasperated people are getting here at the continual worry which that little country causes to Austria under encouragement from Russia.'[76] The Oriental Railway Company in Macedonia, in which Austria-Hungary's government owned a controlling share, was now mostly in Belgrade's hands, so Vienna was forced to negotiate for its sale to Serbia, something not concluded by the outbreak of war in July 1914. The surprisingly crushing Ottoman defeat followed by the equally surprising Bulgarian defeat robbed Austria-Hungary of counterweights to resurgent Serbia. At a meeting of the Austro-Hungarian joint ministerial council, foreign minister Leopold Berchtold noted:

'Today Serbia represents a great attraction, for it is seen that its prestige has risen while ours has fallen. If Serbia develops further, our Yugoslavs will feel further drawn to it ... A reckoning with Serbia and its humiliation are a vital interest of the Monarchy.'[77]

Vienna on 17–18 October 1913 demanded Serbia withdraw from Albania within eight days or face military action. Serbia's government had to comply.[78] It responded to Austro-Hungarian hostility by cultivating sympathetic politicians among the Habsburg South Slavs. The anniversary of the execution of seventeenth-century anti-Habsburg Croatian rebels Nikola Zrinski and Frano Krsto Frankopan on 30 April 1914 was publicly commemorated in Belgrade. The ceremony was attended by Metropolitan Dimitrije and Stojan Novaković, president of the Serbian Royal Academy, and involved Serbian and Croatian students together singing the Croatian national anthem, 'Our Beautiful Homeland'—which in the 1990s became independent Croatia's national anthem. Pro-Serbian enthusiasm among the Croats peaked with Serbia's Balkan War victories. But Pašić remained unwilling to subordinate Serbian national policy to Serbo-Croat cooperation; pan-Yugoslav agitation remained auxiliary to his Serbian- and Russian-oriented strategy. As he wrote to the leaders of the Croat–Serb Coalition at this time, 'Our question of liberation and unification will not be resolved by the politicians of the Serbo-Croat Coalition [sic] but by Serbia with Russia. Neither the one nor the other is yet ready for war.'[79]

Stojadinović recalls: 'All of us then in Serbia were drunk with military victories.' The Serbian press adopted the slogan 'For Kosovo Kumanovo—for Slivnica Bregalnica'.[80] Cvijić wrote that 'the nation and the army are one and the same and have a single task. It is often forgotten that we are a true warrior and military nation and that we have always been so, even in the most difficult Turkish times, and that we have already practised heroism and war without any interruption for several centuries; no other Christian Balkan nation can demonstrate this to such measure.'[81] However, the victory over the Bulgarians had cost the Black Hand dearly; among those killed were its president, Radivojević and the supreme central administration members Jovanović-Čupa and Vasić—the last, as secretary of National Defence, had been particularly important. These deaths, as well as the losses sustained by Serbia's army in general unnecessarily heavy, in Black Hand eyes, on account of the failure to attack Bulgaria pre-emptively—and the withdrawal from Albania at Vienna's demand further embittered the organisation against Pašić and his government.

War against the Albanians

Albanian persecution of Serbs in the Albanian-inhabited lands of the Ottoman Empire since 1876 had fuelled anti-Albanian chauvinism in Serbia on the part of officials and intellectuals, who spoke of the Albanians in terms of 'barbarous tribes', 'lazy savages' and 'wild Albanian animals'.[82] Such stereotypes were central to Serbia's

THE BALKAN WARS AND THE ROAD TO WORLD WAR I

propaganda in 1913, as its aspirations in Albanian-inhabited lands confronted the Habsburg- and Italian-backed Albanian national movement. Vladan Đorđević wrote a tract at the start of 1913, published in German in Leipzig, intended to counter foreign support for Albania's independence in favour of its partition between Serbia, Montenegro and Greece. He claimed the Albanians resembled 'pre-humans from the prehistoric age; those people who, for fear of wild beasts, slept in trees, to which they clung with their tails, in order not to fall. In later millennia, in which the human tail has been used less and less, that organ of the human body has increasingly shrunk, until eventually in the historical era it was reduced to those few bones in the coccyx. Only among the Arnauts does it seem that in the nineteenth century there still lived a few tailed people.'[83] He claimed the 'Arnauts have no national type; they have no common national language; they have no culture of any kind. And now we go further. Do the Arnauts have a national history of their own? They do not.' He lamented: 'And from these beasts Austria-Hungary wants to build a state? Good luck to them!'[84]

Interior minister Protić, in his published polemics against Austro-Hungarian and Italian support for Albanian independence, asked why it was 'that in Cavour and Mazzini's Italy, the uncultured, semi-savage Albanians are being promoted at the expense of the Serbs and their brothers the Montenegrins?!' He complained that Albania was 'a new artificial state that is being raised by Serbia's flank' and that 'the Albanians are unfit for state-right autonomy, and that such an Albania will be a hotbed of new disturbances and frictions in the Balkans'.[85] He denigrated the Albanians to demonstrate this: 'The Albanians have no national literature, no folkloric literature of any kind or value. Literature still less; neither old nor new.' Furthermore, 'In the whole of Albania there is not a single trace of any kind of national culture which could raise itself above the tribal life, even though the Albanians have lived for more than two thousand years on the Balkan peninsula.' In fact, 'Even the Turks, who came from Asia and are not even of Indo-Germanic origin, demonstrated some culture and left behind them some traces of culture and some monuments. Only the Albanians have remained at the same level of development as they were a thousand years ago!'[86]

Armed Albanian resistance to the Serbian occupation, encouraged by Austria-Hungary, continued after the defeat of the regular Ottoman forces. The occupation quickly degenerated into a war against the Albanian population. Lazër Mjeda, Catholic archbishop of Skopje, reported to Rome on 24 January 1913 that Serbian forces had massacred almost the entire Albanian population of Ferizaj in Kosovo: 'The city seems like the Kingdom of Death. They knock on the doors of the Albanian houses, take away the men and shoot them immediately. In a few days, the number of men killed reached 400. As for plunder, looting and rape, all that goes without saying; henceforth the order of the day is: everything is permitted against the Albanians—not merely permitted, but willed and commanded.' By that time, the number of Albanians killed in Kosovo was in the region of 20,000–25,000.[87] Atrocities peaked from September 1913, when Albanian and VRMO rebels launched an uprising against the Serbian forces in Macedonia and Kosovo, briefly capturing towns including Đakovica, Debar and Ohrid. Although they were defeated within ten days, the conflict cost Serbia's army about 1,000 dead and 2,500 wounded. General Mišić was scapegoated for this minor debacle; Apis and the Black Hand still resented him as a former King Aleksandar loyalist who also favoured civilian rather than military rule in the new territories, and they engineered his retirement for the second time.[88] Mišić claims Pašić's government was responsible for the debacle, since it had withdrawn the army from its well-defended front line with Albania for political reasons, leaving it vulnerable to attack, so also needed him as scapegoat.[89]

Chetnik forces accompanied Serbia's regular army and killed and looted Albanian civilians, while Serb civilians from southern Serbia crossed into the newly occupied territories to join in the plunder.[90] The British vice-consuls in Skopje and Monastir reported Serb forces as carrying out arbitrary detentions, beatings, rapes, the burning of villages and outright massacres in the occupied areas in October–November 1913. According to vice-consul Charles Greig, 'It is already abundantly evident that Moslems under Servian rule have nothing whatsoever to expect but periodical massacre, certain expulsion and final ruin.' He subsequently reported that the 'Bulgarian and especially the Moslem population in the districts of Perlepe, Krchevo and Krushevo [were] in danger of extermination by the very frequent and barbarous massacres and pillage to which they are subjected by Servian bands'.[91]

According to Trotsky, 'Did not the facts, undeniable and irrefutable, force you to come to the conclusion that the Bulgars in Macedonia, the Serbs in Old Serbia, in their national endeavour to correct data in the ethnographical statistics that are not quite favourable to them, are engaged quite simply in the systematic extermination of the Muslim population in the villages, towns and districts?' According to a Serbian eyewitness interviewed by Trotsky: 'By five pm we were approaching Kumanovo. The sun had set, it was starting to get dark. But the darker the sky became, the more brightly the fearful illumination of the fires stood out against it. Burning was going on all around us. Entire Albanian villages had been turned into pillars of fire— far and near, right up to the railway lines. Dwellings, possessions accumulated by fathers, grandfathers, and great-grandfathers, were going up in flames. In all its fiery monotony this picture was repeated the whole way to Skoplje.'[92] The Danish journalist Fritz Magnussen reported: 'Serbian military activities in Macedonia have taken on the character of an extermination of the Arnaut population. The army is conducting an unspeakable war of atrocities. According to officers and soldiers, 3,000 Arnauts were slaughtered in the region between Kumanova/Kumanovo and Skoplje and 5,000 near Prishtina. The Arnaut villages were surrounded and set on fire. The inhabitants were then chased from their homes and shot like rats. The Serb soldiers delighted in telling me of the manhunts they conducted.'⁹³ According to the 1914 report of the international commission organised by the Carnegie Endowment: 'Houses and whole villages reduced to ashes, unarmed and innocent populations massacred ... such were the means that were employed and are still being employed by the Serb–Montenegrin soldiery with a view to the entire transformation of the ethnic character of regions inhabited exclusively by Albanians.'⁹⁴

Social Democratic opposition to militarism

Having once opposed the conquest of Great Serbia 'from above' by the army and state, the Radicals in government were now conducting precisely such a conquest of territory in Macedonia—a goal pioneered by their nemesis, Milan. Yet they found themselves opposed by a new generation of left-wing rebels: the Social Democrats. Although these had defended the 1903 putsch and its legacy, they quickly parted company with the conspirators, particularly following the officers' attack on the socialists in the 1904 Kragujevac riot. The Social Democrats had roundly condemned the murder of Milan Novaković, who was, according to Dušan Popović, merely a 'Don Quixote' who 'should not have been killed, not only out of regard for the law but out of regard for ordinary humanity'.⁹⁵ Their persistent campaigning against militarism and exposure of military corruption enraged the army; in parliament on 24 February 1911, war minister Ilija Gojković warned Kaclerović that they would never again be permitted to shout 'Down with the army!' in Terazije, to which Kaclerović replied, 'Today from your military perspective there exists only the officer caste, but it has very little in common with the people, or almost nothing. The people to you are nobody and nothing, and the people have to bow down before you; those people that maintain you.'⁹⁶

The Social Democrats believed they had moved beyond Marković in favour of Marxism, but they continued to uphold his anti-militarist and anti-statist principles. They agitated against military expenditure, calling for a 'people's defence instead of a standing army'.⁹⁷ This gelled with their agitation for universal suffrage, against the army and gendarmerie's role in suppressing industrial unrest and against the monarchy. Popović argued in August 1910 'that the interests of the Serbian dynasties and monarchy have stood in direct opposition to the national ideal of the Serb nation ... the Serbian rulers and the monarchy in general have always been and will always be one of the greatest obstacles to the realisation of the Serb national ideal!'⁹⁸ Faced with this agitation, the Radical government moderated its policy on labour unrest; parliament passed a law in 1910 recognising freedom to unionise which came into force in July 1911.⁹⁹ Repression against the workers nevertheless continued; after another riot between workers and soldiers in Kragujevac occasioned by the 1 May celebrations in 1911, 162 armaments factory workers were dismissed, though once again public anger and agitation led to their reinstatement.¹⁰⁰

SERBIA

At the initiative of the Social Democratic Party of Serbia, the first inter-Balkan conference of socialist parties occurred in Belgrade on 7–9 January 1910, which resolved in favour of Macedonia's autonomy as an alternative to the Balkan governments' predatory competition over it. With the outbreak of the Balkan Wars, Serbian socialist anti-militarism was further reinterpreted according to international socialist principles, in a manner exceptional even by European standards. The Social Democratic deputies in Serbia's parliament in June 1912 voted against war credits. Their publication, *Radničke novine* (Workers' Newspaper), stated on 1 February 1913 that the freedom and equality of nations could only be achieved 'not by the conquest of Macedonia by Bulgaria, Serbia and Greece and not by its partition between them, but by full freedom of the Macedonian population to constitute itself nationally and as an equal member join a Balkan federation. Be it understood that that applies also to Thrace and Albania.'[101]

Dimitrije Tucović provided the most detailed exposition of Social Democratic anti-militarism. He combined opposition to Austro-Hungarian imperial expansion into the Balkans with opposition to Serbia's own expansion at the Albanians' expense. He reaffirmed Marković's principle that in seeking a solution to the national question, a popular rebellion be counterposed to the government's plans for military conquest: 'We, Social Democrats, view the power of resistance of the people in national defence; in national rebellion. And in this we significantly differ from those who, in several squads of the regular army, in the cumbersome and expensive state apparatus, which have been built and which maintain themselves and are used against the great majority of the nation, lead the precious security of national defence.'[102] He noted subsequently that the ruling Radical party had long abandoned its struggle to free Serbia's people from bureaucratic rule and had become 'the most determined, most conscious agents of capitalism', which had 'today made peace with the bureaucracy, placing itself in its unlimited service, and those one-time fighters for self-management are ever more finally suppressing, one by one, every organ of self-management'.[103] In contrast to the Serbian regime's bureaucracy and militarism, embodied in its 'standing army', which represented a 'negative influence' that 'undermines and defeats the people's power of resistance', Tucović championed the old ideal of the 'defensive power of the entire nation, in its competence with which it completely and with enthusiasm, on the model of the French *la levée en masse*, pledges to the end the defence of its freedom'.[104]

Tucović consequently campaigned fiercely against the Serbian government's war against the Albanian population, a 'conquering campaign against which every healthy conscience must rebel'; the work of 'our bourgeoisie which, deprived of every national regard, seeks only ever more territory, ever more piazzas, an ever-larger producing and expendable mass which it will exploit'.[105] He echoed the accusations of systematic mass extermination: 'The Serbian army exterminated the Albanians in Old Serbia and Albania, and the Bulgarian army the Turks in Thrace, and the Greek army the

THE BALKAN WARS AND THE ROAD TO WORLD WAR I

Turks and Albanians in Devol, in the criminal belief that they were thereby executing a "national" act; that, by removing that innocent population from the face of the earth, they were ridding themselves of an enemy with which it would in the future be difficult to deal.'[106] In his essay 'Serbia and Albania', he described in detail the nature of the 'colonial struggles' that Serbia's army was waging against the Albanian people:

> The Albanian revolt of September [1913], because of which Serbia had to mobilise again three divisions, is a classic example of how colonial wars are provoked. The occupation of the Serbian army stretched from the east to the very gates of the cliffs and gorges. It separated the plough from the fields, the cattle from the pastures, the flock from the watering hole, the village from the water mills, buyers and sellers from the piazzas, the hinterland from the towns, and whole mountain settlements from their economic centres and food granaries. An Albanian on that side was not allowed to set foot on his land which remained on this side. All sources of life were cut off. In desperation and hunger, the people first begged for free access to the marketplaces, and when they were denied this, between death from starvation and death from the bullet they chose the latter ... And when the revolt broke out, the government via the representative of the ministry of foreign policy announced that the Albanians would be 'punished in an exemplary manner'; the bourgeois press sought extermination without mercy; and the army carried it out. Albanian villages, from which the men had fled in good time, were turned into ruins. These simultaneously became barbaric crematoria in which hundreds of women and children were burned alive.[107]

Tucović inveighed against Protić and Đorđević as hypocritical representatives of the 'bourgeoisie': 'at the same time as they fight against the politics of conquest of Austria-Hungary and Italy [in Albania], they advocate and defend the politics of conquest of Serbia'. But 'In proclaiming this policy, the Serbian bourgeoisie has now for the first time removed from the face of the Serb nation the mask of an oppressed nation which is fighting for its liberation.'[108] Tucović supported Macedonia and Albania's self-rule in a Balkan federation as the only just alternative to their annexation to or partition between particular Balkan states, which could only mean new oppression for some of their inhabitants alongside liberation for others.[109] This reflected Marković's ideas. But unlike another of Marković disciples, Pašić, who sought to achieve Serbia's goals through an alliance with Russia, Tucović viewed his projected Balkan union as an alternative to Serbia's subordination to Russian policy: 'Against those politics, Social Democracy asserts its programme: a political and economic union of all the peoples of the Balkans, not excepting the Albanians, on the basis of full democracy and complete equality.'[110]

Priority question

Serbia's territorial acquisitions of 1912–1913 further retarded its democracy while fuelling the power struggle between the Radical government and Black Hand.

SERBIA

Both agreed that the predominantly ethnic Albanian and ethnic Macedonian population of the new territories should not enjoy full civic or democratic rights in the short term; the Black Hand and Serbian military elite in particular feared their full emancipation would facilitate Serbia's destabilisation in territories still disputed with Bulgaria and Albania, which were backed by Austria-Hungary and Germany.[111] But while the government favoured imposing on them a police regime lasting up to ten years, the army and its supporters, particularly the Liberals, favoured military rule. Interior minister Protić, chief advocate of the first option, argued that the conquered population was politically and culturally inferior to Serbia's population, therefore should not be consulted on how it was ruled. The Radical government feared that the extension of full political rights to the population in the new territories would lead to the emergence of a Muslim opposition bloc in Serbia's parliament.[112] The Independents likewise supported a special regime under a governor in the new territories; Stojanović suggested it should last ten years, 'until these people feel themselves to be Serbian citizens, moreover that they become Serbs, for not even a quarter of the population there are Serbs'.[113] Those—Progressives and Social Democrats—who advocated that the population of the new territories be immediately granted full civic and democratic rights constituted a small, ineffectual minority. According to the 1914 Carnegie Endowment report, 'The new citizens were not to possess the franchise for fear lest a new "Macedonian" party should thus be brought into the Skupshtina [parliament] to upset all the relations between the contending parties in the kingdom and form the mark of common jealousy.' Consequently, 'Macedonia had thus to be viewed as a dependency, a sort of conquered colony, which these conquerors might administer at their good pleasure.'[114]

The conquered territory was placed under administration by the inspector of the police department, Milorad A. Vujičić, the Serbian government's civil commissioner at the army's supreme command. He was directly subordinate to the army's chief of staff and indirectly to the war ministry. This reflected the power-sharing in the new territories between the regime's two wings, Radicals and conspirators. The okrug administrations of Kumanovo, Skopje, Priština, Novi Pazar and Prizren received a directive on 7 November 1912: 'For the presidents, village headmen and councillors it is necessary to choose men who are undoubtedly loyal to the Serbian worldview and who are in every regard upright and enjoying the respect of their fellow citizens. Candidates for these jobs should be sought above all from among the schoolteachers, priests and other figures who have already been and are today in our service.' Two days later, Protić sent a list of eligible individuals who were to be appointed superintendents of the okrugs and districts.[115] Power was thus handed to the trusted pro-Serbian minority among an overwhelmingly non-Serb population.

The regime in the conquered territories combined state terror with forced Serbianisation. The Serbian government on 4 October 1913 issued a decree on public security: 'The decision of the police authorities, published in the respective communes, is sufficient proof of the commission of crime ... Any person accused of rebellion in terms of the police decision and who commits any crime shall be punished with death.' Furthermore, 'Where several cases of rebellion occur in a commune and the rebels do not return to their homes within ten days from the police notice, the authorities have the right to deport their families whithersoever they find convenient.'[116] Meanwhile, Bulgarian-oriented schoolteachers, Exarchist priests and other local notables were systematically killed, beaten, imprisoned, expelled or forced to declare themselves Serbs, causing thousands of Macedonians to flee to Bulgaria. The government sought to ensure that the officials imposed on the new territories were Radical supporters, with the ultimate aim of converting the new population into part of its voting bloc.[117] A decree was enacted on 5 March 1914 to settle Serb colonists on land confiscated from the local population, while others were permitted to buy such land very cheaply; Pašić himself acquired 3,000 hectares near Priština, although the Serbian government's plans for agrarian reform did not progress very far by the time World War I began.[118] Oppression of the local population was compounded by the often poor quality of the officials administering them; according to one account, a typical official 'thought that he had gone to America for temporary work, from where he ought to return with a golden money belt'.[119]

The acquisition of these vast new territories opened a new arena for the power struggle between the Radicals and the Black Hand and Independents. The Kingdom of Serbia's annexation of the territories was proclaimed by royal decree on 20 November 1913, violating Serbia's constitution, Clause 4 of which required that a great national parliament be convened to validate changes to Serbia's borders.[120] Protić used the constitutionally uncertain status of the new territories to justify the unconstitutional character of his emergency regime there; 'what we have taken ... that is Old Serbia, not the Kingdom of Serbia'.[121] The Black Hand challenged the government's control of the new territories, accusing the Radicals of seeking to establish a police dictatorship there; it agitated instead for continued military rule over them, a goal supported by the officer corps as a whole.

Conflict between government and army erupted following a reception at the Russian consulate in Bitola in Macedonia on 12 December 1913, when the Serbian okrug president arranged with the consul to toast the Tsar and a Serbian army colonel objected, claiming he had priority over a civilian who during the war had only been a sergeant. Thus was posed the so-called 'priority question' as to whether civilian or military authorities were to have pre-eminence in the new territories. The dispute endangered Serbia's international position, for the government rejected war minister and Black Hand supporter General Miloš Božanović's request at the end of 1913 for a budget to maintain 51,000 troops under arms and supply them with new equipment, for fear of strengthening the army. The conflict with Božanović led the government on 12 December to postpone its new budget and seek to extend part of the previous budget until March. Since this meant further extending a budget already extended since 1912, it was unconstitutional and bitterly denounced in unison by the opposition parties, who even staged a parliamentary walkout in protest. The illegal measure was nevertheless passed. The government finally put its budgetary bill before the parliament on 3 February 1914, four months later than permitted by the constitution. The embittered opposition consequently obstructed parliamentary business over the subsequent weeks.

The prominent conspirators Major Vemić and Colonel Popović—the latter was restored to duty in the army in 1912 in violation of the agreement with the British to retire him—had proven militarily incompetent during the war, responsible for military debacles involving heavy losses for their troops. Yet their careers continued to blossom thanks to the Black Hand's grip on the army.[122] Popović had been appointed to the command of Serbian forces in Albania as a result of the Black Hand's intervention and the acquiescence of its friend, chief of staff Putnik; his incompetence resulted in a bloody Serbian defeat at Brdica near Shkodër on 8–9 February, with 1,600 soldiers killed. He was heavily criticised in the Serbian press for this but, instead of accepting responsibility, he lashed out at his senior, the Black Hand's old bugbear, General Mišić, Putnik's aide-de-camp, whom he falsely accused of being behind the press attacks.[123] Popović was then promoted to general and appointed senior officer in charge of the new territories.

Vemić personally shot to death in cold blood a soldier who refused to obey an order, pumping multiple bullets into the father of two as he begged for mercy. Božanović unilaterally pardoned Vemić. The Social Democratic deputies Lapčević and Kaclerović submitted an interpellation to Božanović in June 1913, seeking appropriate punishment for Vemić. Under public pressure, Vemić was retried by the Supreme Court, sentenced to ten months' imprisonment, pardoned by Petar under army pressure and decorated.[124] Dušan Popović castigated the Radical government for its failure to confront and crush the conspirators and their militarism: 'Instead of these days witnessing some form of revolution, there has been played out a revolutionary parody … The first greater attempt of the Serbian bourgeoisie to emancipate itself from the unbearable terrible pressure of the officers has turned out comically.'[125] The Radicals nevertheless forced Božanović's resignation on 15 January in response to the Vemić affair. This created a furore among the Black Hand and precipitated a crisis in relations between government and army, at which point it was clear even to foreign ambassadors that the army had its own vision of foreign policy that was not necessarily the government's.[126]

Pašić wished to appoint Protić defence minister in Božanović's place but desisted following threats from the Black Hand, which instead secured the appointment of an officer acceptable to it, Colonel Dušan Stefanović. As their conflict with the army escalated, the Radicals, in particular Protić, openly attacked its 'praetorianism' in the press. The conflict spread to the parliament in February; Protić claimed that a clique of officers existed who 'want to hold under their control not only the entire officer corps, but want to tie up the government and legislative body as well'.¹²⁷ The police were given orders to employ live ammunition if officers attempted a putsch.¹²⁸ Yet the Radicals found themselves undermined by the Independents and Liberals, who considered the Radicals rather than the conspirators their main enemy, with the Liberals openly backing the conspirators in the power struggle.¹²⁹ The Liberal leaders Veljković and Ribarac even sought Austro-Hungarian financial support for a political campaign against Pašić and the Radicals.¹³⁰

The government's Decree on the Priority of Government of 8 March 1914 assigned formal priority to civilian over military authorities in public functions in the new territories. Black Hand pressure on and intimidation of government ministers increased; when the Black Hand supporter and Macedonian guerrilla fighter Major Aleksandar Blagojević issued a report criticising a police official in Macedonia, Protić condemned Blagojević's report in parliament, whereupon Blagojević challenged Protić to a duel. According to *Pijemont*'s account, Blagojević sent his seconds to Protić's cabinet office where, 'surprised and frightened', Protić attempted to apologise, but Blagojević nevertheless subsequently attacked him with a whip at Terazije.¹³¹ Popović, military commander in the new territories, refused to recognise the Priority Decree so was pensioned off once again on 15 April 1914. *Politika* announced on 9 May that the government had submitted a decree for the pensioning of Apis, Tankosić and two other conspirators to Petar, but he had refused to sign it.

Pijemont wrote on 19 May that 'the government and its followers represent a bunch of state anarchists who from behind the cover of good positions and bad laws and decrees damage the state interest, ruin morale, kill authority and plunder the treasury ... These days in our fatherland a struggle is being waged between the government and the army ... the Radical pear has been so ripe already for so long that the King must squash it with his staff as soon as possible. A far-seeing Ruler who cares for the army will certainly do that soon.'¹³² This was justified also by the oppression the government was inflicting on the inhabitants of the new territories. *Pijemont* wrote on 21 May 1914: 'In the newly liberated territories there is true hell. Stojan's police officials, defended by their all-powerful minister, have become robbers and brigands. There is not a place in New Serbia that has not been plundered by these uniformed brigands ... To avoid the danger that in this country rebellion and anarchy should arise, this regime must not be endured a moment longer ...'¹³³

The dispute united all army officers against the government, even those who were not Black Hand supporters. Under pressure from Putnik, acting at the Black Hand's behest, King Petar attempted to dismiss Pašić, who consequently submitted his resignation on 2 June 1914. General Petar Bojović, the new commander in the new territories, who was subsequently associated with the White Hand, sent a formal dispatch on 3 June to the war minister, on behalf of the divisional commanders in the new territories, demanding action to protect the officer corps from the supposed attacks of the civilian authorities and press, including the repeal or alteration of the Priority Decree, and, if this were not forthcoming, threatening disturbances in the army.[134] The Black Hand's plans in respect of the Radical leaders became increasingly extreme; Tankosić proposed to the organisation that he personally employ violence against Pašić and Protić. He even threatened Petar not to support the Radicals; slapping the king's close friend Balugdžić, he told him that he was a 'nobody' who 'performed a nobody's jobs'.[135]

Apis was by the start of June working to mobilise both the army and, with Putnik's blessing and in his name, Independent and Liberal politicians to topple the government. He met with Independent leaders several times to discuss a coup, and some of them, such as Drašković and Prodanović, may have approved the idea; Drašković himself may even have joined the Black Hand. Although just what this coup would have involved is disputed, the essence would have been to crush the Radicals and replace them in government with politicians under the control of the Black Hand, which would thereby have seized control of the state without formally taking power in its own name. Apis admitted to writing to his supporters in the military in Skopje, suggesting that they 'expel some of the district and okrug governors in the new territories with their suitcases to Belgrade, while here in Belgrade it would be our concern to bring things under control', with the intention of suspending the civilian authorities in the new territories and using these territories as a springboard for an attack on and overthrow of the Radical government.[136] However, the plan was not well received by leading members of the officer corps in the new territories and failed when Apis's own circle refused to execute it.[137] Apis ultimately lacked the decisiveness to carry out the plan and could not marshal his allies among the opposition politicians behind it.[138]

When the Independents offered to Petar to form a government, the Black Hand intervened in the discussion to put forward its own candidate for foreign minister, Jovan M. Jovanović-Pižon, which would have cemented its control over policy. But Hartwig put great pressure on Petar to retain Pašić and, perhaps more importantly, persuaded the conflicted Crown Prince Aleksandar, who was hostile to the Black Hand but sympathised with the army against the government, to throw his weight behind Pašić.[139] Consequently, Petar asked Pašić to withdraw his resignation and permitted him to form a new government on the 11th. Pašić's dependence on Russia for his political survival recalled his old adversary King Milan's dependence on Austria-Hungary. Typically, Pašić bought his continued premiership with a concession to his enemies: the Priority Decree was modified so that the civilian government would only have automatic priority over the military on formal occasions when the government was representing itself politically, while on all other occasions the relative priority of civilian and military officials would be determined according to rank and pay. Petar, for his part, was caught between the Black Hand and Radicals and was unable to stand the pressure from both sides; Damjan Popović allegedly warned him that 'blood would be spilled if he did not replace this government'. Petar consequently announced on 25 June that he was resigning his royal duties, on grounds of illness, in favour of Aleksandar as regent and commander-in-chief. This was a cover for his abdication, which French and Austro-Hungarian observers attributed to the machinations of Russian diplomacy but which was primarily the outcome of Serbia's internal conflict.[140]

The acquisition of a large portion of Macedonia at the expense of Bulgaria also widened the gulf between Pašić and the Black Hand over the question of further national expansion. Pašić knew that in any war against Austria-Hungary, Serbia would need Russian support, in return for which Russia would require Serbia to make territorial concessions to the Bulgarians in Macedonia, in order to get them on board. He therefore wished to postpone the showdown with Austria-Hungary until Serbia's portion of Macedonia had been irreversibly integrated into the Serbian state. He recalled in 1923 that on the eve of the First Balkan War, his government's policy had been 'that we first need to liberate Kosovo and South Serbia, and when we have liberated that, that there should then pass fifteen, possibly twenty years, in order for our people across the Sava and Danube to be prepared for unification.'[141] Meanwhile Serbia's government signed a concordat with the Vatican on 24 June 1914, recognising the right of Catholics in Serbia to freedom of worship and their own religious schools in return for Serbia's right to approve the appointment of the Catholic archbishop in Belgrade and the bishop in Skopje, and of any foreigners to church positions in Serbia. By permitting Catholic clergy in Serbia direct relations with the Vatican, Serbia's government eliminated Vienna as an intermediary, thereby removing its control over Serbia's Catholics and potentially increasing Belgrade's influence over South Slav Catholics in Austria-Hungary. Vienna viewed this as a defeat.[142] The Concordat was formally ratified on 20 March 1915.

Sarajevo assassination and outbreak of World War I

Serbia's increasing instability pushed it inexorably toward a military catastrophe unprecedented since the Ottoman suppression of the First Serbian Uprising. Pašić worked hard to maintain good relations with Vienna and encouraged Pribićević's Croat–Serb Coalition to ally with Hungary's government, to reduce the danger that the South Slav question in Austria-Hungary would lead to war.[143] But Apis and the Black Hand's adventurism derailed Pašić's strategy. The plot to murder Austrian Archduke Franz Ferdinand, fateful for world history, may have been embarked on deliberately to undermine Pašić's foreign policy; when Tankosić was arrested in Serbia following the assassination and was asked by a general why he had arranged it, he replied, 'To spite Pašić.'[144]

Following its establishment in 1911, the Black Hand founded a training school at Prokuplje near Niš for guerrillas, the majority of whom were recruited from Bosnia-

Hercegovina. The graduates conducted terrorist activities in Austria-Hungary, particularly in Croatia and Bosnia-Hercegovina. Following an agreement with the Serbian army's general staff, the Black Hand could position its agents at the border stations facing Austria-Hungary and the Ottoman Empire, where they assisted guerrilla activities. These culminated in the assassination of Franz Ferdinand on 28 June 1914, which was planned by Apis and Tankosić and executed using Bosnian agents, with the teenager Gavrilo Princip firing the fatal shots, though there is some dispute over whether Princip was formally a member of the Black Hand.[145] Franz Ferdinand was chosen for assassination, in part because he was viewed as a supporter of a 'trialist' solution to the Austro-Hungarian national question, whereby the empire would have been transformed from a dual to a tripartite monarchy, with its South Slavic lands forming the third unit alongside Austria and Hungary. Such a solution threatened to satisfy the Habsburg South Slavs' aspirations within the Habsburg framework, thereby ending their desire to unite with Serbia.[146] Another reason for the assassination may have been that Apis had been informed that Franz Ferdinand was planning a military attack on Serbia. According to Antonije Antić, Apis had not expected the assassination attempt actually to succeed, but intended it merely to frighten the archduke.[147] However, Franz Ferdinand was hardly unique in having been targeted by Apis for assassination: the enthusiastic regicide who had plotted King Aleksandar's murder also sent an assassin to Vienna in July 1911 to murder Emperor Franz Joseph; he plotted with Bulgarian revolutionaries in February 1914 to murder Tsar Ferdinand; and during 1916 he sent assassins to Athens to murder King Constantine and to Paris to murder Montenegro's King Nikola. He even planned to assassinate Germany's Kaiser Wilhelm.[148]

Apis resolved in about January 1914 to murder the archduke. The plan appears to have originated with Rade Malobabić, a Serb from Croatia and a National Defence agent. Tankosić recruited three young Belgrade-based Bosnian revolutionaries to perform the task: Princip, Trifko Grabež and Nedeljko Čabrinović. The trio agreed by April to perform the assassination and were trained in shooting during May. Princip was the best shot of the three since he had previously trained at Tankosić's guerrilla school in Prokuplje. The Black Hand's contact with the youth occurred mostly through Tankosić's agent Milan Ciganović, a Bosnian who had been a guerrilla under his command against the Bulgarians. There were thus two links in the conspiratorial chain between the assassins and Apis so as to protect the latter from exposure by any police interrogation of the assassins. On 27 May Ciganović provided the assassins with the guns and bombs with which they were to kill the archduke, as well as cyanide capsules which they were then to swallow if they could not shoot themselves first.[149] They left Belgrade the next day. Assisted by the Black Hand's puppet Frontier Guard, they reached the border, whence, assisted by the Black Hand's underground network, they travelled to Sarajevo, arriving on 3 June. Their passage was facilitated by the fact that the Black Hand's network spanned both sides of the Austro-Serbian border, over which Serbia's government had no effective control.[150]

Serbia's government, informed of the plot, attempted unsuccessfully to prevent the assassins crossing into Bosnia, and Pašić subsequently ordered war minister Stefanović to open an investigation into Apis's dispatch of the armed youths across the border. Although Pašić wished to prevent the assassination and avert possible war with Austria-Hungary, warning Vienna of the plot would, firstly, have revealed to it the Serbian government's awareness of the terrorist activities being organised on its own soil and, secondly, discredited him in the Serbian public's eyes if his warning became known. Serbia's ambassador in Vienna, Jovanović-Pižon, met with Austria-Hungary's minister of finance Leon Biliński on 5 June and gave him a coded verbal warning that the assassination was pending, but Biliński failed to understand it. When Apis informed the Black Hand's supreme central administration of the plot for the first time on 14 June, it voted to cancel the assassination, overriding Apis, but he was either unable or unwilling to halt the assassins.[151] In Sarajevo, Princip's collaborator Danilo Ilić recruited three more would-be assassins: Muhamed Mehmedbašić, Vasa Čubrilović and Cvijetko Popović. As local recruits, their involvement served to obscure the plot's genesis in the Black Hand in Belgrade, of which they knew very little.[152]

The archduke and his wife Sophie, Duchess of Hohenberg, visited Sarajevo on 28 June and were warmly received by the citizenry. The assassination barely succeeded: Mehmedbašić, Čubrilović, Popović and Grabež failed to act while Čabrinović hurled his bomb at the royal car but succeeded only in wounding an adjutant of Lieutenant General Oskar Potiorek, military governor of Bosnia-Hercegovina. The archduke bravely ordered his convoy to proceed. After visiting the Sarajevo city hall, he decided to change his itinerary in order to visit the wounded adjutant in hospital. But his driver was not informed of the change of itinerary, so he followed the original route. When Potiorek, seated with Franz Ferdinand in the car, realised the error and told the driver to change his route, the car was stopped by chance alongside Princip, the last assassin. Princip shot the archduke and, aiming at Potiorek but missing, accidentally shot the duchess, mortally wounding them both.

Serbia's destiny was by this point wholly enmeshed in the politics of confrontation between the Austro-German alliance and the Entente powers of Britain, Russia and France, while Great Power politics were conversely at the mercy of Balkan developments. Russian-backed Serb irredentism was as threatening to Austria-Hungary as a possible Austro-Hungarian crushing of Serbia and descent into the Balkans were to Russia. After diplomatic defeats in the Moroccan crises of 1905–1906 and 1911 and defeat in its naval race with Britain, the Balkans and Near East remained Germany's last possible path of significant imperial expansion, from which the French and Russians threatened to exclude it.[153] But the German interest in the Ottoman Empire was equally threatening to St Petersburg. Following Russia's and

Germany's respective diplomatic humiliations in the annexation and Moroccan crises, both felt compelled to support unconditionally their respective allies in the Austro-Serbian conflict. Aware it was losing its arms race with France and Russia and that Austria-Hungary was its only significant, dependable ally, Berlin was ready to risk war to defend Vienna.[154] Meanwhile, the dynamics of the Franco-Russian alliance and Britain's ententes with France and Russia resulted in firm French support, with British encouragement, for Russian intransigence in the Balkans. The rigid two-bloc Great Power system focused tension at its most vulnerable spot—the Austro-Serbian conflict—where a small spark caused the explosion.[155]

Though the crisis had been engineered by the Black Hand rather than by Serbia's legitimate government, the latter was also a reason for the war because Pašić's unconditional loyalty to Russia ensured Vienna would not trust him but would pursue an uncompromisingly severe line.[156] Austria-Hungary's ambassador presented Serbia's government with an ultimatum on 23 July, claiming the 'Sarajevo crime was formulated in Belgrade' and that 'the arms and explosives, with which the murderers were supplied, were given to them by Serbian officers and officials'. It demanded the suppression of all irredentist activity and public discourse in Serbia, including National Defence; the dismissal of Serbian officials implicated in such activity or in the assassination plot; the investigation and punishment of those responsible for the assassination; the arrest of Tankosić and Ciganović; and the participation of Austro-Hungarian organs in these steps. National Defence, rather than the Black Hand, was wrongly fingered by Vienna as the culprit behind the assassination; the Black Hand's use of the broader 'cultural association' as a cover for its activities in Bosnia-Hercegovina had successfully concealed its own responsibility.

Serbia's government responded to the ultimatum on 25 July, claiming that it was 'convinced that this reply will remove the misunderstanding that threatens to cloud the good neighbourly relations between the Austro-Hungarian monarchy and the Kingdom of Serbia'. It accepted most of its terms but 'as regards the participation in that investigation [into the involvement in the assassination of all those on Serbian territory] of the organs of the Austro-Hungarian authorities, which the imperial and royal government would delegate for that purpose, the Serbian royal government cannot accept their participation, because it would thereby be violating the constitution and law on judicial proceedings over criminal acts'.[157] Pašić was keen to avoid war or to provide Vienna with a pretext for it, and as he later said, 'Our response to the Austrian ultimatum went much further than was permitted by the national honour of an independent country', but he feared the implications for Serbian security of permitting entry into Serbia of Austria-Hungary's investigators and police, probably backed by military forces, which could potentially take control of an investigation involving Serbian officers.[158] Even Kaiser Wilhelm felt Serbia's response to the ultimatum was acceptable, amounting to 'a great moral success for Vienna', which had thereby achieved its aims, while the few remaining points of dispute could be resolved by negotiation, though he believed Austria-Hungary should still occupy Belgrade to guarantee Serbia's compliance.[159] Yet Prince Regent Aleksandar and Serbia's government, more realistically appreciating Vienna's intent, decided upon this incomplete acceptance of the ultimatum knowing it probably meant war.[160] Austria-Hungary indeed declared war on Serbia on 28 July. Serbia, with a population of about 4,550,000, stood momentarily alone against an empire with a population of 51,390,223.

Most Serbian parties united in patriotic readiness to stand behind their government and army in defence of the country. Serbia's parliament assembled at an extraordinary session at Niš on 31 July and received the text of Aleksandar's address to it, appealing for the deputies to support the government's measures to defend the country. Only Lapčević, in the name of the Social Democrats, dissented and called for a peaceful resolution of the conflict, accusing the government of 'serving as a toy in the hands of certain Great Powers' which were pursuing their own imperialist goals. Lapčević and the other Social Democratic deputy, Kaclerović, were the only two to vote against the government's reply to the prince regent, pledging support for the war effort, and to vote against war credits.[161] They also asserted that 'all dark organisations, which worsen our foreign relations and which represent a danger for internal peace, need to be disempowered'.[162] They feared the war would grow into a general European inter-imperialist war, and it did. Great Power interests meant the Austro-Serbian war could not remain localised. Germany declared war on Russia on 1 August and on France on the 3rd, and Britain declared war on Germany on the 4th. Montenegro declared war on Austria-Hungary on 5 August and Serbia itself declared war on Germany on 6 August, as did Montenegro on the 8th. Although the Social Democrats had opposed the war, they unanimously resolved to participate along with the rest of the Serbian people in defence of their country. Many died fighting, including party secretary Tucović on 20 November.

Serbia's victory in the Balkan Wars, involving its acquisition of a large territory in the Sanjak, Kosovo and Macedonia, was an act of military conquest 'from above' of the kind that Marković had inveighed against. The victory appeared to vindicate the model of a standing army led by professional officers that Milan had pioneered and that Pašić and the Radicals had traditionally opposed. In presiding over such an enterprise, the Radicals moved a long way from the ideology of their founder to reconcile themselves with the old military-bureaucratic elite. Yet the partnership between the old and new Serbian elites remained unstable as the power struggle continued between the Radicals and the Black Hand supported by the Independents and Liberals. The acquisition of new territory fuelled this power struggle by expanding its arena. Meanwhile, Serbia's expansion heightened Austro-Hungarian enmity, yet Pašić could not navigate this perilous situation successfully because he could not restrain the Black Hand. The Sarajevo assassination and Serbia's descent into a disastrous war with Austria-Hungary were the logical outcome of these conflicts.

PART III

NATIONAL UNIFICATION AND YUGOSLAVIA

13

DEFEAT AND OCCUPATION

1914–1917

Serbia in 1914 was forced to wage a war of survival against Austria-Hungary, a far larger and more powerful predatory neighbour. This was, for the Serbian political classes, a moment of both extreme vulnerability and extreme ambition. It appeared an opportunity finally to wage the revolutionary national struggle anticipated since Svetozar Marković's day, to liberate and unite with, or annex, the Habsburg South Slav lands, with the Russian ally substituting for the general Balkan uprising as the force to bring victory. Yet Serbia was constrained by its own limited strength, the diplomacy of its Great Power allies and its ongoing conflicts with other Balkan states and peoples. The skill of its commanders and bravery of its soldiers impressed the world and fired the radicalism of its war aims. But they alone could not bring victory, which depended on the outcome of World War I as a whole, and until late in the day this did not tilt decisively in favour of the Entente powers.

Self-defence and revolutionary war

The unsought outbreak of war with Austria-Hungary in 1914 resulted in a re-radicalisation of Serbian state policy. Pašić and his supporters were determined that the South Slav lands should be unified under Serbia's leadership and on the basis of its political and constitutional order, to constitute effectively an enlarged Serbia. Pašić tended to use 'Great Serbia' as a synonym for 'Yugoslavia', a name he disliked and generally avoided using on the grounds that it 'smelled of Austrianism'.[1] The Radical journalist Milan Đorđević elaborated on this in his post-war book about Serbian wartime policy: "'Yugoslavia', 'State of Yugoslavia', 'Yugoslav nation' etc. are not new terms … they were the heralds of the extension of the Habsburg tyranny to those parts of our people who were not under the Habsburg sceptre. The name "Yugoslav", in the first place, was intended to erase from the face of the earth the name "Serb", which remained as the only counterweight to Habsburg intentions against our people.'[2] Pašić also referred to the projected state as the 'Serbo-Croat and Slovene state' or simply 'Serb state' or 'new state', and during the war came to use the term 'Serbian three-named nation, Serbs, Croats and Slovenes'. For Pašić, Serbia's acquisition of Bosnia-Hercegovina and an outlet on the Adriatic took precedence over wider South Slav unification. Should the latter occur, it would happen though annexation of the Habsburg South Slav lands to Serbia as the South Slav Piedmont, not through their unification as equals.[3] From this perspective, Yugoslav unification was simply an ambitious form of pan-Serb unification. The idea of national unity of Serbs, Croats and Slovenes was an ideological concept that Pašić and other Serbian politicians and intellectuals upheld, but never at the expense of the idea of national unification of Serbs—the nation that, unlike the 'Yugoslavs', existed in their hearts.

Prince Regent Aleksandar, in his speech to Serbia's army on 4 August 1914, spoke of 'the groans of millions of our brothers, which have reached us from Bosnia and Hercegovina, from the Banat and Bačka, from Croatia, Slavonia, Srem and from our sea, stout Dalmatia', concluding: 'Into battle for the freedom and independence of the Serb nation!', which suggested the 'brothers' in questions were only Serbs rather than South Slavs in general.[4] The speech made clear that Serbia's war aims were not purely defensive but sought liberation of at least some Habsburg subjects. Aleksandar favoured a Great Serbia incorporating all Habsburg territories with a Serbian Orthodox majority; he believed religious differences between Catholics and Orthodox overrode ethno-linguistic kinship, so had reservations about possible union with Croats and Slovenes.[5] As with Pašić, 'The creation of the Yugoslav state union in 1918 was not a primary aim of Aleksandar's. Rather it was but one possible alternative', according to his biographer Branislav Gligorijević.[6]

Serbia's government intended from the start to combine conventional military activity by its regular armies with an uprising of the Serbs and other South Slavs against Austria-Hungary, centred on Bosnia-Hercegovina. The government resolved on 7 August 1914 that the army's supreme command should organise volunteer detachments to engage in guerrilla warfare with the particular goal of launching an uprising in Bosnia-Hercegovina. Already prior to this, on 28 July, the war minister decreed the formation of a special command for volunteer units. Volunteer detachments were then organised under Apis's supervision and sent by him to fight on the Drina. Four Chetnik detachments were established on 4 August, each under the command of a leading Black Hand officer, thereby perpetuating the secret organisation's established leadership in the field of irregular warfare. These detachments were predominantly Serb, consisting in particular of Serbs from East Bosnia who had fled before the Austro-Hungarian offensive. But they included other South Slavs as well, including Muslim Bosniaks. Serbian soldiers that autumn sang Croatian national hymns including 'Our Beautiful Homeland' and shouted 'Long live Serbo-Croat unity', so as to encourage desertions among South Slav soldiers in Austria-Hungary's army.[7] However, the danger of such defectors being punished for treason in the event they were captured while fighting for Serbia led the supreme command to deploy them in garrison and border duties in the newly acquired Macedonian and Kosovar territories instead of against Austria-Hungary.[8]

Serbia's ambitions were nevertheless constrained by the fact that it entered the war as a junior partner in a coalition dominated by three Great Powers: Britain, France and Russia. Serbia was, in their eyes, a small state whose interests could be legitimately compromised for the sake of their grand strategy. The Russians, in particular, treated Serbia as a pawn. They sought to bring Bulgaria into the war on their side, which necessitated offering it much of the Macedonian territory that Serbia had seized in 1912–1913. Serbia's government did not consider the promise of Austro-Hungarian territory to be adequate recompense for surrendering something Serbia already had, particularly since the Entente powers were also seeking to draw Italy into the war with the promise of parts of Dalmatia to which Serbia also aspired and were not yet contemplating the empire's complete destruction, which precluded the achievement of Serbia's maximum territorial goals to the west and north. The Entente powers similarly sought to bribe Romania to enter the war on their side with the offer of territory Serbia wanted: part of Vojvodina adjacent to Belgrade, which was needed to provide Serbia's capital with a defensive hinterland.

Serbian diplomatic and propaganda agitation for South Slav unification was therefore a way of influencing the Entente powers away from awarding territory they held or wanted to other states. Furthermore, Russia sought to re-establish the Balkan union of the First Balkan War, involving both Serbia and Bulgaria, which would have subordinated them to its system of control and left it arbiter of their destinies; consequently, the creation of a large state including the Habsburg South Slav lands was a means for Serbia to evade this subordination. Conversely, the Russians feared such unification would mean Serbia's immersion in a largely Catholic state, so weakening their influence over it; given Russian reservations, Pašić himself, as the inveterate Russophile, was somewhat torn over the question.[9] Finally, the proclaimed goal of unification was intended to pre-empt possible Entente support for the reorganisation of the Habsburg Empire along federal lines or for Croatian independence, either of which would have obstructed Serbia's territorial ambitions westward. Pašić and Aleksandar both feared an independent Croatia would compete with Serbia over disputed lands much as Bulgaria competed with it over Macedonia.[10] From the start, Pašić responded to news that Catholic circles in the allied states were working to establish Croatia and Slovenia as a state union separate from Serbia by declaring: 'We must begin to work in a Great Serbian sense and put forward our viewpoint.'[11] In response to possible Entente backing for an independent Croatia, raised in French and Italian diplomatic circles in September 1914, he resolved that any such state should be denied Bosnia-Hercegovina, Dalmatia, Srem, Slavonia and Lika, so reducing it to a minuscule rump.[12] Given Russia's reservations, Serbia turned to France and Britain, marketing unification as a bulwark against future

German penetration of the Balkans. Russian hostility was paralleled by increasing British sympathy.

Serbia's foreign ministry assembled at the end of August several leading intellectuals to advise it on the goal of unification, including Jovan Cvijić, Nikola Stojanović, Slobodan Jovanović and Aleksandar Belić.[13] Pašić announced to the Entente governments on 4 September 1914 that Serbia's goal was 'a strong south-west Slavic state, in which would be included all Serbs and all Croats and all Slovenes'.[14] In a note of 21 September 1914 to Serbia's ambassador to Russia, Pašić set out highly ambitious territorial aspirations, encompassing not only most of the territory to the north and west of Serbia that was eventually included in Yugoslavia, including Istria (which he considered dividing with Italy), but also territories that after World War I went to Romania, Hungary and Austria, including the towns of Timişoara, Baja and Leibnitz, though he stressed that his overriding goal was Banat (eastern Vojvodina).[15] Nevertheless, when the Entente powers signed the Pact of London on 5 September 1914, pledging that none of them would make a separate peace with the Central Powers, Serbia was not immediately recognised formally as a member of the alliance. It would have to work hard to make its voice heard by its allies.

Initial victory and Niš Declaration

Following the declaration of war, Serbia's principal state organs were relocated from militarily vulnerable Belgrade to Niš, deep in its interior. Austria-Hungary invaded Serbia in August 1914, crossing the Drina and Sava rivers on the 12th. For the first time since the Second Serbian Uprising, Serbia was fighting a genuinely defensive war to protect clear borders from a predatory enemy recognisable as a threat to virtually its entire population. During their occupation of part of north-western Serbia in August 1914, Austro-Hungarian forces perpetrated systematic atrocities, including burning homes, looting and plundering villages, torturing prisoners and executing civilians, including women and children.[16] They shelled civilian targets in Belgrade and, during their brief occupation of the city in December, publicly hanged a youth in Terazije as a warning to the population after he was found with a revolver in his pocket; laughing Austro-Hungarian soldiers periodically pulled the corpse's legs to set it swinging and the body was left dangling until the next morning.[17] The Austro-Hungarians massacred about 4,000 old people, women and children in Mačva, Jadar and Posavina in August 1914 alone. General Horststein, commander of the Austro-Hungarian 9th Army, declared: 'Towards such a population, humanity and generosity of any kind have no place whatsoever; indeed they are damaging, for such stances in war, otherwise sometimes justified, in this case greatly endanger the security of our troops.'[18] Hundreds of thousands of Serbian civilians fled before the enemy into the interior of Serbia.[19] Meanwhile, the Habsburg authorities in Croatia, Dalmatia and particularly Bosnia-Hercegovina embarked upon a policy of systematic persecution of the Serb population. Serb cultural organisations were closed, the Cyrillic alphabet and the Serb name banned and Serb civilians deported from strategically sensitive areas and imprisoned in their tens of thousands in concentration camps, or lynched or executed.[20] The Serbian and Montenegrin armies also carried out atrocities against Bosnia-Hercegovina's Muslim population during their operations on Bosnian territory that year; Muslim homes and farms were burned and looted and many thousands of refugees sent fleeing.[21] Nevertheless, Serbian soldiers knew they were fighting a war of national survival and Serbia's army consequently performed extremely well throughout the conflict.

Austria-Hungary, by contrast, was fighting an aggressive war for which its population and soldiers felt little enthusiasm. Its military operations were seriously dislocated by its confused switch from its initial plan to fight a localised war against Serbia alone to a plan for a more general military effort with Russia as its principal enemy. Its force sent to invade Serbia numbered around 400,000 at the time of its first invasion, which included reserve and garrison units of dubious quality, and peaked at 450,000 in the summer of 1914, giving it no numerical edge over the opposing Serbian army numbering over 400,000.[22] Some of the Austro-Hungarian corps sent against Serbia were themselves as much as 20–25 per cent Serb and 50 per cent Croat in composition, which did not necessarily make them disloyal or unwilling to fight Serbia but may have dampened their martial spirit.[23] For its part, Serbia's army had not recovered from its losses during the Balkan Wars in trained personnel, equipment and livestock; it was under-equipped and its rifles and artillery were a mishmash of different models, several of them obsolete. These disadvantages were outweighed by the higher motivation of its troops and superior skill of its high command: Austria-Hungary's Lieutenant General Potiorek would be completely out-marshalled by Serbia's chief of staff Vojvoda Putnik, with the assistance of some outstanding generals, above all Živojin Mišić, Stepa Stepanović, Pavle Jurišić-Šturm and Petar Bojović.[24] Serbia's attempts at inciting an uprising in Bosnia-Hercegovina and other Habsburg South Slav lands were unsuccessful; as Ekmečić remarks, 'For the Bosnian peasant, a leader such as Karađorđe is more suitable than one such as Apis.'[25] But the Austro-Hungarian military's fear of such an uprising led it to concentrate its offensive against western Serbia, across the Drina from East Bosnia, rather than across the Sava against Belgrade and the principal Serbian railway communications in the Morava valley, which contributed to its failure.[26]

At the Battle of Cer in north-western Serbia on 15–19 August, Serbia's 2nd and 3rd Armies under Stepanović and Jurišić-Šturm decisively defeated the Austro-Hungarians, who pushed back across the Drina and Sava. Although the subsequent Serbian counter-offensive against Habsburg Srem and Bosnia was unsuccessful, a second Austro-Hungarian offensive across the Drina, beginning on 6 September, was temporarily halted by Serbia's 2nd and 3rd Armies at the Battle of the Drina. Serbian forces defending Belgrade forayed across the River Sava on 10 September and captured Zemun, to the jubilation of many of its South Slav inhabitants; they briefly set up a Serbian administration there, which renamed streets after King Petar, Prince Aleksandar and the Serbian commander of the Belgrade front, General Mihailo Živković. The Serbian forces hosted a visit to the town by Živković and Prince Đorđe before retreating from it on the 14th.[27] The Battle of Mačkov Kamen, a plateau near Krupanj in north-western Serbia, from 19 to 22 September, was the bloodiest engagement of the Balkan theatre in 1914; the Austro-Hungarians pushed Serbia's army back with heavy losses on both sides. Serb soldiers fought bravely in both armies: 'In the Battle of Mačkov Kamen in September 1914, fighting on one side was the Fourth Regiment of Užice and on the other a regiment from Lika including a large number of Serbs from that area whose forebears had for centuries been the most faithful soldiers of the Habsburg emperors. Commander Purić of the Užice regiment led his men in fourteen charges, to which the men from Lika responded with lightning-like counterchanges. In one of these Purić shouted to them, "Surrender, don't die so stupidly", and they replied, "Have you ever heard of Serbs surrendering?"'[28]

With a third offensive across the Drina beginning on 6 November, the Austro-Hungarians succeeded in occupying much of north-western Serbia and in taking Belgrade at the start of December. Serbia's desperate military situation produced a division of opinion among its leadership over how to react; this was a further manifestation of the power struggle between the Black Hand and Pašić and the Radicals. Whereas Pašić placed all his bets on the alliance with Russia and continuing the fight alongside it, the Black Hand viewed a separate peace with the Central Powers as a means both to extricate Serbia from defeat and to bring down the Radicals. Apis's close ally, Serbian diplomat Miloš Bogičević, was an actual agent of the Central Powers and possible conduit for such peace talks.[29] At a joint session of Serbia's government and supreme military command on 9 November, chaired by Aleksandar, the Black Hand's protégé Putnik proposed a separate peace.[30] Aleksandar, himself under direct pressure from Russia, rejected this, deciding the issue in favour of Pašić's government. Nevertheless, Russia was immediately informed that the supreme command had proposed a separate peace—a warning of the consequences of its pressure regarding Macedonia. Russia's foreign minister responded by recommending that the allies reassure Serbia that its interests would be respected.[31] At a secret session of parliament on 16 November, Pašić was then compelled by the Black Hand to accept the formation of an all-party government, to unify the nation and put him and the Radicals under a measure of restraint. This was eventually formed on 5 December as a coalition of the Radicals, Independents and Progressives, while the Liberals chose to remain in opposition. Pašić remained prime minister, but, at the Black Hand's insistence, those to whom it particularly objected were excluded, including Protić and the White Hand's Colonel Dušan Stefanović.[32]

DEFEAT AND OCCUPATION

Meanwhile, Austria-Hungary's military operations had exhausted its troops. After the Serbian army's retreat to the right bank of the Kolubara River, the 1st Army under General Živojin Mišić spearheaded a full-scale counter-attack by all three armies against the more numerous Austro-Hungarians on 3 December. The Battle of the Kolubara was the greatest Serbian victory of the war, with the Austro-Hungarians heavily defeated and again driven out of Serbia. On the 15th Serbia's army re-entered Belgrade, where Aleksandar hailed his troops: 'With powerful blows you have destroyed the enemy and struck the solid foundations of a Great Serbia.'[33] An Austro-Hungarian flag was laid out at the royal palace for Petar to drive over, after which the flag was laid on the palace steps so the king could personally step on it, to the cheers of the assembled crowds.[34] Thus concluded the first phase of the war—a Serbian victory which, while impressive, cost it about 120,000 casualties including 22,000 dead. The losses were unsustainable and left the army seriously depleted when the Central Powers resumed the offensive against it the following year.[35]

In the euphoria of victory, the government on 7 December announced to the parliament its first formal statement of war aims, subsequently known as the Niš Declaration: 'The government of the Kingdom deems as its principal and, in these fateful moments, only task to be the successful conclusion of this great war which, in the moment when it began, became also a struggle for the liberation and unification of all our unfree brother Serbs, Croats and Slovenes.'[36] This radical Yugoslavism reflected the influence of the Independents within the coalition government; its most likely author was Drašković. It may also have been aimed at pressing the Entente powers to acknowledge Serbia's maximum war aims.[37] Pašić himself was reluctant to abandon a purely Serbian defensive programme, while resistance from conservative Radicals had led to the omission of any mention of the Slovenes from the Declaration's first draft in favour of narrower Serbo-Croat unification. That unification with the Slovenes along with the Croats was eventually included reflected the influence of Cvijić and Protić, among others, as well as Pašić's less idealistic calculation that the Slovenes could serve as a counterweight to the Croats.[38]

The parliamentary deputies greeted the Niš Declaration with great enthusiasm. It implied a righteous struggle for the liberation of fellow South Slavs—Croats and Slovenes as well as Serbs. Yet by turning Yugoslav unification into a unilateral Serbian war aim rather than something arrived at consensually through agreement between Serbia and the Habsburg South Slavs, it laid the basis for the eventual unilateral imposition of a Serbian-centred, unitarist form of unification.[39] Parliament endorsed the Declaration, in doing so arguably overstepping its competencies, as it had been elected before the war when 'liberation and unification' of Serbs, Croats and Slovenes had not been an issue, and it was uncertain that Serbia's people would have endorsed it now. Conversely, Serbia's allies among the Great Powers all rejected outright or failed to support the Declaration, wishing to preserve flexibility regarding war outcomes. Britain and France still envisaged Austria-Hungary's survival while Russia opposed the Serbs' unification with so many Catholics.[40] Meanwhile, Aleksandar, in his speech to the army on 28 December 1914, pledged that the peace settlement would 'decently reward the sacrifices for our Great Serbia.'[41]

Serbia's government intended to publish an authoritative statement of war aims written collectively by a body of leading Serbian scholars. Though this did not happen, individuals involved in the project did publish individual statements, exhibiting an idealistic belief in Serb–Croat–Slovene unity and its role in the better world that was to follow victory.[42] One such was 'Serbia and the Yugoslav question' by the philologist Aleksandar Belić, published by Serbia's state publisher and dated 30 December 1914, which rejected Karadžić's attempted demarcation of a national border between Serbs and Croats on the basis of difference in dialects, in favour of the concept of 'one language with two names; one nation with two denominations'. Belić insisted: 'The founding of a common state of Slovenes, Croats and Serbs is not only the result of their aspirations in the past; not only an expression of their national-ethnographic unity', but 'also of the direct need for their self-defence from surrounding nations' and for them to serve as a 'bulwark against the Austro-German penetration into the Balkan peninsula, allied to Hungarian imperialist ambitions ... There cannot be European peace and progress without peace in the Balkans.'[43] Similarly, 'What does Serbia want?' by Stanoje Stanojević, a historian close to the Radicals, was published by Serbia's state publisher and dated 18 May 1915. It claimed: 'Serbs, Croats and Slovenes are one nation by origin and by language ... The free Serbian kingdom, true to the traditions of the Serb past, wishes to liberate from foreign rule all its co-nationals, Serbs, Croats and Slovenes, and unite them in a single, unified and simple state whole' in order 'to work full-strength for the achievement of the great ideal of the whole of humanity: that all peoples and all nations be free, healthy, enlightened, materially secure and, as much as possible, happy and contented'.[44]

The Niš Declaration closely followed the formation on 22 November of the Yugoslav Committee in Florence by a group of anti-Habsburg South Slav politicians. It was set up with the approval of Pašić's Serbian government to counter attempts to establish an independent Croatia or annex Dalmatian territory to Italy. It assembled Croatian politicians seeking to fulfil Croatian aspirations within a Yugoslav framework, most notably the Dalmatian Croats Ante Trumbić and Frano Supilo and Bosnian Serb politicians who stood at the frontier between Yugoslavist and pan-Serb politics, most notably Dušan Vasiljević, president of the principal Bosnian Serb party, the Serb National Organisation, and Nikola Stojanović. The latter was Pašić's principal agent in the project but was not simply his cipher. Pašić had first privately explained his concept of South Slav unification to Stojanović and Vasiljević on 27 October: extension of Serbia's constitution to the Habsburg South Slav lands; establishment of a new constitutional order by a (quintessentially Serbian) great national parliament rather than a constituent assembly; symbolic recognition of the 'tribal' individuality of the Croats and Slovenes by incorporating their traditional national names, flags and coats of arms in the emblems and laws of the new state; guaranteed status for the Latin script, Catholic religion and Slovene language; and, as the maximum possible concession, a 'special Croatian provincial assembly'.⁴⁵ At a meeting in Niš on the eve of the Yugoslav Committee's formation, Pašić instructed Vasiljević and Stojanović to work for a unified South Slav state in which the Croats and Slovenes could be 'given concessions that do not spoil the unity of the state and do not hinder the final crystallisation of a unified nation', including recognition of Croatia's historic individuality and symbols and Slovenia's language, possibly extending to their own provincial assemblies.⁴⁶ The Serbian government and Yugoslav Committee would both collaborate and compete throughout the war in pursuing different models for unification and attempts to win Entente support for them. Serbia's government would not accept that any body from among the Habsburg South Slavs had the right to represent them internationally or that Serbia's unification with them should be conditional upon the approval of such a body, since this would prejudice Serbia's territorial claims.

Third Balkan War

Even as it fought for survival, Serbia's conflicts over territory and influence with other states in the region continued. One threat came from Albania, where civil war had raged from May 1914 between the regime of the newly appointed German prince, Wilhelm of Wied, backed by Austria-Hungary, and rebels under Esad Pasha Toptani, backed by Serbia. The conflict spread into Serbian-held Kosovo, where Prince Wilhelm mobilised rebels, while Vienna, even before its formal declaration of war against Serbia, sought to organise, arm and finance a Kosovo Albanian uprising.⁴⁷ Wilhelm's regime collapsed and he left Albania on 3 September 1914, while the victorious Esad Pasha travelled to Niš, where he signed a formal alliance with Serbia on the 17th.

The Ottoman Empire entered the war on the Central Powers' side on 29 October, and the Sultan on 14 November declared a jihad against the Entente powers. This potentially threatened to mobilise the large Muslim population within and adjacent to Serbia's new southern borders against it. CUP agents were sent to these territories for this purpose, while Constantinople worked to overthrow the Esad Pasha regime and Vienna continued to arm and finance Kosovo Albanian rebels. Serbia's government considered military intervention in Albania to counter this threat and defend its client Esad Pasha, while continuing to harbour further territorial ambitions at Albania's expense. Serbia and Greece reached a renewed understanding to divide Albania between them. Ekmečić writes: 'This was no longer a question of routes to the Adriatic nor of something that could be considered the lost medieval homeland, but of outright conquest that would deprive them of the arguments concerning that which, in that regard, they had already achieved and wanted to achieve.'[48] It provoked opposition from Italy and aroused Entente fears about alienating Italy.

Pašić, however, came under countervailing pressure from another source: General Damjan Popović, commander of Serbian troops in the 'New Territories' and close to the Black Hand, favoured a hard line against Albania, even its complete occupation.[49] Meanwhile, Greece invaded southern Albania in October 1914, prompting an Italian counter-invasion of the Vlorë region in the south-west, which in turn spurred Serbia's government to assert its position in northern Albania. Serbia invaded Albania in May 1915 to prevent Esad Pasha's defeat and pre-empt any Austro-Hungarian action, occupying Elbasan in central Albania and threatening Tirana, and undertaking repressive measures against sections of the population supportive of the anti-Esad rebellion. In Ekmečić's words: 'If he had written a new book about Albania, the Social Democratic leader Dimitrije Tucović would have had additional material on the savagery of the Serbian corporals against the Albanians, to whom there was not even proclaimed liberation from the feudal authority of their beys.'[50] The invasion prompted a rebuke from Russia and pressure from the Entente powers to withdraw.[51] Meanwhile, the rivalry between the Radicals and Black Hand extended to Albania, with Pašić's government supporting Esad Pasha while Popović assisted his rival, Ahmed bey Zogolli, later king of Albania, adding to the pressure that the beleaguered Albanian ruler and his Serbian protectors already faced from hostile Austro-Hungarian and Ottoman agents.[52]

Montenegro was both Serbia's ally and rival. Under pressure from pan-Serb public opinion and a powerful annexationist opposition, Montenegro's government had proclaimed to its parliament in January 1914 that it would pursue 'common military and diplomatic action with Serbia in all questions', so that it could 'invest all our energy and all our strength in the defence of Serb interests'; upholding the 'national unity of Serbs and Croats', it would 'work for Yugoslav solidarity and union'. But simultaneously, as King Nikola explained shortly afterwards to his son-in-law King Petar, this was to be on the basis of the 'independence and equal rights of our States and Dynasties'. Montenegro joined the 'holy war for the freedom of Serbdom and Yugoslavdom', in the words of Nikola's proclamation of July 1914, but it retained major territorial ambitions which, as its ambassador in Niš informed Italy's ambassador in October 1914, encompassed 'Hercegovina up to Metković and Shkodër up to the mouth of the Drim'.[53] Such independent expansionism threatened to obstruct Montenegro's absorption into Serbia, which consequently opposed it.

Serbia and Montenegro thus entered the war with a common pan-Serb, pan-Yugoslav ideology but also with rival dynasties each seeking pre-eminence. Serbia's government viewed Montenegro's annexation as a crucial but purely Serbian affair to be kept separate from Yugoslav unification. Consequently, even as Serbia fought for its national survival, Pašić's government worked with Montenegro's annexationists to engineer the downfall of Nikola, the Petrović-Njegoš dynasty and Montenegrin independence. This involved isolating Montenegro diplomatically from the Entente powers and persuading them to approach Montenegrin issues only through Serbia's government, while portraying Nikola's regime as disloyal to the Allied cause. In this, Serbia's government enjoyed the sympathy of Russia, which having long supported Nikola's regime as a counterweight to the Obrenović regime, now considered it expendable in the cause of promoting Karađorđevićite Serbia as its principal Balkan satellite. Conversely, Italy, which before the war had favoured Serbo-Montenegrin union as an anti-Austro-Hungarian measure, now supported Nikola's resistance given its own rivalry with Serbia.

Under Russian pressure, Nikola in August 1914 appointed Serbia's General Janković, head of Serbia's military mission at Cetinje, as chief of the supreme staff of Montenegro's army, while other Serbian officers were placed in key positions in it. Hence Montenegro's army fell under increasing Serbian control. For its part, Montenegro's supreme command appointed Brigadier General Jovan Bećir as its representative at the Serbian army's supreme command. The linking of the military commands of two independent states produced much friction. Serbia's supreme command resented the Montenegrin army's continuing operational independence, which resulted in military moves that undermined Serbian operations; the Montenegrin withdrawal from Sarajevo's vicinity in late October 1914 forced Serbian forces to retreat across the Drina, provoking considerable bitterness among Serbia's military and political leadership.[54] Meanwhile, Serbia's leaders put pressure on Montenegro's supreme command, making it withdraw Montenegrin forces from towns in south-east Bosnia, including Goražde and Foča, which they had occupied in 1914.[55]

Bećir resigned from Serbia's high command on 13 October, outraged by open talk among Serbian officers—particularly Black Hand supporters—of annexing Montenegro. He complained that Black Hand officers attempted to recruit him to their plots for the overthrow of the Petrović-Njegoš dynasty. Another Montenegrin officer attached to Serbia's supreme command, Captain Radivoje Milošević, wrote that in early 1915 Apis had attempted to persuade him to assassinate Nikola.[56] Annexationist officers in Montenegro's army also agitated against the Petrović-Njegoš dynasty and for Montenegro's annexation to Serbia. Serbia's invasion of Albania in May 1915 was deemed a threat by Cetinje, which consequently occupied Shkodër the following month to secure its own position in northern Albania, which Belgrade in turn tried to prevent.[57] Pašić responded to the occupation of Shkodër by inducing Janković's resignation as Montenegrin chief of staff. He was succeeded by Petar Pešić, a former Serbian guerrilla commander in Macedonia and a much more overtly political general, readier to use the post to pursue Serbia's interests.[58] When Serbia's supreme command demanded in July 1915 that Montenegro place its Army of the Sanjak under the command of Serbia's Užice Army, Nikola rejected this for fear of losing what remained of his military independence. Pešić reported to

Serbia's supreme command that the rejection reflected Nikola's collaboration with Austria-Hungary.[59]

The Treaty of London, which Britain, France and Russia signed with Italy on 26 April 1915 to bring it into the war, promised it Istria, northern Dalmatia, most of the eastern Adriatic islands and a protectorate over Albania. This represented an embarrassment for Serbia's government and a blow to its aspirations. Not only had Italy been promised territory that Serbia wanted, but it was an imperial competitor in Albania, moreover Italy's king Victor Emmanuel III was married to King Nikola's daughter Jelena; thus it represented an obstacle to Serbia's absorption of Montenegro. Italy's opposition to Serbia's unification with the Croats and Slovenes discouraged the Entente powers from supporting this Serbian war aim. Italy was thus on several grounds an unwelcome ally for Serbia, which protested against the Treaty of London, requesting that the Entente powers guarantee the right of the Serbs, Croats and Slovenes to unify in a single state. To bolster this request, on 6 May 1915 they organised natives of the Habsburg South Slav lands resident in Serbia as a Yugoslav Congress, which proclaimed 'the complete and indissoluble unity of the Serbs–Croats–Slovenes'. Italy declared war on Austria-Hungary on 23 May. Serbia's parliament on 10 August declared its 'determination to continue the struggle for liberation and unification of the Serb–Croat–Slovene people'.[60] That month, Italy and Russia vetoed a British proposal for Serbia formally to join the Pact of London as a full member of the Allied coalition; Italy did not want to strengthen Serbia's hand over the disputed Austro-Hungarian territories while Russia did not consider Serbia should have the same status as the Great Powers.[61]

The most dangerous regional threat to Serbia, after Austria-Hungary itself, was posed by Bulgaria, whose conflict with Serbia over Macedonia had continued surreptitiously following the formal end of hostilities in August 1913. Seeking as it did to encourage irredentism in Macedonia directed against the Serbian occupier, Bulgaria's position was analogous to Serbia's in relation to the Austro-Hungarian occupier of Bosnia-Hercegovina, with the difference that popular rejection of the occupier was greater in Macedonia's case. The Serbian police inspector in Bitola wrote at the time of the newly acquired population: 'We have indeed liberated it from Turkish slavery, but if we want to speak frankly, it has not seen much advantage from freedom.'[62] The Macedonian population was denied full civil and political rights and placed under the administration of a largely incompetent and corrupt class of new officials selected primarily for their loyalty to the Radical regime. It was subjected to higher taxation than under the Ottomans and to military service, which the Ottomans had largely spared it. Macedonians fled across the border into Bulgaria to avoid the draft. Macedonian recruits in the Kragujevac garrison were reported to be extremely hostile to Serbia and sympathetic to Austria-Hungary, and on the eve of war a group of them fled across the Drina to take refuge in Habsburg territory. Serbian state repression following the outbreak of war hit particularly the Muslim population in Macedonia, whose horses were especially targeted for requisitioning.

The Bulgarians and Ottomans were able in these circumstances to organise a joint network of pro-Bulgarian and Muslim guerrilla bands in Serbian Macedonia. In November 1914, a Bulgarian–Turkish band destroyed a bridge on the River Vardar at Udovo in the south-eastern portion of the territory.[63] Facing both this insurgent threat in its rear and the readiness of its Great Power allies to sell its Macedonian territories to Bulgaria, and needing Macedonian conscripts, the Serbian government felt compelled to extend its emancipatory promises from the west to the south. On 25 December 1914, parallel to the Niš Declaration, it issued the so-called Macedonian Declaration, promising to the inhabitants of the new southern territories 'all political and constitutional attributes of the liberator Serbia. The first regular national parliament following the conclusion of the peace will resolve all the necessary measures, to bring them all into practice.'[64]

Bulgaria was courted during 1915 by both the Entente and Central powers at Serbia's expense. The four principal Entente powers issued a joint memorandum to Serbia on 4 August 1915, demanding it cede the zone of Serbian Macedonia promised to Bulgaria in the 1912 agreement; Russia withheld its war subsidy from Serbia to coerce it to comply. It promised Serbia in return Bosnia-Hercegovina and additional territory on the Adriatic coast and elsewhere. Pašić was unimpressed, complaining bitterly that 'it remains for Serbia to fight to its last strength not only with Austria but with its own allies to defend its homeland and vital interests … They are disposing of and dealing with Serbia as if it were an African colony.'[65] The frustration was mutual; Grigorii Nikolayevich Trubetskoy, head of the Near Eastern Department of Russia's foreign ministry, lamented: 'Express chauvinism among the Serbs periodically manifests itself as amusingly exaggerated self-worth. Many Serbs sincerely believe that they are the first nation in the world and that they have the best army in Europe. They think the same about their literature and learning.'[66] When Trubetskoy warned Pašić of the danger that 'in seeking everything he does not lose that which he could get', and telling him 'the Serbs now needed to choose between Macedonia and Yugoslavism', Pašić replied, 'We will choose Macedonia.'[67] Nevertheless, Serbia's government on 1 September 1915 promised to cede Bulgaria Macedonian territory on the basis of the 1912 agreement, with modifications to ensure Serbia's control of Skopje, Prilep and its border with Greece. In return, it demanded for Serbia formal membership of the Allied coalition, unification with Croatia including Rijeka, annexation of western Banat and the right of the Slovene lands to self-determination. The Entente powers were unwilling to accept these terms, yet on 14 September promised Bulgaria, in return for entering the war on their side, the part of Serbian Macedonia in question: all territory east and south of a line from Eğri Palanka through Veles to Ohrid, including Bitola, but only at the war's end and provided Serbia received compensation in Bosnia-Hercegovina.[68]

SERBIA

Against this, the Central Powers promised Bulgaria immediate possession of all Serbian Macedonia plus part of Serbia proper: the southern Morava valley, Toplica and all eastern Serbia up to the South Morava river, amounting to 59 per cent of Serbia's entire territory.[69] Since the Central Powers, moreover, matched the Entente's offer of Ottoman Eastern Thrace, while requiring Bulgarian military action merely against Serbia rather than against Austria-Hungary and the Ottoman Empire, they easily outbid the Entente. The clinching factors for Sofia were the Central Powers' conquest of Lemberg, Warsaw, Vilna and Kovno from the Russians in June and July and the failure of the Entente powers' Gallipoli offensive in August, which seemed to presage a Central Powers victory. Bulgaria consequently signed a secret treaty of alliance with Germany and Austria-Hungary on 6 September, sealing Serbia's military fate.[70] In these circumstances, at the instigation of Aleksandar and Vojvoda Mišić, Serbia's government during September sought permission from the Entente powers for a pre-emptive strike against Bulgaria, but retreated from this given their opposition, particularly that of Russia, which still hoped to turn Bulgaria around.[71]

Central Powers conquer Serbia

The military tide turned against Serbia after Bulgaria mobilised on 24 September 1915 and prepared to enter the war and after Germany took over command of Central Power operations in the Balkans, launching a major offensive against Serbia on 6 October 1915. Anglo-French forces landed in Salonika in Greek Macedonia on 5 October, violating Greek neutrality much as the Germans had violated Belgian neutrality and prompting the fall of the pro-Entente Greek prime minister Eleftherios Venizelos, but they were unable to prevent the Central Powers from conquering Serbia. The Central Powers mustered up to about 800,000 German, Austro-Hungarian and Bulgarian troops under Field Marshal Anton Ludwig August von Mackensen, facing approximately 300,000 Serbian and 50,000 Montenegrin troops. As well as being outnumbered, Serbia's army was greatly inferior in terms of artillery and air force.[72] It was a quirk of history that among Serbia's commanders was General Jurišić-Šturm, Mackensen's fellow Prussian veteran of the Franco-Prussian War.

Mackensen's forces took Belgrade on 9 October. Bulgaria invaded Serbia on 11 October and formally declared war on the 14th, capturing Kumanovo on the 20th and Skopje on the 22nd and severing Serbia's links with the Aegean Sea. Albanian rebel bands fought alongside Bulgaria's army. In response to these defeats, Serbia's supreme command removed Popović as commander for the New Territories.[73] Bishop Nikolaj Velimirović wrote on 29 October to the historian Robert William Seton-Watson, a prominent British champion of the South Slavs: 'Will England send a help [sic] to Serbia? Serbia is not fighting only for Serbia but at the the same time for India and Egypt. She is not fighting in this moment for a Greater Serbia, but for a greater World, for a greater Humanity and Christianity. I speak out perhaps the last

DEFEAT AND OCCUPATION

cry [*sic*] of the dying Serbia: come and help us, you, the most christian [*sic*] people of the World. Remember your duty before God! We are your unique friend between Hamburg and Baghdad. *Drang nach Osten* is at its beginning. God's and your cause is at stake.'[74]

To avoid encirclement, Serbia's army retreated south-westwards, entering Kosovo in mid-November. Its supreme command resolved on 25 November to retreat over the mountains of Albania and Montenegro to the Adriatic coast. This decision, momentous for Serbia's wartime destiny and subsequent national mythology, was fiercely opposed at a meeting of the commanders of Serbia's four armies by Mišić, hero of Kolubara and commander of the 1st Army, for whom it indicated the supreme command's collapse, given that Putnik was incapacitated by illness. Mišić sought to enlist General Stepanović, commander of the 2nd Army, to seize control of the army and organise a counter-attack against the Central Powers. If such a counter-attack did not happen or failed, Mišić suggested requesting a ceasefire. His opposition to the withdrawal plan may have been linked to his personal resentment of Putnik. Mišić's insubordination was opposed by the other commanders and resulted in his suspension from duty until the following autumn.[75]

The retreat, involving many civilians and soldiers, came to be known as the Albanian Golgotha owing to their huge effort and suffering, with many dying through exposure, hunger and exhaustion. Considerable losses were also inflicted by continuing Albanian guerrilla action; 200 Serbian soldiers were massacred in their sleep in a monastery at the village of Korishë near Prizren. Overall, around 150,000 Serbian soldiers and civilians may have perished in only two months while many survived as little more than 'living corpses'.[76] The retreat was also effectively a death march for most of the 70,000 Austro-Hungarian prisoners of war whom the Serbians took with them; only 23,000 would reach the coast alive.[77] Petar remained at the front during the retreat, allegedly trying to be killed so that he would not be accused of being a deserter like his grandfather Karađorđe after fleeing Serbia in 1813.[78] Zarija Vukičević, a sixteen-year-old army volunteer, recorded in his diary the misery of the retreat:

> Soldiers are collapsing ... They don't have bread; they don't have warm clothes; the cold destroys them, hunger crushes them ... Albania swallows the young Serbian heroes. As soon as we began to march uphill, the wind began. We moved forward tormented by the snow that the wind threw in our faces. A narrow path frozen and slippery. We fall frequently and continue with much difficulty. The more we approached the summit of the hill, the more strongly the wind blew. It blew so strongly against our breasts that we had to pause every ten metres and, finding new strength, move onward.[79]

Katarina Kostić, a former teenage refugee, recalled: 'Terrible sights on the journey: the corpses of killed and robbed refugees, stripped naked and covered in leaves;

prisoners who strip the meat off killed horses piece by piece. They put them briefly in the fire—and eat. Numb from exhaustion and hunger, they don't look at us.'[80]

The end of the march brought no quick respite. Trubetskoy noted that 'it is difficult to imagine the tragic picture that the Serb people are now offering, when at the price of unimaginable sacrifices they have reached the sea, and now beside it suffer hunger, without roofs, without fire beside which they could warm themselves, half barefoot and with their future uncertain'. General Jean de Montdésir, head of a French military mission of assistance, everywhere saw 'pitiful people, women, children, old people, soldiers wounded and mutilated, even the dying' suffering 'without shelter, in rags, with the hungry wailing for help'.[81] Josip Jeras, a Slovene volunteer in the army, described arriving in Shkodër, in Albania: 'We are all alike: thin, darkened, with wild and dirty hair covering our cheeks, with the look of martyrs, in torn, burned clothes. All day we roam the streets and look for bread, bread, bread. Only one word is heard from our mouths, is before our eyes: bread!' And when Christmas came: 'At the international port reigned the peace of Christmas Eve. Thousands of refugees lay on the cold ground under the roof of the endless heavens. Gentle death passed unheard from one to the other and handed out salvation ... Midnight came. We completely forgot about Christ, about his birthday and his suffering, for what were they compared to the suffering of thousands of martyrs on the retreat across Albania!'[82]

Representatives of the Entente general staffs met at Chantilly in France on 5–7 December 1915. The French accepted Entente responsibility for Serbia's defeat but it was resolved to maintain the Balkan front. Colonel Stefanović, on behalf of Serbia, submitted a study suggesting that the relocation of Serbian and Montenegrin forces to the Salonika front could enable the Entente to launch a successful offensive in Macedonia.[83] Consequently, in another violation of Greek neutrality, the French occupied the Greek island of Corfu in January 1916 to establish a haven for the Serbian survivors. After reaching the Albanian coast at Shkodër and Durrës, somewhere between 110,000 and 150,000 military survivors and approximately 20,000 civilians were eventually evacuated by the Entente to Corfu and surrounding islands in Greece and to Bizerte in French North Africa. The conquest of Serbia had cost the Central Powers about 67,000 casualties: 12,000 Germans, 18,000 Austro-Hungarians and the rest Bulgarians.[84]

The evacuation to Bizerte began on 4 January; by the 28th, when it was completed, there were about 10,000 Serbian soldiers there, over half of them sick or wounded, of whom 507 died under the sun within three months and were buried by their comrades. By the start of June, there were 1,200 graves in the Serbian military graveyard at Ferryville (today Menzel Bourguiba) in Bizerte, where they remain to this day; the entrance was marked with the words, in French and Serbian, 'They fell for the salvation of the fatherland!'[85] The spirits of the survivors were maintained, in the months and years following, with sporting competitions, theatrical performances

DEFEAT AND OCCUPATION

and musical concerts, with the soldiers both playing and watching.[86] The evacuation to Corfu began in mid-January 1916, with Serbia's government arriving there on the 18th and was completed by 5 April. 123 out of 166 Serbian parliamentary deputies went into exile following the occupation, of whom 108 eventually convened on Corfu on 10 September 1916 as a reconstituted parliament. A Serbian shanty town arose on Greek soil, with butcher's shops, cafes, canteens selling pies and grilled meat, and theatres.[87] But the bitter struggle between government and opposition had resumed already in January of that year; the latter considered that the former had 'fled disgracefully' from Serbia, abandoning the army, prince regent and even the state treasury; there were demands that Aleksandar appoint a new government in place of the one that had 'abandoned in cowardly manner' its duty.[88]

French protection on Corfu proved something of a mixed blessing. Serbia's army was reorganised into three armies, each containing two divisions: the Morava, Drina, Danube, Šumadija, Timok and Vardar. But the French and Serbians were unable to agree on which of them should hold the position of Allied commander of the Balkan front. Aleksandar and his government considered it a matter both of prestige and of national independence that he should be Allied commander. With the French still negotiating with the Bulgarians to detach them from the Central Powers, the Serbians feared that French control of their army could see their interests and even territory sacrificed for the sake of French wartime strategy. But the French likewise considered it essential for their prestige to hold the command and considered Aleksandar to be 'Russia's man'. After months of negotiation, it was eventually agreed that a French general would be supreme commander on the Salonika front in the name of Prince Regent Aleksandar and the allies, while Serbia's army would maintain its internal autonomy, be deployed in accordance with Serbian national interests and, in case of success, would participate in operations on Austro-Hungarian territory.[89]

While Serbia's government remained in Corfu until the war's end, its army was reassembled and reorganised, then transported to the Greek Aegean coast, alongside the Entente forces already on the Salonika front, between March and May 1916. Serbia's army was positioned in the central section of the front, principally between Mount Kosuf and Lerin. In this region, according to Bulgarian military reports, Serbian and French troops burned down Macedonian villages on the Greek side of the border to prevent them supplying military information to Bulgaria's army.[90] Serbia's army bore the brunt of a Bulgarian offensive on 17 August against the Allied forces in Greece and helped repel it. This was followed by an Allied counter-attack in mid-September; in the Battle of Kajmakčalan, which lasted from the 12th to the 30th, the Serbians under Mišić defeated the Bulgarians, captured the Kajmakčalan peak on the Serbian–Greek frontier and re-entered Serbian territory on 30 September. Serbian and French troops fought their way into the town of Bitola by 19 November, in south-western Serbian Macedonia.

SERBIA

Meanwhile, following Serbia's occupation by the Central Powers in autumn 1915, its government sought to ensure Montenegro did not remain unconquered either, since an intact Montenegrin state and army would have posed a serious obstacle to Serbian annexationist plans. Thus, General Pešić concentrated Montenegrin forces in Hercegovina and the Sanjak and used Montenegro's army to cover the Serbian retreat. This left Montenegro defenceless before Austria-Hungary's forces, which consequently occupied the country and surrounded its army. Pešić refused to order the Montenegrin army's retreat across Albania as its Serbian counterpart had done, ensuring that the Petrović-Njegoš dynasty would lose its military underpinning. Under pressure from Pašić's government and on Pešić's advice, Nikola sued for a separate peace, discrediting himself in the eyes of Montenegro's soldiery and people and the Entente powers.[91] Despite a valiant Montenegrin victory at the Battle of Mojkovac in defence of Serbia's retreating army, the Austro-Hungarians had by January 1916 effectively occupied the country. After presiding over the Montenegrin army's capitulation, Pešić abandoned it and fled Montenegro with his Serbian officers. He subsequently justified himself: 'Did you ever consider what would have been the situation for our entire people if King Nikola had not sent Franz Joseph that note and that there had been, on the Salonika front beside the Serbian supreme command, the Montenegrin supreme command, and upon the breaching of that front and entry into the fatherland, beside King Petar, also King Nikola?'[92] Two days after Pešić, Nikola himself fled Montenegro via Shkodër to Italy, completing his disgrace. Despite Serbia's temporary defeat, it had taken a big step toward annexing Montenegro.

Serbia under Central Power occupation

The Central Powers occupied Serbia, intending that it should forever disappear as an independent state. It was divided into Austro-Hungarian and Bulgarian zones, with the River Morava as the border, the Austro-Hungarians occupying thirteen okrugs including Belgrade and the Bulgarians also receiving Serbian Macedonia and part of Kosovo. The country formed part of a wider area occupied by the Central Powers; along with Montenegro, Albania was mostly conquered by them during 1916, with Esad Pasha fleeing abroad. The Central Powers therefore controlled most of the western Balkans, facing Entente forces occupying southern Albania and part of northern Greece. In Serbia, different occupation policies reflected the different goals of the Austro-Hungarians and Bulgarians. The Austro-Hungarian military authorities aimed to suppress Serbian national life in their part of the country, with a view eventually to annexing it to their empire, within which some controlled form of Serbian national existence would be permitted. The Bulgarians sought to erase Serbian national identity altogether in the territories they ruled, with a view to annexing them as integral Bulgarian lands and forcibly assimilating the population

DEFEAT AND OCCUPATION

so that they became ethnically Bulgarian. Sofia officially maintained that Serbia no longer existed.

Some Serbian politicians chose not to retreat from the country with the army and were ready to collaborate with the Austro-Hungarians, above all Liberals and Obrenović-era Austrophiles. Vukašin Petrović visited Mackensen's staff to offer his collaboration even before the fighting ended. Stojan Ribarac, Vojislav Veljković and Vladan Đorđević awaited the arrival of the Austro-Hungarians at the town of Vrnjačka Banja in central Serbia.[93] The Austro-Hungarians established a municipal council for Belgrade, headed by Veljković from March 1916, with other members including the quixotic Živojin Perić, who favoured Serbia joining the Habsburg Monarchy and resolving the South Slav question within its framework; Pavle Denić, formerly construction minister in Cincar-Marković's government; and Colonel Antonić, foreign minister under both Cincar-Marković and his predecessor, Velimirović. Perić and Denić were both sworn enemies of the 1903 conspirators. The Austro-Hungarians offered another enemy of the conspirators, former prime minister Svetomir Nikolajević, the governorship of Serbia, which he rejected, but his son Božidar became civil governor of the Požarevac okrug.[94] Antonić became president of Belgrade's municipal council on 18 July 1917, remaining so until the last days of the occupation.[95] However, the Austro-Hungarians left very little room even for willing collaboration. Belgrade's council was intended to be a purely administrative body. When Jovan Avakumović suggested in mid-January 1916 to General Johann von Salis-Seewis that they issue a joint proclamation calling for peace and order, the general considered it an affront to his authority and ordered Avakumović's arrest. Even Perić and his fellow councillor Jovan B. Jovanović complained to Vienna that 'Austria-Hungary is arresting Austrophiles the same as Radicals'.[96]

Austria-Hungary's commanders sought to re-create in Serbia the Habsburg bureaucratic-absolutist regime of the mid-nineteenth century, uncorrupted by modern national politics. All political, professional, cultural and sporting organisations were suppressed along with all existing Serbian newspapers, which were replaced with a regime newspaper, *Beogradske novosti* (Belgrade News). Schools operated, albeit with strictly circumscribed curricula and using only the Latin alphabet, except for religious studies for Orthodox pupils, for which Cyrillic was permitted. However, the Austro-Hungarians sought in general to remain within the bounds of what they perceived to be both their own and international law. They saw themselves as defenders of Serbia's civilian population against corruption, lawlessness and, eventually, the anti-occupation Serbian guerrillas (komitadis or komitas). Despite their absolute animosity toward Serbia's political classes and exaggerated fear of popular Serbian nationalism, they came during their occupation to value Serbia as an agricultural producer. They sought to promote Serbia's agriculture, even protect it from excessive demands from Habsburg civilian officials who sought to exploit it to offset food shortages in the empire. Ironically, this meant civilian rations in

Serbia were frequently higher than in the empire itself.[97] Nevertheless, the devastated country suffered particularly severe hunger for half a year from autumn 1915, during which the Austro-Hungarian foreign minister István Burián reported that 'Serbia is directly standing before death from starvation', after which food was sent to alleviate the situation, though not before a considerable number had died from hunger, climbing to 8,000 by the start of September 1917, according to Red Cross figures.[98] Still deadlier was a typhus epidemic that the Austro-Hungarians brought with them, infecting ultimately around 400,000 people in the country, killing 100,000 civilians, 35,000 soldiers, 30,000 war prisoners and half of Serbia's medical personnel, with the death toll peaking in February 1915.[99]

Many Serbs felt hatred for the Serbian regime, now in exile, that had led them to disaster, something expressed in frequent denunciations of fellow Serbs to the occupation police, which were also used to settle scores from the pre-war period.[100] Warfare between the Serbs who served the occupiers and those who rose as komitadis against them amounted to a Serbian civil war, which largely bypassed the Austro-Hungarian army.[101] The latter's own fearful negative stereotype of Serbia's civilian population, as nationalistically indoctrinated and prone to fight against an occupier in violation of the rules of civilised warfare, mirrored the model the Radicals themselves upheld.[102] The Austro-Hungarians sought to contain this supposedly recalcitrant population by imposing draconian punishments for even minor crimes and misdemeanours, which frequently amounted to judicial murder. Furthermore, many military-age men and others feared as possible sources of disorder were interned, totalling 20,000–25,000 by autumn 1915. Following the launch of Russia's Brusilov Offensive on 4 June 1916 and Romania's declaration of war on Austria-Hungary on 27 August, the empire's occupying forces in Serbia began increasingly to fear a popular rebellion, prompting their further mass internment of military-age men. These Serbian internees, held at camps in Austria-Hungary, numbered 70,000 by the end of 1916.[103] Meanwhile, in the territory of the Sanjak acquired by Serbia in the First Balkan War, the Austro-Hungarians more readily sought collaborators among the region's large Muslim population, kindred of the generally *kaisertreu* Muslims of neighbouring Bosnia-Hercegovina. They restored much of the land and privileges to the Muslim landlords that Serbia's government had appropriated from them following its annexation of the territory and established a wholly Muslim administration in the regional capital of Novi Pazar. Consequently, Muslim notables from across the Sanjak gathered at the town of Sjenica in August 1917 and voted for the region to secede from the 'parasitic' kingdoms of Serbia and Montenegro and unite with Habsburg Bosnia-Hercegovina. Other Sanjak Muslims joined volunteer units fighting for the Ottomans.[104]

The Bulgarians divided their zone of Serbia into two military districts with commands in Niš and Skopje respectively. For all the rhetoric of South Slav unity and anti-Germanism, when push came to shove, Serbians were happier under

DEFEAT AND OCCUPATION

Austro-Hungarian than under Bulgarian occupation. As Avakumović put it, 'The idea of leaving the fatherland I already completely excluded. The only dilemma was: whether to remain in that part of Serbia where I was and, by misfortune, could be occupied by Bulgaria, or to move somewhere which would not be part of the sphere of Bulgarian occupation but under Austria with Germany. But, knowing the Bulgarians as brutal, uncivilised and without character or scruples, I did not even consider remaining under their rule.'[105] The Bulgarians forcibly changed Serbian surnames to Bulgarian equivalents, banned baptising children with Serbian names, forbade Serbian folk-dress, replaced school textbooks with Bulgarian ones and suppressed public use of the Serbian language. The Vranje okrug's governor, citing instructions from Bulgaria's interior ministry, warned his subordinates on 6 December 1916: 'I have decided to punish those guilty of using Serb words in speech and writing. You are called upon to demonstrate a definite influence on the people and not allow it to fall under the influence of that brigand language.'

The Bulgarians carried out deportations, executions and forced conscriptions aimed at neutering and decapitating the Serbian nation. The Bulgarian governor-general in occupied Serbia on 14 December 1916 ordered that 'all soldiers from 18 to 50 years of age who have served in the Serbian army, all officers, former teachers, priests, journalists, former deputies, military officials and all suspect persons must be arrested and interned in the interior of the [Bulgarian] empire'.[106] Serbian priests were killed or expelled and replaced in churches by Bulgarian priests, icons and frescoes in Serbian churches were desecrated or replaced by Bulgarian ones and the celebration of Serbian saints' days was banned. Post-war inquiries determined, for example, that at least 100 Serbian priests were summarily killed by the Bulgarians in the regions of Niš, Surdulica and Zaječar and that around 3,500 men were killed by them in the district of Vranje alone, including 500 intellectuals.[107] James A. Drayton, who investigated Bulgarian atrocities after the war, wrote regarding Surdulica near the Bulgarian border in south-east Serbia: 'The country round that village must be one vast cemetery, for during November–December–January–February 1915–16, every day from 200–400 Serbs were led off *en route* for Bulgaria, a large portion of each day's quota being murdered.'[108] Around 100,000 people from Serbia and Serbian Macedonia were interned by the Bulgarians during the course of the war; only about half of these ever returned.[109]

Armed resistance to the occupiers in Serbia began in autumn 1916 in the form of action by small, spontaneously formed guerrilla bands recalling the hajduks of old. In mid-September, the news that Romania had entered the war and the Austro-Hungarian response of interning civilians as a preventive measure, as well as false rumours that Serbia's army was returning, combined to produce an uprising in the Kragujevac region, when 2,000 or 3,000 peasants, some armed, gathered spontaneously in the village of Borač and discussed organising resistance. Austria-Hungary's army responded immediately and following brief combat the uprising was crushed: according to the official report, 23 were executed, 14 houses burned, 760 arrested and 4 ringleaders sentenced to death in absentia, after which their homes and properties were destroyed.[110]

Guerrilla activity was strongest in the Bulgarian zone of occupation in southern and eastern pre-1912 Serbia. The most prominent Chetnik veterans of the pre-World War I period had either retreated from the country with Serbia's army in 1915 or died in combat, but enough Chetnik veterans remained for them to dominate resistance to the Bulgarians, particularly since they came disproportionately from the Bulgarian-occupied areas of Serbia as well as from the lands acquired in the Balkan Wars, though no functional Chetnik organisation remained.[111] With so many older Chetnik leaders dead or in exile, the man who emerged as resistance leader, Kosta Vojinović, was a young man of 25 whose family originated in Kosovo and who had been a protégé of the legendary Vojin Popović ('Vojvoda Vuk'), a Black Hand supporter killed fighting the Bulgarians in late 1916. A Serbian guerrilla detachment was also established in Turnu Severin in Romania, numbering nearly 160 men, by the second half of September 1916, but Serbia's supreme command forbade it to enter Serbian territory, possibly because its leading officers, Lieutenant Colonel Aleksandar Srb and Lieutenant Colonel Božin Simić, were Black Hand supporters.[112]

Serbia's supreme command feared that this guerrilla activity could provoke massive reprisals against Serbia's population. Many Chetnik leaders were closely linked to the Black Hand, which was attempting to expand its influence over the guerrilla movement, so the supreme command may also have feared a successful uprising would have given the Black Hand control of Serbia.[113] Consequently, it sent a commander to occupied Serbia, without informing Serbia's government that it was doing so, to restrain local guerrilla leaders and establish some control over them. He was directed to channel resistance activity toward small-scale acts of diversion and sabotage against enemy communications, while awaiting an Allied offensive from the Salonika front and the supreme command's order for the general uprising.[114] Kosta Pećanac, a veteran of the guerrilla struggle in Macedonia, had suggested the idea and volunteered for the mission, and for the supreme command he was a natural choice. Subsequently described by Protić as 'an extremely vulgar, wild person', he may have volunteered to go to Serbia to escape the pressure from both the Black Hand and White Hand to pick a side in their struggle.[115] He was dropped by aeroplane in the village of Mehane in the Toplica region of southern Serbia. He met with Vojinović on 8 November 1916 at the village of Gornje Spance near the town of Blace and the two issued a proclamation summoning guerrillas to participate in a general uprising—but only when Pećanac so ordered. Independently of his plans, his arrival appears to have emboldened local guerrillas, resulting in their increased activity across southern Serbia between October 1916 and February 1917, which in turn provoked further harsh repression. Austro-Hungarian reports of January 1917 mention 30–34 Serbs executed and 55–57 houses burned down.[116]

DEFEAT AND OCCUPATION

The Bulgarian occupation authorities announced on 14 February the enrolment of male inhabitants of their zone of Serbia aged between 19 and 40 into Bulgaria's army. Yet the Serbian peasantry had a long history of resistance to military authorities, and the measure provoked the so-called Toplica uprising. This erupted on 21 February, when a gathering of about 300 komitadis met by the village of Obilić near Leskovac; those supporting an uprising, headed by Vojinović, with thirteen votes, easily outvoted those opposed, primarily Pećanac, with only two. The uprising was nevertheless already breaking out independently of the komitadi leaders and grew to involve at least 4,000 armed rebels and perhaps about 15,000 participants in total. The Obilić gathering's resolution mentioned a guerrilla 'central committee', though no such body functioned in practice. Contrary to the instructions given him by Serbia's supreme command, Pećanac was forced to support the call for a general uprising and to accept leadership of it to maintain his standing among the rebels, though he sought to restrain it by avoiding military engagements with the occupiers and trying to pacify rather than arouse the rebels and the population in his public statements. The uprising involved coordinated action by the guerrilla commanders across south-central and south-eastern Serbia, beginning with Kuršumlija on 26 February and Prokuplje the following day. It resulted in the liberation of a considerable part of south-eastern Serbia between Kruševac and Niš in the north and Priština and Vranje in the south, inhabited by several hundred thousand people. The rebels established civilian organs of government: municipalities, courts, hospitals and post offices, though without a functioning central authority; it was, in the words of the historian Milivoje Perović, a 'komita state'.[117]

The uprising was suppressed between 12 and 25 March by Bulgarian, Austro-Hungarian and German troops, with at least three divisions diverted from other fronts. They engaged in massive, systematic reprisals against the civilian population; at least 20,000 civilians were killed during the Bulgarian occupation and killings peaked during and after the uprising's suppression, when thousands more men were deported and dozens of villages destroyed. The Bulgarians burned women and children alive in their homes; for example, they burned and destroyed the village of Gajtan, massacring 200 people, mostly women and children; they herded 42 people, including a woman and ten children, in the village of Barje into a house, set it on fire and burned them to death. Civilians were widely tortured and women raped; the Bulgarian bishop Melentije allegedly encouraged rapes of women by soldiers on the grounds that 'even if they become pregnant by them, that isn't bad', while pregnant women were struck in the stomach with bayonets, 'so that they do not bear those Serbian dogs!' Bulgarian Colonel Kalkandjiev was accused in Skopje in February 1918 of murdering a Jew; his defence was: 'I have killed many priests, national notables and other civilians, never wondering if they were Serbs, Jews, Gypsies or Turks, because I have full authorisation from my government to kill anyone who could be damaging or simply suspicious for Bulgaria.'[118]

Resistance subsequently degenerated into uncoordinated, lower-intensity guerrilla action in which the region's population bore the brunt of komitadi terror and pillaging, while the occupiers recruited counter-guerrilla militias to hunt the komitadis down while continuing their harsh reprisals. Fighting continued for the rest of 1917 and into 1918. Pećanac responded to a supposed Entente advance on the Balkan front by carrying out an incursion on 1 May 1917 across the pre-war border into Bulgaria, attacking the town of Bosilegrad: 'We absolutely wholly burned down the town so that it ... was turned into a pile of ashes.' Those few Bulgarian civilians who had not fled before the komitadis were massacred and the area thoroughly plundered; in his own words, 'We killed and slaughtered them as they had done to us.' The Bulgarians responded with further retaliation against Serbian civilians. Pećanac then retreated into Serbia and refrained from combat until autumn 1918.[119] He reached an agreement for collaboration with the Bulgarians, whereby they would refrain from action against one another, while Pećanac executed Serbs who resisted his authority and the Bulgarians concentrated on action against the rebels who still resisted them. Pećanac's family was meanwhile protected in Bulgarian-occupied Niš.[120] Vojinović would eventually accuse him of being a 'coward' and a 'person corrupted in body, spirit and character'.[121] The occupiers exploited such divisions, offering amnesties to rebel leaders who stopped fighting and bounties for the assassinations of others. The population increasingly turned against the komitadis in response to the repression they provoked and their requisitioning of peasant grain.[122] Vojinović was hunted down and killed by the Bulgarians near the village of Grgur on 23 December 1917. The Bulgarian occupation authorities issued a directive on 29 May 1918, stating: 'In order to be able to Bulgarianise the Morava oblast, it is necessary to destroy in advance all that is Serbian, then, on the ruins of Serbianism, build Bulgaria.'[123]

Volunteer units

The Yugoslav Committee sought to recruit forces from the South Slav diaspora or from Habsburg South Slav prisoners of war in Entente hands and attach them to Serbia's army as distinct units. Pašić, however, insisted that any such foreign volunteers be merely absorbed into Serbia's regular military units. He did not wish any autonomous 'Yugoslav' military forces to emerge that could obstruct Serbia's exclusive military control over South Slav military space. A volunteer division recruited from Austro-Hungarian prisoners of war, named the 1st Serbian Volunteer Division and comprising mostly Serbs from Bosnia, Croatia and Vojvodina, but with a predominantly Croatian and Slovene officer cadre, was established in Russia in February 1916 as a part of Serbia's army. It numbered nearly 18,000 by mid-August 1916. A second such unit, the 2nd Serbian Volunteer Division, was established in June 1916, containing many Croats, Slovenes and Muslim Bosniaks as well as

DEFEAT AND OCCUPATION

Serbs.[124] 'Volunteer' was a misnomer; only ethnic Serbs were ready to volunteer in significant numbers and many of the 'volunteers' were forcibly conscripted to the divisions by the Russians. The two divisions together formed the Serbian Volunteer Corps commanded by General Mihailo Živković. Pašić visited the 1st Division at Odessa on 16–17 May 1916. He approved the decision of its commander, Stevan Hadžić, to require the volunteers to take the Serbian army's oath of allegiance, which seriously alienated its Croatian and Slovene officers, whose loyalty was to the Yugoslav ideal rather than to Serbia.[125]

Given the real or suspected residual loyalty of the 'volunteers' to the Habsburg emperor, officers from Serbia tended to view them with suspicion and hostility and subjected them to extremely harsh discipline, which sometimes blended into outright chauvinistic cruelty, involving brutal corporal punishment, that compounded the misery of life on a bloody war front. An attempt by officers of the 2nd Regiment of the 1st Division to reorganise their regiment as the Yugoslav Volunteer Corps, formally separate from Serbia's army and under Yugoslav rather than Serbian flags and insignia, was ruthlessly suppressed by Živković. Volunteers consequently deserted in large numbers.[126] At the Serbian government session on 6 April 1917, Pašić responded to the discontent by suggesting that Croatian and Slovene battalions and regiments be permitted to carry the Croatian and Slovene names and that eventually the corps be renamed the Volunteer Corps of Serbs, Croats and Slovenes. But he rejected the possibility that it carry the Yugoslav name, 'because the Bulgarians, who are Yugoslavs, are not with us'. He felt that if Croat and Slovene volunteers were not happy with their unit's name, they should be turned over to the Russian authorities to do with as they wished: 'And ours who remain loyal to us can found a Serb corps.'[127]

The 'volunteers' were required to fight on the Dobrudja front between Romania and Bulgaria, which was highly unpopular with them. Incorporated in a Russian corps in turn subordinated to Romania's army, armed with largely ineffective captured Austro-Hungarian weapons and receiving orders in Russian, Romanian and French, they suffered heavy losses.[128] Over a third of them—12,735 men, including thousands of Serbs—deserted by the end of May 1917, partly influenced by the Russian Revolution's anti-war mood, leaving a corps of about 20,000, overwhelmingly Serbs.[129] Nevertheless, the Volunteer forces in Russia were eventually relocated to the Salonika front, augmented by recruits from among the South Slav communities of the United States and finally formed into a Yugoslav Division after Prince Regent Aleksandar had approved the idea. But by mid-1918, Pašić's escalating conflict with the Yugoslav Committee caused him to fear it could use the volunteers to obstruct his government's plans, so he wound down their recruitment.[130] Meanwhile, the mistreatment of the recruits had become something of a cause célèbre for Croat opponents of Yugoslav unification. Aleksandar Horvat of the Party of Pure Right submitted an interpellation to Croatia's parliament on 6 July 1918 that spoke exaggeratedly of 'tens of thousands of Croatian soldiers whom the

SERBIA

Serbians murdered and threw into the Black Sea'.[131] The unhappy experience of the volunteer corps foreshadowed in miniature the experience of the first Yugoslav state.

The outcome of the war by 1917 retrospectively vindicated Pašić's policy, derailed by the Black Hand, of avoiding conflict with Austria-Hungary: Serbia was occupied and on the brink of destruction as an independent state, while Russia, on which Pašić and others had placed so much hope, was losing on the battlefield and undergoing a revolution that would soon knock it out of the war altogether. Bulgaria's intervention, aimed at reversing the outcome of the Second Balkan War, ensured Serbia's defeat and occupation and threatened to annihilate Serbian nationhood in the more than half of the country it occupied. Yet the military reforms undertaken since King Aleksandar Obrenović's time had not only produced impressive initial victories for Serbia's army, contrasting starkly with its dismal performance in the wars of 1876–1877 and 1885–1886, but enabled it to survive the defeat of 1915–1916, preserving the kernel of Serbian statehood and the possibility of a revival once the tide of the war turned.

14

LIBERATION AND UNIFICATION

1917–1918

Serbia's political and military leadership, in exile on Greek territory, remained at the start of 1917 bitterly divided three ways between Prince Regent Aleksandar and his White Hand, Prime Minister Pašić and his Radicals, and the mutually sympathetic Black Hand and Independent Radicals. Despite Serbia's setbacks, Pašić retained his ambitious plans for South Slav unification under Serbia's leadership, for which he waged careful diplomacy with the Entente allies and representatives of the Habsburg South Slavs, above all in the Yugoslav Committee, with whom he had major differences. Inevitably, Serbia's internal divisions extended into its negotiations on South Slav unification as the Independents sought allies among the Habsburg South Slavs to offset Radical hegemony, leading them to embrace a more Yugoslavist approach to unification in opposition to Pašić's Serbia-centred approach.

Salonika trial

The struggle over policy between the government and Black Hand continued following the outbreak of war. Apis continued to expand the Black Hand, relying in particular on Bosnians, mostly Serbs, mobilised in irregular formations and often trained in Tankosić's Chetnik school. Whereas the government formally articulated a Yugoslavist ideology in which the individuality of the Croats was acknowledged and unification with the Slovenes sought, the Black Hand, through its newspaper *Pijemont*, was more narrowly Great Serbian: Croatian individuality was downplayed or disregarded; the Serbo-Croat speaking lands, including Croatia proper, simply treated as Serb lands; and the Slovenes excluded from the project for unification.[1] As in 1913, so in 1915, the Black Hand favoured a pre-emptive strike against Bulgaria and resented Pašić's deference to Russia's opposition to this.[2] However, like the rest of the army, the Black Hand had suffered grievous losses in the war, including Tankosić's death. According to the military historian Velimir Ivetić, of its original 180 or more officers, only about 30 were still alive in 1917.[3]

Aleksandar meanwhile strengthened his control over the army as the war progressed. His prestige as acting supreme commander had greatly risen owing to the initial victory over Austria-Hungary. He consequently demanded in early 1915 that chief of staff Putnik seek his approval for all future orders on military operations and that Putnik transfer to him authority to allocate officers to duties. Putnik refused, reaffirming his own authority in both regards. Pašić then brokered a compromise whereby the chief of staff would fully retain the right to determine military operations but Aleksandar would assume the right to allocate officers. Aleksandar exploited his new power in early March to move Apis from the supreme command to a more peripheral position in the Užice Army's staff.[4] That month, Petar Živković, Jurišić-Šturm, Aleksandar's secretary Đurđe Jelinić and other opponents of the Black Hand met to discuss the establishment of their own officers' group to counteract the organisation by all means, including physical elimination of its members. This group's goal was: 'Germany has created Great Wilhelm and now it is creating Great Germany; so will we create Great Aleksandar so that he can create Great Serbia.'[5] According to Aleksandar's supporter General Milan Nedić, from 'that moment Regent Aleksandar took the army in his own hands. His influence was from then of fateful significance for further developments.'

Apis was dismissed as chief of military intelligence in autumn 1915. With Putnik incapacitated, Bojović replaced him as chief of staff in December 1915 with Pešić as his assistant, while Božidar Terzić became war minister—both were hostile to the Black Hand.[6] With the Entente powers' blessing, Black Hand supporters and sympathisers, particularly deputy chief of staff Živko Pavlović, were transferred to less important posts and the key posts filled by White Hand or apolitical officers.[7] The power struggle reached the Volunteer forces in Russia, where the revolutionary spirit among the population affected the troops, making them fertile ground for Black Hand agitation against Serbia's leadership.[8] Colonel Stevan Hadžić was appointed divisional commander of the 1st Serbian Volunteer Division at the White Hand's instigation; his chief of staff was the former contra Colonel Vojin Maksimović. General Mihailo Živković, close to the White Hand, was in June 1916 appointed commander of the Volunteer Corps at the instigation of Aleksandar's circle, but he came under Black Hand influence and switched policy, securing the removal of Hadžić and Maksimović. After the Volunteer forces were transferred to the Salonika front and Živković's actions uncovered, he was pensioned off.[9] Ultimately, four Black Hand officers in the Volunteer forces, Božin Simić, Vojislav Gojković, Aleksandar Srb and Radoje Janković, deserted to avoid deportation back to Salonika; the first three defected to the Bolsheviks and Simić and Gojković eventually joined Tito's Partisans in World War II.[10]

Serbia's catastrophic military defeat discredited Pašić's government in the eyes of many. Exiled on Corfu and surrounded by soldiers, it was in a weak position.

LIBERATION AND UNIFICATION

As Serbia's battered army reconstituted itself, Black Hand members in early 1916 agitated against the government, blaming it for the defeat. Discontented officers may have looked to the Liberal politicians, still in Serbia and traditionally friendly to the Black Hand on anti-Radical grounds.[11] Apis consequently revived plans for a *coup d'état*. The brilliant constitutional-law scholar Slobodan Jovanović had served in the Serbian army's press bureau, which was under the jurisdiction of military intelligence whose chief Apis had been, and he worked with Apis and other Black Hand members in 1916 on a statute to replace Serbia's constitution in the event of a Black Hand putsch. Jovanović subsequently recalled a series of discussions with Apis, in which he warned him of the danger that Aleksandar and Pašić might unite against him and urged him to pre-empt this by reaching an accommodation with whichever of the two was most receptive.[12] Apis in Corfu meanwhile continued plotting assassinations of foreign monarchs; in early 1916, he planned to send Bosnian terrorists to kill Tsar Ferdinand of Bulgaria, Kaiser Wilhelm of Germany and King Constantine of Greece—much as he had used Princip to kill Franz Ferdinand. As King Constantine was head of a neutral state, this threatened further international complications for Serbia.[13]

A plot was hatched from the end of February 1916 by the Progressive newspaper editor Svetolik Jakšić, in collaboration with Slobodan Jovanović and assistant foreign minister Jovanović-Pižon. These were idealistic but elitist representatives of the 'young intellectuals' who had come of age opposing Aleksandar Obrenović's regime. Jakšić aimed to overthrow Pašić's government and replace it with a non-parliamentary 'neutral' military-bureaucratic regime—a 'National Council' of about twenty people, headed by Vojvoda Mišić on account of his great prestige, which would reconcile the Black Hand and White Hand to restore military unity. However, the government learned of the plot and raised an outcry among the Serbian emigration and Entente powers, whose great confidence Pašić enjoyed. Supporters of Apis and Aleksandar subsequently each fingered the other as the force behind it. Aleksandar did meet repeatedly with Jakšić, Slobodan Jovanović and other members of their circle, but according to Jovanović, although Aleksandar was plotting to oust Pašić, Apis refused involvement on the grounds that 'we did not kill Aleksandar Obrenović so that Aleksandar Karađorđević could rule in the same way that he ruled'. Aleksandar's sympathetic biographer Gligorijević claims, however, that his meeting with the people in question had been aimed at restoring unity in the army and at monitoring and restraining Apis, and that he had never intended to strike against Pašić. Conversely, Kazimirović concludes that Aleksandar had indeed mooted a putsch in alliance with the Black Hand. Whoever was behind it, Jakšić's plot may have spurred the frightened Radical ministers to join with Aleksandar finally to crush the Black Hand.[14]

While Serbia's army was engaged in its first offensive on the Salonika front, shots were apparently fired at Aleksandar's motor car near Lake Ostrovo in Greek

Macedonia on 25 September 1916. The Serbian authorities' investigation quickly concluded that this had been an attempt on his life by the Black Hand. This provided the occasion for its destruction, engineered by Aleksandar, Pašić, interior minister Ljubomir Jovanović and White Hand leaders Petar Živković, Petar Mišić and Josif Kostić. Apis, then assistant chief of staff of the 3rd Army, was arrested on 16 December 1916 followed by Vemić on the 19th; documents discovered in the possession of these two provided the basis for the case against the Black Hand leadership. In his memorandum to the war minister of 25 December, Ljubomir Jovanović accused them of violating their oaths as officers to defend the dynasty and constitution by plotting to assassinate Aleksandar and Pašić, overthrow the Karađorđević dynasty and the constitutional order and establish a praetorian dictatorship. Jovanović stressed in particular Apis's attempts to mobilise irregular forces from Bosnia-Hercegovina, Old Serbia and Macedonia to spearhead the putsch.[15] Widespread summary arrests and internments were carried out of real and suspected Black Hand members and sympathisers. These were often arbitrary; those arrested were frequently denied any preliminary hearing or informed of the charges against them. Prisoners were interned at Loutra to the south of Salonika and at Bizerte.[16] Nevertheless, the authorities deliberately chose not to pursue everyone implicated in the Black Hand's illegal activities, as this could have been an almost open-ended process encompassing much of the officer corps, up to and including former chief of staff Putnik.[17]

Following a three-month investigation, twelve members of the Black Hand and its circle were tried on 20 March 1917 before a military tribunal, accused of attempting to assassinate Aleksandar and of forming an illegal conspiratorial-terrorist organisation aimed at subverting the constitutional order. The tribunal comprised two specially formed courts: a military court of first instance to try the accused and a great military court of second instance to confirm the sentences. The first was headed by General Petar Mišić, who after the 1903 putsch had become chief of the general department at the war ministry and a highly influential figure at Petar's court. He had numerous grievances against Apis, who had threatened his life when he had attempted to back out of participation in the putsch, forced his retirement from the army in 1906 to appease the British and backed Schneider-Creusot in the 'gun question', costing Mišić, as Škoda's agent, much money. Mišić had then become a politician in the Radical party and its consultant on military affairs—personification of the court–military–Radical nexus.[18] The second court was headed by the former contra General Mirko Milisavljević with White Hand leader Josif Kostić as one of his judges. These two were undoubtedly selected to ensure the conviction of the accused.[19] The court proceedings were further manipulated to ensure the desired outcome: defendants could not freely choose their own counsels but had to select them from a list of officers given them by the court, which did not permit any defence witnesses to testify.[20] Some defendants were also ready to betray others;

during the trial, Milan Milovanović-Pilac denounced Apis to his supervising officer as a 'coward' and said of him: 'He must be crazy and that will cost him his head. Let them kill him, but why all of us?', while Vemić denounced Apis in court as a 'liar', complaining bitterly, 'You, Dragutin, have deceived me a hundred times during my life and I should have abandoned you long since.'[21]

Historians dispute whether there had really been an attempt on Aleksandar's life and the extent of Apis's anti-constitutional plans. The prosecution pinned on him the Jakšić plot, but his responsibility for this is hotly disputed by his nephew Milan Živanović, in his classic but not entirely objective historical study of the Salonika trial, who instead claims Aleksandar was behind Jakšić. Živanović nevertheless admits that Apis had planned to overthrow the government in June 1914 and that political organisations within the army like the Black Hand were illegal. Yet members of the White Hand circle and high-ranking officers of the army in general, including chief of staff Bojović, were undoubtedly complicit in the Black Hand's illegal activities in spring 1914. Thus, the trial was, to an extent, a case of the pot calling the kettle black.[22] Nevertheless, the court of first instance on 5 June sentenced nine of the defendants to death (Apis, Ljubomir Vulović, Rade Malobabić, Vemić, Milovanović-Pilac, Vladimir Tucović, Radoje Lazić, Čedomir Popović, Bogdan Radenković) and two to prison terms of fifteen years each (Damjan Popović, Muhamed Mehmedbašić); the twelfth (Vitomir Cvetković) had died in detention. The court of second instance on 18 June commuted the death sentences on Čedomir Popović and Radenković to twenty-year prison terms and raised Damjan Popović's term to twenty years. Protić remarked at the time about Apis, 'Better to kill him now than have him kill me later.'[23]

The sentences provoked an outcry among the non-Radical government ministers, with the Independents Davidović and Drašković appealing for clemency. Aleksandar was allegedly so angered by Davidović's intercession that, upon receiving it, he immediately made him step out of the royal car, forcing him to walk a long way, while when Drašković appealed 'Your highness, only not to blood', the prince regent replied, 'Now not to blood, but when it was my blood in question you did not consider it necessary to worry about it.'[24] Petar agreed with his son; when asked if the condemned should receive clemency, he replied, 'Kill them.'[25] The Independent ministers resigned in protest, after which the sole Progressive minister, Vojislav Marinković, was unwilling to remain alone in government with the Radicals. Pašić consequently formed a purely Radical government on 23 June. The Salonika sentences may have been merely the pretext for the Independents' resignations, motivated primarily by foreign policy differences with the Radicals, including those over the Yugoslav question. It has been suggested that the resignations were deliberately provoked by Pašić to rid his government of them.[26] The old inter-party viciousness emerged at sessions of the exiled parliament, at which opposition deputies labelled Pašić a 'murderer', 'bandit' and 'demon of Serbia' (two decades previously the title of a Radical pamphlet attacking Milan).[27]

Aleksandar agreed under pressure to commute to prison terms the death sentences of all the accused except Apis, Vulović and Malobabić. Indeed, the death sentences on the other four may have been cynically imposed to enable the prince regent later to pardon them as a concession to demands for clemency while ensuring that the trial's real target—Apis—would be safely executed. Apis, along with Vulović as his right-hand man and Malobabić as the supposed assassin and Austro-Hungarian double agent, was consequently executed on 26 June. Apis wrote his final testament on 24 June: 'Although condemned by both courts and denied the mercy of the Crown, I die innocent in my conviction that my death was needed by Serbia for several reasons ... and the pain I feel because I will die by Serb guns will be eased by the conviction that the gun pointed at my breast is for the good of Serbia; for the good of Serbia and the Serb Nation, to which I have devoted my entire life.'[28] On the 26th, Aleksandar forced the condemned men to stand for two hours beside their open graves prior to execution while their sentence was read out.[29] Facing the firing squad, Apis declared 'With brother God I die; I die with the wish that there be a Great Serbia, in particular Yugoslavia', or according to another account 'Long live Great Serbia; long live Yugoslavia!'[30]

Apis had on 28 March signed a statement confessing to having organised the Sarajevo assassination. On his way to the execution site, he apparently claimed he was being executed because of his confession. Critics of the trial averred subsequently that his execution was intended to remove an obstacle to a separate peace between Serbia and Austria-Hungary.[31] Yet there is no documentary evidence to support this conclusion. Serbia's leadership was not privy to the secret negotiations of 1917 between the Entente powers and Austria-Hungary over a possible separate peace.[32] It was probably unaware of Apis's involvement in the Sarajevo assassination until it was revealed during his trial.[33] In Gligorijević's words: 'The real reason why the organisation of the assassination in Sarajevo was treated as Apis's worst crime was the firm determination of the government and the regent to make impossible once and for all that the national politics of Serbia be led by a terrorist organisation or that it influence its international relations, and it was the assassination of the Austrian archduke that had led Serbia to lose its national territory and the people to endure the most terrible suffering.'[34]

Many other Black Hand supporters were investigated. Antonije Antić was the only leading conspirator to have remained on friendly terms both with the Black and the White Hand, but not with Aleksandar, who dismissed him at the investigation's start, ending his military career.[35] Of the original 120 officer-conspirators of 1903, about 40 were still alive in 1917, including 1 dismissed, 8 pensioned, 22 interned in Bizerte and 10 part of or close to the White Hand.[36] Colonel Milutin Lazarević, a 1903 conspirator, was convicted by the military court in autumn 1917; his sentence was then upheld by the great military court now headed by Colonel Dobrosav Pavlović, son of the war minister murdered in the putsch and a former contra.[37] Overall, 13 Black Hand officers were convicted and 57 retired from the army.[38] The show trial shocked some foreign observers, such as Seton-Watson, who complained in a Foreign Office memorandum: 'Executions are certainly contrary to Allied interests and would tend to discredit Serbia's reputation abroad.'[39] According to Panta Draškić, a former Black Hander who became Aleksandar's supporter, 'The Black Hand affair seriously disgraced us in the eyes of foreigners, and that at a time when the whole world was marvelling at us.'[40] Nevertheless, when the new Yugoslav state arose in December 1918, its army, formed around Serbia's army, would be essentially free from Black Hand meddling. By contrast, the star of the White Hand, its ranks swollen by former contras and other favourites of Aleksandar, was rising.

Corfu Declaration

Differences between the Serbian government and Yugoslav Committee over the process and outcome of South Slav unification were increasingly apparent as the war progressed. The leading Croats in the Yugoslav Committee, Supilo and Trumbić, agitated for a form of unification that would preclude Serbian hegemony. Supilo advocated the name 'Yugoslavia' for the common state to prevent the Serb appellation being imposed upon the non-Serbs, and indicated that Zagreb could be its future capital. Such proposals were viewed by Pašić as obstructing Serbia's goals.[41] However, international developments by spring 1917 made a pro-Yugoslav policy more pressing for Serbia's government. The fall of the Tsarist regime in March 1917 made Russia a less reliable ally; Pašić was sufficiently concerned already on the 24th of that month to raise with Aleksandar possible Entente intervention against the Russian Revolution to keep Russia in the war.[42] But Pavle Milyukov, foreign minister in Russia's new provisional government, announced on the same day his support for a 'solidly organised Yugoslavia'—a departure from the Tsarist government's suspicion of the Yugoslav project. The United States entered the war on 6 April 1917; President Woodrow Wilson explicitly rejected the politics of annexation in favour of the right of nations to self-determination. And the influence and agitation in Britain of pro-Yugoslav elements, in particular Seton-Watson and the *Times* correspondent Henry Wickham Steed, were growing; Britain was increasingly sympathetic to the idea of a Yugoslav state with a large non-Orthodox component as a check on Russian influence in the western Balkans.[43]

The threat to Serbia of a solution to Austria-Hungary's South Slav question occurring within the Habsburg imperial framework arose again with the so-called May Declaration. Politicians of the new Yugoslav Club in the Austrian imperial parliament on 30 May, through their president, the Slovene Anton Korošec, announced that they 'on the basis of the national principle and Croatian state right request the unification of all lands of the Monarchy, in which live Slovenes, Croats and Serbs, in one independent state body free of all domination by foreign nations and founded on a democratic basis under the sceptre of the Habsburg-Lotharingian Dynasty'.[44] Pašić consequently made overtures to the Yugoslav Committee, and from 15 June to 20 July delegates of the Committee and of Serbia's government held a conference on Corfu to formulate a declaration on their projected Yugoslav union. On this occasion, Trumbić demanded that the Habsburg South Slav lands be granted autonomy in the future state involving the retention of their existing parliaments, while Serbia's delegates all rejected this, insisting on a unitarist constitutional order and the extension of the most important aspects of Serbia's existing constitutional order to the new state.[45] For Pašić, unitarism—the principle that the state be organised as a single unit with a uniform administration and power devolved from the centre, rather than as a federation—was non-negotiable. Decentralisation would have made the common state, in his view, a 'new Austria'.[46] The Yugoslav Committee's other members largely supported the unitarist position, leaving Trumbić isolated.

The decision to name the projected state 'Kingdom of Serbs, Croats and Slovenes' rather than 'Kingdom of Yugoslavia' reflected the unwillingness of Serbia's delegates at Corfu to abandon the Serb name for what they considered an artificial Yugoslav nationhood. All the delegates from Serbia at Corfu, including the Independents and Progressives, backed Pašić's rejection of the Yugoslav name, particularly Protić, who argued that 'the name Yugoslavia is artificial; it even seems to me that it does not accord with the spirit of the language. The people say: Southern Slavs [Južni Sloveni], not Yugoslavs [Jugosloveni]. The people of the eastern territories do not care for it. It was created in the West, as if aimed against the Serb name.'[47] The Yugoslav Committee members were, however, reluctant to abandon the Yugoslav name. The name 'Kingdom of Serbs, Croats and Slovenes' was proposed as a compromise by Vojislav Marinković, who as a Progressive from Serbia represented the centre ground.[48] The conference's decision in favour of a unitarist South Slav national state without the Yugoslav name reflected the imbalance in the strength of the two signatories, with the Yugoslav Committee much weaker than Serbia's government. Nevertheless, the conference accepted Trumbić's view that the actual constitutional order be left to a future constituent assembly.

The conference produced a statement subsequently known as the Corfu Declaration, dated 20 July 1917, signed by Pašić as Serbia's prime minister and foreign minister and Trumbić as Yugoslav Committee president. The preamble stated 'that this our three-named nation is one and the same by blood, by spoken and written language, by the feeling of its unity, by the contiguousness and wholeness of its territory, on which it lives indivisibly, and on the basis of the common vital interests of its national survival and comprehensive development of its moral and material life'. The Declaration announced:

1. The Kingdom of the Serbs, Croats and Slovenes, known also under the name of the South Slavs or Yugoslavs, shall be a free, independent Kingdom with a single territory and single citizenship. It shall be a constitutional, democratic and

parliamentary monarchy headed by the Karađorđević dynasty, which has given proof that it is not separated from the people in its ideas and feelings and that it places the freedom and will of the people above all else.

2. This state shall be called: the Kingdom of Serbs, Croats and Slovenes, and its ruler: the King of the Serbs, Croats and Slovenes.

The Declaration recognised the equality and freedom of use or practice of the Serbian, Croatian and Slovene flags, of the Serb, Croat and Slovene names, of the Cyrillic and Latin alphabets, and of the Orthodox, Roman Catholic and Mohammedan religions. The Declaration rejected 'every partial solution' for 'national liberation and unification' of the Serbs, Croats and Slovenes: 'Our people pose as an indivisible whole the question of their liberation from Austria-Hungary and their unification with Serbia and Montenegro in a single state. According to the principle of free national self-determination, no one part of this whole can be rightfully separated and joined to any other state without the agreement of the people themselves.'

The Declaration ended by stating that the constitution would be 'the source and the point of departure for all authority and rights, and it shall determine the entire life of the state'. It was to be 'accepted in its entirety by a numerically qualified majority of the Constituent Assembly'.[49] The Declaration promised 'the people the opportunity to develop their individual energies in self-governing units as defined by natural, social and economic circumstances'. But by assuming the national unity of Serbs, Croats and Slovenes (and the inclusion of the Muslim Bosniaks, Montenegrins and Macedonians within these groups) and by granting to the constitution of the entire state the absolute sovereign right to determine law for the entire state, it militated against federalism. The Declaration also pre-empted any solution of the question of the Habsburg South Slavs within the Habsburg Empire or any surrender of large South Slav territories to Italy, either of which would have prevented Serbia achieving its territorial ambitions. Nevertheless, acceptance that Serbia would be merged within a Yugoslav whole, thereby abandoning its separate statehood, was a major concession by Pašić. The insistence that the South Slav question could only be resolved in its entirety through simultaneous unification of all Serb, Croat and Slovene lands on the basis of equality ruled out, in principle, any prior enlargement of Serbia's territory at the expense of the Habsburg South Slav lands, thereby restricting, in principle, Pašić's room for manoeuvre on this score. Formally, Yugoslav unification had ceased to be simply a Serbian war aim and had become a consensual project involving different Yugoslav parties. Pašić remained ambiguous about this, and the failure of Serbia's parliament to endorse the Declaration gave him some room to retreat from the commitment.[50]

The reduction of Entente troop strength on the Salonika front and Russia's military collapse during 1917 weakened both Serbia's position and prospects for

Yugoslav unification. The Entente powers remained formally committed to Austria-Hungary's continued existence and during 1917 tentatively explored a possible separate peace with it. The resignations of the Independent ministers in June of that year removed the most hardline champions of Yugoslav unification from Serbia's government; the Independents and Progressives now increasingly viewed the Yugoslav Committee as an ally against their traditional Radical foe. This raised the danger that the Habsburg South Slavs would combine with Serbia's opposition to defeat Pašić's Great Serbian politics in favour of a pluralistic Yugoslav solution. When the Bolshevik Revolution of November 1917 deprived Serbia of its principal protector among the Entente powers and removed Russian imperialism from British and French calculations, the establishment of the large Serbian-dominated South Slav state that Pašić wanted seemed significantly less likely.[51] Austria-Hungary and Germany won a crushing victory over Italy at the Battle of Caporetto ending on 19 November, capturing over a quarter of a million prisoners; Habsburg South Slav soldiers, fighting to defend their lands from Italian conquest, contributed significantly to this success. Pašić's government, despite its continued formal support for Yugoslav unification, consequently retreated to pursuing a narrower, purely Serb unification and limited territorial gains for Serbia. Pašić began to view Serbia's annexation of Bosnia-Hercegovina as an acceptable minimum in the event of peace and as compensation for the cession of Macedonian territory to Bulgaria. On 18 January 1918, he instructed Colonel Stefanović, at the Entente powers' supreme command in Versailles, to compose a memorandum 'that relates to our demands for the future borders of Yugoslavia or Great Serbia'.[52]

Pašić's retreat was opposed by the Yugoslav Committee, which remained committed to full South Slav liberation and unification, and by leading Serbian statesmen and diplomats. Trumbić sought to persuade Aleksandar to summon an all-Yugoslav 'general national assembly' in London or Paris composed of delegates of the Serbian parliament, Yugoslav Committee and Montenegrin Committee and representatives of the army and volunteers to counter the Entente powers' statements accepting Austria-Hungary's continued existence and reaffirm the principle of Yugoslav unity. This was rejected by Aleksandar and Pašić.[53] Pašić wished to retain his government's freedom of manoeuvre and was in principle opposed to dissolving Serbia's statehood and constitutional order in such an all-Yugoslav body.[54] According to Pašić, 'Serbia wants to liberate and unify the Yugoslavs, not drown in the sea of a single Yugoslavia: Serbia does not want to drown in Yugoslavia, but Yugoslavia in her.'[55] He claimed that whenever a nation unified, it was always the name of the 'strongest part of the nation' that was taken for the whole (ignoring the fact that this had not been true of the English and Britain, Savoyards or Piedmontese and Italy or Prussians and Germany).[56] He tried and failed to persuade Stojanović to campaign in the Yugoslav Committee solely for Bosnia-Hercegovina's unification with Serbia outside the Yugoslav framework.[57] Pašić complained that 'our Serbs in the Yugoslav

LIBERATION AND UNIFICATION

Committee have lost every Serb characteristic and become more Yugoslavs'.[58] He appeared lost even in the eyes of his friends, his long-term strategy having collapsed.[59]

Bolshevik Russia signed the Treaty of Brest-Litovsk with the Central Powers on 3 March 1918, definitely ending its involvement in the war. Austrophiles in Serbia including Živojin Perić, Vukašin Petrović and Jovan B. Jovanović responded by submitting a plan to the Austro-Hungarian occupation authority in Belgrade for the convening of a constituent assembly that would formally repudiate Serbia's government and parliament in exile and the Karađorđević monarchy, establish a pro-Austrian government with an Austrian archduke as the new Serbian monarch and sign a separate peace; they were ready to cede Macedonia to Bulgaria in exchange for the return of the Bulgarian-occupied part of pre-1912 Serbia. The Austro-Hungarians considered the plan but rejected it, for fear of alienating Bulgaria and because they doubted such a puppet regime would have sufficient authority among Serbia's population.[60] That month, the Western Entente powers retreated from the war aim of dismembering Austria-Hungary in favour of merely reforming it; the prospect of South Slav liberation appeared to recede.

Serbia's military fortunes subsequently rose again, but Pašić maintained a twin-track approach. He sought the outright annexation to or retention by Serbia of lands he considered purely Serbian or of vital interest—Montenegro, Macedonia, Vojvodina and an outlet on the Adriatic—but also broader Yugoslav unification with the Slovene and Croatian lands, with Bosnia-Hercegovina falling somewhere in between. When Entente policy shifted in mid-1918 away from supporting Austria-Hungary's continued existence, Serbia's government resisted any attempt by the Yugoslav Committee to assume any legal status as official representative of the Habsburg South Slavs, so as to reserve for Serbia the status of sole international representative for all Serbs, Croats and Slovenes. Pašić continued to conflate Yugoslav with pan-Serb unification; his draft memorandum to the Entente governments, submitted to Serbia's ambassador on 31 March 1918, stated: 'The Serb three-named nation—Serbs, Croats and Slovenes—wishes, strives and works always for this; that it be liberated from the Austro-Hungarian yoke and united in a national state numbering 11 to 12 million inhabitants.'[61] In a speech to Serbia's parliament on 27 April, he recalled a conversation with a German student during his student days in Zurich:

> On the occasion of the uprising in Krivošije [in 1869 in Austria-Hungary on the border with Montenegro], he asked me, 'who are those people of Krivošije; who are they?' I replied that they were Serbs. He then agitatedly asked me, 'who are those Hercegovinians?' I again replied: Serbs. He then asked me who are those: Bosnians, people of Boka, Montenegrins? I again replied: Serbs. He asked who are those 'Croats'? I replied that they too were: Serbs. 'So how come that I am an Austro-Hungarian student but I don't know that they are all Serbs?' I then explained to him that that was Austrian politics and that it has deceived not only its students and its

people, but the whole of the rest of the world, which has not greatly concerned itself with these questions. Thus, of the Serb–Croat–Slovene nation, which is one and the same, it has made so many administrations in its country and given it so many names, and has never wanted the Serb nation to be called by its one name.[62]

Serbia's opposition attacked Pašić for his apparently weak diplomatic pursuit of Yugoslav unification. It sought in early March 1918 to topple his government and replace it with a coalition government from which he would be excluded. When that failed, owing to Aleksandar's refusal to support it, the opposition continued to agitate for a coalition government under Pašić in which he would at least not be foreign minister. A bitter session of Serbia's parliament ended on 27 April with its failure to grant the government an additional war credit. The opposition walked out and denounced Pašić's 'unparliamentary' government to the prince regent. Serbia's parliament would never meet again, except for its formal convocation to proclaim the Yugoslav state some months later. The opposition was supported by British advocates of the Yugoslav cause, Seton-Watson and Steed. Seton-Watson published an article on 22 August accusing Pašić of persecuting the opposition, using police methods and violating Serbia's constitution, citing the dismissal of Putnik, the Salonika trial and the failure to support the Yugoslav Committee. These influential British figures encouraged Serbia's opposition in its linking of parliamentarism and Yugoslavism in opposition to the Radicals.[63]

Collapse of the Central Powers

As the Austro-Serbian conflict over Bosnia-Hercegovina had sparked World War I, so the Balkan states' conflict over Macedonia precipitated the final defeat of the Central Powers. The surrender by Greece's pro-German king Constantine of Fort Rupel in Greek Macedonia to the Bulgarians without a struggle on 26 May 1916, followed by Bulgaria's occupation of Greek Macedonian territory east of the River Struma in August, fired the nationalism of Venizelos's supporters, who were in particular Greeks from newly acquired lands such as Macedonia and Crete. Venizelist officers staged a coup in Entente-occupied Salonika on 30 August and Venizelos established a rebel pro-Entente government there in October.[64] Anglo-French forces attacked the royalist Greek government in Athens in December and the Entente powers recognised Venizelos's government as Greece's only lawful government. Britain and France forced Constantine to abdicate on 11 June 1917 and Greece formally entered the war on the Entente side on 2 July. Meanwhile, the withdrawal of most German military forces from the Macedonian front in spring 1918 for participation in General Erich Ludendorff's great push on the Western Front seriously undermined Bulgarian morale.[65] The shift in the balance of forces on the Salonika front did not immediately bring dividends for the Entente powers: while the Serbian supreme command agitated for an offensive from Salonika, this was long resisted by its

LIBERATION AND UNIFICATION

French counterpart, which wanted to concentrate its resources on the Western front. Conflict over strategy between the French and Serbian supreme commands prompted Bojović's resignation as Serbian chief of staff and his replacement on 1 July 1918 with Živojin Mišić.[66]

Eventually, following the failure of the last German offensive on the Western front, the arrival of US forces in the West in strength and reinforcement of the Macedonian front by the Entente powers, the latter launched a major offensive on that front on 14 September 1918. Greece's entry into the war added at least 135,000 troops to the Entente forces there, now numbering approximately 628,000. The Serbian army and Yugoslav volunteers contributed approximately 150,000, with Bojović commanding the 1st Serbian Army and Stepanović the 2nd. Serbian, French and Greek forces under Mišić and General Louis Franchet d'Espèrey attacked and defeated the heavily outnumbered and demoralised Bulgarians on 15–19 September in the decisive Battle of Dobro Pole, though the Bulgarians succeeded simultaneously in defeating the British and Greeks at the simultaneous Battle of Doiran. With mutinies now erupting in Bulgarian ranks, the Serbians and French advanced rapidly, capturing Skopje on the 29th, on which date the Bulgarians signed an armistice marking their exit from the war. Kaiser Wilhelm wrote angrily to Tsar Ferdinand: 'Disgraceful! 62,000 Serbs decided the war.' It was not an inaccurate assessment.[67] The Bulgarians' defeat by the Entente was due to strategic surprise; they had not believed their opponents capable of mounting an offensive on such a scale and with such intensity, then following it up so aggressively, so did not plan accordingly. Serbia's supreme command deserved particular credit for the victory, for relentlessly pursuing its offensive despite the overall Entente commander, Franchet d'Espèrey, wanting to halt it following the defeat at Doiran.[68]

Bulgaria's capitulation was a significant factor in the overall defeat of the Central Powers, though one often underemphasised by historians. The British followed it up by advancing eastwards to threaten Constantinople, prompting the Ottomans to sign an armistice on 30 October. The French and Serbians meanwhile advanced northwards against the Central Powers into Serbia itself, entering Vranje on 5 October, Leskovac on the 7th and Niš on the 12th, a victory after which, General Nedić later recalled with perhaps some exaggeration, 'the press of the whole world once again declared that Aleksandar I Karađorđević as a war-leader was equal to Napoleon Bonaparte'.[69] The Allies liberated Belgrade on 1 November and expelled the last enemy soldiers from the country two days later, with the assistance of the civilian population, part of which even joined in the fighting. A French officer recalled: 'We were excited, looking at those poor people, deprived of everything, who offered their liberators a little water or a late flower. The way that they did this was touching. With tears in their eyes they followed the parade of Serbian and French flags, welcoming us to villages that the enemy had only just abandoned ...'[70] Serbia's army then pushed on into Vojvodina, entering Vršac and Novi Sad on 9–10

437

November. The Italians, stiffened by British, French and American forces and aided by mass South Slav desertions from the Austro-Hungarians' ranks, finally defeated them at the Battle of Vittorio Veneto ending on 3 November, prompting Austria-Hungary to capitulate and sign an armistice the same day, followed by Germany on the 11th. The German leadership's readiness to capitulate occurred not because it lost the military capacity to resist but because its morale collapsed, in part owing to abandonment by its allies.[71] The Hungarian government rejected the Austro-Hungarian armistice and delayed signing its own armistice until the 13th, by which time Serbia's army had captured Subotica and Sombor, key Hungarian towns in what was to become Vojvodina.

South Slav leaders in Austria-Hungary on 6 October proclaimed a National Council of Slovenes, Croats and Serbs, based in Zagreb and claiming to represent the South Slav people inhabiting the empire (essentially in the territories of Styria, Carinthia, Carniola, Croatia, the Austrian Littoral, Rijeka, Dalmatia, Baranja, Bačka, the Banat and Bosnia-Hercegovina, which broadly correspond to present-day Slovenia, Croatia, Vojvodina and Bosnia-Hercegovina). The State of Slovenes, Croats and Serbs, headed by the National Council, declared independence on 29 October and was recognised by Habsburg emperor Charles I. Thus, Serbia's final military victory coincided with the appearance of a new rival body for leadership of the Habsburg South Slavs, which immediately sought recognition from the Entente powers while authorising the Yugoslav Committee to represent it internationally. Serbia's opposition, for its part, made clear to Pašić that, in the event of a break between his government and the Yugoslav Committee, it would support the latter. Yet Pašić opposed the quest of the State of Slovenes, Croats and Serbs for international recognition: 'The Serbian government, like any other, must take care that it is not excluded at the moment when the question of our people is being determined. If our brothers in A[ustria]-Hungary and our allies will not recognise our right to represent all three "tribes" then they cannot take away from us the right to represent the Serb nation in Austria-Hungary. It cannot be held that a lasting peace and brotherly union are being established if Serbia is excluded; if another Yugoslav state is established from which Serbia and Montenegro are excluded.'[72]

At the time of the armistice with Austria-Hungary, Serbia's army had barely begun to enter Habsburg territory in what is today Vojvodina; it crossed the border into Bosnia-Hercegovina on the day the armistice was signed. Meanwhile, Italy's army rapidly occupied the South Slav territory promised to it in the Treaty of London, and more besides: Istria, northern Dalmatia including the cities of Zadar and Šibenik, islands including Krk, Cres, Vis, Hvar, Korčula and Lastovo, the Pelješac peninsula and parts of Carinthia and Carniola. Local resistance kept it out of Split and Trogir, while a force of several hundred Serbian soldiers released from Austro-Hungarian captivity kept it out of Ljubljana. Responding to appeals for help from the National Council and in order to claim and defend territory it considered rightfully belonging

LIBERATION AND UNIFICATION

to the Serb–Croat–Slovene state, Serbia's army occupied the southern Dalmatian towns of Kotor on 8 November, Herceg-Novi on the 12th, and Dubrovnik on the 13th. A Serbian battalion under the command of Colonel Maksimović entered Rijeka on 15 November, confronting the Italians. It withdrew three days later in return for an Italian promise not to occupy the city; this was broken and the Italians occupied Rijeka as soon as the Serbians left. However, Serbia's army entered Split on the 19th together with the French.[73]

Serbian leaders would subsequently present Serbia as having 'liberated' the Habsburg South Slavs and saved them from Italy, a claim serving as a foundational legend for the new Yugoslav state, but this was an exaggeration. The Habsburg South Slavs were 'liberated' by the collapse of Austria-Hungary brought about by the Entente victory; while Serbia's army had fought bravely and contributed significantly to this victory, it did so only as part of a coalition with much stronger states. Serbia had itself been wholly occupied by the Central Powers and was liberated by its Entente allies. As Pribićević noted, 'Then, if Serbia liberated the Croats, I ask myself who liberated the Czechs and the Poles? If the expression "liberated" is already being used, it would be more accurate to say that the Western democracies (France and England) together with the United States of America liberated us (Yugoslavs from Austria-Hungary) and you (Serbia).'[74] Whether the formerly Austro-Hungarian South Slavs were actually freer or better off in the Yugoslav kingdom than they had been under Habsburg rule is a moot point. As regards the Italians, they were only able to threaten the Habsburg South Slav lands in the first place because the Entente powers and Serbia defeated Austria-Hungary. Serbia's army did help to stem the Italians' advance into them in 1918, but only after they had already occupied most of the territory they wanted. It was Allied diplomacy in the peace negotiations that forced Italy to withdraw from some of these occupied territories while permitting it to annex others—substantial Croat- and Slovene-inhabited land that Serbia's statesmen were largely willing to sacrifice in return for concessions elsewhere.[75] Only in World War II was the Italian imperialist occupation of and threat to the South Slav lands defeated, when Tito's Yugoslav Partisans liberated all those Italy had seized since World War I, except for Trieste.

Pašić, upon hearing of the armistice with Austria-Hungary, immediately ordered Serbia's army to occupy Bosnia-Hercegovina, Srem and Banat in order to achieve Serbia's principal war aims and present the Habsburg South Slavs with a fait accompli.[76] The territory whose occupation Pašić prioritised above all—present-day Vojvodina—was predominantly inhabited by non-South-Slavs, primarily ethnic Hungarians, Germans, Romanians and Slovaks. This territory was deemed vital as a defensive hinterland for Belgrade, but was disputed with Romania, so its rapid acquisition was prioritised. Here, Serbia's army advanced rapidly with French support, though, despite the subsequent mythologising of Franco-Serbian military cooperation, relations between the allies remained difficult. Continuing disagreement over strategy and French lack of enthusiasm for action on this front weakened Serbia's advance, while French troops committed acts of plunder, assaults on women and other mistreatment of civilians in Serbian Macedonia, about which Aleksandar complained to the British.[77]

Geneva Declaration

The State of Slovenes, Croats and Serbs was in a weak position owing to Italy's occupation of part of its territory and to the failure of the Entente powers, under pressure from Italy and Serbia, to recognise its independence. But Pašić was also under pressure from Britain and from Serbia's parliamentary opposition to reach an agreement with the leadership of the newly proclaimed state. Serbia's opposition increasingly sided with the latter as a counterweight to Pašić and the Radicals, seriously constraining Pašić's pursuit of purely Serbian national goals.[78] Representatives of the National Council, Serbian government, Serbian opposition and Yugoslav Committee consequently met in Geneva on 6–9 November to resolve outstanding issues; above all, the questions of international recognition of the State of Slovenes, Croats and Serbs and of the form that would be taken by the future unified South Slav state. With the negotiations now between four parties comprising six Serb, three Croat and three Slovene delegates, the balance was less favourable to Pašić than it had been at the Corfu talks of June 1917.[79] Consequently, Pašić was forced, under pressure from the other delegates and from the French, to recognise the National Council as 'the lawful government of the Serbs, Croats and Slovenes', though he reversed the order in which the three people's names appeared in the name of their self-declared state.[80]

Pašić was then outvoted by the other delegates and forced on 9 November to sign with them a document subsequently known as the Geneva Declaration, according to which 'representatives of the government of the Kingdom of Serbia and its parliamentary groups, representatives of the National Council in Zagreb and representatives of the Yugoslav Committee in London, assembled in Geneva, the town of freedom, are happy that they are able unanimously, solemnly and before the whole world to conclude their unification in the State of Serbs, Croats and Slovenes'. Composed by Trumbić and supported in the National Council's name by him and Korošec, it was a plan for unification on a provisionally confederal basis, whereby the Kingdom of Serbia and the State of Slovenes, Croats and Serbs, pending the convening of a joint constituent assembly, would remain distinct, self-governing entities, united by a cabinet of ministers delegated by both entities that would have jurisdiction over matters relevant to both: foreign affairs, defence, the navy and merchant fleet, the convening of the constituent assembly and other limited fields.[81] This would have meant that the Serbs of Austria-Hungary, instead of being directly annexed to Serbia, would be linked with it only through a state and government centred on Zagreb

LIBERATION AND UNIFICATION

and predominantly non-Serb in composition. It would have effectively recognised Zagreb's sovereignty over all South Slav lands west of the Drina.

The Radical minister of construction Momčilo Ninčić wrote at the time: 'We in Belgrade are increasingly gaining the impression that certain Croatian circles have as their plan to separate Serbia and Montenegro from the rest of our provinces and in this manner: instead of a unitary state in which they fear that the Serbs might have the main say, to create a purely Austrian combination. It even lacks any originality but simply copies the relation between Austria and Hungary.'[82] Consequently, although Pašić had personally been forced to sign the Geneva Declaration, it was rejected by deputy prime minister Protić and opposed by Aleksandar owing to its failure to recognise the Karađorđević dynasty's status. In the Serbian government's view, unification according to the Geneva Declaration would mean that 'the Serbs of Bosnia and Hercegovina, Srem and Slavonia, Dalmatia and Lika, Bačka, the Banat and Baranja be separated from Serbia and used to establish a front against Serbia'.[83] Pašić informed the Geneva conference on 10 November of the Serbian government's repudiation of the agreement. This was followed by the National Council's own repudiation of the agreement, at the initiative of its vice-president, Pribićević, who was a hardline unitarist determined to pursue unification in close collaboration with Serbia's government.[84]

After the conference's failure, South Slav unification was accomplished by bilateral negotiations between the governments in Belgrade and Zagreb. The National Council's delegation met on 8 November first Bojović, commander of the 1st Army, then Aleksandar himself, following which the Serbian supreme command sent Lieutenant Colonel Dušan Simović as its delegate to the National Council. Upon arriving in Zagreb, Simović warned the Council that Serbia would not permit the establishment of an independent State of Slovenes, Croats and Serbs west of the Drina and north of the Sava that would separate the former prečani Serbs from the Serbs of Serbia, and that were such a state to be established, Serbia would retain the formerly Habsburg territory it wanted:

> Serbia, which has in this war given between 1 and ½ million lives for the liberation and unification of its brothers of a single blood across the Danube, Sava and Drina, cannot in any circumstances permit that on its borders be formed some new state, which would within its composition take all its co-nationals, or that—after a four-year torment and the complete defeat of the enemy—it remain in the background and surrender all the fruit of the achieved victory to another, which participated in the war on the opposing side. To Serbia—by right of arms, on the basis of the peace agreement with Hungary which was signed by Vojvoda Mišić, as plenipotentiary of the commander of the Allied army on the Salonika front, General Franchet d'Espèrey—belongs the following territory: Banat up to the line Oršava-Karansebeš-R Maroš-Arad beneath Segedin; Bačka up to the line Horgoš-Subotica-Baja; Baranja up to the line of the railway line Osek-Đakovo-Šamac; the whole of Bosnia-Hercegovina and

441

Dalmatia up to the cape Planka. Outside of that territory, you can decide as you wish: to go with Serbia or form a separate state.

This proposed line, separating territory considered unconditionally Serbian by right of conquest from that which Serbia would allow to determine its own future, was decided upon by chief of staff Mišić following consultations with advisers, though Simović himself would have preferred taking a larger slice of Slavonia.[85] Mišić subsequently advised Aleksandar to exclude Croatia from the common state on the grounds that the Croats did not want to be part of it and that this was necessary if it were to be stable. Aleksandar rejected this, asking rhetorically 'Are we really going to leave all that to Italy?' He feared that an independent Croatia, however small, supported by other Catholic states, would be a threat to Serbdom, so it was necessary to integrate the Croats in the common state.[86] Meanwhile, on 16 November, Protić negotiated the formation of a coalition government with Serbia's opposition, at the price of Pašić giving up the post of foreign minister, which was assumed by the diplomat Mihailo Gavrilović.

Annexation of Montenegro

Serbia's government negotiated hard with the Habsburg South Slavs for unification on its terms, but sought Montenegro's outright annexation without negotiation. This was to be achieved through collaboration with Montenegro's annexationists and the marginalisation of King Nikola. The king, following his flight from Montenegro in January 1916, appointed a new government-in-exile in May of that year under the moderate annexationist Andrija Radović, who worked with some success to repair the king's reputation. But in August 1916, Radović submitted to Nikola a proposal for a compromise solution to the dynastic conflict, whereby Serbia and Montenegro would be united as a single state, Nikola would abdicate in favour of Aleksandar and the succession would pass to each dynasty's heir in turn. Nikola refused this proposal, and in September, with Italian encouragement, began working to mobilise a new military force among expatriate Montenegrins. Pašić, a master at destabilising governments, responded by enlisting his agent in Radović's government, justice minister Janko Spasojević, to engineer its resignation. Spasojević failed to achieve this and resigned alone. Nevertheless, after Nikola rejected his memorandum a second time, under pressure from Serbia's government and in agreement with its diplomats, Radović resigned in January 1917.[87]

Pašić established a Montenegrin Committee for National Unification under Radović in Geneva in February 1917, to supplant Nikola's regime. From April it began openly working for unification independently of the king. Pašić thereupon ended contact with Montenegro's official government and began treating the Montenegrin Committee as Montenegro's legitimate representative; the

Committee in turn endorsed all Serbia's moves towards outright union between the two countries. Nevertheless, Pašić was unhappy with the proclamation issued by the Montenegrin Committee immediately after its launch, since it spoke of 'unification of Montenegro with Serbia and Yugoslavia'. He informed it: 'In the declaration—proclamation—of the Montenegrin Committee, there should not be used the word "Yugoslavia" nor "Yugoslav" nor any related formulation or sentence. The Committee is working with us on the joining of Montenegro to Serbia and on the unification of the Serb nation without regard to the other Yugoslavs.' He added: 'Let the Montenegrin Committee use this formulation in its declaration: "Unification of Montenegro and Serbia with the other Serb lands".'[88]

Serbia's government endeavoured systematically through bribes, persuasion and pressure to deter any politician from serving in Montenegro's government. Following Radović's resignation, Nikola offered the premiership to Vojvoda Sima Popović, but Serbia's government persuaded him to refuse, promising to provide for his and his family's livelihood. Nikola then formed a government under Brigadier Milo Matanović. But in May he resigned, as he had come to view Nikola as an obstacle to unification, a view which Serbia's government was propagating with increasing success among the Montenegrin elite, and because Serbia's government undertook to continue paying him his ministerial salary along with those of his ministers who resigned alongside him.[89] Simultaneously, Serbia's government, assisted by the French military authorities, undermined Nikola's efforts at organising a Montenegrin army-in-exile. Serbian government agents waged a propaganda campaign among Montenegrin soldiers at Bizerte, Lipari and Salonika to discredit Nikola and recruit them to Serbia's army. The French authorities gave Montenegrin soldiers unwilling to serve in either Serbia's army or the French Foreign Legion the choice between manual labour service or internment as prisoners of war. A Montenegrin Battalion had been present for a while at Salonika, but its existence was not tolerated by the Serbian authorities; it was forced to remove its Montenegrin name and insignia and employed as cannon fodder, while some of its officers loyal to Nikola were imprisoned. Eventually, in summer 1916, it was transported away from the front, to Corsica. There, the Montenegrin soldiers were brutally exploited as slave labour by rich Corsicans until in May 1918 they were transferred for service in Serbia's army. Thus, the war ended with Nikola lacking any independent Montenegrin armed force.[90]

The division over Montenegro between annexationists following Serbia's government and autonomists following Nikola's regime dovetailed with the division between Pašić and his Yugoslavist opponents, both inside and outside Serbia. Pašić was determined, as he said in April 1918, that 'the unification of Serbia and Montenegro must be carried out, regardless of whether there is Yugoslavia or not' and that Serbian–Montenegrin unification be separated from Yugoslav unification.'[91] Nikola, meanwhile, avoided committing himself to any definite arrangements for how Montenegro would unite with Serbia prior to his return to the country following its military liberation. To counter Serbia's annexationist campaign, he and his government by summer 1918 abandoned talk of Serbdom and Serb unity in favour of 'liberation and unification of all Yugoslavs', in his own words. This was welcomed by the pro-Yugoslav politicians of the Habsburg South Slavs, whom Nikola courted because of their own conflict with Pašić. But Serbia's government successfully opposed both Trumbić's attempt to include the Montenegrin question in the Geneva conference and Montenegro's attempt to participate in it.[92]

Montenegrin soldiers and citizens rose against the collapsing Austro-Hungarian occupation during October 1918 and succeeded in rapidly liberating the country. In these circumstances, special forces were established by Serbia's army, known initially as the Skadar Troops and subsequently as the Adriatic Troops, to commandeer the country and prevent Nikola's return. They took Shkodër on 31 October following a two-day battle, to prevent its use by the Italians in aid of Nikola.[93] By the time they entered Montenegro, the struggle against Austria-Hungary was already almost won; regular Serbian forces' only engagement with the Austro-Hungarians there was their participation in the liberation of Podgorica on 31 October, alongside Montenegrin forces, although a detachment of Chetniks, under Pećanac's overall command, liberated Nikšić on the 20th. Serbia's first troops entered Cetinje on 4 November, having been invited by a citizens' delegation headed by Metropolitan Gavrilo (Dožić).[94] With the completion of military operations, Serbia's army moved to disband the Montenegrin armed units and ensure that the new local authorities were loyal to the annexationist cause.

The Serbian government's delegate Svetozar Tomić and the Montenegro Committee for National Unification's representative Janko Spasojević, having entered Montenegro with Serbia's army, established the Central Executive Committee for the Unification of Serbia and Montenegro in the town of Berane on 25 October 1918, headed by Tomić as president. They organised a mass rally at the town of Andrijevica on 2 November in support of annexation, while similar rallies took place across Montenegro. Their message stressed that unification was occurring in a broader Yugoslav context; thus, the Central Executive Committee's statement called upon Montenegrins 'to accept the idea of national unification, as has already been done by all Serbs, Croats and Slovenes, and proclaim the unification of Serbia and Montenegro, as we have done, so fulfil the age-old Serb wish and committed dream of our ancestors'.[95] With Italian troops menacingly present at Kotor on the Montenegrin coast, the Central Executive Committee hurriedly held elections on 19 November for a new Montenegrin parliament—the 'Great National Parliament'—to produce a fait accompli. Nikola's supporters were largely kept out of the country, suppressed or prevented from agitating freely, the voting was indirect and public, Serbia's army provided an umbrella and existing Montenegrin laws and state bodies were disregarded, so the outcome was an inevitable victory for the annexationist

LIBERATION AND UNIFICATION

'Whites' over the autonomist 'Greens'—the names deriving from the colours of the paper on which their respective candidate lists were printed.[96] This was not a contest over whether unification should occur, since both sides agreed it should, but over whether Montenegro should preserve a degree of autonomy in the new state. As one Green was quoted at the time: 'I too am, indeed we are, for unification, but conditional unification; that Montenegro join unified Yugoslavia as an independent kingdom, just as Serbia will join and other provinces; then Yugoslavia in union will give the form of the new state.'[97] The Whites, supporters of unconditional unification, ensured that it would be prepared and carried out extremely quickly.[98]

The Great National Parliament convened on 24 November at Podgorica, away from the Petrović-Njegoš dynasty's traditional capital of Cetinje. Two days later, by a vote of 163–0 in favour with three deputies absent, it proclaimed the deposition of Nikola and the Petrović-Njegoš dynasty and Montenegro's unification with Serbia under the Karađorđević dynasty on exclusively Serb-nationalist grounds: 'The Serb nation in Montenegro is of one blood, one language and one aspiration, one religion and custom with the nation that lives in Serbia and other Serb areas; they share a glorious past which they rejoice in; common ideals; common national heroes; common suffering; common everything that makes a nation a nation.' Montenegrin–Serbian unification was to occur prior to and distinct from the broader Yugoslav unification, though arguably conditional upon it happening: 'That Montenegro with fraternal Serbia unite in a single state under the Karađorđević dynasty, and thus united enter the common Fatherland of our three-tribe nation of Serbs, Croats and Slovenes.'[99] The assembly elected an executive national council to administer Montenegro in the interim and dispatched a delegation to Belgrade to negotiate unification.

Establishment of Yugoslavia

In the South Slav lands to the west of the Drina, the drive of particular regions for unification sometimes exceeded that of the National Council in Zagreb, either owing to fear of the Italians, fear of social unrest and anarchy or outright Serb irredentism. The Serb and Croat inhabitants of the ethnically diverse territories of Baranja, Bačka and Banat, which Serbs collectively termed 'Vojvodina', began in the autumn to express demands to secede from Hungary and Habsburg rule. However, they soon divided between supporters of all-Yugoslav unification through the National Council and supporters of unilateral unification with Serbia. A meeting in Subotica on 2 October 1918 resolved on behalf of the 'Serbs and Croats of Southern Hungary' that 'only the Peace conference is relevant with regard to the Yugoslav question and in connection with Bačka, Banat and Baranja as future constituent parts of the free common state of all Yugoslavs'. It received a positive response from the National Council. However, these Yugoslavists were quickly outflanked by local Radicals led by Jaša Tomić, who opposed collaboration with the National Council and demanded immediate unification of Vojvodina with Serbia. On 8 October, a Radical representative from the neighbouring territory of Srem in the easternmost part of Croatia-Slavonia joined the National Council but by the end of the month was agitating for Serbia's direct annexation of Srem along with the whole of Vojvodina. The annexationists enjoyed the support of Pribićević and of Pašić's government and believed Vojvodina's unilateral unification with Serbia would strengthen Belgrade's negotiating position vis-à-vis the National Council. Their advantage became still greater with the arrival in the first half of November of Serbia's army, which on the 9th of that month entered Novi Sad, disarmed the militia that local Serbs had established and introduced censorship of the press and post.[100]

Supporters of union established their own national council for Vojvodina at the start of November. On the 13th, Serbia signed a ceasefire with Hungary and imposed a demarcation line with its forces, effectively establishing the new border between the two countries, hence establishing Vojvodina as the territory taken from Hungary. Vojvodina's national council held elections for a regional assembly; women as well as men were allowed to vote, perhaps to increase the size of the South Slav political nation. The assembly convened on 25 November at the town of Novi Sad, representing Bačka, Baranja and Banat and comprising 757 deputies: 578 Serbs, 89 Croats, 62 Slovaks, 21 Ukrainians, 6 Germans and 1 Magyar. The underrepresentation of Germans and Magyars and the complete absence of Romanian deputies were due to the organisers' attempt to exclude from voting members of the nations considered enemies, which included Romania owing to its territorial pretensions regarding Banat.[101] Although a minority called for unification to occur in conjunction with the National Council in Zagreb, the majority demanded immediate unification with Serbia.[102] The assembly consequently proclaimed: 'We are joining the Kingdom of Serbia, whose work and development up till now guarantees freedom, equality and progress in every direction, not only to us, but to all Slavic as well as non-Slavic peoples who live together with us.' The assembly elected from its ranks a 50-member Great National Council, which appointed a National Administration that governed Vojvodina during the unification process.

Serbia's government immediately accepted the union. Vojvodina along with the adjacent territory of East Srem would be the only formerly Habsburg territory whose union with Serbia was successful and permanent. Nevertheless, the Vojvodinians' proclamation of annexation to Serbia explicitly stated: 'This our request desires to assist at once the aspiration of all Yugoslavs, for it is our earnest desire that the Serbian government, associated with the National Council in Zagreb, does everything so that there should come about the creation of a united state of Serbs, Croats and Slovenes under the leadership of King Petar and his dynasty.' Furthermore, to facilitate Yugoslav unification, the proclamation stated that the Vojvodinian assembly was sending two delegates to serve the National

Council in Zagreb and two to serve Serbia's government, making clear it was working toward Yugoslav unification, not just annexation to Serbia.[103] Meanwhile, an assembly of representatives of Srem convened on 24 November in the town of Ruma and demanded the National Council immediately establish 'a unified common government of the new Yugoslav state', otherwise they would vote for 'direct annexation' to Serbia. In the event, they did not need to carry out their threat and Srem entered Yugoslavia as part of Croatia.[104]

Bosnia-Hercegovina's entry into Yugoslavia was conditioned by differences between its elite's Yugoslavist and Serb nationalist wings. The initially dominant, conservative wing of the Bosnian Serb elite, whose senior figure was Gligorije Jeftanović and whose stronghold was Sarajevo, was heir to the Serb autonomist resistance to the Austro-Hungarian occupation. Following Bosnia-Hercegovina's annexation, the Habsburg regime felt secure enough to grant the Bosnian Serbs concessions that largely satisfied Jeftanović's autonomists, who consequently became essentially *kaisertreu*. But after the Bosnian Serb national movement was formally constituted in 1907 as the Serb National Organisation, the older autonomists lost ground to a new, more liberal, Yugoslavist and Mostar-based generation, whose leading figures included Stojanović and Atanasije Šola. Members of this current dominated the national government of Bosnia-Hercegovina appointed by the National Council on 30 October 1918, with Šola as prime minister; it pursued national unification on an all-Yugoslav basis in preference to Bosnia-Hercegovina's outright annexation to Serbia.

The Bosnian Serb population, however, which had suffered heavy wartime repression at Habsburg hands, remained more Serb nationalist in its orientation, resulting in grass-roots pressure for outright annexation. Consequently, 42 out of 54 of the district-level 'national councils' formed in Bosnia-Hercegovina by supporters of separation from Austria-Hungary voted unilaterally to unite with Serbia, bypassing Šola's Bosnian government. This irredentist movement was strongest in the Serb-majority region of Bosanska Krajina (western Bosnia); its epicentre was the city of Banja Luka, whose national council resolved that 'Bosnia-Hercegovina is deemed a constituent and inseparable part of the body of the Kingdom of Serbia, subject solely to King Petar and his government in Belgrade, and all other governments cease to function in their own name'.[105] Serbia's government and army put heavy pressure on the Bosnian government to join this movement and declare Bosnia-Hercegovina's unilateral unification with Serbia. Serbia's supreme command ordered its detachment in Sarajevo to 'assist the National Council in view of unification with Serbia' and Serbia's army everywhere disbanded units of the national guard that Bosnia-Hercegovina's government had established. The Serbian army's detachment in Sarajevo forced Bosnia-Hercegovina's government to return a group of senior officers sent by the National Council to direct military affairs in Sarajevo, asserting its exclusive right to military authority in the country.[106] Nevertheless, Bosnia-

Hercegovina's government resisted the pressure. Consequently, unlike Vojvodina, Bosnia-Hercegovina did not unilaterally unite with Serbia prior to the establishment of Yugoslavia, nor thereafter.

The central committee of the National Council of Slovenes, Croats and Serbs resolved on 26 November to send a 28-member delegation to Belgrade to negotiate unification of the State of Slovenes, Croats and Serbs with the Kingdom of Serbia, on the understanding that the state's definite organisation would be decided subsequently by a constituent assembly.[107] The government of Dalmatia, a territory overwhelmingly ethic Croat but targeted by Italian expansionism, threatened the National Council in late November that if it did not carry out unification of the State of Slovenes, Croats and Serbs with Serbia within five days, it would unite with Serbia unilaterally. Dalmatia's government on 30 November sent a telegram to Serbia's government to inform it that, 'in the name of the entire population of Dalmatia ... formal and definite unification of all South Slavs from the Adriatic to the Vardar in a unified state' must be carried out 'without further hesitation'.[108]

The National Council's delegation arrived in Belgrade on 28 November and on 1 December presented an 'Address to the Throne' to Prince Regent Aleksandar, setting forth the request for unification with Serbia and Montenegro, under King Petar and Aleksandar. A single national representative body was to be formed pending the election of a constituent assembly, while existing governmental bodies in the individual South Slav lands would remain until a new constitutional order was established. Aleksandar formulated his response so as to dilute its Yugoslav dimension and avoid any acknowledgement of the legitimacy of the State of Slovenes, Croats and Serbs. He thus proclaimed Serbia's unification not with the latter as a whole, but with each of the individual lands within it: 'in the name of His Majesty King Petar I, I proclaim the unification of Serbia with the lands of the independent state of Slovenes, Croats and Serbs in the unified Kingdom of Serbs, Croats and Slovenes'. He did not mention Montenegro, assuming its unification with Serbia had already been achieved and had nothing to do with all-Yugoslav unification.[109] The National Council of Slovenes, Croats and Serbs announced the end of its own sovereignty on 3 December, briefly retaining an administrative function until the formation of the common Yugoslav government.

This marked the birth of the state subsequently called Yugoslavia. Serbia's political classes, though greatly divided, agreed that this form of unification had arisen not from any agreement between different peoples or territories but as an expression of a single people's self-determination. They viewed the division of the formerly Habsburg South Slav territories between different lands, such as Croatia-Slavonia, Dalmatia or Bosnia-Hercegovina, as an unnatural legacy of foreign rule, and any assertion of a separate or autonomous identity of these territories as consequently undermining national unity. This placed them at loggerheads with the Slovenes, Muslim Bosniaks and above all Croats, whose sense of national identity was inseparable from their particular territories.[110] Nevertheless, the act of unification did not immediately create a truly unitary state: the provincial governments of the constituent lands of the State of Slovenes, Croats and Serbs—Slovenia, Croatia (including Slavonia and Srem), Bosnia-Hercegovina and Dalmatia—in the short term remained in place. By contrast, those territories directly annexed to Serbia—Vojvodina and Montenegro—enjoyed no such temporary autonomy beyond short-lived councils, so in practice came immediately under the unmediated rule of Serbia's government. This amounted to the establishment of an enlarged or 'Great' Serbia within the new state, made up of Serbia in its pre-1914 borders plus Vojvodina and Montenegro.[111]

Serbia entered the union as a devastated country: around a million of its citizens had been killed or died owing to the war, including about 370,000 soldiers—more than half of those mobilised—and 600,000 civilians, the latter primarily due to disease, hunger and exposure. This amounted to about 21–22 per cent of the country's pre-war population—proportionally the highest loss of any country in the war.[112] The population of Serbia's pre-1912 territory was only 2,595,430 in 1921 compared with 2,911,701 in 1910. Without the war, its population could have been expected to reach 3,406,690 in 1921—a demographic deficit of 43 per cent.[113] The loss of much of the country's workforce together with the occupiers' massive plunder and devastation of Serbia's agriculture and industry, including the loss of most of the country's livestock and the widespread destruction of its factories, mines, mills, farms, orchards and forests, was an economic as well as a humanitarian catastrophe.[114] Liberation and unification had come at a heavy price.

Unification of the South Slav lands to form a kingdom with power centralised in Belgrade was a historical accident, produced by the war ending fortuitously with Serbia on the winning side while Austria-Hungary collapsed completely. Serbia's leaders embraced the cause not merely of pan-Serb but of South Slav unification, for tactical reasons: to pre-empt the establishment of a rival independent South Slav state on, or Italy's acquisition of, territory they considered rightfully theirs. Yet this maximalist extension of Serbian power all the way to the borders of the new, rump Austria and Hungary was a pyrrhic victory. It resulted in rule over non-Serbian territory and peoples so extensive that not only could Serbia not digest them, but Serbia's acquisition even of territories it could reasonably have expected to absorb, above all Montenegro and Bosnia-Hercegovina, was fatally jeopardised. These problems became apparent only later: in the short term, unification on Serbia's terms and under its leadership appeared a tremendous victory, leaving the Radical model of nationhood hegemonic and the prince regent, his popularity and self-confidence cemented by his central role in the victorious wars of 1912–1918, as the leading actor in the new state.

15

ESTABLISHMENT OF THE YUGOSLAV STATE

1918–1921

Unification of the South Slav lands to form the new Kingdom of Serbs, Croats and Slovenes did not fundamentally change the nature of the political conflicts in Serbia. Serbia imposed its hegemony on the new state, but the monarch, Radicals and their party-political opponents now sought allies from among the new lands with which to counteract each other, so that Serbia exported its political divisions to these new lands while importing theirs. Meanwhile, the acquisition of new territories by Belgrade meant ongoing territorial disputes with neighbours—Italy, Hungary, Bulgaria, Albania—that spilled over into internal conflicts within Yugoslavia; Serbian expansionism was thus replaced by a defensive struggle against the irredentism of neighbouring states.

International position of the new state

The Yugoslav state's participation in the Paris peace negotiations was conditioned by the wartime differences between Serbia and both the Habsburg South Slavs and its wartime allies, especially Italy. Italy initially hoped to acquire the Yugoslav territories promised it in the Treaty of London, so objected to international recognition of the new state that included these territories, hoping to limit its diplomatic clout. More generally, Serbia's wartime allies viewed the former Habsburg South Slav lands as parts of a former enemy state, so they were resistant to recognising Yugoslavia given it included them. They recognised its foreign minister Trumbić only as foreign minister of Serbia, though he was a Croat from Dalmatia.[1] Yugoslavia's delegates to the peace conference were treated as delegates of Serbia. But with Pašić heading the delegation and Trumbić as foreign minister, the Yugoslavs were divided among themselves, for Trumbić's primary interest was resisting Italian territorial claims on Slovenian and Croatian territories while Pašić focused on asserting Serbia's borders vis-à-vis Romania, Bulgaria and Albania.[2] In particular, Trumbić and Croatia prioritised retaining the Croatian–Hungarian port of Rijeka (Fiume), which Rome sought as compensation for the conference's failure to honour the Treaty of London, while Pašić and Serbia prioritised pursuing Serbia's claim on Shkodër, coveted for decades as a supposedly historic Serbian port. This split weakened Yugoslavia's negotiating position: it failed to obtain Shkodër but lost to Italy in the north as well.

The new state comprised both former states that had fought on the Entente side (Serbia and Montenegro) and lands that had been part of one of the Central Powers (Slovenia, Croatia, Dalmatia, Vojvodina, Bosnia-Hercegovina). The peace conference eventually resolved that the formerly Habsburg Yugoslav lands would not be liable for Austria-Hungary's reparations payments and that these would be borne solely by Austria and Hungary themselves, which alone would be considered by the victors as enemy states. But they (except for Bosnia-Hercegovina) remained liable for their share of Austria-Hungary's state debt and were required in addition to pay a 'tribute for liberation'. Since Serbia and Montenegro were due reparations payments from the former Austria-Hungary, in practice the Entente powers expected these reparations to be offset against what the former Austro-Hungarian territories of Yugoslavia owed.[3]

President Wilson initiated international recognition of the new state on 10 February 1919. When inter-Allied tensions led Italy to boycott the peace conference in May, the other Powers took the opportunity to recognise it formally too. It consequently signed the peace treaties in its own name: the Treaty of Versailles with Germany on 28 June 1919 was signed by Pašić, Trumbić and Milenko Vesnić as representatives of the 'Serb–Croat–Slovene State' and of 'His Majesty the King of the Serbs, the Croats and the Slovenes', marking the kingdom's international recognition. This was followed by its signature of the Treaty of Neuilly with Bulgaria on 27 November 1919 and the Treaty of Trianon with Hungary on 20 June 1920. The Treaty of Saint-Germain between Austria and its wartime opponents was signed on 10 September 1919, but Yugoslavia did not immediately sign because the Serbians objected to being bound by its minority rights provisions.[4] In particular, Yugoslavia acquired territory from Bulgaria, Strumica in Macedonia and Tsaribrod and Bosilegrad on the old Serbo-Bulgarian border, both inhabited predominantly by ethnic Bulgarians, and Belgrade feared the minority rights provisions would enable Bulgarian irredentists to safeguard the existence there of the Bulgarian language and Exarchate church. But it eventually conceded and signed on 5 December. The acquisition of these territories significantly strengthened the Yugoslav strategic position vis-à-vis Bulgaria.[5]

Belgrade used force to assert its territorial claims in the peace settlement. Yugoslavia acquired territory from Hungary that became Vojvodina—the Banat, Baranja and Bačka—with large ethnic Hungarian, German, Romanian and Slovak minorities, including the large town of Subotica with a population divided roughly equally between Serbs and Croats on one hand and Hungarians on the other. Banat was definitely acquired only after a threat of military conflict with Romania had been averted thanks to French support for Belgrade.[6] These territories, except Strumica and Baranja, would become part of Serbia following its re-establishment as a state in 1944–1946. Hungary's borders with the Slovene- and Croat-inhabited parts of the Yugoslav state were established in favour of the latter, which acquired Medimurje and Prekmurje. But large Croat and Slovene irredentas remained in Italy and Austria. In the latter case, fighting over the disputed territory of Koruško between Austrian and Slovene forces from the former Austro-Hungarian army eventually led in May 1919 to a Yugoslav military offensive, which resulted in the defeat of the Austrians and the occupation of Klagenfurt on 6 June.[7] However, in the Carinthian plebiscite of 10 October 1920 many ethnic Slovenes voted to join Austria in preference to Yugoslavia (22,025 votes to 15,279), partly in response to the poor behaviour of Yugoslav (Serbian) occupying forces in the region and possibly also owing to the German government's financial support of the pro-Austrian campaign. This drew the border to the south of the line held by the Yugoslav army, leaving Klagenfurt in Austria.[8]

The country emerging from the peace settlement was much bigger and more diverse than Serbia had been. It had, according to a census of 31 January 1921, a population of 12,017,323. Of these, 4,129,638 inhabited pre-1914 Serbia. The census listed 5,602,227 of the inhabitants as Serbian Orthodox, 4,735,154 as Catholic and 1,337,687 Muslim, with smaller numbers of Protestants, Jews and Greek Catholics. It also gave 8,946,884 of the inhabitants as speaking Serbo-Croat and 1,024,761 Slovene. There were somewhat over half a million German-speakers, somewhat under half a million speakers each of Hungarian and Albanian and somewhat under a quarter of a million Romanians or Kutzovlachs. Although the new state was established under Serbia's leadership, this did not involve Serbian economic or demographic preponderance. Belgrade in 1921, with a population of 111,739, was barely larger than Croatia's capital of Zagreb, with 108,674, and Zagreb would be the financial capital of the new state.[9] The country was overwhelmingly agricultural: in 1921, 75.9 per cent of the working population was employed in agriculture, animal husbandry, forestry and fishing and only 9.8 per cent in industry and crafts.[10] Some 79.83 per cent of Yugoslavia's population lived in villages. Serbia (defined narrowly by its pre-1912 borders plus the adjacent territory taken from Bulgaria in 1919) was the most rural of Yugoslavia's constituent lands, with 85.71 per cent of its population inhabiting villages.[11] Yugoslavia had one of the lowest literacy rates in interwar Europe. Its inhabitants tended to be less well educated and literate the further south and east they lived, except for western Bosnia, which had the lowest literacy rate in the country. In January 1921, 35.57 per cent of the population of Serbia was literate (55.44 per cent of the male population and 16.49 per cent of the female population), whereas almost all Slovenia's population was literate.[12]

SERBIA

The Yugoslav state acted as a pillar of the Versailles order imposed on Europe by the victorious Entente powers. One centre of resistance to this order was Russia's Bolshevik regime. In response to the Bolshevik Revolution, Serbia's government had offered to send 30,000 Serbian volunteers to fight the Bolsheviks, provided the Entente powers provided supplies, transportation and equipment.[13] The offer was not taken up, but Aleksandar responded positively in early 1919 to a request for military assistance from the White Russian generals Kolchak and Denikin and sought to dispatch a Yugoslav expeditionary force of 40,000 to assist them. This too came to nothing given insufficient means and the Entente powers' unwillingness to provide the necessary support.[14] Serbian troops nevertheless served during the Russian Civil War alongside the British and French against the Bolsheviks in northern Russia. In the Murmansk region, by mid-July 1918 the Allied force of about 10,000 under British command included the Additional Battalion of the Volunteer Corps of Serbs, Croats and Slovenes—consisting mostly of Serbs and with a Serb commander—which originally numbered about 1,200. This unit helped suppress the Soviet authorities in the Kandalashsky and Murmansk regions. Serbian troops also engaged in heavy but unsuccessful fighting against Bolshevik forces near Archangel. The Additional Battalion was withdrawn from Russia by autumn 1919.[15] Yugoslavia refused to recognise the Soviet government until 1940 and took in as many as 31,000 White Russian refugees by April 1921, after which an additional 40,000—former soldiers of General Wrangel's defeated White army—were admitted by agreement. The Russian Orthodox Church's hierarchy also found refuge in Yugoslavia.[16] This became a factor in the hostility of the Communist International (Comintern) to the Yugoslav state, which had major consequences for Yugoslavia from 1941.

Hungary constituted another centre of opposition to the new European order. When Béla Kun's short-lived Communist regime in Budapest attempted to repudiate the Treaty of Trianon in 1919 through military offensives against Romania and Czechoslovakia, Yugoslavia mobilised to fight it. This was linked to harsh repression of social unrest in the Yugoslav territories bordering Hungary—Slovenia, Croatia and Vojvodina—and apparently inspired by its revolution; elements in the Yugoslav military considered establishing concentration camps.[17] A Hungarian irredentist uprising erupted in Subotica on 21 April 1920. Yugoslavia signed an alliance with Czechoslovakia against Hungary on 14 August 1920 and, after Charles, the last Habsburg emperor and king, returned to reclaim its throne, the allies issued an ultimatum to it on 3 April 1921. Romania then signed on to the ultimatum and, under pressure also from the Great Powers, Charles left Hungary on 5 April. Romania signed alliances with Czechoslovakia on 23 April and Yugoslavia on 7 June, creating a three-way system of alliances that became known as the Little Entente. The alliances obliged each partner to defend the other in case of unprovoked attack by Hungary and were intended to frustrate both Magyar irredentism and a Habsburg restoration. After Charles returned to Hungary on 21 October to try again, Yugoslavia and

ESTABLISHMENT OF THE YUGOSLAV STATE

Czechoslovakia mobilised, the Entente powers intervened once more, and the Hungarians were forced to dethrone the Habsburg dynasty and intern Charles.[18] The Yugoslav–Romanian alliance was directed also against Bulgaria and was strengthened by Aleksandar's marriage to Princess Maria of Romania on 8 June 1922. Relations with Greece remained good and on 10 May 1923 Athens and Belgrade agreed to establish a Yugoslav free zone at Salonika. These arrangements ultimately depended upon French leadership in Europe to maintain the Versailles order.

Yugoslavia and Italy signed the Treaty of Rapallo on 12 November 1920 and the Pact of Friendship of 27 January 1924. The latter, signed by Benito Mussolini, Pašić and foreign minister Ninčić, committed the parties to cooperate in maintaining the Versailles settlement, remain neutral if either were attacked without provocation by a third party, offer diplomatic and political support if the other's interests and security were endangered by a foreign attack and coordinate in the event of an international conflagration. The treaties allowed Italy to retain significant South Slav territories: in Carniola and the Austrian Littoral (which today comprise Istria and western Slovenia), the great ports of Trieste and Rijeka, the Dalmatian city of Zadar and the Adriatic islands of Cres, Lošinj, Palagruža and Lastovo. Rijeka was surrendered to Italy because Ninčić and Aleksandar believed Serbia had no particular interest in acquiring such a port in the northern Adriatic, which would divert Yugoslavia's trade away from Serbia, Vojvodina and Bosnia, and that Belgrade should instead develop its principal port at the Bay of Kotor in the south.[19] This would be a major Croatian grievance against Belgrade.

Yugoslavia and France signed a treaty of friendship on 11 November 1927 reaffirming Belgrade's commitment to the anti-revisionist bloc. Nevertheless, Yugoslavia had reservations about this alignment; its government, represented by Ninčić, had been slow to sign for fear of antagonising Italy, while Aleksandar himself had a jaded view of the French given their wartime behaviour as allies, so opposed the presence of a French military mission in his country.[20] Overall, Belgrade perceived Yugoslavia as having only one serious adversary on its borders (Italy), while other states were either weak (Austria, Hungary, Bulgaria, Albania) or friendly (Romania, Greece) and Yugoslavia was protected by regional alliances (the Little Entente and, from 1934, the Balkan Pact). This disincentivised any investment in modernising Yugoslavia's armed forces and arms industry, which eventually undermined its security.[21]

Yugoslav unification on a Serbian model

Yugoslavia's creation was unconstitutional. By proclaiming unification through direct agreement with the delegation of the National Council of Slovenes, Croats and Serbs, Aleksandar bypassed the other South Slav leaders—Serbian prime minister Pašić, Yugoslav Committee president Trumbić, the State of Slovenes, Croats and Serbs' president Korošec and the Serbian opposition. He thereby asserted his primacy in the new state.[22] His declaration of a 'unified Kingdom of Serbs, Croats and Slovenes' without reference to its provisional character disregarded the request of the National Council's delegation that the definite organisation of the state be decided only by the constituent assembly. It conflicted also with Serbia's constitution, which specified that only a great national parliament could execute such an act. Aleksandar thereby pre-empted the constituent assembly's competence to resolve, in particular, the question of the monarchy. His declaration was then treated by supporters of the new order as a 'super-constitutional' act that the subsequent constituent assembly could not overturn. It meant the new state was from the start founded on an unconstitutional and undemocratic basis, hinting at Aleksandar's future autocratic evolution.[23]

The act of unification was thus a royal putsch similar to those executed by the previous King Aleksandar in 1894 and 1901. Serbia's leading constitutional law scholar, Slobodan Jovanović, who had come of age opposing Aleksandar Obrenović's regime of successive putsches, noted that in the act of unification, the National Council had acted 'outside the law' while the prince regent had acted 'contrary to the law', and that the Kingdom of Serbia had been abolished and replaced by a new state of Serbs, Croats and Slovenes without authorisation from any appropriate constitutional body.[24] More recently, the historian Ljubodrag Dimić has noted that 'the very act of unification by its very nature contradicted the constitution of the Kingdom of Serbia. Had the constitution been respected, unification could not have been executed in the way in which it was done, nor would it have been possible to form the government and the Provisional National Legislature in the way in which they were formed.' This was necessitated, too, by the Serbian leadership's rejection of the request of the National Council of Slovenes, Croats and Serbs that unification be conducted through agreement between two state entities: the Kingdom of Serbia and the State of Slovenes, Croats and Serbs. This was to ensure the complete erasure of the latter's statehood but required the corresponding erasure of Serbia's own statehood and constitutional order. Consequently, 'The constitutional-legal chaos provided the opportunity for the monarch (regent) and government to rule, essentially, without any constitutional limitation.' Rule by government decree replaced the rule of law.[25]

In the circumstances of national exuberance among Serbia's political classes, however, this royal putsch was received more warmly than most previous ones. Yugoslavia's first prime minister, Protić, addressing the Serbian parliament on 29 December, admitted that this 'great historical act' was 'executed without your formal participation' but asserted that 'we were convinced you were with us'.[26] Indeed, Serbia's parliament then 'unanimously accepted and affirmed the unification of Serbs, Croats and Slovenes in a common state'.[27] This was again arguably unconstitutional, since the Kingdom of Serbia and its parliament had formally ceased to exist on 1 December, but it did lend the new state democratic legitimacy in Serbia. Unfortunately for the government, politicians in Croatia including Stjepan

ESTABLISHMENT OF THE YUGOSLAV STATE

Radić (1871–1928), whose party, soon named the Croat Republican Peasant Party (HRSS), rapidly emerged as the principal Croat party in Yugoslavia, then demanded that Croatia's parliament similarly be allowed to ratify the act of union. Since the government was not confident of the outcome it did not allow this, so the new state lacked from the start the democratic legitimacy in Croatia that it had in Serbia.[28] The parties to the unification had accepted the need for a provisional all-Yugoslav legislature, but its formation was not agreed upon prior to unification, given the opposition of Serbia's leaders to forming any provisional legislature whose delegates from the former Habsburg lands would be appointed by Habsburg-era legislatures. Thus, unification gave the new kingdom a common monarch but in the immediate term no common government or parliament. There was no constitution covering the new state until the constituent assembly completed its work in June 1921; the government applied Serbia's constitution across the new kingdom when convenient but at other times disregarded it, with the result that Yugoslavia's government was non-constitutional for its first two and a half years.[29]

Several factors combined to ensure Serbia's hegemony in the new union. Serbs were easily the largest national group in the new state and the most widely dispersed geographically, inhabiting in significant numbers all the constituent provinces of the state except the Slovene territories in the extreme north-west. The overwhelming majority of Serbs in the former Habsburg lands of Vojvodina, Croatia-Slavonia, Dalmatia and Bosnia-Hercegovina gave their support to political parties favouring a unitarist constitutional order for the new state, therefore to strong control by the Belgrade government over the entire country. Other than Montenegro, whose independence and statehood were extinguished by Serbia prior to Yugoslav unification, Serbia was the only country in the new state possessing a recent tradition of independent statehood or its own army. The western South Slavs were constrained by their fear of Italy as well as fear that Serbia itself might conduct a narrower form of unification—Great Serbian rather than Yugoslav, as per Simović's threat—that would leave a vulnerable rump Croatia along with Slovenia outside the union. Finally, the massive outbreak of social unrest engulfing the Habsburg South Slav lands in 1918, closely following the Bolshevik Revolution, prompted the National Council to seek the Serbian army's protection of the social order, at the price of further weakening its hand vis-à-vis Belgrade.

The Army of the Kingdom of Serbs, Croats and Slovenes was formed around Serbia's former army, which in December 1918 numbered 120,494 soldiers and 6,936 officers. The new army peaked in size at 437,664 mobilised soldiers and 13,795 officers in July 1919 and averaged just over 200,000 soldiers up to May 1920; nearly half its officers—including all its naval officers—had fought on the Central Powers' side, primarily in Austria-Hungary's armed forces. By March 1922, 26.08 per cent of the new state's generals and admirals were veterans of the Habsburg forces. However, officers from the former Montenegrin and particularly Austro-Hungarian armies were discriminated against in terms of both military rank and nationality. This ensured the hegemony within the new army, throughout the kingdom's existence, of the old Serbian army's officer corps and of Serbs from Serbia generally. Students in the Military Academy were 60 per cent Serb in 1919, rising to 84 per cent in 1928, although naval officers remained predominantly Croat and Slovene.[30] Although at least some elements within the Yugoslav army's military and veterans' associations attempted to be inclusive toward former Austro-Hungarian officers, their efforts came up against the army's dominant military culture, which identified entirely and solely with the legacy of Serbia's army and its struggle against the Central Powers.[31] Thus, for example, Field Marshal Svetozar Borojević von Bojna, an ethnic Serb who had commanded Austro-Hungarian forces in the defence of the empire's South Slav lands from the Italians, so could reasonably be considered a Serb and Yugoslav military hero, was not welcome in Yugoslavia and died in poverty in Austria. Likewise, members of the old Austro-Hungarian gendarmerie were purged while the old Serbian gendarmerie was extended to encompass all the new kingdom, constituting another tool in the hands of Belgrade for controlling the population of the former Habsburg lands.[32]

The clinching factor ensuring Serbian hegemony over the former Habsburg territories was support for a centralist constitutional order on the part of these territories' Serbs; the prečani acted as the linchpin of Belgrade's rule west of the Drina. This alignment of the Serbs outside Serbia with those inside was not simply conditioned by their Serb nationality, but reflected the political and historical circumstances in which the various Serb groups found themselves. The Serb political classes of Vojvodina and Srem, immediately to the north of Belgrade, had long constituted a vocal irredenta that looked directly toward Serbia. Their principal party, the Radical Party, was the sister party of the Radicals in Serbia and merged formally with them following unification. The Serb political classes of the Croat-majority lands of Croatia-Slavonia and Dalmatia, personified by their dominant figure Pribićević, had long sought protection of the Serb minority's status vis-à-vis the Croat majority. This had led them, before 1914, to align themselves with Hungary against the Great Austrian Catholic circle around Franz Ferdinand, whose most hardline Croat supporters were bitterly anti-Serb. Pribićević and his followers subsequently sought to guarantee the Croatian Serbs' position by uncompromising support for Yugoslav unitarism, whereby Croatia's autonomy would be eliminated and with it any possibility of Croatian oppression of the Croatian Serbs. The Bosnian Serb political classes, meanwhile, initially sought to maintain unity with their Bosnian Croat and Muslim counterparts against the danger of social unrest and inter-communal strife which in 1918 threatened to overwhelm Bosnia-Hercegovina. Over and above their desire, as Serbs, to be united with Serbia, their support for Yugoslav unitarism was an extension of their support for inter-religious Bosnian unity.

ESTABLISHMENT OF THE YUGOSLAV STATE

The Serb political classes of Vojvodina, Croatia-Slavonia, Dalmatia and Bosnia-Hercegovina consequently came together in the new kingdom to ensure its organisation on a unitarist and centralist basis under effective domination by Belgrade and Serbia. The manner in which they did so helped transform the domestic balance of forces in Serbia itself—part of the wider transformation that entry into the common South Slav state produced. For 1918 saw both unification of Serbs in a single state and broader South Slav unification, and Serbia's political classes were forced to adapt to belonging to a multinational state while broadening their ranks to include Serbs from very different political traditions. Ultimately, Yugoslav unification exacerbated differences not just between the political classes of Serbs and non-Serbs and of Serbs of Serbia and prečani Serbs, but between different factions in Serbia itself. In the short term, however, the three principal and previously mutually antagonistic elements in Serbia's politics—the prince regent and his court, the Radicals and the anti-Radical parliamentary opposition (Independent Radicals, Liberals/Nationalists and Progressives)—along with the political classes of the Serbs outside Serbia, closed ranks against all federalist and autonomist currents among non-Serbs.

Negotiations between representatives of the National Council and Serbia's parties resulted in a projected first Yugoslav government under Pašić, but Aleksandar refused to grant him the mandate out of animosity toward him and because he wanted to mollify the Serbian opposition. This royal fiat created a very negative impression on politicians from the former Habsburg lands.[33] Aleksandar instead appointed Yugoslavia's first government on 20 December 1918 under Protić as prime minister with Trumbić as foreign minister, dismissing Serbia's old government on the same day. Eight portfolios in the new government went to ministers from Serbia, four to ministers from Croatia-Slavonia, three to ministers from Bosnia-Hercegovina, two to ministers from Slovenia, one to a minister from Dalmatia and one to a minister from Montenegro. Of these twenty ministers, thirteen were Serbs, four Croats, two Slovenes and one a Muslim Bosniak. Pribićević became interior minister, thereby controlling administrative and police muscle in the new state.[34] He had been nominated for the post by the National Council's delegates in the belief that, as a Serb from Croatia with a proven record of defending Croatia under Austria-Hungary, he would bring the Serbs of Serbia and Croats together.[35] Instead, his brand of centralist repression proved more extreme than what any of Serbia's leading politicians favoured. Serbian domination was thus assured at the start of the transition period prior to promulgation of the constitution, during which centralism was ruthlessly implemented.

The government on 22 December formally confirmed the name of the new state, 'Kingdom of Serbs, Croats and Slovenes', and decreed its flag would be a tricolour of blue, white and red horizontal stripes while the coat of arms would be formed of the Serbian two-headed eagle holding a shield, on the right of which would be the

Serbian four-Cs emblem, on the left the Croatian chequerboard and on the bottom an emblem representing old Illyria and Slovenia, with a crescent moon and three stars.[36] The symbolism acknowledged the heritage of each of the three recognised Yugoslav tribes, with the Serbian one predominating. The National Council of Slovenes, Croats and Serbs was almost immediately abolished as an administrative body while the national governments of Croatia, Bosnia-Hercegovina, Dalmatia and Slovenia were dismissed on 7 January 1919 and replaced with more limited administrations named 'country governments' (zemaljske vlade) rather than national governments, to avoid any implication that they possessed rights as states. Their competencies were subordinated to the relevant ministries of the Belgrade government. The governor (ban) of Croatia was replaced on 18 January; the new ban, a prominent member of Pribićević's Croat–Serb Coalition, stated upon his appointment that Croatia's government would have no state-right role but merely execute its functions 'according to the directives and under the control of the central government' in Belgrade.[37] Sections of Serbian criminal law pertaining to crimes against the king, royal house, state and constitutional order were extended across Yugoslavia on 25 February 1919, as was the authority of Serbian military courts over civilians in the former Habsburg lands on 28 April.[38] The ministries of internal affairs and justice required state officials and judges to pledge allegiance to the king; this was widely resisted in Croatia.[39]

Under pressure from Belgrade, the Yugoslav Committee on 12 February 1919 renounced its mandate to represent the formerly Austro-Hungarian South Slavs,[40] dissolving itself altogether on 2 May. Montenegro's Great National Parliament on 20 April 1919 transferred power from its executive national council to a representative of the Belgrade government, then dissolved both itself and the executive national council. Montenegro soon lost all remaining vestiges even of provincial administrative particularity. The Great National Council of Vojvodina was already dissolved on 20 December 1918, followed by the National Administration on 11 March 1919, and the region's administration transferred to the Belgrade government. Eventually, after the constitution's proclamation in June 1921, the country governments would be downgraded again to 'provincial administrations'; this would last until 1924 when the individual Yugoslav lands lost all traces of administrative autonomy. However, they remained divided into six legal regions: Slovenia and Dalmatia, Croatia and Slavonia, Bosnia-Hercegovina, Vojvodina, Montenegro and pre-1914 Serbia. Above these were four supreme courts: the Belgrade Court of Cassation with a chamber in Novi Sad and separate courts of appeal in Belgrade and Skopje, the Chamber of Seven in Zagreb with separate chambers for Croatia-Slavonia and for Slovenia-Dalmatia, the Supreme Court of Bosnia-Hercegovina in Sarajevo and the Great Court of Montenegro in Podgorica.[41]

State control of religious-political affairs was ensured by a decree on the organisation of the Ministry of Religion of 31 July 1919, subordinating all religious establishments in the new kingdom to state control. The unification of the Orthodox churches within Yugoslavia to form the new Serbian Orthodox Patriarchate of the Kingdom of Serbs, Croats and Slovenes was proclaimed on 12 September 1920 with the Patriarchate in Constantinople's blessing, thereby restoring the Serbian Patriarchate dissolved in 1766. This formally unified the members of five different autocephalous churches: the metropolitanate of the Kingdom of Serbia; the metropolitanate of the Kingdom of Montenegro; the metropolitanate of Karlovci (to which the Serbs of Croatia-Slavonia and Vojvodina had belonged); the metropolitanate of Bukovina-Dalmatia (to which Serbs in the Austrian part of Austria-Hungary had belonged); and the Ecumenical Patriarchate of Constantinople (to which the Serbs of Bosnia-Hercegovina and the territories conquered by Serbia and Montenegro in the Balkan Wars had belonged). Nevertheless, the church remained fragmented in its allegiances; in Bosnia-Hercegovina it supported the Radicals but in Croatia-Slavonia it did not. This undoubtedly contributed to the much greater Radical electoral success in the former than in the latter. When the synod of the newly unified church elected the sitting Metropolitan of Serbia, Dimitrije Pavlović, as its first Patriarch on 28 September, the government rejected this method of selection and passed a law on 23 October ruling that an 'electoral body' presided over by the king had the right to select the Patriarch from a choice of three candidates submitted by the synod. Even though the Orthodox Church was eventually formally separated from the state by a law of 8 November 1929, the state retained significant control over it, including the right to dispose of its property and the king's right to confirm or veto the election of the Patriarch and bishops.[42]

Governmental power in Yugoslavia was thus rapidly concentrated exclusively in the Belgrade government's hands. Serbs from Serbia comprised twelve out of fourteen prime ministers who held office in the Yugoslav kingdom and almost always held the key ministries of the interior, army and navy, foreign affairs and justice. The Serbian Ekavian dialect was imposed as Yugoslavia's official language—as Skerlić had advocated but without his quid pro quo of the Serbs' adoption of the Latin alphabet, so Cyrillic remained the principal official alphabet. The construction of this big centralised state involved a huge expansion of the bureaucracy: pre-war Serbia had had 40,000 bureaucrats, while by 1925 Yugoslavia had 280,000, despite having a population only three times larger.[43] Paradoxically, it was the traditionally anti-bureaucratic Radicals who oversaw this. Nevertheless, as was long the case with Serbia, with state expansion came modernisation, now catalysed by union with more developed formerly Habsburg territories. The government passed a law on 23 January 1919 formally adopting the Gregorian calendar for all Yugoslavia, replacing the Julian calendar previously used in Serbia, which was synchronised with the rest of Europe. Serbia had also lagged behind Western and Central Europe regarding social security; since the Yugoslav constitution adopted in June 1921 guaranteed basic rights of social security for workers, the government in August 1921 passed a law providing security in cases of incapacity, old age and death, which came into force in Serbia and Montenegro on 1 January 1922. It was extended later that year to provide security for invalids, tenants and those suffering a death in the family. Workers' security extended to medical assistance and sick pay.[44] Thus, the two sides of monarchical government—modernisation and authoritarianism—persisted.

Repression in the periphery

Belgrade sought to maintain the diverse new state's unity through repression, whose character varied according to Serbia's particular relationship with each territory in question. When Radić sent a memorandum to the Paris peace conference rejecting as illegitimate Croatia's inclusion in Yugoslavia under the Karađorđević dynasty, on the grounds that it had not been sanctioned by Croatia's parliament, he was arrested on Pribićević's initiative on 25 March 1919 and detained for nearly a year. Other Croat politicians who resisted the new order were also jailed. In response to the demand of the Croat Union, representing the moderate wing of the Croatian opposition, for restoration of the Croatian Home Guard as an autonomous Croatian military force, a royal edict in September 1919 extended Serbian military law across the new state's entire territory. The army's compulsory registration of draught animals through branding sparked a major peasant revolt near Zagreb in September 1920, which according to local officials aimed at establishing a 'Croat peasant republic'. The army and gendarmerie suppressed it at the cost of at least fifteen peasants' lives, with others subjected to corporal punishment.[45] The army acted to protect landlords in the former Habsburg lands from the widespread peasant unrest, suppressing not only revolutionary agitation but any seen as anti-Serbian, and widely treating the Croatian and Bosnian population, in particular, as an enemy in need of disciplining. Soldiers inflicted corporal punishment on peasants who expressed subversive views, assaulted civilians for minor or imagined transgressions and confiscated property arbitrarily. But Croat resistance would prove unbreakable, permanently destabilising the Yugoslav state.

In Bosnia-Hercegovina, former Austro-Hungarian officials were purged and replaced by bureaucrats imported from Serbia, a process assisted by interior minister Pribićević and by Šola's Serb-dominated Bosnian government.[46] Members of irregular or paramilitary Serb groups—former volunteers from Russia and Chetnik guerrillas—engaged in widespread terrorising and looting of civilians, particularly Muslim Bosniaks. A Serb peasant uprising against the Muslim landlords erupted as the Habsburg regime collapsed, growing into a rampage against the Muslim population as a whole involving vandalism, assault and murder. By September 1920, approximately 2,000 Muslim Bosniaks had been killed in the new state.[47] Not only landlords but Muslim peasants were targeted and their land usurped by Serb peasants and Serbian army volunteers. Muslim Bosniaks responded by closing ranks behind a single political party, the Yugoslav Muslim Organisation (JMO). At Husino in the Tuzla region of north-east Bosnia, an uprising of predominantly Croat miners broke out on 25 December 1920, as the culmination of a Bosnian miners' strike. The authorities suppressed it by mobilising a purely Serb militia while the Radical press denounced the strike as Croat, anti-Serb and anti-Yugoslav. Seven miners were killed.[48] Likewise, the Muslim population of the part of the Sanjak previously annexed by Montenegro suffered massive violence in November 1924, when the assassination of the governor of the Kolašin district, a strong unionist, was blamed on Muslims, prompting a massacre by local Montenegrins of about 600 Muslims in Šahovići and the surrounding area. Continuing anti-Muslim violence in the Sanjak prompted many Muslims to emigrate to Bosnia-Hercegovina, Macedonia or Turkey, consolidating the Serb ethnic and economic hold over the area.[49]

Peasant discontent in Bosnia-Hercegovina and other parts of Yugoslavia was partially accommodated by the government. An Interim Decree on Land Reform was issued on 25 February 1919 for all Yugoslavia, abolishing serfdom and transferring ownership of the lands to the former serfs, while also stipulating that the former landlords should be indemnified. This reflected also the Serbian leadership's need to fulfil its October 1912 promise to the Macedonian peasantry regarding social and economic liberation. A promise made on 20 February 1917, to provide plots of land to all military and non-military volunteers (primarily from Austria-Hungary) of five and three hectares apiece respectively, was fulfilled by a government decree of 8 November 1919, which also sought to ensure volunteers would not support revolutionary politics.[50] However, successive Yugoslav governments struggled to steer agrarian reform between the conflicting landlord and peasant lobbies, and the agrarian question—at all times less important in pre-1912 Serbia than in most other parts of Yugoslavia—was never fully resolved in the kingdom. The rural population therefore continued till the end to include both impoverished holders of uneconomic micro-holdings and large landowners who evaded redistribution.[51] In response to the Husino uprising, the government issued a decree on 29 December known as the Pronouncement (Obznana) banning all Communist organisations, meetings, newspapers and manifestations. It also authorised expulsion from state service of all bureaucrats and from the country of all foreigners who propagated Bolshevism, removed stipends from Communist students and banned in Belgrade 'all manifestations of a subversive or incendiary character' while the constituent assembly was in progress.[52]

With repression came exploitation. At the time of Yugoslavia's unification, five different currencies were circulating on its territory: the Austro-Hungarian crown, German mark, Bulgarian lev, Montenegrin perper and Serbian dinar. Every owner of crowns had 20 per cent of them confiscated by the government on 5

September 1919 as an alleged deflationary measure, yet the government then put the confiscated crowns back into circulation to cover its expenses, thereby exacerbating the very inflation which the confiscation was supposed to have combated. Instead of replacing crowns with dinars at the time of unification when the exchange rate was 1:2 in favour of the crown, the government conducted the replacement only between 16 February and 3 April 1920. By this time, the exchange rate was 4:1 in favour of the dinar, largely owing to the government's own encouragement of the crown's inflation. This amounted to a material loss for the former Habsburg lands of 1.4 billion crowns and significantly increased Serbia's purchasing power at their expense.[53]

Vojvodina (Banat, Bačka and Baranja), one of the richest parts of the new state alongside Slovenia, was subjected to particularly harsh exploitation. At the time of unification, it possessed 20 per cent of the state's industrial enterprises and 25 per cent of its railway network as well as its best agricultural land. Yet the majority of its population was non-Slavic and disenfranchised.[54] Subsequently, for the first five months of 1925, it constituted 11.5 per cent of Yugoslavia's population but contributed 36.9 per cent of the state budget, compared with pre-Yugoslav Serbia including the territories acquired in the Balkan Wars plus Montenegro, which constituted 37 per cent of the population but contributed only 16.9 per cent of the budget. A peasant in Vojvodina in 1926 paid a 20 per cent higher direct tax than a peasant in Serbia, while a teacher's salary in Vojvodina was significantly lower than in Serbia. Overall, Vojvodina contributed over 25 per cent of the state's total taxes in 1920–1928 and, though this imbalance was corrected somewhat thereafter, it continued to pay disproportionately in the 1930s. Agrarian reform hit Vojvodina, as a region with a disproportionate number of large landholdings, particularly hard; the non-Slavic ethnic minorities (Germans, Hungarians, Romanians) were excluded from redistribution. Consequently, many families, particularly from these minorities but even Serbs and other Slavs, were financially ruined. The region's agriculture declined: in 1921–1929 the number of heads of cattle fell from about 47,000 to 27,000 and of swine from about 1,000,000 to 600,000. Vojvodina's local bureaucracy was massively purged, in particular of ethnic Germans and Hungarians, and colonised by officials from Serbia. The Vojvodinian Serb writer Vasa Stajić wrote in 1922 that 'they came without love for Vojvodina, revolted by the ethnic diversity of its population, convinced that they were doing a patriotic act by plundering and degrading it'. Or as the famous writer Miloš Crnjanski, a Hungarian Serb, wrote in 1925, Vojvodina's people had 'an old, nice, sunny impression. That which will change the picture for Banat, and alienate it, will be the system of taxes. Taxes, huge taxes. It isn't known who pays, or how much. It isn't written anywhere. It happens roughly and by surprise. A horseman arrives in the village and, like a Turk, seeks a head-tax.' The system was enforced through harassment and repression of local members of the opposition, who were regularly beaten by the police while their supporters were barred from voting.[55]

ESTABLISHMENT OF THE YUGOSLAV STATE

Montenegro was treated more as an occupied than as a liberated country, with its population subject to curfew and other restrictions on liberty. Montenegro's flag, which had continued flying under Austro-Hungarian occupation, was now removed from public buildings, and those who expressed a Montenegrin national identity or loyalty to King Nikola were regularly imprisoned. The purge of his supporters from the administration, the imposition of an alien administration headed by Svetozar Tomić, a Serbian foreign ministry functionary, and the systematic denigration of the former king and dynasty helped push many Montenegrins into active opposition, in a context of widespread poverty and hunger.[56] Consequently, a Green uprising erupted in Montenegro at the start of 1919, on the eve of Orthodox Christmas—hence known as the Christmas Uprising—led by Jovan Plamenac and Krsto Popović, with the date chosen to recall the mythical 1702 massacre of Muslims immortalised in Njegoš's *The Mountain Wreath*.[57] Rebel forces surrounded Cetinje and other Montenegrin towns; though they were defeated outside the Cetinje region within a couple of days, fighting around Cetinje itself peaked on 5–7 January, when the rebels attempted unsuccessfully to enter the town.

The rebel leadership—the Ustasha (Rebel) Council—accepted Montenegro's inclusion in Yugoslavia but demanded the annulment of the acts of the Podgorica Great National Parliament as contrary to Montenegro's constitution and that Montenegro's status be decided at Yugoslavia's constituent assembly.[58] The Italians, who as part of a multinational Entente force had troops on the Montenegrin coast, encouraged the revolt. For the first time, supporters of the rebellion, in an appeal to the League of Nations, claimed the Montenegrins were a nation distinct from the Serbs.[59] The rebellion was effectively defeated by mid-January, but guerrilla resistance continued. Yugoslav forces supported by White paramilitaries employed extreme brutality to crush the resistance, often beating, torturing and killing members of the rebels' families and burning and plundering their homes and farmsteads. Families and even whole villages visited by the rebels were interned, including women and children.[60] According to a contemporary Serbian source, some 5,000 Montenegrin homes were thus burned between 1919 and 1924, when guerrilla resistance finally ended.[61]

The final act in Montenegro's annexation occurred on 29 April 1919, when the Great National Parliament met for the last time and voted to transfer all executive powers in Montenegro to an administrator appointed from Belgrade. However, so alienated was much of Montenegro's population from the new order that the Communists won the constituent assembly elections there with 37.99 per cent of the vote. Montenegro's government-in-exile, meanwhile, was excluded from the Paris peace conference and the French, British and Americans terminated relations with it in 1920–1921. The Italians dissented from this policy and in May 1919 permitted the government-in-exile to organise a new armed force at Gaeta on Italian territory, following which an armed detachment of Montenegrin exiles from Italy led by Popović landed on the Montenegrin coast in July to join the resistance.[62] But the Montenegrin army in Italy was merely a pawn in Rome's conflict with Belgrade. Ultimately falling victim to Italian–Yugoslav rapprochement, it was disbanded during 1921.[63] After Nikola's death on 1 March of that year, the Montenegrin government-in-exile, abandoned by Italy, finally collapsed by the end of 1922. The Green émigrés were amnestied in 1925 and their leader, Plamenac, returned to Montenegro and became a Radical. Yet Montenegrin opposition to the new order persisted and a federalist Montenegrin Party was founded in 1925.[64]

The Albanian-inhabited territory conquered in the Balkan Wars was reoccupied by Serbia's army from autumn 1918, involving massacres of Albanians and destruction of their homes and villages. The resulting Albanian minority in Yugoslavia numbered 439,657 of whom 288,900 were in Kosovo, according to the 1921 census, although the real figure was probably significantly larger, probably about 700,000–800,000.[65] Pećanac was tasked with forming a gendarmerie in Peć following its reoccupation by the Serbian army; the gendarme commander in the town subsequently admitted: 'A gendarmerie formed in this way not only did not live up to its calling but was a haven for thieves and bandits, for whom only identification papers were needed to show that they were gendarmes.' Local people were indiscriminately arrested and robbed by those tasked with establishing order.[66] Even Adam Pribićević, Svetozar's brother, when he settled in Kosovo after the war, was physically harassed and threatened with a gun by the municipal president, who told him, 'You shot at us across the Drina' and 'Go back to your Franz Ferdinand'. Adam commented: 'And my party was then in government and my brother a minister! It can be imagined what the police did to the unfortunate peasants, when they attacked me like this.'[67]

Albanians engaged in armed resistance to Yugoslavia in the form of the Kaçak movement, whose forces numbered around 10,000 armed rebels by 1919. A Committee for the National Defence of Kosovo was established in Shkodër in November 1918 under Hasan Prishtina's leadership to support this resistance. It ordered a full-scale rebellion on 6 May 1919; this was crushed, but armed resistance continued. The authorities resorted to forming armed bands from local Serbs and to interning the families of suspected rebels in camps in central Serbia.[68] Belgrade also incited its own Albanian factions in northern Albania to rebel against the Tirana regime, seeking to defeat the resistance in Kosovo by neutralising its hinterland across the border; a pro-Yugoslav north Albanian leader consequently proclaimed a Republic of Mirdita. A conflict zone between Albania and Yugoslavia thus emerged, approaching outright military conflict by summer 1920, with troops from each state crossing into the territory of the other. Since the border between the two states was not finalised until November 1921, this was also an outright conflict over territory.

Serbian troops in Kosovo killed 6,040 people and destroyed 3,873 houses in January–February 1919. One Albanian source claimed that by 1921 the figure had reached 12,371 killed, 22,110 imprisoned and 6,000 houses destroyed. Although perhaps exaggerated, these figures would have been surpassed by the time Albanian armed resistance was finally crushed.[69] About 40,000 Albanians fled or were expelled to Albania by 1921, with a more gradual exodus of Albanians to Turkey numbering about 45,000 by 1939.[70] Serb and Montenegrin colonists, including people who had participated in the repression, were settled on land confiscated from rebels.[71] This policy was promoted especially by Yugoslavia's Democratic Party while in government, linked to its support for agrarian reform; in principle, this benefited poorer Albanians too, but they received smaller plots than the Serb colonists.[72] By the late 1930s, about 60,000 colonists, mostly Serbs, had been introduced into the Kosovo region.[73] The passage of the interim decree on land reform of 25 February 1919 prompted tenants in 'South Serbia' (Kosovo, Macedonia and the Sanjak of Novi Pazar) to cease paying rent to their mostly Muslim landlords. Land reform was not fully legally regulated until the 1930s and the reform process was still incomplete when Yugoslavia entered World War II in 1941.[74] However, during the interwar period as a whole, 200,000 hectares of agricultural land in Kosovo—over a third of the total amount of agricultural land there—were confiscated from the original owners, of which half was distributed to colonists, while about 90,000–150,000 Albanians and other Muslims emigrated from the territory.[75]

Serbia's constitution was extended to South Serbia at the start of August 1919, and on 21 February 1921 the provisional legal state in the region was annulled and the Kingdom of Serbia's regular laws came into effect there.[76] However, Belgrade did not respect the terms of the peace settlement requiring it to respect minority rights. Albanian-language education was actively suppressed; Albanian schools were closed or converted into Serbian schools, so that by 1930 there were no Albanian-language schools in the country, except for some clandestine ones. The initial policy of educating Albanians in Serbian-language schools was eventually dropped for fear of creating educated opponents of the regime, in favour of the policy of discouraging public education for Albanians altogether, except in mektebs (Islamic seminaries). The share of Albanians among high school pupils in Kosovo fell to 2 per cent. All Albanian-language publications were suppressed. This contrasted with the treatment of other national minorities—Germans, Hungarians, Czechs, Turks, Russians—which were permitted their own schools and newspapers. The goal was forcible assimilation of the Albanians on the grounds that they were Albanianised Serbs.[77]

Stability in Kosovo was contingent upon Belgrade's relations with Tirana. The irredentist politician Hasan Prishtina briefly became prime minister of Albania in December 1921 but was overthrown by interior minister Ahmed Zogolli, who soon renamed himself Ahmet Zogu. He sought reconciliation with Yugoslavia; diplomatic relations were finally established in March 1922 and the violence in Kosovo subsided. But Albania remained a battleground for influence between Yugoslavia and Italy. In June 1924, Zogu was overthrown and a left-wing government took power under Fan Noli, backed by the Soviet Union and showing irredentist aspirations. Belgrade responded by arming rebels under Zogu, who consequently overthrew Fan Noli in December and re-established an initially pro-Yugoslav regime. Zogu suppressed the Committee for the National Defence of Kosovo and systematically killed or scattered its activists, eventually assassinating Hasan Prishtina in 1933.[78] But he also rapidly transformed Albania into Italy's satellite, ensuring continued rivalry between Rome and Belgrade over it. Tirana's support for Albanian irredentism resumed with Italian encouragement. Zogu's assumption on 1 September 1928 of the name and title Zog I, 'King of the Albanians', implied an irredentist claim on Yugoslavia's Albanian-inhabited territories.

Belgrade also pursued the forcible assimilation of the ethnic Macedonian population, imposing upon it Serbian laws and Serbian officials with Serb nationalist credentials. The Orthodox community was transferred to the Serbian Orthodox Church's authority in September 1920 and all links with the Greek or Bulgarian churches suppressed. Exarchist priests and Bulgarian-oriented schoolteachers were once again expelled and all Bulgarian clubs and societies closed. Serbian was declared the official language of education and administration and writing or publishing was forbidden in the population's native language (close to Bulgarian, it would be standardised after World War II as Macedonian). Bulgarian-language signs and books were removed. Bulgarian surnames were forcibly Serbianised, with Stankov becoming Stanković and Atanasov becoming Atanacković. Popular alienation from the new state was reflected in the constituent assembly elections in which 36.72 per cent of Macedonian votes went to the Communists. Meanwhile VMRO, based in Bulgarian Macedonia where it formed a state within a state, waged a guerrilla struggle in Yugoslav Macedonia which escalated in spring 1922, with 1,675 active komitas operating there by 1923. The authorities registered 467 VMRO attacks between 1919 and 1934 that killed 185 Yugoslav officials and wounded 253 while killing or wounding 268 civilians, including the massacre of 20–30 Serb colonists at Kadrifakovo on 16 January 1923, while acts of counter-terror included the massacre of all male villagers from Garvan in March of the same year on the orders of the Bregalnica district chief. Macedonia became the most heavily garrisoned territory in Yugoslavia, home to around 50,000 or more soldiers, gendarmes, military policemen and state-sponsored members of the Association Against Bulgarian Bandits. Belgrade planned to settle 50,000 Serbian families in Macedonia, in particular on land bought from emigrating Ottoman landowners, and to use them both to fight VMRO and to Serbianise the territory. This failed, and only 4,200 households had settled there by 1940.[79] Meanwhile, Yugoslav Macedonia suffered economically from its separation from the rest of historic Macedonia, and its road and railway connections remained underdeveloped throughout the interwar period, partly for supposed strategic reasons.[80] The region, along with Kosovo, had the worst literacy rate in Yugoslavia after western Bosnia. Half its schools were closed because the state either could not afford to pay for teachers or paid them so little they abandoned their posts.[81]

ESTABLISHMENT OF THE YUGOSLAV STATE

VMRO's terrorist activities in Macedonia eventually prompted a warning from Aleksandar to the Bulgarian ambassador that 'insofar as you are not in a position to guarantee order on your territory, I will go to establish it myself'.[82] There followed a joint Yugoslav–Romanian–Greek ultimatum to Bulgaria in September 1922, demanding it resettle from its border territories into the interior those refugees collaborating with the guerrillas. Bulgaria's anti-militarist prime minister Aleksandar Stamboliyski genuinely wanted reconciliation with Belgrade and signed the Treaty of Niš on 23 March 1923, committing Sofia to suppressing VMRO. But this helped trigger his overthrow by VMRO and other right-wing nationalists on 9 June; he was brutally tortured and the hand with which he had signed the treaty symbolically amputated, after which he was murdered and his headless corpse thrown into the River Maritsa. The new government, under Aleksandar Tsankov, repudiated the Treaty of Niš and the VMRO terrorist campaign in Yugoslav Macedonia escalated, peaking with the assassination of a Yugoslav general in Štip on 7 October 1927. Yugoslavia responded by heavily fortifying its border with Bulgaria, restricting access through it and signing a treaty of friendship with Greece on 17 August 1926.

Formation of the Democratic Party

While Belgrade's hold on the new state's territory was repressively enforced, Serbia's political parties sought to co-opt political factions from outside Serbia. The more conservative Serb factions in Croatia and Bosnia-Hercegovina, which were more narrowly Serb nationalist and had been more pro-regime under the Habsburgs, tended to unite with the Old Radicals, while the more oppositional and Yugoslavist factions tended to unite with the Independents and their Progressive and Liberal allies. A conference in Sarajevo on 15–16 February 1919, under Pribićević's leadership and the auspices of Šola's Bosnian government, was held to unite unitarist currents in Yugoslavia behind Pribićević's project of a new Yugoslav centralist party. On that occasion, Pribićević stated: 'The beginning of this great creation, so I believe, is that we create our great national personality, that we build it united, that there should disappear not only formally, but that there should completely disappear Croatia, Serbia, Bosnia and Dalmatia and that there arise a completely unified Kingdom of Serbs, Croats and Slovenes.'[83] Most Bosnian political currents participated in this meeting, along with Pribićević's Croat–Serb Coalition from Croatia and a party of liberal unitarists from Slovenia, but the principal Bosnian Croat and Muslim factions refused to join the new party given its extreme centralism. Formally founded at this conference as the Democratic Party, it was consequently Serb-dominated, uniting the principal unitarists among the Croatian Serb and Bosnian Serb elites with some minor unitarist factions among Croats, Slovenes and Muslims. The Democratic Party would contribute 30 of the 42 delegates in the Provisional National Legislature of the new kingdom allotted to Bosnia-Hercegovina.[84]

It proved impossible to unite the new Democratic Party in the former Habsburg lands with the Old Radicals in Serbia to form a single party, comprising all significant Serb factions and wholly dominating the new state, despite their common support of a centralised, unitary Yugoslavia and some mutual goodwill. This reflected the structural difficulty, if not impossibility, of achieving Serb territorial unification, particularly in conjunction with Yugoslav unification. The Radicals were unwilling to submerge themselves in a new party based in lands outside Serbia that they privately considered to be newly annexed provinces. Conversely, Pribićević, dominant among the prečani Serbs and the most powerful politician from the former Habsburg lands, was unwilling to sacrifice this pre-eminence through his own absorption in the Radicals. He also feared that merging with the overtly Great Serbian Radicals would compromise the Democrats' purported all-Yugoslav character, weaken their appeal among non-Serbs and unite Croats against them. The Radicals unilaterally expanded into the former Habsburg lands following unification, becoming competitors of Pribićević's own party-building project; their unification with the Radical organisation in Vojvodina prompted Pribićević to break with them formally so as to free his hands to compete with them openly. Finally, a Democrat–Radical merger and, with it, a purer form of Serb political unification succumbed to the long-standing power struggle in Serbia between court and Radicals, as Aleksandar opposed it out of fear of such a powerful party emerging, influencing Pribićević against it too.[85]

The Democrats merged instead with the anti-Radical opposition bloc from Serbia comprising the Independents, Progressives and Liberals (Nationalists), uniting with the first two of these parties on 11 April 1919 and the third, under Veljković, on 15 April. The Independents were dominant within this bloc and their Yugoslavist orientation, developed in opposition to the Old Radicals' Great Serbianism, made them Pribićević's natural partners. The Liberals and Progressives, for their part, were Obrenović-era court parties that could no longer compete independently with either Radical faction. Ironically, therefore, though the Independents had once mocked the Old Radicals as 'fusionists' because of their 1901–1903 alliance with the Progressives, it was they who eventually fused with the Progressives. Ribarac rejected the merger and stood in the constituent assembly election for a separate Liberal Party, but he was its only candidate—elected, narrowly, in his home district of Požarevac. After his death, the Požarevac Liberals voted on 14 September 1924 to join the Democratic Party.[86] However, the Yugoslav unitarism of the new party's Serbian wing was not as hardline as Pribićević's; two of its leading figures, the former Independents Milan Grol and Kosta Kumanudi, had during the war even advocated a federal Yugoslavia.[87] For at least some Democrats from Serbia, the new party's principal purpose was to continue the struggle against the Old Radicals.[88] They were consequently ready, following the constitution's promulgation in June 1921, to offer the Croats and Slovenes concessions over autonomy. By contrast, Pribićević's political base was weaker in Croatia and Slovenia than the Democrats' two principal rivals in those lands, the HRSS and the Slovene People's Party (SLS) respectively. He therefore sought to compensate for this through close collaboration with other elements in Serbia—the court and Radicals –and was unwilling to compromise on the question of provincial autonomy.[89] Thus, the Democrats were from the start an unstable coalition between prečani and Serbian wings, whose local interests prescribed conflicting political strategies.

The Provisional National Legislature was authorised by a decree from the prince regent and appointed by the new Yugoslav government based on agreed quotas of delegates from the National Council of Slovenes, Croats and Serbs, the Serbian parliament, Montenegro, Vojvodina and the Yugoslav Committee. It first met on 1 March 1919 and selected as its provisional president its oldest member, Jeftanović, former leader of the Bosnian Serb autonomist movement under Austria-Hungary. It was supposed to comprise 296 delegates, of whom 108 were to be from Serbia including Macedonia, 24 from Baranja, Bačka and Banat (Vojvodina), 12 from Montenegro, 42 from Bosnia-Hercegovina, 32 from the Slovene lands, 12 from Dalmatia, 4 from Istria and 62 from Croatia-Slavonia. The actual number attending the opening and subsequent sessions was slightly lower, with only 84 delegates from Serbia proper and those from Macedonia selected a month later. The relevant provincial representative bodies of the individual lands were supposed to select their delegates, though not all of these were legally constituted bodies with proper procedural rules. Consequently, those elements dominant in these bodies had undue influence in selecting the delegates at the expense of their local rivals. The system for electing delegates varied between different lands, with varying degrees of official manipulation.[90] In practice, the central government, through its minister for the constituent assembly, and the provincial governments played a decisive role in the selection. This made the procedure contrary to parliamentary principles, provoking objections from across the new country.[91] In Serbia's case, its 84 seats were divided between the parties through agreement, with 39 for the Old Radicals, 20 for the Independent Radicals, 11 for the Liberals, 6 for the Progressives, 6 for a breakaway Radical faction, 1 for the Social Democrats and 1 going to a Radical dissident.[92]

The Democrats, with 115 delegates, were the largest party in the Provisional National Legislature, followed by the Radicals with 69 delegates (from Serbia, Vojvodina, Srem and Bosnia-Hercegovina). This gave the Democrats eleven governmental ministers against the Radicals' three and a strong presence across Yugoslavia, with 31 delegates in Croatia, 30 in Bosnia-Hercegovina and 11 in Slovenia. The Democrats appeared poised to become Yugoslavia's leading party,[93] but they were prone to splits from the start. A left-wing faction led by the former Independents Stojanović, Prodanović and Žujović, whose republican sympathy was of long standing and which was too embittered by the Salonika trial to accept the Democratic Party's support for the Karađorđević monarchy, founded on 27

January 1920 the Republican Democratic Party, subsequently renamed the Yugoslav Republican Party. They prioritised opposition to the dynasty and were more strongly committed to the early Radical legacy embracing anti-centralism and federalism; both Stojanović and Žujović prior to unification supported a federal Yugoslavia.[94] The Republican party consequently initially supported decentralised unitarism and formally declared for federalism in 1924. Insignificant for years, it would assume some importance after two decades, when the Yugoslav kingdom was approaching its demise.

People's Radical Party expands beyond Serbia

The Radicals were the principal champions within the new state of integral Serb nationalism and attracted Serbs outside Serbia on this basis. In their campaign for the constituent assembly elections, they rejected the concept of a unitary Yugoslav nation that sought 'overnight to re-knead the Serb bread into a Yugoslav cake' as even more dangerous than that of a federal Yugoslavia. They supported a centralised state for pragmatic reasons: autonomy for Bosnia-Hercegovina and Croatia would be unacceptable since it would mean that the Serb inhabitants of those lands might be outvoted by non-Serb majorities, while any redrawing of internal borders to include all Serbs within a single federal unit would be difficult given the geographical intermingling of Serbs and Croats.[95] Yet the Serb nation in the new state did not constitute as seamless a whole as Radical ideology suggested. Serbs of the different Yugoslav territories all possessed their own political, religious and cultural organisations; Serbs outside Serbia mostly adhered to the Radical party through these organisations, rather than as individuals. Thus, the Radical party's expansion involved co-opting, in different ways, a variety of Serb organisations to produce a bigger, more heterogeneous party. Whereas in the 1920s Radical electoral candidates in pre-1912 Serbia were still drawn predominantly, though not overwhelmingly, from the inhabitants of the villages, in all other Yugoslav lands they were drawn predominantly from inhabitants of towns: merchants, members of the liberal professions and other middle-class elements. There was hence a socio-economic split between the old Serbian and new prečani sections of the party.[96]

The Radical leadership in 1918 focused expansion primarily on Vojvodina and Bosnia-Hercegovina.[97] This was spurred by the threat posed by the appearance of the Democratic rival, and it hoped to find new bases of support to compensate itself for the decline of its political hegemony in Serbia.[98] The Radical party in Croatia had, as we have seen, been a conservative pro-regime party under Jaša Tomić's leadership. It was strongest in Srem, the part of Croatia-Slavonia closest to Serbia, in contrast to Pribićević's Serb Independent Party, which had been strongest in western Croatia (Lika, Kordun, Banija).[99] Spurred by the Democratic Party's foundation in Sarajevo some days earlier, a congress of Radicals from Slavonia and Vojvodina convened in

Novi Sad on 27 February 1919 and elected a council to negotiate unification with Radicals in other Yugoslav lands.[100] The Radicals won 30 per cent of the vote in Vojvodina in the constituent assembly elections, compared with 12 per cent for the Democrats. Their victory was partly due to the disenfranchisement, at interior minister Pribićević's initiative, of the non-Slavic majority of the population (ethnic Germans, Hungarians, Romanians and Jews), making them easily the region's most popular party. Subsequently, their share of the vote rose to 46.7 per cent in the 1925 elections, and though it fell to 38.3 per cent in the 1927 elections, this was still comfortably ahead of the Democrats at 17.1 per cent.[101]

The Radicals' success in becoming the principal party of Vojvodinian Serbs was partly due to support from the Serbian Orthodox Church in the region and the involvement of clergymen in the party. Following the enfranchisement of the non-Slavic minorities, the Radicals had to compete with political parties representing them, but on the other hand they were able to recruit some members of these minorities themselves.[102] Of 513,472 ethnic Germans in Yugoslavia (4.21 per cent of the total population), 328,173 lived in Vojvodina, where they had shared with the South Slavs their second-class status vis-à-vis the Magyar population in the former regime. This made them natural allies of the new regime against Hungarian irredentism, and Germans were permitted wide freedom to organise schools, societies and publications. The Radicals helped them win permission to establish the Schwäbischer-Deutscher Kulturbund as a German cultural society covering all Yugoslavia; its founding conference occurred in June 1920 in Novi Sad. Eventually, in June 1922, a Party of the Germans in the Kingdom of Serbs, Croats and Slovenes was established too.[103] Further westward, in Croatia-Slavonia, the Radicals were able to find some support in Serb-inhabited localities; their organisations were generally formed around defectors from Pribićević's former Serb Independent Party.[104] But in this territory, even among Serbs, they remained less popular than the Democratic Party and, subsequently, its successor, the Independent Democratic Party.

The Radical party in Bosnia-Hercegovina grew out of Jeftanović's conservative wing of the Serb National Organisation and out of the 1918 grass-roots movement for Bosnia-Hercegovina's unilateral annexation to Serbia. Its leading figure was Milan Srškić, Jeftanović's son-in-law and formerly Pašić's agent in the Yugoslav Committee. Initially, Srškić helped found the Democratic Party in Bosnia-Hercegovina along with other leading Bosnian Serb politicians, intending that it merge with the Radicals in Serbia. Pribićević's decision to merge instead with the anti-Radical opposition in Serbia led Srškić's faction to split and form the Bosnian Radical organisation.[105] Its formation began with two mass rallies held in Banja Luka and Sarajevo in January 1919 to demand Bosnia-Hercegovina's annexation to Serbia, in opposition to the Yugoslavist policy of Šola's Bosnian government. It then grew as an appendage of the Radical party in Serbia. Of 49 Radical candidates in Bosnia-Hercegovina for the constituent assembly, 10 were from Serbia. Pašić himself headed the Radical list for the Banja Luka okrug while three of the remaining five heads of the party's okrug lists in Bosnia-Hercegovina were other distinguished Radicals from Serbia.[106]

The Radicals, champions of Bosnia-Hercegovina's outright annexation to Serbia, emerged as the largest party among Bosnian Serbs. Their position there was weakened, however, by the appearance of another predominantly Serb party: the League of Farmers (Savez Zemljoradnika), subsequently renamed the Farmers' Party, founded on 25 October 1919 by Mihailo Avramović, pioneer of Serbia's peasant cooperative movement, who had begun as a Radical. It sought to represent the sectional interests of Yugoslavia's rural population, i.e. all those who farmed or worked the land, including landless labourers. Social change in Serbia meant that, whereas once the entire rural population would have felt its interests represented by the Radical party, there was now space for a party that viewed the peasantry not as the nation but as a section of the nation needing sectional representation. Avramović founded his party in conjunction with sympathetic factions in other parts of Yugoslavia, of which the most important was the most radical wing of the former Serb National Organisation in Bosnia-Hercegovina, once led by Petar Kočić and centred on Banja Luka, which under Austria-Hungary had agitated for more radical agrarian reform and a more aggressive reckoning with the Muslim landlords. In the constituent assembly elections, three-quarters of the party's votes came from Serb voters, of which slightly over half were from Bosnia-Hercegovina.[107] Nevertheless, the potential radicalism of this party was tamed by the entry into it of Jovanović-Pižon and Milan Gavrilović, diplomats formerly involved with the Chetnik campaign in Macedonia and once close to Pašić; the first was a Radical and the second an Independent and alleged former Black Hand member.[108] They joined apparently at the instigation of Aleksandar himself, who feared the party's potential republicanism. Taking control of it, they prompted Avramović's withdrawal.[109] The Farmers would be the distant third choice for voters in pre-1912 Serbia and a marginal force in Slovenia and Dalmatia. But by championing more radical agrarian reform at the Muslim landlords' expense, they won a large proportion of Serb votes in Bosnia-Hercegovina, where they emerged as serious competitors of the Radicals.

The Democrats in Bosnia-Hercegovina were champions of cooperation between the Serb, Croat and Muslim Bosniak elites and of the unity of the Habsburg South Slav elites generally, therefore opponents of Bosnia-Hercegovina's annexation to Serbia. They could thus appeal to the Bosnian Serb masses neither on a nationalist basis like the Radicals nor on a class basis like the Farmers. Consequently, in the constituent assembly elections, the Radicals won 17.17 per cent of the Bosnian vote, the Farmers 16.65 per cent, the Democrats only 5.59 per cent and the JMO, principal party of Muslim Bosniaks, 33.5 per cent.[110] The JMO won more votes than the Radicals again in 1923, and though in 1925 the Radicals in coalition with Pribićević's Independent Democrats came first with 40.4 per cent of the vote, in the 1927 election the JMO exceeded the Radical vote once more by 30.8 per cent to 27.5

per cent.[111] Thus, although Serbs formed the largest single nationality in Bosnia-Hercegovina—43.87 per cent of the population in 1921 was Orthodox compared with 31.07 per cent Muslim and 23.48 per cent Catholic—their division between different parties meant the JMO came first in elections there. Even within the Radical party itself, Serb national unification was not seamless. Srškić, head of the Bosnian Radical organisation, supported, like the Farmers, a radical championing of the interests of the Bosnian Serb peasantry vis-à-vis the Muslim landlords. He rejected the moderate stance on agrarian reform favoured by the party's national leadership, ultimately resigning as Bosnian prime minister over the issue.

Unlike Bosnia-Hercegovina, 'South Serbia' was under firm and exclusive, albeit not stable, control by Serbia and was considered by the Radicals to be part of Serbia in the narrow sense. There they felt secure enough to pursue a more moderate strategy of allying with the Džemijet, the party representing the Muslim (ethnically Bosniak, Albanian and Turkish) čaršija, or elite, of the region.[112] Furthermore, the Radicals' conservative policy on agrarian reform and opposition to the programme of colonising South Serbia with Serb settlers enabled them to draw local Muslims into their own party.[113] Thus, in South Serbia, of 420 Radical electoral candidates in the period 1920–1927, 294 were Orthodox Serbs while 124 were Muslims of different ethnic groups; by contrast, in Bosnia-Hercegovina, of 254 candidates, 225 were Orthodox Serbs and only 16 Muslims.[114] This policy contrasted with that of the Democrats, who initially favoured radical agrarian reform and supported colonisation.

The alliance with the Džemijet enabled the Radicals to dominate South Serbia; the two parties together won over 70 per cent of the vote in the 1923 parliamentary elections. The alliance subsequently collapsed owing to its unpopularity among Muslims, given the extent of repression; leading Džemijet politician Ferat Draga visited the HRSS's party congress in October 1924 with the intention of taking his party over to the anti-centralist opposition. This prompted Pašić to move against the Džemijet. He sent his regional strongman Puniša Račić, previously a joint Radical–Džemijet candidate in Tetovo, to coordinate with local Serbs a campaign of obstruction and intimidation against it.[115] Consequently, the Radicals crushed the Džemijet and cemented their dominance in the region through state repression and electoral manipulation. Draga was arrested along with other party activists and sentenced to twenty years in prison. In the 1925 parliamentary elections, the Radicals and their partners won over 54 per cent of the vote while the Džemijet was reduced to 6.7 per cent of the vote and no seats. The Džemijet soon ceased to function altogether; its newspaper was suppressed, several more of its leaders arrested, and one of them assassinated in May 1927. The Radicals retained the largest number of votes in the region in the 1927 elections, though their lead slipped to 52.8 per cent against 39.3 per cent for the Democrats.[116]

In Montenegro, by contrast, the Radicals struggled to establish a strong presence. The mainstream annexationist faction behind Andrija Radović and the Montenegrin Committee for National Unification joined the Democrats, leaving the Radicals without a strong body of supporters in old Montenegro. Instead, they penetrated old Montenegro from the adjacent coastal area of the Bay of Kotor, formerly part of Habsburg Dalmatia, where the Serb Orthodox population identified itself purely as Serb rather than as Montenegrin, and from the Sanjak, divided between Serbia and Montenegro during the Balkan Wars. The eminent Radical politician Ljubomir Jovanović hailed from the Bay of Kotor and his personal base there acted as the party's launchpad in Montenegro.[117] Nevertheless, the Radicals only began to organise seriously in Montenegro in September 1920 and won only 9 per cent of the vote in the constituent assembly elections, placing them fourth behind the Communists, Democrats and Republicans. In the 1923 elections, enjoying the administrative advantages that being in government conferred, they won 25 per cent of the vote, putting them marginally behind the Democrats with 25.8 per cent and marginally ahead of the Montenegrin federalists with 24.3 per cent. In the 1925 elections, they slipped back into third place with 21.9 per cent of the vote, behind the federalists with 25.7 per cent and Democrats with 22.3 per cent. Finally, in the 1927 elections, thanks to their use of state terror against the federalists and the latter's collapse, the Radicals won convincingly with 34.7 per cent of the vote against the Democrats' 29.9 per cent.[118]

Therefore, the tendency in every Yugoslav land outside pre-1912 Serbia considered exclusively Serbian or with an ethnic-Serb majority or plurality—Vojvodina, Bosnia-Hercegovina, South Serbia, Montenegro—was for the Radicals steadily to become the leading party among the Serbs and, except in Bosnia-Hercegovina, among the population as a whole.

Yugoslav Communist Party

The Socialist Workers' Party of Yugoslavia (Communists) was formed through unification of the Social Democratic parties of Bosnia-Hercegovina and Serbia in their entireties, the great majority of members (but not the leaderships) of the Social Democratic parties of Croatia-Slavonia and Dalmatia, and a Social Democratic faction from Vojvodina. At its first congress (the 'Congress of Unification') on 20–23 April 1919, Filip Filipović was elected secretary and the party was organised territorially on the basis of six provincial executive committees whose jurisdictions broadly corresponded to the historic South Slav lands: Belgrade (Serbia and Macedonia); Novi Sad (Vojvodina); Zagreb (Croatia-Slavonia); Split (Dalmatia); Ljubljana (Slovenia); and Sarajevo (Bosnia-Hercegovina and Montenegro). Belgrade's jurisdiction over Macedonia reflected the absence of an existing indigenous Communist organisation in that territory. At the party's second congress, held at

Vukovar in Croatia on 20–25 June 1920, it was renamed the Communist Party of Yugoslavia (KPJ). Its membership was then about 65,000. However, at this congress the more reformist elements loyal to the ideals of the Second International split under Živko Topalović's leadership, eventually constituting themselves as the Socialist Party of Yugoslavia on 18 December 1921. In the constituent assembly elections, the KPJ won 198,736 votes, coming fourth behind the Radicals, Democrats and HRSS, with most of its votes drawn from the most repressed and unrepresented regions of the new state: Montenegro, Macedonia and Kosovo.

Having inherited the national ideology of the pre-war Serbian Social Democrats, the KPJ initially shared the ruling parties' belief that the Yugoslavs formed a single nation and supported a unitary state.[119] However, the KPJ also stood in the anti-state, anti-centralist traditions of the early Serbian socialists and Radicals, so it opposed the repressive regime of the Serbian centralist parties and Karađorđević monarchy. The founding congress noted: 'Unification of the Yugoslavs in a single national state was realised not through revolutionary struggle of the impoverished masses but as the result of great wars in Europe and the Balkans. Consequently, the Yugoslav bourgeoisie, with the goal of safeguarding itself, formed an alliance with reactionary militarism and bureaucracy.'[120] At its second congress, the party advocated a 'Soviet Republic of Yugoslavia' and 'people's army' in which 'all workers and poor peasants who are competent to carry weapons will be armed'.[121] In this phase, the party effectively ignored the national question in favour of demands for democracy and social justice and against state repression.

Opposition to the tyrannical centralising regime nevertheless pushed the Communists away from unitarism and toward sympathy for the national aspirations of the non-Serb Yugoslavs. Sima Marković, leader of the KPJ deputies to the constituent assembly and Serbia's leading Marxist theorist, in his speech before the constituent assembly's constitutional council on 8 February 1921, argued that 'the gentlemen who have forced centralist politics from Belgrade' were the ones who have 'ruined instead of built national unity', since this policy had 'wholly naturally inspired the interpretation that behind it, very skilfully, is hidden the hegemonist aspiration of the Serbian, or to put it better, Serb bourgeoisie', which had 'inspired counter-aspirations, so created diverse tendencies that have for two years rent and are still rending apart our national unity'.[122] Consequently, the early Serbian Communists favoured a decentralised state made up of six administrative entities based on the historical South Slav lands: Croatia, Slovenia, Serbia with Macedonia, Montenegro, Vojvodina, and a sixth entity made up of Dalmatia and Bosnia-Hercegovina. Since Macedonia had been effectively annexed by Serbia prior to World War I, the merger of Dalmatia and Bosnia-Hercegovina was the KPJ's only departure from the principle of retaining historical provinces.

Marković subsequently elaborated on this position in his essay 'The national question in the light of Marxism', published in 1923, arguing that 'a cursory look at the history of the Serbs, Croats and Slovenes in the 19th century shows that the Serbs, Croats and Slovenes have all, completely independently of each other, developed independently into modern nations'. Since the Serb bourgeoisie was using the centralised Yugoslav state to enforce its pre-eminence, 'the Serb theory of the national unity of Serbs, Croats and Slovenes is just a mask for Serb imperialism'. Consequently, 'the Marxist proletariat recognises the unlimited right of the Croats and Slovenes to self-determination; that is, the right to independent state existence'. Since, however, the Croat and Slovene proletariat's interest lay in 'the fullest unity' with the Serb proletariat, and given that the three nations lived intermingled with each other and that the Croat and Slovene bourgeoisies anyway did not want to secede, Marković concluded that 'from the viewpoint of the working class, provincial autonomy, on the basis of fullest democracy, would be the best solution to the constitutional question, a solution that could completely satisfy all nations and national minorities which have declared the wish to remain in a state union'. Marković identified this autonomist solution with the Slovene position, lying midway between Serb centralism and Croat federalism, and with Stojan Protić's position,[123] arguing that Yugoslavia should be part of a wider 'fraternal union of Balkan peoples', including an 'autonomous Macedonia in borders determined by plebiscite'.[124] However, as Marković elaborated in another text published that year, he interpreted provincial autonomy very broadly to include 'the right to secede from the current state'—a position thus close to federalism. Moreover, 'The principle of self-management is to be enacted through lower administrative units ...'[125]

The Third Country Conference of the KPJ on 1–4 January 1924 consequently called for 'the realisation of full self-determination of nations to overthrow the hegemony of the Serb bourgeoisie and its militarist clique, which is today one of the main bases of counter-revolution in the Balkans', so as to replace Yugoslav centralism with 'voluntary federative (federal) state unification'.[126] However, for the Comintern, which fiercely opposed the Versailles order and the Kingdom of Serbs, Croats and Slovenes with it, and which upheld the Leninist principle of the right of nations to self-determination, Marković did not go far enough. Meanwhile, other Yugoslav Communists, particularly from western Yugoslavia, agitated for outright support of the non-Serb national movements of resistance to Belgrade. Consequently, under the Comintern's guidance, the KPJ moved during the 1920s steadily further from support for Yugoslav unity. Marković, who both supported Yugoslav unity and was ready to resist Stalin and the Comintern, was increasingly marginalised within the party and eventually expelled from it.[127]

Radical–Democrat conflict and collaboration

At the central government level, the Democrats' merger with the anti-Radical bloc from Serbia gave them eleven out of seventeen ministers against the Radicals' three;

the latter included Protić as prime minister. The Radicals were not prepared to play so secondary a role in a government dominated by elements from outside Serbia and by their own traditional rivals. Consequently, Protić resisted Pribićević's ultra-centralist model, including his attempts to reduce the autonomy of the provincial governments of Slovenia, Croatia and Bosnia-Hercegovina, and sought instead to preserve the country's existing internal administration pending the convening of the constituent assembly. He advocated broadly preserving the traditional South Slav lands in a somewhat looser unitary Yugoslavia, and approached the Croat and Slovene parties as potential allies. He feared, presciently, that wholly suppressing Croatian demands for autonomy would ultimately produce a police state in Croatia that would gradually extend across Yugoslavia, creating an Obrenović-type royal tyranny.[128] Meanwhile, the Radicals attempted to establish their own local organisations in the former Habsburg lands, generating fierce rivalry on the ground with the Democrats which escalated to violence, particularly by Radicals against Democrats in Bosnia-Hercegovina. The Radicals denounced their rivals as anti-monarchical, anti-Karađorđević, even anti-Serb.[129] Their alliance with the Croat Union deprived the government of a stable parliamentary majority.

The Radical–Democrat conflict toppled Protić's coalition government on 1 August 1919. It was replaced by a new Democrat-dominated coalition government under the Democratic leader Davidović, including the Social Democrats. This coalition reflected the Democrats' centre-left orientation and prioritised addressing the social question over the national question. The new government's position was weak, inasmuch as it was opposed by 'the strongest Serb, the strongest Croat and the strongest Slovene party', as one contemporary noted.[130] Conversely, the Radicals in early October attempted to form a government coalition with a moderate Croat faction, the National Club, by means of an agreement that would have restored a degree of administrative authority to the governments in Croatia and Bosnia-Hercegovina, thereby potentially reconciling somewhat the Croats to the new state, but this was sabotaged by the opposition of Aleksandar and the Democrats, with the Democrats claiming that even the Radicals' minor concession to the National Club would mean the 'establishment of a new Austria on our kingdom's territory'.[131] Thus, internal Serb and Serbian power struggles undermined the attempt of both principal Serb factions to order the new state as they wished.

Davidović's government sought to strengthen its position by dissolving the Provisional National Legislature and holding immediate elections for the constituent assembly, but Aleksandar opposed this, seeking instead to unite government and opposition to form a combined government to safeguard the state's internal order and external borders. Consequently, the government resigned. Its replacement by a Radical-led coalition government under Protić on 19 February 1920 led to the dismissal of Pribićević as interior minister and a softening of Belgrade's rule west of the Drina. But Protić's government was replaced on 16 May by one headed by his fellow Radical Milenko Vesnić, who, supported by Pašić and Aleksandar, was readier to support Pribićević's project of a strictly centralised state. This heralded a Radical–Democrat modus vivendi and the formation of a coalition government on 18 May to push through a centralist constitution under the court's auspices. This coalition government also reflected a hardening of the mainstream Serb parties against manifestations of social radicalism; the Democrats abandoned their support for radical agrarian reform and ditched their Social Democratic partners in preparation for a confrontation with the labour movement. The Croat Union and SLS, initially part of the governing coalition, rapidly passed into opposition, while their ally Protić resigned as minister for the constituent assembly in June after his constitutional draft, which would have granted limited autonomy to provinces based on Yugoslavia's historic constituent lands, was rejected by the prime minister.

The Provisional National Legislature was dissolved on 22 October 1920. Elections for the constituent assembly were held on 28 November, presided over by Vesnić's coalition government, which manipulated the results by various administrative means, including underrepresentation, in terms of number of parliamentary deputies, of the Croatian lands; varying degrees of police harassment and suppression of electoral campaigning by non-Serb political parties; and the disenfranchisement of most non-Slavs. In the territories conquered by Serbia in the Balkan Wars, effectively only parties supporting centralism were permitted to function.[132] Suffrage was restricted to all men aged 21 or over, except those on active military service. The demand for female suffrage had been raised already in 1912 in a memorandum to Serbia's parliament from the recently formed Serbian National Women's Union, which included the Women's Society and other women's organisations. This campaign was interrupted by the outbreak of the Balkan Wars, but it accelerated after 1918. On the day the constituent assembly opened, 8 May 1921, a large gathering in Belgrade of representatives of all women's organisations in the capital and of others from Ljubljana, Zagreb, Sarajevo, Banja Luka, Dubrovnik, Skopje, Niš and Požarevac demanded female enfranchisement.[133] But whereas the opposition supported female suffrage, the government parties rejected it. The Radicals were most opposed, partly reflecting their claim to uphold traditional peasant society. Opposition was justified partly on the grounds that women had no independent political views of their own but reflected external influences—including the influence of the Catholic Church in Slovenia, of Islam in Bosnia-Hercegovina and of their husbands in Serbia. The Radicals' opposition to female suffrage may therefore have been influenced by the cold calculation that it would have increased other parties' votes more than their own. The Democrats had supported female suffrage when in coalition with the Social Democrats; their turn against it was opportunistic.[134]

The Democrats and Radicals, as the two principal Serb-dominated parties, won 19.88 per cent and 17.71 per cent respectively of the total Yugoslav vote, giving them 92 and 91 deputies respectively out of the constituent assembly's 419—a strong but not quite sufficient base with which to promulgate their desired centralist constitution. The two parties' electoral success was essentially confined to Serbia proper, Vojvodina, the Serb-majority areas in Croatia-Slavonia (where Serbs voted mainly for the Democrats) and Bosnia-Hercegovina (where Serbs voted mainly for the Radicals and Farmers). The Democrats were also victorious in Kosovo-Metohija and the Sanjak, where both they and the Radicals collaborated with the Džemijet. But in Macedonia and Montenegro, the KPJ outpolled both Democrats and Radicals.[135] The Communists overall received 12.4 per cent of the vote and 58 seats, making them the third-largest party in the assembly. The Croats of Croatia and Dalmatia, disenchanted with the new state, mostly voted for Radić's hardline HRSS rather than the moderate Croat Union; the former consequently won 14.3 per cent of votes and 50 seats, ensuring the government's constitutional project would face tough opposition. The next largest parties were the League of Farmers (9.4 per cent of votes and 39 seats), JMO (6.9 per cent of votes and 24 seats) and SLS (3.7 per cent of votes and 14 seats). The Social Democrats won 2.9 per cent of votes and 10 seats, Džemijet won 1.9 per cent and 8 seats, and the Republicans 1.1 per cent and 3 seats, of which 2 were in Montenegro.[136] The centralist parties would therefore need to manoeuvre to promulgate the constitution.

St Vitus's Day Constitution

The constituent assembly convened on 12 December 1920. Its sovereign right was prejudiced from the start since Serbia's monarchy had already been imposed by fiat on the new state. In the government's view, the constituent assembly was thus not a sovereign body, since there existed prior to it the prerogative of the king, who had the power to delay it. In response to the HRSS's electoral success, the assembly's provisional rules of procedure imposed by the government on 8 December 1920 required deputies to pledge loyalty to the king, thereby abrogating the right of the assembly to determine whether indeed the state was to be a monarchy or not. In response to objections from the opposition, ministers expressed the opinion that 'the constituent assembly is not sovereign' and that the people did not have the right to remove the king or monarchy.[137] Unwilling to prejudice their rights in this way, the most powerful opposition bloc of deputies—made up of the KPJ, National Club and Yugoslav Club—boycotted parliament in protest at these provisional rules of procedure; their absence gave the Radicals and Democrats a majority in the vote for formal rules of procedure, which were adopted at the end of January 1921 and which likewise required deputies to pledge allegiance to the king. A rule opposed by the Croat, Slovene and Muslim Bosniak parties empowered the constituent assembly to pass the constitution with a majority of 50 per cent of deputies plus one.[138] In order to participate in the assembly, the opposition bloc then resolved to take the pledge to the king.

A new government under Pašić of Radicals and Democrats, each with five ministerial portfolios, assumed office on 1 January 1921. The Radical–Democrat coalition then forced their draft constitution for a centralised Yugoslav state, modelled on the 1903 Serbian constitution, through the constituent assembly. This centralist constitution represented the logical culmination of Pašić's anti-pluralism: he identified Yugoslavia with Serbia, Serbia with the Radical party and the Radical party with himself. He had largely reversed traditional Radical support for the principle of self-management; as Slobodan Jovanović complained, 'The viewpoint of Pašić's government is that not only federalism but even self-management is dangerous for state unity.'[139] As Lazar Marković, justice minister and former minister for the constituent assembly recalled, 'the Radical party, advocating the need for broad self-management in the municipalities and oblasts [the largest administrative-territorial subdivision of the kingdom], emphasised that self-managing oblasts must not, by their size or their competence, be such as to bring into question the state's unitary character.'[140] The constitutional draft thus granted the king the power to appoint the oblast governors.

Protić noted that 'the proposals for the constitution of Mr Vesnić and Mr Pašić's government contain within them much bureaucratism and bureaucratic centralism and insufficient expression of the principle of self-management which is today increasingly being eroded and which is the old banner of the People's Radical Party.'[141] He criticised the government's constitutional draft on the grounds that it failed to safeguard adequately parliamentary sovereignty, limit the monarch's power, guarantee personal and press freedom and subject military personnel to civilian courts in cases of ordinary crimes—i.e. that it betrayed traditional Radical principles.[142] Protić supported the state's organisation on the basis of self-governing provinces corresponding to Yugoslavia's historic lands: 'The provinces are these: Serbia; Old Serbia with Macedonia; Croatia and Slavonia with Rijeka, Istria and Međimurje; Bosnia; Montenegro with Hercegovina, Boka and Primorje; Dalmatia; Srem with Bačka; Slovenia with Prekomurje.'[143] His proposals won considerable support particularly in Vojvodina, both from local Radicals and from members of the Croat and Slovak minorities; this marked the early stirrings of the Vojvodinian autonomist opposition.[144]

To pass the constitution, the Radical–Democrat bloc needed the votes of the principal Muslim Bosniak party, the JMO. This party preferred in principle a constitutional order preserving the autonomy of Bosnia-Hercegovina and other historic lands, but the Radical–Democrat bloc bought its votes with two concessions in an agreement on 15 March 1921. The first was a decree on 12 May 1921, modifying the terms of the agrarian reform somewhat in favour of the Muslim landlords at the expense of the Bosnian Serb peasants. The reform still amounted to a massive transfer of economic power in Bosnia-Hercegovina from the former to the latter, and would reduce many Muslim landlord families to poverty.[145] The second concession involved recognising a special administrative status for Bosnia-Hercegovina: according to Clause 135 of the constitution, the kingdom's division into oblasts was to be realised, regarding Bosnia-Hercegovina, without changing its historic external borders; this meant that no part of Bosnia-Hercegovina would be merged in an oblast with non-Bosnian territory and the country would be preserved as a distinct administrative region. Furthermore, its six historic okrugs were to function as oblasts pending the kingdom's final division into oblasts. Subsequently, the law of 26 April 1922, dividing the kingdom into thirty-three oblasts, preserved Bosnia-Hercegovina's six historical okrugs (Sarajevo, Tuzla, Mostar, Vrbas [Banja Luka], Bihać and Travnik) as oblasts in the new state and provided institutional safeguards for their continued existence that oblasts elsewhere in Yugoslavia lacked. Both concessions to the JMO prompted the Farmers to vote against the constitution.[146]

The Serbian historian Stanoje Stanojević warned against the administrative arrangement for Bosnia-Hercegovina in a front-page polemic in *Politika*, published the day before the constitution's promulgation. He argued that the provisions of Clause 135 amounted to the 'complete autonomy of Bosnia-Hercegovina and its special status within the state', i.e. the creation of a 'state within a state'. In Stanojević's opinion, 'there is absolutely no reason, neither historical nor ethnographic nor political nor economic, to single out Bosnia-Hercegovina and preserve it as a special entity within the state', something that would mean 'that the state be thrown into new and inescapable chaos and the nation into endless discord and convulsion'.[147] This was an exaggeration, but the constitution indeed restricted Serbia's ability to absorb Bosnia-Hercegovina, even though its acquisition had been a Serbian goal since Ilija Garašanin's time. This was a price the Serbian political classes paid for their extension of centralised rule by Belgrade all the way to Slovenia, a country in which Serbian nationalists had little interest. Pursuit of maximal national goals undermined the achievement of more realisable ones.

The hardline HRSS refused to participate in the constituent assembly while the deputies of the moderate Croat and Slovene autonomist parties walked out of it on 13 June in opposition to the way the Radical–Democrat bloc forced through the constitution. They were closely preceded by the Communists, who had abandoned the assembly two days earlier in protest at the repression they faced. On this decidedly non-consensual basis, the centralist constitution was passed by a slim majority in the constituent assembly on St Vitus's Day, the anniversary of the Battle of Kosovo, 28 June 1921—hence nicknamed the St Vitus's Day Constitution. Of 419 elected deputies, only 285 of whom were actually present, 223 voted for the constitutional committee's draft, 35 voted against and 161 opponents of the draft boycotted the vote. This was a majority of only 13 above the minimum required for the vote to pass (210).[148] The parties voting for the constitution were the Democrats, Radicals, JMO and Džemijet; those voting against were the Farmers, Republicans, Social

Democrats and the independent Ante Trumbić. Pašić's personal role in ensuring the constitution's adoption was huge, perhaps decisive.[149]

The St Vitus's Day Constitution, proclaimed jointly by King Petar and Prince (King) Aleksandar, carried Aleksandar's signature. It strangely defined the official language of the kingdom as 'Serbo-Croat-Slovene' and guaranteed citizens' equality before the law; freedom of the press, association and expression; freedom and equality of religions; and independence of the courts. Legal affairs related to family or inheritance among Muslims were to be decided by sharia courts. The constitution guaranteed personal liberties, including freedom from unlawful arrest, the right to form trade unions, security of private property, prohibition of the death penalty for political crimes (other than attempted or successful assassinations of the monarch or members of his family) and the right of citizens to prosecute state or local bodies. All ranks of state service were equally open to all citizens, but only if they were of 'Serb–Croat–Slovene nationality'. The state assumed certain economic and social obligations toward its citizens such as in the fields of welfare, health care and education, while citizens had corresponding duties toward the state, including the duty to defend it. The constitution decreed that free, direct and secret elections for a single-chamber national parliament were to occur every four years, with a deputy for every 40,000 inhabitants; all citizens aged 21 or over were to have the suffrage, while the question of female suffrage was open to future legislation. Deputies represented the whole nation, not merely their constituents. The right of state officials to stand for parliament was restricted. Out of 313 parliamentary deputies, pre-1914 Serbia would have 112, Croatia-Slavonia 66, Bosnia-Hercegovina 48, Vojvodina 34, Slovenia 25, Dalmatia 16, Montenegro 7, Belgrade 2, Zagreb 2 and Ljubljana 1.

The constitution vested considerable powers in the monarch—legislative powers in conjunction with parliament and executive powers through his ministers. Laws could be proposed by the government or individual ministers with the king's authorisation or by members of parliament and were passed by parliament with the king's signature. Judicial verdicts were reached and executed in his name. He confirmed and proclaimed laws, appointed state officials and granted military ranks. He was supreme commander of all military forces and bestowed military orders and other decorations. He appointed the oblast governors (great župans). He had the power to grant amnesties. He represented the state in all its relations with foreign states, though foreign treaties required parliamentary approval. He declared war and concluded peace, though, unless the state was attacked or war was declared against it, this required parliamentary consent. He summoned parliament and opened and concluded its sessions, though dismissals of parliament had to contain a deadline of three months for new elections and four months for the summoning of the new parliament. Budgets were approved annually, but if the parliament were dissolved without having approved the budget, the previous year's budget could be extended by decree for up to four months. The king enjoyed immunity before the law. The government, known as the ministerial council, was appointed by him and responsible both to him and to parliament. All exercise of royal powers required the responsible minister's countersignature. The king could propose changes to the constitution, as could parliament with the approval of three-fifths of its deputies.[150]

The king's power thus went considerably beyond that of a figurehead. Governments were assembled by the court, not by parliament, and during the period when the constitution operated, they were almost invariably toppled by the king rather than by parliament, while the king regularly gave mandates to governments without parliamentary majorities.[151] This was important given the character of the man who would be king for over two-thirds of the kingdom's existence. Old King Petar, frail and sickly at the time of Yugoslavia's creation, played virtually no role in its politics. He did not return from his wartime exile until mid-July 1919, and on 11 March of that year, at his court in Athens, he signed an act of abdication, copies of which were sent to Aleksandar and to prime minister Protić.[152] This was kept secret from the public so that the new king, Aleksandar, continued to present himself to the public as prince regent while official documents still named Petar as king until his death on 16 August 1921. Unlike his father, Aleksandar was determined to rule as well as reign and made full use of his constitutional powers.

Communists retaliated against state repression with acts of terrorism. Spasoje Stejić, a Bolshevik returnee from Soviet Russia, threw a bomb on 29 June 1921 at the car containing Aleksandar and Pašić, just after the king had formally pledged allegiance to the new constitution; neither was hurt but several bystanders were injured. Stejić was subsequently defended at his trial by Dragiša Vasić, a Black Hand sympathiser and Republican. Drašković, author of the Pronouncement, was assassinated on 21 July by members of the Red Justice, a Communist youth faction from Bijeljina in north-east Bosnia. The notorious Law for the Protection of Public Security and Order in the State, codifying the Pronouncement, was then passed on 1 August, though the Social Democrats, Republicans and SLS voted against it while the Farmers and JMO voted in favour but with great reservations. The law criminalised Communist and anarchist political activities, thereby banning the Communist party. The mandates of the Communist parliamentary deputies were consequently nullified.[153] The Independent Workers' Party of Yugoslavia, through which the Communists sought to remain active, was likewise banned on 11 July 1924. Drašković's assassin Alija Alijagić was sentenced to death and hanged on 8 March 1922, in violation of the constitutional prohibition of the death penalty. Other conspirators received long prison sentences, including Rodoljub Čolaković, subsequently first prime minister of the People's Republic of Bosnia-Hercegovina at the end of World War II.

The law of 26 April 1922, dividing the state into oblasts, each with its own elected assembly and governing council, was imposed by the government by decree, without consulting parliament. It resulted in Serbia being administratively subdivided into more and smaller oblasts than other parts of the country. Thus, the territory of pre-1914 Serbia including Serbia's part of the Sanjak and Kosovo was divided into fourteen oblasts: Belgrade, Podunavlje, Podrinje, Valjevo, Požarevac, Užice, Šumadija, Morava, Timok, Raška, Kruševac, Kosovo, Niš and Vranje. Banat was divided between the Belgrade and Podunavlje oblasts, the latter with its capital in Smederevo, to promote integration of this strategically crucial territory into Serbia. By comparison, Croatia-Slavonia was divided into only four oblasts, including Srem, which was preserved as a unit (alongside Osijek, Zagreb and Primorje), western Vojvodina into one (Bačka), Slovenia into two (Maribor and Ljubljana), Dalmatia into two (Split and Dubrovnik), Bosnia-Hercegovina into the aforementioned six, Macedonia into three (Skopje, Bregalnica and Bitola) and Montenegro was broadly preserved as a single unit (Zeta). The more numerous oblasts in Serbia corresponded to its traditional pre-Yugoslav okrugs and existing party organisations and aimed to maximise administrative control by the central state and Serbian parties, letting them field more party lists. The larger size of oblasts elsewhere was a small concession to the non-Serb opposition.[154]

As regards Serbia's constitutional order, unification of Yugoslavia in 1918 via the prince regent's fiat was a royal putsch in the tradition of those of 1894 and 1901. Thus, the achievement of unification by Serbia's court and army, and the subsequent use of its army and gendarmerie to suppress dissent, meant the perpetuation and strengthening of royal authoritarianism, now recovering from its 1903 defeat. The three anti-Radical parties in Serbia (Independents, Progressives and Liberals) united with Pribićević's extreme centralists from former Austria-Hungary to form the Democratic Party while the Radicals expanded into Yugoslavia outside Serbia, with the result that Serbia's party-political struggle now extended across the new state. The two parties managed to set aside their differences to push the centralist constitution through the constituent assembly despite strong opposition from left-wing, Croat, Slovene and even some predominantly Serb parties, but this was merely an interlude in their rivalry. The power struggle between Serbia's political classes would continue in Yugoslavia much as before, but with the parties enjoying relatively smaller majorities and the new state held together by force, the balance of power shifted back toward the crown.

16

REIGN OF THE SECOND KING ALEKSANDAR

1921–1934

Cooperation between the main parties representing Serb voters, enabling the passage of the St Vitus's Day Constitution, did not last. Solidarity between prečani Serbs and Serbians began to fracture almost immediately. The first sign of this was the defection from the Serb front of the largely Bosnian Serb League of Farmers, which voted against the constitution. Pribićević succeeded briefly in acting as a bridge between Serbia and the former Habsburg lands, but since this role arose fortuitously it was unsustainable. His brutally centralist policies rapidly alienated non-Serbs. In the constituent assembly elections, the Democrats in Pribićević's native Croatia-Slavonia won only 17.87 per cent of the vote against 52.55 per cent for Radić's HRSS. In other prečani-inhabited lands, except for Vojvodina, the Democrats' showing was still weaker; they won only 10.38 per cent of the vote in Dalmatia and, as we have seen, were crushingly defeated in Bosnia-Hercegovina. In Vojvodina, the Democrats won 19.45 per cent of the vote but were heavily defeated by the Radicals, who won 47.4 per cent.[1] Pribićević was revealed as a giant with feet of clay, whose genuine base of support lay only among Croatian Serbs. This reduced his indispensability in the eyes of political elements in Serbia.

Collapse of prečani-Serbian unity

After the constitution's promulgation, the HRSS united with two smaller Croat parties, the Croat Union and Croat Party of Right, to form the Croat Bloc, emphasising Croat national unity against the new order. By contrast, the Radical–Democrat coalition crumbled as the two partners began struggling over control of government and policy, with the Radicals seeking to acquire the interior ministry while the Democrats sought amnesty for the Black Handers convicted in Salonika. A further catalyst was the government's passage of a new electoral law in June 1922 aimed at reducing the proportional element of parliamentary representation by excluding smaller parties that achieved low votes. This was aimed at strengthening the parliamentary representation of the governing parties, but it favoured parties that enjoyed a concentration of seats in particular areas over those whose votes were geographically more evenly distributed, thus strengthening the Radicals against the Democrats.[2] King Aleksandar sought to maintain the Radical–Democrat coalition to isolate the Croatian opposition, even suggesting that the two principal Serb parties fuse, but this was rejected by both, with the Radicals in particular viewing it as a ploy to maintain the Democrats in government.[3]

The Democrats' own unity meanwhile cracked as their two principal wings— Pribićević's prečani Serbs and the Serbian bloc dominated by Davidović and the former Independents—pursued conflicting policies. Davidović's bloc focused on its traditional power struggle with the Radicals. This led it to conciliate Croat Democrats increasingly alienated by Pribićević's hardline politics and to seek allies among the Croatian opposition itself, which meant softening its stance on centralism. It drew support from Bosnian Serb Democrats whose Yugoslavism had traditionally involved close collaboration with Bosnian Croats and who did not see the loosening of centralism in such existentially dangerous terms as their Croatian Serb counterparts did. By contrast, for the Croatian Serbs in Pribićević's bloc, resolutely upholding the St Vitus's Day Constitution and centralist order remained paramount. Davidović's faction convened a congress in Ilidža in Bosnia on 28–29 June 1922 that assembled Democrats, supporters of the wartime Yugoslav Committee, JMO supporters and other moderates to condemn the polarising politics of both government and Croat opposition and call for a constitutional compromise; this gelled with the sentiments of Protić's Radical faction. Another congress in Zagreb on 10 September also assembled moderate Democrats and others, and issued a resolution calling for 'administrative deconstruction', 'people's self-management' and the revision of the law dividing the state into oblasts. Among those attending were Davidović himself and Ivan Ribar, a Croat Democratic politician and president of the Yugoslav parliament. These gatherings offended hardline centralists, in particular Pribićević's Democrats and Srškić's Bosnian Serb Radicals.[4] Under pressure from Pribićević and his supporters, Davidović was forced to resign as Democratic Party president. The party's two factions advanced rival candidates for president of parliament and on 20 October 1922, with Aleksandar's backing, Pribićević's bloc and the Radicals voted the former's candidate into the post, defeating Davidović's ally Ribar in what was another victory for the hardliners.[5]

These tensions led to the resignation of Pašić's coalition government on 12 December and Aleksandar's dissolution of parliament nine days later, thereby preventing the HRSS deputies from entering parliament as allies of Davidović's Democrats.[6] Aleksandar was alienated by the Serbian Democrats' approaches to the Croatian opposition, their support for constitutional revision and continued agitation over the Salonika trial question. He consequently gave Pašić the mandate to form a purely Radical government, which was achieved on 16 December. The Radicals purged the Yugoslav administration of the Democrats' supporters, particularly policemen; about 3,000 officials were sacked between December 1922 and January 1923.[7] Aleksandar meanwhile strengthened his grip on power on 6 January 1923 by promoting to general seventeen colonels without the necessary qualifications, mostly White Hand supporters.[8] In the parliamentary elections on 18 March, the first following the constituent assembly, the government employed systematic administrative manipulation and police terror against the Democrats' supporters in the territory of pre-1914 Serbia. They also fully exploited the royal favour they then enjoyed by presenting a vote for them as a 'vote for the king'. Their use of such methods elsewhere and against other parties was generally less ruthless, except where these parties were seen as encroaching on their domain—for example, the HRSS in Vojvodina.[9] Since the Democrats were split and Davidović's faction had not yet made the case for decentralisation, the Radicals appealed to the electorate as the only credible centralists. Consequently, the Democrats' share of the Yugoslav vote fell further: they won 400,342 votes, 18.4 per cent of the total, down from 19.88 per cent in 1920. The Radicals won 562,213 votes, 25.8 per cent of the total, up from 17.71 per cent in 1920. This gave the Democrats 51 seats in parliament against 108 for the Radicals. In the territory of pre-1912 Serbia, the Radicals won 241,312 votes (49.3 per cent) and 50 seats against 157,626 (32.2 per cent) and 21 for the Democrats and 57,818 (11.8 per cent) and 2 for the Farmers. Among Serb voters outside Serbia, the Radicals decisively defeated the Democrats in Vojvodina and Dalmatia, crushed them in Bosnia-Hercegovina, overtook them in Macedonia, Kosovo and the Sanjak, were marginally outvoted by them in Montenegro and lost to them decisively only in Croatia-Slavonia, where Pribićević's authority among Serbs was supreme. In Bosnia-Hercegovina and Dalmatia, the Farmers outpolled the Democrats among Serb voters and came a respectable second to the Radicals.[10]

The election did not give the Radicals a parliamentary majority, but they remained the sole governing party thanks to the opposition's divisions and the acquiescence or collaboration of parts of it. The three principal parties representing the three principal non-Serb peoples from former Austria-Hungary, the HRSS, JMO and SLS, now united to form the Federalist Bloc, in which Radić's voice was strongest. However, on 12–13 April 1923, in a cynical move that would become characteristic of the way the constitutional question was subordinated to the power struggle between factions in Serbia, the Radicals negotiated a deal with the HRSS, JMO and SLS, known subsequently as Marko's Protocol after the president of the Radicals' parliamentary deputies' club, Marko Đuričić, who negotiated it. The division of Croatia, Bosnia-Hercegovina and Slovenia into oblasts, which the HRSS opposed as amounting to Croatia's fragmentation, would be suspended and their provincial governments replaced by ones acceptable to the Federalist Bloc. In return, the HRSS's deputies would stay outside parliament and the Federalist Bloc would not collaborate with the Democrats but remain neutral between government and opposition. The HRSS hoped this deal would be a step toward constitutional revision, but Pašić viewed it as a short-term expedient. He was consequently able to form a pure Radical government on 2 May.

Marko's Protocol rapidly unravelled owing to differences between the parties over the question of constitutional revision, Radić's continued aggressive rhetorical attacks on the Serbian political classes and fierce criticism from Pribićević's Democrats of the Radicals' collaboration with 'rebels'. Pašić consequently again turned against the HRSS and ensured his continued parliamentary majority by blocking the verification of its 67 deputies on the grounds that they refused to recognise the constitution. He then bolstered the Radicals' 108 deputies through pacts with the Džemijet and the ethnic German party, giving him a majority of 130 out of 245 verified deputies. Such ploys exacerbated the Serb–Croat conflict.[11] After leaving the parliament on 27 June, Pašić was lightly wounded in his car in an assassination attempt by a young former functionary of the foreign ministry embittered by his dismissal the previous year; that the news of it was published on the following day, St Vitus's Day, likely added to the public excitement. In the fraught atmosphere, one Radical newspaper blamed the attempt on the HRSS.[12] The Radicals then abandoned any attempt to reach an agreement with the HRSS, Radić fled abroad on 21–22 July and parliament resolved on the 25th to prosecute the parliamentary deputies belonging to the HRSS presidency.[13] Yet repression could not solve the Croat question; in Slobodan Jovanović's words, 'In the struggle with the Croats, Pašić fell into the same error in which King Milan had been during his struggle with the Radicals: he thought he was dealing with a party when in fact he was dealing with a nation.'[14]

Power within the Democratic Party meanwhile shifted in favour of Davidović's faction. Pribićević resigned from the party's general council in mid-December 1923. Immediately after the elections, the SLS, HRSS and JMO reconstituted the Federalist Bloc. Pašić's break with the HRSS and his reaffirmation of absolute commitment to the St Vitus's Day Constitution led Pribićević to gravitate toward the Radicals whereas Davidović's Democrats gravitated toward the federalist opposition to offset Radical dominance. This prompted Pribićević's wing of the Democratic Party to secede altogether to form the Independent Democratic Party—essentially a party for Croatian Serbs. The Independent Democrats signed an agreement with the Radicals on 27 March 1924 to form what they called the National Bloc, referred to informally as the P-P (Pašić–Pribićević) government. This bloc did not enjoy a parliamentary majority, so again attempted to obstruct verification of the HRSS deputies' mandates to ensure its position. When its contrived majority nevertheless began crumbling, the P-P government resigned on 12 April, whereupon Pašić received a new mandate from the king and reconstituted the P-P government on 21 May. When he could no longer prevent the HRSS deputies' verification—which occurred on 27 May, thereby depriving his government of its majority—he arranged parliament's dissolution. This pushed the Democrats into an Opposition Bloc alongside the HRSS, JMO and SLS.[15] Thus, the traditional rivalry between Radicals and Democrats pushed one in a hardline, centralist, anti-parliamentarian and anti-Croat direction and the other into an alliance with the non-Serb opposition that threatened the centralist order.

Radić and the HRSS's thorough alienation from the Yugoslav state led them to approach revisionist foreign powers hostile to it. The self-exiled Radić negotiated in late 1923 with representatives of Mussolini's Italy and Admiral Miklós Horthy's Hungary, even reaching an informal agreement on 23 November with Hungary for its recognition of Croatia's independence in return for Croatian support for the Hungarian reacquisition of Vojvodina. Since Radić knew the Italians and Hungarians were negotiating about the potential partition of Croatia between them in the event it left Yugoslavia, this was probably just a manoeuvre to strengthen his position vis-à-vis Belgrade. Still more dramatic was Radić's two-month stay in Moscow in June–August 1924 and the affiliation of the HRSS to the Soviet Union's Peasant International, at a time when the Comintern was advocating self-determination for Croatia and other non-Serbian Yugoslav lands. Thus, the Croat question, like its Macedonian and Kosovo Albanian counterparts, grew from an internal Yugoslav to an international question.

Given its inability to form a parliamentary majority, the P-P government resigned in mid-July 1924, whereupon Davidović's Democrat–JMO–SLS bloc formed a government on the 27th. Radić meanwhile returned from exile and the HRSS deputies ended their boycott of the Yugoslav parliament, assumed their parliamentary seats and lent their support to Davidović's government. As a concession to the Croatian opposition, the government restored the provincial administration in Croatia-Slavonia, halting the previous government's attempt to liquidate it, and permitted free use of the Croatian flag and free formation of Croatian national organisations.[16] The government negotiated the HRSS's entry into the government, but this was blocked by Aleksandar with Pašić's support, given the HRSS's anti-monarchical, anti-militarist politics, its refusal to recognise the constitution and its insistence on Croatia's sovereignty. Pašić mobilised the Radical apparatus to agitate among the population against the government, which was accused of being not only 'federalist' but 'Turkish'—owing to its inclusion of the JMO's Mehmed Spaho. Radical pamphlets portrayed Davidović in a Turkish vizier's headdress.[17]

Aggressive Radical tactics against the Democrats in Serbia gelled with the Serb–Croat and Serb–Muslim conflicts in Croatia, Dalmatia and Bosnia-Hercegovina to make Yugoslav politics increasingly violent, with parties forming or co-opting paramilitary organisations. Under Pribićević, the Democrats established a paramilitary organisation, the Organisation of Yugoslav Nationalists (ORJUNA), which particularly targeted HRSS supporters in Croatia-Slavonia and Dalmatia as well as JMO and Radical supporters. ORJUNA's methods of violence and intimidation encouraged the emergence of Croat and Serb nationalist counterparts, the Croat Nationalist Youth and Serb Nationalist Youth, the second of these being the Radical party's paramilitary wing.[18] In Bosnia-Hercegovina, the violence of the Serb Nationalist Youth and its Muslim affiliate Osman Đikić was primarily directed against the JMO, viewed by the Bosnian Radicals as their principal enemy. This paramilitary activity periodically resulted in injuries and deaths. While in government, the Radicals directed state terror against their Democratic rivals in Serbia rather than against the non-Serb parties outside Serbia, they nevertheless granted ORJUNA a certain leeway to use terror against the HRSS and Croat Nationalist Youth.[19]

For the Democrats in Serbia, reliance on paramilitary forces evolved naturally from their long association with the Black Hand, which their right wing continued to nurture. Meanwhile, Chetnik veterans of the guerrilla struggle in Macedonia, the Balkan Wars and World War I formed organisations linked to the political parties. The first of these, the Association of Chetniks for the Freedom and Honour of the Fatherland, was established in 1921, led by Chetniks close to the Black Hand, linked to the Democrats and under ORJUNA's influence. Resistance among Chetniks to this alignment was spearheaded by the Radical politician Puniša Račić, a Black Hand defector and veteran of guerrilla action in Macedonia and Kosovo. The Chetnik organisation split in 1924 at Račić's instigation, facilitated by the court, Radicals and White Hand supporters within its ranks, in response to the Democrats' pivot toward the HRSS. The split spawned two new rival pro-Radical Chetnik organisations: the United Serb Chetniks for King and Fatherland and, under Račić's direction, the larger United Serb Chetniks 'Petar Mrkonjić', which was explicitly Great Serbian in orientation. All three Chetnik organisations were founded in Serbia then spread to western Yugoslavia where they acted violently against their rivals. The two pro-Radical Chetnik organisations were particularly active in Macedonia, Vojvodina and Bosnia-Hercegovina, targeting both non-Serb parties and the Radicals' Serbian rivals, the Democrats and Farmers.[20] They merged in July 1925 into the Association of Serb Chetniks 'Petar Mrkonjić' under Račić's leadership.

Pašić and the White Hand leader Petar Živković met secretly in early October 1924 to coordinate policy; so close was this alliance that Pašić seriously considered making Živković his successor as Radical leader.[21] Davidović's government was then toppled by the resignation of the war minister, Army General Stevan Hadžić, in protest at the 'defeatist work of the HRSS', in particular Radić's demands for a reduction in the size of the army and condemnation of its possible intervention in Albania. Hadžić was the king's first adjutant and his wife Ela was Queen Marija's first lady-in-waiting.[22] He was aggrieved at the apparent support given these demands by the government's Slovene and Bosnian Muslim members. He visited the royal court and informed the king that he intended to resign, whereupon the king advised him to 'do what his conscience required'. Aleksandar viewed Davidović's desire for a rapprochement with Radić in terms of the traditional anti-monarchical tendencies of his Democrats, as former Independents, dovetailing with the HRSS's republicanism.

He therefore used his extra-constitutional influence over the senior officer corps to topple Davidović's government.[23] While Davidović wanted to replace Hadžić with a different minister on the grounds that his government enjoyed the confidence of parliament, Aleksandar insisted on his government's resignation.[24] He allegedly informed Davidović on 15 October: 'Your understanding of democracy, your understanding of monarchy and your understanding of the Crown's prerogatives are such that, if they triumphed, I could not remain king in this country ... And my understanding of the Crown's prerogatives is again such that, if it triumphed, you could not remain prime minister. In such circumstances, only two things are possible: ... either you look for another king, or I look for another prime minister.' Davidović reluctantly resigned the same day.[25]

Aleksandar offered the new governmental mandate on 6 November to Pašić, who returned to power once more in a coalition with Pribićević without a parliamentary majority. The restored P-P government resumed repression of the Croatian opposition using the anti-Communist law of 1 August 1921, justified by reference to the HRSS's flirtation with Moscow. The Davidović government's restoration of Croatia's provincial administration was nullified. The HRSS was banned, its political activity suppressed and Radić and five associates arrested on 5 January 1925, though the party's candidates were still permitted to participate in the subsequent parliamentary elections of 8 February 1925. The Opposition Bloc, including the Democrats, protested against the arrests.[26] The coalition of Radicals and Independent Democrats, running as the National Bloc, won 43.4 per cent of the vote in the February 1925 elections, giving them 163 out of 315 parliamentary seats. This was thanks in part to its administrative harassment and intimidation of opposition politicians and voters.[27] In Davidović's words, 'The heaviest pressure was employed against people, without any regard for the law and the constitution ... These elections are a disgrace to our state.'[28] This was essentially a victory for the Radicals, who won 141 seats, while their Independent Democrat partners won 22. Davidović's Democrats won 11.8 per cent of the vote and 37 seats, and the HRSS 22.3 per cent and 67. In Serbia, the Radicals won 55.2 per cent of the vote against the Democrats' 27 per cent and the Farmers' 9.7 per cent. The Radicals were decisively victorious in southern Yugoslavia (Macedonia, Kosovo and Sanjak) and in Vojvodina, winning an absolute majority of seats in both territories. They won a plurality of seats in Bosnia-Hercegovina, again helped by administrative repression and paramilitary violence. In Montenegro, however, the federalists won the most votes, despite the government and Radicals' use of similar measures.[29]

The Radicals therefore reaffirmed their primacy over their Serbian rivals and Pribićević's marginality was confirmed, while the HRSS was definitely established as the most powerful non-Serb political force in the country, with which Serbia's politicians would have to contend. The Opposition Bloc during February 1925 transformed itself into the Bloc of National Agreement and Peasant (People's)

Democracy, which the HRSS joined. However, the HRSS's increasing moderation allowed it to escape confinement to the opposition. Radić's nephew Pavle announced in the Yugoslav parliament on 27 March 1925 that it had accepted Croatia's inclusion in the Yugoslav state, the St Vitus's Day Constitution (subject to revisions) and the ruling dynasty; the party would hence rename itself the Croat Peasant Party (HSS), dropping the adjective 'Republican'. Although this did not mark a radical shift in HRSS/HSS policy which had been evolving in a moderate direction for months, the conciliatory announcement signalled a revolution in parliamentary alliances. Pavle then met with Aleksandar, reassuring him of the HSS's new-found moderation, after which Aleksandar brokered a meeting between him and Pašić. Finally, Aleksandar apparently received a statement from Stjepan Radić on 24 April reaffirming his party's conversion. This led to a Radical–HSS alliance, publicly announced on 2 July. Charges against Radić and the other imprisoned HSS politicians were dropped on 18 July 1925 and the HSS and Radicals formed a coalition government—the so-called R-R (Radicals–Radić) government, with Radić as education minister.

Both Aleksandar and Pašić understood that repressing the HSS was only boosting its prestige in the Croat public's eyes and that they needed to retreat from confrontation if they wanted to salvage the Yugoslav project. But the price of reconciliation—the sacrifice of the HSS's *bête noire*, Pribićević—was one that both were reluctant to take. In Gligorijević's words, 'neither Pašić nor the king wanted to accept responsibility for that great sacrifice. They passed that hot potato one to the other.'[30] The Radical–HSS coalition gave the HSS local administrative control over much of western Yugoslavia, enabling it to purge officials appointed there by Pribićević and his supporters, who were thus now discarded by the second Serbian faction. Meanwhile, the opposition was in disarray after its abandonment by the HSS. The Bloc of National Agreement collapsed and in October 1926 the Democrats and JMO formed a narrower coalition, the Democratic Union. The biggest winner was Aleksandar: the HSS's capitulation marked his personal triumph and gained him a degree of acceptance in Croatia: the royal family was given a warm reception on its visit to Zagreb on 15 August 1925, to celebrate the millennium of the founding of the medieval Croatian state.[31]

The court finally breaks Pašić and the Radicals

From the Yugoslav state's birth, ultimate power was held by Aleksandar through his control of the army, assured by the creation and promotion within it of the White Hand and crushing of the Black Hand. He further strengthened this control on 4 March 1919, when his supreme command ordered the formation of a new Royal Guard. This was an elite force composed predominantly of Salonika front veterans from pre-1912 Serbia in whose complete loyalty Aleksandar trusted and which would protect his regime from the sort of putsch the Black Hand had threatened.[32] It was headed by Živković, who consolidated his position as the paramount figure in Aleksandar's military establishment.[33] In the period 1920–1922, many of the most successful and popular older members of the army's top brass died or retired with honour, in particular Janković, Stepanović, Živojin Mišić, Jurišić-Šturm and Bojović. This left the army securely in the control of Aleksandar's officer-protégés.[34]

At one remove from the party-political fray, Aleksandar was viewed by the Serbian parties as the guarantor of Serbian pre-eminence in Yugoslavia and by the non-Serbian parties as a potential defence against it. Politicians' increasing quest for royal assistance against each other weakened and discredited parliamentary politics while strengthening his hand and encouraging him to view himself as arbiter. By 1925, he had found in the HSS a new counterweight to Pašić and the Radicals, while the latter had lost their status as the sole dependable defender of the constitutional order.[35] He was now free to refocus on the good old fight of the monarch's struggle with the Radicals. According to Pašić's biographer Vasa Kazimirović, 'the fact is incontestable that Radić had an important role in everything and that Aleksandar so much more easily decided on a final break with Pašić because Radić stood with him without reservation'.[36] Conversely, Pašić now sought Croatian allies against Radić; his Radicals therefore began collaborating with the Croat extreme right. Pašić himself met with the leader of the Croat Party of Right, Ante Pavelić, future Nazi-puppet ruler of the Independent State of Croatia. The Radical newspaper *Balkan* (The Balkans) commented that Pavelić was 'a good man and a good Croat' and that 'it is known to us that no Croat has ever known better to specify the Croatian viewpoint and bring about a complete turn-around than Mr Pavelić succeeded in doing in conversation with Nikola Pašić'.[37]

The Radicals having evolved into a court party, they increasingly enjoyed the fruits of office. This involved corruption, from which Serbian politics suffered much more than they had in the pre-Yugoslav era. Davidović claimed Pašić had already been bribed by the court to the tune of 40,000 dinars for his mea culpa at the time of the trial for the St John's Day attempt. Pašić's claim for compensation for war damages—reflecting not his entire wealth but just what was actually damaged during the war—was reported in December 1921 as including two houses in Belgrade and three in his native Zaječar, property in Kosovo with 130 houses, around 800 bottles of wine dating back to the 1900s and 1890s plus vintage šljivovica and komovica (a type of grape brandy), two guns with silver-embossed butts that had allegedly belonged to the fifteenth-century Albanian lord Skenderbeg, a jewel-encrusted box given him by the Russian Tsar, pictures of King Petar and the Romanian and Bulgarian kings in valuable frames and other jewellery, with a total value of 1,594,784 dinars. Pašić's son Radomir trod a path followed by many spoilt children of powerful statesmen, both in Serbia and elsewhere, becoming a pioneer in multiple corrupt business ventures.[38] Meanwhile, the unification of a vast new state on a legally dubious basis greatly increased the distribution of patronage on the part of the government and court, consequently the scope of corruption. This turned Pašić and his Radical ministers into easy targets for scandals by which their opponents, backed by Aleksandar, could destroy them.

The scandal that began Pašić's undoing arose because the Radical finance minister Milan Stojadinović had delayed paying the Yugoslav state debt owed to the Czechoslovak company Adamstal for repairs to Yugoslavia's railway stock until the company had paid him and his friends a bribe to the value of 16 million dinars; the delay in payment resulted in an effective loss to the Yugoslav treasury of 122 million dinars due to depreciation of the dinar against the Czech crown in the interval. The bribe was paid through Radomir Pašić as intermediary, using an account at the Slavonic Bank, whose director was his friend Ljubomir Milin. But when Milin died in the course of the transaction, Radomir tried to avoid paying his widow her share of the bribe, leading her to appeal for help to the inspector of the trade ministry, Dragiša Stojadinović (not related to Milan Stojadinović), who was the son-in-law of Ljubomir Jovanović—president of parliament, vice-president of the Radical party and the emerging leader of Aleksandar's anti-Pašić Radical faction. Like several of the men who acted against Aleksandar's enemies in this period, Dragiša was a veteran of the Chetnik campaign in Macedonia. He informed the press of Radomir's scam on 30 June 1924. So began a feud within the Radical party that would steadily escalate over the next two years into a major political crisis.[39]

The Radicals and HSS—Serb and Croat nationalists respectively—made uneasy bedfellows, and relations between them in government rapidly frayed. Following the publication of a further article in the press by Dragiša Stojadinović exposing Radomir's Adamstal scam, Davidović in the opposition's name submitted on 24 March 1926 a parliamentary interpellation regarding the affair, to which Nikola Pašić responded by attempting to adjourn parliament. Prompted by Aleksandar, Radić abandoned his alliance with Pašić and sided with the opposition over the corruption affair. This compelled Pašić to resign as prime minister on 4 April 1926. He was replaced by Nikola Uzunović, a Radical enjoying Aleksandar's trust, who inherited the coalition with the HSS. However, when Uzunović reconstituted his government on 15 April, Radić and the mainstream HSS were excluded in favour of dissident HSS politicians supported by the king. Aleksandar's strategy was to create a parliamentary bloc of pro-centralist factions, under his personal aegis, based upon Democrats, HSS politicians and particularly Radicals loyal to himself. This revived the strategy of his namesake, Aleksandar Obrenović, of attempting to neutralise Pašić, turn the Radicals into a tame pro-regime party and build a pro-regime coalition by splitting the existing parties. The second King Aleksandar had the advantage, however, that while some among the Serbian political classes were concerned at his growing influence in political life, this was balanced by their appreciation of him as a bulwark against Croatian separatism.[40]

REIGN OF THE SECOND KING ALEKSANDAR

Aleksandar thus promoted Jovanović, who had served him well as interior minister during the Salonika trial, as head of a Court Radical faction against Pašić and his supporters. Encouraged by the opposition, which was fully exploiting the corruption scandal, Jovanović's faction began investigating Radomir's corrupt activities, and parliament eventually established a committee of inquiry on 3 June. Meanwhile, Pašić retaliated and on 26 April narrowly succeeded in having the Radical general council expel Jovanović from the party, though several prominent Radical politicians refused to support this, partly out of awareness of Aleksandar's hostility to Pašić and their consequent unwillingness to sacrifice their own standing at court for his sake. This led to the formation of a dissident ten-member Radical parliamentary faction under Jovanović. Pašić's influence in his own party fell. Under pressure from Aleksandar, his supporters first postponed then abandoned plans to hold a grandiose public celebration of his 80th birthday.[41]

Pašić and his supporters forced Uzunović to resign as prime minister on 7 December. Pašić met with the king on 9 December, requesting that, as leader of the largest parliamentary party, he be allowed to form a new government, but Aleksandar replied, 'You are under surveillance. Until you cleanse yourself of the accusations relating to your son's affairs, you cannot head the government!' According to his supporter Milan Stojadinović's account, Pašić was crushed. He returned home, refusing to eat with his family: 'You have dinner, and I will go and lie down. I don't feel well ...' He died of a stroke the following day. Stojadinović claims he visited Pašić's home in the early hours following his death and Pašić's wife Đurđina showed him her husband in his deathbed, telling him 'There, you see, they've succeeded ... He's dead ...'[42] The news quickly spread that Pašić's death was linked to his meeting with the king; rumours even circulated that he had been poisoned.[43] His death crippled his party, a development which Aleksandar facilitated by promoting his own faction within it, headed first by Jovanović, subsequently by Velimir Vukićević. Aleksandar similarly factionalised the Democrats, promoting against Davidović's leadership a faction led by Vojislav Marinković and other former Progressives.

Pašić had survived innumerable scrapes and cliff-hangers but finally met his Waterloo. He had allegedly said that 'the Court is like a hot hell-furnace: if you are too close you will burn yourself; if you are too far you will get cold and freeze'.[44] His tumultuous life justifies this aphorism. He was Yugoslavia's Bismarck: apparently spectacularly successful in achieving national unification in his lifetime, he was eventually brought down by his ambitious younger monarch, while his model of national unification proved deeply flawed and largely transient. The Germany Bismarck unified lost two world wars and a third of its original territory, while his Prussia disappeared. The Yugoslavia Pašić unified disappeared while his Serbia lost all the territory he had gained for it except Vojvodina, the Sanjak and some minor enclaves and ended the twentieth century as a defeated, pariah state.

SERBIA

Assassination of Stjepan Radić

Following Pašić's death, Aleksandar reinstated Uzunović as prime minister. With the two now determining government policy, the Radical–HSS partnership was short-lived. It collapsed by early 1927 owing to differences over agrarian reform in Dalmatia (with the Radicals defending the interests of the large landowners) and standardisation of taxation across Yugoslavia (with the Radicals defending Serbia's privileged position), and to the Radicals' obstruction, through the interior ministry, of HSS electoral campaigning, particularly in Bosnia-Hercegovina and Vojvodina.[45] In February, with Aleksandar's approval, Uzunović abandoned the HSS, dismissed Radić as education minister and formed a coalition with the SLS. Thus, the Radicals discarded Radić and the HSS as they had Pribićević and the Independent Democrats. Uzunović selected as transport minister General Svetislav Milosavljević, chief of the general staff's transport service. When Miša Trifunović, a leading Radical, complained to the king that it was inappropriate to appoint an army officer to government, Aleksandar retorted 'Was it only you politicians who fought for this country and the soldiers didn't? Do only you politicians have the right to participate in the administration of this country and the soldiers not?'[46]

Aleksandar replaced Uzunović's cabinet on 17 April 1927 with one headed by Vukićević, Marinković and the JMO leader Spaho. As Vukićević and Marinković did not control their respective parties, their government depended entirely upon Aleksandar, who dissolved parliament to enable his protégés to govern without its interference for five months. This coalition was widely suspected of presaging the establishment of a 'fourth party', in allusion to Aleksandar Obrenović's project, through which the king would establish his personal regime.[47] The subsequent elections of 11 September 1927—the last to be held in the Kingdom of Serbs, Croats and Slovenes—were characterised by government manipulation, extreme police harassment of the opposition and its voters and internal Radical feuding. The Radicals' share of the vote and particularly of parliamentary seats consequently fell significantly, to 50.9 per cent and 41 in Serbia respectively, while the Democrats' share there rose to 35.3 per cent and 31. The Radicals' vote declined everywhere outside Serbia as well, except Montenegro. Nevertheless, they received the most votes in Yugoslavia as a whole of any party; and of their 117 seats, 100 went to Vukićević's faction and only 17 to the former Pašić loyalists grouped behind the party's general council, reflecting the king's great success in subordinating Serbia's principal party to his control.[48] Vukićević's government now rested on the support of an unstable parliamentary majority of the Radicals, Democrats, SLS, JMO and the German minority's party, while it was bitterly attacked by the opposition over its abusive electoral practices.

In these circumstances of increasing royal control of politics through a tamed Radical party, the previously hostile HSS and Independent Democrats united to form the principal opposition bloc in parliament, the Peasant–Democrat Coalition, on 10 November 1927. This was essentially an all-Croatian (i.e. Croat and Croatian Serb) alliance against the dominant political classes of Serbia; although intended to take in the Democrats and JMO, this failed to occur. The new bloc expressed the newly apparent division of interests between Serbians and prečani Serbs. Pribićević acknowledged this, claiming subsequently that, in a conversation they had on 22 July 1928, Aleksandar had accused him of having established a 'prečani front' that would threaten the state's unity.

> I replied to the King that he was mistaken if he believed that, on that question, all Serbs were on his side. I added that in the country there existed not only the Croat question (as well as perhaps the Slovene, although Dr Korošec was in the government), but also the question of the prečani Serbs. Their position is absolutely the most difficult. Every Serbian, deep down, after all sometimes thinks that it is necessary to reach an agreement with the Croats, but not one believes that the prečani Serbs too are a factor in the state and that they too need to be satisfied. In Belgrade, it is commonly believed that they must listen and that the Serbians speak in their name. I warned the king that this had already become an unavoidable issue ...[49]

In Pribićević's opinion, 'For official Belgrade, the Serb national idea consists of all Serbs outside Serbia having to work for its supremacy like ordinary functionaries who do not even have any kind of right to participate in carrying out state policy, except completely subordinate to the leadership of official Belgrade.'[50]

Croatian feeling against the regime was embittered by the government's territorial and economic concessions to Italy, culminating in the 20 July 1925 Nettuno Convention granting concessions to Italian landlords in Dalmatia and to Italian immigrants, which appeared to threaten Croatian economic and national interests. Obstruction of its ratification became a central plank of Croatian parliamentary opposition strategy. The confrontation in parliament between the Serbian-dominated government's deputies and the Croatian opposition bloc became constant and ferocious, even physical. The opposition brought parliamentary proceedings to a standstill through filibustering while vicious insults flew back and forth between deputies on either side. In one debate on 12 March 1928, Radić accused Čedo Radović, minister for social policy, of being an 'ignoramus' and a 'thief in a minister's chair'; Radović retorted that Radić was a 'drunkard'.[51] Although Radić's hostility had previously focused alternately on Aleksandar and Pribićević, he now directed his animosity against the Serbian political classes, above all the Radicals. In a personal audience with Aleksandar on 19 February 1928, he proposed that the king establish a non-party military regime that would be 'against the Great Serbian parties'.[52] The same proposal had been made by Pribićević in his own audience with the king the day before and was endorsed by some senior Radicals, including Bosnia's Srškić. It greatly damaged relations between the HSS and Democrats, prompting the latter to join

Vukićević's government on 22 February to form a new Radical–Democrat coalition. Once again the king managed to split the opposition.

Aleksandar had thus succeeded, using divide-and-rule tactics involving the Croatian opposition, in weakening Serbia's principal political parties—Radicals and Democrats—and in strengthening his influence over them. But the principal parties from Croatia, the HSS and Independent Democrats, successfully resisted his control and remained firmly united, thus obstructing his consolidation of power. The king therefore resorted to more extreme measures to complete the establishment of his personal regime.[53] In this, he enjoyed strong backing from the army, National Defence and veterans' and Chetnik organisations, where there was extreme discontent with the nationally fractured party-political system which was contrasted unfavourably with the patriotic unity of Serbia's wartime armed forces. This was a constituency that Aleksandar could rely upon to support his overthrow of the parliamentary order in favour of an authoritarian regime that would continue the struggle for unification for which the soldiers and guerrillas had fought up to 1918.[54]

The ferocity of the confrontation between government and opposition peaked in mid-1928. Radić was excluded from a parliamentary session on 4 May because of his insult to Radović. The Independent Democrat Sava Kosanović was assaulted in parliament the following day. Violence was inflicted not only on the Croatian opposition; on 29–30 May, students from Belgrade University demonstrated against the Nettuno Convention and were beaten by the police, prompting a complaint in parliament from a Farmers' deputy.[55] Fighting erupted on 10 June when the gendarmerie attempted to remove Radić forcibly from parliament. A vicious campaign against the opposition in the pro-government press reached a climax on 14 June, when the government's newspaper *Jedinstvo* (Unity), in a front-page article written by its editor Vladimir Ristović, issued a thinly veiled call for violence against the opposition deputies entitled 'It is only possible to talk with swine in their own language'. The article warned Pribićević that 'heads of traitors and rogues will fall, if it proves necessary, but order in the land and the authority of parliament will be held up high', then went on to threaten Pribićević and Radić that they had by their actions 'placed themselves outside the law, in the eyes both of those who are called to defend the legal order and of those who will, in the emergency thus brought about, feel personally called upon to pass judgement themselves and for their own account'.[56] There followed five days of deadlock in parliament over the government's rejection of the opposition's demand that the name of the deputy president of parliament, the Muslim Halid-beg Hrasnica, be rewritten 'Halid Hrasnica' on the grounds that the term 'beg' was an aristocratic title whose use was forbidden by the constitution. It was characteristic of the intransigence on both sides that neither would back down over this triviality.[57]

Radić recorded on 19 June having been told by a senior Radical that 'Velja Vukićević was so furious that he was ready to do anything' and that 'what his newspaper *Jedinstvo* wrote, that Radić and Pribićević have to be killed, is not unfortunately merely an empty threat'.[58] During another confrontation in parliament that day, Radić asked the president of parliament, Ninko Perić, 'Are you president of the parliament or a keeper of cattle?' He was then violently threatened by the Radical deputies Joca Selić, who shouted 'You donkey! You drunk! We'll break his head!', and Toma Popović, who shouted 'Patience must come to an end! His head will roll one of these days, there! Cattle must be taught a lesson by beating! Dead heads will roll here one of these days! But they, not the Serbs, will be to blame!' Popović had to be restrained from attacking Radić. Another Radical deputy, Puniša Račić, shouted that 'Radić has to get a beating!'[59] On that day, Račić submitted a proposal to the president of the parliament, signed by an additional 23 deputies, demanding that Radić be medically examined to determine 'if he is sane', and that if he turned out to be, he should be punished to the maximum, so 'that undesired consequences be avoided, which otherwise may occur as the result of this sort of behaviour by Mr Radić'.[60]

Another verbal confrontation occurred on the parliamentary floor on 20 June between Račić, who spoke menacingly, and an HSS deputy, Ivan Pernar, who heckled him. Račić proclaimed: 'I, sir, as a Serb and a national deputy, when I see the danger facing my nation and Fatherland, openly say that I will employ other weapons, which are needed to protect the interests of Serbdom...', which several opposition deputies interpreted as a violent threat. When Pernar accused Račić of having 'plundered the begs [i.e. Muslim landlords]' in Kosovo, Račić pulled out a revolver, strode towards him and demanded that he retract the accusation.[61] When Pernar failed to do so immediately, Račić shot him, followed by four other HSS deputies, including Stjepan Radić. Račić was assisted by Dragutin Jovanović ('Vojvoda Lune'), another veteran of guerrilla action in Kosovo, albeit a Democrat, who drew his own revolver and stood at Račić's side to deter anyone from intervening, while another two Radical deputies and personal friends of Račić's, Dragan Bojović and Toma Popović, apparently also stood alongside him. Following the crime, Račić shouted in front of some of the ministers and pro-government deputies, 'Long live Serbia! Long live Great Serbia!'[62] He then made his way to a get-away car provided by Bojović (who had also obtained for him the gun used in the assassination) but surrendered to the authorities later that day.[63] Two of the deputies who were shot, Pavle Radić and Đuro Basariček, were killed immediately while three of them, Stjepan Radić, Ivan Pernar and Ivan Granđa, were wounded.

Controversy has remained over whether Račić acted on his own accord or at the behest of higher state or political elements. Račić was a protégé of Vukičević and had been involved in the Black Hand's terrorist activities against King Nikola's regime in Montenegro. He had subsequently testified against Apis at the Salonika trial and been a principal organiser of post-war counter-insurgency repression of the civilian population of Kosovo and Macedonia. He was thus a typical enforcer of the

White Hand, which was widely suspected of being behind the assassination. The Croatian sculptor Ivan Meštrović, who moved in elite Belgrade circles at the time and knew Aleksandar personally, claimed to have been told by the minister of court that on the day of the assassination Račić had come directly to parliament from the royal palace, which suggests the king's complicity.[64] But Meštrović is a notoriously unreliable witness.[65] In any event, Račić was tried in June 1929 and received a sentence of only twenty years in prison; the court accepted his argument that he had acted without premeditation, in defence of his own honour.[66] The proceedings against his accomplices Lune and Popović were dropped. For many Croats, the trial and sentence strengthened the impression that the assassination had some measure of official blessing.

The assassination was nevertheless widely condemned by Serbs. The Radical deputy Milutin Tomić visited the opposition's parliamentary club on the day after the assassination and with 'unqualified revulsion condemned the bloody and terrible crime that occurred yesterday in the national assembly', while the *Niški glasnik* (Niš Herald) stated three days later: 'All we true Serbians, in our ancestors' blood, at this terrible moment feel the same deep pain for the loss of the virtuous representatives of the people, and we deplore the savage, barbarous act of such a bandit as Puniša Račić'. According to *Zastava*, a Radical newspaper from Novi Sad, 'the public cannot find either excuse or justification for this crime of Puniša Račić's'.[67] The Association of Chetniks for the Freedom and Honour of the Fatherland published a statement on 23 June, claiming that Račić's role in the Chetnik guerrilla struggle had been minimal and inglorious and stating: 'The Association of Chetniks, revolted by the terrible crime, most ardently shares the heavy national pain, which has deeply shaken the patriotic heart of the whole of our people and sincerely regrets the innocent lives and spilled blood of our Croat brothers.'[68] The Radical politician Lazar Marković wrote some years later of 'the horrible crime of the Montenegrin deputy Puniša Račić, whose consequences must today be borne by the whole country'.[69]

The Croatian opposition bloc withdrew from the parliament following the shooting. Aleksandar then attempted to establish a 'neutral', cross-party government under former war minister General Stevan Hadžić, for which he had the Croatian opposition's blessing. But Hadžić was unable to muster the necessary parliamentary support. The king then let the SLS politician Anton Korošec reconstitute Vukićević's cabinet under his own leadership—the only time in Yugoslavia's interwar history that a non-Serb led a government. In this government, a greater role was given to ministers from outside Serbia, from the ranks of the SLS and JMO as well as a Croat member of the Democratic Party—this was intended to counter the opposition's complaint of Serbian hegemony. However, when parliament reopened on 1 August, the HSS and Independent Democrat deputies formed their own assembly in Zagreb and declared that since the 'act of 1 December 1918 and Constitution of 28 June 1921 were used to ensure the hegemony of the former Kingdom of Serbia over all other lands and national parts', and the existing state order had been wholly negated by the assassinations in the parliament, the Peasant–Democrat Coalition would 'wage a most decisive struggle for a new state order which would guarantee full equality to all mentioned individualities'. It repudiated the rump Yugoslav parliament's authority: 'All conclusions which would create in particular financial obligations, which would be imposed upon the people, we declare null and void and non-obligatory for the prečani territories, which we represent.'[70] The HSS leadership by now viewed the political parties from Serbia, rather than the king, as the obstacle to constitutional reform and the normalisation of political life; it indicated that it saw no possible solution coming from parliament and that its preference was for the king to form a non-parliamentary government, even if dictatorial.[71]

As the 1920s were drawing to a close, Yugoslavia appeared to be close to collapse. Radić symbolically left Belgrade and returned on 8 July to Zagreb, where he died of his injury on 8 August; his death was avenged the same day when Ristović, author of the *Jedinstvo* article that had incited the murder, was shot dead in Zagreb by a Croat nationalist. The Croatian deputies' departure from the parliament permitted the ratification of the Nettuno Convention on 13 August 1928, by a single vote, which seemed to many Croats to add insult to injury. Radić's funeral in Zagreb on the same day was attended by vast crowds numbering perhaps 300,000 in a great manifestation of Croat popular support for his politics.[72] The Serbian political classes remained bitterly divided over how to respond to the crisis, with Davidović and the Democrats dissenting from the government's hardline policy toward the opposition. Meanwhile, the Communists were becoming increasingly militant in their support for the national movements of the non-Serb Yugoslav peoples against Belgrade. In 1927, Sima Marković was arrested and the seat of the Central Committee of the KPJ was transferred from Belgrade to Zagreb. A certain Josip Broz was arrested in Zagreb on 4 August 1928 after distributing a leaflet calling upon the people to condemn the assassination in the parliament, and bombs and guns were discovered at his home. The KPJ on 1 September called explicitly for the formation of 'free and independent worker-peasant republics of Croatia, Slovenia, Serbia, Macedonia, Montenegro, Bosnia-Hercegovina and Vojvodina!'[73] On the tenth anniversary of the state's foundation, 1 December 1928, there was a bloody clash between police and student protesters in Zagreb's central square, with armed KPJ activists playing a leading role in the disturbances.

The Communist and Croatian nationalist threats to Yugoslavia thus threatened to converge; the regime faced a peasant revolutionary popular opposition in Croatia akin to those that Serbian monarchs had periodically suppressed since Miloš's day. The clash in Zagreb prompted the government to install the White Hand protégé and former contra Colonel Maksimović as great župan of Zagreb.[74] But it also prompted Davidović to dissent from the government's policy: on 27 December, he stated his opposition to Maksimović's appointment and opposed the government's demand for special powers of repression to deal with the alleged threats to the state. He instead demanded from Korošec that the government negotiate with the Peasant–Democrat Coalition and concede its demand for the dissolution of parliament and new elections. Since Korošec and the rest of the government rejected these demands, it was forced to resign the same day.[75]

Aleksandar summoned Pribićević and Vladimir Maček, Radić's successor as HSS leader, to discuss a solution to the crisis; this occurred in separate meetings at the royal palace on 4 January. Maček insisted on constitutional revision and the establishment of Yugoslav federalism based on the seven 'historic lands' of Slovenia, Croatia, Bosnia-Hercegovina, Vojvodina, Serbia, Montenegro and Macedonia. Pribićević informed the king that 'my position is wholly in accordance with the stance of the Croats and Maček, to the end and in everything', to which Aleksandar replied, according to his own account, 'You have become a federalist; you have struck a knife in the back of the other Serbs.' The following day, Aleksandar again met with Maček, who urged him to form a 'non-political government' while softening his demands to include the retention by Serbia of Macedonia and the division of Bosnia-Hercegovina between Serbia and Croatia. However, Aleksandar then met with constitutional law professor Slobodan Jovanović, who advised him against accepting constitutional revision on this basis on the grounds that it represented dualism on the Austro-Hungarian model.[76] Consequently, the royal court chancellery announced that day that, because of the inability of Yugoslavia's politicians to agree on a solution to the crisis, 'there is no possibility for any kind of parliamentary solution whatsoever which might guarantee the maintenance of full state and national unity'.[77]

6 January Regime

The experience of the 1920s demonstrated that all of the principal Serb political parties in turn—Democrats, Radicals and even Pribićević's initially ferociously centralist Independent Democrats—were ready to collaborate with the Croatian opposition at the price of at least considering constitutional reform along lines it favoured. According to the logic of Yugoslav parliamentary politics, such constitutional reform would eventually occur, leaving the HSS allied to the Independent Democrats political masters in Croatia and the Radicals and Democrats between them controlling Serbia, curtailing King Aleksandar's room for manoeuvre. Given the opposition of most of the non-Serb political classes to unitarism and the unwillingness of their Croatian wing to permit the parliamentary regime to function on a unitarist basis, a federal solution was the only way in which both Yugoslavia and parliamentarism could have been saved. For Aleksandar, conversely, an aggressive reassertion of a unitarist political order was the only way to avoid his gradual demotion to a figurehead monarch and to reassert his primacy.

REIGN OF THE SECOND KING ALEKSANDAR

This did not mean that Aleksandar was in principle opposed to Croatia's separation from Yugoslavia. After the shootings in parliament, Aleksandar offered to grant Croatia independence by its 'amputation' from the rest of Yugoslavia, believing that this was preferable to a federal Yugoslavia. According to Pribićević, Aleksandar said to him, 'But I don't want a federation; I shall never agree to a federation. I would rather have partition than a federation.' He apparently offered to leave Yugoslav troops on independent Croatia's borders to protect it from Italy. Pribićević nevertheless rejected the idea on principle, asking the king 'If you are, therefore, considering amputation, the question is posed: who will hold the handle of the knife by which the state will be cut up?'[78] This was the stumbling block: Aleksandar could not agree with the Croatian opposition on where, if Croatia were to separate from Serbia, the border between them should lie. Maček demanded Croatia-Slavonia and Dalmatia within their historic borders and at least part of Bosnia-Hercegovina and Vojvodina. Aleksandar's private response to this was allegedly 'And then, what would the Serbs say if the Croatian oblast bordered on Belgrade, and it must not be forgotten that I am also a Serb? ... The Croats exaggerate their importance, for if all other parts are gathered around the matrix then the Croats and Croatia are only a detail ...'[79] Furthermore, with an aggressive Italy continuing to harbour designs on Yugoslavia's territory and on Albania, there seemed to be an acute danger of Italian co-option of an independent Croatia as an anti-Serbian cat's paw, just as there had been during the war.

Following Maček and Pribićević's rejection of the offer of amputation, Aleksandar proclaimed a royal dictatorship on 6 January 1929, ending the Yugoslav parliamentary regime. The constitution was suspended and parliament dissolved. According to the royal court's official announcement: 'The time has come, when between the people and the King there cannot and may no longer be an intermediary ... Instead of parliamentarism developing and strengthening the spirit of national and state unity, it—such as it is—is beginning to lead to spiritual disintegration and national fragmentation. It is my holy duty to defend state and national unity by all means.'[80] This proclamation was composed primarily by Uzunović, Srškić and Božidar Maksimović.[81] Yet the putsch may initially have had the blessing of the HSS leadership, for it chimed with Radić and Maček's preference for the overthrow of the St Vitus's Day Constitution and the concentration of the union between Croatia and Serbia purely in the king's person.[82]

The dictatorship ('the 6 January Regime') was justified by the need to save Yugoslavia. Its ideology was centred on the concept of integral Yugoslav nationhood for the sake of which the individual nationhoods of Serbs, Croats and Slovenes were to be suppressed. However, this ideology was adopted for pragmatic reasons and lacked deep roots. Centralism accompanied repression. The Law on Royal Power and Supreme State Administration, enacted on the day the dictatorship was proclaimed, stated that 'the king is the bearer of all power in the country' and could proclaim laws, appoint officials and distribute military ranks; he was commander of the army, had the power of amnesty for all crimes, represented the state in all its relations with foreign states, declared war and concluded peace, enjoyed immunity and could not be prosecuted, and chose the cabinet and prime minister, who were responsible to him alone.[83] The revised Law for the Protection of the State, enacted the same day, banned the writing, publication or distribution of texts that 'threaten public peace or bring into question the public order'; all public gatherings not authorised by the authorities; all parties or associations 'that make propaganda or persuade others, that it is necessary to change the existing order in the state'; and all parties that 'carry a religious or tribal label'.[84] The Press Law of 11 January gave the state major powers to suppress newspapers, including those that provoked 'hatred against the state as a whole or religious or tribal discord'.[85] The trade union movement and all existing political parties were suppressed. Elected municipal and oblast councils and assemblies were replaced by administrations appointed by the oblast governors (great župans) or, in the case of the Belgrade, Zagreb and Ljubljana municipalities, by the king himself on the interior minister's advice.

The new regime's foundation was the White Hand, with Živković as prime minister and interior minister in the 'non-partisan' government appointed following the coup. The regime's second military strongman was Hadžić; appointed minister of the army and navy in December 1926, he remained so until his death on 23 April 1931. As with the 1903 putsch, the putschist officers in 1929 ousted their rivals within the army: in the spring of 1929, there was a major redistribution of military posts in favour of those loyal to Aleksandar and against those of suspect loyalty. In April–May 1929, 35 generals or officers of equivalent rank, 41 colonels, 26 lieutenant colonels and 10 majors were pensioned off.[86] Beyond that, just as King Aleksandar of Serbia had presided over a 'fusion' of Radicals and Progressives and considered establishing a 'fourth party', so King Aleksandar of Yugoslavia sought to handpick loyalists from the various Yugoslav parties to create a new, loyalist political elite and a controlled form of parliamentarism, also largely led by former Old Radicals and Progressives. Živković's government was dominated by Serbs, who made up ten of the sixteen ministers as against five Croats and one Slovene. Five of the Serb ministers were Radicals and three Democrats. With Srškić as justice minister, Kumanudi as minister of posts and telegraphs and Marinković as foreign minister, the key posts relating to security were in Serb hands, whereas Croats dominated the posts relating to the economy: the ministries of finance, trade and industry, and agriculture and water. Korošec held the transport ministry.[87] Meanwhile, according to Stojadinović, 'King Aleksandar, as Uzunović tells me, never wanted to hear of the Muslims' and rejected all suggestions to include the JMO in his dictatorship's governments.[88] JMO members were purged from local government in Bosnia-Hercegovina and replaced with Radicals, while the dictatorship promoted Muslim Bosniaks from previously marginal pro-Serb, non-JMO groups. One such, Srškić's supporter Hamdija Karamehmedović, was appointed minister without portfolio on 2 July 1932, becoming the regime's leading Muslim figure.[89]

Aleksandar's principal aim was to establish his personal domination over Serbia and its political classes, including those territories that he and his entourage considered 'Serb lands'. He viewed in effect the Yugoslav state as an expanded Serbia; at the tenth anniversary celebrations of the Battle of Kumanovo on 24 October 1922, he had announced that 'the struggle, which began in 1804, under my exalted great-grandfather, was resumed in 1912, when the cannon shots of September announced that the moment had arrived for our final liberation. Those cannons do not fall silent right up until 1918, when the heroic muscles of our sons *surround our extended Fatherland*' (emphasis in original).[90] Although the confrontation between the Croatian and Croatian Serb parties on the one hand and the Serbian parties on the other was the most visible source of the political crisis, for Aleksandar's regime the threat represented by the former also provided a convenient pretext for suppressing the latter. His contempt for politicians and parties transcended the Serb–Croat conflict; he established the dictatorship because he believed that 'the politicians have wrecked and abused parliamentarism for the sake of pathetic party purposes'.[91] Meanwhile, it was primarily Serb politicians who initially objected to the dictatorship. Maček was optimistic following its proclamation: 'The St Vitus's Day Constitution, which has for over seven years tormented the Croatian nation, is demolished.' He expressed the hope that 'given the great wisdom of His Majesty the King, I hope he will succeed in establishing for us the idea of the Croat nation: that the Croat be master in his free Croatia'.[92]

According to Pribićević, writing from exile, 'The dictatorship was introduced to realise the Yugoslav idea. But that was just a mask behind which hid exclusively Great Serbian politics, or to be more precise, the politics of the Serbians.'[93] It would have been more accurate to say the politics of the Serbian court. Despite the Yugoslavist veneer, the administration remained overwhelmingly Serb-dominated; for example, in 1932, Serbs and Montenegrins accounted for 39 per cent of the Yugoslav population but 89 per cent of the staff at the interior ministry, 85 per cent at the justice ministry, 90 per cent at the ministry of social policy and national health, and 96 per cent at the education ministry.[94] However, Queen Draga's sister Ana Milićević Lunjevica, an exile like Pribićević, noted: 'Today the Serbs, through the dictatorship, have had all their traditions plundered down to their very name— for the Kingdom of Serbia, as such, does not exist under the murderous regime in Serbia! They are manufacturing Serb history now, so they want to take away her history: no history, no tradition, no name any longer! Everything that is hers has been changed by the crime: country, name, nation! No longer Serbia and Serbs, just Yugoslavia and Yugoslavs.'[95] Pribićević and Milićević Lunjevica expressed two sides of the truth about the dictatorship: it paradoxically represented both Serbian hegemony and the erasure of Serbia.

SERBIA

Aleksandar's regime consequently enacted on 3 October 1929 its most infamous act, the Law on the Naming and Division of the Kingdom into Administrative Territories. The Kingdom of Serbs, Croats and Slovenes was renamed the Kingdom of Yugoslavia and divided administratively into nine units, each of which went by the Croatian term 'banovina' and was named after a river (except for the Primorje Banovina, whose name meant 'sea coast'). Although the historiography has traditionally presented this arrangement as intended to erase the traditional borders between the constituent parts of Yugoslavia along with their identities, this was only partly true. The north-westernmost unit, the Drava Banovina, corresponded to Slovenia. Croatia-Slavonia, shorn of Srem and part of eastern Slavonia, was broadly preserved as the Sava Banovina; its border with the Drava Banovina was Croatia-Slavonia's traditional north-western border while its southern and south-eastern border broadly corresponded to Croatia-Slavonia's traditional border with Bosnia. The Sava Banovina was easily the most populous of the banovinas and the second largest by territory; its formation was intended to mollify Croatian opinion.[96] Northern and central Dalmatia were united with western Hercegovina and adjacent areas of south-western and central Bosnia to form the Primorje Banovina, constituting a second Croat-majority unit.

The remaining six banovinas were the Vrbas Banovina, comprising western and north-central Bosnia; the Drina Banovina, comprising eastern Bosnia, part of eastern Slavonia, part of Srem and western Serbia; the Danube Banovina, comprising Vojvodina, the rest of Srem and central Serbia; the Zeta Banovina, comprising Montenegro, southern Dalmatia, south-eastern Bosnia-Hercegovina, the Sanjak and part of Kosovo; the Morava Banovina, comprising eastern and part of southern Serbia and part of Kosovo; and the Vardar Banovina, comprising the rest of southern Serbia, most of Kosovo and Yugoslav Macedonia. Belgrade and its surroundings formed a separate, tenth unit, in the manner of Washington DC: the Administration of the City of Belgrade. A 'ban' (governor) was appointed for each banovina. General Milosavljević, formerly transport minister in Uzunović's government, the White Hand's retired Army General Krsto Smiljanić and retired General Svetomir Matić were, with the king's approval, appointed bans of the Vrbas, Zeta and Danube Banovinas respectively.

The arrangement gave the Orthodox a majority in six and the Serbs a majority in five out of nine banovinas—if the view, then dominant, that Montenegrins were Serbs is accepted. On the assumption that the Vardar Banovina, which incorporated most of the non-Serb territory conquered in the Balkan Wars, could eventually be assimilated, the arrangement secured for the Serbs ownership and control over six banovinas, against two for the Croats and one for the Slovenes. This included Serbia itself, most of Bosnia-Hercegovina, Vojvodina, Srem, part of eastern Slavonia, southern Dalmatia (including Dubrovnik), Montenegro, the Sanjak, Kosovo and Macedonia. As Gligorijević notes, 'It should be said that at the time of the formation of the banovinas, account was taken of the national interests of the Slovenes, Croats and above all Serbs.'[97] Yet it was Serbia itself along with Bosnia-Hercegovina that was primarily eviscerated. Among Serbia's population, the administrative arrangement was unpopular, indeed viewed as negating Serbia's statehood. Pre-1912 Serbia was divided between four different banovinas of which only the Morava Banovina had its capital in Serbia, so that Serbians in the Danube, Drina and Vardar Banovinas who needed to visit their banovina capital had to travel to Novi Sad, Sarajevo and Skopje respectively.[98] Vojvodina, where non-Serbs were in the majority, was subsumed within the Danube Banovina, which had a safe Serb majority and where the influence of local autonomist Serbs was diluted. Not coincidentally, the architect of this arrangement and the most powerful civilian member of Aleksandar's regime was no Serbian but justice minister Srškić, leader of Bosnia-Hercegovina's Radicals, whose bitter struggle with the JMO for domination in Bosnia-Hercegovina paralleled in some ways Aleksandar's struggle with Serbia's political classes. Srškić belonged to Aleksandar's closest circle and was Živković's personal friend.[99] He thereby achieved his goal of partitioning Bosnia-Hercegovina four ways, ensuring Serb control of three parts, Croat control of the fourth and the dispersal of the Muslims as a minority in each of the four. Indeed, Aleksandar allegedly told Meštrović that Bosnia had been partitioned because of the Muslims.[100] The latter were further weakened by the regime's establishment of a unified, all-Yugoslav Islamic Religious Community, with its seat in Belgrade and subordinated to the justice ministry. A new reis-ul-ulema, Ibrahim Maglajlić, was installed from the ranks of the pro-Serbian Muslims to head it. The ban on parties with a religious affiliation was primarily directed against Srškić's *bête noire*, the JMO.

Like other authoritarian regimes in contemporary Europe, Aleksandar's dictatorship promoted mass organisations to inculcate loyalty among its citizens. The autonomous Falcon (Sokol) sports societies that existed in the individual Yugoslav lands were abolished on 4 December 1929 in favour of a new Union of Falcons of the Kingdom of Yugoslavia; this mass organisation was intended to encourage among the citizenry both a common Yugoslav identity and respect for authority, discipline and collective work, and to prepare them for military service. The new Falcons' union, whose activities extended beyond sport to lessons of direct ideological indoctrination, was supposed to create a new 'Yugoslav type of culture' on the principle that 'whoever is a Falcon is a Yugoslav'. The king obtained the defection of the HSS's vice-president Dragutin Karla Kovačević and sought to build around him a pro-regime faction of the party.[101] He was appointed head of the Yugoslav Peasant Movement, which was intended to win peasant loyalty to the king and to Yugoslavia by means of carefully choreographed, police-supervised rallies.[102] The Yugoslav National Workers' Union was established with a monopoly on labour organisation, supposedly to protect working-class interests, paralleling the Fascist trade unions of Mussolini's Italy.

The regime passed a law on secondary schools on 31 August 1929, followed by a law on elementary schools on 5 December, imposing a uniform school system on the entire kingdom aimed at inculcating belief in Yugoslav national and state unity.[103] A law was passed on 1 January 1930 by which the judiciaries and criminal legal codes of the diverse parts of the kingdom, that had been inherited unchanged from the entities that entered it in 1918, were now finally unified. A new Law on the Naming and Division of the Kingdom into Administrative Territories was passed on 28 August 1931, modifying the banovinas' borders in a manner perhaps intended to appease Croat opinion. Thus, the principal Croatian banovina, the Sava Banovina, was enlarged to incorporate all of eastern Slavonia—the towns of Vukovar, Vinkovci and Županja—while the second Croat-majority banovina, the Primorje Banovina, gained the Dalmatian island of Korčula and a larger share of Hercegovina, while losing the predominantly Muslim town of Travnik in central Bosnia.

The regime aimed formally to suppress Serb, Croat and Slovene nationhood in favour of a broader, manufactured Yugoslav nationhood. This meant that Yugoslavism was treated less as a synthesis or compromise between the Serb, Croat and Slovene (sub)nations and increasingly as a hegemonic ideology and state religion, which gradually served to delegitimise it as opposition to the regime grew.[104] The Serbian regimental flags of the Yugoslav army were abolished on 6 September 1930 and replaced by Yugoslav flags. This policy failed. Though the Serbian parliamentary parties were successfully weakened, Serb nationalism found other, less democratic outlets. As in Ottoman times, the Serbian Orthodox Church acted as the bearer of the Serb national idea; whereas the Croatian flag was banned by the regime, the Serbian flag was permitted as the flag of the Serbian Orthodox Church. Nevertheless, the regime consolidated its control over the church. A law of 8 April 1930 gave king and state great influence on the election of the Patriarch. The Serbian church introduced a new constitution on 16 November 1931 requiring Orthodox priests, like other state officials, to swear allegiance to the king, who retained the right to confirm or reject the selection of the Patriarch and bishops.[105]

The regime's integral Yugoslavism had a definite Serbian flavour. The king based his patriotism on the Serbian military tradition or, in his words, 'my sacred duty to which I am directed in this difficult moment by the oath of the victims of Kolubara, Albanian Golgotha and Kajmakčalan'.[106] The establishment of an Orthodox metropolitanate in Zagreb and the opening of Orthodox churches in Slovenia, to serve the needs of Orthodox soldiers stationed there, undermined the official Yugoslavism by extending the reach of a specifically Serb national organisation and by provoking a Croat reaction. In December 1928, on the eve of the dictatorship's establishment, the government elevated the Day of St Sava, founder of the Serbian church, to an all-Yugoslav national holiday and put pressure on non-Serbs to celebrate it, provoking significant discontent among them, including Bosnia-Hercegovina's reis-ul-ulema and Zagreb's Catholic archbishop. Although the regime also celebrated the day of the Croatian pioneer of Yugoslavism, Bishop Strossmayer, this did not receive nearly as much official emphasis as St Sava's Day. The regime also privileged the use of the Cyrillic alphabet over the Latin and the Ekavian dialect over the Ijekavian used by western Yugoslavs.[107] Economic policy continued to favour Serbia: for example, in the period 1925–1934, 63.3 per cent of state investment in public works went to Serbia (including the territory gained in the Balkan Wars), 10 per cent to Bosnia-Hercegovina, 9 per cent to Croatia, 6.1 per cent to Montenegro, 4 per cent to Vojvodina, 3.9 per cent to Slovenia and 3.7 per cent to Dalmatia.[108]

The regime retreated somewhat from naked royal absolutism on 3 September 1931, when the king promulgated a new constitution, authored by himself, Živković, Marinković, Srškić and Ninko Perić.[109] This vested executive power exclusively in the king's hands through his ministers; the constitution defined him as the 'carrier of national unity and state wholeness' and 'guardian of their everyday interests', and all his powers as specified in the St Vitus's Day Constitution were retained or expanded. Whereas the St Vitus's Day Constitution specified that acts of royal authority were not valid without a minister's countersignature, now ministers were simply required to countersign them. The constitution established a national representative body that was to consist of a national parliament, elected every four years, sharing power with a senate whose members were to be drawn in equal numbers from royal appointees on the one hand and senators elected to six-year mandates on the other, with elections for half the elected senators to be held every three years. This was a throwback to Aleksandar Obrenović's April Constitution. Every member of the national representative body was required to pledge allegiance to the king and to 'safeguard above everything the unity of the nation, the independence of the state and the wholeness of the state oblasts', and to 'safeguard the Constitution and have before his eyes the good of the nation'.

The king had the power to proclaim and veto legislation and the exclusive power to summon and dismiss the national representative body and to call elections. Judicial verdicts and rulings were made in his name, though the courts remained independent. He could reach agreements with foreign states without approval from the representative body. The government was the principal bearer of the right to propose legislation, which a member of the representative body could only do if he had the backing of one-fifth of members of either the national parliament or senate. Legislation had to be approved by both parliament and senate; if they could not agree over it, the king would decide the matter. Bans were appointed by the king on the proposal of the president of the council of ministers (prime minister). Parliament had the right to determine the annual budget; if parliament were dissolved without the budget's approval, the budget of the previous budgetary year would be extended for up to four months, after which, if it were still not approved, the king could extend the budget by decree until the end of the new budgetary year. Most significantly of all, Article 116 of the constitution granted the king major emergency powers:

'In case of war, mobilisation, disorder or rebellion that would jeopardise the public order and security of the state or in general when the public interest is endangered to a sufficient measure, the King may, in those exceptional circumstances, order by decree that extraordinary, necessary measures are temporarily taken in the whole Kingdom or in one part of it, independently of constitutional and legal regulations.' This article made the king so powerful that it was known as the 'little constitution'. Nevertheless, individual rights and freedoms were guaranteed, including freedom from arbitrary arrest and of speech, expression, religion and association, though association of a party-political nature on a religious, tribal or regional basis was prohibited. The representative body's members retained the right to propose changes to the constitution if supported by three-fifths of the parliament or senate. As under the St Vitus's Day Constitution, legal affairs related to family or inheritance among Muslims were to be decided by sharia courts.[110]

The number of national representatives and senators, and the means by which they were to be elected, were established by an electoral law on 10 September, which aimed to disenfranchise parties based on particular nations or regions, such as the Radicals, HSS, JMO and SLS. To stand in an election, a party had to field a list of candidates for each of the 368 districts in the country. The leader of the country list had to have it endorsed by 60 voters from every district while the district candidates had to be endorsed by an additional 200 voters from their district; thus every country list had to assemble 95,680 signatures, which had to be confirmed by the district courts. Of the eventual 306 parliamentary deputies, two-thirds would go to the country list with the largest number of votes, apportioned for the banovinas according to where the votes had been cast; if it won an absolute majority of votes, it would receive in addition an equivalent proportion of the remaining one-third of deputies. This effectively guaranteed control of parliament by the government's party, since the regime party could mobilise the state-appointed district and municipal governors to drum up the necessary support. The remaining third of candidates would be divided only among parties receiving 50,000 votes or more. The candidates were to be elected by direct universal male suffrage involving open rather than secret ballot. The subsequent parliamentary elections of 8 November 1931 were understandably boycotted by all the opposition parties, resulting in a parliament wholly dominated by the government's deputies. This was followed by elections to the senate on 3 January 1932, in which 46 senators were elected indirectly by the banovinas through an electoral body composed of parliamentary deputies, banovina councillors and municipal presidents. The king immediately appointed an additional 26 senators.[111] This electoral system failed in its goal of preventing parties representing individual nations from standing; it simply forced them to unite in larger opposition blocs.

REIGN OF THE SECOND KING ALEKSANDAR

Socio-economic change and Radical decline

Gone were the days when the Serbian peasantry solidly identified with the Radicals. The decade of rule by parliamentary parties since 1918 had widely discredited them in the populace's eyes, so that their replacement by a royal dictatorship won wide approval, particularly among those too young to remember the Obrenovićes.[112] The Radicals contributed more members to the dictatorship's supporters than any other party. Their decline was manifested also in the passing of the generation of politicians who had brought them to pre-eminence. Apart from Pašić, this included Milenko Vesnić (d. 1921), Stojan Protić (d. 1923), Mihailo Gavrilović (d. 1924), Jovan Jovanović (d. 1926), Nastas Petrović (d. 1928), Jovan Đaja (d. 1928) and Ljubomir Jovanović (d. 1928). Their deaths were part of a broader process of change in the party reflecting wider social changes.[113] World War I was a demographic disaster, with particularly heavy losses among the young adult males that had comprised the Radicals' most dynamic constituency, and the war's effect was to accelerate the long-term trend of increasing differentiation of the peasantry on the basis of wealth. War reparations did not in practice compensate peasants for the occupation's ruinous effects; for example, livestock that Bulgaria was forced to surrender, instead of being distributed to those peasants whose own livestock had been confiscated, was sold to those who could afford to buy it, and the money deposited in the state's war-damages account.[114] Yugoslavia's population growth from 11,984,911 in January 1921 to 15,703,000 at the end of 1939, due to a high birth rate, was virtually Europe's highest, with the Serb population growing faster than that of other Yugoslav peoples. Around 40 per cent of the Yugoslav population in 1921 was younger than 14. The population of pre-1912 Serbia rose from just over two and a half million to approach four million by the end of the 1930s. Yugoslavia and Serbia were still predominantly agricultural but suffering from increasing rural overpopulation, for which there was limited outlet, given relatively slow industrialisation and urbanisation and the limited possibilities of emigration, particularly after immigration restrictions effectively ended emigration to the United States by 1922.[115] The population's educational level remained poor owing to official neglect: only 2–5 per cent of the peacetime annual state budget went to education and culture.[116]

The Great Depression began in 1929 and hit Yugoslavia in full by mid-1930. The country's exports fell to a third of their 1929 level by 1932, by which time the state's foreign debt reached 38.8 billion dinars. The peasantry was worst hit; the price of agricultural produce collapsed and there was a corresponding steep rise of peasant indebtedness and an exodus of rural poor flocking to find work in the towns, while possibilities for emigration ended altogether. The disintegration of the zadrugas accelerated as members went their separate ways seeking work, while the guild handicrafts also declined in favour of the cheaper unauthorised handicrafts in which many peasants engaged for survival. The number of peasant homesteads grew in Serbia by 74 per cent between 1897 and 1931 as the population rose and the zadrugas were divided, meaning a further steep rise in the number of families with land insufficient to support them, or wholly landless.[117] Thus, the peasantry's decline as a class accelerated. The conditions in which part of the peasantry lived was described by a local newspaper from Leskovac in 1927: 'The land is not used rationally; the agricultural branches of fruit growing, poultry farming and gardening are underdeveloped; women, besides illiteracy, do not know well how to cook, nor to knead, nor to wash; in whole areas everyone sleeps on the floor because there are no beds; in some more mountainous villages, children sleep in the same section as the livestock; in the rooms are rarely found wooden floors; windows are small and made with paper, lavatories exist only exceptionally; nobody uses a pocket handkerchief nor knows what one is, etc.'[118]

Women in the countryside were increasingly unready to accept their complete subordination to men; young wives, traditionally lowest-ranking in the zadruga, increasingly rebelled against the authority of their parents-in-law, drawing their husbands with them, while the husband's authority over his wife greatly declined and he was increasingly likely to consult her about family affairs. Peasant women in Serbia were much readier to rebel in this manner than those in most other parts of Yugoslavia. The flip-side was that young women and girls were less valued and protected by the community; for example, the custom of bride purchase was dying out and there was less pressure on young men to marry lovers whom they had impregnated and more likelihood of peasant women ending up unmarried or in poverty. Abortion, prostitution and husbands' extra-marital affairs occurred much more frequently. Wife-beating was very widespread, significantly more so in Serbia than in other parts of Yugoslavia, indicating tension and conflict arising from the transition in gender relations. Overall, Serbian peasant women widely regretted the decline of the traditional social order.[119]

The industrial sector, where impoverished peasants increasingly sought work, was underdeveloped by European standards owing to the country's primitive infrastructure, dearth of investment capital and poorly educated population. Only 9 per cent of pre-1912 Serbia's population in 1931 was engaged in industry and handicraft.[120] The poverty of the industrial working class was as bad as the peasantry's; a report of the chamber of labour of Belgrade for the period 1926–1931, based on an investigation of many factories and workshops in the capital city and provinces, concluded: 'The least care was taken over hygiene and diet. In the majority of workshops, 8, 10 and more trainees slept in a single room of less than 20 cubic metres square. Their beds were mostly boards covered with a little straw, husks or some rags, full of every kind of filth. A single pillow and cover is for two, even three boys who sleep together. The inspectors came across many cases of itching and the scratching of the body, caused by filth and lice bites.' The use of child labour remained widespread; an official investigation in 1931 of 7,149 companies with 139,346 workers uncovered 479 child-workers younger than fourteen and 17,047 aged fourteen to seventeen, figures that did not improve during the life of the Yugoslav kingdom.[121]

The effects of the Great Depression hit the industrial sector somewhat later than the agricultural sector, with factories ceasing production and many workers made unemployed. Export-oriented branches were particularly hard hit, especially timber (Yugoslavia's most important export industry) and cement, as were construction, milling and the food industry, while manufacturing, mining and smelting also declined. The number of registered unemployed in Yugoslavia more than quadrupled between 1930 and 1939, to over 650,000, though the real number of unemployed was undoubtedly much higher. Companies responded by uniting in cartels, allowing them to reduce wages. The textile industry actually benefited from the collapse of foreign competition and tripled its production between 1931 and 1935, yet its workers' wages by 1938 had fallen to 40 per cent of their 1931 level. Unwaged labour, solely for food and accommodation, became more widespread. Nevertheless, Serbia along with Montenegro was hit by the crisis later and recovered sooner than other parts of Yugoslavia.

Already before the start of the Great Depression, women were entering the industrial workforce in increasing numbers, and the Depression, by hitting hardest the more male-dominated higher-skilled and higher-paid sectors of the workforce, actually increased the relative representation of women as well as of children.[122] The female proportion of the workforce peaked at 30 per cent in 1934–1935, dropping only slightly below that for the rest of the decade. Female representation was particularly high in the textile industry, where in 1934 women constituted 64 per cent of unskilled and 44 per cent of skilled workers as well as 34 per cent of management officials.[123] Thus, impoverishment occurred alongside modernisation. Despite the Depression, perhaps over 400 new factories may have been built on the territory of pre-1912 Serbia between 1918 and 1938, while the value of industrial and mining output rose by 83.2 per cent between 1923 and 1939. Socio-economic changes produced a class of peasant-workers—those who lived partly or wholly in the countryside but worked in industry, forming roughly 60 per cent of Yugoslav industrial workers in the 1930s.[124] As a new, economically insecure class, they were less ready to support the conservative Radicals and perhaps more receptive to radical politics, even to the Communists.[125]

Belgrade expanded as the modern, cosmopolitan capital of a large multi-ethnic state, more than doubling its population between 1921 and 1931, from 111,739 to 238,775—a tenfold increase since full Serbian control had been established over it in 1867. Its transformation into the Yugoslav capital left its architectural mark. The two greatest Yugoslav sculptors of the interwar period were both from present-day Croatia—Ivan Meštrović (1883–1962) and Toma Rosandić (1878–1958). Meštrović created the monument 'Victor', a muscular nude male with a sword atop a pillar, originally made in 1913 during the pan-Yugoslav euphoria of the Balkan Wars and finally erected at Kalemegdan in 1928. It came to symbolise its city as the Eiffel Tower or Statue of Liberty did. Meštrović also built the 'Monument to the Unknown Soldier', a World War I memorial, at Mount Avala, overlooking Belgrade, which was unveiled in 1938. Rosandić sculpted the 'Weary Fighter', a reclining male nude unveiled at Kalemegdan in 1935, and 'Black Horses at Play', two equine statues unveiled in 1938 that flank the entrance to the national parliament in Belgrade. These monuments symbolised Serbia's social and cultural modernisation.

A cultural milestone was reached on 1 October 1924 when Radio Belgrade began broadcasting; for one hour every evening on Tuesdays, Thursdays and Saturdays, it would transmit news reports, musical concerts, service reports, adverts and stock-market news.[126] Another milestone was reached on 16 February 1939, when novelist Isidora Sekulić (1877–1958), a Hungarian Serb, became the Serbian Royal Academy's first female member. At the same time the number of educated native Serbian woman was rapidly increasing; in the school year 1926–1927, 1,235 out of 4,688 students enrolled at the university were women and in the philosophy faculty they even outnumbered male students (707 to 469).[127] This modernisation existed alongside great poverty. A working-class family in Belgrade in 1931 on average had only 1.5 and, two years later, 1.3 rooms at its disposal. In the newly arisen sprawling suburban slums, people lived and children played among unpaved roads, rubbish piles and ditches used as toilets, the streams that supplied their water contaminated with waste and in conditions so filthy that town officials and doctors refused to visit them, while conditions in other Serbian cities such as Šabac, Leskovac and Niš were as bad or worse. Tuberculosis, typhus and other diseases were widespread in Serbia.[128] The death rate for children in Belgrade in the years 1930–1933 was 20.33 per cent while for other parts of the country it was 23–26 per cent, owing to the absence of adequate health care, poor diet and widespread disease.[129] Mortality among children and youth was three or four times higher in Serbia than in the countries of Western and Central Europe. The average lifespan in 1931 was about 46.51 years for men and 49.57 for women.[130]

Economic development and social diversification had therefore, by the end of the 1920s, altered the character of the previously relatively homogeneous, predominantly rural Serbian population. Peasant resistance to the Serbian state, present since its birth, was finally subsiding as the peasantry declined. The Radicals could no longer successfully pose as the natural representatives of Serbia's population, whose aspirations now pulled in different, conflicting directions, but no other party emerged in this period to replace them. The Depression accelerated these trends; although it increased the reservoir of popular discontent, it also depressed spirits and channelled politics in a more conservative direction. A political vacuum was emerging that would be filled in the 1940s by the Communists, but in the short term socio-economic change helped tilt the balance of power away from the political parties and toward the court.

Both as a reflection of its own ethos and in response to the largely peasantist character of the opposition led by the HSS and Farmers, the Yugoslav government responded to the Depression with an economic policy prioritising state support for agriculture over and above industry. It established an economic council on 12 February 1932 to advise on state support for economic activity; 24 of its 60 members were representatives of agriculture, agricultural cooperatives and forestry and only 16 of trade, industry, crafts, transport, banking and mining, 15 of public workers and 5 of the working class and private employees.[131] A moratorium on peasant debts became effective from 19 April 1932, as a result of which a large portion were cancelled outright and the remainder consolidated and made payable at a reduced rate of interest over a period of twelve years, beginning in 1936.[132] The state, for so long viewed by the peasants as the enemy, was now presented as their saviour.

Resistance and repression under the dictatorship

The dictatorship united the greater part of Yugoslavia's political classes in opposition to it, but parties representing different nationalities responded in different ways. The Croats further united politically behind the goal of self-rule, predominantly behind the HSS. State repression was disproportionately directed against Croats; according to available figures, Catholics, mostly Croats, made up the majority of those tried for crimes against the state for every year of the dictatorship.[133] Repression particularly hit the Communists. Overall, in the period of outright dictatorship, thousands were imprisoned, around 400 killed in prison and about 1,500 sentenced under the Law for the Protection of the State.[134] The Yugoslav police murdered the KPJ's secretary Đuro Đaković and its affiliate Red Aid's secretary Nikola Hećimović on 25 April 1929, followed on 17 August by Pajo Marganović, secretary of the Communist youth organisation.

Pribićević was arrested on 17 May 1929 and interned in Brus, deep in the Serbian interior, subsequently in the state hospital in Belgrade. He was released over two years later after he had started a hunger strike and the French and Czechoslovak governments had intervened on his behalf; subsequently, he was permitted to leave the country, though he lost his pension. A group of Croat youths was arrested in December 1929 on suspicion of planning acts of terrorism, after which Maček himself was arrested on the 21st, accused of aiding it financially. He was subjected to a show trial before the dictatorship's new State Court for the Protection of the State in the spring of 1930 on charges relating to terrorism; this failed to result in a conviction, although thirteen of the accused terrorists tried alongside him, who apparently had links with the exiled Pavelić, were convicted and sentenced to prison terms of between six months and fifteen years.[135] Maček's adviser, the eminent Croatian scholar Milan Šufflay, was assassinated on 18 February 1931, apparently with official complicity. Meanwhile, the Slovenes and Muslims remained united behind their principal parties, the SLS and JMO. Korošec resigned from the government on 28 September 1930 while Spaho remained aloof from it from the start. With the Radicals' decline, the Democrats under Davidović emerged as the leading Serbian party of opposition to the regime, thereby achieving the Independent Radicals' old goal of becoming the party of the Serbian people's democratic aspirations.[136] The Farmers meanwhile replaced the Radicals as the voice of Serbian peasant resistance and, more than any other Serbian party, found themselves targeted by repression. Dragoljub Jovanović, leader of the Farmers' left wing, was the only top-ranking party politician apart from Maček to be tried before the State Court for the Protection of the State. He was arrested on 4 April 1929, released following a failed prosecution, rearrested in September 1930 and sentenced to twenty days in prison. His crime was to have criticised the state's financial policy and the importation of agricultural produce to serve military needs.

The Serbian political classes' ferocious struggle with Radić and Pribićević's Croatian bloc had nevertheless helped lessen the once-bitter tension between the Serbian parties and the court. In Gligorijević's words, 'The relations between that opposition and the court never developed in the direction of the formation of two enemy camps which would struggle to mutual destruction. On the contrary, there was tolerance and understanding on both sides for that which each of them undertook.' The restoration of a semblance of constitutionality in September 1931 encouraged further defections to the regime of members of the old Serbian political parties who had until then remained in opposition. Meanwhile Živković, rather than Aleksandar, was the focus of anti-regime hostility. Students at Belgrade University rioted in November–December 1931, demanding his resignation. Aleksandar was consequently ready to reconcile with the Serbian opposition by taking another step in the pretence of restoring constitutional life, with Živković's dismissal as prime minister and his replacement with Marinković, the veteran Progressive, on 4 April 1932. Živković, the face of the dictatorship, was left in command of the Royal Guard but fell into disfavour and was kept under surveillance. In his own words, 'My relations with King Aleksandar, following my dismissal as prime minister, were not good in the slightest. I was only some sort of commander of the Royal Guard, and in reality I was a prisoner of that Guard.'[137]

The idea of a new court party drawn from loyal factions of the old parties, once considered by Aleksandar Obrenović, was now attempted by Aleksandar Karađorđević. The Živković government had resolved on 4 July 1930 to establish a regime party, in order 'definitely to destroy the traces of the former parties'.[138] This party was finally established under Marinković, supposedly uniting the principal elements of mainstream Yugoslav politics, with a correspondingly clumsy name:

the Yugoslav Radical Peasant Democracy (Jugoslovenska Radikalna Seljačka Demokratija or JRSD), with Uzunović as its president. It was formed primarily from the pro-regime parts of the Radical and Democratic parties as well as part of the SLS. The regime began to prepare its foundation properly in August 1931, and in April 1932 a 'provisional general council' was formed. The regime's parliamentary deputies, senators and ministers were centrally involved in the party's formation; it was conducted by means of many rallies and conferences in localities in which a warlike atmosphere was engendered; opponents of the new party and of integral Yugoslavism were threatened with a 'war to extermination'.[139] According to one parliamentary deputy's report to the interior ministry, district governors 'went through the villages and municipalities, threatening, punishing, arresting particular citizens' while emphasising that every citizen 'who doesn't want to join the JRSD is against the state, because the JRSD is the state party'.[140]

Marinković, probably through consultation with his former Democratic colleagues, hoped to liberalise the regime further to the point of genuine parliamentarism. To this end, at a JRSD conference at Niš on 8 May 1932, he suggested a referendum to seek the Yugoslav citizenry's endorsement of the unitarist constitutional order and definite rejection of federalism. Yet his position was weak, owing to his regime's heterogeneous character. He was opposed by two groups within it: the young guard of enthusiastic supporters of the dictatorship who resented the pre-eminence of the old order's politicians—they met in the Hotel Bristol, so were nicknamed 'Bristollers'—and conservative former Radicals who wished to restore the Radical party as the monarchical regime's principal mainstay. Both groups attacked Marinković for jeopardising the unitarist order.[141] Aleksandar initially approved Marinković's plan, but Marinković's failed attempt to reach an agreement with Mussolini's Italy heightened the king's fear of any appearance of weakness, inclining him to listen to the hardliners. He consequently replaced Marinković by one such critic, Srškić, on 2 July 1932—the only time a Serb from outside pre-1912 Serbia served as prime minister in the Yugoslav kingdom.[142] This amounted to a victory for the Bristollers.

Jovanović was arrested again on 2 May 1932 after speaking at a rally at Kragujevac and sentenced in September to a year in prison. Also in May 1932, the Farmers organised illegal rallies in various locations in Bosanska Krajina at which the regime was repeatedly denounced. A crowd of around a thousand peasants raided a food depot at Prijedor, resulting in the killing of a guard and injuries on both sides. 121 people were consequently prosecuted in the biggest political trial in Yugoslavia in ten years.[143] Agitation by Farmers that spring and summer under Miloš Tupanjanin provoked gendarme assaults; a clash at Ub in northern Serbia on 1 July resulted in three dead and the arrest of fifteen people, including Tupanjanin.[144]

The Peasant–Democrat Coalition published a statement on 7 November 1932, known as the Zagreb Points, denouncing the dictatorship as the 'culmination' of the

SERBIA

'Serbian hegemony that was, already from the start, imposed on Croatia and on all our lands on this side of the Drina, Sava and Danube'. It demanded revocation of the constitutional order, the withdrawal of soldiers and officials from Serbia from territories to the west and north of the Sava, Drina and Danube rivers and a 'return to the year 1918'. Thus, it potentially negated not only Yugoslav unification, but Serbia's unification with Montenegro and Vojvodina as well.[145] The Serbian opposition parties, Radicals and Democrats, thus found that the Peasant–Democrat Coalition conflated them with the hegemonist regime while the regime conflated them with the separatist prečani opposition. The Radicals interpreted talk of 'Serbian hegemony' as indicative of the Peasant–Democrat Coalition's intention 'that all Croats be brought together while the Serbs be split between Bosnia, Montenegro, Serbia, Vojvodina and maybe Macedonia.'[146] In response to the Points, Maček and several of his collaborators were arrested on 31 January 1933. Maček himself was convicted by the State Court for the Protection of the State in Zagreb on 29 April 1933 and sentenced to three years in prison. The HSS vice-president Josip Predavec was murdered on 14 July 1933; regime complicity was again suspected. The SLS and JMO issued their own statements calling for the Yugoslav state to be reorganised on the basis of self-governing units, and as a result members of both parties, including Korošec and Spaho themselves, were arrested on 31 January 1933 and interned or imprisoned.

Members of the Radical, Democratic and Farmers' parties on 14 February 1933 issued a protest at the arrests of the Peasant–Democrat members. The Zagreb Points galvanised sections of the Serbian opposition, above all the Democrats and the Farmers' left wing, to retreat from supporting unitarism. But although the three principal Serbian opposition parties—Radicals, Democrats and Farmers—could unite behind the demand for a restoration of parliamentary democracy, they were unable to agree on a solution to Yugoslavia's national question, which prevented their forming a solid opposition bloc with the Peasant–Democrat Coalition. The Democrats in 1934 resolved in favour of a federation of four units: Slovenia; Croatia including northern Dalmatia; Serbia including Vojvodina, Montenegro and Macedonia; and a Serbo-Croat buffer zone comprising Bosnia-Hercegovina and southern Dalmatia. But the Radicals rejected all such federalist concessions, remaining implacably committed to the unitary kingdom. They were divided between those favouring collaboration with the rest of the opposition and those favouring a return to power through agreement with the court.[147] These divisions in the opposition, particularly in Serbia, ensured the regime's survival.

The oppressiveness of the centralist dictatorship spurred the regionalist movement in Vojvodina. Agrarian reform to divide Yugoslavia's large estates, promised by the interim decree of 25 February 1919, was finally executed by the Law on Agrarian Reform on Large Estates of 19 June 1931: 720 such estates were affected, of which 369 were owned by private individuals, 50 by private corporations, and the rest mostly by municipalities and other communes, churches, monasteries and the central government. This involved their loss of 33.3 per cent of their land to expropriation and a further 10.1 per cent to elective purchases; the land taken was primarily cultivated while what was left to them consisted disproportionately of forests and pastures. Of the 369 private landowners affected, 310 were foreign nationals. The beneficiaries were over 200,000 landless and small landowner families. This amounted to a transfer of wealth in Vojvodina from the ethnic minorities to the South Slavic population but it inevitably created losers as well as winners. The redistribution largely just formalised unilateral expropriations that peasants had conducted after 1918. The long period of legal uncertainty this involved had negatively affected agricultural productivity, which was also hurt by the increasing loss, due to tariff barriers, of the traditional export markets in other parts of former Austria-Hungary.[148] These factors contributed to widespread discontent in Vojvodina.

The veteran Vojvodinian Radical Joca Lalošević lamented, in a speech before the Radical party's committee in Vojvodina on 17 April 1932, that 'Vojvodina, when it became part of the new state, was a rich, orderly, bounteous and advanced province, economically, culturally and socially'; but 'today Vojvodina is a squeezed lemon; ruined, dispersed, economically reduced to the beggar's staff and nationally wounded to the heart and completely disappointed'. The judgement was damning enough to elicit the sympathy of leading Radicals from Serbia, Miloš Trifunović and Milan Stojadinović, who joined with Lalošević and representatives of the Hungarian and German minorities to issue the so-called Sombor resolution in July, demanding 'that in the framework of the borders of our state be immediately put into practice the principle "Vojvodina for the Vojvodinians", with the same rights that other provinces will have and with the same administrative system that will be introduced in other provinces'. These were Radicals, and they did not go so far as to embrace autonomy. Nevertheless, on 11 December 1932, in response to the Zagreb Points, 33 members of the Vojvodinian opposition from twelve districts of the region, primarily Radicals and Independent Democrats but also Democrats and HSS members, assembled in Novi Sad for several days of discussion at which demands were raised for Vojvodina to have autonomous control over its own economic resources ('Autonomy of government and money!'). The conference issued its own statement, subsequently known as the Novi Sad declaration, which was intended to represent both the province's unitarist and autonomist currents; it repeated the Sombor resolution's demand for Vojvodina's equality with other provinces. The regime responded by arresting and imprisoning the meeting's host, Aleksandar Moč.[149] But eventually, in August 1935, the Novi Sad resolution would be made public and a Movement for Vojvodina formally launched, with the Independent Democrat Žarko Jakšić demanding, in its name, that 'for Vojvodina, we decisively seek absolutely the same position that Croatia is seeking for itself'.[150]

SERBIA

Pavelić left Yugoslavia immediately after the dictatorship's establishment to pursue more radical activities in exile. He organised among the Croatian anti-Yugoslav emigrations in Vienna and Budapest and visited Sofia to establish links with the VMRO before travelling to Italy to put his fledgling radical separatist organisation at Mussolini's service. He established in Italy the Ustasha (Insurgent)—Croatian Revolutionary Organisation, which mimicked the fascism of its hosts and aspired to establish an independent Croatian state incorporating all the alleged 'Croatian lands': Croatia-Slavonia, Dalmatia, Bosnia-Hercegovina and parts of what are today Serbia and Montenegro. Armed Ustasha organisations were established in both Italy and Hungary. Following the collapse of Italian–Yugoslav negotiations in autumn 1932 and Mussolini's decision to pursue an actively anti-Yugoslav course, the Ustashas embraced terrorism. A band of armed Ustashas left Italian-held Zadar on the Dalmatian coast on 7 September to launch an uprising in Croatia. They attacked the police station at Brušane, near Gospić in Lika, but were easily repelled.

To pacify opposition, the regime modified the electoral law on 24 March 1933 so that parties in elections would be obliged to find endorsements from only 30 voters in at least half the electoral districts, rather than 60 in all of them.[151] The JRSD held the first of an intended series of rallies in each of the banovina's capitals, at Niš, capital of the Morava Banovina, on 23 April 1933. The central government's machinery was mobilised to produce a giant gathering drawn from all parts of the kingdom; supporters were transported by train from across the country to attend, with particular pressure put on state employees to participate. One report implausibly claimed the number of participants reached 200,000. Several government ministers were present, including prime minister Srškić. However, many of the attendees were members of the opposition who took the opportunity to travel, at the state's expense, to the centre of the banovina and protest before the authorities; there were cries not only of 'Long live Yugoslavia!' but of 'Long live Great Serbia, down with [JRSD leader] Uzunović, down with his government!' With rain spoiling the rally, Aleksandar was reportedly greatly disappointed by the event, moving him to change course politically.[152] The JRSD was renamed the Yugoslav National Party (Jugoslavenska Nacionalna Stranka JNS) in June 1933, by which time it was already failing.

Aleksandar continued to pursue his opponents through the courts. Investigation into the so-called Našička affair began in 1934—the largest corruption scandal in interwar Yugoslav history, involving embezzlement, bribery and tax evasion on the part of the managers of the Zagreb affiliate of the Našička joint-stock company, Europe's largest timber company. The crime, in which leading ministers, particularly Radicals, were implicated, involved the theft of hundreds of millions of dinars, partly at the expense of a bank owned by the king. In 1935, 107 people were eventually indicted, including the company's directors Aleksandar Sohr and Adolf Schlesinger and former justice minister Nikola Nikić, and hundreds more were implicated. However, by this time Aleksandar was dead, and the judicial proceedings finally ended when one of the Radical politicians implicated in the affair, Milan Stojadinović, was prime minister. The final outcome was that most of the accused were acquitted, including Nikić, while Sohr and Schlesinger received sentences of only seven and eight months respectively.[153]

Foreign policy of the 6 January Regime

Aleksandar attempted to restore friendly relations with Fascist Italy, albeit unsuccessfully owing to Mussolini's hostility. His self-confidence was strengthened by the signing of the Pact of Organisation of the Little Entente in Geneva on 16 February 1933, motivated by Yugoslavia, Czechoslovakia and Romania's common fear regarding the direction in which Europe was heading. It converted the loose alliance system into a unified tripartite community with a permanent consultative council, binding each of its members to obtain the approval of the others before signing any new political treaty or economic agreement.[154] Yugoslavia also signed the Balkan Pact with Romania, Greece and Turkey on 9 February 1934, aimed at preserving the territorial status quo in the Balkans and directed particularly against Bulgaria. This threatening re-creation of the Second Balkan War coalition, emphasising Bulgaria's isolation, helped trigger a putsch in Sofia on 19 May 1934 by the Zveno faction, whose agenda was to improve relations with Yugoslavia. The new Zvenari regime consequently deployed the army to suppress the VMRO, effectively ending its major raids into Yugoslavia and Greece, its terrorism within Bulgaria and its influence over Bulgarian foreign policy.[155] Aleksandar's visit to King Boris in Sofia on 27 September of that year apparently set the seal on the reconciliation. Army General Milan Nedić, a favourite of Aleksandar within the army, subsequently described the king's policy: 'He led a Balkan policy. He wanted to guarantee the Balkans to the Balkan peoples. With that goal he went everywhere and met with many politicians from Romania and Greece, and he was in Turkey and in Bulgaria.' In the event of another war between Germany and the Western democracies, 'the Balkans, in the interests of its peoples, must remain neutral'.[156] Nevertheless, the regime's insecurity and dependence on the military both at home and abroad resulted in a vast military budget, taking up more than two-sevenths of state expenditure in 1933–1934.[157]

Faced with the Italian threat, Aleksandar turned to Nazi Germany; he was also motivated by his desire to avoid sole dependence on France—thereby again replicating the policy of the last Obrenović ruler, who abandoned his father's Austrian alignment for a more balanced policy towards Austria-Hungary and Russia. Aleksandar had preferred the Nazis coming to power in Germany to a restoration of the Hohenzollerns, which he feared might presage a Habsburg restoration in Austria. He subsequently preferred a German Anschluss with Austria to such a restoration, to Austria's domination by Italy or to its unification with Hungary on a neo-Habsburg basis. He consequently refused to join France and Italy in opposing the Anschluss.¹⁵⁸ This attitude alienated France but was favourably received by Hitler, and on 1 May 1934 Germany and Yugoslavia signed a commercial treaty granting Yugoslavia most-favoured-nation status. Aleksandar's agrarian orientation chimed with the Nazi view of the Balkans as an agricultural region, making his regime a natural economic partner for the Reich.¹⁵⁹ The agreement of 1 May was the first of a series that would turn Yugoslavia during the 1930s into Germany's economic satellite. It was accompanied by an agreement between the two countries establishing special clearing accounts in their respective national banks, whereby the importer would pay for imports into the exporter's clearing account, creating credit which the exporter could then use to buy good from the importer, with each party reimbursing its own producers. This obviated the need for any actual exchange of hard currency or gold. The arrangement seemed to favour Yugoslavia, allowing it to dispose of agricultural produce that, in the conditions of the Great Depression, it was struggling to export. In practice, it allowed Germany to obtain huge quantities of agricultural produce from Yugoslavia and other East Central European countries on credit, which these countries struggled to redeem and could only do so by buying from Germany. It thereby locked them into a system of German economic control. Yugoslavia's participation from late 1935 in League of Nations sanctions against Italy over its invasion of Ethiopia decimated its trade with this major economic partner, a breach which Germany filled.¹⁶⁰ By the end of the 1930s, half of Yugoslavia's foreign trade was tied to Germany, from which it was obtaining most of its armaments, while Germany absorbed up to a quarter of all Yugoslav produce and enjoyed, through the clearing mechanism, almost unlimited access to Yugoslav mineral resources, which were crucial for its military needs.¹⁶¹

Aleksandar's replacement of Srškić with Uzunović as prime minister on 27 January 1934 marked the start of a possible retreat from authoritarianism. The king moved toward a compromise with the opposition, aiming at the appointment of a broad-based government in which all the major Serb, Croat and Slovene parties would have been represented while Croatia would have received 'broad autonomy'. He held talks to this end, either in person or through intermediaries, with Maček, Korošec, the Radical leader Aca Stanojević and other opposition politicians. But he did not have long to develop this policy, since his destruction was being plotted by his most extreme opponents—the Ustashas. Pavelić met in August with VMRO leader Vanča Mihailov in Rome, in the presence of the Italian political police's general secretary, to plan the king's assassination; the pair were then received by Italian foreign minister Count Ciano.¹⁶² On 9 October 1934, Aleksandar disembarked at Marseilles for a state visit intended to develop the Franco-Yugoslav alliance. Given that the Yugoslav police was aware that the Ustashas were plotting his death, a responsible government arguably would not have let him travel to France in the absence of proper security measures, but, like Prince Mihailo, he was an autocrat who tolerated no restraints and was blasé about his personal safety.¹⁶³ Sitting in a car alongside French foreign

REIGN OF THE SECOND KING ALEKSANDAR

minister Louis Barthou, he was assassinated by a VMRO terrorist from Bulgaria, Veličko Dimitrov Kerin aka Vlado Chernozemski. The assassination and resulting fracas also claimed the lives of Barthou and the chauffeur. Unlike his predecessors Prince Mihailo and King Aleksandar of Serbia, who were murdered in Serbia by Serbs, King Aleksandar of Yugoslavia had proven impervious to Serbian opposition; it required the conjunction of Croat and Macedonian terrorism supported by Italy, Hungary and Bulgaria and the extraordinary incompetence of French security to destroy him. The pivot towards Germany nevertheless continued after his death; Hermann Göring attended Aleksandar's funeral in Belgrade and laid a wreath at his grave, dedicated 'to their sometime heroic opponent as a sign of pain and sorrow—from the army and navy of the German Reich'. Before leaving Belgrade, Göring told a reporter from London's *Daily Mail*: 'The existence of a strong Yugoslavia at the entrance door to the Balkans represents an element of peace. Germany is a supporter of a strong Yugoslavia.'[164] That month, October 1934, Hitler ended relations with the Croatian opposition and ordered the suppression of the Croatian émigré press in Germany.

For all the emphasis of historians on the national question as the reason for interwar Yugoslavia's instability, it is remarkable how little it changed the nature of the political struggle in Serbia. King Petar turned out to represent not the start of constitutional monarchy but a mere interlude arising from the temporary destruction of royal authority in 1903. Serbia's immersion in Yugoslavia shifted the balance of power in the state back toward the crown, giving it a much larger range of parties to play off against each other and much more plausible internal enemies against which to mobilise the Serbian population, while socio-economic change weakened the once mighty Radical party. The establishment of Aleksandar's dictatorship marked the culmination of the authoritarian, elitist policies pursued by Serbian monarchs since the Obrenović era. His much greater use of violence than previous Serbian monarchs reflected the difference between dominating a small, ethnically homogeneous state and dominating a large multinational one with many unwilling subjects. Nevertheless, Aleksandar's was still a personal regime like Mihailo's and the first Aleksandar's, so his murder meant not just a change of ruler but a change of regime.

17

FASCISM AND COURT RADICALISM

1934–1939

King Aleksandar's death, like the death or fall of previous Serbian monarchs, began the transition to a more liberal regime, but once again this was a question of degrees as the regime remained one of controlled parliamentarism in which power remained with the court. In the aftermath of the assassination, the king's clique closed ranks, with prime minister Uzunović appointing the regime's other three former prime ministers, Živković, Marinković and Srškić, to his government. The government then implemented Aleksandar's secret will, naming a three-man regency to succeed him until such time as his son and heir, King Petar II, attained his majority on 6 September 1941. This provided a pretext for the regime to postpone discussion of constitutional revision until then. The regency was headed and solely controlled by Aleksandar's first cousin, Prince Pavle Karađorđević (1893–1976), son of Petar I's brother Arsen, while its nominal second and third members, education minister Radenko Stanković and the ban of the Sava Banovina Ivan Perović, were mere window dressing. Like Aleksandar Obrenović after breaking with Milan in 1900, Pavle sought to sideline hardline authoritarian and militarist elements and share power with Radical and other civilian politicians enjoying a degree of popular support. Again, the transition to a gentler regime created enemies from among the authoritarian elements without mollifying the pro-parliamentary opposition. And again, the regime's supposed 'betrayal' of Serbian national interests catalysed opposition to it.

Serbia's far right

Aleksandar's dictatorship was characterised by Communists as 'monarcho-fascist', though it had more in common with traditional Balkan monarchical absolutism than with contemporary Fascist and Nazi regimes.[1] Its authoritarianism backed by mass organisations resembled other regimes of East-Central and South-Eastern Europe of the interwar period, but whereas the regimes of King Carol in Romania and Ioannis

Metaxas in Greece, for example, emulated domestic or foreign fascist movements, in Yugoslavia it was the king's authoritarian-populist regime that spawned independent or semi-independent fascist parties. The regime permitted several pro-regime 'loyal opposition' parties to emerge which followed the nationalist-authoritarian model. At the end of 1932, a group of JSRD parliamentary deputies seceded on Živković's initiative to form the Yugoslav People's Party (Jugoslavenska Narodna Stranka), headed by Svetislav Hođera, Živković's former chief of cabinet. This party would develop consciously along fascist lines; its members donned a blue-shirted uniform and mimicked the Nazi style. A second, short-lived regime-established 'loyal opposition' was the Radical Social Party, formed from the Radicals' pro-regime wing.

By smashing the system of established Yugoslav parties and engaging in an apparently revolutionary experiment in nation-building, Aleksandar inspired the enthusiasm of some radical right-wingers, catalysing their ideological evolution along fascist lines. These were above all Serbs but included some non-Serb integral Yugoslav nationalists. Miloš Crnjanski (1893–1977), an eminent Hungarian Serb novelist, journalist and professor, served as Yugoslav cultural attaché in Berlin in 1928–1929; his adulation of the man he referred to as the 'Blessed Chivalric King Aleksandar I the Unifier' approached a personality cult:

> The contours of His achievements are already being denigrated. The lines of a great soldier who never abandons his soldiers; the lines of a great statesman who looked at people and built above them a state, disregarding human weakness. And above all, with some bitterness about his lips—although His smile was always so cheerful—He will mean in every account the highest belief in the idea that the same blood ran for ages from the Alps to Strumica and that for one and the same nation is built, so painfully, a state that He carried first, until his last breath, as his extraordinary vision in his wise, deep and dark eyes.[2]

Building upon Aleksandar's suppression of the Yugoslav political parties and creation of a regime party and inspired by Mussolini, Crnjanski embraced fascist ideas of the non-parliamentary corporative state: 'The characteristic contours of our political parties, our parliamentary life in general are, without doubt, fairly negative ... Wherever parties exist, even covertly, there exist tribal boundaries, separatist instincts. And what is worse, what is often overlooked, is cultural provincialism.' By contrast, 'Corporations could mean, above all, a deep break in our political history. And it is difficult to imagine that without such a break we could achieve something new and better.'[3] Crnjanski rejected the concept of 'patriot' as inadequate: 'We need a much firmer and more permanent phenomenon of nationalist. The problem is not yet in the party programme, for programmes do not fall from the heavens, but in the gathering and assembling of such people of all nuances.'[4] This flowed from Aleksandar's strategy of building his regime using supporters from different political parties.[5]

FASCISM AND COURT RADICALISM

Aleksandar promoted radical rightists in place of the ousted traditional politicians, but some of these individuals and groups moved into opposition to a regime which they considered insufficiently radical. The early 1930s saw the appearance of Yugoslav Action, led by Velibor Jonić, a former Farmer who served as National Defence's secretary under Aleksandar's dictatorship, which advocated a 'total state' and directed its agitation against the Croatian-centred federalist opposition and against the ruling JNS;[6] the Association of Fighters of Yugoslavia, organised by Yugoslav-nationalist Slovenes, which saw itself as a 'link in a chain of Associations of warriors for a whole state'; and 'ZBOR' in Hercegovina under Ratko Parežanin and Radmilo Grđić. The word 'ZBOR' means 'assembly' in Serbo-Croat, and was chosen on the grounds of the importance of people's assemblies in Serb tradition and because 'ZBOR' formed an acronym that stood for 'cooperative, combative, association, work'.

The most important radical rightist was Dimitrije Ljotić, son of the early Serbian socialist Vladimir Ljotić. Aleksandar relied upon such Karađorđević dynastic loyalists to staff his dictatorship. The histories of the Karađorđević and Ljotić families were, as we have seen, closely interwoven, and dynastic loyalty was central to Ljotić. So was deep, inherited religiosity. After the Ljotić family emigrated from what later became Greek Macedonia to the village of Krnjevo in Serbia in the early eighteenth century, the devout Dimitrijević brothers, Đorđe (known as Ljota) and Toma, founded a church in 1750, dedicated to the family saint, St George, before moving to Smederevo at the end of the eighteenth century. Ljota adopted Toma's son Đorđe, who thereby gained the surname Ljotić. Đorđe's son Dimitrije himself founded a church in Smederevo dedicated to St George.[7] Vladimir parted ways with his socialist comrades at the time of the Bosnian uprising in the 1870s over his loyalty to the Karađorđevićes.[8] He was also a loyal, lifelong friend of Pašić; the two had closely collaborated as fellow exiles in the 1880s.[9] Vladimir returned to Serbia in 1889 following Milan's abdication and the establishment of the Radical government. As a Radical, he was appointed Serbia's consul in Salonika in 1890, possibly in part because of his Macedonian roots. He formed part of a powerful Karađorđevićite Radical circle based in his native Smederevo, which was centrally involved in Avramović's peasant cooperative movement. Dimitrije would later pay tribute to Avramović as a teacher and inspiration.[10] As president of the Smederevo municipality, Vladimir was a member of the state delegation that travelled to Geneva after the 1903 putsch to bring Petar Karađorđević back to Serbia.[11]

Dimitrije went through a youthful phase of Tolstoyan pacifism; unwilling to fight in the Balkan Wars, he served instead in the volunteer front-line medical corps. Spending nine months in Paris, he was influenced by the ideas of the French far-right ideologue Charles Maurras (1868–1952).[12] But he then served as an NCO and reserve officer in Serbia's army during World War I, remaining in military service until June 1920. As commander of the railway station in Bakar in Croatia, he actively participated in suppressing a Communist-inspired railwaymen's strike in April 1920, arresting 36 strikers according to his own testimony.[13] Despite reservations about its commitment to parliamentary democracy, he was persuaded by a friend to join the Radical party in 1920 and became head of its youth organisation, leaving it when the dictatorship was established. Aleksandar appointed him justice minister on 16 February 1931. Invited by the king to work on the new Yugoslav constitution, according to his own account Ljotić composed a plan for 'an organic, constitutional and hereditary monarchy, undemocratic and non-parliamentary, based on the mobilisation of live national forces, organised on the basis of economic, corporative, cultural and benevolent societies, with political responsibility of the government only to the King and privately before the King and before the assembly with decentralised self-government'.[14] Aleksandar rejected this, resolving instead to set up a regime party, to which Ljotić strongly objected.[15] He consequently resigned his ministerial portfolio and went into loyal opposition. With Aleksandar's blessing, Ljotić gathered the small fascist groups around him: Yugoslav Action, Association of Fighters of Yugoslavia and ZBOR. They formally fused on 6 January 1935—the anniversary of the dictatorship's establishment. The new party was named Yugoslav National Movement—ZBOR.

Ljotić stated: 'We openly say that ZBOR has no other task but to complete the works begun on 1.12.[1918] and 6.1.[1929].'[16] Preponderant within it were the same war veterans who had formed such an important constituency of support for Aleksandar's dictatorship and whose patriotism and martial valour Ljotić hoped to mobilise for Yugoslavia's renewal along authoritarian lines.[17] ZBOR's symbol was a shield displaying a head of corn emblem, behind which was a sword.[18] The party competed in Yugoslav elections and aspired to be a pan-Yugoslav movement, but attracted only a tiny proportion of the Yugoslav electorate. It manifested Alexandrine integral Yugoslav nationalism of a Serb flavour, fired by Orthodox Christian mysticism and anti-materialism, and advocated an organic state and society on a non-democratic, non-parliamentary basis. It was rhetorically strongly anti-Western and anti-capitalist and favoured a planned economy. In an undated booklet entitled *What Does ZBOR Want?*, Jonić expounded an ideology whose debt both to Aleksandar's dictatorship and to the Radical party was clear.

> The state must be the supreme controller and regulator of all relations, but it must not thereby restrain the beneficent living forces of the nation. Therefore we say: 'Only in those functions which relate to the life of the nation as a whole must the state authority be centralised; in others, self-management must be developed.' By self-management, true and real, the state will unburden itself of those tasks which it is not in a condition to accomplish as they should be, among other things, because the needs of life today are multiple and complex. Apart from that, it will establish thereby a necessary control over the bureaucracy, which always has a tendency to equate itself with the state ... Only the king is untouchable.

On the one hand, 'The village will be the measure of Yugoslav social politics'—Jonić lamented mainstream politicians' lack of 'respect for our national traditions' and society's 'rejection of patriarchal morals'. On the other hand, 'Autochthonous Yugoslav culture, in the spirit of its traditions and on the basis of humanity, builds a people of free creativity. The protector of this creative aspiration is the Yugoslav state.' ZBOR thus reconciled Serbia's monarchical-statist and Radical anti-statist traditions under the banner of integral Yugoslav nationalism.[19]

Ljotić argued in 1938 that under capitalism, 'people have not seen that they have created an order in which stands the phrase "liberty, equality, fraternity" and that behind that phrase the possibility is offered to money that it rule humanity ... Democracy enables the rule of money.' Ljotić called instead for an 'all-state, all-nation politics' to ensure the 'rule of the people', based not on parties, which he deemed artificial and divisive, but on traditional socio-economic orders (staleži): farming, industrial labour, craft, trade and so on.[20] There would be a parliament based on the orders, with legislative functions but no role in the executive or administration.[21] He believed that such an 'organic' organisation of the state, rejecting the 'mechanistic' models of centralism, unitarism and federalism, would resolve the Yugoslav national question.[22] 'We have Yugoslavia. That Yugoslavia comprises Serbs, Croats and Slovenes and it should comprise the Bulgarians. That is a true, final, permanent and, we hope, eternal Yugoslavia ... Our movement is a Yugoslav movement.'[23] His ideas thus reflected Italian Fascist ideas of a corporative state as well as those of the early Serbian socialists and Radicals, who had rejected social and economic modernisation along Western lines in favour of a social harmony based on indigenous Serbian social institutions. Ljotić also resuscitated their ideal of Balkan solidarity, advocating a Yugoslav policy of bringing together Romania, Bulgaria, Greece and Turkey in order to keep the Balkans out of the European war.[24] His close associate Ratko Parežanin, one of ZBOR's founders, established the Balkan Institute in March 1934 with generous financial assistance from King Aleksandar, motivated by the belief that 'our cultural imitators of the West are the poison of our common public life'. It sought to promote instead 'the community and solidarity of the Balkan nations; their economic raising and cultural advancement; the better and more certain destiny of the people of the Balkans in the future'.[25]

Ljotić's ideology was, however, much more religious than that of the early socialists and Radicals: 'Slavic religious organisations must and should be welcomed everywhere in the country with due recognition' as an alternative to 'an atheist and lay state, which, in our understanding, means the fall of the people'.[26] He was also more anti-Semitic, arguing that the Jews had 'thanks to their influence over the economy succeeded in taking control, in the purely economic domain, of every nation', as well as of 'the great manifestations of spiritual life of every nation', including, he claimed, at least three-quarters of the world's film industry. He blamed the Jews for the outbreak of the war in 1939: 'In the drama whose execution they direct, they have given everyone an appropriate role, and so cunningly that a Hitler, for whom we believe that he had very well perceived the Jewish plans, acted very well, albeit unconsciously, the way Israel needed.'[27]

Ljotić's movement dovetailed with existing political tendencies within the Serbian Orthodox Church. These had been catalysed by the appearance of a Protestant Nazarene heresy among the Serbs of Austria-Hungary during the second half of the nineteenth century, which spread to Serbia and appeared to threaten the established position of the Orthodox Church. Orthodox churchmen responded by equating Serbdom with Orthodoxy, arguing that the latter was the only true national religion among Serbs. Their Counter-Reformation initially took the form of the Bogomoljci (Worshippers of the Lord) revivalist movement, inspired by Bishop Nikolaj Velimirović, which established its headquarters in Kragujevac in 1920. The establishment of Yugoslavia in 1918, with its religious and ethnic heterogeneity, strengthened among Orthodox clerics their sense of themselves as bearers and defenders of Serbdom in this alien state, as they had been in the Ottoman Empire. Aleksandar's dictatorship was broadly welcomed among the Orthodox clergy as heralding Yugoslav spiritual unification under the Orthodox Church's leadership. But instead of this happening, the enforced Yugoslav identity seemed to threaten the Serbian Orthodox identity. Patriarch Gavrilo (Dožić) recalled a fraught conversation he had as a bishop and member of a church delegation to prime minister Živković in which the premier warned that 'besides the Serbian church there are other religions, which have the same rights by law as the Serbian church. It is my duty strictly to take that into account.' Dožić consequently considered Živković's government 'unnational and damaging to the people's interests'.[28]

The 6 January Regime, followed by its collapse in 1934, produced an Orthodox clerical reaction in Svetosavlje, a political ideology expressing itself in the cult of St Sava, who was consequently elevated to a central place in Serbian national iconography for the first time. This religious revivalist movement extended beyond the clergy to encompass leading Serb intellectuals, who thereby marked their disillusionment with the Yugoslav idea and a return to identification with a specifically Serbian and Orthodox tradition. Crnjanski complained: 'Serbdom gave everything, entering herein, head held high, renouncing its name, state being, its flag and, what is more, its victories, pride and morality', while Croats and others pursued their own separatist politics.[29] Consequently, 'The need is for a purely Serb outlook on things; Serb egoism and a turn away from an emotional and otherworldly discussion of things, to a realistic outlook and standpoint, in accordance with the interests of Serbdom. Otherwise, this tedious comedy will continue and will end once more as a Serb tragedy.'[30] With the 700th anniversary of St Sava's death approaching, Crnjanski in 1934 published a book about him which concluded: 'Sava's legend and Sava's work, however, will remain the most celebrated and most exalted that have arisen through the centuries on the bitter land of the Balkans, to illuminate for us always with their rays from the past.'[31]

Svetosavlje fused Orthodox piety and Serb nationalism on an anti-liberal, anti-materialist, anti-secular, anti-Catholic and anti-Islamic basis.[32] Velimirović delivered the movement's keynote speech in Belgrade on 17 March 1935, entitled 'The nationalism of St Sava', praising St Sava for establishing a 'national church', which Velimirović contrasted positively with an 'international or non-national church' like the Catholic Church, since it possessed 'one single national independent church organisation with its central authority from the people and among the people; with national priests, national language and the national customary expression of its faith', and served as the foundation for the Serbian national state and dynasty. Furthermore, 'According to the understanding of St Sava, the people's life is one indivisible whole, both physically and spiritually and morally.' Velimirović saw a kindred spirit in 'the current Leader of the German people. With great difficulty, his struggle still unfinished, he has managed to organise over the past two years, from only the Protestant part of the German people, something resembling a national church.' Svetosavlje's leading theorist, Archimandrite Justin Popović, would describe its principles most explicitly a few years after World War II, in his text *Svetosavlje as a Philosophy of Life*, which argued that the West had fallen after rejecting God in favour of materialist and anthropocentric principles. Salvation for the Serbs meant 'accepting St Sava's enlightenment and wholly implementing it in all schools, from the lowest to the highest, and in all educational, national and state institutions from the first to the last'.[33]

Patriarch Varnava (Petar Rosić) himself espoused an anti-materialist, anti-Communist religious philosophy. In this context, Ljotić sought to penetrate the Serbian Orthodox clergy. From 1935, he sat on the Braničevo eparchy's council, whose seat was in Požarevac, and was a member of the Patriarchal Council of the Serbian Orthodox Church in Belgrade. He built a close relationship with Velimirović, whose followers joined ZBOR.[34] Ljotić's movement also sought to penetrate the officer corps, succeeding in recruiting Colonel Kosta Mušicki, who had served as King Aleksandar's adjutant, and Colonel Miloš Masalović, chief of cabinet to General Milan Nedić, one of the army's most senior officers and formerly a key Aleksandar loyalist. Nedić himself was related to Ljotić; the two met frequently to discuss domestic and international politics. It was through Ljotić that German Intelligence made contact with Nedić; this would have important consequences after the German occupation of Yugoslavia in 1941 when the two emerged as the principal Serbian quislings, while Mušicki became commander of the elite quisling Serbian Volunteer Corps.[35] Mušicki was a Serb from Croatia; the Yugoslav nationalism Ljotić espoused was attractive for many Croatian Serbs, even for some Yugoslav-nationalist Croats.

Chetnik associations also evolved and expanded during and after Aleksandar's rule. Following the dictatorship's establishment, the Association of Serb Chetniks

'Petar Mrkonjić' was dissolved and its members soon rejoined the original Chetnik organisation, the Association of Chetniks for the Freedom and Honour of the Fatherland. This was headed in 1928–1932 by Ilija Trifunović-Birčanin, who in 1932 became president of National Defence, after which the Chetnik organisation's leadership passed to Pećanac, subsequently head of the quisling Chetnik forces in Serbia during World War II. With the blessing of King Aleksandar, who appreciated his loyalty, Pećanac greatly expanded the Chetnik organisation to include new members with no particular connection to the Chetnik past; it explicitly defined its purpose as the defence of the Serbs against their domestic enemies.[36]

After Aleksandar's assassination, when they were no longer restrained by him, Pećanac's Chetniks became increasingly rogue, assaulting non-Serbs in Croatia and Bosnia-Hercegovina.[37] The number of its subcommittees in Yugoslavia rose from 150 in 1934 to 430 in 1935, by which time it had 213,210 members. By 1938, its general council claimed to have a thousand subcommittees and over half a million members.[38] Pećanac's Chetnik organisation was heavily influenced by the paramilitary organisation ORJUNA, which was anti-Semitic, hostile to multiparty democracy and openly sympathetic to Nazi Germany and Fascist Italy. The Chetnik organisation's paper *Jugoslovenska straža* (Yugoslav Guard) said of the Jews on 27 October 1935: 'Today, we can say freely that Hitler was then in the right when he acted against them so mercilessly and bit by bit expelled them. Hitler was in the right when he went so far as to expel even those who, in their most distant roots, had Jewish blood. Hitler was in the right when he pushed that base sect out of Germany.' The Chetnik organisation demanded that the Jews be likewise expelled from Yugoslavia.[39]

Milan Stojadinović and the Court Radical renaissance

The establishment of the regency, according to Milan Stojadinović, was a quiet putsch by Uzunović and Pavle in which the former ensured the latter's installation as regent despite his prior political marginality; Uzunović was compelled to do so given Pavle's support in court and military circles.[40] Uzunović sought to uphold the legacy of Aleksandar, whom parliament posthumously awarded the title of 'King-Unifier'. But the enforced state mourning Uzunović decreed was excessive; by banning cinema, theatre and musical performances and ordering the draping of black flags on buildings and the wearing of black armbands by the populace, he rapidly alienated much of it.[41] He was forced from office on 20 December 1934 by the resignation of foreign minister Bogoljub Jevtić, who was Živković's relative by marriage, a Radical and former minister of the court under the dictatorship. This marked an attempt by Pavle to turn from the dictatorship's prominent politicians to less compromised individuals. Jevtić's car had been immediately behind Aleksandar's in the fateful convoy in Marseilles, and Jevtić had approached the dying king, who he claimed (probably falsely) had begged him with his last words, 'Look after Yugoslavia'. Jevtić promoted his government as upholding the legacy of the martyred king and retained Živković as war minister; Živković assumed he would be the dominant figure in a government nominally headed by his younger relative. But Jevtić's attempt to perpetuate the dictatorship's hardline rule, combined with his unwillingness to defer to Živković, in turn doomed his government.

Jevtić raised the question at the League of Nations of foreign states' responsibility for Aleksandar's assassination. Given French and British intimations to Belgrade that it could not count on their support for action against Italy, Jevtić's memorandum of 22 November 1934 ignored the latter. It focused instead on little Hungary, demanding the League discuss its responsibility for hosting Ustasha terrorists. But it still failed to elicit meaningful French support. The League limited itself to holding the Hungarian authorities responsible for failure to take sufficient measures to prevent the assassination and to demanding that it inform them of the measures it would take to punish those responsible. The resolution thus reduced Hungary's responsibility to a sin of omission on the part of its security forces, rather than an active pro-terrorist policy on the part of its government.[42] Hungary paid only lip service to the resolution. According to Stojadinović, Jevtić's failure convinced Pavle to replace him as prime minister. Paris's failure to support Belgrade disillusioned the Serbian public in their traditional French ally, whose security failures were responsible for Aleksandar's death in the first place, pushing Yugoslavia further toward the fascist states.[43]

Prince Regent Pavle, the new reigning dynast was, unlike Aleksandar, a civilian educated in Britain (at Christ Church, University of Oxford) who had rejected a military career. He was averse to militarism, autocracy and centralism and sympathetic to a federal solution for Yugoslavia.[44] According to Maček, after his first meeting with Pavle, 'I judged that he was a man, although with a strong hint of aristocracy, absolutely cultured in the European sense of that word. I immediately saw that, unlike his late cousin Aleksandar, he had not a trace of Serb chauvinism.' Allegedly, when Maček tactfully said that the Croats had nothing against a monarchy on the British model, Pavle agreed: 'Be assured that the British type of monarchy is most sympathetic to me,' but added, referring contemptuously to several politicians from Serbia, 'I ask you whether those are British?'[45]

Pavle could not and would not base his rule on the circles that had formed the mainstay of Aleksandar's regime: court generals, above all the White Hand, and an unrepresentative amalgam of court politicians. He consequently pursued a gentler political course. The day after the appointment of Jevtić's government, he pardoned Maček. He mended fences with the less oppositional segments of the authentic Yugoslav political classes, particularly those in Serbia, above all the Radicals. These had been less hardline in their opposition to the Alexandrine dictatorship than the Democrats or Farmers and unwilling to embrace federalism. While the Democrats and Farmers were oriented toward alliance with the hardline opposition of the Peasant–Democrat Coalition, the Radicals had edged instead toward alliance with other more moderate opposition parties, the JMO and SLS. Though they were not permitted to operate legally by the regime while Aleksandar was alive, and their request for legalisation in August 1933 was rejected, they continued to seek an accommodation with it after his assassination. They formed an alliance with the SLS in November 1934 which, it was envisaged, would be joined also by the JMO. The partners discussed with Jevtić a possible coalition government, but they failed to agree.[46] Nevertheless, at Pavle's personal request, Stojadinović, a member of the Radical party's general council, joined Jevtić's government in December 1934 as finance minister, without the general council's authorisation but without incurring its displeasure.

Milan Stojadinović (1888–1961) personified the younger generation of Radicals who had come of age after the 1903 putsch, when their party was no longer the party of opposition to monarchical despotism but the principal party of government and the elite. He was a wealthy businessman, one of the richest men in Serbia, and had been a university professor in economics and president of the Belgrade stock exchange. He had been a protégé of Pašić, whom he described in his memoirs as 'the greatest statesman to whom the Serbian land had ever given birth'.[47] He served as finance minister under Pašić, leaving government in 1928 and remaining in opposition under the dictatorship. However, his opposition was not as unconditional as that of some others, and the king appointed him, in the final months of his life, intermediary in negotiating a reconciliation between the Court Radicals who served the dictatorship and the Radical general council. According to Stojadinović, Aleksandar's aim was to retreat from dictatorship in alliance with the Radicals, but this policy was aborted by his assassination.[48] Stojadinović and Pavle had meanwhile formed a political friendship as two out-of-favour members of the elite who were moderate in their criticisms of the regime.[49] Stojadinović was therefore uncompromised by collaboration with the dictatorship yet moderate enough in his opposition to be an acceptable partner for the regime. He thus become the Court Radical through whom Pavle sought to manage a transition resembling that which Serbia had undergone under Aleksandar Obrenović after his break with Milan in 1900.

Jevtić's government dissolved parliament on 6 February 1935. An election was held on 5 May and the results officially announced the same day: the government's list had won 62.6 per cent of the vote and 320 seats; the principal opposition bloc headed by Maček, uniting the HSS, Independent Democrats, JMO, Democrats and Farmers under the name United Opposition, won 35.4 per cent and 48 seats; while the minor lists led by Božidar Maksimović, a defector from the government bloc, and by Ljotić failed to win any seats. The Radicals and SLS did not participate in the election. Jevtić formed a government of the JNS and his own clique, the

FASCISM AND COURT RADICALISM

Patriotic Youth Front. However, the official results provoked an outcry that forced the government to stage a recount, whose results were announced on 22 May: now the government's list allegedly won 60.6 per cent of the vote and 303 seats, Maček's opposition list 37.4 per cent of the vote and 67 seats, and the Maksimović and Ljotić lists still no seats. This failed to mollify the Democrats, Farmers and Peasant–Democrat Coalition, which on 30 May declared a boycott of parliament. Two days later, the Peasant–Democrat Coalition announced that 'the further survival of the state is possible only if the justified demands of the Croatian nation are satisfied'.[50] Thenceforth it pursued an autonomous opposition policy while the JMO moved toward collaboration with the regime; consequently, the United Opposition was reduced to the Democrats and Farmers.[51]

Jevtić's moral defeat in the elections provided the occasion for Pavle, finance minister Stojadinović and war minister Živković to oust him, since they were agreed he was not competent to remain prime minister. Živković, veteran praetorian, sought a new, more pliant front man through whom he could dominate government while Pavle and Stojadinović wanted to avoid alienating the powerful court general; thus, after they had offered the premiership to Živković and he had refused, the three agreed it should go to Stojadinović.[52] In intense talks held in May and June 1935, the Radicals, JMO and SLS agreed to merge to form a new ruling party, the Yugoslav Radical Union (JRZ), to be headed by an executive council comprising Stojadinović and the leaders of the three constituent former parties: Stanojević, Korošec and Spaho.[53] Živković, Stojadinović and the three Croat ministers resigned on 20 June, toppling Jevtić's government. His fall marked the final defeat of the Alexandrine system, whereby the regime ruled in opposition to the Serbian civilian elite.

Stojadinović formed a government on 24 June 1935. It initially retained Živković as war minister. Its formation signified, in fact, the Radicals' re-emergence as the court's preferred partner, once again edging aside the military elite. They came to power through their alliance with the other two moderate opposition parties, the JMO and SLS. The Radical leadership viewed this transition as marking a return to the democratic order it had traditionally favoured. It supported the government on the understanding that it would pass laws to restore democracy by means of elections free of government manipulation, freedom of association including the right freely to organise political parties and freedom of the press with the end of censorship.[54] As Lazar Marković of the general council wrote on 30 June, 'The People's Radical Party, faithful to its traditional principles of freedom and parliamentarism, modelled on the most enlightened nations of Western Europe, sincerely rejoices in such a turnabout in our internal politics.'[55] He explained to a Radical meeting in Sarajevo a few days later that they had reached agreement with the JMO and SLS for the sake of restoring normal democratic conditions and achieving a compromise with the Croats.[56]

SERBIA

The new tripartite party, the JRZ, was formally registered on 19 August 1935. Unlike the JNS, which was formally a wholly new, all-Yugoslav party, the JRZ was a coalition of three pre-1929 political parties, and Stojadinović's regime would be less avowedly innovative than Aleksandar's, marking a retreat from the Alexandrine model of integral Yugoslavism. Živković's three allies among the minsters resigned following the JRZ's registration, in what Stojadinović considered an attempt by the White Hand chief to derail his policy.[57] According to the JRZ manifesto, published on 20 August, the unity of state and nation, monarchy and Karađorđević dynasty would be upheld, but the party appreciated 'that the territories, of which our state is composed, lived in the past their particular lives, and over a long period of time developed particular customs: administrative, political and other…respect for the three names of our people, Serb, Croat and Slovene, and their equality; respect for recognised religion, as for both alphabets; respect for tradition—all that needs to be protected'. The unitary state would be preserved but 'self-government' would be promoted as 'the best system of ordering the state administration'.[58]

Stojadinović presented himself and his wing of the new composite party as the representatives of Serbia rather than of Yugoslavia as a whole, ceding to Spaho and the JMO the leadership of the Bosnian Muslims and dominance in Bosnia-Hercegovina and to Korošec and the SLS the leadership of the Slovenes and dominance in Slovenia. Since most of the Bosnian wing of the Radicals had followed Srškić into the JNS, what was left was a very weak rump, and Stojadinović, in building his coalition to replace the JNS, had little choice but to rely on the Muslims. But this came at the price of abandoning any significant support among Bosnian Serbs.[59] Stojadinović's surrender of power in Bosnia-Hercegovina to the JMO marked a reversal of Aleksandar's policy, which had been to ally with Srškić and the Bosnian Radicals and weaken the Muslims. The divergence of interest between the political classes of Serbia and of the Bosnian Serbs was thereby confirmed. Stojadinović meanwhile hurried to establish JRZ organs in Serbia, Vojvodina, Montenegro and Macedonia—both to give himself a base equivalent to Spaho's in Bosnia-Hercegovina and Korošec's in Slovenia and to present himself as leader of the majority of Serbs, as Spaho, Korošec and Maček were of the Bosnian Muslims, Slovenes and Croats respectively.[60] The field was left open for a compromise with the Croatian opposition grouped behind Maček.

Stojadinović thus recognised the authorities of the principal non-Serbian parties while seeking to monopolise power in Serbia itself through the marginalisation of the Serbian opposition parties.[61] His regime represented a Serbian reaction against the previous regime's authoritarian Yugoslavism, a reassertion of Serbia's political identity and voice vis-à-vis Yugoslavia, another attempt at reconciliation between court and Radicals and a return to the Radicals' traditional policy of seeking political hegemony for themselves within Serbia, now limited in practice to the areas where the JRZ's Serbian wing was active: pre-1912 Serbia, Vojvodina, the Sanjak, Montenegro, Kosovo and Macedonia. Yet just as Pavle dismantled the court's structure of authoritarian rule in the White Hand and army, so Stojadinović watered down the Radical party. The union with the JMO and SLS involved importing these two parties' tenets into the common party programme, diluting the Radicals' voice. Meanwhile, Stojadinović attempted to expand the base of his wing of the JRZ, incorporating both former collaborators of the dictatorship and those who had never been Radicals. His policies thus further threatened the Radical party's identity and the authority of its old guard grouped in and around the general council under Stanojević. The resulting conflict was both a power struggle between Stojadinović and the Radical old guard and a battle over the party's character and purpose. The Radicals' two representatives in government resigned in August 1935 in an attempt at destabilising Stojadinović's fledgling regime, but they merely succeeded in consolidating it. The conflict culminated in the general council's repudiation of Stojadinović in a memorandum on 18 December 1935, with Stanojević complaining that the proposed laws restoring free elections, freedom of association and freedom of the press had not been passed and 'ever more among the people has the conviction arisen that the government of Mr Dr Stojadinović is a continuation of the regime of the last six–seven years'.[62] This was immediately followed by a police raid on the JRZ's Belgrade premises controlled by the general council and the cancellation of the council's government subsidy, which instead was transferred directly to the JRZ organisation controlled by Stojadinović.[63]

This quarrel, between Court Radicals wishing to compromise with the court for the sake of power and Radicals outside government opposing any such dilution of the party's principles, was the latest stage of a conflict that had been intrinsic to the party since the late 1880s. It marked the third major split in the Radical party, following the 1901–1904 secession of those who became the Independents and the 1928–1929 secession of those who supported Aleksandar's dictatorship and joined the JNS. Even before Stojadinović and the general council finally split, the struggle for control of the new JRZ between the two led to cases of parallel JRZ organisations being established in the same localities in Serbia. This weakened both. The JRZ behind Stojadinović remained feebly organised as a party and attracted relatively few members, despite the administrative means employed by the government to assist it.[64] In Bosnia-Hercegovina, the break with the general council left the JRZ still more dominated by the JMO.[65] But the fortunes of the Radicals loyal to the general council fell still further, marking their definite end as Serbia's principal party. At the start of 1936 they joined the Democrats and Farmers in the United Opposition, but the Democrats replaced them as Serbia's leading opposition party, supported by the greater part of the Serbian intelligentsia.[66]

The majority of parliament members recruited by Jevtić transferred their allegiance to the JRZ and remained with Stojadinović after his break with the general council. At the time of its formation on 21 October 1935, the JRZ's parliamentary club comprised 116 deputies while 33 more continued to support the government but did not join the JRZ. The club's deputies increased to 153 by January 1936 and would grow further thereafter. Stevan Ćirić, president of parliament and a JNS member, defected to the JRZ on the grounds that 'the Serb part of the Yugoslav nation today is not gathered in a single larger party or organisation' and that it was necessary to remedy this deficit by means of the JRZ.[67] Nevertheless, the JRZ's hold on Serbia remained uncertain; 64 of its parliamentary deputies in January 1936 were from the territories that would be included in Serbia from 1945 (including Vojvodina, Kosovo and the Sanjak), rising to 82 by October 1938. If other supporters of the government outside the JRZ club are included, this meant that only 61.8 per cent of parliamentary deputies from the territory of post-1945 Serbia supported the government by October 1938.[68] Indeed, Bosnian Muslims voted for the JRZ rather more solidly than did Serbs in Serbia and much more solidly than did Serbs outside Serbia; according to the JMO newspaper *Pravda* (Justice), in the Yugoslav municipal elections of December 1936, 91 per cent of Muslims voted for the JRZ against 72.3 per cent of Slovenes and 70 per cent of Serbs.[69]

Stojadinović relaxed press censorship and police harassment of opponents of the government and amnestied a number of political prisoners. The JNS's youth organisation, Yugoslav National Youth, was banned. The government established a regime trade-union organisation, the Yugoslav Workers' Union (JUGORAS), inspired by the regime labour associations in Fascist Italy and Nazi Germany and headed by the minister for social policy and national health Dragiša Cvetković. As Stojadinović recalls, members were required to wear blue uniforms and blue shirts and to give the 'fascist salute', which was intended to bring about the 'fascisisation of the country'.[70] A decree on a minimum wage was issued on 15 April 1937, followed by a decree on state social security for the poor, old and disabled on 1 September. According to Cvetković, Stojadinović proposed establishing the institution of 'führer', whereby Pavle would be the führer of the state, Stojadinović political führer of the country, and Cvetković führer of the workers, but Pavle vetoed this.[71] A 'new economic course' involved the pursuit of autarky, deflation and balanced trade, with increased state intervention in support of economic enterprises. A decree on the liquidation of peasant debts on 25 September 1936 completed the process begun under Aleksandar, resulting in the writing off of 50 per cent of the principal of these debts. The government reduced unemployment through large-scale public works; it launched a major programme of railway and road building and opened dozens of new factories for textiles, food, aluminium and paper. Increased armaments production both reduced unemployment and served the regime's foreign policy goals. The antiquated mining complex at Bor in the Timok region was modernised and expanded to become Europe's leading producer of copper outside Germany. The lead and zinc mines at Trepča in Kosovo were likewise modernised and a sulphuric acid factory opened at Šabac. The copper and lead in particular were hungrily absorbed by Nazi Germany.[72]

FASCISM AND COURT RADICALISM

Stojadinović's authority was constrained by the fact that his parliament had been elected under Jevtić, so contained large numbers of Jevtić's supporters. Živković had opposed the JRZ's formation as something that would reduce his own authority, and began to collaborate dangerously with Jevtić against the government, in which he still sat. The senate was packed with members of the JNS installed there under the dictatorship, and on 11 November 1935 a group of 59 of them sent Stojadinović an interpellation accusing him of 'returning to the old party life and the renewed division of national powers on the basis of tribal, regional and confessional characteristics', thereby leading the country to 'complete anarchy'.[73] Meanwhile, the relaxation of repression, combined with the continued failure to restore genuine parliamentary democracy or reach a compromise with the Croats, prompted Maček and the HSS from mid-1935 to establish paramilitary organisations, the Croat Civic Defence and Croat Peasant Defence, which rapidly spread across Croatia-Slavonia and Dalmatia and, in generally weaker form, the Croat-inhabited areas of Bosnia-Hercegovina.

Damjan Arnautović, a deputy from among Jevtić's supporters, attempted to assassinate Stojadinović in parliament on 6 March 1936. The attempt bore some resemblances to the Radić assassination: the would-be assassin had served in the southern Yugoslav territories (as a schoolteacher in Macedonia); he was linked to the White Hand; and he fired several shots at his target with a revolver. Stojadinović responded by sacking Živković, ending the White Hand's grip on power.[74] The government used the incident to burnish its credentials as a democratising force that was facing down the remnants of the dictatorship.[75] Stojadinović was indeed at this point actually more afraid of the politicians of the former dictatorship than he was of his democratic opponents in the United Opposition. With support from Živković's rivals among the generals formerly loyal to Aleksandar, Stojadinović purged the army of Živković's supporters. Stojadinović's military allies were, in particular, Nedić, who had served as chief of the general staff for a year from 1 June 1934 then become a member of the military council on 9 March 1935, and Ljubomir Marić, who had succeeded Nedić as chief of the general staff from 12 May 1935 and now replaced Živković as war minister, serving in that post until August 1938.[76] Meanwhile, the Chetnik organisations were frowned upon by the JRZ government. In Bosnia-Hercegovina, the ruling JMO restricted their activities as instigators of anti-Muslim violence. Stojadinović did so too throughout Yugoslavia since he viewed them as competitors of his own projected mass paramilitary organisation.[77] Interior minister Korošec, working with the ban of the Drava Banovina, likewise ordered the disbanding of the National Defence organisation there, though Stojadinović resisted this.[78]

Stojadinović's politics represented a new, centrist course between the Alexandrine dictatorship's integral Yugoslav nationalism and the Radical party's traditional Serbian nationalism. To present himself and his party as the national leader and party of Serbia and the Serbs, he pragmatically sought to maximise his basis of support by courting the ethnic minorities in pre-1912 Serbia and the adjacent lands: the ethnic

Germans, Hungarians and Romanians of Vojvodina and, initially at least, even the Albanians of Kosovo and Macedonia.[79] He moderated anti-Croat repression, thereby earning unremitting attacks from elements in the JNS, army and Orthodox Church. This was a difficult path to steer; on 16 April 1936, after a HSS politician was murdered by a prisoner on parole, angry peasants lynched six members of the JRZ in the Croatian village of Kerestinec, which appeared to vindicate Stojadinović's hardline critics.[80] Yet he did not let this derail his policy of moderation.

Concordat crisis

As part of his efforts to appease Croat opinion and because it was sought by his Catholic clericalist partner Korošec, Stojadinović promoted a concordat between Yugoslavia and the Vatican to regulate the Catholic Church's status in Yugoslavia. The Vatican was already pressing for a new, uniform concordat to replace the four existing concordats that, inconsistently with one another, regulated the church's position in four different parts of Yugoslavia, dating back to when they were internationally separate entities: the formerly Habsburg lands of Croatia, Dalmatia, Slovenia and Vojvodina; Bosnia-Hercegovina; Montenegro; and Serbia. The new concordat was signed on 25 July 1935, but Stojadinović delayed presenting it to the parliament for ratification until July 1937, when he felt his authority was more secure. The Concordat promised that 'the Catholic Church is recognised, in all of its rituals, the full right freely and publicly to carry out its mission in the Kingdom of Yugoslavia'. It granted the Holy See the right to select Yugoslavia's Catholic bishops from the ranks of its citizens in consultation with the government; the bishops in return would pledge allegiance to the Yugoslav king and his heirs. It granted full freedom in Yugoslavia for Catholic religious orders and organisations, freedom and state support for Catholic seminaries and theological colleges under church control, freedom to establish and maintain religious schools, compulsory religious education for Yugoslav Catholic youth with syllabi supervised by the church, and the regulation of the content and character of school education in general for Yugoslavia's Catholic population in accordance with Catholic values, with its teachers required to be Catholics as far as possible.[81]

The proposed Concordat proved a major miscalculation. It offended hardline Serbian Orthodox sensibilities on multiple counts: it promised the re-establishment of a Catholic diocese in Niš, state recognition of the Catholic Action movement, state funding for all the Catholic Church's seminaries and catechetical schools and the withdrawal of priests of all denominations from political life. The Holy Episcopal Synod of the Serbian Orthodox Church viewed it as abolishing religious equality and making the Catholic Church Yugoslavia's dominant church; its representation to the government on 3 December 1936 stated that 'it would be compelled by its holy vow and its holy duty, in unison with its clergy and its pastors, to fight with all available means against the acceptance of such a law in our Fatherland'.[82] Patriarch Varnava, in his New Year's Day speech on 14 January 1937, bitterly denounced the proposed Concordat as the work of Yugoslav leaders 'without sense or honour' who had 'made an agreement with the black chief of the Black International'—the Pope—leading to the 'triumph of that chief over the Balkans, for which they had been striving for five hundred years'. Varnava even compared Stojadinović's government unfavourably with the Ottomans:

> The Turks knew of the false character of that International and did not allow it in the Balkans. The Turks knew of its destructive activity in the state; they knew that that international did not refrain from any means nor from any plot or intrigue and they did not enter into any compromise with it. The Orthodox religion the Turks sometimes persecuted, but they deemed it a religion and respected it as a religion. But they looked upon that Black International not as a religion but as political. And there you have it, my brothers; our holders of government are entirely opening the gate to that unscrupulous political organisation and permitting it to stand with firm feet on the Balkans. And who is doing this? Not any foreigners but the christened sons of St Sava's Church ... Honour to the Turks and shame on such Orthodox and such Serbs.[83]

According to Stojadinović, Bishop Platon objected to the Concordat's recognition of the right of the Catholic Church to pursue its mission across the whole of Yugoslavia on the grounds that 'Our country is proclaimed a *"terra infidelium"*, as if it were a question of Africa, where the Catholic Church had to Christianise wild blacks.'[84] Varnava also praised Hitler's policy toward the Catholic Church in an interview with a German newspaper in May 1937, citing it as an example of decisiveness that Yugoslavia should emulate.[85]

During the struggle over the Concordat, Dožić recalls, 'We were conscious of our power, for the whole nation was with their Church.'[86] A special session of the Holy Episcopal Synod met on 8 July at the same time as the parliamentary committee deliberating on the Concordat commenced its sitting. That evening, a prayer was held at all Belgrade's Orthodox churches for the health of the ailing Patriarch Varnava, amounting to a well-organised attempt by the church to put pressure on the government, in which many former ministers and opposition politicians participated. Prayers for Varnava were then held throughout the country.[87] Subsequently, the requirement that priests withdraw from politics, in particular, may have prompted two Orthodox priests and parliamentary deputies of the JRZ Club, Vojislav Janjić and Archimandrite Nikanor Grujić, to vote against the Concordat on 14 July when it came before the parliamentary committee set up to examine it, of which Janjić was president. The Concordat was consequently rejected by the committee at the first vote. It passed the next day after Stojadinović replied in detail to the criticisms, after which it was put before parliament. Janjić, Grujić and fourteen other parliamentary deputies were expelled from the JRZ club owing to their opposition to it.

SERBIA

The Belgrade city administration on 19 July banned public meetings and marches in an attempt to suppress the Orthodox Church's political mobilisation against the Concordat. Gendarmes clashed that day with a procession departing from the Belgrade cathedral; Simeon Stanković, bishop of Šabac, was seriously injured. This sparked protests from the Holy Episcopal Synod and other Serbian organisations; black flags were hung outside the Patriarchate and Belgrade's churches. The disturbances in Belgrade's streets continued over the following days.[88] Parliament approved the Concordat on 23 July against JNS opposition, but this opposition prompted Stojadinović to postpone its ratification in the senate until feelings in Serbia had calmed. Varnava's death on the day that parliament approved the Concordat then sparked a further Orthodox Church revolt. The Synod rejected a state funeral for Varnava and on 8 August imposed sanctions on the government ministers and deputies who had voted for the Concordat, in anticipation of their excommunication. Nevertheless, the governor of Belgrade, Milan Aćimović, strove to ensure that the church funeral would not occasion any further violence or disorder; he feared it would discredit the authorities to rely on the army, so he arranged with Pećanac for the Chetnik organisation to provide security. The funeral consequently took place peacefully.[89] Stojadinović announced on 9 October that the Concordat would not be put before the senate and on 1 February 1938 withdrew it altogether, after which the Synod lifted its sanctions against the offending ministers and deputies. The anti-Concordat revolt reflected Serb nationalist opposition to a regime widely viewed as too Yugoslav and discordant with Serbia's traditions.

The leaders of the Peasant–Democrat Coalition (Maček of the HSS and Adam Pribićević of the Independent Democrats) and of the United Opposition (Stanojević of the Radicals, Davidović of the Democrats and Jovanović-Pižon of the Farmers) had meanwhile united in the National Agreement Bloc, informally still called the United Opposition, which published a joint proclamation on 8 October 1937 condemning the existing Yugoslav order as illegitimate: the 1921 constitution had been promulgated 'without the Croats'; the 1931 constitution was 'in opposition to basic democratic tenets and promulgated not only without the Croats and against the Croats but without the Serbs and against the Serbs'; while the government 'has no authority either among the Croats or among the Serbs'. The proclamation therefore called for a 'new constitutional order' that would be 'established as the common work of the Serbs, Croats and Slovenes' and declared that 'the last chance has been reached, for all undemocratic systems and regimes to be dispensed with once and for all, and that the Croats, Serbs and Slovenes be enabled to organise their state union on the basis of agreement, to the equal satisfaction of the Serbs, the Croats and the Slovenes'.

Consequently, the future 'Constituent Assembly should promulgate the constitution on the basis of a majority in which will be a majority of Serb, a majority of Croat and a majority of Slovene national representatives of the Constituent

Assembly'. In fact, as Miloš Trifunović, Radical general council member and architect of this policy made clear, the Slovenes were only included pro forma and it was 'a matter only of the Croats and Serbs and their mutual agreement ... if the majority of Serbs and the majority of Croats agree and in the parliament draw up an internal organisation [of the state] then this will be added to the already accepted constitution and all disputes between the Serbs and Croats are resolved'.[90] According to Marković, 'Of the state of Yugoslavia as a hereditary, constitutional and parliamentary monarchy, as of the Karađorđević dynasty from which King Petar II has assumed the throne, between us Serbs and between the Croats there thus exists, according to this agreement, complete consensus.'[91] This proclamation thus marked the Serbian opposition parties' departure from unitarism and their acceptance that the future Yugoslav constitutional order would require Croat consent.

Green shirts and new friendships

Faced with this opposition challenge, Stojadinović attempted to bolster his regime by further emulating Europe's fascist regimes. He established his own green-shirted paramilitary force for holding fascist-style marches and rallies, which employed a fascist-style salute and addressed him as 'Vođa' (Leader)—chanted repeatedly, it unfortunately sounded like 'đavo' (devil). Although he had been in opposition under the 6 January Regime, he promoted the cult of the murdered King Aleksandar to which other fascist and pro-fascist politicians subscribed, describing him in his speeches as 'not an ordinary King' but the people's 'Chivalrous King Aleksandar the Unifier', 'its Great King, its Great Leader', who 'carried the whole burden of state politics upon his shoulders'. He employed the slogan 'One king, one people, one state', which resembled the Nazis' 'Ein Volk, ein Reich, ein Führer'.[92]

Stojadinović further reoriented Belgrade toward Germany and Italy while maintaining the traditional alliance with France, a policy he described as 'old and new friendships'.[93] This was justified as improving upon Serbia's traditional policy of linking its destiny with just one great power—Russia up to World War I, then France—and as a sign that Yugoslavia had reached maturity as a state.[94] Consequently, from the second half of 1936, Germany stepped in as Yugoslavia's protector against its revisionist neighbours, Italy and Hungary, and put pressure on Italy to reach an accommodation with it. Yugoslavia signed a pact of 'perpetual friendship' with Bulgaria on 24 January 1937, followed by a treaty of friendship and non-aggression with Italy on 25 March 1937, which required Italy to recognise Yugoslavia's territorial integrity, grant her most-favoured-nation status in trade and suppress Ustasha activity on its soil, while Yugoslavia accepted Italian primacy in Albania. Germany's Krupp firm opened a steel mill in Zenica in Bosnia on 2 October 1937, after Stojadinović awarded it a contract in preference to its French and Czech competitors. This facilitated Yugoslavia's further economic colonisation by Germany.[95]

Stojadinović visited Berlin in January 1938 and assured Hitler that 'as regards Yugoslavia, I can declare that it will not in any circumstances join a pact directed against Germany. The Serbs and the Germans were not in the last world war bitter enemies but honourable opponents.' Hitler agreed, stating: 'Germany desires, in its own interest, the existence of a strong and consolidated Yugoslavia.'[96] Recalling past German–Yugoslav relations, Stojadinović remarked that 'if there had been any discord, that was only when the Yugoslav government looked at Germany through foreign spectacles. Yugoslavia has now taken off those spectacles and looks at all things realistically, through its own eyes.'[97] He received Hitler's guarantee of Yugoslavia's territorial integrity in return for its acquiescence in Germany's Anschluss with Austria. Stojadinović recalls: 'I deemed that the "Anschluss" was the lesser evil for Yugoslavia. Thereby would all hopes be destroyed of our foreign and internal enemies with the *K.u.K.* [*Kaiser und König*—Emperor (of Austria) and King (of Hungary)] mentality, that there could ever again be, in any form, restored the deceased Austro-Hungarian Monarchy, which could have meant a mortal danger for Yugoslavia's survival.'[98] However, the Anschluss, subsequently proclaimed on 12 March 1938, gave Yugoslavia a land border with Germany, increasing its vulnerability, while the Munich Agreement of 30 September, whereby Germany dismembered Czechoslovakia with the acquiescence of Britain and France, made the latter two's unwillingness to risk war for the sake of the states of Eastern and Central Europe brutally apparent. These events confirmed to many in Belgrade the necessity of continuing the policy of rapprochement with Germany and other revisionist states.

In the international climate of ascendant radical authoritarian nationalism, Stojadinović increased the persecution of Yugoslavia's Albanian minority. Since 1933, the Yugoslav and Turkish governments had seriously discussed the possible deportation of huge numbers of Yugoslav Albanians to Turkey, and from the mid-1930s land confiscations were stepped up, with the goal of removing the means of subsistence from Albanians to force them to emigrate. The historian Vasa Čubrilović, formerly one of Gavrilo Princip's fellow Sarajevo assassins, delivered a speech to the nationalist Serb Cultural Club on 7 March 1937, presenting a plan for 'expulsion of the Arnauts', which was subsequently written up and submitted as a memorandum to Yugoslavia's government. It lamented that official bodies had, 'in the turbulent and bloody Balkans, forgetting where they were, wanted to use Western methods for resolving major ethnic problems', pointing out that 'when Germany can expel tens of thousands of Jews and Russia can move millions from one part of the continent to the other, a world war will not occur because of some hundreds of thousands of expelled Arnauts'. Čubrilović advocated 'the use of the law to make survival of the Albanians among us as difficult as possible', including 'the merciless use of all police regulations', 'refusal to recognise old land deeds', 'persecution of clergy', 'destruction of cemeteries', 'Chetnik action' and 'the secret burning of villages and Arnaut town quarters', after which the vacated lands were to be settled with Serbs from poorer areas, above all Montenegrins.⁹⁹

Stojadinović's government thought along those lines. It initialled an agreement with Turkey on 11 July 1938 for the latter to take 40,000 families, with Yugoslavia's government paying 500 Turkish pounds for each of them but confiscating in return all their land. The plan was to have been executed between 1939 and 1944.¹⁰⁰ Stojadinović even discussed with Italy's foreign minister Galeazzo Ciano in January 1939 the possible partition of Albania itself; this would, he later admitted, have meant the Italian occupation of most of the country with Yugoslavia receiving a small slice as compensation—probably the extreme north including Shkodër, Serbia's traditional territorial goal.¹⁰¹ Yugoslav foreign ministry officials believed such a partition would end the irredentist threat that independent Albania posed and facilitate the assimilation or exodus of Yugoslavia's Albanians.¹⁰² Stojadinović also encouraged Italian expansionism elsewhere. During his visit to Yugoslavia, after going on a hunt with him, Ciano recorded in his diary on 20 January 1939: 'Went hunting in the forest. Good news from Spain. Stoyadinovich received it shouting: "Corsica, Tunis, Nice!"'¹⁰³ Conversely, when a Croat envoy from Maček arrived in Berlin on 20 February, Hitler and Göring refused to meet with him, with Göring sending him a message that 'Germany does not have any kind of plans or intentions against the integrity of friendly Yugoslavia'.¹⁰⁴

Yugoslav senate elections on 6 February 1938 resulted in the government's defeat of the United Opposition in Serbia but an opposition victory in the Sava and Primorje Banovinas, after which the opposition continued to boycott the upper chamber. Yugoslavia's parliament concluded its work on 17 March and was not thereafter reconvened, and on 11 October Stojadinović called elections for 11 December. He mobilised his green-shirts to drum up support during the election campaign, relying also on Hođera's blue-shirts—Hođera himself would join the government following the election.¹⁰⁵ The Serbian wing of the opposition was subjected to heavy police terror and repression. State employees, including workers in state-owned factories, were required to vote for the government list, and the government asked the banovina authorities to submit to it the names and addresses of Jews who voted against it.¹⁰⁶ The United Opposition was further weakened by poor organisation, failure of coordination and mutual antagonism between its component parties: the Democrats and Radicals were traditional rivals and the latter in particular jealously guarded their tradition as a stand-alone party and sole legitimate representative of Serbia's population, while the Farmers viewed themselves as a class party of the peasantry hostile on socio-economic grounds to both Radicals and Democrats.¹⁰⁷ There was no equivalent government repression in Croatia, where the HSS's paramilitary forces successfully manipulated the elections.¹⁰⁸

The elections of 11 December 1938 produced a heavy moral defeat for the government, which was perceived by the Yugoslav public as having lost. Its list won

SERBIA

1,643,783 votes (54.1 per cent) and 306 seats against 1,364,524 votes (44.9 per cent) and 306 seats for the opposition. The latter defeated the government in the Sava and Primorje Banovinas while the government won decisively in every other banovina except Vrbas. However, according to one contemporary analysis, Stojadinović's list won its strongest support among Serbs in the Sava Banovina while also doing well among Serbs in Dalmatia. Thus, 74 per cent of the Serb vote in Croatia-Slavonia and 59 per cent in Dalmatia voted for Stojadinovć's list, compared with 66 per cent in pre-1912 Serbia, 62 per cent in Vojvodina (Banat, Bačka and Baranja) and 65 per cent in South Serbia. This partly reflected the alienation of much of the Serb population in Croatia from its traditional party, the Independent Democrats, owing to their pro-Croatian autonomist orientation. In Bosnia-Hercegovina and Montenegro, by contrast, the majority of Serb (i.e. Serbian Orthodox, including Montenegrin) votes went to the opposition: 59 per cent and 55 per cent respectively. Overall, 62.19 per cent of Yugoslavia's Serbs, 90.34 per cent of Muslims, 78.26 per cent of Slovenes and 93.55 per cent of members of the smaller ethnic groups (i.e. those not considered Serbs, Croats or Slovenes) voted for Stojadinović's list, while 96 per cent of Croats voted for the opposition.[109] Stojadinović blamed interior minister Korošec for treating the opposition too liberally during the election—particularly in the Sava Banovina—and dismissed him. The two also fell out over Korošec's opposition to Stojadinović's tolerant policy toward the German national minority. Without Korošec, the cabinet was reduced to a body effectively representing only the eastern half of Yugoslavia plus the Bosnian Muslims. Stojadinović appointed Aćimović as the new interior minister and attempted to toughen policy vis-à-vis the Croats and the opposition generally.

Pavle was by now ready personally to take over the reins of power. He was unhappy both with his premier's increasingly authoritarian behaviour, perceived as threatening the authority of the Karađorđević dynasty and Pavle personally, and with his failure to reach an agreement with the Croats. British diplomacy aimed at removing the pro-German Stojadinović may also have encouraged the pro-British Pavle to move against him. Pavle appointed the ousted Korošec as senate president while the Muslim ministers were ready to help topple Stojadinović. The occasion was provided on 3 February 1939, when Bogoljub Kujundžić, Stojadinović's hardline education minister, made an aggressively anti-Croat statement, concluding: 'The Serb nation has suffered too many losses ever to permit the idea of Kupinec [Maček's birthplace in Croatia] to be stronger than Oplenac [the Karađorđević family crypt]!' Five other ministers responded by resigning: Pavle's new protégé Cvetković, the JMO's Spaho and Džafer Kulenović, and the Slovenes Miha Krek and Franc Snoj; they claimed Kujundžić's outburst showed that the government was obstructing a compromise with the Croats and that such a compromise was imperative.[110] Stojadinović had to resign and Cvetković replaced him as prime minister on 5 February 1939. Cvetković later attributed Stojadinović's fall to Pavle's objection to his fascist ambitions: 'That intention of Dr Stojadinović brought about his later fall from government when he, although warned, continued to prepare the introduction of a fascist regime.'[111] Yugoslavia's strongest prime minister of the 1930s had been no more successful than Aleksandar in building an enduring stable regime with solid popular support. Following his resignation, Ciano recorded in his diary: 'With the removal of Stoyadinovich the Yugoslav card has lost for us 90 per cent of its value.'[112]

Stojadinović briefly remained JRZ president, and he and his supporters attempted to stage a come-back, agitating against Cvetković and denouncing the basis on which he was pursuing agreement with Maček and the HSS. Cvetković responded by summoning a JRZ general council session on 9 July 1939, at which Stojadinović and several of his closest collaborators and former ministers were expelled from the party and Cvetković replaced him as party president. Stojadinović continued agitating against the government, eventually founding a new party, the Serbian Radical Party.[113] His bitter polemics against Cvetković and Pavle followed the Radical tradition of presenting the Serbian ruler and his supporters as being nationally alien, un-Serb. Thus, of Cvetković, who was of partly Cincar background, Stojadinović wrote in his memoirs: 'There was among the people a widespread belief that he was of gypsy background. Certainly, his physical appearance confirmed that viewpoint, as did his actions and personal and private life.' In reference to Cvetković's role in his overthrow, Stojadinović commented: 'That national proverb of ours is known: "Give a Gypsy power and he will first hang his own father!"' A leaflet that Stojadinović's supporters distributed on his initiative, dated 2 April 1940, referred to 'the race, that Mr Dragiša Cvetković belongs to'. Of Pavle, Stojadinović wrote in his memoirs in reference to his foreign, English, upbringing that he 'hated the Serbs—I don't know why—from the bottom of his soul'; that he 'never fitted in in our milieu, in which he felt like a foreigner. The Serbs did not like him at all'; and that he attempted to play 'not a Yugoslav but an English prince—with a bowler hat on his head and an umbrella in his hand'. He even hinted strongly that Pavle was not genuinely Prince Arsen's son but the love child of Finland's commander-in-chief Carl Mannerheim. Leaflets attacking Pavle on these grounds were found by the police in Stojadinović's office shortly after the distribution of his racist leaflet attacking Cvetković, though Stojadinović claimed the police had planted them there to discredit him.[114] Stojadinović was arrested on 19 April 1940.

Cvetković–Maček Agreement

Dragiša Cvetković (1893–1969) was a former mayor of Niš and Radical, who had first entered national government in 1928. His position as prime minister was weak, being dependent on Pavle's personal backing and on Korešec and Spaho's support, while his own party, the JRZ, was seriously damaged by the internecine conflict between his supporters and Stojadinović's. Through his predominantly JRZ government, the Serbian royal court finally established a wholly subordinate regime based on the Radical tradition. Cvetković was ideologically loyal to the Radical legacy, and spoke at the unveiling of a monument on 10 November 1940 to the Timok rebels of 1883, at the execution site at Kraljevica outside Zaječar, attributing Yugoslavia's unification to their spirit.[115] He was also a suitable man to resolve the Croat question, having in the early 1920s been close to Protić and greatly influenced by his opposition to the St Vitus's Day Constitution and his advocacy of compromise with the Croats.[116] His government included Nedić as defence minister and Aleksandar Cincar-Marković as foreign minister; the latter was Dimitrije Cincar-Marković's nephew and had been Pašić's secretary during the Paris peace negotiations.

The government declared on 16 February before parliament that 'the Royal government believes that an agreement with the Croats over the Croat question must be its clear and decisive policy'.[117] The United Opposition of Radicals, Democrats and Farmers consequently sought from Pavle authorisation itself to conduct the negotiations with the Croats, i.e. with the Peasant–Democrat Coalition. The Farmers' leader Jovanović-Pižon discussed this possibility with Pavle on 16 March and asserted that, in any negotiated territorial division of Yugoslavia, the United Opposition considered South Serbia (Kosovo, the Sanjak and Macedonia), Montenegro, Bosnia-Hercegovina, Vojvodina, Srem and Dubrovnik to belong rightfully to Serbia.[118] But the United Opposition was marginalised because the Peasant–Democrat Coalition on the one hand and the court and government on the other preferred each other as negotiating partners. Pavle did not want to accede to the United Opposition's demand for a restoration of parliamentary democracy while the latter's insistence that such a restoration occur before any solution to the Croat question alienated the HSS. The United Opposition's ability to work with the Croatian opposition was obstructed by the resistance of the Radicals, in particular, to any reform of the state along federal lines.[119] It feared that a settlement of the Croat question prior to a settlement of the question of democracy would weaken its bargaining position vis-à-vis the regime, but its failure to support the Croats simply ensured that they would seek friends elsewhere. Maček preferred to support a regent and government that were ready to grant Croatian demands immediately.[120]

Slovakia seceded from Czechoslovakia on 14 March 1939—an ominous precedent for Yugoslavia. Italy invaded and occupied Albania on 7–12 April, further weakening Yugoslavia's strategic position. Pavle responded by cultivating good relations with Germany. He visited Berlin on 1 June, where Hitler received him in grandiose style, holding a banquet in his honour at which the Führer noted that although Germany and the Yugoslav nation had been on opposite sides in World War I, Germany at the time respected the Yugoslav nation's heroism. He gave Pavle a guarantee of Yugoslavia's territorial integrity, whose violation he promised not to permit by anyone, meaning Italy.[121] Meanwhile, Maček considered other options in case Belgrade continued to obstruct the resolution of the Croat question, so approached Mussolini's regime to explore a possible anti-Yugoslav agreement.[122] Nevertheless, the pro-British Pavle was not ready to align entirely with Germany, and the menacing international situation further convinced him and others in Belgrade of the need to resolve Yugoslavia's internal conflict. Consequently, Maček and Cvetković negotiated the first draft of an agreement between 22 and 27 April 1939. This initially envisaged an autonomous Croatia comprising the Sava and Primorje Banovinas plus the town and district of Dubrovnik, with further borders decided by plebiscite in the disputed areas of Srem, Vojvodina, Bosnia-Hercegovina and Dalmatia. Pavle rejected this out of opposition to the idea of territorial demarcation by plebiscite, after which Maček agreed to limit the area of the plebiscite to Srem and Bosnia-Hercegovina. But the resulting revised draft agreement, reached on 27 April, remained unacceptable to Pavle.[123] Finally, at the end of June, Maček and Cvetković agreed on the projected territorial demarcation of an autonomous Croatia. After this, progress toward an agreement proceeded smoothly, encouraged by Britain and France, which feared the unresolved Croat question would weaken Yugoslavia's ability to resist the Axis powers.

The influential law professor Mihailo Konstantinović submitted a lengthy memorandum suggesting that Clause 116 of the constitution, permitting the king emergency powers in cases of threats to the 'public order and security of the state', be used to divide the kingdom into three banovinas—effectively, to make it a federation of a Slovene, a Croat and a (much larger) Serb unit. This amounted to a suggestion that the government divide up the Yugoslav lands and impose a new constitutional order without consulting the representatives of the Yugoslav peoples.[124] Nevertheless, Cvetković would justify the establishment of the Croatian banovina: 'because the public order in Croatia was under threat; because of the Croat nation's refusal to participate in affairs of state, the king was empowered to carry out an alteration of the banovina units and, through the joining of the Sava and Primorje banovinas, to satisfy the Croat nation's demands by establishing an autonomous Croatian unit, thereby guaranteeing the peace and the threatened public order'. He claimed the establishment of the Serb and Slovene units would have to await a new parliament elected on the basis of a new democratic electoral law, subsequently justifying the failure to establish such units immediately on the grounds that there were no threats to public order in the Slovene and Serb lands that would have permitted the invocation of Clause 116, that the Croatian banovina and its borders were purely a provisional solution to the immediate Croatian crisis, and that the agreement required ratification by the Yugoslav parliament.[125]

Maček and Cvetković finally reached agreement and received Pavle's blessing on 24 August. The Agreement, with British and French blessing, was published on the 26th, when Pavle appointed a new government under Cvetković. The Peasant–Democrat Coalition received six ministerial portfolios (five going to the

HSS and one to the Independent Democrats), with Maček becoming deputy prime minister and Juraj Šutej finance minister. Army General Milan Nedić, a former favourite of Aleksandar's, became minister of the army and navy (defence). Three portfolios went to members of the opposition—the Farmers' Branko Čubrilović and the Radicals' Marković and Maksimović—while the remainder went to JRZ members.[126] The Agreement stated: 'The Sava and Primorje Banovinas and the districts of Dubrovnik, Šid, Ilok, Brčko (Derventa), Gradačac, Travnik and Fojnica will be united in a single unit that will be called the Banovina of Croatia.' The Banovina of Croatia would have authority over agriculture, trade and industry, forestry and mines, construction, social policy, national health, physical education, justice, education and internal affairs, while all other affairs of state including defence and internal security would remain with the central government. The territorial demarcation of the Banovina of Croatia and the division of competencies between it and Belgrade would be provisional pending establishment of a new constitutional order for Yugoslavia, on which occasion 'municipalities and villages that do not have a Croat majority and that are annexed to the Banovina of Croatia would be separated from the aforementioned districts'. The king and the Croatian parliament (Sabor) would jointly exercise legislative authority in the Banovina, while administrative authority would be exercised by the king through a governor (ban) responsible both to the king and to the Sabor.[127] These tenets were elaborated upon in the Decree concerning the Banovina of Croatia, promulgated and published on the same day as the Agreement.

The finance and defence ministers of the new government soon clashed over the budget, with Šutej seeking money for the Croatian banovina's administration and Nedić for the armed forces; Šutej considered the army's financial demands ruinous while Nedić feared the Croatian banovina was taking money needed for the army and would use it to strengthen its own militias, the Croat Civic Defence and Croat Peasant Defence.[128] These militias, previously armed only with staffs, now gained the right to carry firearms and act alongside the police in maintaining order.[129] But they did so inconsistently. In the months after the agreement, Croats in the Banovina, newly empowered, inflicted retribution on Yugoslav officials and the Belgrade regime's supporters. A gendarme corporal in a village near Varaždin in northern Croatia was beaten up on 10 September, as was the former mayor and president of the Serbian Orthodox community of the town of Vis on the island of the same name. Falcon organisations, associated with Aleksandar's dictatorship, were particularly targeted; a prominent member of the Falcon organisation in Zagreb was murdered on 2 September while the premises of the Falcon organisation in Crikvenica in north-western Croatia were forcibly appropriated by the Peasant Defence the following day. Although the HSS leadership was not directly involved in these attacks, the newly established Croatian local authorities frequently either participated in them or took no action against their perpetrators. The Agreement also prompted the return of many Ustasha emigrants, including 213 to the territory of the former Primorje Banovina already by mid-October.¹³⁰

The Agreement raised the question of how Yugoslavia outside the Croatian banovina would be reorganised. While there was broad agreement that the Drava Banovina should be transformed into an autonomous Slovenian banovina, the Serb and Bosnian questions proved harder to agree upon owing to the conflicting goals of Serb and Muslim politicians. Konstantinović had on the eve of the Agreement mooted to Cvetković the possibility that the projected tripartite Yugoslavia be modified to include the establishment of a fourth, Bosnian-Hercegovinian banovina. This was to have comprised the Vrbas Banovina and the Bosnian and Hercegovinian portions of the Drina and Zeta Banovinas (i.e. all Bosnian territory outside the Banovina of Croatia), on the grounds that demographic intermingling between Serbs and Croats made the drawing of a border between them impossible to carry out, particularly given their further intermingling with the Muslims and the unwillingness of Bosnian Serbs to be incorporated into the Croatian banovina. He also considered separation of the Bugojno, Konjic and Stolac districts and part of the Mostar district from the Primorje Banovina and their inclusion in the Bosnian rather than the Croatian banovina, so that 'the Muslims, because of whom this province is partly to be established, should fall within a single province'. The Bosnian banovina thus formed would not be an 'Orthodox Serb territory' but rather a 'mixed province'.¹³¹ This suggestion found no place in the negotiations with the HSS. The Agreement thus left the Bosnian question open.

The Yugoslav government held discussions on 3 and 6 November 1939 on further state reorganisation. The Farmers' Milan Gavrilović declared for a Yugoslavia comprising Slovenian, Croatian and Serbian units with a special status for Bosnia-Hercegovina within the Serbian unit; Cvetković confirmed this would be acceptable provided the Croats returned those districts they had taken from Bosnia-Hercegovina. Konstantinović confirmed that the HSS representatives were in principle ready to accept the return of the Croatian-annexed parts of Bosnia-Hercegovina on condition that 'apart from Croatia and Slovenia be formed a fourth unit'.¹³² Kulenović, who had become JMO leader and JRZ vice-premier following Spaho's death on 29 June, demanded that Bosnia-Hercegovina be established as a separate unit, but Gavrilović objected that this would mean 'fragmentation of the Serbs'.¹³³ Consequently, Kulenović announced at a press conference on 6 November the Muslim demand that 'a fourth territorial unit be established besides the first three, besides the Serbian, Croatian and Slovenian', i.e. that an autonomous Bosnian-Hercegovinian banovina be established.¹³⁴ This marked the launch of the Muslim Movement for the Autonomy of Bosnia-Hercegovina, which encompassed much of the Bosnian Muslim elite. Facing increasingly vocal Serb opposition to the idea of Bosnian autonomy, Cvetković felt compelled on 20 November to instruct the government's central press bureau that 'there must no longer be let out a single word about the autonomy of Bosnia-Hercegovina'.[135] Nevertheless, he came to envisage a compromise involving Bosnia-Hercegovina's autonomy within the projected Serb banovina. Writing from exile in 1954, he claimed that the idea had been to establish a composite Serb unit comprising five autonomous provinces: Serbia, Montenegro, Bosnia-Hercegovina (minus the parts that went to the Croatian banovina), Macedonia and Vojvodina.[136]

With an autonomous Croatia established, the SLS began agitating for an immediate transfer of power to the Drava Banovina to create an equivalently autonomous Slovenia. Among the Serbian members of the government, opinion was initially divided over whether to proceed immediately to resolving the rest of the Yugoslav national question through the establishment of Slovenian and Serb banovinas or first to hold elections. With the Democrats and other Serbian opposition parties and groups agitating for the former option, the JRZ's general council under Cvetković likewise voted on 24 January 1940 in favour of it. They hoped that by quickly establishing a Serb banovina they would pre-empt Croat demands for more territory or Muslim demands for a Bosnian banovina while appeasing Serb nationalist critics and boosting their weak standing among the Serb public. Conversely, the HSS government ministers opposed the immediate establishment of a Serb banovina because they did not want their further territorial demands pre-empted and sought to retain influence over the non-Croatian banovinas.[137] If the rump Bosnia-Hercegovina were not made an autonomous entity but annexed to a future Serb banovina, the HSS politicians intended to demand additional Bosnian territory, in particular the mining areas of Zenica, Visoko and Žepče in which many Croats lived.[138] The JRZ's decision led to the formation of a commission of three legal experts including Konstantinović, minister without portfolio and soon to become justice minister, all of whom had worked on Cvetković's behalf on the decree concerning the Croatian banovina. According to its draft, 'The Vrbas, Drina, Danube, Morava, Zeta and Vardar Banovinas are joined as a unit under the common name of Serb Country (Srpska zemlja), whose seat is in Skopje. What up till now have been banovinas are converted into oblasts, retaining their names and their seats.' The proposed competencies of the Serb Country broadly corresponded to those of the Croatian banovina, though instead of a governor there would be a government called the Country Council.[139] Meanwhile, just as Maček sought to obstruct the formation of the Serb banovina to maximise his and the HSS's influence in Yugoslavia, so Cvetković sought to extend his own and the JRZ's influence into the Croatian banovina by competing with the Independent Democrats for the Croatian Serb vote.

The Agreement therefore did not end the power struggle in Yugoslavia between Serbia and Croatia while it exacerbated political strife in Bosnia-Hercegovina. Belgrade's sacrifice of the Bosnian Muslims, through partitioning Bosnia-Hercegovina, led pro-Serb Muslim notables to abandon pro-Serb politics and arise in opposition to the Belgrade regime. The Bosnian Serbs' fear that Belgrade would sacrifice them to appease the Muslims—which Konstantinović's proposal of a fourth banovina suggests was not groundless—prompted them to mobilise in their own movement, known as Serbs Assemble! In turn, the regime's apparent readiness to sacrifice Serb possession of Bosnia-Hercegovina to appease a significant non-Serb Yugoslav constituency exacerbated nationalist opposition in Serbia to the Yugoslav regime.

18

END OF THE YUGOSLAV KINGDOM

1939–1941

The Cvetković–Maček Agreement was reached as the clouds of war were gathering over Europe. The day before, 23 August 1939, the German and Soviet foreign ministers surprised the world by signing a non-aggression pact securing Germany's rear in preparation for its conflict with the Western democracies. Germany invaded Poland on 1 September, triggering declarations of war by Britain and France that are traditionally taken as marking the start of World War II. For the next two years, as its strategic position worsened, Yugoslavia's government endeavoured to sustain its neutrality and stay out of the war, but this was undermined and ultimately sabotaged by the domestic opposition in Serbia. This opposition culminated in a military putsch on 26–27 March 1941, led by air-force officers Army General Dušan Simović and Brigadier General Borivoje Mirković, triggered by the government's attempt to avert a German invasion by joining the Tripartite Pact of Germany, Italy and Japan. This was a reprise of the 1903 putsch and it would plunge Yugoslavia into World War II as the earlier putsch, albeit less directly, had set Serbia on the road to World War I.

Serb-nationalist backlash

The Cvetković–Maček Agreement was reached by a government with very limited legitimacy in the Serbian people's eyes. Cvetković's party base, the Serb wing of the JRZ, was merely a Radical splinter holding power through court patronage while opposed by both the Radical general council and Stojadinović's supporters. Cvetković himself was a politician of limited standing, entirely dependent on Pavle, who in turn was not a king, merely a regent. The regime had been established undemocratically through suppression of the principal Serbian parties yet was not even supported by all the military and political circles that had backed Aleksandar's dictatorship. Consequently, it had a weak mandate to conclude an agreement that, in the eyes of most politically conscious Serbs, awarded the Croats too much territory and autonomy. It therefore faced overwhelming opposition from the Serbian opposition parties and intelligentsia. This opposition was spurred by its increasing authoritarianism; the government took control of Radio Belgrade on 14 August 1940 and, shortly afterwards, of Radio Zagreb.[1] The stage was set for a Serb nationalist backlash.

The Radical party had been crippled by successive splits. Although more strongly committed to a unitary Yugoslavia than either the Democrats or Farmers, it was also less oppositional vis-à-vis the regime. During 1939 it sought an accommodation with the regime involving potentially its entry into the government and its own reunification, i.e. of those grouped behind the general council with those in the JRZ. As one Radical supporter of reunification, justice minister Marković, wrote on 15 February 1940, the Radicals 'need to feel they must unite if they want to play that role in state life that the Radical Party had and particularly if they want to defend the interests of Serbdom and the Serb nation'.[2] Nothing came of this and the Radicals remained the most passive of the principal Serbian parties for the remainder of the kingdom's existence. The Farmers, meanwhile, accepted the Agreement and permitted their representative Branko Čubrilović to join the government, while the party's left wing under Dragoljub Jovanović seceded to found a new People's Peasant Party on 15 March 1940.

It was consequently the Democrats, under Milan Grol's leadership after Davidović's death on 19 February 1940, that spearheaded mainstream Serbian opposition to the Agreement. As the old Liberal and Progressive politicians had mostly died, left politics or defected to King Aleksandar's regime, the Democratic Party was effectively the old Independent Radical Party, its Yugoslav unitarist window dressing increasingly shed in favour of a return to outright Serb nationalism. As it stated, 'The Serbs are this time struck twice. For while the Croats, under the leadership of their indisputably mandated representatives, are, in full freedom, by the will of the people organising their Banovina of Croatia and asserting themselves in the mixed border zones vis-à-vis the Serbs, *the Serbs are standing on the sidelines, bound hand and mouth, as if this were a matter that had nothing to do with them*' (emphasis in original).[3] The Democrats objected to the Agreement on the grounds, firstly, that it violated the terms of the 8 October 1937 joint declaration of the United Opposition and Peasant–Democrat Coalition, whereby the latter was supposed to remain united with the former in seeking a comprehensive solution to the constitutional question; and secondly, because the Croatian question had been resolved without a general constitutional settlement or any resolution of the Serbs' position in Yugoslavia. Although the Democrats had declared for federalism in 1933, the Banovina of Croatia's competencies and borders went beyond what it considered acceptable. The Democrats were particularly aggrieved that territory left outside the Croatian banovina (excluding the Drava Banovina, which everyone understood to be Slovene) was not recognised as Serb land and was open to further Croatian territorial demands.[4]

END OF THE YUGOSLAV KINGDOM

The Democrats consequently reprised the Independent Radicals' traditional role of principled parliamentary opposition to the court–Radical regime. Yet the fracturing of the United Opposition between those willing to join the government and those determined to resist it weakened the mainstream opposition, so the initiative passed to more extreme elements whose militancy recalled the Black Hand's hardline extra-parliamentary activities. On the far right, Ljotić denounced the Agreement from a Yugoslav unitarist perspective: 'The state according to this agreement in the economic and social sense does not constitute a unified territory. Accordingly, no planned economic and social politics is possible.' Yet he attributed the Croat question to the Serbs' own moral failing ('Serb sin').[5] He even proposed that 'if the Serbs do not know how to govern, let Mr Maček govern, but not with one quarter, but with the whole', appealing to him to 'declare for Yugoslavia' since 'the whole of Croatian history leads towards Yugoslavism'.[6] From late 1940, Ljotić and ZBOR resolved to overthrow the regime, enthrone Petar II and establish a fascist order. But the Germans did not support this plan; they were mostly content with Pavle's regime.[7] Yugoslav nationalist objections to the Agreement remained a fringe phenomenon beside a burgeoning integral Serb nationalist opposition.

Serb Cultural Club

The most vocal manifestation of this opposition was provided by the Serb Cultural Club (SKK), informally established in late 1936 and formally approved by the interior ministry on 15 January 1937. As the civilian conspirators of 1903 had predominantly comprised Liberals and hardline anti-Radical supporters of the Obrenović regime, so the SKK's members were largely Democrats or their sympathisers by background, but above all opponents of the Radicals. In particular, they were sympathisers of the former Black Hand and opponents of the court–Radical alliance from the time of the Salonika trial (Slobodan Jovanović, Dragiša Vasić) and Bosnian Serbs from the ranks of the Democrats and Young Bosnia (Nikola Stojanović, Vladimir Ćorović, Vasa Čubrilović).[8] In particular they were men like Jovanović who had not previously engaged in party-political life. Their sense of standing above party divisions in the national interest recalled the ethos of the elite shaped under Aleksandar Obrenović.[9] They represented a reaction against Serb nationalism's subordination to Yugoslavism, which they believed had disunited and unfocused the Serbs in their pursuit of their national goals while allowing other Yugoslavs, particularly the Croats, to unite and pursue theirs—hence the unification of almost all politically active Croats within a single party, the HSS, and their extraction of the Croatian banovina from the weak regime in Belgrade. The regime's attempt to reach a Concordat with the Vatican in the period 1935–1938 catalysed both the SKK's formation and its leadership's decision, by mid-1938, in favour of a putsch to overthrow Pavle's regime—one inspired by the 1903 putsch.

The SKK published a newspaper, *Srpski glas* (Serb Voice), subtitled 'Strong Serbdom—Strong Yugoslavia', whose first issue appeared on 16 November 1939. It countered Aleksandar's ideology of merging the Serb, Croat and Slovene nations within an integral Yugoslav nationhood with a radically different position: that Yugoslavia could only be strong if based upon a strong Serbia that maintained its national distinctiveness and cohesion:

> The time has come to hear a pure Serb voice ... Thus, we have decided to base ourselves on the healthy Serb instinct that from the Belgrade pashaluk created Šumadija and Serbia, and later Yugoslavia. It is necessary at once that there be heard the Serb voice free of all foreign theories and party prejudices, so that a strong Serbdom can permeate Yugoslavia with its fighting spirit and pass down to it as a testament to future generations ... In Yugoslavia the Serbs are the most numerous and have the most experience in statecraft. Consequently, the other Yugoslavs have recognised their right to be first among equals ... The Serb national revival is imminent and with it the revival of Yugoslavia.[10]

This ideology drew upon the long tradition of oppositional Serb nationalism since the 1850s, pioneered by the Old Liberals and most fully expressed by the early Radicals, of viewing the regime in Belgrade (first of the Constitutionalists, later of the Obrenovićes), as un-Serb, alien and unwilling to fulfil the national mission, and the opposition as needing to articulate an authentic Serbness, not merely to oppose the regime but to bring about the Serbs' revitalisation; furthermore, that opposition to the regime was the expression, not of any particular party but of the nation, within which there must be no divisions. Slobodan Drašković, son of murdered Democratic politician Milorad Drašković, wrote that 'for Yugoslavia it is essential not only that the Serbs die defending it from armed attack from without but that their presence in the state be felt; that with their strength they mercilessly strike against all enemies, open and skilfully camouflaged, of whatever colour and whatever evil they have prepared ... The Serbs, divided, blinded by partisanship and disorganised like this, cannot come to expression within Yugoslavia. Therefore Yugoslavia must become Serb. And Croat and Slovene, be it understood. But Serb.'[11] Although directed against Croat nationalism, *Srpski glas* saw it as a model to be emulated, for 'when the question is raised of mutual relations between Serbs and Croats', then 'just as the Croats have a unified outlook on those relations and just as the Croats do not view those relations from a party standpoint, but from a national standpoint, so should the Serbs.'[12] According to Dragoljub Srranjaković, a member of the SKK's executive council from Belgrade, speaking at a 'Serb cultural-national council' held in Sombor in Vojvodina on 29 October 1939: 'When today the reorganisation of our state is being carried out, the Serbs more than ever must be conscious of their task and their role in it. To be able to fulfil their tasks, they must assemble and form themselves into solid ranks, not on a party but on a national basis, and from their midst bring to the fore the most competent and honourable people for their representatives, regardless of party identification or religious membership.'[13] Drašković and other leaders of the SKK's youth wing viewed it as heir to the United Serb Youth and Young Bosnia.[14]

The SKK believed the establishment of the Banovina of Croatia opened the question of establishing an equivalent Serb banovina, whose territorial extent they viewed in maximal terms: the whole of eastern Yugoslavia (pre-1912 Serbia, Macedonia, Kosovo, Montenegro, Vojvodina), all Bosnia-Hercegovina, not just eastern but also western Srem (the districts of Vukovar, Vinkovci and Dalj, today part of Croatia), southern Dalmatia and, potentially, all areas of present-day Croatia where Serbs lived, following the principle 'wherever there are Serbs—there is Serbia'.[15] The SKK consequently sought to agitate and form committees among the Serbs of Bosnia-Hercegovina and Croatia to work for the inclusion of their areas in the projected Serb unit.

Slobodan Jovanović, SKK president and founder, was a constitutional law scholar, historian and son of the Old Liberal Vladimir Jovanović. He had been close to Apis in the years preceding the Salonika trial and had conspired with him against Aleksandar and the Radicals. Ideologically, he was a Westerniser who nevertheless sought to combine Western and native Serbian traditions.[16] He claimed to have decided to found the SKK following a visit to Bosnia, when he noticed the Bosnian Serb population's cultural stagnation. He blamed this on the fact that, whereas under Austria-Hungary the Bosnian Serbs had fought to affirm Serb culture and identity, under Yugoslavia they left this to the state, which was not a Serb state.[17] Konstantinović noted, after meeting with Jovanović in September 1940: 'Slobodan surprises me when he says that it is possible to reach agreement with the Germans but not with the Croats ... He is, in fact, a bitter Serb chauvinist.'[18] Konstantinović himself was an SKK member, though a more moderate Serb nationalist than Jovanović or most other members; his project of a 'Serb Country' probably reflected SKK ideology. Ironically, Jovanović's brilliant, monumental six-volume history of nineteenth-century Serbia showed enormous sensitivity to the reality of the country's diverse political currents, but this did not translate into a political ideology similarly respectful of the differences between them.

Jovanović recruited as SKK co-founder his friend and fellow lawyer Vasić, who became its vice-president. He was a long-standing militant opponent of the Belgrade regime; a former army officer and cousin of Ljubomir Vulović, executed alongside Apis. The friendship between Jovanović and Vasić dated from the time they had resided together on Corfu and served on the Salonika front during World War I, when Vasić had been a reserve officer. The friendship had been strengthened by the Salonika trial about which they had shared the same legal and moral opinions. Vasić was decisively influenced by his impression of the ordinary Serbian soldier's heroism set against the tyrannical, corrupt character of the regime of court and Radicals.[19] After World War I, he joined the Republican party. This was formed partly in response to the Salonika trial by the most militant Independents on an anti-Karađorđević basis, and remained close to the surviving Black Handers; one of the leading Republicans, Jaša Prodanović, was their strongest supporter among Yugoslav politicians, and the apartment of his son Bora became the centre at which they gathered.[20] One convicted Black Hander, Vojislav Gojković, after serving three and a half years in prison, became a prominent member of the party.[21] Vasić himself established close links with former Black Hand members and, as a lawyer in the so-called St Vitus's Day trial of 1922, even defended Communists accused of attempting to assassinate Aleksandar. On that occasion, concluding his defence, he vented his loathing of the existing order: 'Among other things, Your Honour, if these men were corrupted and worthless as the prosecutor suggests, they would not today be sitting here in the dock, surrounded by the bayonets of the authorities, but in warm offices somewhere, and many of them as inspectors and chiefs with grand desks, at which today sit innumerable charlatans who do nothing, who don't know how to do anything and who, on the basis of their abilities, would not ever be able to reach them.'[22] After the establishment of Aleksandar's dictatorship, Vasić again intervened on behalf of persecuted Communists. He was editor of *Srpski glas* until the regime banned it in June 1940.

The SKK's prominent Bosnian Serb members included Stojanović as vice-president, Čubrilović as secretary and Ćorović as intellectual motor. Stojanović had been a youthful Serb nationalist in Bosnia-Hercegovina and author of the provocative article 'To your or our extermination', which had portrayed the Croat national idea as weak and subservient to foreign influences, thus destined to succumb to the superior Serb national idea.[23] Its publication had triggered the anti-Serb riots in Croatia of August 1902. But he then evolved in a more moderate direction. Čubrilović as a Young Bosnia activist, Stojanović as a Yugoslav Committee member and Ćorović as a representative of the Bosnian organisation of the National Council of Slovenes, Croats and Serbs all upheld, prior to Yugoslavia's formation, the principle of Serbo-Croat cooperation in place of integral Great Serb nationalism.[24] Stojanović and Ćorović's enthusiastic Yugoslavism led them to become founding members of the Democratic Party. Participation in the SKK represented, for these Bosnian Serbs, a disillusioned retreat from their youthful idealistic Yugoslavism and reversion to integral Serb nationalism, aimed particularly at securing Serb possession of their Bosnian homeland. Bosnian Serb SKK members were at the forefront of the movement Serbs Assemble!, which was aimed both at preventing the establishment of an autonomous Bosnian banovina and at revoking the Agreement. A particularly prominent role was played by Stevan Moljević, the SKK's leading agent in Banja Luka and the Vrbas Banovina, the centre of its irredentist activity in Bosnia-Hercegovina.[25]

Another SKK founder and senior figure was Dr Mladen Žujović, a former army officer from a distinguished Serbian military family. His paternal grandfather had been chief of military administration under Miloš and his uncle Jovan Žujović was an early socialist, first cousin of the socialist pioneer Živojin Žujović and acquaintance of Svetozar Marković. Jovan became a leading Serbian academic before falling into disfavour following the St John's Day assassination attempt, then in turn a fierce critic of Aleksandar Obrenović's regime, foreign minister in Ljubomir Stojanović's Independent Radical government and a founder of the Republican party. Mladen was one of several Yugoslav officers from Serbia who resigned in 1920 in protest after officers of their own rank from the former Austro-Hungarian army, incorporated into the newly formed Yugoslav army, were allegedly promoted above them for political reasons.[26] This professional frustration recalled that of the 1903 conspirators, who had resented the favouritism shown in the army to Queen Draga's brothers. After leaving the army, Mladen became Vasić's law partner and joined the Republican party alongside him.

The SKK and Serbs Assemble! were twin precursors of Draža Mihailović's World War II 'Yugoslav Army in the Fatherland', better known as the Chetnik movement. Mihailović established a Central National Committee for this movement in August 1941 after the Axis occupation of Yugoslavia, with an executive council comprising Vasić, Moljević and Žujović. Another prominent Republican, SKK member and law partner of Vasić's, Vojislav Vujanac, also became a member of the Central National Committee. In turn, as prime minister of Yugoslavia's wartime government-in-exile, Slobodan Jovanović would appoint Mihailović minister of the army, navy and air force on 11 January 1942.[27] That leading Republicans became leading members of the overtly Karađorđevićite Chetniks was the latest iteration in Serbia of loyalties to monarchs or dynasties representing opportunistic factional banners rather than core ideologies.

Reborn military conspiracy

The elite rebellion against Pavle's regime dovetailed with the growing opposition to it among current and former army officers, re-creating the civilian–military conspiracy of 1901–1903 and involving some of the same individuals. At an SKK meeting at Žujović's house in Belgrade in July or August 1938, chaired by Jovanović, the regime's overthrow was plotted, with instructions on illegal organisation, based on Black Hand practice, presented by two prominent 1903 conspirators, Antonije Antić and Velimir Vemić, and adopted by the participants. An executive council to direct this secret activity was set up comprising Vasić, Žujović and another lawyer, Milan Nikolić. The plan involved establishing cells within each army unit.[28] Other members of this conspiratorial network linked to the Black Hand or the 1903 conspiracy included Živojin Balugdžić, Vasić's son-in-law Major Srba Popov of the air force,[29] Apis's former good friend Srđan Budisavljević of the Independent Democrats and Drašković, whose father Milorad had conspired with Apis and resigned from the government in protest at his execution.

The conspiratorial network once again expanded owing to army officers' political and professional frustrations. General Bogoljub Ilić was one example. According to his memoirs, he had approved of the 1903 putsch but been critical of subsequent activities of both the Black and White Hand. After Aleksandar's 1929 coup, he told prime minister Živković that he disapproved of his policies, causing him to fall into official disfavour and be repeatedly moved between posts. After Pavle became regent in 1934, Ilić continued criticising the government and the supreme command. As the army's supreme inspector, he fell into disfavour with Pavle in mid-1940 and was transferred from his post to the command of the 5th Army in Niš, which he angrily rejected, triggering his removal from active service. He was particularly critical of the government's failure to deal with what he saw as the anti-Yugoslav activities of the non-Serbs, claiming it ruled on the assumption that 'Serbs are worthless' while delegating absolute power in the banovinas to the leaders of the Slovenes, Croats and Muslims: 'Korošec was God in Slovenia', 'Mr Dr Maček was all and everything in the Croatian banovina', and Spaho similarly dominated the Drina Banovina, while 'Dragiša was a toy in their hands' and 'about the Serbs in the Drina Banovina and in Bosnia in general nobody cared'. Ilić told Simović several times of the discontent in the army and among the people, and Mirković informed him of his plans for the putsch a whole year before Yugoslavia joined the Tripartite Pact. The putsch leaders intended 'to show the whole world that the Serbs did not approve either the internal or the external policies of Prince Pavle or of the government of Dragiša Cvetković'.[30]

Another example was Colonel Dragoljub 'Draža' Mihailović, subsequently famous during World War II as leader of the Chetnik movement. Early in World War I, in September 1914, he was accused of failing to follow an order for which he was punished with fifteen days' disciplinary confinement—in his view unfairly— at the initiative of White Hand leader Lieutenant Colonel Josif Kostić. When he was subsequently denied promotion, he attributed it to that incident,[31] even though Kostić had favoured his promotion: 'I was passed over by Josip [sic] Kostić, who has all through my life been my enemy.' He became Apis's sympathiser.[32] In 1920 he fell into disfavour with the authorities again after celebrating New Year's Eve at a tavern in the company of a friend and fellow officer who openly toasted the Bolsheviks; when his friend was threatened by some of those present, Mihailović drew his revolver to defend him. An officer who had testified against Apis in Salonika then intervened in the confrontation, causing Mihailović again to be punished with fifteen days' disciplinary confinement.[33] He subsequently continued incurring disfavour through his self-willed behaviour. Appointed military attaché in Sofia in 1935, he was transferred away at the Bulgarian government's request because of his links with officers opposed to the Bulgarian royal dynasty. As commander of the 39th Infantry Regiment based in Celje, Slovenia, he submitted to his superiors in early 1939 a plan for reorganising Yugoslavia's army based on nationality and territory—Serb, Croat and Slovene. For this he was punished with thirty days' arrest. He was again punished in November 1940 with thirty days' arrest for attending without permission a meeting organised by Britain's military attaché in Belgrade. He subsequently joined Simović and Mirković's putschist circle.[34]

The putsch's structural basis was nevertheless broader than simply the Black Hand and its sympathisers. Stojadinović's dismissal of Živković in March 1936 and subsequent purge of his supporters from the army meant that former members of the White Hand, too, would be among the malcontents; Živković himself joined the conspiratorial circle along with his brother General Dimitrije Živković. More generally, the depoliticisation of the army under Stojadinović and its removal from political leadership in the state in favour of civilians, from Stojadinović and Pavle downwards, increased the officer corps' resentment. Memory of the 1903 putsch was fresh in everyone's minds, and the coup leaders of 1941, Simović and Mirković, were only a few years younger than men like Antić and Vemić. Mirković, the conspiracy's initiator, later claimed to be inspired by the 1903 putsch when, in response to the Concordat, he began plotting in 1937. He had links to British Intelligence.[35] His fellow conspirators were concentrated especially among junior and reserve air-force officers and among career officers of the general staff school. Prominent among the school's officers was Major Živan Knežević, formerly chief of cabinet to Simović when he had been chief of staff. Živan's brother Professor Radoje Knežević had been secretary of the Democratic Party's executive committee and Petar II's French tutor, until he fell out with Pavle and his wife Princess Olga, and was dismissed. As Patriarch Gavrilo wrote of Radoje, 'As a young person he was left on the street with his family, because in 1937 he was pensioned. His patriotism and national feelings were hurt.' His dismissal left him free to devote himself to political meddling.[36] Radoje was an SKK member, so the Knežević brothers linked the civilian and military wings of the putschist circle, much as Antić and his uncle Genčić had linked the two wings of the 1903 conspiracy. Mirković in early 1941 recruited to the conspiracy the ambitious Simović, the recently appointed air-force chief who had played an important role in Yugoslavia's establishment in 1918.[37] Simović had been dismissed as chief of staff in January 1940 at the initiative of then defence minister Army General Milan Nedić; Simović later claimed Nedić had done so at Pavle's request, allegedly because of his anti-German sentiments.[38] Army General Petar Kosić, Petar II's tutor, became the new chief of staff.

Patriarch Gavrilo, a known opponent of the regime who had defeated it over the Concordat, was naturally receptive when Simović sought support for his projected putsch. Simović met with Gavrilo repeatedly and received his blessing; this strengthened his resolve while drawing the Patriarch into the putschist circle.[39] Major Ilija Trifunović-Birčanin, head of National Defence, was a veteran of the guerrilla campaign in Macedonia and head of the Chetnik association until 1932; his strong objection to the Concordat made him bitter and vocal in his opposition to the regime. Following Patriarch Varnava's death, Trifunović-Birčanin made a speech at his graveside claiming that 'armed organs of the government' were waging a 'bestial' war against the Orthodox Church.[40] He met with Mirković on the evening of the putsch, 26 March, to place National Defence at his disposal.[41] He was subsequently commander of Mihailović's Chetnik forces in western Bosnia and Dalmatia during World War II. Božin Simić was a 1903 conspirator, veteran of the guerrilla campaign in Macedonia and former Black Hand member. Assigned to organise Yugoslav volunteers in Russia during World War I, he had defected to the Bolsheviks to avoid prosecution at Salonika. He was supported in exile by the Salonika trial convict and fellow 1903 conspirator Vladimir Tucović, returned to Yugoslavia in 1935 and became an SKK collaborator. Appointed as a Yugoslav delegate in Moscow, he returned to Yugoslavia again in March 1941 to help organise the putsch.[42]

The conspiracy of 1941 was therefore not a response to any single political grievance but an expression of the enduring power struggle, dating back to before World War I, between the two wings of the Serbian elite: the court–Radical nexus and the nexus of Independents and 1903 conspirators, the latter now reborn as a nexus of new military conspirators and Democrats and Republicans. The government's signing of the Pact was merely the pretext and occasion for the putsch: the path to it led from the 1903 putsch via the Salonika trial, the rise and fall of King Aleksandar's regime, the Concordat, the Agreement and the decline of the United Opposition.[43] Radoje Knežević apparently said after the war that 'if there had been a government with true Serbian representatives, like the Croatian and Slovenian representatives, the Pact would not have mattered, if there had been no alternative'.[44] Jovanović reportedly told Konstantinović that the Pact might have been acceptable if the internal regime had been changed.[45] One of the most vocal critics of the putsch, Ljotić's cousin and supporter Milan Fotić, wrote after the war that which side supported the Pact and which the putsch was simply a matter of circumstance: 'If Dragiša [Cvetković] had been in opposition in March 1941 and Grol in government, Dragiša would have been among those carrying out the putsch and Grol would have signed the Pact.'[46]

Return to official anti-Semitism

Anti-Semitism among the Serbian population had by the 1930s been steadily declining for decades. The Serbian Jewish community was historically small, numbering only 2,049 in 1874, living almost entirely in the towns and mostly in Belgrade, rising to 4,160 a decade later and to 5,997 by 1910. Jewish municipalities were established in several of the principal towns, providing community organisation and leadership in religious, educational, cultural and humanitarian activities. The community was highly integrated into Serbian society and mostly comprised families that had been in the country since Ottoman times. Ashkenazi Jews, culturally more distinct from native Serbians, arrived in Serbia in the nineteenth century, mostly from the Habsburg Empire, and had their own Jewish organisation recognised by the state in 1869 but numbered only 600 in the country by 1911. Consequently, anti-Semitism did not assume such political importance as it did in some other Eastern and Central European countries such as Poland or Romania. The constitution of 1889, revoked in 1894 but restored in 1903, definitely abolished discrimination against Jews.

Mihailo was the last Serbian ruler to uphold anti-Semitic measures. Both kings Milan and Petar in particular were sympathetic to the Jews—Petar personally laid the foundation of a new Belgrade synagogue on 10 May 1907. The Radicals' early anti-Semitism was abandoned after they became a governing party, when they became increasingly inclusive of Jews. The Progressives had been the first party to embrace integrated Jews, while the Liberals were conversely the party in the 1880s most prone to anti-Semitic rhetoric—their papers attacked the supposed 'Jewish influence' over the Progressives. Nevertheless, assimilation proceeded smoothly. Jews Serbianised their names so that Avram became Avramović, David became Davidović and so forth. About 600 Jews fought as soldiers and officers for Serbia in the Balkan Wars and World War I. From 1919 the Democrats, like the Radicals, were inclusive of Jews and both principal Serbian parties included people of Jewish background, although not in leadership positions. Whereas in 1895, only 3.88 per cent of Belgrade Jews identified Serbian as their first language while 77.2 per cent identified Ladino and 17.02 per cent German, by 1931 54.2 per cent identified Serbian and only 29.72 per cent Ladino.[47] Zionism was consequently comparatively slow to develop among Serbia's integrated Sephardim, in contrast to the Ashkenazim of the western and northern South Slav lands; when the Union of Zionists of the Kingdom of Serbs, Croats and Slovenes was founded in Yugoslavia in 1919, its seat was in Zagreb. Nevertheless, the Serbian-Jewish law student David Albala founded a Zionist organisation in Belgrade in 1905. He went on to serve as a Serbian army captain during World War I and joined Serbia's wartime mission to the United States to agitate among American Jews for Serbia's cause. The mission's chief, Milenko Vesnić, issued Albala with a letter warmly supporting the goal of a Jewish national homeland in Palestine.[48]

After Yugoslavia's establishment, Jews still constituted only a small minority of 64,159 in 1921, according to the census—considerably fewer than ethnic Germans, Hungarians, Albanians, Romanians, Czechs and Slovaks (when treated as one group) or Turks. The prominence of the national question in the new state inevitably drowned out any supposed Jewish question. The founding congress of the Union of Jewish Religious Municipalities, which united Jews from all the Yugoslav lands, took place on 1 July 1919. Although Yugoslav Jews had mostly been treated as members of a non-Yugoslav minority and were disenfranchised in the constituent assembly elections in 1920, this policy was quickly reversed following protests from the Union of Jewish Religious Municipalities. Thereafter Yugoslavia did well in observing Jewish rights by Central and Eastern European standards, although it still sought to restrict the emigration to Yugoslavia of foreign Jews, even when their skills were needed, as with Jewish doctors.[49] King Aleksandar was sympathetic to the Jews, and on 14 December 1929 the Law on the Religious Community of Jews in Yugoslavia guaranteed them individual and collective civic rights. State funding to the community was generous and Aleksandar opened honorary consulates in Tel Aviv and Haifa. The pro-Zionist policy was continued after Aleksandar's death but was ambiguous in its motivation, which in part was to encourage emigration by members of the non-Slavic minorities. Yet only 800 Jews emigrated to Palestine between 1919 and 1939, about 1 per cent of Yugoslavia's Jewish population. This was a third of the European average, testimony to the relatively favourable conditions for Jews in Yugoslavia.[50]

Nevertheless, assimilation only went so far; no Jew became a leading politician in the Yugoslav kingdom or an army officer of higher rank than colonel. The Belgrade regime was sympathetic to Serbian Jews but tended to view Jews from the Austro-Hungarian lands with suspicion, so promoted Serbian Jews within the community such as Isak Alkalai of Belgrade, Aleksandar's personal friend, appointed Yugoslavia's chief rabbi in 1932. Yugoslavia's multinational character facilitated the development of a Jewish national consciousness parallel to the identities of its other constituent peoples, and Zionism became the dominant national orientation among Yugoslav Jews by the 1930s. Meanwhile, as Europe descended into far-right domination in the 1930s, Yugoslavia was affected by the international spirit; groups such as ORJUNA and ZBOR emulated the anti-Semitism of foreign far-right groups, which resonated also with some currents of Orthodox religious thinking. Anti-Semitism was also present to varying degrees in Slovene, Croat and Bosnian Muslim national politics, above all in far-right and Catholic clericalist currents, of which Korošec in particular was an exponent. Expressions of anti-Semitism became more common in newspapers in Serbia and other parts of Yugoslavia as the 1930s ended and the 1940s began and as Belgrade drew closer to Nazi Germany.

The Stojadinović and Cvetković governments—to curry favour with Germany, or under pressure from it and from Britain, which sought to restrict emigration of Jews to Palestine—increased restrictions on the entry of foreign Jewish emigrants into Yugoslavia or their transit across its territory. Patriarch Varnava made anti-Semitic statements at the funeral of a Russian metropolitan in August 1936, identifying Jews with Bolshevism, and the following May, in the aforementioned interview with a German newspaper, called for an alliance of Germany and Yugoslavia against the Bolshevik menace. Bishop Velimirović, politically close to Ljotić, made repeated anti-Semitic statements during the 1930s. In late 1938, at the request of Simović in his capacity as army chief of the general staff, the army's organisational department prepared a study suggesting that Yugoslavia's national minorities should be considered potentially disloyal in case of war; this included the Jews, although they were not classified as 'dangerous' as were the ethnic Germans, Hungarians and Albanians, and Jews continued to be better represented in the Yugoslav officer corps than other non-Slavic national minorities.

Stojadinović indicated in an interview with a French newspaper in January 1939 that Jews in Yugoslavia enjoyed 'perfect equality' but that 'an absence of loyalty on their side could change the situation'. After his fall, Cvetković ordered the distribution of a pamphlet accusing him of being in league with Jews and Freemasons, which was aimed at discrediting him in German eyes. Finally, at the initiative of education minister Korošec, supported by Cvetković, the government issued its first anti-Semitic decrees on 5 October 1940. Jewish-owned businesses dealing in foodstuffs were to be submitted for review by the local authorities which would be empowered to forbid such businesses to continue operation or to assign commissaries to the enterprises, paid for at the latter's expense, to 'concern themselves with the correctness of the operation of the enterprise'. The numbers of Jewish students and pupils enrolled at universities, high schools with the status of universities and higher, and middle, normal and other vocational schools were to be limited, while foreign Jews were to be banned altogether from enrolling as pupils or students. These measures were opposed by justice minister Marković and minister without portfolio Konstantinović, while Maček and the Croatian ministers expressed reservations. They were the occasion of a genuine power struggle, with Konstantinović seeking to mobilise his colleagues and Pavle for the purpose of ousting Korošec. When this failed, Konstantinović participated in implementing the decrees, though with Maček's support and by threatening his resignation he succeeded in blocking further anti-Semitic decrees sought by Korošec. Meanwhile, the Serbian Orthodox Church's leaders expressed their opposition to the increasingly anti-Semitic and pro-German Yugoslav government by switching to a more philo-Semitic discourse: Patriarch Gavrilo met with delegations of both the Ashkenazi and Sephardic communities during his visit to Sarajevo in September 1940 and expressed his appreciation of Sarajevo's Jews, while Velimirović became increasingly critical of Hitler and, in his Christmas Eve epistle on 6 January 1939, asked his flock to fast one day for the Jews.[51]

Yugoslavia joins the Tripartite Pact

Yugoslavia's already weak strategic position progressively worsened after the outbreak of World War II. Fearing Germany, the government on 5 March 1940 rejected further military cooperation with France, Serbia's World War I ally.[52] Germany in May–June invaded and defeated France, which capitulated on 22 June. This immediately prompted the Soviet Union to force France's and Yugoslavia's ally Romania to cede to it the disputed territories of Bessarabia and northern Bukovina. Additional large Romanian territories, northern Transylvania and southern Dobrudja, were annexed by Hungary and Bulgaria respectively in late August and early September 1940, whetting their appetites for further expansion. Romania was greatly weakened and now wholly dependent upon German protection. Germany, Italy and Japan signed the Tripartite Pact on 27 September 1940, joined by Hungary on 20 November and Romania on 23 November. Milan Jovanović Stoimirović, the Yugoslav government press chief, noted in his diary on 26 October: 'The small nations, observing that struggle of titans around them, are petrified with fear, like children who see their parents quarrelling and know that children can in the course of this get heavy beatings although they are not guilty of anything.'[53]

Yugoslavia attempted to repair relations with the Soviet Union, with which it signed a commercial treaty on 11 May 1940 and established diplomatic relations on 24 June, hoping thereby to obtain Soviet support in the event that Yugoslavia were attacked.[54] Yet the noose around Yugoslavia's neck continued to tighten. German troops entered Romania on 7 October. Italy invaded Greece on 28 October, bringing the war to the Balkans. Greece's successful resistance increasingly ensured Germany would have to intervene militarily to rescue its ally. Bulgaria joined the Tripartite Pact on 1 March 1941 and German troops entered Bulgaria the following day. In these circumstances, despite Pavle's pro-Allied sympathies, the Serbian officer corps's pro-French traditions and the widespread anti-Axis sentiment among the Yugoslav public, German pressure for Yugoslavia to join its fold became increasingly irresistible and the strategic imperative for a German–Yugoslav agreement increasingly clear, despite the British anger this would incur.

Yugoslavia's crown council, including Pavle, Cvetković, foreign minister Cincar-Marković, minister of court Milan Antić, war minister Nedić and chief of staff Kosić met on 28 October, the day Italy attacked Greece. It resolved to prevent, at all costs, an Italian occupation of Salonika, given its crucial military and economic importance to Yugoslavia. The following day, Antić instructed Cincar-Marković and Nedić to raise with the Germans the possibility of Yugoslavia occupying Salonika. Yugoslavia's military attaché in Berlin received a telegram from Nedić on 1 November expressing Yugoslavia's interest in acquiring Salonika—sent apparently without the general staff's knowledge. This followed informal requests from SKK members for German approval of Yugoslavia's acquisition of Salonika when Petar II came of age. Hitler was receptive and expressed to Ciano his belief that Yugoslavia could be won for the Axis and would gain Salonika after Greece's defeat.[55] Italian planes bombarded Bitola in Yugoslav Macedonia on 5–6 November; Yugoslavia's armed forces, under Nedić's direction, made no response.

Nedić nevertheless resigned as war minister at this time at Pavle's request, in consequence of his extremely pro-German orientation, his apparent manoeuvring to bring Yugoslavia into the war on Germany's side and his collaboration with Ljotić. He was replaced by General Petar Pešić, the court general who had engineered Montenegro's surrender to Austria-Hungary in 1915, who was just as convinced as Nedić that Germany would win the war and that it therefore had to be

END OF THE YUGOSLAV KINGDOM

accommodated.[56] Nedić's resignation followed the government's banning of ZBOR on 24 October, the pretext for which was a physical attack by its members on left-wing students at the Technical Faculty in Belgrade the day before. ZBOR's close links with German Intelligence were well known. Over 160 ZBOR supporters were arrested during October and November.[57] Following Nedić's resignation, Simović was appointed air-force commander with Mirković as his assistant. The Yugoslavs followed a balanced policy, providing valuable military assistance to the Greeks, which incurred German displeasure,[58] and signing a treaty of friendship and non-aggression with Hungary on 12 December 1940.

Germany and Britain each endeavoured to bring Yugoslavia into the war on its side, but it was Germany that could bring military pressure to bear, particularly after its army's entry into Bulgaria. Pavle travelled to Berchtesgaden on 4 March 1941 to meet Hitler, who insisted that Yugoslavia join the Pact. Pavle brought Hitler's demand on 6 March before Yugoslavia's crown council, which comprised himself, his fellow regents Stanković and Perović, Cvetković, Cincar-Marković, Pešić, Antić and vice-premiers Maček and Franc Kulovec. Cincar-Marković made clear that refusal to sign the Pact would mean war with the Axis. Pešić then explained that, if war occurred, the Germans would rapidly occupy northern Yugoslavia including Belgrade, Zagreb and Ljubljana, after which Yugoslavia's army would have to withdraw to the mountains of Bosnia-Hercegovina, where it could hold out for about six weeks before capitulating, given that Britain was incapable of providing significant support. Maček and Kulovec made it clear that from the Croatian and Slovenian perspectives such a sequence of events was unacceptable: they were not prepared to sacrifice their countries to inevitable German occupation.[59] The general councils of the Radical, Democratic and Yugoslav National parties had, since at least late 1940, been themselves agitating with Pavle in favour of a policy of friendship with Germany.[60]

The crown council consequently voted to join the Pact. It did so unanimously, with the exception of Pavle, who did not vote; he had established the crown council and sought the vote to ensure responsibility for the fateful decision was shared by his ministers. While agreeing to join, the crown council laid down the conditions that Yugoslavia's territorial integrity be guaranteed, that it not be required to join the war or permit the transit of Axis troops or war material across its territory and that Hitler support its acquisition of Salonika. The Yugoslavs' demands subsequently hardened as they both procrastinated and sought maximum guarantees. Cincar-Marković reported to the crown council on 12 March that Berlin insisted on full rather than partial Yugoslav adherence to the Pact, meaning acceptance of Article 3 requiring full military cooperation. This was accepted by Pešić and Kulovec but rejected by Cvetković and Stanković on the grounds that it would drag Yugoslavia into the war. The crown council resolved to expel former premier Stojadinović from the country. At a further meeting on 17 March, the crown council made explicit that Yugoslavia's acquisition of Salonika should include a territorial link to the Aegean Sea.

After both the German and Italian ambassadors had intervened on Stojadinović's behalf, on 18 or 20 March 1941 he was handed over on the Greek border to British troops, who interned him, as a dangerous pro-German figure, on the island of Mauritius, thereby preventing his future use by the Germans.[61] Cincar-Marković on 20 March put the proposal for Yugoslavia's adherence to the Tripartite Pact before Yugoslavia's government, prompting the immediate resignations of social welfare minister Budisavljević and agriculture minister Branko Čubrilović, while justice minister Konstantinović submitted but then withdrew his resignation. Disquiet among senior army officers prompted Pešić to convene a meeting of senior commanders in Belgrade, including Simović, at which he described Yugoslavia's adherence to the Pact as 'a great success of our policy' which guaranteed Yugoslavia's independence at a time when it could not resist the Axis militarily.[62] British pressure to keep Yugoslavia from signing the Pact was relentless but unavailing; as Pavle said to the US minister at the time, 'You big nations are hard, you talk of our honour but you are far away.'[63] Faced with Germany's ultimatum, Cvetković and Cincar-Marković finally signed the protocol for Yugoslavia's membership of the Pact on 25 March in Vienna with representatives of Germany, Italy and Japan, but on the crown council's aforementioned terms. The German record of the event noted: 'The Führer, in the further course of the discussion, emphasised that he had always been a sincere friend of Yugoslavia', while 'Cvetković thanked the Führer for his words. The Yugoslav nation knows that the Führer has always been amicably disposed towards it.'[64] On the same day, German foreign minister Joachim von Ribbentrop wrote to Cvetković to confirm that 'on the occasion of the new determination of borders in the Balkans, it is necessary to take account of the interest of Yugoslavia in a territorial link with the Aegean Sea through the extension of its sovereignty to the city and port of Salonika'.[65]

Putsch of 26–27 March and government of Dušan Simović

London had applied heavy pressure on Pavle and his government to dissuade them from signing the Pact. By the time it was signed, Britain's Special Operations Executive (SOE) was working with Serbian officers, politicians and parties to facilitate a putsch against them. One of SOE's tools against Pavle's regime was the Farmers' party, which was actively opposed to the Pact. Both the Farmers' leader Gavrilović and his predecessor, Jovanović-Pižon, who died on 20 June 1939, had been active supporters of the Chetnik guerrilla campaign in Macedonia before World War I, in which Gavrilović had personally participated, after which he became an early Black Hand member, though he was subsequently critical of it. The Farmers were subsidised by SOE, whose collaborators in the party included Gavrilović, Miloš Tupanjanin and possibly Čubrilović. SOE also subsidised the Independent Democrats, among whom Budisavljević was its collaborator. Another SOE friend was the Radicals' Mirko Kosić, while it had additional contacts in all significant primarily Serb parties—Radicals, Democrats, Independent Democrats, Farmers and JNS—including Grol.[66]

According to his aide-de-camp Captain Dragiša N. Ristić's account, Simović met with Pavle on 23 March and threatened that signing the Pact would provoke an armed rebellion in the air force. He told him he was planning to convene a meeting of army leaders in Belgrade to discuss the situation. A confrontation followed at Pavle's office between Simović and chief of staff Kosić, who dismissed Simović's threat and warned that Yugoslavia had no option but to sign the Pact. Pešić, too, was summoned to meet with Pavle at the palace, where he likewise dismissed the threat.[67] On 25 March, following the radio announcement of Yugoslavia's adherence to the Pact, the SKK hosted a meeting of delegates of the youth wings of various parties and bodies: the Democratic, Farmers' and Yugoslav National parties; the Union of Falcons; the Belgrade merchants; and its own. The delegates proclaimed the establishment of a Front for the Defence of the Fatherland. The Radicals' youth organisation did not join.[68] Demonstrations against the Pact took place in Belgrade, Kragujevac, Kraljevo and other towns in Serbia and elsewhere in Yugoslavia. A detachment of soldiers of the Knjaževac garrison staged a small uprising in the town, taking control of the post office and the municipal and district offices. The captain of the mutineers spoke before a demonstration in the town alongside the KPJ's district secretary, though the revolt was quickly suppressed and several left-wing officers and soldiers arrested.[69]

Tom G. Mapplebeck, a British Intelligence agent in Belgrade and close friend of Mirković, visited him in the afternoon of 26 March and insisted that the putsch be executed within 48 hours.[70] Ironically, the putsch would succeed in part because the pro-British Pavle had not allowed the British legation or its officials or communications to be monitored, thereby giving British Intelligence freedom to operate.[71] The United States, too, agitated for rejection of the Pact by Yugoslavia and its politicians. US supporters of intervention in the war lauded the spirit of Serb heroism and martial prowess; half a century later, it would ironically be US opponents of military intervention in the 1990s war in the former Yugoslavia who would laud this spirit.[72] Meanwhile, after the re-establishment of diplomatic relations between Yugoslavia and the Soviet Union, Gavrilović had been made ambassador to Moscow. At least two Black Hand members, Simić and Mustafa Golubić, were Soviet agents in contact with the conspirators, and Simić met with Simović on 26 March, the day before the putsch, to inform him of Soviet dispositions. Vasić was in close contact with Golubić.[73]

The military plan for the putsch was devised at the air force command at Zemun, on Belgrade's outskirts. Mirković launched the putsch late in the evening of 26 March. Putschist forces, numbering around 8,000 in total, moved to commandeer the airport, royal court, government building, Belgrade city administration building and other key points of the capital, marching under the slogan 'For king and fatherland'.⁷⁴ By the early hours of the following day, Mirković's forces had commandeered central Belgrade and arrested the government. It was a virtually bloodless takeover, except for a single policeman who was shot dead when he refused to hand over control of the radio station in Belgrade's Makiš neighbourhood. There was some attempt at resistance, notably by General Kosić, who was in no doubt that 'the Pact in fact did not cause the putsch, which had different causes. The Pact was only to some extent the direct occasion of the putsch.' He testified later that the king had approved the signing of the Pact and, when Kosić woke him at the royal villa on the morning of the 27th to inform him that a putsch was in progress, ordered him to mobilise troops to suppress it. Yet Kosić's resistance failed since his officers largely either supported the putsch or were unwilling to resist it, and he was arrested at the base of the Royal Guard, which made no effort to defend him.⁷⁵

Pavle was travelling to a holiday in Slovenia and was informed of the putsch when his train stopped in Zagreb. There, he was escorted to the Palace of the Ban by vice-premier Maček, who urged him to arrest the commander of the predominantly Croat 4th Army, install in his place the Croat General August Marić and use this force to crush the putschists. General Marić endorsed this plan, but Pavle, broken by the news of the putsch, rejected it. He feared that to act upon it would constitute an act of rebellion against King Petar and lead to civil war, and perhaps feared also for his family's safety in putschist-controlled Belgrade. He apparently even urged Maček to join the putschist government so as to preserve national unity and avoid war. He then meekly returned by train to Belgrade. There he was greeted by Simović, who escorted him to the war ministry where, along with the other two regents, he signed a decree of resignation. Cvetković and other senior figures of the regency regime were arrested. Pavle was allowed to go into exile in Greece, where relatives of his wife lived; there, like Stojadinović before him, he was taken into custody by the British, who eventually interned him in Kenya.⁷⁶

Major Knežević arrived at the royal palace at Dedinje, known as the White Palace, to obtain Petar's signature to a document declaring that he had acceded to the throne and that he authorised Simović's appointment as prime minister. Although Knežević did not find the king at the palace, the commander of the external palace guard was quickly won over to the putsch and suggested to Knežević that they proceed as if the king had actually signed the document.⁷⁷ Consequently, on the morning of 27 March, Petar was declared to have come of age and a putschist officer impersonating him went on air with a 'proclamation to the people'. The new king noted in his memoirs: 'To my great surprise I listened as a voice similar to my own gave the following proclamation ...' Written by Slobodan Jovanović, it claimed that 'at this difficult moment for our nation I have decided to take the royal government into my hands', called upon 'all Serbs, Croats and Slovenes to gather round the throne' and 'carry out their duty towards the king and fatherland', and announced that a new government had been appointed under Simović. That afternoon, Pavle visited the king at the White Palace to inform him he had resigned and that royal power was now in his hands; the king, having thus become the putschists' puppet, signed the proclamation he had heard earlier on the radio as well as a decree appointing Simović prime minister.[78] Petar was seventeen; like Aleksandar Obrenović, he illegally assumed formal power before coming of age. This putsch appropriated the tradition of the royal putsches of 1893 and 1929, though this time the king was figurehead rather than executor. Fotić would comment wryly that 'it is not difficult to carry out a putsch, least of all in our country'.[79]

The putsch occasioned demonstrations in Belgrade under subsequently famous or infamous slogans: 'Better war than the Pact'; 'Better the grave than a slave'; 'No war without Serbs'. Ljotićite counter-demonstrators reversed the first of these to 'Better the Pact than war'.[80] Anti-Pact, pro-putsch demonstrations erupted throughout Yugoslavia, in particular in Serbia as well as in Split and Ljubljana. Patriarch Gavrilo, for his part, had responded to the news that Yugoslavia was joining the Pact by summoning the Holy Episcopal Synod, which consequently convened on 27 March to welcome the putsch: 'Before our nation these days, fate has again posed the question of which empire shall we declare for. This morning at dawn a response was given to that question: we have chosen the heavenly empire, that is God's empire true and just, of national unity and freedom.'[81] Simović visited the Synod the day after the putsch to thank the bishops for their support, informing them: 'Yesterday morning, following the act carried out on 27 March, you were the first to take upon yourself the difficult role and carry out your duty to the end, raising the standard of the cross that had truly been toppled under the weight of dust, and so clearly state that the Empire of heaven is the Serb way, how and why 27 March came about and the initiatives that led to it.'[82] The SKK newspaper *Srpski glas* re-emerged on the day of the putsch to publish the royal proclamation and pledge that it would 'more than ever be the true expression of the thoughts and feelings of the Serb nation which has now, in its most difficult moment, demonstrated all its consciousness and greatness'.[83] The newspaper published also a proclamation of the Front for the Defence of the Fatherland, whose signatories apparently included the youth organisations of the Radical, Democratic, Farmers', Yugoslav National and Socialist parties and of the SKK, National Defence, Chetniks and other associations,[84] along with a proclamation of the 'Council of Serb cultural and economic organisations and institutions', signed by a list of individuals including the SKK's Ćorović, Stojanović and Vasić.[85]

The putschists were divided over the political system to be introduced, with some, including Mirković and possibly Radoje Knežević and Simović, favouring a cabinet of generals heading an authoritarian regime modelled on Ion Antonescu's dictatorship in Romania, in which Simović would be 'Administrator of the State'.[86] But they reluctantly deferred to others who insisted upon a formal return to democratic government based on the St Vitus's Day Constitution. The new government's composition was consequently decided at a meeting at the general staff headquarters in the early morning of 27 March, attended by Simović, Jovanović, Trifunović-Birčanin and representatives of the main pre-1935 Serb parties, summoned to be informed that Simović was forming the new government, allegedly at the king's request, and to rally them behind him. Branko Čubrilović and Tupanjanin (wearing his pyjamas) represented the Farmers; party leader Grol, Božidar Vlajić, Božidar Marković and Radoje Knežević, the Democrats; Miša Trifunović and Mirko Kosić, the Radicals; Budisavljević, the Independent Democrats; and Jovan Banjanin and Petar Živković, the JNS.

Simović arrived at the meeting with Maček and Kulovec's agreement for the HSS and SLS to join the new government, despite the fact that the HSS politicians were convinced that the putsch had been motivated by Serbian opposition to the Agreement. Maček later claimed that they had joined the putschist government because the alternative was 'automatically to join with Hitler'.[87] The new government consequently included ten former ministers of the Cvetković–Maček government, including all four Croats except Maček himself, who agreed to join only on 3 April. The putschists secured this adherence by promising not only to respect the Agreement but to increase the competencies of the Croatian banovina, granting it very broad autonomy in the fields of the police, gendarmerie and internal security. The attendees were divided over the question of whether they were for peace or war; Tupanjanin fiercely argued, 'What do you mean by peace? Those are stupidities! This is a national revolution and after it comes a national war.'[88] But the others were mostly for peace, partly because Maček, who feared Croatia being dragged into the war, made his inclusion in the government conditional upon adherence to the Pact, while the putschists feared national disunity if the Croats were excluded.[89] According to Ilija Jukić, a Yugoslav diplomat at the time, 'The senior members of the cabinet, prompted by Maček's message from Zagreb, realised that Hitler and Mussolini had to be placated. After examining the documents in the top-secret files connected with the previous government's accession to the Tripartite Pact, they found that the treaties were not so bad after all.'[90]

The Radical Momčilo Ninčić was appointed foreign minister; a former chairman of the Italian–Yugoslav, German–Yugoslav and Hungarian–Yugoslav societies, he was viewed as an appointment that might mollify Berlin. Simović unilaterally chose Budisavljević as interior minister and General Ilić as war minister. Representatives of all the above-mentioned parties would join the government: Trifunović as education minister, Grol as minister of social policy and national health, Marković as justice minister, the Independent Democrats' Sava Kosanović as minister of supplies and nutrition and Branko Čubrilović as agriculture minister. Jovanović became second vice-premier. Bogoljub Jevtić of the JNS became minister of transport. The Croats were represented by Maček as first vice-premier, Šutej as finance minister, Ivan Andres as minister of trade and industry, and Josip Torbar as minister of posts, telegraphs and telephones. The Slovenes from the previous government were also retained, with Kulovec as construction minister and Miha Krek as minister without portfolio. So was the JMO's Kulenović as minister of forestry and mines. Other ministers without portfolio were Bariša Smoljan, Marko Daković, Jovan Banjanin and Gavrilović. It was therefore a government that included representatives of most significant political parties in the country.

Mirković himself apparently never imagined the putsch could lead to a German invasion.[91] He kept a signed photo of fellow aviator, Marshal Hermann Göring, in a place of honour in his quarters.[92] The putschist government declared in favour of peace with Germany and Simović assured Germany's ambassador that Yugoslavia's policy toward Germany would remain unchanged and that the putsch had not been directed against it but was a response to domestic political factors. He claimed: 'He had always been a friend of Germany, and was proud of his acquaintance with the Reichsmarschall [Göring] and with [Luftwaffe] Field Marshal Milch, and he requested that his regards be conveyed to them.'[93] One of the government's first acts was to amnesty the political prisoners held by Pavle's regime. These included Ljotić's supporters, who were consequently released from prison; Ilić even invited Ljotić himself to join the government. However, the amnesty was not applied consistently; many Communists and their sympathisers, particularly in Croatia and Slovenia, remained incarcerated until the Axis invasion in April, when they consequently fell into the hands of the Nazis, Fascists and their collaborators.[94] On the other hand, the putschist government intended to rehabilitate Apis and the other Salonika trial defendants.[95]

Though the putsch had been fuelled by opposition to the Agreement and occasioned by adherence to the Pact, the putschist regime was thus ironically compelled to uphold both the Agreement and the Pact and to extend both Croatian autonomy and collaboration with the Axis. During the 1930s and early 1940s, the threat posed to the Yugoslav regime internally by the Croatian opposition and externally by the Axis powers had given it two options: either to seek accommodation with Germany and Italy in order to maintain the existing unitarist order against the Croatian opposition, or to accommodate Croatian demands so as to reduce internal Yugoslav strife and present a more united front vis-à-vis Germany and Italy. Stojadinović had pursued the first strategy and Pavle and Cvetković the second.[96] The putschists wanted to have their cake and eat it but they ended up doing neither. Years later, Fotić commented: 'And that myth of Apis and legend of democracy dragged Yugoslavia to 27 March. Again, as in 1893 ... and in 1903, there appeared a rogue marriage between democracy and army. The army overthrew the regency and surrendered government to the democracy and, as in 1914, by its act dragged the country into war.'[97]

Yugoslavia's envoy in Berlin, Ivo Andrić, visited the German foreign ministry on 29 March to give assurances that the putsch had been related purely to internal political factors and that Yugoslavia's new government had ordered the suppression of all anti-German manifestations.[98] Ninčić on 30 March handed a statement to the German ambassador in Belgrade: 'The present Royal Yugoslav Government remains true to the principle of respect for international treaties which have been concluded, among which the Protocol signed on the 25th of this month in Vienna belongs. It will insist in the most determined fashion on not being drawn into the present conflict. Its chief attention will be devoted to the maintenance of good and friendly relations with its neighbours the German Reich and the Kingdom of Italy.'[99] Ninčić notified all Yugoslav missions abroad on 1 April that Yugoslavia remained committed to the Pact. Simić and Golubić were dispatched to Moscow on the same day to obtain an agreement with the Soviet Union; the Yugoslav ambassador in Moscow eventually signed a Treaty of Friendship and Non-Aggression with the Soviets on the morning of 6 April.

Hitler, however, responded to the putsch on the same day by issuing his directive to attack Yugoslavia. He viewed the putsch, carried out immediately after the signing of the Pact, as a personal affront. Nedić, subsequently installed on 29 August by the Germans as prime minister of the quisling Government of National Salvation in occupied Serbia, claimed that Hitler told him: 'If the Pact had remained in force, you in the course of this war would have become rich as Croesus. Yugoslavia as a whole was in Germany's interest. However, you gave the German nation a slap, and you twice wounded my heart. I then ordered that the Serb nation be exterminated and that it be hit with a crusade.'[100] The cabinet met on 5 April, with the majority led by Ninčić willing to accept an Italian offer to intercede on Yugoslavia's behalf with the Germans if the Yugoslavs would agree to occupy the Greek–Yugoslav border to prevent British and Greek troops from entering Yugoslavia. Yet Simović, apparently convinced that Yugoslavia was capable of resisting Germany militarily, took the occasion to deliver a fiery nationalist speech recalling the Battle of Kosovo and Serbia's history of struggle against the Turks. No decision was reached on the Italian offer by the time Germany began its military assault on Yugoslavia on the morning of 6 April.[101]

April War

Yugoslavia by the spring of 1941 was paradoxically both groaning under the weight of military expenditure yet wholly unable to defend itself. The army absorbed 22.6 per cent of state expenditure in 1939–1940; Yugoslavia was consequently Europe's most indebted state by late 1940. It possessed a limited military industry, with state-owned factories at Kragujevac, Kruševac and Čačak in Serbia and at Kamnik in Slovenia, Zagreb and Sarajevo, which supplied some basic military needs, but it was dependent upon imports for more high-tech military supplies.[102] At the end of 1938, Germany granted Yugoslavia a credit of 200 million marks to purchase warplanes, artillery and other military supplies, after which in July 1939 the two states signed a

END OF THE YUGOSLAV KINGDOM

secret protocol, compelling Yugoslavia to pay for 50 per cent of its arms imports from Germany with strategic raw materials while granting it also a concession to exploit its gas reserves. A further secret protocol was signed in October 1939, involving further German deliveries of arms to Yugoslavia in exchange for huge quantities of copper, lead, aluminium and other raw materials.[103] Paradoxically, therefore, Yugoslavia was wholly dependent for armaments on the state that posed the gravest military threat to it.

The Army of the Kingdom of Yugoslavia was, since the state's establishment in 1918, a Serbian-dominated army with officers from the old Serbian army preponderant in the general staff and Serbs from Serbia in the officer corps overall. The establishment of the Croatian banovina and apparent moves toward the state's federalisation increased the distrust felt by the high command for the non-Serb rank and file, which they viewed as a potential fifth column. Consequently, at the end of the 1930s, the general staff began organising Chetnik detachments—irregular forces whose task was to monitor and control the activities of Croatian soldiers and civilians. This had the effect of increasing the alienation of Croatian soldiers from the army, whose morale deteriorated further.[104] Meanwhile, as the government struggled to finance rearmament, it resorted to increased printing of money by the National Bank, causing retail prices to rise by 65 per cent and wholesale prices by 87 per cent between August 1939 and the end of 1940, with the cost of food and clothing particularly affected, thereby lowering the population's standard of living. The government established a new ministry of food and supply in January 1941 and attempted to impose price controls, but these failed to bring results, so popular discontent rose rapidly just when national unity was most needed.[105]

Yugoslavia's defence plans since the late 1930s assumed an attack by Germany, Italy and Hungary against its northern and north-western borders. However, they were successively modified in line with the Axis powers' steady encroachment into the Balkans, starting with Italy's occupation of Albania in April 1939. The latest plan, R-41, was composed in February 1941 in response to the entry of German troops into Romania and their likely entry into Bulgaria. This plan was not sent to the army group commanders until 31 March, leaving them with less than a week to implement it, so that the country's defence, such as it was, was largely organised on the basis of the earlier plan, R-40. This envisaged an initial defence on all borders followed by the army's retreat south-eastwards towards Greece, through which it would eventually retreat to link up with the Greeks and British. The fact that this envisaged the rapid abandonment of Slovenia and Croatia to Axis occupation influenced Slovene and Croat attitudes to the possibility of war and resistance.

The putsch wrecked the previous government's strategy of avoiding invasion through collaboration with Germany, without producing a government willing to avoid invasion by determined military preparations for resistance. Immediately after the putsch, the general staff recommended general mobilisation, but the government rejected this for fear of providing a pretext for Germany's invasion, which it hoped could be averted or at least delayed by diplomacy. Instead, secret mobilisation was ordered on 30 March and began on 3 April, just three days before the invasion commenced, by which time it was far from complete.[106] At the time of the invasion, Yugoslavia's army of about 30 divisions had about 700,000 men in arms, of whom about 400,000 were poorly trained recruits who had been in uniform for under a month. These forces were organised into four army groups comprising seven armies. None of the divisions had achieved full mobilisation of its manpower or military preparedness, largely owing to widespread draft-dodging. Furthermore, Yugoslavia's national tensions sapped its combat readiness. Mobilisation on the territory of the Croatian banovina initially did not involve the requisitioning of livestock and carts so as not to antagonise the peasant population, rendering it largely ineffective; when the order eventually came on 3 April to purchase livestock and carts, the peasantry effectively obstructed it. The army did not trust the approximately 122,000 conscripts from the ranks of the national minorities—ethnic Albanians, Hungarians and Germans—so was lumbered with many troops it had no use for; conversely, trusted troops from Serbia were deployed to garrison areas inhabited by minorities, taking them away from duties elsewhere.[107]

The Wehrmacht invaded its Yugoslav ally on 6 April, beginning with the Luftwaffe's bombardment of Yugoslavia's airbases and capital city. Yugoslavia's government had declared Belgrade an open city prior to the war's start, yet its terror-bombing by Germany, codenamed Operation Punishment, struck schools, hospitals and residential quarters, claiming between 2,000 and 3,000 civilian lives and causing massive material damage, including the total destruction of the National Library with over 300,000 books and the damaging of around 10 per cent of houses in the city. The Jewish quarter at Dorćol was singled out for attack, with 70–80 per cent of its buildings burned along with many of their inhabitants and the Bet Yizrael synagogue set on fire.[108] Among those killed was construction minister Kulovec. The Luftwaffe immediately took control of Yugoslavia's airspace and cut communications between Yugoslavia's supreme command and its armies in the field. The destruction of the Belgrade radio station prevented Petar's planned broadcast calling upon Serbs, Croats and Slovenes to resist the attack.[109] Yugoslavia's government and supreme command moved on the same day from Belgrade to the village of Sevojno near Užice.

Hitler had had no plan to attack Yugoslavia prior to the March putsch, so one had to be improvised quickly, but his forces were in full combat readiness, well trained and experienced and superior to the Yugoslavs in quality and armaments. Italian and Hungarian troops also participated in the conquest. The combined invasion force amounted to 24 German, 23 Italian and 5 Hungarian divisions. The Germans attacked first from all four countries where their troops were based: Austria (now part of Germany), Hungary, Romania and Bulgaria. Invading Yugoslav Macedonia from Bulgaria, they took Skopje on the 7th. By the 9th, Yugoslav forces were retreating southwards from Slovenia and northern Croatia. On the 10th, German forces from western Hungary attacked south-westwards and captured Zagreb. Shortly before they entered the city, Ustasha officer Slavko Kvaternik, acting on SS instructions, proclaimed the Independent State of Croatia. Yugoslav deputy prime minister Maček called upon the 'Croat people' to 'collaborate with the new government'. On the same day, Slovene politicians organised as the National Council, directed by Marko Natlačen, ban of the Drava Banovina, likewise declared the end of Yugoslav rule over Slovenia and sought command over Yugoslav army units in the banovina. These events encouraged widespread defeatism and demoralisation in the army and population, and the desertion particularly of Croat troops.[110] Meanwhile, the Italians invaded from the north-west on 7 April and, meeting little resistance, captured Ljubljana on the 12th. The Hungarians joined the attack on the 11th and occupied with little resistance areas in Vojvodina that Hitler had assigned to them. German forces launched a multi-pronged attack towards Belgrade from Romania, Hungary and, after capturing Niš on the 9th, upwards from southern Serbia. This powerful German thrust in the south cut off Yugoslav forces from possible retreat southwards to link up with the Greeks and British.

Yugoslav resistance collapsed ignominiously. The Yugoslav government, faced with defeat on all fronts, except the Albanian front where its forces achieved a forlorn advance, moved on 11 April to Pale (the future base of Radovan Karadžić's Bosnian Serb rebels in the 1990s) in the mountains outside Sarajevo, on the half-hearted assumption that they could organise continued resistance in the mountainous interior. Belgrade fell without a struggle to a single SS infantry platoon of ten men on the 12th, when the mayor surrendered the city to it.[111] As one eyewitness noted, 'The Germans came into possession of Belgrade without expending, directly themselves, a single rifle bullet!'[112] Another described the aftermath: 'The situation in Belgrade was terrible. Ruins everywhere, soot, broken glass in the streets, the city without water and on top of that a ban on the use of water closets. It was particularly difficult for us to watch our soldiers who, under the guard of the Germans, swept the streets, repaired the sewers, piled up the bricks of the ruined houses ...'[113] Simović, as prime minister and chief of the general staff, without consulting the cabinet, transferred the latter post to Army General Danilo Kalafatović on the 13th, along with instructions that he seek a ceasefire and capitulation since further resistance was impossible 'due to events in Croatia and Dalmatia'.[114] He thus sought a scapegoat for defeat in Croat treachery—the alleged disloyalty of Croat officers and fifth-columnist activities of the HSS paramilitary forces and Ustashas.

Kalafatović convened a meeting of the staff of the supreme command on 14 April, at which he informed his colleagues that 'because of failure on all fronts' and 'the complete collapse of our army in Croatia, Dalmatia and Slovenia' he had come to the conclusion that 'all further military resistance is impossible' and that it was consequently necessary to seek 'an honourable ceasefire with the German and Italian troops with the aim that we lighten for the army and people all consequences of this undesired war'. His location of the army's collapse in the Croatian and Slovenian lands obscured the fact that the collapse was occurring throughout the country.[115] However, the Germans and Italians rejected the consequent request for a ceasefire, demanding unconditional capitulation. Consequently, the supreme command surrendered unconditionally to the Germans on the 15th. Simović intended this to be a purely military capitulation, enabling the Yugoslav government formally to continue resistance. Petar fled by plane from an airport near Nikšić in Montenegro to Greece on the 14th. Simović, Ninčić, Mirković and most members of the putschist government followed him out of the country the following day. The Germans took Kalafatović prisoner in Sarajevo on the 16th. It was left to General Radivoje Janković, the operational department chief on the staff of the supreme command, along with the indignant former foreign minister Cincar-Marković—who had had no role in creating the catastrophe but was now recruited to mitigate it—to sign the capitulation in Belgrade on the 17th on his behalf. The government's fiction that it was agreeing to a ceasefire rather than an unconditional surrender prevented the Yugoslav commanders from disbanding their units in time to avoid capture. Consequently, a very large number—approximately 398,000—of Yugoslav troops were taken into captivity as prisoners of war, mostly by the Germans; these were predominantly Serbs, as Yugoslav soldiers of other nationalities including Montenegrins were mostly spared. Subsequently, a large proportion of the Serbs were also released: those from the territory of the new Croatian puppet-state or from the areas occupied by Italy, Hungary and Bulgaria, and eventually some Serbs from Serbia ready to collaborate. The number of prisoners consequently dropped to about 210,000.[116]

Yugoslavia's defeat and occupation took the Germans eleven days and cost them 151 dead. One German officer remarked that 'from the German point of view the conquest of Yugoslavia was virtually a military parade'.[117] Simović, in exile with his government in Athens on the day the capitulation was signed, blamed the ignominious rout on 'Croat treason', provoking a bitter dispute among the ministers.[118] The supreme command's deliberate and rapid withdrawal of Yugoslavia's army from the country's north, its rapid defeat in eastern Yugoslavia when attacked from the eastern Balkans and the surrender of Belgrade without a struggle exposed this excuse as false. The establishment of the Independent State of Croatia had indeed sapped military morale in Croatia, Dalmatia and Bosnia, and there had been cases of outright treason by Croat troops under Ustasha influence. Thus, the 108th Infantry Regiment in Bjelovar in northern Croatia, under the influence of pro-Ustasha elements including the town mayor, rebelled against the staff of the 4th Army on the night of 7–8 April and was subsequently joined by the 40th Supplementary Regiment and part of the 42nd Infantry Regiment. The rebels took control of Bjelovar and arrested the garrison, prompting the commander of the 4th Army to threaten the bombardment and destruction of the town. Such instances contributed to the rapid collapse of the

END OF THE YUGOSLAV KINGDOM

4th Army. The national conflict in Yugoslavia therefore continued within the army's ranks during the invasion.[119] However, the military situation had been no better on other fronts: the German advance in the south had caused desertion among the troops and panic among many commanders.[120] The Germans captured Skopje, defended primarily by Serb troops from Serbia, before they captured Zagreb, something which in turn weakened morale on the northern front. That Simović had placed the defeatist Nedić in command of the 3rd Army in Macedonia was symbolic.[121]

At the government-in-exile's session on 28 April in Jerusalem, whither it had moved from Greece, Simović admitted the Yugoslav generals' defeatism: 'Almost all generals were opposed to resistance ... When the generals wanted a ceasefire as soon as possible, so that they could return to their families, what could be expected of the rank and file?'[122] In reality, few of any nationality were very willing to die for the Yugoslav kingdom. In Stojadinović's words, 'The Croats did not defend it, nor did the Serbs, for it was in particular they who were resentful ...' As a result of the Agreement, 'the Croats were not satisfied and the Serbs were resentful'.[123] According to the military historian Velimir Terzić, 'conscious of the lack of heterogeneity and obvious weaknesses of the Yugoslav army, the majority of commanders did not see any perspective in fighting and the successful offering of resistance, so that they, like Prince Pavle and the royal government, accepted the Tripartite Pact, although in the majority they sympathised with the Allies from the First World War.'[124] Nedić vented his grievances over the war and defeat in a public proclamation later that year in his capacity as Serbia's quisling prime minister: 'Where was England in April? Why didn't it come to your aid? Not a single Englishman wanted to die to save Yugoslavia, just as not one wanted to come to Serbia's aid in 1915 either.'[125] Given Britain's role in instigating the putsch that triggered the invasion and its subsequent inability to provide meaningful support to Yugoslavia's defence, his complaint was not completely groundless.

Germany invaded Greece at the same time as it did Yugoslavia. Because it could now attack Greece across Yugoslavia's territory, bypassing the Greeks' defensive Metaxas line, Yugoslavia's entry into the war actually accelerated the defeat of Greece and the British forces there. Some historians have since claimed that Germany's invasion of Yugoslavia and Greece resulted in a delay of several weeks to the launch of Operation Barbarossa, consequently the Wehrmacht could not reach Moscow before winter set in; hence Germany lost the war because of Greek or Yugoslav resistance in 1941. In fact, Barbarossa was delayed owing to logistical problems unrelated to the Balkans; the campaign there did not affect it. Yugoslavia's entry into the war allowed Germany to transport its troops from Greece back into position for Barbarossa more quickly, across Yugoslav territory.[126] The Axis invasion and occupation would kill over a million Yugoslavs, about half of them Serbs.[127]

The putsch of 26–27 March was the product of Serbian opposition to the authoritarian court regime that had ruled Yugoslavia since 1929, when King

Aleksandar had overthrown the Serbian political parties, and particularly since 1935, when Prince Regent Pavle and prime minister Stojadinović had sidelined the military in favour of the new generation of Court Radicals. It represented the latest counterstrike of essentially the same constellation of forces that had destroyed the Obrenović regime in 1903 and that, in turn, had been defeated in 1917: praetorian officer-conspirators (heirs to the Black Hand) and Democrats and Republicans (heirs to the Independent Radicals). The Concordat, Agreement and Pact had fuelled the opposition that had culminated in the putsch, but they did not cause it, any more than Aleksandar Obrenović's failure to fight the Albanians had caused his overthrow. For all that interwar Yugoslav politics had apparently been dominated by the national question, the act that finally triggered the kingdom's destruction was carried out by Serbs from Serbia against other Serbs from Serbia. It was a chapter in an inter-Serbian power struggle that the unification of Yugoslavia had not fundamentally changed.

CONCLUSION

The first Yugoslavia that existed from 1918 to 1941 is widely viewed as having been brought down by its unresolved national conflict. Yet it was destroyed by a foreign invasion triggered by a putsch that represented merely the latest battle in a long-standing internal conflict between two rival factions of Serbia's elite, in which Croats, Slovenes, prečani Serbs and other non-Serbian Yugoslavs played wholly secondary roles.

Serbia's original modern elite—monarch, bureaucracy and army—arose from the revolution against the Ottomans of 1804–1815 and its aftermath. The elite's exploitation and oppression of the peasant majority caused the latter widely to perceive it as the heir to the Ottoman oppressors. The regime's modernisation of the country, involving onerous taxes and collaboration with the neighbouring Habsburg Empire, combined with the elite's gradual adoption of dress and manners characteristic of Western and Central Europe, catalysed the rise of a populist-nationalist, Russophile opposition that viewed the regime and elite not simply as oppressors but as nationally alien, un-Serb. Viewing the regime as un-Serb or unpatriotic and directing nationalism against it became staples of Serbian opposition politics. When essentially free elections were finally permitted in the 1880s, the peasantry gave their votes to the populist-nationalist, anti-state Radicals, who thereby emerged as a counter-elite. After an outright power struggle, the two elites gradually synthesised from the late 1880s, whereby the king would rule in alliance with at least part of the Radical party. This alliance was opposed by elements in both camps—the 'hard right' of the political elite traditionally allied to the court and the 'hard left' of the Radical party. This produced a counter-synthesis eventually manifested in the alliance between the Black Hand and Independent Radicals. Members of this counter-synthetic elite tradition finally overthrew the supposedly 'un-Serb' regime of the court–Radical synthesis in March 1941, triggering the destruction of the Yugoslav and, by extension, the modern Serbian state. The power struggle between the two factions nevertheless continued: Milan Nedić's Nazi-quisling Government of National Salvation, established on 29 August 1941 on the basis of court generals including White Hand leader Josif Kostić and a cross-party coalition in which Radicals of one type or another featured prominently, represented the residue of the Yugoslav regime of the late 1920s and 1930s, against which stood Draža Mihailović's Chetniks, a nominal resistance movement that quickly began collaborating with the occupiers, heir to the faction of the Black Hand and Independents (Democrats, Republicans), which followed the Black Hand in their use of the skull and crossbones emblem.

The first modern Serbia thus never successfully resolved the tensions inherent in its creation. Prince Miloš's authoritarianism was perpetuated by the succession of princes, regents and kings who followed him, eventually giving rise to the first King Aleksandar's ideology of a regime standing 'above' party politics, which decisively influenced the elite's ethos. The Radical party's ideology reflected the peasantry's socially and culturally homogeneous worldview, lacking the appreciation of pluralism that a socially diverse society potentially produces. Serbia's dynasties, constitutions and laws were too youthful securely to command elite obedience, while the monarchical-bureaucratic-military elite and Radical counter-elite—the two Serbias—could not agree on a pluralistic political order in which competition between factions could be managed constitutionally. The monarchical-elitist ideology of a regime standing above party divisions did not bring national unity. Neither did the Radicals' populist ideology denying the legitimacy of political divisions or alternatives within the nation, which was steadily adopted by most Serbian factions including their opponents. Anti-pluralist ideologies intended to enforce national unity in practice produced crippling disunity and mutually assured destruction.

The failure was perhaps not preordained. The Young Conservative government's well-intentioned decision to hold parliamentary elections in 1880 without police manipulation was too liberal for Serbia's level of development. It enabled the People's Radical Party to emerge as a force unambiguously possessing overwhelming popular support in Serbia, but without any genuine shift of social power away from the old elite, generating an anti-Radical reaction that unfolded destructively over the next six decades. Much of the historical responsibility for the destructive form this reaction took lies with the malevolent, erratic Milan Obrenović. His abdication, continued meddling in Serbian politics, engineering of the 1894 royal coup and, finally, breach with his son fragmented the old elite, poisoned its relations with the Radicals and began the army's factionalisation. This factionalisation gave rise to the Frankenstein's monster of praetorianism, resulting in the putsches of 1903 and 1941 and, in turn, the military disasters of 1915 and 1941, which Serbia was lucky to survive. Mihailović and his Chetnik movement were the final incarnation of this praetorianism which, by attacking Tito's Partisans in November 1941, produced civil war in Serbia in the 1940s before finally leaving the historical stage. While other Serbian leaders lacked Milan's exceptional personal flaws, they share responsibility for the state's failure, including Nikola Pašić, whose hegemonist ideology and practice alienated almost every other significant figure in Serbian and Yugoslav politics outside the ranks of his own supporters; Jovan Ristić, whose anti-democratic putsch in 1892 against the Radical government began the old elite's destructive anti-Radical backlash; and the two King Aleksandars, each of whom reverted to a personal regime when

CONCLUSION

the situation required democratic or constitutional reform. But each of these four reflected the ethos of the structure he headed, and it would have violated this ethos if he had acted differently.

Serbia could perhaps have transcended these structural problems had it not been seemingly blessed but in fact cursed by its fortuitous absolute victory in 1918, leading to the establishment of a big Yugoslav state as an extension of itself, through an act of union that represented another royal coup. The constitutional order that Serbia's political classes imposed on the new state, notorious among historians for its unitarism that disregarded the non-Serbs' national aspirations, expressed the same anti-pluralism as other elements of Radical ideology and monarchical authoritarianism. Royal authority had been destroyed by the 1903 putsch, but the creation of Yugoslavia shifted state power from the politicians back toward the crown. The second King Aleksandar could play off the diverse Yugoslav factions against each other to achieve a hegemony that the first King Aleksandar had never securely enjoyed. The establishment of Yugoslavia therefore derailed Serbia's transition to a democratic constitutional monarchy.

The 1941 putsch, by triggering the Axis invasion, proved the downfall not only of the Serbian and Yugoslav state but of the ideal of pan-Serb unification to produce an enlarged or 'Great' Serbia; otherwise, a 'Great Serbia' in the form of a Serbian banovina would probably have emerged, incorporating Vojvodina, Montenegro, the Sanjak, Kosovo, Macedonia and about 72 per cent of Bosnia-Hercegovina. Subsequent attempts to establish an enlarged Serbian state or entity, by Mihailović's Chetniks and the Nedić regime in the 1940s, were first blocked by the German occupier then definitely defeated when both Serbian anti-Communist factions were crushed by Tito's Partisans assisted by the Allied powers. The Partisans' establishment of a multinational Yugoslav federation involved the incorporation of Vojvodina, Kosovo and most of the Sanjak in the People's Republic of Serbia but proved an insuperable straitjacket to further expansion, as Slobodan Milošević's failure in the 1990s demonstrated. The opportunity to establish a Great Serbia, lost thanks to the 1941 putsch, thus never recurred. Despite the stereotype of Serbia as an excessively nationalistic country, its national goals were in practice sacrificed to its internal power struggle.

The way in which the first modern Serbian state ended should not, however, obscure its achievements. From the verge of national destruction in 1813, Serbia emerged from humble peasant beginnings to become a modern European country with an educated elite, university, schools, theatres, libraries, banks, factories, embassies, cinemas, automobiles and other trappings of modern life common to European states. This achievement was not reversed even by the disasters of 1915 and 1941, and liberation from occupation in 1944 brought a permanent renewal of statehood. As Serbia was cursed by Milan's destructive personality from the 1880s, so it had been blessed by the extraordinary political genius of Miloš, who brought the country from catastrophe in 1813 to recognition as an autonomous principality in 1830 and began the construction of a nation-state. His achievements were augmented by able successors, particularly the Constitutionalists, who made Serbia a *Rechtsstaat*; Prince Mihailo and Ilija Garašanin, who ended the Ottoman occupation of Serbia in 1867; and Jovan Ristić who, despite the blunder of his first anti-Ottoman war, led Serbia to independence in 1878. This state-building process culminated in the first King Aleksandar's reign with the creation—above all, by his father—of a modern army, militarily effective but highly politicised, responsible for the spectacular victories of 1912–1914 and 1918 but also for the tragedies of 1903, 28 June 1914, 1915 and 1941. The ambiguous outcome of Serbia's state-building process thus intersects with the mixed records of the last two Obrenović rulers. The first modern Serbia's story thus has contradictory lessons: a nation will develop inexorably according to its nature, but its destiny is influenced by the character and choices of its leaders, who are responsible for its successes and failures.

NOTES

INTRODUCTION

1. For example, Stevan K. Pavlowitch, *Serbia: The History Behind the Name*, Hurst, 2002; John K. Cox, *The History of Serbia*, Greenwood Press, 2000; Alex Dragnich, *Serbia Through the Ages*, Columbia University Press, 2005; Tim Judah, *The Serbs: History, Myth and the Destruction of Yugoslavia*, 3rd ed., Yale University Press, 2009. Similarly in French: Yves Tomić, *La Serbie du prince Miloš a Milošević*, Peter Lang, 2003.
2. Michael Boro Petrovich, *A History of Modern Serbia, 1804–1918*, v1–2, Harcourt Brace Jovanovich, 1976.
3. Holm Zundhausen, *Geschichte Serbiens*, Böhlau Verlag, 2007; Holm Zundhausen, *Istorija Srbije od 19. do 21. veka*, Clio, 2008.
4. Dejan Djokić, *A Concise History of Serbia*, Cambridge University Press, 2023.
5. For example Dušan T. Bataković, ed., *Nova istorija srpskog naroda*, Naš dom and L'Age d'Homme, 2002; Dragoslav Janković, *Istorija države i prava Srbije u XIX veku*, Nolit, 1955; Sima Ćirković, *Srbi među evropskim narodima*, Equilibrium, 2004; Stanoje Stanojević, *Istorija srpskog naroda*, Book and Marso, 2001; Vladimir Ćorović, *Istorija Srba*, 6th ed., Zograf, 2001; Milorad Ekmečić, *Dugo kretanje između klanja i oranja: Istorija Srba u novom veku (1492–1992)*, Evro-Đunti, 2011; Miloš Blagojević, Dejan Medaković, Radoš Ljušić and Ljubodrag Dimić, *Istorija srpske državnosti*, v1–3, Srpksa akademija nauka in umjetnosti, 2000–2001; Vasa Kazimirović, *Srbija i Jugoslavia 1941–1945*, v1–4, Prizma, 1995; Slavko Gavrilović, Jovanka Kalić, Andrej Mitrović, Radovan Samardžić, Vladimir Stojančević and Sima Ćirković, *Istorija srpskog naroda*, v1–10, Srpska književna zadruga, 1981–1993.

1. SERBIA AND THE SERBS BEFORE THE NINETEENTH CENTURY

1. John V.A. Fine, *The Early Medieval Balkans: A Critical Survey from the Sixth to the Late Twelfth Century*, University of Michigan Press, 1991, 1–13.
2. Božidar Ferjančić, 'Beograd od početka seobe naroda do doseljenja Slovena (175–602)', in Vasa Čubrilović, ed., *Istorija Beograda*, v1, Srpska akademija nauka i umjetnosti, 1974, 105–112.
3. Branka Magaš, *Croatia Through History: The Making of a European State*, Saqi, 2007, 22; Noel Malcolm, *Bosnia: A Short History*, Macmillan, 1994, 4–6.

NOTES pp. [10-14]

4. Fine, *Early Medieval Balkans*, 22-24; Boro Grafenauer, Dušan Perović and Jaroslav Šidak, eds, *Istorija Naroda Jugoslavije*, v1, Prosveta, 1963, 69-70.
5. Ćorović, *Istorija Srba*, 42-43.
6. Traian Stoianovich, *Balkan Worlds: The First and Last Europe*, M.E. Sharp, 1994, 125; Hanna Popowska-Taborska, 'Ślady etnonimów słowiańskich z elementem obcym w nazewnictwie polskim', *Acta Universitatis Lodziensis Folia Linguistica*, 27, 1993, 225.
7. Gy Moravcsik, ed., *Constantine Porphyrogenitus: De Administrando Imperio* (English translation), Pázmány Péter Tudományegyetemi Görög Filológiai Intézet, 1949, 153.
8. Ćirković, *Srbi među evropskim narodima*, xiii.
9. Fine, *Early Medieval Balkans*, 56-57; Vladimir Ćorović, *Istorija Bosne*, Glas Srpski and Ars Libri, 1999, 104.
10. Jozo Tomasevich, *Peasants, Politics and Economic Change in Yugoslavia*, Stanford University Press, 1955, 10.
11. Fine, *Early Medieval Balkans*, 109-110.
12. Tibor Živković, *Sloveni i Romeji: Slavizacija na prostoru Srbije od VII do XI veka*, Istorijski institut Srpske Akademije Nauka i Umetnosti, 2000; Ćorović, *Istorija Srba*, 44-45.
13. Jovan Cvijić, *Balkansko poluostrvo*, 2nd ed., Srpska akademija nauka i umjetnosti, Zavod za udžbenika i nastavna sredstva and Književne novine, 1991, 166-167.
14. Vladimir Ćorović, *Istorija Jugoslavije*, Prosveta, 1989, 28.
15. George Ostrogorsky, *History of the Byzantine State*, 2nd ed., Basil Blackwell, 1968, 235-236.
16. A.P. Vlasto, *The Entry of the Slavs into Christendom: An Introduction to the Medieval History of the Slavs*, Cambridge University Press, 1970, 208-209; Kenneth Morrison and Elizabeth Roberts, *The Sandžak: A History*, Hurst, 2013, 13.
17. Florin Curta, *Southeastern Europe in the Middle Ages, 500-1250*, Cambridge University Press, 2006, 124-125, 215.
18. Živković, *Sloveni i Romeji*, 157-158.
19. Moravcsik, *Constantine Porphyrogenitus*, 161; Muhamed Hadžijahić, *Povijest Bosne u IX i X stoljeću*, Preporod, 2004, 9-23, 85-86.
20. Elizabeth Roberts, *Realm of the Black Mountain: A History of Montenegro*, Hurst, 2007, 54-55; Kenneth Morrison, *Montenegro: A Modern History*, I.B. Tauris, 2009, 15.
21. Miloš Blagojević, *Srbija u doba Nemanjića: Od kneževine do carstva, 1168-1371*, Vajat, 1989, 36; Curta, *Southeastern Europe*, 333-334.
22. Ćorović, *Istorija Jugoslavije*, 199-200.
23. John V.A. Fine, *The Late Medieval Balkans: A Critical Survey from the Late Twelfth Century to the Ottoman Conquest*, University of Michigan Press, 1994, 38.
24. Curta, *Southeastern Europe*, 389-393.
25. Fine, *Late Medieval Balkans*, 47-51.
26. Ibid., 116-117; Ostrogorsky, *Byzantine State*, 431.
27. Fine, *Late Medieval Balkans*, 39-40; Dimitry Obolensky, *The Byzantine Commonwealth: Eastern Europe, 500-1453*, Praeger, 1971, 311.

28. Ćorović, *Istorija Jugoslavije*, 126.
29. Vasa Čubrilović, *Istorija političke misli u Srbiji XIX veka*, Prosveta, 1958, 23–28.
30. Đoko Slijepčević, *Istorija srpske pravoslavne crkve*, v1, JRJ, 2002, 89.
31. Ćorović, *Istorija Jugoslavije*, 24.
32. Curta, *Southeastern Europe*, 396–397.
33. Fine, *Late Medieval Balkans*, 203–204.
34. Tomasevich, *Peasants*, 17–19.
35. Noel Malcolm, *Kosovo: A Short History*, Macmillan, 1998, 52–57.
36. Dušan J. Popović, *Beograd kroz vekove*, Turistička štampa, 1964, 21, 29.
37. Ćorović, *Istorija Srba*, 179.
38. Malcolm, *Kosovo*, 47; Blagojević, *Srbija u doba Nemanjića*, 140; Obolensky, *Byzantine Commonwealth*, 247–248.
39. Ivan Božić, Sima Ćirković, Milorad Ekmečić and Vladimir Dedijer, *Istorija Jugoslavije*, Prosveta, 1972, 69–71.
40. Ostrogorsky, *Byzantine State*, 505; Fine, *Late Medieval Balkans*, 273–274.
41. Fine, *Late Medieval Balkans*, 312–313.
42. Ibid., 290, 309; Malcolm, *Kosovo*, 48.
43. Ostrogorsky, *Byzantine State*, 525.
44. Obolensky, *Byzantine Commonwealth*, 248–249.
45. Ćorović, *Istorija Jugoslavije*, 163.
46. Čedomilj Mijatović, *Servia and the Servians*, Cosimo, 2007, 140–169; Malcolm, *Kosovo*, 49.
47. Fine, *Late Medieval Balkans*, 273–274.
48. Ibid., 378–381.
49. Ibid., 387.
50. Ibid., 389; Blagojević, *Srbija u doba Nemanjića*, 222.
51. Halil İnalcık, *The Ottoman Empire: The Classical Age 1300–1600*, Phoenix, 1973, 13–14.
52. William Stearns Davis, *A Short History of the Near East: From the Founding of Constantinople (330 A.D. to 1922)*, Macmillan, 1923, 200–201.
53. Grafenauer, et al., *Istorija Naroda Jugoslavije*, v1, 422.
54. Fine, *Late Medieval Balkans*, 502–503.
55. Ibid., 525–526.
56. Malcolm, *Kosovo*, 78.
57. Thomas Emmert, *Serbian Golgotha: Kosovo, 1389*, Columbia University Press, 1990, 79–120.
58. Malcolm, *Kosovo*, 66–67.
59. Miodrag Popović, *Vidovdan i časni krst: Ogled iz književne arheologije*, 4th ed., Knjižara krug, 2007, 43–70.
60. Dimitrije Djordjević, 'The tradition of Kosovo in the formation of modern Serbian statehood in the nineteenth century', in Wayne S. Vucinich and Thomas Emmert, eds, *Kosovo: Legacy of a Medieval Battle*, Modern Greek Studies, University of Minnesota, 1991, 309–312.

61. Popović, *Vidovdan i časni krst*, 71–83.
62. Vuk Stefanović Karadžić, *Srpske narodne pjesme*, v2, Prosveta, 1969, 214–215.
63. Ibid., 225–226.
64. Zundhausen, *Istorija Srbije*, 108–112.
65. Anna DiLellio, *The Battle of Kosovo 1389: An Albanian Epic*, I.B. Tauris, 2009, 3–48; Popović, *Vidovdan i časni krst*, 26–32; Emmert, *Serbian Golgotha*, 79–120; Malcolm, *Kosovo*, 70–74.
66. Ćorović, *Istorija Srba*, 338–339.
67. Ćirković, *Srbi među evropskim narodima*, 120–121.
68. Grafenauer et al., *Istorija Naroda Jugoslavije*, v1, 440.
69. Radoš Ljušić, *Kneževina Srbija*, Srpska Akademija Nauka i Umjetnosti, 1986, 47.
70. Malcolm, *Kosovo*, 98.
71. Boro Grafenauer, Branislav Đurđev and Jorjo Tadić, eds, *Istorija Naroda Jugoslavije*, v2, Prosveta, 1960, 24–25; Mustafa Imamović, *Bosnia and Herzegovina: Evolution of Its Political and Legal Institutions*, Magistrat, 2006, 104, 119–123.
72. Olga Zirojević, *Srbija pod turskom vlašću 1459–1804*, Srpski genealoški centar, 2007, 36–37; Mihailo Gavrilović, *Miloš Obrenović*, v2, Davidović, 1909, 361–364; Neda Božinović, *Žensko pitanje u Srbiji u XIX i XX veku*, Pinkpress, 1996, 25.
73. Tomasevich, *Peasants*, 27.
74. Radovan Samardžić, Pavle Ivić, Dimitrije Bogdanović, Miroslav Pantić, Sreten Petković and Dejan Medaković, *Istorija srpskog naroda*, v3.2, Srpska književna zadruga, 1993, 42; Muhammet Zahit Atçıl, 'State and government in the mid-sixteenth century Ottoman Empire: The Grand Vizierates of Rüstem Pasha (1544–1561)', PhD dissertation, Department of Near Eastern Languages and Civilisation, University of Chicago, June 2015, 16–20, 186–187, 206–213.
75. Heath W. Lowry, *The Nature of the Early Ottoman State*, State University of New York Press, 2003, 115–130.
76. Nikolai Todorov, *The Balkan City, 1400–1900*, University of Washington Press, 1983, 52.
77. Zirojević, *Srbija pod turskom vlašću*, 40–41.
78. Radmila Tričković, *Beogradski pašaluk 1687–1739*, Službeni glasnik, 2013, 243–244; Grafenauer et al., *Istorija Naroda Jugoslavije*, v2, 80–88; Avdo Sućeska, *Ajani: Prilog izučavanju lokalne vlasti u našim zemljama za vrijeme Turaka*, Naučno Društvo SR Bosne i Hercegovine, 1965, 35–36.
79. Sućeska, *Ajani*, 100.
80. David Norris, *Belgrade: A Cultural and Literary History*, Signal, 2008, 10.
81. Zirojević, *Srbija pod turskom vlašću*, 131.
82. Evlija Çelebi, *Putopis: Odlomci iz jugoslovenskim zemljama*, Svjetlost, 1967, 71, 326.
83. Milan Đakov Milićević, *Kneževina Srbija*, Državna štamparija, 1876, 23.
84. Nicholas J. Miller, *Between Nation and State: Serbian Politics in Croatia before the First World War*, University of Pittsburgh Press, 1997, 6.
85. Dušan J. Popović, *O Cincarima*, Prometej, 1998, 244–246, 279–285.

86. Miller, *Between Nation and State*, 7.
87. Gunther E. Rothenberg, *The Military Border in Croatia, 1740–1881: A Study of an Imperial Institution*, University of Chicago Press, 1966, 4–10.
88. Malcolm, *Bosnia*, 51–54, 70–71; Muhamed Hadžijahić, *Porijeklo bosanskih Muslimana*, Bosna, 1990, 107; Vasa Čubrilović, 'Poreklo muslimanskog plemstva u Bosni i Hercegovini', in Vasa Čubrilović, *Odabrani istorijski radovi*, Narodna knjiga, 1983, 208–215.
89. Ćorović, *Istorija Jugoslavije*, 306–307.
90. Magaš, *Croatia Through History*, 324.
91. Samardžić,et al., *Istorija srpskog naroda*, v3.2, 46–53; Ćorović, *Istorija Jugoslavije*, 310–311.
92. Samardžić,et al., *Istorija srpskog naroda*, v3.2, 64–71.
93. Magaš, *Croatia Through History*, 325.
94. Ćorović, *Istorija Srba*, 418.
95. Tričković, *Beogradski pašaluk*, 41; Grafenauer et al., *Istorija Naroda Jugoslavije*, v2, 535–536.
96. Benedikt Kuripešić, *Putopis kroz Bosnu, Srbiju, Bugarsku i Rumeliju 1530*, Čigoja, 2001, 43.
97. Milorad Ekmečić, *Stvaranje Jugoslavije, 1790–1918*, v2, Prostveta, 1989, 59.
98. Gligor Stanojević, *Srbija u vreme bečkog rata*, Nolit, 1976, 25.
99. Leften Stavrianos, *The Balkans Since 1453*, Hurst, 1958, 2000, 138–142; Tomasevich, *Peasants*, 32–35.
100. Zirojević, *Srbija pod turskom vlašću*, 36; Grafenauer et al., *Istorija Naroda Jugoslavije*, v2, 1275–1278.
101. Michael Boro Petrovich, 'The role of the Serbian Orthodox Church in the First Serbian Uprising, 1804–1813', in Wayne S. Vucinich, ed., *The First Serbian Uprising, 1804–1813*, Social Science Monographs, 1982, 261–262.
102. Zirojević, *Srbija pod turskom vlašću*, 173–178.
103. Srđan Katić, *Jegen Osman-paša*, APP, 2001, 105–116.
104. Tričković, *Beogradski pašaluk*, 39.
105. Ibid., 19, 469.
106. Miroslav Pavlović, 'Faktičko-pravni položaj smederevskog sandžaka posle 1739. godine', in Srđan Rudić and Lela Pavlović, eds, *Srpska revolucija i obnova srpske državnosti*, Istorijski institut, 2016, 11–12.
107. Tričković, *Beogradski pašaluk*, 469.
108. Ibid., 265–266.
109. Stanojević, *Srbija u vreme bečkog rata*, 170.
110. Ibid., 183–184.
111. Miller, *Between Nation and State*, 13.
112. Radovan Samardžić, Rajko L. Veselinović and Toma Popović, *Istorija srpskog naroda*, v3.1, Srpska književna zadruga, 1993, 103, 544; Dušan J. Popović, *Srbi u Vojvodini*, v1, Matica Srpska, 1957, 326–329.

113. Slijepčević, *Istorija SPC*, v2, 199.
114. Emmert, *Serbian Golgotha*, 81.
115. Fine, *Late Medieval Balkans*, 534, 603; Roberts, *Realm of the Black Mountain*, 95–106.
116. Morrison, *Montenegro*, 17–18; Roberts, *Realm of the Black Mountain*, 15–16, 136–139.
117. Tomasevich, *Peasants*, 33–35.
118. Zirojević, *Srbija pod turskom vlašću*, 215.
119. Grafenauer et al., *Istorija Naroda Jugoslavije*, v2, 1261–1262.
120. Slijepčević, *Istorija SPC*, v1, 370–372.
121. Popović, *Beograd*, 292.
122. Tričković, *Beogradski pašaluk*, 387.
123. Ibid., 445; Popović, *Beograd*, 297.
124. Tričković, *Beogradski pašaluk*, 432.
125. Pavlović, 'Faktičko-pravni položaj smederevskog sandžaka', 9–10; Grafenauer et al., *Istorija Naroda Jugoslavije*, v2, 270.
126. Malcolm, *Kosovo*, 168–171.
127. Petrovich, 'Serbian Orthodox Church in the First Serbian Uprising', 263–265.
128. Slijepčević, *Istorija SPC*, v2, 341; Gavrilović, *Miloš Obrenović*, v2, 657.
129. Božić et al., *Istorija Jugoslavije*, 186–187.
130. Dragoslav Janković, *Srpska država prvog ustanka*, Nolit, 1984, 40; Milenko Vukičević, *Karađorđe*, v1, Državna štamparija Kraljevine Srbije, 1907, 36–37, 47, 66–67.
131. Čubrilović, *Istorija političke misli*, 60.
132. Janković, *Srpska država prvog ustanka*, 43.
133. Gavro Škrivanić, 'The armed forces in Karadjordje's Serbia', in Vucinich, *First Serbian Uprising*, 304–306.
134. Leopold von Ranke, *History of Servia and the Servian Revolution*, De Capo Press, 1973, 94.
135. Ekmečić, *Dugo kretanje*, 145, 150.
136. Zirojević, *Srbija pod turskom vlašću*, 299.
137. Ekmečić, *Dugo kretanje*, 106–107.
138. Duncan Wilson, *The Life and Times of Vuk Stefanović Karadžić 1787–1864: Literacy, Literature and National Independence in Serbia*, University of Michigan Press, 1986, 47–48.
139. Ekmečić, *Dugo kretanje*, 101–105, 150.

2. THE SERBIAN UPRISINGS

1. Vladimir Karić, *Srbija: opis zemlje, naroda i države*, Kraljevska srpska državna štamparija, 1887, 477.
2. Fine, *Late Medieval Balkans*, 577.
3. Cvijić, *Balkansko poluostrvo*, 127–130; Grafenauer et al., *Istorija Naroda Jugoslavije*, v2, 1279–1281.
4. Cvijić, *Balkansko poluostrvo*, 244–247.

5. Ljušić, *Kneževina Srbija*, 75–76.
6. Ibid., 82; Petrovich, *Modern Serbia*, v1, 170.
7. Vladimir Stojančević, Jovan Milićević, Čedomir Popov, Radoman Jovanović and Milorad Ekmečić, *Istorija srpskog naroda*, v5.1, Srpska književna zadruga, 1981, 19.
8. Cvijić, *Balkansko poluostrvo*, 340–341.
9. Vera St. Erlich, *Family in Transition: A Study of 300 Yugoslav Villages*, Princeton University Press, 1966, 42–43.
10. Grafenauer et al., *Istorija Naroda Jugoslavije*, v2, 733–734.
11. Ekmečić, *Dugo kretanje*, 116; Marie Žanin-Čalić, *Socijalna istorija Srbije 1815–1940: Usporedni napredak u industrijalizaciji*, Clio, 2004, 296–297.
12. Vuk Stefanović Karadžić, 'Zakon ili vjera', in Milan S. Filipović, ed., *Sabrana dela Vuka Karadžića*, 17, *Etnografski spisi*, Prosveta, 1972, 357.
13. Karić, *Srbija*, 169–179; Mijatović, *Servia and the Servians*, 66, 98.
14. Erlich, *Family in Transition*, 60–67, 229–232; Božinović, *Žensko pitanje*, 25–26; Karić, *Srbija*, 158.
15. Popović, *Beograd*, 376–379.
16. Erlich, *Family in Transition*, 156–159, 197–206.
17. Radmila Radić, *Narodna verovanja, religija i spiritizam u srpskom drustvu 19. i u prvoj polovini 20. veka*, Institut za noviju istoriju Srbije, 2009, 34.
18. 'Smoking rates by country 2022 ', World Population Review, https://worldpopulation review.com/country-rankings/smoking-rates-by-country, accessed 9 April 2022.
19. Radić, *Narodna verovanja*, 40–77.
20. Grafenauer et al., *Istorija Naroda Jugoslavije*, v2, 752–756.
21. Valentina Izmirlieva, 'Christian hajjis: The other Orthodox pilgrims to Jerusalem', *Slavic Review*, 73, 2 (Summer 2014), 322–346.
22. Tričković, *Beogradski pašaluk*, 220–221.
23. Zirojević, *Srbija pod turskom vlašću*, 260.
24. Janković, *Srpska država prvog ustanka*, 50–51.
25. Vladimir Stojančević, 'Karadjordje and Serbia in his time', in Vucinich, *First Serbian Uprising*, 29.
26. Ibid., 48.
27. Stanford J. Shaw, 'The Ottoman Empire and the Serbian Uprising, 1804–1807', in Vucinich, *First Serbian Uprising*, 72–74.
28. Škrivanić, 'Armed forces in Karadjordje's Serbia', 318–319.
29. Janković, *Srpska država prvog ustanka*, 46.
30. Ekmečić, *Stvaranje Jugoslavije*, v1, 93–94.
31. Shaw, 'Ottoman Empire and the Serbian Uprising', 74–75.
32. Prota Mateja Nenadović, *Memoari*, Rad, 1980, 112.
33. Vukičević, *Karađorđe*, v1, 224–231.
34. Sućeska, *Ajani*, 100.
35. Radoš Ljušić, *Vožd Karađorđe: Biografija*, Zavod za udžbenike i nastavna sredstva, 2005, 12–14.

36. Ibid., 16–23.
37. Vukičević, *Karađorđe*, v1, 47–58.
38. Ljušić, *Vožd Karađorđe*, 30–34.
39. Janicije Đurić, 'Skupština u Orašcu', in Miodrag Maticki, ed., *Čitanka Prvog srpskog ustanka*, Čigoja, 2004, 86.
40. Petrovich, 'Serbian Orthodox Church in the First Serbian Uprising', 269.
41. Shaw, 'Ottoman Empire and the Serbian Uprising', 77–78.
42. Ekmečić, *Stvaranje Jugoslavije*, v1, 97.
43. Ljušić, *Vožd Karađorđe*, 68–69.
44. Vladimir Stojančević, *Miloš Obrenović i njegovo doba*, Prosveta, 1966, 25–26.
45. Alexander Christie-Miller, 'Ada Kaleh: The story of an island', *The White Review*, no. 17 (June 2016); Ljušić, *Vožd*, 73–74.
46. Shaw, 'Ottoman Empire and the Serbian Uprising', 80–81.
47. Janković, *Srpska država prvog ustanka*, 95–104.
48. Ljušić, *Vožd Karađorđe*, 109–113.
49. Janković, *Srpska država prvog ustanka*, 263–264, 271.
50. Ljušić, *Vožd Karađorđe*, 116–123.
51. Škrivanić, 'Armed forces in Karadjordje's Serbia', 309–312; Ekmečić, *Stvaranje Jugoslavije*, v1, 102.
52. Petrovich, 'Serbian Orthodox Church in the First Serbian Uprising', 265–279.
53. Nenadović, *Memoari*, 202.
54. Ljušić, *Vožd Karađorđe*, 141–145.
55. Petrovich, *Modern Serbia*, v1, 49.
56. Vukičević, *Karađorđe*, v2, 1912, 448.
57. Nenadović, *Memoari*, 207.
58. Muhamed Hadžijahić, *Od tradicija do identiteta: Geneza nacionlnog pitanja bosanskih Muslimana*, Svjetlost, 1974, 154–155.
59. Ranke, *Servian Revolution*, 177–179.
60. Wayne S. Vucinich, 'Russia and the First Serbian Uprising', in Vucinich, *First Serbian Uprising*, 102–104; Shaw, 'Ottoman Empire', 84–87; Ljušić, *Vožd Karađorđe*, 165.
61. Vukičević, *Karađorđe*, v2, 468.
62. Popović, *Beograd*, 316–318, 412; Ženi Lebl, *Do "konačnog resenja": Jevreji u Beogradu, 1521–1942*, Čigoja, 2001, 71–73.
63. Janković, *Srpska država prvog ustanka*, 260–261.
64. Vukičević, *Karađorđe*, v2, 468–470.
65. Popović, *Beograd*, 316.
66. Safet Bandžović, 'Muslimani u Smederevskom sandžaku: Progoni i pribježišta (1804–1862)', in Mirsad Arnautalić, ed., *150 godina od protjerivanja muslimana iz Kneževine Srbije*, Medžlis Islamske zajednice Orašje, 2013, 21.
67. Miodrag Popović, *Vuk Stef. Karadžić*, 2nd ed., Polit, 1972, 31.
68. Gavrilović, *Miloš Obrenović*, v2, 717; Radoš Ljušić, *Ljubavi srpskih vladara i političara*, IP Zograf, 2000, 22.

69. Ljušić, *Vožd Karađorđe*, 184.
70. Ibid., 182–191.
71. Ibid., 196–202.
72. Ibid., 208–220.
73. Ibid., 233.
74. Milan Stepanović, 'Jovan Savić, Ivan Jugović: Osnivač Velike Škole u Beogradu i utemeljitelj visokog školstva u Srba', *Norma*, XIII, 1–2 (2008), 211–232.
75. Petrovich, *Modern Serbia*, v1, 49.
76. Ljušić, *Vožd Karađorđe*, 225–227.
77. Janković, *Srpska država prvog ustanka*, 158–159.
78. Ljušić, *Vožd Karađorđe*, 237–239.
79. Ekmečić, *Stvaranje Jugoslavije*, v1, 153.
80. Škrivanić, 'Armed forces in Karadjordje's Serbia', 314–318.
81. Ekmečić, *Stvaranje Jugoslavije*, v1, 141.
82. Ljušić, *Vožd Karađorđe*, 254–265.
83. Ljušić, *Ljubavi srpskih vladara*, 23.
84. Ljušić, *Vožd Karađorđe*, 271–272; Ekmečić, *Stvaranje Jugoslavije*, v1, 148–149.
85. Janković, *Srpska država prvog ustanka*, 166.
86. Ljušić, *Vožd Karađorđe*, 341–346.
87. Stojančević et al., *Istorija srpskog naroda*, v5.1, 73.
88. Ljušić, *Vožd Karađorđe*, 375.
89. Janković, *Srpska država prvog ustanka*, 254–256.
90. Ibid., 187–188.
91. Stojančević, *Miloš Obrenović*, 47.
92. Oto Dubislav Pirh, *Putovanje po Srbiji u godine 1829*, Prosveta, 1983, 44–45.
93. Čubrilović, *Istorija političke misli*, 101.
94. Gavrilović, *Miloš Obrenović*, v1, 1908, 51.
95. Janković, *Srpska država prvog ustanka*, 262.
96. Ljušić, *Vožd Karađorđe*, 429–430.
97. Stojančević, 'Karadjordje and Serbia in his time', 35.
98. Stojančević, *Miloš Obrenović*, 18–27.
99. Gavrilović, *Miloš Obrenović*, v1, 322–325.
100. Ibid., 54-55; Stojančević, *Miloš Obrenović*, 34–36.
101. Gavrilović, *Miloš Obrenović*, v1, 65.
102. Ibid., 116–117.
103. Ibid., 86–92.
104. Ibid., 95–97.
105. Ranke, *Servian Revolution*, 302.
106. Gavrilović, *Miloš Obrenović*, v1, 100–107.
107. Ibid., 132–134.
108. Stojančević, *Miloš Obrenović*, 52–58.
109. Ibid., 60–63; Petrovich, *Modern Serbia*, v1, 94–95.

110. Gavrilović, *Miloš Obrenović*, v1, 190–191.
111. Ibid., 233.
112. Ibid., 230.
113. Stojančević, *Miloš Obrenović*, 64–69.
114. Ibid., 70–73.
115. Norris, *Belgrade*, 38.
116. Radoš Ljušić, *Srpska državnost 19. veka*, Srpska književna zadruga, 2008, 56.
117. Ekmečić, *Stvaranje Jugoslavia*, v1, 77.
118. Slijepčević, *Istorija SPC*, v2, 199.
119. Gavrilović, *Miloš Obrenović*, v2, 260–262.
120. Ekmečić, *Stvaranje Jugoslavije*, v1, 239.
121. Gavrilović, *Miloš Obrenović*, v3, 1912, 189.
122. Čubrilović, *Istorija političke misli*, 249–255, 289–297.

3. PRINCE MILOŠ AND THE FOUNDING OF MODERN SERBIA

1. Gavrilović, *Miloš Obrenović*, v1, 312–317.
2. Stojančević, *Miloš Obrenović*, 90–100.
3. Gavrilović, *Miloš Obrenović*, v1, 359.
4. Popović, *O Cincarima*, 256.
5. Ljušić, *Vožd Karađorđe*, 468.
6. Radomir J. Popović, *Toma Vučić-Perišić*, Istorijski Institute and Službeni glasnik, 2003, 28.
7. Ljušić, *Vožd Karađorđe*, 468–469.
8. Ekmečić, *Stvaranje Jugoslavije*, v1, 211–212.
9. Ljušić, *Ljubavi srpskih vladara*, 61–64.
10. Petrovich, *Modern Serbia*, v1, 209.
11. Ljušić, *Ljubavi srpskih vladara*, 83.
12. Ibid., 64–66.
13. Gavrilović, *Miloš Obrenović*, v1, 718–719.
14. Pirh, *Putovanje po Srbiji*, 78.
15. Božinović, *Žensko pitanje*, 25.
16. Ljušić, *Ljubavi srpskih vladara*, 47.
17. Stojančević, *Miloš Obrenović*, 439–440.
18. Ljušić, *Ljubavi srpskih vladara*, 34.
19. Čubrilović, *Istorija političke misli*, 123.
20. Slobodan Jovanović, *Ustavobranitelj i njihova vlada*, BIGZ, 1990, 49–50.
21. Stojančević, *Miloš Obrenović*, 106–114; Petrovich, *Modern Serbia*, v1, 197–198.
22. Stojančević, *Miloš Obrenović*, 114–120.
23. Gavrilović, *Miloš Obrenović*, v1, 323–325.
24. Stojančević, *Miloš Obrenović*, 74–84.
25. Gavrilović, *Miloš Obrenović*, v1, 264.

26. Gavrilović, *Miloš Obrenović*, v2, 445–446.
27. Gavrilović, *Miloš Obrenović*, v1, 384–385.
28. Ibid., 494.
29. Gavrilović, *Miloš Obrenović*, v2, 503–504.
30. Stojančević, *Miloš Obrenović*, 204–205; Božinović, *Žensko pitanje*, 26.
31. Ljušić, *Kneževina Srbija*, 248.
32. Stojančević, *Miloš Obrenović*, 126–128.
33. Ljušić, *Kneževina Srbija*, 103.
34. Branislav Krivokapić, 'Obrenović branio pušenje', *Blic*, 6 June 2010.
35. Gavrilović, *Miloš Obrenović*, v2, 508.
36. Stojančević, *Miloš Obrenović*, 121–122.
37. Gavrilović, *Miloš Obrenović*, v2, 511.
38. Ibid., 575–577.
39. Vasilije Krestić, 'Knez Miloš Obrenović i Đakova buna', in Vasilije Krestić, *Iz istorije Srba i srpsko-hrvatskih odnosa*, BIGZ, 1994, 26, 36–37.
40. Ranke, *Servian Revolution*, 358–359.
41. Krestić, 'Knez Miloš Obrenović i Đakova buna', 39.
42. Popović, *Toma Vučić-Perišić*, 34–38; Krestić, 'Knez Miloš Obrenović i Đakova buna', 38–39, 42–43.
43. Stojančević, *Miloš Obrenović*, 128–129.
44. Života Đorđević, *Srpska narodna vojska 1861–1864*, Narodna knjiga, 1984, 9.
45. Krestić, 'Knez Miloš Obrenović i Đakova buna', 52.
46. Stojančević, *Miloš Obrenović*, 130–131.
47. Krestić, 'Knez Miloš Obrenović i Đakova buna', 56–60, 65–66.
48. Ibid., 72–76.
49. Gavrilović, *Miloš Obrenović*, v2, 559–560.
50. Milan V. Petković, *Srpski obaveštajci od plunkiste Radovana do pukovnika Apisa*, Gutenbergova Galaksija, 2003, 164.
51. Popović, *Toma Vučić-Perišić*, 50–51.
52. Gavrilović, *Miloš Obrenović*, v2, 164–175.
53. Ljušić, *Kneževina Srbija*, 209–210.
54. Gavrilović, *Miloš Obrenović*, v2, 233–243.
55. Stojančević, *Miloš Obrenović*, 144–147.
56. Gavrilović, *Miloš Obrenović*, v3, 557–559.
57. Gavrilović, *Miloš Obrenović*, v2, 158–162.
58. Gavrilović, *Miloš Obrenović*, v3, 298–299.
59. Ljušić, *Kneževina Srbija*, 291–292; Karić, *Srbija*, 484–487.
60. Gavrilović, *Miloš Obrenović*, v3, 604–607.
61. Stojančević, *Miloš Obrenović*, 148–150.
62. Popović, *Toma Vučić-Perišić*, 116–117, 170–171.
63. Popović, *Beograd*, 440–442, 462.
64. Gavrilović, *Miloš Obrenović*, v3, 332–350.

65. Ahmed S. Aličić, *Pokret za autonomiju Bosne od 1831. do 1832. godine*, Orijentalni Institut u Sarajevu, 1996, 184–187.
66. Gavrilović, *Miloš Obrenović*, v3, 351–372.
67. Stojančević, *Miloš Obrenović*, 153.
68. Gavrilović, *Miloš Obrenović*, v3, 420–434.
69. Ljušić, *Srpska državnost*, 31.
70. Ibid., 315–320.
71. Ljušić, *Kneževina Srbija*, 48–49.
72. Gavrilović, *Miloš Obrenović*, v3, 614–615.
73. Popović, *Toma Vučić-Perišić*, 61–69; Ljušić, *Srpska državnost*, 52.
74. Petrovich, *Modern Serbia*, v1, 105–106.
75. Stojančević, *Miloš Obrenović*, 180–186.
76. Ljušić, *Kneževina Srbija*, 76–78.
77. Ibid., 178–190, 277–278; Tomasevich, *Peasants*, 186.
78. Petrovich, *Modern Serbia*, v1, 171.
79. Ljušić, *Kneževina Srbija*, 303.
80. Ibid., 331–332.
81. Stojančević, *Miloš Obrenović*, 200, 379.
82. Gavrilović, *Miloš Obrenović*, v2, 254.
83. Stevan K. Pavlowitch, *Anglo-Russian Rivalry in Serbia, 1837–1839: The Mission of Colonel Hodges*, Mouton and Co., 1961, 189; Slobodan Jovanović, *Vlada Milana Obrenovića*, v2, BIGZ, 1990, 68.
84. Pavlowitch, *Anglo-Russian Rivalry*, 34.
85. Ljušić, *Kneževina Srbija*, 56–57.
86. Radoš Ljušić, Slađana Bojković, Miloje Pršić and Božidar Jovović, *Oficiri u visokom školstvu u Srbije 1804–1918.*, Vojnoizdavački zavod, 2000, 203–209.
87. Ekmečić, *Stvaranje Jugoslavije*, v1, 239.
88. Petrovich, *Modern Serbia*, v1, 114–119, 205–206.
89. Krestić, 'Knez Miloš Obrenović i Đakova buna', 67–68.
90. Ljušić, *Oficiri u visokom školstvu*, 209–217.
91. Đorđević, *Srpska narodna vojska*, 9–10.
92. Živomir Spasić, *Kragujevačka vojna fabrika 1853–1953*, Vojnoizdavački zavod, 1973, 14–15.
93. Petrovich, *Modern Serbia*, v1, 206–208; Radić, *Narodna verovanja*, 34.
94. Đorđević, *Srpska narodna vojska*, 7–8.
95. Petrovich, *Modern Serbia*, v1, 217–222.
96. Ibid., 190–191, 195–196; Pavlowitch, *Anglo-Russian Rivalry*, 31; Ljušić, *Kneževina Srbija*, 242–243.
97. Gavrilović, *Miloš Obrenović*, v2, 660–661.
98. Slijepčević, *Istorija SPC*, v2, 306–308.
99. Ibid., 321–322.
100. Ibid., 316–318.

101. Norris, *Belgrade*, 44.
102. Petrovich, *Modern Serbia*, v1, 213–216.
103. Slijepčević, *Istorija SPC*, 2, 337.
104. Ljušić, *Kneževina Srbija*, 72–73, 79.
105. Ibid., 333.
106. Žanin-Čalić, *Socijalna istorija*, 43; Stojančević et al., *Istorija srpskog naroda*, v5.1, 140.
107. Gavrilović, *Miloš Obrenović*, v3, 605–606.
108. Stavrianos, *Balkans Since 1453*, 340–341.
109. Popović, *Toma Vučić-Perišić*, 61.
110. Ljušić, *Kneževina Srbija*, 193–194.
111. Leposava Cvijetić, 'Popis stanovništva i imovine u Srbiji 1834 godine', *Miscellanea*, 13, 1984, 11–12.
112. Ljušić, *Kneževina Srbija*, 223–233.
113. David Urquhart, *England, France, Russia and Turkey*, 5th ed. (Kindle), J. Ridgway, 1835, location 1140.
114. Ekmečić, *Stvaranje Jugoslavije*, v1, 224–228, 470–475.
115. Alphonse de Lamartine, *Voyage en Orient 1832–1833*, Librairie de Charles Gosselin, 1843, 304–306.
116. Vuk Stefanović Karadžić, 'Vuk Karadžić Milošu Obrenoviću, Zemun, 24. april 1832.', in Golub Dobrašinović, ed., *Sabrana dela Vuka Karadžića*, 23, *Prepiska IV (1829–1832)*, Prosveta, 1988, 654, 665.
117. Ljušić, *Kneževina Srbija*, 113–117.
118. Popović, *Toma Vučić-Perišić*, 71.
119. Mirjana Marinković, *Turska kancelarija kneza Miloša Obrenovića*, Istorijski institut Srpske akademije nauka i umetnosti, 1999, 29.
120. Popović, *Toma Vučić-Perišić*, 45–46; Ljušić, *Ljubavi srpskih vladara*, 33.
121. Božinović, *Žensko pitanje*, 26.
122. Pavlowitch, *Anglo-Russian Rivalry*, 33.
123. Stojančević, *Miloš Obrenović*, 276–277.
124. Ljušić, *Kneževina Srbija*, 114–127.
125. Popović, *Toma Vučić-Perišić*, 71–75; Ljušić, *Kneževina Srbija*, 127–128.
126. Ljušić, *Kneževina Srbija*, 132–133.
127. Ekmečić, *Stvaranje Jugoslavije*, v1, 230.
128. Miodrag Radojević, ed., *Srpski ustavi od 1835. do 1990. godine sa ustavima Kraljevine SHS I Kraljevine Jugoslavije*, Gramatik, 2004, 31–43.
129. Ljušić, *Kneževina Srbija*, 137–150.
130. Ibid., 215–216.
131. Ibid., 53, 65–71.
132. Petrovich, *Modern Serbia*, v1, 186.
133. Ljušić, *Kneževina Srbija*, 57.
134. Ibid., 273.
135. Gavrilović, *Miloš Obrenović*, v3, 527–528; Ljušić, *Kneževina Srbija*, 280.

136. Gavrilović, *Miloš Obrenović*, v3, 530.
137. Ljušić, *Kneževina Srbija*, 293–294.
138. Marinković, *Turska kancelarija*, 147.
139. Stojančević, *Miloš Obrenović*, 363–364.
140. Pavlowitch, *Anglo-Russian Rivalry*, 38–40.
141. Ibid., 173.
142. Ibid., 128–150.
143. Ljušić, *Kneževina Srbija*, 270.
144. Ibid., 184.
145. Ibid., 188–191.
146. Radojević, *Srpski ustavi*, 55–67; Radoš Ljušić, *Prvo namesništvo, (1839–1840)*, Prosveta, 1995, 52–64.
147. Ljušić, *Kneževina Srbija*, 57.
148. Petrovich, *Modern Serbia*, v1, 279.
149. Jovanović, *Ustavobranitelji*, 27–28; Ljušić, *Kneževina Srbija*, 209–213.
150. Jovanović, *Ustavobranitelji*,121–129.
151. Đorđević, *Srpska narodna vojska*, 10.
152. Popović, *Toma Vučić-Perišić*, 101–102.
153. Ibid., 106.
154. Ljušić, *Prvo namesništvo*, 29–30.
155. Đorđević, *Srpska narodna vojska*, 10–11; Ljušić, *Kneževina Srbija*, 253–254.
156. Petrovich, *Modern Serbia*, v1, 208–209.
157. Stojančević, *Miloš Obrenović*, 460.
158. Nebojša Jovanović, *Dvor Kneza Aleksandra Karađorđevića 1841–1858*, Laguna, 2010, 13.

4. THE CONSTITUTIONALIST ERA

1. Stojančević et al., *Istorjia srpskog naroda*, v5.1, 252–255.
2. Ljušić, *Prvo namesništvo*, 75.
3. Ibid., 40–46.
4. Jovanović, *Dvor Kneza Aleksandra*, 37–49.
5. Ljušić, *Prvo namesništvo*, 130–131.
6. Ibid., 40, 143–145.
7. Ibid., 154.
8. Radoš Ljušić, *Knjiga o Načertaniju: nacionalni i državni program Kneževine Srbija (1844)*, Beletra, 2004, 104–106.
9. Stojančević et al.,*Istorjia srpskog naroda*, v5-1, 255–256; Radoš Ljušić, *Kneginja Ljubica*, SO Gornji Milanovac, Muzej Rudničko-takovskog kraja and Dečje novine, 1997, 150–151.
10. Popović, *Toma Vučić-Perišić*, 128–129.
11. Petar Milosavljević, 'Vlada Ustavobranitelja (1838–1858)', in Čubrilović, ed., *Istorija Beograda*, v2, 116–121; Ranke, *History of Servia and the Servian Revolution*, 435.

12. Stojančević et al., *Istorija srpskog naroda*, v5.1, 242–246.
13. Ibid., 255–260; Stojančević, *Miloš Obrenović*, 421–422; Ljušić, *Kneginja Ljubica*, 151–153.
14. Popović, *Toma Vučić-Perišić*, 135–140.
15. Ibid., 140–143.
16. Ibid., 117–118.
17. David MacKenzie, *Ilija Garašanin: Balkan Bismarck*, East European Monographs, 1985, 19.
18. Nikola Hristić, *Memoari 1840–1862*, Prosveta, 2006, 54.
19. Ranke, *Servian Revolution*, 440–441; Stojančević et al., *Istorjia srpskog naroda*, v5.1, 259.
20. Hristić, *Memoari*, 51.
21. Đorđević, *Srpska narodna vojska*, 12.
22. Popović, *Toma Vučić-Perišić*, 146–151.
23. Hristić, *Memoari*, 65–66.
24. Popović, *Toma Vučić-Perišić*, 155–162.
25. Ljušić, *Knjiga o Načertaniju*, 79–80.
26. MacKenzie, *Ilija Garašanin*, 9–15.
27. Jovanović, *Ustavobranitelji*, 26, 33–34.
28. Ljušić, *Knjiga o Načertaniju*, 114.
29. Dragoljub Živojinović, *Kralj Petar I Karađorđević: u ignanstvu 1844–1903. godine*, v1, 2nd ed., Zavod za udžbenike, 2009, 5.
30. Jovan Avakumović, *Memoari*, Izdavačka knjižarnica Zorana Stojanovića, 2008, 13–14.
31. Jovanović, *Dvor Kneza Aleksandra*, 14, 73.
32. Michael Palairet, *The Balkan Economies c.1800–1914: Evolution without Development*, Cambridge University Press, 1997, 91–99; 109–110; Ljušić, *Srpska državnost*, 46.
33. Žanin-Čalić, *Socijalna istorija*, 43.
34. Petrovich, *Modern Serbia*, v1, 280–281, 342–343.
35. Ekmečić, *Stvaranje Jugoslavije*, v1, 209, 233–234.
36. Karić, *Srbija*, 223.
37. Vladan Đorđević, *Uspomene*, Nolit, 1988, 362, 366–367.
38. Popović, *Vuk Stef. Karadžić*, 342.
39. Ekmečić, *Stvaranje Jugoslavije*, v1, 239; Popović, *Beograd*, 376–380; Jovanović, *Dvor Kneza Aleksandra*, 163–165.
40. Jovanović, *Dvor Kneza Aleksandra*, 166–167.
41. Ibid., 61–63.
42. Ibid., 68.
43. Ibid., 287–293; Živojinović, *Kralj Petar*, v1, 7.
44. Jovanović, *Dvor Kneza Aleksandra*, 17.
45. Ibid., 68, 99, 171–174.
46. Božinović, *Žensko pitanje*, 30–33.
47. Jovanović, *Dvor Kneza Aleksandra*, 259–260.

48. Radojević, *Srpski ustavi*, 63–64.
49. Jovanović, *Ustavobranitelji*, 50–51.
50. Ibid., 66–67; Božinović, *Žensko pitanje*, 56.
51. Gale Stokes, *Legitimacy Through Liberalism: Vladimir Jovanović and the Transformation of Serbian Politics*, University of Washington Press, 1975, 6.
52. Pavlowitch, *Anglo-Russian Rivalry*, 36, 66; Ljušić, *Kneževina Srbija*, 232–242.
53. Žanin-Čalić, *Socijalna istorija*, 40; Stoianovich, *Balkan Worlds*, 255–256.
54. Jasmina B. Milanović, *Žensko društvo (1875–1942)*, ISI, 2020, 22.
55. Jovanović, *Ustavobranitelji*, 35–37.
56. Slijepčević, *Istorija SPC*, v2, 333.
57. Melek Hanum, *Thirty Years in the Harem, or, The Autobiography of Melek Hanum of Kibrizli-Mehemet-pasha*, Chapman and Hall, 1872, 133–150; Jovanović, *Dvor Kneza Aleksandra*, 305–306.
58. Hristić, *Memoari*, 179–186, 201–210; Kosta Hristić, *Zapisi starog beograđanin*, Nolit, 1989, 56–57.
59. Jovanović, *Ustavobranitelji*, 199, 206–207.
60. Ekmečić, *Stvaranje Jugoslavije*, v1, 242, 441.
61. Petrovich, *Modern Serbia*, v1, 191–192.
62. Popović, *Vuk Stef. Karadžić*, 26.
63. Slavko Gavrilović, Vasilije Krestić, Andrija Radenić, Kosta Milutinović, Pavle Ivić, Jovan Kašić, Dragiša Živković and Dejan Medaković, *Istorija srpskog naroda*, v5.2, Srpska književna zadruga, 1981, 311–335.
64. Vuk Karadžić, *Pjesnarica 1814–1815*, Prosveta, 1965, 39.
65. Popović, *Vidovdan i časni krst*, 107–126.
66. Milord Ekmečić, 'The emergence of St Vitus's Day as the principal national holiday of the Serbs', in Vucinich and Emmert, *Kosovo*, 334–336; Malcolm, *Kosovo*, 79–80.
67. Karadžić, 'Vuk Karadžić Milošu Obrenoviću, 24. april 1832.', 660.
68. Petrovich, *Modern Serbia*, v1, 192.
69. Wilson, *Life and Times of Karadžić*, 304–305.
70. Popović, *Vuk Stef. Karadžić*, 397.
71. Svetozar Marković, 'Dopis iz Beograda', in *Celokupna dela*, v1, Narodna knjiga, 1987, 206.
72. Popović, *Beograd*, 410–411.
73. Popović, *Vuk Stef. Karadžić*, 213.
74. Ibid., 235–236.
75. Ibid., 34.
76. Ibid., 108.
77. Dositej Obradović, *Pismo Haralampiju*, Antologija Srpske Književnosti, 2009, 4–5.
78. Ivo Banac, *The National Question in Yugoslavia: Origins, History, Politics*, Cornell University Press, 1984, 79–82.
79. Ivo Banac, 'The Confessional "rule" and the Dubrovnik exception: The origins of the "Serb Catholic" circle in nineteenth-century Dalmatia', *Slavic Review*, 42, 3 (Autumn 1983), 452–453.

80. Popović, *Vuk Stef. Karadžić*, 296.
81. Ibid., 303.
82. Vuk Stefanović Karadžić, 'Srbi svi i svuda', in Filipović, ed., *Etnografski spisi*, 31–32.
83. Popović, *Vuk Stef. Karadžić*, 359–360.
84. Vuk Stefanović Karadžić, 'Srbi i Hrvati', in Miodrag Maticki and Boško Suvajdžić, eds, *Sabrana dela Vuka Karadžića*, v14.2, *O jeziku i književnosti III/2*, Prosveta, 2014, 283.
85. Srdja Pavlović, *Balkan Anschluss: The Annexation of Montenegro and the Creation of the Common South Slavic State*, Purdue University Press, 2008, 48–51.
86. Popović, *Vuk Stef. Karadžić*, 297–298.
87. Petar Petrović-Njegoš, *Gorski vijenac*, Svjetlost, Sarajevo, 1973, 95; translation courtesy of Vasa D. Mihailovich, Project Rastko, https://www.rastko.rs/knjizevnost/umetnicka/njegos/mountain_wreath.html, downloaded 22 March 2022.
88. Gavrilović, *Istorija srpskog naroda*, v5.2, 354.
89. Ljušić, *Knjiga o Načertaniju*, 64.
90. Ibid., 85.
91. Banac, 'Confessional "rule" and the Dubrovnik exception', 456.
92. Ekmečić, *Stvaranje Jugoslavije*, v1, 474–475.
93. Ibid., 478–479.
94. Banac, 'Confessional "rule" and the Dubrovnik exception', 459.
95. Ljušić, *Knjiga o Načertaniju*, 88–89.
96. Ekmečić, *Stvaranje Jugoslavije*, v1, 472–473.
97. Ljušić, *Knjiga o Načertaniju*, 115.
98. Banac, *National Question*, 83–84.
99. Ekmečić, *Stvaranje Jugoslavije*, v1, 369, 479–484.
100. Ilija Garašanin, *Načertanije*, Studio 104, 1998, 71–75, 93.
101. Ibid., 75; Ljušić, *Knjiga o Načertaniju*, 118–119.
102. Garašanin, *Načertanije*, 94–101.
103. Dušan T. Bataković, *The Foreign Policy of Serbia (1844–1867): Ilija Garašanin's Načertanije*, Institute for Balkan Studies and Serbian Academy of Sciences and Arts, 2014, 153, 192–196.
104. Popović, *Vuk Stef. Karadžić*, 367–369, 379.
105. Spasić, *Kragujevačka vojna fabrika*, 16.
106. MacKenzie, *Ilija Garašanin*, 64.
107. Jovan Milinković-Alavantić, *Katanska buna u Šapcu 1844. godine*, Srpska štamparija dra Svetozara Miletića, 1889, 114.
108. Petrovich, *Modern Serbia*, v1, 223–230.
109. Lebl, *Do "konačnog resenja"*, 77–81.
110. Popović, *Beograd*, 413.
111. Nebojša Popović, *Jevreji u Srbiji 1918–1941*, Institut za Savremenu Istoriju, 1997, 17; Milan Koljanin, *Jevreji i antisemitizam u Kraljevini Jugoslaviji*, Institut za Savremenu Istoriju, 2008, 164; Milan Ristović, 'The Jews of Serbia (1804–1918): From princely protection to formal emancipation', in Tullia Catalan and Marco Dogo, eds, *The*

Jews and the Nation-States of Southeastern Europe from the 19th Century to the Great Depression: Combining Viewpoints on a Controversial Story, Cambridge Scholars Publishing, 2016, 27–28; Lebl, *Do "konačnog resenja"*, 81–97; Philip J. Cohen, *Serbia's Secret War: Propaganda and the Deceit of History*, Texas A&M University Press, 1996, 65.

112. Ekmečić, *Stvaranje Jugoslavije*, v1, 508–509.
113. Ibid., 511.
114. Ljušić, *Knjiga o Načertaniju*, 126–137, 224–228.
115. Damir Agačić, *Tajna politika Srbije u XIX. stoljeću*, AGM, 1994, 68–69.
116. Ibid., 72–106; Popović, *Toma Vučić-Perišić*, 193–194.
117. Vasilije Krestić and Radoš Ljušić, eds, *Programi i statuti srpskih političkih stranaka do 1918. godine*, Književne novine, 1991, 11–12.
118. Magaš, *Croatia Through History*, 195–196.
119. Stojančević et al., *Istorija srpskog naroda*, v5.1, 277.
120. Ivan T. Berend, *History Derailed: Central and Eastern Europe in the Long Nineteenth Century*, University of California Press, 2003, 113; Stavrianos, *The Balkans since 1453*, 265.
121. Dimitrije Boarov, *Politička istorija Vojvodine u trideset tri priloga*, CUP, 2001, 56–57.
122. Čubrilović, *Istorija političke misli*, 212–216.
123. Jovan Ristić, *Istoriski spisi*, Srpska književna zadruga, 1940, 32.
124. Jaša Prodanović, *Ustavni razvitak i ustavne borbe u Srbiji*, Geca Kon, n.d., 110–114.
125. Stojančević et al., *Istorjia srpskog naroda*, v5.1, 275.
126. Živan Živanović, *Politička istorija Srbije u drugoj polovini devetnaestog veka*, v1, Izdavačka knjižarnica Gece Kona, 1923, 25; Petrovich, *Modern Serbia*, v1, 279.
127. Agačić, *Tajna politika Srbije*, 51–52.
128. Popović, *Toma Vučić-Perišić*, 195–210.
129. Nenad Urić, 'Dobrovoljci iz Srbije i srpski pokret u Ugarskoj 1848–1849', in Petar Kačavenda, ed., *Dobrovoljci u oslobodilačkim ratovima Srba i Crnogoraca*, Institut za Savremenu Istoriju, 1996, 13.
130. Petrovich, *Modern Serbia*, v1, 239–245.
131. Urić, 'Dobrovoljci iz Srbije', 17.
132. Ibid., 16–19; Stojančević et al., *Istorija srpskog naroda*, v5.1, 279.
133. Ekmečić, *Stvaranje Jugoslavije*, v1, 654.
134. Hristić, *Zapisi starog beograđanin*, 516–517.
135. MacKenzie, *Ilija Garašanin*, 108–109; Ristić, *Istoriski spisi*, 61–63.
136. Spasić, *Kragujevačka vojna fabrika*, 17–23; Ljušić, *Oficiri u visokom školstvu*, 219–224.
137. Petrovich, *Modern Serbia*, v1, 247.
138. Morrison, *Montenegro*, 24–25; Roberts, *Realm of the Black Mountain*, 217–218.
139. Dušan Berić, *Ustanak u Hercegovini 1852–1862*, Srpska Akademija Nauka i Umjetnosti, 1994, 276–279.
140. MacKenzie, *Ilija Garašanin*, 123–124.
141. Spasić, *Kragujevačka vojna fabrika*, 23–47.

142. MacKenzie, *Ilija Garašanin*, 152.
143. Draga Vuksanović-Anić, *Stvaranje moderne srpske vojske: Francuski uticaj na njenoj formiranje*, Vojnoizdavački i novinski centar, 1993, 35–37; Hristić, *Memoari*, 356.
144. MacKenzie, *Ilija Garašanin*, 150; Ristić, *Istoriski spisi*, 128–131.
145. MacKenzie, *Ilija Garašanin*, 146.
146. Đorđević, *Srpska narodna vojska*, 15.
147. Jovanović, *Ustavobranitelji*, 129–133.
148. Ibid., 138–150.
149. Hristić, *Zapisi starog beogradanin*, 52.
150. MacKenzie, *Ilija Garašanin*, 166, 174.
151. Ćorović, *Istorija Jugoslavije*, 505–506.
152. Jovanović, *Dvor Kneza Aleksandra*, 203–204.
153. Hristić, *Memoari*, 228–244; Hristić, *Zapisi starog beogradanin*, 42.
154. Jovanović, *Dvor Kneza Aleksandra*, 325–326.
155. Hristić, *Memoari*, 248–249.
156. Jovanović, *Ustavobranitelji*, 183.
157. Ibid., 195–196.

5. THE NATIONAL LIBERATION STRUGGLE RESUMES

1. Stokes, *Legitimacy Through Liberalism*, 3; Ljušić, *Prvo namesništvo*, 95–96.
2. Ekmečić, *Stvaranje Jugoslavije*, v1, 244.
3. Petrovich, *Modern Serbia*, v1, 285.
4. Jovanović, *Ustavobranitelji*, 74.
5. Stokes, *Legitimacy Through Liberalism*, 6–13.
6. Jovanović, *Ustavobranitelji*, 76.
7. Jovan Milićević, *Jevrem Grujić: Istorijat svetoandrejskog liberalizma*, Nolit, 1964, 10–13, 64–68.
8. Jovan Ristić, *Poslednja godina spoljašnje politike Kneza Mihaila*, Prosveta, 1895, 8.
9. Milićević, *Jevrem Grujić*, 40–45.
10. Milovan Janković and Jevrem Grujić, *Slaves du sud, ou le peuple Serbe avec les Croates et les Bulgares, apercu de leur vie historique, politique et sociale*, Libraire de A. Franck, 1853, 18, 38, 44–45, 125–129, 131.
11. Jovanović, *Ustavobranitelji*, 199, 206–207.
12. Slobodan Jovanović, *Vlada Milana Obrenovića*, v1, BIGZ, 1990, 40.
13. Ljušić, *Knjiga o Načertaniju*, 111.
14. Vladimir Jovanović, *Uspomene*, BIGZ, 1988, 18–19.
15. Ibid., 33–37.
16. Milićević, *Jevrem Grujić*, 8–13.
17. Ljušić, *Ljubavi srpskih vladara*, 68–69.
18. Alimpije Vasiljević, *Moje uspomene*, Srpska književska zadruga, 1990, 72.
19. Popović, *Toma Vučić-Perišić*, 131, 143, 150.

20. MacKenzie, *Ilija Garašanin*, 188.
21. Jovanović, *Ustavobranitelji*, 212-214.
22. Ibid., 238-241.
23. Hristić, *Memoari*, 277.
24. Andrija Radenić, ed., *Svetoandrejska skupština*, Naučno delo, 1964, 228-229.
25. Ibid., 203-204.
26. Vladimir Stojančević, 'Politička istorija 1830-1839', in Čubrilović, *Istorija Beograda*, v2, 96.
27. Jevrem Grujić, *Zapisi*, v2, Srpska kraljevska akademija, 1923, 107.
28. Jovanović, *Ustavobranitelji*, 242-259; MacKenzie, *Ilija Garašanin*, 194-210.
29. Jovanović, *Dvor Kneza Aleksandra*, 344-346.
30. Jovanović, *Ustavobranitelji*, 217-218.
31. Slobodan Jovanović, *Druga vlada Miloša i Mihaila*, BIGZ, 1990, 276-278; Janko Nicović, *Ustavni razvoj Srbije*, Kapital banka, 2000, 119-120.
32. Jovanović, *Druga vlada*, 273-278; MacKenzie, *Ilija Garašanin*, 212-214.
33. Grujić, *Zapisi*, v2, 236.
34. Ibid., 277.
35. Jovanović, *Druga vlada*, 278-285; MacKenzie, *Ilija Garašanin*, 218-219.
36. Milićević, *Jevrem Grujić*, 99-100.
37. Petrovich, *Modern Serbia*, v1, 283-284.
38. Hristić, *Memoari*, 303.
39. Lebl, *Do "konačnog resenja"*, 98-101; Popović, *Jevreji*, 18, 25.
40. Jovanović, *Druga vlada*, 287-293, 323.
41. Milan Piroćanac, *Knez Mihailo i zajednička radnja balkanskih naroda*, Državna štamparija kraljevine Srbije, 1895, 14-15.
42. Živanović, *Politička istorija*, v1, 55.
43. Đorđević, *Srpska narodna vojska*, 18-22.
44. Berić, *Ustanak u Hercegovini*, 641-643.
45. Hristić, *Memoari*, 338-343; Hristić, *Zapisi starog beogradanin*, 436-437.
46. Jovanović, *Druga vlada*, 324-337.
47. Hristić, *Memoari*, 306-308.
48. Jovanović, *Druga vlada*, 318-320.
49. Ibid., 320-321.
50. Ibid., 295-299.
51. Hristić, *Memoari*, 321-322.
52. Jovanović, *Uspomene*, 101-102.
53. Milićević, *Jevrem Grujić*, 133-136.
54. Jovanović, *Druga vlada*, 395.
55. Živanović, *Politička istorija*, v1, 67.
56. Ibid., 65.
57. Popović, *Vuk Stef. Karadžić*, 416.
58. Andrija Radenić, ed., *Dnevnik Benjamina Kalaja*, Istorijski institut, 1976, 37.

59. Lebl, *Do "konačnog resenja"*, 104–106, 119–124; Popović, *Jevreji*, 18–19; Koljanin, *Jevreji i antisemitizam*, 164–167; Cohen, *Serbia's Secret War*, 65–67; Isidore Loeb, *La situation des Israélites en Turquie, en Serbie et en Roumanie*, Joseph Baer, 1877, 33–34.
60. Jovanović, *Druga vlada*, 377–384.
61. Živanović, *Politička istorija*, v1, 69–86; Hristić, *Memoari*, 385–394.
62. Živanović, *Politička istorija*, v1, 79.
63. Nicović, *Ustavni razvoj*, 121.
64. Jovanović, *Druga vlada*, 383–384.
65. Ibid, 359–363.
66. Đorđević, *Srpska narodna vojska*, 120–126.
67. Ekmečić, *Stvaranje Jugoslavije*, v2, 65.
68. Hristić, *Memoari*, 395–413.
69. Jovanović, *Druga vlada*, 366–367.
70. Božinović, *Žensko pitanje*, 58; Milanović, *Žensko društvo*, 26–27.
71. Petrovich, *Modern Serbia*, v1, 352–354.
72. Ibid., 341.
73. Jovanović, *Druga vlada*, 353–357; MacKenzie, *Ilija Garašanin*, 240–242.
74. Piroćanac, *Knez Mihailo*, 19–20.
75. Ibid., 36–39.
76. Hristić, *Memoari*, 356.
77. Jovanović, *Druga vlada*, 414–416.
78. Ibid., 413–421; Jovanović, *Vlada Milana*, v1, 27.
79. Jovanović, *Druga vlada*, 417–418.
80. Đorđević, *Srpska narodna vojska*, 158–159.
81. Jovan Milićević, 'Istorija predaje turskih gradova u Srbiji srpskoj vladi 1867. godine', in Vasa Čubrilović, ed., *Oslobodenje gradova u Srbiji od Turaka 1862–1867. godine*, Srpska Akademija Nauka i Umjetnosti, 1970, 243–249.
82. Hristić, *Zapisi starog beogradanin*, 34–37; Đorđević, *Srpska narodna vojska*, 57–59; Petrovich, *Modern Serbia*, v1, 317.
83. Zorica Janković, *Put u Carigrad: Knez Mihailo, predaja gradova i odlazak Turaka iz Srbije*, IP Beograd and Istorijski muzej Srbije, 2006, 21.
84. Jovanović, *Uspomene*, 112–113.
85. Jovan Ristić, *Bombardanje Beograda (1862. godine)*, Državna štamparija, 1872, 47.
86. Ibid., 95–96.
87. Fikret Karčić, 'Protokol konferencije u Kanlidži 1862.: Pravnohistorijska analiza odredaba o muslimanskom stanovništvu', in Arnautalić, *150 godina od protjerivanja muslimana*, 71–84.
88. Đorđević, *Srpska narodna vojska*, 71–72.
89. Hristić, *Memoari*, 464; Galib Šljivo, 'Protjerivanje stanovništva islamske vjere iz Kneževine Srbije 1830–1878.', in Arnautalić, *150 godina od protjerivanja muslimana*, 63.

90. Hristić, *Memoari*, 446–447, 456–457.
91. Đorđević, *Srpska narodna vojska*, 68–70.
92. Ibid., 91–92.
93. ibid., 114–115.
94. Ibid., 134.
95. Ibid., 164–167.
96. Vuksanović-Anić, Stvaranje moderne srpske vojske, 76–83.
97. See chapter 6, 172–173.
98. Jovanović, *Druga vlada*, 385–389.
99. Ibid., 365–371.
100. Ibid., 371–375.
101. Milićević, *Jevrem Grujić*, 144.
102. Živanović, *Politička istorija*, v1, 100–105; Stokes, *Legitimacy Through Liberalism*, 67–68; Jovanović, *Druga vlada*, 435–440.
103. Hristić, *Memoari*, 480–481.
104. Živanović, *Politička istorija*, v1, 106–107.
105. Ibid., 112.
106. Bataković, *Nova istorija srpskog naroda*, 168; Ljušić, *Srpska državnost*, 428–429; Pavlović, *Balkan Anschluss*, 52.
107. Radoman Jovanović, 'Sukob uticaja Crne Gore i Srbije u hercegovackom ustanku 1875–1878', in Stevo Ćosović, ed., *Slavno doba Hercegovine: spomen knjiga o hercegovačkim ustanku 1875–1878*, Svet knjige, 2005, 153–167.
108. Ljušić, *Knjiga o Načertaniju*, 137–138, 230; Banac, *National Question*, 89–90.
109. Milorad Ekmečić, *Radovi iz istorije Bosne i Hercegovine XIX veka*, Beogradski izdavački-grafički zavod, 1997, 32–36.
110. Hadžijahić, *Od tradicija do identiteta*, 159.
111. Janković, *Put u Carigrad*, 62–82.
112. Ibid., 84–95.
113. Petrovich, *Modern Serbia*, v1, 316; Safet Bandžović, 'Iseljavanje muslimanskog stanovništva iz Kneževine Srbije u bosanski vilajet (1862–1867)', *Znakovi vremena*, 12 (2001), 150–171; Stevan Ignjić, 'Muslimanska imanja u Užicu', in Čubrilović, *Oslobođenje gradova*, 377–386; Edin Hajdarpašić, 'Out of the ruins of the Ottoman Empire: Reflections on the Ottoman legacy in south-eastern Europe', *Middle Eastern Studies*, 44, 5 (September 2008), 721–722.
114. Ekmečić, *Stvaranje Jugoslavije*, v2, 68.
115. Popović, *Beograd kroz vekove*, 347.
116. Milićević, *Kneževina Srbija*, 23.
117. Todorov, *Balkan City*, 337–338.

6. LIBERALS, SOCIALISTS AND NATIONALISM FROM BELOW

1. Vladimir Jovanović, 'Klike i stranke u Srba', in Vladimir Jovanović, *Izabrani spisi*, Službeni glasnik, 2011, 125; Vasiljević, *Moje uspomene*, 71, 74–75, 77, 80, 87–88, 98; Živanović, *Politička istorija*, v1, 123.
2. Vladimir Jovanović, 'Strani consuli u Srbiji', in Jovanović, *Izabrani spisi*, 119–120.
3. Vladimir Jovanović, 'Srpski narod i istočno pitanje', in Jovanović, *Izabrani spisi*, 65–69.
4. Vladimir Jovanović, 'Srbenda i gotovan', in Jovanović, *Izabrani spisi*, 99–106.
5. Jovanović, 'Klike i stranke u Srba', 133, 139.
6. Jovanović, 'Srpski narod i istočno pitanje', 77–79.
7. Svetozar Miletić, *O srpskom pitanju*, Orpheus and Gradska biblioteka, 2001, 115, 126.
8. Živanović, *Politička istorija*, v1, 124.
9. Živanović, *Politička istorija*, v1, 122–125; Avakumović, *Memoari*, 100–101.
10. Stokes, *Legitimacy Through Liberalism*, 88–120.
11. MacKenzie, *Ilija Garašanin*, 289.
12. Piroćanac, *Knez Mihailo*, 83–85; Zdenko Zlatar, 'The last year of Michael of Serbia's foreign policy (1967–68): A reappraisal', *Australian Journal of Politics and History*, 2008, 95–96.
13. MacKenzie, *Ilija Garašanin*, 333–336.
14. Piroćanac, *Knez Mihailo*, 84.
15. Jovanović, *Vlada Milana*, v1, 27.
16. Ibid., 480–485.
17. Živanović, *Politička istorija*, v1, 138–141.
18. Zlatar, 'Last year of Michael of Serbia's foreign policy', 98; MacKenzie, *Ilija Garašanin*, 342–344.
19. Zlatar, 'Last year of Michael of Serbia's foreign policy', 101.
20. Živanović, *Politička istorija*, v1, 148–151.
21. Jovanović, *Druga vlada*, 393.
22. David MacKenzie, *Jovan Ristić: Outstanding Serbian Statesman*, East European Monographs, 2006, 1–9; Jovanović, *Vlada Milana*, v1, 31–36; Vasiljević, *Moje uspomene*, 51–52.
23. Živanović, *Politička istorija*, v1, 125.
24. Stojančević et al., *Istorija srpskog naroda*, v5.1, 300–301; Nicović, *Ustavni razvoj*, 125; Prodanović, *Ustavni razvitak*, 150–161.
25. Vasiljević, *Moje uspomene*, 91.
26. Jovanović, *Druga vlada*, 485–490.
27. Jovanović, *Vlada Milana*, v1, 9, 167–168.
28. Stokes, *Legitimacy Through Liberalism*, 144; Avakumović, *Memoari*, 107.
29. Avakumović, *Memoari*, 90–106.
30. Stokes, *Legitimacy Through Liberalism*, 141–145.
31. Jovanović, *Vlada Milana*, v1, 49–59.
32. Avakumović, *Memoari*, 92.

33. Jovanović, *Vlada Milana*, v1, 46–49.
34. Woodford D. McClellan, *Svetozar Marković and the Origins of Balkan Socialism*, Princeton University Press, 1964, 64.
35. Radenić, *Dnevnik Benjamina Kalaja*, 49.
36. Avakumović, *Memoari*, 57–58, 86, 100.
37. Živojinović, *Kralj Petar*, v1, 52–53, 62–65.
38. Ilija N. Đukanović, *Ubistvo Kneza Mihaila i dogadaji o kojima se nije smelo govoriti*, v2, Beletra, 1990 (Nikola Nikolić, 1935), 154–155.
39. Jovanović, *Druga vlada*, 494–499.
40. Ibid., 499–501.
41. Avakumović, *Memoari*, 78.
42. Živanović, *Politička istorija*, v1, 244.
43. MacKenzie, *Ilija Garašanin*, 377–384; Stokes, *Legitimacy Through Liberalism*, 132–148.
44. Jovanović, *Vlada Milana*, v1, 67–70.
45. Loeb, *La situation des Israélites*, 35–37, 89–90; Lebl, *Do "konačnog rešenja"*, 138–140.
46. Popović, *Jevreji*, 19.
47. Radojević, *Srpski ustavi*, 71–93; Jovanović, *Vlada Milana*, v1, 72–76.
48. Jovanović, *Vlada Milana*, v1, 89–90.
49. Ibid., 76–80.
50. Ibid., 93–94.
51. Ibid., 103–104.
52. Ibid., 110–111.
53. Ekmečić, *Stvaranje Jugoslavije*, v2, 138.
54. Petrovich, *Modern Serbia*, v2, 495–496.
55. Milorad Ekmečić, *Ustanak u Bosni 1875–1878*, 3rd ed., Službeni list SRJ, 1996, 52–58.
56. Ibid., 59–66; Jovan Ristić, *Spoljašnji Odnošaji Srbije novijega vrenema*, v3, Prosveta, 1901, 305–332.
57. Ristić, *Spoljašnji Odnošaji*, v3, 141–146; Jovanović, *Vlada Milana*, v1, 117–119.
58. McClellan, *Svetozar Marković*, 30–31; Jovan Skerlić, *Svetozar Marković*, Portalibris, 2020, 10–12.
59. Ljubica Vl. Ljotić, *Memoari*, Knjižarnica Obradović, 1990, 15.
60. Živojinović, *Kralj Petar*, v1, 83–84.
61. Ljotić, *Memoari*, 49–52.
62. Vasa Kazimirović, *Nikola Pašić i njegovo doba 1845–1926*, v1, Nova Evropa, 1990, 191–192.
63. Jovanović, *Vlada Milana*, v1, 370–371.
64. Živojinović, *Kralj Petar*, v1, 46–48, 86–87.
65. Latinka Perović, *Srpski socijalisti 19. Veka: Prilog istoriji socijalističke misli*, v1, Rad, 1985, 22.
66. Ibid., 154–155.
67. Ekmečić, *Stvaranje Jugoslavije*, v1, 243–244.

68. Perović, *Srpski socijalisti*, v1, 187.
69. Ibid., 191–193.
70. Skerlić, *Svetozar Marković*, 9–18.
71. McClellan, *Svetozar Marković*, 35, 39.
72. Ibid., 51.
73. Jovanović, *Vlada Milana*, v1, 144–145.
74. Svetozar Marković, 'Rešenje istočnog pitanja', *Celokupna dela*, v1, 31–34.
75. Svetozar Marković, 'Partije u Srbiji', *Celokupna dela*, v1, 71.
76. Ibid., 84.
77. McClellan, *Svetozar Marković*, 69.
78. Skerlić, *Svetozar Marković*, 30–31; Slobodan Jovanović, *Svetozar Marković*, 2nd ed., Geca Kon, 1920, 91–92.
79. For example, McClellan, *Svetozar Marković*, 65–66, 146–147, 183–186; Andreja Živković and Dragan Plavšić, 'The Balkan socialist tradition: Balkan socialism and the Balkan Federation, 1871–1915', *Revolutionary History*, 8, 3 (2003), 5–6, 13–16.
80. Svetozar Marković, '"Velika Srbija"', *Celokupna dela*, v1, 186–190.
81. Svetozar Marković, 'Naše sveto pravo', *Celokupna dela*, v1, 157–159.
82. Skerlić, *Svetozar Marković*, 91–95.
83. Jovanović, *Svetozar Marković*, 143.
84. Ibid., 100; Skerlić, *Svetozar Marković*, 199.
85. Svetozar Marković, 'Slovenska Austrija i Srpsko jedinstvo', *Celokupna dela*, v5, 96–101.
86. Svetozar Marković, 'Odgovor dr-u Vladanu Đorđeviću na njegovo "otvoreno pismo" u "Jedinsvtu" od Svetozara Markovića', *Celokupna dela*, v7, 157.
87. Kazimirović, *Nikola Pašić*, v1, 206–211.
88. Svetozar Marković, 'Socijalizam ili društveno pitanje', *Celokupna dela*, v13, 153–154.
89. Svetozar Marković, 'Srbija na istoku', *Celokupna dela*, v8, 11, 20–21.
90. Ibid, 24–26.
91. Ibid., 55, 59.
92. Ibid., 61–69.
93. Gale Stokes, *Politics as Development: The Emergence of Political Parties in Nineteenth-Century Serbia*, Duke University Press, 1990, 51–52.
94. Marković, 'Srbija na istoku', 84–85.
95. Perović, *Srpski socijalisti*, v2, 302.
96. Marković, 'Srbija na istoku', 85, 93–95.
97. Ibid., 96.
98. Stokes, *Legitimacy Through Liberalism*, 149–162.
99. Stokes, *Politics as Development*, 43–44.
100. McClellan, *Svetozar Marković*, 131–132.
101. Ibid., 57–59.
102. Jovanović, *Vlada Milana*, v1, 112–113.
103. Stokes, *Legitimacy Through Liberalism*, 197–212.
104. Milićević, *Jevrem Grujić*, 201, 212.

7. ACHIEVEMENT OF INDEPENDENCE

1. Ljušić, *Srpska državnost*, 216.
2. Zorica Janković, 'Milan i Artemis', *Vreme*, 951 (26 March 2009).
3. Jovanović, *Vlada Milana*, v1, 234.
4. Milan Piroćanac, *Beleške*, Zavod za udžbenike i nastavna sredstva, 2004, 469.
5. Kazimirović, *Nikola Pašić*, v1, 344.
6. Bogdan Bogdanović, *Ukleti neimar*, Feral Tribune, 2001, 59.
7. Piroćanac, *Beleške*, 470.
8. Jovanović, *Vlada Milana*, v1, 158–159.
9. Ekmečić, *Ustanak u Bosni*, 72.
10. McClellan, *Svetozar Marković*, 179–181.
11. Ekmečić, *Ustanak u Bosni*, 73.
12. Ibid., 80.
13. Jovan Mašin, father of Aleksandar Mašin, who played a key role the 1903 putsch. See Stokes, *Politics as Development*, 309
14. Ekmečić, *Stvaranje*, v2, 174.
15. Jovanović, *Vlada Milana*, v1, 177–184; Tomasevich, *Peasants*, 44.
16. Momčilo Isić, *Seljaštvo u Srbiji 1918–1941*, v1, Institut za Noviju Istoriju Srbije, 2000, 14–17.
17. Jasmina Milanović, *Aćim Čumić 1836–1901*, Zavod za udžbenike, 2007, 24–28.
18. Ibid., 82–83; Krestić and Ljušić, *Programi i statuti*, 47–48.
19. Milanović, *Aćim Čumić*, 141–142.
20. Jovanović, *Vlada Milana*, v1, 202–212.
21. Stojančević et al., *Istorija srpskog naroda*, v5.1, 310, 375.
22. Krestić and Ljušić, *Programi i statuti*, 79–80.
23. Kazimirović, *Nikola Pašić*, v1, 149–151.
24. Dejan Djokić, *Pašić and Trumbić: The Kingdom of Serbs, Croats and Slovenes*, Haus, 2010, 15.
25. Milan St. Protić, *Radikali u Srbiiji: Ideje i pokret, 1881–1903*, Srpska akademija nauka i umjetnosti, 1990, 60–76.
26. Kazimirović, *Nikola Pašić*, v1, 173–174.
27. Ljotić, *Memoari*, 55–56, 178–193.
28. Kazimirović, *Nikola Pašić*, v1, 192.
29. Latinka Perović, *Pera Todorović*, Rad, 1983, 60–63.
30. Ibid., 89–91.
31. Spasić, *Kragujevačka vojna fabrika*, 192–193.
32. Živan Živanović, *Politička istorija Srbije u drugoj polovini devetnaestog veka*, v2, Izdavačka knjižarnica Gece Kona, 1924, 125–126.
33. McClellan, *Svetozar Marković*, 207, 214; Jovanović, *Vlada Milana*, v1, 193–197.
34. Živojinović, *Kralj Petar*, v1, 46–48, 86–87; Jovanović, *Vlada Milana*, v1, 197–198.
35. Latinka Perović, *Srpski socijalisti 19. Veka: Prilog istoriji socijalističke misli*, v3, Službeni list SRJ, 1995, 54.

36. Protić, *Radikali u Srbiji*, 112, 132–134.
37. Latinka Perović and Andrej Šemjakin, eds, *Nikola Pašić: Pisma, članci i govori (1872–1891)*, Službeni list SRJ, 1995, 43, 51.
38. Božinović, *Žensko pitanje*, 70–73; Milanović, *Žensko društvo*, 39–41, 99, 119, 298–301, 341–343.
39. Ekmečić, *Ustanak u Bosni*, 149–153.
40. MacKenzie, *Jovan Ristić*, 98.
41. Ekmečić, *Ustanak u Bosni*, 133.
42. MacKenzie, *Jovan Ristić*, 101–102.
43. Živomir Spasić, *Kragujevački crveni barjak 1876*, Radnički univerzitet u Kragujevcu, 1972, 16–18.
44. Dubravka Stojanović, *Kaldrma i asfalt: urbanizacija i evropeizacija Beograda, 1890–1914*, Čigoja, 2008, 197–198.
45. Jovanović, *Vlada Milana*, v1, 247–254; Stokes, *Politics as Development*, 85–88.
46. Stokes, *Politics as Development*, 89–90.
47. Jovanović, *Vlada Milana*, v1, 267–268.
48. Perović and Šemjakin, *Nikola Pašić*, 51–54.
49. Spasić, *Kragujevački crveni barjak*, 46–56.
50. Ibid., 67–111; Jovanović, *Vlada Milana*, v1, 257–258; Stojančević et al., *Istorija srpskog naroda*, v5.1, 375; Spasić, *Kragujevačka vojna fabrika*, 195–197.
51. Stokes, *Politics as Development*, 93–98.
52. Stojančević et al., *Istorija srpskog naroda*, v5.1, 310.
53. Keshko's mother Pulcheria Sturdza was a Moldavian princess and her father Petre Keşcu an ethnic Romanian from Bessarabia and Russian army colonel. Natalija felt herself to be Russian. See Ljubinka Trgovčević, ed., *Moje uspomene: Kraljica Natalija Obrenović*, Srpska književna zadruga, 1999, 33.
54. Jovanović, *Vlada Milana*, v1, 276–277.
55. Andrija Radenić, *Radikalna stranka i timočka buna*, v1, Istorijski arhiv 'Timočka Krajina' Zaječar, 1988, 52.
56. Ekmečić, *Ustanak*, 164–165.
57. Dated 15 July 1876; Ljotić, *Memoari*, 91.
58. Kazimirović, *Nikola Pašić*, v1, 265–266.
59. Ibid., 267–268.
60. Živojinović, *Kralj Petar*, v1, 129–131.
61. Jovanović, *Vlada Milana*, v1, 264.
62. Ibid., 276–295; MacKenzie, *Jovan Ristić*, 114; Stojančević et al., *Istorija srpskog naroda*, v5.1, 379.
63. Stokes, *Politics as Development*, 104–105.
64. Ibid., 107–115.
65. Pera Todorović, *Dnevnik jednog dobrovoljca*, Nolit, 1988, 197–206.
66. Slobodan Branković, *Nezavisnost slobodoljubivih: Velika istočna kriza i Srbija 1875–1878*, Svetska srpska zajednica, Institut srpskog naroda, 1998, 63–74.

67. Ekmečić, *Ustanak u Bosni*, 237–238; Živojinović, *Kralj Petar*, v1, 145.
68. Jovanović, *Vlada Milana*, v1, 351.
69. Suzana Rajić, *Vladan Đorđević: Biografija pouzdanog obrenovićevca*, Zavod za udžbenike, 2007, 19–22.
70. Vukašin M. Antić and Žarko Vuković, 'Vojni sanitet u Prvom srpsko-turskom ratu 1876–1877', *Vojnosanitetski pregled*, 64, 9 (2007), 639–646.
71. Ekmečić, *Ustanak u Bosni*, 258.
72. Ljušić, *Oficiri u visokom školstvu*, 240–241.
73. Vasa Čubrilović, *Bosanski ustanak 1875–1878*, 2nd ed., Službeni list SRJ and Balkanološki institut SANU, 1996, 277–281.
74. Ibid., 264.
75. Ekmečić, *Ustanak u Bosni*, 256.
76. Čubrilović, *Bosanski ustanak*, 182.
77. Nikola Ilić, *Oslobođenje Južne Srbije 1877–1878*, Sloboda, 1977, 20–21; Jovanović, *Vlada Milana*, v1, 300–302; Stojančević et al., *Istorija srpskog naroda*, v5.1, 383.
78. Branković, *Nezavisnost slobodoljubivih*, 417–419.
79. Jovanović, *Vlada Milana*, v1, 315–316.
80. Ibid., 319–324.
81. Branković, *Nezavisnost slobodoljubivih*, 155–159, 167–180; Jovan Ristić, *Diplomatska istorija Srbije za vreme srpskih ratova za oslobodenje i nezavisnost 1875–1878*, v1, Prosveta, 1896, 138–141.
82. Jovanović, *Vlada Milana*, v1, 325–329.
83. MacKenzie, *Jovan Ristić*, 128.
84. Jovanović, *Vlada Milana*, v1, 306.
85. Petrovich, *Modern Serbia*, v2, 389.
86. Ekmečić, *Ustanak u Bosni*, 320.
87. Nikola Babić, *Na putevima revolucije: Članci i rasprave*, Svjetlost, 1972, 14.
88. Milićević, *Jevrem Grujić*, 238–239.
89. Živanović, *Politička istorija*, v1, 348.
90. Radenić, *Radikalna stranka i timočka buna*, v1, 138–142.
91. Jovanović, *Vlada Milana*, v1, 355–364.
92. Živojinović, *Kralj Petar*, v1, 166–167.
93. Ibid., 175.
94. Piroćanac, *Beleške*, 4–22; Milanović, *Aćim Čumić*, 183–194.
95. Jovanović, *Vlada Milana*, v1, 365–375; Stokes, *Politics as Development*, 129–134; Živojinović, *Kralj Petar*, v1, 173–180.
96. Ekmečić, *Stvaranje*, v2, 316.
97. Ilić, *Oslobođenje Južne Srbije*, 34.
98. Živojin Mišić, *Moje uspomene*, Beogradski izdavačko-grafički zavod, 1978, 100.
99. Petrit Imami, *Srbi i Albanci kroz vekove*, Standard 2, 2000, 41–42, 95–104, 117–127.
100. Miloš Jagodić, 'The emigration of Muslims from the new Serbian regions, 1877–1878', *Balkanologie*, 2, 2 (1998), 1–6.

101. Ilić, *Oslobođenje Južne Srbije*, 121.
102. Miloš Jagodić, 'Upadi Albanaca u Srbiji 1879. godine', *Istoriijski časopis*, 51 (2004), 91.
103. Radenić, *Radikalna stranka i timočka buna*, v1, 272.
104. Čedomir Popov, Dimitrije Đorđević, Novica Rakočević, Djordje Mikić, Kosta Milutinović, Vasilije Krestić, Andrija Radenić and Milorad Ekmečić, *Istorija srpskog naroda*, v6.1, Srpska književna zadruga, 1983, 53; Jagodić, 'Emigration of Muslims', 14–15.
105. Stokes, *Politics as Development*, 165–166; Ilić, *Oslobođenje Južne Srbije*, 170; Koljanin, *Jevreji i antisemitizam*, 168; Lebl, *Do "konačnog resenja"*, 141–142.
106. Hristić, *Zapisi starog beograđanin*, 88–89.
107. Jovanović, *Vlada Milana*, v1, 383–384.
108. Mihailo Vojvodić, Dragoljub Živojinović, Andrej Mitrović and Radovan Samardžić, eds, *Srbija 1878. dokumenti*, Srpska književna zadruga, 1978, 52–53.
109. Jovan Ristić, *Diplomatska istorija Srbije za vreme srpskih ratova za oslobođenje i nezavisnost 1875–1878*, v2, Prosveta, 1898, 134.
110. Jovanović, *Vlada Milana*, v1, 385.
111. MacKenzie, *Jovan Ristić*, 178.
112. Ibid., 185–192.
113. Jovanović, *Vlada Milana*, v1, 387.
114. Vojvodić et al., *Srbija 1878.*, 445–450.
115. Ibid., 460.
116. MacKenzie, *Jovan Ristić*, 200–204.
117. Ljušić, *Srpska državnost*, 31, 38.
118. Vojvodić et al., *Srbija 1878.*, 491.
119. Slijepčević, *Istorija SPC*, 381–383.
120. Popov et al., *Istorija srpskog naroda*, v6.1, 52–53.
121. Ibid., 7–8.
122. Žanin-Čalić, *Socijalna istorija*, 48–49.
123. Živojinović, *Kralj Petar*, v1, 207–210.
124. Jovanović, *Vlada Milana*, v1, 397.
125. Vojvodić et al., *Srbija 1878.*, 624.
126. Jovanović, *Vlada Milana*, v1, 31
127. Živanović, *Politička istorija*, v2, 264.
128. Stokes, *Politics as Development*, 141–142.
129. MacKenzie, *Jovan Ristić*, 217.
130. Latinka Perović, ed., *Nikola Pašić u narodnoj skupštini*, Službeni list SRJ, 1997, 78.
131. Jovanović, *Vlada Milana*, v1, 18.
132. Latinka Perović, *Između anarhije i autokratije: Srpsko društvo na prelazima vekova (XIX–XXI)*, Helsinški odbor za ljudska prava u Srbiji, 2006, 284–286.
133. Stokes, *Politics as Development*, 186.
134. Perović, *Između anarhije i autokratije*, 271–279.
135. Ibid., 111–126.

136. Radenić, *Radikalna stranka i timočka buna*, v1, 233–234.
137. Perović, *Nikola Pašić u narodnoj skupštini*, 440.
138. Živanović, *Politička istorija*, v2, 90.
139. Popov et al., *Istorija srpskog naroda*, v6.1, 56–57.
140. Jovanović, *Vlada Milana*, v2, 19–31; Živanović, *Politička istorija*, v2, 108–111.

8. COURT AND RADICALS

1. Perović, *Između anarhije i autokratije*, 188–189; Piroćanac, *Beleške*, VII–IX.
2. Slobodan Jovanović, *Srpsko-bugarski rat: Rasprave iz diplomatske istorije*, Kraljevsko Srpske dvorske knjižare, 1901, 57–58.
3. Perović, *Nikola Pašić u narodnoj skupštini*, 640.
4. Ibid., 650–655.
5. Lazar Vrkatić, ed., *Pojam i biće srpske nacije*, Izdavačka knjižara Zorana Stojanovića, 2004, 438–440; Jovanović, *Vlada Milana*, v2, 52–59.
6. Norris, *Belgrade*, 67–68.
7. Jovanović, *Vlada Milana*, v2, 58–66, 145, 152, 200.
8. Ibid., 148–149.
9. Jovanović, *Vlada Milana*, v2, 97–104.
10. Slijepčević, *Istorija SPC*, v2, 372.
11. Popov et al., *Istorija srpskog naroda*, v6.1, 10–15.
12. Palairet, *Balkan Economies*, 301.
13. Ibid., 117–118, 258–259.
14. Jovanović, *Vlada Milana*, v2, 97.
15. Ibid., 44–51
16. Krestić and Ljušić, *Programi i statuti*, 101–104.
17. Ibid., 107–109.
18. Jovanović, *Vlada Milana*, v2, 66–67.
19. Krestić and Ljušić, *Programi i statuti*, 121–125.
20. Olga Popović-Obradović, *Parlamentarizam u Srbiji od 1903. do 1914. godine*, Službeni list SRJ, 1998, 62–70.
21. Perović, *Srpski socijalisti*, v3, 68.
22. Petrovich, *Modern Serbia*, v2, 416–418.
23. Ibid., 578.
24. Jovanović, *Vlada Milana*, v2, 76.
25. Ibid., 89–94.
26. Stokes, *Politics as Development*, 237.
27. Perović, *Nikola Pašić u narodnoj skupštini*, 759–760.
28. Jovanović, *Vlada Milana*, v2, 142–146.
29. Ibid., 150–151.
30. Stokes, *Politics as Development*, 248–253.
31. Radenić, *Radikalna stranka i timočka buna*, v1, 437.

32. Perović, *Pera Todorović*, 71–72.
33. Ibid., 104–106; Jovanović, *Vlada Milana*, v2, 164–172; Nicović, *Ustavni razvoj*, 164–180.
34. Živojinović, *Kralj Petar*, v1, 242.
35. Radenić, *Radikalna stranka i timočka buna*, v2, 533.
36. Slavica B. Raković-Kostić, *Evropeizacija srpske vojske 1878–1903*, Vojnoistorijski institut, 2007, 78–80.
37. Ibid., 395.
38. Ibid., 100.
39. Radenić, *Radikalna stranka i timočka buna*, v2, 521.
40. Krestić and Ljušić, *Programi i statuti*, 101–103.
41. Perović and Šemjakin, *Nikola Pašić*, 137.
42. Radenić, *Radikalna stranka i timočka buna*, v1, 402.
43. Raša Milošević, *Timočka buna 1883. godine: Uspomene Raše Miloševića, člana glavnog odbora Radikalne stranke*, Štamparija Drag. Gregorića, 1923, 148.
44. Radenić, *Radikalna stranka i timočka buna*, v1, 685.
45. Raković-Kostić, *Evropeizacija srpske vojske*, 157.
46. Nikola Vučo, 'Proletarizacija seljaštva u istočnoj Srbiji', 67–80, in Vasa Čubrilović, ed., *Timočka buna 1883. i njen društveno-politički značaj za Srbiju XIX veka*, Srpska akademija nauka i umjetnosti, 1986, 6–7.
47. Petar Milosavljević, 'Timočka buna 1883 godine', in Čubrilović, *Timočka buna*, 6–7.
48. Rade Panajotović, "Učitelji i sveštenici u timočkoj buni", in Čubrilović, *Timočka buna*, 215–229.
49. Radenić, *Radikalna stranka i timočka buna*, v1, 647.
50. Milosavljević, 'Timočka buna', 8–9.
51. Stokes, *Politics as Development*, 286–288; Radenić, *Radikalna stranka i timočka buna*, v2, 689.
52. Radenić, *Radikalna stranka i timočka buna*, v1, 680.
53. Stokes, *Politics as Development*, 289–290; Jovanović, *Vlada Milana*, v2, 187–189.
54. Radenić, *Radikalna stranka i timočka buna*, v2, 715.
55. Slobodan Jovanović, *Moji savremenici*, Avala, Windsor, 1962, 139–140.
56. Đorđe Stanković, *Nikola Pašić i jugoslovensko pitanje*, v1, Beogradski izdavačko-grafički zavod, 1985, 72–73.
57. Jovanović, *Vlada Milana*, v2, 204–207.
58. Živojinović, *Kralj Petar*, v1, 286–289.
59. Jovanović, *Vlada Milana*, v2, 219–220, 227–230.
60. Ibid., 278.
61. Momir Samardžić, 'Delatnost Milutina Garašanina na organizovanju srpske propagande u Staroj Srbiji i Makedoniji 1885. godine: Koreni i plan', *Istorijski Časopis*, 51 (2004), 115–126.
62. Radenić, *Radikalna stranka i timočka buna*, v2, 806–816, 848–849.
63. Perović, *Između anarhije i autokratije*, 226.

64. Jovanović, *Srpsko-bugarski rat*, 61.
65. Raković-Kostić, *Evropeizacija srpske vojske*, 179; Richard J. Crampton, *Bulgaria 1878–1918: A History*, East European Monographs, 1983, 99–101.
66. Jovanović, *Srpsko-bugarski rat*, 141.
67. Raković-Kostić, *Evropeizacija srpske vojske*, 186–197; Jovanović, *Vlada Milana*, v2, 252–265.
68. Božinović, *Žensko pitanje*, 69.
69. Slobodan Jovanović, *Vlada Aleksandra Obrenovića*, v1, BIGZ, 1990, 92–93.
70. Malcolm, *Kosovo*, 199.
71. Stanković, *Nikola Pašić i jugoslovensko pitanje*, v1, 75.
72. Radenić, *Radikalna stranka i timočka buna*, v2, 819.
73. Perović, *Srpski socijalisti*, v3, 109.
74. Radenić, *Radikalna stranka i timočka buna*, v2, 820–823; Živanović, *Politička istorija*, v2, 298–300.
75. Popović-Obradović, *Parlamentarizam*, 72–74.
76. Jovanović, *Vlada Milana*, v2, 291–292.
77. Ibid., 301–302; Živanović, *Politička istorija*, v2, 302–304.
78. Živojinović, *Kralj Petar*, v1, 317–332
79. Trgovčević, *Kraljica Natalija*, 113.
80. Ibid., 101.
81. Petrovich, *Modern Serbia*, v2, 437–438; Jovanović, *Vlada Milana*, v2, 319–321; Perović, *Između anarhije i autokratije*, 229–230.
82. Radenić, *Radikalna stranka i timočka buna*, v2, 871–872.
83. Ibid., 880.
84. Živanović, *Politička istorija*, v2, 369.
85. Ljušić, *Ljubavi*, 168.
86. Radojević, *Srpski ustavi*, 97–136.
87. Ljušić, *Srpska državnost*, 38, 236.
88. Jovanović, *Vlada Milana*, v2, 345–371.
89. Milošević, *Timočka buna*, 291.
90. MacKenzie, *Jovan Ristić*, 270.
91. Vlado St. Marijan, *Povratak grofa od Takova: Prilog istoriji parlamentarizma u Srbiji*, Službeni glasnik, 2013, 8.
92. Živanović, *Politička istorija*, v4, 1925, 238.
93. Perović and Šemjakin, *Nikola Pašić*, 319–320.
94. Olga Popović-Obradović, 'Koreni antimoderne političke kulture u Srbiji', in Latinka Perović, ed., *Olga Popović-Obradović: Kakva ili koliko drzava; Ogledi o politickoj i drustvenoj istoriji Srbije XIX–XXI veka*, Helsinški odbor za ljudska prava u Srbiji, 2008, 332.
95. Jovanović, *Vlada Aleksandra*, v1, 104.
96. Ibid., 109–110.
97. Popović-Obradović, *Parlamentarizam*, 82.

98. Jovanović, *Vlada Aleksandra*, v1, 38, 44.
99. Ibid., 115.
100. Avakumović, *Memoari*, 252–259.
101. Radenić, *Radikalna stranka i timočka buna*, v1, 145.
102. Jovanović, *Vlada Aleksandra*, v1, 119–121.
103. Ibid., 124–133.
104. Ibid., 19–24.
105. Ibid., 57.
106. Žanin-Čalić, *Socijalna istorija*, 122–129.
107. Vladimir Zarić, 'Sociologija zadrugarstva Mihaila Avramovića', in Slobodan Antonić, ed., *Sto godina sociologije u Srbiji*, Srpsko sociološko društvo, 2012, 140–141.
108. Isić, *Seljaštvo*, v1, 17–18.
109. Jovanović, *Vlada Aleksandra*, v1, 48–53; Slijepčević, *Istorija SPC*, v2, 413–415.
110. Suzana Rajić, *Aleksandar Obrenović: Vladar na prelazu vekova sukobljeni svetovi*, 2nd ed., Srpska književna zadruga, 2014, 420–423.
111. David MacKenzie, *Apis: The Congenial Conspirator; The Life of Colonel Dragutin T. Dimitrijević*, East European Monographs, 1989, 1, 24–25.
112. Savo Skoko and Petar Opačić, *Vojvoda Stepa Stepanović u ratovima Srbije 1876–1918.*, v1, 5th ed., Beogradski izdavačko-grafički zavod, 1984, 159.
113. Živan Živanović, *Politička istorija Srbije u drugoj polovini devetnaestog veka*, v3, Izdavačka knjižarnica Gece Kona, 1924, 31
114. Emmert, *Serbian Golgotha*, 129.
115. Rajić, *Aleksandar Obrenović*, 455.
116. Dejan Djokić, 'Whose myth? Which nation? The Serbian Kosovo myth revisited', in János M. Bak, Jörg Jarnut, Pierre Monnet and Bernd Schneidmueller, eds, *Uses and Abuses of the Middle Ages: 19th–21st Century*, Wilhelm Fink, 2009, 215–233.
117. Popović, *Vidovdan i časni krst*, 157–159.

9. COURT-RADICAL COLLABORATION AND PRAETORIAN REACTION

1. Jovanović, *Vlada Aleksandra*, v1, 137–138.
2. Slobodan Jovanović, *Vlada Aleksandra Obrenovića*, v2, BIGZ, 1990, 142.
3. Jovanović, *Vlada Aleksandra*, v1, 142–143.
4. Petrovich, *Modern Serbia*, v2, 454.
5. Rajić, *Aleksandar Obrenović*, 32; Živanović, *Politička istorija*, v3, 53–54.
6. Jovanović, *Moji savremenici*, 139–140.
7. Popović-Obradović, *Parlamentarizam*, 83–85.
8. Perović, *Između anarhije i autokratije*, 154–155.
9. Mihailo Vojvodić, 'Prva i druga vlada Nikole Pašića (1891–1892)', in Vasilije Krestić, ed., *Nikola Pašić: Život i delo*, Zavod za udžbenika i nastavna sredstva, 1997, 109–110; Kazimirović, *Nikola Pašić*, v1, 512–514; Jovanović, *Vlada Aleksandra*, v1, 112–114.

10. Jovanović, *Vlada Aleksandra*, v1, 145–154.
11. Milanović, *Žensko društvo*, 125–126.
12. Piroćanac, *Beleške*, 483.
13. Đorđe Karađorđević, *Istina o mome životu*, Ivanka Marković Sontić, 1988, 193.
14. Živojinović, *Kralj Petar*, v1, 363.
15. Živanović, *Politička istorija*, v3, 104–105.
16. Marijan, *Povratak grofa od Takova*, 18–22.
17. Ibid., 33, 41, 55–57.
18. Ibid., 59–76.
19. Ibid., 44–45.
20. Ibid., 86–91.
21. Ibid., 95–97.
22. Ibid., 183.
23. Kazimirović, *Nikola Pašić*, v1, 525.
24. Marijan, *Povratak grofa od Takova*, 230–231.
25. Jovanović, *Vlada Aleksandra*, v1, 173–185.
26. Kazimirović, *Nikola Pašić*, v1, 526.
27. Živanović, *Politička istorija*, v3, 130.
28. Avakumović, *Memoari*, 320.
29. Rajić, *Aleksandar Obrenović*, 71–83.
30. Raša Milošević, *Državni udar ozgo: Prvi april 1893; Svrgnuće knjeg kraljevskog namestništva*, Geca Kon, 1936, 24.
31. Marijan, *Povratak grofa od Takova*, 276–277.
32. Ibid., 264–267; Rajić, *Aleksandar Obrenović*, 29–30; Avakumović, *Memoari*, 324–325.
33. Milošević, *Državni udar ozgo*, 41–42, 46.
34. Ibid., 132.
35. Marijan, *Povratak grofa od Takova*, 364.
36. Rajić, *Aleksandar Obrenović*, 87–91; Jovanović, *Vlada Aleksandra*, v1, 220.
37. Jovanović, *Vlada Aleksandra*, v1, 217–219.
38. Rajić, *Aleksandar Obrenović*, 128.
39. Ibid., 92–97; Chedomille Mijatovich, *A Royal Tragedy: Being the Story of the Assassination of King Alexander and Queen Draga of Serbia*, Dodd, Mead and Co., 1907, 51–52.
40. Đorđević, *Uspomene*, 367.
41. Milošević, *Državni udar ozgo*, 32.
42. Marijan, *Povratak grofa od Takova*, 430.
43. Rajić, *Aleksandar Obrenović*, 113.
44. Jovanović, *Vlada Aleksandra*, v1, 249.
45. Kazimirović, *Nikola Pašić*, v1, 536.
46. Jovanović, *Vlada Aleksandra*, v1, 268–273.
47. Ibid., 249–253.
48. Rajić, *Aleksandar Obrenović*, 116.

49. Jovanović, Vlada Aleksandra, v1, 259, 265.
50. Ibid., 266–267.
51. Rajić, *Aleksandar Obrenović*, 129.
52. Ibid., 283.
53. Mihailo Vojvodić, *Srbija u međunarodnim odnosima krajem XIX i početkom XX veka*, Srpska akademija nauka i umjetnosti, 1988, 43–51.
54. Jovanović, *Vlada Aleksandra*, v1, 298, 304–316.
55. Rajić, *Aleksandar Obrenović*, 187–188.
56. Vojvodić, *Srbija u međunarodnim odnosima*, 101–105.
57. Nicović, *Ustavni razvoj*, 227–232; Prodanović, *Ustavni razvitak*, 350–361.
58. Jovanović, *Vlada Aleksandra*, v1, 324–326.
59. Popović-Obradović, *Parlamentarizam*, 85–86.
60. Rajić, *Aleksandar Obrenović*, 166–167.
61. Živanović, *Politička istorija*, v3, 360–361.
62. Vojvodić, *Srbija u međunarodnim odnosima*, 151–153.
63. Stavro Skendi, *The Albanian National Awakening 1878–1912*, Princeton University Press, 2016, 257–286.
64. Djordje Stefanović, 'Seeing the Albanians through Serbian eyes: The inventors of the tradition of intolerance and their critics, 1804–1939', *European History Quarterly*, 35, 3 (July 2005), 469–472.
65. Ilić, *Oslobođenje Južne Srbije*, 219–222.
66. Skendi, *Albanian National Awakening*, 201–202, 293–294.
67. Rajić, *Aleksandar Obrenović*, 271.
68. Jovanović, *Vlada Aleksandra*, v1, 334.
69. Rajić, *Aleksandar Obrenović*, 224.
70. Jovanović, *Vlada Aleksandra*, v1, 364.
71. Ibid., 357–363.
72. Mijatovich, *Royal Tragedy*, 94.
73. Rajić, *Vladan Đorđević*, 79.
74. Jovanović, *Vlada Aleksandra*, v2, 15.
75. Ibid., 18–19.
76. Ibid., 17–24.
77. Kazimirović, *Nikola Pašić*, v1, 558.
78. Jovanović, *Vlada Aleksandra*, v2, 24–32.
79. Ibid., 44–46, 86–87; Raković-Kostić, *Evropeizacija srpske vojske*, 413.
80. Raković-Kostić, *Evropeizacija srpske vojske*, 335–344; Vojvodić, *Srbija u međunarodnim odnosima*, 214.
81. Jovanović, *Vlada Aleksandra*, v2, 66–78.
82. Rajić, *Aleksandar Obrenović*, 468–469.
83. Raković-Kostić, *Evropeizacija srpske vojske*, 391–406.
84. Rajić, *Aleksandar Obrenović*, 242–244.
85. Jovanović, *Vlada Aleksandra*, v2, 100–102.

86. Nikola Pašić, *Moja politička ispovest*, Zadužbina Miloša Crnjanskog, 1989, 158–160.
87. Jovanović, *Vlada Aleksandra*, v2, 102–125.
88. Pašić, *Moja politička ispovest*, 151–155.
89. Ibid., 167.
90. Ibid., 132.
91. Perović, *Izmedu anarhije i autokratije*, 161.
92. Dragiša Vasić, *Devetsto treća (majski prevrat)*, Tucović, 1925, 176–177; Jovanović, *Vlada Aleksandra*, v2, 162–163.
93. Rajić, *Aleksandar Obrenović*, 505.
94. Vasa Kazimirović, *Crna ruka: Ličnosti i dogadaji u Srbiji od prevrata 1903. do Solunskog procesa 1917. godine*, Prometej, 2013, 43.
95. Milanović, *Žensko društvo*, 117, 149–153, 444.
96. Živan Živanović, *Politička istorija Srbije u drugoj polovini devetnaestog veka*, v4, Izdavačka knjižarnica Gece Kona, 1925, 104.
97. Jovanović, *Vlada Aleksandra*, v2, 326.
98. Ana Milićević-Lunjevica, *Moja sestra Kraljica Draga*, Rad, 1995, 115.
99. Vladan Đorđević, *Kraj jedne dinastije: Prilozi za istoriju Srbije od 11 oktobra 1897 do 8 jula 1900*, v3, Štamparija D. Dimitrijević, 1906, 449–450.
100. Ibid., 452.
101. Ibid., 470–484.
102. Ibid., 685–694.
103. Radovan M. Drašković, *Pretorijanske težnje u Srbiji*, Žagor, 2006, 20–21.
104. Đorđević, *Kraj jedne dinastije*, v3, 643–644.
105. Avakumović, *Memoari*, 423–430; Kazimirović, *Nikola Pašić*, v1, 603–604; Rajić, *Aleksandar Obrenović*, 432.
106. Rajić, *Aleksandar Obrenović*, 293.
107. Kazimirović, *Nikola Pašić*, v1, 591–592.
108. Živanović, *Politička istorija*, v4, 228.
109. Jovanović, *Vlada Aleksandra*, v2, 326; Vasić, *Devetsto treća*, 52; Antonije Antić, *Beleške*, Zadužbina 'Nikola Pašić' and Narodni muzej, 2010, 59–61.
110. Rajić, *Aleksandar Obrenović*, 294.
111. Vasić, *Devetsto treća*, 11.
112. Antić, *Beleške*, 43.
113. Marija Cincar-Marković, 'Pred 29 maj 1903: Ženidba Kralja Aleksandra sa Dragom Mašin', *Politika*, 22 October 1926.
114. Stojančević, *Miloš Obrenović*, 203.
115. Jovanović, *Uspomene*, 488.
116. Jovanović, *Vlada Aleksandra*, v2, 168.
117. Đorđević, *Kraj jedne dinastije*, v3, 696.
118. Rajić, *Aleksandar Obrenović*, 296–298; Stanojević, *Istorija srpskog naroda*, 394–395.
119. Pašić, *Moja politička ispovest*, 175.
120. Rajić, *Aleksandar Obrenović*, 303.

121. Vasić, *Devetsto treća*, 53.
122. Raković-Kostić, *Evropeizacija srpske vojske*, 394–397.
123. Vasić, *Devetsto treća*, 12.
124. Vojvodić, *Srbija u međunarodnim odnosima*, 316–317.
125. Živojinović, *Kralj Petar*, v1, 437–439.
126. Mijatović, *Servia and the Servians*, 26.
127. Kazimirović, *Crna ruka*, 67–75.
128. Đukanović, *Ubistvo Kneza Mihaila*, v1, 22–23; Radenić, *Dnevnik Benjamina Kalaja*, 520.
129. Mišić, *Moje uspomene*, 215–216.
130. Prodanović, *Ustavni razvitak*, 377.
131. Ibid., 429–430; Nicović, *Ustavni razvoj*, 238.
132. Rajić, *Aleksandar Obrenović*, 304–314.
133. Nicović, *Ustavni razvoj*, 239–240.
134. Radojević, *Srpski ustavi*, 139–160; Jovanović, *Vlada Aleksandra*, v2, 211–214.
135. Popović-Obradović, *Parlamentarizam*, 87–92.
136. Ibid., 93–94.
137. Jovanović, *Vlada Aleksandra*, v2, 246–247.
138. Rajić, *Aleksandar Obrenović*, 497.
139. Milićević-Lunjevica, *Moja sestra Kraljica Draga*, 125.
140. Marija Cincar-Marković, 'Pred 29 maj 1903: Program i rad kabineta generala Cincar-Markovića', *Politika*, 24 October 1926.
141. Jovanović, *Vlada Aleksandra*, v2, 273–274.
142. Krestić and Ljušić, *Programi i statuti*, 243–245.
143. Perović, *Između anarhije i autokratije*, 355.
144. Rajić, *Aleksandar Obrenović*, 252.
145. Vladimir Ćorović, *Odnosi između Srbije i Austro-Ugarske u XX veku*, Biblioteka grada Beograda, 1992, 25.
146. Velimir Ivetić, 'Politička uloga ministara vojnih Kraljevine Srbije od 1903. do 1914. godine', doctoral dissertation, Faculty of Political Science, University of Belgrade, 2013, 34.
147. Rajić, *Aleksandar Obrenović*, 389.
148. Ibid., 429.
149. Ibid., 369.
150. Ibid., 379–380.
151. Vojvodić, *Srbija u međunarodnim odnosima*, 374–376.
152. Radoje Domanović, *Stradija*, Slovo ljubve, 1980, 51, 58–59, 61.
153. Pašić, *Moja politička ispovest*, 189–198.
154. Rajić, *Aleksandar Obrenović*, 326–328.

10. A ROYAL 'HONOUR KILLING'

1. Antić, *Beleške*, 36. Vojin Čolak-Antić, another officer conspirator, was similarly appointed to the Royal Guard by Milan at the same time.
2. Drašković, *Pretorijanske težnje*, 24.
3. Vasić, *Devetsto treća*, 53.
4. Drašković, *Pretorijanske težnje*, 25–26.
5. Kazimirović, *Nikola Pašić*, v1, 602–609.
6. Rajić, *Aleksandar Obrenović*, 292.
7. Živanović, *Politička istorija*, v4, 334.
8. Kazimirović, *Crna ruka*, 67–75, 101–107.
9. Rajić, *Aleksandar Obrenović*, 439; Antić, *Beleške*, 68–73.
10. Drašković, *Pretorijanske težnje*, 27–28.
11. Kazimirović, *Crna ruka*, 76–86.
12. Vasić, *Devetsto treća*, 63–64.
13. David MacKenzie, *The 'Black Hand' on Trial: Salonika, 1917*, East European Monographs, 1995, 7–24; Wayne S. Vucinich, *Serbia between East and West: The Events of 1903–1908*, Stanford University Press, 1954, 46–59; Petrovich, *Modern Serbia*, v2, 504–507.
14. MacKenzie, *Apis*, 36.
15. Živanović, *Politička istorija*, v4, 343–345; Živojinović, *Kralj Petar*, v1, 454–456.
16. Antić, *Beleške*, 81–83, 188–189; Kazimirović, *Nikola Pašić*, v1, 611.
17. Rajić, *Aleksandar Obrenović*, 442.
18. Jovanović, *Vlada Aleksandra*, v2, 334–335; Kazimirović, *Crna ruka*, 88.
19. MacKenzie, *Apis*, 27.
20. Petar Živković, *Sećanja 1903–1946*, Zadužbina 'Nikola Pašić' and Narodni Muzej 'Zaječar', 2016, 23.
21. Rajić, *Aleksandar Obrenović*, 443.
22. Vojvodić, *Srbija u međunarodnim odnosima*, 462; Kazimirović, *Nikola Pašić*, v1, 610.
23. M. Boghitschewitsch, *Die auswärtige Politik Serbiens 1903–1914*, vol. III: *Serbien und der Weltkrieg*, Brückenverlag, 1931, 7.
24. Kazimirović, *Crna ruka*, 96.
25. Živojinović, *Kralj Petar*, v1, 458–462.
26. Ibid., 439; Kazimirović, *Nikola Pašić*, v1, 611–612.
27. Živojinović, *Kralj Petar*, v1, 444–445; Jovanović, *Vlada Aleksandra*, v2, 274–275.
28. Drašković, *Pretorijanske težnje*, 45.
29. Jovanović, *Vlada Milana*, v2, 128–129.
30. Popov et al., *Istorija srpskog naroda*, v6.1, 10–15.
31. Sergije Dimitrijević, *Socijalistički radnički pokret u Srbiji, 1870–1918*, Nolit, 1982, 29–30; Palairet, *Balkan Economies*, 262–265.
32. Dimitrijević, *Socijalistički radnički pokret*, 22–25.
33. Isić, *Seljaštvo*, v1, 17–19; Petrovich, *Modern Serbia*, v2, 524–530.

34. Palairet, *Balkan Economies*, 99–100.
35. Ibid., 362.
36. Žanin-Čalić, *Socijalna istorija*, 64.
37. Radić, *Narodna verovanja*, 34.
38. Isić, *Seljaštvo*, v1, 15.
39. Ekmečić, *Stvaranje Jugoslavije*, v2, 76–77.
40. Žanin-Čalić, *Socijalna istorija*, 182–187.
41. Petrovich, *Modern Serbia*, v2, 523.
42. Stojanović, *Kaldrma i asfalt*, 117–135.
43. Dubravka Stojanović, *Iza zavese: Ogledi iz društvene istorije Srbije 1890–1914*, Udruženje za društvenu istoriju, 2013, 156–159.
44. Stojanović, *Kaldrma i asfalt*, 297–304.
45. Norris, *Belgrade*, 111.
46. Suzana Luković, '"Satana na četiri točka": Beograđani su od prvog auta u gradu bežali, vlasnik se plašio da ga vozi, a onda je misteriozno nestao', *Blic*, 21 March 2018.
47. Milanović, *Žensko društvo*, 28.
48. Popov et al., *Istorija srpskog naroda*, v6.1, 10–15, 32; Žanin-Čalić, *Socijalna istorija*, 244–254, 282, 288.
49. Perović, *Srpski socijalisti*, v3, 161–171.
50. Latinka Perović, ed., *Dimitrije Mita Cenić: Izabrani spisi*, v1, Rad, 1988, 109–110.
51. Ibid., 187–188.
52. Branko Nadoveza, 'Koncepcije federacije Mite Cenića', in Mihailo Marković, ed., *Socijaldemokratske nasleđe u Srbiji: Dimitrije Cenić*, Zavod za udžbenike i nastavna sredstva, 1995, 214–217.
53. Dimitrije Cenić, *Ispod zemlje ili moja tamnovanja*, Nolit, 1988, 75, 189–190.
54. Perović, *Srpski socijalisti*, v1, 298.
55. Dragiša Stanojević, *Interesi srpstva*, Štamparija Napredne stranke, 1885, 15–23.
56. Ibid., 182–183, 199.
57. Rajić, *Aleksandar Obrenović*, 457.
58. Spasić, *Kragujevačka vojna fabrika*, 199.
59. Dimitrijević, *Socijalistički radnički pokret*, 85–91.
60. Triša Kaclerović, *Radovan Dragović*, Rad, 1954, 21.
61. Triša Kaclerović, *Martovske demonstracije i majski prevrat*, Glavni odbor SSJ za Srbiju, 1950, 32–33.
62. Vasić, *Devetsto treća*, 44.
63. Božo K. Maršićanin, *Tajne dvora Obrenovića*, v2, self-published, 1907, 122.
64. Vasić, *Devetsto treća*, 134–135.
65. Marija Cincar-Marković, 'Pred 29 maj 1903: Martovske demonstracije', *Politika*, 27 October 1926.
66. Jovanović, *Vlada Aleksandra*, v2, 299; Kaclerović, *Martovske demonstracije*, 39–41; Rajić, *Aleksandar Obrenović*, 414–415, 434–435; Maršićanin, *Tajne dvora Obrenovića*, v2, 133.

67. Rajić, *Aleksandar Obrenović*, 436.
68. Kaclerović, *Martovske demonstracije*, 68–69.
69. Rajić, *Aleksandar Obrenović*, 417.
70. Ibid., 418–419.
71. Jovanović, *Vlada Aleksandra*, v2, 310.
72. Maršićanin, *Tajne dvora Obrenovića*, v2, 157–159, 166–170.
73. Jovanović, *Vlada Aleksandra*, v2, 337–338.
74. Rajić, *Aleksandar Obrenović*, 446–447.
75. Jovanović, *Uspomene*, 502.
76. Mladen J. Žujović, *Eseji o ljudima i dogadajima 1903–1959*, Interklima-grafika, 2004, 13.
77. Vasić, *Devetsto treća*, 83; Antić, *Beleške*, 165.
78. Vasić, *Devetsto treća*, 90.
79. Živković, *Sećanja*, 16–21.
80. MacKenzie, *Apis*, 42–43; Antić, *Beleške*, 165.
81. Kazimirović, *Crna ruka*, 16–17.
82. Vasić, *Devetsto treća*, 86–87.
83. Živković, *Sećanja*, 38–39.
84. Vasić, *Devetsto treća*, 95–96.
85. Milićević-Lunjevica, *Moja sestra Kraljica Draga*, 132.
86. Antić, *Beleške*, 170–171.
87. Kazimirović, *Nikola Pašić*, v1, 614; Kazimirović, *Crna ruka*, 16–17.
88. Kazimirović, *Nikola Pašić*, v1, 615.
89. Kazimirović, *Crna ruka*, 18–19.
90. Jovanović, *Uspomene*, 500–501.
91. Živanović, *Politička istorija*, v4, 353–354.
92. Milan Ž. Živanović, *Pukovnik Apis: Solunski process hiljada devetsto sedamnaesta*, self-published, 1955, 105.
93. Kazimirović, *Crna ruka*, 21–24; Christopher Clark, *The Sleepwalkers: How Europe Went to War in 1914*, Penguin, 2013, 96.
94. Antić, *Beleške*, 184.
95. Maršićanin, *Tajne dvora Obrenovića*, v2, VII–XI.
96. Vasić, *Devetsto treća*, 98–100; Živanović, *Pukovnik Apis*, 658; Branko Pejović, 'Neplanirano uz zaverenike u Majskom prevratu', *Politika*, 20 January 1918.
97. Mišić, *Moje uspomene*, 224–225.
98. Rajić, *Aleksandar Obrenović*, 527.
99. Kazimirović, *Crna ruka*, 23, 29.
100. Perović, *Izmedu anarhije i autokratije*, 313.
101. Rajić, *Aleksandar Obrenović*, 451–452.
102. Maršićanin, *Tajne dvora Obrenovića*, v2, XVI.
103. Drašković, *Pretorijanske težnje*, 42.
104. Mijatovich, *Royal Tragedy*, 205–206.

105. Pera Todorović, *Dnevnik*, Srpska književna zadruga, 1990, 424.
106. Perović, *Između anarhije i autokratije*, 168.
107. Milan Stojadinović, *Ni rat ni pakt: Jugoslavija između dva rata*, Glas, 2002, 12.
108. Elinor Glynn, *Three Weeks*, Aegypan Press, 2006, 115–120.
109. 'The murdered archduke', *John Bull*, 11 July 1914; 'To hell with Servia!', *John Bull*, 8 August 1914, reproduced in Henri Pozzi, *Black Hand Over Europe*, Croatian Information Centre, 1994, 260–263.
110. MacKenzie, *'Black Hand' on Trial*, 379.
111. Neil Balfour and Sally Mackay, *Paul of Yugoslavia: Britain's Maligned Friend*, Hamish Hamilton, 1980, 21, 305.
112. Vasić, *Devetsto treća*, 93.
113. Živanović, *Pukovnik Apis*, 661; Kazimirović, *Crna ruka*, 20.
114. Rajić, *Aleksandar Obrenović*, 452.
115. Raković-Kostić, *Evropeizacija srpske vojske*, 427.
116. Đorđević, *Kraj jedne dinastije*, v3, 732.
117. Jovanović, *Vlada Aleksandra*, v2, 349–352.
118. Ibid., 348.
119. Žujović, *Eseji o ljudima i događajima*, 8–9.
120. Drašković, *Pretorijanske težnje*, 13.
121. Ibid., 49; Rajić, *Aleksandar Obrenović*, 440.
122. Kazimirović, *Nikola Pašić*, v1, 615.
123. Kazimirović, *Crna ruka*, 72–74.
124. Karađorđević, *Istina o mome životu*, 197.
125. Norris, *Belgrade*, 104.
126. Kazimirović, *Nikola Pašić*, v2, 5–6.
127. Živojin Perić, *O amnestiji u srpskom krivičnom pravu u vezi sa pitanjm o sudskoj odgovornosti zaverenika*, Izdanja vlasništva Smotre, 1909, 58.
128. Popović-Obradović, *Parlamentarizam*, 98.
129. Pašić, *Moja politička ispovest*, 127–129.
130. Drašković, *Pretorijanske težnje*, 54–56; Popović-Obradović, *Parlamentarizam*, 98–103.
131. Kazimirović, *Crna ruka*, 133–134.
132. Popović-Obradović, *Parlamentarizam*, 106.
133. Dragoljub Živojinović, *Kralj Petar I Karađorđević*, v2, Zavod za udžbenike, 2009, 439–469; Boghitschewitsch, *Auswärtige Politik Serbiens*, 11–18.
134. Živojinović, *Kralj Petar*, v1, 70–75.
135. Todorović, *Dnevnik*, 372.
136. Aleksandar Lukić, *Jugoslovenska Republikanska Stranka u političkom životu Kraljevine Jugoslavije (1920–1941)*, INIS, 2020, 32–38, 61–62, 88.
137. Ivetić, 'Politička uloga ministara vojnih', 191.
138. Popović-Obradović, *Parlamentarizam*, 95–104.
139. Ibid., 119–136; Radojević, *Srpski ustavi*, 97–136, 163–188.
140. Popović-Obradović, *Parlamentarizam*, 144–145, 161.

141. Dubravka Stojanović, *Srbija i demokratija 1903–1914: Istorijska studija o 'zlatnom dobu srpske demokratije'*, Udruženje za društvenu istoriju, 2003, 352–363.
142. Popović-Obradović, *Parlamentariza*m, 113.
143. Todorović, *Dnevnik*, 419.
144. Rajić, *Aleksandar Obrenović*, 5–6.
145. Author's conversation with Latinka Perović, autumn 2006.
146. Dubravka Stojanović, 'Apis: povratak na mesto zločina', *Peščanik*, 8 September 2015.

11. RADICAL–CONSPIRATOR CONDOMINIUM

1. MacKenzie, *Apis*, xiii.
2. Vasić, *Devetsto treća*, 190–191; Ivetić, 'Politička uloga ministara vojnih', 198.
3. Jovanović, *Moji savremenici*, 402.
4. Savo Skoko, *Vojvoda Radomir Putnik*, v1, 2nd ed., BIGZ, 1985, 192–212.
5. Mišić, *Moje uspomene*, 236–237.
6. Kazimirović, *Crna ruka*, 196.
7. Vasić, *Devetsto treća*, 185–188.
8. Ibid., 194–196.
9. Raković-Kostić, *Evropeizacija srpske vojske*, 431.
10. Kazimirović, *Crna ruka*, 197–198.
11. Popović-Obradović, *Parlamentarizam*, 111–112.
12. Popović-Obradović, 'Koreni antimoderne političke kulture', 28–29.
13. Jovanović, *Moji savremenici*, 149–150.
14. Popović-Obradović, *Parlamentarizam*, 168–170; Kazimirović, *Crna ruka*, 131–132.
15. Popović-Obradović, *Parlamentarizam*, 114.
16. Perović, *Srpski socijalisti*, v3, 148.
17. Popović-Obradović, *Parlamentarizam*, 114–115.
18. Drašković, *Pretorijanske težnje*, 70–75.
19. Dušan Popović, 'Revolucionarna parodija', in Dušan Popović, *Izabrani spisi*, Prosveta, 1951, 392–393.
20. Živojinović, *Kralj Petar*, v2, 241–256.
21. Petrovich, *Modern Serbia*, v2, 544–548.
22. Stevan Simić, *Srpska revolucionarna organizacija: Komitsko četovanje u Staroj Srbiji i Makedoniji*, Duška, 1998, 52–59.
23. Momčilo Pavlović and Božica Mladenović, *Kosta Milovanović Pećanac 1879–1944: Biografija*, Institut za Savremenu Istoriju, 2006, 17–21.
24. Simić, *Srpska revolucionarna organizacija*, 123–159.
25. Ćorović, *Odnosi između Srbije i Austro-Ugarske*, 42–44.
26. Pavlović, *Balkan Anschluss*, 48–59.
27. Karađorđević, *Istina o mome životu*, 49–51.
28. Dimitrije-Dimo Vujović, *Ujedinjenje Crne Gore i Srbije*, Istorijski institut Narodne Republike Crne Gore, 1962, 45–46; Morrison, *Montenegro*, 32–33.

29. Roberts, *Realm of the Black Mountain*, 259.
30. Ibid., 273–275; Ivo Banac, *National Question*, 278–280; Drašković, *Pretorijanske težnje*, 160.
31. Stojanović, *Srbija i demokratija*, 111.
32. Jovanović, *Uspomene*, 503.
33. Kazimirović, *Crna ruka*, 183–184.
34. Živanović, *Pukovnik Apis*, 106.
35. Dimitrije Đorđević, *Carinski rat Austro-Ugarske i Srbije, 1906–1911*, Istorijski institut, 1962, 38–39.
36. Živojinović, *Kralj Petar*, v2, 191.
37. Živojin Balugdžić, *Pašić i Paču u službi otadžbine*, Taletova, 1905, 23–39.
38. Đorđević, *Carinski rat*, 66–67, 72; Živojinović, *Kralj Petar*, v2, 192–194.
39. Popović-Obradović, *Parlamentarizam*, 181.
40. Simić, *Srpska revolucionarna organizacija*, 58; Ivetić, 'Politička uloga ministara vojnih', 70.
41. Đorđević, *Carinski rat*, 152–153; Kazimirović, *Nikola Pašić*, v2, 52.
42. Đorđević, *Carinski rat*, 176–178.
43. Violeta Manojlović, 'Defence of national interest and sovereignty: Serbian government policy in the Bosnian crisis, 1906–1909', Master's thesis, Simon Fraser University, November 1997, 33.
44. Drašković, *Pretorijanske težnje*, 96–97.
45. Rajić, *Vladan Đorđević*, 280.
46. Kazimirović, *Nikola Pašić*, v1, 616.
47. Rajić, *Vladan Đorđević*, 274–284; Đorđević, *Carinski rat*, 216–217.
48. Popović-Obradović, *Parlamentarizam*, 285–286.
49. Skoko and Opačić, *Vojvoda Radomir Putnik*, v1, 173.
50. Vasić, *Devetsto treća*, 197–201
51. Spasić, *Kragujevačka vojna fabrika*, 207; Kaclerović, *Radovan Dragović*, 45; Skoko and Opačić, *Vojvoda Radomir Putnik*, v1, 175.
52. Vasić, *Devetsto treća*, 201–209.
53. Popović-Obradović, *Parlamentarizam*, 288.
54. Živojinović, *Kralj Petar*, v2, 283–284.
55. Branislav Gligorijević, *Kralj Aleksandar Karađorđević: U ratovima za nacionalno oslobodenje*, v1, Zavod za udžbenike i nastavna sredstva, 2002, 39; Mile Bjelajac, *Vojska Kraljevine Srba, Hrvata i Slovenaca*, Narodna Knjiga, 1988, 39; MacKenzie, *'Black Hand' on Trial*, 31; Đorđević, *Carinski rat*, 232.
56. Popović-Obradović, *Parlamentarizam*, 202–205.
57. Ibid., 288.
58. Dimitrijević, *Socijalistički radnički pokret*, 144.
59. Stojanović, *Iza zavese*, 26.
60. Popović-Obradović, *Parlamentarizam*, 203.
61. Ibid., 323–324.

62. Kaclerović, *Martovske demonstracije*, 79.
63. Kazimirović, *Crna ruka*, 221–228.
64. Živojinović, *Kralj Petar*, v2, 207.
65. Manojlović, 'Defence of national interest and sovereignty', 35–39.
66. Đorđević, *Carinski rat*, 298.
67. Ibid., 321–331.
68. Ćorović, *Odnosi između Srbije i Austro-Ugarske*, 110–115.
69. Đorđević, *Carinski rat*, 481–506, 513–517.
70. Kazimirović, *Nikola Pašić*, v2, 81.
71. Đorđević, *Carinski rat*, 454.
72. Popović-Obradović, *Parlamentarizam*, 213–222.
73. Andrew Mango, *Atatürk*, John Murray, London, 1999, 76–78.
74. Marko Attila Hoare, *The History of Bosnia: From the Middle Ages to the Present Day*, Saqi Books, 2007, 82.
75. Ekmečić, *Stvaranje Jugoslavije*, v2, 603.
76. Manojlović, 'Defence of national interest and sovereignty', 58.
77. Vrkatić, *Pojam i biće*, 479–480.
78. Manojlović, 'Defence of national interest and sovereignty', 59.
79. Popović-Obradović, *Parlamentarizam*, 374.
80. Vladimir Dedijer, *Sarajevo 1914*, Prosveta, 1978, v2, 91.
81. Živojinović, *Kralj Petar*, v2, 377–378.
82. Petrovich, *Modern Serbia*, v2, 548–557.
83. Dejan Šunjka and Rade Erceg, 'Okupljanje srpske pameti', *Glas Javnosti*, 13 April 2009.
84. MacKenzie, *'Black Hand' on Trial*, 32–33.
85. Manojlović, 'Defence of national interest and sovereignty', 69.
86. Vladimir Jovanović, 'Problem bliskog istoka i pangermanska opasnost', in Jovanović, *Izabrani spisi*, 493, 497, 505–506.
87. Manojlović, 'Defence of national interest and sovereignty', 63–65; Kazimirović, *Nikola Pašić*, v2, 105.
88. Manojlović, 'Defence of national interest and sovereignty', 68.
89. Ljušić, *Srpska državnost*, 436.
90. Ćorović, *Odnosi između Srbije i Austro-Ugarske*, 411–413; Morrison and Roberts, *Sandžak*, 78–86.
91. Ćorović, *Odnosi između Srbije i Austro-Ugarske*, 247–249; Manojlović, 'Defence of national interest and sovereignty', 78–79.
92. Stojanović, *Srbija i demokratija*, 386.
93. Olga Popović-Obradović, 'Živojin Perić između liberalizma i konzervatizma', in Jovica Trkulja and Dragoljub Popović, eds, *Liberalna misao u Srbiji: Prilozi istoriji liberalizma od kraja XVIII do sredine XX veka*, Centar za unapređivanje pravnih studija and Friedrich Naumann Stiftung, 2001, 327–335; Branko Nadoveza, *Politička misao Živojina Perića*, Institut za političke studije, 2005, 17.
94. Krestić and Ljušić, *Programi i statuti*, 493–494.

95. Samuel R. Williamson, *Austria-Hungary and the Origins of the First World War*, Macmillan, 1991, 71; Petrovich, *Modern Serbia*, v2, 561–562.
96. Žanin-Čalić, *Socijalna istorija*, 161.
97. Petrovich, *Modern Serbia*, v2, 562–564.
98. Slijepčević, *Istorija SPC*, v2, 448–449; Živojinović, *Kralj Petar*, v2, 448–450.
99. Dedijer, *Sarajevo*, v2, 85, 105.
100. *Narodna Odbrana*, Izdanje stredišnog odbora Narodne Odbrane, 1911.
101. Popović-Obradović, *Parlamentarizam*, 116.
102. Dedijer, *Sarajevo*, v1, 307–322.
103. Stojanović, *Srbija i demokratija*, 260.
104. Popović-Obradović, *Parlamentarizam*, 226–228.
105. Ibid., 385–389.
106. Petković, *Srpski obaveštajci*, 559–560.
107. Živojinović, *Kralj Petar*, v2, 346–351.
108. MacKenzie, *Apis*, 53, 76–86.
109. Ibid., 78; Živojinović, *Kralj Petar*, v2, 354–355.
110. Gligorijević, *Kralj Aleksandar*, v1, 40.
111. Živojinović, *Kralj Petar*, vol. v2, 379; MacKenzie, *Apis*, 77.
112. Antić, *Beleške*, 208.
113. Karađorđević, *Istina o mome životu*, 221–222, 267–272; Živojinović, *Kralj Petar*, v2, 353–354.
114. Drašković, *Pretorijanske težnje*, 98–99; Dedijer, *Sarajevo*, v2, 94–95; Gligorijević, *Kralj Aleksandar*, 1, 40–41.
115. Jovanović, *Moji savremenici*, 404.
116. Antić, *Beleške*, 248–250, 327–328.
117. MacKenzie, *Apis*, 84–85; Dedijer, *Sarajevo*, v2, 97; Živković, *Sećanja*, 59–65.
118. Dedijer, *Sarajevo*, v2, 86.
119. MacKenzie, *'Black Hand' on Trial*, 36–38.
120. Dedijer, *Sarajevo*, v2, 81–83.
121. 'Ustav organizacije "Ujedinjenje ili smrt"', in Bože Čović, ed., *Izvori velikosrpske agresije*, August Cesarec and Školska knjiga, 1991, 125–127; Drašković, *Pretorijanske težnje*, 120–121.
122. Živanović, *Pukovnik Apis*, 29; Dedijer, *Sarajevo*, v2, 86–87.
123. Dedijer, *Sarajevo*, v2, 81–82.
124. MacKenzie, *'Black Hand' on Trial*, 44.
125. Dedijer, *Sarajevo*, v2, 86.
126. Drašković, *Pretorijanske težnje*, 107.
127. 'Program "Pijemonta"', *Pijemont*, 21 August 1911.
128. Dedijer, *Sarajevo*, v2, 84–85.
129. Drašković, *Pretorijanske težnje*, 151–152.
130. Popović-Obradović, *Parlamentarizam*, 384.
131. Živanović, *Pukovnik Apis*, 27–28.

132. Živojinović, *Kralj Petar*, v2, 387.
133. Bjelajac, *Vojska Kraljevine SHS*, 43; Živanović, *Pukovnik Apis*, 35; Gligorijević, *Kralj Aleksandar*, v1, 50–51.
134. Drašković, *Pretorijanske težnje*, 107–108, 146–147.
135. Gligorijević, *Kralj Aleksandar*, v1, 45.
136. Ekmečić, *Dugo kretanje*, 338.
137. Drašković, *Pretorijanske težnje*, 145–147.
138. Joachim Remak, *Sarajevo: The Story of a Political Murder*, Weidenfeld and Nicolson, 1959, 48.

12. THE BALKAN WARS AND THE ROAD TO WORLD WAR I

1. Banac, *National Question*, 84.
2. Marković, 'Slovenska Austrija i Srpsko jedinstvo', 96–101.
3. Pašić, *Moja politička ispovest*, 131–132.
4. Đorđe Stanković, *Nikola Pašić: Prilozi za biografiju*, Plato, 2006, 185–193.
5. Stanković, *Nikola Pašić i jugoslovensko pitanje*, v1, 89.
6. Stanković, *Prilozi za biografiju*, 271–272.
7. Nikola Pašić, *Sloga Srbo-Hrvata*, Vreme knjige, 1995, 48–52, 60–63.
8. Ibid., 90–94, 100–105.
9. Charles Jelavich, *South Slav Nationalisms: Textbooks and Yugoslav Union before 1914*, Ohio State University Press, 1990, 34.
10. Ibid., 140–141.
11. Ibid., 61–98.
12. Ibid., 74–77.
13. Miller, *Between Nation and State*, 38–42, 103–107.
14. Magaš, *Croatia Through History*, 453–455.
15. Ibid., 456; Miller, *Between Nation and State*, 137–143.
16. Magaš, *Croatia Through History*, 457–461.
17. Mira Radojević, 'O jugoslovenstvu samostalnih radnika', *Istorija 20. veka*, 16, 2 (1998), 17–30.
18. Krestić and Ljušić, *Programi i statuti*, 322.
19. Ekmečić, *Stvaranje Jugoslavije*, v2, 561.
20. Viktor Novak, ed., *Antologija jugoslovenske misli i narodnog jedinstva, 1390–1930*, Autorovo štampa državne štamparije, 1930, 574.
21. Jovan Skerlić, 'Neoslavizam i jugoslovenstvo', in Jovan Skerlić, *Feljtoni, skice i govori*, Prosveta, 1964, 235–237.
22. Banac, *National Question*, 211.
23. Gligorijević, *Kralj Aleksandar*, v1, 377.
24. Cvijić, *Balkansko poluostrvo*, 344–355.
25. Ibid., 344, 348.
26. Jovan Cvijić, 'O nacionalnom radu', in Jovan Cvijić, *Govori i članci*, v1, Napredak, 1921, 54–59.

27. Ibid., 64–71.
28. Jovan Cvijić, *Aneksija Bosne i Hercegovine i srpski problem*, Državna štamparija Kraljevine Srbije, 1908, 16–20, 55, 59, 62.
29. Jelavich, *South Slav Nationalisms*, 74–77.
30. Ljubodrag Dimić, *Kulturna politika u Kraljevini Jugoslavije 1918–1941*, v1, Društvo i država, Stubovi kulture, 1996, 86.
31. Stojanović, *Kaldrma i asfalt*, 352.
32. Clark, *Sleepwalkers*, 259–262, 281–282.
33. Gligorijević, *Kralj Aleksandar*, v1, 353.
34. Mehmet Hacısalihoğlu, 'The Young Turk policy in Macedonia: Cause of the Balkan Wars?', in M. Hakan Yavuz and Isa Blumi, eds, *War and Nationalism: The Balkan Wars, 1912–1913, and Their Sociopolitical Implications*, University of Utah Press, 2013, 100–131; Richard C. Hall, 'Bulgaria and the origins of the Balkan Wars, 1912–1913', in Yavuz and Blumi, *War and Nationalism*, 85–99.
35. Crampton, *Bulgaria 1878–1918*, 404–407.
36. Vrkatić, *Pojam i biće*, 499–504.
37. Kazimirović, *Nikola Pašić*, v2, 156–161.
38. Stefanović, 'Seeing the Albanians through Serbian eyes', 472.
39. Milan Nikšić, 'Stanje u Turskoj na Kosovu i Metohiji za vreme poslednje decenije njihove vladavine', in Dušan T. Bataković, ed., *Savremenici o Kosovo i Metohiji 1852–1912*, Srpska književna zadruga, 1988, 368–369.
40. Milan Rakić, *Konzulska pisma 1905–1911*, Prosveta, 1985, 94.
41. Ibid., 50, 59, 106–107, 280–284, 296–298.
42. Malcolm, *Kosovo*, 242–243.
43. Ibid., 246–248; Ekmečić, *Stvaranje Jugoslavije*, v2, 646–647.
44. Stanković, *Prilozi za biografiju*, 204.
45. Tomasevich, *Peasants*, 125, 346; Milovan Obradović, *Agrarna reforma i kolonizacija na Kosovu (1914–1941)*, Institut za istoriju, Kosova, 1981, 23.
46. Gligorijević, *Kralj Aleksandar*, v1, 353.
47. Leon Trotsky, *The Balkan Wars 1912–13*, Pathfinder Press, 1980, 103–104.
48. Maja Miljković, 'The Serbian view of Macedonia', *South Slav Journal*, 21, 81–82 (Autumn/Winter 2000), 26.
49. Ivetić, 'Politička uloga ministara vojnih', 127–128.
50. Milorad Ekmečić, *Ratni ciljevi Srbije 1914.*, Srpska književna zadruga, 1973, 37–38.
51. Mustafa Imamović, *Historija Bošnjaka*, Preporod, 1997, 458.
52. Imami, *Srbi i Albanci*, 201.
53. Richard C. Hall, *The Balkan Wars 1912–1913: Prelude to the First World War*, Routledge, 2000, 45–55, 86–90.
54. Ljušić, *Knjiga o Načertaniju*, 118, 120.
55. Stanković, *Prilozi za biografiju*, 200–210.
56. Jovan Cvijić, 'Izlazak Srbije na Jadransko more', in Cvijić, *Govori i članci*, v2, 22–23.
57. Malcolm, *Kosovo*, 256.

58. Stanković, *Nikola Pašić i jugoslovensko pitanje*, v1, 111–112.
59. Stanković, *Prilozi za biografiju*, 211.
60. Malcolm, *Kosovo*, 257.
61. Justin McCarthy *Death and Exile: The Ethnic Cleansing of Ottoman Muslims, 1821–1922*, Darwin Press, 1996, 135, 164.
62. Jovan Cvijić, 'Raspored balkansih naroda', in Cvijić, *Govori i članci*, v1, 165–166.
63. Stanković, *Nikola Pašić i jugoslovensko pitanje*, v1, 135.
64. Trotsky, *Balkan Wars*, 366.
65. Stanković, *Prilozi za biografiju*, 213–214.
66. Jovanović, *Moji savremenici*, 165.
67. Dedijer, *Sarajevo*, v2, 98.
68. Kazimirović, *Crna ruka*, 553–556.
69. Drašković, *Pretorijanske težnje*, 164–165.
70. Kazimirović, *Nikola Pašić*, v2, 172.
71. Živojinović, *Kralj Petar*, v2, 505.
72. Dimitrije Djordjević, 'Radomir Putnik', in Peter Radan and Aleksandar Pavkovic, eds, *The Serbs and Their Leaders in the Twentieth Century*, Ashgate, 1997, 123–124.
73. Hall, *Balkan Wars*, 107–125.
74. Stavrianos, *Balkans Since 1453*, 540; Ljušić, *Srpska državnost*, 32, 38.
75. Clark, *Sleepwalkers*, 99–100.
76. Joachim Remak, '1914: The Third Balkan War; Origins reconsidered', in H.W. Koch, ed., *The Origins of the First World War: Great Power Rivalry and German War Aims*, 2nd ed., Macmillan, 1984, 98.
77. Stanković, *Nikola Pašić i jugoslovensko pitanje*, v1, 137–138.
78. Williamson, *Austria-Hungary and the Origins of the First World War*, 154.
79. Stanković, *Nikola Pašić i jugoslovensko pitanje*, v1, 142–143.
80. Stojadinović, *Ni rat ni pakt*, 53.
81. Jovan Cvijić, 'Geografski i kulturni položaj Srbije', in Cvijić, *Govori i članci*, v2, 38.
82. Stefanović, 'Seeing the Albanians through Serbian eyes', 472.
83. Vladan Đorđević, *Arnauti i velike sile*, ANN Istočnik, Prnjavor, 2004, 12.
84. Ibid., 30, 41.
85. Balkanicus, *Srbi i bugari u Balkanskom ratu*, Gece Kona, 1913, 21–22, 83, 99, 148.
86. Balkanicus, *Albanski problem i Srbija i Austro-Ugarska*, Gece Kona, 1913, 11, 18, 31, 62.
87. Malcolm, *Kosovo*, 254.
88. James Lyon, *Serbia and the Balkan Front, 1914: The Outbreak of the Great War*, Bloomsbury, 2015, 76.
89. Kazimirović, *Crna ruka*, 236–240.
90. Stefanović, 'Seeing the Albanians through Serbian Eyes', 475.
91. Clark, *Sleepwalkers*, 44.
92. Trotsky, *Balkan Wars*, 267, 286.
93. Hall, *Balkan Wars*, 137.

94. *The Other Balkan Wars: A 1913 Carnegie Endowment Inquiry in Retrospect with a New Introduction and Reflections on the Present Conflict by George F. Kennan*, Carnegie Endowment for International Peace, 1993, 151.
95. Popović, 'Revolucionarna parodija', 394.
96. Triša Kaclerović, *Militarizam u Srbiji: Afere i skandali u vojsci*, Narodni univerzitet, 1952, 39.
97. Dimitrijević, *Socijalistički radnički pokret*, 137.
98. Dušan Popović, 'Monarhistička legenda', in Popović, *Izabrani spisi*, 194.
99. Dimitrijević, *Socijalistički radnički pokret*, 144–145.
100. Spasić, *Kragujevačka vojna fabrika*, 211–212.
101. Moša Pijade, ed., *Istorijski arhiv Komunističke Partije Jugoslavije*, v3, Istorijskog odeljenje Centralnog komiteta KPJ, 1950, 240.
102. Dimitrije Tucović, 'Naša reč', in Dimitije Tucović, *Sabrana dela*, v2, Rad, 1980, 270.
103. Dimitrije Tucović, 'Protiv tutorstva birokratije', in Tucović, *Sabrana dela*, v3, 254.
104. Dimitrije Tucović, 'Buržoaska i proleterska Srbija', in Tucović, *Sabrana dela*, v4, 163.
105. Dimitrije Tucović, 'Rad s Arbanasima', in Tucović, *Sabrana dela*, v7, 72–72.
106. Dimitrije Tucović, 'Krvna osveta soldateske', in Tucović, *Sabrana dela*, v7, 161.
107. Tucović, 'Srbija i Arbanija', in Tucović, *Sabrana dela*, v7, 98–102.
108. Ibid., 39, 74–79.
109. Dimitrije Tucović, 'Albansko pitanje', in Tucović, *Sabrana dela*, v3, 232–239; Branko Nadoveza, *Srpski socijaldemokrati i ideja balkanske federacije do 1918*, Institut za noviju istoriju Srbije, 2000, 67–91.
110. Dimitrije Tucović, 'Balkanski savez', in Tucović, *Sabrana dela*, v7, 28–31; Tucović, 'Srbija i Arbanija', 110.
111. Stanković, *Prilozi za biografiju*, 214.
112. Ekmečić, *Ratni ciljevi*, 257–258.
113. Gligorijević, *Kralj Aleksandar*, v1, 55.
114. *Other Balkan Wars*, 159.
115. Miljković, 'Serbian view of Macedonia', 27–28.
116. *Other Balkan Wars*, 160.
117. Ekmečić, *Ratni ciljevi*, 258; Banac, *National Question*, 317.
118. Malcolm, *Kosovo*, 279; Tomasevich, *Peasants*, 125.
119. Miroslav Perišić, ed., *Ministarstvo i ministri policije u Srbiji 1811–2001*, Vojna štamparija, 2002, 64–65.
120. Radojević, *Srpski ustavi*, 97–98.
121. Popović-Obradović, *Parlamentarizam*, 404–408; Malcolm, *Kosovo*, 264–265.
122. Gligorijević, *Kralj Aleksandar*, v1, 53.
123. Kazimirović, *Nikola Pašić*, v2, 169.
124. Popović-Obradović, *Parlamentarizam*, 412–413; Clark, *Sleepwalkers*, 96–97; Kazimirović, *Crna ruka*, 543–544.
125. Popović, 'Revolucionarna parodija', 399.
126. Ekmečić, *Ratni ciljevi*, 64–65.

127. Dedijer, *Sarajevo*, v2, 100.
128. Perišić, ed., *Ministarstvo i ministri policije*, 65.
129. Popović-Obradović, *Parlamentarizam*, 413–415.
130. Kazimirović, *Nikola Pašić*, v2, 217–218.
131. Drašković, *Pretorijanske težnje*, 176; Gligorijević, *Kralj Aleksandar*, v1, 58; Kazimirović, *Crna ruka*, 568.
132. Dedijer, *Sarajevo*, v2, 101.
133. Ibid., 101.
134. Živanović, *Pukovnik Apis*, 220–221.
135. Živojinović, *Kralj Petar*, v2, 522.
136. Živanović, *Pukovnik Apis*, 214–220.
137. Jovanović, *Moji savremenici*, 445; Bjelajac, *Vojska Kraljevine SHS*, 43; Dedijer, *Sarajevo*, v2, 101–102.
138. Kazimirović, *Crna ruka*, 597.
139. Dušan T. Bataković, 'Storm over Serbia: The rivalry between civilian and military authorities (1911–1914)', *Balcanica*, 44 (2013), 340–343; Živanović, *Pukovnik Apis*, 225–226.
140. Živojinović, *Kralj Petar*, v2, 528–530.
141. Ekmečić, *Ratni ciljevi*, 64–65.
142. Đorđe Stanković, *Nikola Pašić, saveznici i stvaranje Jugoslavije*, Nolit, 1984, 88–90; Dragoljub Živojinović, *Vatikan, Srbija i stvaranje jugoslovenske države 1914–1920*, Nolit, 1980, 45–47.
143. Miller, *Between State and Nation*, 167.
144. Dedijer, *Sarajevo*, v2, 123–124.
145. Ibid., 86.
146. Mackenzie, *Apis*, 123–137; Remak, *Sarajevo*, 56–57.
147. Antić, *Beleške*, 267–268, 338–339.
148. Drašković, *Pretorijanske težnje*, 267; Remak, *Sarajevo*, 53; Živanović, *Pukovnik Apis*, 278.
149. Remak, *Sarajevo*, 66–68.
150. Clark, *Sleepwalkers*, 57–58.
151. Ibid., 59–63; Remak, *Sarajevo*, 71–78.
152. Remak, *Sarajevo*, 93–96.
153. See Fritz Fischer, 'World policy, world power and German war aims', in Koch, *Origins of the First World War*, 128–188.
154. Niall Ferguson, 'Public finance and national security: The domestic origins of the First World War Revisited', *Past and Present*, 142 (February 1994), 141–168.
155. Clark, *Sleepwalkers*, 293–301, 349–358.
156. Jovanović, *Moji savremenici*, 171.
157. Silvija Ćurić and Vidosav Stevanović, eds, *Golgota i Vaskrs Srbije 1914–1915*, 2nd ed., Zrinski, 1989, 9–17.
158. Kazimirović, *Nikola Pašić*, v2, 286.

159. Gordon Martel, *The Month That Changed the World: July 1914 and WWI*, Oxford University Press, 2014, 265–267.
160. Dragoljub Živojinović, *Kralj Petar I Karađorđević*, v3, Zavod za udžbenike, 2009, 9–11.
161. Vlado Strugar, *Jugoslavenske socijaldemokratske stranke 1914–1918*, Jugoslavenska akademija znanonsi i umjetnosti, 1963, 18–19.
162. Pijade, *Istorijski arhiv KPJ*, v3, 286.

13. DEFEAT AND OCCUPATION

1. Stanković, *Prilozi za biografiju*, 272.
2. Milan Đorđević, *Srbija i jugosloveni za vreme rata 1914–1918*, Biblioteka grada Beograda, 1991, 270.
3. Stanković, *Nikola Pašić i jugoslovensko pitanje*, v1, 207–210; Andrej Mitrović, *Srbija u Prvom svetskom ratu*, 2nd ed., Glasnik, 2015, 388.
4. Vrkatić, *Pojam i biće*, 586–587.
5. Gligorijević, *Kralj Aleksandar*, v1, 354–355.
6. Branislav Gligorijević, 'King Aleksandar I Karađorđević', in Radan and Pavkovic, *Serbs and Their Leaders in the Twentieth Century*, 148.
7. Ekmečić, *Ratni ciljevi*, 153–156.
8. Mitrović, *Srbija u Prvom svetskom ratu*, 107–110.
9. Ekmečić, *Ratni ciljevi*, 86–87; Gligorijević, *Kralj Aleksandar*, v1, 375.
10. Gligorijević, *Kralj Aleksandar*, v1, 370.
11. Ekmečić, *Ratni ciljevi*, 333.
12. Banac, *National Question*, 117.
13. Ekmečić, *Ratni ciljevi*, 87.
14. Dragoslav Janković, *Srbija i jugoslovensko pitanje 1914.–1915. godine*, Institut za Savremenu Istoriju, 1973, 204.
15. Vrkatić, *Pojam i biće*, 597–598.
16. Lyon, *Serbia and the Balkan Front*, 147–148.
17. Miloš Brun, *Belgrade during the Great War: The City Through the Eyes of Those Who Lived in It*, Helion and Company, 2018, 15, 45–46.
18. Mira Radojević and Ljubodrag Dimić, *Srbija u velikom ratu 1914–1918: Kratka istorija*, Srpska književna zadruga, 2014, 127–128.
19. Janković, *Srbija i jugoslovensko pitanje*, 230–231.
20. Ekmečić, *Stvaranje Jugoslavije*, v2, 711–719; Pero Slijepčević, 'Bosna i Hercegovina u Svetskom Ratu', in Pero Slijepčević, ed., *Napor Bosne i Hercegovine za oslobođenje i ujedinjenje*, Narodna Odbrana, 1929, 221–235.
21. Imamović, *Historija Bošnjaka*, 463–465.
22. Richard L. DiNardo, *Invasion: The Conquest of Serbia, 1915*, Praeger, 2015, 16–21.
23. Barbara Jelavich, *History of the Balkans: Twentieth Century*, v2, Cambridge University Press, 1983, 116.
24. Lyon, *Serbia and the Balkan Front*, 74–94, 238–245.

25. Ekmečić, *Ratni ciljevi*, 157.
26. Ibid., 152–153.
27. Brun, *Belgrade during the Great War*, 38–41.
28. Vladimir Dedijer, Ivan Božić, Sima Ćirković and Milorad Ekmečić, *History of Yugoslavia*, McGraw-Hill, 1974, 480.
29. Kazimirović, *Crna ruka*, 536–551.
30. Mitrović, *Srbija u Prvom svetskom ratu*, 93.
31. Ekmečić, *Ratni ciljevi*, 89–90.
32. Stanković, *Nikola Pašić i jugoslovensko pitanje*, v1, 151–153.
33. Gligorijević, *Kralj Aleksandar*, v1, 355.
34. Brun, *Belgrade during the Great War*, 48.
35. DiNardo, *Invasion*, 131–138.
36. Vrkatić, *Pojam i biće*, 599–600.
37. Janković, *Srbija i jugoslovensko pitanje*, 210–211.
38. Stanković, *Nikola Pašić i jugoslovensko pitanje*, v1, 155–156.
39. Ibid., 206.
40. Živojinović, *Kralj Petar*, v3, 60–65.
41. Đorđe Stanković, *Srbija i stvaranje Jugoslavije*, Službeni glasnik, 2009, 75–76.
42. Janković, *Srbija i jugoslovensko pitanje*, 278–288.
43. Aleksandar Belić, *Srbija i jugoslovensko pitanje*, Biblioteka grada Beograda, 1991, 78, 114, 126.
44. Stanoje Stanojević, *Što hoće Srbija?*, Državna štamparija Kraljevine Srbije, 1915, 21, 25, 27.
45. Stanković, *Nikola Pašić i jugoslovensko pitanje*, v1, 203–204.
46. Ekmečić, *Ratni ciljevi*, 333–334.
47. Mitrović, *Srbija u Prvom svetskom ratu*, 175–177.
48. Ekmečić, *Ratni ciljevi*, 404.
49. Mitrović, *Srbija u Prvom svetskom ratu*, 183.
50. Ekmečić, *Ratni ciljevi*, 393.
51. Gligorijević, *Kralj Aleksandar*, v1, 153–154.
52. Mitrović, *Srbija u Prvom svetskom ratu*, 185.
53. Ekmečić, *Ratni ciljevi*, 405–409.
54. Janković, *Srbija i jugoslovensko pitanje*, 151.
55. Vujović, *Ujedinjenje Crne Gore i Srbije*, 114.
56. Ibid., 105; Pavlović, *Balkan Anschluss*, 69.
57. Vujović, *Ujedinjenje Crne Gore i Srbije*, 108–109.
58. Banac, *National Question*, 282.
59. Vujović, *Ujedinjenje Crne Gore i Srbije*, 112.
60. Petrovich, *Modern Serbia*, v2, 630.
61. Janković, *Srbija i jugoslovensko pitanje*, 130.
62. Ekmečić, *Ratni ciljevi*, 264.
63. Ibid., 255–268.

64. Stanković, *Nikola Pašić i jugoslovensko pitanje*, v1, 159–160.
65. Gligorijević, *Kralj Aleksandar*, v1, 362.
66. Ibid., 357.
67. Kazimirović, *Nikola Pašić*, v2, 369.
68. Janković, *Srbija i jugoslovensko pitanje*, 130–131.
69. Andrej Mitrović, *Serbia's Great War 1914–1918*, Hurst, 2007, 118.
70. Crampton, *Bulgaria 1878–1918*, 440–443.
71. Gligorijević, *Kralj Aleksandar*, v1, 161–162.
72. DiNardo, *Invasion*, 22–35.
73. Mitrović, *Srbija u Prvom svetskom ratu*, 200–201.
74. Hugh Seton-Watson, Christopher Seton-Watson, Ljubo Boban, Mirjana Gross, Bogdan Krizman and Dragovan Šepić, eds, *R.W. Seton-Watson and the Yugoslavs*, v1, British Academy, University of Zagreb, Institute of Croatian History, 1976, 251.
75. Gligorijević, *Kralj Aleksandar*, v1, 181–185.
76. Kazimirović, *Nikola Pašić*, v2, 380–381.
77. DiNardo, *Invasion*, 121–130.
78. Mile Bjelajac, 'King Petar I Karadjordjević', in Radan and Pavkovic, *Serbs and Their Leaders in the Twentieth Century*, 107.
79. Zarija Vukičević, 'Iz dnevnika šesnaestogodišnjeg dečaka dobrovoljca', in Silvija Ćurić and Vidosav Stevanović, eds, *Golgota i Vaskrs Srbije 1915–1918*, 2nd ed., Zrinski, 1989, 60.
80. Katarina Kostić, 'Bolna sećanja', in Ćurić and Stevanović, *Golgota i Vaskrs Srbije 1915–1918*, 182.
81. Andrej Mitrović, Pavle Ivić, Dragiša Živković, Predrag Palavestra, Dejan Medaković, Radovan Samardžić and Vladeta Tešić, *Istorija srpskog naroda*, v6.2, Srpska književna zadruga, 1983, 102.
82. Josip Jeras, 'Planina smrti', in Ćurić and Stevanović, *Golgota i Vaskrs Srbije 1915–1918*, 133–134.
83. Petar Opačić, *Srbija, solunski front i ujedinjenje 1918*, 2nd ed., Književne novine, 1990, 29–30; Richard C. Hall, *Balkan Breakthrough: The Battle of Dobro Pole 1918*, Indiana University Press, 2010, 63–64.
84. DiNardo, *Invasion*, 101–120.
85. Predrag Pejčić, *Srpska vojska u Bizerti (1916–1918)*, Zavod za udžbenike, 2008, 9–21.
86. Ibid., 121–140.
87. Božidar Cermanović-Cera, 'Srbi na Krfu', in Ćurić and Stevanović, *Golgota i Vaskrs Srbije 1915–1918*, 337–348.
88. Gligorijević, *Kralj Aleksandar*, v1, 254.
89. Ibid., 209–225.
90. Hall, *Balkan Breakthrough*, 66.
91. Banac, *National Question*, 280–284; Roberts, *Realm of the Black Mountain*, 304–315; Nikola Milovanović, *Vojni puč i 27. mart 1941*, Sloboda, 1981, 281; Dragovan Šepić, *Italija, saveznici i jugoslavensko pitanje 1914–1918*, Školska knjiga, 1970, 149–150.

92. Vujović, *Ujedinjenje Crne Gore i Srbije*, 117–118.
93. Mitrović, *Srbija u Prvom svetskom ratu*, 201–202.
94. Ljubinka Trgovčević, *Naučnici Srbije i stvaranje jugoslovenske države*, Narodna knjiga, 1986, 84–85.
95. Ivetić, 'Politička uloga ministara vojnih', 536–537
96. Mitrović, *Srbija u Prvom svetskom ratu*, 300–309.
97. See Jonathan Gumz, *The Resurrection and Collapse of Empire in Habsburg Serbia, 1914–1918*, Cambridge University Press, 2009.
98. Mitrović, *Srbija u Prvom svetskom ratu*, 310–311.
99. Radojević and Dimić, *Srbija u velikom ratu*, 160–162.
100. Gumz, *Resurrection and Collapse*, 84–86.
101. Ibid., 229–230.
102. Ibid., 116–120.
103. Ibid., 96–98; Mitrović, *Srbija u Prvom svetskom ratu*, 301–304.
104. Emily Greble, *Muslims and the Making of Modern Europe*, Oxford University Press, 2021, 102; Morrison and Roberts, *Sandžak*, 93
105. Avakumović, *Memoari*, 625.
106. Milivoje Perović, *Toplički ustanak*, Kultura, 1988, 27.
107. Mitrović, *Srbija u Prvom svetskom ratu*, 295–297.
108. Perović, *Toplički ustanak*, 44.
109. Ibid., 317.
110. Andrej Mitrović, *Ustaničke borbe u Srbiji 1916–1918.*, Srpska književna zadruga, 1988, 133–135.
111. Ibid., 154–155.
112. Mitrović, *Srbija u Prvom svetskom ratu*, 229; Kazimirović, *Crna ruka*, 705–707.
113. Mile Bjelajac, 'Komandovanje dobrovoljačkim jedinicama i crnorukci', in Kačavenda, *Dobrovoljci*, 122–124.
114. Perović, *Toplički ustanak*, 66–69.
115. Mitrović, *Ustaničke borbe*, 159–161.
116. Ibid., 207–208.
117. Perović, *Toplički ustanak*, 172.
118. Ibid., 215, 315, 317–326.
119. Mitrović, *Ustaničke borbe*, 385–388.
120. Ekmečić, *Stvaranje Jugoslavije*, v2, 781.
121. Perović, *Toplički ustanak*, 44.
122. Mitrović, *Ustaničke borbe*, 422–428.
123. Perović, *Toplički ustanak*, 300.
124. Mitrović, *Srbija u Prvom svetskom ratu*, 227–229.
125. Stanković, *Nikola Pašić i jugoslovensko pitanje*, v2, 88–90; George Grlica, *Odessa in 1917 from a Croatian Perspective*, New York, 2000 [reprinted from the *Journal of Croatian Studies*, 38 (1997)], 13–23.
126. Petrovich, *Modern Serbia*, v2, 634–635; Grlica, *Odessa*, 23–27.

127. Dragoslav Janković, *Jugoslovensko pitanje i krfska deklaracija 1917. godine*, Savremena administracija, 1967, 78; Stanković, *Nikola Pašić i jugoslovensko pitanje*, v2, 97–98.
128. Aleksandar S. Jovanović, 'Uzroci velikih gubitaka 1. srpske dobrovoljačke divizije u Dobrudži 1916.', in Kačavenda, *Dobrovoljci*, 125–134.
129. Janković, *Krfska deklaracija*, 79.
130. Stanković, *Nikola Pašić i jugoslovensko pitanje*, v2, 107–108.
131. Grlica, *Odessa in 1917*, 54.

14. LIBERATION AND UNIFICATION

1. Ekmečić, *Ratni ciljevi*, 108–112.
2. Jovanović, *Moji savremenici*, 421–422.
3. Ivetić, 'Politička uloga ministara vojnih', 122.
4. Živanović, *Pukovnik Apis*, 44–45.
5. Gligorijević, *Kralj Aleksandar*, v1, 249–250.
6. Ibid., 208.
7. Drašković, *Pretorijanske težnje*, 233–235.
8. Branislav Gligorijević, 'Regent Aleksandar Karađorđević i dobrovoljci', in Kačavenda, *Dobrovoljci*, 96–97.
9. Bjelajac, 'Komandovanje dobrovoljačkim jedinicama i crnorukci', 117–118; MacKenzie, *'Black Hand' on Trial*, 352–354.
10. Dragan Bakić, 'Apis's men: The Black Hand conspirators after the Great War', *Balcanica*, 66 (2015), 221–225.
11. Seton-Watson et al., *R.W. Seton-Watson and the Yugoslavs*, v1, 297.
12. Jovanović, *Moji savremenici*, 422–423.
13. Živanović, *Pukovnik Apis*, 278.
14. Jovanović, *Moji savremenici*, 174–175, 425–427, 453–454; Gligorijević, *Kralj Aleksandar*, v1, 255–261; Kazimirović, *Crna ruka*, 681–704.
15. Živanović, *Pukovnik Apis*, 57–58.
16. MacKenzie, *'Black Hand' on Trial*, 87–93; Pejčić, *Srpska vojska u Bizerti*, 159–162.
17. Gligorijević, *Kralj Aleksandar*, v1, 262–263.
18. Živanović, *Pukovnik Apis*, 103–106.
19. Ibid., 101–135.
20. Ibid., 163–164, 168.
21. Mackenzie, *Apis*, 250–251, 264.
22. Živanović, *Pukovnik Apis*, 284–293, 461.
23. MacKenzie, *'Black Hand' on Trial*, 345–346.
24. Gligorijević, *Kralj Aleksandar*, v1, 272.
25. Živojinović, *Kralj Petar*, v3, 262.
26. Živanović, *Pukovnik Apis*, 530–531.
27. Mitrović et al., *Istorija srpskog naroda*, v6.2, 127–128.
28. Živanović, *Politička istorija*, v4, 393.

29. Dedijer, *Sarajevo*, v2, 133.
30. Živanović, *Pukovnik Apis*, 579, 591.
31. Ibid., 568–570; Dedijer, *Sarajevo*, v2, 133.
32. Gligorijević, *Kralj Aleksandar*, v1, 269; Drašković, *Pretorijanske težnje*, 290–299.
33. Mitrović et al., *Istorija srpskog naroda*, v6.2, 131.
34. Gligorijević, *Kralj Aleksandar*, v1, 269–270.
35. Žujović, *Eseji o ljudima i događajima*, 85.
36. Ivetić, 'Politička uloga ministara vojnih', 122.
37. Živanović, *Pukovnik Apis*, 139.
38. Mile Bjelajac, *Generali i admirali Kraljevine Jugoslavije 1918–1941: Studija o vojnoj eliti i biografski leksikon*, INIS, 2004, 30.
39. Mackenzie, *'Black Hand' on Trial*, 382–383.
40. Panta Draškić, *Moji memoari*, Srpska književna zadruga, 1990, 191.
41. Banac, *National Question*, 118–119.
42. Stanković, *Nikola Pašić, saveznici i stvaranje Jugoslavije*, 104–105.
43. Ferdo Čulinović, *Jugoslavija između dva rata*, v1, Izdavački zavod Jugoslovenske akademije znanosti i umjetnosti, 1961, 40–41.
44. Ferdo Šišić, *Dokumenti o postanku Kraljevina Srba, Hrvata i Slovenaca*, Naklada 'Matice Hrvatske', 1920, 94.
45. Janković, *Krfska deklaracija*, 232–248.
46. Stanković, *Nikola Pašić i jugoslovensko pitanje*, v1, 222.
47. Janković, *Krfska deklaracija*, 230.
48. Stanković, *Nikola Pašić i jugoslovensko pitanje*, v1, 217.
49. Vrkatić, *Pojam i biće*, 625–628.
50. Stanković, *Nikola Pašić i jugoslovensko pitanje*, v1, 183.
51. Jovanović, *Moji savremenici*, 176–180.
52. Stanković, *Nikola Pašić i jugoslovensko pitanje*, v1, 200.
53. Gligorijević, *Kralj Aleksandar*, v1, 385–387.
54. Stanković, *Nikola Pašić i jugoslovensko pitanje*, v2, 185–188.
55. Šepić, *Italija, saveznici i jugoslavensko pitanje*, 358.
56. Mitrović, *Srbija u Prvom svetskom ratu*, 386.
57. Nikola Stojanović, *Jugoslovenski odbor (članci i dokumenti)*, Izdanje 'Nove Evrope', 1927, 58.
58. Gligorijević, *Kralj Aleksandar*, v1, 422.
59. Janković, *Krfska deklaracija*, 414.
60. Mitrović, *Srbija u Prvom svetskom ratu*, 394–396.
61. Dragoslav Janković and Bogdan Krizman, eds, *Građa o stvaranju jugoslovenske države (1.I—20. XII 1918)*, Institut društvenih nauka, 1964, 157.
62. Ibid., 177.
63. Kazimirović, *Nikola Pašić*, v2, 480–492.
64. George Th. Mavrogordatos, *Stillborn Republic: Social Coalitions and Party Strategies in Greece, 1922–1936*, University of California Press, 1983, 282–285; Thomas W. Gallant, *Modern Greece*, Hodder Education, 2016, 129–134.

65. Hall, *Balkan Breakthrough*, 109–110.
66. Gligorijević, *Kralj Aleksandar*, v1, 284–287, 294–296.
67. James Lyon, 'The Battle of Dobro Polje: The forgotten Balkan skirmish that triggered the end of WWI', *Military History Now*, 12 October 2020, https://militaryhistorynow.com/2020/10/12/knock-out-blow-at-dobro-polje-six-facts-about-the-obscure-battle-that-ended-ww1/, accessed 11 April 2022.
68. Opačić, *Solunski front*, 298–301.
69. Milan Nedić, *Kralj Aleksandar I Ujedinitelj; Kao vojskovod*, Privrednik, 1935, 11.
70. Opačić, *Solunski front*, 366.
71. Niall Ferguson, *The Pity of War*, Allen Lane, 1998, 284–286, 386–387.
72. Gligorijević, *Kralj Aleksandar*, v1, 403.
73. Šepić, *Italija, saveznici i jugoslavensko pitanje*, 379–400; Magaš, *Croatia Through History*, 493–495; Opačić, *Solunski front*, 418–428; Aleksa Ignjatović, 'Pukovnik Stevan Švabić: Šumadinac koji je odbranio Ljubljanu', *Nedeljne novine kragujevačke*, 16 November 2022.
74. Svetozar Pribićević, *Diktatura kralja Aleksandra*, Globus, 1990, 36.
75. Magaš, *Croatia Through History*, 501–506. For details of the territorial settlement with Italy, see Chapter 15, 455.
76. Stanković, *Nikola Pašić i jugoslovensko pitanje*, v2, 214.
77. Gligorijević, *Kralj Aleksandar*, v1, 292–297.
78. Jovanović, *Moji savremenici*, 176–178.
79. Stanković, *Nikola Pašić i jugoslovensko pitanje*, v2, 207–208.
80. Petrovich, *Modern Serbia*, v2, 668.
81. Vrkatić, *Pojam i biće*, 659–666.
82. Petrovich, *Modern Serbia*, v2, 674.
83. Gligorijević, *Kralj Aleksandar*, v1, 408.
84. Petrovich, *Modern Serbia*, v2, 674–675.
85. Bogdan Krizman, *Hrvatska u Prvom svjetskom ratu*, Globus, 1989, 336–337.
86. Gligorijević, *Kralj Aleksandar*, v1, 437.
87. Vujović, *Ujedinjenje Crne Gore i Srbije*, 157–163.
88. Ibid., 219.
89. Ibid., 163–167.
90. Ibid., 180–205.
91. Gligorijević, *Kralj Aleksandar*, v1, 413.
92. Vujović, *Ujedinjenje Crne Gore i Srbije*, 174–178.
93. Gligorijević, *Kralj Aleksandar*, v1, 414.
94. Vujović, *Ujedinjenje Crne Gore i Srbije*, 309.
95. Ibid., 313.
96. Banac, *National Question*, 284–285.
97. Vujović, *Ujedinjenje Crne Gore i Srbije*, 321.
98. Nicović, *Ustavni razvoj*, 277–278.
99. Vrkatić, *Pojam i biće*, 673–674; Nicović, *Ustavni razvoj*, 279.

100. Boarov, *Politička istorija Vojvodine*, 109.
101. Ibid., 111.
102. Čulinović, *Jugoslavija*, v1, 119–124.
103. Vrkatić, *Pojam i biće*, 669.
104. Radojević and Dimić, *Srbija u velikom ratu*, 280.
105. Gligorijević, *Kralj Aleksandar*, v1, 426.
106. Ibid., 423–425; Nusret Šehić, *Bosna i Hercegovina 1918–1925*, Institut za istoriju u Sarajevu, 1991, 18, 21–22.
107. Čulinović, *Jugoslavija*, v1, 104–119.
108. Šišić, *Dokumenti o postanku Kraljevina SHS*, 263.
109. Ibid., 280–283; Gligorijević, *Kralj Aleksandar*, v1, 436.
110. Đorđe Stanković, *Nikola Pašić i Hrvati (1918–1923)*, BIGZ, 1995, 142.
111. Ljubodrag Dimić, *Istorija srpske državnosti: Srbija u Jugoslaviji*, Srpska akademija nauka i umetnosti, 2001, 53.
112. Mitrović, *Srbija u Prvom svetskom ratu*, 482.
113. Tomasevich, *Peasants*, 224–225.
114. Isić, *Seljaštvo*, v1, 28–33; Žanin-Čalić, *Socijalna istorija*, 204.

15. ESTABLISHMENT OF THE YUGOSLAV STATE

1. Gligorijević, *Kralj Aleksandar*, v2, 12–13.
2. Ibid., 16–17.
3. Gligorijević, *Kralj Aleksandar*, v2, 24–25.
4. Djokić, *Pašić and Trumbić*, 127–134.
5. Gligorijević, *Kralj Aleksandar*, v2, 25–26.
6. Djokić, *Pašić and Trumbić*, 138.
7. Branko Petranović, *Istorija Jugoslavije 1918–1988*, v1, Nolit, 1988, 88.
8. Čulinović, *Jugoslavija između dva rata*, v1, 300; Ekmečić, *Stvaranje Jugoslavije*, v2, 827.
9. Petranović, *Istorija Jugoslavije*, v1, 74, 167.
10. Smiljana Đurović, *Državna intervencija u Jugoslaviji, 1918–1941*, Institut za Savremenu Istoriju, 1986, 28.
11. Isić, *Seljaštvo*, v1, 37.
12. Momčilo Isić, *Seljaštvo u Srbiji 1918–1941*, v2, Institut za Noviju Istoriju Srbije and Službeni glasnik, 2009, 227; Petranović, *Istorija Jugoslavije*, v1, 324–325.
13. Ilya Somin, *Stillborn Crusade: The Tragic Failure of Western Intervention in the Russian Civil War, 1918–1920*, Transaction Publishers, 1996, 54.
14. Gligorijević, *Kralj Aleksandar*, v2, 85.
15. George Stewart, *The White Armies of Russia: A Chronicle of Counter-revolution and Allied Intervention*, Russell and Russell, 1933, 89–92; Nikola B. Popović, *Srbi u građanskom ratu u Rusiji, 1918–1921*, Institut za savremenu istoriju, 2005, 147–150.
16. Gligorijević, *Kralj Aleksandar*, v2, 97–98.
17. Čulinović, *Jugoslavija između dva rata*, v1, 285.

18. Gligorijević, *Kralj Aleksandar*, v3, 19–20.
19. Ibid., 37.
20. Ibid., 65–66.
21. Velimir Terzić, *Slom Kraljevine Jugoslavije 1941: Uzroci i posledice poraza*, v2, Narodna knjiga, 1983, 153.
22. Stanković, *Nikola Pašić i jugoslovensko pitanje*, v2, 224.
23. Čulinović, *Jugoslavija između dva rata*, v1, 147–150.
24. Nebojša Popović, *Slobodan Jovanović i jugoslovenska država*, Institut za Savremenu Istoriju, 2003, 98, 111.
25. Dimić, *Srbija u Jugoslaviji*, 38, 58–59, 63–64.
26. Šišić, *Dokumenti o postanku Kraljevina SHS*, 295.
27. Gligorijević, *Kralj Aleksandar*, v2, 8.
28. Čulinović, *Jugoslavija između dva rata*, v1, 177–178.
29. Branislav Gligorijević, *Parlament i političke stranke u Jugoslaviji, 1919–1929*, Institut za Savremenu Istoriju, 1979, 17–24.
30. Petranović, *Istorija Jugoslavije*, v1, 88–91; Dimić, *Srbija u Jugoslaviji*, 84–85; Bjelajac, *Generali i admirali*, 13.
31. John Paul Newman, *Yugoslavia in the Shadow of War: Veterans and the Limits of State Building, 1903–1945*, Cambridge University Press, 2015, 67–68.
32. Banac, *National Question*, 145–153.
33. Neda Engelsfeld, *Prvi parlament Kraljevstva Srba, Hrvata i Slovenaca: Privremeno narodno predstavništvo*, Globus, 1989, 38.
34. Ibid., 39–40; Banac, *National Question*, 216–217.
35. Branislav Gligorijević, *Demokratska stranka i politički odnosi u Kraljevini Srba, Hrvata i Slovenaca*, Institut za savremenu istoriju, 1970, 23.
36. Šišić, *Dokumenti o postanku Kraljevina SHS*, 291–292.
37. Engelsfeld, *Prvi parlament Kraljevstva SHS*, 31; Gligorijević, *Demokratska stranka*, 83–86.
38. Gligorijević, *Demokratska stranka*, 86–89.
39. Gligorijević, *Kralj Aleksandar*, v2, 78–79.
40. Gligorijević, *Demokratska stranka*, 27–29.
41. Imamović, *Bosnia and Herzegovina*, 291–293.
42. Slijepčević, *Istorija SPC*, v2, 559–565; Gordana Krivokapić-Jović, *Oklop bez viteza: O socijalnim osnovama i organizacionoj strukturi Narodne radikalne stranke u Kraljevini Srba, Hrvata i Slovenaca (1918–1929)*, Institut za Novijoj Istoriji Srbije, 2002, 190.
43. Petranović, *Istorija Jugoslavije*, v1, 137.
44. Žanin-Čalić, *Socijalna istorija*, 217–218.
45. Banac, *National Question*, 254–255; Gligorijević, *Demokratska stranka*, 195–197.
46. Atif Purivatra, *Jugoslavenska Muslimanska Organizacija u političkom životu Kraljevine Srba, Hrvata i Slovenaca*, 2nd ed., Svjetlost, 1977, 42–43.
47. Imamović, *Historija Bošnjaka*, 490.
48. Hoare, *History of Bosnia*, 161.

49. Morrison and Roberts, *Sandžak*, 97–98.
50. Tomasevich, *Peasants*, 346; Obradović, *Agrarna reforma i kolonizacija*, 92.
51. Čulinović, *Jugoslavija između dva rata*, v1, 226–231.
52. Vrkatić, *Pojam i biće*, 765–767.
53. Engelsfeld, *Prvi parlament Kraljevstva SHS*, 68–69.
54. Boarov, *Politička istorija Vojvodine*, 119, 123–124.
55. Ibid., 129–131; Dragomir Jankov, *Vojvodina: Propadanje jednog regiona*, Dragomir Jankov, 2005, 58–69.
56. Vujović, *Ujedinjenje Crne Gore i Srbije*, 331–349.
57. Roberts, *Realm of the Black Mountain*, 324.
58. Vujović, *Ujedinjenje Crne Gore i Srbije*, 359–361.
59. Ekmečić, *Dugo kretanje*, 370–371.
60. Vujović, *Ujedinjenje Crne Gore i Srbije*, 485–489, 510–517; Banac, *National Question*, 286–287.
61. Pavlović, *Balkan Anschluss*, 164–168.
62. Vujović, *Ujedinjenje Crne Gore i Srbije*, 483.
63. Ibid., 393–399.
64. Banac, *National Question*, 289–291.
65. Ibid., 297–298.
66. Ljubodrag Dimić and Đorđe Borozan, eds, *Jugoslovenska država i Albanci*, v1, Službeni list SRJ, 1998, 197.
67. Adam Pribićević, *Moj život*, Prosvjeta, 1999, 81.
68. Malcolm, *Kosovo*, 273–275.
69. Ibid., 273, 278.
70. Vladan Jovanović, *Jugoslovenska država i južna Srbija 1918–1929: Makedonija, Sandžak, Kosovo i Metohija u Kraljevini SHS*, Institut za Noviju Iistoriju Srbije, 2002, 205.
71. Obradović, *Agrarna reforma i kolonizacija*, 145–147.
72. Malcolm, *Kosovo*, 280–281.
73. Stefanović, 'Seeing the Albanians through Serbian eyes', 480.
74. Tomasevich, *Peasants*, 358–361.
75. Malcolm, *Kosovo*, 281, 286.
76. Dimić, *Srbija u Jugoslaviji*, 64–65.
77. Malcolm, *Kosovo*, 267–268; Banac, *National Question*, 298–299.
78. Banac, *National Question*, 305.
79. Ibid., 318–324; Andrew Rossos, *Macedonia and the Macedonians: A History*, Hoover Institution Press, 2008, 137–138.
80. Petranović, *Istorija Jugoslavije*, v1, 79, 170.
81. Ibid., 325–326.
82. Gligorijević, *Kralj Aleksandar*, v3, 28.
83. Hrvoje Matković, ed., *Svetozar Pribićević: Izabrani politički spisi*, Golden Marketing and Narodne novine, 2000, 171.

84. Gligorijević, *Demokratska stranka*, 54–56; Šehić, *Bosna i Hercegovina*, 126.
85. Gligorijević, *Demokratska stranka*, 58–64.
86. Živanović, *Politička istorija*, v4, 364.
87. Trgovčević, *Naučnici Srbije*, 269.
88. *Istorija građanskih stranaka u Jugoslaviji*, v1, SUP, 1952, 146–147; Gligorijević, *Demokratska stranka*, 16.
89. Gligorijević, *Demokratska stranka*, 79–80.
90. Gligorijević, *Parlament i političke stranke*, 26–34.
91. Čulinović, *Jugoslavija između dva rata*, v1, 202–206.
92. Dimić, *Srbija u Jugoslaviji*, 57.
93. Gligorijević, *Kralj Aleksandar*, v2, 44.
94. Trgovčević, *Naučnici Srbije*, 259–269; Lukić, *Jugoslovenska Republikanska Stranka*, 97–99.
95. Gligorijević, *Parlament i političke stranke*, 74.
96. Krivokapić-Jović, *Oklop bez viteza*, 393.
97. Ibid., 37.
98. Pašić, *Moji savremenici*, 181.
99. Miller, *Between Nation and State*, 93–94, 114.
100. Krivokapić-Jović, *Oklop bez viteza*, 404.
101. Gligorijević, *Parlament i političke stranke*, 84–85, 191, 239.
102. Krivokapić-Jović, *Oklop bez viteza*, 307–348.
103. Petar Kačavenda, *Nemci u Jugoslaviji 1918–1945*, Institut za Savremenu Istoriju, 1991, 12–15.
104. Krivokapić-Jović, *Oklop bez viteza*, 374.
105. Tomislav Kraljačić, 'Organizacija i struktura Radikalne stranke u Bosni i Hercegovini', *Godišnjak društva istoričara Bosne i Hercegovine*, 19 (1970–1971), 209–214.
106. Tomislav Kraljačić, 'Narodna Radikalna Stranka u Bosni i Hercegovini na izborima za ustavotvorno skupštinu', *Prilozi*, 5 (1969), 211.
107. Banac, *National Question*, 191.
108. Dragoljub Jovanović, *Ljudi, ljudi ... Medaljoni 94 političkih, javnih, naučnih i drugih savremenika*, Filip Višnjić, 2005, 24–26, 37.
109. Momčilo Isić, 'Miloš Moskovljević o vodstvu Saveza Zemljoradnika 1929–1941. Prvi deo: Vreme šestojanuarske diktature 1929–1934', *Tokovi istorije*, 2 (2013), 12–13.
110. Banac, *National Question*, 389.
111. Gligorijević, *Parlament i političke stranke*, 145, 192, 239.
112. Obradović, *Agrarna reforma i kolonizacija*, 70–71.
113. Krivokapić-Jović, *Oklop bez viteza*, 163–187.
114. Ibid., 396.
115. Malcolm, *Kosovo*, 270–271.
116. Gligorijević, *Parlament i političke stranke*, 142–144, 189–190; Stefanović, 'Seeing the Albanians through Serbian eyes', 480; Greble, *Muslims and the Making of Modern Europe*, 179.

117. Krivokapić-Jović, *Oklop bez viteza*, 297–298.
118. Gligorijević, *Parlament i političke stranke*, 84, 144–145, 190–191, 238.
119. Banac, *National Question*, 332–339.
120. Moša Pijade, ed., *Istorijski arhiv Komunističke Partije Jugoslavije*, v2, Istorijskog odeljenje Centralnog komiteta KPJ, 1950, 12–13.
121. Ibid., 35.
122. Sima Marković, 'Diskusija dr Sime Markovića u načelnoj debati o nacrtu Ustava u Ustavom odboru Ustavotvorne skupštine 8. februara 1921. godine', in Desanka Pešić, ed., *Sima Marković: Tragizam malih Naroda; Spisi o nacionalnom pitanju*, Filip Višnjić, 1985, 16.
123. See below, 482.
124. Sima Marković, 'Nacionalno pitanje u svetlosti marksizma', in Pešić, *Sima Marković*, 78–87.
125. Sima Marković, 'Ustavno pitanje i radnička klasa Jugoslavije', in Pešić, *Sima Marković*, 101–102.
126. Pijade, *Istorijski arhiv KPJ*, v2, 69–70, 75.
127. Kosta Nikolić, *Boljševizacija KPJ 1919–1929: Istorijske posledice*, Institut za Savremenu Istoriju, 1993, 116–125; Branislav Gligorijević, *Kominterna jugoslovensko i srpsko pitanje*, Institut za savremenu istoriju, 1992, 286–313; Hoare, *History of Bosnia*, 163–171.
128. Jovanović, *Moji savremenici*, 216.
129. Gligorijević, *Demokratska stranka*, 94–104.
130. Ibid., 112.
131. Ibid., 128–130.
132. Banac, *National Question*, 387–392; Krivokapić-Jović, *Oklop bez viteza*, 38.
133. Milanović, *Žensko društvo*, 185–187, 229.
134. Gligorijević, *Parlament i političke stranke*, 68–70.
135. Ibid., 82–84.
136. Čulinović, *Jugoslavija između dva rata*, v1, 309.
137. Ibid., 313–314.
138. Gligorijević, *Parlament i političke stranke*, 89–93, 113.
139. Popović, *Slobodan Jovanović*, 122
140. Lazar Marković, *Jugoslovenska država i hrvatsko pitanje*, Geca Kon, 1935, 128.
141. Stojan Protić, *Vladin predlog ustava: Jedna kritika*, Pantić i drug, 1921, 8.
142. Ibid., 15–41.
143. Ibid., 52–53.
144. Boarov, *Politička istorija Vojvodine*, 126.
145. Hoare, *History of Bosnia*, 108.
146. Ibid., 109–111.
147. Stanoje Stanojević, 'Autonomije Bosne', *Politika*, 27 June 1921.
148. Banac, *National Question*, 393–405.
149. Stanković, *Nikola Pašić i Hrvati*, 104–105.

150. Ibid., 232–233; Radojević, *Srpski ustavi*, 191–224.
151. Dimić, *Srbija u Jugoslaviji*, 104.
152. Živojinović, *Kralj Petar*, v3, 279–282.
153. Gligorijević, *Demokratska stranka*, 242–243.
154. Dimić, *Srbija u Jugoslaviji*, 116–117; Stanković, *Nikola Pašić i Hrvati*, 150–154.

16. REIGN OF THE SECOND KING ALEKSANDAR

1. Banac, *National Question*, 389.
2. Gligorijević, *Demokratska stranka*, 252–253.
3. Gligorijević, *Kralj Aleksandar*, v2, 202.
4. Ivan Ribar, *Politički zapisi*, v1, Prosveta, 1948, 109–111; Čulinović, *Jugoslavija između dva rata*, v1, 398–401; Stanković, *Nikola Pašić i Hrvati*, 185–192.
5. Stanković, *Nikola Pašić i Hrvati*, 206–214.
6. Ibid., 234–235.
7. Ibid., 253.
8. Gligorijević, *Parlament i političke stranke*, 117–128; Gligorijević, *Demokratska stranka*, 345–346.
9. Gligorijević, *Parlament i političke stranke*, 132–133.
10. Ibid., 139–150.
11. Čulinović, *Jugoslavija između dva rata*, v1, 416–425; Dimić, *Srbija u Jugoslaviji*, 122–123; Stanković, *Nikola Pašić i Hrvati*, 287–296.
12. 'Atentat na predsenika vlada g. Pašića', *Politika*, 28 June 1923; Slobodan Kljakić, 'Atentati na Aleksandra i Pašića', *Politika*, 28 June 2008; Stanković, *Nikola Pašić i Hrvati*, 315–316.
13. Stanković, *Nikola Pašić i Hrvati*, 319–321.
14. Jovanović, *Moji savremenici*, 184.
15. Čulinović, *Jugoslavija između dva rata*, v1, 426–429.
16. Gligorijević, *Parlament i političke stranke*, 171.
17. Stojadinović, *Ni rat ni pakt*, 199.
18. Branislav Gligorijević, 'Organizacija jugoslovenskih nacionalista (ORJUNA)', *Istorija XX. veka: Zbornik radova V*, Institut društvenih nauka, Odeljenje za istorijske nauke, 1963, 345–346.
19. Gligorijević, *Parlament i političke stranke*, 133.
20. Nusret Šehić, *Četništvo u Bosni i Hercegovini (1918–1941): Politička uloga i oblici djelatnosti četničkih udruženja*, Akademija nauka i umjetnosti Bosne i Hercegovine, 1971, 80–94; Newman, *Yugoslavia in the Shadow of War*, 105–107.
21. Gligorijević, *Demokratska stranka*, 417.
22. Bjelajac, *Generali i admirali*, 157.
23. Newman, *Yugoslavia in the Shadow of War*, 69–70; Gligorijević, *Kralj Aleksandar*, v2, 251–252.
24. Stojadinović, *Ni rat ni pakt*, 200.

25. Gligorijević, *Kralj Aleksandar*, v2, 254.
26. Čulinović, *Jugoslavija između dva rata*, v1, 442–446.
27. Dimić, *Srbija u Jugoslaviji*, 127–128.
28. Čulinović, *Jugoslavija između dva rata*, v1, 447.
29. Gligorijević, *Parlament i političke stranke*, 188–193.
30. Gligorijević, *Kralj Aleksandar*, v2, 275.
31. Mark Biondich, *Stjepan Radić, the Croat Peasant Party, and the Politics of Mass Mobilization, 1904–1928*, University of Toronto Press, 2000, 232.
32. Bjelajac, *Vojska Kraljevine SHS*, 75–76.
33. Mackenzie, *Apis*, 299.
34. Bjelajac, *Vojska Kraljevine SHS*, 45.
35. Gligorijević, *Parlament i političke stranke*, 201–207
36. Kazimirović, *Nikola Pašić*, v2, 638.
37. Ibid., 642–643.
38. Zvonimir Kulundžić, *Politika i korupcija u Kraljevini Jugoslaviji*, Stvarnost, 1968, 24–27.
39. Ibid., 265–272.
40. Biondich, *Stjepan Radić*, 231.
41. Gligorijević, *Parlament i političke stranke*, 207–210.
42. Stojadinović, *Ni rat ni pakt*, 249–250.
43. Kazimirović, *Nikola Pašić*, v2, 655.
44. Živković, *Sećanja*, 96–97.
45. Gligorijević, *Parlament i političke stranke*, 225–227.
46. Gligorijević, *Kralj Aleksandar*, v2, 292.
47. Gligorijević, *Demokratska stranka*, 474–476.
48. Gligorijević, *Kralj Aleksandar Karađorđević*, v2, 294.
49. Pribićević, *Diktatura kralja Aleksandra*, 75.
50. Ibid., 163; Ljubo Boban, *Svetozar Pribićević u opoziciji (1928-1936)*, Sveučilišta u Zagrebu, Institut za Hrvatsku povijest, Zagreb, 1973, 38–39.
51. Čulinović, *Jugoslavija između dva rata*, v1, 519–520.
52. Gligorijević, *Kralj Aleksandar*, v2, 300.
53. *Istorija građanskih stranaka*, v2, 44–46.
54. Newman, *Yugoslavia in the Shadow of War*, 69–79.
55. Čulinović, *Jugoslavija između dva rata*, v1, 521–522.
56. Zvonimir Kulundžić, *Atentat na Stjepana Radića*, Stvarnost, 1967, 300–301.
57. Ibid., 312.
58. Ibid., 328.
59. Ibid., 318.
60. Gligorijević, *Kralj Aleksandar*, v2, 306.
61. Kulundžić, *Atentat na Stjepana Radića*, 355–364.
62. Ibid., 400.
63. Ibid., 274–276, 403.

64. Ivan Meštrović, *Uspomene na političke ljude i dogadaje*, Matica Hrvatska, 1969, 184–185.
65. See Branko Miljuš, ed., *Ivan Meštrović i antisrpska klevetnička propaganda*, Avala, 1970.
66. Christian Axboe Nielsen, *Making Yugoslavs: Identity in King Aleksandar's Yugoslavia*, University of Toronto Press, 2014, 94.
67. Kulundžić, *Atentat na Stjepana Radića*, 469–470.
68. Kulundžić, *Politika i korupcija*, 440–441.
69. Marković, *Jugoslovenska država i hrvatsko pitanje*, 309.
70. Čulinović, *Jugoslavija izmedu dva rata*, v1, 535.
71. Ljubo Boban, *Maček i politika Hrvatska Seljačka Stranka 1928–1941*, v1, Liber, 1974, 30–43.
72. Biondich, *Stjepan Radić*, 241.
73. Hoare, *History of Bosnia*, 168.
74. Gligorijević, *Kralj Aleksandar*, v2, 337–338.
75. Ibid., 347.
76. Ibid., 349–351.
77. Nielsen, *Making Yugoslavs*, 71; Boban, *Maček i politika HSS*, v1, 43.
78. Pribićević, *Diktatura kralja Aleksandra*, 68–69.
79. Meštrović, *Uspomene*, 188–189. This quotation is considered plausible by the fullest, highly sympathetic biography of King Aleksandar: Gligorijević, *Kralj Aleksandar Karadordević*, v2, 357–358.
80. Branislav M. Stepanović, *Nacionalni testament Kralja Aleksandra I*, Brastvo, 1936, 257–258.
81. Gligorijević, *Kralj Aleksandar*, v2, 356.
82. Ibid., 352–353.
83. Čulinović, *Jugoslavija izmedu dva rata*, v2, 11; Nielson, *Making Yugoslavs*, 79.
84. Vrkatić, *Pojam i biće*, 782–785.
85. Nielsen, *Making Yugoslavs*, 175–176.
86. Bjelajac, *Generali i admirali*, 38.
87. Nielsen, *Making Yugoslavs*, 81–82.
88. Stojadinović, *Ni rat ni pakt*, 301.
89. Zlatko Hasanbegović, *Jugoslavenska Muslimanska Organizacija 1929.–1941. (U ratu i revoluciji 1941.–1945.)*, Bošnjačka nacionalna zajednica za grad Zagreb i Zagrebačku županiju, Institut društvenih znanosti Ivo Pilar and Medžlis Islamske zajednice Zagreb, 2012, 140.
90. Gligorijević, *Kralj Aleksandar*, v2, 208.
91. Ibid., 355.
92. Čulinović, *Jugoslavija izmedu dva rata*, v2, 15.
93. Pribićević, *Diktatura kralja Aleksandra*, 106.
94. Sabrina Petra Ramet, *The Three Yugoslavias: Statebuilding and Legitimation, 1918–2005*, Indiana University Press, 2006, 90.
95. Milićević-Lunjevica, *Moja sestra Kraljica Draga*, 169.

96. Ivana Dobrivojević, *Državna represija u doba kralja Aleksandra*, Institut za Savremenu Istoriju, 2006, 107.
97. Gligorijević, *Kralj Aleksandar*, v3, 192; Bjelajac, *Generali i admirali*, 29.
98. Dobrivojević, *Državna represija*, 112.
99. Nedim Šarac, *Uspostavljanje šestojanuarskog režima 1929. godine sa posebnim osvrtom na Bosnu i Hercegovinu*, Svjetlost, 1975, 188.
100. Meštrović, *Uspomene*, 213.
101. Boban, *Maček i politika HSS*, v1, 51.
102. Nielsen, *Making Yugoslavs*, 113–145; Dimić, *Kulturna politika*, v1, 432–439.
103. Dimić, *Kulturna politika*, vol. 2: *Škola i crkva*, 122–124, 154–156.
104. Dimić, *Srbija u Jugoslaviji*, 141–142.
105. Slijepčević, *Istorija SPC*, v2, 565–568.
106. Nielson, *Making Yugoslavs*, 155.
107. Ibid., 124–131.
108. Đurović, *Državna intervencija*, 180.
109. Todor Stojkov, *Opozicije u vreme šestojanuarske diktature 1929–1935*, Prosveta, 1969, 111.
110. Radojević, *Srpski ustavi*, 227–252.
111. Dobrivojević, *Državna represija*, 67–68; Čulinović, *Jugoslavija između dva rata*, v2, 45; Imamović, *Istorija Bošnjaka*, 511.
112. Dobrivojević, *Državna represija*, 52–53.
113. Krivokapić-Jović, *Oklop bez viteza*, 53–91.
114. Isić, *Seljaštvo*, v1, 79.
115. Tomasevich, *Peasants*, 288–341; Žanin-Čalić, *Socijalna istorija*, 281.
116. Dimić, *Kulturna politika*, v1, 86.
117. Žanin-Čalić, *Socijalna istorija*, 222–232.
118. Isić, *Seljaštvo*, v2, 238.
119. Erlich, *Family in Transition*, 197–198, 225–226, 236–279, 292–293, 316–341, 416–420; Peđa J. Marković, *Beograd i Evropa 1918–1941: Evropski uticaji na proces modernizacije Beograda*, Savremena administracija, 1992, 55–63.
120. Žanin-Čalić, *Socijalna istorija*, 399.
121. Ibid., 250, 281–282, 289.
122. Ibid., 332–377; Đurović, *Državna intervencija*, 108–110. Marković, *Beograd i Evropa*, 54–55.
123. Žanin-Čalić, *Socijalna istorija*, 244–248.
124. Ibid., 209, 213, 232–237, 398.
125. If the experience of neighbouring Bosnia-Hercegovina is anything to go by. See Marko Attila Hoare, *Genocide and Resistance in Hitler's Bosnia: The Partisans and the Chetniks, 1941–1943*, Oxford University Press, 2006, 47–53.
126. 'Istorija duga 90 godina', *RTS*, 1 October 2013.
127. Milanović, *Žensko društvo*, 28.
128. Žanin-Čalić, *Socijalna istorija*, 314–324.

129. Dimić, *Kulturna politika*, v1, 72–73.
130. Žanin-Čalić, *Socijalna istorija*, 250, 281–282, 289.
131. Đurović, *Državna intervencija*, 167–168.
132. Tomasevich, *Peasants*, 413.
133. Dobrivojević, *Državna represija*, 148.
134. Čulinović, *Jugoslavija između dva rata*, v2, 17.
135. Gligorijević, *Kralj Aleksandar*, v3, 188-189; Boban, *Svetozar Pribićević u opoziciji*, 63–68.
136. Stojkov, *Opozicije*, 90–91.
137. Ibid., 114; Gligorijević, *Kralj Aleksandar*, v3, 204–205.
138. Gligorijević, *Kralj Aleksandar*, v3, 192–194.
139. Dobrivojević, *Državna represija*, 127.
140. Ibid., 128.
141. Stojkov, *Opozicije*, 140–141.
142. Čulinović, *Jugoslavija između dva rata*, v2, 55; Gligorijević, *Kralj Aleksandar*, v3, 205–206. Milan Srškić was by chance born in Belgrade when his father briefly moved there, but his family was from Sarajevo, where he was schooled and, after studying law in Vienna, lived and worked until World War I.
143. Stojkov, *Opozicije*, 172.
144. Dobrivojević, *Državna represija*, 236–240.
145. Vrkatić, *Pojam*, 793–794; Boban, *Maček i politika HSS*, v1, 87–97.
146. Stojkov, *Opozicije*, 227–228.
147. Ibid., 225–230.
148. Tomasevich, *Peasants*, 362–382.
149. Boarov, *Politička istorija Vojvodine*, 142–148; Branislav Milić-Šumarov, 'Izlaganja', in Vladislav Radaković, ed., *Nova vojvođanska ustavna inicijativna*, Vojvođanski klub, 2012, 90–91; Stojkov, *Opozicije*, 219–220.
150. Boarov, *Politička istorija Vojvodine*, 142–148
151. Čulinović, *Jugoslavija između dva rata*, v2, 84.
152. Dobrivojević, *Državna represija*, 132–133; Nielsen, *Making Yugoslavs*, 231.
153. Kulundžić, *Politika i korupcija*, 71–215.
154. Keith Hitchins, *Rumania 1866–1947*, Clarendon Press, 1994, 432.
155. Richard Crampton, *Bulgaria*, Oxford University Press, 2007, 243–247.
156. Military Archive, Belgrade, Nedić Collection, box 68, folder 4, doc. 1.
157. Đurović, *Državna intervencija*, 330.
158. Gligorijević, *Kralj Aleksandar*, v2, 135–136; Stojkov, *Opozicije*, 227–228, 263.
159. Đurović, *Državna intervencija*, 105–106.
160. Frank C. Littlefield, *Germany and Yugoslavia 1933–1941: The German Conquest of Yugoslavia*, East European Monographs, 1988, 25–35.
161. William S. Grenzebach, Jr, *Germany's Informal Empire in East Central Europe*, Franz Steiner Wiesbaden GMBH, 1988, 44, 68, 171–172; Đurović, *Državna intervencija*, 204, 213, 283–285.

162. Gligorijević, *Kralj Aleksandar*, v3, 285.
163. Ibid., 291–293.
164. Stojadinović, *Ni rat ni pakt*, 321.

17. FASCISM AND COURT RADICALISM

1. Šarac, *Uspostavljanje šestojanuarskog režima*, 287–289.
2. Miloš Crnjanski, 'Konture životopisa Blaženopočivšeg Viteškog Kralja Aleksandra Prvog Ujedinitelja', in Miloš Crnjanski, *Politički spisi*, Sfairos, 1989, 49–53.
3. Miloš Crnjanski, 'Korporacije sa nacionalističkog gledišta', in Crnjanski, *Politički spisi*, 80–83.
4. Miloš Crnjanski, 'Socijalna baza našeg nacionalizma', in Crnjanski, *Politički spisi*, 92–95.
5. Olivera Milosavljević, *Percepcija fašizma u beogradskoj javnosti 1933–1941*, Helsinški odbor za ljudska prava u Srbiji, 2010, 82, 92–93, 421.
6. Jovanović, *Ljudi, ljudi ...*, 221.
7. Ljotić, *Memoari*, 13–15.
8. Ibid., 89–92.
9. Ibid., 55–56, 178–193.
10. Dimitrije Ljotić, 'Govor Dimitrija Ljotića, bivšeg ministra i pretsednika Saveza reparskih zadruga u Smederevu', in Dimitrije Ljotić, *Sabrana dela*, v1, Nova Iskra, 2003, 80–82.
11. Krivokapić-Jović, *Oklop bez viteza*, 60, 89–90.
12. Dimitrije Ljotić, 'Iz moga života', in Ljotić, *Sabrana dela*, v1, 43–52.
13. Mladen Stefanović, *ZBOR Dimitrije Ljotića, 1934–1945*, Narodna knjiga, 1984, 19–20; Ljotić, 'Iz moga života', 48–49.
14. Ljotić, 'Iz moga života', 125.
15. Ibid., 133–134.
16. Ibid., 145.
17. Newman, *Yugoslavia in the Shadow of War*, 228–229.
18. Stefanović, *ZBOR*, 21–28.
19. Velibor Jonić, *Šta hoće 'ZBOR'?*, Jugoslovenski narodni pokret 'ZBOR', n.d., 3–7, 10.
20. Dimitrije Ljotić, *Naš put*, Vihora, 1938, 10, 17, 26–27.
21. Dimitrije Ljotić, 'Staleški parlament', in Ljotić, *Sabrana dela*, v3, Nova Iskra, 2003, 149–151.
22. Dimitrije Ljotić, 'Ni centralizam, ni unitarizam, ni federalizam', in Ljotić, *Sabrana dela*, v3, Zadruga, 2001, 130–131.
23. Ljotić, *Naš put*, 27.
24. Đoko Slijepčević, *Jugoslavija uoći i za vreme Drugog svetskog rata*, Iskra, 1978, 188–189.
25. Ratko Parežanin, *Za balkansko jedinstvo: Osnivanje, program i rad Balkanskog Instituta u Beogradu (1934–1941)*, 2nd ed., Iskra, 1980, 10–17.
26. Dimitrije Ljotić, *Poruka fašističkom šegrtu*, 2nd ed., self-published, 1923.
27. Dimitrije Ljotić, *Drama savremenog čovječanstva*, ZBOR, 1940, 26–27, 36–37.
28. Milan Mladenović, ed., *Memoari patrijarha srpskog Gavrila*, Sfairos, 1990, 35–39.

29. Miloš Crnjanski, 'Tragedija srpstva', in Crnjanski, *Politički spisi*, 77.
30. Miloš Crnjanski, 'Do tog mora doći', in Crnjanski, *Politički spisi*, 64.
31. Miloš Crnjanski, *Sveti Sava*, Politika, Klub Privrednik and Zadužbina Miloša Crnjanskog, 2011, 155.
32. Bojan Aleksov, *Religious Dissent between the Modern and the National: Nazarenes in Hungary and Serbia, 1850–1914*, Harrassowitz Verlag, 2006, 155–162, 170–178; Zundhausen, *Istorija Srbije od 19. do 21. veka*, 315–318.
33. Justin Popović, *Svetosavlje kao filosofija života*, Manastir Ćelije, 1993, 83, 119–120.
34. Stefanović, *ZBOR*, 30–31.
35. Ibid., 40, 57, 65–66.
36. Pavlović and Mladenović, *Kosta Milovanović Pećanac*, 161–162.
37. Newman, *Yugoslavia in the Shadow of War*, 232.
38. Šehić, *Četništvo u BiH*, 68–69; Jozo Tomasevich, *War and Revolution in Yugoslavia, 1941–1945: The Chetniks*, Stanford University Press, 1975, 119.
39. Šehić, *Četništvo u BiH*, 122–125.
40. Stojadinović, *Ni rat ni pakt*, 314–318.
41. Ibid., 322.
42. Gligorijević, *Kralj Aleksandar*, v3, 330.
43. Stojadinović, *Ni rat ni pakt*, 355–359.
44. Balfour and Mackay, *Paul of Yugoslavia*, 84–85.
45. Vladko Maček, *Memoari*, Hrvatska seljačka stranka, 1992, 122.
46. Mira Radojević, *Udružena opozicija 1935–1939*, Institut za Savremenu Istoriju, 1994, 38–39.
47. Stojadinović, *Ni rat ni pakt*, 251.
48. Ibid., 298–307.
49. Ibid., 297.
50. Stojkov, *Opozicije*, 315–316; Čulinović, *Jugoslavija između dva rata*, v2, 92–93.
51. Radojević, *Udružena opozicija*, 42–43.
52. Stojadinović, *Ni rat ni pakt*, 332–336.
53. Dragan Tešić, *Jugoslovenska radikalna zajednica u Srbiji, 1935–1939*, Institut za Savremenu Istoriju, 1997, 28–29.
54. Archive of Yugoslavia, Collection 37, M. Stojadinović, 11-64; 11-51.
55. Archive of Yugoslavia, Collection 37, M. Stojadinović, 11-64; 11-52.
56. Archive of Yugoslavia, Collection 37, M. Stojadinović, 11-64; 11-53.
57. Stojadinović, *Ni rat ni pakt*, 351.
58. Tešić, *Jugoslovenska radikalna zajednica*, 40.
59. Hasanbegović, *Jugoslavenska Muslimanska Organizacija*, 258–259.
60. Todor Stojkov, *Vlada Milana Stojadinovića (1935–1937)*, Institut za Savremenu Istoriju, 1985, 85.
61. Tešić, *Jugoslovenska radikalna zajednica*, 7–8.
62. Archive of Yugoslavia, Collection 37, M. Stojadinović, 11-64; 11-57.
63. Tešić, *Jugoslovenska radikalna zajednica*, 47–58.

64. Stojkov, *Vlada Milana Stojadinovića*, 141–142.
65. Hasanbegović, *Jugoslavenska Muslimanska Organizacija*, 297–298.
66. Radojević, *Udružena opozicija*, 80–83.
67. Tešić, *Jugoslovenska radikalna zajednica*, 77–79.
68. Ibid., 95–96.
69. Stojkov, *Vlada Milana Stojadinovića*, 178.
70. Stojadinović, *Ni rat ni pakt*, 589, 666–667.
71. Vidosav Petrović, ed., *Dragiša Cvetković (Njim samim: Članci, govori, intervjui, polemike, memoari...)*, Punta, 2006, 397.
72. Đurović, *Državna intervencia*, 197–213, 260–285; Žanin-Čalić, *Socijalna istorija*, 382–393.
73. Stojkov, *Vlada Milana Stojadinovića*, 158.
74. Tešić, *Jugoslovenska radikalna zajednica*, 46–47.
75. Bojan Simić, 'Atentat u narodnoj skupštini marta 1936. Godine: Pozadine, sudski proces, posledice', in Jasmina Šaranac-Stamenković, Ljiljana Skrobić, Mirjana Ilić and Milena Kaličanin, eds, *Novi pravci istraživanja u društvenim i humanističkim naukama*, Filozofski fakultet, 2020, 163–174.
76. Stojkov, *Vlada Milana Stojadinovića*, 151.
77. Šehić, *Četništvo u BiH*, 205.
78. Stojkov, *Vlada Milana Stojadinovića*, 146–147.
79. Tešić, *Jugoslovenska radikalna zajednica*, 289–311.
80. Stojkov, *Vlada Milana Stojadinovića*, 182–183.
81. Vrkatić, *Pojam i biće*, 804–816; Ramet, *Three Yugoslavias*, 94–99.
82. Slijepčević, *Istorija SPC*, v2, 580–581.
83. Milovanović, *Vojni puč*, 161–162.
84. Stojadinović, *Ni rat ni pakt*, 524.
85. Koljanin, *Jevreji i antisemitizam*, 331–332.
86. Mladenović, *Memoari patrijarha srpskog Gavrila*, 115.
87. Milovanović, *Vojni puč*, 167–168.
88. Ibid., 171–174; Slijepčević, *Istorija SPC*, v2, 585–586.
89. Mladenović, *Memoari patrijarha srpskog Gavrila*, 114–115.
90. Archive of Yugoslavia, Collection 37, M. Stojadinović, 11-64; 11-127.
91. Archive of Yugoslavia, Collection 37, M. Stojadinović, 11-64; 11-124.
92. Milan Stojadinović, *Jedan Kralj, jedan narod, jedna država*, Sekcija za unutrašnju propagandu JRZ, 1939, 5–7, 38, 46.
93. Ibid., 8.
94. Stojadinović, *Ni rat ni pakt*, 463.
95. Littlefield, *Germany and Yugoslavia*, 51–53; Stojadinović, *Ni rat ni pakt*, 454–460.
96. Stojadinović, *Ni rat ni pakt*, 498–499.
97. Ibid., 502.
98. Ibid., 501.
99. Vasa Čubrilović, 'Iseljavanje Arnauta', in Čović, *Izvori velikosrpske agresije*, 106–124.

100. Malcolm, *Kosovo*, 283–286; Greble, *Muslims and the Making of Modern Europe*, 186–187.
101. Stojadinović, *Ni rat ni pakt*, 566–574.
102. Imami, *Srbi i Albanci*, 263.
103. Hugh Gibson, ed., *The Ciano Diaries 1939–1943*, Doubleday, 1946, 12–14.
104. Terzić, *Slom Kraljevine Jugoslavije*, v1, 1982, 59.
105. Petranović, *Istorija Jugoslavije*, v1, 282–283.
106. Tešić, *Jugoslovenska radikalna zajednica*, 216–217.
107. Radojević, *Udružena opozicija*, 110–111.
108. Ljubo Boban, *Sporazum Cvetković-Maček*, Institut društvenih nauka, 1965, 54.
109. Tešić, *Jugoslovenska radikalna zajednica*, 248–249.
110. Boban, *Sporazum Cvetković-Maček*, 79.
111. Petrović, *Dragiša Cvetković*, 397.
112. Gibson, *Ciano Diaries*, 24.
113. Tešić, *Jugoslovenska radikalna zajednica*, 396–401.
114. Stojadinović, *Ni rat ni pakt*, 619, 625, 641, 667–670.
115. Petrović, *Dragiša Cvetković*, 273–275.
116. Ibid., 378–379.
117. Boban, *Sporazum Cvetković-Maček*, 121.
118. Ibid., 137.
119. Radojević, *Udružena opozicija*, 165–167, 238.
120. Boban, *Sporazum Cvetković-Maček*, 153–156.
121. Ferdo Čulinović, *Dvadeset sedmi mart*, Jugoslavenska akademija znanosti i umjetnosti, 1965, 58–60.
122. Čulinović, *Jugoslavija*, v2, 136–147.
123. Boban, *Maček i politika HSS*, v2, 47–49.
124. Mihailo Konstantinović, *Politika sporazuma*, Agencija 'Mir', 1998, 507–516.
125. Petrović, *Dragiša Cvetković*, 366–367, 384–385.
126. Boban, *Sporazum Cvetković-Maček*, 188–190.
127. Ibid., 403–404.
128. Bjelajac, *Generali i admiral*, 46.
129. Čulinović, *Jugoslavija*, v2, 109.
130. Dejan Djokić, *Elusive Compromise: A History of Interwar Yugoslavia*, Columbia University Press, 2007, 212–222.
131. Konstantinović, *Politika sporazuma*, 516, 518–519.
132. Hasanbegović, *Jugoslavenska Muslimanska Organizacija*, 605–606.
133. Ibid., 606.
134. 'Ministar g. Kulenović smatra da pored hrvatske, slovenačke i srpske banovine, treba stvoriti i četvrta jugoslovensku banovinu, koju bi činile Bosna i Hercegovina', *Politika*, 7 November 1939.

135. Hasanbegović, *Jugoslavenska Muslimanska Organizacija*, 622.
136. Petrović, *Dragiša Cvetković*, 388–389.
137. Boban, *Sporazum Cvetković-Maček*, 307–319.
138. Boban, *Maček i politika HSS*, v2, 145–146; Dana Begić, 'Pokret za autonomiju BiH u uslovima sporazuma Cvetković-Maček', *Prilozi*, 2 (1966), 188–189.
139. Boban, *Sporazum Cvetković-Maček*, 412–414.

18. END OF THE YUGOSLAV KINGDOM

1. Ranka Gašić, *Beograd u hodu ka Evropi - kulturni uticaj Britanije i Nemačke na beogradsku elitu 1918–1941*, Institut za savremenu istoriju, 2005, 110.
2. Archive of Yugoslavia, Collection 82, M. Jakovljević, 1-3.
3. Radojević, *Udružena opozicija*, 193.
4. Boban, *Sporazum Cvetković-Maček*, 218–241.
5. Dimitrije Ljotić, 'Sporazum', in Dimitrije Ljotić, *Sabrana dela*, v5, Nova Iskra, 2003, 44.
6. Archive of Yugoslavia Collection 85, L. Marković, 2.
7. Milovanović, *Vojni puč*, 378–379.
8. Nebojša A. Popović, 'Srpski Kulturni Klub', *Istorija 20. veka*, 7, 1–2 (1989), 112–114.
9. Popović, *Slobodan Jovanović*, 211–217.
10. 'Naša reč', *Srpski glas*, 16 November 1939.
11. Slobodan Drašković, '"U Srbiji nema mesta srbovanju"', *Srpski glas*, 16 May 1940.
12. 'Naša reč'.
13. 'Rad Srpskog Kulturnog Kluba u Beogradu', *Srpski glas*, 16 November 1939.
14. Popović, *Slobodan Jovanović*, 216.
15. Dimić, *Srbija u Jugoslaviji*, 197–206.
16. Dimitrije Đorđević, 'Historians in politics: Slobodan Jovanović', *Journal of Contemporary History*, 8, 1 (1973), 24–27.
17. Dimić, *Kulturna politika*, v1, 508–509; Popović, *Slobodan Jovanović*, 213.
18. Konstantinović, *Politika sporazuma*, 177.
19. Nikola Milovanović, *Dragiša Vasić: Od građanskog buntovnika do kontrarevolucija*, Nova Knjiga, 1986, 188–190.
20. Bakić, 'Apis's men', 225–226.
21. Ribar, *Politički zapisi*, v4, 93.
22. Milovanović, *Dragiša Vasić*, 171.
23. Nikola Stojanović, 'Do istrage vaše ili naše', in Čović, *Izvori velikosrpske agresije*, 99–105.
24. Hoare, *History of Bosnia*, 90–98.
25. Ibid., 137–145.
26. Teodora Žujović, 'Biografija Mladena J. Žujovića', in Mladen J. Žujović, *Ratni dnevnik 1: Srbija u i svetskom ratu*, Interklima-grafika, 2004, 6.
27. Fikreta Jelić-Butić, *Četnici u Hrvatskoj 1941–1945*, Globus, 1986, 16–17; Lukić, *Jugoslovenska Republikanska Stranka*, 377, 394–395.
28. Milovanović, *Dragiša Vasić*, 226–227.

29. Čulinović, *Dvadeset sedmi mart*, 248–249.
30. Bogoljub Ilić, *Memoari armijskog generala 1898–1942*, Srpska književna zadruga, 1995, 138–149, 167, 171–174, 180–183; Milovanović, *Vojni puč*, 383.
31. Miloslav Samardžić, *General Draža Mihailović i opšta istorija četničkog pokreta*, v1, Pogledi, 2005, 21–23.
32. Miodrag Zečević, ed., *Dokumenti sa suđenja ravnogorskom pokretu 10 juni–15 juli 1946. god.*, v1, SUBNOR Jugoslavije, 2001, 293.
33. Dragoljub M. Mihailović, *Rat i mir denerala: izabrani ratni spisi*, v2, Srpski reč, 1998, 372.
34. Tomasevich, *Chetniks*, 130–131.
35. J.B. Hoptner, *Yugoslavia in Crisis, 1934–1941*, Columbia University Press, 1962, 247–253.
36. Mladenović, *Memoari patrijarha srpskog Gavrila*, 221–223.
37. Simović subsequently disputed with Mirković which of them had been the principal organiser of the putsch, but Mirković's claim enjoys better documentary support (Tomasevich, *Chetniks*, 44–46).
38. Milovanović, *Vojni puč*, 265–268.
39. Mladenović, *Memoari patrijarha srpskog Gavrila*, 226–234.
40. Newman, *Yugoslavia in the Shadow of War*, 234–235.
41. Dragiša N. Ristić, *Yugoslavia's Revolution of 1941*, Pennsylvania State University Press, 1966, 88.
42. Živković, *Sećanja*, 90–91.
43. Hoptner, *Yugoslavia in Crisis*, 247–253.
44. Ilija Jukić, *The Fall of Yugoslavia*, Harcourt Brace Jovanovich, 1974, 86.
45. Ibid., 86.
46. Milan A. Fotić, *Izgubljeni put: Pravno-politička i ideološka rasprava*, v1, A.Ž. Jelić, 2001, 77.
47. Popović, *Jevreji*, 19–27, 151; Ristović, 'The Jews of Serbia', 30–37.
48. Popović, *Jevreji*, 73–83; 119–121; Koljanin, *Jevreji i antisemitizam*, 70.
49. Koljanin, *Jevreji in antisemitizam*, 190–192.
50. Ibid., 74–80, 95–96.
51. Ibid., 331–341, 388, 403, 420–430; Popović, *Jevreji*, 127–143; Harriet Pass Freidenreich, *The Jews of Yugoslavia: A Quest for Community*, Jewish Publications Society of America, 1979, 153–181, 239–242; Konstantinović, *Politika sporazuma*, 181, 186–189, 194–195, 208–209; Lebl, *Do "konačnog resenja"*, 276–285.
52. Bjelajac, *Generali i admirali*, 48.
53. Milan Jovanović Stoimirović, *Dnevnik 1936–1941*, Matica Srpska, 2000, 396.
54. Littlefield, *Germany and Yugoslavia*, 77–78.
55. Ferdo Čulinović, *Slom stare Jugoslavije*, Školska knjiga, 1958, 120.
56. Milovanović, *Vojni puč*, 366.
57. Hoptner, *Yugoslavia in Crisis*, 183–187; Stefanović, *ZBOR*, 84–89.
58. Hoptner, *Yugoslavia in Crisis*, 190–192; Littlefield, *Germany and Yugoslavia*, 90–91.

59. Balfour and Mackay, *Paul of Yugoslavia*, 227–228.
60. Milovanović, *Vojni puč*, 353–354.
61. Čulinović, *Dvadeset sedmi mart*, 124–134, 155–159; Hoptner, *Yugoslavia in Crisis*, 218–229.
62. Čulinović, *Dvadeset sedmi mart*, 179–180.
63. Hoptner, *Yugoslavia in Crisis*, 236.
64. Antun Miletić and Fabijan Trgo, eds, *Aprilski rat 1941.*, v2, Vojnoistorijski institut, 1987, 312–315.
65. Ibid., 325.
66. Heather Williams, *Parachutes, Patriots and Partisans: The Special Operations Executive and Yugoslavia, 1941–1945*, Hurst, 2003, 27–32.
67. Ristić, *Yugoslavia's Revolution*, 74–78.
68. Milovanović, *Vojni puč*, 415–416.
69. Ibid., 420.
70. Williams, *Parachutes, Patriots and Partisans*, 32; Tomasevich, *Chetniks*, 45.
71. Balfour and Mackay, *Paul*, 258.
72. Ivo Tasovac, *American Foreign Policy and Yugoslavia, 1939–1941*, Texas A&M University Press, 1999, 108–140.
73. Milovanović, *Dragiša Vasić*, 229–230.
74. Čulinović, *Dvadeset sedmi mart*, 268–273.
75. Branko Petranović and Nikola Žutić, eds, *27. Mart 1941.: Tematska zbirka dokumenata*, Nicom, 1990, 367–372.
76. Ibid., 375; Čulinović, *Dvadeset sedmi mart*, 280–286.
77. Balfour and Mackay, *Paul of Yugoslavia*, 246.
78. Petranović and Žutić, *27. Mart 1941.*, 372–377; Čulinović, *Dvadeset sedmi mart*, 278–279; 'Živeo kralj! Proklamacija njegovog veličanstva Kralja Petra Drugog svima Srbima, Hrvatima i Slovencima', *Srpski glas*, 27 March 1941.
79. Fotić, *IZGUBLJENI PUT I deo 27.-mi mart 1941 – Objavljeno u emigraciji*, Fototipsko, 2001, 76.
80. Milovanović, *Vojni puč*, 418.
81. Ljubomir Durković-Jakšić, *Učešće Patriarha Gavrila i Srpke pravoslavne crkve u događajima ispred i za vreme 27. Marta 1941. i njihovo stradanje u toku rata*, Sveti arhijerejski sinod Srpske pravoslavne crkve, 1980, 18–19.
82. Petranović and Žutić, *27. Mart 1941.*, 403.
83. 'Danas, na dan 27 marta 1941, na dan nacionalnog preporoda ponovo se pokreće "Srpski glas" koji je bila zabranila protivnarodna i protivdržavna vlada 13 juna 1940.', *Srpski glas*, 27 March 1941.
84. 'Proglas Omladinskog fronta za odbranu Otadžbina', *Srpski glas*, 27 March 1941.
85. 'Proglas Saveta patriotskih, srpskih kulturnih i privrednih organizacija i ustanova', *Srpski glas*, 27 March 1941.
86. Petranović and Žutić, *27. Mart 1941.*, 84–85, 367; Čulinović, *Dvadeset sedmi mart*, 267.

87. Maček, *Memoari*, 153.
88. Milovanović, *Vojni puč*, 49.
89. Čulinović, *Dvadeset sedmi mart*, 292–303.
90. Jukić, *Fall of Yugoslavia*, 62.
91. Hoptner, *Yugoslavia in Crisis*, 263–267; Boban, *Sporazum Cvetković-Maček*, 371–373.
92. Hoptner, *Yugoslavia in Crisis*, 253.
93. Ristić, *Yugoslavia's Revolution*, 113–114.
94. Milovanović, *Vojni puč*, 522–523.
95. Mackenzie, *Apis*, 303–304.
96. Boban, *Sporazum Cvetković-Maček*, 383.
97. Fotić, *27-mi mart 1941*, 39.
98. Čulinović, *Dvadeset sedmi mart*, 345.
99. Tomasevich, *Chetniks*, 51.
100. Military Archive, Belgrade, Nedić Collection, box 68, folder 4, doc. 1.
101. Hoptner, *Yugoslavia in Crisis*, 266–285.
102. Đurović, *Državna intervencija*, 330, 333–334, 345.
103. Ibid., 283–284.
104. Hoptner, *Yugoslavia in Crisis*, 161.
105. Žanin-Čalić, *Socijalna istorija*, 396–397.
106. Terzić, *Slom Kraljevine Jugoslavije*, v2, 219–221.
107. Ibid., 174, 218, 222–224.
108. Koljanin, *Jevreji i antisemitizam*, 500.
109. Čulinović, *Slom stare Jugoslavije*, 193.
110. Terzić, *Slom Kraljevine Jugoslavije*, v2, 369–377.
111. Čulinović, *Slom stare Jugoslavije*, 277–278.
112. Milan Banić, *Agonija Jugoslavije: Dani sloma 1941*, Srpska Kultura, Željko Jelić and Slobodna knjiga, 1998, 71.
113. Boško N. Kostić, *Za istoriju naših dana: Odlomci iz zapisa za vreme okupacije*, Jean Lausier, 1949, 17.
114. Čulinović, *Slom stare Jugoslavije*, 282–283.
115. Terzić, *Slom Kraljevine Jugoslavije*, v2, 439–441.
116. Ibid., 468–469.
117. Tomasevich, *Chetniks*, 72.
118. Terzić, *Slom Kraljevine Jugoslavije*, v2, 461.
119. Ibid., 329–331, 342–347, 503.
120. Čulinović, *Jugoslavija između dva rata*, v2, 239–240.
121. Terzić, *Slom Kraljevine Jugoslavije*, v2, 654–658.
122. Ibid., 510–511.
123. Stojadinović, *Ni rat ni pakt*, 660–661.
124. Terzić, *Slom Kraljevine Jugoslavije*, 2, 654.
125. Military Archive, Belgrade, Nedić Collection, box 1, folder 2, doc. 1.

126. Martin van Creveld, *Hitler's Strategy 1940–1941: The Balkan Clue*, Cambridge University Press, 1973, 170–183.
127. Vladimir Žerjavić, *Gubici stanovništva Jugoslavije u drugom svjetskom ratu*, Jugoslavensko viktimološko društvo, 1989, 61–63; Bogoljub Kočović, *Žrtve drugog svetskog rata u Jugoslaviji*, Veritas Foundation Press, 1985, 65–70.

SELECT BIBLIOGRAPHY

Archives

Archive of Yugoslavia, Belgrade

Military Archive, Belgrade

Published primary sources

Avakumović, Jovan, *Memoari*, Izdavačka knjižarnica Zorana Stojanovića, Sremski Karlovci and Novi Sad, 2008

Belić, Aleksandar, *Srbija i jugoslovensko pitanje*, Biblioteka grada Beograda, Belgrade, 1991

Ćurić, Silvija and Vidosav Stevanović, eds, *Golgota i Vaskrs Srbije*, vols. 1–2, Zrinski, Čakovec and Beograd, Belgrade, 1989

Domanović, Radoje, *Stradija*, Slovo ljubve, Belgrade, 1980

Garašanin, Ilija, *Načertanije*, Studio 104, Belgrade, 1998

Hristić, Nikola, *Memoari 1840–1862*, Prosveta, Belgrade, 2006

Janković, Milovan and Jevrem Grujić, *Slaves du sud, ou le peuple Serbe avec les Croates et les Bulgares, apercu de leur vie historique, politique et sociale*, Libraire de A. Franck, Paris, 1853

Jovanović, Vladimir, *Uspomene*, BIGZ, Belgrade, 1988

Jovanović, Vladimir, 'Srbenda i gotovan', in Jovanović, Vladimir, *Izabrani spisi*, Službeni glasnik, Belgrade, 2011, pp. 99–106

Karadžić, Vuk Stefanović, *Srpske narodne pjesme*, vols 1–4, Prosveta, Belgrade, 1969

Karadžić, Vuk Stefanović, 'Srbi svi i svuda', in Filipović, Milan S., ed., *Sabrana dela Vuka Karadžića*, vol. 17, *Etnografski spisi*, Prosveta, Belgrade, 1972, pp. 31–48

Krestić, Vasilije and Radoš Ljušić, eds, *Programi i statuti srpskih političkih stranaka do 1918. godine*, Književne novine, Belgrade, 1991

Ljotić, Dimitrije, *Naš put*, Vihora, Split, 1938

Marković, Svetozar, 'Srbija na istoku', *Celokupna dela*, vol. 8, Narodna knjiga, Belgrade, 1987

Miletić, Antun and Fabijan Trgo, eds, *Aprilski rat 1941.*, vols. 1–2, Vojnoistorijski institut, Belgrade, 1987

SELECT BIBLIOGRAPHY

Nenadović, Prota Mateja, *Memoari*, Rad, Belgrade, 1980

Obradović, Dositej, *Pismo Haralampiju*, Antologija Srpske Književnosti, Belgrade, 2009

Pašić, Nikola, *Sloga Srbo-Hrvata*, Vreme knjige, Belgrade, 1995

Petranović, Branko and Nikola Žutić, eds, *27. Mart 1941.: Tematska zbirka dokumenata*, Nicom, Belgrade, 1990

Petrović-Njegoš, Petar, *Gorski vijenac*, Svjetlost, Sarajevo, 1973

Popović, Justin, *Svetosavlje kao filosofija života*, Manastir Ćelije, Valjevo, 1993

Pribićević, Svetozar, *Diktatura kralja Aleksandra*, Globus, Zagreb, 1990

'Program "Pijemonta"', *Pijemont*, 21 August 1911

Protić, Stojan, *Vladin predlog ustava: jedna kritika*, Pantić i drug, Belgrade, 1921

Radenić, Andrija, ed., *Svetoandrejska skupština*, Naučno delo, Belgrade, 1964

Radojević, Miodrag, ed., *Srpski ustavi od 1835. do 1990. godine sa ustavima Kraljevine SHS i Kraljevine Jugoslavije*, Gramatik, Belgrade, 2004

Šišić, Ferdo, *Dokumenti o postanku Kraljevina Srba, Hrvata i Slovenaca*, Naklada 'Matice Hrvatske', Zagreb, 1920

Stanojević, Dragiša, *Interesi srpstva*, Štamparija Napredne stranke, Belgrade, 1885

Stojadinović, Milan, *Ni rat ni pakt: Jugoslavija između dva rata*, Glas, Belgrade, 2002

Tucović, Dimitije, 'Srbija i Arbanija', in Dimitrije Tucović, *Sabrana dela*, vol. 7, Rad Belgrade, 1980

Vrkatić, Lazar, ed., *Pojam i biće srpske nacije*, Izdavačka knjižara Zorana Stojanovića, Sremski Karlovci and Novi Sad, 2004

Secondary sources

Banac, Ivo, *The National Question in Yugoslavia: Origins, History, Politics*, Cornell University Press, Ithaca and London, 1984

Blagojević, Miloš, Dejan Medaković, Radoš Ljušić and Ljubodrag Dimić, *Istorija srpske državnosti*, vols. 1–3, Srpksa akademija nauka in umjetnosti, Novi Sad, 2000–2001

Boarov, Dimitrije, *Politička istorija Vojvodine u trideset tri priloga*, CUP, Novi Sad, 2001

Boban, Ljubo, *Sporazum Cvetković-Maček*, Institut društvenih nauka, Belgrade, 1965

Boghitschewitsch, M., *Die auswärtige Politik Serbiens 1903–1914*, vol. III: *Serbien und der Weltkrieg*, Brückenverlag, Berlin, 1931

Božinović, Neda, *Žensko pitanje u Srbiji u XIX i XX veku*, Pinkpress, Belgrade, 1996

Ćorović, Vladimir, *Istorija Jugoslavije*, Prosveta, Belgrade, 1989

Ćorović, Vladimir, *Odnosi između Srbije i Austro-Ugarske u XX veku*, Biblioteka grada Beograda, Belgrade, 1992

Čubrilović, Vasa, *Istorija političke misli u Srbiji XIX veka*, Prosveta, Belgrade, 1958

SELECT BIBLIOGRAPHY

Čulinović, Ferdo, *Jugoslavija između dva rata*, vols. 1–2, Izdavački zavod Jugoslovenske akademije znanosti i umjetnosti, Zagreb, 1961

Cvijić, Jovan, *Balkansko poluostrvo*, 2nd ed., Srpska akademija nauka i umjetnosti, Zavod za udžbenika i nastavna sredstva, Književne novine, Belgrade, 1991

Dedijer, Vladimir, *Sarajevo 1914*, Prosveta, Belgrade, 1978

Dimić, Ljubodrag, *Kulturna politika u Kraljevini Jugoslavije 1918–1941*, vols. 1–3, Društvo i država, Stubovi kulture, Belgrade, 1996

Dimitrijević, Sergije, *Socijalistički radnički pokret u Srbiji, 1870–1918*, Nolit, Belgrade, 1982

Đorđević, Dimitrije, *Carinski rat Austro-Ugarske i Srbije, 1906–1911*, Istorijski institut, Belgrade, 1962

Đorđević, Života, *Srpska narodna vojska 1861–1864*, Narodna knjiga, Belgrade, 1984

Drašković, Radovan M., *Pretorijanske težnje u Srbiji*, Žagor, Belgrade, 2006

Đurović, Smiljana, *Državna intervencija u Jugoslaviji, 1918–1941*, Institut za Savremenu Istoriju, Belgrade, 1986

Ekmečić, Milorad, *Ratni ciljevi Srbije 1914.*, Srpska književna zadruga, Belgrade, 1973

Ekmečić, Milorad, *Stvaranje Jugoslavije, 1790–1918*, vols. 1–2, Prostveta, Belgrade, 1989

Emmert, Thomas, *Serbian Golgotha: Kosovo, 1389*, Columbia University Press, 1990

Erlich, Vera St., *Family in Transition: A Study of 300 Yugoslav Villages*, Princeton University Press, Princeton, 1966

Gavrilović, Mihailo, *Miloš Obrenović*, vols. 1–3, Davidović, Belgrade, 1909

Gavrilović, Slavko, Jovanka Kalić, Andrej Mitrović, Radovan Samardžić, Vladimir Stojančvić and Sima Ćirković, *Istorija srpskog naroda*, vols. 1–10, Srpska književna zadruga, Belgrade, 1981–1993

Gligorijević, Branislav, *Kralj Aleksandar Karađorđević*, vols. 1–3, Zavod za udžbenike i nastavna sredstva, Belgrade, 2002

Gumz, Jonathan, *The Resurrection and Collapse of Empire in Habsburg Serbia, 1914–1918*, Cambridge University Press, Cambridge, 2009

Hoptner, J.B., *Yugoslavia in Crisis, 1934–1941*, Columbia University Press, New York and London, 1962

Ilić, Nikola P., *Oslobođenje Južne Srbije 1877–1878*, Sloboda, Belgrade, 1977

Janković, Dragoslav, *Jugoslovensko pitanje i krfska deklaracija 1917. godine*, Savremena administracija, Belgrade, 1967

Janković, Zorica, *Put u Carigrad: Knez Mihailo, predaja gradova i odlazak Turaka iz Srbije*, IP Beograd and Istorijski muzej Srbije, Belgrade, 2006

Jelavich, Charles, *South Slav Nationalisms: Textbooks and Yugoslav Union before 1914*, Ohio State University Press, Columbus, 1990

SELECT BIBLIOGRAPHY

Jovanović, Nebojša, *Dvor Kneza Aleksandra Karađorđevića 1841–1858*, Laguna, Belgrade, 2010

Jovanović, Slobodan, *Druga vlada Miloša i Mihaila*, BIGZ, Belgrade, 1990

Jovanović, Slobodan, *Ustavobranitelj i njihova vlada*, BIGZ, Belgrade, 1990

Jovanović, Slobodan, *Vlada Aleksandra Obrenovića*, vols. 1–2, BIGZ, Belgrade, 1990

Jovanović, Slobodan, *Vlada Milana Obrenovića*, vols. 1–2, BIGZ, Belgrade, 1990

Kazimirović, Vasa, *Nikola Pašić i njegovo doba 1845–1926*, vols. 1–2, Nova Evropa, Belgrade, 1990

Koljanin, Milan, *Jevreji i antisemitizam u Kraljevini Jugoslaviji*, Institut za Savremenu Istoriju, Belgrade, 2008

Krivokapić-Jović, Gordana, *Oklop bez viteza: O socijalnim osnovama i organizacionoj strukturi Narodne radikalne stranke u Kraljevini Srba, Hrvata i Slovenaca (1918–1929)*, Institut za Novijoj Istoriji Srbije, Belgrade, 2002

Kulundžić, Zvonimir, *Atentat na Stjepana Radića*, Stvarnost, Zagreb, 1967

Ljušić, Radoš, *Kneževina Srbija*, Srpska Akademija Nauka i Umjetnosti, Belgrade, 1986

Ljušić, Radoš, *Knjiga o Načertaniju: nacionalni i državni program Kneževine Srbija (1844)*, Beletra, Belgrade, 2004

Ljušić, Radoš, *Vožd Karađorđe: Biografija*, Zavod za udžbenike i nastavna sredstva, Belgrade, 2005

Malcolm, Noel, *Kosovo: A Short History*, Macmillan, London, 1998

Marijan, Vlado St., *Povratak grofa od Takova: Prilog istoriji parlamentarizma u Srbiji*, Službeni glasnik, Belgrade, 2013

Milanović, Jasmina B., *Žensko društvo (1875–1942)*, ISI, Belgrade, 2020

Mitrović, Andrej, *Srbija u Prvom svetskom ratu*, 2nd ed., Glasnik, Belgrade, 2015

Nicović, Janko, *Ustavni razvoj Srbije*, Kapital banka, Belgrade, 2000

Palairet, Michael, *The Balkan Economies c.1800–1914: Evolution without Development*, Cambridge University Press, Cambridge, 1997

Pavlowitch, Stevan K., *Anglo-Russian Rivalry in Serbia, 1837–1839: The Mission of Colonel Hodges*, Mouton and Co., Paris and La Haye, 1961

Perović, Latinka, *Srpski socijalisti 19. Veka: Prilog istoriji socijalističke misli*, vols. 1–2, Rad, Belgrade, 1985; vol. 3, Službeni list SRJ, Belgrade, 1995

Perović, Milivoje, *Toplički ustanak*, Kultura, Belgrade, 1988

Petranović, Branko, *Istorija Jugoslavije 1918–1988*, vol. 1, Nolit, Belgrade, 1988

Petrovich, Michael Boro, *A History of Modern Serbia, 1804–1918*, vols. 1–2, Harcourt Brace Jovanovich, New York and London, 1976

Popović, Dušan J., *Beograd kroz vekove*, Turistička štampa, Belgrade, 1964

SELECT BIBLIOGRAPHY

Popović, Miodrag, *Vuk Stef. Karadžić*, 2nd ed., Polit, Belgrade, 1972

Popović, Radomir J., *Toma Vučić-Perišić*, Istorijski Institute and Službeni glasnik, Belgrade, 2003

Popović-Obradović, Olga, *Parlamentarizam u Srbiji od 1903. do 1914. godine*, Službeni list SRJ, Belgrade, 1998

Radenić, Andrija, *Radikalna stranka i timočka buna*, vols. 1–2, Istorijski arhiv 'Timočka Krajina' Zaječar, Zaječar, 1988

Rajić, Suzana, *Aleksandar Obrenović: vladar na prelazu vekova sukobljeni svetovi*, 2nd ed., Srpska književna zadruga, Belgrade, 2014

Ranke, Leopold von, *History of Servia and the Servian Revolution*, De Capo Press, New York, 1973

Slijepčević, Đoko, *Istorija srpske pravoslavne crkve*, vols. 1–3, JRJ, Belgrade, 2002

Stanković, Đorđe, *Nikola Pašić i jugoslovensko pitanje*, vols. 1–2, Beogradski izdavačko-grafički zavod, Belgrade, 1985

Stojančević, Vladimir, *Miloš Obrenović i njegovo doba*, Prosveta, Belgrade, 1966

Stojanović, Dubravka, *Kaldrma i asfalt: Urbanizacija i evropeizacija Beograda, 1890–1914*, Čigoja, Belgrade, 2008

Stokes, Gale, *Legitimacy Through Liberalism: Vladimir Jovanović and the Transformation of Serbian Politics*, University of Washington Press, Seattle and London, 1975

Terzić, Velimir, *Slom Kraljevine Jugoslavije 1941: Uzroci i posledice poraza*, vols. 1–2, Narodna knjiga, Belgrade, 1983

Tomasevich, Jozo, *Peasants, Politics and Economic Change in Yugoslavia*, Stanford University Press, Stanford, 1955

Tričković, Radmila, *Beogradski pašaluk 1687–1739*, Službeni glasnik, Belgrade, 2013

Trotsky, Leon, *The Balkan Wars 1912–13*, Pathfinder Press, New York, 1980

Vasić, Dragiša, *Devetsto treća (majski prevrat)*, Tucović, Belgrade, 1925

Vujović, Dimitrije-Dimo, *Ujedinjenje Crne Gore i Srbije*, Istorijski institut Narodne Republike Crne Gore, Titograd, 1962

Vukičević, Milenko, *Karađorđe*, vols. 1–2, Državna štamparija Kraljevine Srbije, Belgrade, 1907

Žanin-Čalić, Marie, *Socijalna istorija Srbije 1815–1940: Usporedni napredak u industrijalizaciji*, Clio, Belgrade, 2004

Živanović, Milan Ž., *Pukovnik Apis: Solunski process hiljada devetsto sedamnaesta*, self-published, Belgrade, 1955

Živanović, Živan, *Politička istorija Srbije u drugoj polovini devetnaestog veka*, vols. 1–4, Izdavačka knjižarnica Gece Kona, Belgrade, 1923

Živojinović, Dragoljub P., *Kralj Petar I Karađorđević*, vols. 1–3, 2nd ed., Zavod za udžbenike, Belgrade, 2009

INDEX

1 April Dinner (1893), 273–5, 307, 313
6 January Regime (1929–34), 5, 504–25, 530, 532, 545
Abdul Hamid II, Ottoman Sultan, 350, 372
Abdula, Marko Todorović, 71
Abdulmejid I, Ottoman Sultan, 102, 103–4, 107
abortion, 514
absolutism, 65, 76, 87, 90, 96–7, 108, 118, 132, 133, 146, 153, 159, 298, 511, 527
Abu-Bekir Pasha, 41, 45
Aćimović, Milan, 544, 548
Action Ministry
    First (1875), 210, 213, 214
    Second (1876), 214–15
Ada Kaleh, Romania, 45
Adamstal, 496
Additional Battalion, 454
Adrianople, Thrace, 9, 374-6, 379
    Battle of (378), 9
    Siege of (1912–13), 374-6
    Treaty of (1829), 77, 87
Adriatic Sea, 11, 14, 15, 57, 118, 140, 313, 349, 353, 374-5, 377, 400, 407, 410, 411, 413, 435, 448, 455
Adriatic Troops, 444
Aegean Islands, 161, 412
Aegean Sea, 161, 412, 415, 572
von Aehrenthal, Alois Lexa, 349–50, 351, 354
Aganlija Husein, 42, 45, 50
agas, 168

agriculture
    Kingdom of Serbia (1882–1918), 284, 309-10, 314, 387, 417, 449
    Ottoman Serbia (1459–1815), 38
    Principality of Serbia (1815–1882), 69, 109–10, 113, 147, 204, 230, 237, 234, 238, 246
    Yugoslavia (1918-41), 453, 463–4, 467, 480, 513-5, 517, 518, 520-1, 524
Ahmed bey Zogolli, 408, 467–8
Ahmedi, 20
Akkerman Convention (1826), 76–7
Alavantić, Rade, 308
Albala, David, 567
Albania
    Cenić and, 313
    Independent Albania (1912–14), 375, 377, 380
    Italy, relations with, 468, 505, 579
    Karić and, 366
    Kingdom of (1928–39), 505
    medieval (to c. 1431), 15–16
    Mihailo and, 161
    Plan (1844) and, 124, 125
    Principality of (1914–25), 407–8, 410, 413–14, 416, 455, 467–8
    Ottoman (c. 1431–1912), 30, 28, 49, 372, 374, 375
    Republic of Mirdita (1921), 466
    Serbian vice-royalty plan (1848), 128
    World War I (1914–18), 407–8, 410, 413–14, 416, 510
    World War II (1939–45), 579, 581
Albanian language, 222, 372, 467

INDEX

Albanians, 9, 13, 20–21, 79, 122, 161, 216, 567, 569
   Aleksandar I of Serbia and, 299–301
   Balkan Wars (1912–13), 373, 374, 379, 380-3, 384-5
   expulsions of (1878), 222–4
   Gopčević on, 253
   in Kosovo, 371–2, 380–83, 407, 413, 466–8, 475, 542
   in Macedonia, 542
   Kaçak movement (1918–24), 466–7
   Mürzsteg Agreement (1903), 338
   national movement, 282, 375, 380–81
   Stojadinović and, 546-7
   uprising (1913), 382–3, 384–5
   World War I (1914–18), 407–8, 410, 412, 413–14
   World War II (1939–45), 580
Aleksandar, Prince of Serbia (1842-58), 107–8, 112, 186, 294
   accession (1842), 107–8
   April Circular (1852), 133, 134
   Austria, relations with, 126, 136–7, 149
   Austrian Serbs, relations with, 136–7
   background, 102
   Belgrade Konak, 112, 113
   cannon foundry establishment (1853), 134
   civil code (1844), 114, 139
   Council and, 135–7, 144
   deposition (1858), 141, 144–6
   dress, 111
   foreign students and, 139
   Garašanin's dismissal (1853), 134
   garrison decree (1845), 109
   Hussar Rebellion (1844), 126, 142, 178, 308
   Illyrian Movement, relations with, 128
   Kragujevac commune and, 208
   Law on Crafts (1847), 110
   Law on Spiritual Authority (1847), 114
   Mihailo's assassination (1868), 179, 180
   Ottomans, relations with, 115, 149
   Persida's coup plot (1863), 166
   Plan (1844), 123
   Radovanović, relationship with, 179
   Revolutions (1848–9), 130–32
   Russia, relations with, 134
   Slav Society and, 126
   St Andrew's Day parliament (1858), 141, 143–7, 148, 166, 285, 297
   St Peter's Day parliament (1848), 130–31, 195
   Tenka's plot (1857), 137
Aleksandar I, King of Serbia, 1, 5, 184, 256, 258, 264–5, 267–302, 303–25
   anointment (1889), 264–5
   armed forces, 263–4, 276, 280, 281, 284–5, 292–4, 297, 299, 424
   assassination (1903), 303–8, 319–25, 330, 331, 342
   Austria-Hungary, relations with, 265, 285, 292, 294, 300, 307
   authoritarianism, 276, 278, 279, 283, 284–6
   Balkan tour (1896–7), 281
   Bulgaria, agreement with (1897), 281
   Čebinac conspiracy (1894), 277, 279
   constitution (1901), 295–7, 326, 327
   constitution revocation (1894), 277–8
   coup d'état (1893), 273–4, 307, 313
   coup d'état (1903), 303–8, 317–25, 331
   Draga, relationship with, 279, 283, 288–95, 297–8, 301
   fusion coalition (1901–2), 295–301
   government of generals (1902–3), 299, 301–2
   Kosovo monument erection (1889), 264
   Law on Marriage of Officers (1901), 293–4
   March disturbances (1903), 314–17
   mother, relationship with, 267–70, 279, 280, 283
   parents, exile of (1891), 269–70, 277
   Progressives, relations with, 278
   Radicals, views on, 283

INDEX

Regime of 11 October (1897–1900), 283–6, 291, 293, 314
Russia, relations with, 265, 285, 289, 292–3, 294
St John's Day attempt (1899), 286–7, 289, 292, 313, 344, 495
tour (1893), 275
wedding (1900), 288–95
Wedding Cabinet (1900–1901), 291–2, 295, 346
Aleksandar I, King of Yugoslavia, 356–8, 449, 494–5
6 January Regime (1929–34), 5, 504–25
amputation offer (1928), 505
assassination (1934), 524–5, 533, 534–5, 562
assassination attempt on (1916), 427–31
assassination attempt on (1921), 485
Balkan Wars (1912–13), 373, 374
Black Hand investigation (1911), 360
Bulgaria visit (1934), 523
Chetniks, relations with, 534
coalition government (1921–2), 488
colonels, appointment of (1923), 489
constitution (1921), 484, 485, 511
Croatian opposition and, 488, 491, 494, 495, 499–500, 505
far right politics, 527–34
foreign policy, 523–5
France, relations with, 455
Franz Ferdinand assassination (1914), 395
Geneva Declaration (1918), 441, 442
Italy, relations with, 455, 524, 535
Jewish community, relations with, 568
JMO, relations with, 506
JRSD and, 519, 522
Maria, wedding to (1922), 455
Našička affair (1934–5), 522–3
National Club and, 479
National Council delegation (1918), 448

nationalism, 370–71, 373, 400, 401
Pašić, relationship with, 495, 496–7
Peasant–Democrat Coalition and, 499
personality cult, 528
Pribićević, audience with (1928), 499
priority question crisis (1914), 390
Radić assassination crisis (1928), 504–5
Radović, audience with (1928), 499
regency (1914–21), 390
Royal Guard formation (1919), 494
Russia, memorandum to (1912), 370
Russian Civil War (1917–22), 454
Salonika trial (1917), 319, 323, 428–31
Treaty of Niš (1923), 469
VMRO conflict, 469
White Hand, *see* White Hand
World War I (1914–18), 400, 401, 404, 412, 415, 423, 426–31, 437, 440
Yugoslavia, establishment of (1918), 441–2, 448, 455–6, 459
Živković, relationship with, 356–7
Aleksinac, Serbia, 79, 80, 215, 247, 255
Alexander I, Emperor of Russia, 47, 50, 51, 58, 75, 76
Alexander II, Emperor of Russia, 160, 219, 231, 311
Alexander III, Emperor of Russia, 251
Alexander of Battenberg, Prince of Bulgaria, 251
Alexandria, Egypt, 349
Alexandru, Dominator of Romania, 202
Ali Pasha of Janina, 29, 216
Alijagić, Alija, 485
Alimpić, Ranko, 142, 145, 153, 164, 210, 214, 216, 217
Alkalai, Isak, 568
All-Yugoslav Islamic Religious Community, 509
Alliance Israélite Universelle, 155
Altenburg, Hungary, 140
aluminium, 540, 579
anarchism, 188, 389, 485
Anastasijević, Miša, 143, 152
Anđeljković, Koča, 35

INDEX

Anđelović, Mahmud-pasha, 22
Andonović, Jevrem, 279, 286
Andrássy, Gyula, 175, 226
Andres, Ivan, 576
Andrić, Ivo, 577–8
animal husbandry, 11, 38, 71, 109-10, 453, 309
Ankara, Battle of (1402), 18
anti-Semitism, *see* Jews
anti-state ideologies, 147, 188, 261, 262, 270, 284, 308, 360, 477
Antić, Antonije, 303–7, 316, 317, 318, 320, 356, 360, 392, 430, 563, 565
Antić, Milan, 570-1
Antonescu, Ion, 575
Antonić, Vasilije, 301, 342, 417
Antwerp, Belgium, 349
Apis, *see* Dimitrijević, Dragutin
apothecaries, 84, 172, 216
April Circular (1852), 133, 134
April Constitution (1901), 3, 295–7, 326, 511
aqueducts, 310
Arambašić, Stanko, 42, 44
Aranđelovac, Serbia, 44
Aranđelović, Radomir, 304, 305
aristocracy, 16, 22, 118, 195, 202
armed forces
    Aleksandar's reign (1842–58), 108, 109, 111, 126, 128, 133
    Aleksander I of Yugoslavia's reign (1921–34), 468, 492, 494-5, 498, 500, 506, 510
    Aleksandar I of Serbia's reign (1889–1903), 263–4, 276, 280, 281, 284–5, 292–4, 297, 299, 424
    First Serbian Uprising (1804-1813), 47-8, 53
    Mihailo's reign, first (1839–42), 105, 106–7
    Mihailo's reign, second (1860–68), 157–8, 161–5, 166, 176, 373
    Milan's reign (1868–89), 182, 184, 211, 215, 220, 239, 241, 244, 246, 252
    Miloš's reign, first (1815–39), 74, 83–4, 87, 97–8, 157–8
    Miloš's reign, second (1858–60), 145, 150
    Petar I's reign (1903–21), 335–6, 340, 345–6, 399–416, 422–4, 425–31, 455, 457-8, 462, 468, 563
    Petar II's reign (1934–45), 539, 541, 552, 563–6, 570-3, 578–83
    Pre-1804, 29, 30, 42, 44
    see also national militia
Armenians, 22
Arnautović, Damjan, 541
Arsenije III, Patriarch, 29, 30, 32
Arsenije IV, Patriarch, 32
Arsenijević-Batalaka, Lazar, 152, 160
Artillery School, Belgrade, 133, 147, 148, 161, 216, 244
Ashkenazim, 566-7, 569
Association Against Bulgarian Bandits, 468
Association for Serb Liberation and Unification, 203
Association of Chetniks for the Freedom and Honour of the Fatherland, 492, 534
Association of Fighters of Yugoslavia, 529, 530
Association of Serb Chetniks 'Petar Mrkonjić', 492, 502, 533–4, 565
Assumption Day parliament (1864), 167
Atanacković, Jovan, 290-1, 295, 304–6, 320-1, 325, 333, 336, 343, 344, 347
Atatürk, Mustafa Kemal, 252
Athens, Greece, 281, 392, 436, 485, 582
Austria, pre-1804, *see* Habsburg Empire
Austria, post-1918, 402, 452, 456, 580
    Anschluss (1938), 523–4, 546
    Koruško conflict (1919), 453
Austria-Hungary (1867–1918), *see* Habsburg Empire
Austrian Empire (1804–1867), *see* Habsburg Empire
Austrian Serbs, 37, 44–5, 46, 56, 58, 82, 94
    Aleksandar, relations with, 136–7

674

INDEX

artisans, 81, 117
bureaucrats, 62, 113, 148
Cenić and, 312
employment decree (1839), 101
Garašanin and, 136–7
Hussar Rebellion (1844), 126, 142, 178, 308
intellectuals, 115
Karadžić and, 115–18, 120
language and, 116
Liberal purge of (1859), 148
military service, 74
nationalist project and, 123, 126
Orthodox Church and, 237
Peasant–Democrat Coalition, 499
shopkeepers, 81
St Peter's Day parliament (1848), 130, 195
teachers, 84–5, 116
United Serb Youth, 173
Vučić-Perišić and, 126–7
Yugoslav unification (1918–21), 441, 458, 459, 470, 487
autocracy
    Aleksandar I's reign (1921–34), 5, 456, 504–25
    Mihailo's second reign (1860–68), 154, 155, 157, 158, 171, 174
    Milan's reign (1868–89), 201, 206
    Miloš's first reign (1815–39), 70, 75, 87, 91, 92, 93, 99, 108, 170
    Miloš's second reign (1858–60), 146, 147, 149, 153, 154, 157, 170
automobiles, 310, 587
Avakumović, Jovan, 109, 260, 261
    Aleksandar's wedding (1900), 290
    April Constitution (1901), 296, 297
    conspirator resignations affair (1903), 333
    election boycott (1895), 278
    May putsch (1903), 305, 306
    Mihailo's assassination (1868), 179
    National Liberal split (1904), 340
    Ottoman garrison clash (1862), 109

Pelagić's imprisonment (1893), 313
Pig War outbreak (1906), 344
prime minister, first term (1892–3), 271, 273, 313
prime minister, second term (1903), 325
Radicals, relations with, 275, 277–8
World War I (1914–18), 417, 419
Avars, 9, 10, 11
Avramović, Mihailo, 263, 474, 529
Azanja, Serbia, 221

Baba-Dudić family, 145, 152, 178, 179, 180, 181
Bačka region, 113, 125, 129, 140, 366, 369, 400, 438, 441, 445, 452, 464, 471, 482, 486
Baja, Hungary, 402
Bakar, Croatia, 529–30
baklava, 25
Bakunin, Mikhail, 129, 206-7, 358
Balkan ('The Balkans'), 495
Balkan federation, 191, 192, 195, 248, 367, 384, 385, 478, 531
Balkan Institute, 531
Balkan Pact (1934), 455, 523
The Balkan Peninsula (Cvijić), 368
Balkan Wars, 244, 318, 359, 361, 372, 384, 461, 464, 466, 476, 480, 492, 508, 511, 516, 529, 567
    First (1912–13), 285, 318, 359, 361, 373–7, 388, 391, 401, 403, 418, 420
    Second (1913), 318, 359, 361, 377–82, 424, 523
Balugdžić, Živojin, 307, 315, 340–41, 343, 344, 345, 347, 390, 563
Ban, Matija, 109, 113, 123, 126, 152, 153, 209
Banat region, 27, 36, 113, 125, 129, 132, 140, 366, 369, 400, 411, 438, 439, 441, 445, 452, 464, 471, 486
Banija, Croatia, 88, 472
Banja Luka, Bosnia, 447, 473, 474, 480, 562

675

INDEX

Battle of (1739), 33
Banja, Serbia, 54, 246
Banjanin, Jovan, 576, 577
banking, banks, 184, 186, 206, 241, 294, 349, 496, 517, 522, 524, 579, 587
banovinas, formation of (1929), 508-9
Baptised Serbia, 10-11
Bar, Montenegro, 12
Barajevo, Serbia, 106
Baranja region, 129, 369, 438, 441, 445, 452, 464, 471
Barje, Serbia, 421
Barlovac, Mihailo, 162
Barthou, Louis, 525
Basariček, Đuro, 501
bashibazouks, 175
Batočina, Battle of (1689), 30
Bayezid I, Ottoman Sultan, 17-18
Bayezid II, Ottoman Sultan, 23
Bayraktar Mustafa Pasha, 42, 51
Bečej, Serbia, 129
Bećir, Jovan, 409
Bela Crkva, Serbia, 131
Bela Palanka, Serbia, 104, 217
Belgium, 230, 265, 349, 412
Belgrade,
    Dar ul Jihad, renamed as, 24
    medieval, 15, 18, 21, 32, 33
    Kingdom of Serbia (1882–1918), *see* Belgrade in the Kingdom of Serbia
    Ottoman (1521–1815), *see* Belgrade in the Ottoman Empire
    Principality of Serbia (1815–1882), *see* Belgrade in the Principality of Serbia
    Serbian Uprising (1804–13), 45, 48, 49, 50, 56, 77
    Singidunum, 9
    Treaty of (1739), 33
    Yugoslavia (1918-1941), *see* Belgrade in Yugoslavia
Belgrade in the Kingdom of Serbia (1882–1918)
    aqueduct, 310
    automobiles, 310
    Bosnian crisis (1908–9), 351, 352
    cinemas, 310
    coup d'état (1893), 274, 275, 313
    coup d'état (1903), 317–25
    demographics, 310
    elections (1892), 272
    Mihailo's statue, 235
    Natalija's return (1895), 279
    Radical national congress (1896), 280
    sewers, 310
    Society of Serbs demonstration (1902), 299–300
    street lights, 310
    student protests (1906), 348
    synagogue, 567
    trams, 310
    University, 310
    World War I (1914–18), 402–5, 412, 416–17, 437
Belgrade in the Ottoman Empire (1521–1815), 24–5, 30, 41, 56, 59
    churches, 41
    Great School, 52
    Habsburg occupation (1688–90), 29, 30
    Habsburg occupation (1717–39), 32–3
    Habsburg–Ottoman war (1788–91), 34, 35
    janissary conflict (1800–1801), 42–3
    Jewish community, 25
    massacre (1815), 59
    mosques, 33
    pashaluk established (1687), 29
    Treaty of Sistova (1791), 35, 41
    women in, 39
    Uprising, First (1804–13), 45, 48, 49, 50, 56, 77, 113
    Uprising, Second (1815), 59–60
    viziers, 41, 46, 58, 60
Belgrade in the Principality of Serbia (1815–1882), 68, 69, 87, 88, 98, 109
    Aleksandar's accession (1842), 107
    apothecaries, 84

INDEX

Artillery School, 133, 147, 148, 216
bombardment (1862), 151, 162, 166, 167, 174
cannon foundry, 132-3
capital status, 98, 103, 104
Čarapić revolt (1827), 75
cathedral, 86
churches in, 78
class in, 110
constitution (1838), 95
consulates, 94, 98, 115, 172
craftsmen in, 87
Đak's rebellion (1825), 72, 73
employment decree (1839), 101
Great School, 84, 85, 159, 165, 170, 172, 174, 178, 188, 204, 238
Greek rebellion outbreak (1821), 71
gymnasium, 85, 110, 140
hatt-ı şerif (1830), 77-8, 80
house numbers introduced (1844), 109
Jewish community, 110, 127, 149, 155, 162
Josimović's redevelopment of, 170
Jovan's rebellion (1839), 97
Konak, 112, 113
Kükürt Çeşme crisis (1862), 162-3, 166, 167
liberation (1867), 168-70
lycée, 113, 123, 140, 159, 177, 187, 205
metropolitanate, 78, 85, 85, 111-12
Mileta's rebellion (1835), 91
Muslim community, 80, 81, 82, 114-15, 151
National Library, 84, 159
National Theatre, 160
Obrenovićite–Constitutionalist conflict (1839-42), 103
Ottoman garrison, *see* Ottoman garrisons
population growth, 170
riots (1860), 151
Serb quarter, 86, 109, 115
Slav Society, 126
Society of Serb Youth, 140
smoking laws, 71
street lamps introduced (1856), 109
telegraph introduced (1855), 109
Terazije bombing (1871), 203
Turkish quarter, 109
viziers, 71, 73, 77, 95, 105, 115
Belgrade in Yugoslavia (1918–41)
  April War (1941), 580-581
  architecture, 515-16
  banovina, 508
  Communist Party in, 476
  Concordat crisis (1937), 544
  constituent assembly (1920–21), 463
  constitution (1921), 463, 484
  coup d'état (1941), 573-4
  courts, 460
  German invasion (1941), 581
  Nettuno Convention protests (1928), 500
  oblast, 486
  Operation Punishment (1941), 580
  Patriarchal Council, 533
  population, 453, 515
  riots (1931), 518
  slums, 516
  Tripartite Pact protests (1941), 573
  University, 518
  ZBOR violence (1940), 571
Belgrade Credit Office, 184
Belgrade Workers' Society 314
Belić, Aleksandar, 402, 406
Belimarković, Jovan, 145, 151, 152, 156, 164, 174, 222, 223, 258, 260, 273
Belogradiček, Bulgaria, 222
Beogradske novosti ('Belgrade News'), 417
Berchtold, Leopold, 379-80
Berlin, Germany, 349
  Treaty of (1878), 224, 225, 226-7, 250, 251
Bervi-Flerovsky, Vasily, 207
Bessarabia, 58, 225, 569
  Serbian emigration in, 66, 71, 72, 75, 102, 112
beys, 22, 23, 168

677

INDEX

Biarritz, France, 279
Bijeljina, Bosnia, 53, 217
Biliński, Leon, 393
bishoprics, 11, 14, 16, 31, 227, 250, 263, 279, 281, 284, 299
von Bismarck, Otto, 160, 227, 497
Bitola, Macedonia, 374, 379, 387, 486, 570
Bizerte, Tunisia, 414, 428, 443
Bjelovar, Croatia, 582
Blace, Serbia, 420
Black Hand, 4, 5, 314, 334, 355, 357–61, 363, 391–5
    Aleksandar assassination attempt (1916), 427–31
    Balkan Wars (1912–13), 378, 380, 382
    coup d'état (1941), 563-5, 566, 572, 573
    Democrats, relations with, 487, 492
    Franz Ferdinand assassination (1914), 322, 391–5, 430
    Prokuplje training school, 391–2
    Salonika trial (1917), 319, 323, 428–31, 436, 471, 487, 497, 501
    Serb Cultural Club and, 559, 561-2
    territorial acquisitions (1912–13) and, 385–6, 387, 389, 390
    World War I (1914–18), 404, 408, 420, 424, 425–31, 501
Blagojević, Aleksandar, 389
Blanc, Louis, 207
Blaznavac, Milivoje Petrović, 145, 152, 161, 165, 175–7, 180–1, 203, 204, 295
Bloc of National Agreement, 493–4
blue-shirts, 528, 547
Bobovište, Serbia, 218
Bochkaryov, Ivan, 190
Bogičević, Miloš, 404
Bogomoljci movement, 532, 533
Bogosavljević, Adam, 208, 210, 211, 229–30
Bois-le-Conte, 89, 92
Bojna, Croatia, 214
Bojović, Dragan, 501

Bojović, Petar, 294, 374, 389, 403, 426, 429, 437, 441, 495
Boka Kotorska, 12, 19, 140, 361, 435, 482, 439, 444, 476
Boljevac, Serbia, 246
Bolsheviks, 248, 423, 426, 431, 433, 434, 454, 457, 485, 568
bombardment of Belgrade (1862), 151, 162, 166, 167, 174
Bontoux, Paul Eugène, 241
bookshops, 84, 184
bootmakers' guild, 117
Bor, Serbia, 540
Borač, Serbia, 419
Borak, Serbia, 46
Boris III, Tsar of Bulgaria, 523
Borojević von Bojna, Svetozar, 458
Bosanska Krajina, Bosnia, 209, 447, 519
Bosilegrad, Serbia, 422, 452
Bošković, Pavle, 345
Bošković, Stojan, 153, 155, 176
Bosnia(-Hercegovina),
    Austro-Hungarian rule (1878–1918), *see* Bosnia-Hercegovina, Condominium of
    medieval (to 1463), 10, 12, 13, 14, 17, 18, 21, 25
    Ottoman (1463–1878), *see* Bosnia in the Ottoman Empire
    People's Republic of (1946–63), 485
    in Yugoslavia (1918-41), *see* Bosnia-Hercegovina in Yugoslavia
Bosnia-Hercegovina, Condominium of (1878–1918),
    Aleksandar and, 370–71, 400
    annexation crisis (1908–9), 350–55, 358, 369
    Black Hand in, 358, 359, 361, 391–2
    Chief Educational Council on, 366
    Congress of Berlin (1878), 226
    Cvijić on, 38, 369
    Franz Ferdinand assassination (1914), 322, 391–5
    Geneva Declaration (1918), 441

INDEX

Hercegovina rebellion (1882), 235, 310
Karić and, 366
Metropolitan Mihailo and, 236
Milan and, 235, 242, 249
Milovanović and, 361
Muslim emigration from, 27, 371
Muslim National Organisation in, 350
Pašić and, 238, 349, 364, 400, 401
Petar Karađorđević and, 307
sea links and, 349, 400, 407
Serb National Organisation in, 350, 406, 447, 473, 474
Varešanin assassination attempt (1910), 355
World War I (1914–18), 402, 403, 409, 410, 416, 422, 428, 438-9
and Yugoslav unification (1918), 438-9, 441, 447-8, 449
Bosnia-Hercegovina in Yugoslavia (1918-41), 4, 5
6 January Regime (1929–34), 506, 519
amputation offer (1928), 505
banovinas, division between, 508, 509
bureaucracy, 462
Chetniks in, 534, 541
Communist Party and, 476-7
constitution (1921), 482–3, 484, 487
country government, 460
Cvetković–Maček Agreement (1939), 550, 551, 553, 554–5
Democratic Party in, 469, 473
federalism in, 472, 489–91
German invasion (1941), 581, 582
Husino uprising (1920), 463
Ilidža congress (1922), 488
investment in, 511
Islam in, 474–5, 480
JRZ in, 540
Maček and, 504, 505
Marko's Protocol (1923), 489
National Club and, 479
oblasts, 486, 489
Paris Peace Conference (1919–20), 452
peasant's revolt (1918–20), 462
People's Radical Party in, 473–4
Pribićević's centralism and, 479
provincial administration, 460, 489
Provisional National Legislature (1919–20), 471
Serbs in, 457, 458, 475, 481
World War II (1939–45), 581, 582
Yugoslav Muslim Organisation, *see* Yugoslav Muslim Organisation
ZBOR, 529, 530
Bosnia in the Ottoman Empire (1463-1878), 23, 25–7, 28, 31, 45
ayans, 24, 43
Constitutionalists and, 128
Cvijić on, 38
education in, 168
emigration from, 55, 227
Garašanin and, 124, 125, 140, 168
Gradaščević rebellion (1831–2), 79, 95
Great Power negotiations (1870), 185–6
Grujić and Janković on, 140
Habsburg-Ottoman Wars, 33, 34, 35
immigration to, 82, 169
Karadžić on, 119-20
Marković on, 192
Mihailo and, 161, 168, 176
Miletić and, 203
Miloš's invasion plan (1859), 151
refugee crisis (1834), 82
Reichstadt agreement (1876), 216–17
Šafárik on, 119
Serb schools in, 185
Serbian Orthodox Church in, 26–7
Serbian Uprising, First (1804–13), 48–9, 53
Serbian Uprising, Second (1815), 60
Serbian vice-royalty plan (1848), 128
uprising (1875–8), 201, 208, 209–15, 216–17, 219–20
Žujović and, 188
Bosniaks, 4
Balkan Wars (1912-13), 374, 376

679

INDEX

in Ottoman Empire (1463-1912), 61, 82, 161
Cvetković–Maček Agreement (1939), 553, 554
Kingdom of Serbs, Croats and Slovenes (1918-29), 459, 462–3, 469, 474, 475, 481, 482, 492, 506
Kingdom of Yugoslavia (1929-41), 538, 540, 548, 568
Serb national politics and, 118-20, 125, 161, 185, 195
World War I (1914-18), 400, 422
Yugoslav unification (1914-18), 433, 448
Bosnian Croats, 118-20, 458, 463, 469, 488
Bosnian Muslims, see Bosniaks
Bosnian Serbs, 14, 118-20, 185, 209, 406, 447, 458, 461–2, 473, 488, 538, 559, 561, 581
Botorić, Svetozar, 310
boyars, 83, 87
Božanović, Miloš, 360, 387, 388
Bozarović, Gligorije, 84
Brăila, Romania, 349
Braničevo, Serbia, 15, 533
Branko, father of Vuk Branković, 17
Branković, Đorđe, 29, 31
Branković, Đurađ, 18, 19, 21
Branković, Vuk, 17, 18, 20
Brankovina, Serbia, 44
Brčko, Bosnia, 552
Brdica, Battle of (1913), 388
Bregalnica, Macedonia, 468, 486
  Battle of (1913), 379, 380
Bregalnica River, 379
Brest-Litovsk, Treaty of (1918), 435
Breznik, Bulgaria, 226, 251
brigandage, 32, 38, 43, 44, 48, 52, 59, 69, 261, 419
Bristollers, 519
Brušane, Croatia, 522
Brusilov Offensive (1916), 418
Brussels, Belgium, 349
Bucharest, Romania, 102, 143, 281

Treaty of (1812), 55, 62, 76
Treaty of (1913), 379
Buda(pest), Hungary, 25, 29, 128, 454, 522
  Eyalet of (1541–1686), 25, 28, 29
Budimlja, bishopric of, 14
Budisavljević, Srđan, 563, 572, 573, 576
Bugojno, Bosnia, 553
Bukovina, 569
Bukovina-Dalmatia, metropolitanate of, 461
Bulgaria,
  Exarchate Church, 185, 224, 227, 452, 468
  Kingdom of (1908–46), see Bulgaria, Kingdom of
  medieval (to 1393), 10, 11-12, 13, 15-16, 17
  Ottoman (1393–1878), see Bulgaria, Ottoman
  Principality of (1878–1908), see Bulgaria, Principality of
Bulgaria, Kingdom of (1908–46), 2, 371, 391, 455
  Balkan League agreements (1912), 371, 373
  Balkan Wars (1912–13), 374, 376, 377–80, 382, 384
  Dobrudja annexation (1940), 569
  Ferdinand assassination plots, 392, 427
  Ljotić and, 531
  Treaty of Friendship (1937), 545
  Treaty of Neuilly (1919), 452
  Treaty of Niš (1923), 469
  Tripartite Pact accession (1940), 570
  VMRO in, 469, 523, 524–5
  World War I (1914–18), 401, 410–22, 425, 434, 435, 436, 437
  World War II (1939–45), 570, 579, 580
  Yugoslavia invasion (1941), 580
  Zveno, 523
Bulgaria, Ottoman (1393–1878), 18, 42, 85
  Congress of Berlin (1878), 227
  Exarchate establishment (1870), 185
  Garašanin and, 124, 129, 160–61

INDEX

Grujić and Janković and, 140
Habsburg War (1683–99), 30
Jovanović and, 173
Marković and, 192
Miletić and, 203
Miloš and, 105, 151
nationalists and, 119
population, 170
rebellion (1841), 104, 105
rebellion (1867), 176
rebellion (1876), 201
Russia, relations with, 219
Serbian Committee in, 160–61
Slav Society and, 126
Stambolov government (1887–94), 279
Bulgaria, Principality of (1878–1908), 224–5, 228, 235, 249–52, 253, 287
    Eastern Rumelia annexation (1885), 281, 371
    Macedonia, claims to, 250, 281, 285, 299, 336, 341, 349–50
    monarchy, 287, 305
    Pašić on, 365
    Pig War outbreak (1906), 343
    Plovdiv annexation (1885), 250
    Radical manifesto (1881) and, 239
    railway convention (1883), 237
    Serbia, agreement with (1897), 281
    Serbia, agreements with (1904–5), 337
    Serbian War (1885–6), 250–52, 253, 256, 263, 265
    Russia, relations with, 219, 224, 265
Bulgarian Exarchate, 185, 224, 227, 452, 468
Bulgarian language, 452, 468
Bulgarians, 24, 228, 392
    Middle Ages (to 1393), 4, 10, 12, 15, 18, 20
    in Ottoman Empire (1393-1878), 105, 185, 224, 227
    rebels in Ottoman Empire, 105, 201, 209, 215, 219, 279, 299, 336-7, 371, 372

    and Serbian expansionist plans, 122, 124, 126, 160-161, 176, 281
    Serbo-Bulgarian war (1885-6), 249-53
    and South Slav unity, 119, 192, 365, 367, 423, 531
    under Belgrade's rule (1912-41), 387, 411, 452, 468
buljubašas, 43
Buonarroti, Philippe, 358
bureaucracy, 585
    Aleksandar's reign (1842–58), 108, 110, 111, 112, 113, 133, 140, 141, 146
    Aleksandar I's reign (1889–1903), 262, 284
    Mihailo's reign, first (1839–42), 101, 103
    Mihailo's reign, second (1860–68), 154, 156, 165
    Milan's reign (1868–89), 197, 238
    Miloš's reign, first (1815–39), 62, 68, 72, 84, 86, 88, 90, 98, 193
    Miloš's reign, second (1858–60), 147–9, 152, 156
    Petar's reign (1903–21), 461, 462, 464
Burián, István, 351, 418
Burke, Edmund, 330
Bursa, Anatolia 109
Byzantine Empire (395–1453), 9–13, 15, 16, 259

Čabrinović, Nedeljko, 392, 393
Čačak, Serbia, 58, 60, 73, 84, 85, 88, 103, 272, 346, 578
Čakavian dialect, 120
Candlemas Parliament (1835), 92
cannons, 35, 83-4, 102, 106, 107-8, 132-4, 158, 252, 281, 318, 507
capitalism, 117, 187, 194, 206, 208, 312, 313
Capitulations, 127
Caporetto, Battle of (1917), 434
Čarapić, Đorđe, 75
Čarapić, Marko, 75

INDEX

Čarapić, Vasa, 75
Carinthia, 438, 453
Carnegie Endowment, 383, 386
Carniola region, 438, 455
Čarnojević, Arsenije III, 29
Carol II, King of Romania, 527
Cartwright, Fairfax, 379
Časlav, Prince of the Serbs, 12
Çatalca, Thrace, 374, 376
Catargiu, Elena Maria, 202
'Catechism of a Revolutionary' (Nechayev), 358
Catholic Action, 542
Catholicism, 13, 14, 216
    6 January Regime (1929–34), 517
    Albanians and, 337, 381
    anti-Semitism and, 568
    in Bosnia, 27, 124, 168, 185, 475
    census (1921), 453
    Concordat crisis (1937), 542–4, 559, 565, 584
    Croats and, 26, 270, 365, 400, 401, 406, 407, 433, 442, 517
    Garašanin and, 124
    in Habsburg Empire, 27, 32, 33, 113, 118, 123, 154, 292, 401
    Kosovo legend and, 19
    in Macedonia, 381, 391
    Military Border, 26
    Ottomans and, 26, 27, 33
    Slovenes and, 400, 401, 406, 407, 480, 433
    Vatican Concordat (1914), 391
    Vatican Concordat (1937), 542–4, 559, 565, 584
Cavour, Camillo Benso, Count, 190, 214, 361, 381
Čebinac, Mihailo, 277, 279
Čegar, Battle of (1809), 53, 54, 89
Çelebi, Evliya, 25
Celje, Slovenia, 564
Ćelović, Luka, 336-7
Cenić, Dimitrije, 208, 308–9, 311–13
Cenić, Đorđe, 182

censuses
    1834, 86
    1884, 227
    1921, 453, 466, 567
Central Council, 314
Central National Committee, 563
Central Revolutionary Council, 373
Central Revolutionary Liberation Committee, 203
Central Revolutionary Secret Council, 336
centralism, 458–9, 480–86
    6 January Regime (1929–34), 505, 520
    bureaucracy and, 461
    Communist Party and, 477–8
    constitution (1921), 480–86
    Democratic Party and, 469–70, 486, 487, 488
    Džemijet and, 475
    Pribićević and, 459, 469, 479, 480, 486, 487, 488, 504
    Protić and, 479, 480
    Republican party and, 472
Cer, Battle of (1914), 403
Cetinje, Montenegro, 31, 203, 214, 281, 338, 409, 444, 445, 465
Chamil Pasha, 105, 107
Chantilly conference (1915), 414
Charlemagne, Holy Roman Emperor, 11
Charles I, Emperor of Austria, 438, 454–5
Charles V, Holy Roman Emperor, 26
Charykov, Nikolai, 298, 301
Cherkess people, 68
Cherniaev, Mikhail Grigorievich, 214, 217-9
Chernozemski, Vlado, 525
Chernyshevsky, Nikolay, 190
Chetniks
    Albanians, repression of, 546
    anti-Semitism, 534
    Association of Serb Chetniks, 492, 500, 502, 533–4, 541, 565
    Balkan Wars (1912–13), 373–4, 382, 492
    Black Hand and, 425, 492

INDEX

Bosnia, repression in, 462, 534
Macedonia (1902–12), 299, 336-7, 373, 474, 492, 496, 565, 572
National Defence establishment (1908), 352
United Serb Chetniks, 492, 500, 544
United Serb Chetniks – Petar Mrkonjić, 492, 500, 533–4, 544
World War I (1914–18), 400, 420-2, 444, 492
World War II (1939–45), 563, 564, 566, 575, 579
Chief Educational Council, 240, 365–6
child labour, 311, 514–15
chopping of the knezes (1803), 43, 44, 59, 145
Christ Church, Oxford, 535
Christianity, 11–12
Catholicism, *see* Catholicism
Cyril and Methodius' mission (863), 11
folk Christianity, 14, 39
forced conversion to, 50
Orthodox Church, *see* Serbian Orthodox Church
Christmas Uprising (1919), 465
Christmas, as celebrated by Serbs, 39
church law
1830s, 86
1862, 159
1883, 236, 263
1890, 263, 284
Ciano, Gian Galeazzo, 524, 547, 549, 570
Ciganović, Milan, 392, 394
Cincar-Marković, Aleksandar, 550, 570, 571, 572, 582
Cincar-Marković, Dimitrije, 285, 299, 301–2, 306, 347
Aleksandar's marriage (1900), 290, 291, 293, 295, 298
government of generals (1902–3), 299, 301–2, 306, 347
Macedonia operations (1902), 299
March disturbances (1903), 315, 316
May putsch (1903), 318, 323, 332, 346

Cincars, 22, 25–6, 31, 50, 66, 109, 115, 177, 216, 252, 264, 283, 344, 549
cinemas, 310, 531, 534
Circle of Serbian Sisters, 336
Ćirić, Ilija, 273
Ćirić, Stevan, 540
City Library of Belgrade, 84
civil code (1844), 114
clothing, 62, 82–3, 111, 113, 133, 141, 158, 170, 311–12, 419, 585
coat of arms,
Black Hand, 358
Obrenović dynasty, 264
Russian, 55,
Serbian, 34, 55, 78, 94, 97
Yugoslav, 459–60
coinage, 160–1, 204, 229
Čolak-Antić, Vojin, 325
Čolaković, Rodoljub, 485
Comintern, 454, 478, 491
Committee of Union and Progress (CUP), 350–1, 372, 407
Communist Manifesto (Marx and Engels,), 187
Communist Party of Yugoslavia (KPJ), 463, 476–8, 515, 516, 527
Aleksandar's assassination (1934), 562
assassinations of leadership (1929), 517
Congress of Unification (1919), 476
constituent assembly (1920–21), 481
Country Conference, Third (1924), 478
coup d'état (1941), 577
national question, 477–8
Pronouncement and (1920, 1921), 463, 485, 493
Radić assassination (1928), 503
railway strike (1920), 530
Concordat crisis (1937), 542–4, 559, 565, 584
Congress of Berlin (1878), 224, 225, 226–7
Congress of Unification (1919), 476
Conservative Party (1914), 354

683

INDEX

Conservatives
    Milan's reign (1868–89), 181, 182, 197, 204, 220, 221, 233, 237–8
    Miloš's second reign (1858–60), 142, 146, 149, 152–3
    Mihailo's assassination (1868), 179, 180, 197
    Mihailo's second reign (1860–68), 154–6, 158, 162, 171–3, 177
    Ottoman Wars (1876–8), 220, 221
conspirator question, 331–6, 339–40, 343–4, 345, 361, 388, 389
Constantine (missionary), 11
Constantine I, King of Greece, 392, 427, 436
Constantine VII, Byzantine Emperor, 10, 12
Constantinople
    anti-Greek pogrom (1821), 75
    Austrian embassy, 19
    Balkan Wars (1912–13), 374, 376
    British embassy, 94, 122
    Byzantine (to 1453), 13, 16
    constitution delegation (1838), 95
    garrison withdrawal agreement (1867), 168–70
    Greek rebellion outbreak (1821), 71, 75
    Kanlice Palace conference (1862), 162
    Mihailo's visit (1839), 102, 169
    Mihailo's visit (1867), 169
    Milan's visit (1874), 205
    Miloš's visit (1835), 93–4
    Ottoman conquest (1453), 21
    Petar's visit (1910), 355
    Plan (1844), 123–6
    Polish émigrés in, 108, 122–3
    railway links, 227
    Russian embassy, 92, 94
    Serbian rebel delegation (1815), 60
constitution
    1835 constitution, 3, 89–94, 118
    1838 constitution, 3, 88, 95–7, 118, 157, 172, 295
    1869 constitution, 3, 181–4, 195–7, 201, 204–6, 213, 277–9, 295, 327
    1883 draft constitution, 240, 243, 280, 295
    1889 constitution, 3, 257–8, 259, 271, 277, 295, 297, 301, 326–7
    1896 draft constitution, 280, 295
    1901 constitution, 295–7, 326, 327, 511
    1903 constitution, 3, 326–9, 331
    1921 constitution, 463, 467–88, 461-2, 481–4, 488, 461-462, 490, 494, 502, 505, 507, 511, 512, 550, 575
    1931 constitution, 511–12
Constitutionalist era (1842–58), 112, 122
    April Circular (1852), 133, 134
    Aleksandar, deposition of (1858), 141, 144
    armed forces, 108, 109, 111, 126, 128, 133
    bureaucracy, 108, 110, 111, 112, 113, 133
    civil code (1844), 114
    education, 113
    garrison decree (1845), 109
    Hussar Rebellion (1844), 126, 142, 178, 308
    Law on Crafts (1847), 110
    Law on Spiritual Authority (1847), 114
    Plan (1844), 89, 123–6, 140, 160, 171, 222
    police law (1850), 133
    Revolutions (1848–9), 128–32
    St Andrew's Day parliament (1858), 141, 143–7, 166, 285, 297
    St Peter's Day parliament (1848), 130
    Tenka's plot (1857), 137
Constitutionalists
    Aleksandar's reign (1842–58), 107–38, 139–46
    Austria, relations with, 105–6, 107, 122, 126–7, 133–7
    Austrian Serbs, relations with, 126–7, 136

INDEX

Council and, 135–7, 139
France, relations with, 133, 134
Hussar Rebellion (1844), 126, 142, 178, 308
Jewish community, relations with, 127, 149
Karadžić, relationship with, 117
Mihailo's reign (1839–42), 103–7, 122
Miloš, deposition of (1839), 96–8
Ottomans, relations with, 102–9, 128, 133, 140–41, 150
Plan (1844), 89, 123–6, 140, 160, 171, 222
Revolutions (1848), 128–32
Russia, relations with, 104, 107–8, 122, 126, 133–5, 137
St Andrew's Day parliament (1858), 141, 143–7, 166, 285, 297
Tenka's plot (1857), 137
consulates, 94, 98, 111, 115, 128, 134, 169, 172, 252-3, 372, 387, 568
contras, 333, 345–6, 352, 355, 360, 426, 428, 430-1, 503
copper, 540, 579
Corfu, Greece, 414, 415, 426, 427, 432, 440, 561
Corfu Declaration (1917), 431–6
Ćorović, Vladimir, 11, 16, 27, 559, 562, 575
corporal punishment, 74, 75, 113, 158, 165, 184, 204, 220
Corsica, 443, 547
cotton, 309
Council
  Aleksandar's reign (1842–58), 127, 130, 135–7, 139, 144
  Aleksandar I's reign (1889–1903), 260–61, 271, 281, 296
  Mihailo's reign, first (1839–42), 102–3, 106, 108, 109
  Mihailo's reign, second (1860–68), 155, 157, 159, 162, 164, 172
  Milan's reign (1868–89), 181, 182, 183, 211, 236, 239, 258
  Miloš's reign, first (1815–39), 75, 88, 89, 90, 91, 93, 95–8, 295
  Miloš's reign, second (1858–60), 146–7, 148, 149, 150
  Uprising, First (1804–13), 46-8, 51, 52-5, 56, 58, 191
Counter-Reformation, 532
Court Liberals, 177–82, 197, 205, 238, 279, 290, 497
Court of Cassation, 114, 146, 147, 277, 460
Court Radicals, 275–6, 280, 301, 302, 316, 497, 536, 539
court
  Habsburg Empire (to 1918), 179, 367
  Kingdom of Serbia (1882–1918), 236, 247, 249, 258, 275, 277, 278, 286, 306, 333, 346, 355, 388, 428-30
  Principality of Serbia (1815–1882), 67, 69, 74–5, 86, 91–2, 93, 96, 114, 126, 133, 137, 146, 149, 151, 165, 177, 166–7, 183, 212, 206, 228
  Yugoslavia (1918-41), 460, 482, 484, 510, 517, 518, 520
craftsmen, 49, 82, 87, 110, 117, 127, 155, 208, 309, 310–11, 313
Cres, Croatia, 438, 455
Crete, 168, 281, 350, 436
Crijević, Ludovik, 19
Crikvenica, Croatia, 552
Crimean War (1853–6), 134–5, 136, 173
Crna Reka, Serbia, 80, 258
Crnjanski, Miloš, 464, 528, 532-3
Crnojević, Ivan, 31
Crnorecki, Serbia, 246
Croat Bloc, 487
Croat Civic Defence, 541, 552, 581
Croat Nationalist Youth, 492
Croat Party of Right, 355, 487, 495
Croat Peasant Defence, 541, 552, 581
Croat Peasant Party (HSS), 512, 517, 549
  abandonment of republicanism, 494
  Aleksandar I and, 495, 500, 503-5, 509
  April War (1941), 581
  banovina debate (1940), 554

685

constitution declaration (1937), 544
coup d'état (1941), 576
Cvetković–Maček Agreement (1939), 550-55, 559
formation of Peasant-Democrat Coalition (1927), 498-9
Kerestinec riots (1936), 542
in National Agreement Bloc, 544
Novi Sad declaration (1932), 521
paramilitary forces, 541, 547, 552
Predavec assassination (1933), 520
Radicals and, 494, 496, 498
Radić assassination (1928), 498–504
in United Opposition, 536, 544
see also Croat Republican Peasant Party

Croat Progressive Party, 366

Croat Republican Peasant Party (HRSS), 457, 471, 475, 481, 483, 487, 489–90, 491, 492–4
see also Croat Peasant Party

Croat Union, 462, 479, 480, 481, 487

Croat–Serb Coalition (1905–18), 366-7, 380, 391, 460, 469

Croatia, 4, 10, 363–4
Aleksandar on, 400
Austria-Hungary period (1868–1918), 314, 380, 391, 392, 401, 562
Balkan Wars (1912–13), 380
Belić and, 406
Black Hand and, 358, 392
Cenić on, 312–13
Chief Educational Council on, 366
Communist Party and, 477
Corfu Declaration (1917), 433
flag, 407, 433, 491, 510
Garašanin and, 124
Geneva Declaration (1918), 441, 442
Habsburg period (1527–1918), 26, 31, 120, 125, 128–30, 167, 191
Independent State of (1941–5), 495, 581, 582
Karić and, 366
Kingdom of (925–1527), 25, 314, 494
Marković and, 191, 478
Milovanović and, 361
Niš Declaration (1914), 405
Paris Peace Conference (1919–20), 452
Pašić and, 364–7, 380, 400, 401, 431
Skerlić and, 368
state right, 191, 431, 460
World War I (1914–18), 403, 406–7, 422–4, 431, 438–9
in Yugoslavia (1918-41), *see* Croatia in Yugoslavia
Yugoslav Committee, 406
Yugoslav unification (1918), 438, 446-9, 456-7

Croatia in Yugoslavia (1918-41),
6 January Regime (1929–34), 506, 507, 519–20
amputation offer (1928), 505
anti-Semitism in, 568
banovinas, 508, 550–55
Chetniks in, 534
Communist Party in, 476
constitution (1921), 482, 483, 484, 487
country government, 460
coup d'état (1941), 576, 577
Cvetković–Maček Agreement (1939), 550-55, 557-8, 579
Democratic Party in, 470–71
federalism in, 472, 478, 488, 489–91
flag, 491
German invasion (1941), 581–2
Hungarian conflict (1919), 454
investment in, 511
Maček's federalist proposals (1929), 504-5
Marko's Protocol (1923), 489
National Club, 479
Nettuno Convention (1925), 499, 500, 503
oblasts, 486, 489
ORJUNA in, 491
Orthodox Church in, 461
Paris Peace Conference (1919–20), 451–2

INDEX

Peasant–Democrat Coalition, 499, 503, 519–20
provincial administration, 460, 489, 491, 493
Provisional National Legislature (1919–20), 471
Radicals in, 472–3
Serbs in, 457, 458, 459, 481, 487
Ustasha, 522, 535
World War II (1939–45), 571, 579, 581–2
Zagreb Points (1932), 519–20
Croatian Home Guard, 462
Croatian language, 119, 120, 140, 312–13, 368, 453
Croats, 4,
April War (1941), 580-3
in Bosnia, 458, 463, 469, 488
Garašanin and, 124, 130
in Dalmatia, 406, 448, 481
in Italy, 453
Karadžić and, 119-20, 406
Kingdom of Serbs, Croats and Slovenes (1918-29), 459, 469-71, 472, 476, 478-9, 481, 488, 490, 499, 502-5, 506
Kingdom of Yugoslavia (1929-41), 508-9, 510, 517, 520, 532, 533, 535, 537, 538, 541, 544-5, 548, 550, 552-4, 557-61, 564, 568, 574, 576, 579
Middle Ages, 10
Mihailo and, 161
national identity, 448
repression of, in Yugoslavia (1914-18), 490
Revolutions (1848-9), 128–30, 132
Serb nationalism, 161, 364-5
South Slav unity, 5, 119, 120, 161, 361, 363, 364-5, 367-9, 380, 400, 531
in Vojvodina 446, 452
in Volunteer units, 422-3
World War I, 403

Yugoslav unification and (1914-18), 402, 405-7, 408, 410, 425, 431, 433, 435, 439, 440-2, 444-9, 456
Čubrilović, Branko, 552, 558, 572, 573, 576
Čubrilović, Vasa, 68, 393, 546, 559, 562
cuisine, 25, 39, 172, 540
Čukarica, Serbia, 348
Cukić, Kosta, 153, 154, 158, 165
Cukić, Pavle, 65-6, 154, 234
Čumić, Aćim, 204, 205, 206, 221, 234, 237
Ćuprija, Serbia, 35, 41, 46, 54, 87, 97, 174, 255
Čurćija, Ilija, 178
currency, 160–61, 204, 229, 463–4
Cuza, Alexandru Ioan, 202
Cvetković, Dragiša, 540, 548–55, 557, 564, 566, 568, 569, 570, 571-2, 574, 577
Cvetković, Vitomir, 429
Cvetković–Maček Agreement (1939), 550–55, 557–8, 579
Cvijić, Jovan, 38, 367–70, 371, 375, 376–7, 402, 405
Cyril, Saint, 11
Cyrillic alphabet, 11, 120, 125, 368, 403, 417, 433, 461, 511
Czajkowski, Michal, 122, 123
Czartoryski, Adam, 89, 122, 123
Czechoslovakia, 454, 496, 517, 523, 545, 546
Czechs, 123, 124, 129, 439, 467, 567

Dabar, bishopric of, 14
Dacians, 9
dahijas, 29, 42–6, 49, 246
Daily Mail, 525
Đaja, Jovan, 247, 268, 270, 283, 287, 336, 513
Dajbog, 19, 39
Đak, Miloje Popović, 72-3
Đak's rebellion (1825), 72–4, 76, 91, 146, 158, 208, 246
Đaković, Đuro, 517
Daković, Marko, 577
Đakovica, Kosovo, 375, 376, 382

687

INDEX

Dalj, Srem, 84, 561
Dalmatia, 4, 364
   Aleksandar and, 400
   Baptised Serbia, 10
   Black Hand and, 358
   Cenić on, 312
   Chief Educational Council on, 366
   Communist Party and, 477
   Croatian claims to, 366
   Cvijić and, 369
   Garašanin and, 125, 129, 140
   Geneva Declaration (1918), 441
   Karadžić and, 118, 119, 120
   Kingdom of Serbia (1217–1346), 14
   Maček and, 504, 505
   Marković and, 191
   Napoleonic Italy (1806–14), 49
   National Council of Slovenes, Croats and Serbs, 438
   Niš Declaration (1914), 406
   Orthodox Church in, 26
   Ottoman-Habsburg War (1683–99), 31
   Paris Peace Conference (1919–20), 452
   Pašić and, 401, 406
   sea outlet and, 349
   Venetian Dalmatia (1409–1797), 27
   Treaty of London (1915), 410
   World War I (1914–18), 402, 406, 410
   in Yugoslavia (1918-41), *see* Dalmatia in Yugoslavia
   Yugoslav unification, 448
Dalmatia in Yugoslavia (1918-41),
   agrarian reform, 498
   amputation offer (1928), 505
   banovinas, 508, 510
   Communist Party in, 476
   constitution (1921), 482, 484
   country government, 460
   Cvetković–Maček Agreement (1939), 550, 551
   Farmers' Party in, 474
   German invasion (1941), 581, 582
   investment in, 511

Nettuno Convention (1925), 499, 500, 503
   oblasts, 486
   provincial administration, 460
   Provisional National Legislature (1919–20), 471
   Serbs in, 457, 458, 459
   World War II (1939–45), 581, 582
Damjanović, Radovan, 137, 143
Daničić, Đuro, 159
Danilo, Prince-Bishop of Montenegro, 121
Danilo I, Prince of Montenegro, 133, 161
Danube Banovina, 508, 509, 554
Danube Division, 251, 273, 320, 415
Danube River, 15, 17, 21, 25, 38, 52, 54, 82, 94, 169, 220, 237, 391, 441, 520
Danubian Principalities, *see* Moldavia; Wallachia
Danubian vilayet (1864–1878), 170
Dar ul Jihad, Belgrade renamed as, 24
   see also Belgrade, Ottoman
Davidović, Dimitrije, 62, 75, 77, 84, 87, 92, 113, 118
Davidović, Ljubomir, 489, 490, 497, 518
   Adamstal scandal (1926), 495, 496
   annexation crisis (1908–9), 351, 352
   Atanacković's resignation (1906), 343
   constitution declaration (1937), 544
   death (1940), 558
   decentralisation and 489, 490, 492–3
   Grujić government (1903–4), 339
   Ilidža congress (1922), 488
   May putsch (1903), 337
   Nettuno Convention (1925), 503–4
   prime minister, first term (1919–20), 479
   prime minister, second term (1924), 491, 492–3
   Salonika trial (1917), 429
Day of St Sava, 510
Deak, Pavle Nestorović, 29, 30
Debar, Macedonia, 185, 224, 355, 375, 379, 382
Dečani, Kosovo, 15, 337, 376

INDEX

Dedinje, Belgrade, 574–5
deforestation, 110, 309
Deligrad, Serbia, 49, 54, 216, 218, 219
   Battle of (1806), 48-9
Democratic Party, 4, 467, 469–72, 473, 558–9
   6 January Regime (1929–34), 518, 520
   Black Hand, relations with, 487, 492
   centralism, 469–70, 486
   constituent assembly (1920–21), 480–86
   coup d'état (1941), 575
   Cvetković–Maček Agreement (1939), 558–9
   Davidović government, first (1919–20), 479
   Davidović government, second (1924), 491, 492–3
   federation plan (1934), 520
   HRSS/HSS, relations with, 491, 492, 499
   Ilidža congress (1922), 488
   Independent split (1923), 490
   Jevtić government (1934–5), 535
   JRSD formation (1931–2), 519
   Novi Sad declaration (1932), 521
   Opposition Bloc, 491, 493
   ORJUNA, 491–2, 534, 568
   Pašić government (1921–4), 482, 487–8, 491–3
   Pašić government (1924–5), 493
   People's Radical Party, relations with, 478–81
   Radić assassination (1928), 503
   Serb Cultural Club and, 559, 562
   Tripartite Pact (1940), 571, 573
   United Opposition, 536, 537, 539, 541, 544, 547, 550
   Vukičević government (1928), 500
   Zagreb congress (1922), 488
   Zagreb Points (1932), 520
Democratic Union, 494
demographics
   Kingdom of Serbia (1882–1918), 309–10, 311
   Ottoman Serbia (1459–1815), 22, 23, 24, 38, 61
   Principality of Serbia (1815–1882), 86–7, 98, 110, 170, 222–4, 227
   Yugoslavia (1918-41), 449, 453, 475, 513–14, 567
Demotika, Battle of (1352), 16
Denić, Pavle, 315, 345, 417
Denikin, Anton, 454
Denmark, 349
Derventa, Bosnia, 552
Desa, Župan of Raška, 12
desetak (tenth), 23, 69, 70
Despotović, Mileta, 217, 219
Devol, Albania, 385
deys, 29, 42–6, 49, 246
Didić, Ljubomir, 246
Dimić, Ljubodrag, 456
Dimitrije, Serbian Patriarch, 380, 461
Dimitrijević, Đorđe (Ljota), 529
Dimitrijević, Dragutin 'Apis', 264, 356, 357–9
   Aleksandar, relationship with, 357, 361
   Balkan Wars (1912–13), 378, 382
   Black Hand formation (1911), 358
   conspirator retirements (1906), 347, 361
   coup d'état (1941), 577
   Crown Prince Đorđe, relationship with, 357
   Franz Ferdinand assassination (1914), 391, 392, 430
   intelligence division appointment (1913), 359
   March disturbances (1903), 315
   May putsch (1903), 303–7, 316, 317, 318, 321–2
   Mišić, Petar, relationship with, 361, 382
   Priority Decree (1914), 389, 390
   Salonika trial (1917), 429, 430, 501
   World War I (1914–18), 425, 426, 427, 428

INDEX

Dimitrijević, Toma, 529
Dinaric type, 368
dirges, 280, 321
Djokić, Dejan, 1
Dnevnik (*Daily*), 295
Dobrnjac, Petar, 52, 54
Dobrnjac, Stevan Todorović, 71
Dobro Pole, Battle of (1918), 437
Dobrudja region, 225, 423, 569
Doiran, Battle of (1918), 437
Dokić, Đuro, 320
Dokić, Lazar, 110, 268, 273-6
Domaćica (*Housewife*), 209
Domanović, Radoje, 299, 300-1
Dorćol, Belgrade, 164, 580
Đorđe, Crown Prince of Serbia, 325, 328, 338, 351, 352, 356-357, 404
Đorđević, Gerasim, 85
Đorđević, Jovan, 201
Đorđević, Katarina, 159, 209
Đorđević, Mihailo, 348
Đorđević, Milan, 399
Đorđević, Vladan, 110–11
    Albanians, views on, 381, 385
    Aleksandar's marriage (1900), 288–90, 291, 292
    End of a Dynasty (1906), 288–9, 344
    healthcare plan (1879), 229
    imprisonment (1906), 344
    May putsch (1903), 306, 308, 313, 324, 329
    Pig War outbreak (1906), 343
    prime minister (1897–1900), 283, 286, 288, 290, 306, 347
    Red Cross founding (1876), 216
    Simić, criticism of, 282
    United Serb Youth, 174, 203
    Vienna Group, 344
    World War I (1914–18), 417
Dožić, Gavrilo, 444, 532, 543, 565, 569, 575
draft constitution
    1883, 240, 243, 280, 295
    1896, 280, 295
    1921, 482-3
Draga (Draginja), Queen of Serbia, 279, 283, 297–8, 301, 303–5
    assassination (1903), 303–5, 319–25, 330, 342, 563
    background and character, 288-9
    March disturbances (1903), 315, 316
    marriage to Aleksandar (1900), 288–95
    pregnancy revelation (1901), 297–8, 304
Dragović, Rade, 314, 329
Dragutin, King of Serbia, 15
'Drang nach Osten', 352, 365, 365, 413
Draškić, Panta, 431
Drašković, Milorad, 378, 390, 405, 429, 485, 560, 563
Drašković, Radovan M., 321–2, 324
Drašković, Slobodan, 560-1, 563
Drava Banovina, 508, 541, 553, 554, 558, 581
Drayton, James A., 419
Drenica, Kosovo, 21
Dresden, Battle of (1813), 56
dress, 62, 82–3, 111, 113, 133, 141, 158, 170, 311–12, 419, 585
Drina Banovina, 508, 509, 553, 554, 564
Drina Division, 251, 294, 320, 415
Drina River, 26, 53, 54, 65, 82, 209-10, 218, 400, 402–4, 409, 410, 441, 466
    Battle of the (1914), 403–4
Dubrovnik, Croatia, 12, 15, 19, 57, 78, 109, 120, 140, 270, 361, 439, 480, 486, 508, 550, 551, 552
ducatists, 153, 177
Duda, Baba, 145
Duklja, 11, 12, 14, 31
Dulić, Dragutin, 304
Dumba, Konstantin, 340
Đunis, battle of (1876), 219
Đurađ Branković (play), 160
Đuričić, Marko, 489
Durrës, Albania, 15, 374, 414
Dušan, Emperor of Serbia, 15–16, 17, 140, 314, 370

INDEX

Dušanovac, Belgrade, 272
Džemijet, 475, 481, 483, 490

Eastern Rumelia (1878–1885), 227, 251, 281, 371
economy
    Aleksandar's reign (1842–58), 117
    Aleksandar I of Serbia's reign (1889–1903), 262, 309, 310–11
    Aleksandar I of Yugoslavia's reign (1921–34), 511, 513–17
    Kingdom of Serbia (1217–1346), 14
    Mihailo's second reign (1860–68), 155
    Milan's reign (1868–89), 184–5, 187, 230, 234, 246
    Miloš's first reign (1815–39), 71, 80, 81–2, 87
    Ottoman Serbia (1459–1815), 37, 42
    Petar I's reign (1903–21), 343–4, 348–50, 354–5
    Petar II' reign (1934–45), 540
Edhem Pasha, 137, 141
education
    Aleksandar's reign (1842–58), 113, 116, 139
    Aleksandar I of Serbia's reign (1889–1903), 262, 284
    Aleksandar I of Yugoslavia's reign (1921–34), 510, 513
    Mihailo's first reign (1839–42), 105
    Mihailo's second reign (1860–68), 159
    Milan's reign (1868–89), 187, 204, 211, 229, 240–41, 365–6
    Miloš's first reign (1815–39), 84–5
    Miloš's second reign (1858–60), 148
    Petar I's reign (1903–21), 366, 370, 453, 468, 484
Eğri, Eyalet of (1596–1661), 28, 29
Eğri Palanka, Macedonia, 411
Egypt, 42, 80, 95, 252, 350
Ekavian dialect, 368, 461, 511
Ekmečić, Milorad, 28, 45, 61, 115, 403, 407
Elbasan, Albania, 408
elections, 148, 262, 487, 512, 522

1859 parliamentary elections, 149, 152
1869 parliamentary elections, 182
1874 parliamentary elections, 205, 208
1875 parliamentary elections, 210
1877 parliamentary elections, 220
1880 parliamentary elections, 238
1882 top-up election, 242
1883 parliamentary elections, 245–6
1884 parliamentary elections, 248
1887 parliamentary elections, 255; top-up election, 255
1888 parliamentary elections, 256
1892 Belgrade municipal elections, 272
1893 parliamentary elections, 271, 272–3, 274
1895 parliamentary elections, 295
1897 parliamentary elections, 281
1898 parliamentary elections, 284
1901 parliamentary elections, 297
1903 parliamentary elections, 334
1905 parliamentary elections, 342
1906 parliamentary elections, 347
1908 parliamentary elections, 350
1923 parliamentary elections, 489
1925 parliamentary elections, 475, 493
1927 parliamentary elections, 474, 475, 498
1931 parliamentary elections, 512
1932 senate elections, 512
1935 parliamentary elections, 536
1938 senate elections, 547; parliamentary elections, 547–8
electoral law
    1870, 182
    1890, 262
    1922, 487
    1931, 512
    1933, 522
Elias, Saint, 19
Elijah's Day Uprising (1903), 336–7
Emin-efendi, 107
End of a Dynasty (Đorđević), 288–9, 344
Engels, Friedrich, 187
Entente Cordiale (1904), 350, 394

INDEX

Epirus, 161, 374
Equality of Citizenry decree (1859), 149
Esad Pasha, 407–8, 416
Ethiopia, 524
Eugene of Savoy, 30
expansionism, 2, 16
   Aleksandar I's reign (1889–1903), 281, 285
   Black Hand, 357–61
   Mihailo's second reign (1860–68), 160–65
   Milan's reign (1868–89), 185, 249–50, 252–3
   Miloš's first reign (1815–39), 80, 81, 93, 98, 124, 226
   Miloš's second reign (1858–60), 150–51
   Ottoman Wars (1876–8), 222–5
   Petar I's reign (1903–21), 336–9, 370-80
   Plan (1844), 89, 122–6, 140, 160, 171, 222
Falcon societies, 370, 509, 552, 573
far-right politics, 527–34
Farmers' Party, 474, 489, 493, 518, 535, 539, 544, 547
6 January Regime (1929–34), 518, 519, 520, 535–6
   Chetniks and, 492
   constitution (1921), 481, 483, 487
   coup d'état (1941), 575
   Cvetković–Maček Agreement (1939), 550, 552, 558
   federalism and, 520, 535
   foundation (1919), 474
   Great Depression (1929–39), 517
   Law on Public Security (1921), 485
   Nettuno Convention (1925), 500
   fascism, 360, 522, 527–8, 530, 535, 540, 545–9
   federalism, 459, 470, 472, 482, 489–91, 504, 505, 520
   Communist Party and, 477-8
   in Croatia, 478, 488–91
   in Montenegro, 466, 476, 493

Federalist Bloc, 489–90
Ferat Draga, 475
Ferdinand I, Holy Roman Emperor, 25, 26
Ferdinand I, Tsar of Bulgaria, 280, 378, 392, 427
Ferizaj, Kosovo, 381
Ferryville, Bizerte, 414
Feth-i Islam, 82, 162
feudalism, 11, 14–15, 17–18, 24, 26, 80, 81, 83, 93, 463
fez, 102, 111, 133, 141
fiefdoms, Ottoman, 22, 31
Filiki Eteria, 66, 71
Filipović, Filip, 476
Filipović, Josip, 162
Filipović, Todor, 46
films, 310, 531, 534
First Serbian Bank, 184, 186
First Serbian Uprising (1804–13), 2, 19, 35, 43–59, 65, 66, 71, 75, 78, 90, 91, 107, 108, 113, 115, 120, 126, 131, 135, 157, 172, 186, 191, 193, 216, 222, 223, 234, 325, 391
flags,
   Croatian, 407, 433, 491, 510
   Montenegrin, 465
   Serbian, 44, 48, 97, 169, 239, 321, 358, 405, 407, 423, 433, 437, 510, 532
   Slovene, 407, 433
   Yugoslav, 459, 491, 510
Foča, Bosnia, 409
Fojnica, Croatia, 552
folk beliefs, 14, 19, 39, 40
folk healers, 40
food, 25, 39, 172, 540
forests, 32, 37, 38, 101, 105, 110, 131, 151, 204, 309, 449, 521
Fort Rupel, Greek Macedonia, 436
Fotić, Milan, 566, 575
'Foundation of a Serbian Administration' (1807), 51, 60

INDEX

Franasović, Dragutin, 254
France
    Aleksandar I's assassination (1934), 535
    Anschluss, opposition to (1934), 523–4
    Balkan Wars (1912–13), 376
    civil code, 114
    Constitutionalists, relations with, 133, 134
    Crimean War (1853–6), 134–5, 136
    Croatia, relations with, 401
    Cvetković–Maček Agreement (1939), 551
    Egypt and Syria campaign (1798–1801), 42, 43
    Entente Cordiale (1904), 350, 393, 394
    fashion, 111
    First Serbian Uprising (1804–13), 54
    Greek War of Independence (1821–9), 77
    Italian War of Independence (1859), 190, 214
    Jewish expulsions crisis (1861), 155
    Kükürt Çeşme crisis (1862), 163
    Mihailo, relations with, 160, 163
    Milan, relations with, 181
    military training, 161, 165
    Montenegro, relations with, 465
    Moroccan crises (1905–6/1911), 393–4
    Munich Agreement (1938), 546
    Mürzsteg Agreement (1903), 337, 350
    Napoleonic Wars (1803–15), 19, 49, 51, 53, 55, 56
    Niš Declaration (1914), 405
    Paris Commune (1871), 186
    parliamentarism, 299
    Petar's resignation (1914), 391
    Polish émigrés, relations with, 122
    Pribićević intervention (1931), 517
    Principality of Serbia, relations with, 89, 92
    Prussian War (1870–71), 216, 244, 412
    Radicals, 206–7
    Radicals, relations with, 362
    Reval agreement (1908), 350
    Revolution (1789–99), 35
    Revolution (1848), 128
    Russian Civil War (1917–22), 454
    Schneider-Creusot, 281, 340–1, 343, 349, 428
    Stojadinović, relations with, 545
    tariff agreement (1907), 349
    Tenka's plot (1857), 137
    Treaty of Friendship (1927), 455
    World War I (1914–18), 395, 401–2, 405, 410, 414–15, 436–40, 443
    World War II (1939–45), 569
Franchet d'Espèrey, Louis, 437, 441
Franciscans, 21, 125, 168
Franco-Hungarian Bank of Pest, 186
Frankopan, Frano Krsto, 380
Franz Ferdinand, Archduke of Austria-Este, 322, 344, 391–5, 427, 430, 458, 466
Franz Joseph I, Emperor of Austria, 132, 134, 281, 392
Free Corps, 34–5, 42, 44, 46, 48, 90, 108
freedom of association, 240, 248, 257, 260, 296, 297, 484, 512, 537, 539
freedom of expression, 240, 257–8, 260, 296, 328, 484, 512, 537, 539
freedom of religion, 26, 49, 78, 124-5, 127, 372, 391, 484, 512
Freemasons, 569
French Foreign Legion, 443
French language, 154, 202, 207, 328
Friedjung, Heinrich, 367
Friedland, Battle of (1807), 51
Front for the Defence of the Fatherland, 573, 575
Frontier Guard, 361, 392
furniture, 38, 39, 109, 115
furriers' guild, 127
'fusion' (1901–2), 295–301, 316, 470, 506

Gabler, Wilhelm, 111
Gaeta, Italy, 465
Gaj, Ljudevit, 120, 121, 128

693

INDEX

Gajtan, Serbia, 421
Gallipoli, Thrace, 17
Garašanin, Ilija, 98, 109, 111-12, 122–6, 128–30, 132, 133–4, 364, 373
    Aleksandar's deposal (1858), 146
    April Circular (1852), 133, 134
    Austrian Serbs, relations with, 136–7
    on Bosnia, 483
    background, 108
    Bulgarian conflict (1867), 176
    cannon foundry establishment (1848), 132
    Croats, relations with, 167
    death (1874), 233
    Hercegovina rebellion (1851–2), 133
    Hungarian conflict (1848–9), 130
    Kükürt Çeşme crisis (1862), 162–3
    Law on Parliaments (1859), 146
    marriage controversy, views on, 175–6
    Mihailo's assassination (1868), 179
    Mihailo's second reign (1860–68), 154, 158, 160
    Miloš's restoration (1858–9), 141, 144, 145, 146, 147, 153
    Montenegro, relations with, 133, 167
    Plan (1844), 89, 122–6, 140, 160, 171, 222, 375
    police law (1850), 133
    Russia, relations with, 134, 175, 176, 181
    Serbian Committee establishment (1862), 160
    St Andrew's Day parliament (1858), 141, 144, 145
    Tenka's plot (1857), 137
    uprising plans, 128–30, 133
Garašanin, Luka, 104, 106
Garašanin, Milutin (Ilija's son), 205, 233, 235, 248, 251–5, 257, 261, 273, 284, 334
Garašanin, Hadži Milutin Savić, 40, 55, 59, 72, 103-6, 108
Garašanin, Svetozar, 178
Garaši, Serbia, 55, 108
Garibaldi, Giuseppe, 165, 190, 361
Garvan, Macedonia, 468
Gauls, 10
Gavrilo V, Serbian Patriarch, 444, 532, 543, 565, 569, 575
Gavrilović, Jovan, 158, 181
Gavrilović, Mihailo, 62, 442, 513
Gavrilović, Milan, 474, 553, 572, 577
Gedik Ahmed Pasha, 22
Genčić, Đorđe
    Aleksandar's marriage (1900), 290, 291, 294, 324
    Balugdžić's resignation (1905), 341
    conspiracy against Aleksandar (1900-03), 303-7, 324, 340, 565
    Đorđe's succession renounced (1909), 357
    May putsch (1903), 318, 320, 325, 329, 344, 357
    Minister of Internal Affairs (1899–1900), 286, 290
    Minister of National Economy (1903), 325
    March disturbances (1903), 318
    Milan, relations with, 282, 324
    Pig War outbreak (1906), 344
General Military Administration, 150, 161
General Union, 241, 242
General Workers' Union, 329
Geneva, Switzerland, 327, 349, 440-1, 442, 444, 523, 529
Geneva Declaration (1918), 440–2
Gepids, 9
German Empire (1871–1918), 248
    Aleksandar I's anointment (1889), 265
    Balkan Wars (1912–13), 376, 377
    Bosnian crisis (1908–9), 354
    capital investment, 349
    Franz Ferdinand assassination (1914), 394
    military, 244, 245, 285
    monarchy 296, 305

INDEX

Moroccan crises (1905–6/1911), 393–4
Reval agreement (1908), 350
Serbo-Ottoman Wars (1876–8), 216
Social Democrats, 348
Timok rebellion (1883), 248
Wilhelm assassination plot (1916), 392, 427
World War I (1914–18), 2, 395, 401–2, 412–22, 436–8
German language, 118, 132
Germans, 132, 439, 446, 452, 464, 467, 473, 490, 498, 521, 542, 567, 569, 580
Germany, 10, 452, 118, 248
    German Empire (1871–1918), *see* German Empire
    Nazi Germany (1933–45), *see* Germany, Nazi
    unification (1866–71), 160, 364, 497
Germany, Nazi (1933–45), 2, 302, 495, 523, 527
    Aleksandar's assassination (1934), 524–5
    Anschluss plan (1934), 546
    anti-Semitism, 568, 569
    armaments funding (1938), 578
    Catholicism in, 543
    commercial treaty (1934), 523
    France, invasion of (1940), 569
    Krupp steel mill in Zenica (1937), 545
    Maček's visit (1939), 547
    mineral imports, 540
    Molotov–Ribbentrop Pact (1939), 557
    Munich Agreement (1938), 546
    ORJUNA and, 534
    Poland, invasion of (1939), 557
    Romania, invasion of (1940), 570
    Soviet Union, invasion of (1941), 583
    Stojadinović, relations with, 545–6
    Tripartite Pact (1940), 557, 564, 566, 570–72, 576
    Yugoslavia occupation (1941–5), 533, 563, 578–84
Geršić, Gliša (Giga), 166, 247
Gevgelije, Macedonia, 374
Glagolitic, 11
Glavaš, Stanoje, 43, 44, 52, 59
Gligorijević, Branislav, 400, 427, 430, 494, 508, 518
Gligorijević, Hadži Prodan, 58
Glynn, Elinor, 322
'God of Justice', 201
Gođevac, Milorad, 299, 337
Gojković, Ilija, 361, 383
Gojković, Vojislav, 426, 562
Golubić, Mustafa, 573, 578
Gołuchowski, Agenor Maria, 281
Gopčević, Spiridon, 253
Goraćići, Serbia, and massacre at (1893), 272, 325
Goražde, Bosnia, 409
Göring, Hermann, 525, 547, 577
Gornja Dobrinja, Serbia, 57
Gornje Spance, Serbia, 420
Gornji Karlovac, Croatia, 85
Gornji Matejevac, Serbia, 104
Gornji Milanovac, Serbia, 205
Gospić, Croatia, 522
Goths, 9
government of generals (1902–3), 299, 301–2, 306
Grabež, Trifko, 392, 393
Gradačac, Croatia, 552
Gradaščević, Husein-kapetan, 79, 95
Grahovac, Battle of (1858), 161
Granđa, Ivan, 501
Grdelica gorge, Serbia, 223
Grđić, Radmilo, 529
Great Depression, 513–14, 515, 516–17, 524
Great Migration (1690), 30
Great Moravia, 11
Great School
    First Serbian Uprising (1804–1813), 52
    Principality of Serbia (1815–1882), 84, 85, 159, 165, 170, 172, 174, 178, 204, 238

INDEX

Kingdom of Serbia (1882–1918), 250, 252, 268, 310
Greece, 13, 15–16, 287, 455
    Balkan League agreements (1912), 373
    Balkan Pact (1934), 455, 523
    Balkan Wars (1912–13), 374, 376, 377, 379, 384
    Bosnian uprising (1875–8), 215
    Cenić on, 313
    Constantine assassination plot (1916), 392, 427
    coup d'état (1917), 436
    German invasion (1941), 583
    Italian invasion (1940), 570, 571, 579
    Karić and, 366
    Ljotić and, 531
    Metaxas regime (1936–41), 527–8
    Mihailo, relations with, 161, 175, 176
    monarchy, 287, 305
    Ottoman War (1897), 281
    Salonika agreement (1923), 455
    Serbian-Ottoman Wars (1876–8), 219
    Serbo-Greek convention (1861), 161
    Treaty of Friendship (1926), 469
    War of Independence (1821–9), 62, 66, 71, 75, 76, 77
    World War I (1914–18), 412, 414, 436, 437
    World War II (1939–45), 570, 571, 579, 582, 583
Greek language, 11, 25, 90, 170
Greek Orthodox Church, 120, 121, 468
Greeks, 9, 13, 16, 18, 22, 24, 50
    Phanariots, 66, 71
    Serbian Orthodox Church and, 32, 33–4, 48, 85, 236
    travelling doctors, 40
green-shirts, 545, 547
Gregorian calendar, 2, 19, 461
Greig, Charles, 382
Grgur, Serbia, 422
Grol, Milan, 470, 558, 566, 573, 576
Grujić, Jevrem, 140–45, 147, 152, 153, 155, 158, 166, 174, 181, 209, 210

Grujić, Nikanor, 543
Grujić, Sava, 165, 188, 190, 207, 212, 215, 256–7, 267–9, 275–6, 334, 336, 345
Grujović, Boža, 46
Grujović, Mihailo, 55
Gruža, Serbia, 73, 90, 106
guilds, 76, 87, 110, 117, 127, 262, 311, 513
gun question, 340–41, 343, 344, 345, 348–9, 428
Gurgusovac, Serbia, 88, 107
gymnasiums, 36, 85, 86, 110, 140, 148, 188, 284, 285
Győr, Eyalet of (1594–1598), 28
gypsies, 22, 45, 86, 110, 169, 421, 549
'gypsying', 110

Habsburg Empire (1282–1918), 3, 19, 25, 26, 27, 28–36, 37, 78, 175
    Albanians, relations with, 282, 380, 381, 385
    Aleksandar I of Serbia, relations with 265, 285, 292, 294, 300, 307–8
    Aleksandar (Prince of Serbia, 1842-58), relations with, 126, 136-7
    Ausgleich (1867), 175
    Balkan Wars (1912–13), 374–5, 376, 377, 379–80
    Bosnia negotiations (1870), 186
    Bosnia, rule over (1878–1918), *see* Bosnia-Hercegovina, Condominium of
    Bosnian uprising (1875–8), 210, 219-20
    civil code (1811), 114
    condominium agreement (1897), 281, 286
    conspirator question and, 336, 340, 347, 362
    Constitutionalists, relations with, 105–6, 107, 122, 126–7, 133–7
    Croat–Serb Coalition (1905–18), 366, 391
    education in, 118

INDEX

Franz Ferdinand assassination (1914), 322, 391–5, 430
French Revolutionary Wars (1792–1801), 35
Greek War of Independence (1821–9), 75
gun question (1904–7), 340–41, 343, 344, 345, 348–9, 428
Hercegovina rebellion (1882), 235, 310
Italian War of Independence (1859), 214
Kosovo legend and, 19
Kotor annexation (1814), 19
Kükürt Çeşme crisis (1862), 163
Liberals in, 173, 195
Marković on, 191
May Declaration (1917), 431–2
migration to, 37, 44–5, 46, 56, 58, 62, 162
Mihailo, relations with, 160, 162, 171, 175
Milan, relations with, 181, 185, 230–1, 233–5, 237, 250, 254, 256, 283
Mileta's rebellion (1835), 92
Miloš, relations with, 63, 66, 74, 75, 78, 84–5, 92, 94
Mürzsteg Agreement (1903), 337, 350
Napoleonic Wars (1803–15), 19, 53
Ottoman War (1683–99), 28–31, 35
Ottoman War (1716–18), 32
Ottoman War (1737–9), 32–3
Ottoman War (1788–91), 34–5, 40
Paris Peace Conference (1919), 452
Petar I, relations with, 227, 336, 347, 391
Pig War (1906–11), 343–4, 348-9, 350, 354
postal services agreement (1869), 185–6
Prussian War (1866), 168, 173, 174, 352
railways, 196, 226, 227, 230, 237, 241
Reval agreement (1908), 350
Revolutions (1848–9), 111, 120, 128–32, 187
Secret Convention (1881), 235, 280
Serbian language in, 116
Serbian Uprising, First (1804–13), 45, 46, 54, 55, 56, 58, 65
Serbian Uprising, Second (1815), 59, 60
Serbo-Bulgarian War (1885–6), 251
Serbo-Ottoman Wars (1876–8), 216–17, 225–6
Škoda company, 340, 343, 348–9, 428
Slavic kinship in, 119–20
St John's Day attempt (1899), 286
swine fever outbreak (1895), 279
Tenka's plot (1857), 137
Timok rebellion (1883), 248
trade agreement (1881), 230, 234
trade war (1878–9), 229
trade war (1906–11), 343-4, 348–9, 350, 354
United Serb Youth, 173-4, 181, 195-6
World War I (1914–18), 2, 4, 395, 399, 412-22, 434-5, 438, 439
Zagreb treason trial (1909), 366–7
hacılık, 40
Hadži-Toma family, 177–8, 306
Hadži-Toma, Nikola, 249, 305, 306, 341
Hadži-Toma (Opulos), 177
Hadžić, Ela, 492
Hadžić, Jovan, 114, 117
Hadžić, Stevan, 423, 426, 492–3, 502, 506
hajduks, 32, 38, 43, 44, 48, 52, 59, 69, 261, 419
hajj, 40
Hartwig, Nikolai, 370, 378, 390
has, 23
hatt-ı şerif, 76, 131
    1829, 77
    1830, 3, 77–9, 83, 84, 85, 87, 89, 96, 98, 102, 193
    1833, 80, 81, 93, 98, 124
    1838, 95, 193

INDEX

healthcare, 40, 84, 206, 216, 229, 484, 516, 552
hećimi, 40
Hećimović, Nikola, 517
Heraclius, Byzantine Emperor, 10
Herceg-Novi, Montenegro, 439
Hercegovina
    Austro-Hungarian rule over, *see* Bosnia-Hercegovina, Condominium of
    Cvijić and, 38
    Garašanin and, 125, 140, 160, 167–8
    Marković and, 189, 190, 191, 192
    medieval (to 1482), 10-11, 14, 15
    Mihailo and, 176
    Miloš and, 122, 151
    Montenegro and, 167, 408
    Orthodox migration to, 26
    rebellion (1851–2), 133–4
    rebellion (1861), 161
    rebellion (1875–8), 201, 208, 209–15
    rebellion (1882), 235, 310
    Serbian Committee and, 160
    Serbo-Greek convention (1861), 161
    in Yugoslavia (1918-41), *see* Bosnia-Hercegovina in Yugoslavia
    Žujović and, 188
    see also Bosnia in the Ottoman Empire
Herder, Johann Gottfried, 119
Herzen, Alexander, 165
Hilandar monastery, Mount Athos, 13
Hitler, Adolf, 524, 525, 532, 534, 543, 546, 547, 550, 569, 570, 571, 576, 578, 580, 581
Hođera, Svetislav, 528, 547
Hodges, George, 94
Hohenzollern dynasty, 523
Holy Roman Empire (800–1806), 25, 26, 28–36, 37
    French Revolutionary Wars (1792–1801), 35
    Ottoman War (1683–99), 28–31, 35
    Ottoman War (1716–18), 32
    Ottoman War (1737–9), 32–3
    Ottoman War (1788–91), 34–5, 40

Serbian Uprising, First (1804–13), 45, 46
Horststein, General, 402
Horthy, Miklós, 491
Horvat, Aleksandar, 423
Horvatović, Đura, 219, 222
hospodars, 87
Hotel Bristol, Belgrade, 519
Hozrev Pasha, 103
Hristić, Artemis, 254
Hristić, Filip, 153, 155, 156, 158, 209
Hristić, Kosta, 224
Hristić, Nikola
    Aleksandar's reign (1842–58), 115, 126, 137, 144, 178
    Aleksandar I's reign (1889–1903), 278, 290
    Mihailo's assassination (1868), 179
    Mihailo's first reign (1839–42), 106
    Mihailo's second reign (1860–68), 154, 155, 156, 159, 161, 177, 178
    Milan's reign (1868–89), 184, 245–6, 256, 258
    Miloš's second reign (1858–60), 151, 153
    prime minister, first term (1867–8), 177–9, 181, 184
    prime minister, second term (1883–4), 245–6
    prime minister, third term (1888–9), 256, 258
    prime minister, fourth term (1894–5), 278
Hum, 11, 12, 14
Hum, bishopric of, 14
Hungarian language, 128
Hungarian Royal Academy, 52
Hungarians, *see* Magyars
Hungary, 12, 13, 15, 17, 18, 19, 20, 21, 26, 27, 37, 46, 125, 191, 402, 452, 454–5
    Charles I's return (1921), 454–5
    education in, 139, 140
    HRSS, relations with, 491
    Illyrian Court Commission and, 34

INDEX

intellectuals in, 36, 113, 115
Matica Srpska founding (1826), 119
Ottoman (1541–1699), 25, 27, 31
Revolution (1848–9), 120, 128, 129–32
Royal Academy, 52
Soviet Republic (1919), 454
Stojadinović, relations with, 545, 546
Transylvania annexation (1940), 569
Treaty of Friendship (1940), 571
Tripartite Pact accession (1940), 570
Ustashas in, 535
Vienna War (1683–99), 29, 30, 31
Yugoslavia invasion (1941), 580, 581
Hunyadi, Julija, 154, 175, 292, 324
Huns, 9, 11
Huršid Ahmed Pasha, 53, 60
Husino, Bosnia, 463
Hussar Rebellion (1844), 126, 142, 154, 178, 308
Hussein Pasha, 79
Hvar, Croatia, 438
Hvosno, bishopric of, 14

Ibar Army, 374
Ibrahim Pasha, 49, 60
Ičko, Petar, 49
Ijekavian dialect, 120, 511
Ilić, Bogoljub, 564, 576, 577
Ilić, Danilo, 393
Ilić, Jovan, 143, 144
Ilić, Mihailo, 348
Ilić, Stevan, 295, 315
Ilić, Vojislav, 370
Ilidža congress (1922), 488
Illyria, 9, 10, 30, 460
Illyrian Court Commission, 34, 36
Illyrian Movement, 120, 123, 128
Illyrian Provinces, 53
Illyrians (pre-Slavic inhabitants of Balkans), 9, 10
Ilok, Croatia, 86, 552

Independent Democratic Party, 473, 474, 490, 493, 498, 500, 502, 504, 521, 536, 544, 548, 552, 554, 573, 576
Independent Radical Party, 3–4, 287, 298, 302, 331, 339–41
  Avakumović government (1903), 325
  Bosnian crisis (1908–9), 353, 355
  conspirators, relations with, 337, 340
  constitution (1901), 296, 297
  constitution (1903), 327
  contra pardoning affair (1908), 352
  Democratic Party merger (1919), 470, 486
  Elijah's Day Uprising (1903), 337
  Grujić government (1903–4), 334
  Grujić government (1906), 345
  gun question (1904–7), 340–41
  Niš Declaration (1914), 405
  March disturbances (1903), 314, 316
  May putsch (1903), 4, 306, 308, 321, 328
  'Our first word' (1902), 298
  Pašić government (1906–8), 347
  Petrović inquiry (1911), 356
  Provisional National Legislature (1919–20), 471
  Radical terrorism against, 355, 362
  Salonika trial (1917), 429
  St John's Day attempt (1899), 286–7, 289, 292, 313, 344
  Stojanović government (1905–6), 342, 345
  territorial acquisitions (1912–13) and, 389, 390
  White Hand, relations with, 362
  World War I (1914–18), 404, 425
  Yugoslav Committee, relations with, 434
  Yugoslav nationalism, 363, 367–70
  Yugoslavia, establishment of (1918), 459
Independent State of Croatia (1941–5), 495, 581, 582
Independent Workers' Party, 485

INDEX

industrialisation, 117, 134, 138, 204, 208-9, 213, 230, 234, 308-9, 311, 349, 354, 449, 513, 514-15, 540
Inoćentije, Metropolitan of Belgrade, 291, 321
Interim Decree on Land Reform (1919), 463
Internal Macedonian Revolutionary Organisation (VMRO), 336-7, 342, 358, 371, 468-9, 474, 522, 523, 524-5
International Criminal Tribunal for the former Yugoslavia, 342
Ioannina, Greece, 375, 376
Isailović, Dimitrije, 84
Islam; Muslims, 4, 22
    6 January Regime (1929-34), 506, 509, 510
    Akkerman Convention (1826), 76-7
    Albanian expulsions (1878), 222-4
    Balkan Wars (1912-13), 382
    Bosnian peasant's revolt (1918-20), 462
    census (1921), 453
    Corfu Declaration (1917), 433
    Cvetković-Maček Agreement (1939), 553, 554
    Democratic Party and, 469
    Džemijet, 475, 481
    emigration from Bosnia-Hercegovina, 27, 371
    expulsions (1833-4), 81-3, 98, 118
    hajj, 40
    hatt-ı şerif (1830), 78, 79, 98
    JRZ and, 540
    Kanlice Palace conference (1862), 162
    Kosovar Albanians, 467, 475
    Miloš's restoration (1858-60), 150, 151
    Montenegro Christmas massacre (1702), 121, 465
    mosques, 33, 50, 62, 170, 224
    Ottoman withdrawal (1867), 168-70
    reis-ul-ulema, 509, 510
    Šahovići massacre (1924), 463
    sharia law, 22, 484, 512
    St Peter's Day parliament (1848), 131
    women's suffrage and, 480
    World War I (1914-18), 418
    Yugoslav Muslim Organisation, *see* Yugoslav Muslim Organisation
Istria, 140, 364, 366, 369, 402, 410, 438, 455, 471, 482
Italy, 160, 457, 509, 522, 527, 534, 540
    Albania, relations with, 282, 375, 381, 385, 468, 505, 547
    Albania invasion (1939), 579
    Aleksandar's assassination (1934), 524, 535
    Anschluss, opposition to (1934), 523-4
    Austrian War (1866), 174, 352
    Balkan Wars (1912-13), 375
    Bitola bombing (1940), 570
    Croatia, relations with, 401
    Cvetković-Maček Agreement (1939), 551
    Ethiopian War (1935-7), 524
    Greece, invasion of (1940), 570
    HRSS, relations with, 491
    Jewish expulsions crisis (1861), 155
    Libyan War (1911-12), 371
    Montenegro, relations with, 465
    Napoleonic Kingdom (1805-14), 49
    Nettuno Convention (1925), 499, 500, 503
    Pact of Friendship (1924), 455
    Paris Peace Conference (1919-20), 451-2
    Piedmont-Sardinia (1720-1861), 160, 173, 190, 214, 358, 359, 361, 364
    Stojadinović, relations with, 545, 547, 549
    trade agreement (1880), 230
    trade agreement (1907), 349
    Treaty of Friendship (1937), 545
    Treaty of Rapallo (1920), 455
    Tripartite Pact (1940), 557, 564, 566, 570-72, 576
    War of Independence, Second (1859), 190, 214

INDEX

War of Independence, Third (1866), 174
World War I (1914–18), 401, 410, 434, 438, 439
   Yugoslav Committee founding (1914), 406
   Yugoslavia invasion (1941), 578, 580
Ivankovac, Serbia, 46
   Battle of (1805), 46
Ivanović, Jakov, 147
Ivanović, Katarina, 113
Ivetić, Velimir, 426
Ivković, Marinko, 246, 247
Ivković, Vidoje, 178, 180
Izvolsky, Alexander, 351

Jadar, Serbia, 79, 80, 402
Jagodina, Serbia, 62, 74, 87, 88, 113, 205, 233
Jakšić, Svetolik, 299, 427, 429
Jakšić, Žarko, 521
Jamnica, Croatia, 213, 214
janissaries, 23, 28, 31, 35, 40–45, 49, 51, 61, 347
Janj, Bosnia, 53
Janjić, Vojislav, 543
Janković, Aleksa, 126, 131, 136
Janković, Božidar, 318, 333, 352, 359, 374, 409, 495
Janković, Dragoslav, 47
Janković, Milovan, 140–41, 147, 152, 153, 155, 157, 166
Janković, Radivoje, 582
Janković, Radoje, 426
János Hunyadi, Voivode of Transylvania, 19
Japan, 350, 557, 570, 572
Jasenica, Serbia, 72, 74, 166
Javnost (Public), 207
Jedinstvo (Unity), 500–501, 503
Jeftanović, Gligorije, 447, 471, 473
Jelačić, Josip, 120, 128, 130
Jelinić, Đurđe, 426
Jenko, Davorin, 201
Jeras, Josip, 414

Jeremić, Gaja, 152
Jerusalem, Palestine, 40, 583
Jevtić, Bogoljub, 534–7, 539, 541, 576
Jews, 22, 24, 25, 50, 127, 149, 155, 421, 566–9
   anti-Jewish law (1846), 127, 149, 183
   anti-Jewish laws (1861), 155, 183
   army and, 183, 567
   Ashkenazim, 566, 569
   census (1921), 453, 567
   Congress of Berlin (1878), 227
   constitution (1869), 183
   emigration, 127, 155, 183, 568
   integration of, 566-8
   Kükürt Çeşme crisis (1862), 162
   Ljotić and, 531
   murders (1865), 155
   Niš annexation (1878), 224
   ORJUNA and, 534
   population numbers, 86, 110, 127, 155
   Radical anti-Semitism, 234-5, 243
   Sephardim, 25, 567, 569
   Yugoslav government anti-Semitism, 547, 568-9
   Zionism, 567-8
Joaquin III, Patriarch, 227
John Bull, 322
Jonić, Velibor, 529, 530–1
Jošanica, Serbia, 88
Joseph II, Holy Roman Emperor, 36
Josimović, Emilijan, 170
Jovan's rebellion (1839), 97
Jovanović, Aleksa, 110, 291-2, 295, 297
Jovanović, Đorđe, 265
Jovanović, Dragoljub, 518, 519, 558
Jovanović, Dragutin, 501, 502
Jovanović, Jovan B., 417, 435, 513
Jovanović, Ljubomir, 337, 357, 428, 476, 496, 497, 513
Jovanović, Pantelija, 152, 180
Jovanović, Pavle, 86, 90 111–12, 114, 147, 152
Jovanović, Risto, 145
Jovanović, Slobodan, 135, 141–2, 299, 563

INDEX

on Aleksandar's marriage to Draga, 283, 288, 292, 293, 324
and Apis, 427
on British parliamentary model, 334
on conspirators, 332
on constitutional revision (1928), 504
on Constitutionalists, 135, 141
on Council, 135
coup d'état (1941),563, 566, 574, 576
on Draga, 283, 288, 292
on dress, 141
on Austro-Hungarian invasion of Bosnia (1878), 227
on HRSS, 490
on Marković, 188, 191
on May putsch (1903), 324, 332
on Milan, 181, 191, 250, 292
on Natalija, 283
on Obrenovićes and women, 324
on Ottoman Wars (1876–8), 219
on peasants, 241, 260
on Piroćanac, 234
on Progressives, 239
Serb Cultural Club, 559, 561, 563
on Serbian Orthodox Church, 237
on St Vitus's Day constitution (1921), 482
World War I (1914–18), 402, 427
on Yugoslavia, establishment of (1918), 456
Jovanović, Viđentije, 33
Jovanović, Vladimir, 140-2, 172–4, 177, 196, 218, 561
    Action Ministries (1875; 1876-8), 210, 218
    Bosnian crisis (1908–9), 352
    Conservatives, views on, 172, 173
    critique of Serbian elite culture, 172-3
    Great School dismissal (1864), 165, 172
    on Hussar Rebellion (1844), 142
    Law on Bureaucrats (1865), 166
    Marković, relationship with, 188-9, 196
    May putsch (1903), 317, 319

Mihailo's assassination (1868), 179
Narodna Skupština proposal, 155
Society for Serbian Letters speech (1864), 165
Srbske novine editor, 153
United Serb Youth and, 173–4, 196
Jovanović-Brkić, Vasilije, 33
Jovanović-Cukić, Stojan, 126
Jovanović-Čupa, Ljubomir, 314, 333, 337, 358, 378, 380
Jovanović-Pižon, Jovan, 299, 390, 393, 427, 474, 544, 550, 572
Jovanović Stoimirović, Milan, 570
judiciary
    Kingdom of Serbia (1882–1918), 249, 277, 278, 286, 306
    Principality of Serbia (1815–1882), 67, 69, 74–5, 114, 133, 151, 166–7, 206, 228
    Yugoslavia (1918-41), 460, 482, 484, 510, 517, 518, 520
Jugoslovenska straža (*Yugoslav Guard*), 534
Jugović, Ivan, 52
Jukić, Ilija, 576
Julian calendar, 2, 461
Julija, Princess of Serbia, 154, 175, 292, 324
Jurišić-Šturm, Pavle, 244, 403, 412, 426, 495
Justinian I, Byzantine Emperor, 9, 321
Jusuf-Muhlis Pasha, 95

Kaçak movement (1918–24), 466
Kaclerović, Triša, 314, 315, 348, 357, 360, 383, 388, 395
kadis, 22, 41, 62
Kadrifakovo, Macedonia, 468
Kajkavian dialect, 120
kajmakamlije, 172
kajmakams, 144
Kajmakčalan, Battle of (1916), 415, 510
Kalafatović, Danilo, 581, 582
Kalemegdan fortress, Belgrade, 109, 112
    Aleksandar's accession (1842), 107, 148
    Aleksandar's deposition (1858), 144

INDEX

anti-Constitutionalist uprising (1840), 103
bombardment of Belgrade (1862), 162
constitution presentation (1839), 95
Đak's rebellion (1825), 73
Elijah's Day Uprising (1903), 336
Mihailo's accession, first (1840), 102
Mihailo's accession, second (1860), 154
militia mutiny (1862), 164
Miloš's accession (1858–9), 148, 152
Ottoman withdrawal (1867), 169, 170
protests (1848), 115
Weary Fighter sculpture (1935), 516
Victor monument (1928), 516
Kalinik II, Patriarch, 33
Kaljević, Ljubomir, 178, 196, 205, 210–11, 212, 213, 216, 227, 288, 325
von Kállay, Benjamin, 155, 176, 179, 186, 307
Kallipolis, *see* Gallipoli
Kamnik, Slovenia, 578
Kanizsa, Eyalet of (1600–1686), 28, 29
Kanlıce Palace conference (1862), 162–3
kapetanijas, 88
Karabiberović, Živko, 152, 181, 182-3
Karaburma, Belgrade, 309
Karađorđe, 35, 42–59, 60, 61, 62–3, 104, 108, 113, 373
 assassination (1817), 66–7, 69, 70
 background, 43-4
 beats up Milovanović (1809), 53-4
 becomes Serbian uprising leader (1804), 44
 biopic film (1911), 310
 character, 43-4, 48, 51, 52, 57
 flees Serbia (1813), 56
 in Free Corps, 42, 44
 grave, 275
 kills Maričević (1804), 45
 massacre of Muslims, 49, 50, 56
 Miloš and, 52, 55, 57-8
 opposition to, 47, 50-1, 52-3, 54-5, 56, 58

Karađorđević, Aleksa (Karađorđe's great-grandson), 307
Karađorđević, Aleksa (Karađorđe's son), 52, 75, 143
Karađorđević, Aleksandar, *see* Aleksandar I, King of Yugoslavia
Karađorđević, Aleksandar, *see* Aleksandar, Prince of Serbia
Karađorđević, Arsen, 527, 549
Karađorđević, Božidar, 307
Karađorđević, Đorđe (Crown Prince), *see* Đorđe, Crown Prince of Serbia
Karađorđević, Đorđe (Karađorđe's grandson), 143
Karađorđević, Kleopatra, 112
Karađorđević, Olga, 323, 565, 574
Karađorđević, Pavle, *see* Pavle, Prince Regent of Yugoslavia
Karađorđević, Persida, *see* Persida, Princess of Serbia
Karađorđević, Petar, *see* Petar I, King of Serbia
Karađorđević, Petar, *see* Petar II, King of Serbia
Karađorđević, Poleksija, 128
Karađorđević, Sarka, 143
Karađorđević, Zorka, 244
Karađorđević dynasty, 4–5, 113, 154, 182, 294, 357, 428, 445, 529, 538, 545, 548
 Communist Party of Yugoslavia and, 477
 Corfu Declaration (1917), 432-3
 Croatia and, 462
 Democratic Party and, 471
 Geneva Declaration (1918), 441
 installation (1842), 102, 107-8
 May putsch (1903) and, 305-6, 325-8
 opposition to Obrenović regime, 159, 166, 179, 180, 187, 221, 254
 overthrow (1858), 144-6, 186
 restoration (1903), 325-8
 Secret Convention (1881) and, 235
 socialists and, 186-7
Karađorđević Star, 328

703

INDEX

Karađorđevićites, 145–6, 154, 164, 166, 179, 180, 186-7, 207-8, 220-1, 235, 262, 277, 306, 307-8, 529
Karadžić, Radovan, 581
Karadžić, Vuk Stefanović,
    Austrian Serbs, views on, 115–18, 120
    background, 52, 115-16
    Bay of Kotor visit (1835), 19
    constitution proposal (1832), 89
    dress, 111
    Garašanin and, 126
    linguistic nationalism, 115–22, 123, 124, 138, 366, 406
    Mihailo's second reign (1860–68), 154, 155, 158-9
    on Miloš and Muslims, 60
    orthography, 116, 120, 159
    on peasants, 38, 41, 82
    poetry anthologies, 19, 116
    von Ranke and, 49
    Slavic Congress (1848), 129
    on townsmen, 82
Karamehmedović, Hamdija, 507
Karanovac, Serbia, 46
Karić, Vladimir, 37, 110, 366
Karlovac, Croatia, 46, 116
Karlovci, metropolitanate of, 461
Karlowitz, Treaty of (1699), 30
Kavadar, Macedonia, 379
Kazan Cathedral, St Petersburg, 321
Kazimirović, Vasa, 304, 427, 495
Kenya, 574
Kerestinec, Croatia, 542
Kerin, Veličko Dimitrov, 525
Keşcu, Petre, 615
Keshko, Natalija, *see* Natalija, Queen of Serbia
de Kéthely, Júlia Hunyady, *see* Julija, Princess of Serbia
Kikinda, Serbia, 129, 195
Kingdom of Serbs, Croats and Slovenes, *see* Yugoslavia
Kirk Kilisse, Battle of (1912), 374
Kladovo, Serbia, 54, 82, 162

Klagenfurt, Austria, 453
Klonimirović, Časlav, 12
kmets, 39, 41, 43, 47, 60, 70, 74, 76, 88, 91, 96, 98, 145, 148, 149, 211, 228, 249, 255, 271
knezes
    Ottoman period (1459–1815), 24, 29, 33, 41–5, 47, 53, 56, 58–9, 145
    Principality of Serbia (1815–1882), 65, 68, 70–74, 87–8, 90, 91, 98
Knežević, Radoje, 565, 566, 574, 575, 576
Knežević, Timotije, 126, 147
Knežević, Živan, 565
knežinas, 41, 43, 47, 48, 53, 55, 56, 68, 71, 74, 88, 90, 157
Knić, Serbia, 58, 73
Knićanin, Stevan Petrović, 81, 106, 126, 130, 131, 132, 133, 165
Knićanka, Jelena, 243
Knjaževac, Serbia, 54, 107, 217, 234, 246–7, 573
Koča's Krajina, 35
Kočić, Petar, 474
Kolaković, Stevan, 357
Kolašin, Montenegro
    massacre at (1901), 282
    Šahovići massacre (1924), 463
    Affair (1909), 338-9
Kolchak, Alexander, 454
Kolubara, Serbia, 103
Kolubara River, 405
    Battle of the (1914), 405, 413, 510
komitadžis, 417, 418, 419–22
komovica, 495
Konjic, Hercegovina, 553
Konstantinović, Anka, 175–6, 177, 178
Konstantinović, Katarina, 175, 177, 178
Konstantinović, Mihailo, 551, 553-5, 561, 566, 569, 572
Kopiliq, Kosovo, 21
Kopitar, Jernej, 119, 121
Koprivnica, Zaječar, 229
Korčula, Croatia, 438, 510

704

INDEX

Kordun, Croatia, 472
Korishë, Kosovo, 413
Korošec, Anton, 456, 499, 506, 518, 564
   anti-Semitism, 568, 569
   arrest (1933), 520
   Concordat crisis (1937), 542
   Geneva Declaration (1918), 440
   JRZ formation (1936), 537, 538
   May Declaration (1917), 432
   prime minister (1928–9), 502, 504
   Stojadinović government (1935–9), 538, 541, 548
   Uzunović government (1934), 524
Koruško conflict (1919), 453
Kosanica region, Serbia, 223
Kosanović, Sava, 500
Kosić, Mirko, 573, 576
Kosić, Petar, 565, 570, 573, 574
Kosovo
   Balkan Wars (1912-13), 374-7, 380-3, 391, 395
   Battle of, First (1389), 17, 18–21, 116, 121, 259, 264, 280, 380, 483, 578
   Battle of, Second (1448), 19
   Congress of Berlin (1878), 226
   Cvijić and, 369, 371
   Karić and, 366
   Kingdom of Serbia (1217–1346), 15
   Kingdom of Serbia (1912–1918), 379, 380–3, 385–91, 401, 407, 413
   Ottoman period (1455–1912), *see* Kosovo in the Ottoman Empire
   Raška period (1091–1217), 12
   Yugoslavia (1918–41), *see* Kosovo in Yugoslavia
   World War I (1914–18), 407, 413, 416
Kosovo in the Ottoman Empire (1455–1912), 30, 55, 79, 222, 226, 282, 337, 371
Kosovo in Yugoslavia (1918-41), 5, 377, 466–8
   Albanian population, 466–8
   banovinas, 508
   constitution (1921), 482
   Democratic Party in, 481
   JRZ in, 538, 540
   Kaçak movement (1918–24), 466–7
   land reform (1919), 467
   oblast, 486
   People's Radical Party in, 475
Kosovo myth, 116, 264, 265, 280, 578
Kosovo Polje, 374
Kosovo War (1998–9), 6, 377
Kosovska Mitrovica, 225, 372
Kossuth, Lajos, 129, 130
Kostić, Josif, 317, 357, 360, 428, 564
Kostić, Katarina, 413–14
Kostić, Ljubomir, 317, 318, 319, 347
Kostić, Petar, 250
Kotor, Montenegro, 12, 19, 140, 361, 435, 482, 439, 444, 476
Kovačević, Dragutin Karla, 509
Kovno, Lithuania, 412
Kragujevac,
   Central Powers occupation (1916–18), 419
   Kingdom of Serbia (1882–1916), *see* Kragujevac in the Kingdom of Serbia
   Ottoman Empire (1459–1815), 35, 47, 58, 59, 61
   Principality of Serbia (1815–1882), *see* Kragujevac in the Principality of Serbia
   Yugoslavia (1918-41), 519, 532, 573, 578
Kragujevac in the Kingdom of Serbia (1882–1918), 309, 310
   armaments factory, 281, 338
   Bomb Affair (1907), 338
   constitution (1889), 257
   contra conspiracy (1907), 346
   craftsmen association, 313
   gymnasiums, 284
   Ilić, attack on (1907), 348
   Macedonians in, 410
   riots (1904), 346, 383

INDEX

Kragujevac in the Principality of Serbia (1815–1882)
  Aleksandar's deposition (1858), 144
  armaments factory, 161, 206
  Assumption Day parliament (1864), 167
  cadets, 83–4
  cannon foundry, 133, 134
  constitution (1869), 182
  capital status, 103
  commune (c. 1873–6), 206–8, 211–13
  court of appeals, 74
  craftsman–merchant class, 87
  Đak's rebellion (1825), 72, 73
  Jovan's rebellion (1839), 97
  Michaelmas parliament (1867), 176
  Mihailo's deposition (1842), 106
  Mileta's rebellion (1835), 91
  Miloš's court, 68, 69, 74
  Miloš's deposition (1839), 98
  nahija, 87
  Nativity of Mary's Day parliament (1859), 149, 151
  parliaments, 76
  Radical congress (1881), 243
  Red Flag affair (1876), 213
  Revolutionary Liberation Committee, 204
  St Peter's Day parliament (1848), 130–31, 195
  teacher training college, 184, 206
  Transfiguration Day parliament (1861), 156
Krajina, Serbia, 80, 257
Kraljevo, Serbia, 13, 46, 573
Krek, Miha, 548, 577
Kriva Palanka, Macedonia, 371
Krk, Croatia, 438
Krnar, Naum, 66-7, 325
Krnjevo, Serbia, 529
Krupp, 545
Krušedol, Serbia, 31, 294

Kruševac, Serbia, 17, 46, 79, 80, 88, 90, 97, 219, 247, 257, 264, 265, 280, 285, 421, 486, 578
Küçük-Ali, 42
Kujundžić, Bogoljub, 548
Kujundžić, Milan, 166, 176, 205
Kükürt Çeşme crisis (1862), 162–3
Kulenović, Džafer, 548, 553, 577
Kulovec, Franc, 571, 576, 577, 580
kuluk, 23, 24, 38, 47, 68, 70–71, 72, 80, 90, 92, 93, 95, 96, 131, 241, 247
Kumanovo, Macedonia, 223, 374, 379, 380, 382, 386, 412
  Battle of (1912), 374, 380, 507
Kumanudi, Kosta, 470, 506
Kun, Béla, 454
Kupinec, Croatia, 548
Kuripešić, Benedikt, 19, 28
Kuršumlija, Serbia, 222, 282, 421
Kutuzov, Mikhail, 55
Kutzovlachs, 453
Kvaternik, Slavko, 581

Ladino, 25, 567
Lalošević, Joca, 521
de Lamartine, Alphonse, 89
languages
  Albanian, 222, 372, 467
  Bulgarian, 452, 468
  Čakavian dialect, 120
  Croatian, 120, 140, 312–13, 368, 453
  Cyrillic alphabet, 11, 120, 125, 368, 403, 417, 433, 461, 511
  Ekavian dialect, 368, 461
  French, 154, 202, 207, 328
  German, 118, 132
  Glagolitic, 11
  Greek, 25, 170
  Hungarian, 128
  Ijekavian dialect, 120, 511
  Kajkavian dialect, 120
  Ladino, 25, 567
  Latin alphabet, 9, 120, 125, 368, 407, 433, 461, 511

INDEX

Macedonian, 468
Old Church Slavonic, 11
Russian Church Slavonic, 116, 119
Serbian, 25, 116–22, 124, 159, 170, 312–13, 419, 453
Slovene, 407
Štokavian dialect, 120
Turkish, 25, 109, 120, 170, 222
Vienna Agreement (1850), 120
Lapčević, Dragiša, 314, 348, 388, 395
Larkin, Philip, 324
Lassalle, Ferdinand, 206
Lastovo, Croatia, 438, 455
Latin alphabet, 9, 120, 125, 368, 407, 433, 461, 511
Lavrov, Pyotr, 207
Law on Agrarian Reform (1931), 520
Law on Bookshops (1870), 184
Law on Bureaucracy (1861), 156
Law on Crafts (1847), 110
Law on Garrison Military (1845), 126
Law on Handicrafts (1910), 311
Law on Marriage of Officers (1901), 293–4
Law on Municipalities (1866), 166
Law on Naming and Division of the Kingdom (1929), 508
Law on Organisation of Public Instruction (1844), 114
Law on Organisation of the Council (1839), 97
Law on Parliaments (1859), 146, 149, 156
Law on Parliaments (1861), 156
Law on Protection of Public Security (1921), 485
Law on Protection of the State (1929), 506, 517
Law on Public Security (1904), 339
Law on Public Security (1921), 485
Law on Reclamation of Land (1839), 96
Law on Religious Community of Jews (1929), 568
Law on Royal Power (1929), 505
Law on Schools (1929), 510
Law on Spiritual Authority (1847), 114

Law on Succession to the Throne (1861), 157
Lazar, Autocrat of the Serbs, 17, 19–21, 31, 116, 259, 264
Lazarević, Dobrivoje, 333
Lazarević, General Luka, 290, 295, 304, 320, 322, 325, 333, 347
Lazarević, Reverend Luka, 48, 55, 325
Lazarević, Luka I., 345
Lazarević, Milutin, 319, 324–5, 333, 430
Lazarević, Vasilije, 114
Lazić, Radoje, 429
lead, 540, 579
League of Farmers, *see* Farmers' Party
League of Nations, 465, 524
Ledru-Rollin, Alexandre, 206
Leibnitz, Austria, 402
Lemberg, Ukraine, 412
Lenderbank, 241
Leopold I, Holy Roman Emperor, 26, 30
Leopold II, Holy Roman Emperor, 36
Lepenica, Serbia, 74
Leserf, Emilija, 78
Lešjanin, Ljubomir, 333
Lešjanin, Milojko, 217, 222
Lešjanin, Rajko, 166, 179
Leskovac, Serbia, 104, 222, 223, 225, 309, 310, 421, 437, 514, 516
la levée en masse, 384
Lezhë, Albania, 374
Liberal Democratic Party, 340
Liberal Party (Požarevac), 470
liberalism; Liberals, 139–43, 238
  anti-Semitism, 567
  Baba-Dudić family and, 145, 152, 178, 179, 181
  Bosnia crisis (1871), 203
  Bosnian uprising (1875–8), 210, 214, 215
  bureaucracy and, 238
  constitution (1869), 3, 181–4, 195–7, 201, 204–6, 213, 277–9, 295, 327
  Court Liberals, 177–82, 197, 205, 238

INDEX

Hadži-Toma family, 177–8
independence struggle (1872–82), 201
Marković and, 188, 189, 190
Miloš's restoration (1858–60), 141–9, 152, 153, 156–7
Mihailo's assassination (1868), 178–80, 197
Mihailo's reign (1860–68), 156–8, 160, 162, 164–6, 170, 171–8
Milan's accession (1868), 181
National Liberal Party, *see* National Liberal Party
nationalism, 130, 140–41, 171–4, 210
Ottoman Wars (1876–8), 218, 220, 228
Radicals split with (1870), 196
railway convention (1880), 230
Topola uprising (1877), 221, 227, 234, 261
United Serb Youth, *see* United Serb Youth
Libya, 371
life expectancy, 309, 516
Lika, Croatia, 401, 404, 441, 472, 522
Lim River, 10, 14
Lipari, Italy, 443
literacy, 45, 61, 111–14, 140, 178, 310, 453, 468, 514
literature
 Austrian Slavs, 31, 115, 367
 Despotate of Serbia (1402–1459), 18
 Kingdom of Serbia (1882–1918), 411
 Principality of Serbia (1815–1882), 112, 115–16, 125, 191
Lithuania, 412
Little Entente
 1921, 454–5
 1933, 523
livestock, 38, 42, 57, 58, 71, 82, 96, 101, 309, 449, 464, 513
 state farm, 263
 trade wars, 229, 279, 280, 294, 343
 see also pigs
Ljočić, Draga, 252

Ljočić, Đura, 196, 205, 214, 252
Ljotić, Dimitrije, 529–32, 537, 559, 568, 570, 577
Ljotić, Dimitrije (Vladimir's father), 186, 529
Ljotić, Đorđe, 186, 529
Ljotić, Ljubica, 187
Ljotić, Vladimir, 186–7, 207, 214, 215, 529
Ljubibratić, Mićo, 168
Ljubica, Princess of Serbia, 67-8, 73, 90, 103, 105, 142
Ljubljana, Slovenia, 313, 369, 438, 476, 480, 484, 486, 480, 506, 571, 575, 581
Ljušić, Radoš, 51, 53, 103
London, England, 320, 349, 434
 Treaty of (1913), 376, 377
 Treaty of (1915), 410, 438, 451, 452
London peace conference, 1912-3, 375
Longworth, John Augustus, 164
Lošinj, Croatia, 455
Loubris, Charles, 134
Louis Philippe I, King of the French, 128
Loznica, Serbia, 115, 126, 368
Lubenau, Reinhold, 25
Ludendorff, Erich, 436
Luftwaffe, 577, 580
Lukavčević, Jovan, 135, 145–6
Lule Burgas, Battle of (1912), 374
Luma, Albania, 375
Lune, Vojvoda, 501, 502
Lunjevica, Ana (Vojka) Milićević, 298, 507
Lunjevica, Nikodije, 294, 304, 318
Lunjevica, Nikola (Draga's brother), 294, 318
Lunjevica, Nikola Milićević (Draga's grandfather), 292, 293
Lunjevica, Panta, 312
Lusatia, 10
lycée, Serbian, 85, 113, 123, 140, 148, 159, 177, 187, 205

Macedonia, 4, 5, 10, 38, 55, 119, 226
 Albanian uprising (1913), 382–3, 384–5

INDEX

Aleksandar and, 370–71
Archbishopric of Ohrid, 13, 27
Balkan Wars (1912–13), 373, 374, 376–80, 383, 384
Black Hand and, 358
Cenić and, 313
Communist Party and, 477
Congress of Berlin (1878), 226
Corfu Declaration (1917), 433
Cvijić and, 369
Garašanin and, 122, 160
Karić and, 366
Kingdom of Serbia (1217–1346), 15
Kingdom of Serbia (1912–1918), 376, 378, 379, 382, 385–91, 401, 496
Maček and, 504
Milan and, 249, 252–3
Raška (1091–1217), 12
Ottoman Macedonia (c. 1389–1912), see Macedonia in the Ottoman Empire
Principality of Bulgaria (1878–1908), 224
Serbian Empire (1346–1371), 15, 16, 17, 27
Serbo-Greek convention (1861), 161
Social Democrats and, 384–5
Tucović on, 385
World War I (1914–18), 410–12, 414, 416, 434, 435, 436
World War II (1939–45), 572
Yugoslavia (1918-41), see Macedonia in Yugoslavia
Macedonia in the Ottoman Empire (c. 1389–1912), 27, 206, 224, 225, 252–3, 341
Balkan War (1912), 373, 374
Black Hand in, 358, 361
Bulgarian claims to, 250, 281, 285, 299, 336, 341, 349, 371
Congress of Berlin (1878), 226, 227
Elijah's Day Uprising (1903), 336–7
emigration, 227
Great Powers' withdrawal (1911), 371
Habsburg War (1683–99), 30
Mürzsteg Agreement (1903), 337, 350
Orthodox church in, 250, 252, 279, 281
railways, 252–3
rebellion (1841), 104–5
Reval agreement (1908), 350
Serbian schools in, 185, 252–3, 279, 281
Serbian Uprising, First (1804–13), 55
VMRO, 336–7, 342, 358, 371
Macedonia in Yugoslavia (1918–41), 463, 468–9, 491, 501, 504, 541
April War (1941), 580, 583
banovinas, 508
Communist Party and, 476, 477, 478, 481, 503
constitution (1921), 482
elections in, 477, 481, 489, 493
German invasion (1941), 580
Italian bombing (1940), 570
JRZ in, 538, 542
land reform (1919), 467
oblasts, 486
People's Radical Party in, 475
Provisional National Legislature (1919–20), 471
Serbian views of 520, 550, 554, 561
VMRO in, 468–9
Macedonian Declaration (1914), 400
Macedonian language, 468
Macedonians, 4, 119, 415
national identity, 377
in Serb national politics, 253, 377, 386, 411, 433, 463, 468
Social Democrats and, 384
under Belgrade's rule (1912-41), 372, 376, 386-7, 410-11, 468
VMRO, see Internal Macedonian Revolutionary Organisation
Maček, Vladimir (Vladko), 538, 541, 547, 548, 549, 559, 564
Aleksandar and (1929), 504-5, 507, 524
anti-Semitic decrees (1940), 569
coup d'état (1941), 574, 576

709

INDEX

Cvetković–Maček Agreement (1939), 550–55
  establishment of Independent State of Croatia (1941), 581
  German invasion threat (1940-41), 571
  in opposition to Yugoslav regime, 517,518, 520, 536, 537, 544
  Pavle and, 535
von Mackensen, Anton Ludwig, 412, 417
Mackenzie, David, 356–7
Mačkov Kamen, Battle of (1914), 404
Mačva, Serbia, 402
Magazinović, Stevan, 148
Maglajlić, Ibrahim, 509
Magnussen, Fritz, 382
Magyars, 119, 128, 129, 370, 439, 446, 454, 464, 467, 473, 521, 542, 567, 569, 580
Mahmud II, Ottoman Sultan, 51, 56, 83, 92, 93, 95, 252
Majstorović, Antonije, 106, 145, 146, 152, 166, 179
Majstorović, Ranko, 90, 91, 106
Majstorović's Conspiracy (1863), 166, 179
Maksimović, Nićifor, 85
Maksimović, Vojin, 346, 426, 439, 503–4, 505, 536, 537, 552
Mali žurnal (*Little Journal*), 333, 344
Mali Zvornik, Serbia, 81, 205, 225, 226
Malobabić, Rade, 392, 429, 430
Malta, 349
Manasija monastery, Serbia, 18
Manastir, Battle of (1912), 374
Manchester, England, 309
Mandl, Leopold, 359
Mannerheim, Carl, 549
Manuel I Comnenus, Byzantine Emperor, 12
Mapplebeck, Tom, 573
Maraşli Ali Pasha, 60-2, 65, 66, 67, 69, 70, 71
March disturbances (1903), 314–17
Marganović, Pajo, 517
Maria (Marija), Queen of Yugoslavia, 455, 492

Maria Theresa, Holy Roman Empress, 34
Maribor, Slovenia, 486
Marić, August, 574
Marić, Jovan, 152
Marić, Lazar, 178, 179, 180
Marić, Ljubomir, 541
Maričević, Teodosije, 44, 45
Marinković, Dimitrije, 295
Marinković, Milan, 304, 317, 323
Marinković, Pavle, 295, 327, 347, 348, 360
Marinković, Vojislav, 337, 346, 429, 432, 497, 498, 506, 511, 518, 519, 527
Marinović, Jovan, 134, 136, 153, 158, 163, 179, 181, 204, 205, 206, 233
Maritsa, Battle of (1371), 17, 18
Marko, King of Serbia, 17, 18
Marko's Protocol (1923), 489–90
Marković, Božidar, 576
Marković, Jelena 'Ilka', 243
Marković, Jevrem, 165, 187, 203, 205, 215, 221, 227, 243, 261
Marković, Koča, 87
Marković, Lazar, 482, 502, 537, 545, 552, 558, 569
Marković, Radoje, 186
Marković, Sima, Marxist theorist, 477–8, 503
Marković, Vojvoda Sima, 46, 55, 66
Marković, Stefan, 136
Marković, Svetozar, 186–7, 205, 210, 308, 313, 368, 385, 395, 563
  on Austrian Serbs, 117
  background, 188
  beginnings of Radical party, 195-6, 206-8, 231, 238
  Bogosavljević, relationship with, 229
  Bosnian uprising (1871-8), 203, 209, 213
  Cenić, influence on, 312
  death (1875), 208, 314
  Karađorđević restoration plans, 187
  and Kragujevac, 204, 206–8, 212

INDEX

nationalism, 188–95, 196, 364, 367, 399
   political thought, 188-95
   Social Democrats and, 383, 384
Marmara, Sea of, 374
marriage laws, 86, 114, 211
Marseilles, France, 349
Maršićanin, Božo, 315, 317, 320, 321
Martinović, Obren, 57
Marx, Karl, 187, 192, 195, 208
Masalović, Miloš, 533
Mašin, Aleksandar, 274, 295, 304, 317, 318, 321, 325, 332, 341, 344, 347
Mašin, Draga, *see* Draga, Queen of Serbia
Mašin, Jovan, 295
Mašin, Svetozar, 289, 295
Masurica, Vranje, 223
Matanović, Milo, 443
Matejić, Ranko, 145, 146
Matić, Dimitrije, 153, 184
Matić, Svetomir, 508
Matica Srpska (Serb Framework), 119, 173
Mauritius, 572
Maurras, Charles, 529
May Declaration (1917), 431–2
May putsch (1903), 4, 5, 303–8, 317–25, 331, 335, 338, 345, 356, 363, 364, 557, 559, 563, 564, 565, 566, 577
Mazzini, Giuseppe, 361, 381
McCarthy, Justin, 376
Mecca, 40
Međimurje, Croatia, 453, 482
Mehane, Serbia, 420
Mehmed II, Ottoman Sultan, 21, 22, 23
Mehmed Foça-oglu, 42
Mehmedbašić, Muhamed, 393, 429
mektebs, 467
Melek Hanum, 115
Menzel Bourguiba, Bizerte, 414
merchants
   Albanian, 224,
   Ottoman Bosnia, (1463-1878) 168, 209

Ottoman Serbia (1459–1815), 34, 42, 43
Kingdom of Serbia (1882-1918), 262
Principality of Serbia (1815–1882), 71, 82, 83, 87, 93, 96, 105, 124, 127, 155, 193-4
Ragusan, 15
Yugoslavia (1918-1941), 472, 573
Meštrović, Ivan, 502, 509, 515–16
Metaxas, Ioannis, 527–8
Methodius, Saint, 11
Metohija, 140, 369, 481
metric system, 204
metropolitanates, 16, 31, 32, 34, 36, 78, 85, 111–12, 358, 461, 510
von Metternich, Klemens, 75, 94, 117, 128
Michaelmas parliament (1867), 176
Mihailo I, King of Duklja, 12
Mihailo, Metropolitan of Belgrade, 147
   anti-Jewish laws (1861), 155
   autocephaly recognition (1879), 227
   church law (1862), 159
   church law (1890), 263, 284
   ducatist movement (1859–60), 153
   exile (1883–9), 237, 248
   Karađorđevićes, relations with, 249
   Kosovo monument erection (1889), 264
   Kükürt Çeşme crisis (1862), 163
   Mihailo's marriage, views on, 176
   Ottoman Wars (1876–8), 215
   Radicals, relations with, 236–7, 248
   reinstatement (1889), 263
   Russia, relations with, 236
Mihailo Obrenović III, Prince of Serbia, 73, 90, 102–7, 141, 144, 154–70, 171–80, 184, 324
   accession, first (1839), 102–4
   armed forces, 157–8, 161–5, 373
   assassination (1868), 178–80, 186, 197, 306, 324, 325
   Assumption Day parliament (1864), 167
   Austria, relations with, 160, 171, 175

711

INDEX

bombardment of Belgrade (1862), 151, 162, 166, 167, 174
Bulgarian conflict (1867), 176
bureaucracy, policies on, 156, 165
church, law on (1862), 159
constitution, views on, 157
Constitutionalist conflict (1839–42), 103–7, 144
Council, law on (1862), 159
deposition (1842), 106–7, 142
Dorćol mutiny (1863), 164
ducatist movement (1859–60), 153
equestrian statue, 235
expansionism, 160–65
French language, 154
Great Powers, relations with, 155, 160, 162, 163
Jewish community, relations with, 155
Julija, marriage to, 175, 177, 178, 292, 324
Karadžić, relationship with, 117
Kükürt Çeşme crisis (1862), 162–3, 166, 167
Liberals and, 141, 156–7, 160, 162, 164–6, 171–80
Majstorović's Conspiracy (1863), 166
Marković and, 190
Michaelmas parliament (1867), 176
militia uprising (1866), 174
Law on Municipalities (1866), 166
Law on Succession to the Throne (1861), 157
military service law (1861), 158
Niš rebellion (1841), 104–5
Ottoman withdrawal (1867), 168–70, 174, 296
pro-Miloš rising (1840), 105
Russia, relations with, 104, 105, 134, 160, 175, 176, 179
United Serb Youth, relations with, 174–5

Mihailov, Vanča, 524
Mihailović, Dragoljub 'Draža', 563, 564, 566
Mihailović, Konstantin, 20
Mihailović, Mićić, 107
Mihailović, Pavle, 247
Mihailović, Stevča, 177
   Aleksandar's deposition (1858), 145, 146
   Assumption Day parliament (1864), 167
   bureaucrats, purge of (1858–60), 147
   Kanlice agreement (1862), 163–4
   Karađorđevićes, relations with, 159
   Mihailo's deposition (1842), 107, 142
   Miloš, relationship with, 153
   Ottoman Wars (1876–8), 218
   prime minister, first term (1875), 210
   prime minister, second term (1876–8), 214
   railway convention (1880), 230
   St Andrew's Day parliament (1858), 143
   Transfiguration Day parliament (1861), 156, 158
Mihaljević, Mihailo, 35
Mijatović, Čedomilj, 176, 205, 209, 233, 235, 250, 264, 283, 322
Milan I, King of Serbia, 167, 180–86, 197, 202–6, 233–58, 324, 373
   abdication (1889), 258, 323
   Aleksandar I's reign (1889–1903), 267–70, 284–5, 292, 293
   armed forces, 184, 211, 214, 215, 220, 239, 241, 244, 246, 252
   assassination attempt (1873), 311
   assassination attempt (1882), 243
   assassination attempt (1899), 286–7, 289
   Austria, relations with, 181, 185, 230–31, 233–5, 250, 254, 256, 283
   background and character, 202-3
   Bosnia and, 185–6, 203–4, 209–10, 211, 214
   Bulgarian War (1885–6), 250–52, 253, 256, 263, 265

INDEX

commander-in-chief (1897–1900), 284–5, 292, 293, 297
Conservatives and, 204, 233, 237–8
Constantinople visit (1874), 205
constitution (1869), 3, 181–4, 195–7, 201, 204–6, 213, 277–9, 295, 327
constitution (1889), 3, 257–8, 259, 271, 277, 295, 301, 326–7
death (1901), 294, 324
Draga, relationship with, 289, 292
exile, first (1891–4), 269–70, 277
exile, second (1895–7), 279, 282
exile, third (1900), 290–91
expansionism, 185
French language, 202, 328
Kingdom proclaimed (1882), 235
Kragujevac protests (1873), 207
Kragujevac conflict (1875–6), 213
Law on Bookshops (1870), 184
Liberals, relations with, 204, 278
majority (1872), 201
municipal self-government law (1875), 211
Natalija, marriage to, 213, 254, 256, 258, 267–70, 324
national anthem and, 202
Niš address (1897), 282
Ottoman Wars (1876–8), 185, 215–24
Regime of 11 October (1897–1900), 283–6, 291, 293, 314
Russia, relations with, 181, 185, 213–14, 218–19, 231, 233–4, 244, 250, 285
Secret Convention (1881), 235, 280
Smederevo incident (1871), 203
Terazije bombing (1871), 203
Timok rebellion (1883), 245–9, 253, 263, 265, 275, 306, 324, 550
top-up election (1882), 242
Topola uprising (1877), 221, 227, 234, 261
Milan Obrenović II, Prince of Serbia, 46, 54, 57, 90, 98, 101–2, 103
Milch, Erhard, 577

Mileševa monastery, Serbia, 14
Mileta's rebellion (1835), 91–2, 93
Miletić, Svetozar, 173, 174, 179, 195, 203, 366
Milica, Queen regent of Serbia, 17, 78
Milićević, Milan Đakov, 25, 170
Milin, Ljubomir, 496
Milinković, Jovan, 207
Milisavljević, Mirko, 428
Military Academy, 83, 133, 244, 264, 276, 285, 307, 458
Military Border, 19, 26–7, 34, 48, 129, 130
militia,
    Habsburg Serb auxiliary, 29-30
    national, *see* national militia
    Stanković's, 147
Miljković, Jovan, 316, 318
Mill, John Stuart, 187
millet system, 24
Milojković, Radivoje, 177, 179, 181, 182, 183, 184, 210, 220, 255, 261, 306
Miloš Obrenović I, Prince of Serbia, 3, 42, 50, 52, 55, 57–63, 65–99, 112, 324, 373
    abdication (1839), 85, 98
    absolutism, 65, 76, 87, 90, 96–7, 108
    Akkerman Convention (1826), 76–7
    Albanian lords, conflict with (1832), 79–80
    armed forces, 74, 83, 150
    Austria, relations with, 63, 66, 74, 75, 78, 84–5, 94
    background, 57-8
    Bessarabia émigrés, relations with, 66, 71, 72, 75
    bureaucrats, purge of (1858–60), 147–9, 152
    Čarapić revolt (1827), 75
    censorship decree (1832), 78
    civil code and, 114
    constitution (1835), 3, 89–94, 118
    constitution (1838), 3, 88, 95–7, 118, 157, 172, 295
    Council, formation of (1827), 75

INDEX

Đak's rebellion (1825), 72–4, 76, 91, 146, 158, 208, 246
death sentences, 69, 152
Equality of Citizenry decree (1859), 149
expansionism, 150–51
firman rejection (1820), 70, 71
'Great' soubriquet (1898), 285
hatt-ı şerif (1830), 3, 77–9, 83, 84, 89, 102, 193
hatt-ı şerif (1833), 81, 93, 124
hereditary prince status, 67, 70, 77–8, 92, 96, 150, 153
Hungarian Revolution (1848), 131
illiteracy, 61, 65, 101
Jewish community, relations with, 127, 149, 155
Jovan's rebellion (1839), 97
Karađorđe, execution of (1817), 66–7, 69, 70
Karadžić, relationship with, 117
Law on Parliaments (1859), 146, 149, 156
liberals and, 140, 152
Marković on, 193
Mihailo's reign (1839–42), 102, 103, 105
Mileta's rebellion (1835), 91–2
mistresses, 67–8, 324
Muslim expulsions (1833–4), 81–3
National Library founding (1832), 84
nationalism, 151
Orthodox Church, relations with, 85–6
parliamentary elections (1859), 149
Presentation Parliament (1835), 92
rebellion (1821), 71–2
restoration (1858–9), 145–53
Russia, relations with, 69–70, 72, 76–7, 83, 88–9, 90, 92–5, 122
Russo-Ottoman War (1828–9), 77
Serbian Uprising, First (1804–13), 57–9

Serbian Uprising, Second (1815), 59–63, 308
sipahis, relations with, 74–5
Srpske novine and, 153
Tenka's plot (1857), 137
United Kingdom, relations with, 88–9, 94
Wallachian estates, 202
women, treatment of, 67-8, 90
Milosavljević, Svetislav, 498, 508
Milosavljević, Svetozar, 275, 277
Milošević, Radivoje, 409
Milošević, Raša, 208, 223, 247, 252, 258, 274, 275, 276
Milošević, Slobodan, 149
Milovanović, Milovan, 295, 351, 352, 353, 355, 361, 370, 371, 378
Milovanović, Mladen, 51, 52, 53, 54, 55, 75, 102
Milovanović-Pilac, Milan, 429
Milovuk, Katarina, 159, 209
Milutin, King of Serbia, 15
Milyukov, Pavle, 431
minimum wage decree (1937), 540
mining 14, 15, 18, 246, 309, 311, 354, 449, 463, 515, 517, 540, 554
Mirdita, Republic of (1921), 466
Mirko, Grand Duke of Grahovo, 306
Mirković, Borivoje, 557, 564, 565, 566, 571, 573-4, 575, 577, 582
Miroslav, Župan of Hum, 12
Mišar, Battle of (1806), 48
Mišić, Petar, 295, 304, 307, 317–19, 321, 325, 333, 340, 346, 347, 361, 428
Mišić, Živojin, 222, 294, 320–21, 332, 346, 379, 382, 388, 403, 405, 412, 413, 415, 427, 437, 441, 442, 495
Mišković, Jovan, 268, 282, 293
misogyny, 288-9, 292, 315, 319, 321-3, 333
Mizija, 30
Mjeda, Lazër, 381
Moč, Aleksandar, 521
modernisation

INDEX

Kingdom of Serbia (1882–1918), 241, 252, 262, 285, 310
Principality of Serbia (1815–1882), 81, 109, 139, 147, 159, 170, 194, 196, 204, 230, 233–4
Yugoslavia (1918-41), 461–2, 515–16
Modruša, Croatia, 25
Mohács, Battle of (1526), 25, 26
Mohács, Battle of (1687), 29
Mojkovac, Battle of (1916), 416
Moldavia, 49, 50, 66, 71, 87, 202
Moler, Pavle Nikolajević, 65–6, 154
Moljević, Stevan, 562, 563
Molotov–Ribbentrop Pact (1939), 557
Monasterlija, Jovan, 31
Monastir, Macedonia, 382
Mondain, Hippolyte Florentain, 134-5, 161, 163, 164
de Montdésir, Jean, 414
Monte Carlo, Monaco, 327
Montenegrin Committee, 442–5, 476
Montenegrin Party, 466, 476, 493
Montenegrins, 4, 79, 463, 507, 508, 548
    annexationists, 338-9, 408-9, 442-5
    colonists, 467, 547
    federalists, 466, 476, 493
    Greens, 444-5, 465-6
    national identity of, 338, 433, 435, 465
    Nikola's supporters, 442-5, 465-6
    in Serb national politics, 118-19, 121, 161, 189, 381
    Šafárik and, 119
    soldiers, 219, 383, 403, 409, 412, 414, 416, 443, 444, 457-8, 465-6, 582
    Whites, 444-5, 465
Montenegro, 4, 5, 10, 11, 12, 13, 14, 16, 19, 38, 174, 181, 188
    Aleksandar I of Serbia and, 280
    Aleksandar I of Yugoslavia and, 370–71
    Balkan League agreements (1912), 373
    Balkan Wars (1912–13), 374, 375, 376
    Battle of Grahovac (1858), 161
    Berlin Congress (1878), 227
    Black Hand and, 358
    Bomb Affair (1907), 338
    Bosnian crisis (1908–9), 351, 353
    Bosnian uprising (1875–8), 210, 214–15
    Cenić and, 312, 313
    Communist Party and, 477
    Corfu Declaration (1917), 433
    flag, 465
    emigration from, 227
    Garašanin and, 124, 125
    Great National Parliament (1918–19), 444–5, 465
    Grujić and Janković and, 140
    Habsburg–Ottoman war (1788–91), 34
    Karadžić and, 118, 120, 121
    Hercegovina rebellion (1882), 235
    Karić and, 366
    Kolašin Affair (1909), 338–9
    Maček and, 504
    Marković and, 191, 192, 195, 367
    Mihailo and, 161
    Milan and, 167, 244, 249
    Miletić and, 203
    Miloš and, 122
    Ottoman War (1861–2), 161
    Ottoman Wars (1876–8), 215, 219
    Paris Peace Conference (1919–20), 452
    Pašić's visit (1886), 254
    People's Radical Party and, 239, 242
    Prince-Bishopric (1516–1852), 19, 34, 43, 55, 79, 108, 121–2, 133
    Sanjak of (1513–1528), 31
    Serbian alliance (1866), 167
    Serbian vice-royalty plan (1848), 128
    World War I (1914–18), 395, 408, 412, 416, 435, 442–5, 501
    Zeta (1451–96), 21, 31
    Žujović on, 188
    in Yugoslavia (1918-41), *see* Montenegro in Yugoslavia
Montenegro in Yugoslavia (1918-41), 442–5, 449, 457, 465–6
    Christmas Uprising (1919), 465

INDEX

Communist Party in, 476, 481
constitution (1921), 482, 484
federalism in, 466, 476, 493
German invasion (1941), 582
Great Depression (1929–39), 515
Green movement, 444–5, 465, 466
investment in, 511
JRZ in, 538
oblasts, 486
Paris Peace Conference (1919–20), 452, 465
People's Radical Party in, 475
provincial administration, 460
Provisional National Legislature (1919–20), 471
Šahovići massacre (1924), 463
World War II (1939–45), 582
Zagreb Points (1932), 520
Zeta banovina established (1929), 508
Monument to the Kosovo Heroes, 264, 265
Morava Banovina, 508, 522, 554
Morava Division, 251, 333, 415
Morava River, 12, 71, 84, 216, 218, 257, 416, 422
Morava oblast, 486
Moravia, 11
Moravica, bishopric of, 14
Moroccan crises (1905–6; 1911), 393
mosques, 25, 33, 50, 62, 109, 170, 224
most-favoured-nation status, 230, 234, 524
Mostar, Hercegovina, 447, 483, 553
Mostić, Vasilije, 290, 293
Mount Athos, Greece, 13
Mount Avala, Serbia, 75, 516
The Mountain Wreath, (Petar II), 121–2, 465
Movement for Vojvodina, 521
Mraović, Teodosije, 236, 256, 263
Mrcajlović, Đorđe, 178, 179
Muhammad Ali, Wāli of Egypt, 80, 95, 252
Mülla Yusuf, 42
Munich, Germany, 113
Munich Agreement (1938), 546

Murad I, Ottoman Sultan, 17, 20, 21
Murad II, Ottoman Sultan, 21
Mürzsteg Agreement (1903), 337–8, 350
Musa Efendi, 103–4
müsellim, 22, 41, 60, 62
music, 40, 112, 169, 173, 201-2, 380, 414-5, 516, 534
Mušicki, Kosta, 533
Mušicki, Lukijan, 85
Muslim National Organisation, 350
Muslims, *see* Islam; Muslims
Mussolini, Benito, 455, 491, 509, 522, 523, 528, 551, 576
Mustafa IV, Ottoman Sultan, 50, 51
Mustafa Pasha, Hadži, 41–2, 43, 44, 49, 73–4

nahijas
  Ottoman Serbia (1459–1815), 22–3, 33, 41, 47, 48, 53, 56, 58
  Principality of Serbia (1815–1882), 68, 69, 74, 76, 79–80, 87–8, 124
Naples, Italy, 349
Napoleon I, Emperor of the French, 49, 51, 53, 55, 56, 60, 437
Napoleon III, Emperor of the French, 134
Napoleonic Wars (1803–15), 19, 49, 51, 53, 55, 56
Narodna Skupština (*National Parliament*), 155
Narodnaya Volya (People's Will), 311
Narodni glasnik (*People's Herald*), 227
Narodnik movement (1860s–70s), 207, 311
Našička affair (1934–5), 522–3
Natalija, Queen of Serbia, 292, 324
  custody dispute, 256, 258
  Draga, relationship with, 283, 290, 291, 292
  ethnicity, 615
  exile, first (1891–5), 267–70, 279
  exile, second (1900–41), 291
  marriage (1875), 213
  Timok rebellion (1883), 248

INDEX

separation from Milan (1887), 254
Simić appointment (1896), 280
return to Serbia (1895), 279
Women's Society patronage, 288
nation-in-arms, 74, 84, 135, 157–8, 164, 165
National Agreement Bloc, 544
national anthem, Croatian, 380
national anthem, Serbian, 201
National Bank, 241, 579
National Bloc, 490, 493
National Chancellery, 61, 65, 66, 69, 84, 87
National Club, 479, 481
National Council (1918–19), 438, 440–42, 445–8, 455–6, 457, 460, 471
National Defence, 352, 355, 361, 380, 534, 541, 565
   1941 putsch, 565-6
   6 January Regime (1929–34), 500, 529
   Black Hand and, 358, 359, 361
   Bosnian annexation crisis (1908–9), 354
   foundation (1908), 336, 352
   Franz Ferdinand assassination (1914), 392, 394
   Organisation of Ottoman Serbs, 372
   Varešanin assassination attempt (1910), 355
   World War II (1939–45), 575
National Liberal Party, 195, 239, 241
   Aleksandar, relations with, 260–61, 276
   amnesty (1894), 277
   anti-Semitism, 567
   Avakumović government, first (1892–3), 271–3, 277
   Avakumović government, second (1903), 325
   Bosnian crisis (1908–9), 353, 355
   coalition government (1887–8), 255–6
   conspirator question, 339–40, 361
   constitution (1889), 258
   constitution (1901), 295–7
   constitution (1903), 327
   coup d'état (1893), 273–4, 275

   People's Radical Party, pact with (1886), 254
   Petrović inquiry (1911), 356
   Radical terrorism against, 355, 362
   Royal Serbian Academy and, 262–3
   split (1904), 339–40
   territorial acquisitions (1912–13) and, 386, 389
   White Hand, relations with, 362
   World War I (1914–18), 404
   see also National Party
National Library, 84, 159, 580
national militia,
   Aleksandar's reign (1889-1903), 261, 263, 276
   Constitutionalist regime (1839-58), 97, 98, 106, 131, 135
   First Serbian Uprising (1804-13), 53
   Mihailo's second reign (1860-8), 157-8, 161-5, 166, 174, 176, 177
   Milan's reign (1868-89), 188, 205, 207, 211, 212, 215, 216, 220, 239, 244, 245–6, 251, 254, 256, 258
   Miloš's first reign (1815-39), 73-4, 84, 97
   Miloš's second reign (1858-60), 150
   Ottoman period (to 1804), 42, 44
National Museum, 114
National Party, 459, 471
   formation of, 339–40,
   merger with Democratic Party, 470, 486
National Salvation, Government of (1941), 302, 578
National Salvation proclamation (1891), 269
National Theatre, 160, 174, 211, 235, 351
nationalism, 2, 6, 119–32, 138, 171–4, 363–70
   Aleksandar I of Serbia and, 285, 308
   Aleksandar I of Yugoslavia and, 370–71, 373, 400, 401
   Belić and, 406
   Black Hand, 357–61, 425

717

INDEX

Cenić, 311–13
Corfu Declaration (1917), 431–6
Garašanin, 89, 123–6, 140, 160, 171, 222
    Independent Radicals and, 363, 367–70
    Karadžić and, 119–22, 123, 124, 138, 366, 406
    Kosovo myth, 116, 264, 265, 280, 578
    language and, 119–22, 124, 312–13, 366, 406
    liberals and, 130, 140–41, 171–4, 210
    Marković and, 188–95, 196, 364, 367, 399
    Mihailo and, 184, 279
    Milan and, 242, 373
    Miloš and, 122, 151, 373
    Niš Declaration (1914), 405
    Pašić, 206, 364, 391, 400, 401–2, 425
    People's Radical Party, 239, 241, 243, 248, 264, 265, 281, 383, 406
    Revolutions (1848–9), 128–32, 187
    socialist, 188–96
    Žujović, 187–8
Nativity of Mary's Day parliament (1859), 149, 150, 152
Natlačen, Marko, 581
Naumović, Mihailo, 317, 318, 325
Navarino, Battle of (1827), 77
Nechayev, Sergey, 311, 358
Nedić, Milan, 302, 426, 437, 523, 533, 541, 550, 552, 565, 570–1, 578, 583
Negotin, Serbia, 50, 51, 54, 84, 88, 222, 247, 272
Negotinac, Serafim, 247
Nemanja, Župan of Raška, 12–13
Nemanjić, Ratko, *see* Sava, Saint,
Nemanjid dynasty (1166–1371), 12–17
Nenadović, Aleksa, 35, 42, 43, 44, 47
Nenadović, Aleksandar, 135, 136, 152
Nenadović, Atanasije, 152
Nenadović, Jakov, Petar I's adjutant, 307, 308, 340–1, 343, 344, 345
Nenadović, Vojvoda Jakov, 45, 46, 52, 53, 54-5, 102
Nenadović, Jevrem, 135
Nenadović, Kosta, 135, 145
Nenadović, Ljubomir, 275
Nenadović, Marija, 186
Nenadović, Mateja, 44–8, 52, 54, 65, 95, 98, 103, 104, 126, 129, 186
Nenadović, Mladen, 178, 179
Nenadović, Persida, *see* Persida, Princess of Serbia
Nenadović, Sima, 179
Nenadović, Svetozar, 179, 275
Neškov Vis, Serbia, 252
Nestorović Deak, Pavle, 29, 30
Nettuno Convention (1925), 499, 500, 503
Neue Freie Presse (*New Free Press*), 367
Neuilly, Treaty of (1919), 452
newspapers, *see* press
Nicaea, Anatolia, 13
Nice, France, 327
Nicholas I, Emperor of Russia, 76, 77, 89, 92, 107–8, 133, 160
Nicholas II, Emperor of Russia, 292, 301, 370, 371, 378, 387
Nikić, Nikola, 522–3
Nikola I, King of Montenegro, 161
    annexation of Montenegro (1918), 443–5, 465
    assassination plot (1916), 392
    Belgrade visit (1896), 280
    Bomb Affair (1907), 338
    Bosnian uprising (1875–8), 210, 215
    death (1921), 466
    deposed (1918), 445
    guerrilla raids (1884), 249
    Kolašin Affair (1909), 338–9
    May putsch (1903) and, 306
    militia uprising (1866), 174
    Ottoman War (1861–2), 161
    Pašić's visit (1886), 254
    Russia, relations with, 181, 280, 409
    Serbian alliance (1866), 167
    United Serb Youth and, 203
    World War I (1914–18), 408, 416, 442–5

INDEX

Nikolajević, Božidar, 417
Nikolajević, Konstantin, 128-9, 136
Nikolajević, Nikola, 72
Nikolajević, Svetomir, 241, 252, 268, 277, 278, 279, 334, 345, 417
Nikolić, Atanasije, 113, 123, 147, 160
Nikolić, Dimitrije, 320, 323, 334, 345
Nikolić, Milan, 563
Nikolić, Sergije, 140
Nikšić, Melentije, 48, 60, 66, 85, 86
Nikšić, Milan, 371–2
Nikšić, Montenegro, 444, 582
Ninčić, Momčilo, 441, 455, 576, 578, 582
Niš
    Battle of (1689), 30
    Battle of (1878), 222
    Bulgarian crisis meetings (1885), 250
    Bulgarian occupation (1915–18), 418, 419, 437
    de-Ottomanisation, 224
    Grujić and Janković on, 140
    May putsch (1903), 308, 332, 346
    Milan, address to (1897), 282
    Milan–Radicals summit (1886), 253
    Ottoman (1448–1878), 30, 32, 71, 89, 104–5, 185, 217, 222
    parliamentary sessions in, 248, 278–9
    population growth, 310
    Principality of Serbia (1878–1882), 222, 224, 225, 226, 227, 228, 300
    Raška (1091–1217), 12, 13
    Sanjak of (1448–1878), 30, 32, 71, 89, 104–5
    Serbian Uprising, First (1804–13), 46, 53
    Skull Tower of Niš, 53, 89
    Treaty of (1923), 469
    World War I (1914–18), 395, 402, 408
    Yugoslavia (1918-41), 480, 486, 519, 522, 542, 581
Niš Declaration (1914), 405–6, 411
Niški glasnik (*Niš Herald*), 502
Njegoš tribe, 31
Noli, Fan, 467–8
North Atlantic Treaty Organisation (NATO), 6, 377
Norway, 349
Nova Varoš, Serbia, 53
Novaković, Aleksa, 304–6
Novaković, Milan, 332–3, 345, 346, 348, 355–6, 383
Novaković, Nikola, 67
Novaković, Stojan, 233, 344
    April Constitution (1901), 296
    Constantinople envoy (1897–1900), 284
    draft constitution (1896), 280, 295
    education minister, first term (1874), 205
    education minister, third term (1880–83), 236, 365
    on Karađorđe, 53
    Metropolitan Mihailo's dismissal (1881), 236
    prime minister, first term (1895–6), 279–80
    prime minister, second term (1895–6), 354, 355
    United Serb Youth, 174
    Vienna group, relations with, 344
    Zrinski-Frankopan commemoration (1914), 380
Novi Pazar, Serbia,
    Austro-Hungarian occupation (1915-18), 418
    Balkan Wars (1912–13), 374, 379
    Kingdom of Serbia (1912–18), 386
    Plan (1844), 140
    Raška (1091–1217), 11, 12
    Serbian Uprising, First (1804–13), 53
    Sanjak of (1865–1912), *see* Sanjak of Novi Pazar
    Yugoslavia (1918–41), 467
Novi Sad, Serbia
    Austria-Hungary (1867–1918), 196, 203, 209, 265
    Austrian Empire (1804–67), 114, 131, 159, 172, 173–4, 265

INDEX

Yugoslavia (1918-41), 437, 446, 460, 472-3, 476, 502, 509, 521
Novine Srbske (Serb Newspaper), 84, 152-3
Novo Brdo, Kosovo, 22

Obilić, Miloš, 19-21, 116, 121
Obilić, Serbia, 421
Obradović, Dositej, 36, 49, 52, 55, 113, 118, 119
Obrenovac, Serbia, 321
Obrenović, Aleksandar, *see* Aleksandar I, King of Serbia
Obrenović, Jevrem, 68, 73, 84, 90, 95, 98, 103, 105, 180, 202, 329
Obrenović, Jovan, 72, 84, 97
Obrenović, Julija, *see* Julija, Princess of Serbia
Obrenović, Ljubica, *see* Ljubica, Princess of Serbia
Obrenović, Mihailo, *see* Mihailo Obrenović III
Obrenović, Milan II, 67, 90, 98, 101-2, 103
Obrenović, Milan IV/I, *see* Milan I, King of Serbia
Obrenović, Milan (Miloš's half-brother), 46, 54, 57
Obrenović, Miloš (Jevrem's son), 202
Obrenović, Miloš, *see* Miloš Obrenović I
Obrenović, Natalija, *see* Natalija, Queen of Serbia
Obrenović, Tomanija, 178
Obrenović dynasty, 4, 5, 75, 96, 98, 103, 112, 139, 141, 142, 171, 323
   Aleksandar I (1889-1903), 1, 5, 184, 256, 258, 264-5, 267-302, 303-25
   destruction (1903), 317-25
   Mihailo III, first reign (1839-42), 73, 90, 102-7, 141, 142, 144
   Mihailo III, second reign (1860-68), 154-70, 171-80
   Milan II (1839), 46, 54, 57, 90, 98, 101-2, 103
   Milan IV/I (1868-89), 180-97, 201-58

Miloš, first reign (1815-39), 3, 42, 50, 52, 55, 57-63, 65-99, 112
Miloš, second reign (1858-60), 145-53
   overthrow (1842), 105-7
   restoration (1858), 144-6, 186
Obrenovićites
   Aleksandar's reign (1842-58), 117, 126, 130, 142-6, 178, 308
   Mihailo's first reign (1839-42), 103, 105, 106, 107, 144
   Mihailo's second reign (1860-68), 157, 159, 166, 167, 171
   Miloš's second reign (1858-60), 152, 153, 238
Obznana (1919, 1921), 463, 485, 493
Odessa, Ukraine, 159, 423
Odjek (Echo), 262, 298, 314, 321, 349, 351
Officers' Club, 317
Ogulin, Croatia, 25
Ohrid, archbishopric of, 13, 27
Ohrid, Macedonia, 371, 374, 375, 382, 411
Okan, Niko, 185
okrugs, 88, 96, 114, 143, 161, 206, 228, 257, 271, 341, 386
Okupović, Rustem-pasha, 23
Old Church Slavonic, 11
Old Liberals, 179-80, 196, 205, 212, 218, 230, 238, 269, 321, 560
Old Radicals, 4, 299, 326-8, 331, 334, 337, 339, 340, 342, 469, 470, 471, 506
Old Serbia, 185, 371, 375, 387
   Albanians and, 282, 299, 337, 382, 384
   Aleksandar on, 370
   Balugdžić on, 341
   Balkan Wars (1912-13), 374, 375, 379, 387
   Black Hand and, 358
   Cenić on, 312
   Chief Educational Council and, 366
   Cvijić on, 369
   Ekmečić on, 61
   Jovanović on, 173
   Mihailo and, 185
   Milan and, 224, 242, 249-50, 253

INDEX

Pašić on, 242
Olga of Greece and Denmark, 323, 565, 574
oligarchy, 172
    Aleksandar's reign (1842–58), 112, 133, 137, 138, 141, 146, 154, 172
    Mihailo's first reign (1839–42), 103
    Mihailo's second reign (1860–68), 154, 170
    Milan's reign (1868–89), 197
    Miloš, first reign (1815–39), 96–7, 99, 101, 108
Omar Pasha Latas, 161, 162
On Liberty (Mill), 187
Operation Barbarossa (1941), 583
Operation Punishment (1941), 580
Opozicija (*Opposition*), 340
Orahovica, Salvonia, 108
Orašac, Serbia, 44
Orbini, Mavro, 19, 78
Order of Prince Lazar, 264
Organisation of Ottoman Serbs, 372
Organisation of Yugoslav Nationalists (ORJUNA), 491–2, 534, 568
Oriental Railway Company, 379
Orşova, Romania, 90, 94, 111
Osijek, Croatia, 441, 486
Oslobođenje (*Liberation*), 207
Osman Đikić (paramilitary organisation), 492
Osman Pasha, 217
Ostružnica, Serbia, 45
Otok, Croatia, 25
Ottoman Empire (1299–1922), 2–3, 9, 14, 17–36, 37–63, 119
    Abdul Hamid's deposition (1909), 372
    Akkerman Convention (1826), 76–7
    Balkan Wars (1912–13), 373–80
    Battle of Ankara (1402), 18
    Battle of Batočina (1689), 30
    Battle of Maritsa (1371), 17, 18
    Battle of Mohács, First (1526), 25, 26
    Battle of Mohács, Second (1687), 29
    Battle of Kosovo, First (1389), 17, 18–21, 116, 121, 259, 264, 483, 578
    Battle of Kosovo, Second (1448), 19
    Battle of Varna (1444), 21
    Bosnian crisis (1908–9), 351, 353, 354
    Bosnian rebellion (1831–2), 79, 95
    Bosnian rebellion (1875–8), 201, 208, 209–15, 216–17, 219–20
    Bulgaria, conquest of (1393), 18
    Bulgarian conflict (1867), 176
    Bulgarian rebellion (1876), 201
    Capitulations, 127
    Constitutionalists, relations with, 102–9, 128, 133, 140–41, 150
    Cretan revolt (1866–9), 168
    Crimean War (1853–6), 134–5, 136
    educational reform (1856), 168
    Egyptian War (1831–3), 80, 95, 252
    French invasion (1798–1801), 42
    Gallipoli, capture of (1354), 17
    garrisons, *see* Ottoman garrisons
    grand viziers, 22, 23, 27
    Greek War (1821–9), 62, 66, 71, 75, 76, 77
    Greek War (1897), 281, 282
    Habsburg War (1683–99), 28–31
    Habsburg War (1716–18), 32
    Habsburg War (1737–9), 32–3
    Habsburg War (1788–91), 34–5, 40
    hatt-ı şerif, 76, 77–9, 81, 83, 84, 87, 93, 102, 193
    Hercegovina rebellion (1851–2), 133
    Hercegovina rebellion (1861), 161
    Italian War (1911–12), 371
    janissaries, 23, 28, 31, 40–46
    Jewish community, relations with, 155
    Kosovo border conflict (1899), 282
    Kükürt Çeşme crisis (1862), 162–3
    Macedonian uprising (1903), 336–7
    Mihailo's expansionism and, 162
    Milan I, relations with, 181
    Mileta's rebellion (1835), 92
    millet system, 24

INDEX

Montenegro War (1861–2), 161
Mürzsteg Agreement (1903), 337, 350
Niš rebellion (1841), 104–5
Peace of Szeged (1444), 21
railways, 196, 227, 237, 252–3
Reval agreement (1908), 350
Russian War (1806–12), 49–51, 53, 54, 55
Russian War (1828–9), 77, 87
Russian War (1877–8), 217, 220–21, 222
Serbian schools in, 185, 252–3, 279, 281–2, 285
Serbian Uprising, First (1804–13), 2, 3, 19, 35, 43–59, 113, 120, 191, 585
Serbian Uprising, Second (1815), 59–63, 308, 585
Serbian Wars (1876–8), 185, 220–24, 300
sharia law, 22, 62
taxation in, 18, 22, 23, 24, 28, 38, 45, 47, 61
Tenka's plot (1857), 137
Tripolitania revolt (1835–58), 95
Siege of Vienna (1529), 25
Siege of Vienna (1683), 29
Young Turk Revolution (1908), 350–51, 358
World War I (1914–18), 407, 412, 418, 437
Ottoman garrisons in Serbia,
Aleksandar's deposition (1858), 144
Aleksandar's reign (1842-58), 109, 114-15, 135, 137, 141
British consul assault (1858), 115
First Serbian Uprising (1804-15), 45, 49
Jovan's rebellion (1839), 97
Kükürt Çeşme crisis (1862), 109, 162–4, 167
Liberals and, 141, 174
Miloš's first reign (1815–39), 61, 62, 69, 73, 76, 78, 80-1, 82, 83, 97

Ottoman period (to 1804), 29, 35, 42, 43
riots (1860), 151
Second Serbian Uprising (1815), 60
withdrawal (1867), 168–70, 175, 185, 189, 296
'Our Beautiful Homeland', 380, 400
Ozerović, Avram, 234–5

P-P government, first (1924), 490-1
P-P government, second (1924-5), 493
Pact of London (1914), 402, 410
Paču, Lazar, 339, 341, 349, 355, 370
paganism, 14, 19, 39, 40, 116, 265
Palagruža, Croatia, 455
Pale, Bosnia, 581
Palestine, 40, 155, 567, 568, 583
Palež, Bosnia, 59
Palilula, Belgrade, 71
  barracks, 164, 178
Palmerston, Henry John Temple, 3rd Viscount, 94
Pančevo, Serbia, 106, 131, 162
panduri, 24, 96
Pantelić, Stevan, 264
paper, 38, 224, 514, 540
Paraćin, Serbia, 35, 88, 113, 234, 309
paramilitary organisations, 333-4
  bashibazouks, 175
  Black Hand, *see* Black Hand
  blue-shirts, 528, 547
  Bosnian, 400, 425, 462
  Chetniks, *see* Chetniks
  Croat Civic Defence, 541, 552, 581
  Croat Nationalist Youth, 492
  Croat Peasant Defence, 541, 552, 581
  Free Corps, 34–5, 42, 44, 46, 48, 90, 108
  green-shirts, 545, 547
  Habsburg Serb auxiliary, 29–30
  Montenegrin White, 465
  National Defence *see* National Defence
  national militia, *see* national militia
  Organisation of Ottoman Serbs, 372

INDEX

ORJUNA, 491-2, 534, 568
Radical, 492, 493
Serbian Volunteer Corps, 533
Stanković's militia 147,
Ustashas, 522, 524, 535, 545, 553, 581, 582
VMRO, *see* Internal Macedonian Revolutionary Organisation
White Hand, *see* White Hand
Parežanin, Ratko, 529, 531
Paris, France, 111, 122, 128, 134, 136, 139, 140, 186, 202, 233, 234, 241, 311, 327, 332, 341, 355, 392, 434, 529
    Peace Conference (1919–20), 451–4, 462, 465, 550
    Treaty of (1856), 127, 135, 136, 143
parliaments
    Aleksandar's reign (1842–58), 107, 108, 143
    Aleksandar I of Serbia's reign (1889–1903), 276, 278–9, 284
    Aleksander I of Yugoslavia's reign (1921–34), 487–8
    Miloš's reign, first (1815–39), 68, 74, 75, 76–7, 88, 97, 98
    Miloš's reign, second (1858–60), 146, 149
    Mihailo's reign, first (1839–42), 102, 103–4
    Mihailo's reign, second (1860–68), 156–7, 167, 176
    Milan II's reign (1839), 101
    Milan IV/I's reign (1868–89), 182, 183–4, 205, 206, 208, 239, 243, 257
    Petar I's reign (1903–21), 328, 484–5
Party of Pure Right, 423
Pašić, Đurđina, 497
Pašić, Nikola, 3, 4, 5, 206–9, 238, 240, 245, 269, 275
    Adamstal scandal (1926), 496
    Albanian massacre (1913), 382
    Aleksandar, relationship with, 495

Aleksandar's assassination (1903), 306–7, 326
Aleksandar's wedding (1900), 293
armed forces, views on, 245
assassination attempt on (1892), 272
assassination attempt on (1921), 485
assassination attempt on (1923), 490
Austrian trade agreement (1881), 234, 242
Balkan Wars (1912–13), 373–5, 376, 377, 378
Bosnia crisis (1908–9), 352, 353
Bosnian uprising (1875–8), 208, 211–12, 214
Bulgaria, relations with, 341, 371
Bulgarian War (1885–6), 250–52
coalition government (1901–2), 301
coalition government (1908–9), 353–4
conspirators, dismissal of (1904), 336
constitution (1901), 297
constitution (1921), 484
Corfu Declaration (1917), 431–6
coup d'état (1893), 273–4
coup d'état (1903), 306–7, 326
Croatia and, 364–7, 380, 391, 400, 401, 431
Croatian right, relations with, 495
death (1926), 497, 513
Džemijet, repression of (1924), 475
Franz Ferdinand assassination (1914), 393, 394
Geneva Declaration (1918), 440–42
Grujić government (1903–4), 334
gun question (1904–7), 340–41, 349
HRSS, relations with, 491
imprisonment (1897–8), 283–4
Italy, relations with, 455
Karađorđevićes, relations with, 249
Kosovo Albanians, agreement with (1912), 372
Kosovo estate, 387
Kragujevac congress (1882), 243
Ljotić, relationship with, 529
Macedonia policy, 253, 349–50, 391

723

INDEX

Marko's Protocol (1923), 490
Milan's abdication (1889), 259
Montenegro, relations with, 254, 408, 442–5
Natalija's deportation (1891), 269–70
National Bloc government (1924), 490
national congress (1896), 280
National Defence, relation with, 359
nationalism, 206, 364, 391, 400, 402, 425
Niš Declaration (1914), 405
Niš meeting (1886), 253–4
Ottoman withdrawal (1867), 169
press law, views on, 228
prime minister, first term (1891–2), 269–71
prime minister, second term (1904–5), 339–42
prime minister, third term (1906–8), 345, 346, 347, 349–50
prime minister, fourth term (1909–11), 355, 366–7
prime minister, fifth term (1912–18), 370, 382, 388, 389, 390, 404
prime minister, sixth term (1921–4), 482, 487–90
prime minister, seventh term (1924–6), 493, 494–6
priority question crisis (1914), 388, 389, 390
property, 495
Radical party formation (1870), 196
railway convention (1880), 230
Russia, relations with, 248, 340, 401, 404
Russian Revolution (1917), 431
Salonika trial (1917), 319, 323, 428–31, 436
socialism and, 309
St John's Day attempt (1899), 286–7, 495
St Petersburg envoy (1893), 275
Timok rebellion (1883), 247
Treaty of Versailles (1919), 452

United Serb Youth and, 174
Western society, view on, 213
World War I (1914–18), 399, 401–2, 404, 405, 408, 422–4, 431, 439
Yugoslav Committee founding (1914), 406
Yugoslav nationalism, 206, 364–7
Yugoslav unification (1918–21), 473–4, 484
Yugoslavia, establishment of (1918), 440–42, 443–4, 446, 451, 455, 459
Živković, relationship with, 492
Pašić, Radomir, 495, 496, 497
Passarowitz, Treaty of (1718), 32
pastoralism, 11, 38, 71, 109-10, 453, 309
Pasvanoglu Osman Pasha, 41–2, 43
Patriarchate of the Yugoslav kingdom, 461, 510, 533, 544, 575
Patriarchate of Constantinople, 32, 33, 75, 96, 85–6, 227, 237, 250, 355, 461
Patriarchate of Peć (1346–1766), 16, 17, 27, 29, 31, 32, 34, 376, 461
Patriotic Youth Front, 537
Paulucci, Philip, 50–51
Pavelić, Ante, 495, 517, 522, 524
Pavle, Prince Regent of Yugoslavia, 527, 534–9, 557, 584
  coup d'état (1941), 5, 559, 563–6, 572–8
  Cvetković–Maček Agreement (1939), 550, 551, 557, 558
  führer proposal (1937), 540
  Hitler, meeting with (1941), 571
  May putsch (1903), 323
  Stojadinović's ouster (1939), 548–9
  Tripartite Pact accession (1941), 571, 583
Pavlović, Dimitrije, 461
Pavlović, Dobrosav, 430
Pavlović, Melentije, 75, 85
Pavlović, Milovan, 111, 277, 301, 315, 316–17, 318, 320, 323, 430
Pavlović, Teodor, 119
Pavlović, Živko, 426

INDEX

Peace of Szeged (1444), 21
peasant cooperatives, 263, 474, 529
Peasant International, 491
Peasant–Democrat Coalition, 499, 503, 504, 519–20, 536, 537, 544, 550, 551, 558
peasantry
    Aleksandar's reign (1842–58), 109–10, 114, 140
    Aleksandar I of Serbia's reign (1889–1903), 260, 261, 262, 263, 309–10
    Aleksandar I of Yugoslavia's reign (1921–34), 513–16
    First Serbian Uprising (1804-13), 45, 47
    medieval Serbia (to 1459), 14-15, 18
    Mihailo's second reign (1860–68), 164–5, 166
    Milan's reign (1868–89), 196, 204, 206, 207, 208, 213, 241, 246–9
    Miloš's first reign (1815–39), 70–71, 72, 80, 81, 83, 93, 96
    Miloš's second reign (1858–60), 151
    Ottoman era (1459-1804), 17–18, 19, 23, 24, 28, 32, 34, 38-40, 41, 42
    Petar I's reign (1903–21), 462–4, 474–5, 480, 482, 503, 509, 513–19, 521, 529
    Petar II's reign (1934–45), 540, 542, 547, 580
Peć, Archbishop of, 16
Peć, Kosovo, 372, 375, 376
Peć, Patriarchate of (1346–1766), 16, 17, 27, 29, 31, 32, 34, 376, 461
Pećanac, Kosta, 337, 420, 421, 422, 444, 466, 534, 544
Pečić, Dragutin, 342
Pelagić, Vaso, 187, 203, 205, 210, 213-4, 227, 313
Pelješac, Croatia, 438
People's Peasant Party, 558
People's Radical Party, 3–5, 88, 165, 196, 197, 201, 206–9, 238–41, 259, 265, 275, 513

    Aleksandar's assassination (1903), 306–7
    anti-Semitism, 234-5, 567
    anti-state ideology, 261, 262, 270, 308, 360
    armed forces, relations with, 335
    Austrian trade agreement (1881), 234
    Bogosavljević's death (1880), 229–30
    Bosnian crisis (1908–9), 351, 352, 353, 355
    Bosnian uprising (1875–8), 208, 211–12, 215
    British parliamentary model and, 334
    Bulgarian War (1885–6), 250–52
    centralism, 489
    Chetnik organisations, 492
    coalition government (1887–8), 255–6
    coalition government (1901–2), 295–301
    coalition government (1908–9), 353–4, 355
    coalition government (1909–11), 355
    coalition government (1920–21), 480
    conspirator question, 331–6, 339–40, 343–4, 345, 361
    constituent assembly (1920–21), 480–86
    constitution (1889), 3, 257–8, 259, 271, 277, 295
    constitution (1901), 295–7, 326
    constitution (1903), 327–9, 331
    contra pardoning affair (1908), 352
    Corfu Declaration (1917), 431–6
    coup d'état (1893), 273–4, 307
    coup d'état (1903), 325–6, 331
    coup d'état (1941), 575
    Court Radicals, 275–6, 280, 301, 302
    Croatian right, relations with, 495
    Cvetković–Maček Agreement (1939), 558
    decline of, 513, 515
    democratic ideology, 260, 280
    Democratic Party, relations with, 478–81

725

INDEX

federation debate (1934), 520
Grujić government, first (1888), 256
Grujić government, second (1889–91), 259–65, 267–9, 297
Grujić government, third (1893–4), 276–7
Grujić government, fourth (1903–4), 334–9
healthcare proposal, opposition to (1879), 229
HRSS, relations with, 491
Independents split (1904–5), 339–41
Jevtić government (1934–5), 536
JRSD formation (1931–2), 519
JRZ formation (1935), 537, 539
Karađorđevićes, relations with, 249, 277
Kragujevac commune (1873–6), 206–8, 211–13
Kragujevac congress (1882), 243
Liberals, pact with (1886), 254
low-tax ideology, 281, 292, 316
March disturbances (1903), 316
Milan, relations with, 255–6
Milovanović government (1911–12), 355, 360, 361
Natalija's deportation (1891), 269–70
national congress (1896), 280
'National Salvation' proclamation (1891), 269
nationalism, 239, 241, 243, 248, 264, 265, 281, 383, 406
Nikolajević government (1894), 277–8
Niš Declaration (1914), 405
Niš meeting (1886), 253–4
Novi Sad congress (1919), 472–3
Novi Sad declaration (1932), 521
Ottoman Wars (1876–8), 215, 220, 221
Pašić government, first (1891–2), 269–71, 297
Pašić government, second (1904–5), 339–42
Pašić government, third (1906–8), 345–50

Pašić government, fourth (1909–11), 355, 366–7
Pašić government, fifth (1912–18), 370, 382, 388, 389, 390, 404
Pašić government, sixth (1921–4), 482, 487–90
Pašić government, seventh (1924–6), 493, 494–6
Petrović inquiry (1911), 355–6
Progressives, relations with, 241–4, 255, 261
Protić government, first (1918–19), 456, 459, 479
Protić government, second (1920), 479
Radić assassination (1928), 498–504
railway convention (1880), 230
Russia, relations with, 281
Salonika trial (1917), 319, 323, 428–31, 436, 471, 487, 497, 501
Serb Nationalist Youth, 492
Simić government, first (1894), 277
Simić government, second (1896–7), 280, 282
socialism and, 308–9, 313
St John's Day attempt (1899), 286–7, 289, 292, 313, 344, 495
Stojadinović government (1935–9), 537
territorial acquisitions (1912–13) and, 385–91
terrorism, 355, 362
Timok rebellion (1883), 245–9, 253, 259, 263, 265, 275, 306, 324, 550
Tripartite Pact (1940), 571
unification debate (1940), 558
United Opposition, 544, 547, 550
Uzunović government (1926–7), 496, 498
Velimirović government, first (1902), 350
Velimirović government, second (1908–9), 350, 353

INDEX

Vesnić government (1920–21), 480, 482
Vukičević government (1927–8), 498, 500, 502
Wedding Cabinet (1900–1901), 291–2, 295, 346
White Hand, relations with, 361
women's high school, opposition to (1879), 229
World War I (1914–18), 404, 425
Yugoslav Committee founding (1914), 406
Yugoslav unification (1918–21), 470, 473
Yugoslavia, establishment of (1918), 445–6, 449, 451, 455, 459
Zagreb Points (1932), 520
People's Republic of Bosnia-Hercegovina (1946–63), 485
People's Republic of Serbia (1946–63), 2, 587
People's Will, 311
Perić, Ninko, 501, 511
Perić, Živojin, 295, 326, 334, 354, 417, 435
Pernar, Ivan, 501
Perović, Ivan, 527, 571
Perović, Latinka, 194, 311, 330
Perović, Milivoje, 421
Persida, Princess of Serbia, 102, 112, 113, 115, 126, 135, 166, 178, 179
Pešić, Petar, 409, 416, 426, 570–72, 573
Pest, Hungary, 84, 119, 128, 173, 179
  see also Budapest
Petar (knez), 41
Petar I, King of Serbia, 110–11, 186, 294–5
  abdication document (1919), 485
  accession (1903), 325–30
  automobile purchase (1906), 310
  background and character, 327–8, 356
  Balkan Wars (1912–13), 374, 378
  Bosnian uprising (1875–8), 210, 214
  conspirator question, 331–6, 339–40, 343–4, 345, 361, 388, 389
  constitution (1903), 3, 326–9, 331
  constitution (1921), 484–5
  contra pardoning affair (1908), 352
  Cvijić's speech (1907) and, 368
  death (1921), 485
  Decree on Officers (1904), 335–6
  French language, 328
  gambling habit, 327
  gun question, 340–41, 343, 344, 345, 348–9, 428
  internment (1878), 227
  Konak demolition (1904), 112
  May putsch (1903), 305, 307, 319
  Mihailo's assassination (1868), 180
  National Council delegation (1918), 448
  Ottoman Wars (1876–8), 216, 221
  Pašić, agreement with (1886), 254
  Pašić's resignation (1914), 389, 390
  priority question crisis (1914), 389–91
  resignation of duties (1914), 391
  Russia, relations with, 335, 370
  Salonika trial (1917), 429
  succession, 356–8
  synagogue opening (1907), 567
  United Serb Youth and, 187
  World War I (1914–18), 404, 405, 408, 413
  Zorka, marriage to, 244
Petar I, Prince-Bishop of Montenegro, 121
Petar II, King of Yugoslavia, 527, 545, 559
  coup d'état (1941), 574
  German invasion (1941), 580, 582
  majority (1941), 527, 570
Petar II, Prince-Bishop of Montenegro, 121–2
Petar, Metropolitan of Belgrade, 86, 90 111–12, 114, 147, 152
Peter I, Emperor of Russia, 30
Petronijević, Avram, 90,
  Aleksandar's reign (1842–58), 108, 111, 112, 122
  death (1852), 133, 136

727

INDEX

Mihailo's reign (1839–42), 102, 103, 104, 107
Miloš's reign (1815–39), 78, 79, 83, 89, 90, 91, 95, 98
Petrovaradin, Serbia, 32
Petrović family, 31
Petrović-Njegoš dynasty, 31, 121, 338, 408–9, 416, 445
Petrović, Đorđe, 179
Petrović, Karađorđe, *see* Karađorđe
Petrović, Lazar, 290, 294, 295, 316, 318, 319, 323
Petrović, Marinko, 48
Petrović, Milan, 304
Petrović, Miloje, 54
Petrović, Mojsije, 32
Petrović, Nastas, 348, 355–6, 513
Petrović, Vukašin, 290, 306, 329, 343, 344, 417, 435
Petrović Era, Milutin, 90, 106, 131
Petrovich, Michael Boro, 1, 67
Phanariots, 66, 71
Piedmont-Sardinia (1720–1861), 160, 173, 190, 214, 358, 359, 361, 364, 367, 400
Pig War (1906–11), 343–4, 348-9, 350, 354
pigs, 37, 38, 42, 43, 52, 61, 310
    acorns and, 37, 101, 105, 110, 111, 309
    sacrifice of, 39
    swine fever outbreak (1895), 279
    trade sanctions and, 229, 279, 280, 294, 343, 349
Pijemont (Piedmont), 357, 359–60, 378, 389, 425
von Pirch, Otto, 56, 68
Piroćanac, Milan, 251, 270, 284
    background, 233-4
    on Milan, 202-3
    prime minister, 202, 233-6, 242, 248, 249
Pirot, Serbia, 104, 185, 217, 222, 225, 226, 227, 233, 237, 247, 251, 252, 257, 273
    Battle of (1878), 222

Plamenac, Jovan, 465, 466
Plan (1844), 89, 123–6, 138, 140, 160, 171, 222, 375
Platon, Bishop of Banja Luka, 543
Plevna, siege of (1877–8), 217, 220–1
Pliva River, 10
Pljakić, Petrija, 67
Pljevlja, Montenegro, 379
Plovdiv, Bulgaria, 250
plums, 237
Podgorica, Montenegro, 444, 445, 460, 465
Podhorski, Ljudevit, 328
Podrinje region, 81, 84, 88, 106, 257, 486
Podunava okrug, 257
Podunavlje region, 486, 486
Poland, 10, 286, 567
    German invasion (1939), 557
    Jagiellonian dynasty (1385–1572), 20, 21
    partition period (1795–1918), 88, 108, 122–3
policing
    Aleksandar's reign (1842–58), 109, 114, 133, 145
    Aleksandar I of Serbia's reign (1889–1903), 260, 261–2, 269, 271–3, 277–8, 284, 300, 315, 316
    Aleksandar I of Yugoslavia's reign (1921–34), 464, 468, 489, 498, 500, 503, 509, 517, 522, 524
    Mihailo's first reign (1839–42), 103
    Milan's reign (1868–89), 204, 208, 211, 216, 228, 238, 240–43, 245, 248, 254–7, 265
    Miloš's first reign (1815–39), 83, 85, 96, 98
    Petar I's reign (1903–21), 335, 342, 346–8, 351, 386–7, 389, 392, 410, 458, 459, 466, 479, 480
    Petar II's reign (1934–45), 540, 546–7, 549, 552
Politika (Politics), 329, 373, 389
polygamy, 39, 67
Popov, Srba, 563

728

INDEX

Popović, Čedomir, 315, 338, 429
Popović, Cvijetko, 393
Popović Ðak, Miloje, 72-3
Popović, Damjan
    Aleksandar's marriage, views on, 290, 295, 304
    Balkan Wars (1912-13), 388
    Balugdžić's resignation (1905), 341
    conspirator question and, 325, 333, 341, 344, 347
    coup plot rumours (1909), 357
    gun question, views on, 344
    May putsch (1903), 304, 307, 317, 325
    ministerial crisis (1903), 333
    Montenegro annexation (1919), 466
    priority question and, 389, 390–91
    retirement (1906), 347
    Salonika trial (1917), 429
    World War I (1914-18), 408, 412
    World War II (1939–45), 408, 412, 429
Popović, Dušan, 315, 335, 383, 388
Popović, Jovan Sterija, 113-4
Popović, Justin, 533
Popović, Krsto, 465-6
Popović, Miodrag, 118
Popović, Nikodije, 304
Popović, Sima, 443
Popović, Toma, 501-2
Popović, Vojin, 337, 420
Popović-Obradović, Olga, 260, 355
populism, 3
    Karadžić, 116, 117
    liberals, 158
    Miloš, 105, 147, 148, 149, 151
    People's Radical Party, 3, 239, 261, 262
    Obrenovićites, 143, 146
    Radical party, 196, 208, 211
    Vučić-Perišić, 126, 131, 133, 138, 141
Portugal, 349
Posavina, Serbia, 402
posela, 112-3
postal services, 109, 185-6
Potiorek, Oskar, 393, 403
Požarevac, Serbia

Kingdom of Serbia (1882–1918), 255, 257, 310, 313, 417
Ottoman Serbia (1459–1815), 35, 42, 45
Principality of Serbia (1815–1882), 61, 68, 71, 72, 83, 84, 87, 91, 105, 174, 183
Serbian Uprising, First (1804–13), 45, 48, 55
in Yugoslavia (1918-41), 480, 486, 533
Požarevac Liberals, 470
Požega, Serbia, 57, 58, 87
Prague, Bohemia, 129, 367
Prahovo, Serbia, 54
Pravda (Justice), 373, 540
Predavec, Josip, 520
Prekmurje, Slovenia, 453
Preodnica (Morning Star), 173
Presentation Parliament (1835), 92
Preslav, Bulgaria, 11
press, newspapers,
    Aleksandar's reign (1842–58), 117, 130
    Aleksandar I of Serbia's reign (1889–1903), 260, 262, 268–9, 274, 276–7, 284, 291, 295, 296–7, 298, 314, 316
    Aleksandar I of Yugoslavia's reign (1921–34), 475, 490, 495, 500, 501, 502, 506, 514
    Habsburg Empire (to 1918), 36, 117, 125, 174, 213, 227, 291, 367, 417
    Mihailo's second reign (1860–68), 155, 156, 173, 176, 184, 188
    Milan's reign (1868–89), 196, 203, 204–5, 207-8, 211, 212, 213, 215, 220, 228, 238, 239–42, 247, 248, 256–8, 308-9
    Miloš's first reign (1815–39), 78, 84
    Miloš's second reign (1858–60), 152-3
    other European, 322, 332, 543, 568, 569
    Ottoman Empire (1299–1922), 153, 250, 373

729

INDEX

Petar I's reign (1903–21), 329, 333–4, 335, 339, 340, 344, 345, 346, 349, 350, 357, 359, 367, 417, 425, 463, 467, 482, 484
Petar II's reign (1934–45), 537, 540, 560, 575
Pribićević, Adam, 466
Pribićević, Svetozar
   6 January Regime (1929–34), 507, 517, 518
   amputation offer (1928), 505
   Aleksandar, audience with (1928), 499
   arrest (1929), 517
   centralism, 459, 469, 479–80, 486, 487, 488, 504
   coalition government (1924), 490
   coalition government (1924–5), 493
   constitution (1921), 487
   constitution declaration (1937), 544
   Croat–Serb Coalition (1905–18), 366, 367, 391, 460
   Davidović, conflict with (1922), 488
   Geneva Declaration (1918), 441
   imprisonment (1929–31)
   interior minister (1918–20), 459, 462, 469–71, 479
   Marko's Protocol (1923), 490
   ORJUNA, 491–2
   Peasant–Democrat Coalition, 499
   purge (1925), 494
   Radić arrest (1919), 462
   Radić assassination crisis (1928), 504, 505
   Sarajevo conference (1919), 469
   Serb Independent Party, 366, 472
   World War I (1914–18), 391, 439
   Yugoslav unification (1918–21), 441, 446, 458, 459, 462, 469–71, 486
Prijedor, Bosnia, 519
Prijepolje, Serbia, 53
Prilep, Macedonia, 411
Primorje Banovina, 508, 510, 547, 548, 551-3
Primorje region, 140, 358, 482, 486
Princip, Gavrilo, 355, 392, 393, 427, 546
printing, 36, 78, 124, 125, 168, 184, 207, 333
Priority of Government, Decree on the (1914), 389
priority question, 387–91
Prishtina, Hasan, 372, 466, 467–8
Priština, Kosovo, 140, 253, 282, 372, 374, 379, 382, 386, 387, 421
Prizren, Kosovo, 12, 13, 28, 140, 372, 375, 379, 386, 413
   Sanjak of (1455–1913), 28
Prodanović, Jaša, 269, 298, 321, 337, 390, 471, 562
Prokuplje, Serbia, 222, 391, 392, 421
Pronouncement (1919, 1921), 463, 485, 493
property rights, 69, 75, 83, 114, 152, 180, 184, 204
prostitution, 192, 514
Protestantism, 453, 532, 533
Protić, Đorđe, 87, 90, 91, 95, 103, 105
Protić, Kosta, 218, 222, 258, 271
Protić, Stojan, 208, 280, 347, 370, 478
   administrative divisions and, 342
   Albanians, views on, 381, 385
   April Coup (1893), 274, 275
   authoritarianism, 280
   Balugdžić's resignation (1905), 341
   Bosnian crisis (1908–9), 351, 354
   British parliamentary model and, 334
   coalition toppling (1911), 355
   conspirators question and, 335, 360
   constitution (1921), 482, 550
   Corfu Declaration (1917), 432
   death (1923), 513
   Dnevnik editor, 295
   Geneva Declaration (1918), 441
   Ilidža congress (1922), 488
   labour unrest law (1906), 348
   May putsch (1903), 325
   Pećanac, relationship with, 420
   Petar's abdication (1919), 485
   press law (1904), 335

INDEX

prime minister, first term (1918–19), 456, 459, 479
prime minister, second term (1920), 479
public security law (1904), 339
Regime of 11 October (1897–1900), 283
resignation (1907), 348
St John's Day attempt (1899), 286-7, 292
territorial acquisitions (1912–13), 386, 388-9, 390
Yugoslavia name, views on, 432
Proudhon, Pierre-Joseph, 188
Provisional National Bosnian Government, 219
Provisional National Legislature (1919–20), 456, 469, 471, 479–80
Prozorovsky, Alexander, 51–2
Prussia, Kingdom of (1701–1918), 160, 165
  Austrian War (1866), 168, 173, 174, 352
  French War (1870–71), 216, 244, 412
  German unification (1866–71), 160, 364
  Jewish expulsions crisis (1861), 155
  press law, 228
Putnik, Radomir, 332, 333, 347, 374, 379, 388, 389-90, 403, 404, 413, 426, 428, 436

R-40 plan, 579
R-41 plan, 579
R-R government (1925–6), 494, 496
Račić, Puniša, 339, 475, 492, 501–2
Rački, Franjo, 167
Radenik (Worker), 196, 203
Radenković, Bogdan, 358, 361, 373, 429
Rađevina, Serbia, 79, 80
Radić, Pavle, 494, 501
Radić, Stjepan, 456–7, 462, 481, 489, 490, 492, 493-6, 505, 518
  assassination (1928), 498–504, 541

Radical Democracy, 287
Radical Party, *see* People's Radical Party
Radical Party (Croatia), 366, 458, 472
Radical Social Party, 528
Radio Belgrade, 516, 558
Radio Zagreb, 558
Radivojević, Ilija, 319, 358, 380
Radivojević, Ranko, 221
Radničke novine (Workers' Newspaper), 384
Radnik (Worker), 308–9
Radojević, Mirka, 218
Radojković, Mileta, 90-1
Radosavljević, Teodor, 115, 135, 136
Radovanović, Đorđe, 178, 179
Radovanović, Kosta, 178, 179
Radovanović, Ljubomir, 178, 179
Radovanović, Pavle, 156, 178, 179
Radovanović, Petar, 85
Radović, Andrija, 442, 443, 476
Radović, Čedo, 499, 500
Rafajlović, Živojin, 299, 337
Ragusa, 12, 15, 19
  see also Dubrovnik
railways
  Kingdom of Serbia (1882–1918), 237, 241–2, 252–3, 262, 309, 312, 339, 341, 349, 353, 379, 403
  Principality of Serbia (1815–1882), 196, 205, 226, 227, 230, 234, 237
  Yugoslavia (1918–41), 464, 468, 496, 529-30, 540
Rajačić, Josif, 129, 132
Rajcija, 30
Rajović, Cvetko, 78, 89, 148
Rajović, Dragomir, 247, 253, 306
Rakić, Milan, 372
Rakovića, Serbia, 98
von Ranke, Leopold, 49, 59, 73
Rapallo, Treaty of (1920), 455
rape of women, 23, 33, 48, 217–18, 223, 323, 381, 382, 421
Rašić, Mihailo, 360
Raška (1091–1217), 11–14, 26, 124
Raška oblast, 486

731

INDEX

Raška, bishopric of, 14, 26
Raška-Prizren, bishopric of, 279
Ravanica monastery, Serbia, 19, 31
Rechtsstaat, 70, 101
Red Aid, 517
Red Cross, 216, 418
Red Justice, 485
Regency Constitution (1869), 3, 181–4, 195–7, 201, 204–6, 213, 277–9, 295, 327
Reichsstadt agreement (1876), 216–17
Renaissance (c. 1400 – c. 1600), 27
Republic of Mirdita (1921), 466
Republic of Venice (697–1797), 12, 19, 27
Republican Democratic Party, *see* Republican party
republicanism, 474, 492, 305, 339, 471, 492
Republican party, 471-2, 476, 481, 483, 485, 561-2, 563, 566, 584
Resavac, Milisav Zdravković, 90, 91
Reshid Pasha, 103
Reval agreement (1908), 350
Revolutions of 1848–9, 111, 120, 128–32, 187
Ribar, Ivan, 488
Ribarac, Stojan, 271, 273, 278, 296, 297, 307, 340, 343, 355, 389, 417, 470
von Ribbentrop, Joachim, 572
Ribeaupierre, Alexander, 62
Ribnikar, Vladislav, 329
Rijeka, Croatia, 369, 411, 438, 439, 452, 455, 482
Ringstrasse, Vienna, 170
Ristić, Dragiša N., 573
Ristić, Jovan
    Action Ministry, First (1875), 210
    Action Ministry, Second (1876), 214–15
    Aleksandar's reign (1842–58), 111
    Austrian trade negotiations (1880), 230–31
    Avakumović appointment (1892), 270–71
    background, 177

    Bosnia, policies on, 186, 203–4
    Bulgaria, views on, 225
    coalition government (1887–8), 255–6
    Congress of Berlin (1878), 225–7
    constitution (1869), 182, 184, 205
    constitutional council (1888–9), 257
    death (1899), 284, 286
    family, 306
    Karađorđevićes, relations with, 249
    Mihailo's second reign (1860–68), 163, 168, 177
    Milan's accession (1868), 181
    Miloš's second reign (1858–60), 152–3
    National Liberal Party registration (1883), 240
    Niš annexation (1878), 228
    Ottoman Wars (1876–8), 214–15, 218, 220, 225–6
    Pašić, relationship with, 238, 269
    pension, 334
    Progressives, purge of (1887), 255
    resignation (1880), 231, 233
    St John's Day attempt (1899), 286
    Timok rebellion (1883), 248
Ristić Džervinac, Mihailo, 319, 324, 337
Ristović, Vladimir, 500, 503
Rizvanbegović, Hamzaga, 168
Rodofinikin, Konstantin, 51–2, 54
Rogić, Stanoje, 178, 179
Roman Empire (27 BCE – 395 CE), 9–10
Romania, 313, 366, 455
    anti-Semitism in, 567
    Antonescu regime (1940–44), 575
    Balkan Pact (1934), 455, 523
    Balkan War (1913), 379
    Charles I ultimatum (1921), 454
    fascism in, 527, 575
    Little Entente (1921), 454–5
    Little Entente (1933), 523
    Ljotić and, 531
    monarchy, 287, 305
    Serb nationalists and, 313, 366
    trade agreements, 343, 349
    Tripartite Pact (1940), 570

INDEX

United Principalities (1862–1881), 176, 202, 215, 219, 227
World War I (1914–18), 401, 402, 418, 419, 420, 423, 439, 452–3
World War II (1939–45), 569–70, 579, 580
Yugoslavia invasion (1941), 580, 581
Yugoslavia, establishment of (1918), 446, 451, 452–3
Romanians, 71, 86, 119, 132, 439, 452, 453, 464, 473, 542, 567
romanisation, 9
Romantic Period (1798–1837), 117-8, 130
Rosandić, Toma, 515–6
Rosić, Petar (Varnava), 355, 533, 543-4, 565, 568
Royal Guard, 303, 494, 518, 574
Royal Serbian Academy, 254, 262–3
see also Serbian Royal Academy
Rudnik, Serbia, 48, 58, 59, 68, 72, 87, 97, 103, 247, 258
Rudovci, Serbia, 59
Rumelia, Eyalet of (1365–1867), 21, 23, 25, 33, 42, 60, 77
Rushchuk, Bulgaria, 176
Russia,
  Akkerman Convention (1826), 76–7
  Aleksandar, relations with, 107–8
  Aleksandar I of Serbia, relations with, 265, 285, 289, 292–3, 294
  Aleksandar's memorandum (1912), 370
  Anglo-Russian Entente (1907), 350, 393, 394
  Balkan Wars (1912–13), 374, 375, 378, 379
  Bosnia negotiations (1870), 185
  Bosnian crisis (1908–9), 351, 352, 354
  Bosnian uprising (1875–8), 208, 210, 214, 219–20
  Bulgaria, relations with, 219, 224, 265, 371
  Civil War (1917–22), 454
  condominium agreement (1897), 281, 286
  conspirators question and, 335
  Constitutionalists, relations with, 104, 107–8, 122, 126, 133–5, 137
  Crimean War (1853–6), 134–5, 136
  Franz Ferdinand assassination (1914), 394
  Garašanin, relations with, 134, 175, 176, 181
  Great Game (c. 1813–1907), 94
  Greek War of Independence (1821–9), 75, 77
  Japanese War (1904–5), 350
  Jewish expulsions crisis (1861), 155
  Kükürt Çeşme crisis (1862), 163
  liberalism and, 187
  Marković and, 188, 190
  Mihailo, relations with, 104, 105, 134, 160, 175, 176, 179
  Milan, relations with, 181, 185, 213–14, 218–19, 231, 233–4, 244, 250, 285
  Mileta's rebellion (1835), 92
  Miloš, relations with, 69–70, 72, 76–7, 83, 88–9, 90, 92–5, 122
  Montenegro, relations with, 181, 280, 409
  Moroccan crises (1905–6/1911), 393–4
  Mürzsteg Agreement (1903), 337, 350
  Napoleonic Wars (1803–15), 49, 51, 55, 56
  Narodnik movement (1860s–70s), 207, 311
  Niš Declaration (1914), 405
  oligarchy and, 172
  Ottoman War (1806–12), 49–51, 53, 54, 55
  Ottoman War (1828–9), 77, 87
  Ottoman War (1877–8), 217, 220–21, 222
  People's Will (1879–87), 311
  Petar I, relations with, 335, 370, 391

733

INDEX

Polish Uprising (1830–31), 88, 108, 122
Progressives, relations with, 279
Radicals, relations with, 249, 335, 362
Revolution (1917), 248, 423, 426, 431, 433, 434, 457
Secret Convention gifting (1896), 280
Serbian Uprising, First (1804–13), 46, 50, 51–2, 58, 65
Serbian-Ottoman Wars (1876–8), 216–17, 218–19, 225–6
Serbo-Bulgarian alliance (1912), 371
socialists and, 208
Soviet, *see* Russia, Soviet
St John's Day attempt (1899), 286
tariff agreement (1907), 349
Timok rebellion (1883), 248
trade agreement (1880), 230
Treaty of Unkiar-Skelessi (1833), 80, 92
Tucović on, 385
Vučić-Perišić, relations with, 133, 134
Western education and, 187
World War I (1914–17), 395, 401, 402, 405, 410, 412, 414, 418, 423
Russia, Soviet (1917–91), 248, 423, 426, 431, 433, 434
Bessarabia occupation (1940), 569
Civil War (1917–22), 454
commercial treaty (1940), 570
HRSS, relations with, 491, 493
Molotov–Ribbentrop Pact (1939), 557
Peasant International, 491
Treaty of Brest-Litovsk (1918), 435
Treaty of Friendship (1941), 578
Russian Church Slavonic, 116, 119
Russian Orthodox Church, 321, 454
Russians in Yugoslavia, 454, 467

Šabac, Serbia
Aleksandar's reign (r. 1842–58), 126, 127, 142
Aleksandar I of Serbia's reign (1889–1903), 284, 308, 310, 321

Aleksandar I of Yugoslavia's reign (1921–34), 516
Mihailo's first reign (1839–42), 103
Mihailo's second reign (1860–68), 155, 162
Milan's reign (1868–89), 183, 237, 263
Miloš's first reign (1815–39), 82, 84, 85, 87, 88
Ottoman period (1459–1815), 41, 48, 50
Petar II's reign (1934–45), 540
Šafárik, Jan, 123, 159
Šafárik, Pavel Josef, 119, 123, 129
Šahovići massacre (1924), 463
Saint-Germain, Treaty of (1919), 452
saints, in Serb custom, 39
Šajkača Battalion, 129
Sakar, Serbia, 81
von Salis-Seewis, Johann, 417
Salonika, 10, 11, 227, 242, 252, 349, 353, 369, 529
Balkan Wars (1912–13), 377
World War I (1914–18), 412, 443
World War II (1939–45), 570, 571–2
Salonika front (1915–18), 415, 420, 423, 426, 427, 433, 494
Salonika trial (1917), 319, 323, 428–31, 436, 471, 487, 488, 497, 501, 559, 561-2, 564, 566, 577
salt, 71, 261, 262, 271
Samouprava (*Self-management*), 238, 242, 247, 329, 355
Sanjak of Novi Pazar
Medieval period, 10, 11, 14
Ottoman period, 53, 217, 222, 224, 226, 227, 235
Kingdom of Serbia (1882–1918), 351, 353, 369, 371, 374, 416, 418
Yugoslavia (1918-41), 463, 467, 476, 481, 486, 489, 493, 497, 508, 538, 540
San Stefano, Treaty of (1878), 222, 225, 250
Sarajevo, Bosnia

734

INDEX

Franz Ferdinand assassination (1914), 392-5, 430, 546
Jewish community, 127, 569
Ottoman period (1463–1878), 57, 127, 169
World War I (1914–18), 409
World War II (1939–45), 569, 578, 581, 582
Yugoslavia (1918–41), 447, 460, 469, 472, 473, 476, 480, 483, 509, 537
Sarmatians, 9
Sava (Ilija Garašanin's grandfather), 108
Sava, Saint, 13-14, 27, 78, 147, 363, 510-1, 532-3, 543
Sava Banovina, 508, 510, 527, 548, 551
Sava River, 12, 15, 25, 38, 79, 82, 113, 151, 155, 169, 237, 247, 391, 402, 403-4, 441, 520,
Savić, Jovan, 52
Schlesinger, Adolf, 522–3
Schneider-Creusot, 281, 340–41, 343, 349, 428
Schönbrunn, Treaty of (1809), 53
School of Agriculture and Forestry, 184, 211
Schwäbischer-Deutscher Kulturbund, 473
Second International (1889–1916), 313, 477
Second Serbian Uprising (1815), 59–63, 68, 71, 74, 85, 90, 91, 107, 108, 157, 170 193, 222, 223, 234, 278, 308, 402
Secret Convention (1881), 235, 279, 280
Sekulić, Isidora, 516
Selevac, Serbia, 72, 73
self-management, 188, 530
    Aleksandar's reign (1842–58), 140
    Aleksandar I of Serbia's reign (1889–1903), 260, 261, 271, 297, 316
    Aleksandar I of Yugoslavia's reign (1921-34), 478, 488
    Habsburg occupation (1717–39), 32, 33
    Marković and, 190, 191, 194, 195
    Milan's reign (1868–89), 205, 210-11, 212, 213, 238-9, 240, 244, 249, 257
    Miloš's first reign (1815–39), 68, 71, 88, 96
    Miloš's second reign (1858–60), 148
    Ottoman period (1459–1804), 32, 33, 41, 43
    Petar I's reign (1903-21), 384, 482
    Petar II's reign (1934-45), 538
    Radicals and, 207, 210-11, 212, 238-9, 240, 244, 257, 260, 261, 297, 316, 384, 482, 538
    in Serbian Uprisings (1804–15) 53, 56
Selić, Joca, 501
Selim I, Ottoman Sultan, 23
Selim III, Ottoman Sultan, 40–46, 47, 49-50
Sephardim, 25, 567, 569
Serb Cultural Club, 546, 559–63
    coup d'état (1941), 5, 563–6, 575
    Salonika annexation plan (1940), 570
    Tripartite Pact (1941), 573
Serb Independent Party, 366-7, 472, 473
Serb National Organisation, 350, 406, 447, 473, 474
Serb Nationalist Youth, 492
Serbia, Baptised, 10-11
Serbia, Despotate of (1402–1459), 18–21, 29
Serbia, Kingdom of (1217–1346), 13–16, 124
Serbia, Kingdom of (1718–1739), 32-3
Serbia, Kingdom of (1882–1918)
    administrative divisions, 341
    Aleksandar's assassination (1903), 303–8, 319–25, 330, 331–2
    Aleksandar's wedding (1900), 288–95
    armed forces, *see* armed forces
    Balkan League agreements (1912), 373
    Balkan Wars (1912-13), 285, 318, 359, 361, 373–82, 388
    Bosnian crisis (1908-9), 350–55, 358
    Bulgaria, agreement with (1897), 281

INDEX

Bulgaria, agreements with (1904–5), 337
church law (1890), 263, 284
conspirator question, 331–6, 339–40, 343–4, 345, 361, 388, 389
constitution (1889), 3, 257–8, 259, 271, 277, 295, 297, 301, 326–7
constitution (1901), 3, 295–7, 326, 327
constitution (1903), 3, 326–9, 331
contras affair (1903), 333
Corfu Declaration (1917), 431–6
coup d'état (1893), 273–5, 307, 313
coup d'état (1903), 4, 5, 303–8, 317–25, 331–2
Decree on Officers (1904), 335–6
Decree on the Priority of Government (1914), 389
demographics, 309–10, 311
economy, 262, 309, 310–11
electoral law (1890), 262
gun question, 340–41, 343, 344, 345, 348–9, 428
Law on Handicrafts (1910), 311
Law on Marriage of Officers (1901), 293–4
Milan's abdication (1889), 258, 323
modernisation, 310
peasant cooperatives, 263, 310
political parties, 237–41
proclamation of (1882), 235
public security law (1904), 339
railways, 237, 241–2, 262
Regime of 11 October (1897–1900), 283–6, 291, 293, 314
Salonika trial (1917), 319, 323, 428–31, 436, 471, 487, 497, 501
taxation in, 262
territorial acquisitions (1912–13), 385–91
trades unions law (1911), 383
World War I (1914–18), 2, 4, 395, 399–424, 425–38
Serbia in the Ottoman Empire (1459–1815), 2–3, 6, 14, 22–36, 37–63

Battle of Batočina (1689), 30
Battle of Slankamen (1691), 30
Battle of Zenta (1697), 30
Christianity in, 22–34, 36, 50
devşirme system, 23
emigration, 25–6, 30, 33, 34, 38, 57
First Serbian Uprising, *see* First Serbian Uprising
folk beliefs in, 14, 19, 39, 40
Great Migration (1690), 30
Great Migration (1739), 33
Islam in, 22, 23, 24, 35, 45, 50
janissaries, 23, 28, 31, 40–46
Jewish community, 22, 24, 25, 50
kmets, 39, 41, 43, 47
knezes, 24, 29, 33, 41–5, 47, 53, 56, 58–9
kuluk, 23, 24, 38
land in, 22–3, 28
medicine in, 40
millet system, 24
nobility, 22, 23
pastoralism, 38
peasantry, 23, 28, 38–40
pilgrimage in, 40
sharia law in, 22
sipahis, 22, 23, 28, 31, 41, 43, 45, 46
taxation in, 22, 23, 24, 28, 38, 45, 47, 61
Treaty of Karlowitz (1699), 30
Uprising, First (1804–13), 2, 3, 19, 35, 43–59, 113, 120, 191, 585
Uprising, Second (1815), 59–63, 308, 585
women in, 23, 39
zadrugas, 38–9
Serbia, Principality of Moravian (1371–1402), 17
Serbia, Principality of (1815–1882), 3, 6, 65–99, 101–38, 139–70, 171–97, 201–31, 233–5
Action Ministry (1875), 210, 213, 214
administrative divisions, 87–8, 96
Akkerman Convention (1826), 76–7
armed forces, *see* armed forces

INDEX

cannon foundry, 132–3, 134
censorship in, 78, 130
census (1834), 86–7
census (1884), 227
chancellery, 65, 66, 69, 84, 87
Christianity in, 69, 71, 73, 81–2, 85, 86–7, 113
civil code (1844), 114
Congress of Berlin (1878), 224, 225, 226–7
constitution (1835), 3, 89–94, 95, 118
constitution (1838), 3, 88, 95–7, 118, 157, 172, 295
constitution (1869), 3, 181–4, 195–7, 201, 204–6, 213, 277–9, 295, 327
consulates, 94, 98, 115, 172
corporal punishment in, 74, 75, 113, 158, 165, 184, 204, 220
Council, *see* Council
courts, 67, 69, 74–5, 114, 133, 151, 166–7, 206, 228
craftsmen in, 87, 110, 117, 127, 141, 155, 170, 208
currency, 160–61, 204, 229
death penalty in, 69, 152
education in, 84–5, 105, 113, 139, 148, 159, 229
Equality of Citizenry decree (1859), 149
garrisons decree (1845), 109
hatt-ı şerif (1830), 3, 77–9, 83, 84, 89, 102, 193
hatt-ı şerif (1833), 81, 93, 124
healthcare in, 84, 216, 229
immigration, 81, 82
Jewish population, *see* Jews
knezes, 65, 68, 70–74, 87–8, 90, 91, 98
kuluk in, 70–71, 72, 80, 90, 92
land in, 69, 83, 96, 113, 114, 118, 204
Law on Bookshops (1870), 184
Law on Bureaucracy (1861), 156
Law on Crafts (1847), 110
Law on Garrison Military (1845), 126
Law on Organisation of the Council (1839), 97
Law on Parliaments (1859), 146, 149
Law on Parliaments (1861), 156
Law on Reclamation of Land (1839), 96
Law on Spiritual Authority (1847), 114
market economy, 81
municipal self-government law (1875), 211
Muslim population, *see* Islam; Muslims
Orthodox Church in, *see* Serbian Orthodox Church
Ottoman garrisons, *see* Ottoman garrisons
Ottoman Wars (1876–8), 185, 220–24
parliaments, *see* parliaments
peasantry, *see* peasantry
policing, *see* policing
press law (1875), 228
printing in, 78
railways, 196, 226, 227, 230
Russia, relations with, *see* Russian Empire
smoking laws, 71
taxation in, *see* taxation
trade in, 71–2, 155
trade agreements in, 230
women in, 90, 111, 114, 209, 229
Serbia, in Yugoslavia (1918-41), *see* Yugoslavia
Serbia in the East (Marković), 192-4
Serbian Committee, 160
Serbian Commune, 188
Serbian Empire (1346–1371), 15–17, 121, 124, 140, 314
Serbian language, 25, 116–22, 124, 159, 170, 312–13, 419, 453, 461
Serbian Learned Society, 165, 262
Serbian Medical Society, 216
Serbian Museum, 114
Serbian National Women's Union, 480
Serbian Orthodox Church, 13–14, 18
  in Austria, 86

INDEX

autocephaly recognition (1879), 227, 236
bishoprics, 14, 16
Bogomoljci movement (c. 1920 – c. 1945), 532
in Bosnia, 14, 26–7, 475
church law (1862), 159
church law (1883), 236, 263
church law (1890), 263, 284
Concordat crisis (1937), 542–4, 559, 565, 584
constitution (1838), 96
constitution (1869), 182
coup d'état (1941), 575
flag, 510
Jewish community, relations with, 568, 569
Kosovo legend and, 20
Kostić mission (1884–5), 250
Law on Spiritual Authority (1847), 114
Leopold I's recognition (1690), 30
meat consumption and, 73
in Macedonia, 250, 252, 279, 281
metropolitanates, 16, 31, 32, 36, 78, 85–6, 263, 461
Mihailo's reforms (1862), 159
Miloš and, 85–6
nationhood and, 119
Niš Sanjak (1448–1878), 104–5
in Old Serbia, 250
Ottoman period (1459–1817), 24–34, 36
Patriarchate (1920–), 461
Patriarchate of Peć (1346–1766), 16, 17, 27, 29, 31, 32
Progressives and, 236
Radicals and, 211
saints, 39
Serbian nationalism and, 510, 530
Tripartite Pact accession (1941), 571
Varnava's death (1937), 566
Yugoslav identity and, 532–3
Yugoslav unification (1920), 461, 468

Serbian Progressive Party, 205, 253–5, 344
6 January Regime (1929–34), 506
Aleksandar, relations with, 276, 306
constitution (1889), 258
constitution (1901), 295–7
constitution (1903), 329
contra pardoning affair (1908), 352
Democratic Party merger (1919), 470, 486
Đorđević government (1897–1900), 283, 286
draft constitution (1883), 240, 243, 280, 295
establishment of regime of (1880), 233-234
Garašanin government (1884–7), 248–55, 316
Jewish community, relations with, 567
manifesto (1881), 239
Novaković government (1895–6), 279–80, 295, 296
Pašić government (1906–8), 347–8
Petrović inquiry (1911), 356
Piroćanac government (1880–83), 238, 241–5, 316
Provisional National Legislature (1919–20), 471
Radical terrorism against, 355, 362
Radicals, relations with, 249, 255, 260, 261
reconstitution (1906), 344
Russia, relations with, 279
territorial acquisitions (1912–13) and, 386
World War I (1914–18), 404
Yugoslav Committee, relations with, 434
Yugoslavia, establishment of (1918), 459
coalition government (1901–2), 295–301
Bosnian crisis (1908–9), 352, 353, 354, 355
Serbian Radical Party, 549

INDEX

Serbian Red Cross, 216
Serbian Revolutionary Organisation, 336–7
Serbian Royal Academy, 262–3, 264, 380, 516
    see also Royal Serbian Academy
Serbian Social Democratic Party, 281, 314, 329, 335, 339, 348, 357, 383–5, 477
    coalition government (1919–20), 479
    constituent assembly (1920–21), 481
    constitution (1921), 483
    militarism, opposition to, 383–5
    territorial acquisitions (1912–13) and, 386
    World War I outbreak (1914), 395
Serbian vice-royalty plan (1848), 128
Serbian Vojvodina (1848–9), 129–32, 177
Serbian Volunteer Division, 1st, 422, 426
Serbian Volunteer Division, 2nd, 422
    Serbo-Greek convention (1861), 161
Serbs and Popinjays (Jovanović), 165, 172–3
Serbs Assemble!, 555, 562, 563
Serčesmi, Ali-aga, 58
Serres, Macedonia, 17
Seton-Watson, Robert, 412, 431, 436
Sevojno, Serbia, 580
sewers, 310, 581
sharia law, 22, 41, 62, 484, 512
Shashit Pasha, 41
Shkodër, Albania, 28, 49, 79, 125, 375, 376, 388, 408, 409, 414, 416, 444, 452, 466, 547
Sanjak of (1479–1913), 28, 49
Shtime, Kosovo, 79
shops
    Aleksandar's reign (1842–58), 109, 114, 117, 127
    Aleksandar I's reign (1889–1903), 262, 314, 315
    Mihailo's first reign (1839-42), 101
    Mihailo's second reign (1860–68), 155, 170
    Milan's reign (1868–89), 184–5

    Miloš's first reign (1815–39), 80, 81, 91, 93, 96
    Ottoman period (1459–1815), 25
    World War I (1914-18), 415
Šibenik, Croatia, 438
Šid, Croatia, 552
Sigismund, King of Hungary, 18
Silistria, 30
Simeon I, Tsar of Bulgaria, 12
Simeon, Saint, 13
Simić, Aleksa, 75, 83, 90, 112, 134, 136, 141
Simić, Božin, 308, 420, 426, 566, 573, 578
Simić, Đorđe, 112, 277, 280, 282, 283
Simić, Stojan, 83, 90, 91, 95, 98, 112, 131, 277
Simović, Dušan, 441–2, 457
    appointment as air-force commander (1940), 571
    coup d'état (1941), 557, 564, 565–6, 572–8
    German invasion (1941), 581-3
    minorities study (1938), 568
    Yugoslav unification (1918), 441–2
Sinđelić, Vojvoda Stevan, 53
Singidunum, 9
sipahis, 22, 23, 28, 31, 41, 43, 45, 46, 49, 62, 69, 74–5, 80
Sistova, Treaty of (1791), 35, 41, 44
Sjenica, Serbia, 53, 56, 217, 337, 418
Skadar Troops, 444
Skenderbeg, 495
Skerlić, Jovan, 314, 328, 339, 352, 367–8, 461
Škoda, 340, 343, 348–9, 428
Skopje, Macedonia
    Bulgarian occupation (1916–18), 412, 418, 421, 437
    Kingdom of Serbia (1912–16), 374, 374, 377, 379, 382, 386, 390, 411
    Raška (1091–1217), 12, 13
    Serbian Empire (1346–1371), 16

INDEX

Ottoman Empire (1392–1912), 46, 104, 185, 224, 252, 281, 299, 358, 361, 372
Yugoslavia (1918-41), 460, 480, 486, 580, 583
Skopljak, Süleyman Pasha, 58
Skull Tower of Niš, 53, 89
Slankamen, Battle of (1691), 30
Slav Society, 126, 130
slavenosrpski, 116
slavery, 21, 50, 68, 218, 443
Slaves du sud (Grujić and Janković), 140
Slavic Congress (1848), 129
Slavic Union, 207
Slavonia, 4, 25, 26, 34, 84, 108, 120, 129, 140, 364, 366, 505
    Black Hand and, 358
    Central Revolutionary Liberation Committee (c. 1872), 203
    Chief Educational Council on, 366
    Geneva Declaration (1918), 441, 442
    World War I (1914–18), 400, 401
    Yugoslav (1918-41), *see* Slavonia in Yugoslavia
Slavonia in Yugoslavia (1918-41), 441, 446, 448, 449, 483
    banovinas, 508, 510
    Communist Party in, 476
    oblasts, 486, 489
    ORJUNA in, 491
    Orthodox Church in, 461
    provincial administration, 460, 489, 491, 493
    Radicals in, 472–3
    Serbs in, 457, 458, 459, 481, 487
Slavonic Bank, 496
Slavonic Serbian, 116, 118
Slavs, arrival in Balkans, 9–11
Slivnica, Battle of (1885), 252, 350, 380
šljivovica, 38, 68, 495
Slobozia, Romania, 51
Slovaks, 129, 439, 446, 452, 482, 567
Slovene People's Party (SLS), 471

6 January Regime (1929–34), 512, 518, 519, 520
banovina debate (1940), 554
constitution (1921), 481
coup d'état (1941), 576
Davidović government (1924), 491, 492–3
electoral law (1931), 512
Federalist Bloc, 489, 490
Jevtić government (1934–5), 536
JRZ formation (1935), 537
Korošec government (1928–9), 502
Law for Protection of Public Security (1921), 485
Opposition Bloc, 491
Stojadinović government (1935–9), 538, 539
Uzunović government (1926–7), 498
Vesnić government (1920–21), 480
Slovenes, 4
    April War (1941), 580, 581
    Carinthian plebiscite (1920), 453
    in Italy, 453
    Kingdom of Serbs, Croats and Slovenes (1918-29), 459, 469, 470, 478-9, 486, 492, 505, 506
    Kingdom of Yugoslavia (1929-41), 508-9, 510, 518, 424, 528, 529, 538, 540, 544-5, 548, 551, 558, 560, 562, 564, 568, 574, 577, 579
    South Slav unity, 119, 361, 363, 365, 367, 369, 400, 531
    unification of Yugoslavia (1914-18), 402, 405, 406, 407, 410, 425, 431, 433, 435, 444, 445, 446, 448, 456
    in Volunteer units, 422, 423
Slovenia, 4, 10, 364
    Black Hand and, 358
    Bulgarian agreement (1915), 411
    Corfu Declaration (1917), 433
    Maček on, 504
    Milovanović and, 361
    Niš Declaration (1914), 405

INDEX

World War I (1914–18), 401, 405, 407, 411, 433, 438
  in Yugoslavia (1918-41), *see* Slovenia in Yugoslavia
Slovenia in Yugoslavia (1918-41), 449, 451, 452–3, 455
  6 January Regime (1929–34), 506
  anti-Semitism in, 568
  Association of Fighters of Yugoslavia, 529, 530
  banovina debate (1940), 554
  banovina, 508
  Communist Party in, 476, 477, 478
  constitution (1921), 482, 483, 484
  country government, 460
  coup d'état (1941), 577
  Cvetković–Maček Agreement (1939), 550, 551, 553
  Democratic Party in, 470–71
  Farmers' Party in, 474
  federalism, 489–91
  German invasion (1941), 581
  Hungarian conflict (1919), 454
  investment in, 511
  Koruško conflict (1919), 453
  Marko's Protocol (1923), 489
  oblasts, 486, 489
  Pribićević's centralism and, 479
  provincial administration, 460, 489
  Provisional National Legislature (1919–20), 471
  World War II (1939–45), 571, 579, 581–2
Slovenski Jug (*Slavic South*), 367
Smederevo, Serbia
  Kingdom of Serbia (1882–1918), 259, 263, 272, 529
  Ottoman Empire (1459-1815), 27, 35, 42, 47, 186, 529
  Principality of Serbia (1815–1882), 69, 70, 72, 73, 82, 87, 106, 118, 162, 166, 183, 203, 221, 237,
  Sanjak of (1459–1817), 22–5, 29, 33–7, 41, 42, 292

Uprising, First (1804–13), 45, 46, 57, 58
Uprising, Second (1815), 60
Serbian Despotate (1402–1459), 21
Yugoslavia (1918-41), 486
Smiljanić, Krsto, 508
smoking, 40, 71, 276, 356
Smoljan, Bariša, 577
Smoljinac, Serbia, 272
Smutekovac park, Belgrade, 347
Snoj, Franc, 548
Social Democratic Party (Croatia), 366, 476
Social Democratic Party (Serbia), *see* Serbian Social Democratic Party
Social Democratic Party (Vojvodina), 476
socialism, 6, 110, 117, 178, 180, 186–96, 203, 205, 308–13, 314–17
  Cenić's movement, 308–9, 311–13
  Dragović's movement, 314
  March disturbances (1903), 314–17
  Marković's movement, *see* Marković, Svetozar
  Radicals and, 208–9, 211–13, 262, 308–9
Socialist Party of Yugoslavia, 477
Socialist Workers' Party of Yugoslavia, 476
Society for the Legal Settlement of the Conspiratorial Question, 334, 345, 346
Society for Serbian Letters, 113, 117, 165
Society of Cyril and Methodius, 252
Society of Serb Youth, 140, 177
Society of Serbs from Old Serbia and Macedonia, 299–300
Society of Shoemaking Workers, 313
Society of St Sava, 252-3
Sofia, Bulgaria, 21, 217, 228, 251, 252, 281, 341, 366, 379, 522, 523, 564
Sohr, Aleksandar, 522–3
Soko, Serbia, 81, 82, 87, 162, 163, 169
Sokol nahija, 68
Sokol (Falcon), 370, 509, 552, 573
Sokolović, Mehmed-pasha, 23, 27
Šola, Atanasije, 447, 462, 469, 473

741

INDEX

Solarević, Leonid, 290, 293, 295, 304, 320
Sombor, Serbia, 52, 84, 438, 560
Sombor resolution (1932), 521
Sophie, Archduchess of Austria, 129
Sophie, Duchess of Hohenberg, 393
Sorbs, 10, 244
Soviet Union, *see* Russia, Soviet
Spaho, Mehmed, 491, 498, 518, 520, 537, 538, 548, 549, 553, 564
Spain, 25, 547
Spasojević, Janko, 442, 444
Special Operations Executive (SOE), 572–3
Split, Croatia, 438, 439, 476, 486, 575
Sracimir, 12
Srb, Aleksandar, 420, 426
Srbija (*Serbia*), 176
Srebrenica, Bosnia, 18, 53
Srećković, Mihailo, 111, 293
Sredojević, Sreten, 346
Srem, 15, 25, 29, 43, 125, 136, 140
    Kingdom of Serbia (1882–1918), 312, 358, 366, 400, 401, 403, 439, 441, 446-7
    Sanjak of (1541–1699), 29
    Yugoslavia (1918-41), 449, 458, 471, 472, 482, 486, 508, 550, 551, 561
Sremska Mitrovica, Serbia, 84, 115, 308
Sremski Karlovci, Serbia, 30, 31, 32, 34, 78, 84, 86, 115, 118, 129, 130, 132, 236
Srpske novine (*Serb Newspaper*), 84, 152–3
Srpski glas (*Serb Voice*), 560, 562, 575
Srpski književni glasnik (*Serb Literary Herald*), 300
Srškić, Milan, 473, 475, 488, 499, 505, 506–7, 509, 511, 519, 522, 524, 527, 538, 655
St Andrew's Day parliament (1858), 141, 143-8, 156, 166, 177, 285
St John's Day attempt (1899), 286–7, 289, 292, 306, 313, 344, 495, 563
St Mark's Church, Belgrade, 319
St Nicholas Committee (1868–9), 182, 236
St Peter's Day parliament (1835), 93
St Peter's Day parliament (1848), 130–31, 195
St Petersburg, Russia, 46, 78, 89, 188, 190, 221, 225, 270, 275, 281, 308, 321, 357
St Sava's Day, 147, 511
St Vitus's Day, 19, 265, 483, 490
St Vitus's Day constitution (1921), 481–4, 461-2, 488, 490, 494, 502, 505, 507, 511, 512, 550, 575
St Vitus's Day trial (1922), 562
Stajić, Vasa, 464
Stamboliyski, Aleksandar, 469
Stambolov, Stefan, 265, 279
Stamenković, Andrija, 144
Štampa (*Press*), 373
Stanković, Filip, 147, 151, 159, 163, 166, 179
Stanković, Radenko, 527
Stanković, Simeon, 544, 571
Stanojević, Aca, 208, 246, 249, 277, 286, 524, 537, 539, 544
Stanojević, Dragiša, 110, 178, 179, 186, 187, 269, 312, 313
Stanojević, Jakov, 152
Stanojević, Jeremija, 152, 179, 186
Stanojević, Nikola, 402
Stanojević, Stanoje, 406, 483
Stanovljanske Polje, Serbia, 221, 346
Stara Gradiška, Croatia, 213
Stari Vlah, Serbia, 53, 80
Staro Oslobođenje (*Old Liberation*), 212
State Court for the Protection of the State, 517, 518, 520
Statuta Valachorum (1630), 26
Steed, Henry Wickham, 307, 431, 436
Stefan Dečanski, King of Serbia, 15
Stefan Dragutin, King of Serbia, 15
Stefan Dušan, Emperor of Serbia, 15–16, 17, 18, 140, 314, 370
Stefan Lazarević, Despot of Serbia, 17–18
Stefan Milutin, King of Serbia, 15
Stefan the First Crowned, 13–14, 264
Stefan Uroš I, King of Serbia, 14-15
Stefan Uroš V, Emperor of Serbia, 16–17

INDEX

Stefanović, Danilo, 204, 209–10
Stefanović, Dušan, 388, 393, 404, 414, 434
Stefanović Tenka, Stefan, 103, 131, 135, 137, 204
Stejić, Spasoje, 485
Stepanović, Stepa, 294, 346, 351, 360, 374, 403, 413, 437, 495
Štip, Macedonia, 224, 379, 469
Stoimirović, Milan Jovanović, 570
Stojadinović, Dragiša, 496
Stojadinović, Milan, 322, 380, 496, 497, 506, 521, 523, 534–50, 557, 565, 577, 583, 584
    Albanians, persecution of, 546
    assassination attempt (1936), 541
    Concordat crisis (1937), 542–4, 559
    constitution declaration (1937), 544
    expulsion from Yugoslavia (1941), 571–2, 574
    fascism, 545–9
    Jewish community, relations with, 568-9
Stojančević, Vladimir, 57
Stojanović, Dubravka, 330
Stojanović, Ljubomir, 298, 321, 325–6, 337, 339, 342-3, 345, 346, 347, 367, 386, 472, 563
Stojanović, Milan, 322
Stojanović, Nikola, 402, 406–7, 434, 447, 471, 559, 562, 575
Stojanović, Tihomir, 321
Stojanović-Čosa, Stevan, 84
stojanovština, 347
Stojimirović, Frano, 28
Stojković, Milenko, 45, 50, 52, 53, 54, 55, 68
Štokavian dialect, 120, 366
Stokes, Gale, 194
Stolac, Hercegovina, 553
Stradija (Domanović), 300-1
Stranjaković, Dragoljub, 560
Stratimirović, Stevan, 46, 86, 116
street lights, 109, 310
Stroganov, Grigory Alexandrovich, 70
Strossmayer, Josip Juraj, 167, 511
Struma River, 436
Strumica, Macedonia, 452-3, 528,
Studenica, Serbia, 13, 85, 88, 264
Sturdza, Pulcheria, 615
Styria, 438
Subotica, Serbia, 438, 441, 445, 452, 454
Südbahn, 241
Šufflay, Milan, 518
Šugrin, Serbia, 233
Süleyman Pasha, 45, 49, 50
Süleyman Pasha Skopljak, 58–60
sulphuric acid, 540
Šumadija, 37-8, 40, 45, 58, 84, 97, 103, 116, 368, 486, 560
Šumadija Division, 251, 346, 415
Šumatovac, Serbia, 218
    Battle of (1876), 218
Sundhaussen, Holm, 1
Supilo, Frano, 406, 431
Supreme Court, 114, 137, 166–7, 388, 460
Supreme Military Council, 299
Supreme Military Court, 333, 346
Surdulica, Serbia, 419
Šutej, Juraj, 552, 576
Svest (Conscience), 329
Svetosavlje as a Philosophy of Life (Popović), 533
Svetosavlje, 532-3
Sweden, 349
Switzerland, 190, 206, 207, 230, 252, 349
Syrmia, 15

Taborište, Serbia, 91
tailors' guild, 127
Tajsić, Ranko, 210, 269, 275, 277, 286–7
Takovo, Serbia, 59, 308
Tankosić, Vojislav, 318, 337, 338, 352, 389, 390, 391, 392, 394, 425
Taušanović, Kosta, 208, 247, 261, 275, 283, 286–7, 292, 298
taxation
    Aleksandar's reign (1842–58), 110, 130, 141

INDEX

Aleksandar I of Serbia's reign (1889–1903), 261, 262, 292
Aleksander I of Yugoslavia's reign (1921–34), 464, 498, 522
Ottoman period (1459–1817), 22, 23, 24, 28, 38, 45, 47, 61
Milan's reign (1868–89), 182, 228, 241, 249, 257
Miloš's reign, first (1815–39), 3, 69, 70, 72, 74, 83, 93, 96
Miloš's reign, second (1858–60), 151
Mihailo's reign (1839–42), 105
Mihailo's reign, second (1860–68), 174
Petar I's reign (1903–21), 328, 410
Petar II's reign (1934–45), 498
Uprising period (1804–17), 47
telegraph, 109, 273
telephones, 310, 318, 320
Temesvár, 25, 28, 29, 36, 140, 402
Eyalet of (1552–1716), 28, 29
Tenka's plot (1857), 137
Teodorović, Atanasije, 84
Teodorović, Lazar, 72, 87, 98, 103, 104
Teodosije, Metropolitan of Belgrade, 236-7, 256, 263
Terazije bomb (1871), 203
Terazije, Belgrade, 112, 203, 273, 334, 383, 389, 402
Terzić, Božidar, 426
Terzić, Velimir, 583
Tetovo region, Macedonia, 206, 377, 379, 475
textiles, 81, 309, 515, 540
theatre, 160, 174, 203, 211, 235, 351, 415, 534
Theodora, Byzantine Empress, 321
Thessaloniki, *see* Salonika
Thessaly, Greece, 161
Thrace, 16, 161, 374, 384, 412
Thracians, 9, 10
Three Weeks (Glynn), 322
Tihomir, 12
Tilsit, Treaty of (1807), 51
timars, 22, 28, 31, 83

Timișoara, Romania, 25, 28, 29, 36, 140, 402
Timok Division, 251-2, 415
Timok, Serbia, 54, 188, 206, 258, 324, 486, 540
rebellion (1883), 246-9, 253, 259, 263, 265, 272, 275, 278, 306, 324, 550
Timur, Timurid Emperor, 18
Tito, Josip Broz, 377, 426, 439, 503, 586-7
tobacco, 40, 71, 256, 261, 262, 271, 276
Todorović Abdula, Marko, 71
Todorović, Pera, 207, 208, 212, 215, 243, 246, 247, 253, 256, 316, 322, 328, 329, 335
Todorović, Petar, 55
Todorović, Poleksija, 209
Todorović, Stevan, 71
Todorović, Velimir, 318, 323
Tomaš, King of Bosnia, 21
Tomašević, Stjepan, 21
Tomić, Jaša, 446, 472
Tomić, Milutin, 502
Tomić, Svetozar, 444, 465
Topalović, Živko, 477
Topčider, Serbia, 103–4, 178, 181, 305
Toplica, Serbia, 12, 14, 223, 226, 258, 412
uprising (1917), 420-2
Topola, Serbia, 43, 48, 52, 72, 112, 166, 208, 275
uprising (1877), 221, 227, 234, 261, 286, 346
Toptani, Esad Pasha, 407–8, 416
Torbar, Josip, 576
torture, 59, 69, 107, 346, 402, 421, 465, 46
trade unions, 310-11, 315, 383, 484, 506, 509, 540
trams, 310
Transfiguration Day parliament (1861), 156, 158, 178
Transylvania, 90, 569
Travnik, Bosnia, 483, 510, 552
Travunija, 14
Trepča, Kosovo, 540
Trešnja, Serbia, 97

744

INDEX

Trianon, Treaty of (1920), 452, 452
Trieste, 140, 364, 369, 439, 455
Trifković, Marko, 370
Trifunović, Miloš (Miša), 498, 521, 545, 576
Trifunović-Birčanin, Ilija, 534, 565, 576
Tripartite Pact (1940), 557, 564, 566, 570–78, 583, 584
Tripolitania revolt (1835–58), 95
Trn, Bulgaria, 225, 226, 251
Trnava, Serbia, 58
Trogir, Croatia, 438
Trotsky, Leon, 373, 377, 382
Tršić, Serbia, 115
Trubetskoy, Grigorii, 411, 414
Trumbić, Ante, 406, 431, 432, 434, 440, 444, 451, 452, 455, 459, 484
Tsankov, Aleksandar, 469
Tsaribrod, Serbia, 452
tuberculosis, 75, 98, 101, 207, 516
Tucaković, Arsenije, 174
Tucaković, Petar, 84, 142
Tucaković, Todor, 142, 152, 156, 174, 181, 182, 230
Tucović, Dimitrije, 314, 315, 384–5, 395, 408
Tucović, Vladimir, 315, 429, 566
Tupanjanin, Miloš, 519, 572, 576
turbans, 62, 78, 491
Turkey, Republic of (1922–), 252
    Albanian and Muslim migration to 463, 467, 546, 547
    Balkan Pact (1934), 523
    Ljotić and, 531
Turkish dress, 62, 78, 82, 111, 113, 133, 141, 491, 585
Turkish language, 25, 109, 120, 170, 222
Turkish minority in Yugoslavia, 467, 475, 567
Turkish Revolution (1908), 350–51, 358, 372
Turnu Severin, Romania, 420
Tuzla, Bosnia, 463, 483
Tvrtko I, King of Bosnia, 17

typhus, 418, 516

Ub, Serbia, 48, 519
Udovo, Macedonia, 411
Uglješa, despot of Serres, 17
Ugričić, Jeftimije, 146
Ukrainians, 129, 446
Ulcinj, Montenegro, 12
Unification or Death, *see* Black Hand
Union of Falcons, 509, 573
Union of Jewish Religious Municipalities, 567
Union of Zionists, 567
United Kingdom
    Aleksandar I of Serbia's anointment (1889), 265
    Aleksandar I of Yugoslavia's assassination (1934), 535
    Balkan Wars (1912–13), 376
    Bosnia negotiations (1870), 185
    conspirators crisis (1905), 343–4, 361, 428
    Constitutionalists, relations with, 122
    consul, assault on (1858), 115
    coup d'état (1941), 572–3, 583
    Crimean War (1853–6), 134–5, 136
    Cvetković–Maček Agreement (1939), 551
    Entente Cordiale (1904), 350, 393, 394
    Great Game (c. 1813–1907), 94
    Greek War of Independence (1821–9), 77
    Jewish community, relations with, 155
    Kükürt Çeşme crisis (1862), 163
    May putsch, reaction to (1903), 342
    Mihailo, relations with, 155, 162, 163
    Montenegro, relations with, 465
    Moroccan crises (1905–6/1911), 393–4
    Munich Agreement (1938), 546
    Niš Declaration (1914), 405
    parliamentarism, 299, 334
    Petar I, relations with, 335
    Polish émigrés, relations with, 122

INDEX

Principality of Serbia, relations with, 88–9, 94
Russian Civil War (1917–22), 454
Russian Entente (1907), 350, 393, 394
Serbian-Ottoman Wars (1876–8), 216
tariff agreement (1907), 349
trade agreement (1880), 230
World War I (1914–18), 395, 401, 402, 405, 410, 414, 436–8
United Opposition, 536, 537, 539, 541, 544, 547, 550, 558, 559, 566
United Serb Chetniks for King and Fatherland, 492
United Serb Youth, 173–5, 177, 186, 188, 205, 561
Belgrade congress (1867), 174, 177, 190
Bosnia operations (1871), 203
Karađorđevićes and, 187
Kikinda congress (1869), 195
Mihailo's assassination (1868), 180
Novi Sad congress (1866), 173
Russia, relations with, 188, 190
Veliki Bečkerek congress (1868), 181, 190
Vršac congress (1871), 196
United States, 423, 431, 437, 438, 439, 465, 513, 567, 573
'Unity of the Serbo-Croats' (Pašić), 365
University of Belgrade, 310, 500, 518
Unkiar-Skelessi, Treaty of (1833), 80, 92
Uroš I, King of Serbia, 14
Uroš V, Emperor of Serbia, 16–17
Urovci, Serbia, 42
Urquhart, David, 88-9, 122
Ustasha Council, 465
Ustashas, 522, 524, 535, 545, 553, 581, 582
Užice Army, 409, 426
Užice, Serbia, 50, 82, 85, 87, 162, 163, 169–70, 242, 258, 309, 322, 346, 404, 486, 580
Uzunović, Nikola, 496-7, 498, 505, 506, 508, 519, 522, 524, 527, 534

Valjevo, Serbia, 47, 59, 68, 87, 178, 257, 275, 320–21, 357, 486
Varaždin, Croatia, 26, 552
Vardar Banovina, 508, 509, 554
Vardar Division, 415
Vardar River, 411, 448
Varešanin, Marijan, 355
Varna, Bulgaria, 21, 349
Battle of (1444), 21
Crusade of (1443–4), 21
Varnava I, Serbian Patriarch, 533, 543, 544, 565–6
Vasić, Dragiša, 485, 559, 561-3, 573, 575
Vasić, Milan, 352, 358, 359, 380
Vasić, Miloš, 291, 293, 346, 360
Vasiljević, Alimpije, 164, 172, 174, 176, 177, 180, 195, 210, 218
Vasiljević, Dušan, 406–7
Vatican, 365, 391, 542–4, 559, 565, 584
Velbužd, Battle of (1330), 15
veiling, 39
Veles, Macedonia, 185, 224, 355, 411
Veliki Bečkerek, Hungary, 181
Veliki Izvor, Serbia, 217
Veliki Šiljegovac, Battle of, (1876), 219
Velimirović, Nikolaj, 412, 532, 533, 568, 569
Velimirović, Pera, 196, 208, 301, 350, 353, 417
Veljko, Hajduk, 42, 43, 52, 54, 131
Veljković, Stojan, 165, 205
Veljković, Vojislav, 307, 325, 340, 343, 389, 417, 470
Vemić, Velimir, 308, 319, 320, 323, 335, 357, 358, 388, 428-9, 563, 565
Venice, Italy, 57
Venice, Republic of (697–1797), 12, 19, 27
Venizelos, Eleftherios, 412, 436
Versailles, France, 434
Treaty of (1919), 452, 455, 478
Vesnić, Milenko, 452, 480, 482, 513, 567
Victor Emmanuel III, King of Italy, 410
Victor monument, Kalemegdan, 515-6
Vittorio Veneto, Battle of (1918), 438

746

INDEX

Vidin, Bulgaria, 42, 53, 104, 222, 224, 250, 251, 252, 313, 366
Vienna, Austria, 38, 84, 113, 121, 132, 133, 154, 170, 191, 221, 225, 241, 308, 320, 325, 340, 344, 367, 392, 393, 522, 655
    fashion, 111
    Milan in, 209–10, 231, 235, 256, 290, 291, 294
    railway links, 227
    revolution in (1848-9), 120-1, 128
    Serbian students in, 118, 139, 216,
    Siege (1529), 25
    Siege (1683), 29
    Tripartite Pact (1941), 572, 578
    Zora, 173
Vienna Agreement (1850), 120
Vienna Group, 344
Vilna, Lithuania, 412
Vinkovci, Croatia, 510, 561
Vis, Croatia, 438, 552
Višegrad, Bosnia, 53
Viševac, Serbia, 43
Višnjić, Filip, 53, 116
Visoko Dečani monastery, Kosovo, 15
Visoko, Bosnia, 554
Vlachs, 11, 15, 24, 25–6, 27, 85, 118, 202, 203, 244, 453
vladanovština, 291, 347
Vlajić, Božidar, 576
Vlastimir, Župan of Raška, 11
Vlorë, Albania, 408
Vojinović, Kosta, 420, 421, 422
vojvoda, introduction of rank, 293
Vojvodina in the Habsburg Empire (1699–1918), 4, 5, 25, 27, 29, 30, 31, 34, 36, 125, 312
    Black Hand and, 358
    emigration from, 227
    Great National Council (1918), 446, 460
    Illyrian Court Chancellery, 36
    Karić and, 366
    Ottoman War (1716–18), 32
    Ottoman War (1788–91), 34
    Revolutions (1848–9), 129–32, 177
    World War I (1914–18), 401, 422, 435, 437, 438, 439
Vojvodina in Yugoslavia (1918-41), 439, 445–7, 449, 464
    6 January Regime (1929–34), 520–21
    agrarian reform, 464
    autonomist movement, 482, 520-1
    banovinas, 508
    Communist Party and, 476, 477
    constitution (1921), 482, 484, 487
    Cvetković–Maček Agreement (1939), 550, 551
    economy, 464
    Great National Council (1918), 446, 460
    Hungarian claims to, 454, 491
    Hungarian conflict (1919), 454
    Hungarian invasion (1941), 581
    investment in, 511
    JRZ in, 538, 540
    Maček and, 504, 505
    oblasts, 486
    Orthodox Church in, 473
    Paris Peace Conference (1919–20), 452
    People's Radical Party in, 472–3
    provincial administration, 460
    Provisional National Legislature (1919–20), 471
    Radicals in, 470
    railways, 464
    Serbs in, 457, 458, 459
    taxation in, 464
    World War II (1939–45), 581
    Zagreb Points (1932), 520
Voljavča monastery, Serbia, 47
Vračar, Serbia, 107, 163
Vranje, Serbia
    Battle of (1878), 222
    Kingdom of Serbia (1882–1918), 237, 250, 253, 257, 285, 337, 342, 419, 421, 437
    Ottoman Serbia (1459–1815), 22

INDEX

Principality of Serbia (1815–1882), 104, 185, 222-7, 230
Yugoslavia (1918-41), 486
Vranov, Serbia, 263
Vrbas Banovina, 508, 548, 553, 554, 562
Vrnjačka Banja, Serbia, 417
Vršac, Serbia, 196, 437
Vučić-Perišić, Toma, 66-7, 90, 111
    Aleksandar's reign (1842–58), 107, 122, 126
    Austrian Serbs, relations with, 126–7
    death (1859), 152
    Karađorđe, execution of (1817), 66–7
    Mihailo's reign (1839–42), 102, 103, 104, 105, 106–7, 206, 208
    Miloš's reign, first (1815–39), 66–7, 73, 75, 81, 83, 87, 90, 91, 95, 97
    Miloš's reign, second (1858–60), 145, 147, 151–2
    Revolutions (1848), 130–31
    Russia, relations with, 133, 134
    Slav Society, relations with, 126
    St Andrew's Day parliament (1858), 141, 143, 145
    Tenka's plot (1857), 137
Vujić, Mihailo, 295, 298, 301, 302, 308
Vujičić, Milorad A., 386
Vukan, Župan of Raška, 12, 13
Vukašin, King of Serbia, 17
Vukićević, Milenko, 49, 50
Vukićević, Velimir, 497, 498, 500–502
Vukićević, Zarija, 413
Vukovar, Croatia, 476-7, 510, 561
Vuličević, Petar, 72
Vuličević, Vujica, 55, 66-7, 72
Vulović, Ljubomir, 320, 337, 429, 430, 561

Wallachia
    boyars in, 83, 87
    Bulgarian rebellion (1841), 105
    emigration from, 82
    Greek Rebellion outbreak (1821), 66, 71, 72

Jews, 127
Milan and, 202
Miloš and, 102, 105, 148, 202
Obrenović estates, 202
political system, 83, 87
Russo-Ottoman War (1806–12), 49, 50
salt trade, 71
Serbian exiles in, 55
Warsaw, Poland, 412
Weary Fighter sculpture, Kalemegdan, 516
Wedding Cabinet (1900–1901), 291–2, 295, 346
Western culture, 111, 117, 133, 195, 197, 206, 208, 233, 252, 365
What Does ZBOR Want? (Jonić), 530-31
White Hand, 389, 489, 494, 564, 585
    6 January Regime (1929–34), 506, 508
    Black Hand investigation (1911), 360
    Chetniks and, 492
    coup d'état (1941), 565
    formation, 356-8, 360-2
    JRZ formation (1935), 538
    Pašić, relations with, 492
    Pavle and, 535, 538–9
    Radić assassination (1928), 501-2
    Salonika trial (1917), 428-30
    Stojadinović assassination attempt (1936), 541
    World War I (1914–18), 404, 420, 425, 426–31
    Zagreb riots (1928), 503
White Palace, Belgrade, 574–5
White Russians, 454, 467
Wilhelm II, German Emperor, 392, 394, 426, 427, 437
Wilhelm of Wied, Prince of Albania, 407
Wilson, Woodrow, 431, 452
witchcraft, 40
women
    abduction of, 40, 79, 155, 372
    dress, 62, 111, 170, 311
    health, 309-10, 516
    legal subordination to husbands, 114
    marriage laws and, 86, 211

INDEX

Miloš's treatment of, 67-8, 90
misogyny, 288-9, 292, 315, 319, 321-3, 333
prostitution, 192, 514
Radical party and, 229, 262, 480
schools for girls and, 113, 148, 159, 207, 209, 229, 284
sexual abuse of, 33, 44, 48, 50, 56, 217-8, 223, 381-2, 421, 440, 514
social deprivation, 309-10, 514
socio-economic change and, 112-3, 310, 311, 514-5, 516
social position in Ottoman era, 39-40
suffrage, 182, 328, 446, 480
organisations, 209, 269, 288, 336, 480
witchcraft, 40
'women's work', 23, 70, 90
Women Workers' School, 209
Women Workers' Society, 329
Women's Society, 209, 269, 288, 480
wool, 309
World War I (1914–18), 4, 5, 294, 332, 395, 399–424, 425–38
    Albanian Golgotha (1915), 413, 510
    armistices (1918), 437–8
    Battle of Caporetto (1917), 434
    Battle of Cer (1914), 403
    Battle of Dobro Pole (1918), 437
    Battle of Doiran (1918), 437
    Battle of the Drina (1914), 403–4
    Battle of Kajmakčalan (1916), 415
    Battle of the Kolubara (1914), 405, 413
    Battle of Mačkov Kamen (1914), 404
    Battle of Mojkovac (1916), 416
    Bizerte evacuation (1915), 414
    Brusilov Offensive (1916), 418
    Chantilly conference (1915), 414
    Corfu evacuation (1915), 414, 415
    Dobrudja front (1916–18), 423
    Greek entry (1917), 436
    guerrilla warfare, 400, 409, 411, 413, 417, 419–22, 425
    Niš Declaration (1914), 405
    Pact of London (1914), 402, 410
    Salonika front (1915–18), 415, 420, 423, 426, 427, 433, 494
    Toplica uprising (1917), 420-2
    Treaty of Brest-Litovsk (1918), 435
    Treaty of London (1915), 410
    typhus epidemic (1914–15), 418
    United States' entry (1917), 431
    Volunteer units, 422–4
World War II (1939–45), 5
    Albania, Italian invasion of (1939), 579
    France, German invasion of (1940), 569
    Greece, German invasion of (1941), 583
    Greece, Italian invasion of (1940), 570, 571, 579
    Operation Barbarossa (1941), 583
    Poland, German invasion of (1939), 557
    Romania, German invasion of (1940), 570, 579
    Romanian annexations (1940), 569–70
    Soviet Union, German invasion of (1941), 583
    Tripartite Pact (1940), 557, 564, 566, 570–72, 576
    Yugoslavia, Axis invasion of (1941), 533, 563, 578–84
Wrangel, Pyotr, 454

Yeğen Osman-pasha, 29
Young Bosnia, 559, 561, 562
Young Conservatives, 205, 221, 233, 237-8, 265
Young Turk Revolution (1908), 350–51, 358, 372
Young Turks, 350–51, 372, 407
Ypsilantis, Alexander, 71
Yugoslav Academy of Sciences and Arts, 167
Yugoslav Action, 529, 530
Yugoslav Army in the Fatherland, 563, 564, 566, 585-6, 587
Yugoslav Club, 367, 431, 481

INDEX

Yugoslav Committee, 406-7, 422, 423, 425, 431, 432, 434-6, 438, 440, 455, 460, 471, 473, 488, 562
Yugoslav Muslim Organisation (JMO), 463
  6 January Regime (1929-34), 506, 509, 512, 518, 520
  Bosnian banovina, 553,
  Chetniks and, 541
  coalition government (1924), 491
  constitution (1921), 474-5, 481, 482, 483, 485
  Democratic Union, 494
  Federalist Bloc, 489-90
  Ilidža congress (1922), 488
  Jevtić government (1934-5), 536
  JRZ formation (1935), 537
  Korošec government (1928-9), 502
  Marko's Protocol (1923), 489
  ORJUNA, 491-2
  Peasant-Democrat Coalition and, 499
  self-government, statement on (1933), 520
  Simović government (1941), 576-7
  Stojadinović government (1935-9), 538-41, 548
  Vukičević government (1927-8), 498
Yugoslav National Movement-ZBOR, 530-32, 533, 559, 568, 571
Yugoslav National Party (JNS), 522, 529, 536, 538, 539-42, 544, 571, 573, 575, 576
Yugoslav National Workers' Union, 509
Yugoslav nationalism, 4-5, 119-20, 123-4, 363-70, 399-402, 405-7
  Aleksandar and, 370-71, 373, 400, 401
  Belić and, 406
  Black Hand and, 357-61, 425
  Cvijić and, 368-70, 405
  Corfu Declaration (1917), 431-6
  Garašanin and, 89, 123-6, 140, 160, 167-8, 171, 222
  Independent Radicals and, 363, 367-70
  Ljotić and, 530-1

  Marković and, 188-95, 196, 364, 367
  Milan and, 242
  Niš Declaration (1914), 405
  Pašić and, 206, 364, 391, 400, 401-2, 425
  Pribićević and, 441, 458, 469
  Revolutions (1848-9), 128-32
  Skerlić and, 367-8
  Žujović and, 187-8
Yugoslav Peasant Movement, 509
Yugoslav People's Party, 528
Yugoslav Radical Peasant Democracy (JRSD), 519, 522, 528
Yugoslav Radical Union (JRZ), 537-55, 557, 558
  Concordat crisis (1937), 542-4, 559, 565, 584
  Cvetković government (1939-41), 548-55
  Cvetković-Maček Agreement (1939), 550-55
  formation (1935), 537-40
  Stojadinović government (1935-9), 537-48
Yugoslav Republican Party, *see* Republican party
Yugoslav Succession, War of (1991-5), 1, 6, 377
Yugoslav Volunteer Corps, 423
Yugoslav Workers' Union (JUGORAS), 540
Yugoslavia (1918-92), 2, 4-5, 6
  6 January Regime (1929-34), 5, 504-25, 532
  administrative divisions, 483, 486, 508
  Aleksandar's assassination (1934), 5
  Aleksandar's proclamation (1918), 448, 455-6
  anti-Communist law (1921), 493
  armed forces, 455, 457-8, 462, 468, 492, 494-5, 498, 500, 506, 510, 539, 541, 552, 563-6, 570-3, 578-83
  Balkan Pact (1934), 455, 523
  census (1921), 453, 567

INDEX

centralism, *see* centralism
Charles I ultimatum (1921), 454
coat of arms, 459–60
constitution (1921), 448, 456–7, 461–2, 463, 467–88, 502, 505
constitution (1931), 511–12
country governments, 460
coup d'état (1941), 5, 563–6, 572–8
currency, 463–4
Cvetković–Maček Agreement (1939), 550–55, 557–8, 579
electoral law (1922), 487
emigration, 513, 568
flag, 459
Geneva Declaration (1918), 440–42
German occupation (1941–5), 533, 563, 578–84
Hungarian conflict (1919), 454
Hungarian uprising (1920), 454
Kaçak movement (1918–24), 466–7
language policies, 511
Law on Naming and Division (1929), 508
Law on Protection of Public Security (1921), 485
Law on Protection of the State (1929), 506, 517
Law on Religious Community of Jews (1929), 568
Law on Royal Power (1929), 505
Ministry of Religion, 460–61
Press Law (1929), 506
provincial administrations, 460
Provisional National Legislature (1919–20), 471, 479–80
Radić assassination (1928), 498–504
Tripartite Pact accession (1941), 557, 564, 571, 573, 576
unification of (1918), 448-9
VMRO conflict, 468–9
Za Otadžbinu (*For the Fatherland*), 345–6
Zach, František Aleksandr, 111, 123–4, 133, 147, 160, 161, 216, 217, 364
Zadar, Croatia, 57, 438, 455, 522

zadrugas, 38–9, 81–2, 114, 173, 192, 311, 313, 513-4
Zagreb, Croatia, 131, 140, 168, 453, 486, 522, 552, 574, 576
  6 January Regime (1929-34), 506, 510, 520
  Chamber of Seven, 460
  Communist Party in, 476, 503
  constitution (1921), 484
  Corfu Declaration (1917), 431
  Democratic congress (1922), 488
  German invasion (1941), 578, 581, 583
  German threat to (1940), 571
  metropolitanate, 510
  National Council (1918–19), 438, 440-1, 445, 446, 447
  peasant revolt (1920), 462
  population, 453
  Radić assassination crisis (1928), 502, 503
  Revolutions (1848), 131
  royal visit (1925), 494
  treason trial (1909), 366–7
  Union of Zionists, 567
  women's organisations in, 480
Zagreb Points (1932), 519–20, 521
Zahumlje, 14
Zaječar, Serbia
  in the Kingdom of Serbia (1882–1918), 246, 247, 251, 255, 284, 419
  in the Principality of Serbia (1815–1882), 85, 88, 147, 188, 206, 208, 217, 222, 229
  in Yugoslavia (1918-41), 495, 550
Zastava (*Flag*), 174, 288, 502
ZBOR, 529, 530–31, 533, 559, 568, 571
zeâmets, 22
Zemun, Serbia, 45, 56, 84, 97, 107, 108, 109, 114, 146, 162, 247, 341, 404, 573
Zenica, Bosnia, 545, 554
Zenta, Battle of (1697), 30
Žepče, Bosnia, 554
Žerajić, Bogdan, 355
Zeta Banovina, 508, 553, 554

INDEX

Zeta, 12, 13, 14, 16, 21, 26, 31
Zeta, bishopric of, 14, 16
Žiča monastery, Serbia, 13, 264
zinc, 540
Živanović, Milan, 429
Živanović, Milosav, 323
Živanović, Živan, 156, 228, 256, 286, 288, 293, 303, 304, 306, 307, 336, 337
Živić, Milan, 221
Živković, Dimitrije, 565
Živković, Ljubomir, 287, 298, 306, 325, 339
Živković, Mihailo, 374, 404, 423, 426
Živković, Petar
   6 January Regime (1929-34), 506, 509, 511, 518, 532, 564
   Aleksandar relationship with, 356–8
   Black Hand, relations with, 358, 360, 426, 428
   coup d'état (1941), 565, 576
   Jevtić government (1934–5), 535, 537
   JRZ foundation (1935), 538, 541
   May putsch (1903), 317, 318, 325, 356
   Pašić, relationship with, 492
   prime minister (1929–32), 506, 511, 518, 532, 564
   Royal Guard, 495
   Salonika trial (1917), 428
   Stojadinović government (1935–9), 537, 538, 541, 565
   Uzunović government (1934), 527, 534
   White Hand, 358, 360, 426, 428, 506, 541, 565
   Yugoslav People's Party, 528, 576
Znorić, Antonije, 29
Zog I, King of the Albanians, 408, 467–8
Zora (Dawn), 173
Zrinski, Nikola, 380
Žujović, Jovan, 298–9, 321, 324, 328, 342, 343, 378, 471, 472, 562
Žujović, Mladen, 324, 562-3
Žujović, Živojin, 187–8, 563
Županja, Croatia, 510
župans, 10–11
Zurich, Switzerland, 190, 191, 196, 206, 207, 252, 435
Zveno, 523
Zvonimir, King of Croatia, 314
Zvornik, Bosnia, 81, 151
Zwierkowski, Ludwik, 122-3